D1604712

FOR REFERENCE

Do Not Take From This Room

Twentieth-Century
Literary Criticism

Guide to Gale Literary Criticism Series

For criticism on	Consult these Gale series
Authors now living or who died after December 31, 1999	*CONTEMPORARY LITERARY CRITICISM (CLC)*
Authors who died between 1900 and 1999	*TWENTIETH-CENTURY LITERARY CRITICISM (TCLC)*
Authors who died between 1800 and 1899	*NINETEENTH-CENTURY LITERATURE CRITICISM (NCLC)*
Authors who died between 1400 and 1799	*LITERATURE CRITICISM FROM 1400 TO 1800 (LC)* *SHAKESPEAREAN CRITICISM (SC)*
Authors who died before 1400	*CLASSICAL AND MEDIEVAL LITERATURE CRITICISM (CMLC)*
Authors of books for children and young adults	*CHILDREN'S LITERATURE REVIEW (CLR)*
Dramatists	*DRAMA CRITICISM (DC)*
Poets	*POETRY CRITICISM (PC)*
Short story writers	*SHORT STORY CRITICISM (SSC)*
Black writers of the past two hundred years	*BLACK LITERATURE CRITICISM (BLC)* *BLACK LITERATURE CRITICISM SUPPLEMENT (BLCS)*
Hispanic writers of the late nineteenth and twentieth centuries	*HISPANIC LITERATURE CRITICISM (HLC)* *HISPANIC LITERATURE CRITICISM SUPPLEMENT (HLCS)*
Native North American writers and orators of the eighteenth, nineteenth, and twentieth centuries	*NATIVE NORTH AMERICAN LITERATURE (NNAL)*
Major authors from the Renaissance to the present	*WORLD LITERATURE CRITICISM, 1500 TO THE PRESENT (WLC)* *WORLD LITERATURE CRITICISM SUPPLEMENT (WLCS)*

ISSN 0276-8178

Volume 125

Twentieth-Century Literary Criticism

**Criticism of the
Works of Novelists, Poets, Playwrights,
Short Story Writers, and Other Creative Writers
Who Lived between 1900 and 1999,
from the First Published Critical
Appraisals to Current Evaluations**

Janet Witalec
Project Editor

GALE®

THOMSON
GALE

Detroit • New York • San Diego • San Francisco • Cleveland • New Haven, Conn. • Waterville, Maine • London • Munich

Twentieth-Century Literary Criticism, Vol. 125

Project Editor
Janet Witalec

Editorial
Jenny Cromie, Scott Darga, Kathy D. Darrow, Julie Keppen, Ellen McGeagh, Linda Pavlovski

Research
Nicodemus Ford, Sarah Genik, Tamara C. Nott, Tracie A. Richardson

Permissions
Lori Hines

Imaging and Multimedia
Robert Duncan, Leitha Etheridge-Sims, Lezlie Light

Product Design
Michael Logusz

Composition and Electronic Capture
Carolyn Roney

Manufacturing
Stacy L. Melson

LIBRARY OF CONGRESS CATALOG CARD NUMBER 76-46132

ISBN 0-7876-5939-8
ISSN 0276-8178

Printed in the United States of America
10 9 8 7 6 5 4 3 2 1

Contents

Preface vii

Acknowledgments xi

Literary Criticism Series Advisory Board xiii

Preface

Since its inception more than fifteen years ago, *Twentieth-Century Literary Criticism* (*TCLC*) has been purchased and used by nearly 10,000 school, public, and college or university libraries. *TCLC* has covered more than 500 authors, representing 58 nationalities and over 25,000 titles. No other reference source has surveyed the critical response to twentieth-century authors and literature as thoroughly as *TCLC*. In the words of one reviewer, "there is nothing comparable available." *TCLC* "is a gold mine of information—dates, pseudonyms, biographical information, and criticism from books and periodicals—which many librarians would have difficulty assembling on their own."

Scope of the Series

TCLC is designed to serve as an introduction to authors who died between 1900 and 1999 and to the most significant interpretations of these author's works. Volumes published from 1978 through 1999 included authors who died between 1900 and 1960. The great poets, novelists, short story writers, playwrights, and philosophers of the period are frequently studied in high school and college literature courses. In organizing and reprinting the vast amount of critical material written on these authors, *TCLC* helps students develop valuable insight into literary history, promotes a better understanding of the texts, and sparks ideas for papers and assignments. Each entry in *TCLC* presents a comprehensive survey on an author's career or an individual work of literature and provides the user with a multiplicity of interpretations and assessments. Such variety allows students to pursue their own interests; furthermore, it fosters an awareness that literature is dynamic and responsive to many different opinions.

Every fourth volume of *TCLC* is devoted to literary topics. These topics widen the focus of the series from the individual authors to such broader subjects as literary movements, prominent themes in twentieth-century literature, literary reaction to political and historical events, significant eras in literary history, prominent literary anniversaries, and the literatures of cultures that are often overlooked by English-speaking readers.

TCLC is designed as a companion series to Gale's *Contemporary Literary Criticism,* (*CLC*) which reprints commentary on authors who died after 1999. Because of the different time periods under consideration, there is no duplication of material between *CLC* and *TCLC*.

Organization of the Book

A *TCLC* entry consists of the following elements:

■ The **Author Heading** cites the name under which the author most commonly wrote, followed by birth and death dates. Also located here are any name variations under which an author wrote, including transliterated forms for authors whose native languages use nonroman alphabets. If the author wrote consistently under a pseudonym, the pseudonym will be listed in the author heading and the author's actual name given in parenthesis on the first line of the biographical and critical information. Uncertain birth or death dates are indicated by question marks. Single-work entries are preceded by a heading that consists of the most common form of the title in English translation (if applicable) and the original date of composition.

■ A **Portrait of the Author** is included when available.

■ The **Introduction** contains background information that introduces the reader to the author, work, or topic that is the subject of the entry.

■ The list of **Principal Works** is ordered chronologically by date of first publication and lists the most important works by the author. The genre and publication date of each work is given. In the case of foreign authors whose works have been translated into English, the English-language version of the title follows in brackets. Unless otherwise indicated, dramas are dated by first performance, not first publication.

- Reprinted **Criticism** is arranged chronologically in each entry to provide a useful perspective on changes in critical evaluation over time. The critic's name and the date of composition or publication of the critical work are given at the beginning of each piece of criticism. Unsigned criticism is preceded by the title of the source in which it appeared. All titles by the author featured in the text are printed in boldface type. Footnotes are reprinted at the end of each essay or excerpt. In the case of excerpted criticism, only those footnotes that pertain to the excerpted texts are included.

- A complete **Bibliographical Citation** of the original essay or book precedes each piece of criticism.

- Critical essays are prefaced by brief **Annotations** explicating each piece.

- An annotated bibliography of **Further Reading** appears at the end of each entry and suggests resources for additional study. In some cases, significant essays for which the editors could not obtain reprint rights are included here. Boxed material following the further reading list provides references to other biographical and critical sources on the author in series published by Gale.

Indexes

A **Cumulative Author Index** lists all of the authors that appear in a wide variety of reference sources published by the Gale Group, including *TCLC*. A complete list of these sources is found facing the first page of the Author Index. The index also includes birth and death dates and cross references between pseudonyms and actual names.

A **Cumulative Nationality Index** lists all authors featured in *TCLC* by nationality, followed by the number of the *TCLC* volume in which their entry appears.

A **Cumulative Topic Index** lists the literary themes and topics treated in the series as well as in *Classical and Medieval Literature Criticism, Literature Criticism from 1400 to 1800, Nineteenth-Century Literature Criticism,* and the *Contemporary Literary Criticism* Yearbook, which was discontinued in 1998.

An alphabetical **Title Index** accompanies each volume of *TCLC*. Listings of titles by authors covered in the given volume are followed by the author's name and the corresponding page numbers where the titles are discussed. English translations of foreign titles and variations of titles are cross-referenced to the title under which a work was originally published. Titles of novels, dramas, nonfiction books, and poetry, short story, or essay collections are printed in italics, while individual poems, short stories, and essays are printed in roman type within quotation marks.

In response to numerous suggestions from librarians, Gale also produces an annual paperbound edition of the *TCLC* cumulative title index. This annual cumulation, which alphabetically lists all titles reviewed in the series, is available to all customers. Additional copies of this index are available upon request. Librarians and patrons will welcome this separate index; it saves shelf space, is easy to use, and is recyclable upon receipt of the next edition.

Citing *Twentieth-Century Literary Criticism*

When writing papers, students who quote directly from any volume in the Literary Criticism Series may use the following general format to footnote reprinted criticism. The first example pertains to material drawn from periodicals, the second to material reprinted from books.

George Orwell, "Reflections on Gandhi," *Partisan Review* 6 (Winter 1949): 85-92; reprinted in *Twentieth-Century Literary Criticism,* vol. 59, ed. Jennifer Gariepy (Detroit: The Gale Group, 1995), 40-3.

William H. Slavick, "Going to School to DuBose Heyward," *The Harlem Renaissance Re-examined,* ed. Victor A. Kramer (AMS, 1987), 65- 91; reprinted in *Twentieth-Century Literary Criticism,* vol. 59, ed. Jennifer Gariepy (Detroit: The Gale Group, 1995), 94-105.

Suggestions are Welcome

Readers who wish to suggest new features, topics, or authors to appear in future volumes, or who have other suggestions or comments are cordially invited to call, write, or fax the Project Editor:

Project Editor, Literary Criticism Series
The Gale Group
27500 Drake Road
Farmington Hills, MI 48331-3535
1-800-347-4253 (GALE)
Fax: 248-699-8054

Acknowledgments

The editors wish to thank the copyright holders of the criticism included in this volume and the permissions managers of many book and magazine publishing companies for assisting us in securing reproduction rights. We are also grateful to the staffs of the Detroit Public Library, the Library of Congress, the University of Detroit Mercy Library, Wayne State University Purdy/Kresge Library Complex, and the University of Michigan Libraries for making their resources available to us. Following is a list of the copyright holders who have granted us permission to reproduce material in this volume of *TCLC*. Every effort has been made to trace copyright, but if omissions have been made, please let us know.

COPYRIGHTED MATERIAL IN *TCLC*, VOLUME 125, WAS REPRODUCED FROM THE FOLLOWING PERIODICALS:

African American Review, v. 31, Summer, 1997 for review of "The Memphis Diary," by Gabrielle Forman. Reproduced by permission of the author.—*Anglia,* v. 112, 1994. Reproduced by permission.—*Annali d'Italianistica,* v. 15, 1997. Reproduced by permission.—*Black Scholar,* v. 24, Winter, 1994. Reproduced by permission.—*Canadian Forum,* v. 27, August, 1947 for "Italian Villages," by G. J. Wood. Reproduced by permission of the author.—*Christian Science Monitor,* v. 50, November 10, 1958. Reproduced by permission.—*The Commonweal,* v. 46, May 2, 1947; v. 54, August 10, 1951. Reproduced by permission.—*English Literature in Transition,* v. 31, 1988. Reproduced by permission.—*ETC: A Review of General Semantics,* v. 37, no. 4, Winter, 1980. Reproduced by permission of the International Society for General Semantics, Concord, California.—*Hudson Review,* v. 4, Autumn, 1951. Reproduced by permission.—*Italica,* v. 56, Summer, 1979; v. 72, Summer, 1995. Reproduced by permission.—*Journal of Humanistic Psychology,* v. 35, Fall, 1995 for "The Application of Rogerian Theory to Literary Study," by Samuel J. Sackett; v. 59, Winter, 1992 for "'Howards End' Revisited," by Alfred Kazin. © 1992 by Alfred Kazin. Reproduced by permission of Sage Publications and The Wylie Agency respectively.—*Modern Fiction Studies,* v. 10, Winter, 1964-65. Reproduced by permission.—*The Nation,* v. 164, May 24, 1947; v. 173, July 21, 1951; v. 194, June 2, 1962. Reproduced by permission.—*The New Republic,* v. 122, April 3, 1950; v. 125, July 30, 1951. Reproduced by permission —*New York Herald Tribune Book Review,* September 7, 1958; March 11, 1962. Reproduced by permission.—*Papers on Language and Literature,* v. 21, Summer, 1985. Southern Illinois University Board of Trustees. Reproduced by permission.—*Partisan Review,* v. 18, September-October, 1951 for "The Miraculous Ayme and Others," by Delmore Schwartz. Reproduced by permission of the author.—*Psychology Today,* v. 1, December, 1967. Reproduced by permission.—*Quarterly Journal of Speech,* v. 72, November, 1986 for "Style and Content in the Rhetoric of Early Afro-American Feminists," by Karlyn Kohrs Campbell. Reproduced by permission of the publisher and the author.—*Rhetoric Review,* v. 8, Sprint, 1990. Reproduced by permission.—*Rhetoric Society Quarterly,* v. 17, Winter, 1987. Reproduced by permission.—*Saturday Review of Literature,* v. 30, April 19, 1947; v. 33, February 25, 1950; v. 34, June 30, 1951. Reproduced by permission.—*The Saturday Review,* v. 41, September 6, 1958. Reproduced by permission.—*Style,* v. 31, Summer, 1997 for "'Only Connecting' with the Family: Class, Culture and Narrative Therapy in E. M. Forster's 'Howards End,'" by Kenneth Womack. Reproduced by permission of the publisher and the author.—*Texas Studies in Literature and Language,* 35:3, pp. 347-62, Fall, 1993 for "E. M. Forster's Prophetic Vision of the Modern Family in 'Howards End,'" by Jeane N. Olson. Copyright © 1993 by the University of Texas Press. All rights reserved. Reproduced by permission of the publisher and the author.—*Times Literary Supplement,* December 13, 1928. Reproduced by permission.—*Twentieth Century Literature,* v. 31, Summer-Fall, 1985; v. 45, Spring, 1999; v. 46, Fall, 2000. Reproduced by permission.—*The Writer,* v. 54, December, 1941; v. 63, November, 1950. Reproduced by permission.

COPYRIGHTED MATERIAL IN *TCLC*, VOLUME 125, WAS REPRODUCED FROM THE FOLLOWING BOOKS:

Born, Daniel. From "Private Garden, Public Swamps: 'Howards End' and the Revaluation of Liberal Guilt," in *The Birth of Liberal Guilt in the English Novel: Charles Dickens to H. G. Wells*. University of North Carolina Press, 1995. Copyright © 1995 by University of North Carolina Press. All rights reserved. Reproduced by permission of the publisher.—Braxton, Joanne M. From "Crusader for Justice: Ida B. Wells," in *Black Women Writing Autobiography: A Tradition within a Tradition* as it appears in *Black Women Writing Autobiography*. Temple University Press, 1989. Copyright © 1989 by Temple University Press. All rights reserved. Reproduced by permission of Temple University Press.—Daleski, H. M. From "'Howards End': Goblins and Rainbows," in *Unities: Studies in the English Novel*. University of Georgia Press,

PHOTOGRAPHS AND ILLUSTRATIONS APPEARING IN *TCLC*, VOLUME 125, WERE RECEIVED FROM THE FOLLOWING SOURCES:

Literary Criticism Series Advisory Board

The members of the Gale Group Literary Criticism Series Advisory Board—reference librarians and subject specialists from public, academic, and school library systems—represent a cross-section of our customer base and offer a variety of informed perspectives on both the presentation and content of our literature criticism products. Advisory board members assess and define such quality issues as the relevance, currency, and usefulness of the author coverage, critical content, and literary topics included in our series; evaluate the layout, presentation, and general quality of our printed volumes; provide feedback on the criteria used for selecting authors and topics covered in our series; provide suggestions for potential enhancements to our series; identify any gaps in our coverage of authors or literary topics, recommending authors or topics for inclusion; analyze the appropriateness of our content and presentation for various user audiences, such as high school students, undergraduates, graduate students, librarians, and educators; and offer feedback on any proposed changes/enhancements to our series. We wish to thank the following advisors for their advice throughout the year.

Bess Streeter Aldrich
1881-1954

(Also wrote as Margaret Dean Stevens) American novelist and short story writer.

INTRODUCTION

Best known for her novels set in the early settlement days of the American Midwest, Aldrich has been honored for her realistic portrayals of the American pioneering experience. Used often as supplemental reading in American history classes, Aldrich's novels and short stories are driven by their characters, many of them strong, fearless, and hardworking women. Her stories of pioneers were inspired by the experiences of both her mother's and father's pioneer families and are set in the prairies of the Midwest. Aldrich took special care to acknowledge the strength, hardiness, and loving sacrifices of pioneer women, and her protagonists are usually female paragons for whom family is of the highest importance.

BIOGRAPHICAL INFORMATION

Born in Cedar Falls, Iowa, in 1881, Aldrich's family had a history of pioneering. Her grandparents, whose stories appear in her books, traveled with their families from Illinois to settle in Iowa when it was still a wilderness. Aldrich began to write at an early age, and at fourteen won a camera in a short-story contest. She earned her first writer's fee at the age of seventeen when the *Baltimore News* bought one of her short stories for five dollars. After training as a teacher at Iowa State Teachers College, Aldrich taught in high school and college for several years before her marriage, writing articles for teachers' magazines and short stories under the name of Margaret Dean Stevens.

In 1907 she married Charles Aldrich, and they moved to Nebraska. Her husband encouraged her to write under her married name, and she did so, publishing her first collection of short stories, *Mother Mason*, in 1924 and her first novel, *The Rim of the Prairie*, in 1925. Her husband died suddenly of a heart attack in 1925 when the youngest of their four children was four years old. Subsequently, Aldrich supported her family with her writing, publishing a book every two years and writing a total of 168 short stories. From 1930 she also served as book editor for the *Christian Herald*. She died of cancer in 1954 at the age of seventy-four. After her death, the street in Lincoln, Nebraska, where she had lived was renamed Aldrich Road in

her honor. A greater posthumous honor came in 1973 when she became the seventh person inducted into the Nebraska Hall of Fame.

MAJOR WORKS

Aldrich's most famous book, *A Lantern in Her Hand* (1928), became a worldwide best seller. It was written to honor her mother, embodied in the central character, and is based on stories Aldrich heard as a child from her parents, grandparents, aunts, and uncles, and stories sent to her by others who had experienced the pioneer life. Its sequel, *A White Bird Flying* (1931), was one of the three top-selling books of the year, along with Willa Cather's *Shadows of the Rocks* and Pearl Buck's *The Good Earth*. *Miss Bishop* (1933), about a spinster teacher who devotes her life to her family and her students, was made into a film, *Cheers for Miss Bishop*, in 1941. Aldrich's last novel, *The Lieutenant's Lady* (1942), was based on the diaries of an army officer and his wife and also became a best seller.

Many of Aldrich's books are collections of her short stories. *Mother Mason* and *The Cutters* (1926) contain series of stories about pioneer families. Others, such as *The Man Who Caught the Weather* (1936) and *Journey into Christmas* (1949), are collections of stories first published in various periodicals.

CRITICAL RECEPTION

Aldrich's novels and short stories were extremely popular during the 1940s and 1950s, and her work was in much demand by periodicals such as *Woman's Home Companion, McCall's, Cosmopolitan, Good Housekeeping, Saturday Evening Post, Collier's,* and *Harper's Weekly*. Although her writing was not critically acclaimed for its artistry, she enjoyed a wide readership who loved her simple, sentimental stories about hope and struggle, hardship and romance. She sold every story she wrote, although some of them were rejected many times before their sale. Her work was considered wholesome, uplifting, and cheerful, reflecting her personal attitude about life, but while she wrote of love and personal sacrifice, she avoided the subjects of sexual passion and the sordid and seamy aspects of humanity. Her work has been faulted for this, and for her insistence that marriage, family, and the rearing of children is woman's highest and most satisfying calling. These ideals were, however, those that she believed in firmly and exhibited in her own life.

PRINCIPAL WORKS

Mother Mason (short stories) 1924
The Rim of the Prairie (novel) 1925
The Cutters (short stories) 1926
A Lantern in Her Hand (novel) 1928
A White Bird Flying (novel) 1931
Miss Bishop (novel) 1933
Spring Came On Forever (novel) 1935
The Man Who Caught the Weather (short stories) 1936
Song of Years (novel) 1939
The Drum Goes Dead (short stories) 1941
The Lieutenant's Lady (novel) 1942
Journey into Christmas and Other Stories (short stories) 1949
The Bess Streeter Aldrich Reader (short stories) 1950
A Bess Streeter Aldrich Treasury (short stories) 1959
Across the Smiling Meadow and Other Stories (short stories) 1984
The Home-Coming and Other Stories (short stories) 1984

CRITICISM

Times Literary Supplement (review date 13 December 1928)

SOURCE: Review of *A Lantern in Her Hand,* by Bess Streeter Aldrich. *Times Literary Supplement* (13 December 1928): 992.

[*In the following brief review of* A Lantern in Her Hand, *the critic notes the novel's "absorbing interest."*]

There is imaginative power in this story [*A Lantern in Her Hand*] of pioneering days in Iowa and Nebraska, and even the most homely and trivial happenings in the eighty years of Abbie Deal's life are so dramatically treated as to give the chronicle of her struggle against an adverse destiny an absorbing interest. Abbie herself is a memorable figure, with her sturdy loyalty and romantic longings, the heritage of her aristocratic Scotch and peasant Irish ancestors. Jolting in the covered wagon as it made its slow advance westward over the prairies from the little village of Chicago, the child Abbie listened avidly to her sister's oft-told tale of the lovely lady, Isabelle Anders-Mackenzie. All through her maidenhood the legend of Isabelle, made concrete in the shape of a string of pearls, a family heirloom, acted as a beacon to Abbie's thoughts of fame as singer, writer, or painter. When she was nineteen, just after the Civil War, Abbie refused a chance of going to New York and married Will Deal. The Deals took the trail westward from Cedar Falls to the young State of Nebraska, where Abbie reared her six children with indomitable courage through all the hard years of famine and drought, grass-hopper plagues and snow, until the determination of the early settlers bore its fruit in rolling miles of rich cornland and wealthy cities.

Bess Streeter Aldrich (essay date December 1941)

SOURCE: Aldrich, Bess Streeter. "The Story Germ." *The Writer* 54, no. 12 (December 1941): 355-7.

[*In the following essay, Aldrich illustrates how to build character and a story line by describing how she created Miss Bishop.*]

Several times in the past years your editor has asked me to contribute an article and each time I have been too busy, or thought I was, which is nearly the same thing. This morning another pleasant request has arrived and in the same mail a letter from a young woman with that old query: "Can you help a beginning writer? Where do you get your ideas? How can . . . ?" etc., etc. I wouldn't go so far as to say it is the hand of Fate, but the simultaneous arrival of the two causes me to put aside the desk work of the moment and do that article for *The Writer.*

Now I have written and sold about one hundred and sixty short stories and have had ten books published with their by-products of serialization, syndication, English sales, foreign translations, plays, and a movie or two. But I still do not know just how to go about helping a young person in his own story writing. It is the greatest lone-wolf profession in the whole category.

One of my sons, home from the University for vacation, is at this moment across the hall in his room engaged in the throes of evolving a story. Brought up in the writing atmosphere of our home, he expects no help but maternal encouragement. If he has not gained anything from his mother about actual construction, he has learned how to do his work diligently, to rely upon himself, and to take those frequent and sickening doses of rejection slips with something approaching equanimity.

"Where do you get your ideas?" the correspondent queries.

Another young person interviewing me once, asked: "When you are writing one story and another just clamors to be told at the same time, what do you do?" With compassion I eyed her and with patience I answered: "Oh, but they never clamor. If I had two ideas at the same time or ever a few weeks apart, I would think it too good to be true."

Fresh ideas do not flock to a writer's head (not to *this* head) like birds to a martin house. One has to labor very hard to catch them. No doubt there are writers who see themes and plots so clearly that they do not have to put the strain on themselves which some of us do. A few times, but so few that they are almost negligible, I have visioned the skeleton of a story in its entirety or have been haunted by some theme which would not down. For those few times I have thanked the gods and hastily sketched the outlines of the stories. But for the most part I have worked hard, walking the floor at times as one would in physical pain, trying to get hold of an idea which would only elude me. Because I know so well in what labor most stories are written, I discount the sincerity of nine out of ten people who say they want to become a writer more than anything in the world. What they want is the satisfaction of seeing their stuff in print, the checks, and that bit of prestige which curiously attaches itself to anyone associated with the business. But they would not want to pay the price,—to spend hours of writing only to tear the story to pieces, or to bear all the early disappointments so familiar to those of us who have come up the hard and slippery way.

Back to the question,—how may we get story ideas when they refuse to present themselves to us as well-defined plots? *By putting intensive thought upon a small idea which, in its tiny form and limited feeling, has not enough substance for a story.*

Personally, I have found that whenever I am emotionally disturbed, there is the germ of a story in that disturbance,—but *only a germ.* Which means, given the cause of that disturbance for a beginning idea, I must work on it, change it, add to it, until the final story may be very far removed from the original nucleus.

If I am moved to laughter over the naive actions of an adolescent, a funny experience of a friend, an item in the newspaper, there is reason to believe that I can draw a smile from my readers with any of those episodes from which to plan. If I feel a suspicious moisture in my left eye over some small happening, there is reason to think I may be able to draw a surreptitious tear from some reader's eye with that bit of an anecdote upon which to work. And *work* is the word, not just a passive attitude, hoping that the story will inspirationally write itself.

Now, a concrete example: I open a newspaper from my old home town and see the headlines: OLD BUILDING TO BE RAZED. WORK BEGINS JUNE FIRST. And, because the editor is an alumnus of the school in question, there is a sentimental third line: GOOD-BYE TO OLD CENTRAL.

I am emotionally disturbed. It brings back a flood of youthful memories and a certain tender regret that the old building is to stand there among the trees no more. After June, the only thing remaining of the rambling brick building will be the memory of it in the minds and hearts of hundreds of men and women. And then, with an eye to business, I begin to wonder how I can work out a story from that uncomplicated emotion of regret at knowing the old building is to be torn down. For the tearing down of a condemned building is not a story nor the son of a story. It

is only an incident. And a story must be more than an incident. It must have people in it, real people with hopes and fears. It must have life and color and movement. It must give forth odors and sounds. And something must happen, something to hold the interest or stir the blood, to bring that laughter or that tear.

So I begin the process of fumbling in the dark, putting out tentacles, as it were, from that center of my emotion.

I reason: If I am disturbed, countless other old students will be moved, too. Old teachers, also. I begin to recall some of those instructors, especially those who gave so much of themselves to their students. I'll do the story of a teacher—one who saw the opening of the college and lived through its growth—who will be there at the end of the old building as she was at the beginning. And now I have left the world of reality and slipped into the world of fancy, for my teacher is not to be any particular one but a fictitious person whose characteristics shall embody something from them all. Soon I have named her so that she may seem more real to me. I decide on "Miss Bishop," and some old-fashioned first name,—Ella. That suits her, for living in the seventies,—"Ella Bishop."

This Ella Bishop is becoming very real, so that I understand how lonely and sad she is in her old age without much to show in a material way for all her good works. A new president of the college will ask her to resign. If she is to be pictured as sad and lonely and hurt over the loss of her position, she ought at some time in the story to be quite the opposite, for the greatest characteristic of drama is contrast. And all contrast has a touch of the dramatic in it. The contrasting activities of "Dr. Jekyll" and "Mr. Hyde"—of "Faust" and "Mephistopheles"—of "Jesus" and "Judas"—these are the things of which drama is made. I ponder over the question of what can be done for contrast. The old students must rally to her. They must give her one exalted hour, one evening of adulation. It shall be in the old building itself, the night before it is to be torn down. A satisfactory climax: The alumni coming back to pay her homage—the old building's last appearance—and Ella Bishop's supreme moment after despair.

Perhaps I have not yet written a word, only visualized a woman and a situation. But the climax is there, a point toward which I can now work. I go back to pick up the threads of her life. Why did she never marry? Was her life always as barren as it must appear to the modern student? All this to be worked out, and research to be done for the accuracy of a midwestern college background in its evolution. (This latter, a very exacting phase of story writing, but not under discussion here.)

By this time I am writing,—much of the climax first so that later I may work toward it. Ella Bishop has grown as familiar to me as my next door neighbor. To live the lives of his characters, crawling into their very skins, is the writer's prerogative, almost his duty. He must be an actor,—an actor who plays all the parts.

Enough of detailed description. **Miss Bishop** went on the best seller list several years ago and on the screen this year through a fine interpretation of the actress, Martha Scott,—a story and a photoplay which had their beginnings in a very small germ, the momentary emotion caused by reading a headline: OLD BUILDING TO BE RAZED.

I hope this has not sounded pedantic. There are other ways to develop a story. This one is mine. And while there is very little which an older writer can do to help a beginner (for each one must "gae his ain gait," as my Scotch mother used to say) there is always the chance that the telling of a personal experience or the explaining of an individual method will find its interested young reader.

Bess Streeter Aldrich (essay date November 1950)

SOURCE: Aldrich, Bess Streeter. "Working Backward." *Writer* 63 (November 1950): 350-53.

[*In the following essay, Aldrich uses her story "Journey into Christmas" to show how she builds a story and characters.*]

A number of years ago I wrote an article for *The Writer* titled **"The Story Germ."** Several young writers were kind enough to tell me it was helpful to them. In that article I stressed the point that plots for stories seldom come to one in their entirety, but that, given some small situation or dramatic moment or distinctive human trait, one can work out a story based on that little happening or emotional period or outstanding characteristic.

With the editor asking for another article I can think of nothing more practical than to follow that lead with a detailed account of how one can work backward in developing a short story. Any similarity between this article and the former will harm no one, for those who read the other, written so long ago, no doubt have become sure-fire authors by this time or have given up the literary ghost.

People who have had no experience in writing often hold the idea that turning out a story must be the easiest thing in the world. A story reads smoothly. The people in it seem natural. Events move forward in regular and interesting sequence. It comes to a surprising or satisfactory climax. And there you are. Nothing could be easier. Or so they think. But they do not know with what knitting of brows, chewing of pencils and discarding of wordage that easily read story is constructed. For more often than not, it is the outgrowth of some little happening, too small in itself to constitute a whole story, which has become one after intensive work.

Over many years of writing I have evolved two methods for the development of short stories. For a character story—one which stresses the person rather than the plot—I begin by getting mentally acquainted with that fictitious character, dwelling on his appearance, traits, mental processes and emotional reactions, until he takes upon himself the semblance of such reality that automatically he moves into action. In this way *The Man Who Caught the Weather* was constructed; a story which was rejected by twenty-eight magazines before it was purchased by the old *Century Magazine*. It was chosen for the O. Henry Award volume of that year, has been used in several anthologies, syndicated, resold to a British magazine and read on various radio story hours. I insert that item for the benefit of young writers who lose their courage over a second or third rejection and who, like the ship wrecked brother, "hearing, may take heart again."

The second method—which is the line this little article is taking—is the constructing of a story from some dramatic incident or interesting contrast between two settings or ideas, and working backward from that point. With fine disregard for the law of gravity, I start with the capstone of the structure, slip another stone under it, and another one under that, until solid ground is reached.

Naturally the story which I shall use as an illustration should be read in its entirety if a detailed analysis is to be understood. It was in the 1948 Christmas number of *The Saturday Evening Post* and titled **"Star across the Tracks."** Also it is to be found in my book *Journey into Christmas,* a compilation of short stories. Bearing down heavily on the Christmas atmosphere, it has the simplest of plots, but even so, it entailed a great deal of planning, for the little plot grew out of a mere setting upon which this backward method was used.

Very briefly, the story is this: An old day laborer is the yard man for three families who live in a fine residential district of a midwestern city in which there is a city-wide contest for the best outdoor Christmas decorations. The old man assists his three families in putting up their elaborate decorations, but wins the first prize himself with a simple nativity scene at his own little home across the tracks.

The origin of the story was this: On a Christmas night we were taking one of my sons to his train after his holiday visit with us. Our city had gone in extensively for outdoor decorations and as we drove from our suburban section we passed any number of elaborately decorated yards. There were lights in brilliant landscaping effects, picturesque Santa Clauses, and life-sized reindeer, expansive and expensive. At the station we found the train had changed time, and there would be quite a wait, but not long enough to drive back home. It was a mild evening, in contrast to some of our midwestern holiday weather, and we drove leisurely through a section of town beyond the station where the Christmas touch was evident, if on a less extravagant scale. Then we came to it: a hayfilled manger, evidently made from packing-boxes, by the side of a small cottage, a white-robed figure bending over it and lighted with a single faint glow.

The son, who was a young newspaperman, said: "There's a story for you, Mother. That's right up your alley . . . elaborate decorations up town and this little manger scene here across the tracks."

Now any incident which brings laughter or tears, or which calls forth one's sympathy, anger, admiration, in fact, anything which touches the emotions has the germ of a story in it. The sight of the crude manger and the white pasteboard figure here by the little house, far away from those brilliantly lighted ones, touched us all. And I knew, as my son had suggested, there *was* a story in it waiting to be developed if it could be worked out.

But a story is more than a scene and more than the contrast between two settings. There is nothing static about it. Something must happen. Characters must come to life. People must live and move across the pages of the magazine so that the reader lives and moves with them. A few days later I was starting the mental machinery by which a story could be evolved from the small germ of that little manger across the tracks. *And working backward.*

In other words, the climax was to be that the simple scene by the cottage would win a citywide first prize away from all that uptown splurge. But as almost all stories change from fact into fancy, even though based on reality, instead of the mere manger of boxes, I find myself visualizing a shed with open front to the street, a cow and team of horses munching on the hay, pigeons fluttering on the roof, a star overhead, and the Babe and Mother in that stable setting. (Immediately I am thinking this is a bit incongruous in a city which prohibits stock in its limits, so make a note to state casually, early in the story, that this is the only section where stock can be kept.)

Now, the people who live there—in the story, of course—who are they? What do they do? Some old man and his wife, hard working and obviously with a religious trend. Almost at once I have named them: *Mr. Harm Kurtz* and his wife. Pa Kurtz and Mamma. For fictitious characters immediately named come more readily to life. The rest of the family, if any, stays vague, for I may want to create characters to fit the story needs.

Mr. Kurtz will be a day laborer. Why not connect him in some way with one of those big highly decorated homes? At once he becomes the yard man for three of the well-to-do families, and they are named, too, so they will begin to seem real: the Scotts, the Dillinghams and the Porters. I see them in their homes with Pa Kurtz helping to put up all those brilliant lights, then see Pa going home to his small house across the tracks on an unpaved street, telling the day's happenings to Mamma and fixing up his own shed, with its cow and horses, for the nativity scene. But something there doesn't ring true,—the incongruity of Pa

Kurtz, tired to death of the whole thing, coming home and entering into the decorative contest. No, it will be Mamma with the religious bent who arranges the stable scene.

And here is a knotty problem: our midwestern climate so cold at times, and a shed for stock standing open toward the street? One can't state an incongruity and let it go at that, if one's stories are to ring true. Each step must be the natural outgrowth of that which has gone before. So for some reason the one side of the shed has to come off temporarily. Why not have Pa Kurtz yank off the boards in anger? Mamma has chided him for the old shed looking so decrepit. She is expecting Christmas company and her pride will be hurt. Immediately, I am creating a daughter coming home with her little boys, and Mamma is saying: "Just as plain as I'm standing here I can remember your telling Carrie you'd have the new lumber on that old shed by next time she comes." At that, Pa flares up with: "I'll have that new lumber on by the time Carrie comes if it's the last thing I do." And he begins yanking off the siding, exposing the manger, the cow, the horses, the hay. That problem over, I'm trying to think what can be used for the Mother Mary. A mannikin from a store would be just right, but one doesn't simply go into a house and bring out a mannikin.

I digress here to say that nothing is so irritating in a story as the parenthetical statement. As a judge for one of the monthly reading club's books, I recently read a submitted manuscript which was rather good, had it not been for that amateurish dragging in by the hair of the head, so to speak, of properties and people which never had been presented to the reader until the moment they became useful. So, to have a mannikin handily in the house, I create another daughter, Lillie, who works in a department store, and immediately the store belongs to one of those well-to-do families, thus making the little plot more compact.

In order that it will not escape me, I write that part at once, even though the story is not under construction. "Lillie was a whiz with the needle. She made her own dresses at home and tried them on Maisie the mannikin. That was one of the store's moronic-looking models which had lost an arm and sundry other features and Lillie had asked for it when she found they were going to discard it. Now she hung her own skirts on Maisie to get their length. That was about all the good the mannikin did her, for Lillie's circumference was fully three times that of the model."

So, early in the story I plant the mannikin and when the time comes for Mamma to want something for the figure of the Madonna, there is no incongruous break.

There must be a star above the shed, and because Pa is only a grouchy onlooker, not entering into the decorative scheme at all, I create a son, Ernie, who is a mechanic. Lillie says to him: "Mamma wants you to fix a star up over the stable. Mrs. Dillingham gave an old one to Pa." I am writing this also before starting the real construction of the story: "Ernie had been a fixer ever since he was a little boy. Not for his looks had the River City Body and Fender Wreck Company hired Ernie Kurtz. So, after his warmed over supper, he got his tools and a coil of wire and fixed the yellow bauble high over the stable, the wire and the slim rod almost invisible, so that it seemed a star hung there by itself."

And now I have the causes and effects of several movements in the story to come: Pa home from helping with all those elaborate decorations . . . Mamma chiding him about the dilapidated shed . . . his yanking off the boards in anger . . . Mamma seeing how like the Bethlehem scene the old stable looks . . . going into the house to get Lillie's mannikin, draping it with sheets into the form of the Mother Mary, saying: "I ain't doin' this for show like Pa's families he's been helpin'. I'm doin' it for Carrie's little boys. Something they can see when they drive in . . . something they'll never forget, like's not, as long as they live."

This much will suffice to show the working backward method sometimes used by writers. By working that way I have created a substantial reason for every stone which is going into the structure. Now I can begin to work from the first, putting in the atmospheric descriptive matter, conversation, all the human touches a story needs: the arrival of the children for Christmas . . . the drive up through the fine residential sections of town . . . the family's utter enjoyment of the elaborate lighting effects there, with no thought that their own scene is more effective . . . their wagering among themselves as to which of the big houses will get the prize . . . hearing over the radio the next day that their own has won it . . . the hundreds of cars driving down the little unpaved street on Christmas night . . . the open shed . . . the horses pulling at the hay . . . the cow gazing moodily into space . . . the pigeons on the ridgepole in a long feathery group . . . white Mary bending over the manger . . . and overhead the star.

And then to end on some substantial Christmas thought. With Mamma asking Pa why he can't get to sleep and his saying: "Keep thinkin' of everything. All that prize money comin' to us. Attention from so many folks. Children all home. Folks I work for all here and not a bit mad. You'd think I'd feel good. But I don't. Somethin' hangs over me. Like they'd been somebody real out there in the shed all this time. Like we'd been leavin' 'em stay out there when we ought to had 'em come in. Fool notion . . . but keeps botherin' me."

And then Mamma gave her answer. Comforting, too, just as he knew it would be. "I got the same feelin'. I guess people's been like that ever since it happened. Their consciences always hurtin' 'em a little because there wasn't no room for Him in the inn."

This resumé of the constructing of a story plot has been written for beginning writers, as experienced ones will have worked out their own methods. There is little enough one can do to assist another in the writing line, for it is a lone wolf business if ever there was one. But sometimes a frank personal experience from one who has been at work in it for a long time will strike a helpful note. I know, for thirty-five years ago I was a beginner, avidly searching for all the helps in constructing, and advice for short cuts I could read. Occasionally I ran across some of the helps. But never a short cut could I find.

Abigail Ann Martin (essay date 1992)

SOURCE: Martin, Abigail Ann. "Bess Streeter Aldrich." In *Bess Streeter Aldrich*, pp. 5-41. Boise, Idaho: Boise State University, 1992.

[*In the following essay, Martin provides a critical discussion of Aldrich's major works.*]

"Nebraska," wrote Bess Streeter Aldrich, "is only the state of my adoption, but I am sure that I feel all the loyalty for it which the native-born bears . . . while I am not a native Nebraskan, the blood of the midwestern pioneer runs in my veins and I come rightly by my love for the Nebraska pioneer and admiration for the courage and fortitude which he displayed in the early days of the state's history . . ." (Introduction to *The Rim of the Prairie*).

Certainly both love and admiration are apparent in Aldrich's finest work, *A Lantern in Her Hand* (1928). This novel alone is enough to give her a place among distinguished writers of the American West. Her feeling for—and appreciation of—the Midwest shine out in much of her other fiction, but primarily it is for *Lantern* that she is to be honored. Few other writers have presented so detailed and vivid a picture of pioneer life.

Born on 17 February 1881, in Cedar Falls, Iowa, she was the daughter of James Wareham and Mary Anderson Streeter. Her childhood as the youngest of a large and lively family was a happy one, and during her impressionable years she was imbued with the values and mores of small-town life, values and mores which greatly influenced her writing. From her numerous aunts and uncles she often heard tales of life in pioneering days, for both her parents had, in their youth, come to Iowa from "the East." Her parental grandfather, Zimri Streeter, had been a member of the Iowa Territorial Legislature, his salty character making him a prominent figure among his colleagues.

Educated in the public schools of Cedar Falls, she went on to Iowa State Teachers College in the same town, graduating in 1901. For five years she taught primary grades in Boone and Marshalltown, Iowa, and in Salt Lake City, Utah, and for a short time she was assistant supervisor of the primary training school at Iowa State Teachers College.

In September 1907 she married Charles S. Aldrich, banker and attorney of Tipton, Iowa, where the couple lived until after the birth of their first child, Mary Eleanor, in 1909, when the family moved to Elmwood, Nebraska. Here Aldrich's husband became cashier of the American Exchange Bank, and here the three Aldrich sons were born: James, Charles, and Robert. Here too Charles Aldrich, husband and father, died suddenly on 5 May 1925. And here Aldrich's literary career began in earnest.

She had been writing from an early age. At fourteen she sold a children's story to the Chicago *Record* and received a five-dollar camera as a prize. At seventeen, hearing that the Baltimore *News* was paying five dollars for stories, she wrote a love story, received the five dollars, and promptly spent it for a black chiffon parasol!

For some years she had been producing articles for teachers' magazines, stories for young children, and a goodly number of short stories for the *American Magazine* and *The Ladies Home Journal*. Her story **"The Little House Next Door"** won a prize of $175 offered in 1911 by the latter magazine. Two collections of magazine stories had been published as well as a novel, *The Rim of the Prairie* (1925).

All this success had been pleasant, of course, but not economically necessary. Her husband's death gave her the impetus to make money, and producing fiction thus became her life work.

This work flourished in the midst of her growing children and their activities, interrupted often by household tasks and emergencies. She is quoted as answering a query about housekeeping: "Three huge meals three times a day for a girl and three boys with the largest appetites in the world. I could take a prize for patching at the county fair" (Marble 10).

Again, she remarks, "I have written with three babies tumbling over my feet, with a house of paperdolls under my desk and their five-year-old owner demonstrating a cyclone with them, with one eye on a cooking meal and the other on the story in hand, with grammar grade boys making kites and bows and arrows around me" (Marble 5).

Beginning under such conditions—and persisting—Aldrich in the end produced 160 short stories and seven novels. Some of this fiction has been serialized, syndicated, sold in England, and translated into Dutch, Danish, Hungarian, Swedish, Spanish, and French. All of her books have been published in Braille.

Aldrich's novels and stories obviously grew out of her background, her environment, her circumstances. And because they all bear the decided impress of her Midwestern life they are worth examining and evaluating. Both the strengths and the weaknesses of her fiction have regional overtones.

Near the end of her first novel, *The Rim of the Prairie,* she describes the way one of the characters writes of the Midwest. Here she seems to be expressing her own credo: "Warner Field writes of the mid-west. He does not credit it with having in its air either the crispness of the mountains or the salt tang of the sea . . . nor will he discredit the sorcery of the odors of loam and sod and subsoil, of dewy clover, and ripening corn and the honey-sweetness of lavender alfalfa. He does not pretend that it is idyllic . . . nor will he speak of it as bleak and uninteresting. He does not assert that it has attained to great heights of culture and art . . . nor will he sell it for thirty pieces of silver. But in some way Warner Field catches in his writings the gleam of the soul of the wide prairie, dim and deep and mysterious. For here, as everywhere, drama ebbs and flows like the billowing of the seas of yellow wheat" (351-52).

In the wider perspective of history, Bess Streeter Aldrich will be remembered for her pioneer fiction—four novels and several short stories that tell of the settling of the Midwest. Actually, her first real prominence as a writer came with the publication of *A Lantern in Her Hand* (1928). Those critics are unperceptive who say it was something of an anomaly, this novel about struggling "dirt farmers" that was published in the roaring twenties when flaming youth, bootlegging, and a kind of shrill prosperity dominated the scene. They overlook society's always undiminished interest in its beginnings, in its own local (or national) development.

This interest Aldrich exploited in ways both innocent and clever. It was innocent because, as she said somewhere, she simply wanted to honor the pioneer women who, as her own mother had, had come to a raw country, lived through appalling hardships and poverty, and had never lost their buoyancy of spirit or their sense of values.

On the other hand she was clever. She was careful to research her material meticulously, making use of bona fide records, papers, anecdotes. As a result the novel is richly detailed and true.

On the very first page of *Lantern* the reader is caught up in the story and senses its authenticity. More, the book is infused with Aldrich's warm admiration for the pioneers who, because of almost unbelievable labor, and in the face of devastating frustrations, disappointments, and suffering, settled one of the richest and most productive states of the union.

Her admiration is not only, or even principally, for their strength and perseverance; it is for their unfaltering courage. The note is struck in Joyce Kilmer's verse from which the novel's title is taken:

> Because the road was steep and long,
> And through a dark and lonely land,
> God set upon my lips a song
> And put a lantern in my hand.

The central figure in the book is Abbie Deal, born Mackenzie, whom the reader meets at the age of eight, just coming to Iowa from the East with her widowed mother and her brothers and sisters. The story takes Abbie swiftly through her growing-up years, her emergence as an exquisite young woman with a delightful voice and a dreamy imagination, to her courtship by sturdy Will Deal, and their marriage.

Sometime after the birth of their first child, a son, when she is pregnant with her second child, Abbie learns that Will is eager to go west to the new territory, Nebraska. By "homesteading" he can acquire a fine profitable farm. All it will require is work, and he is suited to that. For Abbie it requires more than work: it requires courage. The land they are going to is new—and lonely. There will be just a handful of people making a settlement. And these people, destined to be her only neighbors and friends, are as yet strangers. She must leave all that she cares for and venture into who knows what perils. (Childbirth will be completely without medical assistance, or even the aid of her own mother and sister.) There will be no school, no church, no stores, no newspaper.

There is as yet no house for them, of course, nor for their few animals. Shelters will have to be hastily constructed of sod, for the country has no stones for building, and for wood only such trees as grow along the small stream near which they will live.

Very little is there to protect them when the bitter winter comes, when raging winds sweep unimpeded over the prairies, and fierce snows make the country blinding and treacherous. In the summers there will be brutal heat, the sun pouring its terrible radiance down through air as clear and dry as glass. There will be crops destroyed in an hour by drought or by insects; there will be, at times, the debilitating lack of ordinary decencies: even sufficient soap, even the most rudimentary things beloved by women— fabrics for sewing, little toys for their children.

There will be moments when life will cease to be worth living, when the fatigue of each day seems to yield nothing in the way of progress or prosperity. And for a long, long time there will be overwhelming nostalgia, the craving of a tender, affectionate heart for her own people, for her familiar surroundings.

All this is shown in Aldrich's lengthy novel. As the narrative of one woman and her family in pioneer conditions, *Lantern* is complete.

Thus it is much more than the story of one woman. It is a piece of social history, showing how Nebraska, and in particular one town, grew through the years. Interesting statistics help give the aura of authenticity referred to above. For instance, Will Deal buys "railroad land" at $2.00 an acre in 1868, when Nebraska had been a state just under a year. The town which he and Abbie and a few other families found is located "35 miles from Nebraska City, and ten miles from Weeping Water." At this time Omaha has a population of 15,000, and contains eleven churchs, five schools, five banks, five breweries, sixty saloons, and a

hoop factory. Lincoln had just been designated the state capital, a place, Abbie says, which is "away out on the prairie with just two or three log houses."

Abbie and Will endure a great many crises and hard times. They know what it is to have crop failures: the land is rich and good, but often rain is scanty. In an effort to increase moisture-retention, they drive to Nebraska City to get cottonwood seedlings to plant. Will never loses his faith in the land, and Abbie, worn with work and childbearing and discouragement, stands by him.

Eventually, of course, times improve, and those settlers who have "stuck it out" live to see their state flourish, with fine modern cities and universities and many cultural amenities. Abbie and Will rear children who are a credit to them: a prosperous banker, a successful lawyer, a prominent singer, a university professor. Their oldest daughter marries a physician who becomes one of Lincoln's most distinguished doctors. Through everything the two keep their love for each other and for the land.

In a way—and surely intentionally—Aldrich makes the Deals to stand as symbols of the pioneer spirit that has made her adoptive state great. Abbie is "Everywoman"— that is, the archetype of the pioneer mother whose tired and ravaged body contains the living spirit of enterprising courage and will.

Spring Came on Forever (1935), though not as sweeping in scope as *Lantern*, is also a graphic presentation of frontier life. Here the pioneers are German, leaving Illinois for Nebraska, enduring all the hardships of settling on a raw, untamed land. And, of course, becoming prosperous. There is the blizzard of 1888, the devastating flood of the early 1930s. There are setbacks and grim, unrelenting labor. But there is an undisturbed, a profound, feeling for the land.

The story itself is uncomplicated. Matthias Meier, a hearty young blacksmith, goes into the new land, makes his way brilliantly, and ends up wealthy and respected. As a young man he falls in love with Amalia Stolz, whose overbearing father forbids their marriage. She must become the wife of a coarse, hardworking man, and she ends up a tiny, shrivelled-up woman with very little to show for a life of pitiless toil and privation. Somehow Neal and Hazel, descendants of Matthias and Amalia, meet and fall in love. When they marry they elect to stay on the land, because the love of it is part of their lives.

The title is taken from Vachel Lindsay's poem "The Chinese Nightingale."

> Who shall end my dream's confusion?
> Life is a loom, weaving illusion . . .
> One thing I remember:
> Spring came on forever . . .

Song of Years (1938-39) also tells of pioneer days. This long and lively tale concerns the ebullient Martin family: the father, Jeremiah; the mother, Sarah; their two sons and seven daughters; and their friends. They are early settlers in Iowa, and the story presents an excellent picture of life in the young country beginning in June 1854 and ending just after the Civil War.

The colorful detailed narrative describes the girls' love affairs (especially that of Suzanne). These are full of incident, for the Martin daughters are given to coquetry. More important, the book gives a clear picture of the impact of the Civil War on the everyday life of the little settlement. Because coffee is a dollar a pound, women try many substitutes: these range from rye, wheat, and bran mixed with molasses to sweet potatoes chipped and browned in sugar. Gold and silver suddenly disappear; "money" becomes printed paper, little slips worth ten, fifteen, twenty-five, or fifty cents. The whole is a vivid picture of the settling of the Midwest, obviously modelled on the reminiscences of Aldrich's grandparents.

Then in 1942 when the country was at war, Aldrich published a "pioneer" novel quite different from the three previously described. *The Lieutenant's Lady* tells of the life (full of hardships, danger—and a bit of glamour) lived by the wife of an Army officer. This is, Aldrich explains on the first page, a "fictionalized version of a real diary," and the reader is led to see that the diary tells a complete story.

Linnie Campbell journeys from New York to Omaha in the 1860s, and Omaha, at the time the territorial capital of Nebraska, was, to put it simply, a very primitive place: "Already the young town had begun to put on airs by denying the privilege of stacking hay in the streets and passing an ordinance that any hogs found running loose were to be impounded and sold." The fight to change Nebraska's status from territory to state is told in detail, followed by a description of the dissension over the location of the state capital. Those who wanted it out on the prairie and those who wanted it named Lincoln were finally victorious, but the struggle was long and bitter.

Linnie and Lieutenant Norman Stafford are married after some rather interesting complications, and they go to live at Fort Berthold, in Dakota Territory, and later at Camp Cook in Montana Territory. Conditions of army post living are described vividly: the loneliness, the ever-present fear of Indian uprisings, and the lack of cultural amenities. (Linnie sets up a little school for the children of personnel.)

Hardships abound (as in any pioneer living), but Linnie and Norman never lose spirit and courage and pride of country. Norman remains a career Army man all his life, and Linnie goes with him faithfully as he is moved about. In very trying circumstances they bring up four children.

The book seems to be a tribute to Army wives, as well as to the Army. Significantly, as it was brought out in 1942, Aldrich carefully confirms its timeliness: "The lieutenant's lady lived to be very old, so old that she had seen her son and two of her grandsons in the United States Army and a toddling great-grandson marching and counter-marching with a wooden gun."

Secondary in importance among Aldrich's works are three novels that may be described as "romances," though each is more than that. Their central figures are women who suffer—and find joy—in love. *The Rim of the Prairie* (1925) was the first of all the Aldrich novels; *A White Bird Flying* (1931) takes up the story of Abbie Deal's granddaughter; and *Miss Bishop* (1940), the most nearly comprehensive character portrait of all, details the long life of a college teacher. This latter book proved so popular that it was made into a movie equally appealing, *Cheers for Miss Bishop* (1941) starring Martha Scott and Paul Muni.

Though each of these novels derives its interest from its heroine, they differ as to setting and era. In *The Rim of the Prairie* the reader becomes intimately acquainted with a small Midwestern town, a town full of "characters." Many of the older people have been pioneers, have seen the town grow, and have retained memories of older, harsher times. There is a mystery to be brought to light near the end; there are emotional moments a-plenty; and, of course, there is the triumph of love over what had seemed insurmountable difficulties. The plot is rather more complicated than in any of the following Aldrich novels, and the main character, Nancy Moore, is a vivid young woman surrounded by a number of colorful people—rich and poor, old and young.

A White Bird Flying is much simpler in concept. Readers familiar with *A Lantern in Her Hand* find it interesting because so many of the characters are known in the earlier book. This one tells of Laura Deal, lovely, talented granddaughter of Abbie and Will. From a very early age she is close to her grandmother, and after Abbie's death she finds inspiration in her memory. Her ambition is to become a great writer, to carry out one of Abbie's cherished dreams.

The story takes her through adolescence and university years to her love for Allen Rinemiller, whose grandparents had come to the prairie country with the Deals. A great opportunity for advancement along her chosen career is offered Laura, and she is forced to choose between a glamorous future and marriage. Here, as has been noted before in Aldrich's tales, a flavor of the "early days" can be sensed; here are people linked with the past, "modern" though they may be.

The third of these romances, *Miss Bishop,* is notable for its strong central character. Ella Bishop is one of the most forceful women Aldrich ever created. Her story may be told in a short paragraph.

One of the thirty-two students who attend the first year of what will later be a great university, Ella dominates the situation wherever she is. Graduating, she is taken on as a member of the faculty and spends the rest of her life giving herself to others: to her students, to her friends, to her family. An ecstatic love affair is brutally ended, and Ella later resists the temptation to enter into another with a married man. All her life she keeps steadily at work, depriving herself of one pleasure after another to help various members of her family and to inspire her students. In the end she is accorded enthusiastic appreciation by the university and has acquired a wide circle of friends. There are some dramatic moments in **Miss Bishop,** well calculated to please the Hollywood of the early 1940s, but the main concern of the reader is the character and personality of Ella herself, as well as her impact on those about her.

A great share of Aldrich's writings may be subsumed under the heading "Small-Town Fiction." Such periodicals as *Ladies Home Journal, American Magazine, Good Housekeeping, Women's Home Companion, Delineator,* and *Saturday Evening Post* welcomed these bright tales of "ordinary" people. Because of their popularity many were gathered into collections—six in number.

The first of these is **Mother Mason** (1924). All the stories here are concerned with the doings of the Mason family, including not only Tillie, the hired "help," but also the daughter-in-law. A great many things go on in the lively Mason household. Mother feels so beset that she takes a few days off to go to the city all by herself. Her pretext is exceedingly flimsy, but it satisfies her family, and she has a wonderful (if solitary) time. Each of the three daughters encounters love and reacts characteristically. Junior, the troublesome pre-teenager, gets into an amusing scrape. Tillie decides to embark on a life of her own, only to return crestfallen a short time later. Whatever happens, the Masons never know a dull moment.

The Cutters (1926) is another collection of stories about a single family, with the focal point Nell, the young mother. Nell's marriage is happy, and her energetic children are bouncingly healthy, but she nevertheless has problems to solve and obstacles to overcome. Many of these problems and obstacles are internal: they show her seeking to come to terms with herself, to adjust her values. She is envious of an old school friend's great success in the business world; she is overawed by an older matron's complacent efficiency; she is pricked by an insistent ambition to write; she feels the strain of entertaining an enviably rich businessman and his wife. Some of Nell's experiences are sheer comedy: her entering a "contest" involving a word puzzle; her working on a gala dinner to honor a "home grown" celebrity; her decision about disciplining her two maddening small sons.

Through both these collections breathes the atmosphere of small-town middle America. In them the life of these towns during the 1920s comes vividly to life.

Throughout the 1930s and into the 1940s, Aldrich produced a large number of stories having to do with a variety of characters. Her locale never changes. No matter what name she gives, it is the small town she has known (and loved) all her life. Many of these stories were published in **The Man Who Caught the Weather** (1936), **The Drum Goes Dead** (1941), **Journey into Christmas and Other Stories** (1949), and **A Bess Streeter Aldrich Reader**

(1950). **A Bess Streeter Aldrich Treasury** (1959), **The Home-Coming and Other Stories** (1984), and **Across the Smiling Meadow and Other Stories** (1984) have been brought out posthumously.

All the plots are uncomplicated. An old man keeps tabs on the weather and goes to his wife's grave to comfort her during an electrical storm. A youngish businessman has his hope for the future renewed at a Christmas celebration. All the citizens of a town join in welcoming a returning "boy who made good"—and he finds his childhood sweetheart waiting for him. Near death, a mother comes to a realization of the value of life. A middle-aged couple celebrates a wedding anniversary. Always in the end there is an upward swing: the men and women, the boys and girls, come to a greater appreciation of life—and of each other. Aldrich's endings may not be exactly "happily ever after," but they are definitely upbeat. Her reader leaves her people contentedly, seeing them wrapped in serenity and satisfaction, or at least knowing they will somehow work things out. In these stories Aldrich has definitely caught and reproduced the American longing for security and for fun.

She has done more. As Victor P. Hass, *World Herald* Book Editor, says, "The core of her writings is family. She has few superiors in American writing in showing, through action, the meaning of family in human life. Her families—the Masons, the Cutters, the Moores, the Deals—were complete. They, and thousands like them, were intensely important because they were the foundation on which the American Dream was built".

Children play important parts in Aldrich's family stories, and it is obvious that she is fond of them. We have seen that she worked with her very lively sons and daughter around her. (When he was small, her youngest, Robert, thought that all mothers wrote.) They and their activities formed a very important part of her everyday life. So it is not surprising that some of her best and most amusing remarks concern boys and girls.

Consider, for instance, small Jakie Cohen in **Rim of the Prairie**: "Because of his great curiosity over a firecracker," he is "the possessor of a glass eye which he would remove for the edification and entertainment of anyone who paid him a cent." Or observe Nell Cutter's skirmish with her obstreperous sons as they put off feeding their rabbits.

As all popular authors are, she was frequently asked to write articles or give statements concerning her philosophy of creative writing, her methods, etc. Her answers were never ambiguous: the reader is left in no doubt as to what she was trying to accomplish and why.

Discussing **A Lantern in Her Hand** she observes that though it was written in the "roaring 20's" it was far from "sophisticated," seemingly apart from the flamboyant life of the times. And she adds, "That it has made new friends each year since that day might be a bit of a lesson for young writers: *Regardless of the popular literary trend of* *the times, write the thing which lies close to your heart"* (Italics hers; **"The Story behind *A Lantern in Her Hand*"** 241).

When it comes to writing of life in a modern setting, she has very clear convictions, convictions which any of her readers may see are amply illustrated by her work: "In regard to the modern novel being a true mirror of the American home, the trend, of course, has been to write of the fast, high-strung, disintegrating home. That type of home is as American as the type I write about, but no more so. It no more represents all of America than does my type. But it is heard from far more than the type that I represent. After all, there are not very many of us who are writing of the small-town, financially-comfortable, one-man-for-one-woman, clean, decent and law-abiding families. As stories call for something dramatic, I suppose the idea is that there isn't much drama in that sort of family. But there is birth there, and love and marriage and death and all the ups-and-downs which come to every family in every town, large or small" (Marble 3).

She goes on to say, "If you have lived life deeply, touched bottom, as it were, it takes away any inclination to sit and wade through pages of sex stuff, or even wearily to follow somebody's ponderous mental reactions. They call it real life; at least, if it's decent, it's bunk. Are indecency and slime all that constitute real life?" (Marble 13).

One notes here what is obviously one of Aldrich's most deeply rooted convictions: "clean and decent" are divorced from "sex stuff"; furthermore, anything not "law-abiding" or "one-man-for-one-woman" must perforce be "sordid." And the work of the artist may be geared to the "clean and decent" and "law-abiding" as justifiably as to the "sordid."

Besides her uncomplicated credo that "clean" and "everyday life" have their drama—and are preferable to the "sordid"—she has a very firm conviction that character portrayal is the foundation of fiction. One must understand and sympathize with people, she says. A writer must empathize completely with his people; only then can he write truly of experiences as they live them. "When I have mentally constructed a personality about whom I wish to write, I find myself somewhat lost in that personality, crawling back into the character's skin, so to speak, and viewing life from his standpoint" (Marble 12).

Aside from her deeply felt convictions as to kinds of life to present and characters to create, she holds one about writing as *work*. That is what it is for her and, she implies, for any serious writer. At times she actually walked the floor as if in physical pain, "trying to get hold of an idea which would only elude me" (**"The Story Germ"** 355).

Interestingly, she illustrates how the "germ" of a story came to her in a news item about an old college building that was to be razed. Working from the simple fact of the demolishment of a landmark, she gradually evolved the novel *Miss Bishop,* one of her greatest successes (**"The Story Germ"** 356-57).

Her finest work, *A Lantern in Her Hand,* had an unusual beginning. It is rooted in the history of her mother's and father's families. Her mother's tart answer to commiseration about the hardships of pioneer life was, "Oh, save your pity. We had the best time in the world." Aldrich never forgot those words, thinking of them as she read—too often—how writers depicted the frontier women as "gaunt, brow-beaten creatures, despairing women whom life seemed to defeat" (**"The Story behind *A Lantern in Her Hand*"** 240).

And so she determined to write a novel that would amount to a tribute to her mother and others like her, women of intrepid spirit, courage, humor, and strength who had helped settle a wide and fertile land. It was to be more than a tribute: it was to be an authentic account of life on the plains during the early years.

Her research was enterprising. In 1927, at the request of the editor of the *Nebraska State Journal,* she spoke over the radio on the subject "The Pioneer in Fiction." At the end of her speech she requested listeners to send her any anecdotes or facts about frontier living they might have. In reply she was flooded with material: newspaper clippings, diaries, letters, scrapbooks. In addition she interviewed many elderly people who could remember their pioneering days.

As a result *A Lantern in Her Hand* is a book rich in vivid—and homely—detail, a book so informative that it has frequently been used as supplementary reading in schools. From it the student gains not only knowledge, but a kind of awed admiration and respect for people like the Deals and their friends. For these people worked with what seems almost superhuman strength. They founded towns and built roads, established schools, staked out cemeteries. And they defied a grim and relentless Nature that time and again burned their crops with scorching sun or lashed at their poor homes with brutal blizzards.

As noted above, Aldrich lets her own attitudes toward life guide her writing. One easily sees, in novel after novel, short story after short story, exactly what values she holds. And these values are clearly recognizable as those of Midwestern rural and small-town society during the first half of the century.

The stories are free from profanity and any other sort of coarse language. As Robert Louis Stevenson was able to write a pirate tale without a single "cussword," so Aldrich manages to give a sense of reality to life on the prairie without one. More, she can write of "modern" young people, university students, who speak clear unadorned English. Their slang is another matter, as will be noted later.

A few people in the Aldrich world smoke (males only), but no one ever drinks anything headier than coffee. As far as sex goes, it is as well hidden as in any Victorian novel. People fall in love; Aldrich tells us they do—indeed, she insists on it. But it is mostly a friendly "let's be partners" type of love. Once in a while a mild hint of something a bit earthier is evident, but this is not protracted. One senses, for instance, pure lust as Ed crushes young Abbie to him and begs her to marry him.

One senses it also in *Miss Bishop* when Delbert is courting Ella. His ardor vaguely worries her. When he yearns, "You're a cool little piece, aren't you, Ella? You *do* love me, don't you?" she assures him she does. She just wants to be "so sure." Love is such a big thing; she wants to understand it. Delbert embraces her passionately, saying, "It's this!"

Aldrich goes on, "But Ella knew better—Ella Bishop knew her love was something more than that—something more deeply beautiful—something infinitely more delicate" (63-64).

Here the reader sees clearly that for Ella Bishop sex per se is unclean. True, the treachery of Delbert and Amy is a hideous thing. But the actual sex act would today be viewed as incidental. The 1870s (when Ella is young) of course saw this in a different light, and Aldrich is probably correct in her depiction of Ella's attitude, when she has her say witheringly to the little flirt who has seduced her fiancé: "You little *animal*." But the reader understands clearly that Aldrich is in agreement.

In *A White Bird Flying* when Laura thinks of Allen Rinemiller, there seems to be physical desire. She loves him. She loves being with him, for he is the one person she can talk to. But because of her ambition she at first refuses his offer of marriage. She is going to New York, to a writing career! Neither he nor she gives a thought to extramarital sex.

When Kathy's and Jimmy's marriage is imperilled, no indication is given as to what effect on their sex life their disagreements have. Physical passion simply has no place in Aldrich's concept of "family fiction."

There are no divorces in Aldrich's world, either, though there may occasionally—very occasionally—be a reference to an unhappy marriage. A case in point is that of Uncle Harry and Aunt Carolyn in *A White Bird.*

One of the most strongly held convictions of Aldrich's life is her theory of the place of women in society. The subject is one of crucial interest in our day; when Aldrich was writing it was coming disturbingly to the forefront. She has drawn some engaging women: Mother Mason, Nell Cutter, Abbie Deal, Linnie Stafford, and many, many more. Of her whole feminine galaxy only one career woman stands out: Ella Bishop, the teacher.

Ella is shown to be self-sufficient, courageous, energetic—in the end completely fulfilled. But she is alone. Though Grace Deal of *A White Bird* is also a self-sufficient

and energetic single woman, she reveals in an uncharacteristic speech that her life has not been all she wished.

Nowhere has Aldrich put her case for "woman's place" so clearly as in *The Cutters.* Entertaining a former classmate who has become a successful businesswoman, Nell voices her envy. Her friend speaks: "Nellie," she says gravely, "for everything in this world we pay the price. You bought your lovely family with your freedom; and the price I pay for freedom is—heartache. I have an infinite capacity for love—and no husband. I have the heart of a mother—and no child. We say the world progresses, and it does. Women have come up out of slavery and serfdom; they can stand shoulder to shoulder now with the men of the business, scholastic, and political world. But there are some fundamentals to which normal women will always look with longing eyes. In the last analysis, nothing can take the place of them. Love, home, children. I've put my heart and soul into the business, and results show it. I'm rather justly proud of what I've accomplished. And yet—all I really want is a corner of my own, green and shady and restful, where I may sit and . . . rock the baby I never had" (101).

There is an echo of these sentiments, couched in much crisper language, in the advice Grace Deal, a successful university professor, gives her niece Laura. Don't do as I did, she says in effect: don't turn down love and home and family for a career!

Thus Aldrich vividly illustrates what Betty Friedan, decades later, was to call "the feminine mystique." And Aldrich's attitude is neatly summarized in what Friedan says of Helene Deutsche: "This brilliant feminine follower of Freud states categorically that the women who by 1944 in America had achieved eminence by activity of their own in various fields had done so at the expense of their feminine fulfillment" (121).

But Carol Fairbanks remarks that, cheerful and optimistic as Aldrich's *Lantern* is, her Abbie Deal is barred from developing her artistic and musical talents; she must see them flower in her children and grandchildren (107). Thus Abbie "is the archetypal nineteenth-century woman who sets aside her personal needs and arranges finances so that her daughters realize their dreams" (202).

Fairbanks further points out that Aldrich has underscored the position of women in pioneering days. In *Spring Came on Forever* the German immigrant expects to get ahead because he has land, a good team of horses, and a woman. Said woman must work hard and be as unobtrusive as possible in order to escape his wrath.

Contrast the personality of Nell's friend with Willa Cather's Alexandra Bergson, a woman who is stronger than her brothers and who, with superb ability and great labor, carves a fine farm from the rich Nebraska country. Her life, at the end of the story, is to be completed by her marriage with Carl.

Or turn to Ruth Suckow and see how she handles a similar theme in her novel *Cora*. Cora has done well in the business world, has become one of the successful women of the city: "She could hold her own among them. She was almost 'at the top.' She had wanted to attain this—life would have been a failure if she hadn't done so. Now she struggled fiercely to enjoy what she had won.

"But there was something wrong . . . There had to be something else . . . something *inside* of things . . . she did not know how to put it."

In spite of obvious similarities, Aldrich differs—I believe fundamentally—from other women who have written of the Midwest, precisely in this question of feminine values. Certainly, as has been noted, she shows strong women, women of courage and perseverance, with a decided bent toward independence. But unlike Cather's Alexandra and Ántonia and Thea, and Suckow's Cora, their strength and fulfillment come from *womanliness*.

They come, not from meeting the world in the manner of a man, not from managing farms and ranches, or climbing the corporate ladder, or buying and selling. Mother Mason, Nell Cutter, Abbie Deal, and other Aldrich women characters do not lead easy lives, are certainly not immune to physical and emotional suffering. But theirs is not the suffering of marketplace competition nor the frustration of political losses. It is not even the turmoil of the artistic life, the grueling labor and almost intolerable pressures of careers on the stage, the painstaking work of the writer or the painter.

No, Aldrich's women find their greatest satisfaction in being sturdy daughters, devoted wives, strict and compassionate mothers. For instance, we see Laura Deal giving up her writing plans to be happy as wife and mother. We see Abbie sorrowful when her daughter Isabelle tells her she and her husband plan not to have children so they can both pursue their musical careers. And how much more sorrowful Abbie is when daughter Grace announces that she will remain single!

A much more important difference between Aldrich and other Midwest writers is that she never questions the basic assumptions of "moral" middle-class life. She sees heroism in this life, and she sees humor, but she never really probes beneath its surface.

Ruth Suckow, on the other hand, has an uneasy awareness that something is amiss in the structure of middle-class society. She has a sense of unsatisfactory aspects in the relations of the sexes, for example. Willa Cather, with all the poetry of her narratives, feels keenly—and transmits to her readers—some of the profound problems of "normal" people: jealousy, hatred, revenge, ambition. Mari Sandoz, aware as she is of the beauty and promise of the Great Plains, is devastatingly truthful about showing the ugliness that can flourish in the midst of it all. Helen Hooven Santmyer, demure as she seems in her sweeping novel *And La-*

dies of the Club, shows what meanness can lie beneath the surface of a quiet Ohio town. Examples can go on and on. Something in the very makeup of society is askew, as American writers have insisted from James Fenimore Cooper on through Mark Twain to our own time.

Since about the beginning of the present century, which signaled the start of the "revolt from the village" movement, small-town life has been a popular theme. From E. W. Howe's *Story of a Country Town* to Sinclair Lewis's *Main Street* down to *And Ladies of the Club* and Garrison Keillor's *Lake Wobegone Days,* writers of fiction have delighted in exposing the faults, the meannesses, the unlovely provincialism, of many Winesburgs and Gopher Prairies. Such fiction has often been scathing, often cynical, occasionally satirical. Aldrich, on the contrary, looks at little towns with loving eyes and warm sympathy. And she is adept at finding amusing incidents in the lives of her characters.

True, she does admit that "culture" is regarded suspiciously. And in one story, **"Welcome Home, Hal,"** she departs from her usual attitude to remark, "A small Midwestern town through alien eyes is sometimes not a lovely thing."

Her basic feeling, however, is illustrated by Nell Cutter's outburst: "All our modern authors have just two types of people in their small town writings: the discontented kind, or the dull, stolid kind who are too dumb to know enough to *be* discontented. I'm not either one—and there are a lot of us—and I'd like to have Miss Duffield know it. We're not all dowdy and we're not all crude."

After all, Aldrich says, "What were the fundamentally big things of life, the things that were eternal? Knowledge . . . appearances . . . sophistication? Or truth . . . friendship . . . love?" (*Cutters* 200-01).

Though she wrote during and after the World War I years, Bess Streeter Aldrich has nothing to say about war hysteria, "the red menace," labor troubles, breadlines, voices both loud and quiet who insist that something is amiss, that some sectors of the population are wronged, are restless, are demanding redress.

Her Cutters and Masons, her modern Deals—her businessmen and bankers and university instructors—live their emotional and financial lives apparently untouched by the world around them. Nowhere is there evidence that this author had read and enjoyed Jane Austen, but a reader can conclude that she would have sympathized with her as she kept her characters out of the turbulence of their era.

A rather curious attitude occasionally surfaces in Aldrich's fiction; one feels almost discourteous in mentioning it, for it is so obviously unconscious. This is her feeling against the American East. It stands to reason, of course, that she would be enthusiastic about the Midwest. Never has anyone loved a place more, nor felt so joyous in the love of it.

That love breathes through every line of *Lantern,* for instance, the novel written as a tribute to pioneer women. It is everywhere in *Rim of the Prairie,* in *Miss Bishop,* in *A White Bird Flying.* But often it is accompanied by something almost like veiled hostility toward the East.

This hostility is mainly implied. Young Abbie Deal's flashy suitor, Dr. Ed, begs her to come with him to New York. There he can give her cultural advantages, have her lovely voice trained. Her granddaughter Laura has a chance to go to New York to be a companion to her wealthy uncle and aunt (and eventually to inherit their fortune) while taking advantage of the cultural atmosphere to develop her writing talent. Both girls refuse because they love their honest farmer sweethearts more than they crave the "opportunities" of the East.

A White Bird Flying contains one scene that is rather explicit about the East-Midwest problem. Several college girls are discussing the attitude of Easterners toward Nebraska, their ignorance of the state, and their condescension. One tells of the Easterner who, when a story in the *Saturday Evening Post* is mentioned, says, "Oh, do they have the *Saturday Evening Post* in Nebraska?" And, "I would expect the trees here look odd to you?" one visiting Nebraskan is asked.

Another tells of a newspaper woman who, visiting in New York, counters the obvious condescension of her hosts by pointing out that the author Willa Cather, the comedian Harold Lloyd, and the sculptor Gutzum Borglum are all Nebraskans. She finishes by saying she'll be delighted to visit Coney Island—it was designed by a "Nebraska boy."

Laura and Allen (in *White Bird*) argue about the Midwest versus the East. She tells him there's no "atmosphere" in the Midwest; as one of her professors has said, "no spiritual uplift." Allen asks where she could find "more substantial people," and she counters with the remark that "substantial people" are poor literary material.

According to her professor, there is no "great beauty" in the Midwest—no sea, no mountains, etc. The landscape is "monotonous." Allen answers with the Bad Lands of Dakota, the blue sky over the Nebraska sand hills, the Minnesota lakes and birches.

Thus, here and there in her fiction, Aldrich seems to be on the defensive as far as the Midwest is concerned, repelling possible attacks, as it were. And, as has been noted, her love of her native region is so deep that it permeates her work.

It certainly is apparent in her descriptions of nature. Probably no American writer has been more delightfully graphic when it comes to settings. In her pictures of the country, Aldrich rivals Willa Cather, Mari Sandoz, Ruth Suckow. One *feels* the country as she spreads it before one. Observe her description of spring: "Spring came over the prairie—not softly, shyly, but in great magic strides. It

was in the flush of grass on the alders and willows of Stove Creek. It was in the wind,—in the smell of loam and grasses, in the tantalizing odor of wild plums budding and wild violets flowering . . ." (*Lantern* 82-83).

Compare that passage with Willa Cather's spring day: "It was a beautiful blue morning. The buffalo peas were blooming in pink and purple masses along the roadside, and the larks, perched on last year's dried sunflower stalks, were singing straight at the sun, their heads thrown back and their yellow breasts aquiver. The wind blew about us in warm, sweet gusts" (*My Ántonia* 127-28).

Aldrich's feeling for the plains, for Nebraska, is more than simple love; it is a vital empathy. Because of this she is as forceful in her descriptions of the frightening aspects of the land as in its more gracious moods. For her, as for Cather and Sandoz, it is a living, breathing presence.

When it comes to making the reader experience the white terror of a plains blizzard, she is a powerful artist. Her storm scenes have all the dreadful actuality of Sandoz's. And probably no one has described a tornado more impressively than she has in *Rim of the Prairie.* Her words are worthy of being quoted at length:

> Above the trees an immense yellow-black smoke whirled up into the sky, spiraling, rotating, in great volume . . . it was no fire but a more cruel thing. Greenish clouds had whipped themselves into the bowl of a huge wine-glass. . . . There was no sound anywhere. No wind in the trees. No bird sang. No cock crew. There was silence everywhere save in the frenzied heart of the Thing that moved swiftly across the prairie. It boiled and crackled and roared. It was heavy. But it was not clumsy. Gracefully it moved. Almost daintily it picked its way in and out of the farmlands. It bent and swayed and sung. The stem stretched and pulled away from the bowl. But it did not break. It sucked at the ground and whatever it touched, living or inanimate thing, answered its wild call and was pulled up into the cloud glass to make wine for the fallen gods.
>
> (332)

One may note an egregious mixing of metaphors here, and one may object to the prolixity. But no reader can escape a feeling of breathless immediacy. One is *there* living the terror, overwhelmed with the realization of the sheer strength of elemental powers.

Aldrich's easy, almost conversational style lends itself to humor, and here she is distinctive. Her reader is always conscious of a sunny temperament, one that takes pleasure in the small amusements of life, that finds laughter in day-to-day happenings. Life, whether on the grim frontier or in a small Midwestern town, is filled with little chuckles, brief moments of laughter.

Some of the humor seems off-hand. For instance, in *The Cutters* one finds a bit of totally unconscious irony in Grandma's description of the successful careers of her six sons. She ends her statement with the remark that Robbie, the "rascallyest" one of all, is the new governor of the state.

But unfortunately, in Aldrich's amusement she is inclined to go too far. She not only laughs; all too often she points up her laughter with references that make her remarks seem dangerously close to wisecracks.

As an example, see how she describes a committee planning a function: "Over the dinner itself there was enough discussion to have filled a book the size of the classic which Mr. Webster wrote" (*Cutters* 185). And the reader winces as an old Civil War veteran remembers Christmas in Atlanta, when they burned the city "before startin' out with Sherman on that little hoofin' jaunt we took to the sea."

Miss Bishop yields several noteworthy examples. Here she remarks that "hundreds of little towns grew to their full size of two or five or ten thousand, paused in their growth, and admitted that none of them by taking Chamber-of-Commerce thought could add one cubit to its stature" (3). When Midwestern College holds its opening ceremony, "There was [sic] prayers, in which the president informed the Lord of the current events of the morning" (11).

Further, "Professor Carter made an heroic attempt to initiate the novices into the mysteries of Chaucer" (20). And, "A Professor O'Neill, representing Messrs Caesar, Ovid, and Livy, taught for a single year, as his radical views on the origin of the human race, which he so often found occasion to wedge in between the Aquitanians and the Belgae, proved his undoing, and he was summarily dismissed" (136).

Often, too, Aldrich is guilty of an embarrassing affectation: she is fond of parodying famous lines of poetry. *The Rim of the Prairie* contains a statement about a young teacher: "By the next night Nancy's head, pedagogically speaking, was bloody but unbowed" (106). And in *The Cutters* another teacher, near the end of summer, remarks that "in one week I go like the quarry slave at night, scourged to the dungeon of his schoolroom" (245). A very little of this kind of thing goes a long way, and regrettably Aldrich overdoes it.

Some readers might find the conversations of her young girls excessively irritating. Many of these girls seem interchangeable, from Nancy Moore of *Rim*, through Katherine Deal of *White Bird* to Gretchen of *Miss Bishop*. All of them exhibit an airy flippancy supposed to be funny, but which all too often ends in making one flinch.

Nancy says to Aunt Biny, "Real love, Aunt Biny, belongs to another generation. It went out with rubber-tired buggies and castors for centerpieces" (*Rim* 55). And she assures the worried little woman about her engagement: "I'll try to idolize Mr. Farnsworth. He's getting a bit bald on the north mansard roof slope of his head and he's a little too short and a little too fat and a lot older than the hero ought to be. But I'll do my best to moon over him" (58). Abbie Deal's granddaughter Kathy flaunts a like breezy cynicism, though she does marry for love.

In *White Bird* Laura's college friends, discussing campus affairs, show a studied cleverness. Jealousy is "acid raisins"; an assignment in a literature course is "a date with the Russian writer Tchekov"; Shakespeare is always "Billy."

The most egregious case of strained flippancy can be found in the character of Gretchen, Ella Bishop's foster grand-niece. This young woman is hardly bearable. Utterly uninhibited, she seems never to express a worthwhile idea. Not only are all male professors "papa" to her, she can apparently take nothing—and no one—seriously. Rummaging in an old trunk, she finds poor Ella's unfinished wedding gown, and without permission tries it on. "Am I not *perfect*?" she says, coming before her aunt. "Isn't it the answer to a maiden's prayer? May I wear it? What does the sweet old auntie say? . . . You're stunned speechless at my gorgeousness, aren't you? . . . What's the answer, sweet pumpkin?" (280-81).

When Ella supplies the money so Gretchen can live in the sorority house, the girl expresses her appreciation with, "I think you're a luscious old peach. I suppose I ought to be noble and say I couldn't think of accepting the offer, but I'm crazy to do it, and will take you at your word that you really want me to" (283). Later on she tells Ella, "You're an old smoothy,—in fact you're probably the noblest soul that ever trod over campus dandelions" (296).

If humor lightens Aldrich's narratives, an irritating tendency toward didacticism gives occasional heavy moments. This writer simply cannot keep from pointing a moral—and too often it is a moral that readers are quite capable of finding for themselves. Further, most of her "moral" passages are interwoven with a sugary sentimentalism quite unworthy of so gifted a teller of tales.

An excellent example may be quoted from a Christmas story, **"The Drum Goes Dead"**: "And so suddenly that it seemed a new thought—though it was as old as the silent stars—a bright-colored strand wove itself across the gray warp of his mind. *The world was not in chaos to these children.* Through their eyes it was still the same world of limited dimensions he and these other burdened people had known as children, and because this was so, it was still a good world.

"Humanity must hang fast to its faith and its hope. It must never let them go as long as there remained in the world a child and a song,—a gift and a star" (65; emphasis Aldrich's).

This didacticism sometimes extends to descriptions of characters. Aldrich presents many interesting people; even her minor actors are colorful. However, she feels obliged to discuss them with the reader; they would do very well if she just left them alone. An especially vivid example is that of Nancy Moore, of *Rim.* She is charming, but her author is not content to show us that she is; she must tell us: "She could no more have abandoned that gay little way of hers than she could have changed the color of her eyes" (21).

Despite flaws such as these, Aldrich's style is smooth and lucid, shot through with the good-natured humor of a pleasant, good-natured personality. Her readers are both soothed and gently amused.

As I have attempted to show, Bess Streeter Aldrich gives faithful pictures of frontier life. The bulk of her work, however, concerns small-town families living according to the tenets of what George Bernard Shaw once called "middle class morality." Clearly she has presented what she sees as truth about life. Indeed, one interviewer has observed that "perhaps her strength has been in the fact that she has not lost contact at any time with the *real people* in this land" (Sherlock 29). If her vision has been affected by her own sunny disposition and the values she learned as a child, she is no different from many other earnest writers of fiction. She has a right to be called a realist according to her own lights.

But the term is not technically applicable to her work. Her predilection is for a pleasant romanticism, a deft veiling of the darker aspects of life. She certainly knew they existed; every now and then a reference is made (in some cases almost reluctantly) to lust, to greed, to sorrow, to frustration. But the overall picture is one of satisfaction in being alive, in doing one's work well, and, above all, in loving one's family and friends.

A critic is wrong to fault a writer for not doing what he or she did not intend to do, and Aldrich has said plainly that she did not intend to write of sophisticated people, of perverts, of "sin." "Life has been wholesome, sane and happy for me," she writes, ". . . I have set down life as I have found it, knowing that many, many people in the world have known it as I have—a thing of mingled happiness and sorrow, little pleasures and little disappointments, deep courage, high faith, grief, laughter, and love" (Marble 41).

In a very revealing article, **"Why I Live in a Small Town,"** she is almost militant: "Why quarrel with a writer over realism and idealism? After all, an author is glass through which a picture of life is projected. The picture falls upon the pages of the writer's manuscript according to the mental and emotional contours of that writer. It is useless to try to change those patterns. If one writer does not see life in terms of grime and dirt, adulteries and debaucheries, it does not follow that those sordid things do not exist. If another does not see life in terms of faith and love, sympathy and good deeds, it does not follow that those characteristics do not exist. I grow weary of hearing the sordid

spoken of as real life, the wholesome as Pollyanna stuff. I contend that a writer may portray some of the decent things of life around him and reserve the privilege to call that real life too. And if this be literary treason, make the most of it" (21).

A publisher's note confirms her words; speaking of how she "sought to convey the sturdy cheerful realism of her mother," it points to her "intelligent optimism that has illumined all of her . . . work, setting her apart from the mass of current writers, who tend too often to view the American scene darkly and despondently" (*The Bess Streeter Aldrich Reader* v).

And a bit of grudging—almost reluctant—praise occurs in the entry devoted to her in *Twentieth Century Authors* (1942): "Her typical book covers the entire life, from youth to age, of a Middle Western woman, and her thesis is that love, marriage, and children are the most important things in life. Her intense feeling for nature, a natural gift for characterization, and her humor place her work in a rather higher category than its philosophy might indicate" (17).

A less gracious reviewer acknowledging the virtues of *Lantern,* observes that "Mrs. Aldrich does make the settlement of the West seem an epic accomplishment. . . . She does make bearing children and loving them, and teaching them, and cheerfully giving up all the world that they might have it instead, seem worth doing." This is obviously written tongue in cheek, for the writer adds sneeringly, "Novels will go on telling about these things forever, and people will read them, and laugh over them, and cry over them. And it will do people no harm" (*Saturday Review of Literature* 17 Nov. 1928: 371).

One excellent proof of her views concerning writing is the fact that for a while she read book manuscripts for a monthly book club called "The Family Bookshelf." The object was to eliminate literature not suitable for children. (Other members of the reading committee were Drew Pearson, Dr. Daniel Poling, and Edwin Balmer, editor of *Redbook.*)

Certainly many readers found her outlook on life and literature congenial. When the Lincoln Kiwanis Club honored her, one tribute began, "Books that sneer at the frailties of mankind, or books that discourage human aspiration, will always impress me as nothing better than bad books. It is the glory of Nebraska, I think, that we have a writer who has never been touched by the frost of what is cynical or bitter. She walks bravely with a lantern in her hand, always a mellow light shines from her fiction. Sanity and a gracious spirit are the soul of her work."

However, even those who agree with Aldrich's convictions might feel a little restless when reading some of her fiction. *Miss Bishop,* for example. This is a charming novel in many ways, and colorful in its delineation of the start and growth of a great university. Ella Bishop is a likeable heroine—except for the fact that she has no flaws. Time after time she gives up her desires for other people, mainly her family. One of her more painful decisions is consenting to rear the child of her faithless lover and the woman with whom he has betrayed her.

Yearning to go to Europe, she twice relinquishes her plans for a trip abroad. On the first occasion her aged mother is ailing, and on the second her supremely selfish foster niece needs money in order to live in a sorority house. Later Ella sends the girl on a trip to Europe to escape a disastrous love affair. In all the crises of her life, Ella Bishop's first thought is for someone else.

But how one would have liked to see her, if only a few times, succumb to selfishness, to irresponsibility, yes, to passion! If only just once she had told her selfish family that she was going to do as *she* wished! (As a matter of fact, many of her sacrifices are made over the protests of her family and friends.)

One wishes she had had at least one glorious, ecstatic night with John Stevens, instead of refusing him because he is married (even though she knows his wife gives him nothing), and because she must stay "pure" so she can, in her own eyes, be a proper role model for her students. One would have liked her to be a little indiscreet, occasionally, and perhaps been rapped over the knuckles for it. One wishes, in sum, that she hadn't constantly been loving and giving and idealistic—and always with a merry quip at her own expense!

Miss Bishop may be an extreme example, but the romanticism that suffuses it may be seen here and there in all Aldrich's work. Nor is she above a bit of gentle mysticism. A good instance of this can be found in **Lantern.** It occurs at the end of the chapter telling of the ingenious ways Abbie and Will, in spite of crushing poverty, made Christmas for their little children.

The youngsters, before going to bed, look out at the silent, snowy night and see a star which, they say gleefully, is stopping right over their house. Aldrich meditates:

> Historians say, "The winter of 'seventy-four to seventy-five was a time of deep depression. . . ." Deep depression? To three children on the prairie it was a time of glamour. There was not much to eat in the cupboard. There was little or no money in the father's flat old pocketbook. The presents were pitifully homely and meager. And all in a tiny house,—a mere shell of a house, on a new raw acreage of the wild, bleak prairie. How could a little rude cabin hold so much white magic? How could a little sod house know such enchantment? And how could a little hut like that eventually give to the midwest so many influential men and women? How, indeed? Unless . . . unless, perchance, the star *did* stop over the house?
>
> (116)

Twin to romanticism is a certain innocence that crops up now and then in her work. One is amused to read of college-educated Nell Cutter's failed attempt at short-story writing. Her first effort is rejected by an editor who tells her to "go into the technical construction of story work." Nell's reaction is amazement: "Technical!" she says. "Whoever dreamed that there was any technical construction to a story? I thought when popular writers wrote they just sat down and *wrote*. It looks so easy, as thought it just rolled off their pens" (213).

And Laura Deal, just out of the University, thinks there's not enough "scope" for the creative writer in the Midwest. The people are "ordinary," the scenery "uninspiring." It is as if she'd never heard of Madame Bovary, or the one passion and four walls of Dumas, as if she were ignorant of the dramatic possibilities inner conflicts can present.

However, for all the flaws in style—the excesses of overdone humor, of didacticism, of sentimentality—Bess Streeter Aldrich remains a notable figure, fully worthy to be ranked as one of the gifted writers of Midwestern fiction—a group including Willa Cather, Mari Sandoz, Ruth Suckow, Martha Ostenso, to name a few of the women. Fairbanks links her with Cather and Laura Ingalls Wilder as one of "three prairie women writers" (188).

In Abbie Deal, Aldrich has created a woman to compare favorably with Cather's Alexandra Bergson and Ántonia Shimerda. With her courage and spirit Abbie is very like Sandoz's Dr. Morissa Kirk in her resourcefulness, in the practical way she makes use of the materials about her. She never flinches at hardship or pain, though she has moments, as is natural, of feminine longing and resentment, moments when life seems too hard to bear. But she always straightens her shoulders and goes on. She is, when all is said, the epitome of the courage, the endurance, and the ethical constancy which Americans like to think make up the spirit of the pioneer. *A Lantern in Her Hand* accomplishes what Aldrich planned it should: it pays tribute to the intrepidity and fearlessness of the women who left their homes to accompany their men to an unsettled land fraught with unknown dangers.

Perhaps Aldrich knew the writings of contemporary Midwestern authors such as Cather, Sandoz, Suckow, and Ostenso, but no indication of such knowledge exists. Perhaps she would have felt a distance between her and these women, all of whom refuse to ignore the sordid aspects of rural life. None of them has the determined cheerfulness that wins out in Aldrich's fiction.

But it may be that very element of cheer that made her appreciated by so many readers—surprisingly different readers. For instance, Admiral Chester Nimitz wrote her that he and his officers gained courage reading *A Lantern in Her Hand* during the worst days of World War II in the Pacific. And his is only one of many letters expressing like sentiments.

One is struck by the tone of some of these letters. They seem to attest to the charm of Aldrich's personality, the pleasant graciousness that one senses between the lines of her stories. Acknowledging biographical materials Aldrich has sent her, one woman says, "It means a great deal to my friends and myself to discover that a person who knows fame and success, could be interested in just ordinary folks."

Again, a fifteen-year-old girl writes with adolescent emotion, "It seems funny—we have never seen each other, you didn't even know I existed and yet you are one of my best friends—one to whom I tell my secrets to [sic]—one who I feel will understand me . . . I love you, Mrs. Aldrich, because you know and can put into beautiful words all that I feel within me."

Near the end of his detailed critique of one of Sarah Orne Jewett's short stories, Louis A. Renza inserts a significant quotation. Jewett, in one of her letters, says, "I often think that the literary work which takes the least prominent place, nowadays, is that belonging to the middle ground. Scholars and so-called intellectual persons have a wealth of literature in the splendid accumulation of books that belong to all times, and now and then a new volume is added to the great list. Then there is the lowest level of literature, the trashy newspaper and sensational novels, but how seldom a book comes that stirs the minds and hearts of the good men and women of such a village as this" (178).

These words seem peculiarly apropos to Aldrich's work if we read "village" to mean "just ordinary folks." Indeed these are precisely the people for whom Bess Streeter Aldrich felt the greatest affinity, and for whom she wrote.

Besides her writing, which seems to have been a real labor of love as well as a means of livelihood, she enjoyed activities in her church (Methodist), Order of Eastern Star, Nebraska Writers Guild (of which she was for a time president), the Nebraska Press Association, the Omaha Women's Press Club, Altrusa of Lincoln, and the honorary societies Chi Delta Phi (national literary fraternity) and Theta Sigma Phi (national journalistic sorority).

In 1934 she was awarded an Honorary Doctorate of Literature by the University of Nebraska for her achievements as homemaker, author, citizen, and one giving distinguished service to Nebraska. And in 1939 the Lincoln Kiwanis Club honored her with the Distinguished Service Medal as "Homemaker, Citizen, and Author."

After her death on 3 August 1954, 52nd Street, where her Lincoln home stood, was renamed "Aldrich Road." Eleven years later in the small town of Elmwood, a Nebraska Historical Marker sponsored by the Elmwood Library Board was dedicated to her. It stands in Elmwood Park, across the street from the house in which she lived for many years.

In 1973 she was elected to the Nebraska Hall of Fame, the second woman to be so honored; only Willa Cather preceded her. And in 1976, at the celebration of the nation's Bicentennial, she was named one of the Ten Mothers of Achievement from Nebraska.

An unusual honor was bestowed upon her as recently as 1984. The unique publishing company, Amereon House (Mattituck, New York) reprinted *The Home-Coming and Other Stories* and *Across the Smiling Meadows and Other Stories*. Joanna Paulson, the editor, says in a preface to the latter volume that the purpose of the publishers is "to preserve and distribute the efforts of authors of quality and popularity that have fallen between the cracks [sic] in our modern, fast-paced society" (7).

One cannot see Bess Streeter Aldrich as a "forgotten" literary figure. In 1987 Elmwood, her home town, honored her memory with an "Aldrich Day." The "Bess Streeter Aldrich Foundation," formed in 1977, seeks to promote her work and is ambitious to raise money for a "permanent memorial."

One of the most significant examples of the praise she has received may be found in the 1949 poll by a group of scholastic magazines. Asked to name the ten books which have done the best job of telling about American life, the readers included *A Lantern in Her Hand*—the only one of the ten not filmed.

Certainly Bess Streeter Aldrich's work is a faithful, if not a complete, picture of American life. Readers can turn with confidence to her richly detailed and authentic account of pioneering on the prairies, of everyday life in small towns, to restore their faith in the spirit of their country.

Carol Miles Petersen (essay date 1995)

SOURCE: Petersen, Carol Miles. Introduction to *The Collected Short Works 1907-1919*, pp. vii-xiii. Lincoln, Neb.: University of Nebraska Press, 1995.

[*In the following introduction to a collection of Aldrich's short works, Petersen gives a critical overview of Aldrich's writing.*]

In describing how to write a short story, Bess Streeter Aldrich noted the author must "live the lives of his characters, crawling into their very skins. . . . He must be an actor. More than that, he must play all the parts."[1] In playing "all the parts," Bess Streeter Aldrich brought to her readers the pleasure of well-written stories that reflect her own personality: her positive outlook on life, her humor, her understanding of people. The stories further offer the pleasure of recognizing characters and incidents that reappear in Aldrich novels: the revised Mason and Cutter family stories became the books *Mother Mason* (1924), and *The Cutters* (1926); and Zimri Streeter appears as **"Grandpa Statler"** in the 1915 story of that name, in the 1925 novel

The Rim of the Prairie, in the 1939 *The Song of Years,* and as the hero of the 1944 short story **"Soldier Vote of '64".** The character of the school teacher in **"The Madonna of the Purple Dots"** (1907) and in **"The Cat Is on the Mat"** (1916) appears as that of the protagonist in *The Rim of the Prairie.*

Many of these stories are reprinted for the first time since their original publication. I have included two that were sold but not published—one, **"The Madonna of the Purple Dots,"** because the magazine went out of business and the other, **"Concerning the Best Man,"** because of an editorial policy change. Aldrich wrote more than one hundred short stories and was able to claim the enviable record of never writing a story she did not sell. Many of her stories were syndicated after first publication and many were sold to British magazines; her readership was enormous. All of her novels are in print.

This book contains stories that Aldrich wrote from the start of her career through 1919. That year she turned thirty-eight, and had accomplished a great deal both in her personal life and in her writing. After graduating from college in 1901 she taught for three years, received a second teaching degree, married, moved three times, bore three children and was pregnant with her fourth child, was active in church work, organized the first Women's Club and helped start the first Public Library in Elmwood, Nebraska, and wrote and sold twenty-six stories plus miscellaneous articles. All of this demonstrates the truth of a comment in 1920 by one of her editors that hers was "a case of stored up energy."[2]

Bessie Genevra Streeter was born in Cedar Falls, Iowa, on 17 February 1881, the youngest of eight children. With ten years separating Bess from her nearest brother and fourteen from her nearest sister, Bess learned to rely on her reading and her own imagination for entertainment; she said that the characters she met in books became as familiar to her as the neighbors. Reading meant curling up in the large friendly armchair in the living room or tucking a book under her apron as she went upstairs in the morning to make the beds, knowing that if she got her chores done quickly she could then read until someone began to wonder where she was. Favorite authors included James M. Barrie, whose humor she enjoyed, and Charles Dickens, whose characterizations she appreciated. Along with her personal favorites, there was the Bible, a staple of her Scots-Presbyterian family. From it, she learned the moral principles by which she would live and which her writing would reflect. She also learned Bible verses, which occasionally surface in her novels, rephrased, but with cadences intact.

Relishing stories as she did, Bess began creating her own—sometimes in the playhouse that her father had built for her in the backyard. Probably from about the age of nine or ten and using a lead pencil as she always would for first drafts, Bess wrote fanciful stories; she knew even as a child that "when words are put together right they're just like singing."[3] Also in the playhouse, pedaling with furious speed on a broken treadle sewing machine, she transported herself on adventurous trips; playing with neighborhood friends, she wove tales of exciting balls, beautiful gowns, and handsome knights with their ladies. One of these friends, Grace Simpson, recalls how Bess would begin telling a story peopled by herself and all of her listeners; she would describe the setting, the dazzling people, and her own exquisite dress; then turning to Grace, Bess would say it was Grace's turn. Grace, lacking a flowing imagination, would respond, "Oh, I don't know, Bess, you tell me."[4] And Bess would describe Grace's and any of the other children's costumes in detail. In all likelihood Grace Simpson was reincarnated as Josephine Cutter's friend, Effie Peterson, in **"Josephine Encounters a Siren"** (*The American Magazine,* December 1922).

Bess won her first writing prize, a camera, at the age of fourteen, later admitting, "It was then I first tasted blood; for the intoxication of seeing my name in print was overwhelming." At seventeen she entered a contest with a story she later described as "heavy as a moving van. It oozed pathos. It dripped melancholy."[5] It won five dollars for her, which she used to purchase a showy umbrella she thought made her look sophisticated and which would later appear as a humorous object in her writing. She wrote articles throughout her college career at Iowa State Normal School, now known as the University of Northern Iowa, from which she graduated in 1901. She then went on to teach in Boone and Marshalltown, Iowa, and then Salt Lake City, Utah. She returned to Cedar Falls, Iowa, in 1906, working as Assistant Supervisor of the Primary Department on the equivalent of her master's degree, which she received the following year. While she taught and worked on her second degree, she wrote articles and published children's stories and had a story accepted for publication just weeks before her wedding.

However, after her 1907 marriage to attorney Charles Sweetzer Aldrich and their subsequent move from Cedar Falls to Tipton, Iowa, she found little time for writing. In 1909 the Aldriches, their two-month-old daughter Mary Eleanor, Bess's mother, and her sister Clara and brother-in-law John Cobb moved to Elmwood, Nebraska, where the Aldriches and the Cobbs had purchased the American Exchange Bank. For the next two years, Aldrich spent her time as wife and mother and became an active member of her new community. Then, in 1911, she saw an advertisement in the *Ladies Home Journal* asking readers to send in stories for a contest the *Journal* was sponsoring. Aldrich's desire to write resurfaced, and the next few afternoons while the baby napped, Aldrich wrote her story. She took it to the bank to type, and when one of the clerks needed to use the typewriter, Bess took out her story, waited until he was done, and then sat down to pick out the letters again until the next interruption. The contest attracted more than two thousand entrants, apparently exceeding what was anticipated, for the magazine dropped the contest idea and instead purchased six of the submitted stories. Aldrich's **"The Little House Next Door"** was one of those. When the $175 check came, her mother, who was living at the Aldrich home at the time, said, "Look again, Bess, it must be a dollar seventy-five!"[6] It was, indeed, one hundred seventy-five.

Bess Streeter Aldrich then began the transition from occasional to full-time author. With the excitement and impetus of this important sale, she began immediately on another story, sandwiching writing time between the tasks of caring for her husband, her children, and her home. She explained that "the blood that had come from the people who crossed the Mississippi on the ice with oxen began to assert itself, and I determined that if keeping constantly at writing would eventually land one somewhere, I would begin writing in earnest. From that time on I had a manuscript on the road" almost constantly. The next story "wandered around from magazine to magazine making twenty-three trips before it found an editor who would buy it, and it brought only twenty dollars." Because some of her stories went out so often, they became dog-eared, and Aldrich would retype the first and last pages to create the impression that the story was on its first trip. She said that she was "selling one just often enough to encourage me."[7]

In order to sell, Aldrich knew she had to work on the details and techniques of writing; thus she did whatever gave her the opportunity to practice. She entered and won a few newspaper contests, submitted a recipe to *Armour Cookbook* that was accepted, sent a couple of comments to *The Delineator* and received one dollar for each, and wrote some other miscellaneous materials, only two of which are included in this collection. The first is **"My Life Test"** and the second is **"How I Knew When the Right Man Came Along."** These both have the Aldrich cadence and character types, and, to the best of my knowledge, are Aldrich's writings; however, they were published anonymously, and no conclusive evidence proving they are hers has come to my attention. Both are recorded in her financial journal.

Every acceptance, whether it garnered one dollar or many times that amount, was recorded in Aldrich's financial journal. In four years, she had earned a total of $638 for her writings; only three sales had exceeded $100. She continued to work at her craft by taking correspondence lessons from a writing school whose director told her that inasmuch as she had already had some success in publishing, he would take her on as his private pupil and read her work himself. It was not long before he told her that she was a born writer and that her work was so good there was little he could teach her, although he would be glad to continue to read and critique any material she might choose to send him. Acceptances for her work increased.

The year 1918 was an important one for Aldrich. Until this time, describing it as a form of writer's print fright much like an actor's stage fright, Aldrich had written as Margaret Dean Stevens, a combination of her two grand-mothers' names. She was now confident enough to use Bess Streeter Aldrich. Proof of her increasing success came in 1918 when *McCall's* accepted **"The Box behind the Door,"** and *The People's Home Journal*, another solid magazine of the time, bought **"Their House of Dreams."** The letter from *The American Magazine* for **"Mother's Dash for Liberty"** must have been the most exciting acceptance since the *Journal* had published **"The Little House Next Door"** in 1911. Aldrich felt this sale was her turning point, for she had long been trying to break into the highly regarded *American*, which had rejected some of her stories that other magazines, such as *McCall's*, had subsequently accepted. *The American* reflected the optimistic ideals of its editor, John M. Siddall, who chose only well-written and upbeat stories. Evidently Siddall understood his subscribers, for by November of 1919 *The American*'s paid circulation was more than 125 million.[8] **"Mother's Dash"** appeared in the December issue. Shortly thereafter, a soldier stationed in Germany wrote that his buddies had worn out his copy of *The American* because **"Mother's Dash"** reminded them so much of home and their own mothers; he asked for more of these stories. Aldrich already had the next one at the editor's office.

In 1920 her fourth and last child was born, giving Bess and Charles one daughter and three sons. Fortunately, Charles gave Bess "help and encouragement . . . pressed [her] to take more time for writing, encouraged [her] in every way." Continuing to find the time to write was not easy, however, and she struggled with obstacles: "I wrote when the meals cooked, when babies tumbled over my feet, and while I was ironing, in the old days. The hand that rocked the cradle was often the left one, while the right was jotting down a sentence or two. I have had the first draft of many a story sprinkled liberally with good old sudsy dishwater."[9] Nor did the writing itself necessarily come easily, and Aldrich speaks of "walking the floor" in distress over an idea as she would of walking the floor with a baby in distress, and in so doing she reveals how for her the private and the professional, the domestic and the literary, were one.[10]

Not surprisingly, Aldrich's principles for her fiction were those by which she lived. Her writing must be acceptable to everyone, she determined. Her stories are about decent people saying and doing decent things. There is no swearing in Aldrich stories, no sex, no divorce, none of the seamy side of life; indeed, "decent" and "seamy" are Aldrich's terms. She wrote,

> Why quarrel with a writer over realism and idealism? After all, an author is a glass through which a picture of life is projected. The picture falls upon the pages of the writer's manuscript according to the mental and emotional contours of that writer. It is useless to try to change these patterns. If one writer does not see life in terms of dirt and grime and debaucheries, it is no sign that those sordid things do not exist. If another does not see life in terms of faith and love, courage and good deeds, it does not follow that those characteristics

do not exist. . . . I claim that one may portray some of the decent things about him and reserve the privilege to call that real life too.[11]

By similar principles, Aldrich chose to write of domestic rather than of political conflicts. As a granddaughter, a wife, and a writer she knew of war: during the Civil War her grandfather, in his sixties, had gone to Atlanta to bring the Iowa soldiers' votes back to their state to be counted in the 1864 presidential election, and, because all contact with the North had been cut, he had had to endure with Sherman's troops the terrible march to the sea. Her husband had served in the Spanish-American War and had almost died; and Aldrich wrote and published stories during World War I. War was the single topic for which Aldrich expressed unequivocal hatred, and in her own way she devoted herself to eradicating it. As if willing a future free of war, she joined others in believing that World War I would end all wars; and as if erasing it from the present, she expunged it from her fiction. The **"Rosemary of Remembrance,"** published in the *Black Cat Magazine* in 1917, contains no direct mention of the conflict—nor do any of her stories. Only in the subtext of metaphors does armed violence erupt: words are "like a hand grenade" and "shrapnel."[12] The "hand grenade" metaphor also appears in a 1918 story and rain is compared to "shrapnel" in another 1918 story. Perhaps the metaphors took her unaware, for Aldrich consciously dedicated herself to the belief that people read to escape, and that as a writer she should offer an enjoyable respite from war's horrors. It was a principle of literary nonviolence, one might say—a principle Aldrich retained throughout her career. Years later she explained to an editor that she could not believe that during a war people wanted to read about conflict in their leisure time.[13]

An observer of life and people, Aldrich recognized that much of life is lived through feelings. She said that "my type of story is a story of emotion rather than of the intellect. I try to make the reader feel."[14] She also wanted to promote understanding of rural lives by her urban readers. Aldrich lived and wrote in a village, and her stories ring with the life of small towns: the kensingtons (church women's groups), the school activities, the functions and celebrations that were combined efforts of all the townspeople, and the sense of personal history they had about each other. In her stories, Aldrich is protective of and supports those who remain on the farms; her message is that farmers are becoming well educated and often may be college graduates and that the wives are becoming chic and up to date, much as their urban sisters. One reason her work was so in demand was that she offered to her readers the feel of the country, the best of their memories of rural homes known or imagined. As one editor wrote to Aldrich, he and his wife were "small town folks—the big cities are full of us. . . . You don't merely create characters, you create people with whom we are familiar."[15] Aldrich was a fighter for what she believed in, although something of a velvet-gloved fighter, and there was little that could raise

her ire as quickly as someone insulting her beloved Midwest, which she inevitably defended. Aldrich believed in the farmers and villagers and in their lives, knew that they experienced the same emotions as their urban relatives, and, while recognizing that they were not perfect, wrote of them with respect and affection.

Always conscious of the distinctions that a choice of language makes, she rejected academic classifications and described herself as a realist, explaining that "sentiment" (that is, emotion) was part of reality:

> Sentiment doesn't lie in soil, or in climate, or latitude, or longitude. It lies in the hearts of people. Wherever there are folks who live and work and love and die, whether they raise hogs in Iowa or oranges in California or the sails of a pleasure boat at Palm Beach, there is the stuff of which stories are made.[16]

My own label for Aldrich's writing is "romantic realist," for she was a writer who affirmed the goodness that exists in everyday living.

Even in these early years as a writer, Aldrich was firm in her principles, but she never felt it her duty to force her ideas on others. She offered her thoughts and words as possibilities or examples, but let each choose her or his own path. She was consistent in her ideals.

Notes

1. Bess Streeter Aldrich, cards on how to write a short story, Box 10, archives of Nebraska State Historical Society, Lincoln, Nebraska, hereinafter NSHS.

2. John M. Siddall to Bess Streeter Aldrich, 22 June 1920, Box 4, NSHS.

3. Bess Streeter Aldrich, *The Cutters* (New York: D. Appleton & Company, 1926), p. 110.

4. Julie Bailey, "Bess Streeter Aldrich, Her Life and Work," May 1965, p. 7, Cedar Falls Historical Society, Cedar Falls, Iowa.

5. Bess Streeter Aldrich, "How I Mixed Stories with Do-Nuts," *The American Magazine,* February 1921, p. 33.

6. Item 20, n.p., n.d., NSHS.

7. Bess Streeter Aldrich, Box 10, NSHS. Box 10, File Misc. and Mss., p. 5, NSHS.

8. John M. Siddall to Bess Streeter Aldrich, 19 November 1919, Box 4, NSHS.

9. "Nebraska Woman Gains Fame as Author," *Fillmore County (Neb.) News,* 12 May 1926.

10. Box 10, File Misc. and Mss., p. 4, NSHS.

11. "There Are Two Viewpoints . . . ," Box 10, File Misc. and Mss., p. 2, NSHS.

12. Bess Streeter Aldrich, "The Rosemary of Remembrance," *The Black Cat Magazine,* 1917.

13. John L. B. Williams to Bess Streeter Aldrich, 18 September 1941, Box 7, Bus. Corres. File 1941, NSHS.

14. Draft of talk "And There Are Times When . . . ," Box 10, File Misc. and Mss., p. 1, NSHS.

15. John M. Siddall to Bess Streeter Aldrich, 22 January 1920, Box 4, NSHS.

16. Lillian Lambert, "Bess Streeter Aldrich," *Midland Schools* (Des Moines, Ia.) 42:8 (April 1928), University of Northern Iowa Archives, p. 299.

FURTHER READING

Bibliography

Peterson, Carol Miles. *Bess Streeter Aldrich: The Dreams Are All Real.* Lincoln, Neb.: University of Nebraska Press, 1995, 237 p.
    Includes a complete bibliography of Aldrich's work.

Biography

Meier, A. Mabel. "Bess Streeter Aldrich: A Literary Portrait." *Nebraska History* 50, no. 1 (1969): 67-100.
    Biographical chronology of Aldrich's life and writings.

Additional coverage of Aldrich's life and career is contained in the following sources published by the Gale Group: *Children's Literature Review,* Vol. 70; and *Literature Resource Center.*

Howards End

E. M. Forster

INTRODUCTION

English novelist, short story writer, essayist, critic, and biographer.

The following entry presents criticism on Forster's novel *Howards End* (1910). For additional coverage of his life and works, see *CLC,* Volumes 1, 2, 3, 4, 9, 10, 13, 15, 22, 45, and 77.

In *Howards End* (1910) Forster explored the often violent and disturbing struggle for survival and dominance among English social classes in the first years of the twentieth century. Ultimately arguing in favor of the fundamental integrity of the individual and the primacy of personal relations, *Howards End* focuses largely on the simplicity of its famous dictum: "Only connect!"

PLOT AND MAJOR CHARACTERS

Howards End begins with the depiction of a series of seemingly unrelated encounters and events that soon cause the lives of individuals in three distinct English social classes to intertwine, with permanent and sometimes shocking consequences. Margaret and Helen Schlegel are sisters who represent the middle level of the English middle class. Financially independent but not wealthy, the Schlegel sisters are categorized as intellectual humanists, devoted to the arts and literature rather than the capitalist interests of the upper-middle-class Wilcox family, who cannot be bothered with intellectual or emotional issues because they are entirely focused on rigid financial and social pursuits. A third class level is illustrated by Leonard Bast, a lower-middle-class clerk at an insurance company who loses his job and is cast into poverty because of some advice he takes from Henry Wilcox. It is primarily Margaret Schlegel who serves as the bridge among the three social groups. Margaret befriends Henry Wilcox's first wife, Ruth, who is the inheritor of the country house Howards End and who feels an affinity for Margaret that she does not have with any of her family; eventually, she tries to bequeath Margaret the house in her will. Margaret also becomes closely acquainted with Henry, whom she eventually marries. Helen has a child with Leonard Bast, who dies from heart failure after receiving a beating from Henry's son Charles. After a series of misunderstandings and separations, the three main characters—Margaret, Helen, and Henry—are reunited at Howards End, where they all choose to live, along with Helen and Leonard's child.

Margaret's famous plea, "Only connect," beseeching others to observe and unite the various aspects of life—the mundane and the extraordinary—serves as a unifying theme among the disparate classes and characters.

MAJOR THEMES

Forster's themes in *Howards End* are many and varied. Most important is the antagonism among the classes in Edwardian England. The second half of the nineteenth century in England—as well as in America—saw a burgeoning of the middle and upper-middle classes, as industrial spread and businesses, particularly factories, grew. This business class, which had money but few family or social connections to the gentry, was known for its pragmatic approach to living, valuing material acquisition over patronage of the arts and liberal education. The tension between the Wilcoxes and the Schlegel sisters revolves around these differing values. By making the sisters part

German, Forster also called to attention to sociopolitical relations between England and Germany at the turn of the century. The sisters' relationship with each other also is important to understanding Forster's themes. With each sister involved with men of different classes, they represent a separate facet of class awareness. The central symbolic image in the novel is Howards End, the house itself, which serves as a symbol of unity and community in an unstable and chaotic social world.

CRITICAL RECEPTION

Howards End is acknowledged as one of Forster's greatest achievements in fiction. Critics have noted, however, that Forster seemed uneasy about representing physical relationships. The events that occur between Helen Schlegel and Leonard Bast have received the most negative commentary, with many critics finding their relationship baffling. Nonetheless, opinion of *Howards End* generally places it among Forster's most important commentaries on Edwardian society.

PRINCIPAL WORKS

Where Angels Fear to Tread (novel) 1905
The Longest Journey (novel) 1907
A Room with a View (novel) 1908
Howards End (novel) 1910
The Celestial Omnibus, and Other Stories (short stories) 1911
Alexandria: A History and a Guide (nonfiction) 1920
The Story of the Siren (short stories) 1920
Pharos and Pharillon (nonfiction) 1923
A Passage to India (novel) 1924
Aspects of the Novel (criticism) 1927
Abinger Harvest (essays) 1936
Two Cheers for Democracy (essays) 1951
The Hill of Devi: Being Letters from Dewas State Senior (nonfiction) 1953
Marianne Thornton: A Domestic Biography (biography) 1956
Maurice (novel) 1971

CRITICISM

James Hall (essay date 1963)

SOURCE: Hall, James. "Family Reunions: E. M. Forster." In *The Tragic Comedians: Seven Modern British Novelists,* pp. 11-30. Bloomington: Indiana University Press, 1963.

[*In the following essay, Hall argues that Forster presents a conservative view of family dynamics in* Howards End.]

The breakup and continuance of the family are such consistent themes in E. M. Forster's novels that every reader must understand them in a way. But, asked anything specific about them, he is unlikely to understand much more than that they exist, and even less likely to understand their relation to other themes to which critics have given a more prominent place. So my turning Eliot's title to Forster's feeling for family continuity does not mean to be whimsical but to focus an apparent paradox. Most critics of Forster have made much of his liberalism. But, unlike Eliot, the avowed conservative, who in his plays distrusts a return to family roots, Forster in every novel but one uses a sense of family continuity to make reconciliation with the adult world possible. A conservatism about the family sustains his liberalism about other institutions—though *sustains* is a simple word for a more dynamic process.

Roughly, two of Forster's novels are about breaking away from the family, two about trying to restore it, and the fifth about trying to live without it. *Where Angels Fear to Tread* and *A Room with a View* do show rebellions against the passive acceptance of family values. *The Longest Journey* is Ricky's struggle to accept members of his family whom he cannot readily accept—mother, wife, brother—and ends in partial acceptance and a promise of reconciliation in a new generation. *Howards End* deals with the estrangement of two sisters who are eventually reconciled with another promise of fuller reconciliation in a new generation. *A Passage to India,* his most pessimistic and searching novel, carries the resolution in *Howards End* through a sterner test and concludes on the most skeptical note about personal relations in Forster. (Margaret's defense of Helen in a crisis—the defense of a social outcast by an uncomfortable member of the comfortable class—leads to a "happy" ending. *A Passage to India* tests the community of spirit induced by an uncomfortable Englishman's defending a Mohammedan doctor in a British Indian court, and finds it successful during the crisis but no basis for understanding because interests diverge too far.)

But each main action has a counteraction. When *Where Angels Fear to Tread* and *A Room with a View* are read only as rebellions in favor of a freer, more natural life, the family becomes a restrictive conspiracy opposing growth and intruding into the hero or heroine's adult life an archaic set of *don'ts*. But this restrictiveness is only one side. In both novels the scenes from family life also give a base of habitual affections and resentments on which the Archimedean main figure can stand. And the characters in both novels make more sense as groups than as individuals. By themselves they are startlingly incomplete. In *A Room with a View* George needs Mr. Emerson and his theories for his own brooding naturalism to mean anything, Lucy needs Charlotte and Mr. Beebe to give direction to the passive side of her nature. In Italy Lucy resists some of Charlotte's ideas and is bewildered by others, but Charlotte is Lucy's conscience and is obeyed, disobeyed, liked, and disliked in about the way consciences can expect. Without Charlotte's negatives and hesitations, Lucy would be only the girl who plays Beethoven with a little too much enthusiasm. And if Lucy's marriage to George were a straightforward rebellion against the family *don't's,* she should in all logic slough off Charlotte, who as chaperon constantly reminds Lucy that she speaks for her mother. But, although by *Howards End* Forster can say that "conversion is an idea peculiarly appealing to half-baked minds," *A Room with a View* ends with two conversions—of Lucy and the chaperon. And active cooperation, not merely passive assent, is required from Charlotte for the marriage to take place. Lucy and George, separated by misunderstandings, can be married only when Charlotte has been converted to the fuller life and passively conspires in the arrangements with Mr. Emerson.

A similar conversion of the chaperon happens in *Where Angels Fear to Tread.* Philip finds a freer, more natural way of life in Italy, but again the spinster loosely attached to the family must be converted before Philip can believe in his own experience. (Forster, like Mr. Beebe, is a connoisseur of spinsters.) Caroline Abbott, the chaperon who has tried to atone for her previous failure by making sure that Philip carries out the family mission, leads him to see that the "rescue" of Gino's baby is wrong, though Philip has been seeing that in a way all along. The discovery of Italy is a tourist's discovery in both novels and must be absorbed by the more meaningful life in England. It is not enough for Lucy and Philip to rebel. Without the chaperon's participation the rebellion has no standing or promise of endurance. In both his novels about breaking away from the family, Forster's conservatism leads him to carry the family authority along with the rebels.

But these chaperons are not so much "authority" as Forster's special way of by-passing the problems of authority. Since the fathers are dead in his novels, the chaperons are the nearest approaches to moral authority; but, though they have a set of imperatives, they have a happily limited power of enforcing them. Charlotte's position as a poor relation makes her power equivocal, and Caroline and Harriet cannot make Philip do anything. But these spinsters, whose lives are arrested and who ape the older generation, are far sterner than the mothers. The mothers in these novels are more motherly and less saintly than the withdrawn, dying ones in the last two novels. They are comfortable, irritating, complaining, fussy, lovable. Philip's relation with his mother has added the value of a permissive disregard. She gives him a comfortable way of living, nags him, but, except for the trip to Italy, leaves him free to do as he pleases. She objects, but her objections have become conventionalized and can be disregarded without consequence to their relation.

This conservatism about the family even in the novels of rebellion forecasts a stronger conservatism in *Howards End. Howards End* shows the reasons for the breakup of the Schlegel family, the efforts to establish individual ways of life, and the reconciliation on a basis which allows for adult experience. At the beginning of the novel the Schle-

gel sisters have no problem of breaking away from parents—they are as free as people can be. They have money, friends, intelligence, and apparent stability. The novel treats the further difficulty in personal relations caused by different views of human nature.

Howards End involves a dichotomy between structure and texture or, to use other terms, between formal and sympathetic structures. Everyone who writes on Forster must respect Lionel Trilling, but Forster's plots are among the most diagrammable in English literature and Trilling's interest in a modulated liberalism makes him emphasize the formal structure of *Howards End*—intellectual versus businessman versus underdog—at the expense of the sympathetic structure. The truly interested writing in *Howards End,* like the truly interested writing in Trilling's own *The Middle of the Journey,* is about intellectual versus intellectual—the split between Margaret and Helen over how life should be lived and their reconciliation by including something from both their values. (There is a second, though weaker, kind of vitality in Forster's condescension to Leonard Bast, the clerk who aspires to the Schlegel values, knows he will not achieve them, and becomes morally significant in rejecting a sentimental, quickie view of the possibilities of experience. Leonard cannot achieve anything positive, but he can discover that an all-night walk in the woods is painful, not romantic.)

In saying this I do not mean that a reasonable structure of the novel cannot be set up through the conflict between activist, intellectual, and underdog. But a telling point in a "comedy" of manners is, when is it comic? *Howards End* can be comic about Leonard's puzzling over Ruskin's "Seven miles to the north of Venice. . . ." But Forster says that the greatest feeling is the sense of space and, by the criterion of free movement, the comic and telling parts of *Howards End* are in the Schlegels' tone about serious matters. The scene where Margaret urges Tibby to choose a career has this kind of ease. Tibby's significance lies in his commitment to being uncommitted. But Margaret has been thinking of marriage and the Wilcoxes, and would like to impose a little Wilcox spirit on Tibby. What comes out is a community-in-difference:

> Did he at all know where he wanted to live? Tibby didn't know that he did know. Did he at all know he wanted to do? He was equally uncertain, but when pressed remarked that he should prefer to be quite free of any profession. Margaret was not shocked, but went on sewing for a few minutes before she replied:
>
> "I was thinking of Mr. Vyse. He never strikes me as particularly happy."
>
> "Ye-es," said Tibby, and then held his mouth open in a curious quiver, as if he, too, had thought of Mr. Vyse, had seen round, through, over, and beyond Mr. Vyse, had weighed Mr. Vyse, grouped him, and finally dismissed him as having no possible bearing on the subject under discussion. That bleat of Tibby's infuriated Helen. But Helen was now down in the dining-room preparing a speech about political economy. At times her voice could be heard declaiming through the floor.

"But Mr. Vyse is rather a wretched, weedy man, don't you think? Then there's Guy. That was a pitiful business. Besides"—shifting to the general—"every one is better for some regular work."

Groans.

"I shall stick to it," she continued, smiling. "I am not saying it to educate you; it is what I really think. I believe that in the last century men have developed the desire for work, and they must not starve it. It's a new desire. It goes with a great deal that's bad, but in itself it's good, and I hope that for women, too, 'not to work' will soon become as shocking as 'not to be married' was a hundred years ago."

"I have no experience of this profound desire to which you allude," enunciated Tibby.

"Then we'll leave the subject till you do. I'm not going to rattle you around. Take your time. Only do think over the lives of the men you like most, and see how they've arranged them."

"I like Guy and Mr. Vyse most," said Tibby faintly, and leant so far back in his chair that he extended in a horizontal line from knees to throat.

But Tibby, apparently downed, sees through Margaret and craftily turns the talk to marriage and the Wilcoxes.

Forster varies his community-in-difference theme skillfully through a scene as different as Helen's story about Mrs. Bast:

As she spoke, the door was flung open, and Helen burst in in a state of extreme excitement.

"Oh, my dears, what do you think? You'll never guess. A woman's been here asking me for her husband. Her what?" (Helen was fond of supplying her own surprise.) "Yes, for her husband, and it really is so."

"Not anything to do with Bracknell?" cried Margaret, who had lately taken on an unemployed of that name to clean the knives and boots.

"I offered Bracknell, and he was rejected. So was Tibby. (Cheer up, Tibby!) It's no one we know. I said, 'Hunt, my good woman; have a good look round, hunt under the tables, poke up the chimney, shake out the antimacassars. Husband? Husband?' Oh, and she so magnificently dressed and tinkling like a chandelier."

"Now, Helen, what did happen really?"

"What I say. I was, as it were, orating my speech. Annie opens the door like a fool, and shows a female straight in on me, with my mouth open. Then we began—very civilly. 'I want my husband, what I have reason to believe is here.' No—how unjust one is. She said 'whom,' not 'what.' She got it perfectly. So I said, 'Name, please?' and she said, 'Lan, Miss,' and there we were."

"Lan?"

"Lan or Len. We were not nice about our vowels. Lanoline."

"But what an extraordinary—"

"I said, 'My good Mrs. Lanoline, we have some grave misunderstanding here. Beautiful as I am, my modesty is even more remarkable than my beauty, and never, never has Mr. Lanoline rested his eyes on mine.'

"I hope you were pleased," said Tibby.

"Of course," Helen squeaked. "A perfectly delightful experience. Oh, Mrs. Lanoline's a dear—she asked for a husband as if he were an umbrella. She mislaid him Saturday afternoon—and for a long time suffered no inconvenience. But all night, and all this morning her apprehensions grew. Breakfast didn't seem to be the same—no, no more did lunch, and so she strolled up to 2, Wickham Place as being the most likely place for the missing article."

"But how on earth—"

"Don't begin how on earthing. 'I know what I know,' she kept repeating, not uncivilly, but with extreme gloom. In vain I asked her what she did know. Some knew what others knew, and others didn't, and if they didn't, then others again had better be careful. Oh dear, she was incompetent! She had a face like a silkworm, and the dining-room reeks of orris-root. We chatted pleasantly a little about husbands, and I wondered where hers was too, and advised her to go to the police. She thanked me. We agreed that Mr. Lanoline's a notty, notty man, and hasn't no business to go on the lardy-da. But I think she suspected me up to the last."

In comparison, when Forster sets Schlegels against Wilcoxes, the intellectual woman against the new rich, his scenes become angry and he is almost always outside his characters. He is edgy with Charles Wilcox even about Charles' liking for automobiles. He treats Evie's sporting life and Dolly's talk to her child as equal absurdities. He makes Mr. Wilcox foolish for thinking about subletting instead of worrying about Leonard, whom Mr. Wilcox does not know. In showing the new rich, Forster loads the situations so much that the writing becomes satiric and often too irritable to be telling. Right quarrels with wrong, and the reader is uncomfortable with the easy distinction.

The interesting conflict in *Howards End,* then, is not between right and wrong, but between two rights—which ought to be complementary and are not. Forster portions out between Margaret and Helen attitudes and qualities he admires with a minimum of reservation. Both are right, their tone is right, and the family scenes work in a way that the diagrammable scenes do not. And scenes of the Schlegels with Leonard work, though in a different way.

The family conflict and reconciliation has a structure of its own, with turning points different from those of the class conflict. The novel opens with the family unity upset by Helen's attraction to and quick revulsion from the Wilcoxes. The first part—to the time the Schlegels are forced to leave the house in Wickham Place so that new apartments can be built—shows the family unity being subjected to the strain of interests changing with age. Forster places Margaret's drama at the moment in her life when she is losing interest in the "life of lectures and concerts."

She is reluctant to part from the banter and enthusiasm of life at Wickham Place, but her own restiveness is the inner wish which matches the threat from outside—the tearing down of the house in the name of "progress." She wants to make other arrangements, and is being forced to. Her weariness with lectures and concerts comes out explicitly after her marriage.

> As for theatres and discussion societies, they attracted her less and less. She began to "miss" new movements, and to spend her spare time re-reading or thinking, rather to the concern of her Chelsea friends. They attributed the change to her marriage, and perhaps some deep instinct did warn her not to travel further from her husband than was inevitable. Yet the main cause lay deeper still; she had outgrown stimulants, and was passing from words to things. It was doubtless a pity not to keep up with Wedekind or John, but some closing of the gates is inevitable after thirty, if the mind itself is to become a creative power.

At the time Margaret responds both to Mrs. Wilcox's withdrawn quality and to her complete concern with her family. And in marrying Mr. Wilcox later, Margaret works out her lived myth, trying to put herself in the place of a mother figure even to the point of marrying the father figure and, like Mrs. Wilcox, feeling uncomfortable everywhere except in the atmosphere of quiet, renewal, and continuity represented by the farm at Howards End. Entirely aside from the Wilcoxes' cheating, Margaret is not ready to inherit Howards End at the time Mrs. Wilcox leaves it to her. She can truly inherit it only after she has in her way gone through Mrs. Wilcox's experiences with Mr. Wilcox and worked out a *modus vivendi* suited to her own personality. She never feels comfortable with Mr. Wilcox. He is always the problem, to be handled by a compromise of good sense but never accepted as the ideal father which Margaret's talk about her own father and her decision to marry imply she is searching for. She is still talking about her own father near the end of the novel.

The basis for estrangement between Helen and Margaret is set up in the opening scenes, which seem at the time to lead toward greater solidarity. Helen at first likes the sense of masculine sureness which the Wilcoxes all apparently have. But she can live with this assurance only so long as she believes it to be complete. Every man should be ideally courageous, every woman ideally beautiful. Helen is not ideally beautiful, but she holds Paul to a standard of ideal courage and, when she sees him as the frightened son in a patriarchal system, feels betrayed and rejects all Wilcoxes totally. Aunt Juley's blundering rescue brings Helen back to the family and Aunt Juley's argument that Schlegels are better than Wilcoxes, foolishly carried on and foolishly answered, still makes Helen's point.

Margaret supports Helen in her flight from the Wilcoxes. But she herself comes on them from another side and her friendship with Mrs. Wilcox is an enthusiasm not shared by Helen or their intellectual friends. The estrangement between the sisters arises from a divergence of sympathies rather than quarrels of the Lawrence sort. They do what people with ideals about "personal relations" can to smooth over the divergence, but Helen rejects the managing, authoritarian spirit so thoroughly that she can like only the underdog Leonard Bast. Trying to hold to the existing arrangement, she opposes Margaret's marriage violently:

> "Don't," sobbed Helen, "don't, don't, Meg, don't!" She seemed incapable of saying any other word. Margaret, trembling herself, led her forward up the road, till they strayed through another gate on to the down.
>
> "Don't, don't do such a thing! I tell you not to—don't! I know—don't!"
>
> "What do you know?"
>
> "Panic and emptiness," sobbed Helen. "Don't!"
>
> Then Margaret thought, "Helen is a little selfish. I have never behaved like this when there has seemed a chance of her marrying." She said: "But we would still see each other very often, and—"
>
> "It's not a thing like that," sobbed Helen. And she broke right away and wandered distractedly upwards, stretching her hands towards the view and crying.
>
> "What's happened to you?" called Margaret, following through the wind that gathers at sundown on the northern slopes of the hills. "But it's stupid!" And suddenly stupidity seized her, and the immense landscape was blurred. But Helen turned back.
>
> "Meg—"
>
> "I don't know what's happened to either of us," said Margaret, wiping her eyes. "We must have both gone mad." Then Helen wiped hers, and they even laughed a little.

Forster says that Helen's brief affair with Leonard is loveless, a combination of impulse and principle. But in the earlier scenes at Wickham Place Helen takes a different interest in him from Margaret's. Margaret tries to deal humanely with his immediate problem, but takes no great personal interest. Helen baits him, jokes at him when she knows he cannot answer in kind.

> An air of evasion characterized Mr. Bast. He explained again, but was obviously lying, and Helen didn't see why he should get off. She had the cruelty of youth. Neglecting her sister's pressure, she said, "I still don't understand. When did you say you paid this call?"
>
> "Call? What call?" said he, staring as if her question had been a foolish one, a favourite device of those in midstream.
>
> "This afternoon call."
>
> "In the afternoon, of course!" he replied, and looked at Tibby to see how the repartee went. But Tibby, himself a repartee, was unsympathetic, and said, "Saturday afternoon or Sunday afternoon?"
>
> "S—Saturday."
>
> "Really!" said Helen; "and you were still calling on Sunday, when your wife came here. A long visit."

"I don't call that fair," said Mr. Bast, going scarlet and handsome. There was fight in his eyes. "I know what you mean, and it isn't so."

. . . "Mr. Bast, you're a born adventurer," laughed Margaret. "No professional athlete would have attempted what you've done. It's a wonder your walk didn't end in a broken neck. Whatever did your wife say?"

"Professional athletes never move without lanterns and compasses," said Helen. "Besides, they can't walk. It tires them. Go on."

"I felt like R.L.S. You probably remember how in 'Virginibus—'"

"Yes, but the wood. This 'ere wood. How did you get out?"

But Helen becomes obsessed with the idea that something must be done for him. Her illusion is that a mothering, instinctive helpfulness can triumph over all the "little things" that thwart Leonard and separate him and her as people. She and he have both been let down by the practical, managing people, by Margaret as well as by the Wilcoxes.

For Margaret's marriage to Mr. Wilcox is not merely an identification with Mrs. Wilcox or a desperate determination to be protected by a fatherly man. She and Mr. Wilcox deserve each other in another way. They are both managers of life and the emotions rather than followers of them. The main threat of the novel is not, as Trilling says, that the Wilcoxes may inherit England, but that they may inherit Margaret. She feels this threat herself and sees the marriage as one of opposites in which she must maintain a willingness to compromise, but also keep her individuality.

> By quiet indications the bridge would be built and span their lives with beauty.

> But she failed. For there was one quality in Henry for which she was never prepared, however much she reminded herself of it: his obtuseness. He simply did not notice things, and there was no more to be said. He never noticed that Helen and Frieda were hostile, or that Tibby was not interested in currant plantations; he never noticed the lights and shades that exist in the greyest conversation, the finger-posts, the milestones, the collisions, the illimitable views.

From the point of view of the novel, Margaret's commitment to Mr. Wilcox is wrong, but real. To preserve it she refuses Helen's arguments after the discovery of Mr. Wilcox's affair with Jackie, and the estrangement from Helen, hitherto kept within bounds, becomes an actual separation.

> They spent their honeymoon near Innsbruck. Henry knew of a reliable hotel there, and Margaret hoped for a meeting with her sister. In this she was disappointed. As they came south, Helen retreated over the Brenner, and wrote an unsatisfactory postcard from the shores of the Lake of Garda, saying that her plans were uncertain and had better be ignored. Evidently she disliked meeting Henry. Two months are surely enough to accustom an outsider to a situation which a wife has accepted in

two days, and Margaret had again to regret her sister's lack of self-control. In a long letter she pointed out the need of charity in sexual matters: so little is known about them; it is hard enough for those who are personally touched to judge; then how futile must be the verdict of Society. . . . Helen thanked her for her kind letter—rather a curious reply. She moved south again, and spoke of wintering in Naples.

Helen settles in Germany and conceals her pregnancy because she can no longer count on complete sympathy from Margaret.

My point so far is that Forster's imagination is more fully engaged when he writes about the articulate and self-conscious members of an intellectual family than when he writes about people who, whether for Leonard's or Mr. Wilcox's reasons, are less articulate and self-conscious. But the point would hold true further: he writes better about Aunt Juley than about Evie or Charles Wilcox, though both are more important to the formal structure of the novel than she is. These second-generation Wilcoxes, the furthest removed from the Schlegel sisters' concern with the complexities of experience and their own natures, are puppets illustrating arrogance, jealousy, suspicion, and cupidity. But it would be foolish to deny Forster's interest in his class conflict. A page count would prove that even if the text did not insist on it. So the serious question becomes, what is the relation between the class conflict and the family conflict?

Again roughly, Forster's major tension is between the desire to shape life by what seems best and possible in the present and the desire to maintain the meaning of the formative past. The Schlegel sisters want to master the adult world and yet keep the child's sense of identity and continuity. Such balances seldom come out even, but Forster's individuality shows most in the way he tries to balance. The conflict of Wilcoxes, Schlegels, and Basts establishes the primary moral line—tells us what value to put on people with sharply different temperaments and aims. The action of the novel rewards and punishes in these terms. Margaret and Helen, who provide the moral center of this drama, inherit and live at Howards End. The second-generation Wilcoxes are routed. Charles is imprisoned, all are separated permanently from their father. Mr. Wilcox, the patriarch, is shorn—for defending his children's and his own rules of conduct against Margaret's. Charles' killing Leonard with the old sword caricatures the Wilcox claim to descent from the warrior class as well as the Schlegel ideal of the warrior-philosopher. Charles has overrated himself and Margaret has been tempted to overrate Mr. Wilcox. The ending is a *Jane Eyre* one: the offenders are punished severely and the husband is gelded, needing thereafter only a nurse. Conversely, Leonard, who could never fit in at Howards End but wanted to, is given an absurd but good death while trying to do a last "right thing." The Schlegel sisters inherit because they have deserved to, but the high barriers to community of spirit remain barriers. Helen and Margaret both try to reach understanding with people of extremely different backgrounds, temperaments, and hopes. The novel yields no ground at all to this possibility.

But all this was in the cards, though the reader does not see that until the end. Too great differences are separative and, at close quarters, produce only the urge to destroy or an ineffective sympathy. But the drama of estrangement and reconciliation within the family cannot be resolved by an either/or. The Schlegel sisters have enough understanding and sympathy to make for some solidarity. But both for a time face a feeling of uprootedness, of self-searching, that makes their own activities and their friends' seem superficial. Their decisions during this period come from sympathies, hitherto submerged, toward people outside their group. They want to identify with people who are different, but they do not agree on different-in-what-way. Their alienation is built up slowly and comes to a crisis through their acting on these submerged sympathies. Margaret goes along with Mr. Wilcox and sees that he cannot be a rescuer for Leonard Bast. Helen believes that he is Leonard's destroyer. She asks that a man whose life and aspirations are drastically out of kilter be put right by individual responsibility and action.

So in the more personal conflict the outsiders, Wilcox and Bast, become objects of attraction fitting Margaret's and Helen's immediate needs. But since they do not successfully work as protector and protégé—Margaret is caring for Henry at the end, Helen "cannot love a man"—they contribute to a reconciliation only in an oblique way. The question can fairly be raised whether the characters who fit the primary moral line of the novel have a lasting part in the lives of the more self-aware characters.

But they do. In the end the family is reconstituted on a new basis. One way is, of course, by exclusion. Of those belonging before, Aunt Juley, with her nominal position as the senior Schlegel, and Tibby, with his indifference and limited possibilities, have dropped out. Of those who might have become members, Mr. Wilcox has been subdued and Leonard had already been excluded by his own limitations before his death. The child is the symbolic reminder, though, that Leonard has been meaningful. Margaret has come into her delayed inheritance from Mrs. Wilcox not only by physically taking over Howards End, but by accepting Mrs. Wilcox's sense of experience. She has been Margaret's example of an independence arising from a sense of what she is and what is possible for her, combined with a tolerance for others' feelings. Mrs. Wilcox rejects Margaret's letter about Helen early in the novel without rejecting Margaret herself. By the end Margaret has found that, for her, there can be no such thing as being protected, though she can help to defend Helen. She achieves her kind of independence backed by her sense of reliving, but reliving in a "fairer" way, the life of Mrs. Wilcox in Mrs. Wilcox's own home, where the physical symbols constantly remind her that such a life is possible. Early in their relation Margaret tries to express the meaning behind one of Mrs. Wilcox's unexpandable ideas on life:

"I almost think you forget you're a girl."

Margaret was startled and a little annoyed. "I'm twenty-nine," she remarked. "That's not so wildly girlish."

Mrs. Wilcox smiled.

"What makes you say that? Do you mean that I have been gauche and rude?"

A shake of the head. "I only meant that I am fifty-one, and that to me both of you—Read it all in some book or other; I cannot put things clearly."

"Oh, I've got it—inexperience. I'm not better than Helen, you mean, and yet I presume to advise her."

"Yes. You have got it. Inexperience is the word."

"Inexperience," repeated Margaret, in serious yet buoyant tones. "Of course, I have everything to learn—absolutely everything—just as much as Helen. Life's very difficult and full of surprises. At all events, I've got as far as that. To be humble and kind, to go straight ahead, to love people rather than pity them, to remember the submerged—well, one can't do all these things at once, worse luck, because they're so contradictory. It's then that proportion comes in—to live by proportion. Don't begin with proportion. Only prigs do that. Let proportion come in as a last resource, when the better things have failed, and a deadlock—Gracious me, I've started preaching!"

"Indeed, you put the difficulties of life splendidly," said Mrs. Wilcox, withdrawing her hand into the deeper shadows. "It is just what I should have liked to say about them myself."

Later, old Miss Avery, in her clairvoyant confusion, insists on Margaret's obligation to a renewal which will set things right:

"Mrs. Wilcox, it has been mistake upon mistake for fifty years. The house is Mrs. Wilcox's and she would not desire it to stand empty any longer."

To help the poor decaying brain, Margaret said:

"Yes, Mrs. Wilcox's house, the mother of Mr. Charles."

"Mistake upon mistake," said Miss Avery. "Mistake upon mistake."

"Well, I don't know," said Margaret, sitting down in one of her own chairs. "I really don't know what's to be done." She could not help laughing.

The other said: "Yes, it should be a merry house enough."

"I don't know—I dare say. Well, thank you very much, Miss Avery. Yes, that's all right. Delightful."

"There is still the parlour." She went through the door opposite and drew a curtain. Light flooded the drawing-room and the drawing-room furniture from Wickham Place. "And the dining room." More curtains were drawn, more windows were flung open to the spring. "Then through here—" Miss Avery continued passing and repassing through the hall. Her voice was lost, but Margaret heard her pulling up the kitchen blind. "I've not finished here yet," she announced, returning.

"There's still a deal to do. The farm lads will carry your great wardrobes upstairs, for there is no need to go into expense at Hilton." . . .

"You think you won't come back to live here, Mrs. Wilcox, but you will."

"That remains to be seen," said Margaret, smiling. "We have no intention of doing so for the present. We happen to need a much larger house. Circumstances oblige us to give big parties. Of course, some day—one never knows, does one?"

Miss Avery retorted: "Some day! Tcha! Tcha! Don't talk about some day. You are living here now."

"Am I?"

"You are living here, and have been for the last ten minutes, if you ask me."

It was a senseless remark, but with a queer feeling of disloyalty Margaret rose from her chair.

And, in the shotgun communion which reconciles Margaret and Mr. Wilcox, Margaret accepts the necessity of earning the meaning of her predecessor's experience:

Then it was Dolly's turn. Anxious to contribute, she laughed nervously, and said: "Good-bye, Mr. Wilcox. It does seem curious that Mrs. Wilcox should have left Margaret Howards End, and yet she got it, after all." . . .

Margaret saw their visitors to the gate. Then she returned to her husband and laid her head in his hands. He was pitiably tired. But Dolly's remark had interested her. At last she said: "Could you tell me, Henry, what was that about Mrs. Wilcox having left me Howards End?"

Tranquilly he replied: "Yes, she did. But that is a very old story. When she was ill and you were so kind to her she wanted to make you some return, and, not being herself at the time, scribbled 'Howards End' on a piece of paper. I went into it thoroughly, and, as it was clearly fanciful, I set it aside, little knowing what my Margaret would be to me in the future."

Margaret was silent. Something shook her life in its inmost recesses, and she shivered.

"I didn't do wrong, did I?" he asked, bending down.

"You didn't, darling. Nothing has been wrong."

But Forster's feeling for the contradictoriness of experience enters in even here. Margaret values most in herself a capacity for decision based on a broad and humane understanding of experience. But in dealing with the arbitrary authority of Mr. Wilcox, she wins by an impulsiveness that is like Helen's. The impulse is not finally inconsistent, but it overrides her immediate principle of give-and-take because Mr. Wilcox will not give as he takes. For Margaret, the action of the novel means discovering, under the stress of change in herself and her circumstances, what she wants and does not want to do.

For Helen, the action reveals what her generous impulsiveness can and cannot do. Her effort to mother Leonard fails, but she can mother the child and can enter into the promise he represents. The pessimism about the great barriers of class and background prevails, though mitigated. Helen and Margaret both find that they can live with another person whose values are similar no matter how great the temperamental difference—and that temperamental differences can be complementary. But neither could have known this with certainty without the attempts at the impossible combination. Both find events and people more inflexible and more unpredictable than they had believed, and return to earlier loyalties. For all the talk about personal relations, the novel is not optimistic about the possibility of having them with people outside the group who have been reared to have similar values. The "inner life" has more inflexible rules than either Margaret or Helen had hoped, but at the end they are prepared to live with this inflexibility in themselves and other people as they were not willing to in the beginning. The novel looks toward the permanent separation between people of *A Passage to India*; the fates of Leonard and Mr. Wilcox are real and forceful. But this pessimism goes along with the concluding scene of stable family life. A family of two middle-aging women, an old man, and a child is a limited prospect, but it fulfills the urgency in the novel to reestablish the threatened unity. Margaret has lost her uprootedness and established a feeling of continuity. Helen has stopped being the outcast she has chosen to be and the Wilcoxes have obligingly treated her as, and begins to think of "such a crop of hay as never."

Treating the Wilcoxes and Leonard Bast in relation to the Schlegel sisters perhaps obscures a qualitative difference. Leonard's interest as a character comes from a brilliant double vision. In one view he is the man blundering toward understanding and culture, an understanding and culture which Forster allows the reader to take for granted as his own. But the barrier is permanent and this is a promised land Leonard can never enter. His interest comes from his desire and his inability to do so. But in most of Forster's work two moral views are honored: one would lead toward the fuller, more natural life, and one would recognize what is not natural to the individual. For Leonard, Ruskin is unnatural. And this negative vision is of the highest importance because so much of ordinary life assumes that everything is possible for anyone. In *A Room with a View* Forster gives a measure of credit to Cecil for recognizing the necessities of his personality. Tibby gets similar credit in *Howards End,* but in both cases there is too little struggle, the acceptance comes too readily, to create a rounded character. The special combination of affection and irony that Forster has for Leonard is one of his best achievements.

Mr. Wilcox does not measure up to the role the novel demands of him. It is never clear that he has even as much character as Margaret sees in him. He is the creature of her need and Forster's hostility. But one quality of the Wilcoxes as a group does contribute to the novel. I have treated the second-generation Wilcoxes as puppets and they are, but as a family they have an inverted vitality. Their confidence in their rules and actions is enough to diminish Margaret from a flexible to a completely rebellious personality. They have a capacity for making Margaret not herself, but the problem they see her to be. The episode about running over the cat is the grosser treatment of this, but almost any passage where Margaret is with them shows this ability, which, more than anything else, leads to Margaret's shift from compromise to rebellion in the final scenes. She rebels directly against Mr. Wilcox when he and Charles insist on classifying Helen as merely another problem to be handled with a morally timid firmness.

Camus' book *The Rebel* distinguishes between rebellion, which everyone engages in, and revolt, which he symbolizes in the French revolutionaries' step of killing the king. There is a great deal of revolt in Forster's novels, notably in his treatment of Mr. Wilcox. But over-all his chief characters are rebels. In *Where Angels Fear to Tread* the hero comes to a changed view of the possibilities of life; in *A Room with a View* a changed view leads to a change of status, a romantic marriage. But, in both, the main characters want to modify the family authority rather than dispense with it. In *Howards End* the desire for family continuity causes the revolt against an outside authority. But the reconciliation between Helen and Margaret comes as they arrange the books, the furniture, and the old sword from Wickham Place at Howards End. Their common memories and attitudes unite them just before the final quarrel with Mr. Wilcox:

> "But the chairs show up wonderfully. Look where Tibby spilt the soup."
>
> "Coffee. It was coffee surely."
>
> Helen shook her head. "Impossible. Tibby was far too young to be given coffee at that time."
>
> "Was father alive?"
>
> "Yes."
>
> "Then you're right and it must have been soup. I was thinking of much later—that unsuccessful visit of Aunt Juley's, when she didn't realize that Tibby had grown up. It was coffee then, for he threw it down on purpose. There was some rhythm, 'Tea, coffee—coffee, tea,' that she said to him every morning at breakfast. Wait a minute—how did it go?"
>
> "I know—no, I don't. What a detestable boy Tibby was!"
>
> "But the rhyme was simply awful. No decent person could have put up with it."
>
> "Ah, that greengage tree," cried Helen, as if the garden was also part of their childhood. "Why do I connect it with dumbbells? And there come the chickens. The grass wants cutting. I love yellow-hammers—"
>
> Margaret interrupted her. "I have got it," she announced.
>
> "'Tea, tea, coffee, tea,

> Or chocolaritee!'
>
> "That every morning for three weeks. No wonder Tibby was wild."
>
> "Tibby is moderately a dear now," said Helen.
>
> "There! I knew you'd say that in the end. Of course he's a dear."

The sisters quarrel because they are what they are, but the hostility toward alien authority and the ineffective sympathy for the underdog are both resolved in family terms—a dependent husband for Margaret, a child for Helen. The rebellion and sympathy which make up Forster's liberalism are enveloped by the theme of family continuity.

There are other implications in these reunions, of course. One is the strong feminine identification in all the novels of manners. Too, Forster's way of using the past has, as Mann would say, its dark side. He often does not incorporate an understanding of the past into the present so that the present can be lived more effectively, as some recent novelists do, but rather in *Howards End* comes close to using the past as a resistance to the present. At times Margaret and Helen are nearer a frantic effort to restore the older family pattern than they are to understanding. Forster's conservatism about the family works on one hand to deepen the sense of identity and reality. But it also leads to the distrust of experience which is so strong in *A Passage to India*. *A Passage to India* is based not on the tension between restrictiveness and the natural life, but upon fear of attack. The distinction between reality and fantasy is less clearly maintained than in the novels of manners. The melodramatic side of the novel treats fears as representative reality. And it is by too much design that the spinster initiates the attack and is capable of conversion only to the negative honesty of a Leonard Bast.

Barry R. Westburg (essay date winter 1964-65)

SOURCE: Westburg, Barry R. "Forster's Fifth Symphony: Another Aspect of *Howards End*." *Modern Fiction Studies* 10, no. 4 (winter 1964-65): 359-65.

[*In the following essay, Westburg interprets Helen Schlegel's response to hearing Beethoven's Fifth Symphony as indicative of her feelings about the various dichotomies the novel suggests.*]

Helen Schlegel, one of E. M. Forster's characters in *Howards End,* envisions "heroes and shipwrecks in the music's flood" when she hears Beethoven's Fifth Symphony at a Queen's Hall concert; and she goes on to imagine "gusts of splendour, gods and demi-gods contending with vast swords, colour and fragrance broadcast on the field of battle, magnificent victory, magnificent death!" (p. 33).[1] Purists of the arts would perhaps object to Helen's response to the symphony, because she here interprets music partially in terms of visual—and, as the word "fragrance" suggests, olfactory as well—sensations, a type of "confusion of genres" that Lessing, for one, warned against in his *Laocoon.* Lessing argued, it will be remembered, that there are essentially two kinds of art: plastic and narrative. Painting and sculpture, he says, differ from poetry and music in that, while the former arts make use of "forms and colors in space," the latter are based upon "articulate sounds in time"; and one of these distinct modes of expression cannot profitably be interpreted in terms of the other.[2] This aptitude of Helen's for mixing genres—in this instance, seeing pictures where she should only be hearing sounds—is worth noticing because we know that it is Forster's economy rarely to introduce an idea, object, or action for no purpose whatsoever; something he mentions once should be remembered, and if he brings it up again, it should be investigated. It happens that Forster makes a great deal out of Helen's reaction to the Fifth Symphony.

First of all, lest there be any doubt as to the importance of the Fifth Symphony to Forster himself (he calls it in **Howards End** "the most sublime noise that has ever penetrated into the ear of man"), it is interesting how frequently he alludes to it in his other works. In one of his essays, he discusses the typical emotional evocations of some of the various keys, and concludes: "more interesting than any, because it moved so often through the mind and under the fingers of Beethoven, is the key of C minor. . . . The catalogue of the C minor items is a familiar one. Heading it is the Fifth Symphony." And he says that this key "fuses the sinister and the triumphant."[3] Another essay, **"Not Listening to Music,"** mentions Beethoven's "love, when tragic, for the key of C minor."[4] In *Aspects of the Novel,* in his discussion of "rhythm," he apostrophizes the Fifth Symphony for having the sort of rhythm worthy of emulation by novelists. He asks, "Is there any effect in novels comparable to the effect of the Fifth Symphony as a whole, where, when the orchestra stops, we hear something that has never been played?"[5]

Returning to Helen, let us consider the occasions whereupon she violates Lessing's dictum. Actually, the only instance given in the action of the novel is the one already mentioned, taking place in Chapter V. (Forster, with his characteristic attention to symbolic detail, devotes almost all of Chapter V to depicting this performance of Symphony V.) But we can assume that we are here shown one of Helen's characteristic tendencies, because Margaret, in the scene at the New English Art Club meeting, recalls a similar occurrence. "'Helen, who will muddle things, says no, it's like music. The course of the Oder is to be like music. It's obliged to remind her of a symphonic poem. The part by the landing-stage is in B minor. . . . There is a slodgy theme in several keys at once, meaning mudbanks, and another for the navigable canal, and the exit into the Baltic is in C sharp major, pianissimo," (p. 75). This is a reversal, by the way, of what Helen did before (at the concert); now she experiences plastic objects in terms of narrative (musical) art.

Again, in Margaret's first interview with Leonard, she becomes more explicit on the same subject. She asks Leonard,

"Do you think music is so different to pictures?"

"I—I should have thought so, kind of," he said.

"So should I. Now, my sister declares they're just the same. We have great arguments over it. She says I'm dense; I say she's sloppy. . . . What *is* the good of the arts if they're interchangeable? What *is* the good of the ear if it tells you the same as the eye? Helen's one aim is to translate tunes into the language of painting, and pictures into the language of music. . . . If Monet's really Debussy, and Debussy's really Monet, neither gentleman is worth his salt. . . ."

                                                        (p. 39)

Then she speculates about the cause of this tendency that she (and Lessing) objects to: "'The real villain is Wagner. He has done more than any man in the nineteenth century towards the muddling of arts. . . . The wells [of thought] . . . communicate with each other too easily now, and not one of them will run quite clear. That's what Wagner's done'" (pp. 39-40).

These remarks by Margaret are echoed in the 1939 essay, **"Not Listening to Music,"** in which Forster, while admitting his own predisposition for giving a program to whatever music he hears, reflects upon the problem of interpreting one art in terms of another. Wagner's leitmotivs compel this manner of interpretation, Forster writes (in a passage that parallels quite closely the above observations by Margaret), but

I accepted this leitmotiv system much too reverently and forced it on writers it did not suit, such as Beethoven. . . . I thought that music must be the better for having a meaning. . . . I think so still, but am less clear as to what a meaning is. In those days it was either a non-musical object, such as a sword [one of the objects Helen envisages, by the way] or a blameless fool, or a non-musical emotion, such as fear. . . . When music reminded me of something which was not music, I supposed it was getting me somewhere. "How like Monet!" I thought when listening to Debussy, and "How like Debussy!" when looking at Monet. I translated sounds into colours, saw the piccolo as apple-green, and the trumpets as scarlet. The arts were to be enriched by taking in one another's washing. I still listen to some music this way.[6]

Admittedly, we cannot glean much from this last quotation except the realization that, while Forster does recognize the limitations of her outlook and does have Margaret point these out, essentially his response to music has been like Helen's. And even Margaret shows in one place that she herself cannot entirely accept the extreme of too pure an appreciation of music, when she says, "'I wonder if the day will ever return when music will be treated as music. Yet I don't know. There's my brother. . . . He treats music as music, and oh, my goodness! he makes me angrier than anyone, simply furious'" (p. 39). The fact that Helen more closely resembles the author in this respect should not obscure her position in the novel, though. Margaret is the central figure—there can be no doubt of that, though even she is not simply a mouthpiece for Forster. But Helen—and this is important to bear in mind for what will follow presently—is a sort of catalyst; she is responsible, in one way or another, for whatever significant action takes place. If Helen had not left her umbrella at Queen's Hall, the sisters would never have met Leonard. If she had not brought Leonard and Jacky to Oniton, her sister would never have discovered Henry's infidelity to the late Mrs. Wilcox, and, most important, Helen would not have found an occasion to give herself to Leonard. Helen's return to Howards End for books was partly responsible for her and Margaret's decision to remain there, which, in turn was indirectly the cause of Leonard's death and Charles' imprisonment.

Now, since the major theme of the novel deals with the attempt to "connect the prose and the passion," matter and spirit, "Beast and Monk," outer reality and inner reality, and a number of other apparently irreconcilable polar opposites (masculinity and *Ewigweibliche,* England and Germany), Helen's position is crucial. She is ostensibly of the Schlegel camp, and hence is on the side of reflectiveness, "passion" (as opposed to "prose" in Forster's dichotomy), spirit—in short, the inner life. But she is also active (witness her effect on the action) and she eventually gains enough worldly knowledge (witness her unwedmotherhood) to act, especially later on in the novel, as a bridge to the outer world—the Wilcox world. And perhaps her greater energy compensates for the deficiency in Schlegelian good sense she shows in some of her dealings with Leonard Bast. (It might appear that Margaret, on account of her marriage to Henry, does the most for merging the two outlooks, but she does not establish a real rapport with him until the end of the novel, after Helen has provided the opportunity for exposing Henry's deceit, and thus has done much to knock the props from under the Wilcox smugness and moral obtuseness. Henry is forced to undergo some rigid self-examination, and, as a result, is drawn a little closer to the Schlegels—as his final residence at Howards End seems to indicate.)

There is, then, a dialectic to the novel, involving an attempt to synthesize what is worthwhile from the Schlegel point of view with what may be good in the Wilcox outlook, and this process takes place as much on the symbolic as on the literal level. And Helen's hearing of Beethoven's Fifth is the occasion whereupon some of the more important of these symbols are introduced. At the Queen's Hall concert, when the Schlegels and a few friends hear the symphony, Forster describes the reactions of the several auditors with a view to contrasting their characters—especially with a regard for contrasting their respective abilities for connecting outer and inner life. Tibby, who has the musical score in his lap, responds to the music on its purest plane; he is completely intellectual about it, "profoundly versed in counterpoint." He is at the

extreme verge of Schlegelism—so much so that he will never be able to "connect," to enter the flux of life in the world, which demands embracing at least a few Wilcox traits. Margaret "can see only the music," but she is a few floors lower than Tibby in the ivory tower of pure aestheticism, for, after all, she does not need the highly abstract medium of a printed score to aid her ear. Her response is more spiritual than intellectual, but she does not, as Helen does, create something not given in the music *per se.* Margaret does not project a fantasy or a vision between herself and the music. However, in a sense, her sister Helen's tendency to meet the music halfway by imposing a creation of her own, a personal program, upon the pure form of the music is in keeping with her predominantly creative role throughout the book. One need only recall again her function as an engine of the plot and as the mother of a child.

The other listeners exhibit a wide variety of possible responses to music, all different from the more sensitive attitudes of the sisters. Mrs. Munt can experience only the most salient feature of music, so she "taps surreptitiously." Fräulein Mosebach hears even less than Mrs. Munt; she only "remembers Beethoven is *echt Deutsch.*" And Herr Leisecke "can remember nothing but Fräulein Mosebach." Leonard Bast is incapable of appreciation at present; he is distracted by economic concerns, such as the loss of his umbrella, and the cost of the concert. The same can be said of his upper middle class counterparts, the Wilcoxes, who are conspicuous by their absence. They, too, are distracted by economic concerns from participating in "cultural activities."

Before returning to Helen, and in order to understand her more fully, we must consider the concept of "culture" as it is developed in *Howards End.* The Fifth Symphony is an artifact of culture in the usual sense of the word—as the word applies to the "appreciation" of art, literature, and so on—but it is also a *means* to culture in a profounder sense. This deeper kind of culture enables one to "see life whole"; it has a cosmopolitanizing effect, which enables one to transcend class and national boundaries, and to see beyond one's own life, own condition, into the spheres of such diverse peoples as Basts and Wilcoxes. Margaret and Helen, to different degrees, attain this sort of culture. Contrarily, the uncultured Wilcoxes (excluding the first Mrs. Wilcox who is cultured in her own way), who embody the business virtues of regularity, dependability, and industriousness—as well as hardness and blindness to the problems of others—"see life steadily." "To him steadiness included all praise," says the narrator about Henry Wilcox; "He himself . . . was in appearance a steady man" (p. 90). The real aim of mankind—and supposedly only the truly cultured person can understand this—is to combine these two positive, yet incomplete, principles and to "see life steadily and see it whole" (p. 269).

As the episode at the concert shows, though, not everyone can make use of the arts as a guide, a "sign post," to show the way to this highest human goal. Tibby, for example, cultured as he is in the ordinary sense, uses the symphony only to isolate himself from human problems—hence he cannot even see life whole, and it follows that he is not cultured, according to Forster's broader application of the word. This statement applies to Leonard as well, as his clumsy attempt to "talk literature" with the Schlegels proves.

If we want to know for whom the concert has the most significance as a cultural guidepost to the highest kind of existence, we must, in fact, exclude anybody for whom the symphony is merely a terminal experience—that is, anybody who simply hears the music for its own sake. Here the book, touching on the broader question of art for art's sake versus art as a social and moral force, seems to be implying that the latter view of art is the more valid. The music must have an effect in the world of action, and in particular, it must help bring about a "drowning and a breaking of the dykes that separate man from man" (to borrow Yeats's phrase), and to do so it must signify something beyond itself, beyond its pure arrangement of sounds. Now we have the key to Helen's creativity, her implicit potency in spite of her apparent weakness and failure. Now we understand why the author has her contradict Margaret (and Lessing) by seeing in the music what apparently was not given. "The music summed up to her all that had happened or could happen in her career," Forster says. She sees a "program," while aesthetes and Philistines alike see nothing; and this program, a revelation or vision of what is later to happen in the novel, encompasses both social commentary and a particular prophecy—the prophecy, couched in an ironic symbolism, of Leonard's death. "Gods and demi-gods contending with vast swords"—is this not a mock heroic foreshadowing of Charles' absurd attack on Leonard with the "vast sword" of the late Mr. Schlegel? As the scion of a wealthy capitalist family, Charles is a twentieth-century "god"; as an unemployed clerk with one-time cultural aspirations, the ineffectual Bast qualifies as a "demi-god" by comparison. "Magnificent victory, magnificent death!"—Charles wins with the flat of the blade as Leonard dies pathetically, of a weak heart.

The commentary on human life which is part of Helen's vision occurs in the following passage: "The music started with a goblin walking quietly over the universe, from end to end. Others followed him. They were not aggressive creatures; it was that that made them so terrible. . . . They merely observed in passing that there was no such thing as splendour or heroism in the world. After the interlude of elephants dancing, they returned. . . . Panic and emptiness! Panic and emptiness! The goblins were right" (p. 33). The goblin theme, which Forster expands throughout the novel as a sort of Wagnerian leitmotiv (in spite of the fact that he has Margaret condemn Wagner for inventing the technique), is an important adjunct to the Schlegelian attitude. Were the goblins "only the phantoms of cowardice and unbelief"? In the widest sense, they represent the element of "sinisterness," of falsity, that is inevitably implicit in any standpoint, any thesis, no matter how "triumphantly" that thesis is propounded. Only a cultured person

is capable of making this necessary observation, of seeing that there are no absolutes, no moral or intellectual positions that are completely justifiable. And it is Wilcoxism—uncritical, always thrusting forward without looking back at the ruin in its wake—which is the particular target of the goblins, who do not disappear in spite of the declamations of the Wilcoxian "heroes." "They were only the phantoms of cowardice and unbelief? One healthy impulse would dispel them? Men like the Wilcoxes, or President Roosevelt, would say yes. Beethoven knew better. The goblins really had been there" (p. 34).

The goblins are begotten in the "squalor" created heedlessly by the Wilcox ilk. They appear to the Schlegels only when the latter come into contact with Basts, who are the victims of the Wilcox will to power, the living indictment of the crimes of the "gods and heroes." The incident with Leonard's umbrella brings this fact to the attention of both sisters rather vividly: "It [the incident] remained as a goblin footfall, as a hint that all is not for the best in the best of all possible worlds, and that beneath these superstructures of wealth and art there wanders an ill-fed boy . . ." (p. 45).

So it becomes the spiritual mission of the sisters, especially Helen, in her way, to try to bring the Wilcoxes to pause a moment in their "outer lives of telegrams and anger," so that the latter may look deeply enough within themselves, and widely enough around themselves, to see their fundamental weaknesses and responsibilities to the rest of mankind; and eventually, aided by love, with its source in the inner life, they may connect, among other dualities, spirituality and materialism. The movement of Mr. Wilcox, and particularly the sisters Schlegel, is toward (but always only *toward*—Forster is here interested in depicting plausible gains for man, not impossible ones) the unified consciousness that "sees life steadily while seeing it whole." And it is, as we can now see, Helen's ability to feel "articulate sounds in time" partly as "forms and colors in space" (and *vice versa*) in synaesthetic, creative, and prophetic experience—in particular, her hearing of the Fifth Symphony—which symbolizes, and in some respects actuates the overall movement in ***Howards End*** towards synthesis of opposites into this steady and whole vision of life. The questionable aesthetic experience of *synaesthesia* (questionable, at least to Lessing) is thus used by Forster to reflect within its more limited sphere the equally doubtful, but highly desirable, experience of *synthesis,* of unity of being won through encompassing all of life—even life beyond the concert hall.

Notes

1. All page numbers in parentheses refer to the Vintage paperback edition of *Howards End* (New York, 1954).

2. Trans. by Ellen Frothingham (New York, 1961), p. 91.

3. "The C Minor of That Life," in *Two Cheers for Democracy* (New York, 1951), p. 125.

4. *Two Cheers for Democracy,* p. 130.

5. "Pattern and Rhythm," in *Aspects of the Novel* (New York, 1954), p. 168.

6. *Two Cheers for Democracy,* p. 128.

George H. Thomson (essay date 1967)

SOURCE: Thomson, George H. "*Howards End.*" In *The Fiction of E. M. Forster,* pp. 170-99. Detroit: Wayne State University Press, 1967.

[*In the following essay, Thomson examines the symbolic objects in* Howards End.]

> Rigidity and Chaos, these two forms of the negative are directly opposed to the creative principle, which encompasses transformation, hence not only life but also death. Across the diabolical axis of rigidity and chaos cuts the transformative axis of life and death.
>
> —Erich Neumann

The center of our attention in *Howards End* is to be the object as archetype rather than the character as archetype. But if we are properly to understand the symbolic objects of the novel, we will have first to take some notice of Mrs. Wilcox, for every one and every thing is a fragment of her mind (p. 331). She is the most inclusive of all the symbols of totality. Knowing this, we may find it especially interesting to observe the way she is first described and the way she first breaks into the action.

Helen Schlegel writes her sister Margaret that early in the morning she saw Mrs. Wilcox walking in the garden. "Then she walked off the lawn to the meadow. . . . Trail, trail, went her long dress over the sopping grass, and she came back with her hands full of the hay that was cut yesterday . . ." (p. 4). When Mrs. Wilcox next appears, it is a moment of crisis. Helen's Aunt Juley has let Charles Wilcox know that his brother Paul and Helen are secretly in love. Helen speaks first:

> "Aunt Juley . . . I—I meant to stop your coming. It isn't—it's over."

> The climax was too much for Mrs. Munt. She burst into tears.

> "Aunt Juley dear, don't. Don't let them know I've been so silly. It wasn't anything. Do bear up for my sake."

> "Paul," cried Charles Wilcox, pulling his gloves off.

> "Don't let them know. They are never to know."

> "Oh, my darling Helen—"

> "Paul! Paul!"

> A very young man came out of the house.

> "Paul, is there any truth in this?"

> "I didn't—I don't—"

> "Yes or no, man; plain question, plain answer. Did or didn't Miss Schlegel—"

> "Charles dear," said a voice from the garden. "Charles, dear Charles, one doesn't ask plain questions. There aren't such things."

> They were all silent. It was Mrs. Wilcox.

> She approached just as Helen's letter had described her, trailing noiselessly over the lawn, and there was actually a wisp of hay in her hands. She seemed to belong not to the young people and their motor, but to the house, and to the tree that overshadowed it. One knew that she worshipped the past, and that the instinctive wisdom the past can alone bestow had descended upon her—that wisdom to which we give the clumsy name of aristocracy.
>
> (pp. 22-23)

Mrs. Wilcox is an Earth-Mother figure but that is not what makes her entry into the story so strangely powerful and compelling. The hush that surrounds her, the aura of timelessness and mysterious strength, creates an extraordinary effect; an effect like that of a perfectly spinning top which without moving sustains all motion.

Here we have a subdued awareness of something like a moment of ecstasy. The moment arises from the encounter with the house and tree as well as from the encounter with Mrs. Wilcox. Though the effect is naturally less extraordinary when repeated, Mrs. Wilcox creates much the same impression in later scenes. Forster allows us to see her close up but always from the outside. He gives her only a few characteristics but they are notable ones. She is consistently associated with certain objects, she moves in a slow but irresistible—almost ghost-like—way, suggesting a timeless figure, and she does not think or scheme, her effect is that of being. Her full significance can only be developed by the full novel. But from the beginning we may apprehend her as a form which contains all other symbols and is itself contained only within the totality of the novel.

Howards End has another containing symbol. It takes shape in Helen Schlegel's visual imaginings as she listens to the third and fourth movements of Beethoven's Fifth Symphony. This symphony becomes her special symbol. "The music had summed up to her all that had happened or could happen in her career" (p. 36). But its significance extends beyond the limits of her own career. Indeed, Beethoven's music emerges as a symbol of the whole of life and the whole of the novel.

The third movement opens with goblins walking over the universe. They remind Helen of her affair with Paul Wilcox. Panic and emptiness! It closes in joyous splendor, reminding the reader of Helen rushing in from the hayfield at the close of the novel. The music does not, however, specifically parallel the story.[1] Rather, it defines two poles of human experience. One may feel there is splendor and poetry and love in the world; one may feel there is "no such thing as splendour or heroism in the world" (p. 34), that even love and hatred have decayed (p. 121); and like Helen one may feel now the one, now the other. Moreover, Forster's Beethoven shows no desire to assert that heroic splendor exists in any absolute sense. It exists, as does its negation, in man's experience. No other reality is insisted upon. The symphony, then, defines the scope and nature of the experiences to be encountered by the characters of *Howards End.*

If one were to ask what **Howards End** is about, the answers would probably be as varied as if one were to ask what the Fifth Symphony is about. The novel is about the Schlegel sisters, young ladies of independent means and cultivated taste. Of them it might be said: "the imaginative life is distinguished by the greater clearness of its perception, and the greater purity and freedom of its emotion." It is about the Wilcoxes, men of business with plenty of money and not much independence or taste. Of them it might be said: "do we not feel that the average business man would be in every way a more admirable, more respectable being if his imaginative life were not so squalid and incoherent?"[2] It is even about Leonard Bast, the clerk with one foot on the slippery first rung of the middle-class ladder, who is a displaced yeoman and so another version of the decline of the yeoman class as symbolized in the dying out of Mrs. Wilcox's family, the Howards.

From the point of view of plot, the novel is about the attempt to connect the two main families through the marriage of Margaret Schlegel and Henry Wilcox and so unite the practical competence, the expertise, and the immense energy of the Wilcoxes with the thoughtfulness, the self-analysis, and the culture of the Schlegels. Like the marriage itself, the attempt to connect the outer and the inner life moves toward ruin when it is intersected by another plot which has as its center the one-night love affair of Helen Schlegel and Leonard Bast. This plot culminates in a violent crisis and brings all the characters together in a final confrontation at Howards End.

There are many ways of indicating what the novel is about, but the most effective is to say it is about Howards End. The story begins and ends there. To Mrs. Wilcox the place is sacred. When shortly before her final illness she asks Margaret to come down to Howards End with her, a lasting bond is established between the two women. Her dying wish that Margaret should have Howards End creates a crisis for the Wilcoxes. They respond in a business-like way, for they are—however much coarsened—the true descendants of Forster's own ancestors, the Thorntons.

When the Thornton family declined and Battersea Rise, which had been their home for over one hundred years, fell vacant, "London knocked and everything vanished—vanished absolutely, and has left no ghost behind, for the Thorntons do not approve of ghosts." They do not approve of ghosts because they have "no sense whatever of the unseen."[3] So it is with the Wilcoxes. A house—even such a house as Howards End—means nothing to them. It is simply a possession and they mean to keep it. Judged from a

legal or practical point of view, they may be said to have acted correctly. Mrs. Wilcox had been looking for a spiritual heir to Howards End, and a consideration of this kind cannot be muddled up with the practical business of transferring property. At least, so the Wilcoxes think. But the little fact that cannot be got round remains: they have ignored the last wish of a woman whom they had reason to value. The Schlegels would not have ignored such a wish.

Now that Mrs. Wilcox is dead, a series of coincidences bring Margaret and Henry Wilcox together. Yet after their marriage Howards End still eludes Margaret as a home. Instead it becomes the place where the furniture from Wickham Place is stored and where, on her own initiative, it is convincingly arranged by Miss Avery. And so, unknown to any of the principal characters, the house is now in readiness. Helen, who is pregnant, returns from Germany. She longs to spend one night with Margaret, surrounded by their possessions from Wickham Place. Henry refuses permission, Margaret revolts, Charles asserts himself, Leonard dies, Henry breaks down. The result, Margaret is after all to inherit Howards End and from her it is to go to Helen's son. For Margaret has drawn Henry and Helen and the child together, assisted by the benign influence of Howards End with its meadow, its house, its tree, and, overarching all, the unseen presence of Ruth Wilcox.

Within this context we may define, in a preliminary way, the symbolic import of hay, house, and tree. The hay symbolizes individual life; the house, individual life in relation to family, that is to ancestors and heirs; the wych-elm, individual life in relation to the total life of man rooted in an unknown past and branching into an unknown future.

The word *life* is prominent in these formulations. But death is everywhere implicit. Hay is dead grass, and ancestors and the whole of man's past life are dead too. At the same time we notice that death, the most inescapable of evils, is conspicuously associated with the heroic splendors of Beethoven. Its meaning for man is supremely ambiguous: "Death destroys a man: the idea of Death saves him" (p. 253). This statement, out of the mouth of Michelangelo,[4] is the key that unlocks the symbolic mysteries of hay, house, and tree, and at the same time relates them to the theme of "Only connect." Putting first things first, then, we may begin with this theme.

In his 1907 paper on Dante, Forster commented on the barrier that exists between body and soul: "Most modern thinkers realize that the barrier eludes definition. . . . and the wisest of our age, Goethe for example, and Walt Whitman, have not attempted to find it, but have assayed the more human task of harmonizing the realms that it divides."[5] Or as Margaret says in writing of the seen and unseen: "Our business is not to contrast the two, but to reconcile them" (p. 109). In Forster's scheme of things to reconcile or connect is to harmonize; and to harmonize is to attain proportion. The body of the world was created out of four elements, says Plato, "and it was harmonized by proportion, and therefore has the spirit of friendship."[6]

Like Plato, Forster will arrive at friendship or comradeship as the end to be attained through proportion. But first he observes with reference to the division between body and soul, between seen and unseen: "The business man who assumes that this life is everything, and the mystic who asserts that it is nothing, fail, on this side and on that, to hit the truth." And truth is not halfway in between. Rather, it is "to be found by continuous excursions into either realm, and though proportion is the final secret, to espouse it at the outset is to insure sterility" (p. 206).

We will have a better understanding of what Forster means by proportion if we relate this statement to his later analysis of love and truth. In the passage just quoted truth means the answer or the final secret—which is proportion. In the later passage it is used more precisely. Love is the acceptance of things as they are. Truth is the yearning for things as they ought to be. Only through love, which is acceptance, can a man make useful excursions into the realm of the seen; and only through truth, which is yearning for what ought to be, can he make useful excursions into the realm of the unseen. And out of many such excursions, balancing each other, emerges proportion, the final secret. The warfare of love and truth may seem eternal, the whole visible world and all of life may rest on it, but proportion brings them together, harmonizes them, introduces the spirit of friendship or comradeship. To begin with proportion is to begin with an abstract formula. It is to begin without love or truth, without making sorties into the realms of body and soul, seen and unseen, what is and what ought to be. And so it can result only in sterility (p. 243).

For each man, the first and inescapable division is that between body and soul. Continual excursions into each realm result in that development of the inner life symbolized by the ability to say "I." The ability to say "I" is to the inner life what proportion is to the outer life. It is the final secret to be attained through prolonged and honest effort. The Wilcoxes cannot say "I." They have evaded the realities of the inner life and are hollow in the middle. They are muddled and when the crisis comes all within is panic and emptiness. The inner life of proportion which results in personal relations and the outer life of proportion which results in comradeship are equally beyond their reach. But to someone like Margaret there are "moments when the inner life actually 'pays,' when years of self-scrutiny, conducted for no ulterior motive, are suddenly of practical use. Such moments are still rare in the west; that they come at all promises a fairer future" (p. 206).

It is now apparent that Forster's terms are more precise than they may at first have seemed. Body and soul, seen and unseen, love and truth, the inner life that says "I" and the outer life of proportion can be precisely defined in relation to the theme of man's divided nature and the necessity to connect.

The theme becomes more complex and requires new terms and a new definition of love when the divided individual experiences sexual love. Then the beast and the monk emerge and it is necessary to connect them. The connection robs them of life and establishes the rainbow arch of love. Mr. Wilcox illustrates the failure to achieve such a connection, for he is beastly in his relations with Mrs. Bast and monk-like in his distrust of the flesh (pp. 196-97, 194). Beast and monk, though at odds, do not represent a real polarity. Rather they are alike in that each in its own way places value upon the flesh as such. The essential conflict here is between beast-monk whose materialistic nature degrades the flesh, and love whose spiritual nature transcends and redeems the flesh.

The half-life of the divided beast-monk is clarified by another set of terms: "Margaret greeted her lord with peculiar tenderness on the morrow. Mature as he was, she might yet be able to help him to the building of the rainbow bridge that should connect the prose in us with the passion. Without it we are meaningless fragments, half monks, half beasts, unconnected arches that have never joined into a man" (p. 196). And a little later: "Only connect! That was the whole of her sermon. Only connect the prose and the passion, and both will be exalted, and human love will be seen at its height" (p. 197). It is not particularly fruitful to parallel beast with passion and monk with prose. But observe that the missing term in beast-monk is love, while the missing term in prose-passion is poetry. Here poetry, like love, signifies the spirit's power to transform and exalt. In sexual love, the law of the spirit must triumph, the flesh must be redeemed. For the law of the flesh, if it triumphs, leaves behind it lust and shame, passion and final drabness.

Forster's basic division is between flesh and spirit. But if we extend the logic of the image in which beast and monk are robbed of life and transformed through love, it should follow in the case of the broader conflict of matter and spirit, seen and unseen, that matter will be transformed through spirit into a reality of another kind. Forster does not, of course, entertain such a possibility. The material things of the world, as Margaret so often tells us, are to be accepted. The freedom and culture of the Schlegel sisters is made possible by the islands of money upon which they stand. Ruth Wilcox makes the same point in a different way when she twice asserts that a house cannot stand without bricks and mortar (p. 81).

The flesh is the only part of material existence which Forster sees as directly subject to the spirit. In the context of the flesh, love means transformation. In other contexts it means attachment to things as they are. And always, I think, it has a third meaning. It is libido, the energy or power that impels us both to accept things as they are and to yearn for things as they ought to be, that impels us to make sorties into the realms of the seen and unseen. Love in this sense is a kind of preliminary connection which in its higher and more self-conscious form expresses itself as proportion and comradeship.

The theme of the epigraph, only connect, and the various usages of the word love are most richly illustrated in the failures and triumphs of the Schlegel sisters. In the central portion of the novel we discern a sharp contrast in their development. Helen, who has the kind of qualities Forster admires—"spontaneity, natural gaiety, recklessness"[7]—through a failure to connect, remains spiritually stagnant. The drab intellectual companion of her European stay is proof of her inner condition. Yet when she returns to England, Howards End nourishes a spectacular evolvement, a sudden opening out, like a flower, into the fresh air and sunshine of the clear spirit. In contrast, Margaret makes a steady, non-spectacular progress toward the same goal.

It is in the realm of sexual love that Helen fails to connect. She misinterprets Wilcox prose and is willfully deluded by Paul Wilcox's momentary passion. Her later reaction of hate is inverted passion, while her devotion to Leonard Bast is founded in another misinterpretation of prose. "There's an odd notion . . . running about at the back of her brain" Margaret tells us, "that poverty is somehow 'real'" (p. 191). Helen's divided nature reveals itself in her confusion and error. But the division is apparent only in a sexual context. When she returns to Margaret's love and the strong associations of the past, intelligibility and joy triumph.

Helen's failure to establish a meaningful or durable relationship with a man is not disastrous. Human beings may have defects, limited areas of failure (Margaret, for instance, cannot love children), but they are not on that account debarred from bliss. Indeed, imperfectness, by fixing limits to the range and direction of growth, becomes an important source of individuality. Thus variety characterizes the human scene, relieving the monotony of life's daily grey. The Schlegel sisters are the best illustration of that variety, and the best assurance that in moving toward proportion the individual does not thereby move toward monotony.

Margaret, differing from her sister, shows us how love and connection can lead to a series of spiritual triumphs, each more far-reaching than its predecessor. It is true that she is modest about her accomplishments. When she visits Oniton before her marriage to Henry Wilcox, she notes that it is imperfect like herself: "Its apple-trees were stunted, its castle ruinous. It, too, had suffered in the border warfare between the Anglo-Saxon and the Kelt, between things as they are and as they ought to be" (p. 244). Nevertheless, her love for Henry Wilcox establishes a bridge, albeit a shaky one, between his worldliness and her own spiritual insight. Her love for Ruth Wilcox connects her with Howards End and from loving Howards End she comes to love the countryside and all England. And through the final secret of proportion she is able to achieve a broader vision, her "unexpected love of the island . . . connecting on this side with the joys of the flesh, on that with the inconceivable" (p. 216). Later, visiting the farm near Howards End, she perceives that "the graver sides of life, the deaths, the partings, the yearnings for love, have their deepest expression in the heart of the fields." Yet at this moment nature is filled with the happiness of light and

sound and color. "It was the presence of sadness at all that surprised Margaret, and ended by giving her a feeling of completeness. In these English farms, if anywhere, one might see life steadily and see it whole, group in one vision its transitoriness and its eternal youth, connect—connect without bitterness until all men are brothers" (pp. 283-84). Margaret is more than once referred to as heroic. Here then is her final and heroic goal, and love's highest destiny—the brotherhood of man. The word for it is comradeship, a word to be considered in a later place.

The countryside has a prominent role in Margaret's vision of brotherhood. As in the previous novels, the living world of vegetable nature supports the spirit of man. But how long it may do so is now in doubt. "Under cosmopolitanism . . . we shall receive no help from the earth. Trees and meadows and mountains will only be a spectacle, and the binding force that they once exercised on character must be entrusted to Love alone. May Love be equal to the task!" (p. 275) Love here may be presumed to have its full complement of meanings.

Forster does not assert that alone love will be equal to the task since the binding force of earth is still at work. But he comes close to such an assertion by establishing death, which is meaningful in purely human terms, as the most powerful influence in strengthening the wings of love. The significance of death is enforced by two memorable passages in the novel. The first is from the scene in the Hotel at Oniton and represents, fairly directly, the thoughts that Helen tries to express in her talk with Leonard Bast:

> "Death destroys a man: the idea of Death saves him." Behind the coffins and the skeletons that stay the vulgar mind lies something so immense that all that is great in us responds to it. Men of the world may recoil from the charnel-house that they will one day enter, but Love knows better. Death is his foe, but his peer, and in their age-long struggle the thews of Love have been strengthened, and his vision cleared, until there is no one who can stand against him.
>
> (p. 253)

The second passage concerns Leonard as, eight months later, he walks to Howards End:

> To Leonard, intent on his private sin, there came the conviction of innate goodness elsewhere. . . . Again and again must the drums tap, and the goblins stalk over the universe before joy can be purged of the superficial. It was rather paradoxical, and arose from his sorrow. Death destroys a man, but the idea of death saves him—that is the best account of it that has yet been given. Squalor and tragedy can beckon to all that is great in us, and strengthen the wings of love. They can beckon; it is not certain that they will, for they are not love's servants. But they can beckon, and the knowledge of this incredible truth comforted him.
>
> (p. 342)

The idea of death strengthens a man's power to love and to connect because it shows him (in Helen's words) "the emptiness of Money" (p. 252), the emptiness of all things material, and it shows him that death destroys the flesh and that the destiny of the flesh is neither heroic nor splendid. Thus squalor and tragedy and death, by saving a man from exclusive fixation on material things, invite him to respond to the unseen as well as to the seen, to things of the spirit as well as things of the flesh. They beckon to his capacity for love and joy and at the same time purge his love and joy of the superficial.[8]

"Death destroys a man: the idea of Death saves him." We may now go on to see how this theme is associated with the symbols of hay, house, and tree.

The hay. Perhaps the most tantalizing passage in **Howards End** is that in which Margaret protests against the "jangle of causes and effects": "Here Leonard lay dead in the garden, from natural causes; yet life was a deep, deep river, death a blue sky, life was a house, death a wisp of hay, a flower, a tower, life and death were anything and everything, except this ordered insanity . . ." (p. 348). To take this statement literally is to compound confusion. What it says is that each of these items is an image of life-and-death. The river of life implies the death of the individual; the blue sky, image of infinity, enforces a recognition of earthbound transience; a flower is as short-lived as it is beautiful; and a tower is reminiscent of both the ruined castle at Oniton (p. 244) and "the Six Hills, tombs of warriors, breasts of the spring" (p. 326). This passage, then, suggests the context within which we will find the meaning of the hay symbol.

Flowers, grass, and hay, the smaller flourishings of vegetable nature, are symbolically associated with the individual human life. The most decisive piece of evidence of this is to be found in Margaret's discussion with Helen about individual differences in the grey world of every day. The most important part of the discussion will be quoted later. It is noteworthy also that these images of grass and hay are never presented in their own right but always in association with one or another of the characters. Both the garden with its flowers and the meadow of hay are persistently associated with Ruth Wilcox. She knows that grass and flowers fall, cradled by the sickle of death. Her devotion to the living plant is revealed to us in the garden image; her devotion to the dead plant, in the hay image. We read: "Ruth knew no more of worldly wickedness and wisdom than did the flowers in her garden, or the grass in her field" (p. 94). More frequently we read of her connection with the hay—already illustrated from the novel's opening scenes.

In contrast we not that Margaret, except in the final scene, is always associated with grass rather than hay. For the moment we shall assert that grass stands as an image for the individual seen under the aspect of life; hay as an image for the individual seen under the aspect of death. The meaning of hay is further defined at the close of the novel.

> Helen took up a bunch of grass. She looked at the sorrel, and the red and white and yellow clover, and the quaker grass, and the daisies, and the bents that composed it. She raised it to her face.

"Is it sweetening yet?" asked Margaret.

"No, only withered."

"It will sweeten to-morrow."

(p. 357)[9]

This image in its structure, in the relation of its parts, directly parallels the structure of the proposition "Death destroys a man: the idea of Death saves him." Facing up to the reality of death, we find our lives sweetened and made meaningful; and we find the lives of those now dead to have freshness and value for us. This has been Ruth Wilcox's experience: "she cared about her ancestors, and let them help her" (p. 23). Her attachment to hay symbolically asserts what she could never find words to express and what she herself now stands for.

The saving power of the idea of death, already elaborated by Helen, is defined in a somewhat different way by Margaret as she contemplates Leonard's death and the manner in which cause and effect "go jangling forward to some goal doubtless, but to none that she could imagine. At such moments the soul retires within, to float upon the bosom of a deeper stream, and has communion with the dead, and sees the world's glory not diminished, but different in kind to what she has supposed. She alters her focus until trivial things are blurred. Margaret had been tending this way all the winter. Leonard's death brought her to the goal" (pp. 350-51). We can now see why Margaret, up to this moment, has been associated only with grass and why she is able shortly after to understand that the hay will sweeten.

Another image is summed up in the hay symbol. In the course of the story many references are made to life's daily grey and to the relieving of its monotony. The passage in which Helen takes up the bunch of grass and looks at the many varieties and colors that compose it comes immediately after Margaret's little sermon on the differences planted in a single family "so that there may always be colour; sorrow perhaps, but colour in the daily grey" (p. 357). The differences arise from variety in the objects of our love; hence the hay represents not just individual man, but man in his individuality.

The hay is associated with the meadow, and a strange meadow it is. A boundary separates it from the garden, and the wych-elm stands on the boundary and leans a little over the house (p. 3). Mrs. Wilcox walks "off the lawn to the meadow" whose corner to the right Helen can "just see" (p. 4). Margaret on her first visit looks into the garden. "Farther on were hints of the meadow and a black cliff of pines. Yes, the meadow was beautiful" (p. 212). And as the novel moves to its close we see the farmer, "amid whirring blades and sweet odours of grass, encompassing with narrowing circles the sacred centre of the field" (p. 354). Here surely we catch a glimpse of the unseen. The meadow confirms Helen's plea that "the Invisible lodges against the Visible" (p. 253). And it confirms the spiritual incapacity of the Wilcoxes. Just as they cannot endure any deep emotion, so they cannot tolerate the unseen. The meadow breaks them up. Shattered and congested by hay fever, they flee the outdoors and seek refuge in the house and in the city. In contrast, Mrs. Wilcox's life was of the garden and the meadow. She was sustained by the unseen, by the spirit. The meadow continues to represent that sustaining power but now it includes Mrs. Wilcox as a part of the unseen. Before her death she says to Margaret: "I cannot show you my meadow properly except at sunrise" (p. 91), thereby implying that the things of the spirit are not subject to decay. Properly seen the meadow belongs to the light and the beginning of things, it belongs to eternal youth.

"'The field's cut!' Helen cried excitedly—'the big meadow! We've seen to the very end, and it'll be such a crop of hay as never!'" The close of the novel asserts the power and the spiritual vision of Ruth Wilcox and the sharing of that vision by the Schlegel sisters. More specifically it is a dramatic counterpart to the proposition that cultivation of the inner life "pays" and that attention to the unseen and to the significance of death "saves."

The house. The meaning of Howards End is clearly established in the early account of Ruth Wilcox, who belonged to the house and the tree, and who worshiped the past and the instinctive wisdom of the past—"that wisdom to which we give the clumsy name of aristocracy" (p. 23).

Clinging to the house is the vine which Ruth Wilcox fought to preserve and which Helen instantly loves. It is Margaret's symbol. When Charles Wilcox heard of his mother's bequest of Howards End to Margaret, he looked at the house—"the nine windows, the unprolific vine. He exclaimed, 'Schlegels again!'" (p. 101) The vine has already been described as encumbering the south wall (p. 98), precisely the word to represent the Wilcox view of Margaret. And, like Margaret, it is unprolific. In reality, of course, the vine is attached to and embraces the house. Margaret is the spiritual heir of Ruth Wilcox and of Howards End. The vine is the physical sign of her heirdom. The fact that it had been there all the time is strangely suggestive. The same is true of the fact that the furniture from Wickham Place fits perfectly into Howards End. When Helen returns from Germany it is her love of the vine and of the books and furniture from their former home that enables her, and also Margaret, to appreciate Howards End in something like the way Mrs. Wilcox had appreciated it. "'Ah, that greengage tree,' cried Helen, as if the garden was also part of their childhood" (p. 315).[10]

"Explanations and appeals had failed; they had tried for a common meeting-ground, and had only made each other unhappy. And all the time their salvation was lying round them—the past sanctifying the present; the present, with wild heart-throb, declaring that there would after all be a future, with laughter and the voices of children" (p. 315). The house gives a new dimension to the proposition that the idea of death saves, emphasizing as it does the wisdom to be gained through those now dead and the hope to be attained through those who have yet to live.

The sense of the ancestral is strengthened by the six Danish tumuli. Margaret settles that beneath the Six Hills "soldiers of the best kind lay buried. She hated war and liked soldiers—it was one of her amiable inconsistencies" (p. 209). The inconsistency is hardly surprising, since her father was a soldier. The Six Hills are Margaret's symbol. They give her a sense of an ancestral background in the vicinity of Howards End. And like Mrs. Wilcox's home, they are associated with the earth (p. 211) as well as the past, and so with the living as well as the dead. Covered with spring herbage (p. 320), they are not only tombs of warriors, but "breasts of the spring" giving promise for the future (p. 326). Margaret and Henry Wilcox sit on one of these hills when Henry, broken by the turn of events, tells her that Charles will go to jail for manslaughter. "Margaret drove her fingers through the grass. The hill beneath her moved as if it was alive" (p. 353). Mrs. Wilcox had found Howards End a continuing source of strength and insight and new life. Margaret finds the Six Hills such a source also.

At this point it will be valuable to look more clearly at the idea of ancestors and the family. Forster's outlook is Greek, and may be summed up in these words of Erwin Rohde:

> All cult, all prospects of a full life and future well-being . . . of the soul on its separation from the body, depends upon the holding together of the family. To the family itself the souls of its former ancestors are, in a limited sense, of course, gods—*its* gods. It can hardly be doubted that here we have the root of all belief in the future life of the soul, and we shall be tempted to subscribe to the belief . . . of those who see in such family worship of the dead one of the most primitive roots of all religious belief—older than the worship of the higher gods of the state and the community as a whole; older even than the worship of Heroes, and of the ancestors of large national groups. . . . Among the Greeks . . . this belief lived on in the shadow of the great gods and their cults, even in the midst of the tremendous increase in the power and organized influence of the state. But these larger and wider organizations cramped and hindered its development.[11]

Even the concluding sentences have ominous relevance. We see Howards End and the Six Hills pitted against the endless advance of the sprawling city, symbol of the superstate.

Yet all is not relevant. If Forster's view of family is much the same as that expressed by Rohde, and if Rohde's view is much the same as that expressed by I. A. Richards—who was the first but not the last to comment at length on this aspect of Forster's work[12]—what are we to make of the fact that Margaret's "ancestors" are ancient Danish soldiers who are not her ancestors at all, and what of the further fact that Howards End is not inherited by a descendant of Mrs. Wilcox, not even inherited by a direct descendant of her spiritual heir, Margaret Schlegel, but rather is inherited by the son of Leonard Bast and Helen Schlegel? I suggest that these two facts make untenable the usual account of Forster's attitude to family. That account suggests that Forster's interest in ancestors and heirs has its basis in genetic inheritance. The truth seems rather to be that he values ancestors because they symbolize the one thing that can give stability, the collective and universal past; and he values children because they symbolize a potential hope and a potential wholeness greater than we know at present. Forster's interest in the living continuity represented by ancestors and descendants is a general rather than a particular interest, it is universal rather than individual. That is why the same novel can encompass ancestor worship, child glorification, and the admirable Margaret Schlegel. That is why it is not supremely important who fathers Helen's child, but is supremely important that there be a child.

Because Forster's values are not restricted to the genetic, his emphasis falls not on the "family tree" but on the house and on the wych-elm which is a universal tree and is the genius of the *place*.[13] This emphasis is confirmed in many ways. Miss Avery, who has been a friend of the Howards, is described as "the heart of the house." And the heart of the house beats "faintly at first," suggesting Mrs. Wilcox, "then loudly, martially," suggesting Margaret. On this, Margaret's first entry into Howards End, a "noise as of drums seemed to deafen her." The drums marked the transition in Beethoven's Fifth Symphony; now Miss Avery, descending the stairs, marks the transition in the house—from Ruth Wilcox to Margaret Schlegel (p. 213). The birth of Helen's child also confirms the importance of the house. There are nine windows in the front of Howards End. They are arranged in three-above-three fashion and each looks from a room. The heir to Howards End is "born in the central room of the nine" (p. 359).

The final meaning and beauty of Howards End as a symbol is to be discovered in its connection with Wickham Place. At the beginning of Chapter 31 Forster, in one of his finest passages of subdued poetry, describes the death and destruction of Wickham Place, the home of the Schlegel family for thirty years. Its death is compared to that of a person from whom "the spirit slips before the body perishes." The phrasing reminds the reader of Ruth Wilcox. During Margaret's visit to her shortly before her final illness, she conveys a haunting impression of dissolution and of withdrawal into the shadows. There was a long pause in their conversation—"a pause that was somehow akin to the flicker of the fire, the quiver of the reading-lamp upon their hands, the white blur from the window; a pause of shifting and eternal shadows" (p. 76). The reader is also reminded that Mrs. Wilcox has spent the thirty years of her married life at Howards End. The description of Wickham Place as "void of emotion, and scarcely hallowed by the memories of thirty years of happiness" (p. 271), suggests the attitude of the Wilcox family to Howards End and to Ruth Wilcox herself.

If the demolition of Wickham Place parallels the physical dissolution of Ruth Wilcox, then Wickham Place living may be said to have the same value for Margaret as Ruth

Wilcox living, while Howards End has the same value for Margaret as Ruth Wilcox dead. This may be put in another way: Wickham Place is to Howards End as grass is to hay. Wickham Place was a house of life and happiness, but as the rented home of an alien adventurer it was, like the flesh, a temporary habitation. The past is concentrated in the movables, the sword, the books, the furniture, which are finally established at Howards End. It is as though this house in the country had been the home of the Schlegel sisters for all their lives, as though Wickham Place, through death and the vision that Ruth Wilcox enforces, had been transformed (sweetened) and had taken to itself a new name and habitation.[14]

But this is only half the truth. The idea of salvation through death or of life through death is paradoxical. Likewise the image of houses is paradoxical. Grass because it is alive is subject to destruction, it is in a state of dying; whereas hay, once it has withered and sweetened, has passed beyond destruction and has a new and permanent value, it is in a state of living. These same descriptions can be applied to Wickham Place and Howards End—but only *after* death and the transformation which it brings has touched Howards End and given it permanent life. In the early part of the novel this has not happened or at least it has not happened for Margaret and Helen. We first see Howards End in the summer haying season, that is to say, at the beginning of harvest time. But our strongest impression, though largely an imaginative one, is associated with Mrs. Wilcox's invitation to Margaret to come and see her house and meadow. It is very late in the fall and Mrs. Wilcox is dying. Here we see Howards End as autumnal and under the aspect of death.

This view is quite transformed when Margaret first comes to the place—it is the moment of her vision of brotherhood—and finds Miss Avery has unpacked the books and arranged the furniture. Now the hedge is "a half-painted picture which would be finished in a few days." Now "Spring has come, clad in no classical garb, yet fairer than all springs" (p. 284). The chapter describing Margaret's next visit to Howards End—Henry has set a trap for Helen—opens this way:

> One speaks of the moods of spring, but the days that are her true children have only one mood: they are all full of the rising and dropping of winds, and the whistling of birds. New flowers may come out, the green embroidery of the hedges increase, but the same heaven broods overhead, soft, thick, and blue, the same figures, seen and unseen, are wandering by coppice and meadow. The morning that Margaret had spent with Miss Avery, and the afternoon she set out to entrap Helen, were the scales of a single balance. Time might never have moved, rain never have fallen, and man alone, with his schemes and ailments, was troubling Nature until he saw her through a veil of tears.
>
> (p. 301)

Howards End now exists for Margaret and Helen under the permanent aspect of spring. Like the hay and like Mrs.

Wilcox it is seen as unalterable in its value and unchanging in its living reality. For this reason it is appropriate that Margaret does not go with Mrs. Wilcox to see Howards End in its autumnal aspect. And it is appropriate that Mrs. Wilcox is connected with Wickham Place, that the living but temporary house which must suffer destruction should offer a parallel to the mortal woman who must die. Wickham Place, says Helen in retrospect, "was a grave" (p. 317).

Grass and flowers, the life and gaiety of a rented house, all have within them the seed of the death that destroys through time and change and flux. But hay and the house and property of Howards End have incorporated death and mastered it. They have passed through death into a condition of permanence and eternal promise. The concept of salvation through the idea of death has been broadened and enriched by the house image which is a physical symbol of the continuity between past and future generations. And participating in that continuity, the individual is for ever the point of juncture through which death and the past are transformed into new life and the future. That is why the idea of the moment, of "now," is so important, and why this idea is linked with the wych-elm, the most universal of all the symbols.

The tree: "every westerly gale might blow the wych-elm down and bring the end of all things" (p. 355). Here then is the Tree of Life. It is under this tree that Helen and Paul Wilcox kiss. It is under it that Helen and Margaret find peace when Helen returns, carrying Leonard Bast's child. Their conversation at this time develops the implications of one of the minor aspects of the tree but one of its most fascinating, namely the pigs' teeth in its bark.[15] Helen has been speaking of her night with Leonard:

> "Oh, Meg, the little that is known about these things!"
>
> She laid her face against the tree.
>
> "The little, too, that is known about growth! Both times it was loneliness, and the night, and panic afterwards. Did Leonard grow out of Paul?"
>
> Margaret did not speak for a moment. So tired was she that her attention had actually wandered to the teeth—the teeth that had been thrust into the tree's bark to medicate it. From where she sat she could see them gleam. She had been trying to count them. "Leonard is a better growth than madness," she said. "I was afraid that you would react against Paul until you went over the verge."
>
> (pp. 330-31)

The tree endures the injury of the teeth, absorbing them into its growth. According to legend, the teeth have a medicinal effect. Similarly, Helen has endured the injury of her brief moment with Paul, and through Leonard she has been able to escape negative reaction and to incorporate the injury into her life. This incorporation, as the further course of the story shows, has its medicinal or beneficent effect. And this not simply psychologically or spiritually,

but also physically. As Leonard grows out of Paul, so the unborn child grows out of Leonard. Helen, like the tree and like life itself, embodies the alien and the injurious and transforms them to beauty and promise.

The power of the wych-elm to absorb and transmute the incidental or individual injury strengthens our impression that the significance of the tree is vast and universal. Forster confirms this impression by his statement that the tree is "symbolical," it is "the genius of the house."[16] The genius of a man is his psyche or other self or spirit, which sustains his life. Similarly, the genius of a place is the spirit which sustains the life of the place—precisely the significance Forster attributes to the wych-elm at Howards End.

The tree, like much else about Howards End, comes very directly from Forster's personal experience. Writing many years later of his childhood and his mother, he says: "The truth is that she and I had fallen in love with our Hertfordshire home and did not want to leave it. . . . The garden, the overhanging wych elm, the sloping meadow, the great view to the west, the cliff of fir trees to the north, the adjacent farm through the high tangled hedge of wild roses were all utilised by me in *Howards End,* and the interior is in the novel too."[17] These words, which reach back through more than sixty years of Forster's experience, are charged with a sense of ecstasy. The same sense of ecstasy gets into the novel where it is more subdued and diffused so that without the sounding of trumpets or the banging of drums it touches everything to life at Howards End. In the process the wych-elm—far from conveying an abstract conception of Life—is transformed and expresses the sense of a living totality.

A great tree is both organic and enduring, for in its living it outlives the generations of man. Its development as a traditional life symbol is a reflection of the natural inclination of the image. It is not surprising that Forster personally encountered such a tree and that he came to apprehend it as a life symbol. Nor is it surprising that his conception of the wych-elm was enriched by tradition. I will restrict myself to three possible examples of such enrichment. From his friend Syed Ross Masood he may have learned that in India the "tree, with its spreading branches and leaves, is the Universe itself." In editing the *Aeneid* he may have been impressed by Virgil's ancient oak cleaving to the rocks, "and as high as it shoots up to the top in the ethereal regions, so deep it descends with its root toward Tartarus." And almost certainly he was influenced by the image in Lowes Dickinson's Sonnet XXV:

> Thou knowest, love, of love's immortal tree
> Strength in the root and tenderness the flower,
> And more luxuriant sweet the bloom will be
> The deeper drawn from elemental power.[18]

Forster ignores the heroic aspect of the symbol. Virgil relates his mighty oak to the unmoved heroic mind, and Dickinson in a letter refers to his sonnet in connection with Wagner's heroic love.[19] Forster says that Howards

End is English and that the wych-elm is an English tree. It is "neither warrior, nor lover, nor god; in none of these rôles do the English excel." Rather its special attributes are comradeship and the peace of the moment.

"It was a comrade, bending over the house, strength and adventure in its roots, but in its utmost fingers tenderness, and the girth, that a dozen men could not have spanned, became in the end evanescent, till pale bud clusters seemed to float in the air. It was a comrade. House and tree transcended any similes of sex . . . to compare either to man, to woman, always dwarfed the vision. Yet they kept within limits of the human" (p. 218). With this compare Margaret's visit to Miss Avery's farm home, which like the surrounding country gives promise of comradeship and the brotherhood of man. Comradeship is the highest and most universal form of human love.

The second meaning of the wych-elm as a symbol is established in the scene between Helen and Margaret during their first evening at Howards End. They are sitting under the tree.

> The present flowed by them like a stream. The tree rustled. It had made music before they were born, and would continue after their deaths, but its song was of the moment. The moment had passed. The tree rustled again. Their senses were sharpened, and they seemed to apprehend life. Life passed. The tree rustled again.
>
> "Sleep now," said Margaret.
>
> The peace of the country was entering into her. It has no commerce with memory, and little with hope. . . . . It is the peace of the present, which passes understanding. Its murmur came "now," and "now" once more as they trod the gravel, and "now," as the moonlight fell upon their father's sword.
>
> (pp. 332-33)

The sisters can apprehend life and know the peace of the present because in their relations they have achieved comradeship and, consequently, are secure in the knowledge that their lives at this moment are contained in a meaningful, that is to say connected, oneness of human life stretching unbrokenly from past to future. Like Stephen Wonham, they guard the paths between the dead who have evoked them and the unborn whom they will evoke. They are the point, the juncture, the living "now" wherein the past lodges against the future. And from such an awareness comes the full acceptance of the moment that is always the present. The wych-elm encompasses all human life. It symbolizes general salvation or comradeship and individual salvation or the peace of the moment. Both are implicit in the idea of death and in the strength of love.

Hay, house, and tree: these great archetypal symbols—life-giving, wholly significant, conveying a sense of totality—are not the result of one or two great moments of ecstatic apprehension but arise from a continuing series of less intense visionary insights. The extraordinary sense of aliveness and wholeness does not adhere to these moments of insight or to the characters who experience them; rather the nouminous quality attaches itself to and remains permanently with the objects. Thus liberated, the power and significance of the symbols can be freely deployed to strengthen and expand the role of Mrs. Wilcox. Such is their destiny, to find unity in her and her love for Howards End.

Mrs. Wilcox is a Great Mother figure. In her highly developed state the Great Mother has two forms or aspects which are often symbolized as separate persons, but in Mrs. Wilcox they are combined. The simpler of the two forms is that of the Earth-Mother or Demeter. She presides over birth and death and all growth and decay. Mrs. Wilcox in her garden and in her devotion to grass and flowers assumes the role of Demeter.

As well as being the source of life, the Great Mother is the source of transformation. At the level of the earth and the womb her power of transformation is both obvious and mysterious. At a higher level—the level that best defines the role of Mrs. Wilcox—her power of transformation is spiritual and encompasses the highest wisdom. Her spirituality is stressed when we speak of the anima (of which more will be said in a moment), her wisdom when we speak of Sophia, the most transcendent of all archetypal feminine figures. Mrs. Wilcox in her meadow and in her devotion to hay assumes the role of Sophia.[20]

At Howards End the tree bends over and sometimes enshadows the house. At other times the house enshadows the tree. But during the night that Helen and Margaret slept at Howards End after hearing the whisper of "now" in the rustling leaves, the house and tree under the moon's light "disentangled, and were clear for a few moments at midnight. Margaret awoke and looked into the garden. How incomprehensible that Leonard Bast should have won her this night of peace! Was he also part of Mrs. Wilcox's mind?" (p. 333) The reader's answer will be affirmative. Leonard sought what Mrs. Wilcox had found, "a real home" (p. 151). Leonard, whom she never knew, is included. Ruth Wilcox's mind is able to connect—"connect without bitterness until all men are brothers." Her symbols are the house and the tree, which between them signify her inclusiveness. The wych-elm by its organic nature enforces her role as Earth-Mother; the house, symbolic of the ancestral wisdom of the past and the joyous promise of the future, her role as Sophia. The two roles complement and support each other. For a moment, at the witching hour, Margaret has an insight into their dual nature.

The wych-elm kept within limits of the human. So does Ruth Wilcox in her Demeter aspect. Otherworldliness is no more than an echo. References to life beyond the grave are attributed to a character or, if Forster's own, are poetically ambiguous. Consider the following: Margaret "knew that out of Nature's device we have built a magic that will win us immortality. . . . We are evolving, in ways that Science cannot measure, to ends that Theology dares not contemplate. 'Men did produce one jewel,' the gods will say, and, saying, will give us immortality. Margaret knew all this . . ." (pp. 254-55). And Forster knows it too. But he is not saying that man will gain immortality in another world or, literally speaking, in this world. Love will win us immortality. When all men are brothers, the individual man will live for ever in the connected continuity of mankind. The "one jewel" may refer to Jesus, not as redeemer of a fallen world, not as dying god, but as a man of love who, like Ruth Wilcox, reveals the promise of human brotherhood.

The death of Ruth Wilcox helped Margaret to see "a little more clearly than hitherto what a human being is, and to what he may aspire. Truer relationships gleamed. Perhaps the last word would be hope—hope even on this side of the grave" (pp. 108-9). Later as Margaret contemplated Howards End and the tree which is a comrade, she understood that their "message was not of eternity, but of hope on this side of the grave. As she stood in the one, gazing at the other, truer relationship had gleamed" (p. 218).

In addition to her role as Demeter, Ruth Wilcox is an anima figure, the feminine image of transformation which in its most transcendent form appears as Sophia. The anima, in keeping with its spiritualized and idealized character, has usually an odd relationship to time and frequently appears as immortal or outside time. Mrs. Wilcox alive is "this shadowy woman" who asks once and will never ask again (p. 89). She is a figure in long trailing skirts who moves slowly, almost automatically, and certainly irresistibly—toward what? And death places her image forever beyond time. Of the dead Forster has written: "their personal yearnings are stilled and so they can help us, as the living cannot; their hatreds and fears are over, their lust for possessions quelled. . . ."[21] And of Mrs. Wilcox he writes: "To her everything was in proportion now . . ." (p. 257). Proportion is the final secret of the inner life that says "I" and the final secret of the outer life that achieves comradeship; it is the establishing of harmony between love, our attachment to things as they are, and truth, our passion for things as they ought to be. Proportion is the union of Demeter and Sophia. Margaret says to her sister: "I feel that you and I and Henry are only fragments of that woman's mind. She knows everything. She is everything. She is the house, and the tree that leans over it. People have their own deaths as well as their own lives, and even if there is nothing beyond death, we shall differ in our nothingness" (p. 331).

Through Mrs. Wilcox all the polarities are reconciled: grass and hay, tree and house, body and soul, matter and spirit, Wickham Place and Howards End, love and truth, Demeter and Sophia. All the polarities are reconciled except one. The city of London is not included in the vision of England, for it negates every value that Howards End and Mrs. Wilcox stand for.

London is a realm of chaos and greyness. That is its insistent image. But on one occasion it is seen in the image of hell. Margaret is returning from her shopping expedition with Mrs. Wilcox and is feeling desolate after refusing the invitation to see Howards End. The exceptional nature of the imagery here is intended to suggest—through Margaret—what London and its way of life mean to Mrs. Wilcox. "The city seemed Satanic, the narrow streets oppressing like the galleries of a mine." It was not the fog that harmed, but a "darkening of the spirit which fell back upon itself, to find a more grievous darkness within." Margaret sees Mrs. Wilcox passing through the glass doors of the lift and, imprisoned, going up heavenward. "And into what a heaven—a vault as of hell, sooty black, from which soots descended!" When Margaret rushes to the station to join Mrs. Wilcox in her expedition to the country, we are told that "the clock of King's Cross swung into sight, a second moon in that infernal sky" (pp. 89-90).

The clock of King's Cross has already appeared at the beginning of the novel and the difference between Margaret's view of it then and her view of it now confirms that in the present case the vision reflects the experience of Mrs. Wilcox. Her own vision is of railway terminals as gates to sunshine and the unknown (p. 12). "To Margaret . . . King's Cross had always suggested Infinity. . . . Those two great arches, colourless, indifferent, shouldering between them an unlovely clock, were fit portals for some eternal adventure . . ." (p. 13).

The adventure will at last take Margaret to Howards End. And Howards End is private and personal and makes possible the experience of the unseen. "It is private life that holds out the mirror to infinity; personal intercourse, and that alone, that ever hints at a personality beyond our daily vision" (p. 86). On the other hand the city is public and offers a false infinity. When Helen, back from Germany, refuses to meet Margaret and instead fades into London's vast indifference, Margaret has a true and desolating vision: "The mask fell off the city, and she saw it for what it really is—a caricature of infinity. The familiar barriers, the streets along which she moved, the houses between which she had made her little journeys for so many years, became negligible suddenly. Helen seemed one with grimy trees and the traffic and the slowly-flowing slabs of mud. She had accomplished a hideous act of renunciation and returned to the One" (p. 296).

The One is characterized by flux, "eternal formlessness; all the qualities, good, bad, and indifferent, streaming away—streaming, streaming for ever" (p. 193); and by greyness, "the grey tides of London" which rise and fall in continual flux (p. 113). Nothing escapes. Even Wickham Place in its quiet backwater falls before the tide and is "spilt . . . back into the grey" (p. 721). One visualizes London "as a tract of quivering grey." It lies beyond humanity. "It lies beyond everything" (p. 114).

One of the committed denizens of this grey realm, one of the kings of chaos,[22] is Henry Wilcox. He has suffered a characteristic fate of the successful man. His conscious mind has lost touch with the emotional, intuitive, and unconscious resources of his nature. The result is isolation, and "Isolation means death."[23] Its outer manifestation is rigidity; its inner manifestation, chaos.

Rigidity is unflagging, unthoughtout, hence meaningless, devotion to the norms of society. "Henry treated a marriage like a funeral, item by item, never raising his eyes to the whole, and 'Death, where is thy sting? Love, where is thy victory?' one would exclaim at the close" (p. 232). Were he to raise his eyes to the whole, the result would be panic and emptiness. For behind rigidity lies chaos. Henry Wilcox has lost the capacity for growth and transformation. When he cannot fall back on conventional formulas he collapses into panic and emptiness. Then begins the process of evasion and muddle until reality is reduced to a kind of grey porridge. "Outwardly he was cheerful, reliable, and brave; but within, all had reverted to chaos . . ." (p. 197).

In this reversion to chaos he is one with the condition of the great city which lies beyond humanity. We know who is responsible for this condition and we know that it spreads far beyond London. Henry Wilcox did indeed buy a house at Oniton. "But the Wilcoxes have no part in the place, nor in any place. It is not their names that recur in the parish register. It is not their ghosts that sigh among the alders at evening. They have swept into the valley and swept out of it, leaving a little dust[24] and a little money behind" (p. 264). Because the Wilcoxes have no part in any place they make no distinctions. And because they make no distinctions, they are "levelling all the world into what they call common sense" (p. 252). The threat is summed up by Helen: "London is only part of something else, I'm afraid. Life's going to be melted down, all over the world" (p. 358).

Though this insight is fearful and oppressive, it is not the controlling vision of the novel. Margaret recognizes that "either some very dear person or some very dear place seems necessary to relieve life's daily grey, and to show that it is grey" (p. 154). Her desire for personal attachment is fulfilled *through* Mrs. Wilcox who, like a great wave, "flowed into her life and ebbed out of it for ever . . . the wave had strewn at her feet fragments torn from the unknown. . . . Her friend had vanished in agony, but not, she believed, in degradation. Her withdrawal had hinted at other things besides disease and pain" (p. 108). The things hinted at, truer relationships, hope this side of the grave, love of England, all come to Margaret during the course of the story.

For Howards End remains—that is the great fact. There Margaret forgets the phantom of bigness with its continual flux as she recaptures "the sense of space, which is the basis of all earthly beauty." Starting from Howards End, she awakes to unexpected love of the whole island (p. 216). The whole island is alive, for like Howards End it is still a part of nature. Along the entire south coast the rising tides pressed inland "and over the immense displacement the sun presided. . . . England was alive, throbbing through

all her estuaries, crying for joy through the mouths of all her gulls, and the north wind, with contrary motion, blew stronger against her rising seas" (pp. 185-86).

In this ecstatic vision of a land embraced by the immense displacement of the tides the vast metropolis of London has no part. The city with its quivering grey reaches is the hell which cannot be included for it is a hideous amorphous monster with a mindless drive to devour the whole island.

Some readers and critics think that, because London and what it stands for cannot be included, the novel is a failure and, in particular, that the happy ending is faked. This way of thinking about the novel ignores two important facts. The first fact is that the terrible monster, the dragon of myth and legend, is never finally destroyed, though it is frequently defeated. Like the goblins of Beethoven's symphony, it rises up again and again, and must be contended with over and over. Psychologically this is a true perception. It is naive to think the goblins can be tidied out of existence. The second fact is that comedy expresses the triumph of light over darkness. Again it is Beethoven's symphony which gives us the best insight into the novel's intention and achievement. For here, more cogently than anywhere else in his fiction, Forster speaks about himself as artist.

Our equation reads: let Beethoven be Forster. After the goblins had twice insinuated their message of despair, Beethoven took them in hand. "He appeared in person . . . he blew with his mouth and they were scattered!" But Beethoven knew the goblins were real and "might return—and they did!" Thus Beethoven's wisdom is affirmed. After describing the reappearance of the goblins, Forster begins the next paragraph emphatically: "Beethoven chose to make all right in the end" (p. 35). Here then is our image of the personal artist—of the narrator who stands openly at the center of his narrative—personal not to the end that he may indulge in egoistic exhibitionism, but that he may manipulate and comment on his creation, making of it a truthful and meaningful representation of life. For this reason we can trust Forster even though we may disagree with him.

It was also his hope that we could trust him for another reason:

> Beethoven chose to make all right in the end. He built the ramparts up. He blew with his mouth for the second time, and again the goblins were scattered. He brought back the gusts of splendour, the heroism, the youth, the magnificence of life and of death, and, amid vast roarings of a superhuman joy, he led his Fifth Symphony to its conclusion. But the goblins were there. They could return. He had said so bravely, and that is why one can trust Beethoven when he says other things.
>
> (pp. 35-36)

The novel, like the symphony, ends in joyous splendor—and for the same reason. Forster chooses to make all right in the end. But the goblins are there. Panic and emptiness, squalor and tragedy—they may return, indeed, they will. And they have a place in the splendor and triumph.

Forster many years later notes his conviction that in the Fifth Symphony and the other works in C minor Beethoven "is engaged in the pursuit of something outside sound—something which has fused the sinister and the triumphant."[25] In his last two novels, Forster sought an effect not unlike this. His words remind us of Elizabeth Bowen's account of the sense of evil in his novels, "the sense of conscious life's being built up over a somehow august vault of horror." This is the sinister echo of panic and emptiness which lies behind the triumphant joy of the final scene of **Howards End.** The happy ending is a fact of comedy, and its permanence is enforced by art. But when the artist has said the thing that is true, he has earned our confidence. Beethoven and his symphony symbolize not simply Forster and his novel but symbolize as well the trust we may place in both.

Notes

1. But it comes close to paralleling the story, especially with reference to Helen's career. This has been ably demonstrated by Johnstone in *The Bloomsbury Group,* pp. 226-28. For another parallel, between Helen's *synaesthesia* and the novel's theme of *synthesis,* see the lively and perceptive article by Barry R. Westburg, "Forster's Fifth Symphony: Another Aspect of *Howards End,*" *Modern Fiction Studies,* X (Winter 1964-65), 359-65.

2. The reader may have guessed from the style—but certainly not from the meaning—that the quoted remarks are not Forster's. They are from "An Essay in Aesthetics" published in 1909 by Roger Fry and show how precisely Forster's thoughts echo those of another member of the Bloomsbury intellectual aristocracy. See *Vision and Design* (London, 1928), pp. 24, 23.

3. *Abinger Harvest,* pp. 285, 281.

4. I am indebted to Mr. Forster for bringing this fact to my attention. The words do not appear in Vasari or Condivi or in Charles Holroyd's *Michael Angelo Buonarroti* (1903). They appear in the following form in John Addington Symonds, *The Life of Michelangelo Buonarroti* (New York, 1962):

   > While still in his seventieth year, Michelangelo had educated himself to meditate upon the thought of death as a prophylactic against vain distractions and the passion of love. . . . "Marvellous is the operation of this thought of death, which, albeit death, by his nature, destroys all things, preserves and supports those who think on death, and defends them from all human passions." He supports this position by reciting a madrigal he had composed, to show how the thought of death is the greatest foe to love:—

> Not death indeed, but the dread thought of death
> Saveth and severeth
> Me from the heartless fair who doth me slay. . . .
>
> (p. 502)

Forster may have been influenced by this association of death and love but the use to which he puts the association is the opposite of Michelangelo's.

5. *Working Men's College Journal,* X, 283.

6. *Timaeus, Dialogues of Plato,* III, 451.

7. *Two Cheers,* p. 299.

8. I distinguish in Appendix A between the life-oriented attitude of Forster and the art-oriented attitude of the French symbolists and the English poets of the nineties. One could hardly find a more apt illustration of this distinction than that which comes from setting Forster's treatment of death in *Howards End* over against Arthur Symons' analysis in *The Symbolist Movement in Literature*:

   > And so there is a great, silent conspiracy between us to forget death. . . . That is why we are active about so many things which we know to be unimportant; why we are so afraid of solitude, and so thankful for the company of our fellow-creatures. Allowing ourselves, for the most part, to be but vaguely conscious of that great suspense in which we live, we find our escape from its sterile, annihilating reality in many dreams, in religion, passion, art. . . . Each is a kind of sublime selfishness, the saint, the lover, and the artist having each an incommunicable ecstasy which he esteems as his ultimate attainment. . . . But it is, before all things, an escape; and the prophets who have redeemed the world and the artists who have made the world beautiful, and the lovers who have quickened the pulses of the world, have really, whether they knew it or not, been fleeing from the certainty of one thought: that we have, all of us, only our one day; and from the dread of that other thought: that the day, however used, must after all be wasted.
   >
   > (*Collected Works* [London, 1924], VIII, 248-49)

   Here we find an impressive mixture of century's-end pessimism and art-for-art's-sake theory, and a striking contrast with Forster's emphasis on the life-enhancing.

9. Cf. "Dolly raised her faded little face, which sorrow could wither but not steady" (p. 360).

10. As so often in Forster's work, this crucial appearance of the greengage tree has been carefully prepared. See pp. 4, 211.

11. *Psyche,* pp. 172-73. This is better than Forster's own account: "The past is not a series of vanished presents . . . it would exercise no effect if it were. It is a distillation, and a few drops of it work wonders. . . . This is not a private fancy of mine: all

races who have practised ancestor-worship know about it, and Ulysses went down into the underworld to acquire better balance for his course in this." See "Recollectionism," *New Statesman and Nation,* N.S., March 13, 1937, p. 405.

12. I. A. Richards, "A Passage to Forster; Reflections on a Novelist," *The Forum,* LXXVIII (1927), 918.

13. In *Marianne Thornton* there is an admirable illustration of how a feeling for place can establish a continuity between past and future generations. See the account of Marianne Thornton's second visit to Paris, and esp. p. 186.

14. Further connection is established in Miss Avery's judgment that Ruth Wilcox should have married "Some real soldier" (p. 290). The father of Margaret and Helen was a soldier and an idealist. A soldier fights to preserve what now exists, thereby showing his love. But a soldier idealist fights also for things as they ought to be—for truth. Mr. Schlegel, I think, would have satisfied Miss Avery's conception of a real soldier. (See esp. pp. 29-31.) Had Ruth Wilcox married this real soldier, Margaret would have been her physical as well as spiritual heir and Howards End would have been her home always.

15. Pigs, of course, were traditionally associated with Demeter. Images of pigs were found in the holy plot of Demeter at Cnidus. See C. T. Newton, *A History of Discoveries at Halicarnassus, Cnidus, and Branchidae* (London, 1862-63), II, 331-32, 385, 390-91.

16. Furbank and Haskell, *Writers at Work,* p. 30.

17. *Marianne Thornton,* p. 301. Opposite p. 302 there is an excellent photograph of the house as a background to "My mother, pony and self in Hertfordshire (about 1885)."

18. The sources for the three quotations are: E. B. Havell, *The Ideals of Indian Art* (London, 1911), p. 59; *The Works of Virgil,* trans. Davidson, rev. T. A. Buckley (New York, 1877), Bk. IV, lines 441 ff.; [Dickinson], *Poems* (London, 1896), p. 54.

19. *G. L. Dickinson,* p. 227.

20. The immensely articulate Margaret Schlegel and her charming and lively sister, though they are not portrayed as archetypal characters, move toward a full sharing of Mrs. Wilcox's experience and significance. Margaret in her association with grass and in her final understanding of hay is the heir of Mrs. Wilcox. Thus in the novel's closing scene the narrator for the first time refers to her by that name. She may not be the equal of the first Mrs. Wilcox but she follows heroically in her footsteps, and like her predecessor, attains proportion. Helen is related to Mrs. Wilcox more indirectly. She represents the same aspects of the Great Mother that Mrs. Wilcox represents, but at a much more elemental level. As an Earth-Mother figure Helen's role is simply biological. As a femi-

nine figure of transformation her role is also primarily biological. Injury becomes promise. Paul Wilcox is transformed into Leonard Bast who is transformed into the child. Of course Helen's experience has psychological and spiritual implications; but as a figure of transformation she remains, in comparison with Mrs. Wilcox, elemental. Her role is reflected in her character: in her lack of interest in any permanent relationship with a man, in her inclination to attract or be attracted, and in her spontaneity and glad animal spirits.

For the various manifestations of the Great Mother, see esp. Jung, *Collected Works,* Vol. XVI: *The Practice of Psychotherapy* (1954), pp. 173-74; and Erich Neumann, *The Great Mother: An Analysis of the Archetype,* trans. Ralph Manheim, Bollingen Series, XLVII (New York, 1963).

21. "The Function of Literature in War-time," *Working Men's College Journal,* XIV (March 1915), 61.

22. To Leonard Bast, "Mr. Wilcox was king of this world, the superman, with his own morality, whose head remained in the clouds" (p. 253). He is a superman because he never says "I," because he is impersonal and so beyond humanity (p. 248). He is also an imperialist and in the very act of building empires he levels all the world. He is a destroyer (p. 342). In this he resembles death. But the comparison with death, as Helen insists, reveals him for the false emperor he is. "Death's really Imperial," and the mention of Death strikes panic into the heart of any Wilcox for it reveals that the destroyer and all that he has built will in turn be destroyed (p. 252). Death reveals also that the false emperor worships false gods, of which the novel offers one memorable example, the Porphyrion Insurance Company. This god was a giant. "A giant was of an impulsive morality—one knew that much. . . . But his true fighting weight, his antecedents, his amours with other members of the commercial Pantheon—all these were as uncertain to ordinary mortals as were the escapades of Zeus" (p. 147). Forster is saying again that London and the London way of life is a caricature of infinity.

23. Forster continues: "And isolation sometimes masks itself behind bustle or worldly success or what passes for civilization." See the Introduction to Donald Windham, *The Warm Country* (London, 1960).

24. The dust is thrown up by the motor cars which the Wilcoxes delight to drive. These cars are a prominent symbol of the Wilcox attitude and way of life. The emergence of the automobile on the roads of England during the first decade of the century aroused a degree of consternation and passion that it is not easy for the modern reader to appreciate. I quote from Lowes Dickinson's "The Motor Tyranny," *Independent Review* (October 1906):

> For some ten years the people of this country—as of all countries—have been groaning un-

der a public nuisance which increases day by day until it has reached a malignity and magnitude altogether unprecedented. Their property has been depreciated; their senses offended; their comfort destroyed; their security invaded. . . . And if it is urged that this nuisance is as yet confined to a few main thoroughfares, it must be remembered that we are only at the beginning; and that, according to any reasonable forecast, in ten years' time, unless some drastic measures are adopted, there will not be a country lane in the kingdom free from dust and stench, nor a field or a common undisturbed by that most odious of sounds, the hooting of the motor horn.

(p. 15)

25. *Two Cheers,* p. 125.

Michael Levenson (essay date summer 1985)

SOURCE: Levenson, Michael. "Liberalism and Symbolism in *Howards End." Papers on Language and Literature* 21, no. 3 (summer 1985): 295-316.

[*In the following essay, Levenson argues that* Howards End "*gives the experience of modernity a turn toward politics and toward mysticism.*"]

Liberalism and symbolism, both unwieldy terms, become more unwieldy when brought together. They seem to belong to such different orders of description and such different strains of modernity that it provokes a small mental shudder to recall that John Stuart Mill and Charles Baudelaire were near contemporaries. Although no one would mistake E. M. Forster for either Mill or Baudelaire, liberalism and symbolism are prominent in his ancestry, and *Howards End* (1910), which occupies a place in both lineages, marks a striking point of connection between political hopes and literary tropes. The only thing more vivid than Forster's perception of social constraint was his perception of imaginative escape. Looking at the world from the standpoint of both historical necessity and visionary possibility, he saw depth in modern experience, but also incongruity, because he saw with one liberal and one symbolist eye. It is necessary to correct for the parallax. *Howards End* gives the experience of modernity a turn toward politics and toward mysticism. It asks what happens to the self when its own modes of understanding come into conflict and it is unsure whether it has sustained a symbolic victory or a political defeat.

In the work of Forster it is possible to glimpse what the development of the English novel might have been if, at the turn of the century, it had endured an evolutionary, rather than a revolutionary, change. Forster belongs neither with the stout Edwardians, Wells, Bennett, and Galsworthy, nor with the lean modernists, Joyce, Woolf, Ford, and Lewis. He shared with the latter a sense of an irrevocable historical transformation that necessarily alters the methods of art, but he could never muster the conviction for a programmatic assault on traditional forms. For this reason he continues to occupy an ambiguous position in the history of modern fiction. His own formal experiments, which are by no means negligible, often appear as involuntary expressions of his own sense of loss, and much of their inspiration can be seen as an attempt to revive a dying tradition.

1

"Oh, to acquire culture!" thinks Leonard Bast, "Oh, to pronounce foreign names correctly."[1] He is walking alongside Margaret Schlegel, who has just pronounced Wagner's name (correctly, one must assume) and who has promised to recover Bast's umbrella, thoughtlessly taken by her sister during a concert at Queen's Hall. Bast stammers, falls silent, takes his umbrella, refuses an invitation to tea, bolts home, and reads Ruskin. Then, reminded of the disparity between the flat of an insurance clerk and the stones of Venice, he lays Ruskin aside with this unhappy thought: "Oh, it was no good, this continual aspiration. Some are born cultured; the rest had better go in for whatever comes easy. To see life steadily and to see it whole was not for the likes of him" (52).

Arnold's formulation was a touchstone for Forster who came back to it repeatedly in *Howards End,* its progressive restatements marking the development of the novel's argument. On this first occasion it broaches the problem of modern character, which for Forster (certainly not uniquely) is a problem of lost unity, lost because of related historical pressures: urbanism, imperialism, cosmopolitanism, bureaucracy, the estrangement of social classes. But there is another implication in Arnold's phrase that has particular bearing on Forsterian characterization: the attention to a form of response (seeing) rather than a form of action.

The initial and decisive characterization of Margaret Schlegel identifies her leading quality as "a profound vivacity, a continual and sincere response to all that she encountered in her path through life" (7). Forster thus endows her not with a desire but with a disposition; he is concerned less with her will to act than with her "sincere response" to what she encounters. Of the boorish Charles Wilcox we are told that "Want was to him the only cause of action" (93). Forster mentions such an opinion only as a way of dismissing it; he himself is primarily interested in neither wants, nor causes, nor indeed actions in their conventional sense. *Howards End,* like so much of Forster's work, suggests that the incidents which determine the broad course of life, both the intimate movements of the soul and the rude spasms of history, exceed the reach of individual will. One is accountable neither for one's desires nor one's epoch. Both exist as ungovernable forces that change particular lives but resist the workings of human agency; and therefore Forster declines to describe them with precision. He prefers to maintain strict attention upon the subject that interests him most: the region of individual experience that lies between the insurgence of the feelings and the oppressions of history. Part of the reason why Forster has come to seem outdated is that the space between history and the emotions has progressively narrowed in our time, but in *Howards End* there is still room to maneuver. Nevertheless, in the face of such powerful antagonists, what is to be done?

One cannot change one's desires; one cannot alter the movement of history. But it is possible to change the form and style of one's response, and here we come to a telling aspect of the novel's method of characterization: its tendency to describe individuals in terms that apply equally to works of art. Leading traits of characters include their predilections toward romance (Helen), irony (Tibby), sincerity (Margaret), sentimentality (Leonard), or prose (Henry). Moreover, these various possibilities reflect Forster's own historical sense, specifically his appropriation of the English literary tradition. Tibby derives from the Wildean nineties; Leonard connects his aspirations to Ruskin, Meredith and Stevenson; the Schlegel sisters (as others have noted) descend from *Sense and Sensibility*; Miss Avery is a late incarnation of a Gothic housekeeper; and the narrator alternately assumes the tones of Thackeray and Trollope. Through a kind of historical ventriloquism Forster displays the novelistic tradition he has inherited. This is more than an exercise in stylistic virtuosity; it serves to underscore an arresting fact, the intimate connection between fictional character and literary mode. Indeed character in *Howards End* is essentially a mode of aesthetic response, where this is understood not as the casual striking of a pose but as the deepest form of one's engagement with experience. That human responses vary so greatly poses perhaps the chief difficulty of the novel: the heterogeneity of modes, the diversity of styles, tones and manners.

Forster, who acknowledged his great debt to Jane Austen, is commonly linked to Austen and James as a novelist of manners. One might better say that he is a novelist of bad manners, who attends less to the shared norms and values which govern a community than to the moral awkwardness that results when incompatible norms and incommensurable values collide. Thus, Helen's "high-handed manner" (177) competes with the "breezy Wilcox manner" (178); Evie develops a "manner more downright" (147), while Tibby remains "affected in manner" (247), and Margaret finds Leonard's class "near enough her own for its manners to vex her" (35). Forster assumes nothing so stable as a coherent system of human conduct; indeed in his most serious purpose, he dramatizes the search for a moral manner, which becomes one with the search for an imaginative mode.

Beethoven's Fifth Symphony provides a comic and anodyne example. It excites a great variety of reactions—Mrs. Munt's surreptitious foot-tapping, Helen's reverie of heroes and goblins, Tibby's attention to counterpoint—but the variety is unthreatening because it overlays a fundamental point of agreement, namely that the "Fifth Symphony is the most sublime noise that has ever penetrated

into the ear of man. All sorts and conditions are satisfied by it" (29). Beethoven, however, is valuable just insofar as he is an exception. Precisely the problem which the novel poses is the difficulty of such agreement and the incongruity of diverse sorts and sundry conditions. When Mrs. Wilcox fails to "blend" with the Schlegel set, when Leonard describes his squalid flat in the style of Ruskin, when Tibby and Charles attempt to converse having "nothing in common but the English language" (396), the painful dissonance establishes an urgent requirement, the need for an appropriate mode with which to confront the facts of contemporary experience. The Arnoldian conception of seeing life steadily and whole represents an ideal mode for the engaged personality but an ideal which seems to have become obsolete. Arnold's phrase, as we will see, has still wider implications, but then so too does the issue of modality.

The agonies of Leonard Bast reflect both the disgregation of the self and the disgregation of its community—the failure of both to advance in the direction which Arnold had so confidently forecast.

> Culture looks beyond machinery, culture hates hatred; culture has one great passion, the passion for sweetness and light. It has one even greater!—the passion for making them *prevail*. It is not satisfed till we *all* come to a perfect man; it knows that the sweetness and light of the few must be imperfect until the raw and unkindled masses of humanity are touched with sweetness and light.[2]

Against such a view, *Howards End* places Bast whose hopes are kindled only at the cost of great pain and who, when he burns, gives off no sweetness and little light. Bast will come to mistrust the healing power of culture, as will Margaret Schlegel who thinks of him and arrives at this post-Arnoldian conclusion:

> Culture had worked in her own case, but during the last few weeks she had doubted whether it humanized the majority, so wide and so widening is the gulf that stretches between the natural and the philosophic man, so many the good chaps who are wrecked in trying to cross it.
>
> (113)

Instead of Arnold's widening isthmus Forster sees a widening gulf. Moreover, the problem does not end here; it goes beyond the "unkindled masses" to infect the privileged few. Halfway through the novel, just before Henry Wilcox proposes marriage to Margaret Schlegel, the two discuss the burdens of house-hunting. Wilcox insists that Margaret is not as unpractical as she pretends, and Arnold's celebrated dictum makes a second appearance.

> Margaret laughed. But she was—quite as unpractical. She could not concentrate on details. Parliament, the Thames, the irresponsive chauffeur, would flash into the field of house-hunting, and all demand some comment or response. It is impossible to see modern life steadily and see it whole, and she had chosen to see it whole. Mr. Wilcox saw steadily.
>
> [158]

At this point we should recall the view of *Howards End* that has dominated the criticism since it was proposed over forty years ago. In an interpretation which first appeared in his book *E. M. Forster* (1943), Lionel Trilling offered a thoroughgoing symbolic reading according to which *Howards End* was to be seen as a "novel about England's fate," "a story of the class war."[3] Under the assumptions of this account, the Schlegels exemplify the predicament of the intellectual situated between the victims and beneficiaries of modern capitalism. Their role is to reach downwards toward a depressed clerical class, as represented by Leonard Bast, and upwards toward a thriving business class, as represented by the Wilcoxes. When Helen bears a child fathered by Leonard and when Margaret marries Henry, the Schlegels symbolically fulfil their historical mission, and at the end of the novel, when Henry, Margaret, Helen, and Helen's son settle at Howards End ("the symbol for England"), the reconciliation among classes has been achieved. According to Trilling, the novel asks the question, "Who shall inherit England?" and it provides its answer in the final image of the child playing in the hay, "a symbol of the classless society."[4]

Trilling offers not merely an interpretation of the novel, but an embrace of certain possibilities within it. Placing himself in a line of descent from both Arnold and Forster, he suggests, in effect, an Arnoldian recovery from Forsterian scepticism. Within the terms of Trilling's account *Howards End* successfully overcomes the division of experience between the self and its community. The symbolic equations between characters and classes—and most notably the allegorical cast of the conclusion—traverse the distance between individual and collective life. Through the resources of symbolism, the private gesture is at the same time a public gesture, and activities as personal as love and marriage become signs of amorousness among economic groups. With that stroke the incongruity between individual and social experience is relieved; the question is whether it can be relieved so easily. Undoubtedly, the symbolic associations which Trilling identifies pertain to the reading of the novel, but the difficulty comes in trying to decide exactly how they pertain to it. To address that issue is to widen our concerns, to acknowledge the problem of the novel's narrator, to consider the formal consequences of Forsterian characterization, and to ask how symbolic experience bears on the experience of politics.

2

Forster's narrator in *Howards End* retains the formal prerogatives of his Victorian antecedents: the freedom to rove through space and time, the detachment from the affairs he chronicles, the access to the minds of his characters, and the privilege of unqualified ethical assessment. Dolly, we are told, "was a rubbishy little creature, and she knew it" (89-90). Here is a definitive judgment in the tradition of the Victorian literary moralists, but here also are signs of diminished power. The trenchant dismissal loses some of its force through those colloquialisms—"rubbishy," "and

she knew it"—which give it more the tone of a personal crochet than an Olympian edict. Later, faced with the weighty question of whether Margaret should have been informed of Ruth Wilcox's bequest, the narrator responds with a mild "I think not" (96). Surely someone who knows that Dolly is a rubbishy little creature might be expected to have a stronger opinion on such a momentous question. But Forster gives us a narrator who constructs the fictional universe with all the resources of a narrating divinity, only to halt suddenly and gape at what he has made with the incomprehension of any other mortal.

Consistently in *Howards End* the represented world seems to recede from the one who ought to know it best. Consider, for instance, the initial description of Jacky, the woman who shares Leonard's shabby life on "the extreme verge of gentility."

> A woman entered, of whom it is simplest to say that she was not respectable. Her appearance was awesome. She seemed all strings and bell-pulls—ribbons, chains, bead necklaces that clinked and caught—and a boa of azure feathers hung round her neck, with the ends uneven. Her throat was bare, wound with a double row of pearls, her arms were bare to the elbows, and might again be detected at the shoulder, through cheap lace. Her hat, which was flowery, resembled those punnets, covered with flannel, which we sowed with mustard and cress in our childhood, and which germinated here, yes, and there no. She wore it on the back of her head. As for her hair, or rather hairs, they are too complicated to describe, but one system went down her back, lying in a thick pad there, while another, created for a lighter destiny, rippled around her forehead. The face—the face does not signify.

[48]

It betrays no disrespect to Forster to say that Jacky disappears within the description. The passage offers too much information and too little; like Jacky herself it depends on effects; it reveals no attachment to detail for its own sake. The ribbons, chains and necklaces represent merely a gloss on the vague epithets "awesome" and "not respectable," as though the accumulation of aphoristic insights might finally amount to a coherent image. Moreover, the narrator keeps withdrawing from the descriptive act, back to the mustard and cress of childhood and, more significantly, to an intense consciousness of the verbal process itself. We are told what is "simplest to say," what is "too complicated to describe," what "does not signify." This mannerism appears persistently; a circumstance is invoked and then held to exceed the reach of language. Having mentioned the "poetry" of Helen's rash kiss, the narrator can only shrug: "who can describe that?" (22). Repeatedly, the novel tells us what we will not be told—"Young Wilcox was pouring in petrol, starting his engine, and performing other actions with which this story has no concern" (14)—with the result that there seems a vast penumbral field that exists just beyond the compass of representation. This raises a vexing formal problem to which we must return, but the opening paragraph of chapter six reveals that it is more than a formal concern.

We are not concerned with the very poor. They are unthinkable, and only to be approached by the statistician
or the poet. This story deals with gentlefolk, or with
those who are obliged to pretend that they are gentlefolk.

[43]

Forster mutes the point with irony, but beneath the irony
sounds an issue of consequence: the narrowing of fictional
domain. What can the novel now include? What has passed
beyond its bounds? Indeed *Howards End* does not concern itself with the very poor, nor for that matter with the
very rich, who, one must suppose, are just as unthinkable.
Thinkable is the middle class or, more precisely, a few
representative individuals of that class. *Howards End*
makes no attempt to survey social diversity, and for a
novel that broods so heavily over urban life, its London is
strikingly depopulated.[5] Forster does not aspire to the ca-
paciousness of the great Victorians: he does not seek to
convey the mass and density of modern existence; his is a
novel, not of three classes, but of three households. In itself, this restriction is not noteworthy or even unusual, but
in Forster it becomes pointed because he retains such a
sharp feeling for what he excludes, because the question
of domain becomes a crux in the novel, and because it is
linked so importantly to the question of Forster's liberalism.

Forster frequently remarked upon the obsolescence of the
liberal ideal, but he always expressed that opinion from
the standpoint of an obsolescent liberal. He placed himself
not beyond the tradition of Victorian liberalism but at its
deliquescence, once describing himself as "an individualist
and a liberal who has found liberalism crumbling beneath
him."[6] It is an odd remark. Presumably, he means to suggest that English individualism remained intact while its
liberalism declined. But it is a surprising political perception that can distinguish liberalism so sharply from individualism, and it is worth asking what exactly Forster
meant.

In 1911, a year after the appearance of *Howards End*, L.
T. Hobhouse published a small book called *Liberalism*
which tersely summarized the state of contemporary liberal theory and which has for us the additional, and more
immediate, virtue of establishing terms in which to approach *Howards End.* Hobhouse, who betrays none of
Forster's waning confidence, sees the progress of liberalism as "a steady stream toward social amelioration and
democratic government," a long course within which he
distinguishes two major phases. The first, the "older liberalism" worked to endow the individual with civil, economic, and political freedom. It challenged "authoritarian
government in church and state," and so constituted "a
movement of liberation, a clearance of obstructions, an
opening of channels for the flow of free spontaneous vital
activity." The 'old' liberalism was thus an essentially negative activity, devoted to the removal of constraints, sure in
the belief that once individuals were allowed to develop
freely, an "ethical harmony" would ensue.[7]

According to Hobhouse, Bentham initiated a second phase
in which the highest value attached not to the individual
but to the community and its collective will. The utilitarian calculus ensured that individual rights did not remain
the sole political consideration; it required an adjustment
of claims in conformity to the greatest happiness principle,
and it looked to the state to harmonize competing interests. This commitment has led to the positive aspect of the
liberal movement: the regulation of behavior, the intervention in markets, the exercise of legal restraints and "social
control," an emphasis which threatens "the complete sub-
ordination of individual to social claims" (Hobhouse, 100,
67). As Hobhouse acknowledges, the collectivist impulse
has led some to see a rending contradiction in liberal
thought: a radical individualism on one side and a state
paternalism on the other.

For Hobhouse, however, no such contradiction obtains. It
is merely a bogey of those who fail to recognize that an
individual right "cannot conflict with the common good,
nor could any right exist apart from the common good."
He denies any "intrinsic and inevitable conflict between
liberty and compulsion," and instead brings together the
two emphases which modern liberalism inherits, an individualism and a collectivism. He regards these as mutually
dependent commitments: "a fulfillment or full development of personality is practically possible not for one man
only but for all members of a community," and the highest
aim is not personal liberty but "liberty for an entire community" (Hobhouse, 127, 147, 128). Hobhouse himself did
not expect any immediate realization of this "harmonic
conception," but he held to a belief in steady progress, a
slow course of mutual adjustment in which the self and
the state would move gradually toward equilibrium. Such
a view gives expression to the best hopes of modern liberalism: a commitment to social reform and an unremitting
respect for personal liberty.

The liberalism that Forster sees crumbling around him is
clearly that New Liberalism which Hobhouse outlines,
with its plans for continued legislative reform on a large
scale. And when Forster holds on to his individualism, he
places himself in effect at an earlier stage of liberal ideology when the emphasis had fallen upon the removal of
constraints rather than the regulation of behavior. Unlike
Hobhouse, Forster retains no confidence in an emerging
balance between these two concerns, personal freedom
and public obligation, and faced with these alternatives, he
unhesitatingly chooses private before public, friend before
country, much as Margaret Schlegel makes this choice:

> Others had attacked the fabric of society—property, in-
> terest, etc; she only fixed her eyes on a few human be-
> ings, to see how, under present conditions, they could
> be made happier. Doing good to humanity was useless:
> the many-coloured efforts thereto spreading over the
> vast area like films and resulting in a universal gray. To
> do good to one, or, as in this case, to a few, was the ut-
> most she dare hope for.

[125]

Later Margaret recalls her sister to this Schlegel creed of
moral immediacy, refusing to be bound by abstract prin-

ciples of justice: "Nor am I concerned with duty. I'm concerned with the characters of various people whom we know, and how, things being as they are, things may be made a little better" (225).

This sentiment reflects the novel's much-discussed commitment to "personal relations," which are what Forster clings to when his liberalism crumbles. But it also bears upon some of its recurrent thematic preoccupations, for instance the lively debate over space and size, an issue which like so many others divides Schlegels from Wilcoxes. When Margaret Schlegel first sees Howards End, she overcomes the "phantom of bigness," remembering "that ten square miles are not ten times as wonderful as one square mile, that a thousand square miles are not practically the same as heaven" (198). Only a few pages later Henry Wilcox, soon to be her husband, insists that "the days for small farms are over": "Take it as a rule that nothing pays on a small scale" (203). Scale is of fundamental concern to Forster who often saw the problem of modernity as a loss of proportion that could only be recovered through a new respect for *genius loci*. Consistently he teaches the virtues of the small scale, the intimacy that is jeopardized in an age of imperialism. While Henry ceaselessly extends his empire of African rubber holdings, Margaret willingly surrenders her "cosmopolitanism" for a house that is "old and little."

A variation on this motif occurs in another issue that follows Wilcox/Schlegel lines, the dispute over the logical categories of experience: types and individuals. After the Schlegels have taken an interest in Leonard Bast, Henry Wilcox tries to intervene: "Miss Schlegel, excuse me, but I know the type," to which Margaret rejoins, "he isn't a type" (144). When Miss Avery frightens Margaret and irritates Henry, the latter erupts: "Uneducated classes are so stupid," and Margaret responds by asking, "Is Miss Avery uneducated classes?" (200). In the last phase of the novel, after the revelation of Helen's pregnancy, Margaret loyally reflects that "Not even to herself dare she blame Helen . . . . Morality can tell us that murder is worse than stealing, and group most sins in an order all must approve, but it cannot group Helen" (309). The narrator concurs, observing that "Preachers or scientists may generalize, but we know that no generality is possible about those whom we love" (273). The singular instance thus eludes the coarse generalization; the defense of the small space becomes one with the defense of the concrete particular; and the farmer joins hands with the nominalist.

At this point it is possible to recognize the congruence between the various features of the novel that have recently been at issue: the weakness of the narrator and the narrowing of fictional domain, the dismissal of large-scale liberal reform in favor of individual relations, the defense of the small space against the imperial cosmopolis, and the commitment to the concrete instance that resists generalization. In all these respects the novel dramatizes a movement from large things to small, in which the surrender of the broad view makes possible a discovery of value in the

rich particular. It should be evident that this emphasis poses insuperable difficulties for a view of the novel as a simple parable of class struggle and national reconciliation. Persistently and passionately, Forster distinguishes between the individual and the class, between "a few human beings" and the "universal gray" of humanity.

And yet no one can dispute that **Howards End** retains grand symbolic aspirations. A novel which finds the very poor unthinkable thinks nonetheless about the state of modern England. A novel which narrows its domain still symbolizes the largest questions that face a culture. How can we square the zeal for the individual with the concern for such high generalities? How does the narrow domain comport with the broadening symbolic reach? How, that is, can a novel which wilfully limits its range dramatize a vision of the social whole? And what do these two commitments imply about character and mode?

We can best address these questions by turning to the novel's third reference to Arnold's maxim. Shortly after her wedding, Margaret travels alone to Howards End. As she walks toward the house, she wanders through the Hertfordshire countryside and experiences a sudden, decisive recognition:

> In these English farms, if anywhere, one might see life steadily and see it whole, group in one vision its transitoriness and its eternal youth, connect—connect without bitterness until all men are brothers.
>
> (266)

This third instance serves as a rejoinder to the previous two. It is possible, after all, to see life steadily and whole, possible to unify, possible to connect. Still, before we surrender to a warm sense of imaginative triumph, we must raise another question. For what kind of whole is this, that ignores the city, that neglects modern life, that retreats to farms which, however lovely, are surely not the whole of England? John Martin raises this difficulty in his bluff dismissal of Trilling's reading of the novel: "Lionel Trilling declares that it concerns England's fate, but it does not, for it leaves too much of England out of account."[8] And yet Margaret's vision at Howards End suggests a way both to answer Martin's charge and to amend the symbolic interpretation, because, paradoxically, it is insofar as Margaret leaves much of England out of account, that she learns to address its fate. Only when she narrows her view from the cosmopolis to the little house does she achieve a wide social vision. Only by retreating to the part does she see the steady whole. Thus, she discloses the novel's presiding symbolic figure, synecdoche.

The novel, one might say, is a long preparation for synecdoche. It withdraws from a broad canvas; it reduces its scale; its battles are all waged among individuals. But in retreating to the partial view, it uses those parts to signify wholes. Helen assails Margaret's decision to marry Henry, and Margaret, defending her choice, moves from one man to many: "If Wilcoxes hadn't worked and died in England for thousands of years, you and I couldn't sit here without having our throats cut" (171). Later, Margaret turns to defend Helen and does so in these terms: "The pack was turning on Helen, to deny her human rights, and it seemed to Margaret that all Schlegels were threatened with her" (286). Wilcox exemplifies Wilcoxes, Helen Schlegel all Schlegels, and when Margaret must challenge her husband, his son, and their doctor, a "new feeling came over her: she was fighting for women against men" (287). This persistent imaginative gesture must be distinguished from that habit of mind which the novel repudiates, the tendency to ignore the individual in favor of the type, or, in the terms of Trilling's reading, to identify a character and a class. Synecdoche, on the contrary, embeds the whole within the part and only achieves its broad amplitude by respecting the concrete instance and by detaching the self from its class.

The history of liberalism is itself a history of negotiations between part and whole, and the "ethical harmony" toward which Hobhouse aims is put in just such terms. His "ideal society" is "a whole which lives and flourishes by the harmonious growth of its parts, each of which in developing on its own lines and in accordance with its own nature tends on the whole to further the development of others" (Hobhouse, 136). But for Hobhouse, it must be stressed, this relationship between part and whole is real, not figural. Individual and community are bound materially, socially, and politically, making society "a living whole." "National and personal freedom are growths of the same root," writes Hobhouse, "and their historic connection rests on no accident, but on ultimate identity of idea." If in the modern age the "individual voter" feels powerless, then the pressing need is to establish "organizations" which will "link the individual to the whole." (Hobhouse, 133, 232-33).

As Margaret approaches Howards End she has a fleeting political insight of her own: "Left to itself . . . this county would vote Liberal" (265). Just here the novel reveals both its lingering attachment to a political ideal and its refusal of a political program. Unlike Hobhouse, Forster's aim is not to secure the bonds that tie the few to the many, but to cut those bonds, leaving the county to itself, in the conviction that one can best aspire to the whole by retreating to a part. It is not that Forster abandons hope of social unity—he hopes indeed to "connect without bitterness until all men are brothers" (266)—but he sees this as possible only through a withdrawal from the large social realm. He does not ask the part to stand with, but to stand for, the whole.

Kermode has identified several areas of contact between Forster and the Symbolist tradition, but one point which he does not mention and which deserves particular emphasis here is Forster's keen feeling for *correspondence*: that connectedness between things that things themselves have established, an order which we can only disclose, never impose.[9] Without abandoning political value, Forster seeks to mortify the political will in the hope that *correspon-*

dences will then reveal themselves to the intelligent eye. He can abandon a large fictional domain, can prefer local roots to cosmopolitan rootlessness, can refuse the general category in favor of the singular instance, and can still address "England's fate," because for him, unlike Hobhouse, the effort to "link the individual to the whole" is a matter not of social organization but of imaginary figuration. Forster avails himself of a visionary possibility rare among his immediate contemporaries, but while we should acknowledge that his technical audacity points beyond the realist norms of early modern fiction, we must also recognize that in *Howards End* the post-realist method is in service of a pre-modern past. Synecdoche allows him to retrieve what he had lost. It gives him a way to retain symbolic connection, even after he has lost hope in political connection. It is the trope of a waning liberalism.

3

Synecdoche, if one may generalize, is a symbolic figure highly congenial to the modernist temperament, which is often more comfortable with the detail than with the panorama, but which is typically unwilling to surrender the broad view. The imaginative task, then, is to cultivate the particular so sedulously that it becomes radiant with meaning, to polish the fragment until it becomes luminous enough to disclose the age. The image, the impression, the epiphany, were each turned to this purpose. And yet, this method of resolution remains hazardous; the risk is that respect for particularity will become lost in an awe of generality and that the signified whole will subsume the signifying part. To read *Howards End* only in terms of its symbolic correspondences, to describe it as essentially a fable of modern England, is to foreclose one of its most provocative lines of reflection.

When Margaret Schlegel and Henry Wilcox first move toward one another in shy steps that will lead to their fateful marriage, they are described as "advancing out of their respective families towards a more intimate acquaintance" (152). From this point the novel, which had traded so heavily on the opposition between Schlegels and Wilcoxes, begins to draw increasingly fine distinctions within the two families. Thus Leonard originally sees "the Miss Schlegels" as "a composite Indian god whose waving arms and contradictory speeches were the product of a single mind" (137), and only gradually comes to realize that "a Miss Schlegel alone was different": "Helen had become 'his' Miss Schlegel" (232-33).

This differentiating of characters would be unremarkable, were it not that it placed such strain on the novel's symbolic machinery. Schlegels and Wilcoxes, as is perfectly evident, exemplify Forster's chief alternatives for the English temperament; in Leavis's paraphrase: "The Schlegels represent the humane liberal culture, the fine civilization of cultivated personal intercourse," while the Wilcoxes "have built the Empire; they represent the 'short-haired executive type'—obtuse, egotistic, unscrupulous, cowards spiritually, self-deceivers, successful."[10] As far as it goes, this view is unexceptionable. It happens, however, that the union between the families, so decisive for the theme of connection, can be realized only by figures who "advance out" of those families. Not just any part will serve to conjure the whole. And it is notable that when the novel moves toward its vision of symbolic union at Howards End, it leaves many characters to the side. The exclusions are certainly plausible. Tibby is too effete, Aunt Juley too inflexible, Charles too unimaginative, Evie too severe, Paul too vague. But the result is that the image of a general synthesis is strikingly particularized. The reader must surely pause over a vision of reconciliation that leaves so much unreconciled.

It is no doubt true, as Trilling says, that Howards End is a symbol for England, but this symbol has a homely material existence; it is "old and little"; and if it suggests the possibility of a transhistorical synthesis, it does so from within the confines of historical exigency. Forster took great pains to establish the occurrent social pressures of Edwardianism: the headlong expansion of imperialism, the homogenization of culture, the increasing sordidness of London, and the extension of its suburbs. Within such a context the farm at Howards End appears as an archaism. Indeed, at the novel's conclusion, at the moment of greatest symbolic promise, the forces of history rudely interrupt. Helen hopes that their stay at Howards End will be permanent; Margaret says she thinks that it will be. "All the same," remarks Helen, "London's creeping," and she points to a line of red rust beyond the meadow.

> "You see that in Surrey and even Hampshire now," she continued. "I can see it from the Purbeck Downs. And London is only part of something else, I'm afraid. Life's going to be melted down, all over the world."
>
> Margaret knew that her sister spoke truly.
>
> [337]

Here suddenly is our symbol for the whole challenged like any other part. Howards End, which is to signify England, is contained and threatened by England; the symbolic vehicle sputters; the house is now, again, merely a house, jeopardized by the appetite of suburbs and the smoke of cities.

Howards End, I have said, self-consciously narrows its domain in the spirit of a disillusioned liberalism that withdraws from "the fabric of Society" to a "few human beings." I have also suggested that synecdoche offers a figure for imaginative retrieval; it will be possible to restore symbolically what has been lost politically. Now it becomes clear that symbolism has its own fragility, created by the exigencies of history. The signifying talisman can fail to signify, and then one is left with an absurd material object, heavy in one's hands, whose aura has fled. Where, then, does the novel leave us? with the vision of a renewed England, classless, harmonious and whole? or with the harrowing presence of an urban civilization macadamizing the only values which might save it?

In an early essay on the novel, Leavis introduced a line of argument that has become familiar, even standard, in assessments of *Howards End.* He distinguished "comic" and "poetic" emphases in Forster and suggested that often in his early work these two manners were imperfectly amalgamated, leading to a "discrepancy or clash of modes or tones."[11] More recently, Alan Wilde has spoken of the novel's "defective articulation of the symbolic and realistic levels."[12] Indeed, the clash of tones is inescapable, and any reading of *Howards End* must confront its rapidly shifting registers. Between the reverential vision of Mrs. Wilcox, "assuredly she cared about her ancestors, and let them help her" (19), and the aphoristic dismissal of Tibby, "dyspeptic and difficile" (28), there yawns a chasm into which less agile sensibilities would surely fall. The ambiguity at the end of *Howards End*—a real house or a symbolic England?—displays the terms of the difficulty, and it is fair for us to demand an explanation.

Here is where Forster's conception of character must affect our reading of the novel as a whole. Character in *Howards End,* as we have seen, is not defined by impulsions from within or compulsions from without; it is conceived in terms of styles, manners, and dispositions. Personalities and personal relationships are habitually interpreted in modal terms, and the very categories which critics use to describe the novel already apply to its characters: sincerity and irony, romance and sentimentality. Margaret tells Helen that "there is the widest gulf between my love-making and yours. Yours was romance; mine will be prose." Henry, she immediately adds, "lacks poetry" (171). Surely, then, it serves little point to object that the novel contains conflicting modes, since Forster conceives human diversity as precisely a diversity in mode.

Early in the novel, Margaret and Helen discuss whether Leonard Bast is "capable of tragedy" (112). Margaret thinks that he may be, but Helen has doubts, and not long afterwards the narrator seems to settle the question in Helen's favor: "His had scarcely been a tragic marriage. Where there is no money and no inclination to violence tragedy cannot be generated" (120). But in the closing movement of the novel, after Leonard's death, Margaret has the final word: "let Squalor be turned into Tragedy, whose eyes are the stars, and whose hands hold the sunset and the dawn" (328). Margaret, in effect, is seeking to change not an event but a mode, and here is the answer to Leavis. What he regarded as a defect in Forster's sensibility—"the clash of modes or tones"—gave the sensibility its shape and provided the subject of *Howards End.*

This essay began by considering the Arnoldian ideal of seeing life steadily and whole, and it can move toward conclusion by recalling a more recent discussion of seeing, Wittgenstein's treatment of 'seeing-as' in the second part of the *Philosophical Investigations.* Within the context of a broad consideration of the problem of meaning Wittgenstein reminds us of a certain distinctive visual experience: the abrupt change in perceptual content that can occur through the dawning of a new aspect, the identification of a different principle of coherence, or the sudden recognition of a figure within the image. Thus we can see an arrangement of lines as convex and then suddenly concave; we can see Jastrow's celebrated design now as a duck, now as a rabbit; we can see a triangle as "a triangular hole, as a solid, as a geometrical drawing, as standing on its base, as hanging from its apex; as a mountain, as a wedge, as an arrow or pointer, as an overturned object . . . and as various other things."[13]

What is distinctive about such cases, observes Wittgenstein, is that the visual object remains unchanged while the visual experience may alter completely: "I *see* that it has not changed and yet I see it differently." It is "quite as if the object had altered before my eyes," as if it "had ended by *becoming* this or that." The connection of this phenomenon to imaginative life should be evident, and Wittgenstein notes in passing that we characteristically attempt to persuade one another of aesthetic judgments by saying, for instance, "you have to see it like *this*" (Wittgenstein, 193, 195, 206, 202).

Here we might profitably recall Margaret's late outburst when her husband refuses to let Helen spend the night at Howards End: "You shall see the connection if it kills you, Henry! You have had a mistress—I forgave you. My sister has a lover—you drive her from the house. Do you see the connection?" Henry Lamely responds that the "two cases are different" (305). The dispute, that is, turns on the ability to see not objects or events but "the connection" which exists nowhere in the world but which, once recognized, alters how the world appears. "When the aspect changes," notes Wittgenstein, "parts of the picture go together which before did not" (Wittgenstein, 208). The essential activity in *Howards End* is the changing of aspects and the attempt to communicate such changes—not, of course, for aesthetic reasons, but as part of the novel's most serious moral purpose. The demand which Wittgenstein records, "You have to see it like *this*," becomes an urgent ethical injunction.

These concerns bear closely on the issue of mode, in particular the issue of changing modes. For when we suddenly change, say, from regarding a passage as awkwardly sentimental to seeing it as delightfully parodic, our response has that peculiar character which Wittgenstein describes. We recognize that nothing in the work has altered, and yet we experience a different work. We have the uncanny feeling of "a *new* perception and at the same time of the perception's being unchanged" (Wittgenstein, 196). Such considerations should remind us that the experience of mode is not simply the passive acquiescence in conventions. To recognize parody, for instance, may require a great imaginative effort, and in moments of interpretive confusion we often find ourselves changing our ascriptions of mode as rapidly as we shift between duck and rabbit in examining Jastrow's drawing. Moreover, we can enjoin others to change their visual perceptions and their emotional experience. When Margaret urges, "Let Squalor be turned into Tragedy" (328), her imperative suggests that mode is not fixed and that through an act of heightened perception we may change what we see.

This last phrase, "change what we see," equivocates between perceiver and world, but in so doing it locates Forster's hope for cultural transformation. He wants us to change *what* we see (the world) by changing what we *see* (the image). To see Leonard as tragic, to see a house as England, to see a marriage as the union of poetry and prose—these are imaginative acts with practical consequences. Learning to live within a different mode is a way to alter one's style of response, one's manner of thought, one's habit of feeling. And to persuade others to share one's mode is to change the life of a community. Forster's political quietism must be set against this literary activism that restlessly alters its bearings in the conviction that it will be a new mode—not a new fact—that will begin to change England.

The ambiguity between the real and the symbolic must then be recognized for what it is: not as a confusion of the author, but as a challenge to his characters.[14] After her first visit to Howards End, Margaret

> recaptured the sense of space, which is the basis of all earthly beauty, and, starting from Howards End, she attempted to realize England. She failed—visions do not come when we try, though they may come through trying.
>
> [202]

Margaret, in other words, engages in her own synecdoche. On the basis of Howards End she attempts to realize England; from a symbolically resonant part she wants to attain the whole; and if she fails here, she will be more successful later. But the passage makes clear that the symbolic correspondence on which the novel depends is not given; it must be achieved. After the death of Mrs. Wilcox, her family puzzles over her wish to leave the house to Margaret: "To them Howards End was a house; they could not know that to her it had been a spirit, for which she sought a spiritual heir" (96). Not all characters, that is, have the gift of symbolic vision, and to Trilling's assertion that the house is a symbol for England, one must agree and then quickly add that it is a symbol only to those who live within the symbolic mode. Parts in the novel do not simply and reassuringly signify wholes. Howards End is no counter standing securely for England. It is an invitation to symbolic activity.

Within *Howards End* there emerges a suggestive homology between the fate of the individual in modern society and the position of character in modern fictional form. The failure of the liberal ideal leaves a party of embattled individuals to assume the task of reconstructing a humane community. At the same time, and no doubt for many of the same reasons, the weakness of the narrator leaves central literary tasks in the hands of the characters. Can one start from a house and realize a nation? We might have expected the narrator to adjudicate such a delicate question, but as the novel moves to its crisis, the narrator remains a liberal sceptic, and it falls to the character, especially to Margaret, to raise finer, wider possibilities. This abdication of the narrator, the virtual muting of his voice in the final pages, indicates the refusal—perhaps the inability—of the novel to tell its readers how to take it. The decisive question of how to construe its final events—whether to read them tragically, ironically, poetically, prosaically—is posed by the characters themselves who exemplify these diverse possibilities. From within its own boundaries *Howards End* suggests competing ways in which it might be read. The conflict between the characters is in its broadest implication a dispute over the mode appropriate to the events of the novel, a dispute over the competing claims of realism and symbolism, irony and tragedy.

The instability of the symbol places a special burden on the reader who by tradition and convention assumes that a symbolic correspondence does or does not hold. Indeed, it is hard to see the point of an intermittent symbol. *Howards End* has suffered from this plausible assumption, for if it is read in terms of a figural calculus and if its historical perceptions are ignored, then it will seem merely to embody a mechanical optimism. But the strength of the novel is that it offers the symbolic relation not as a fact but as an opportunity: if Margaret's individual perception were shared by enough others, then it would cease to be merely figural and would become a powerful literal truth. Thus the refusal to settle the interpretive question is due neither to Forster's loss of nerve nor to his love of paradox; it reflects the necessary ambiguity between what is real and what is possible. Historical probability insists on the obsolescence of the small farm and consigns it to the gaping suburban maw, while symbolic possibility suggests that on the basis of the farm England might be restored.

It has been said that, strictly speaking, there can be only one mood in fictional narrative, the indicative, because "the function of narrative is not to give an order, express a wish, state a condition, etc., but simply to tell a story and therefore to 'report' facts (real or fictive)."[15] But *Howards End* in its undemonstrative manner presents a serious challenge to this assumption. By constructing a coherent historical portrait and a coherent symbolic alternative, it suggests that fiction may escape the confines of the indicative; and there is no better way to describe its fragile visionary prospect than as a reconciliation in the subjunctive mood, the expression of a wish from within the boundaries of fact. The novel concludes with an indicative assertion of social crisis and a conditional hypothesis of cultural renewal; it tells us what is true and what might be true. Logically, thinks Margaret, "they had no right to be alive," and therefore "one's hope was in the weakness of logic" (337)—and, one might add, in the uncertain strength of the symbol.

Howards End concludes by locating the modern individual in the space where history and symbolism meet, each laying claim to supremacy. Within its literal narrative it ends by consigning the visionaries to a form of internal exile in the English heartland. The Schlegel sisters make no attempt to escape their native community; they simply withdraw to a neglected spot within it, where they tend values that keep them at odds with the complacent citizens of radical aspiration, imagines how the relation of exiles and citizens of the contemporary world. But *Howards End,* goaded by its memories of radical aspiration, imagines how the relation of exiles and citizens might be reversed. Within its conditional symbolism, its subjunctive allegory, the individual grows larger than the society, and those outside Howards End become the exiles who have misplaced the center of their culture and have mistaken a passing phase for a permanent truth. If, as Margaret hopes, the house belongs to "the future as well as the past" (337), then the present age becomes an aberration instead of an inevitability. Contemporary history is reduced to a parenthesis; Howards End contains it, instead of it Howards End. Such is the elasticity of experience in this novel: contracting and expanding according to changes in mood and mode, offering visionary historical prospects to those who recede from history, exiling the individual and then placing high responsibility upon that exile who might at any moment be asked to signify the community and symbolize its future.

Notes

1. E. M. Forster, *Howards End,* Abinger ed., vol. 4 (1910; rpt. London, 1973), p. 37. Subsequent references are to this edition and will be included parenthetically in the text by page number.

2. Matthew Arnold, *Culture and Anarchy,* in *The Complete Prose Works of Matthew Arnold,* vol. 5, ed. R. H. Super (Ann Arbor, 1965), p. 112.

3. Lionel Trilling, *E. M. Forster* (1943; rpt. New York, 1964), p. 118.

4. Trilling, pp. 118, 135. Cyrus Hoy in "Forster's Metaphysical Novel," *PMLA* 125 (March 1960): 126, also presents a useful reading of *Howards End* "in terms of conflicting principles whose reconciliation serves to define the novel's meaning."

5. Trilling, p. 118.

6. E. M. Forster, "What I Believe," *Two Cheers For Democracy,* Abinger ed., vol. 11 (1951; rpt. London, 1972), p. 72. See Frederick C. Crews for an exposition of the background to Forster's liberalism. *E. M. Forster: The Perils of Humanism* (Princeton, 1962), pp. 7-36.

7. L. T. Hobhouse, *Liberalism* (New York, n.d.), pp. 224, 134, 54, 47, 129. Subsequent references to this work will be included parenthetically in the text as Hobhouse and by page number.

8. John Sayre Martin, *E. M. Forster* (Cambridge, 1976), p. 109.

9. "He declares for the autonomy of the work; for coessence of form and meaning; for art as 'organic and free from dead matter'; for music as a criterion of formal, purity; for the work's essential anonymity.

Like all art, he thinks the novel must fuse differentiation into unity, in order to provide meaning we can experience; art is 'the one orderly product that our race has produced,' the only unity and therefore the only meaning. This is Symbolist." Frank Kermode, "The One Orderly Product (E. M. Forster)," in *Puzzles and Epiphanies: Essays and Reviews 1958-1961* (London, 1962), p. 80.

10. F. R. Leavis, "E. M. Forster," in *The Common Pursuit* (London, 1952), p. 269. Malcolm Bradbury in *Possibilities: Essays on the State of the Novel* (Oxford, 1973), p. 100, has argued that the standard opposition between "comic" and "poetic" emphases conceals a third form, Forsterian irony, and "that irony is of the essence, for it is a mediating presence between the parts of the book that are pre-eminently social comedy and those concerned with the poetic, which is also the infinite."

11. Leavis, p. 262.

12. *Art and Order: A Study of E. M. Forster* (New York, 1964), p. 123.

13. Ludwig Wittgenstein, *Philosophical Investigations,* 3d ed., trans. G. E. M. Anscombe (New York, 1971), p. 206. Subsequent references to this work will be included parenthetically in the text as Wittgenstein and by page number.

14. Bradbury calls the problem of duality "very close to the entire question of Forster's temperament" and shrewdly compares Forster to Hawthorne on this point.

15. Gerard Genette, *Narrative Discourse: An Essay in Method,* trans. Jane E. Lewin (Ithaca, N.Y., 1980), p. 161.

Pat C. Hoy II (essay date summer-fall 1985)

SOURCE: Hoy, Pat C., II. "The Narrow, Rich Staircase in Forster's *Howards End.*" *Twentieth Century Literature* 31, no. 2-3 (summer-fall 1985): 221-35.

[*In the following essay, Hoy discusses* Howards End *as a record of Forster's disillusionment with nineteenth-century idealism.*]

Forster's earlier novels, as well as *Howards End,* were shaped by his desire to do for modern England what Arnold and Ruskin had tried to do for Victorian England: deliver her from the repressive forces that were destroying her spirituality, her redemptive power. But *Howards End* is different. Earlier, Forster had advocated the body not the mind as the primary source of redemption; yet his was a cry, not for hedonism but for a radical revision of the terms of Progress in modern culture. Implicit in those earlier novels was his rejection of an "enlightened deliverance" growing out of pure rationalism. He kept reminding his readers that the body as well as the mind knows; he did so by setting passion, intuition, feeling, and vitality above reason, intellect, social respectability, and culture.

In *Howards End* Forster imagines a salvational scheme that is more purely English and in so doing rearranges his priorities, tries to set mind above body. He deprives *Howards End* of the saving power of Italy. The mind and its byproduct, the ideal, are paramount. And even though a "faint image of the lost city [of Venice]" does remain hidden below the novel's surface, it too is transformed into yet another English symbol, a house.[1] Southern passion gives way to Northern idealism. Only Leonard Bast can actually journey into "ancient night," and even he is torn between the primitive experience and the culture that wants to help him account for it. Nevertheless, Leonard's centrality, as well as his helplessness, keeps the novel alive today; he affords a study of contrasts. He is the unsung anti-hero. His marriage, which represents that joining of the "submerged" masses with "the fortunate few," is more central to the novel than the other marriage, the one we continue to talk about.[2] His marriage too is important as an idea.

Forster tests the ideals of Culture and Equality, which he associates with both Ruskin and Arnold, against the complexities of modern life and, in so doing, exposes the simplicity and inadequacy of those ideals. This examination, focused on Leonard Bast, includes a consideration of the proper use of literature, the impact of Culture and Equality on the lower middle class, and the difficulties that arise when the upper middle class tries to be charitable to the poor. As a counterpoise to the disruptive change and flux that he associates with modernity, Forster projects his own ideal that embraces Mrs. Wilcox, Howards End, the wych-elm, rural agrarianism, and the "inner life"; it also embraces the Schlegels, Henry, and Leonard. Although neither nineteenth-century ideals nor Forster's two fictional marriages survive the test, Leonard's image remains to remind us of the tragic failure of well-intentioned intellectual schemes for salvation, schemes that do not account for the complexity of giving and receiving in the modern world; that lingering image of Leonard also changes our sense of the house—its rightful owner and the source, in Forster's mind, of its numinousness.

Wilfred Stone does not touch on the subject of nineteenth-century influences in *Howards End.* He simply suggests that Arnold's "sweetness and light" is essentially the same as Mr. Schlegel's "light within."[3] However, "sweetness and light" or "beauty and intelligence" are closely linked to Arnold's sense of perfection: "The pursuit of perfection . . . is the pursuit of sweetness and light." It is also the essence of the Arnoldian gospel of Culture, the ideal developed in *Culture and Anarchy* that was to save England from "machinery," greed, and aristocratic indifference:

> He who works for sweetness and light, works to make reason and the will of God prevail. . . . [Culture] is not satisfied till we *all* come to a perfect man; it knows

that the sweetness and light of the few must be imperfect until the raw and unkindled masses of humanity are touched with sweetness and light.[4]

The people of the nation must work for "sweetness and light," must make available to *all,* not the "ideas and judgments constituting the creed of their own profession or party," but the best that culture can offer:

> [Culture] seeks to do away with classes; to make the best that has been thought and known in the world current everywhere; . . . This is the *social idea*; and the men of culture are the true apostles of equality.

> (V:113)

In the late 70s Arnold sought even more emphatically to transmit his ideal of equality to the aristocratic and business classes. The effects of inequality were quite clear, as he pointed out to the Royal Institution in February 1878:

> [O]ur shortcomings in civilisation are due to our inequality; . . . this constitution of things, I say, has the natural and necessary effect, under present circumstances, of materialising our upper class, vulgarising our middle class, and brutalising our lower class. And this is to fail in civilisation.

> (VIII:299)

This bold suggestion for a radical revision of national values was most assuredly not what his audience wanted to hear.

Forster did not disagree with Arnold's humanistic notions; he too wanted the nation to achieve an inward grace that would resist mechanization, but he was far more practical than Arnold and other nineteenth-century idealists who too easily assumed that their schemes were universally applicable to the nation's problems. When Forster turned in *Howards End* to Arnold's judgment of Sophocles—the judgment that "he saw life steadily and saw it whole"—he did so, I think, with conscious irony. Forster's judgment was that Arnold and other idealists did not project far enough ahead, that they did not see the "modern world" whole, that their ideals were indeed problem-beset. That judgment lies at the heart of *Howards End,* and we can see it reflected years later in **"Does Culture Matter?"** Forster suggests that culture does matter, but he qualifies his response with Arnold clearly in mind:

> What is needed in the cultural Gospel is to let one's *light* so shine that men's *curiosity* is aroused, and they ask why Sophocles, Velasquez, Henry James should cause such disproportionate pleasure. . . . Our chief job is to enjoy ourselves and not to lose heart, and to spread culture not because we love our fellow men, but because certain things seem to us unique and priceless, and, as it were, push us out into the world on their service.[5]

There are subtle changes here in the Arnoldian imperatives. It is not by passing on *ideas* but by demonstrating through our lives the numinous and regenerative quality of those ideas that we are likely to inspire others to be more humane and to care about the "best that has been thought and known in the world." The shift is from ideas to the arousal of curiosity about those ideas through inspirational behavior—a shift from abstract ideals to human models. Forster seems to be trying to reshape Arnold's notions so that they will be more palatable to a modern audience; yet he deflates Arnold's lofty ideals without wholly abandoning them.

What then of Leonard Bast and the Schlegels? Do their roles in *Howards End* reflect Forster's disenchantment with nineteenth-century idealism as well as his disenchantment with the state of the English nation between 1908 and 1910? My judgment is that they do. In this novel about the *ideal,* we must to some degree rid ourselves of the expectations that have grown out of the earlier novels where generalized ideals have been little more than codified notions governing English behavior. Forster pauses here to try to see whole a number of conflicting ideals that serve as alternatives for his characters. We get our best sense of those ideals and Forster's judgment about them by examining their impact on Leonard Bast's life. If, as Forster reminds us, "To see life steadily and to see it whole was not for the likes of [Leonard]," we should feel compelled to ask why (52). Our answer will, of necessity, include a further consideration of Ruskin and Arnold, as well as of the Schlegels and the Wilcoxes; all are to some degree culpable for Leonard's premature death of "heart disease."

Forster's rejection of Ruskin is direct and, in a special sense, quite superficial. He does not attack Ruskinian idealism systematically; he simply reacts to that nineteenth-century "clamour for art and literature" that he explicitly associates with Ruskin in this novel, in *A Room With a View,* and in **"Does Culture Matter?"**[6] By 1908 Forster sees quite clearly that England and her poor need more than a clamor for art; he has become distrustful of idealistic plans for salvation dreamed up by rich esthetes, and Leonard Bast is the creative proof of his dissatisfaction. Leonard tries to read and listen his way into middle-class culture, tries desperately to climb that "ladder" into what he perceives to be a better life. Subconsciously, he longs to follow the Schlegel sisters "up that narrow, rich staircase at Wickham Place, to some ample room, whither he would never follow them, not if he read for ten hours a day" (52).[7]

We sense Leonard's plight when he tries to explain to Jacky his motives for reading Ruskin and attending concerts. "Equally indifferent," she is unable even to share his belief in himself as an "Englishman" who never goes "back on his word"—a sentiment that makes him determined not to "leave her in the lurch" even if it means going against family. Forster implies that Leonard has acquired this false nobility from books; Leonard himself makes this connection:

> I care a good deal about improving myself by means of Literature and Art, and so getting a wider outlook. For

instance, when you came in I was reading Ruskin's *Stones of Venice*. I don't say this to boast, but just to show you the kind of man I am.

(51)

He shows no tenderness, only a false sense of his role as protector. He postures. Only at the end of the novel, after his affair with Helen and the disastrous experiences that follow, do we learn that "He pitied [Jacky] with nobility . . . not the contemptuous pity of a man who sticks to a woman through thick and thin" (315-16). From the beginning, Leonard has no sense of the entrapping nature of culture; he simply pursues it with a vengeance. In a similar way Forster pursues Leonard's culture-hankerings, going out of his way to make Leonard ostentatious and superficial, only to shift the emphasis later to redeem both Leonard and what Leonard is, a yeoman, a man of the earth.

If we look carefully at Forster's use of Ruskin as a literary device, we get a clear sense of his rejection of Ruskinian idealism as well as his adaptation of Ruskin's methods; he transforms the "island church" in Venice into Howards End and Ruskin's language into the language of everyday. Forster obviously shared Ford Madox Ford's conclusion that the "literary Language had grown perfectly unfit for the communication of any kind of daily thought, or indeed for any kind of thought of all."[8] Leonard reads from the Torcello chapter of *Stones of Venice*, Volume II—important in terms of the "island church" (to be considered later) and important too in terms of Leonard. Forster wants us to note the contrast between the "rich man" speaking from the gondola and the relatively poor man listening without fully comprehending in a London flat. The problem is reflected in the style. The "fine sentence" Forster selects from the work seems unsuited for "the needs of daily life"; Leonard cannot modify it so that it is suitable for use in a letter to his brother the lay reader. Ruskin's style is beyond Leonard too. He listens "with reverence" to the voice and wants to undergo a "sudden conversion" to Culture, but there is a problem:

> And the voice in the gondola rolled on, piping melodiously of Effort and Self-Sacrifice, full of high purpose, full of beauty, full even of sympathy and the love of men, yet somehow eluding all that was actual and insistent in Leonard's life. For it was the voice of one who had never been dirty or hungry, and had not guessed successfully what dirt and hunger are.

(47)

Ruskin is too remote to be of value. Even Leonard's belief in "a steady preparation for the change" will not admit him to the Schlegels' upper room (48). He has no "heritage that may expand gradually," and Forster continually emphasizes the folly of trying to bridge too rapidly the gap created by years of civilizing.

Margaret Schlegel's calling card, which marks Leonard's place in the Ruskin volume and later leads Jacky to Wickham Place, "symbolize[s] the life of culture" for Leonard.

Typically, he sees the two Schlegel women as the "denizens of Romance, who must keep to the corner he has assigned them, pictures that must not walk out of their frames" (120). Seeing them as art objects and as grail symbols, he cannot see them as human beings, just as they, for entirely different reasons, have difficulty seeing him as a human being. Like Cecil Vyse, Leonard, although motivated differently, misuses art and literature, and thus separates himself from the greater life around him. Margaret, on occasion, sees around this high culture. On one such occasion, she tells Henry Wilcox that Leonard's "brain is filled with the husks of books, culture—horrible; we want him to wash out his brain and go to the real thing" (142). She reveals her own problem as well as Leonard's. Convinced that she can lead others past "life's daily gray," she eventually helps to ruin Leonard by giving him advice and then by abandoning him after he has lost his job. Of greater significance at this point is the cultural gap between Leonard and the "rich man" in the gondola who inspires him to try to climb the "rich, narrow staircase." Leonard cannot move freely between classes; the distance between him and his guides is so great that neither books nor the intellect nor diligence can deliver this lower middle-class man from cultural bondage.

Leonard would be only a pathetic boob if he simply danced through the pages of this novel in pursuit of culture. But he is not a boob; he is a victim. Ironically, he is one of those people Arnold identifies in *Culture and Anarchy* who, in a special way, stand outside class: "*aliens,* if we may so call them,—persons who are mainly led, not by their class spirit, but by a general *humane* spirit, by the love of human perfection" (V:146). Forster gives Leonard this kind of potential but pits him against the complexities of modernity that work against his humane but naive spirit. He remains compelling because deep down within him there is something fine and genuine, something that wants an outlet. Even his sentimental dedication to the protection of Jacky has something about it that is finer than Henry Wilcox's desire to protect women and finer still than Cecil Vyse's medieval desire to "lead women, though he knew not whither, and protect them, though he knew not against what" (*Room* 132). Leonard has also the capacity for wonder and does, on one occasion, move beyond the cultural role he tries to play. On this occasion, he goes "off the roads" on a symbolic journey into "ancient night." His motivation comes from his reading but, ultimately, the books merely serve as "signpost[s]":

> He had visited the county of Surrey when darkness covered its amenities, and its cosy villas had re-entered ancient night. Every twelve hours [*sic*] this miracle happens, but he had troubled to go and see for himself. Within his cramped little mind dwelt something that was greater than Jefferies's books—the spirit that led Jefferies to write them; and his dawn, though revealing nothing but monotones, was part of the eternal sunrise that shows George Borrow Stonehenge.

(118)

The books show Leonard how to push "back the boundaries," to get outside the stifling influence of Jacky and the basement flat for a brief interlude; he gets "back to the Earth" and his primal origins.

Leonard's walk is not a minor, second-hand cultural "experience," and when he shares it with the Schlegels, they understand perfectly its symbolic importance; they elicit his *humane* instinct. They also encourage him to narrate that experience directly, free of cultural encumbrances; they want to know the facts independent of the books that inspired him. When he is finally able to say to Helen that the dawn was not wonderful (avoiding romantic overstatement), he gains Forster's approval: "Down toppled all that had seemed ignoble or literary in his talk, down toppled tiresome R.L.S. and the 'love of the earth' and his silk top-hat" (117). Leonard begins to speak "with a flow, an exultation, that he had seldom known." That is the value of his experience, and Forster asks us not to take it lightly:

> That the Schlegels had not thought him foolish became a permanent joy. . . . He had hitherto supposed the unknown to be books, literature, clever conversation, culture. One raised oneself by study, and got upsides with the world. But in that quick interchange a new light dawned.

> (122)

As Leonard goes home he takes off his top-hat, the badge of culture, and walks bareheaded down Regent Street; thus freed, he invites unconscious "hostility" from the few people who pass, until, finally, he dons the hat that is so big it bends his ears down. Looking ridiculous, he "escape[s] criticism." Thus Forster defines the cultural yardsticks but shows us something far more genuine. Leonard momentarily transcends culture because the Schlegels have confirmed his worth. Arnold was right: "the extrication of the best self, the predominance of the humane instinct, will very much depend upon its meeting, or not, with what is fitted to help and elicit it" (V: 146).

But Leonard's problem is that culture also works against him. On a later occasion, when the Schlegels invite him to tea and advise him to "clear out" of his business because it is destined to collapse, he is perplexed and disappointed. Talking about the details of everyday life, they destroy the illusion of Romance he has structured around them, and we are reminded that for him "'the Miss Schlegels' still remained a composite Indian god, whose waving arms and contradictory speeches were the product of a single mind" (137). When they try to explain to him the deeper meaning of his entry into "ancient night," he "fail[s] to see the connection" between that experience and his daily life:

> "[W]e hoped there would be a connection between last Sunday and other days. What is the good of your stars and trees, your sunrise and the wind, if they do not enter into our daily lives? . . . [H]aven't we all to struggle against life's daily grayness, against pettiness, against mechanical cheerfulness, against suspicion?"

> (140)

But Leonard *is* suspicious; his class makes him suspicious, and Margaret's speech confuses him.

From the moment we first see Leonard at the Queen's Hall performance of Beethoven's Fifth Symphony, we are aware that he is under some compulsion to "pursue beauty," and we see that his efforts leave him with only fragmented knowledge: "His brain might be full of names, he might even have heard of Monet and Debussy; the trouble was that he could not string them together into a sentence (37). Leonard stands near the "abyss," at the "extreme verge of gentility"—poor but proud and unwilling to "confess any inferiority to the rich." Forster wants us to sense the irony of Leonard's position: he is inferior in a practical sense (he lacks the necessities) and superior in another, more important, sense (he is patronized and victimized by a society that heightens his awareness of class distinctions while teasing him to climb the ladder):

> [H]e was inferior to most rich people, there is not the least doubt of it. He was not as courteous as the average rich man, nor as intelligent, nor as healthy, nor as lovable. His mind and his body had been alike underfed, because he was poor, and because he was modern they were always craving better food.

> (43)

But as that passage progresses, the "angel of Democracy" bears the brunt of the burden for making Leonard "obliged to assert gentility." The civilizing process confounds the problem by heightening the awareness of *inequality*. Forster is not advocating either cultural ignorance or rigid class boundaries; he is simply exposing the too simplistic approach to equality.

Forster shows us quite clearly why "To see life steadily and to see it whole was not for the likes of [Leonard]." And connected with that Arnoldian phrase there is another, hidden, irony. I suspect Forster was aware of it. The phrase was first applied to Sophocles in Arnold's 1849 sonnet "To a Friend" and repeated in the 1857 Inaugural Address when he outlined his hope for "an intellectual deliverance" through ancient literature, specifically that of Sophocles (I:19-20, 28). Leonard cannot see life as Sophocles saw it, and he is perhaps Forster's fictive evidence that neither could Arnold. The complexities of modern life simply militate against an "intellectual deliverance" of the sort Arnold imagined. It is Forster, of course, who sees life steadily and whole, and the deliverance he suggests in *Howards End* is less intellectual than Arnold's was in 1857. Forster's plan is educational but does not depend on a complex, formal educational system; its target is the imagination of the middle class, and, like Arnold's plan, it seeks to recapture the classical past. But the focus is more narrowly fixed on the English past. That is why the "great mythology" of *Howards End* is so important to Forster.

If we go back to that "fine sentence" from Ruskin that Forster used to underscore the gap between the "rich man" and "the boy, Leonard Bast," we get a clearer sense of Forster's scheme of cultural salvation:

Let us consider a little each of these characters in succession; and first (for of the shafts enough has been said already), what is very peculiar to this church, its luminousness.

(47)

Adapting the sentence for Leonard's use results in this initial transformation:

Let us consider a little each of these characters in succession; and first (for of the absence of ventilation enough has been said already), what is very peculiar to this flat, its obscurity.

(47)

And then more appropriately, it becomes,

My flat is dark as well as stuffy.

(47)

Ruskin is writing about the little "island church" at Torcello, and he is describing its "characters" and its cultural origins:

It has evidently been built by men in flight and distress. . . . And it is so consistent with all that Christian architecture ought to express in every age (for the actual condition of the exiles who built the cathedral of Torcello is exactly typical of the spiritual condition which every Christian ought to recognize in himself, a state of homelessness on earth, except so far as he can make the Most High his habitation). . . .

(20-23)

The notion of "homelessness on earth" in a period of "flight and distress" lies at the heart of *Howards End* and is central to Forster's dramatic presentation of the "flux" of a modern "nomadic civilization." "What is very peculiar to this [island] church—its luminousness" stands in stark contrast to "what is very peculiar to [Leonard's] flat—its obscurity." Church/flat and luminousness/obscurity: what Leonard and all of the other sensitive people in this novel seek is a real home in the midst of chaotic change, something luminous and permanent. Howards End becomes that sacred place.

Margaret Schlegel recognizes in Leonard's "ancient night" experience the subconscious aim of his journey: "You tried to get away from the fogs that are stifling us all—away past books and houses to the truth. You were looking for a real home" (140). That Leonard never finds his own "real home" is further evidence of the cultural forces working against the yeoman, but the Schlegels find a "permanent home" and Leonard's child occupies it at the end of the novel. Margaret, trying to see through to a new era, observes:

This craze for motion has only set in during the last hundred years. It may be followed by a civilization that won't be a movement, because it will rest on the earth.

All the signs are against it now, but I can't help hoping, and very early in the morning in the garden I feel that our house is the future as well as the past.

(337)

Howards End is Forster's "island church," designed to capture the "spiritual condition which every [Englishman] ought to recognize in himself"—the spiritual condition, not of homelessness, but of permanence. It represents not a reaching up to the Most High, but a reaching down to the earth, to England. Howards End and the tree represent all the greatness the English past can offer as a stay against the "flux" of modernity. It is an earthbound home, agrarian and stable. Here the sun does shine—a luminescence absent from the Schlegel household the previous thirty years (297)—and in so doing suggests a power and a permanence greater even than Wilcox steadiness and Schlegel wholeness. Places, furniture, and trees endure; they outlast people, and from them, we get our surest sense of the everlasting and the spiritual reality behind the flux.

Mrs. Wilcox's attitude toward the importance of places and Helen's deep sense of the spiritual permanence of invested objects suggest a different if not a totally new sense of priorities for Forster. He was willing to extend his imaginative vision to try to put the English *mind* back on the right track. He was beginning to sense how very difficult it would be to enlighten his nation about the power and the beauty of the body; secular salvation would have to be offered in terms more comprehensible to an English mind out of touch with its primitive instincts. His attempt to capture in furniture and places something more enduring than a human life does not suggest Forster's indifference to the human condition; on the contrary, it suggests a concern about the impact of evolutionary change on humanity in general. He is not trying to arrest change but to find something permanent and spiritually comforting behind the "eternal formlessness" that he associates with London and the modern condition, and he subordinates the merely personal to the everlasting.

Howards End is especially coherent if we recognize that Forster's primary inquiry is conducted on an abstract level. We have already noted that in the end the inquiry leads to a reaffirmation of the "inner life," but that conclusion must wait until a search for something very different fails. Forster tries first to see beyond the finite boundaries of a single life, beyond even the boundaries of an era. He projects England's destiny through a number of "family" groupings that reflect this evolving spectrum: the romantic idealist (Mr. Schlegel) is succeeded by a romantic idealist (Helen), a pragmatic idealist (Margaret), and an effeminate son (Tibby). Ruth Wilcox is succeeded by her modern, intellectual heir Margaret Schlegel. Miss Avery is succeeded by her niece, a "most finished young person" whose notions of "gentility" conflict with those Forster associates with Hilton and with Howards End (265). Mr. Wilcox is succeeded by Charles who in turn is succeeded by his rabbity brood who "may inherit the earth" (182). Given that spectrum of future possibilities, it should come as no surprise that Helen and Leonard produce England's heir; the impetuous romantic and the boy from yeoman stock certainly offer greater possibilities than the Wilcox brood.

On the more realistic level, the relationship simply will not support the symbolic weight Forster places on it. He seems to sense this because, at the end of the novel, he returns to the abstract level as Helen tries to remember Leonard as her lover and cannot: "I tempted him, and killed him, and it is surely the least I can do. I would like to throw out all my heart to Leonard on such an afternoon as this. But I cannot. It is no good pretending. I am forgetting him" (335). Margaret advises Helen to recognize her own unique differences:

> It is part of the battle against sameness. Differences— eternal differences, planted by God in a single family, so that there may always be colour; sorrow perhaps, but colour in the daily gray. Then I can't have you worrying about Leonard. Don't drag in the personal when it will not come. Forget him.
>
> (336)

Again we are back to the impersonal, to that level of abstraction that recognizes that there will always be rich and poor, that an "adventure" for Leonard may be nothing for Helen. Only the house and the "eternal differences" seem changeless. Comfort comes through recognition of those differences.

In Forster's early conception of the novel, Margaret, not Helen, was to have the child.[9] This emphasizes the importance of the symbolic marriage between Margaret and Henry, which was to provide not only a glimpse of the mingling of culture and business but also, perhaps, an heir. By the time Forster actually developed the characters, he had changed his plan. Aware perhaps that the genetically dominant Henry Wilcox had already bred out the finest quality of the Howards, he turned to Helen and Leonard. How appropriate then that within Henry "all had reverted to chaos, ruled so far as it was ruled at all, by an incomplete asceticism" and that Margaret with a "masterly" grip on life is like a "mountain peak, whom all might tread, but whom the snows made nightly virginal" (183, 179). Forster makes the pair sexually barren and offers as one of Margaret's "eternal differences" her inability to love children.

Clearly, the importance of the Schlegel-Wilcox marriage rests solely on the *possibility* of joining the idealist and the business man; it is a marriage that will provide the woman an opportunity to change the man, to make him whole and, therefore, better. In that sense, the marriage is destined to deny Henry his "eternal differences." On a related level, it seems to be a marriage that will produce a better man for England from the *only* man England has left who seems still capable of shaping her destiny. But the marriage fails and in noting the reason for its failure, spoken here by Margaret, we see that Forster turned back to the "inner life" that had served him so well earlier:

> You shall see the connection if it kills you, Henry! You have had a mistress—I forgave you. My sister has a lover—you drive her from the house. Do you see the connection? Stupid, hypocritical, cruel—oh, contemptible!—a man who insults his wife when she's alive and cants with her memory when she's dead. A man who ruins a woman for his pleasure, and casts her off to ruin other men. And gives bad financial advice, and then says he is not responsible. These men are you. You can't recognize them, because you cannot connect.
>
> (305)

Margaret is not talking about the "rainbow bridge" but about connecting the inner life with the outer. Had Henry been able to make the internal connection between Monk and Beast, perhaps he too could have made the other connection as well. But he did not connect, and in this important passage we review all of the Wilcox "sins," the limitations of the outer life. Broken, and shuffling around Howards End, Henry does decide finally to give the home to its rightful spiritual heir, but he does not inspire us to believe that he has developed a genuine sense of the "inner life." Nor can Margaret, with Helen as chorus, inspire us to believe that she loves him in other than an idealistic sense. Deciding not to leave Howards End and England, she takes him back out of pity: "She did what seemed easiest . . ." (332). And even if "she did not see that to break him was her only hope," he is broken in the end by Charles's imprisonment and by her expression of disgust over his failure (331). There is certainly no evidence that the "rainbow bridge" has connected the prose and the passion. The beast and the monk are never killed, and the marriage that promised so much is finally subordinated to the novel's other symbols: the house, the wych-elm, the meadow, the child, and the father.

In the end, Leonard Bast is clearly the most emotionally resonant of those symbols. Not only is he of yeoman stock and therefore more entitled by natural rights to Howards End than either Schlegel or Wilcox, he is also able, from his own limited perspective, to connect his inner life with the outer. He goes to Howards End to accept moral responsibility for doing wrong to Helen, never thinking for once that "Helen was to blame." His "remorse" is wrongheaded, but his desire to confess "did not take an ignoble form" (316). Forster would have us understand the "two bright spots" of Leonard's life:

> He remained alive, and blessed are those who live, if it is only to a sense of sinfulness. . . . And the other bright spot was his tenderness for Jacky. He pitied her with nobility now. . . .
>
> (315)

Leonard, who makes connections, has become a sensitive man.

Forster emphasizes Leonard's connection with the primitive past that gives the "island church" and the country their strange power. In the Tewin Woods, through which Leonard must pass, the novel's opposing forces are brought into sharp focus: the legends of the Tewin churchyard and the hermit are linked to Ruth Wilcox and contrasted with the "businessmen, who saw life more steadily, though with the steadiness of the half-closed eye" (320). Those same businessmen are also contrasted with the Hilton farmers, "[h]alf clodhopper, half board-school prig, [who] can still throw back to a nobler stock, and breed yeomen" (320). Finally comes the contrast between yeoman and Imperialist, who "ever in motion, hopes to inherit the earth":

> But the Imperialist is not what he thinks or seems. He is a destroyer. He prepares the way for cosmopolitanism, and though his ambitions may be fulfilled, the earth that he inherits will be gray.
>
> (320)

Thus Forster pits the Yeoman Leonard against the Imperialist Henry and links Leonard more solidly with England's primitive past.

The sun that streams over Leonard during his journey to Howards End does not "free" him, but his remorse becomes "beautiful," and by the time he arrives he is optimistic and convinced of an "innate goodness elsewhere." He sees beyond the goblins, even beyond death and his own private "sin":

> Again and again must the drums tap and the goblins stalk over the universe before joy can be purged of the superficial. It was rather paradoxical, and arose from his sorrow. Death destroys a man, but the idea of death saves him—that is the best account of it that has yet been given. Squalor and tragedy can beckon to all that is great in us, and strengthen the wings of love. They can beckon; it is not certain that they will, for they are not love's servants. But they can beckon, and the knowledge of this incredible truth comforted him.
>
> (321)

Personally and privately triumphant, he enters Howards End to make his formal confession only to be smitten down by the very forces that have "spilt the precious distillation of the years" (146).

As Leonard confesses, Charles Wilcox beats him with the sword. Leonard is hurt "not where it descended, but in the heart," and the Schlegel books—the "ladder" into the cultural aristocracy—fall "over him in a shower" (321). How masterfully Forster delivers his own final thrusts as the yeoman falls victim to the Schlegel sword used so improperly and for such vile ends by the warrior-imperialist who can think of nothing but thrashing Leonard "within an inch of his life." It is even easier in the end to see why England's heir must be the son of this common man who is victimized by the civilizing forces that are shaping his nation's destiny. Somehow, Margaret's words of assurance to Helen about "eternal differences" fail to relieve her sister of culpability in this death. Margaret herself most assuredly, but unwittingly, worked against Leonard by advising him to follow Henry's suggestion to clear out of the

Porphyrion and by failing to get work for him after the fateful night at Oniton. The final verdict in this case is appropriately "Manslaughter" (331). The yeoman cannot survive the onslaught of culture and imperialism. Perhaps his son can.

Notes

1. Ruskin's recreation of Venice foreshadows Forster's attempted resurrection of a lost nation. See *The Stones of Venice* in *The Works of John Ruskin,* ed. Edward T. Cook and A. D. O. Wedderburn (New York: Longmans, Green, 1904), X, 9.

2. See Herbert Howarth, "E. M. Forster and the Contrite Establishment," *The Journal of General Education,* 17 (1964), 196-206, for Forster's general concern about two English nations—one "possessed of wealth" and opportunity, the other "submerged" (196).

3. *The Cave and the Mountain: A Study of E. M. Forster* (Stanford: Stanford Univ. Press, 1966), p. 240. P. N. Furbank notes that in early 1910, Forster read a paper on Arnold to the local Literary Society in Weybridge; he drew consolation from a passage in Arnold's letter that found Arnold himself "ripening" from an "inward spring"—not unlike Forster's "inner light." See *E. M. Forster: A Life* (London: Secker & Warburg, 1977-78), I, 181; rpt. (New York: Harcourt, 1978).

4. *The Complete Prose Works of Matthew Arnold,* ed. R. H. Super (Ann Arbor: Univ. of Michigan Press, 1965), V, 112. Further references to this collected edition appear within the text.

5. *Two Cheers for Democracy,* Abinger Edition, ed. Oliver Stallybrass, (London, Edward Arnold, 1972), Vol. 3, 104. Emphasis added. Further references within the text and within the notes are from The Abinger Edition of E. M. Forster: *Howards End,* Vol. 4 (1973), and *A Room with a View,* Vol. 2 (1979), both ed. Stallybrass.

6. In *A Room with a View,* Forster looks disdainfully on English tourists who are unable to respond to the charm of Italy without Rev. Beebe, Mr. Ruskin, or their Baedekers; the richer response goes to those who experience Italy and her people firsthand (14-28).

7. There is a faint reminder here of Forster's uneasiness upon first meeting Henry James at Lamb House during the period in which Forster was writing the novel (Furbank, I:165).

8. Ford, *Portraits From Life* (Boston: Houghton Mifflin, 1965), p. 214.

9. Stallybrass, ed., *The Manuscripts of 'Howards End'* (London: Edward Arnold, 1973), Vol. 4a, 187.

Mary Pinkerton (essay date summer-fall 1985)

SOURCE: Pinkerton, Mary. "Ambiguous Connections: Leonard Bast's Role in *Howards End.*" *Twentieth Century Literature* 31, no. 2-3 (summer-fall 1985): 236-46.

[*In the following essay, Pinkerton finds that Forster's treatment of the character Leonard Bast in* Howards End *prefigures his ending of* A Passage to India.]

E. M. Forster, in **"The Challenge of Our Time"** (1946), clarified what he saw as the dilemma of Victorian liberal humanism:

> The education I received in those far-off and fantastic days made me soft, and I'm very glad it did, for I have seen plenty of hardness since, and I know it does not even pay. . . . But though the education was humane, it was imperfect, inasmuch as we none of us realized our economic position. In came the nice fat dividends, up rose the lofty thoughts, and we did not realize that all the time we were exploiting the poor of our country and the backward races abroad, and getting bigger profits from our investments than we should. We refused to face the unpalatable truth. . . .
>
> All that has changed in the present century. The dividends have shrunk to decent proportions and have in some cases disappeared. The poor have kicked. The backward races are kicking—and more power to their boots. Which means that life has become less comfortable for the Victorian liberal, and that our outlook, which seems to me admirable, has lost the basis of golden sovereigns upon which it originally rose, and now hangs over the abyss.[1]

Perhaps there is no better gloss on the ideas and questions raised and explored in *Howards End* [hereafter referred to as *HE*].

Reconciliation is problematic and uncertain, but can best be attempted through personal relations. Forster defines his dilemma: "But in public who shall express the unseen adequately? It is private life that holds out the mirror to infinity; personal intercourse, and that alone that ever hints at a personality beyond our daily vision."[2] The cult of personal relations provides a means of connection. Yet in *Howards End* Forster's ambiguous treatment of Leonard Bast undercuts his vision. In revising the manuscripts, Forster isolates Leonard from the personal relationships of the novel through his use of pronouns. He treats Leonard with increasing irony and distance, deleting Leonard's interior monologues. At the same time, Forster struggles to develop Leonard as a character, and finally he attempts to raise Leonard to mythic stature by making Margaret's reflections upon his death parallel her thoughts upon the death of Mrs. Wilcox. For these reasons, Forster's treatment of Leonard betrays the precariousness of his vision and anticipates the conclusion of *A Passage to India.*

In the revised *Howards End* manuscripts one pattern becomes apparent: Forster inserts hundreds of personal pronouns, underscoring in a concrete grammatical way one theme of the novel—the importance of personal relationships. Forster adds pronouns frequently, deletes them less often. Of a total of 794 changes involving pronouns, 601 are insertions, and 193 are deletions. Forster inserts pronouns more than three times as often as he deletes them. The quantity of these changes is not nearly as significant as the qualitative effect they make upon the tone of the published text. The inserted pronouns are most often possessives usually linked with a noun indicating family relationships (my son, my sister, her brother, his son, etc.). Ruth Wilcox and Margaret Schlegel use these constructions most consistently in their own speech. Likewise, these tags are used to identify them. Forster increases pronominal usage to heighten the theme of connection and relatedness in a concrete grammatical way. Shared experience and the importance of personal relationships provide the theme of the novel and consequently dictate certain stylistic choices.

Several examples indicate the care with which Forster thought over his earlier drafts and revised them accordingly. For example, Miss Avery refers to Ruth Wilcox first as "Mrs. Wilcox," then "her old friend Mrs. Wilcox," and then simply "her old friend."[3] Likewise, Forster will sometimes delete a personal pronoun, replace it with a proper name, only to eliminate that in favor of the possessive pronoun and familial tag. For example, Margaret says "It certainly is a funny world but as long as they govern, it'll never be a bad one—never really bad" (*The Manuscripts of Howards End* [hereafter referred to as *MsHE*] 271:11). In revision "they" becomes "the Wilcoxes" and finally "my husband and his sons" (*MsHE* 271:11). When Margaret suggests that Paul may still have some feelings for Helen, Mrs. Wilcox replies: "Not that I know of" (*MsHE* 66:12). With revision, the personal note is added and the response becomes: "Oh no; *he* often—*my* Paul is very young, you see" (*HE* 66:12).

Not only are personal and familial relationships affirmed through the use of pronouns; true ownership of Howards End becomes a focus through Forster's care in inserting and replacing pronouns. When Mrs. Wilcox suggests the excursion to Howards End, for example, she phrases it this way in the manuscripts: "It is in the morning that *my* house is most itself. I cannot show you *the* meadow properly except at sunrise" (*MsHE* 84:10-11). In revision this becomes: "It is in the morning that *my* house is most beautiful. You are coming to stop. I cannot show you *my* meadow properly except at sunrise" (*HE* 84:10-11). And Miss Avery's niece says to Margaret: "Of course Auntie does not generally look after *the house*" (*MsHE* 263-24). In revision the last two words become "your place" (*HE* 294:8). Even more significant are Forster's changes in Margaret's plea to Henry that Helen be allowed to spend one night at Howards End. In the manuscript version, first Forster writes: "She has the idea that one night in *the* house would give her pleasure and do her good" (*MsHE* 302:32). In revision Forster changes *the* house to *our* house, then *that* house, and finally *your* house. The change is enormously significant.

As established as this pattern of pronoun insertion is, Forster departs from the norm in his treatment of Leonard and Jacky Bast. Forster eliminates personal pronouns, and in so doing he conveys their intensified alienation from each other, from other characters in the novel, and from society at large. Of 193 pronoun deletions, 54 refer to Leonard, Jacky, or both. Predictably, Henry and Charles Wilcox are also affected, though less dramatically, by the deletion of pronouns. Here again, statistics are not the whole story, for it is the quality of the text which results from these changes that is striking. Again, selected examples prove to be representative. Instead of describing Leonard greeting "her" (Jacky), Forster revises the passage to read: "greeting *the apparition* with much spirit, and helping *it* off with *its* boa" (*MsHE* 48:330).

Instead of using personal pronouns to refer to Leonard, he becomes "the boy" (*MsHE* 52:8), "a nice creature" (*MsHE* 141:11), "the victim" (*MsHE* 314:15), "the father" (*MsHE* 313:5; 328:5), "the missing article" (*MsHE* 111:33), and "the fellow" (*MsHE* 188:2). Rather than "her husband," he becomes "the husband" (*MsHE* 228:12). "His sentimentality" becomes "Romance" (*MsHE* 120:22). "His face" becomes "the face" (*MsHE* 122:26). "His commercial training" becomes "a commercial training" (*MsHE* 137:28); "his letter" becomes "a letter" (*MsHE* 315:22); and "his brother" becomes "a brother" (*MsHE* 315:24). Forster also replaces the pronoun with Leonard's proper name (*MsHE* 309:5, 335:19, 336:7), and he deletes "they" to write "the Basts" (*MsHE* 307:29, 314:28, 238:22). All of these changes combine to depersonalize Leonard, setting him apart in a grammatical way from the normal relationships of the novel. And with the deletion of personal pronouns, Leonard is distanced and subjected to increased irony by Forster's narrator. To use Forster's words, "Leonard seemed not a man, but a cause" (*HE,* 309:5-6).

Prior to the death scene, the manuscripts and revisions show Forster struggling to humanize Leonard. In the rejected drafts Leonard is mercenary (*MsHE* 233:17), obsequious (*MsHE* 232:26), lying (*MsHE* 115:4) and incompetent (*MsHE* 221:38). In the published text, Leonard is a victim of economic and social forces which he is unable to comprehend. He tries to maintain his dignity in the face of few options; he is not be blamed. At the same time, Forster curtails his use of interior monologue in characterizing Leonard (see especially *MsHE* 47:29 and the radical reworking of Leonard's thoughts during the aftermath of Oniton [MS p. A6, 7, 8-11], which appears in the published text as the beginning of chapter 41). The manuscripts recount Leonard's thoughts, feelings, and motivation. Forster describes the events of Oniton in a more graphic and emotional manner there than he does in the published text.[4] Narrative comment is kept to a minimum and clearly marked. And in the manuscript version, Forster draws a clear parallel between Helen and Jacky (MS p. A8, *MsHE* 323-324). The cumulative effect of all these changes is to distance the reader from Leonard, to remove references to his thoughts and motivations, and to delete physical details which serve to explain the affair. In the published text, the presentation becomes more abstract, less personal, and more highly ironic in its use of narrative strategy. At the same time Helen is portrayed as thoughtless and "in love with the absolute," and consequently Forster drops the analogy between Helen and Jacky.

This increased narrative distance and heightened ironic tone are consistent with Forster's handling of the prelude to their affair. In the coffee room of the Shropshire hotel, Helen addresses Leonard with condescension. She snaps at Leonard and cuts him off, quite aware that she is snubbing him. Forster writes: "Once or twice during the day she had encouraged him to criticize, and then had pulled him up short. Was she afraid of him presuming? If so, it was disgusting of her" (*HE* 232). In the dialogue which follows, Forster pinpoints the lack of understanding and communication possible between Helen and Leonard.

Since his initial interview with the Schlegel sisters, Leonard has changed. He no longer hungers for literary discussion, nor does he seek adventure by nighttime walks in the woods.

> "Walking is well enough when a man's in work," he answered. "Oh, I did talk a lot of nonsense once, but there's nothing like a bailiff in the house to drive it out of you. When I saw him fingering my Ruskins and Stevensons, I seemed to see life straight real, and it isn't a pretty sight. My books are back again, thanks to you, but they'll never be the same to me again, and I shan't ever again think night in the woods so wonderful."
>
> (*HE* 235)

Nor does Leonard harbor any illusions about Jacky. Leonard has become more pragmatic, realizing that he must secure a job and an income before he can again think about pursuing ideals. So Helen's impassioned speech on the struggle between death and money dramatizes their differences. Cruel circumstance has changed Leonard from a dreamy ineffective romantic into a more pragmatic materialist. Forster writes:

> Leonard looked at her wondering, and had the sense of great things sweeping out of the shrouded night. But he could not receive them, because his heart was still full of little things. As the lost umbrella had spoilt the concert at Queen's Hall, so the lost situation was obscuring the diviner harmonies now. Death, Life, and Materialism were fine words, but would Mr. Wilcox take him on as a clerk?
>
> (*HE* 236)

Leonard feels his own stupidity while Helen sees the paradox of Death with increasing clarity. Her plea rises in a dramatic crescendo: "'So never give in,' continued the girl, and restated again and again the vague yet convincing plea that the Invisible lodges against the Visible. Her excitement grew as she tried to cut the rope that fastened Leonard to the earth. Woven of bitter experience it resisted her" (*HE* 236).

Ironically this provides the only information leading up to the liaison between Helen and Leonard. Their positions are counterpointed to a degree which precludes communication, so it is not surprising that Katherine Mansfield could remark: "And I can never be perfectly certain whether Helen was got with child by Leonard Bast or by his fatal forgotten umbrella. All things considered, I think it must have been the umbrella."[5] It is important to note, however, that Helen is seen as extreme, and in her obsession with absolutes and the "unseen," she is as limited as Leonard is by his narrow vision of material possibilities. The gap between them is poignant, and clearly Leonard is more aware of it.

When Leonard recollects the events of Oniton during its aftermath, Forster downplays "realistic" motivation as well as physical detail as he revises.[6] Instead of beginning with the following morning, Forster separates the events of chapter 41 from Oniton by weeks and months. Instead of emphasizing passion, Forster stresses "remorse." Leonard suffers for his actions, but his suffering is presented with great narrative distance, ambivalence, and irony. The published text is ambiguous about which party had been the sexual aggressor, who was to blame (**HE** 314).

By deleting physical description and developing Leonard's suffering, which is based upon misperceptions, Forster prepares for the events that follow. Leonard's disorientation, described in the chapter opening, anticipates his hallucinations the night before he sets out for Howards End. Only by describing Leonard's intense self-loathing does his desire to meet Margaret and confess become credible. The distanced perspective and the irony, though they contribute to the ironic outcome, do make it difficult to sympathize with Leonard. Leonard must be woebegone and filled with remorse if he is to find his way to Margaret at Howards End in order to speak the truth and beg forgiveness; in revising this section, however, presentation of Leonard's subjectivity and humanity are sacrificed to the demands of the plot.

However, Forster's revisions do indicate some attempt to establish Leonard as a believable character. Instead of detailing Leonard's search for employment and the singularity of his feelings for Helen, the published text presents his strength of character unequivocally. In addition to his newly acquired tenderness for Jacky, which was also developed in the rejected draft, Leonard is presented as "alive" and unmuddled. Leonard grows as a character in these few pages of the published text. He is able to rise above his circumstances in a manner that would have been beyond the character presented in the draft version. There we are given a continuation of his earlier characterization: he is irritable for lack of money (MS p. A9, **MsHE** 324) and once "his stomach was filled" he "was again touched by the world's exasperating beauty" (MS p. A9, **MsHE** 325). Page A10 of the draft shows Leonard brooding upon the sea, home of Romance, still aspiring to walks and excursions with the fishermen (**MsHE** 325). Instead of dwelling upon Leonard as an ineffectual romantic, the published text presents him as an active agent of his fate.

The development of Leonard's character in the published text moves beyond these naive aspirations. Leonard is disillusioned. He goes to St. Paul's "partly to avoid the rain and partly to see a picture that had educated him in former years." Of this experience, we are told: "But the light was bad, the picture ill-placed, and Time and Judgement were inside him now" (**HE,** 316). The following sentence in the manuscripts is: "Death alone, with her poppies, still charmed him—Death contending with (Mammon) Money / for the soul of man, and her lap on which all the generations of men shall sleep" (**MsHE** 316:18). With revision this becomes: "Death alone still charmed him, with her lap of poppies on which all men shall sleep" (**HE,** 316:18). This sentence clearly indicates that Leonard has changed since his discussion at Oniton where all that concerned him was money. Though his family has answered his begging pleas for money, the "blackmail" has created ill will and hatred on both sides.

The emphasis upon death at this point picks up the theme of Helen's impassioned speech and prepares for further development of the plot. But equally important, these many changes make Leonard a character of greater strength and substance. The details that present him as a pitiful victim or a romantic fool have been eliminated. Instead, Leonard is presented as disillusioned, but resigned and admirable. As Forster puts it, "Leonard was driven straight through its torments and emerged pure, but enfeebled—a better man, who would never lose control of himself again, but also a smaller man, who had less to control" (**HE** 313).

Leonard no longer has illusions about himself or his life, and he moves toward his end almost fatalistically. Forster says: "He did not suppose that the confession would bring him happiness. It was rather that he yearned to get clear of the tangle. So does the suicide yearn" (**HE** 316). Leonard now yearns for the absolute. Ironically, his acceptance of his own fallibility has led him to a "conviction of absolute goodness elsewhere." He understands Helen's idea "Death destroys a man, but the idea of death saves him." Forster describes Leonard's state: "As he approached the house all thought stopped. Contradictory notions stood side by side in his mind. He was terrified but happy, ashamed, but had done no sin. He knew the confession: 'Mrs. Wilcox, I have done wrong,' but sunrise had robbed its meaning, and he felt rather on a supreme adventure" (**HE** 321).

Leonard's openness to the absolute and his acceptance of contradictions may help to explain the depersonalization which asserts itself again in the description of his death. Forster attempts to give Leonard's actions archetypal significance. As he enters Howards End, Forster writes, "He entered *a* garden, steadied himself against *a* motor-car that he found in it, found *a* door open and entered *a* house" (**HE** 321). In the manuscript version, Leonard's actions are more particularized by Forster's choice of article: "He entered *the* garden, steadied himself against a motor-car that he found in it, found *the* door open and entered *the* house" (**MsHE** 321:17-18). In the manuscript version, Forster first struggles to capture the experience from Leonard's point of view:

It did not hurt him where it struck him, but in the heart, which was odd. Down fell a book case. Nothing had sense. Faces bent over him—Margaret's, Helen's<— Margaret's nodded, and he died, an old woman's, the faces of all women . . . [*or rather three short dashes* (Stallybrass's italics)] He was fainting.

(*MsHE* 321:27)

This peculiar, inconsistent use of point of view with its abrupt shift from Leonard's interior monologue to the narrator's comment is excised through revision, leaving the description more dignified and less sentimental: "It hurt him, not where it descended, but in the heart. Books fell over him in a shower. Nothing had sense" (*HE* 321:27). Peter Widdowson has also noticed the archetypal quality of this scene, many of the details of which are later explained in realistic terms.[7] The published text treats Leonard's death with greater narrative distance, paralleling the effect of those changes at the chapter opening.

In the "baptism" scene which follows, the manuscripts avoided the use of personal pronouns in reference to Leonard, creating an icyness and objectivity which seem singularly inappropriate: "They laid *the corpse* on the gravel, and Helen poured water over *it*" (*MsHE* 321:33). Although this would have been consistent with Forster's treatment of Leonard elsewhere, Forster may have recognized his own lack of feeling here, so the passage is changed to read: "They laid *Leonard,* who was dead, on the gravel; Helen poured water over *him*" (*HE* 321:33-34). Or, perhaps it is only at his death that Leonard is most a "person," since Death is an ally of the personal.

Forster's strategy in handling this episode marks this as a moment where the novel expands. Forster succeeds in eliminating Leonard, for as Widdowson points out, "Leonard has to die to clear the way for his son to be 'Liberal England's' heir untrammelled by the drab reality of his father's life and class; Leonard himself would not fit into 'Howards End/England' but the child brought up in the right environment will.' And Helen could not credibly 'have married a Bast.'"[8] But Leonard's death does not give closure to the novel; it is not a moment of completion.

Margaret's subsequent meditation upon Leonard's death draws clear connections between his death and Ruth Wilcox's by incorporating the same symbols, language, and antithetical structures to arrive at a comparable conclusion. One of the most carefully structured passages in the novel is Margaret's reflection upon Mrs. Wilcox's death which pairs nouns, phrases, clauses, and sentences to convey the sense of extremes which Mrs. Wilcox has managed to reconcile with her death.[9] Aside from the opening and one short centrally located sentence which was inserted in revision ("She had kept proportion"), every sentence is antithetical in some way. Forster removes the literal introduction of the manuscripts, tightens oppositions through revision, and inserts the telling pronouns so that the passage in the published text reads:

She was parting from these Wilcoxes for the second time. Paul and his mother, ripple and great wave, had flowed into her life and ebbed out of it for ever. The ripple had left no traces behind; the wave had strewn at her feet fragments torn from the unknown. A curious seeker, she stood for a while at the verge of the sea that tells so little, but tells a little, and watched the outgoing of this last tremendous tide. Her friend had vanished in agony, but not, she believed, in degradation. *Her* withdrawal had hinted at other things besides disease and pain. Some leave *our* life with tears, others with an insane frigidity; Mrs. Wilcox had taken the middle course, which only rarer natures can pursue. She had kept proportion. She had told a little of her grim secret to her friends, but not too much; she had shut up her heart—almost, but not entirely. It is thus, if there is any rule, that we ought to die—neither as victim nor as fanatic, but as the seafarer who can greet with an equal eye the deep that he is entering, and the shore that he must leave.

(*HE* 100)

And the passage concludes optimistically:

The death of Mrs. Wilcox had helped her in her work. She saw a little more clearly than hitherto what a human being is, and to what he may aspire. Truer relationships gleamed. Perhaps the last word would be hope—hope even on this side of the grave.

(*HE* 101)

With that comment, Margaret turns her energies toward the survivors.

After Leonard's death, Margaret has a parallel moment of reflection which recalls through its imagery Ruth Wilcox's death, and through its unreasonable paradox the ambiguity of Leonard's final moments:

Events succeeded in a logical, yet senseless, train. People lost their humanity, and took values as arbitrary as those in a pack of playing-cards. It was natural that Henry should do this and cause Helen to do that, and then think her wrong for doing it; natural that she herself should think him wrong; natural that Leonard should want to know how Helen was, and come, and Charles be angry with him for coming—natural, but unreal. In this jangle of causes and effects what had become of their true selves? Here Leonard lay dead in the garden, from natural causes; yet life was a deep, deep river, death a blue sky, life was a house, death a wisp of hay, a flower, a tower, life and death were anything and everything, except this ordered insanity, where the king takes the queen, and the ace the king. Ah, no; there was beauty and adventure behind, such as the man at her feet had yearned for; there was hope this side of the grave; there were truer relationships beyond the limits that fetter us now. As a prisoner looks up and sees stars beckoning, so she, from the turmoil and horror of those days, caught glimpses of the diviner wheels.

(*HE* 327)

This passage also echoes Margaret's reflections upon the tree and the house: "Their message was not of eternity, but of hope on this side of the grave. As she stood in the one, gazing at the other, truer relationships had gleamed" (**HE** 203).

Forster carefully works to integrate Leonard's death imagistically, thematically, and structurally into the novel through the parallel between Leonard and Mrs. Wilcox. But, Leonard's death is not grounded in a web of relationships with people or place. In Mrs. Wilcox's death, Margaret gains a vision of proportion, of mediation. With Leonard's death, she grasps a contradiction: his death was "natural, but unreal." In spite of Forster's efforts to elevate Leonard to mythic stature, he is undercut by his own assumptions and his strategy of revision. Connection can come only through personal relationships of which Leonard has been deprived as the pronoun changes indicate. At the same time, Forster treats Leonard with greater irony and narrative distance as the novel evolves. Both of these strategies create an undercurrent which makes Margaret's moment of vision upon Leonard's death precarious at best. And later in the novel, Margaret remarks to Helen: "Then I can't have you worrying about Leonard. Don't drag in the personal when it will not come. Forget him." The ensuing interchange between the sisters provides the final comment on Leonard. Helen asks,

"Yes, yes, but what has Leonard got out of life?"

"Perhaps an adventure."

"Is that enough?"

"Not for us. But for him."

(**HE** 336)

This final condescension and the refusal to make Leonard a protective genie or an agent of the unseen raises the question of Forster's class consciousness and points to the problematic role of Leonard in the novel. Forster's treatment of Leonard provides an important example of an attempt to combine visionary and realistic elements in a single novel.[10]

Notes

1. E. M. Forster, *Two Cheers for Democracy* (New York: Harcourt Brace & World, Inc., 1951), pp. 56-57.

2. E. M. Forster, *Howards End,* ed. Oliver Stallybrass. Abinger Edition Vol. 4. (London: Edward Arnold, 1973), p. 79. Subsequent references to the novel will appear as internal citations (*HE*). My italics.

3. E. M. Forster, *The Manuscripts of Howards End,* ed. Oliver Stallybrass. Abinger Edition Vol. 4A. (London: Edward Arnold, 1973), p. 16. Subsequent references to the manuscripts will appear as internal citations (*MsHE*). My italics.

4. J. H. Stape, "'Leonard's Fatal Forgotten Umbrella': Sex and the Manuscript Revisions of *Howards End,*" *Journal of Modern Literature,* 9 (1981-82), 124.

5. Katherine Mansfield, *Journal* (London: Constable & Co. Ltd., 1954), p. 121. Curiously enough, John

Middleton Murry deleted this irreverent comment from the earlier edition (1927), and it has not been restored in the most recent American edition (New York: The Ecco Press, 1983). Other critics have found fault with this turn in plot development. Samuel Hynes, for example, says "*Howards End* is the weak novel it is because it has heterosexual relationships at its centre—an engagement, a marriage, and a fornication move the plot—and Forster could not handle any of them convincingly. And so the events that should be fully treated are either shuffled offstage or are brought on so wrapped in rhetoric as to be quite meaningless (all that stuff about 'rainbow bridges,' for instance)." See Hynes, "Forster's Cramp," in *Edwardian Occasions* (New York: Oxford University Press, 1972), 117. John Stape has discussed Forster's revisions of this episode particularly as it is recalled later in the novel, first in Helen's words, and later through Leonard's recorded thoughts and feelings. Stape argues that Forster's initial descriptions were presented with sufficient psychological and physical detail for the time. He dismisses Hynes' hypothesis that Forster was limited by his homosexuality in his presentation of heterosexual relations. Instead, Stape suggests that Forster adopted a more cautious treatment particularly of the Leonard-Helen incident because of his sensitivity to the reading public. See J. H. Stape, note 4 above. See also Forster's concern over the incident as expressed in a letter to his publisher and a diary entry quoted by Oliver Stallybrass, "Editor's Introduction," *Howards End.* Abinger Edition Vol. 4. (London: Edward Arnold, 1973), xiii.

6. Stape, 123-32.

7. Peter Widdowson, *E. M. Forster's Howards End: Fiction as History* (London: Sussex University Press, 1977), 104.

8. Widdowson, 104.

9. John Russell, *Style in Modern British Fiction: Studies in Joyce, Lawrence, Forster, Lewis, and Green* (Baltimore: The Johns Hopkins University Press, 1978), p. 102.

10. My understanding of visionary and prophetic elements in modern fiction has been greatly clarified and influenced by Dan Schwarz of Cornell University who directed an NEH summer seminar "Critical Perspectives on the Early 20th Century British Novel" during the summer of 1984, in which I was a participant.

H. M. Daleski (essay date 1985)

SOURCE: Daleski, H. M. "*Howards End*: Goblins and Rainbows." In *Unities: Studies in the English Novel,* pp. 111-25. Athens, Ga.: University of Georgia Press, 1985.

[*In the following essay, Daleski examines personal fragmentation in* Howards End.]

About midway through *Howards End*—in a passage that is right at its center—the novelist describes a pervading condition of personal fragmentation:

> Margaret greeted her lord with peculiar tenderness on the morrow. Mature as he was, she might yet be able to help him to the building of the rainbow bridge that should connect the prose in us with the passion. Without it we are meaningless fragments, half monks, half beasts, unconnected arches that have never joined into a man. With it love is born . . .
>
> It did not seem so difficult [i.e., for Margaret to help Mr. Wilcox]. She need trouble him with no gift of her own. She would only point out the salvation that was latent in his own soul, and in the soul of every man. Only connect! That was the whole of her sermon. Only connect the prose and the passion, and both will be exalted, and human love will be seen at its highest. Live in fragments no longer. Only connect, and the beast and the monk, robbed of the isolation that is life to either, will die.
>
> (pp. 187-88)[1]

The "sermon" may be Margaret's, but Forster uses its text as the epigraph to the novel, and it is the "salvation" not only of Mr. Wilcox but of "every man" that is at issue. What men have to be saved from is the kind of self-division that is implicit in Mr. Wilcox's sexual attitudes, the split between spirit and flesh that makes him in turn a monk and a beast. The "rainbow bridge" Margaret hopes to help him build in order to connect the everyday casualness of prose with the special intensity of passion is itself—much as in D. H. Lawrence—a symbol of the harmonious reconciliation or integration of opposites. In a meeting of sun and rain, it joins earth and sky and signifies an achieved wholeness in contradistinction to the fragmentation of the "unconnected arches." It is love that resolves the specific opposition referred to, for it is born of the connection of monk and beast, but destroys its progenitors by depriving each of the isolation that is essential to its existence. It issues, indeed, as a tenderness that is the product of the union of flesh and spirit, a "tenderness that kills the monk and the beast at a single blow" (p. 219).

The drama of personal fragmentation is enacted against a background of social disintegration: "the city herself, emblematic of their lives, rose and fell in a continual flux, while her shallows washed more widely against the hills of Surrey and over the fields of Hertfordshire. This famous building had arisen, that was doomed. Today Whitehall had been transformed; it would be the turn of Regent Street tomorrow" (p. 115). It is the lack of stability, the "continual flux" of urban life, that particularly concerns the novelist. The flux is inherent in the city itself. It is the very city that rises and falls as old buildings are destroyed in order to make way for new in a continuous process that spills out over the countryside. The quintessential scene in Forster's London is of "an old house . . . being demolished to accommodate [two blocks of flats]": "It [is] the kind of scene that may be observed all over London, whatever the locality—bricks and mortar rising and falling with the restlessness of the water in a fountain, as the city receives more and more men upon her soil" (p. 59).

Fragmentary buildings, which are to be seen everywhere in London, provide an effective image of the lack of integration that is Forster's theme. Indeed it is in this regard, as well as in relation to the phenomenon of flux, that the city may be viewed as being "emblematic" of the lives of the Schlegels—and of the other characters who inhabit it—for the novelist posits a direct connection between the personal and the social predicament, presenting one as the consequence of the other. When the Schlegels are forced to vacate their home at Wickham Place so that it can be demolished, this is said to "[disintegrate] the girls more than they [know]" (p. 253). What the individual needs in the flux of modern city life is a locus of stability, and this, it is intimated, is best provided by a long-standing home. "Can what they call civilization be right," asks Mrs. Wilcox, "if people mayn't die in the room where they were born?" (p. 93). Margaret does not know "what to say" in reply to this, but the novelist insists that modern man is being reduced to "a nomadic horde" and reverting to a "civilization of luggage." The Schlegels, at all events, are denied what Mrs. Wilcox takes to be their natural right, and so are deprived of that which has hitherto "helped to balance their lives" (p. 154).

Given such a view of life in London, it is not surprising that the novel takes its title from the name of a house, a house in the country. Given such a view, moreover, the plot, which turns on the Schlegels' loss of their home and their search for a new one, readily takes on a symbolic dimension: their loss is representative of a general predicament; and their search is for something more than a house. It is a search for that which can provide a secure anchorage for the self.

That the Schlegels eventually find a new home at Howards End is assertive, on the symbolic level, of more than is actually shown to be accomplished, for true personal stability is as much dependent on an inner cohesion and balance as on a stable environment—and I shall argue that none of the Schlegels achieve that. But the conclusion is indicative of the novel's strong contrapuntal structure: Howards End is set against Wickham Place, the country against the city, wholeness against disintegration. It has, indeed, the kind of musical structure so appreciatively described in the account of Helen's response to the third movement of Beethoven's Fifth Symphony:

> the music started with a goblin walking quietly over the universe, from end to end. Others followed him. They were not aggressive creatures; it was that that made them so terrible to Helen. They merely observed in passing that there was no such thing as splendour or heroism in the world. After the interlude of elephants dancing, they returned and made the observation for the second time. Helen could not contradict them, for, once at all events, she had felt the same, and had seen the reliable walls of youth collapse. Panic and emptiness! Panic and emptiness! The goblins were right. . . .

[Then] as if things were going too far, Beethoven took hold of the goblins and made them do what he wanted . . . he blew with his mouth and they were scattered! Gusts of splendour, gods and demigods contending with vast swords, colour and fragrance broadcast on the field of battle, magnificent victory, magnificent death! . . . [But] the goblins really had been there. They might return—and they did. It was as if the splendour of life might boil over and waste to steam and froth. In its dissolution one heard the terrible, ominous note, and a goblin, with increased malignity, walked quietly over the universe from end to end. Panic and emptiness! Panic and emptiness! Even the flaming ramparts of the world might fall.

(pp. 46-47)

In a work evocative of heroic splendor, Beethoven, it is held, found it necessary to include an antiheroic statement. This counterstatement is comparable structurally to Forster's own assertion, in a world of unconnected arches, of the existence of rainbows. But the images in the quoted passage make the description of Beethoven's procedures in the Fifth Symphony more than an analogue of Forster's in the novel, for his goblins are heralds of disintegration. What they point to is the possibility of breakdown, a falling apart in which even "the reliable walls of youth" and "the flaming ramparts of the world" may disintegrate, a collapse which is a "dissolution," a boiling over and a wasting to steam and froth. The goblins, that is, lead straight to the landlord of Wickham Place, who knocks it down and so spills "the precious distillation of the years" which "no chemistry of his can give . . . back to society again" (p. 155). The kind of collapse the goblins announce, moreover, reveals—amid falling walls and ramparts—an inner hollowness, a nothingness at the heart of things, the "panic and emptiness" that Helen (who serves as the center of consciousness in the quoted passage) has discerned behind the confident facade of Paul Wilcox. It is a hollowness that Conrad had some years earlier found at the core of Kurtz in "Heart of Darkness"; it is the kind of void that Forster himself later has Mrs. Moore memorably peer into in a Marabar cave in *A Passage to India.* It is a "terrible, ominous note" that is sounded by the goblin that quietly walks "with increased malignity . . . over the universe from end to end" because what it prophetically foretells is dissolution on a global scale—and the disintegration in 1914 of the society of those who sit listening in the Queen's Hall to Beethoven. With such goblins loose in the world, Forster may well essay the rainbow. When he chooses "to make all right in the end" (p. 47), as Beethoven does despite the goblins, the question is whether we can trust Forster—as he asserts "one can trust Beethoven," who has bravely said "the goblins [are] there" and "could return" (p. 47).

2

Though it is the monk and the beast who are the focus of Margaret's sermon, it is not with the opposition between spirit and flesh that Forster is directly concerned. His interest is in the contrasted qualities and value systems of two families, the Schlegels and the Wilcoxes, who are posed against each other in an elaborate balance, a point counterpoint, that is the unifying principle of the novel. They figure an opposition between the private and the public self.[2] What is involved in the opposition is neatly brought out in an apparently trivial incident. Margaret is traveling with a wedding party to celebrate Evie Wilcox's wedding at Oniton when the front car in which she is driving suddenly stops. The second car pulls up, and Charles Wilcox is "heard saying: 'Get out the women at once.'" The women are "hustled out" into the second car, which drives off, but at that point a girl comes out of a cottage and "[screams] wildly at them." When the ladies want to know what has happened, Charles says, "It's all right. Your car just touched a dog"; and he adds, "It didn't hurt him" (pp. 211-12).

Charles, we note, at once takes command of the situation. When it comes to acting, the Wilcoxes, as Helen remarks, seem "to have their hands on all the ropes" (p. 41); and this capacity manifests itself in the "public qualities" Margaret believes have produced the material civilization on which they all depend (p. 177). The Wilcoxes, furthermore, seem to Helen to represent a "robust ideal" (p. 38): they are not only "competent" but have great "energy," "grit," and "character" (pp. 37, 41). They are also strongly male: Margaret is glad that in Mr. Wilcox she is marrying "a real man" (p. 176).

The capacity for acting in the world, however, not unexpectedly breeds a less admirable worldliness. Like the landlords who are busy demolishing old houses in London, the Wilcoxes' foremost concern is with making money; and they exemplify the nomadic civilization that is the result of these labors, restlessly moving from house to house and seeming to prize their motor cars above all. For the worldly, moreover, "love means marriage settlements; death, death duties," as Helen asserts (p. 41); and accordingly the way in which the Wilcoxes handle the accident is to dispense "compensation" for the loss of a pet, the chauffeurs being left to "[tackle] the girl" in this respect—and the insurance company to pay (p. 213). In the name of the efficient transaction of the business in hand, the Wilcoxes also naturally accommodate themselves to misleading distortion and suppression of the truth. Margaret, who is a woman and appears agitated, must be treated like a child and told the car "didn't hurt" the dog it ran over; as "a possible tenant," she is not told by Mr. Wilcox of the mews behind his Ducie Street house though as a prospective wife who has to be persuaded not to live there she is informed of its "huge drawbacks." She concludes that such behavior is not really devious and stems from "a flaw inherent in the business mind," the novelist commenting—with a show of objectivity that in its lameness is disquieting—that she "may do well to be tender to it, considering all that the business mind has done for England" (p. 184). But the business mind, it appears, is not prepared to do very much for the girl who has lost her pet. When it comes to her, it shows a total incomprehension that anything other than compensation and a hasty retreat are called for—an incomprehension that is extended to Margaret when, "horrified," she asks Charles to stop the car so that she can go back to the girl; he simply "[takes] no notice" (p. 212). We are told that all the Wilcoxes "[avoid] the personal note in life" (p. 101), but the sort of incomprehension Charles displays on this occasion amounts to a blankness that is expressive of a radical incapacity where the personal is concerned, an inner hollowness.

For the Schlegels such behavior is unthinkable. Margaret's most pronounced quality is said to be "a profound vivacity," which is defined as "a continual and sincere response to all that she [encounters] in her path through life" (p. 25). Such responsiveness makes her place a high value on "personal relations," which she and her sister think are "supreme" and "the real life" (p. 41). Where the Wilcoxes are "practical," they are "intellectual" (p. 151); and they pursue an inner life of cultivated sensibility that may rest, amid the prevailing flux, on the "island" of a private income (p. 72), but otherwise has few material preoccupations. Wickham Place may not have a precise location in *Howards End,* but it would appear to be not very far from Bloomsbury. The Schlegels certainly adhere to a distinctive ethos; and Margaret, who is "not a Christian in the accepted sense," is not without her own religion: "It is private life," she reflects, "that holds out the mirror to infinity; personal intercourse, and that alone, that ever hints at a personality beyond our daily vision" (p. 91).

The vistas of private life, however, are somewhat more restricted when it comes to mundane matters. Margaret admits that she and Helen "have never touched" the "great outer life" in which the Wilcoxes move so confidently, though she suspects it may be "the real one" (p. 41)—and indeed the Schlegels appear to be incapable of acting effectively outside a friendly drawing-room. This incapacity is strikingly shown in their inability to find a new house when they have to leave Wickham Place: "I want a new home in September," Margaret says, "and someone must find it. I can't" (p. 157). There is, in a word, something "bloodless" about the Miss Schlegels (p. 42)—and their effeminate brother Tibby. Nor, when the Schlegel blood is up, does it prove to be any more effective. Sitting in the car as Charles drives away from the scene of the accident, feeling the urgent need to take personal responsibility for what has happened, Margaret is faced by his steady refusal to heed her repeated requests that he stop. What she does is in keeping with the impulsiveness she shares with her sister—it is the only way they can act—and reckless of her own safety: she jumps out of the car. It is a courageous protest, but utterly ineffectual, the rage of impotence. In the end she "[yields], apologizing slightly," and is "led back to the car"—leaving the field to Charles. When it emerges it is a cat that has been killed and not a dog, he exclaims "triumphantly": "There! It's only a rotten cat" (pp. 212-13).

The Wilcox propensity for such distinctions is even more damagingly revealed in what they make of the note Mrs. Wilcox writes from her deathbed, which reads: "To my

husband: I should like Miss Schlegel (Margaret) to have Howards End." It is written in pencil, and has no date and no signature (pp. 105-6). The "question" raised by the note—which the Wilcoxes meet to consider—is one that cuts right across the two worlds of the novel, squarely opposing a personal to a business ethic. The Wilcoxes dispose of the private world of "feminine" caprice that the note discloses to them by simply ignoring its existence. The pressing personal question that the note poses—are they not called upon to honor a dying wish, the last request of a wife and a mother?—is easily avoided because it is not even formulated. Nor is the question—which might have "driven them miserable or mad" (p. 107)—of what is implied by such a wish on Mrs. Wilcox's part. Instead they dodge the personal and the emotional; and, "assuming the manner of the committee-room" (p. 106), convert the question into the public and practical one of the note's legality. In the end, the question is reduced to what should be done with the piece of paper; and since it is "not legally binding" (p. 106), they proceed with characteristic decisiveness to "tear the note up and throw it onto their dining-room fire" (p. 108). The irony is that Margaret, had she been informed of Mrs. Wilcox's wish, would also have "rejected [it] as the fantasy of an invalid" (p. 110). But the fact remains that the destruction of the note, though perhaps not technically criminal, is certainly dishonest. Once again it is disquieting that the novelist should seek to minimize the weakness he has so devastatingly exposed. We are told that "the practical moralist" (who presumably believes the end justifies the means) "may acquit them absolutely"; while he "who strives to look deeper," even if conceding they should not be acquitted altogether, is merely palliative: "For one hard fact remains. They did neglect a personal appeal" (p. 108).

A personal appeal of another kind is productive of the central crisis in the novel when Helen decides to throw the Basts at the Wilcoxes on Evie's wedding day. Storming into the Wilcox domain to repudiate what they stand for, Helen emerges in this scene as the epitome of all that is opposed to their way of doing things. Defiantly dressed in "her oldest clothes" as a measure of her personal identification with the Basts in their difficult circumstances, betraying in her "tense, wounding excitement" the degree of her personal involvement with them (p. 222), she has generously accepted a personal responsibility for their plight. But she is as much given to converting reality to her own terms as the Wilcoxes, declaring the Basts to be starving and thus theatrically heightening their condition, in much the way that the Wilcoxes reduce the significance of the deathbed note. And the moment it comes to remedial action, Helen's admirable motives fade into utter inconsequentiality. What she does—much like Margaret in the car—is to abandon herself to her impulse, not considering at all whether it is wise to take the Basts with her to Oniton. Whereas Mr. Wilcox, when tactfully approached by Margaret, shows himself amenable to helping Bast (p. 228), his unfortunate meeting with Mrs. Bast, his former mistress, makes any further suggestion of such aid out of the question. The net result of Helen's attempt to save the

Basts is that she helps to ruin them, for the expedition "[cripples them] permanently" since she forgets "to settle the hotel bill" and takes "their return tickets away with her"; without a job and evicted from his flat, Bast thereafter "[degrades] himself to a professional beggar" (p. 309).

In her haste to set the world to rights, Helen nearly brings about another unanticipated development. Even Margaret is moved to anger at her "bursting into Evie's wedding" in a manner that might seem calculated to cause everyone distress (p. 223), though nothing is further from her intention. In fact she comes close to destroying the relationship of Margaret and Mr. Wilcox: after the scene with Mrs. Bast, Mr. Wilcox, assuming the worst, releases Margaret from her engagement, and it is only Margaret's decision to regard the matter as Mrs. Wilcox's "tragedy," not hers, that saves the marriage (pp. 230-31). It is, of course, Bast's tragedy, too, and it is when Helen guesses that Mr. Wilcox has "ruined him in two ways," that she gives herself to him (p. 305). The ultimate consequences of the expedition to Shropshire are Helen's pregnancy—and Bast's death (though this last event does not have the painful effect that might be expected since the Basts are so utterly unconvincing in all they do and say, so clearly and in more than one sense beings of a different order of existence from that of the Schlegels and Wilcoxes, that they are never more than discordant creaks in the mechanism of the plot).

In episodes such as the killing of the cat, the destruction of Mrs. Wilcox's note, and the invasion of Evie's wedding party, what it means to be a Schlegel or a Wilcox is effectively revealed, and the attributes of the private and public self clearly established. What is notable is the degree to which, in each case, one aspect of the self is subdued to the other. In the Wilcoxes the private is suppressed by the public to an extent that there is only an emptiness where the personal should be. But in the Schlegels the ability to act is equally missing, and the personal reduces the public self to impotence. In both the Wilcox and the Schlegel personality, therefore, there is a radical deficiency, a blankness—like that into which an unconnected arch gapes.

The driving force of **Howards End** is the search for a means of supplying these deficiencies. But how does one connect a broken arch to a blankness? The novel, not unexpectedly, gives no very clear answer to this question, but does explore certain possibilities. An obvious resource is to attempt to develop the missing capacity. This, it would appear, can best be done in relation to a person who abundantly possesses it. Margaret, for instance, knows that the Wilcoxes are "not 'her sort,'" and that they are "deficient where she [excels]"; but nevertheless "collision with them [stimulates] her": "She desired to protect them, and often felt that they would protect her, excelling where she was deficient" (p. 111). The stimulus Margaret derives from contact with the Wilcoxes is clearly that generated by an opposite; the protection she both wishes to extend and to receive would seem to be not so much practical as a mutual fostering of qualities, an offering from a rich store in the area of the other's deficiency. If such casual provision-

ing might be expected to yield modest results, the best hope of continued supply might be supposed to lie in the maintenance of the closest possible relation with the opposite—in a word, in marriage.

It is a metaphorical union of opposites, at all events, that seems to posit the attainment of completeness—as it is the balance of opposites that integrates the narrative. Margaret experiences such "a feeling of completeness" when she is in the country: "In these English farms, if anywhere, one might see life steadily and see it whole, group in one vision its transitoriness and its eternal youth, connect—connect without bitterness until all men are brothers" (p. 264). And that is what the "peculiar glory" of the wych-elm, which Forster has stated was intended to be "symbolical" and "the genius of the house,"[3] seems to signify: "It was a comrade, bending over the house, strength and adventure in its roots, but in its utmost fingers tenderness, and the girth, that a dozen men could not have spanned, became in the end evanescent, till pale bud clusters seemed to float in the air" (p. 206). As Margaret stands in the house and looks at the tree, "truer relationships" are said to "gleam" (p. 206). Massively rooted in the earth, but "bending over the house," the wych-elm connects the house to the earth of its garden; and the tree itself is indicative of how opposites may be reconciled in indisputable wholeness. The "strength" of its roots counters the "tenderness" of its furthermost shoots; its enormous "girth" is balanced by its floating "evanescence."

What the tree at Howards End represents is given further embodiment in Mrs. Wilcox. Of her, Margaret, who is usually level-headed, says: "She knows everything. She is everything. She is the house, and the tree that leans over it" (p. 305). And on another occasion Mrs. Wilcox gives her "the idea of greatness" and makes her "conscious of a personality" that "transcends" and "dwarfs" the activities of her and her friends (p. 86). Clearly Mrs. Wilcox is one of those characters in Forster—Mrs. Moore in *A Passage to India* is another—who are more impressive to other characters than to the reader, for nothing that Mrs. Wilcox does or is would seem to accord with such estimates. But she would appear, if a little tenuously, to be the one character in the novel who is able to reconcile public and private worlds and achieve something like a state of wholeness.

Perhaps our most vivid impression of Mrs. Wilcox is in one of the early scenes in the novel, when we really see her moving into action. Charles Wilcox, seeking to go straight to the heart of the supposed affair between his brother Paul and Helen, at once asks his brother whether there is any truth in it; and, when Paul dithers, demands a plain answer to a plain question:

> "Charles dear," said a voice from the garden. "Charles, dear Charles, one doesn't ask plain questions. There aren't such things."
>
> They were all silent. It was Mrs. Wilcox.
>
> She approached just as Helen's letter had described her, trailing noiselessly over the lawn, and there was actually a wisp of hay in her hands. She seemed to be-

long not to the young people and their motor, but to the house, and to the tree that overshadowed it. One knew that she worshipped the past, and that the instinctive wisdom the past can alone bestow had descended upon her—that wisdom to which we give the clumsy name of aristocracy. High-born she might not be. But assuredly she cared about her ancestors, and let them help her. When she saw Charles angry, Paul frightened and Mrs. Munt in tears, she heard her ancestors say: "Separate those human beings who will hurt each other most. The rest can wait." So she did not ask questions. Still less did she pretend that nothing had happened, as a competent society hostess would have done. She said: "Miss Schlegel, would you take your aunt up to your room or to my room, whichever you think best. Paul, do find Evie, and tell her lunch for six, but I'm not sure whether we shall all be downstairs for it." And when they had obeyed her she turned to her elder son, who still stood in the throbbing, stinking car, and smiled at him with tenderness, and without saying a word turned away from him towards her flowers.

"Mother," he called, "are you aware that Paul has been playing the fool again?"

"It is all right dear. They have broken off the engagement."

"Engagement—!"

"They do not love any longer, if you prefer it put that way," said Mrs. Wilcox, stooping down to smell a rose.

(pp. 36-37)

Once again Wilcoxes and Schlegels meet in a question; but this time the formulation, "plain question, plain answer," is one to which both in their different ways—no-nonsense and businesslike as against the personally direct and sincere—would subscribe. Mrs. Wilcox, however, is sharply differentiated from all of them, and not merely by her sense of a complexity that will not permit of plainness. They belong, not only the Wilcoxes but—whether they like it or not—the Schlegels also, to the restless present of modern city life, to the life that seems to be epitomized in "the throbbing, stinking car." She "worships the past," the sense of continuity and stability that is derived from being in touch with her "ancestors"—and from belonging "to the house, and to the tree that [overshadows] it." Unlike them, she is in touch with nature: she makes her entry with "a wisp of hay in her hands"—the rhythmic hay that ever since E. K. Brown has been pointed to again and again with admiration—and departs smelling a rose.[4] But she is even more strongly differentiated from them all by what she herself is, by the combination of qualities that in this scene she notably shows herself to possess. She is not clever like the Schlegels and their friends, not an intellectual, but she has an "instinctive wisdom" that expresses itself in a penetrating intuition where people are concerned. Though neither Paul nor Helen has spoken to her about their relationship, she has accurately sized it up, showing a sensitivity and delicacy of perception that are the obverse of the obtuseness the Wilcoxes habitually exhibit in the sphere of the personal. And unlike the Schlegels, who veer between paralysis and an impulsive courting of disaster,

she knows how to act: she shows a real capacity for arriving at a swift decision as to the right action to take—and for carrying it out. In short, in contradistinction to the typical fragmentariness of both Schlegels and Wilcoxes, Mrs. Wilcox here exhibits a serene wholeness of being that may serve as a touchstone among the broken arches. And it is with "tenderness"—the tenderness that connects the monk and the beast—that she smiles at her irate son before turning to her flowers.

3

The marriage of Margaret and Mr. Wilcox seems designed to test the possibility of the achievement of wholeness (of a kind epitomized by Mrs. Wilcox) through the union of opposites. The trouble is that it is difficult to accept the verisimilitude of the marriage on a literal level, it being hard to believe Margaret could marry a man who is so obviously lacking in all the qualities she values most; and since the marriage is a central event in the plot, the status of the fiction as a whole is undermined. Nor does the strenuousness of the novelist's asseverations help us suspend our disbelief: "Some day—in the millennium—there may be no need for [Mr. Wilcox's] type. At present, homage is due to it from those who think themselves superior, and who possibly are" (p. 165).

The superiority is all on Mr. Wilcox's side in the first difference between the couple that materializes after their marriage. When Helen, who is keeping her pregnancy from the family, refuses to see Margaret and Tibby though she is back in England, Margaret finds her behavior so strange as to lead her to believe she must be ill—and turns for help to Mr. Wilcox. He proposes that they trick Helen into going to Howards End, and that Margaret should meet her there. Margaret's immediate response is to reject the plan as "quite impossible" because "it's not the particular language" that she and Helen talk (pp. 277-78). Mr. Wilcox becomes impatient, demanding to know whether she wants his help or not, and (as the wheel comes full circle) requiring a "plain answer" to a "plain question":

> By now Margaret wished she had never mentioned her trouble to her husband. Retreat was impossible. He was determined to push the matter to a satisfactory conclusion, and Helen faded as he talked. Her fair, flying hair and eager eyes counted for nothing, for she was ill, without rights, and any of her friends might hunt her. Sick at heart, Margaret joined in the chase. She wrote her sister a lying letter, at her husband's dictation; she said the furniture was all at Howards End, but could be seen on Monday next at 3.0 p.m., when a charwoman would be in attendance. It was a cold letter, and the more plausible for that. Helen would think she was offended. And on Monday next she and Henry were to lunch with Dolly, and then ambush themselves in the garden.

(pp. 278-79)

What Mr. Wilcox does is to force Margaret to assume the manner of the committee-room, and so transform Helen, who "fades as he talks," from a person into a problem, to be dealt with as effectively as possible. But the ethic of action in the "great outer life" is exposed, as references to the hunt and the chase and ambushes multiply, as the way of the jungle, an ethic drawn, indeed, "from the wolf-pack" (p. 277). Mr. Wilcox's management of the matter is as efficient as ever; when Margaret, however, capitulates to the business mind that dictates the cold, lying letter, she does not so much learn how to supply the deficiency in her own makeup as forfeit all integrity. Her own earlier reflections on Helen's too easy dismissal of "the outer life" are instructive in this regard:

> Perhaps Margaret grew too old for metaphysics, perhaps Henry was weaning her from them, but she felt that there was something a little unbalanced in the mind that so readily shreds the visible. The businessman who assumes that this life is everything, and the mystic who asserts that it is nothing, fail, on this side and on that, to hit the truth. "Yes, I see, dear; it's about halfway between," Aunt Juley had hazarded in earlier years. No; truth, being alive, was not half-way between anything. It was only to be found by continuous excursions into either realm, and though proportion is the final secret, to espouse it at the outset is to ensure sterility.
>
> (pp. 195-96)

It is one of the important passages in the book, an indication of how oppositions within the self which do not admit (like that of the monk and the beast) of resolution through the catalyst of sexual tenderness may be reconciled—a passage, like that on the rainbow bridge which immediately precedes it, that strikingly prefigures D. H. Lawrence's views. No easy balance between the opposed attributes of the self—like that of equal weights on a see-saw—no simple "proportion," is possible. The balance required is that of relationship, the maintenance—as the effort is made to give maximum expression to the opposed aspects of the self by "continuous excursions" into both "realms"—of a connection with the opposite, a connection that is retained at all times, even on an excursion into the furthermost regions of one of the realms. It is such habitual connection, I take it, that leads to "the final secret" of proportion. And it is this connection, as she ventures into the "public" sphere of businesslike action, that Margaret lets drop, for she altogether obliterates the "personal."

On the day of the ambush, however, Margaret suddenly decides that she will have to be "on [Helen's] side" (p. 282); and when she sees her and realizes the explanation of her behavior, her conflict is resolved. She then persuades Mr. Wilcox to leave her alone with Helen, and they are reconciled:

> And the triviality faded from their faces, though it left something behind—the knowledge that they never could be parted because their love was rooted in common things. Explanations and appeals had failed; they had tried for a common meeting-ground, and had only made each other unhappy. And all the time their salvation was lying round them—the past sanctifying the present; the present, with wild heart-throb, declaring

> that there would after all be a future, with laughter and the voices of children. Helen, still smiling, came up to her sister. She said: "It is always Meg." They looked into each other's eyes. The inner life had paid.
>
> (pp. 291-92)

In this passage the novelist begins an astonishing reversal of direction (which he maintains from this point to the end of the narrative), a reversal in which all that has previously been aimed at is quietly abandoned. When the triviality "[fades] from their faces," as Helen previously faded in the making of plans for the ambush, the novelist's impelling desire to reconcile opposites seems to fade too. The "inner life" has not only "paid" but done so in its own coin, routing the other. Though it was previously in the connection of opposites that "salvation" was said to lie, it now appears to inhere in the irresistible pull of like to like. It is now mutuality that is supreme, whose hold is unbreakable and productive of an enduring oneness or wholeness, for it is the fact that they and their love are "rooted in common things" that ensures they "never [can] be parted."[5] As like pulls close to like in negation of a great deal that has gone before, it appears, at least in part, to be because of the pressure of unacknowledged matter which enters the novel at this point—the pressure, we may infer, of Forster's own unacknowledged homosexuality (though of course there are no sexual overtones of any kind in the actual relationship of the sisters). That something like a disturbance of this nature is taking place is subsequently suggested when Helen, who has announced she intends to have her child in Germany and knows nothing of the rupture that has in the meanwhile developed between Margaret and Mr. Wilcox, seems equal to destroying their relationship once again—this time with malice aforethought—for she suddenly, and "seriously," asks Margaret to go to Germany with her (p. 306), to leave her husband, we must assume, for her. Furthermore, if "the past [sanctifies] the present" and begets the reunion of the sisters, the future that the present "declares" (with such a "wild heart-throb") will come "with laughter and the voices of children" proves to be more than niggardly, for Margaret seals it with a declaration of her own: "I do not love children," she tells Helen in the closing pages of the novel. "I am thankful to have none" (p. 327). The laughter, therefore, is confined to one child, the illegitimate child Helen bears after Bast's death, who grows up at Howards End in the ménage of the two sisters and a broken man.

The rupture between Margaret and Mr. Wilcox develops when she goes to ask his permission for Helen and herself to spend the night at Howards End. Mr. Wilcox, it appears, has in no way been prepared by marriage to Margaret for what is to be "the crisis of his life," nor taught how to respond to people. He weighs the request as if it were "a business proposition," and evasively turns it down, finally saying he cannot treat Helen "as if nothing [has] happened," and that he would be "false to [his] position in society" if he did (pp. 298-99). Margaret makes a last effort and asks him to forgive Helen, as he may "hope to be forgiven," and as he has "actually been forgiven":

Perhaps some hint of her meaning did dawn on him. If so, he blotted it out. Straight from his fortress he answered: "I seem rather unaccommodating, but I have some experience of life, and know how one thing leads to another. I am afraid that your sister had better sleep at the hotel. I have my children and the memory of my dear wife to consider. I am sorry, but see that she leaves my house at once."

"You have mentioned Mrs. Wilcox."

"I beg your pardon?"

"A rare occurrence. In reply, may I mention Mrs. Bast?"

"You have not been yourself all day," said Henry, and rose from his seat with face unmoved. Margaret rushed at him and seized both his hands. She was transfigured.

"Not any more of this!" she cried. "You shall see the connection if it kills you, Henry!"

(p. 300)

In his "fortress" Mr. Wilcox remains impenetrable, holding to the public duties of his "position in society" and his role as father and husband of the late Mrs. Wilcox—and also, as he declares to his son, defending "the rights of property" (p. 317). It is evident, moreover, that a sanctimonious and unredeemed monk still peeps from behind the ramparts. Helen, by contrast, is altogether vulnerable in her exposed situation, but asks for nothing more than the right to make her personal choices and lead her private life. When Margaret chooses between the two, she is "transfigured": it is a momentous development, for it marks her abandonment of the role of loyal wife and her recovery of an old self, which insists now on a "connection" that may break rather than make Mr. Wilcox—and is prepared to storm the fortress even "if it kills" him. This self is moved to repudiate him utterly, and she sees him as if for the first time in all his stupidity, hypocrisy, cruelty, and contemptibility (p. 300). The "crime," she will have him recognize at last, is not Helen's but his.

After Margaret has made her way back to Helen at Howards End, she determines to leave her husband and go with her sister to Germany (p. 318). She is prevented from doing so only by Bast's death and—when Charles is sentenced to three years' imprisonment—by Mr. Wilcox's collapse: "Then Henry's fortress gave way. He could bear no one but his wife, he shambled up to Margaret afterwards and asked her to do what she could with him. She did what seemed easiest—she took him down to recruit at Howards End" (p. 325). When the fortress finally gives way, Mr. Wilcox must be thought to disintegrate into nothingness since this is what we have consistently been led to expect. But the novelist seems rather to wish to leave us with the impression that the long-sought "connection" is somehow finally achieved in the marriage, despite the fact that the broken arch has been left to lean on nothing. Helen is made to say enviously to Margaret, "I see you loving Henry, and understanding him better daily, and I know that death wouldn't part you in the least"; and Margaret, with an unaccustomed smugness, is made to say in reply:

"All over the world men and women are worrying because they cannot develop as they are supposed to develop. Here and there they have the matter out, and it comforts them. . . . Don't you see that all this leads to comfort in the end? It is part of the battle against sameness. Differences—eternal differences, planted by God in a single family, so that there may always be colour; sorrow perhaps, but colour in the daily gray."

(pp. 327-28)

As we consider the devastations of the goblins, we cannot help feeling that this late appearance of a rainbow in the daily gray is novelistic legerdemain.

Notes

1. Page references to *Howards End* are to the Penguin Modern Classics edition, ed. Oliver Stallybrass (Harmondsworth, 1975; first published 1910). This text follows that of the Abinger Edition, 1973.

2. The opposition has been variously described. Formulations in some of the best discussions of the novel are: "Bloomsbury liberalism" as against "the great world" (Wilfred Stone, *The Cave and the Mountain: A Study of E. M. Forster* [Stanford, 1966], p. 235); "liberalism" as against "a kind of blunt and humorless materialism" (Frederick C. Crews, *E. M. Forster: The Perils of Humanism* [Princeton, N.J., 1962], p. 105); and "the inner life of intellect and spirit" as against "the outer life of the physical and the sensory" (Cyrus Hoy, "Forster's Metaphysical Novel," *PMLA* 75 [March 1960]: 126).

3. E. M. Forster, interview by P. N. Furbank and F. J. H. Haskell, *The Paris Review* 1 (Spring 1953): 34.

4. See E. K. Brown, *Rhythm in the Novel* (Toronto, 1950), pp. 46-50.

5. James Hall has suggestively drawn attention to this aspect: "For all the talk about personal relations, the novel is not optimistic about the possibility of personal relations with people outside the limited group who have been reared to have similar values" ("Forster's Family Reunions," *ELH* 25 [March 1958]: 75).

N. N. Feltes (essay date 1986)

SOURCE: Feltes, N. N. "Anyone of Everybody: Net Books and *Howards End*." In *Modes of Production of Victorian Novels*, pp. 76-98. Chicago: University of Chicago Press, 1986.

[*In the following essay, Feltes examines the ways in which Forster's narrative strategy in* Howards End *reflects the history of the publishing industry at the time.*]

In her book on Mudie's Library, Guinevere Griest's answer to her own question, "Who killed the three-decker?"

is neither precise nor satisfying. She rightly dismisses the proud claims of individuals, of George Moore or his publisher, Henry Vizetelly, or of other publishers who had independently issued single-volume novels in the 1890s, but she then cites only "years of economic pressure" before shifting her attention completely: "What is remarkable about the end of the three-volume form is the completeness and rapidity of its disappearance."[1] Royal Gettmann, in the other extended study of the sudden disappearance of novels in the three-volume format, is more specific in assigning a cause—"the three-decker was bound to disappear because it had ceased to be profitable to the libraries"[2]—but he then becomes too engrossed in the "pounds, shillings and pence" of Mudie's diminishing profits (257-58). Gettmann's analysis is based on the account books and correspondence of the house of Bentley, so that his explanations tend often to elaborate Bentley's own, or those given in the letters from Mudie. At the end of the chapter on the three-decker he does allude to wider circumstances, to "confusion and uncertainty," "bewilderment and paralysis" in publishing, remarking ambiguously that the abolition of the old form meant, in effect, that "the publisher for the moment could not call the tune or that he was forced to call a new one" (262). But he does not escape the individual publisher's vantage point enough to question what that "tune," old or new, might be. To think through the death of the three-decker novel we again need a more relational, a dialectical point of view, not least because, as Gettmann admits,

> actually the 'nineties was not a bad time for publishers, as may be seen from the number of other new firms which came into existence and flourished at this time— Edward Arnold, Methuen and Company, John Lane, and Duckworth and Company.
>
> (263)

For the disappearance of the three-volume format, while sudden enough to be an "event," is by no means the cause of publishers not being able to "call the tune," but rather a symptom of what was a conjunctural crisis in the production of books, the result, as Gareth Stedman Jones says in another context, of "a temporary fusion of seemingly unconnected long-term and short-term phenomena."[3] The decline in the libraries' profitability, the appearance of new publishers, and the death of the three-decker are all determinate elements in that conjunctural crisis whose "short term," I would argue, extends from Frederick Macmillan's announcement in 1890 of a "net" pricing policy, through the Net Book Agreement of 1899 and the *Times* Book War" of 1906-8, to the inclusion, in 1914, of fiction under the Net Book Agreement. Such empirical observations as that there was a new "buyers' market" in books, or that "the subscription-and rental-library trade . . . was being re-established on a more popular basis," or that "the whole price structure was revised downward,"[4] can take their meaning only in relation to an explanation of that wider crisis.

Griest's account, full as it is of detail, is weakened by her empiricist analysis, which simply allows, it seems, Time to solve all the publishers' difficulties she describes. She mentions the reactions of the interested parties to Mudie's decision, in June 1894, to accept no more three-volume novels, the London Booksellers' Society's endorsement of Mudie's action, the fears of the Society of Authors, and the responses of various publishers, concluding with the "complete and objective" analysis of a correspondent to the *Pall Mall Gazette* (176-88). But neither the *Gazette*'s analyst at the time nor Griest attempts to analyze the demise of the three-decker in its relations to the whole structure of the production of novels in Victorian England. Yet the three-decker had been an integral part of that structure; for the previous half-century or more, the hegemonic structure in novel production had been the initial publication of expensive three-volume novels which were then discounted to the lending libraries, which circulated them to members at a shilling a volume, with cheap reprints in any form being delayed, usually for a year. This production of commodity-books had guaranteed safe profits on all levels, retail booksellers profiting as well on the sale of the eventual reprints of successful novels. Any one of these structural elements admitted variations; a publisher might also adopt the alternative mode of part-issue, or discounts might vary, or reprinting might occasionally occur somewhat sooner, but the combination of a high list price, discounts to the libraries, multiple volumes, and the delay in reprinting, supported by an ideological consensus including the novel-reading public, this set of relations provided the dominant petty-commodity structure of novel production and was seen generally as how novels were best to be produced. Because none of the standard accounts sees this as a structure, the significance of the sudden extinction of the three-decker is obscured or sentimentalized, as it was for his contemporaries by Kipling's poem, which eulogizes the three volume novel as a sort of peaceful "Téméraire":

> . . . spite all modern notions, I found her first and best,
>
> The only certain packet for the Islands of the Blest.[5]

But what was occurring was not the arrival of "modern notions" but rather a radical transformation of the literary mode of production, the historical appearance of a new kind of structure, suited to, demanded, and provided by the larger structures of emergent monopoly capitalism.

The signs of confusion were everywhere in the publishing industry from the mid-80s. The era of "free trade in books," inaugurated in 1852 by the defeat of the London Booksellers' Committee's attempt to regulate retail prices, had been a period of intense retail price competition, as booksellers discounted new books directly to the public. Indeed, because of this, by 1890, when the London Booksellers' Society was founded, "the complete collapse of retail bookselling" seemed imminent.[6] At the same time, the circulating libraries' profits were diminishing because the number of novels published (and the space required to stock three-deckers) was increasing faster than the subscription lists, a pressure that was increased as the publishers more often hurried the date of reprinting at a low price.[7] Individual authors such as George Moore demanded that novels be issued at "a purchasable price," so that they might appeal directly to the public, while authors organized into the Society of Authors in 1883, a move which was thought to be provocative, "trade union" behavior.[8] The Education Act of 1870 had obviously changed the conditions of publishing, as did the Berne Convention on international copyright in 1887 and the American "Chace Act" of 1891:

> The decline of the three-decker from the mid-eighties until its death in the mid-nineties is well known to have resulted from differences between British publishers, booksellers, circulating libraries and the Authors' Society. But it is not altogether fanciful to detect a contributory cause in American copyright law. After 1891 the British publisher was naturally reluctant to go to the expense of printing three volumes at home of a novel which had also to be manufactured as a single volume in America.[9]

From the point of view of the production of books those are but contributions or responses to the larger, conjunctural crisis; the prevailing arrangement, the relations of production and distribution, were clearly blocking realization of the potential for the production of commodity-texts. The crisis entailed changing the system while retaining control; the problem was who was to inherit control of the production of books, and the answer, of course, was the capitalist publishers.

This is not to say that the publishers conspired to establish a new hegemony. Just as Mudie's decision in 1894, and the concurrence of W. H. Smith, had been decisions on the level of "the firm"—Arthur Mudie had written to Bentley that the three-volume novel "serves no useful purpose whatever in our business"[10]—so the decision in 1890 to enforce "net" prices on books had initially been that of one firm, Macmillan (indeed of one man, Frederick Macmillan), and had been addressed specifically to "the evils of underselling and to the possibilities of curing them."[11] A good deal of the ideological strength of Macmillan's proposal in his 6 March 1890 letter to *The Bookseller* derived simply from his invoking "the rationality of the individual firm."[12] As he explained in his letter, Macmillan acted in response to "a number of private communications" from booksellers, and his course of action was to be entirely within the rights of an individual firm. He proposed "a general reduction of retail prices, and the diminution of trade allowances to such a point that the full published ["net"] price may reasonably be demanded and obtained from purchasers," with the further stipulation that Macmillan and Co. would allow trade terms (i.e. even the "diminished" trade allowance) only to "booksellers who would undertake not to break prices."[13] Thus, unlike the booksellers' scheme of forty years earlier to enforce existing high prices by collectively boycotting undersellers, Macmillan's plan satisfied the ideological norms of "free trade," by first enabling him to lower the artificially high price of his books, and by then allowing him to do business only with those booksellers whom he chose. Moreover, initially not all books were to be sold "net"; some were to be sold as "subject" books, subject, that is, to discounting by the bookseller, so that, here too, the charge of an unwarranted, total control was evaded. The crucial managerial decisions as to which books were to be sold "net," and which "subject," were of course, to rest with the publisher (this power was to allow the entrepreneurial experimentation of the next two decades, to which I shall return later). Macmillan's action in the 1890s was not collusive but exemplary, and when his carefully calculated risk in selecting Alfred Marshall's *Principles of Economics* as his first net book proved as successful as he had hoped, other publishers also were prepared to set net prices for books. In 1895 the Associated Booksellers of Great Britain and Ireland was founded (succeeding the London Booksellers) "to support . . . the principle of a net price for books."[14] The Publishers' Association was formed in the same year, and by 1899 the Net Book Agreement had been adopted by the two associations and by the Society of Authors and went into effect the next year.[15] The Net Book Agreement had established a new, consensual "terms of trade"; Frederick Macmillan proudly referred to it in 1924 as "the Magna Charta of the book trade."[16]

But if the Net Book Agreement was the book trade's Magna Charta, the "Book War" was its war of liberation, the struggle by which the new publishing structure established itself ideologically. That controversy from 1906 to 1908 over the practices of the *Times* Book Club both clarified the new terms which the agreement had instituted and showed that they could be defended publicly, that the new ideological consensus was one which not even the *Times* could subvert. The *Times* had been in financial difficulty in the early 1900s: for several years neither its sales, the amount of advertising, nor its profits had grown. Moberly Bell, its editor, believed that it had become impossible to make the *Times* pay, both because he believed that it was increasingly difficult to make even an ordinary newspaper pay and because the *Times* "was neither an ordinary newspaper nor produced in ordinary conditions."[17] In 1898, assisted by two American entrepreneurs, Bell had attempted to boost circulation by marketing a cheap reprint of the ninth edition of the *Encyclopaedia Britannica* in installments. When this scheme proved profitable, the same promoters founded the *Times* Book Club, a subscription system in which a "discount subscriber" to the *Times* might borrow any book, three volumes at a time, delivered and collected without charge anywhere in London. Also, and this was the real issue of the "Book War," the subscriber-member was entitled to purchase at a large discount any book previously borrowed.[18] Clearly, this promise to discount "unspoilt" copies a few weeks after publication side-stepped the Net Book Agreement; as a publishers' pamphlet argued, "a 'spoiled' copy is everywhere recognized as a copy which . . . cannot be sold as a new or fresh copy," and "an 'unspoilt' copy is, therefore, equivalent to a new copy."[19] Edward Bell, the president of the Publishers' Association, stated their case:

It is obvious that such announcements were calculated to divert custom from the regular dealers in new books, and in the case of net books, amounted to an evasion, if not an actual infringement of the Net Book Agreement.[20]

The *Times,* of course, tried to define the terms of the struggle in its own interest:

> Fifty-four years ago the publishers attempted, by restrictions on trade, to maintain the high prices then charged for books, and to create for their own profit a firm and permanent monopoly, to be maintained at the expense of the public.
>
> Today the publishers . . . are trying to control not only the price of new books, but the price of second-hand books.[21]

But the prices were no longer "high," and the issue was no longer perceived as "monopoly"; the new terms of trade constituted by the Net Book Agreement seemed untouched by the *Times'* charges that while they did not formally constitute a trust they nevertheless allowed the publishers to be "so solidly organized that they act as against all outsiders with the unanimity and precision of a trust."[22] "Exclusive dealing" was the term helpfully suggested by the judge in the libel case which so undermined the position of the *Times* and its Book Club.[23] The Booksellers' Association and the Society of Authors[24] sided with the publishers, and when Lord Northcliffe secretly bought the *Times* in 1908 he quickly sued for peace. The settlement not only reasserted the Net Book Agreement "without any modification," but added a provision for a "close time" on Book Club copies, six months on net books and three months on subject books, during which they might not be sold as "second-hand." Thus ended, as Frederick Macmillan recalls, "in a manner most satisfactory to me and to publishers in general, one of the most remarkable quarrels in the annals of the Book Trade."[25] The satisfactory result was to establish the Net Book Agreement definitively as the "terms of trade," and thus to allow the victorious publishers fully to explore the possibilities in these newly structured relations of production and distribution of books.

But what had happened in the book trade was simply what had happened generally in the production and distribution of commodities at the turn of the century. The end of the last and the beginning of the new century, says a standard history of the subject, "saw a decisive change from competitive to associative organization in almost every trade in Britain," as a new form of monopolist organization established itself in retail trade associations like the Publishers' Association. This was "merely a continuation of the development of cartels and trusts in British industry,"[26] in the same way that the Net Book Agreement transformed the hegemony of the three-decker/lending library arrangement by concentrating control in the hands of publishers. The purpose of the agreement (indeed, the "kernel" of all trade associations' policy) was "to eliminate certain phases of competition by imposing on their members certain regulations of trading,"[27] that is, to eliminate "underselling" by

enforcing net prices for books. But the practices of retail price maintenance have a more direct bearing on our understanding of publishing practice following the Net Book Agreement. Hermann Levy discusses the way that manufacturers, given "general agreement about price levels and certain trading conditions," are now constantly faced with the need to devise "new methods of securing [their] retailing customers," and a primary means is that extension of the principle of a *patent* which creates "branded goods," to be sold at advertised (or in the publishers' term, "net") prices.[28] "Manufacturers," Levy writes, "have always been in search of means of creating for their goods some reputation-value, apart from cheapness or quality":

> The manufacturer who wishes to exploit the mass demand of modern retail markets . . . must broaden the sphere of patented goods into a field where the quasi-monopolist feature is not made up by legal rights but by the reputation and good will which his article gains. . . . Generally the manufacturer finds it necessary to approach the consumer directly, and so to create for himself a reliable mass market of the "unknown" customer. If this end is achieved the relationship between manufacturer and retailer may be reversed; it is the manufacturer who by controlling this article of reputation has gained the upper hand.[29]

In the case of publishing, the "legal rights" Levy refers to might be compared to the old arrangement with the lending libraries. But in the new "direct" arrangement, control has passed to the publishers; "the key to the situation," writes another commentator, "lies in the manufacturer's hands."[30] The practice of "branded goods" permits manufacturers not only to "discipline price cutters"[31] but, more importantly, directly "to capture the retailer's customers" by creating what these economic historians call "consumer insistence": "it is this 'consumer insistence' which is intended to create the quasi-monopoly value of the brand."[32] Thus, while publishing may be "a type of business distinct from others in many respects,"[33] in many other respects it is very similar, these practices of retail price maintenance generally explaining the early distinction between "net" and "subject" books, the dynamics of book production under the Net Book Agreement, and the reasons for finally including, in 1914, novels among net books. Since the economics of the "branded article" conform fundamentally with "the necessities of modern mass distribution in general,"[34] in book publishing the "branded article" may be seen as a translation of the function of "class" categories in the "new journalism," interpellating "consumer insistence" from a "class" of "unknown customers." The translation, the ideological categories, and the practices specific to book production may be seen only occasionally in the few historical studies, but quite vividly in publishers' notices in the trade journals of the 1890s and early 1900s.

Alfred Marshall's *Principles of Economics* ("2 vols. 8vo. Vol I. price 12 *s.* 6 *d.* net"), the first net book published by Macmillan, was announced in the *Bookseller* for 7 August 1890, five months after Frederick Macmillan had made his plan public.[35] During the approach to Christmas 1890,

Macmillan offered several more net books of various kinds, with different formats and prices: Lockyer's *Meteoric Hypothesis* (demy octavo, 17 *s.* net) and Bowdler Buckton's *Monograph of the British Cicadae* (2 vols., vol 1, 33/6 net) on 1 November, and then on 15 November two expensive, large paper, super royal 8vo. limited editions: Mrs. Oliphant's *Royal Edinburgh* and a reprint of *The Vicar of Wakefield* with 150 illustrations.[36] On 15 December, Macmillan listed a similar, seven-guinea limited edition and then, in the Christmas number of the *Publishers' Circular,* they advertised a *Library Reference Atlas of the World* (£2. 12 *s.* net), some reprinted works by Lewis Carroll at 2/6, 4*s.,* 4/6, and 7/6 (all net) and a "pocket edition" of Tennyson's *Poetical Works,* morocco binding, gilt edges, 7/6 net.[37] From August 1890 to January 1891, Macmillan had introduced about twenty net books, in various formats at different prices.[38] By April 1891, Heinemann was also advertising net books, and in August 1891 Cassell's announced with some fanfare a "new library of popular works at a 'net price,' to be known as 'Cassell's International Novels.'"[39] This last venture seems to have been premature, perhaps one of that firm's "miscalculations" at that period, for by Christmas 1892 all of the novels in the series, originally priced at 7/6 net, were advertised at six shillings each, with no mention of net prices.[40]

We can see very clearly from this the trial and error through which the system of book distribution was reconstituted in the interest of those who controlled production, the publishers. At the inaugural dinner of the London Booksellers' Society in 1890, David Stott, in the chair, had called Macmillan's recent proposal "a step in the right direction," but his notion of what "net books" might mean was limited by his bookseller's perspective:

> There are some books a bookseller cannot sell, and no persuasion or blandishment can influence the customer to buy them. I refer to books on special subjects— technical or specially scientific books, for instance, such as we only purchase when they are ordered. . . .
>
> But on the other hand I protest against any publisher attempting to do the same thing with cheap books. . . .[41]

And in 1894, the *Bookseller,* responding in "Trade Gossip" to letters to the *Times* about net book prices, was again to specify "the application of the system to certain select classes of books, especially those published at a high price, or which appeal only to a limited class of readers."[42] Macmillan's choice of net books in those early months was clearly to some extent dictated by those considerations; but their very first choice for a net book had been intended from the start to test a more subtle possibility. "It was important that the book chosen should be a good one," Frederick Macmillan recalled,

> because if the first net book did not sell, its failure would certainly be attributed to its *netness* and not to its quality. It so happened that in the spring of 1890, we had in preparation a book on *The Principles of Economics,* by Professor Alfred Marshall, the well-known

economist and then Professor of Political Economy at the University of Cambridge. There was little doubt that this book would at once take a leading place in the literature of Economics, and it suggested itself as a most appropriate subject for the experiment we wished to try.[43]

Here we have the beginning of an experiment in selling books as a new kind of "branded goods"; rather than appealing to a known, limited market for a commodity-book, with Mrs. Oliphant's *Royal Edinburgh,* say, or to the market for gilt edges and morocco bindings, Macmillan is here testing an assumed "quality," a "reputation-value," as a way of interpellating the "unknown" reader prepared to buy a commodity-text. Books advertised as "net" in these first years appear to be of these two types: either they are the sort of books which David Stott and other booksellers could not sell generally, on abstruse topics or in special formats or bindings, or they are books which by some sort of "reputation-value" may be hoped to interpellate an unspecified "class" of unknown readers. Thus "net" books might be either commodity-books or commodity-texts; "subject" books remained commodity-books, subject ultimately to a bookseller's persuasion and blandishment, as well as discount. But it was the possibility of extra profit which was opened up in the "net" category which publishers were to explore and exploit directly.

To assert, then, that "at first the net system was only applied to high priced books, especially books selling at more than 6 *s.,*" is inaccurate, but more importantly it is an assertion which arises out of "free market" assumptions, based on the simple efficacy of "demand." The net system was at first applied only to high-priced books, Russi Jal Taraporevala writes, "presumably because the demand for these books was considered by publishers to be relatively inelastic":

> Hence the increase in price, due to "netting," was not expected to reduce total sales substantially. On the other hand cheaper books, for which the demand was presumably thought to have been more elastic, came within the net system only in its later years.[44]

The problematic of a presumed elasticity/inelasticity of "demand" only obscures the dynamics of the net book system; from the point of view of the production of books (rather than "demand"), the publishers may be seen to have eventually so expanded net books as sophisticated "branded goods" that "demand" became a controlled effect of production. The "reputation-value" at the core of "branded goods" lay in an author's name, as with the "well-known" Professor Marshall, interpellating unknown readers of commodity-texts, creating a new audience, although ideologically it might be explained as "satisfying a demand." Publishers were now in a position in the economic structure to undertake in a controlled way the creation of the kinds of mass audiences which the different careers of Charles Dickens and Charles Knight, seventy-five years earlier, had shown to be accessible to a new literary mode of production, by exploiting systematically the power of a commodity-text to interpellate an infinity of unknown subjects. Neither an author, a printer, nor a bookseller could afford

> to take the risk of promoting books . . . on the scale that was now necessary. Older publishing houses . . . rose to greater prominence, and new ones . . . soon achieved leading positions in the book trade.[45]

Hence "the mad quest for the golden seller" that Henry Holt described in "The Commercialization of Literature" in 1905, "the mad payment to the man who has once produced it, and the mad advertising of doubtful books in the hope of creating the seller."[46]

Raymond Williams has approached this moment of "a bouncing cheeky finally rampant commercialism" from a wholly different direction, concluding nonetheless that "what happened between the 1890s and 1914 is of great critical importance for the novel." He suggests that 1895, the year in which Thomas Hardy stopped writing novels, might serve to mark "a new situation in the English novel." We can see at that time a "visibly altering would," an "emerging deciding dividing world," which manifests itself in the history of the novel in the separating out of "'individual' or 'psychological' fiction on the one hand and 'social' or 'sociological' fiction on the other," and in the coming of "literature," that "working, working over, working through, by the last of the great men, the last hero, the novelist."[47] The editors of the *New Left Review*, interviewing Williams nine years after he wrote this account, were uneasy with it, pointing out that he did not really explore the reasons for the decisive "caesura in the form of the novel."[48] If Williams, in 1970, had been unwilling to associate the "disturbance" with some system, "call it sociology or materialism or technologico-Benthamism"[49] (F. R. Leavis's pejorative formulas in those years), in 1979 he is much more precise about "the political emergence of a new working class, and the cultural segregation of a new bourgeois order, after the 1880s." He speaks not only of the "very deep and successful reorganization of bourgeois cultural and educational institutions," "integrated and confident," insulated within "increasingly standardized and masculine institutions," but he specifies the apparatuses of these ideologies: educational institutions, "a fully extended bourgeois press," and "the modernization of publishing."[50]

It is there, indeed, in those apparatuses, that a materialist explanation of what is signified by the "caesura in the form of the novel" must be based. The particular forms of "modernization" I have been analyzing are not merely new "marketing techniques" but rather a necessary extension of the transformation of the relations of production which constituted fully capitalist book publishing. The process initiated in 1890 by Frederick Macmillan, explored in his own list and expanded to those of other publishers, was precisely the "emerging deciding dividing" process of which Williams writes. It arrives (in passing, of course), as net books become increasingly the rule, in increasingly integrated, confident, standardized, and masculine structures

of capitalist control, "masculine" not only because of the list of agents (Macmillan, John Murray, William Heinemann, or Edward Arnold) but also because of the patriarchal necessity of control, of centralized, purposeful planning (sometimes described as "risk-taking") in the production of commodity-texts. For the disruptions in the form of the novel were produced by these transformations of the relations of novel production; if "the parting of the ways" (Williams's chapter heading in *The English Novel*) may be described on an ideal level as the separating of psychological from sociological fiction, from the point of view of production the separation was determined in the last instance by those very forces which determined the separation of "net" from "subject" books. Even new novels, until 1914 usually sold subject to discount, could not entirely escape "netness," those forces determining the overall net/subject structure, for the whole production process, as well as each sector of it, was inevitably in an overdetermined relationship to the "visibly altering world," the "quite fundamental changes in the economic situation," such as scientific management and the revival of capital export, which were producing also the new unionism, the crisis in the London housing market and in the growth of the suburbs, and, in 1903, the Women's Social and Political Union.[51]

Edward Arnold was one of the first of the new names in publishing in the nineties; although the firm became noted for publishing the standard school books required after the Education Act, fiction was "not uncommon under this imprint" early in the century.[52] Forster came to Arnold with *A Room with a View* in 1908. His first two novels had been published by William Blackwood. Forster had sent a short manuscript entitled "Monteriano" to *Blackwood's Magazine* in 1905 and, as he wrote to his mother, Blackwood offered to publish it in volume form:

> the terms they offer are not at all good—I have written trying to do better, and meantime am trying to find out whether Blackwoods as *publishers* are a good firm, as though I dont mind much about money it's important to be in the hands of people who will advertise you well. Methuen and Heinemann are the firms I should have naturally tried first. The title has to be changed, which is very sad, but I see their point of view.[53]

Blackwood's point of view was that the name "Monteriano" would be detrimental to the sale of the book; a friend of Forster's suggested "Where Angels Fear to Tread" and Blackwood agreed that the change would improve the novel's "already slight chances of success."[54] Forster remained with Blackwood for *The Longest Journey* (1907) but switched to Arnold with *A Room With a View*; the reasons for the change are unknown.[55] In March 1909 Forster sent Arnold a synopsis and "a rough draft" of thirty chapters of *Howards End*.[56] Oliver Stallybrass, the editor of the Abinger Edition of the novels, notes that the firm's readers and Arnold himself were bothered by Helen's sexual encounter with Leonard Bast, perhaps having that episode in mind when they suggested shortening the novel. A month later, when the novel was in proof, Forster indicated to Arnold some agreement about Helen:

I was much struck by your original criticism, and tried to do what I could, but the episode had worked itself into the plot inextricably. I hope however that the public may find the book convincing on other counts.[57]

Edward Arnold published *Howards End* on 18 October 1910, 6 *s.*, crown 8vo., in 2,500 copies with further impressions of 1,000, 3,000 and 2,500 copies in November 1910, and 1,000 more in December; 9,959 copies were sold.[58] P. N. Furbank describes the novel's reception: "The book hit the note of the time. . . . For the first time the word 'great' was bandied about . . . ," and he quotes the *Daily Mail* reviewer's emphasis on the novel's "coherence and connectedness," saying that "only connect" might be Forster's motto "not only for his book but for his method of work":

> the fitting of the perception of little things with the perception of universal things; consistency, totality, *connection*. Mr. Forster has written a *connected novel*.[59]

Clearly one "note of the time" which *Howards End* hit is indicated by the appreciation in the contemporary press for the injunction to "connect," a note which paradoxically seems timeless, given the attention paid by later critics to Forster's concern with "the relationships, and the possibility of reconciliation, between certain pairs of opposites." For just as *A Room with a View* is said to have "resonated" with "interlocking sets of contrasting pairs," so in general Forster is seen to define problems "dualistically," to explore "dichotomies," to find "some new and fruitful antithesis by which to set his convictions in play," and in *Howards End* to unfold an Arnoldian "series of polarities."[60] What is significant is the ideological attraction, for contemporary and later critics alike, of Forster's project. In 1910-11 it was perhaps welcomed as a "liberal" response to perceived "real" divisions in society between "the democratic surface and the private core, the People and the people who counted," or between "individualism (and imperialism) as represented by the Conservative Party and collectivism as typified by the burgeoning labour movement," or between men and women.[61] Since then, as "liberalism" has declined as a public political stance, Forster's ideological position has been taken more privately, as "moral realism," or "judicious imperturbability," a "whole style of patient, synoptic comment on social issues."[62] *Howards End* thus develops its epigraph thematically in its repeated reference to Matthew Arnold's advice to see life steadily and see it whole, and this moral effort is further associated with the place, Howards End, one of "these English farms" where, "if anywhere, one might see life steadily and see it whole, group in one vision its transitoriness and its eternal youth, connect—connect without bitterness until all men are brothers."[63] This vision of connectedness is presented metaphorically again and again in *Howards End,* as when the narrator demonstrates the "wisest course" for showing a foreigner England: to stand on the summit of the final section of the Purbeck Hills, "then system after system of our island would roll together under his feet," and as Forster directs "the trained eye" to these systems,

the reason fails, like a wave on the Swanage beach; the imagination swells, spreads and deepens, until it becomes geographic and encircles England.

(164-65)

Yet such a vision, such imagination, is not accessible to the lower-middle-class Leonard Bast—in a moment of despair Leonard realizes "to see life steadily and to see it whole was not for the likes of him" (52)—nor was it available to a calculating businessman, "who saw life more steadily, though with the steadiness of the half-closed eye" (320). Margaret Schlegel, on the other hand, believing that it is impossible to see "modern life" steadily, had chosen "to see it whole" (158). The novel's "patient synoptic comment" is here vague and ambiguous, the imaginative vision which is its theme being finally only "an impossible, yet heroic, effort to 'see life steadily and see it whole,'"[64] which echoes both wistfully and a little shrilly in the defensive naiveté of its final words:

> "The field's cut!" Helen cried excitedly—"The big meadow! We've seen to the very end, and it'll be such a crop of hay as never!"

(340)

But if Helen's outburst embodies the thematic uncertainty in *Howards End,* ignored or accepted by contemporary and later critics alike, its language, as in the final utterance, also embodies a more profoundly historical contradiction, in the novel's interpellation of its reader-subject. We, too, have "seen to the very end," of *Howards End*; but, then, who are "we"? The novel asks this question, historically crucial, on several levels, some of them more self-reflexive than others. "Who's 'we'?" Henry Wilcox asks his son, "My boy, pray, who's 'we'?" (281) and Wilcox is himself later asked by Margaret, as he is attempting to ensure her personal loyalty, "Who is 'we'?" (301). But in 1910 that question was central for the novelist too; it had a determinate historical weight. For while *Howards End* was published by Arnold "subject to discount," Longman, Chatto, and others were already publishing new fiction "net," in various formats and prices.[65] Forster was inevitably implicated in that continuing project to establish the new structures of net-book publishing; in 1909 he had joined with other authors in an undertaking "not to publish an edition of any novel first published at the price of 6 *s.* in a cheap form at any time within two years from the date of its first publication."[66] And whether a novel was published "net" or "subject," the reading audience as a whole was being reconstituted by the relations of production we have discussed. A novelist might not necessarily be attempting to interpellate a mass audience, but as the relations of production moved ever more towards that possibility it became increasingly difficult for a novelist to imagine who or where another, more specific audience might be. In *Howards End* this difficulty, the determinate presence of the Net Book Agreement, registers itself in the awkward indeterminacy of the narrator's indefinite pronouns, "we" and "one."

The characters in *Howards End* most often use the indefinite "we" in a conventional way, "in general statements in which the speaker includes those whom he addresses, his contemporaries, his fellow countrymen, or the like" (*OED*), as in Mrs. Munt's "what *we* are doing in music" (33), or sometimes by asserting a specifically upper-middle-class "we," as when she wonders if the Wilcoxes are "our sort" (6). Similarly, within the created Schlegel world, "one knows what foreigners are" (12), "one" being "anyone of everybody, including (and in later language often specially meaning) the speaker himself" (*OED*); thus Mrs. Wilcox gently rebukes her son: "one doesn't ask plain questions" (19). But, outside the Schlegel/Wilcox world, the narrator's "we" or "one" is far less confident. It may include the speaker, fellow countrymen, and the like, but the "like" may shift uneasily to include unknown reader/subjects. The narrator's "we" is often clearly English, as when the London railway termini are described as "our" gates to the provinces (9), or when "two members of our race" play at "Capping Families" (18). But while "we" are also occasionally clearly upper-middle-class—"we" visit the country on weekends, and "we" look back with disquietude to the "elder race" which once lived there (266)—the interpellation of that class is often undercut, complicated by a not-quite-assured irony which in its uncertainty acknowledges values and subjects more inclusive and urgent than class-values and class-subjects. Leonard Bast's flat in Camelia Road contains a photograph of "a young lady named Jacky" which had been taken "at the time when young ladies named Jacky were often photographed with their mouths open." Jacky's photograph and smile are condescended to further, but then the tone is disrupted just as the narrator moves directly to enlist the reader:

> Take my word for it, that smile was simply stunning, and it is only you and I who will be fastidious, and complain that true joy begins in the eyes, and that the eyes of Jacky did not accord with her smile, but were anxious and hungry.
>
> (46)

Who, indeed, constitute the "you and I" here, revised from the "you or I" of the manuscript precisely to be inclusive?[67] The narrator is, at first, still ironical about the "stunning" smile, then, as "you and I" is introduced, "fastidious" (and still more ironically "captious" in the manuscript [43]), but then erases "our" ironic privilege by admitting it, as "we" contradictorily acknowledge the anxiety and hunger. At a moment like this the text's "we," the "everybody" which includes "anybody," tries jerkily to expand to include even nobodies like Jacky.

There are other such moments of narrative uncertainty, where "our" uneasiness about who "we" are is signaled by a contradictory indefiniteness or a limp gesture towards inclusiveness.[68] The description, or more accurately the narrator's appropriation, of Helen's experience of "panic and emptiness" in Beethoven's Fifth Symphony concludes with the comment, when "Beethoven chose to make all right in the end," that "that is why one can trust Beethoven when he says other things" (31-32). The shift to the present tense marks the intensity of the interpellation of "one," yet

the confidence of that interpellation is immediately dissipated by the indefinite openness of "other things"; "one" (everybody) can trust Beethoven, the text seems to say, so long as that "one" is prepared to grant "one" (anyone) a blank check.[69] A similar contradictory pull disrupts the opening sentences of Chapter 6: "We are not concerned with the very poor. They are unthinkable and only to be approached by the statistician or the poet" (43). Here the "we" is simply the community of narrator and present reader, but "unthinkable" intrudes again a class position which then quickly is softened by being deferred, placed within the thematic dualism of reason and imagination. But the whole of the structure of Chapter 6 is fraught with the indefiniteness of the audience whom the narrator attempts to interpellate. The chapter addresses precisely the division between rich and poor, "gentlefolk" and "the abyss," and how Leonard Bast is placed between them— Leonard "stood at the extreme verge of gentility. He was not in the abyss but he could see it" (43)—but more importantly the chapter struggles formally with how this division is to be thought. In his flat in Camelia Road Leonard begins to read Chapter 2 of the second volume of *The Stones of Venice*, the "famous" chapter (46) in which Ruskin crosses the lagoon to the islands of Torcello and Murano, and as Leonard listens to "the rich man speaking . . . from his gondola" (46)—"Was there anything to be learned from this fine sentence? Could he adapt it to the needs of daily life?" (47)—the narrator points out the irrelevance of Ruskin to Leonard's daily life. With all its command of "admonition and poetry" (46),

> the voice in the gondola rolled on, piping melodiously of Effort and Self-Sacrifice, full of high purpose, full of beauty, full even of sympathy and the love of men, yet somehow eluding all that was actual and insistent in Leonard's Life. For it was the voice of one who had never been dirty or hungry, and had not guessed successfully what dirt and hunger are.
>
> (47)

What is at first striking in this passage is how the narrator constructs a "Ruskin" so as to imply by contrast, however indistinctly, the desired attitude to the poor; whoever the interpellated subject may be, it is first of all to be distinguished from the text's "Ruskin" ("well-fed Ruskin" in the manuscript [43]). The textual revisions show how the necessary "Ruskin" was constructed: the original voice of "a man who had never guessed what dirt and hunger feel like" (and earlier, "what such sensations may be") is rewritten so that not only are "feelings" and "sensations" replaced by what dirt and hunger "are," but "a man" is generalized to the almost indefinite "one," who may have "not" (instead of "never") guessed these realities. The text has thus moved away from an imagined Ruskin's personal experience to the question of an attitude, the attitude of a less definite "one," perhaps including the reader or the narrator, who had not yet but might still guess successfully what are the actualities of a life like Leonard's.

The chapter continues for a paragraph, alternating Leonard's reading of Ruskin's aesthetic aspirations with the narrator's commentary. Jacky then returns to the flat and after their supper of cheap, ersatz food the chapter concludes with Leonard going back to finish his chapter of *The Stones of Venice*:

> Ruskin had visited Torcello by this time, and was ordering his gondoliers to take him to Murano. It occurred to him, as he glided over the whispering lagoons, that the power of Nature could not be shortened by the folly, nor her beauty altogether saddened by the misery, of such as Leonard.

(53)

Again, the text's discordances, as well as the effort of revision, trace the struggle to interpellate a broadly inclusive vantage point for an unknown subject. Ruskin, in his own sentence about "the power of Nature," had spoken of "the misery of man," his gondola having passed the principal cemetery of Venice.[70] Forster had changed "man" to "Leonard" in the three earlier versions of this paragraph, but each time he had also included a phrase, finally deleted, about Ruskin's meditation: ". . . and this comforted him"; ". . . and he was comforted"; "this comforted him" (manuscript, 49, 50). To have retained this final phrase would have heightened the anomaly of "Leonard" in Ruskin's sentence because it would have pointed the text back to Ruskin's supposed feelings. What the text now does, instead of focusing ironically on a cheaply comforted Ruskin, is to conclude its effort to construct a subject-position, different from Ruskin's, from which one might think the almost unthinkable predicament of "such as Leonard," a position which interpellates an unknown subject, with indistinct class predispositions: gentlefolk perhaps, or those obliged to pretend they are gentlefolk, or those who are neither, but merely "unknown."

This effort which the text of *Howards End* so often makes tentatively to open up the narrator's "we," or the indefinite "one," to an "anyone" of a determinedly inclusive "everybody," is much more historically specific than being merely "the fag-end of Victorian liberalism."[71] It is the effort which the new literary mode of production demands of "net" books, but also of "subject" books (like most novels in 1910), as the new literary market is itself "produced." For while Forster assuredly did not set himself in 1909-10 to write a best-seller in *Howards End,* he nevertheless equally surely wrote within a determinate structure of book production, developed over the preceding twenty years, which enabled publishers to use the new means of production to produce commodity-texts. The "bastsellerism" and "bestsellerdom" to which John Sutherland refers are but ideological labels for the full development in capitalist book production of that internal drive towards "total commercial rationalization" and the "hectic change and turnover" in which capitalism realizes its "general formula."[72] Sutherland finds "good historical reasons" why the modern novel is "necessarily tied to the wheels of progressive technology, commercial management and the dictatorship of the consumer."[73] I have denied the "dictatorship" of the consumer, insisting instead on the control of

the capitalist publisher, but otherwise I have detailed the material conditions of Sutherland's necessities and traced that historical process in a text, not even of a best-seller, but of *Howards End.* For the audience of the old, hegemonic literary mode of production had disappeared with the three-decker; readers were being reagglomerated as "consumers" of commodity-texts by the new, rampant, fully capitalist literary mode of production, with the publishers' sway stretching past the bookseller to "capture the retailer's customers." And because these powerful lines of control extended themselves through the production process the interpellated subject was also transformed. Whatever Forster's political or social "liberalism," whatever its placement within Edwardian ideology generally, the reader addressed by *Howards End,* that novel's peculiarly indistinct interpellated subject, was inevitably determined by these material relations of its production. In the ambiguity of its constructed reader-subject *Howards End* bears the impress of its historical mode of production, encodes within itself, in the ways we have seen, its own record of "how, by whom and for whom it was produced."[74]

Notes

1. Guinevere L. Griest, *Mudie's Circulating Library and the Victorian Novel* (Bloomington: Indiana University Press, 1970), 209-11.

2. Royal A. Gettmann, *A Victorian Publisher: A Study of the Bentley Papers* (Cambridge: Cambridge University Press, 1960), 257.

3. Gareth Stedman Jones, *Outcast London* (Harmondsworth: Penguin, 1976), 152.

4. Richard Altick, *The English Common Reader* (Chicago: University of Chicago Press, 1957), 313.

5. Quoted in Griest, *Mudie's,* 7, and Gettman, *Victorian Publisher,* 245.

6. W. G. Corp, *Fifty Years: A Brief Account of the Associated Booksellers of Great Britain and Ireland, 1895-1945* (Oxford: Basil Blackwell, 1945), 3; see also David Stott, "The Decay of Bookselling," *Nineteenth Century* 36 (1894):932-38.

7. Arthur Waugh, *A Hundred Years of Publishing* (London: Chapman and Hall, 1930), 192; Griest, *Mudie's,* 169-70.

8. Gettmann, *Victorian Publisher,* 256; Griest, *Mudie's,* 189; John Goode has analyzed the place of the Society of Authors in the "more mystified ideology of literary production" in "The Decadent Writer as Producer," in *Decadence and the 1890s,* ed. Ian Fletcher (London: Edward Arnold, 1979), 117-21.

9. Simon Nowell-Smith, *International Copyright Law and the Publisher in the Reign of Queen Victoria* (Oxford: Clarendon Press, 1968), 82.

10. Quoted in Griest, *Mudie's,* 173.

11. Frederick Macmillan, *The Net Book Agreement 1899 and the Book War 1906-1908* (Glasgow: Robert Maclehose, 1924), 4.

12. For the place of this ideology in late Victorian economic thinking, see E. J. Hobsbawm, *Industry and Empire* (Harmondsworth: Penguin, 1968), 187f.

13. Macmillan, *The Net Book Agreement,* 6, 16.

14. W. G. Corp, *Fifty Years,* 5; the London Booksellers' Society had already, in 1894, submitted to selected publishers a memorial supporting net prices. Russi Jal Taraporevala, *Competition and Control in the Book Trade, 1850-1939* (Bombay: D. B. T. Taraporevala and Sons, 1969), 36.

15. R. J. L. Kingsford, *The Publishers' Association, 1896-1946* (Cambridge: Cambridge University Press, 1970), 5-17.

16. Macmillan, *The Net Book Agreement,* 30.

17. [Anon.], *The History of the Times,* vol 3, *The Twentieth Century Test, 1884-1912,* (London: The Times, 1947), 441.

18. *The History of the Times,* 443-48.

19. [Anon.], *"The Times" and the Publishers* (London: privately printed for the Publishers' Association, 1906), 11-12, 7.

20. Edward Bell, "The Times Book Club and the Publishers' Association, an Account of the 'Book War' of 1906-1908," in Macmillan, *The Net Book Agreement,* 31.

21. [Anon.], *Publishers and the Public: Reprinted From the Times of 1852* (London: The Times, 1906), Note, 1.

22. [Anon.], *The History of the Book War: Fair Book Prices Versus Publishers' Trust Prices* (London: The Times, 1907), 36.

23. *John and A. H. Hallam Murray v. Walter and Others* (London: printed for private circulation, John Murray, 1908), 84.

24. The *Times* attacked novelists as "the curled darlings of the fiction market [who] came forth from the lotosland through the looking-glass where they dwell withdrawn from the vulgar battle of commerce, or emerged from the vapourous private Utopias wherein they excogitate phosphorescent millenniums." *The History of the Book War,* 32.

25. Macmillan, *The Net Book Agreement,* 75, 77.

26. Hermann Levy, *Retail Trade Associations: A New Form of Monopolist Organization in Britain* (London: Kegan Paul, Trench, Trubner and Co., 1942), 20, 7.

27. Ibid., 5.

28. Ibid., 63-64.

29. Ibid., 65-66.

30. B. S. Yamey, "The Origins of Retail Price Maintenance: A Study of Three Branches of the Retail Trade," *EJ* 62 (1952):528.

31. Yamey, "Origins," 527-28.

32. Levy, *Retail Trade Associations,* 67, 70.

33. Ibid., 15.

34. Ibid., 71.

35. *The Bookseller,* 383 (7 August 1890):869 (hereafter referred to as *B,* with number, date, and page).

36. *The Publishers' Circular* (1 November 1890):1450; (15 November 1890):1525 (hereafter referred to as *PC*).

37. *PC* (15 December 1890):1622; (Christmas Number, 1890):106, 108.

38. Ian Norrie says sixteen in 1890. F. A. Mumby and Ian Norrie, *Publishing and Bookselling,* 5th ed. rev. (London: Cape, 1974), 244.

39. *B,* 404 (Apr. 1891); *PC* (1 Aug. 1891), 917; Frederick Macmillan lists the publishers in 1891 who were publishing net books, in *The Net Book Agreement,* 18.

40. Simon Nowell-Smith, *The House of Cassell, 1848-1958* (London: Cassell, 1958), 188; *PC* (Christmas Number, 1892):98.

41. *B,* 395 (10 October 1890):1020.

42. *B,* 444 (6 November 1894):1021.

43. Macmillan, *The Net Book Agreement,* 14.

44. Taraporevala, *Competition and Control,* 54.

45. B. W. E. Alford, "Business Enterprise and the Growth of the Commercial Letterpress Printing Industry, 1850-1914," *Business History* 7 (1965):4.

46. Henry Holt, "The Commercialization of Literature," *Atlantic Monthly* 96 (1905):599; the Americans had been listing "best sellers" since 1895. Alice Payne Hackett, *70 Years of Best Sellers: 1895-1965* (New York: R. R. Bowker, 1967), 2.

47. Raymond Williams, *The English Novel from Dickens to Lawrence* (London: Chatto and Windus, 1970), 129, 119, 121, 119-20, 137.

48. *Politics and Letters: Interviews with New Left Review* (London: New Left Books, 1979), 261-62.

49. Williams, *The English Novel,* 130.

50. *Politics and Letters,* 262, 263.

51. Maurice Dobb, *Studies in the Development of Capitalism,* 2d ed. (London: Routledge and Kegan Paul, 1963), 313; Asa Briggs, "The Political Scene," in *Edwardian England, 1901-1914,* ed. S. Nowell-Smith (London: Oxford University Press, 1964), 82; Hobsbawm, *Industry and Empire,* 191.

52. Mumby and Norrie, *Publishing and Bookselling,* 279, 347.

53. Oliver Stallybrass, Editor's Introduction, *Where Angels Fear To Tread,* Abinger ed. (London: Arnold, 1975), xi; *Selected Letters of E. M. Forster,* ed. Mary Lago and P. N. Furbank (London: Collins, 1983), 1:67.

54. Stallybrass, Editor's Introduction, *Angels,* xii; Lago and Furbank, *Letters,* 1:84 n.2.

55. Forster may have decided that "as *publishers,*" Blackwood was not "a good firm," for although he "didn't mind much about money," Blackwood's terms for *Angels* were "really no money at all" (Lago and Furbank, *Letters,* 1:71); on the other hand, Forster may have been uneasy with Blackwood's very public Toryism, or his own company among the "chief Blackwood's writers," who in 1904 included, besides Joseph Conrad, "Zack," Sydney Grier, Mary Skrine, Beatrice Harraden, Storer Clouston, etc. F. D. Tredrey, *The House of Blackwood, 1804-1954* (Edinburgh: Blackwood, 1954), 193.

56. Oliver Stallybrass, Editor's Introduction, *Howards End,* Abinger ed. (London: Arnold, 1973), xii; Edward Arnold had been the reader for *Murray's Magazine* who had refused *Tess of the D'Urbervilles* in 1889 "virtually on the score of its improper explicitness." R. L. Purdy, *Thomas Hardy: A Bibliographical Study* (Oxford: Clarendon Press, 1968), 73.

57. Stallybrass, Editor's Introduction, *Howards End,* xiii.

58. B. J. Kirkpatrick, *A Bibliography of E. M. Forster,* 2d rev. imp. (London: R. Hart-Davies, 1968), 29; Derek Hudson, "Reading," in *Edwardian England,* ed. Nowell-Smith, 315.

59. P. N. Furbank, *E. M. Forster: A Life* (London: Secker and Warburg, 1977), 1:188-89.

60. Stallybrass, Editor's Introduction, *Howards End,* x; Stallybrass, Editor's Introduction, *A Room With a View,* xix; Wilfred Stone, "'Overleaping Class': Forster's Problem in Connection," *Modern Language Quarterly* 39 (1978):386; Cyrus Hoy, "Forster's Metaphysical Novel," *PMLA* 75 (1960):133; Furbank, *Forster,* 1:207; E. Barry McGurk, "Gentlefolk in Philistia: The Influence of Matthew Arnold on E. M. Forster's *Howards End,*" *English Literature in Transition* 15 (1972):215.

61. Asa Briggs, "The Political Scene," 71; Kenneth D. Brown, "The Anti-Socialist Union, 1908-49," in *Essays in Anti-Labour History,* ed., K. D. Brown (London: Macmillan, 1974), 236; Samuel Hynes, *The Edwardian Turn of Mind* (Princeton: Princeton University Press, 1968), 172-211.

62. Lionel Trilling, *E. M. Forster* (London: Hogarth Press, 1951), 17; Peter Widdowson, *E. M. Forster's Howards End: Fiction as History* (London: Sussex University Press, 1977), 26-28; Furbank, *Forster,* 1:210.

63. E. M. Forster, *Howards End,* Abinger ed., ed. Oliver Stallybrass (London: Arnold, 1973), 266; all quotations are from this edition and will be cited in the text.

64. Frederick L. Crews, *E. M. Forster: The Perils of Humanism* (Princeton, N.J.: Princeton University Press, 1962), 34.

65. *B,* 96, n.s. (28 October 1910):52.

66. *The Author* 19, 9 (1 June 1909):241.

67. Oliver Stallybrass, ed., *The Manuscripts of Howards End,* Abinger ed. (London: Arnold, 1973), 43; hereafter referred to as "manuscript."

68. See Widdowson, *Forster's Howards End,* 12.

69. Ibid., 110.

70. John Ruskin, *The Stones of Venice* (vol. 2), in *The Works of John Ruskin,* ed. E. T. Cook and A. Wedderburn (London: George Allen, 1904), 10:37.

71. E. M. Forster, "The Challenge of Our Time," *Two Cheers for Democracy,* Abinger ed., ed. Oliver Stallybrass (London: Arnold, 1972), 54.

72. John Sutherland, *Bestsellers* (London: Routledge and Kegan Paul, 1981), 8; "the valorization of value takes place only within this constantly renewed movement. The movement of capital is therefore limitless." Karl Marx, *Capital,* trans. B. Fowkes (Harmondsworth: Penguin, 1976), 1:253.

73. Sutherland, *Bestsellers,* 21.

74. Terry Eagleton, *Criticism and Ideology* (London: New Left Books, 1976), 48.

Perry Meisel (essay date 1987)

SOURCE: Meisel, Perry. "*Howards End*: Private Worlds and Public Languages." In *The Myth of the Modern: A Study in British Literature and Criticism after 1850,* pp. 166-82. New Haven: Yale University Press, 1987.

[*In the following essay, Meisel explores the influence of major writings and thoughts of the Bloomsbury group on the themes in* Howards End.]

The senior Forster's *Howards End* recapitulates the myth of the modern at the level of story while simultaneously putting it into question at the level of narration. The manifest thematic that leads Forster, quite ironically, to ask that we "Only connect" in the book's epigraph turns out to be evacuated by the conspicuous connections systematically demonstrated by the behavior of its language, especially those between the supposedly sundered realms of the private and the public. Like *The Mayor of Casterbridge,* *Howards End* has a calculating myth of the modern that is the wittingly defensive function of a belatedness that its rhetoric takes into account.

Like *The Waste Land,* however, the novel as a whole appears to be the romance announced at its conclusion, replacing at its terminus the loss of Leonard Bast with the gain of a pastoral child—a lost one now found—who serves as the ideal of a primal harmony that is as wishful as the elf's own ritual invention. Howards End itself, of course, is a garden or paradise regained, with the child's resurrective emergence a symptom of the novel's ironically willful romance rather than a guarantee of the epistemological surety it appears to represent instead. Unlike Hardy's Elizabeth-Jane or Joyce's Rudy/Stephen, Forster's child is still partly privileged in his twin social genealogy, half-rich, half-poor, as though the novel wishes to leave a clear trace of its ambivalence about the impossibility of the ideal of landed or grounded identity that Joyce and Hardy alike plainly eschew. As in Eliot, moreover, the pastoral conclusion emphasizes the ease with which the structure of romance at large contains the redemptive romance of Christianity. But while the two are identifiable ideals for Eliot himself, for Forster they are positioned as structures of irony rather than as assertions of truth. As the book's secular Eden, after all, the property of Howards End is a symbol of that realm beyond culture to which literature may appeal when it is in the kind of crisis required to produce such desire. The book's goals are apparently those "endless levels beyond the grave" (1910:332) that signify an eternal truth represented by the summary figure of "the sacred centre of the field" (335) at the narrative's close. With the "wych-elm" (3) serving as a protective "boundary between the garden and meadow" (3), Forster obviously—perhaps too obviously—grounds a mythical primacy in the figure of the enigmatic Mrs. Wilcox. "'Already in the garden'" (4) in the early morning early in the novel itself, Mrs. Wilcox is located in a fanciful landscape of redemptive origins consonant with her primal beatitude whose light overrides the kind of imaginative despair betokened by Coleridgean twilight or Gastonian dimness. "From the garden," says Forster at the novel's close, "came laughter" (342). The ground or property of Howards End is, in short, consecrated as a center, a home, an origin that the will to modernity uniformly produces as a defense against the belatedness that assails it.

So suspiciously programmatic are Forster's spiritual homologues, however, that not only is Christianity but one token of the generic type of romance. So, too, is the structure of native, pagan religiosity that identifies in sequence the will to modernity in its Renaissance, Romantic, and properly High Modernist forms. Howards End has "goblins" (33-34) as well as a garden, the intimations of Shakespearean romance suggesting in turn the Romantic strategy, as in Blake's early sonnets, of invoking indigenous deities in order to regain original inspiration. By so identifying "folklore" (267) and the "Holy of Holies" as alike "transfigured" (85) in their primacy or simulation of godhead, the novel allows Christian and pagan romance to coalesce. Not surprisingly, then, a "halo" (68) surrounds

Mrs. Wilcox's hands as she lies ill. Like the romance ideals with which she is thematically coincident, she represents, at least in Mr. Wilcox's mind at her funeral, "unvarying virtue" (89), almost absolute "innocence" (89)—in short, a static and eternal ideal of virtue and spirituality, although one that remains in the ground of Howards End even after she dies, since it subsequently transmutes or transfigures itself into Margaret. The origin represented by ground or property—the "end" or telos that Howards End is—is, in the pagan sense, the function of a *genius loci* for which Mrs. Wilcox is but a transient habitation and a name, as Margaret will be too. Mrs. Wilcox's divinity is, of course, a product of the ground of Howards End, not the other way around, its spirit allowing Margaret to become its vessel in her turn, and also situating the novel's overly obvious symbol for lost primacy not in a personality but in actual—not metaphorically philosophical—ground, real estate, property. In fact, once "under the earth" (90), Mrs. Wilcox becomes a double emblem for her representation of the soil, roots, ground to which the novel aspires in its synonymous romantic, Christian, Romantic, and modernist terms.

If the term "genius" means spirit or indwelling of origin, the equivalent aesthetic ideality of originality it also represents is, of course, the formal underbelly of what Howards End and Mrs. Wilcox signify from the point of view of literature proper. A wonderfully reflexive instance of the modernist desire she represents from the point of view of literary belatedness, Mrs. Wilcox predictably "worshipped the past" (22) and has "that wisdom to which we give the clumsy name of aristocracy" (22)—the same name to which Forster's elfin child remains partially attached as well. Like the garden she inhabits both dead and alive, Mrs. Wilcox is the paradise lost of the soil at large and the belated imagination in particular, the latter the former's projective condition of representability. Thus Forster's litany of ideals grows more explicitly literary as the novel proceeds—from "aura" (153) and "supernatural life" (171) to the "nymphs" (197) and "new sanctities" (222) of a "Fairyland" (223) that, says Forster openly, even "Prospero" (230) could have commanded. If Mrs. Wilcox begins the novel as an emblem of modernist literary desire, the Shakespearean conclusion is its balancing reflexive counterpart in the text's almost overcoded disposition of motifs that are ideological objects of scrutiny rather than expressive messages. Preparing us for the novel's climax and functioning also as the prototype for Mrs. McNab in *To the Lighthouse* is the aptly named Mrs. Avery (aery, sprightly), who looks after Howards End after the original Mrs. Wilcox's death and resurrects it for the transmigration of Howards End's genius into the new habitation of Margaret. True to her name, Mrs. A(v)ery is to be found "airing," of all things, the "books" (264), as though the text means to remind us that its ideals are calculated exercises in dealing with a literary problem rather than Forster's personal lament as to the fate of civilization. Forster even admits the real nature of his motivating anxiety:

> Why has not England a great mythology? Our folklore
> has never advanced beyond daintiness, and the greater

melodies about our country-side have all issued through the pipes of Greece. Deep and true as the native imagination can be, it seems to have failed here. . . . England still waits for the supreme moment of her literature—for the great poet who shall voice her, or, better still, for the thousand little poets whose voices shall pass into our common talk.

[267]

Though it is an inversion of this latter possibility from which the idiomatic art of reflexive realism will be made ("common talk" passes into literature rather than the other way around), Forster's implicit identification of "the great poet" with the role of mythologist is of special concern. While a "great poet" may well be a mythologist—a self-evident identity for the pioneers, especially of epic—for the latecomer, by contrast, strong art can no longer be persuasion or belief alone; it is, rather, an interrogation of the categories by which one dreams, not a rank presentation of dreams alone. Forster's novel is, to be sure, just such a metacritical art, taking as its raw materials, not some avowed chaos in or of the real, but the ideological grammar that produces the real—structuring mythologies like Hardy's "ache of modernism" or Pater's "modernity." *Howards End* even looks rather like *The Mayor of Casterbridge* in the efficiency and clarity with which it seeks to catalogue and question the chief ideological assumptions that govern modernist speech and desire in both novelistic discourse and general cultural competence.

Whether religious, romantic, or Romantic, then, *Howards End* is a catalogue of the will to modernity rather than an example of it. It is a meditation on modernism at large, finding among its other players the same structure of assumption to be found in Mrs. Wilcox despite the many differences that otherwise appear to divide them. The world the novel depicts is, in fact, one constituted by the ideology of a will to modernity that the novel itself will attempt to account for by describing the structure that produces it. The buzzing name "Schlegel" is probably the clearest instance of the novel's focus on the structure of the ideology of modernity, particularly its Romantic genealogy. Whether it is a question of "truth" (195), "earth" (199), the "fertility of the soil" or the "intensely green" (200) season of "Easter" (198), all such modernist notions of regenerative primacy—of the "earth and its emotions" (214), in a decidedly deliberate pathetic fallacy—are nonetheless shared notions or representations to which Schlegels, Basts, and Wilcoxes all alike subscribe, even if they differ in their particular interpretations of what living "deeply" (214) may mean. The soil of the colonies is as basic to Paul Wilcox's imperialism as the soil of England is to his mother's romanticism.

Like the "life of the body" trammeled by the unnecessary "appliances" (218) of the moneyed classes, it is the category of the original or the eternal that remains central to almost all the characters' recurrent and shared ideality of regeneration in a world of forms to which they come late. Even Bast has a partially direct connection with the earth

in his ancestry; his forebears are, as he puts it, "'agricultural labourers'" (237) whose roots are in that "unspoilt country" (88) that represents what is left of the natural in the urban sprawl that threatens it. Pop Romantic modernist that he is, Bast wants simply to get "'back to the Earth'" (117), despite the phrase's equal foreshadowing of his subsequent death. Indeed, much as the soil upon which London sits precedes it, so Forster's staged myth of the modern, prescient as it is of Eliot's "dissociation of sensibility" eleven years later, also requires "an elder race" of "rural" folk (268) to whom "we look back with disquietude" (268) because of their more direct relation to the soil than ours. Forster even goes so far as to try to equate, like Wordsworth, the images of the garden and of childhood, both versions of primary innocence that Forster wittingly identifies as the kinds of assumptions that predetermine our ways of thinking and living. It is, in short, "the peace of the country" (315) that makes up the book's set of consistent ideals, all of them based on a notion of truth epistemologically intact beyond history, circumstance, and, apparently, beyond language as well. Margaret gives us the ideal in a compelling summary form: "Her conclusion was," says Forster of her mind's development as a little girl, "that any human being lies nearer to the unseen than any organization, and from this she never varied" (30).

So astute—so scholarly in Pater's sense—is the apparently breezy Forster in his interrogation of the forms the myth of the modern takes as an ideological formation that *Howards End* is almost an encyclopedia of the kinds of permutations its oppositions can produce. The opposition between the aesthetic Schlegels and the worldly Wilcoxes is, of course, only one example among many in the novel's scrupulous catalogue of the dualities that structure the myth of the modern, and one isomorphic with the equally recurrent opposition between nature and culture. Even in Bast's imagination of the composing process, for example, the poet Jeffries must work by having a prior state of feeling that he only subsequently turns into the secondariness or belatedness of writing: "the spirit," as Bast thinks, "that led Jeffries to write" (120). Here, and again symptomatically, the imagination of imagination is figured as identical with the structure of its religious and romance ideals: the certitude of a prior state of nature upon which or against which civilization uneasily sits, and the desire for which the novel readily identifies as a will to modernity defensively understandable but empirically problematic. One's job in life is to get to the "'real thing'" behind the "'husks'" (145), to the "root" of the "earth" (150); to penetrate the "husks" that "enclose . . . emotion" (311). In short, to keep, impossible as the mixture of metaphor already predicts, "'memory green'" (152) in the hope that such a realm beyond culture really exists.

Much as Bast assesses writing as a function of an opposition between the primacy of feeling and the secondariness of language, so the opposition between the Schlegels and the Wilcoxes is likewise one between depth and superficiality, art and business. To the Schlegels early in the novel, the Wilcoxes are a "fraud," with only "emptiness" behind them (26)—affectation as opposed to authenticity or sincerity (10), the "lips" to the "heart" (37), the "eyes" to the "smile" (48). So, too, to see the world "half sensibly and half poetically" (12) not only tells us that Margaret is a balanced and judicious woman, but also that the informing oppositions that allow us to make such a judgment are in turn those between, for example, pose and reality, "'romance'" and "'prose'" (174), "prose" and "passion" (186); hence, too, the notion of a "rainbow bridge" between them (186), one of a number of Forster's phrases to be repeated by Woolf. And along with oppositions such as reason and passion, sense and sensibility, male and female, come other logical permutations, especially the key opposition between outer and inner worlds (174-75), the vaunted separation of "public" and private, the without and the "within" (28), "the outer life" (103) and the inner, one's "head" and "the universe" (50). The opposition between private and public is likewise aligned with the opposition between "surface" and depth (220, 240), much as the narrator distinguishes between "true imagination and false" (121), and, just as paradigmatically, between "Romance" and "work" (138). Epistemologically akin to the split between public and private, the split between civilization and soil also leads to the oppositions between "imprisonment and escape" (86), "trade" and "spirit" (84), body and soul or spirit (102, 115, 186), "cold culture" and real "art" (310); even the "orderly sequence . . . fabricated by historians" as opposed to the "chaotic nature of our daily life" (106). Nor should we fail to note the familiar opposition of "dirty" and "pure" (167) and Forster's accompanying lament about "muddles" (e.g., 308). Thus the differences between Schlegels and Wilcoxes—between spirit and trade, intimacy and "'telegrams'" (103)—also inform the notion that the "stench of motor cars" (15) and "metallic fumes" (53) "cut off the sun" (56) and desecrate the "soil" (47). Even at Howards End, a garage replaces the old pony paddock (71), reminiscent of the various urban technologies that replace the rural ones in Hardy's Wessex. Within such a world, the Schlegels "breathe . . . less of the air" and see "less of the sky" (107). "Nature," in short, "withdrew" (107-08). Indeed, Forster goes so far as to admit his quaintness in maintaining such oppositions, since "the Earth as an artistic cult," as he puts it, "has had its day" (108).

The myth of past freshness is so general in the political unconscious of the contemporary world that the novel depicts (and of which it is itself a function) that even the visit to Simpson's with the Wilcoxes displays the novel's selfsame literary and religious ideals in quotidian form: "Though no more Old English than the works of Kipling, it had selected its reminiscences so adroitly that . . . criticism was lulled, and the guests whom it was nourishing for imperial purposes bore the outer semblance of Parson Adams or Tom Jones" (153). In such a world structured by Romantic or modernist desire in its popular mythology as well as in its literary history, "'Houses are alive'" (155), at least according to the central animating Romantic trope of personification that Ruskin recognized by condemning and trying to outlaw. So different is modern life from the wishful glories of the past that the "nomadic civilization" (261) of modern cities, says the narrator, will "receive no help from the earth" (261), the sacred soil that the urban scorns and seeks to destroy or neutralize.

The novel's most famous trope in the organizing mythology its oppositions produce is surely the "civilization of luggage" (150), the wasteland into which we moderns have fallen and whose coherence as a target of attack relies on still another series of organizing oppositions, chief among them the opposition between transit and rest, hurry and serenity, luggage and home, and, of course, city and country. As though the real had really changed on its own, modern ideas, too, are "portable" (61) rather than secure. People, likewise, are always "'moving'" (137) and speaking "the language of hurry" (109), both counterposed to the natural stability of home, rest, and leisure; of seeing things "steadily" and seeing them "whole" (161), as Forster says in his wittingly Arnoldean refrain (see also "empires of facts" [30]) that is perhaps chief among the officially literary motifs included in the novel's survey of (its) hegemonic ideological presuppositions. Forster even soliloquizes, with hidden irony, upon the metacritical rather than mimetic status of his project through Margaret's maintenance of the familiar myth of the modern that has structured her youth as it does the ideology of modernism at large: "London was but a foretaste of this nomadic civilization which is altering human nature so profoundly, and throws upon personal relations a stress greater than they have ever borne before. Under cosmopolitanism, if it comes, we shall receive no help from the earth" (261). With such oppositions so securely in place and so capable of organizing the world the book represents—a world divided between earth and civilization, steadiness and "flux" (261), private and public—the novel is almost merciless in the thoroughness of its inventories. Forster's catalogue of modernist ideology may therefore be said to formulate a grammar that will account for the symptomatic manifestations of the will to modernity in all its forms. By so isolating the means of production of its wishful primacies, Forster can thereby simulate the reality they engender in his (meta)realism while, at the same time, go on to disassemble it in the simultaneously reflexive arrangements of his prose by which the oppositions upon which the myth of the modern is based are, with equal systematicity, also identified by the language that expresses them.

If we begin to inspect the novel's language in any detail at all, then, we find that Forster's vaunted (and only apparent) thematic intent—his myth of the modern—is simultaneously undermined as programmatically as it is set up by a rhetorical contamination or slippage of the oppositions that put it in place. Central among the novel's dualities is the classic modernist antagonism between self and society, private and public, and one that leads Forster to recommend the Moorish ideal of "'personal relations'" (174) as a means of building that "rainbow bridge" (186) between self and community that turns out to be unnecessary because the two are already conjoined. Even Terry Eagleton remains captive to the belief in a straightforward "Forsterian affirmation of the 'personal'" (1981:138), as though there is no real irony in Forster's art. "Personal relations" is, however, an oxymoron, since, as Pater and Joyce—and even Eliot—have shown, self and world are mutually constitutive in the semiotic play of culture that produces subjects and objects alike in a series of gestures that privileges neither side of what is a productive rhetorical opposition rather than one expressive of a condition in the world. A thorough focus on Forster's vocabulary will show just how the oppositions that organize his manifest myth of the modern also turn into one another so as to wreak semantic havoc with the categories the novel's manifest thematic has erected.

If Bloomsbury is indeed programmatic in its use of the unseen poetic arrangements of ordinary language, the real object of a text such as ***Howards End*** is to join linguistically those colloquial terms that are customarily articulated as oppositions. Thus the novel's oppositions turn out to link, paradigmatically, human and fiduciary relations—private and public, spiritual and material, "personal" and "relations"—in a common set of signifiers, throwing the relationship between denotation and connotation into chaos as one of the numerous side-effects that render privacy a function of its dependence on the publicity to which it is normally counterposed. Most pervasive as well as most focused are the similarities rather than differences between psychic and real economy and their mutual interdependence in the tropology that identifies the vocabulary of business or the Wilcoxes with the vocabulary of private emotion or the Schlegels. Private virtue itself, for example, is thereby always grafted, linguistically at least, to the same terms by which we calculate the world of material value to which it is customarily opposed ("worth . . . ," 165, 259, 262, 292), making it no wonder that an idiom such as "'tender hearts'" (169) suddenly reveals an economic aspect to the figure that cautions the degree of epistemological integrity we like to assign to our private worlds. Thus a surprising parade of tropological identifications: one can be "'worthy'" (66) or "'unworthy'" (244) as a person; "tender" (245) emotionally; repose "trust" (37) in another person (shades, too, of *The Confidence Man*); or take an "interest" (103) in someone else. Even more exactly, Helen's stocks, like her emotions, are characteristically "reinvested" (256), while the contrastingly stable Mrs. Munt possesses stock in her more appropriate style of "safe investments" in "Home Rails" (14). One can, moreover, "cancel . . ." one's "mistrust" (37) in a person by means of the same idiom by which one cancels a check. Thus, too, a "'girl with no interests'" (57) is, like the otherwise comfortable Helen, tropologically at least, nevertheless akin to a girl with no money at all—Jacky, for example, with whom Helen in fact changes places when she becomes Bast's lover. Likewise, "'the will to be interested'" (57) directly implicates the vocabulary of the personal in that of the public. "'The very soul of the world is economic'" (61), admits Mr. Wilcox, not only for the materialist reasons that escape him even in the first instance, but also because of the semiotic spillage that

thwarts his like investment in the absolute difference between what is one's own and what is another's.

The vocabularies of the marketplace and stock exchange, in short, programmatically collide with the vocabulary of personal relations. Even throwaway colloquialisms denoting (connoting?) one's private mood such as "on Helen's account" (70) or to give an "account" (85, 106) of something coincide figurally with the public language of commerce and exchange. Such common or idiomatic usage almost endlessly infects the difference between private and public throughout the novel, whether we "'make a great deal of it'" (75), "evoke our interests" (79) or "withdraw" them (79). Thus an emotional "check . . ." (96, 109) has fiduciary connotations, much, amazingly enough, as does Mrs. Wilcox's extraordinary "tenderness" (89) and what is "tender . . ." (182, 193, 318, 325) in others throughout the novel. The property of Howards End has "tenderness" chief among its manifest atmospheric qualities (206), legal tender as it is of the value of the property as real estate. Indeed, one goes on "trusting" one's "husband" (93) or shows "mistrust . . ." (79) for someone in implicitly economic figures meant to describe the private alone, even when it comes to one's "life interest" (99). Though life is, says Forster, "unmanageable" (107), his descriptions of it are, by contrast, scrupulously managed by a language that joins the "alien associations" of the public discourses of management, finance, and exchange with those we (also) use to describe what is most private to us.

Hence the sudden resonance of apparently innocent idioms such as "'on no account'" (112, 248), "on her account" (162), "on his account" (320); the wish to "'tender . . . apologies'" (116); the economic murmur of phrases describing personal relations such as "'managed him'" (144), "trading on" (147), "deposited" (149), "cost" (158), even the matter-of-fact "owing to" (157). People try in short "to balance their lives" (150) through the management of psychic investments etymologically laced with economic ones such as those that make up Henry's bank balance. Thus Margaret's annoying recollection of "the stock criticism about Helen" (277) raises still another series of economic murmurs in an otherwise purely personal idiomatic signification. Even to be "rent into two people" (315-16) by psychological shock carries the quite alien associations that intimate the settled or unsettled state of one's psyche as a form of tenancy. Late in the novel, Helen's "'interests'" (305) slip between fiduciary and psychological meanings almost overtly, the family "'goods'" (306), like Moore's, both blessed and tainted by the oscillation of philosophical and material meanings in the same signifier. And once Forster describes the condemned Leonard as one who does not "count for much" (311), his fate is sealed tropologically and representationally in the same figure.

Hardly random events in the novel, ***Howards End***'s linkage of the public and private in an exemplary set of shared or common expressions not only projects a Keynesian vision of the interdependencies that represent society as a matrix of relations rather than as a set of autonomous atoms, but also serves as a continual reminder of our nonimmediate relation to the world altogether, whether private or public, a world in which we are always belated because "'some medium of exchange'" (155)—some social mediation—is always required for anything to signify at all. Neither self nor world is in itself either independent or immediate; as a set of representations in the first instance, life is a secondary rather than a direct phenomenon from the start it can never be said properly to have (had). Foreshadowing Woolf's rather more overt vision of a world without a given self, Forster must conclude by implication that nothing exists autonomously, and that autonomy itself—the very token of the will to modernity whose typology and nature as a notion the novel elaborates—is a defensive reaction to its own impossibility within the semiotic grid of a culture to which we come belatedly and as a function of the bewildering overdeterminations of its signs and history. The novel's characters may try to act out the will to modernity in their various quests for the self-erasing ideal of "personal relations" that stands for a directness supposedly lost after an implied Eliotic "dissociation" divides modernity from tradition. As Forster's language shows, however, such acting out fails to work through the paradox of liberation that forever forbids the possibility of immediacy or of any kind of transcendent autonomy at all.

If the self-contamination of Forster's metaphors begins to emerge in the novel's habitual identification of psychic and real economy at the level of language—of "goods" and "goods," "worth" and "worth"—such an identity is even more trenchant and etymologically exacting in the movement of another of the novel's chief tropological systems, that of property. As we have seen in Pater's deconstruction of Arnold's selfsame ideals of originality and cleanliness, "property" is a figure etymologically bound to a series of what are, for Forster as well, epistemologically identical structures of desire: for property as such (as in Mrs. Wilcox's "property" [72] or in simple "possessions" [98]); for propriety in manners and sensibility (refinement and serenity); for the properness or integrity of a work of art; and for that self-possession or stability of ego that we equate with mental health. We should recall that *propre* also means what is clean or unspoiled, the graphic and/or tactile representation of the wishful desire for originality or autonomy central to the will to modernity in art and experience alike. Forster's use of the tropology of "property" is both exact in the novel's enduring deconstruction of its myth of the modern, and exacting in the strategic play of the figure throughout the text. Even one example suggests that behaving "'properly'" (9) and avoiding "impropriety" (13) will result in "self-possession" (17)—the possession of oneself is metaphorically akin to the solidity or ground of epistemological certainty and of plain real estate as well.

The figure's strategic vicissitudes organize the novel's language in a striking way. One wants one's "muddles" or dirt "tidied up" (69), for example, so as to let "self-possession," the propriety of one's own being, take on its apparently proper privacy (hence Bast's role as a grossly

thematic reminder that the state of one's psyche and of one's economy are disastrously intertwined). Similarly, a "sloppy" soul (104) and the physically "untidy" (123) are figurations that epistemologically join what would otherwise be put asunder. Any "truth" is, as the Arnold to whom Forster sometimes alludes would have it, one of "clearness of vision" (182), freed from the haze or uncleanliness of outside influence. Thus Margaret's Arnoldean desire that Leonard "'wash out his brain and go to the real thing'" (145). We are in fact all in a "'mist'" (238), and therefore want our "vision cleared" (239)—we want to make a "clean breast" (247) of things. Even the apparently universal and nonliterary ideal of love is figured in the register of property and cleanliness, too: "She loved him," says Forster of Margaret's feeling for Henry, "with too clear a vision to fear his cloudiness" (220). The metaphorical chain is maintained when, for example, Jacky Bast's affair is described as "one new stain on the face of a love that had never been pure" (236). Of course, in a precise instance of Forster's wit, the last figuration again returns us, not to the will to modernity undiagnosed, but to the structure of modernism that produces its emergence. The origin or home—Jacky—to which Leonard wishes to return is, like Molly, already admittedly stained, the figure contaminating the origin as a precondition of the desire for it, its warmth a function of its distance.

With the categories and structure of modernism Forster's subject, then, ***Howards End,*** otherwise a proto-wastelander picture of London as full of "'rubbish'" (157, 161), "'slime'" (173), and "'heaps'" (175), is neither mimetic transcription nor a rehearsal of Eliot's anxiety about tradition as it will be projected in the ruinous landscape of *The Waste Land.* Instead, Forster's myth of the modern, with all its detailed characteristics, is, like Hardy's, an enormously prescient anticipation and prior critique of the ideology of a High Modernism yet to be misread. To say, then, that "the mind is overtaxed" (321) by the novel is to describe the effect of Forster's apparently flat prose as well as to cite still another example of its surprising spillage that scrambles the oppositions necessary to maintain a myth of the modern without being obvious about it. The privacy of the "mind" is troped as the form of a public system, "taxation." The sanctity of privacy itself—that "paradise within thee happier far" still sustaining English Romantic tradition as late as 1910—can, must be signified, alas, only in relation to that which it is not, the public, the traditional, the outside. Because property is, ironically, privacy, it is public enough for Forster to dub the age itself the "Age of Property" (149). Like "personal relations," "Age of Property" is, however, also an implicit contradiction, implying as it does a shared or communal belief in the kind of privacy such a public articulation forbids.

If, moreover, what is private is available only as a function of what is public, the belated status of modern experience and of the modern imagination are once again redoubled, too. Like literary language, the lineaments of being itself are already used, handed down—woven and rewoven, to recall Joyce. This is why Forster grows reflexive as a direct function of his realism rather than as a reaction against it. If the world itself is already taken to be a world of signs or representations from the start, it not only puts all its denizens in the belated role that the modern writer has toward tradition; it also makes the practice of writing about such a world an inherently reflexive procedure, since narrative representation must thereby be a representation of a world already understood to be a set of representations. As taxonomist and diagnostician of the ideology of modernism, then, Forster finds the lifelike objects of his fiction to be already fictions or representations in their own terms. As with his own burlesque pathetic fallacies, Forster will sometimes even provide us with clues as to just how equivalent life and letters (another version of the supposedly opposed public and private) can get to be, sometimes by affirmation, sometimes by negation. Helen, for example, writes to Margaret very early in the novel that though (as Meg has said) "'life is sometimes life and sometimes only a drama,'" "'it really does not seem life'" at all "'but a play'" (4-5). Tibby's sense of family life as scripted ("a scene behind footlights" [280]) is also in line with the novel's habitual systems of usage by which Forster's reflexive realism represents the real by representing the representations that compose it in the first place. Like his own mock-heroic allusions (e.g., 101), the terms by which everyone lives derive from quite discernible mythologies rather than from a natural expressiveness on Forster's own part. London is a "vast theatre" (129); Mrs. Munt "rehearse[s]" (13) for actual events, expecting her niece to "imitate" (14) her in turn; even Leonard's oaths are "learnt from older men" (49), a rather overt sign that the vocabulary of candor and earthiness, too, is belated because derivative or learned. Margaret's desire to have Ruth Wilcox as a friend is likewise figured in an overtly textual metaphor ("Desiring to book Mrs. Wilcox as a friend, she pressed on the ceremony, pencil, as it were, in hand" [79]), while the mourners surrounding Mrs. Wilcox's "grave" (another recurrent term that connotes writing and links it with death) are described as virtual letters in another writerly metaphor: they "moved between the graves, like drops of ink" (88). The life Forster represents in all its forms is, in other words, represented in the first instance as a system of texts or codes already in place when any new or original subject arrives on the scene.

Woolf and, more especially, Strachey will go on to show us, with even greater precision and far clearer intent, the world itself as a set of texts or representations like the textual representations that represent them. Even the various pastoral landscapes upon which *Howards End* dwells so fondly—and tries to separate from the "theatre" of the "Satanic" (84) city—are figured by Forster as "system after system" (167) in their own right, much as Charles and Dolly's newest child is, however humorously, "a third edition" (185). And while such vocabulary may be taken to suggest the dehumanization of life under technology, the measured repetition of Forster's strategic figurations should remind us instead that his focus is not on a world as such, but on the "reverberations" (23), as he puts it himself, of

the dominant codes or discursive polarities by means of which the discourses of ideology produce rather than merely respond to the real.

What, however, is the point of the elaborate romance machinery at book's end? Does it mean to repress the contamination of its modernist categories in the hidden service of the kinds of ideals it otherwise puts in question? But while the book's modernist wishes may be summed up in Helen's rather Moorish remark that "'One is certain of nothing but the truth of one's own emotions'" (170), we know that "one's own" is hardly certain as a category. Ironically, the aesthetic pleasure of the book's ending is its most enduring source of pain. The ending of *Howards End* is an overcompensatory romance whose desire to soothe despite the horrors involved is sociologically pathetic and, epistemologically, symptomatic of something else. Its attempted (or merely staged) dialectical resolution—the kind of structure made readily apparent in the tripartite shape of the later *Passage to India* (1924)—may or may not be but another programmed moment in a novel that is otherwise really a metatext that represents and interrogates the systematic self-representations of life itself rather than our chaotic experience of them. Not only must we ask why Bast dies, but also why it is Charles who kills him. In fact, Charles kills Bast as the function of a double Oedipal displacement. After all, Charles's father has not once but thrice slept with women Charles himself desires—his real mother (naturally), but also Jacky and Margaret, the latter he once fancies flirting with him early on in the story. Thus Bast, who has a sexual connection to Charles's father through his wife Jacky's affair with him, provides Charles with a reason for investing him with a son's displaced fury. Bast thereby becomes his ironic surrogate father as the husband of the Jacky with whom his father has slept. As a subjective structure, it also has the effect of psychologizing away class differences in favor of personal ones, even though, as we shall see in a moment, Forster's psychoanalysis is political as well as poetical. Symbolically, Bast represents the father that Charles cannot in law kill, though he can—and almost does—ruin him by his attack upon the poorer man. More than that, however, Bast as displaced symbolic father substitutes not just for Mr. Wilcox himself, but, in the process, also suggests, by virtue of his own mobile symbolism, that even the real father is not an immediate origin either. The real father is real because he is a symbol, and a symbol of authority because he is a real father. The father actually represents, not himself, but the law that he serves by symbolizing or substituting for it in the eyes of the futurity that will organize itself retrospectively around his legacy. Even the ambiguity in the possible historical play of the Wilcoxes' Christian names, Charles and Henry (both kings of England, it is up to the reader to fashion a relation in accord with a given interpretation), encourages ambiguities as to whom it is that gains the ultimate, if sad, privilege, and encourages in turn the startling psychoanalytic ambiguities that Forster's Oedipal structure is designed to provoke. The father is himself the symbol or surrogate for something else even more primary than his own supposedly seminal authority. The original original—the father—is belated in relation to himself, ironically prior to himself as father since he can only stand for his purported natural authority by virtue of his symbolism. Even Freud himself (in James Strachey's translation) is momentarily explicit about it. Writing of the Wolf Man, Freud says, "He resisted God in order to be able to cling to his father; and in doing this he was really upholding the old father against the new" (1918:66). "The totem, I maintained, was the first father-surrogate, and the god was a later one, in which the father had regained his human shape" (1918:114).

What is repressed in the killing of Bast, then, is not just an expression of Charles's personal Oedipal rage, but the constitutive protest of subjectivity against its formation through categories that make its autonomy impossible. Thus Forster's machinery at novel's end performs double duty, framing Bast's murder in apparently suavely psychoanalytic terms so as to keep us away from the deeper problem to be repressed, not just in the static sociology of English life, but also in the epistemology of psychoanalytic reasoning (another instance of Forster's early scrutiny rather than expression of modernist ideologies): the failure of the notion of the Oedipus complex itself as a route to original truth. Hence Forster allows us to see just what Arnold has tried to hide more than anyone else: that origins, fathers central among their (ironic) figurations, are themselves but symbols or substitutes for something else absent but supposedly more primary, more original than the father even in the immediacy of his flesh.

Also a caution as to the ease or certainty with which we use the notion of authority at large, the novel's surprising psychoanalytic implications are at the same time at the hinge of the poetics of reflexive realism as a project in its own right. The original father's only symbolic power suggests that, in its narratological counterpart, the immediate—the thing represented—is also already a sign for something else at the very moment that it is what it is. A sign is what it is because it is, by the definition that allows it to signify in the first place, something different from itself to begin with. Hence, too, in both reflexive realism and in the transference that structures the analytic session (at least in the younger Strachey's formulation [1934]), the real is only symbolic, while only the symbolic is real. If Forster's text is reflexive because of its realism—because the world it refers to is already a tissue of signs—Forster's implicit notion of symbolism here suggests in turn that the real is precisely the symbolically authoritative.

Forster's reflexive realism in *Howards End,* then, is, like the later work of Woolf and Strachey (and of Conrad and Hardy before them, along with Ford), implicitly but efficiently pedagogical as well. Taking as his subject the systems by which we exist and the by-products or effects of them that make up our lives, Forster produces an allegory of reading in *Howards End* that asks its reader to decide—or not to—a mode of response within the wide spectrum of possibilities the book's complex operations may detonate reader to reader. If Joyce focuses on the minute

paroles of life, forcing the reader to deduce from them the *langues* or codes that contextualize and so give each the meaning the reader requires them to have, Forster instead appeals directly, if invisibly, to the *langues* or ideological paradigms themselves in a cultural metafiction that sets the model for Bloomsbury prose to come. So organized are the components of the ideology of modernism in Forster's text that we can in the final instance only classify *Howards End* as a novel of classification that in turn asks us to classify it. Much, for example, as one may ask fruitlessly who one really is once the vagaries of "property" are exposed, so, too, may one read the book's famous "wych-elm" (the preeminent sign of fixity and established grace in the novel's myth of the modern) as the rather more transient sign to be found in reading it interrogatively—as a Joycean pun that asks instead, through an inversion of its normative meaning, the reflexive question "which elm?" that both frees the text from its denotative referents while simultaneously reaffirming their coherence by virtue of such educative transgression. The novel thereby demonstrates the ever-shifting possibilities produced by the play of both fixed codes and floating signifiers, enjoying just the kind of pleasure *The Waste Land* in particular cannot.

Like Helen's desire that Margaret "'Burn'" (5-6) her letters at the novel's start, or like the Wilcoxes' decision to "tear the note up" (99) with which Mrs. Wilcox has bequeathed Howards End to Margaret, the novel itself functions—like the psychoanalytic transference—as a double operation that asks us both to absorb and destroy its variously incompatible messages at one and the same time. It wishes to leave "no traces behind" (102), even if its language continues to broadcast both its myth of the modern and the contamination of the dichotomies that sustain it. Such simultaneous absorption and cancellation—a structure also figurally identical with Freud's representation of the unconscious in the "Note upon the 'Mystic Writing-Pad'" (1925)—is a strong and decisive response to the problematic of modernist belatedness. Like psychoanalysis, it secures the wishful primacies its representations of them habitually undercut.

Paul Delany (essay date 1988)

SOURCE: Delany, Paul. "'Islands of Money': Rentier Culture in E. M. Forster's *Howards End*." *English Literature in Transition, 1880-1920* 31, no. 3 (1988): 285-96.

[*In the following essay, Delany discusses Forster's "life-long preoccupation" with the privileged lives of upper-class Britons as revealed in* Howards End.]

When he was eight years old E. M. Forster inherited eight thousand pounds from his great-aunt Marianne Thornton, who came from a well-to-do family of Victorian bankers. His widowed mother had about the same amount of capital, ensuring him a comfortable home, and a Public School and Cambridge education. *The Longest Journey* deals with the emotional consequences of this secure and sheltered upbringing; *Howards End,* though not directly autobiographical, examines Forster's *economic* origins. The novel's motto, "Only connect . . ." is usually read as a plea for emotional openness; but Forster is equally concerned with the subtle connections between a class's mentality and how it gets its means of life. I want to show that Forster had a lifelong preoccupation with the morality of living on unearned income; and that in *Howards End* his aim was to move from his own experience of privilege to a comprehensive judgment on the kind of country Edwardian Britain was, and should be.

Like Marx and Freud before him, Forster is possessed by the idea of *unmasking;* he wants to lay bare the tangled economic roots of complacent liberalism. As wealth piled up in nineteenth-century Britain, the rentier class—those who lived mainly on investment income—had increased steadily in numbers and social influence (the Victorian census even had a special category for the "Independent Classes"). This class produced generous supporters of the arts, philanthropy, and such good causes as the abolition of slavery; at the same time, it could be seen as compromised by its fundamentally parasitic status. "The education I received in those far-off and fantastic days made me soft," Forster wrote in 1946, "and I am very glad it did, for I have seen plenty of hardness since, and I know it does not even pay. . . . But though the education was humane it was imperfect, inasmuch as we none of us realized our economic position. In came the nice fat dividends, up rose the lofty thoughts, and we did not realize that all the time we were exploiting the poor of our own country and the backward races abroad, and getting bigger profits from our investments than we should. We refused to face this unpalatable truth."[1]

What could be the worth or the use, Forster asked himself, of an entire class of people who lived on the labor of others? His part-time teaching at the Working Men's College, from 1902 onwards, helped sharpen his awareness of the gulf between his own comfortable existence and that of his hard-pressed students. In his darker moods he condemned himself as a milksop who lived with his mother, who was sexually backward, and who had been absolved by his inherited wealth from the need to seek a useful career.

Howards End starts from the principle stated by its heroine, Margaret Schlegel: "independent thoughts are in nine cases out of ten the result of independent means."[2] But if this proposition is accepted, it contains an uncomfortable lesson for people in Forster's position. It suggests that independence of mind is not entirely virtuous, because it is one of the privileges that accrue to the owners of capital. Or, to look at it another way: if independent thoughts are the result of something else, then they aren't really independent. Money talks, and money thinks; this is Margaret's claim when she goes on to tell her ladies' discussion group "that the very soul of the world is economic":

> "That's more like socialism," said Mrs. Munt suspiciously.

"Call it what you like. I call it going through life with one's hand spread open on the table. I'm tired of these rich people who pretend to be poor, and think it shows a nice mind to ignore the piles of money that keep their feet above the waves. I stand each year upon six hundred pounds, and Helen upon the same, and Tibby will stand upon eight, and as fast as our pounds crumble away into the sea they are renewed—from the sea, yes, from the sea. And all our thoughts are the thoughts of six-hundred-pounders, and all our speeches; and because we don't want to steal umbrellas ourselves we forget that below the sea people do want to steal them, and do steal them sometimes, and that what's a joke up here is down there reality—"[3]

Margaret's position is indeed "like socialism" in saying that consciousness is determined by its economic base; but neither she nor her creator are ready to jump from this premise to revolutionary conclusions. All they feel obliged to do is to make the connection between the Schlegels' class and those, with very different outlooks, that are on each side of it. Below the Schlegels are the Basts, representing the half-submerged yet aspiring lower middle class; above them are the richer Wilcoxes, go-ahead business people "whose hands are on all the ropes" and who stand for "the robust ideal" (112, 38). The older sister, Margaret, concentrates on trying to understand the class above her; the younger, Helen, on understanding the class below. Each takes her sympathy to the point of sexual connection—Margaret's willed and reasoned, Helen's impulsive.

In defending to Helen her decision to marry Henry Wilcox, Margaret intellectualises her motives. "If Wilcoxes hadn't worked and died in England for thousands of years," she bursts out, "you and I couldn't sit here without having our throats cut. There would be no trains, no ships to carry us literary people about in, no fields even. Just savagery. . . . More and more do I refuse to draw my income and sneer at those who guarantee it" (177-178). Margaret, like Forster, is trying to connect her sheltered and cultured existence with what guarantees it: the organizing power of the Wilcoxes. She has to admit that civility rests on the measured application of brute force, and cultural refinement on economic injustice. To understand the particular resonance of this belief in *Howards End,* it will be useful to look briefly at two earlier works on similar themes: Gaskell's *North and South* (1855) and Shaw's *Widowers' Houses* (1892). Although these works helped to shape Forster's vision of the *rentier* way of life, each had its own mood and period flavor, which were quite different from *Howards End.* As usual, Forster ended up by quietly yet firmly choosing his own path. His novel became a justification of his economic status, and a vindication of the unassuming Schlegels over the ambitious Wilcoxes. The second aim of *Howards End*—and a less successful one—was to project Schlegel values into a compelling vision of what Britain's destiny might and should be.

II

Gaskell's *North and South* sets in opposition the active and the contemplative lives, North and South, men and women. These linked oppositions are all finally reconciled in the union of Margaret Hale, daughter of a Southern vicar, with Mr. Thornton, a rough-hewn Northern manufacturer. Forster may well have been influenced by Gaskell's novel in conceiving **Howards End** for he uses a similar dialectical structure, contrasting the morals and economics of two sets of characters, the Wilcoxes and the Schlegels.[4] Spatially, Forster opposes town to country rather than North to South; but a more important difference between the two novels is that Forster's ends with the triumph of one side of his opposed forces, Gaskell's with a vision of complementarity. Margaret Hale and Mr. Thornton have many disagreements, but at the end they are united both sentimentally and economically. Thornton has gone bankrupt in a trade recession, in spite of his competence and hard work, while Margaret has inherited money and real estate from a family friend who was a don at Oxford. She makes Thornton a formal proposal: "if you would take some money of mine, eighteen thousand and fifty-seven pounds, lying just at this moment unused in the bank, and bringing me in only two and a half percent— you could pay me much better interest, and might go on working Marlborough Mills."[5] Thornton is so moved that he counters with his own proposal, that they should get married. Margaret's acceptance brings together the strong and the sweet, the entrepreneur and the rentier, North and South, industry and finance, in one of the most comprehensive of Victorian happy endings.

Margaret Hale, as a Victorian lady, need feel no qualms about becoming a passive investor in her husband's enterprise. But Forster could not rest easily with the idea of living on the fruits of his capital while others took on for him the struggle in the marketplace. It made him feel as if he were feminised—castrated, even—and his moral misgivings were equally strong. "Ever since I have read *Widowers' Houses*," he wrote in 1934, "I have felt hopeless about investments."[6] He had read the play thirty-five years before as an undergraduate. Its hero is a genteel young man, Harry Trench, who has a private income but is also about to set up a medical practice. He has fallen in love with Blanche Sartorius, but is shocked when he discovers that his prospective father-in-law is a slum landlord. Trench is even more shocked to learn that his own capital is invested in a mortgage on one of Mr. Sartorius's filthy hovels. Sartorius points out to him, however, that if he liquidates the mortgage and puts the money into government bonds, his income will fall from £700 to £250 a year. After consulting his conscience, Trench decides both to marry Blanche and join Sartorius in a speculation that promises to double his capital in two years. Since one cannot belong to the upper middle class without being an exploiter, he feels that he may as well be hung for a sheep as for a lamb.

Widowers' Houses demonstrates that social status is proportional to distance from economic reality. At the bottom of the play's pecking order is the despised Mr. Lickcheese, the man who actually squeezes the money out of the wretched slum-dwellers. Next comes Mr. Sartorius, who owns the buildings but never sets foot in them. At the top are Dr. Trench (and his aunt Lady Roxdale), who have not even troubled to find out where their comfortable private incomes came from.

In his own way, Shaw too is saying "Only connect": that is, acknowledge the economic links that implicate each member of society in the actions of everyone else. The way of the world, however, is that people who eat meat have no desire to live next to a slaughterhouse; and by the time of **Howards End,** the rentiers have removed themselves even further than in *Widowers' Houses* from the actual workings of their capital. The English investor now thinks in global, rather than just regional or national terms. So, on reaching their majority, the Schlegel sisters remove their inheritances from "the old safe investments" and put them into what Forster archly calls "Foreign Things" (28). The safe investments would probably be Consols—British government bonds—which for many decades had yielded a steady two and a half to three and a half percent. If we assume that Forster himself was in the same position as the Schlegels, his £8,000 would have yielded about £240 a year until he reached twenty-five, when he came into control of his money and was free to invest it more adventurously. We know that one of his new investments was in British American Great Southern Railway, one of the major Argentinian railways, which yielded about five percent.[7] The Schlegels' aunt, Mrs. Munt, wants them to keep their money in Britain, if not in bonds. She persuades them to invest a few hundred pounds in her favorite "Home Rails"; unfortunately, "the Foreign Things did admirably and the Nottingham and Derby declined with the steady dignity of which only Home Rails are capable" (28).

The popularity of "Foreign Things" had a powerful influence on British economic development. From about 1855 to 1914, Britain exported capital on a huge scale. New portfolio foreign investment in this period amounted to well over four billion pounds. Capital export had as its correlative the relative deprivation of domestic industry, a central feature of the extended crisis of the British economy that has featured so prominently in recent historiography.[8] Two kinds of impulses promoted the shift of capital overseas. One was the straightforward economic motive that average returns were higher in foreign than in domestic investment. But there was also a cultural aversion to the root-and-branch transformation of society that would have been required to keep pace with Britain's technical and industrial rivals, especially in the United States and Germany. The possession of an Empire made it easier for Britain to avoid a head-on industrial competition with these countries, but did not fully determine that choice. In fact, sixty percent of her overseas investment in this period went to foreign countries, and only forty percent to the Empire.[9] The heart of the matter was that Britain's governing classes preferred a strategy of "external" development, whereby the City of London facilitated the transfer of massive capital resources overseas, at the expense of the traditional manufacturing industries of the North.

So far as Forster is concerned, however, industry has not been deprived enough. He does not question investment in Foreign Things because it is at the expense of Home Rails, but because immoral methods must be used to organise it. When Margaret Schlegel goes to visit Henry Wilcox at his office she sees on his wall a map of Africa, "looking like a whale marked out for blubber" (196). The reader is surely meant to think of Gillray's famous cartoon of Napoleon and Pitt carving up the world like a Christmas pudding.[10] If in *Widowers' Houses* the issue is domestic exploitation, in **Howards End** it is Imperialism, and the application of the Imperial mentality to class rule in Britain.

Henry is a self-deceiving Social Darwinist, who speaks complacently of "the battle of life" and cuts down the salaries of his clerks in the name of the "survival of the fittest" (192-93). Margaret becomes steadily disillusioned with him; she comes to believe that he does not stand for the control of savagery, but is himself an expression of it. Social Darwinism gives Henry an excuse to spurn Leonard Bast, the aspiring but unlucky working man. It encourages him to exploit the "subject races" for England's benefit, affronting Margaret's (and Forster's) anti-imperial or "Little England" sentiments. And at home, the creed of the "battle of life" leads to the destruction of the cherished past, the pollution of the countryside by the noise and stink of the motor car, and the loss to the English people of what they most need—a sense of being securely rooted in their own particular corner of the earth. Margaret begins by contrasting the Wilcoxes' manly vigor with her own lack of worldly purpose; but she ends up repelled by the amoral use that the Wilcoxes make of their strength.

III

Howards End repudiates the Wilcox way of life as hopelessly philistine, materialist, and brutal. But Forster is left with the task of imagining a coherent alternative to the Wilcox culture of "red [i.e. red-brick] houses and the Stock Exchange" (170). He seeks to *dis*connect from "the inner darkness in high places that comes with a commercial age" (322), to find a way for the Schlegels to avoid complicity in any of the Wilcox undertakings—that is to say, with commerce, imperialism, modernity itself. The obvious candidate for an alternative British culture is pastoralism, such as Forster described in the conclusion of "The Abinger Pageant":

> Houses and bungalows, hotels, restaurants and flats, arterial roads, by-passes, petrol pumps and pylons—are these going to be England? Are these man's final triumph? Or is there another England, Green and eternal, which will outlast them? I cannot tell you, I am only the Woodman, but this land is yours, and you can make it what you will.[11]

Martin Wiener has told us how pervasive such sentiments have been in English culture since 1850, and even how constitutive of it. But Wiener says relatively little about the functional linkages between anti-industrialism and such distinctive features of English society as the domi-

nance of the City over industry, the export of capital—that is to say, the displacement of industry overseas—and the emergence of an influential rentier class. This syndrome, if we may call it that, has allowed England to have its cake and eat it too: to enjoy the fruits of modern industry while preserving, in the South at least, an archaic and congenial mode of life modelled on a country-house (or country cottage) ideal.

C. K. Hobson's book *The Export of Capital,* published in 1914,[12] is refreshingly explicit about the structural changes in the British economy that are the direct and intended results of capital export. He notes, for example, that "the decay of British agriculture [was] largely attributable to the development of railways in new countries" (xxv). These are the same railways that Forster personally invested in. Furthermore, the depopulation of the British countryside after the Corn Laws was precisely what made it possible for the bohemian fringe of the middle class to move into their country cottages and play at being rustics. Foreign investment may contribute to the decline of British manufacturing, Hobson notes; but when the profits are repatriated they are "likely to mean an increased demand for labour in certain kinds of industry—*e.g.* for artists, printers, dressmakers, domestic servants, gardeners, chauffeurs" (236). In recent years, the familiar chorus of lamentation about the relative decline of Britain tends to ignore the segment of the economy that is based on internationally-oriented finance capital, and that has continued to be viable, prosperous, and politically dominant.[13] If Britain has been in decline, one can only say that large parts of it are declining in style.

Forster's pastoralism, however, seeks to be a true alternative to modernity, rather than a self-serving myth of finance capital. An essential part of his case against the Wilcoxes, that Imperial family, is that they can enjoy their traditional English comforts by doing their dirty work overseas and out of sight. And if the Schlegels were to invest their capital in British industry rather than in Foreign Things, Forster would only see this as dirty work at home. His problem is how to uphold the civic and cultural virtues intrinsic to the rentier way of life, yet avoid complicity with commerce or technology.

He begins by sidestepping the charge that the rentier is a parasite who consumes, but does not produce. Helen Schlegel believes, like G. E. Moore, that "personal relations are the important thing for ever and ever" (176). Work is thus assigned a purely instrumental value, in providing the comfort and leisure that are required for agreeable personal relations. If one can have the comfort without work, so much the better for "the important thing" in life. The Schlegels' younger brother Tibby *is* stigmatised, but for emotional rather than physical laziness. As his name suggests, he is a rather epicene young man, who warms the teapot "almost too deftly" (55). He is also a surrogate for Forster himself; as with Rickie in **The Longest Journey,** the author passes a stern sentence on those whose deficiencies are closest to his own. Tibby's languid existence contrasts with the striving Wilcoxes, but morally he is no better than them:

> Unlike Charles [Wilcox], Tibby had money enough; his ancestors had earned it for him, and if he shocked the people in one set of lodgings he had only to move into another. His was the leisure without sympathy—an attitude as fatal as the strenuous: a little cold culture may be raised on it, but no art. His sisters had seen the family danger, and had never forgotten to discount the gold islets that raised them from the sea. Tibby gave all the praise to himself, and so despised the struggling and the submerged.
>
> (302)

Tibby is damned for his cold self-sufficiency, whereas his sisters are redeemed by their sympathy, their eagerness for connection with the world. These are specifically female traits, of course, and it is part of the female image that they are not *expected* to work. Middle-class women of this period can be thought of as rentiers by biological destiny; their vocation is to display their accomplishments, to *be* rather than to *do*. No one would expect them to be anything but passive investors.

Still, they have some work to do in the world—of an appropriate kind. One of their callings is to *prevent* change, which in Forster is almost always for the worse. In 1907, the year before he began *Howards End,* the Georgian mansion of the Thornton family, "Battersea Rise," had been torn down and its site "completely covered with very small two-story houses."[14] Forster had given money to a campaign to save the house and garden, but nothing could be done. *Howards End* is named after a house which *is* saved—even if the red tide of semi-detached houses is lapping at its fringes—and which ends up in the hands of those who have the moral right to inherit it, the Schlegels.

What is at stake here is the principle of cultural continuity. Property that is rightly transmitted and cherished from one generation to another has its own "aura" (to borrow Walter Benjamin's term); it contrasts, in the novel, with dwellings that are merely passed around by the marketplace and torn down when they cease to be profitable, like the London house where the Schlegels are living at the beginning of the book. The rentier is a preserver of the aura, the precious "spirit of place" that is threatened by the onrushing chaos of modernity. A society dominated by "new men" would have no traditions, no landmarks to guide the succession of generations; the rentier does not build, but she guards the ancestral rites, like the pigs' teeth embedded in the elm at Howards End.[15] She may live on the wealth amassed by previous generations, but she can mitigate this guilt by being a better custodian of England's heritage than the *nouveaux-riches* Wilcoxes.

In the concluding scene of the novel the Schlegel sisters have gained a far more substantial vocation than their earlier life of concert-going and tea-drinking in London. They have become traditional female providers of nurture: Helen cares for her infant son by Leonard Bast, Margaret cares for her husband, who breaks down after his son's conviction for Bast's manslaughter. They are farmers, raising hay on the meadows around the house. And Margaret will be a philanthropist, giving away half her capital over the next ten years. When she dies the house will pass to her nephew, the living symbol of union between the bourgeois Schlegels and the proletarian Basts. As R. N. Parkinson has pointed out, Forster upholds the principle of inheritance, but according to poetic rather than formal justice: in each generation, Howards End is held by those who morally deserve to have it.[16]

Forster's own life imitated his art. His inherited capital was greatly increased by his earnings as a writer after the success of *Howards End* in 1910; but he gave away much of what he had, either to charities or to his friends.[17] In 1931, after some ups and downs in his financial affairs, he joked that "I am not again making the mistake of investing, or even of letting it lie in the Bank. I shall bury it to be disinterred as wanted."[18] In 1934 he started a lively controversy on the issue of ethical investment in *Time and Tide.*[19] He described how he went to South Africa in 1929 and was appalled by the treatment of black workers in the mines at Kimberley; on his return, he sold his shares in a Belgian mining company. Now, he wanted to encourage the readers of *Time and Tide* to get rid of investments in arms companies. Several readers wrote in to point out flaws in this advice, but Forster stuck to his guns. "You can bowl anyone out on his investment list," he responded, "but I deny that all lists are equally harmful or harmless and that one need not bother, and I think it would be healthier if people talked openly about the contents of their lists and did not conceal them like illegitimate children."[20]

Still, a code of personal conduct does not necessarily provide the basis for a credible vision of society as a whole. The Schlegels' retreat into pastoralism is not really an adequate solution to the "Condition-of-England" issues that are presented in the body of the novel. Margaret's strategy for dealing with the modern world is simply to wait until it renounces its own vital principle:

> "Because a thing is going strong now, it need not go strong for ever," [Margaret] said. "This craze for motion has only set in during the last hundred years. It may be followed by a civilization that won't be a movement, because it will rest on the earth. All the signs are against it now, but I can't help hoping, and very early in the morning in the garden I feel that our house is the future as well as the past."
>
> (239)

Again, the contrast with the more positive outlook of *North and South* is instructive. When she revisits her old village in the South, Margaret Hale is at first dismayed not to find the rural Eden she had remembered in her Northern exile:

> A sense of change, of individual nothingness, of perplexity and disappointment, overpowered Margaret. Nothing had been the same; and this slight, all pervading instability, had given her greater pain than if all had been too entirely changed for her to recognise it. . . .

Wearily she went to bed, warily she arose in four or five hours' time. But with the morning came hope, and a brighter view of things.

"After all it is right," said she, hearing the voices of children at play while she was dressing. "If the world stood still, it would retrograde and become corrupt. . . . Looking out of myself, and my own painful sense of change, the progress of all around me is right and necessary. I must not think so much of how circumstances affect me myself, but how they affect others, if I wish to have a right judgment, or a hopeful trustful heart."

(488-489)

Margaret Schlegel gives **Howards End** its moral center, and she is its most sympathetic character; but her social perspective, at the end, is that of hermit in the Dark Ages. Although she has remained true to her mission of connecting classes and sexes, almost all of the novel's significant actions have been initiated by more vital characters: the Wilcoxes, Leonard Bast, her sister Helen. At the end, Forster turns Henry Wilcox into a cipher in order to remove an inconvenient force from the plot, much like the sudden deaths of unwanted characters in other Forster novels. And Henry's personal defeat is made into a facile allegory of the withering away of the class he belongs to. "I'm broken—I'm ended" he whimpers to Margaret (324); but what he represents surely is not. The device recalls D. H. Lawrence's crippling Clifford Chatterly, to point a similar moral; and it shows the artist's traditional condescension to the managerial classes, denying them any real moral or psychological complexity.[21]

Good liberal that he was, Forster was well aware of the case that could be made against his pet causes. He feared that those on the frontier of scientific thought would "abandon literature, which has committed itself too deeply to the worship of vegetation."[22] We can see another danger too: that English literature would waste away on its vegetarian diet—clinging to archaism and nostalgia while failing to engage the contemporary passions of the ordinary citizen. In his creative career, Forster remained a perpetual Edwardian, even though he lived until 1970. That period was the golden age of rentier culture in England—which is why it figures so prominently in England's nostalgia industry today. Everyone wants "a room with a view"; but England is peculiar in its insistence that the view should be of the eternally sunlit meadows of the past.

Notes

1. "The Challenge of Our Time," in *Two Cheers for Democracy* (Harmondsworth: Penguin, 1965): 65.

2. O. Stallybrass, ed., *Howards End* (Harmondsworth: Penguin, 1975): 134. Citations in the remainder of my article are to this edition.

3. Pp. 72-73. In an earlier draft of the novel Forster gave the Schlegel sisters twice as much income, and Tibby £1500.

4. Forster paid tribute to Gaskell in "The Charm and Strength of Mrs. Gaskell," *Sunday Times,* 7 April 1957, p. 10. He mentions having met Gaskell's daughters when he was a boy.

5. Elizabeth Gaskell, *North and South* (1854-55, Harmondsworth: Penguin, 1970): 529.

6. "Notes On The Way," *Time and Tide,* 2 June 1934, p. 696.

7. P. N. Furbank, *E. M. Forster: A Life* (London: Secker and Warburg, 1977), I, 159.

8. Martin Wiener, *English Culture and the Decline of the Industrial Spirit 1850-1980* (Cambridge University Press, 1981). For an important revision of Wiener's view see also Geoffrey Ingham, *Capitalism Divided: The City and Industry in British Social Development* (London: Macmillan, 1984).

9. Matthew Simon, "The Pattern of New British Portfolio Foreign Investment, 1865-1914," in A. R. Hall, ed., *The Export of Capital From Britain 1870-1914* (London: Methuen, 1968): 24.

10. "The Plumb-pudding in Danger": 1805.

11. *Abinger Harvest* (London: Edward Arnold, 1953): 399.

12. (London: Constable, 1914).

13. For a recent survey of the issue, see Perry Anderson, "The Figures of Descent," *New Left Review,* 161 (Jan/Feb 1987).

14. *Marianne Thornton* (New York: Harcourt, Brace, 1956): 9.

15. The attitude to such rites in *North and South* is quite different. When Margaret Hale goes back to visit her old village in the South, she is shocked to hear that one of the villagers had tried to control the "powers of darkness" by roasting alive her neighbor's cat (477-78). This "practical paganism" is contrasted to the more progressive attitudes of the industrial North.

16. "The Inheritors; or A Single Ticket for Howards End," in *E. M. Forster: A Human Exploration,* ed. G. K. Das and John Beer (London: Macmillan, 1979): 55-68.

17. For example, £10,000 to Bob and May Buckingham in 1964. His major asset, the copyright in his writings, was left to King's College, Cambridge.

18. *Selected Letters of E. M. Forster,* eds. Mary Lago and P. N. Furbank (Cambridge: Harvard University Press, 1985), II, 107. Compare J. M. Keynes on the "gradual disappearance of a rate of return on accumulated wealth" (the "euthanasia of the rentier"): "A man would still be free to accumulate his earned income with a view to spending it at a later date. But his accumulation would not grow. He would simply be in the position of Pope's father, who, when he re-

tired from business, carried a chest of guineas with him to his villa at Twickenham and met his household expenses from it as required." *The General Theory of Employment, Interest and Money* (London: Macmillan, 1973): 221.

19. Issues of 2 through 23 June, with associated letters to the editor.

20. *Time and Tide,* 23 June 1934, p. 797.

21. As usual, Forster himself anticipated this criticism: "there is a huge economic movement which has been taking the whole world, Great Britain included, from agriculture towards industrialism. That began about a hundred and fifty years ago, but since 1918 it has accelerated to an enormous speed, bringing all sorts of changes into national and personal life. . . . It has meant the destruction of feudalism and relationship based on the land, it has meant the transference of power from the aristocrat to the bureaucrat and the manager and the technician. Perhaps it will mean democracy, but it has not meant it yet, and personally I hate it. So I imagine do most writers, however loyally they try to sing its praises and to hymn the machine." *Two Cheers for Democracy*: 278.

22. *Commonplace Book,* ed. P. Gardner, (London: Scolar Press, 1985): 37.

Herbert N. Schneidau (essay date 1991)

SOURCE: Schneidau, Herbert N. "Safe as Houses: Forster as Cambridge Anthropologist." In *Waking Giants: The Presence of the Past in Modernism,* pp. 64-102. New York: Oxford University Press, 1991.

[*In the following essay, Schneidau explores the ways in which* Howards End *evidences "autochthony," or "an ideology of sacred space," as symbolized by the house* Howards End.]

> Can what they call civilization be right, if people mayn't die in the room where they were born?
>
> —Ruth Wilcox

Many agree with Lionel Trilling that *Howards End* is "undoubtedly Forster's masterpiece."[1] *A Passage to India,* written much later, may have reached a wider audience, partly because of the topicality of its antiracist and anticolonialist sentiments, and of course Forster enthusiasts can make cases even for the earlier works. But for those interested in the twentieth-century novel, this creation of "1908-1910" counts as a high-water mark for Forster and the genre. The British novel just before the Great War attained a level it has not, in general, reached again, and the best novels of the 1920s were written by those who had attained maturity and mastery before 1914. The War harrowed English sensibilities and sent several of its writers into spiritual exile, ironically imitating James Joyce's pre-

war remove. Their later works belong to International Modernism, not British literature. There was no surge in the number of new British writers after 1918, as in American, because those writers who stayed at home had trouble assimilating Modernism and especially could not embrace *Ulysses,* its pivotal work. Even Virginia Woolf called it the book of a "queasy undergraduate scratching his pimples," a remark that says nothing about Joyce but tells all about the mental paradigms of Bloomsbury.[2]

By 1918 the urge toward uncompromising "truth telling," the frankest possible presentations of social and sexual issues, was overpowering. The War in its official version (no photos or veridical reports had been allowed from the front), and the society out of which it had grown, were nothing but "old lies and new infamy."[3] This too figures in the ascendancy of the American novel and the stasis of the British: for the former, the uncensored aspect of Modernist writing was congenial to its prophetic-puritanic impulses, while the circumlocutory preferences of the latter, typified by Forster's genteel evasions in matters of sexuality, seemed dated or even duplicitous. Here again *A Passage to India* seems belated, and perhaps the years of novelistic silence before and after it appeared were Forster's tribute money to the presiding spirits of a world that had passed him by. Moreover, Forster's methods did not conform to Flaubertian and Jamesian proscriptions of authorial "comment." Indeed Forster revelled in addresses to "dear readers."

Forster and Modernism were thus sundered by powerful forces and beliefs. But in a cautious way he prefigured the world of Joyce and the others, in his deployment of what T. S. Eliot would later call, in regard to *Ulysses,* the "mythical method."[4] The parallels with mythological episodes in *Howards End* do not call attention to themselves, and there are few obviously classical motifs in the novel, in contrast to Forster's earlier works. But Forster does dramatize, through the motifs of the house and the land around it, an ideology that we can call that of sacred space, or autochthony, that is, the belief that spiritual powers, which Forster reticently calls "the unseen," inhere not in heavens or in ethereal forms but in the earth; that they are beings, incarnate in landforms or dwellings or tombs; and that they forcefully affect even godless lives. In many tribal societies, powers such as conception are credited not solely to sexual intercourse but to ancestral spirits who reside in groves, rocks, trees, and the like. Such was the legacy of autochthony, and it persisted into Hellenistic culture in the cult of the *genius loci,* the spirit of place.[5] After this, it became merely "poetic." Forster wants us to suspend disbelief; without going over into fantasy, he wants it to occur to us that these archaic beliefs are true in ways that we, under the dominance of materialist heritages, cannot acknowledge. He means to persuade us to lower our skeptical guards and to take literally such offhand metaphors as Margaret Schlegel's "'Houses are alive. No?'" For in the story the house is alive—it has a heart, and in a revelatory moment the heart is heard beating—and the land too lives: "England was alive, throbbing through all her estuaries, crying for joy through the mouths of all her gulls, and the north wind, with contrary motion, blew stronger against her rising seas."[6] In context, Forster always gives us the chance to write off such remarks as characters' or author's "fancies," but the totality of the design makes it clear that he intends a "logic of the imagination" to work on us, so that the figures have a cumulative or accretive effect. His personal beliefs are of course not necessarily determinative of the novel's imaginative structure, but he did want to be known as one who had tried various spiritual adventures, and his Clapham Sect ancestors revisited him in the form of an ambition to be a spiritual mentor to his age.

Most of the criticism on *Howards End* has centered on "personal relations," on the epigraph "only connect" and the other mottoes that cue a reading of the work as a bourgeois-liberal drama. "Panic and emptiness," "telegrams and anger," and other phrases are used by the Schlegel sisters to signal their rejection, whether contemptuous or forgiving, of the way of life represented by the Wilcoxes: domineering, crass, impersonal, and complacent; life by the code of the successful businessman and the dutiful colonial, highminded and coarsegrained. Here they are businessmen, in *A Passage to India* colonials; Forster may have said that he wanted to "connect" with such people, but he really wanted to stamp them out. In any case the book is not simply a tragicomedy of manners. "The personal" in this work is absorbed and eventually eclipsed by the drama of "the unseen"; the salvageable characters are separated out from the hopelessly obtuse by their intermittent insights into this development, which in turn involves dim awareness—all that any of them are ever vouchsafed—of the theme of autochthony.[7]

Trilling's elegant reading of the book on the social level is now several decades old but remains typical in many ways. He regrets the "mythical fantasy" of Forster's early stories, remarking that "surely the Greek myths made too deep an impression on Forster," and regrets further the persistence of these elements into the earlier novels. The implication is that *Howards End* advances beyond these by subordinating the mythical elements, reducing them to the dominant social criticism. The truth in this is that the autochthonic theme is implicitly critical of the modern consciousness, but it is misleading to imply that myth is subordinated: actually, it is less obvious but more pervasive. Moreover, Trilling supposes that the motifs of house and land are essentially political.

> *Howards End* is a novel about England's fate. . . . England herself appears in the novel in palpable form. The symbol for England is the house whose name gives the title to the book. Like the plots of so many English novels, the plot of *Howards End* is about the rights of property, about a destroyed will-and-testament and rightful and wrongful heirs. It asks the question, "Who shall inherit England?"[8]

Trilling insufficiently signals his irony. Not only might the unwary suppose that Schlegel liberalism is an adequate an-

swer to Wilcox crudeness, but to frame the question legalistically is wholly inconsonant. The novel asks, "Is it credible that the possessions of the spirit can be bequeathed at all?" (pp. 98-99) The concept of "rights of property" is firmly associated with the Wilcox mentality; and when the odious Charles Wilcox goes to prison for killing a man, his sentence grossly misrepresents the situation: but "the law, being made in his image," (p. 334) is incapable of truth.

Forster does labor to make us fear that Wilcox ideals will overwhelm the modern world, but as for inheriting Howards End, the Wilcoxes were never in the running. They are too stupid and insensitive, and are easily outmaneuvered by the powers immanent in house and land. They are caricatures whose genial or generous moments are somehow the results of misapprehension (except for those female Wilcoxes who "marry in" and are thus not real ones), and projects to "connect" with them are absurdly misplaced charity, at best. Forster's inveterate tendency was to practice novelistic overkill against the type of Englishman he feared and resented: clubbable, self-possessed, aggressively conventional. He will set up such a figure and then kill him off quickly and painfully—the revenge of the timid, sensitive, bullied schoolboy, which Forster remained to the end of his life.[9] The Wilcoxes are so grotesque that we may miss the fact that the Schlegel nostrums for progress and social change are likewise caricatures. The sisters are saved only because their openness gives more scope to the force of "the unseen."

In thus dramatizing mythological themes, Forster connects not only with Modernism in general but specifically provides a link between his friend Hardy and his other friend (despite plebeian origins) D. H. Lawrence, in whose works the whole idea flowered rather showily. For Forster it was thus "in the air." His years at Cambridge are best known for his membership in the Apostles and for other friendships that prefigured the Bloomsbury mystique, but his education in classics also enticed him with its promise of recovering a lost world and turning it into a merely misplaced one. He may even have heard something of Jane Harrison and the other Cambridge anthropologists, though he never manifested firsthand knowledge. In a sense his work uncannily recapitulates Harrison's discovery that underneath the Olympian pantheon there was a layer of chthonic, local traditions, cults, and numens of place.[10] The goal of *Howards End* was even more ambitiously revisionist than was Harrison's: he aimed to change not only our understanding of ancient religions but also our thinking about the nature of our lives and their relation to the earth on which they are carried out.

The grandiosity of these ambitions and their thematic conceptualizations surely gave Forster pause, and hesitancies appear even in the famous diffident opening: "One may as well begin with Helen's letters to her sister." This effete tone—"Oh dear yes, the novel tells a story"—betrays Forster's fear of seeming "hearty," unforgivable in British gentility with its decayed ideal of *sprezzatura*: "A country in love with amateurs . . . where the incompetent have such beautiful manners," as Ezra Pound put it.[11] Forster like other well-bred Englishmen disguises his own seriousness, so that the first episodes are dominated by the sisters' goodhearted playfulness and by the comic distractions of Aunt Juley, the interfering relative whose blunders land both families in an awkward misunderstanding. When Helen Schlegel and Paul Wilcox tryst—Helen being perversely attracted to Wilcox manliness—Aunt Juley and Charles Wilcox, Paul's older brother, turn the affair into a shouting match, a "game of Capping Families, a round of which is always played when love would unite two members of our race. But they played it with unusual vigour, stating in so many words that Schlegels were better than Wilcoxes, Wilcoxes better than Schlegels. They flung decency aside" (p. 21). These early pages of sub-Wildean farce are disguise, distraction, sleight-of-hand; Forster is already insinuating hints that will open out as the story progresses and especially as we reread. The very first pages of the book are disguised as an inconsequential letter from Helen to her sister Margaret, describing the house and its trees and grounds, but every detail comes to be part of the book's spiritual pattern. The letter introduces the person Helen cannot know is the presiding genius of the place, Ruth Wilcox, nee Ruth Howard at Howards End, later prevented from dying there only by her husband's habitual insensitivity and underhandedness (p. 283):

> This long letter is because I'm writing before breakfast. Oh, the beautiful vine leaves! The house is covered with a vine. I looked out earlier, and Mrs. Wilcox was already in the garden. She evidently loves it. No wonder she sometimes looks tired [later we learn that she was dying even at this time]. She was watching the large red poppies come out. Then she walked off the lawn to the meadow, whose corner to the right I can just see. Trail, trail, went her long dress over the sopping grass, and she came back with her hands full of the hay that was cut yesterday—I suppose for rabbits or something, as she kept on smelling it.
>
> (p. 4)

The smelling of the hay, like her lack of concern for her dress, is symbolic of Mrs. Wilcox's affinity for the earth, and in the final chapter the Schlegel sisters enact half-consciously her bequeathed awareness: the chapter is framed by an opening in which the "sacred centre" (p. 335) of the hay field is about to be harvested, and an ending in which Helen says more than she knows: "'The field's cut!' Helen cried excitedly—'the big meadow! We've seen to the very end, and it'll be such a crop of hay as never!'" (p. 343) The "very end" is not only the end of the book but also a long perspective that looks back through and past time, all the way back to the eternal present of ancient man and *la pensée sauvage*, which Forster calls "the Now" (p. 249, cf. pp. 315, 323). Thus the hay participates in a double framing, of the last chapter and of the book, and it identifies the first appearance of Ruth Wilcox in Helen's letter as the theophany of Demeter: the hay is her cereal icon. Demeter was Forster's favorite mythological figure, who "alone among gods has

true immortality."[12] The hay reappears so often that critics who do not grasp autochthony find it obtrusive—Mrs. Wilcox is said to be "a wisp of hay, a flower" (p. 74)—and at the climax the same phrase refers to "death" (p. 330). She therefore represents fructifying, sacrificial death, and in that sense plays the role of Persephone as well as that of Demeter: she disappears to emerge in renewed forms of life, organic and inorganic. She is incarnate in the house and field as well as some of the characters, notably Margaret Schlegel, who becomes "Mrs. Wilcox" and is pointedly so addressed at the end, even by the defeated, hostile Wilcoxes themselves

Not surprisingly, the real Wilcoxes all have hay fever. Helen's letter continues:

> Later on I heard the noise of croquet balls, and looked out again, and it was Charles Wilcox practising; they are keen on all games. Presently he started sneezing and had to stop. Then I hear more clicketing, and it is Mr. Wilcox practising, and then, "a-tissue, a-tissue": he has to stop too. Then Evie comes out, and does some calisthenic exercises on a machine that is tacked on to a greengage-tree—they put everything to use—and then she says "a-tissue," and in she goes. And finally Mrs. Wilcox reappears, trail, trail, still smelling hay and looking at the flowers.
>
> (p. 4)

Much later the book's sibyl, old Miss Avery, cackles maliciously at the thought of the Wilcox hay fever. "There's not one Wilcox that can stand up against a field in June—I laughed fit to burst while he [Henry] was courting Ruth. . . . This house lies too much on the land for them" (p. 273).

To the Wilcoxes, Howards End is merely an ungainly and useless property—"'one of those converted farms. They don't really do, spend what you will on them,'" says Henry Wilcox (p. 135)—and they hold on to it only from a grasping instinct. That the house has been in the Howard family for generations means nothing to Henry; for him it is hay fever and problems. To Ruth, on the other hand, it is "a spirit, for which she sought a spiritual heir" (p. 98), and her "one passion . . . the Holy of Holies" (p. 85), though she herself understands this only vaguely and nonintellectually. Throughout she is characterized as dim, evasive, and remote, out of focus with the everyday and the material, although loving and generous and above all majestic. She is in short a figure from another world. Her wisdom comes from atavism, from the voices of her ancestors sounding in her brain (as in Julian Jaynes's theories of "schizophrenic" ancient man).[13] When Aunt Juley and her son Charles have quarreled bitterly at "Capping Families," she settles all, first defusing Charles's efforts to play inquisitor:

> "Paul, is there any truth in this?"
>
> "I didn't—I don't—"
>
> "Yes or no, man; plain question, plain answer. Did or didn't Miss Schlegel—"

"Charles dear," said a voice from the garden. "Charles, dear Charles, one doesn't ask plain questions. There aren't such things."

They were all silent. It was Mrs. Wilcox.

She approached just as Helen's letter had described her, trailing noiselessly over the lawn, and there was actually a wisp of hay in her hands. She seemed to belong not to the young people and their motor, but to the house, and to the tree that overshadowed it. One knew that she worshipped the past, and that the instinctive wisdom the past can alone bestow had descended upon her—that wisdom to which we give the clumsy name of aristocracy. High-born she might not be. But assuredly she cared about her ancestors, and let them help her. When she saw Charles angry, Paul frightened, and Mrs. Munt ["Aunt Juley"] in tears, she heard her ancestors say: "Separate those human beings who will hurt each other most. The rest can wait."

(p. 22)

Her instincts contrast vividly not only with her family's obtuseness but also with Aunt Juley's self-satisfaction and itch to interfere. After the contretemps,

> Mrs. Munt soon recovered. She possessed to a remarkable degree the power of distorting the past, and before many days were over she had forgotten the part played by her own imprudence in the catastrophe. Even at the crisis she had cried: "Thank goodness, poor Margaret is saved this!" which during the journey to London evolved into: "It had to be gone through by someone," which in its turn ripened into the permanent form of: "The one time I really did help Emily's girls was over the Wilcox business."

(p. 23)

So it is delicious irony that we are introduced to still more symbols of "the unseen" through this unseeing person. On her train trip to the village where Howards End stands, "a series of tiled and slated houses passed before Mrs. Munt's inattentive eyes, a series broken at one point by six Danish tumuli that stood shoulder to shoulder along the highroad, tombs of soldiers" (p. 15). These mounds, called the Six Hills, grow in significance as the novel progresses, and link the landscape's eternal "Now" with the historic past. Margaret Schlegel responds to the Six Hills with instinctive admiration: "Beneath them she settled that soldiers of the best kind lay buried. She hated war and liked soldiers—it was one of her amiable inconsistencies" (p. 198).[14] She looks often at them, "tombs of warriors, breasts of the spring" (p. 309). At the crisis of the book, she is sitting on the "glebe," all that is left of the old farmland: "Henry's kind had filched most of it. She moved to the scrap opposite, wherein were the Six Hills." When Henry confesses to her that the Wilcoxes have been utterly defeated, "Margaret drove her fingers through the grass. The hill beneath her moved as if it was alive" (pp. 333-34).[15] They symbolize the renewing vitality of the earth, again uniting life and a fructifying death. In another connection, Forster notes another local "myth": "Six forest trees—that is a fact—grow out of one of the graves in Tewin churchyard.

The grave's occupant—that is the legend—is an atheist, who declared that if God existed six forest trees would grow out of her grave" (p. 323). If we share the Wilcox mentality, we stick to facts. Henry writes off the Six Hills with a passing remark: "'Curious mounds,' said Henry, 'but in with you now; another time'" (p. 204). He is handing Margaret into his "motor" and has no leisure for tourist speculations, but his "another time" is of course a major dramatic irony: he does not know that he is evoking what he himself so grievously lacks, the sense of the Past, the sense that the modern "restless civilization" that seems to him the *telos* of all the ages is simply a phase in the real life of the earth. For Wilcoxes the time is always out of joint, but they like Mrs. Munt are fatuously unaware of it, "incapable of grouping the past" (p. 259). Henry's "mental states became obscure as soon as he had passed through them" (p. 178).

Forster works many more landscape details, such as trees with "healing powers" and other legendary attributes, into his mosaic of the living land and house, but these examples should suffice; the others can easily be tallied if we reread the book with open minds to what the text pointedly says. The cumulative effect of the motifs is an interesting adaptation of the literary impressionism that is more familiarly associated with Ford and Conrad: it requires us to pay attention to minute details, to remember motifs, to put them together by looking again and again, varying our perspectives.[16] As in *pointillisme* the details can hardly be seen for what they really are until they cohere into Gestalten. Forster's techniques culminate in scenes that suddenly irradiate many details with revelatory significance. Possibly the best managed is the entry of Margaret, after years of strange delays and frustrations, into Howards End. She is not consciously aware that she is entering a sacred space, but is unaccountably moved by the landscape as she stands on the porch. A Hardyesque "fancy" pops into her mind: "How Helen would revel in such a notion! Charles dead, all people dead, nothing alive but houses and gardens. The obvious dead, the intangible alive, and—no connection at all between them! Margaret smiled" (p. 200). Then the house opens itself up to her, though it had seemed locked to Henry (he's gone to get the key), and she enters full of "fancies" she doesn't grasp, like Adela Quested going into the Marabar caves.

> She paced back into the hall, and as she did so the house reverberated.
>
> "Is that you, Henry?" she called.
>
> There was no answer, but the house reverberated again.
>
> "Henry, have you got in?"
>
> But it was the heart of the house beating, faintly at first, then loudly, martially. It dominated the rain.
>
> It is the starved imagination, not the well-nourished, that is afraid. Margaret flung open the door to the stairs. A noise as of drums seemed to deafen her. A woman, an old woman, was descending, with figure erect, with face impassive, with lips that parted and said dryly:

"Oh! Well, I took you for Ruth Wilcox."

Margaret stammered: "I—Mrs. Wilcox—I?"

"In fancy, of course—in fancy. You had her way of walking. Good day." And the old woman passed out into the rain.

(pp. 201-2)

Forster has designed the scene so that with the words *old woman* we are ready for a ghost: "'Did you take her for a spook?'" asks the crude but insightful Dolly Wilcox in the next chapter (p. 202). In consequence, the line, "'I took you for Ruth Wilcox'" might have confused Margaret even more than first appears, because it voices her own reaction to the descending figure. This is no spook but the "eccentric" Miss Avery. The momentary confusion is expertly planned: the three women instinctively share much, and at this point their identities actually interpenetrate. Margaret, we learn, was "clutching a bunch of weeds" (p. 202) when she saw the apparition. Near the end of the book, Margaret—by then being called "Mrs. Wilcox"—senses an even more comprehensive incarnation.

> "I feel that you [Helen] and I and Henry are only fragments of that woman's mind. She knows everything. She is everything. She is the house, and the tree that leans over it. People have their own deaths as well as their own lives, and even if there is nothing beyond death, we shall differ in our nothingness. I cannot believe that knowledge such as hers will perish with knowledge such as mine. She knew about realities. She knew when people were in love [Helen and Paul], though she was not in the room. I don't doubt that she knew when Henry deceived her."
>
> "Good night, Mrs. Wilcox," called a voice.
>
> "Oh, good night, Miss Avery."

(pp. 313-14)

The oracular, disembodied voice of Miss Avery, who also "knows everything," emphasizes the interpenetration of Margaret and Ruth Wilcox, but she is included. In fact, the vagueness of the antecedents in Margaret's sentences gestures toward her.

By the end of the book, Margaret even acts and speaks like Ruth Wilcox, settling disputes and muddles with instinctive, atavistic generosity rather than with her earlier Schlegel liberalism, which tends to victimize its legatees. On being praised for this by Helen, she says, sitting amidst the hay: "'Things that I can't phrase have helped me'" (p. 339). "The wisdom the past alone can bestow" has descended on her, through Mrs. Wilcox. But Miss Avery too is a reincarnation; she appears in the book only after Mrs. Wilcox dies, and gradually we learn of an extraordinary bond between the two, who outwardly have been almost mistress and servant. The country people credit Miss Avery with "prophetic powers," and she foretells the futures of all the key characters and of Howards End. So she carries on the "spirit" of Ruth Wilcox in the ordinary sense, but also becomes the *genius loci*, though the male Wilcoxes

insist on treating her as a simple charwoman. Whereas the "inattentive" Aunt Juley can never get straight the name of Howards End, she knows every inch of the place as if it were her skin, knows that the Schlegels are fated to oust the obtuse Wilcoxes, and knows just what the latter are good for: "'Wilcoxes are better than nothing, as I see you've found,'" she says dryly to Margaret (p. 274).

Miss Avery is not only sibylline and a *genius loci*, but also embodies the idea of "folk" wisdom. Forster does little with the folk except for one memorable scene, the aftermath of Ruth Wilcox's funeral. Without telling us that she had died or even that she was ill—indeed the immediately preceding chapter has her "'fit as a fiddle,'" by her own account (p. 87)—Forster begins Chapter 11 with "The funeral was over." Here the "virtual" narrative consciousness (though not the voice) is that of the country people, and eventually one of them in particular, a young woodcutter who pollards elms while the funeral takes place beneath him. For him and the other villagers the ritual is a sensual experience, not a mock-solemn mummery. "The funeral of a rich person was to them what the funeral of Alcestis, of Ophelia, is to the educated. It was Art; though remote from life, it enhanced life's values, and they witnessed it avidly" (p. 88). For the Wilcoxes, in contrast, the woodcutter and his ilk are merely nuisances; blind to the values of communal ritual, they think of the funeral as their property, which others may mar or mishandle.[17] Through the woodcutter Forster underlines all the previously established connections between fatality and fertility, death and rebirth, which are such regular features of autochthonic ideology.

> The young wood-cutter stayed a little longer, poised above the silence and swaying rhythmically. At last the bough fell beneath his saw. [The very pollarding of the elms emblematizes the ritualistic, sacrificial sense that death is necessary to make way for new life.] With a grunt, he descended, his thoughts dwelling no longer on death, but on love, for he was mating. He stopped as he passed the new grave; a sheaf of tawny chrysanthemums had caught his eye. "They didn't ought to have coloured flowers at buryings," he reflected. Trudging on a few steps, he stopped again, looked furtively at the dusk, turned back, wrenched a chrysanthemum from the sheaf, and hid it in his pocket.

(pp. 88-89)

Later we find it was Margaret who had the instinct to send the chrysanthemums; her act would no doubt have pleased Mrs. Wilcox, but it annoys the conventional-minded family. In the same spirit, Margaret herself attended the funeral but "stood far back among the [village] women" (p. 101)—another instinctively correct gesture, but not because of the implied deference for which the Wilcoxes approve it.

Forster has been accused, with some justice, of romanticizing his yeomen; indeed, this aspect of his autochthonic thinking might be called Tory apologetics. The Wilcoxes are certainly representative of Whiggery: they are climbing, grasping, snobbish without right, vulgarly "modern," and shallow—in short, self-righteous *arrivistes* in their worst form.[18] They have no sense of the land, of the people, of the culture; they care only for commercial success, social appearances, and the rights of property construed suspiciously and legalistically. Forster does not trouble to subtilize their offensiveness: "When Mr. Wilcox said that one sound man of business did more good to the world than a dozen of your social reformers, [Helen, in what can only be called a moral rape-fantasy] had swallowed the curious assertion without a gasp, and had leant back luxuriously among the cushions of his motor-car" (p. 24). The motorcar is a fine touch, for it symbolizes their rootless, thoughtlessly destructive way of life. For Forster, entrepreneurial and imperialist drives are simply rationalized spoliation of the earth. Against these activities he sets a complex of almost feudal values: landedness against mercantilism, instinct against calculation, atavism against sophistication.

Forster's latent Toryism shows up most gracelessly in the unsatisfying treatment of Leonard Bast. In spite of his tepid Bloomsbury leanings, Forster was capable of uttering such disclaimers as this: "We are not concerned with the very poor. They are unthinkable, and only to be approached by the statistician or the poet. This story deals with gentlefolk, or with those who are obliged to pretend that they are gentlefolk" (p. 45). Even his most fervent admirers must squirm at that one. This is by no means the only passage that implies that men were better off when all knew their places: when Wilcoxes treat the lower classes rudely, this is meant to contrast with the noblesse oblige of true aristocracy, under which all ranks prosper amicably. But Forster's political views are not as troublesome as their consequence, which is the inability to make the Basts materialize for us. Leonard remains precisely the theoretical pauper of the women's-club debate that leads the Schlegels to try to help him: the novel patronizes him as remorselessly as the ladies do.[19]

However, Forster's social views are well adapted to engender another important pattern of imagery in the novel. Throughout, the thrusting, exploitative Whiggery of the Wilcoxes is characterized by restless, aimless movements from place to place, house to house; they cannot alight anywhere; unsurprisingly, they approve of developers' demolitions of huge blocks of flats in London, in order to throw up more flats, as "good for trade," whereas Margaret finds the "continual flux" deeply unsettling: "us at our worst—eternal formlessness" and loss of differences (p. 182).

> The feudal ownership of land did bring dignity, whereas the modern ownership of movables is reducing us again to a nomadic horde. We are reverting to the civilization of luggage, and historians of the future will take note how the middle classes accreted possessions without taking root in the earth, and may find in this the secret of their imaginative poverty. [N.B. the implied warning to readers.] The Schlegels were certainly the poorer for the loss of Wickham Place. It had helped to balance

their lives, and almost to counsel them. Nor is their ground-landlord spiritually the richer. He has built flats on its site, his motor-cars grow swifter, his exposures of Socialism more trenchant. But he has spilt the precious distillation of the years, and no chemistry of his can give it back to society again.

(pp. 149-50)

Much of the book is occupied with searches for new houses, as leases expire and other modern barbarisms take effect. Margaret sees the tides of the Thames as emblematic of the condition and of the forgetfulness it brings (p. 137). London in this book always stands for an unsatisfactory blur of hurry and construction, an aimless tide washing this way and that, a pointless aggrandizement (Howards End is small). London engenders a "red rust" creeping out into the country in the form of Suburbia (pp. 15, 167, etc.). Looking at this glow of supposed energy but real decay, Helen mourns: "And London is only part of something else, I'm afraid. Life's going to be melted down, all over the world." To which Margaret can only reply, "This craze for motion has only set in during the last hundred years. It may be followed by a civilization that won't be a movement, because it will rest on the earth" (p. 339). They speak at Howards End—itself a survival, a time capsule of the real England sealed against Suburbia and such threatening forces manifest in Wilcox values. The house itself has maneuvered the Schlegels to victory over the Wilcoxes in order to ensure its own preservation.

The pattern of rest versus movement is admirably expressed in the opposition of house to motorcar: as mentioned earlier, the car represents the unseeing, uncaring, destructive oscillation of Wilcoxes careering back and forth. Every time car journeys are described or mentioned, the danger to children and animals is dwelt on. In the most distasteful incident, Charles Wilcox leads a convoy of cars, one of which runs over a cat; instead of stopping, Charles drives on, and Margaret jumps out of the car.

> No doubt she had disgraced herself. But she felt their whole journey from London had been unreal. They had no part with the earth and its emotions. They were dust, and a stink, and cosmopolitan chatter, and the girl whose cat had been killed had lived more deeply than they.

(p. 214)

Even when not so stupidly lethal, cars rob their occupants of the sense of space—which, given the importance of land and geography, is severe loss. Wilcoxes never notice this, of course, but Margaret does: "She looked at the scenery. It heaved and merged like porridge. Presently it congealed. They had arrived" (p. 198). This journey takes them smack up to the entrance to Howards End, but she cannot grasp this because the car has deprived her of spatial orientation. "A little porch was close up against her face. 'Are we there already?'" (p. 199)

This quality of motor journeys is also used metaphorically, in a passage that contrasts Mrs. Wilcox's slowminded nobility to the mercurial dartings of a representative set of Bright Young People (among whom, interestingly, is a Miss Quested): "Clever talk alarmed [Mrs. Wilcox], and withered her delicate imaginings; it was the social counterpart of a motor-car, all jerks, and she was a wisp of hay, a flower" (p. 74). She says to Margaret, "You younger people move so quickly that it dazes me" (p. 78). Margaret has the wisdom to feel this as a reproof from a spiritual agency she cannot comprehend, "a personality that transcended their own and dwarfed their activities" (p. 76). Mrs. Wilcox's transcendence lies of course in her merger with the earth—literally so at her funeral, after which even her smallminded husband has a glimmer of insight: "Ruth knew no more of worldly wickedness and wisdom than did the flowers in her garden, or the grass in her field" (p. 89). The Biblical imagery joins together the associations of her first name, plus Keats's line about the "alien corn," with the Demeter motif. But Henry's metaphorical thought is ironic—and far more accurate than he realizes—because, as we later learn, behind his reverence for her innocence there is a self-congratulatory smugness; he thinks she never suspected his affair with the improbable Jacky. (Later Margaret and Helen intuit that she knew, but her transcendence must have entailed untroubled acceptance of all things brought to her by atavistic wisdom.) Henry's flash of insight dissipates among his hypocrisies. His world is business and motor-cars: even the furniture he likes consists of "chairs of maroon leather. It was as if a motor-car had spawned" (p. 163). Margaret, at this point about to marry Henry under the delusion that he deserves "connecting" with, sinks into such a chair, just as Helen earlier leaned back in his car when yielding to his preposterous views. The most offensive of all the Wilcoxes, Charles, whose corrosive suspicions twist every act and motive into caricatures, persistently drives or attends to cars throughout the book. No wonder that when Helen most keenly grasps how the Schlegels and Wilcoxes have unwittingly combined to ruin Leonard Bast, she has a vision of him being crushed by a "Juggernaut car" (p. 316).

The automobile imagery is linked to yet another pattern: whereas men in the story are associated with cars and restless proprietorship, women are the vessels of true possession, permanence, and rest. In acquiring property, women react instinctively to places and houses themselves, endowing them with feelings and lives in cheerful acceptance of the pathetic fallacy. Thus feminine discourse provides Forster his opportunities to embed autochthonous figures of speech that provide the thematic backbone of the book. The female Schlegels keep up a drumfire of proleptic remarks about the importance of place and their own dependence on it, even before they see the point of their own understanding. Long before she ever sees Howards End, Margaret says "I quite expect to end my life caring most for a place" (p. 130). The implausibility of the sisters' interest in Leonard Bast is sketchily concealed by giving him a role in this pattern. His pitiable attempts to acquire culture have entailed shallow reading of some of the English travel writers and historians of place, from Ruskin to Stevenson and George Borrow; hence his

failure to transcend these writings can become the occasion for remarks by Margaret: "Haven't we all to struggle against life's daily greyness, against pettiness, against mechanical cheerfulness, against suspicion? I struggle by remembering my friends; others I have known by remembering some place—some beloved place or tree—we thought you one of these" (p. 143).

Even Evie Wilcox, otherwise a hardminded and conventional girl with all the Wilcox suspicion and concern for appearances, responds to places with feminine instinct. She it was who induced her father to buy Oniton Grange, another house that Margaret quickly learns to love, only to have her new husband rent it out from under her. Of Evie and Oniton, Henry says: "Poor little girl! She was so keen on it all, and wouldn't even wait to make proper inquiries about the shooting. Afraid it would get snapped up—just like all of your sex" (p. 260-61). Whereas his own approach, naturally, is businesslike and unsentimental, all calculation and hardnosed beating down of others, with few thoughts about the house itself. "One bit of advice: fix your district, then fix your price, and then don't budge. That's how I got both Ducie Street and Oniton. I said to myself, 'I mean to be exactly here,' and I was, and Oniton's a place in a thousand" (p. 155). As usual, Henry's accounts of the acquisition contradict themselves, but his sense of the difference in the masculine and feminine approaches to house buying is ironically accurate. For him no house will really "do," because of his placeless instincts; he is ingenious in finding reasons for moving. Since the act of acquisition is for him more important than the property itself, he gets his satisfaction from the negotiations, which he no doubt conducts on the model of his rebukes to servants and inferiors. Without bothering to tell his new wife, who had "determined to create new sanctities" there (p. 222), he disposes of Oniton because it is "damp" (p. 260), although Forster lets us understand that in reality the house has purposefully repelled him as an intruder, just as Howards End later does. Indeed, while Evie is getting married from Oniton, Margaret feels that the ceremony is somehow unreal and that "the Norman church had been intent all the time on other business" (p. 222).

We find that the whole pattern of rest and movement, with cars and houses, is sexually polarized, and that the shadowy struggle between Schlegels and Wilcoxes is really between atavistically sensitive females and no-nonsense males. Unsurprisingly, the book brings itself to this question: "Are the sexes really races, each with its own code of morality, and their mutual love a mere device of Nature to keep things going?" (p. 240) This thought occurs to Margaret; she thrusts it down, but it recurs later in unanswerable form when she shuts herself up in Howards End with her fugitive and pregnant sister. "A new feeling came over her; she was fighting for women against men. She did not care about rights, but if men came into Howards End, it should be over her body" (p. 290). Here at last the metaphors coalesce, and the struggle that seemed between families is revealed as sex war, full of overtones of race war. Howards End is not to be the possession of any family—the "ancestors" are ultimately generalized—but a home for refugee women and their nameless, almost parthenogenetic offspring. Women deserve it; while males have striven to dominate the earth and to inherit it in a legalistic sense, the females have been half-consciously serving as guardians and stewards.

Forster was not much of a feminist, but he did see that such devices as chivalry are at best patronizing. Margaret knows this, but pretends not to in deference to Henry: a deference she is obliged to repeat again and again until goaded beyond it by what she sees as Henry's attack on her sister, in his refusal to let the two women spend one night with their ancestral *lares* at Howards End. Men are equally objectionable, whether patronizing or suppressing women. Henry has done his best—fortunately that's not much—to denature Howards End with his improvement projects, undertaken to "please" his first wife: the result is a "series of mistakes," a house disfigured internally by rooms "that men have spoilt through trying to make it nice for women" (pp. 297-98). Always men will rationalize their spoliations with cant about doing it all for wives and families, but they make no effort to grasp female points of view, nor would they be caught dead understanding women. The book is unrelieved by the presence of males who can take even a step beyond themselves to try the female side of any issue. Even Tibby Schlegel is an outsider who can silence feminine play (p. 65), although in her early infatuation with Wilcox maleness Helen compares him unfavorably with them, grumbling that he's not a "real boy" and calling him "Auntie Tibby" (p. 43). In a distracted way men sometimes aid women's projects, to keep them quiet, but underneath the sexes are at eternal cross-purposes.

This view of life has enough truth in it to carry the plot over some gross implausibilities, though it is no profound contribution to the theory of sexual warfare. Forster's males, except for the unconvincing Leonard Bast and the inert Tibby Schlegel, are simply projections of his enemy, the arrogant bullying public-schoolboy, or "Red-blood." And his females, for all their sensitivity, are only vaguely women. They are theoretical in every sense, whether idealized or caricatured. Forster had, after all, only a limited ability to imagine himself in other identities, and just as his portrayal of a clerk on the lowest rungs of gentility lacks all *effet du réel*, his women are substantial only from a distance. They are "Mollycoddles," the opposite of "Red-bloods," in dresses.

Forster's characters serve well enough on a first quick reading, but the trouble is that his quasi-impressionist techniques of accreting images are best savored on rereading, and such scrutiny provokes embarrassing questions not only about the characters but also about the plot. Many critics have found Forster's plots in general, and that of *Howards End* in particular, to depend far too heavily on unlikely coincidences, improbable impulses, strained connections. Given the nature of the Wilcoxes, why would the Schlegels ever have anything to do with them? Forster can

get away with asserting that for a brief period Helen was perversely attracted by their "manliness," but the plot requires continued contact, so they have to turn up literally across the street from the Schlegel's London house: a shameless device. Then comes the celebrated problem of the attraction between Margaret and Henry Wilcox—equally unlikely for either one, given what is established of their characters.[20] Forster does labor to suggest that the motive force of their union is Margaret's desire to "connect the prose with the passion" (p. 186). Henry is certainly prosaic, so Margaret's deference to his supposed strengths and forgiveness of his weaknesses is just barely plausible as an extremely deluded form of generosity. But even if that problem is put aside, many more improbabilities intrude. The Basts have to be dragged in repeatedly, by the handle of Leonard's umbrella. Leonard's overpowering urge to discuss books is the barest contrivance, but not worse than Jacky's unimaginable liaison with Henry in an unlikely past, or Helen's ridiculous invasion of Evie's wedding party with them. Most contrived of all is Leonard's supposed desire to confess to "ruining" a woman of higher station. This brings him on a pre-dawn train ride to Howards End, there to be "thrashed" by the bully Charles Wilcox and to die, most conveniently, of heart disease. Although Forster tries to imply that this trip is a kind of Grail quest for Leonard, it is the last term of an absurd series.

As one reads through the book to see what happens next and why, to see a "story" turn into a "plot" in Forster's own terms, one credits these events provisionally, always hoping for further explanation or insight. On rereading, one finds little more than chatty rationalizations by the narrator or the characters. Yet sometimes Forster can make one problem mask another: for instance, he knew better than to attempt direct transcription of the impossible scene in which Leonard impregnates Helen. No amount of insistence on Helen's sexual impulsiveness or deranged state can make us believe this, and Leonard's acceptance is even more unthinkable (Katherine Mansfield said the umbrella did it).[21] However, we don't learn of this intercourse until the crescendo of final events is already in motion, when Margaret and Henry are pursuing what they suppose to be a "mad" Helen, and the revelation of the pregnancy comes as a nice touch. Then our attention is diverted from the impossible by the merely implausible: Leonard's fatherhood is almost forgotten in the impressionist handling of the death scene.

The thread showing that all the implausibilities are linked together is sexual evasiveness, and this is not surprising given Forster's astonishing ignorance, at the age of thirty, of the physical facts of sexual intercourse.[22] Even the unlucky Jacky's sex life, though several times asserted, is portrayed by no more than half-hearted hints. But Forster's reticence achieves more than conformity with Victorian standards, for it forces us to look elsewhere, to see if sexual energy shows up in deflected forms. And though the sexual lacunae mar the book novelistically, they contribute to the theme of autochthony a sense of ominous and telling silence. Sex becomes an indescribable mystery at the heart of human existence, as fertility is for tribal societies: it is sex that is truly "the unseen" in *Howards End.*

In autochthonous cultures, not only is fertility the great mystery but intercourse also is the model of human relationships with the world of nature and animals, much to the distress of missionaries. On cave walls in France and Spain, on rocks in Australia and Polynesia and America, representations of animals survive that are clearly emblems of power, including sexual power. In some instances the intercourse with humans is portrayed, or mimed in ritual. Totemism is an ideology that is inconceivable without animal ancestors, and the proliferation in mythology of hybrid creatures—Centaurs, satyrs, and the like—is evidence of the ubiquity of this kind of thinking. Western writers cannot touch the theme explicitly, though Lawrence comes close and Faulkner gives us glimpses: one Snopes falls in love with a cow, several characters achieve reverence for a totemic bear, and so on. Forster does little with animals—even later with Hinduism to help him—and presumably would have been horrified by "bestiality," but he preserves the sense of sanctified yet obscene mystery and overpowering curiosity that a child's approach to sex can embody, and which figures in autochthonic art.[23]

There is, however, one exception to the rule of loveless coupling in *Howards End,* one tender and intimate scene, at the end of Chapter 40.

> The peace of the country was entering into her. It has no commerce with memory, and little with hope. Least of all is it concerned with the hopes of the next five minutes. It is the peace of the present, which passes understanding. Its murmur came "now," and "now" once more as they trod the gravel, and "now," as the moonlight fell upon their father's sword. They passed upstairs, kissed, and amidst the endless iterations fell asleep. The house had enshadowed the tree at first, but as the moon rose higher the two disentangled, and were clear for a few moments at midnight. Margaret awoke and looked into the garden. How incomprehensible that Leonard Bast should have won her this night of peace! Was he also part of Mrs. Wilcox's mind?
>
> (p. 315)

Out of context, the only element that would prevent reading "this night of peace" to refer to postcoital languor is the fateful and phallic "father's sword," which is unobtrusive here though manifest later. Notice the images of house and tree, already given as both vital and personal on the first page: while the house pervades the book, even the wych-elm recurs insistently. It has pigs' teeth set in its bark, to cure "toothache." When Margaret first sees it, she identifies it as "a comrade." "Neither warrior, nor lover, nor god," it is beyond "any simile of sex" and yet suggests earthy relationships (p. 206). Now, in the night which she spends alone with Helen in the house, against her husband's express prohibition and with all males barricaded outside, the house-tree relation embodies that of the "com-

rades" Margaret and Helen. As we read the paragraph, we look over the preceding chapters and realize that, as Wilfred Stone says, this reunion is the "only convincing love-scene" in the book.[24] Hence the surprisingly ambiguous phrase "as the moon rose higher the two disentangled." Checking ourselves and the text, we find that no, Forster has not written a scene of lesbian incest, but in one way it would certainly seem fitting if he had, and we pass on with relief or disappointment. Forster was good at these tricky situations: what really happened in the Marabar cave? That in both cases the ambiguities are intentional is not to be doubted. When Margaret and Henry finally trap the "truant" Helen in the house, Margaret has only time to "whisper: 'Oh, my darling—'" before she has to shoo all the males away (289). Then a chapter later, she returns and says "'Oh, my darling!'" and "'My darling, forgive me,'" bolting the door from the inside (p. 292). Forster goes far enough, during the ensuing conversation, to establish that Helen has been living with one Monica, a "crude feminist of the South," that is, Italy (pp. 293-94). Much of "dear," "dearest," "dear old lady," recurs in the sister's talk, along with the earlier noted rhetoric about war between the sexes. Then this:

> And the triviality faded from their faces, though it left something behind—the knowledge that they never could be parted because their love was rooted in common things. . . . Helen, still smiling, came up to her sister. She said: "It is always Meg." They looked into each other's eyes. The inner life had paid.
>
> (p. 299)

With "the past sanctifying the present," the house is their "salvation" because, among other things, it furnishes a redoubt against males. Finally: "'But it would give me so much pleasure to have one night here with you. It will be something to look back on. Oh, Meg lovey, do let's! . . . Why not? It's a moon'" (p. 301). Presumably Helen means a lark, but also a honeymoon. (This theme could then be entitled "Come Back to the House Again, Meg Lovey.") Before the scene of embracing and falling asleep "amidst the endless iterations"—of the murmur of "now," of course, but do we not also think automatically of lovers' protestations?—Helen asks Margaret to flee with her, to leave her husband for life in Germany (in spite of a Monica with whom she would not "get on" [p. 314]) in a most unconventional ménage. Though this flight is obviated by the death of Leonard, the imprisonment of Charles, and the breakdown of Henry, the two sisters in the final chapter are living in the house, in full control of it and of the situation. Helen's unnamed baby who is to become legal heir plays in the hay field, Henry is defeated and so "eternally tired" that he can no longer career about, the Wilcoxes are dismissed, Leonard can barely be remembered, and the sisters are as contented a couple as appears in Forster's work. No more is said about Monica.

Forster had the grace to recognize the greatness of Proust, whose Albertine was really Albert, and whose example suggests that the insights of homosexuals into love can be especially keen. Critics have, it appears, been looking for love in all the wrong places in *Howards End,* just as they have caught the autochthonic theme only fitfully. Forster's transposition of sexes, turning homosexual lovers into sisters, has the effect of making his characters vague as women, but it allows him to treat "passion" with some knowledge. Moreover, he can use it as a screening device: as with Hardy's image of the stiffening corpse, readers were disposed to deny what they saw, even to themselves. But, as with the autochthonic motifs, we have only to read what the text says without Wilcox assumptions. Indeed, the themes are intertwined; it seems likely that the tenderness of the love scene owes something to Forster's imagination of the reunion of Demeter and Persephone. This maiden is with child, a child with no real father—so much the better mythologically. The homosexual's point of view opens up possibilities to Forster that he might otherwise not have explored: knowing that sexual desire cannot always be made to behave in approved ways, he becomes excruciatingly aware of blindnesses of all sorts. "'Oh, Meg, the little that is known about these things!'" (p. 313) If we insist on reducing the novel to a "believable" bourgeois drama, we do violence to the imaginative structure and reveal our own conventionality, in sexual as in spiritual matters.

Given the book's opportunities for *méconnaissance,* its history of misreadings is predictable. Some have been more revealing than others. D. H. Lawrence wrote to Forster that he had made "a nearly deadly mistake in glorifying those *business* people in *Howards End.* Business is no good."[25] What can he have been thinking of? To be sure, Forster makes some efforts to persuade us that Margaret's love for Henry is not hopelessly inconceivable, and Margaret is made to give a few rationalizations of modern capitalism. More to the point, Forster makes Schlegel liberalism boomerang: every time Margaret and especially Helen try to help the Basts, they pauperize or degrade them a little more, from the umbrella business to the unpaid hotel bill at Oniton. Helen's ultimate gift, of herself, leads directly to Leonard's death, in a reversal of the myth of Zeus and Semele (so much for heterosexual love). Yet these touches of grim comedy don't really balance the treatment of the Wilcoxes, which is surely a caricature and not a glorification. In Lawrence we should probably diagnose a case of willful blindness, along the lines that Harold Bloom and the late Paul de Man have sketched out. Lawrence's own interest in autochthonic themes was already developed—his fondness for the Pluto-Persephone myth, with a dark male from underground carrying off a pale virgin, has been remarked—and was to grow obsessive.[26] Perhaps he could not see *Howards End* because similar ideas were consuming him, in other forms. But whereas he, like Hardy, embraced primitivistic emphases, neither used autochthony as an actual plot element as Forster does. Nor, on the other hand, does either offer a brittle comic surface over which casual readers can skate, avoiding the deeper reverberations as "some mystic stuff." Hence *Howards End* can be read without the mythological meanings, whereas Lawrence's work can hardly be mistaken for bourgeois drama.

Some critics, feeling the tension between readings, have argued that *Howards End* is seriously flawed by a confusion between the realistic conventions of the traditional novel and the "mystic" or "fabular" elements.[27] This seems imprecise, for the convention is not the book's problem. *Howards End* is a realistic novel but with certain premises that the modern mind is not disposed to accept; in fact it could be said that the book dramatizes just this weakness, as Forster sees it. Wilcox offensive behavior is a consequence of spiritual poverty. But with the autochthonic premises accepted—or at least disbelief suspended, for after all this is fiction—the book makes quite good sense in its own terms. Its problems arise not from its convention but from Forster's limitations as a novelist. As I have argued, these problems catch up with the book when it is reread; yet the rereading is necessary to savor the themes fully. The difficulties are there, but do not prevent the book from being a significant novel, and at least a timid precursor of Modernist developments.

Aside from its place in relation to the Modernist concern with mythology, there are interrelations of *Howards End* with texts by other writers, in ways not easily discerned and almost surely indirect. Two curious examples can be taken from T. S. Eliot and F. Scott Fitzgerald. Forster was well acquainted with Eliot, as they had met at Bloomsbury salons and on Garsington weekends. Forster declined however to contribute to a volume of appreciations of Eliot on grounds of insufficient sympathy.[28] Possibly he felt Eliot's churchiness to be a problem, and certainly Eliot could not have liked the dismissal of "poor little talkative Christianity" in *A Passage to India.* But consider this section from *Howards End,* one of several in which Forster sets Nature against London:

> Nature, with all her cruelty, comes nearer to us than do these crowds of men. A friend explains himself: the earth is explicable—from her we came, and we must return to her. But who can explain Westminster Bridge Road or Liverpool Street in the morning—the city inhaling; or the same thoroughfares in the evening—the city exhaling her exhausted air?
>
> (p. 108)

Westminster Bridge naturally suggests Wordsworth, who found the city beautiful when asleep and uncrowded, and his sonnet's currency made it easy for Forster to play with the image of the city as sleeping giant. A natural progression leads to some of the most unforgettable lines of *The Waste Land:*

> A crowd flowed over London Bridge, so many,
> I had not thought death had undone so many.
> Sighs, short and infrequent, were exhaled,
> And each man fixed his eyes before his feet.
>
> (ll. 62-65)

The exhalation is displaced into the crowd of clerks, of Leonard Basts, but the force is the same. The clock delivers its "dead" sound, and Stetson is queried about the corpse planted in his garden—a touch of English murder-mystery macabre that opens into an autochthonic motif. Eliot of course put the Cambridge anthropologists to the most vigorous use of any Modernist. He covered over his poem's heteroclite origins in prophetic rhetoric ("voices singing out of empty cisterns and exhausted wells" is from a very old layer, and "I John saw these things, and heard them" was excised) with a "mythical method."[29] The passage on London Bridge reads as if Eliot had been badly depressed while watching early newsreels: the crowds move spectrally and jerkily. But in the light of the *Howards End* passage, several possible points of contact show up, starting with the image of exhalation. Eliot returned to it in the third section of *Burnt Norton*:

> Men and bits of paper, whirled by the cold wind
> That blows before and after time,
> Wind in and out of unwholesome lungs
> Time before and time after.
> Eructation of unhealthy souls
> Into the faded air, the torpid
> Driven on the wind that sweeps the gloomy hills of
>   London. . . .

Another displacement, but the same Dantesque adaptation as in *The Waste Land*: the crowds are dead souls, blown aimlessly over a hellish landscape. Even if these lines do not derive directly from Forster's passage, they certainly show a similarity of vision. The mythology of earth and place is after all the organizing principle of the *Four Quartets*. Especially at the beginning of *East Coker* ("Mirth of those long since under earth / Nourishing the corn") and at the end of *The Dry Salvages,* Eliot acknowledges "The life of significant soil"; but Frazer and Jane Harrison and even Jessie Weston are implicit throughout.[30] If *Howards End* served as mediator, it added several chips to the mosaic of intertextuality in Eliot's work.

The response of Forster with Fitzgerald is of a different order, less spiritual and more mechanical, in several senses. *The Great Gatsby* can be read as an American piracy of *Howards End,* in the vein of San Simeon or London Bridge in Arizona. But the autochthonous themes are transmuted beyond recognition; the house of the novel, no longer small and sacred, has hypertrophied into Gatsby's garish mansion, "a factual imitation of some Hotel de Ville in Normandy"—the book mocks what it enacts.[31] Geography is vital in *Gatsby* but not in Forster's way, although the dialectic of country versus London reappears in the theme of "Westerners" who are "subtly unadaptable to Eastern life" (p. 177).[32] Eastern life is flashy, impersonal, pseudosophisticated, like the Wilcoxes transplanted. It is in pursuit of a "vast, vulgar, and meretricious beauty" (p. 99), in contrast to more earthy Western ways. The towns beyond the Ohio are "bored, sprawling," and smallminded (p. 177), but they are at least free of the specious glitter of New York and its satellite communities. The problem with this geographical pattern is that Fitzgerald confuses it by mixing in his own obviously cherished memories of New York's "meretricious beauty" and its romantic appeal to his permanently adolescent sensibility. He remained entranced with the "incomparable milk of wonder" that leads us to pursue "the green light, the orgastic future" long after he knew he should have outgrown it (pp. 112, 182).[33]

Paradoxically, it is the transparent, innocent quality of his own breathless wonder at riches and success that makes Fitzgerald ultimately palatable. Like Gatsby, he is admirable because, not in spite of, the "colossal vitality of his illusion." As Hugh Kenner has remarked, the story of Gatsby is Fitzgerald's attempt at the theme of metaphysical ambitions "to be as gods," which were reborn in our cultural tradition with the grandiose promises of the Renaissance, and which America both lives out and symbolizes: the land is the "fresh, green breast of the new world [that] had once pandered in whispers to the last and greatest of all human dreams," the last goal—he did not think of space—"commensurate to [man's] capacity for wonder" (p. 182).[34] The novel, like Gatsby's project, is only a partial success, but as such serves all the better as a parable of the American fetishization of illimitable ambition.

The means that Gatsby uses to achieve his ends are as vague as those in a Horatio Alger novel, or as Heathcliff's in *Wuthering Heights*. But the enabling act is the creation of a new identity, sprung "from his own Platonic conception of himself," that makes him a "son of God" instead of a product of his "shiftless and unsuccessful" parents (p. 99). In unrooted America, especially the West, the Family Romance becomes as valid as any other genealogy. Indeed, parents themselves nurture the Family Romance by planting fantasies that their offspring will emerge as *wunderkinden,* cancelling their own ordinariness (cf. Mr. Gatz). We Americans are under an unspoken command to succeed, to prove ourselves, and the usual mark of success is to outdo our parents spectacularly. Hence Walker Percy suggests, "Imagine that you have lived your entire life in the house where you were born. For an American, an uncanny, even an unsettling fantasy."[35] Gatsby is the antithesis of Ruth Wilcox.

Gatsby also has no access to the simple homebound pleasures that Ruth's life at Howards End affords. Indeed, his own fetishization of ambition turns him into a typical American anhedonist, unable to enjoy what he's worked so hard for. He could never have enjoyed Daisy; so much is evident from his wistful attitude toward his car, his speedboat, his pool, his shirts, his house ("I have been glancing into some of the rooms," he says absently in reply to Nick's wonder at its illuminated splendor). The watchful sobriety that keeps him from enjoying his own parties—fittingly, since their only purpose is to serve as lure for the Buchanans—characterizes him. Throughout, he watches over others, but his voyeurism has no hint of the sensual. (Americans like to think that they have a powerful streak of sensuality, but this is merely a Puritan self-accusation: they are far more inhibited, in spite of their eroticized environments, than those of other behavioral traditions, and frank, luxuriant hedonism is much rarer than the confusion between needs and desires, means and ends, that leads to acquisitiveness.) A torrid affair with Daisy would have satisfied him were desire his motive force, but he must acquire and possess, and therefore lose. At least he got a swim in.

Living the life of a socialite partygoer himself, Fitzgerald imagined what happens to poor sons of God/bitches (the transformation is accomplished in the words that were Gatsby's and his own eulogy) who don't get rich enough to marry their Ginevras or Zeldas until too late. Although he had acquired both money and princess, Fitzgerald remained haunted by the fear of failure—naturally enough, since he couldn't see why he had earned them. So he sympathized as Nick Carraway does with those who futilely chase success in New York, such as "poor young clerks who loitered in front of windows waiting until it was time for a solitary restaurant dinner—young clerks in the dusk, wasting the most poignant moments of night and life" (p. 57). This pseudopathos about America's Leonards betrays a juvenile romanticism that obtrudes everywhere, in raptures about the "racy, adventurous feel" of New York, and of course in the building up of Gatsby.

If Gatsby is an Americanized Leonard Bast, devoted to self-improvement, Tom and Daisy Buchanan have a full measure of Wilcox nomadism and exploitiveness. They "drifted here and there unrestfully wherever people played polo and were rich together. . . . I felt that Tom would drift on forever seeking, a little wistfully, for the dramatic turbulence of some irrecoverable football game" (p. 6). They also have the Wilcox attitude toward servants and inferiors; Tom is concerned to preserve the "Nordic" race against "the colored" and all immigrants and *arrivistes.* Like Charles Wilcox he is often found in automobiles, though he affects horsiness as a form of defiant nostalgia: "'I'm the first man who ever made a stable out of a garage'" (p. 119). Fitzgerald adopts Forster's vision of the "Juggernaut car," but for him it does not signify merely the onrush of Philistinism. He sees it as a glamorous but lethal weapon, destroying not only our geographical mooring and orientations but very often life itself, and raising grave questions of responsibility. The key question in the book is: Who was driving?

Several critics have commented on the patterns of movement and drift in *Gatsby,* but the elaborate structure of "driving" imagery that holds the book together is not often noticed, although Nick's head is full of it.[36] On his thirtieth birthday he thinks, "Before me stretched the portentous, menacing road of a new decade" (p. 136). He gets involved with the "incurably dishonest" Jordan Baker, and his first insight into her coincides with finding that she was a "rotten driver." Chastised about this, she gives a Wilcox retort. "'They'll keep out of my way,' she insisted. 'It takes two to make an accident.'" This mentality augurs trouble, although it will come from Daisy rather than Jordan. Nick muses further: "Her gray, sun-strained eyes stared straight ahead, but she had deliberately shifted our relations, and for a moment I thought I loved her. But I am slow-thinking and full of interior rules that act as

brakes on my desires . . ." (p. 59). Fitzgerald sensed as early as anyone that American was becoming a culture in which the locus of romance and sexual initiation is likely to be a car: the earliest recorded tryst of Gatsby and Daisy is in her "white roadster" (p. 75). Fittingly, on his honeymoon with Daisy, Tom has an injurious, adulterous auto accident in Santa Barbara, breaking the arm of the girl with him, a chambermaid (like Henry Wilcox, Tom likes his liaisons with the lower classes).

The climax of *Gatsby* comes not with a runover cat but with a hideous accident to Tom's most recent mistress. The preposterously energetic "Myrtle Wilson, her life violently extinguished, knelt in the road and mingled her thick dark blood with the dust." This near-Homeric simile degenerates into a gross evocation of an Aztec sacrifice: "Her left breast was swinging loose like a flap, and there was no need to listen for the heart beneath" (p. 138). Daisy was the driver, we finally learn, although Gatsby with foolish chivalry takes the responsibility and literally dies for her, in a shooting that is as grotesque a mistake as is Charles Wilcox's "murder" of Leonard Bast. But there is a poetic justice in the verdict against Charles, for Wilcoxes bear collective guilt, whereas in *Gatsby* the unpunished real culprit is the callous Wilcox-like indifference of both Buchanans: "They were careless people, Tom and Daisy—they smashed up things and creatures and then retreated back into their money or their vast carelessness, or whatever it was that kept them together, and let other people clean up the mess they had made" (pp. 180-81).

Not many readers observe that Fitzgerald has prepared for the climactic accident by inserting a parodic anticipation of it, in a "bizarre and tumultuous scene" created by the drunken guests leaving a Gatsby party. In a ditch next to the road rests a coupe, "violently shorn of one wheel." Out steps a man in a long duster, who says to spectators:

> "I know very little about driving—next to nothing. It happened, and that's all I know."

> "Well, if you're a poor driver you oughtn't to try driving at night."

> "But I wasn't even trying," he explained indignantly, "I wasn't even trying."

> An awed hush fell upon the bystanders.

> "Do you want to commit suicide?"

> "You're lucky it was just a wheel! A bad driver and not even *try*ing!"

> "You don't understand," explained the criminal. "I wasn't driving. There's another man in the car."

The real driver appears, much drunker than his passenger: "'Wha's matter?' he inquired calmly. 'Did we run outa gas?'" When the "amputated" wheel is pointed out to him, he remarks:

> "At first I din' notice we'd stopped."

A pause. Then, taking a long breath and straightening his shoulders, he remarked in a determined voice:

"Wonder'ff tell me where there's a gas'line station?"

At least a dozen men, some of them a little better off than he was, explained to him that the wheel and car were no longer joined by any physical bond.

"Back out," he suggested after a moment. "Put her in reverse."

"But the *wheel's* off!"

He hesitated.

"No harm in trying," he said.

(pp. 55-56)

This driver's inability to see reality proleptically parodies Gatsby and his intoxicated dream: "'Can't repeat the past?' he cried incredulously. 'Why of course you can!'" (p. 111). And the confusion over apparent and real drivers grotesquely foreshadows Daisy's repellent irresponsibility. With this scene in mind, we can more fully appreciate observations contained in the famous catalog of Gatsby's guests, that Miss Claudia Hip came "with a man reputed to be her chauffeur" and that Ripley Snell "was there three days before he went to the penitentiary, so drunk out on the gravel drive that Mrs. Ulysses Sweet's automobile ran over his right hand" (pp. 62-63). That right hand had long forgotten its cunning, probably. Fitzgerald sees us as alternately obsessed with and maimed by our cars, endlessly led on; so the green light at the end of the Buchanan dock that stands for "the orgastic future" appears as a transcendent traffic signal, beckoning treacherously. It links the "boats against the current" of the book's very last image with the careening automobiles that have replaced war as our way of eliminating surplus young men. The car is linked to us by unbreakable bonds of desire, however, so we can't get rid of it. Fitzgerald shrewdly links the "Dutch sailors'" fateful vision of the New World with the romantic intoxication of the world seen from cars: "The city seen from the Queensboro Bridge is always the city seen for the first time, in its first wild promise of all the mystery and beauty in the world" (p. 69). Hart Crane saw the American myth in bridges, Fitzgerald in the vehicles upon them.

Musing on American self-contradictions, Walker Percy wonders "whether it is a coincidence that this country is not only the most Christian and most eroticized of all societies but also the most technologically transformed and the most violent."[37] *Gatsby* articulates a vision in which Americans combine "romantic readiness" with violence—especially if it can be produced by technology—in the service of projects not only to repeat the past but also to correct and purge it, to pursue a future that is really a retreat: we are "borne back ceaselessly into the past" (p. 182). Fitzgerald's vision marks him as the product of a culture that is haunted, even for its Catholics, by an ambivalent Calvinism that distrusts great cities, great desires, great projects, and yet feeds on them at the same time.

This makes him very different from Forster, whose Biblical thinking is much less obvious. Indeed, Forster's very classicism represents among other things an embarrassment with "Hebraism," which in England means Dissent, not Jews, and with the evangelism of his forebears. In his day, Greek and Latin, gentility, public school education, and the Established Church were the marks of privilege; to be a scion of evangelistic traditions was (at least latently) socially precarious. No wonder Forster's autochthonous ideology smacks of Tory apologetics. He borrows, however, the rhetoric of the prophets of Israel against all human pride and pretension, against all imperialism and massive power structures, in indirect and disguised ways. Surely his denunciations of Wilcoxery owe something to the prophets' assurances that all great works, rich cities, and mighty armies will end where we all began: in the dust.

Forster sometimes invoked this idea as a Mephistophelean spirit of Denial. It appears in *Howards End* as "goblin footfalls" emanating from Beethoven's Fifth Symphony, or at least from Helen's synesthetic fantasy about it. "[The goblins] were not aggressive creatures; it was that that made them so terrible to Helen. They merely observed in passing that there was no such thing as splendour or heroism in the world" (p. 33). For Helen this represents a sudden collapse of ideals, connected to her disillusionment about the Wilcoxes. Later she arrives at a more engaging paradox, in which the goblins of Denial become the force of mortality itself. "'Death destroys a man; the idea of Death saves him.'" The idea of Death, undercutting all human ambitions but especially those swollen with pride, triumphs because it

shows me the emptiness of Money. . . . men like the Wilcoxes are deeper in the mist than any. Sane, sound Englishmen! Building up empires, levelling all the world into what they call common sense. But mention Death to them and they're offended, because Death's really Imperial, and He cries out against them for ever.

(pp. 238-39)

This rhetoric is not however totally compatible with autochthonic premises, which may be why *A Passage to India* embodies a harsher vision. The earth of India transcends and precedes even the mythical powers invested in it. "The high places of Dravidia have been land since land began. . . . They are older than anything in the world, [they are] flesh of the sun's flesh."[38] As such "they are older than all spirit" (pp. 116-17). The Marabar caves are not holy, have no particular powers; they are so primal that they precede all attributes. "Nothing, nothing attaches to them" (p. 117). Their smooth polished surfaces have no carvings, paintings, not even bats' or bees' nests, and their famous echo wipes out all distinctions, reduces all words to "ou-boum." "A Marabar cave can hear no sound but its own" (pp. 145-46). For Mrs. Moore the echo destroys Christianity—"All its divine words from 'Let there be light' to 'It is finished' only amounted to 'boum'" (p. 141)—and all Western certainties. In this landscape the incursions of all conquerors—Hindu, Muslim, or English—are fatuous illusions. The English invasion is comically symbolized by the right-angled streets, mentioned in the first pages, that fit so poorly in the landscape of Chandrapore, "symbolic of the net Great Britain had thrown over India" (p. 11). But the earth of India mocks such ludicrous impositions. "How can the mind take hold of such a country? Generations of invaders have tried, but they remain in exile. The important towns they build are only retreats, their quarrels the malaise of men who cannot find their way home" (p. 128). The lives of plants and animals are almost undisturbed. "It matters so little to the majority of living beings what the minority, that calls itself human, desires or decides. Most of the inhabitants of India do not mind how India is governed" (p. 105). The heat, beginning in April, produces in men "irritability and lust" (p. 201) and spreads infectious, impersonal evil among them, but it awakens life in the very rocks. Thus Adela, climbing up to her cave, feels the sun quickening the soil under her feet: "The temperature rose and rose, the boulders said, 'I am alive,' the small stones answered, 'I am almost alive'" (p. 142).

But there are comparatively few metaphors for the animate earth in the novel, compared to *Howards End*. This time what interests Forster is not life, but death. In the cave is "something very old and very small . . . the undying worm itself" (p. 198). Like the goblins it mocks all large ideas, all heroism, all generosity, all achievement, even our ideas of "Heaven, Hell, Annihilation": "No one could romanticize the Marabar, because it robbed infinity and eternity of their vastness, the only quality that accommodates them to mankind" (p. 141). Thus the echo that can reduce even "the tongues of angels" to a meaningless reverberation tells Mrs. Moore: "Pathos, piety, courage—they exist, but are identical, and so is filth. Everything exists, nothing has value" (p. 140). This is true levelling. Indian earth is purposive, but not in the services of Eros: at the end it thrusts itself between the horses of Aziz and Fielding in spite of their desire, just as the mirrored surface of the cave prevents the struck match and its image from uniting. "The two flames approach and strive to unite, but cannot, because one of them breathes air, the other stone. A mirror inlaid with lovely colours divides the lovers" (pp. 117-18). (Forster's vision of human love varies that of Aristophanes in Plato's *Symposium*.) So the ideology of *A Passage* cannot be called autochthonous; nevertheless, here as in *Howards End* geography is destiny, a point that several of the characters apprehend but in ironic or misleading forms, usually racist.

There are no houses of importance in the later novel, for even the most magnificent buildings are mocked by the Indian landscape, and the bungalows of the conquerors seem pathetic. The land is deeply and essentially jungle, absorptive and proteiform; its boundaries flow, and forms of life spring up and fall back, escaping human classification: "Nothing in India is identifiable, the mere asking of a question causes it to disappear or to merge in something else" (p. 78). Adela, as her last name indicates, is always searching and asking; this is why she seems a prig to Fielding, as if always taking notes, and why she cannot grasp India. To the inhabitants of the jungle, other than human, a house is simply "a normal growth of the eternal jungle, which alternately produces houses trees, houses trees" (p. 29). Mrs. Moore's wasp is found inside, having "no sense of an interior."

There is autochthony in India, as in the cult of "Esmiss Esmoor" that springs up at her death, and in Hinduism and related ideologies it goes far toward grasping the essence of things, but it remains a posteriori to what is in the cave. Though it cannot answer final questions, it gives Indians clear spiritual advantages. One of the most important is their sensitivity to poetry:

> Of the company, only Hamidullah had any comprehension of poetry. The minds of the others were inferior and rough. Yet they listened with pleasure, because literature had not been divorced from their civilization. The police inspector, for instance, did not feel that Aziz had degraded himself by reciting, nor break into the cheery guffaw with which an Englishman averts the infection of beauty.
>
> (p. 97)

In *Howards End* the role of India is played by Germany. The German characters and material are trivial and forgettable, and seem to represent some unassimilated personal experiences of Forster's (he lived in Germany for a few months), although he is able to get off a few sadly prophetic remarks about the looming conflict of the countries. But if we start from the clue given by the Schlegels' name—relating them to the propounders of Romantic, organicist aesthetics—the major pattern becomes clear. A German does

> take poetry seriously. . . . He may miss it through stupidity, or misinterpret it, but he is always asking beauty to enter his life, and I [Margaret] believe that in the end it will come. At Heidelberg I met a fat veterinary surgeon whose voice broke with sobs as he repeated some mawkish poetry. So easy for me to laugh—I, who never repeat poetry, good or bad, and cannot remember one fragment of verse to thrill myself with.
>
> (p. 73)[39]

Forster is here rebuking the English more than praising the Germans—he had a deeper admiration for Indians—and the issue concealed an important facet of his own sense of alienation from his culture. Indeed, he put himself into the novel under a German name—just as Shakespeare hid himself among puns on "will" in his sonnets and plays. One of the book's most ironic passages concerns Helen, who had a proposal from a German that seemed to her merely comical; he was "Herr Forstmeister" (literally, "forest master") who "lived in a wood" (p. 105).

> "It is sad to suppose that places may ever be more important than people," continued Margaret.
>
> "Why, Meg? They're so much nicer generally. I'd rather think of that forester's house in Pomerania than of the fat Herr Forstmeister who lived in it."
>
> (p. 130)

"Fat" was a sufficient disguise, but the play with "forester" leaves little doubt about what is going on—in fact the passage suggests, appropriately, that Forster is the house, not the character. This self-exile places Forster himself in the milieu, here Germany, where "literature and art have what one might call the kink of the unseen about them" (pp. 77).

Even before Wilcoxes and other imperialists went about their business of trying to crush venerable civilizations, there was a spirit of pragmatism in the English heritage that Forster identifies as the root of his own self-estrangement.

> Why has not England a great mythology? Our folklore has never advanced beyond daintiness, and the greater melodies about our countryside have all issued through the pipes of Greece. Deep and true as the native imagination can be, it seems to have failed here. It has stopped with the witches and the fairies. It cannot vivify one fraction of a summer field, or give names to half a dozen stars. England still waits for the supreme moment of her literature—for the great poet who shall voice her, or, better still, for the thousand little poets whose voices shall pass into our common talk.
>
> (p. 267)

Plaintive hopefulness is evident, but Forster also knows that even if he becomes one of the "little poets" he will still be a "Mollycoddle" to most of his countrymen. One must keep this poignant passage in mind to know how Forster felt personally about the theme of autochthony; it was not mere scaffolding for him. In some earlier passages, we might be tempted to underestimate the irony:

> To speak against London is no longer fashionable. The earth as an artistic cult has had its day, and the literature of the near future will probably ignore the country and seek inspiration from the town. One can understand the reaction. Of Pan and the elemental forces the public has heard a little too much—they seem Victorian, while London is Georgian—and those who care for the earth with sincerity may wait long ere the pendulum swings back to her again.
>
> (p. 108)

This is related to the dismissals of "Borrow, Thoreau, and sorrow," and also serves to forestall criticism of the more labored mythology of his earlier work. "Pan" was truly too arty, too colorful, too decorative. Houses that can seem to live are a far more appropriate motif. Any Englishman can be made to respond, even against his instincts for real-estate development if necessary, to Ruth Wilcox's plaint about being allowed to die in the room where one was born. Gatsby would never want that, but even Leonard might have found it a comfort. For those who understand autochthony, it becomes a mighty theme, expressive not merely of *pietas* and continuity, but also of "only connecting" to those spirits of place that can give our lives wholeness. Henry's frustration of his wife's dying wish is the lowest of his mean tricks.

Forster plants the phrase "safe as houses" several times on Henry Wilcox's lips, and it encompasses the book's irony: Henry means it of course in the most reprehensible sense, turning spirits into investments. If he had only tried to understand why his wife wanted to die in her house, he would have had a glimpse into a world in which houses offer safety of a kind that mocks the rise and fall of fortunes and empires. His lack of a sense of the past, and of its religious insights into earth's tenure of us, does him in. For Forster, the past can transform our ineffectual liberalisms into social harmonies, redeem our greedy commercialism, and so on. Had he had more of Lawrence's ruthlessness, Forster might like his friend have been drawn closer to an atavistic vision that is hard to distinguish from an idealized Fascism.

Notes

1. *E. M. Forster* (New Directions, 1943), p. 114.

2. Woolf, quoted in Richard Ellmann, *James Joyce* (Oxford University Press, 1959), p. 542.

3. Ezra Pound, "Hugh Selwyn Mauberley," IV.

4. "Ulysses, Order, and Myth," *Dial* 75 (1923): 483.

5. See my *Sacred Discontent: The Bible and Western Tradition* (Louisiana State University Press, 1976), pp. 69-77. See also Geoffrey Hartman, "Romantic Poetry and the Genius Loci," in his *Beyond Formalism: Literary Essays 1958-1970* (Yale University Press, 1970), pp. 311-36. Hartman covers the older literary allusions to the idea but does not bring in autochthony. See also Jane Chance Nitzsche, *The Genius Figure in Antiquity and the Middle Ages* (Columbia University Press, 1975), which also knows nothing of autochthony.

6. *Howards End* (Vintage Books, n.d.; originally published, 1910), pp. 155, 175. Subsequent page references in the text are to this convenient edition.

7. See p. 338: "Don't drag in the personal when it will not come." Critics should heed Margaret's advice.

8. *E. M. Forster,* pp. 38, 118.

9. The obvious example is Gerald Dawes in *The Longest Journey.*

10. *Prolegomena to the Study of Greek Religions* (see note 44 to the Introduction).

11. "The Prose Tradition in Verse" in T. S. Eliot, ed., *Literary Essays of Ezra Pound* (New Directions, 1954), p. 371.

12. Forster, "Cnidus," in *Abinger Harvest* (Harcourt Brace, 1936), p. 176.

13. *The Origin of Consciousness in the Breakdown of the Bicameral Mind* (Houghton Mifflin, 1976).

14. Miss Avery says that Ruth should have married a "real soldier" (p. 275) instead of Henry, the degenerate imperialist descendant of "warriors of the past."

15. Even critics trying to illuminate Forster's mysticism frequently ignore such passages: for example, Denis Godfrey, in *E. M. Forster's Other Kingdom* (Oliver & Boyd, 1968), though alert to the "instinctive mysticism of the English soil," does not quote it (pp. 137ff.).

16. A textbook example of impressionism is this passage from Joseph Conrad's *Heart of Darkness,* in which Marlow's steamboat is ambushed by natives: "Sticks, little sticks, were flying about. . . . Arrows, by Jove! We were being shot at!" Bruce Harkness, ed., *Conrad's* Heart of Darkness *and the Critics* (Wadsworth, 1960), p. 39. Compare the passage in which Leonard, about to be struck by a sword, sees only a "stick, very bright," descend (p. 324).

17. Compare p. 219: "Henry treated a marriage like a funeral, item by item." Naturally the Wilcoxes are unaware of the fructifying power of Leonard's death, which is manifested in the hay harvest of the last pages.

18. Malcolm Bradbury makes the connection with Whiggery in his essay on *Howards End* in *Forster: A Collection of Critical Essays* (Prentice-Hall, 1966), p. 132.

19. See the later comparison of Leonard with Fitzgerald's Gatsby.

20. As Frederick C. Crews puts it: "Both Margaret and Forster struggle unconvincingly to remind themselves of the Wilcox virtues." *E. M. Forster: The Perils of Humanism* (Princeton University Press, 1962), p. 108. F. R. Leavis, remarking that "nothing in the exhibition of Margaret's or Henry Wilcox's character makes the marriage credible or acceptable," discusses the problem helpfully: see his essay in Bradbury, *Critical Essays,* pp. 40-41.

21. Quoted in Francis King, *E. M. Forster and His World* (Thames & Hudson, 1978), p. 49.

22. See P. N. Furbank, *E. M. Forster: A Life* (Secker & Warburg, 1977), vol. 1, p. 37.

23. See again my *Sacred Discontent,* pp. 60-62, 92-93. The one touch in which Forster shows some awareness of this motif is having young Tom, of Miss Avery's lineage, charmingly confuse humans and rabbits (p. 300).

24. *The Cave and the Mountain: A Study of E. M. Forster* (Stanford University Press, 1966), p. 265.

25. *Letters of D. H. Lawrence,* ed. Aldous Huxley (Viking, 1932), p. 558.

26. See George H. Ford, "The 'S' Curve: Persephone to Pluto," in Julian Moynahan, ed., *Sons and Lovers: Text, Background, and Criticism* (Viking, 1968; originally published, 1913), pp. 577-96.

27. For example, Peter Widdowson, *E. M. Forster's* Howards End: *Fiction as History* (Sussex University Press, 1977), pp. 14-15, 55, 97-98. Forster's chapters on "Fantasy" and "Prophecy" in *Aspects of the Novel* (Harcourt Brace, 1954) are apropos here, especially the latter. The world of *The Brothers Karamazov* or *Moby Dick,* Forster says, "is not a veil, it is not an allegory. It is the ordinary world of fiction, but it reaches back" (p. 134). The oracular phrase is clear if we remember what the Past means to Forster. He does not claim a place for his own work with that of Dostoevsky, Melville, D. H. Lawrence, and Emily Bronte, yet his discussions of them strongly suggest that he aspired, if wistfully, to this status.

28. King, *Forster and His World,* p. 52. See also Forster's essay on Eliot in *Abinger Harvest.*

29. See Valerie Eliot, ed., *The Waste Land: A Facsimile and Transcript of the Original Drafts* (Harcourt Brace Jovanovich, 1971), pp. 9, 75.

30. On Eliot's debt to the Cambridge anthropologists, see Chapter 5 of this book.

31. *The Great Gatsby* (Scribner, 1953; originally published, 1925), p. 5.

32. Fitzgerald deliberately has Gatsby place San Francisco in the Middle West (p. 65) as part of his Family Romance, but the operational moral geography of the novel can be described by adapting the remark attributed to John Barrymore: Outside New York, every place is Bridgeport.

33. Fitzgerald insisted on "orgastic," as he believed it to be "the adjective for orgasm." See Jennifer E. Atkinson, "Fitzgerald's Marked Copy of *The Great Gatsby*" in Matthew J. Bruccoli and C. E. Frazer Clark, Jr., eds., *Fitzgerald/Hemingway Annual 1970* (NCR Microcard Editions [Washington, D.C.], 1970), pp. 30-31.

34. See Hugh Kenner, *A Homemade World: The American Modernist Writers* (Knopf, 1975), pp. 26-31.

35. Walker Percy, *Lost in the Cosmos: The Last Self-Help Book* (Pocket Books, 1983), pp. 146-47.

36. Compare Gale H. Carrithers, Jr., "Fitzgerald's Triumph," in Frederick J. Hoffman, ed., *The Great Gatsby: A Study* (Scribner, 1962), p. 316: he observes that "images of drift, flutter, or rush, the figure of purposeless action" run through the novel. This aligns even the billowing skirts of Daisy and Jordan (p. 8) with the driving imagery.

37. Percy, *Lost in the Cosmos,* p. 177.

38. *A Passage to India,* ed. Oliver Stallybrass (Arnold, 1978; originally published, 1924); subsequent page references are to this text.

39. That Germans are the mediums of poetry here relates to the Germanic wordplay on his own name. The Schlegels are half German, and this spirit in them is part of the reason that they are the true heirs of

Howards End. Thus the complex of meanings that inhere in the house in the novel—based on Forster's own childhood in a house named Rooksnest—seems also to include his own interlude in Germany as a tutor in a castle. Only the name is then unexplained; on that, no one seems to have noticed that there is a tiny place called Howletts End not far from Cambridge.

On Forster's view of poetry, see his remark in *Aspects of the Novel,* p. 93: "Hardy seems to me essentially a poet," even in his novels. This relates to the discussion in Chapter 1 of this book.

Alfred Kazin (essay date winter 1992)

SOURCE: Kazin, Alfred. "*Howards End* Revisited." *Partisan Review* 59, no. 1 (winter 1992): 29-43.

[*In the following essay, Kazin examines* Howards End *from the perspective of historical events of the later twentieth century.*]

Howards End appeared in 1910, a date that explains an idealism important to our understanding of the book. It was E. M. Forster's fourth novel. He had written in rapid succession *Where Angels Fear to Tread* (1905), *The Longest Journey* (1907), and *A Room with a View* (1908). *Howards End* was the last novel he was to publish for fourteen years. The next, *A Passage to India* (1924), was certainly worth waiting for, but it is not as serene and hopeful as *Howards End.* The "Great War," the most influential event of the twentieth century and the onset of all our political woe, had intervened between Forster's two major novels and certainly darkened the second. The reality of British imperialism, bringing the threat of racial politics to Forster's belief in personal relationships as the supreme good, was something unsuspected in *Howards End.*

In 1910 Forster was thirty-one. In the next sixty years he was to publish only one novel more. *Maurice,* a novel about homosexual love that had been circulating privately for years, was published soon after Forster's death in 1970. All these dates and gaps in Forster's record as a novelist have their significance. He was a wonderfully supple and intelligent writer for whom the outside world was a hindrance and even a threat to his identification of himself and his art with "relationships." Everyone knows that he wrote in *Two Cheers for Democracy,* "I hate the idea of causes, and if I had to choose between betraying my country and betraying my friend, I hope I should have the guts to betray my country." But what—as happened so often in World War Two—if my friend betrayed *me* for an ideology he considered his only "country"?

So the date of *Howards End* has a certain poignancy now. The most famous idea in it is "Only connect! That was the whole of her sermon. Only connect the prose and the pas-

sion, and both will be exalted, and human love will be seen at its height. Live in fragments no longer. Only connect, and the beast and the monk, robbed of the isolation that is life to either, will die." No one with the slightest sense of twentieth-century history can read that in the 1990s without thinking (not for the first time) how far we have traveled, in liberal, generous, above all religious instinct, from 1910. *Howards End* is a shapely and beautiful novel, extremely well thought out. One has to read it now as a fable about England at the highest point of its hopes in 1910, while at its center rises up before us, as always, England's eternal Chinese wall of class distinctions, class war, class hatred—a world in which people stink in each other's nostrils because of their social origins or pretensions: in which a poor young man, who has lost his job and is in the depths of despair because of his home life, encounters hostility because he walks down Regent Street without a hat. But *Howards End* resolves this war between the English, tries to lift away this winding-sheet of snobberies and taboos, in the only way it has ever been resolved—in a beautiful theory of love between persons. This extends just as far as love ever extends. Meanwhile social rage keeps howling outside the bedroom.

Howards End is a novel of ideas, not brute facts; in many respects it is an old kind of novel, playful in the eighteenth-century sense, full of tenderness toward favorite characters in the Dickens style, inventive in every structural touch but not a modernist work. A modernist work—*Ulysses* will always be the grand, cold monument—is one that supplants and subsumes the subject entirely in favor of the author as performer and total original. This is hardly the case in *Howards End.* Forster cares; he cares so much about the state of England and the possibility of deliverance that what occupies him most in working out the book is a dream of a strife-torn modern England returning to the myth of its ancient beginnings as a rural, self-dependent society. It is typical of an undefeatable tenderness (almost softness) in Forster's makeup that the book ends in a vision of perfect peace right at the old house in Hertfordshire, Howards End, that is the great symbol throughout the book of stability in ancestral, unconscious wisdom. Even in 1910 this was absurd—hardly an answer to the class war. But fairy tales thrive on being of another world.

The class war is hardly an English prerogative, but the English have been so good at picturing it that it is no wonder they cannot do without it. Where but in England would that quirky refugee Karl Marx have found so perfect a ground, a text, for his belief in the long-established war between the classes? As I write, I notice in a review by Sir Frank Kermode of Sir V. S. Pritchett's *Collected Stories,* that Pritchett once had a conversation with H. G. Wells "in which they considered the question of whether lower-class characters could ever be treated in other than comic terms." It is noteworthy that Kermode finds it entirely natural to write of "lower-class characters" and "suburban little people." These are phrases that seem comic to an American—not because America is less divided than England but because, torn apart as it is by race, fear, and hatred, its gods are equality and social mobility.

How different the case in England. Dickens, though he lent pathos and occasionally even dignity (if not heroism) to his lower-class characters, certainly delighted in "treating" them in comic terms just as much as Shakespeare did. It is hard to think of any first-class English novelist before Thomas Hardy who identifies so much with the "lowly" and who gave characters at the bottom like Jude and Tess so much love and respect.

George Orwell in 1937: "Whichever way you turn, this curse of class differences confronts you like a wall of stone. Or rather it is not so much like a wall of stone as the plate glass pane of an aquarium." This American was for some months near the end of World War II in close contact with "other ranks" in the British army. Even when lecturing at Cambridge after the war, he came to see how the college servants lived, as well as the incomparable beauty of the public surface. These experiences gave glimpses of a side of life in England that explained the rancor and frustration of postwar English writing—but also its violent humor. As Edmund Wilson said, the English Revolution was made in America.

I hasten to add—and *Howards End* is in many respects specifically about England—that as a subject single and entire of itself, blissful to the literary imagination, England—

> This royal throne of kings, this scept'red isle,
> This earth of majesty, this seat of Mars,
> This other Eden, demi-paradise,
> This fortress built by Nature for herself
> Against infection and the hand of war,
> This happy breed of men, this little world,
> This precious stone set in the silver sea

awakens an honest glow in its writers. America is too vast, heterogeneous, and spiritually mixed up to appear before its writers as a believable single image. F. Scott Fitzgerald in his notebooks: "France was a land, England was a people, but America, having about it still that quality of the idea, was harder to utter—it was the graves at Shiloh and the tired, drawn, nervous faces of its great men, and the country boys dying in the Argonne for a phrase that was empty before their bodies withered. It was a willingness of the heart."

America certainly has been harder to utter—except in the most grandiose and boastful terms. By contrast, here is Forster in Chapter Nineteen of *Howards End.* The Schlegel sisters' German cousin is with them on a tour of the countryside, and because one of the signal points of this novel is that the characters are all representative—the English of conflicting attitudes and cultures, the Germans of different sides of Germany—Forster here "interrupts" himself to speak with felt emotion about England, his England, everyone's England, summed up as "our island":

> If one wanted to show a foreigner England, perhaps the wisest course would be to take him to the final section of the Purbeck Hills, and stand him on their summit, a

few miles to the east of Corfe. Then system after system of our island would roll together under his feet. . . . How many villages appear in this view! How many castles! How many churches, vanished or triumphant! How many ships, railways, and roads! What incredible variety of men working beneath that lucent sky to what final end! The reason fails, like a wave on the Swanage beach; the imagination swells, spreads, and deepens, until it becomes geographic and encircles England.

A few pages on, he inserts into a scene of conflict between the Schlegel sisters on the incredible thought (to Helen) that Margaret could even *consider* marrying the overbearing businessman Henry Wilcox:

> England was alive, throbbing through all her estuaries, crying for joy through the mouths of her gulls, and the north wind, with contrary emotion, blew stronger against her rising seas. What did it mean? For what end are her fair complexities, her changes of soil, her sinuous coast? Does she belong to those who have moulded her and made her feared by other lands, or those who had added nothing to her power, but have somehow seen her, seen the whole island at once, lying as a jewel in a silver sea, sailing in a ship of souls, with all the brave world's fleet accompanying her towards eternity?

Earlier, Forster had written of "our race," and later he was to write of his countrymen and women as "comrades." So the attentive reader comes to see that behind the rivalry and final, ironic conjunction of Schlegels and Wilcoxes (meaning Margaret and her defeated husband Henry Wilcox) is Forster's yearning hope (as of 1910) that this grievously class-proud, class-protecting, class-embittered society may yet come to think of some deeper, more ancient "comradeship" as one of its distinguishing marks. Where Forster's belief in "personal relationships" was founded on Bloomsbury and the *Principia Ethica* (1903) of its Cambridge sage G. E. Moore, Forster's invocation of "comradeship" no doubt owes much to Edward Carpenter, a strong defender of homosexuality who was one of the first English disciples of Walt Whitman.

But "comradeship" aside for the moment, English literature's advantage over American literature, so it appeared to the American critic who helped to make Forster famous in America, Lionel Trilling, is that the class war, class distinctions of every kind, social rivalries of the most minute (and even nastiest) kind, are great for literature. As conflict seems to be the first rule in life, so conflict taken seriously enough, without sentimental hopes of easy deliverance, is comedy, is tragedy, is dialogue, is history, is FORCE. Only an Englishman would have opened Chapter Six of *Howards End* with:

> We are not concerned with the very poor. They are unthinkable, and only to be approached by the statistician or the poet. This story deals with gentlefolk, or with those who are obliged to pretend that they are gentlefolk.
>
> The boy, Leonard Bast, stood at the extreme verge of gentility. He was not in the abyss, but he could see it.

This would have enraged the California novelist and pioneer socialist, Jack London, who in 1902 went down into the "horror" of London's poor to write *The People of the Abyss,* a powerful document not likely to interest anyone in England but the Salvation Army. Because *Howards End* is rooted not even in Fabian socialism but in the dream of "personal relationships," one of the felt tensions in the book is the fear of war between England and Germany. The Schlegels' father (now dead) was a German idealist who fought for Prussia before it took Germany over, and in disgust left for England and married an Englishwoman. Even the famous German literary name of "Schlegel," connected with August Wilhelm von Schlegel's translation of Shakespeare, is representative. Margaret and Helen Schlegel are relative outsiders in English society not only because they are "not really English," but because they have been dangerously infected by some old idealism from the Germany of poets and philosophers.

So much for the background of *Howards End* and what we may fairly take to be Forster's ruling concerns. One must be careful not to make the book more solemn in tone than it actually is. It begins with one of the most informal and delightful openings in modern fiction, a thoroughly unexpected way of proceeding that shows just how far 1910 has departed from Victorian heaviness. (The Queen had died just nine years before.) "One may as well begin with Helen's letters to her sister." This is so Forsterian—easy in its approach, altogether unpretentious, of course wily—that it is not until one goes back over the book, with the house, Howards End, staying in mind as the embodiment of Forster's image of a traditional and supposedly "safe" England, that one realizes how altogether clever the opening is.

Helen Schlegel's first excited letter from Howards End, occupied by the bustling, proprietary Wilcoxes, who do not understand all it means to its original and true owner, their wife and mother Mrs. Wilcox, nevertheless firmly posits the house as the thematic center of the book. The house alone—with Mrs. Wilcox as its frail but presiding spirit—is England. The sisters are, at the beginning, as far from the soul of the house as the Wilcoxes are. But a story has to begin somewhere, anywhere, so this story begins with Helen's innocent rapture at getting away to the country from Wickham Place in London. What is oldest and most meaningful about the house's significant surroundings—the great wych-tree and the pig's teeth long ago driven into its trunk—are to Helen only unusual and charming. Yet one day, amazingly enough, this house will become the home of Margaret and Helen and Helen's son by the unfortunate Leonard Bast, dead at the hand of Charles Wilcox hammering him with the flat of a sword that is itself a memorial of "old" England.

The opening is a fairy tale, in all naiveté and innocence, because of Helen's premature joy in the house and her crush on Paul Wilcox, the younger brother. The resolution of the book will be another fairy tale, all too set up and thinly prophetic, about the final, strange, tragically en-

forced occupation of Howards End by the sisters, Helen's son, and Margaret's husband Henry Wilcox, crushed by his son's imprisonment for manslaughter.

Between the brief, illusionary idyll of the opening and the *willed* idyll of the end (a problem for any reader who knows how little England lived up to the rosiness of the book's conclusion) we get the delicious social comedy of the first conflict between the Wilcoxes and the Schlegels. They met as tourists in the Rhineland, looking at—or was it looking for?—medieval castles. An invitation to Howards End ensued. We are now to see acted out "the rift in the lute," as one English historian described the many distinctions that make one English person so routinely despise another. For all the idealism among some of the educated in 1910, the distinctions were bright and distinct (sometimes as lethal) as ever. It is true that 1910—to judge by the sunny moral atmosphere that prevails in *Howards End*—was a period of hope. Forster, like all his Cambridge friends, had indeed taken to heart the precious words from G. E. Moore's *Principia Ethica*: "By far the most valuable things . . . are . . . the pleasures of human intercourse and the enjoyment of beautiful objects; it is they . . . that form the rational, ultimate end of social progress." All this allowed Forster to weave possibilities around his famous injunction—"Only connect!" Fourteen years later, after the most terrible slaughter of Englishmen in a single day at the Somme, Forster evidently found it harder to say of his English and Hindu protagonists in *A Passage to India,* "Only connect!" His beloved India itself stood in the way.

There is even a half-spoken religious touch to *Howards End,* characteristic of this very conscientious writer descended from members of the nineteenth-century Evangelical Clapham Sect. Early in the book Margaret Schlegel says of the already ominous English-German rivalry, "Her conclusion was that any human being lies nearer the unseen than any organization, and from this she never varied." Mrs. Wilcox haunts the book because her sense of tradition is involuntary and subliminal, involved with the "unseen." She represents spiritual qualities not evident to the chattering sophisticates Margaret uselessly tries to involve at a luncheon party.

The comedy so rich in *Howards End* begins with the Schlegels' intrusive Aunt Juley taking it on herself to go down to Howards End when word comes from impulsive Helen that she and Paul are in love. "Love" in 1910 means engagement, engagement marriage, marriage the entwining of families perhaps not meant to be entwined. Aunt Juley may be a fool, but she is a proper Englishwoman who knows how serious are the implications jutting out of the juvenile words, "Paul and I are in love—the younger son who only came here Wednesday." We have the house, Howards End, described from the outside by Helen soon after her visit. And now we have Aunt Juley's confrontation with the older brother, Charles Wilcox, as they come on each other at the railway station.

Barriers everywhere. Charles Wilcox is totally peremptory, Aunt Juley more than slightly befuddled. She can barely make clear her concern about her niece, and Charles, who has had some initial difficulty grasping the fact that his very own brother Paul is involved, is insufferable in his superiority. We are in the comedy country of English folk viscerally unable to tolerate each other on sight. Aren't Charles and Aunt Juley both gentlefolk? Even in her first illusory enchantment with Howards End, Helen had admitted to Margaret, "We live like fighting cocks." "Mr. Wilcox says the most horrid things about women's suffrage so nicely, and when I said I believed in equality he just folded his arms and gave me such a setting down as I've never had."

There is no different of opinion between Charles and Aunt Juley. Both are against any possible engagement between Helen and Paul. The issue between them is that they are prepared to mistrust and misunderstand each other. The world of "distinctions" is made ever more graphic by Charles Wilcox's exasperation with the old station porter for not fetching a package to him immediately he calls for it. In his unbridled *hauteur* he cannot take it in that Aunt Juley even thinks him Paul. And Charles is too proprietary about his "motor" even when there is no way of getting rid of Juley besides inviting her to get into it. This Wilcox "motor" is quite a presence in the book. No motor, no status. No status, no Wilcoxes. Schlegels (at least in 1910) cannot possibly have a motor. Henry and Aunt Juley exchange insults by "'Capping Families,' a round of which is always played when love would unite two members of our race. But they played it with unusual vigour, stating in so many words that Schlegels were better than Wilcoxes, Wilcoxes better than Schlegels. They flung decency aside." Earlier, we have had a hint that love between Paul and Helen is easily thwarted. Helen writes to Margaret that Paul "is mad with terror in case I said the wrong thing." But now, as Henry and Aunt Juley descend from the motor at Howards End in unseemly anger, a voice from the garden reproves, calms, and because of who she is, blesses. It is Mrs. Wilcox.

Mrs. Wilcox, who dies early in the book, leaving her spirit to descend upon her family without their quite knowing or using it, is the representative character in the book who is deepest and speaks the least. Her spirit, already so rooted in Howards End, becomes essential to Margaret, who tries to understand her mysterious authority and perhaps never does so fully even when *she* becomes Henry Wilcox's wife and comes to occupy Howards End. As has often been noted, E. M. Forster "had a thing about old ladies." It is extraordinary how Mrs. Wilcox comes to dominate the book. She is far more impressive than the easily befuddled Mrs. Moore in *A Passage to India.* She embodies natural inheritance, not the solicited kind, and certainly not the frantic striving for property and position so central to her husband and children. Over whom she has not the slightest influence! Who and what is she that she is so important to Forster? She is what does not need to be explained and totally cannot be—the transmission of spirit, not of biological life. The ancientness of the wych elm and the folklore embodied in the pig's teeth driven into the

tree (it was long believed that a piece of the bark would cure toothache) represent the agelessness of a simple truth that cannot be put into words. One can only live it, so very briefly, as Mrs. Wilcox dies in her fifties, and with the fragility of the dying pass it on, sibyl-like, as in a shadowy note from the hospital in which she indicates that "Margaret Schlegel is to have Howards End."

The great thing about Mrs. Wilcox is that she does not know all she knows. She is above or below the fever and the fret of modern English life, which is typified by a lasting insecurity about where to live next. When Margaret and Helen have to move from Wickham Place in London (they never find another London flat, since Howards End is their destiny), Mrs. Wilcox is horrified. "To be parted from your house, your father's house—it oughtn't to be allowed. It is worse than dying. I would rather die than— Oh, poor girls! Can what they call civilization be right if people mayn't die in the room where they were born?"

Forster allows us to infer that Mrs. Wilcox is not unwilling to die in a world fundamentally unintelligible to her. I should add that her virtue consists in her seeming insignificant to her own family. Leaving Howards End to Margaret, a comparative stranger, proves to the Wilcoxes how very odd their mother was. And of course they even suspect Margaret of conniving at the suspect and baffling bequest. But does Mrs. Wilcox's strange wish mean that the "inheritance" of the house—by implication, England—is now safe in the hands of "intellectuals" like the Schlegels, whose most noteworthy characteristic, not always honored in the novel, is their ample supply of abstract good will? This is the optimism of 1910, this is perhaps even Bloomsbury (Forster was not central to it), with its cardinal optimism that persons may yet be stronger than institutions. Still, Forster's fairy tale rests on Margaret, Helen, and Helen's baby by Leonard Bast occupying Howards End at the last. This is certainly an ideal ending of sorts. But isn't Forster too shrewd to allow the reader to take this as anything more than a dream of peace?

And there is this problem with Mrs. Wilcox. Her dying so early in the book, though crucial to the plot, may also be taken as the weakness of such wonderful "old" ladies, like the befuddlement of Mrs. Moore at the caves of Marabar in *A Passage to India* that results in so much trouble for innocent Dr. Aziz and poisons him against the English. "Mrs. Wilcox has left few indications behind her," Forster writes with double-edged irony about a woman deep without being clever. Can it be that Mrs. Wilcox is in her total self-containment without intellect of the pushing, urban, altogether modern kind? To Mrs. Wilcox alone is it not necessary or urgent to say, "Only connect!"? She *is* connection, of the most wonderful silent kind. Typical of Forster, in a passing aside, to tell us that Mrs. Wilcox is a Quaker, while Henry Wilcox and his family, originally Dissenters, are now safe and proper in the Church of England. Mrs. Wilcox is important because she is Other. Far, far from Howards End and its tutelary mistress are the social rivalries and distinctions and snobberies that dispossess fellow human beings. Which is why the poor, easily floored clerk Leonard Bast is in all his cultural confusions and social strivings so important to the book.

Leonard is not a character E. M. Forster knows by heart, as he does Margaret, Helen, and even their laid-back little brother Tibby. Nor is he a character like Henry Wilcox whom Forster knows from the hard social evidence around him. The rising Henry Wilcoxes were—now are—everywhere. Poor little Leonard at the bottom of the lower—lowest!—middle class is a mere clerk, the kind Bloomsbury knew only across a very wide gulf. Virginia Woolf, on *Ulysses,* in her diary for 1922, saw it all as:

> a queasy undergraduate scratching his pimples. . . . An illiterate, underbred book it seems to me, the book of a self-taught working-man, & we all know how distressing they are, how egotistic, insistent, raw, striking & ultimately nauseating. When one can have cooked flesh, why have the raw?

And then there was John Maynard Keynes writing to Duncan Grant some years earlier, "I must go to tea now to meet some bloody working men who will be I expect as ugly as men can be." But Leonard Bast is not even a working man. Bloomsbury could not have imagined a working man, since such did not—certainly not in 1910—listen to Beethoven's Fifth at the Queen's Hall or try to follow Ruskin's verbal ecstasies over architecture in *The Stones of Venice.* Leonard was imaginable to Forster because he was "an illiterate, underbred" striver after CULTURE, and Forster and friends certainly had a lot of that. When Forster said in his splendid book, **Aspects of the Novel,** that a character is real to the reader when the novelist knows all about the character, he was perhaps congratulating himself for knowing Leonard up and down as a social type—the hanger-on where he does not belong, the ultimate in pathos and powerlessness. Why so much of both? Why so *much* wretchedness without respite to Leonard Bast? Because of his being neither bourgeois nor working man but a clerk in an insurance company looking to better himself. A snob without justification, always looking up the backsides of those he finds it natural to idealize, he is the type a mandarin of culture finds unbearable. He is the type the English most easily sacrifice and dismiss. Leonard has no party and no friends or associates. He is uneasy with his live-in "companion," Jacky, who is lower-class all right but somehow contemptible because she lives with the likes of *him.*

Let us face it: Leonard Bast does not know his place, and that is far worse than having *some* place, even at the bottom. Meeting Margaret Schlegel at the concert hall where Beethoven's Fifth will manifest "panic and emptiness" in its growling ups and downs and finally wonderful resurgence of the human spirit over its private terror, Leonard becomes a bother from the very first because of his social unsureness. "She wished that he was not so anxious to hand a lady downstairs, or to carry a lady's programme for her—his class was near enough her own for its manners to vex her." Near enough her own? Remember that

Leonard was early defined by Forster by class or near-class as standing "at the extreme verge of gentility. He was not in the abyss, but he could see it." Leonard is not so much created as *defined.* That is the advantage to a novelist of a class system. Leonard is the sort of hard-luck character the English happily accept in literature because one—isn't one?—is so easily resigned to such a fate, to the abyss. Leonard has no hope about anything. He was meant from all eternity to be squashed. Before long, thanks to the Schlegels transmitting Henry Wilcox's ill-founded belief in the instability of the Porphyrion Insurance Company, Leonard resigns his job, and soon he will have no other.

What is irking about Leonard is that he is all too easily defined. Nobody in the book, beginning with himself, believes in Leonard. Jacky's acquaintance with him is limited to the bedroom. Forster—like the academic critics who, discussing **Howards End,** also smirk over this—has his fun describing Leonard's ridiculous efforts to follow Ruskin's *Stones of Venice.* Culture is the only property some academics have, and as Plato said, property is the greatest passion. Still, nobody, even in a novel, can be so ignorantly pretentious without ceasing to exist. What saves Leonard for Forster is *a)* Leonard is a social specimen defined by his irritating all the other classes—remember the hostility he encounters when, in the greatest distress, he walks down Regent Street without a hat!—and *b)* he is the sacrificial victim all the others demand—even Helen, who bears his child—so that Forster can get on with his plot.

Forster's plot depends on Leonard being discardable. So, in the end, Leonard is the victim of Henry Wilcox's hypocritical self-righteousness (Jacky was once Henry's mistress) and of Charles Wilcox's ferocious sense of class superiority. It is nothing but his sense of rightful domination that leads him to knock down Leonard with the flat of the ancestral sword that has hung so long on the wall at Howards End. This induces Leonard to fall against the bookcases in such a way as to bring the books tumbling down all over him (a nice touch), and he dies of a heart attack! Poor poor Leonard! Yet such is the neatly calculated hierarchical structure at the essence of the novel that without Leonard's intrusion into Howards End and his dying there, Charles Wilcox would not be imprisoned for manslaughter, and his father would not collapse. This leaves Margaret and Helen and Helen's baby by Leonard (it was the supposed "seduction" of Helen by a lower-class type that so outraged the Wilcoxes) free to occupy Howards End. This answers the question said to be at the heart of the book—Who will inherit England? The Schlegels have triumphed over the Wilcoxes—why not say over all Wilcoxes? Which is lovely nonsense.

Forster was a clever plot-maker, and, not altogether surprisingly, very fond of getting things moving by way of a little violence now and then. There is a lot of plot in **Howards End** because there are a lot of class barriers to move past in a society that on the surface, at least, is constructed of barriers. If Leonard in his pursuit of cultural improvement had not gone to hear Beethoven at the Queen's Hall, Helen Schlegel would not have mistakenly gone off with his umbrella. Margaret therefore has to take him back to Wickham Place for the umbrella. Whereupon Margaret and Helen sort of take him up, a little out of pity, much out of the intellectual liberalism suitable to the freshening winds of 1910. When Leonard brokenly describes an ecstatic solitary walk at night, they are stirred, amused, not unmixed with curiosity about such a social specimen. Finally, when on Henry Wilcox's arrogant say-so, Leonard is encouraged by the sisters to give up his clerkship, he soon finds himself unemployable.

Better not to ask why Leonard then gives up in total despair. There is a formula to such things in the English novel, which contains no Huckleberry Finns "lighting out for the territory" when they are held in by civilization. The adjustment of accident to circumstance being everything in a novel so thoroughly plotted, it turns out that Jacky was carnally known to Henry Wilcox, which gives Margaret a moral advantage over Henry. Helen is so torn with pity for Leonard that she comes to bear his son, and this is necessary so that Leonard will die, almost ritually, by sword, making Leonard's son and *his* descendants the heirs of—"England"? Paul Wilcox, preparing to go back to Africa on imperial business, crudely refers to "piccaninnies." The word means "a Negro child—said to be offensive." So Leonard's class ignominy, transferred to the child's illegitimacy, has become one of race.

Paul Wilcox may rant as he likes, but the inheritance on which the book ends is romantic. And indeed there are many romantic and vaguely "mystical" touches to the book, in the form of apothegms or asides by Forster himself. "Only connect!" "Personal relations are the important thing for ever and ever, and not this outer life of telegrams and anger." "Only connect! That was the whole of her sermon. Only connect the prose and the passion, and both will be exalted, and human love will be seen at its highest." And this—almost Dostoyevskian—"Death destroys a man; the idea of death saves him."

The force behind these noble sentences is that they *are* noble and reminds us of a certain pre-1914 spirituality, even of the D. H. Lawrence in his Biblical and utopian phase who was when still in England so friendly to Forster and *Howards End.* But in what sense can "Only connect!" be taken as a solution to the war of the classes, the war of social distinctions, the war between good manners and manners that are merely observant of better manners?

Important as the phrase was to Forster himself, it can be said that while this was an injunction he obeyed as a man and made the basis of his intimate life, he also distrusted it—it could become too special. Bloomsbury believed in "personal relations" because it consisted of friends and lovers. Forster may not have been a genius like Virginia Woolf. Her genius lay in her ability to give consistency to her hallucinatory sense of consciousness, her ability as a novelist to show us the actual rhythms through which the mind at its deepest levels moves. By contrast, Forster the novelist is worldly. He was a man of exquisite *social* sensibility, well aware of conflict as the space through which we must always move. Along with this went a highly developed kindliness toward all creatures that probably arose from his sense of his own difficult sexuality, his identification with women (ancestral and "old"-seeming women). He endured many slights as a man, as a writer many reproaches for seeming altogether too sinewy and inconsistent in the style of his beloved Montaigne. He was in Bloomsbury without being altogether of it—he had conscience.

Though Forster said he preferred Montaigne and Erasmus to Moses and St. Paul, he certainly believed in righteousness as well as personal grace. The problem he faced in *Howards End*—the social war, the class war, the manners war, the war of historic English hardness and even cruelty between the classes, was something that demanded a solution of him as it did not of his friends in Bloomsbury. They were preoccupied not only with "personal relations" but with modernism in art and psychology. Because of Cézanne and Freud, it seems, Virginia Woolf could say that human nature had "changed" around 1908. Forster was not a modernist in this sense, *her* sense. She was preoccupied with style as the structure necessary to narratives of interior consciousness. *Howards End* is not an experimental novel. The transitions and unexpected violence in it are surprising and in a sense delightful; they are there to move the story, not to reflect the author's originality. The style is not only subliminal, it is a form of conversation with the reader. And the reader, not stunned by Forster as he is by Joyce or Woolf, happily joins in. *Howards End* is a classical English novel, more like Jane Austen than like Virginia Woolf. The subject is classical—the social distrust between people, some of whom actually love each other but because of "differences" cannot easily live together. All handled with ingenuity, a bracing comic sense, a certain degree of what we now call "mysticism" (we are so unfamiliar with religious feeling in novelists), but which was just Forster's manifest sense of decency, his strong ethical sense, disarming in its casual tone. *Howards End* is a superb and wholly cherishable novel, one that admirers have no trouble reading over and again.

One problem remains—how are we to take the fairy-tale resolution of the novel? How seriously are we to take this as any kind of solution or culmination? Max Beerbohm, who loved the first part of the book, was scornful of the rest. No doubt he thought it sentimental, much too willed. This is an understandable point that admirers of the book can accept without suffering, since they are so delighted with the intelligence of the book as a whole. This is particularly true of Americans, whose novels can never resemble *Howards End* in the slightest, and who can be as uncritical of the book as they are of the English countryside at its best. The novel is a lovely shapely object, a triumph of brilliant plotting and human sensibility that well disguises the fact that the savage reality of society has escaped it.

This has occurred to English readers and observers. An American feeling about *Howards End,* inspired by Lionel Trilling's influential little book on Forster (1943), is that the novel is a genial, beautifully proportioned work of art that American literature should envy. In the introduction to the 1964 edition of his book, Trilling proudly noted that his book had positively made Forster in America. He added:

> I have no doubt that I was benefited by the special energies that attend a polemical purpose. To some readers it will perhaps seem strange, even perverse, to have involved Mr. Forster in polemic, but I did just that—I had a quarrel with American literature at the time it was established, against what seemed to me its dullness and its pious social simplicities I enlisted Mr. Forster's vivacity, complexity, and irony. It was a quarrel that was to occupy me for some years; from the title of the introductory chapter of this book I took the name of my first volume of essays, The Liberal Imagination. The occasion of that cultural contention no longer exists, at least not in its old form, but it was an event of some importance in my intellectual life, and I would not wish to interfere with what I said in the course of it.

The "dullness and pious social simplicities" Trilling "quarrelled" with in American literature of the time surely could not have referred to such powerful talents as William Faulkner, Theodore Dreiser, F. Scott Fitzgerald, Robert Frost, Wallace Stevens, John Dos Passos, Edmund Wilson—and a host of others. What bothered Trilling was not American literature but his own now discarded American radicalism, especially among his fellow members of the New York intelligentsia who had been disabused by Stalinism and were slowly but unmistakably making their way to the intellectual "neoconservatism" that has become a striking mode among New York children of East European immigrants, born in the first years of the twentieth century, who since the 1940s have become a major force in American intellectual life.

Forster himself, not the most bravura and self-confident talent in the world, was so encouraged by Trilling's book that he beamed on all Americans he met, saying, "Your Mr. Trilling has made me famous!" There was little reason for him to appreciate the situation *outre mer.* To Trilling and many other Americans weary of the corruption of the liberal imagination by the radical tradition—the unspoken premise behind Trilling's argument—Forster's England in *Howards End* resembled a moral paradise. Or a prig's?

Bernard Shaw liked to say "it's the common language that divides us." No, it's just the American difference. There was nothing in common between the England that presides over *Howards End* and the England that Forster's American admirers liked to see as a relief from their own more openly turbulent society. In a way the social problem in America is more hopeless, for the differences founded on race, the lasting wounds of slavery and unfashionable "national origin" may be harder to cross over than the differences between Schlegels and Wilcoxes—who at the end of

the book do get to live in the same ancestral house. The only figures in America comparable to the first Mrs. Wilcox in deep unconscious wisdom, rooted to the earth, crazy about the earth long ago taken from them by white predators, are "native Americans." And they live not in the middle of the most respected society, like Mrs. Wilcox, but in segregated, horribly poor, isolated "reservations."

We in America have lots of Wilcoxes—they are the go-go boys who become corporation executives, Wall Street financiers and the rest. Nor do they look down on the culture of the Schlegel type, all museum curators and professors. They subsidize museums, concert halls, grants for writers, dancers, painters, performers of every stripe; culture adds to the prestige of their cities. And if Leonard Bast is at all imaginable and locatable in America it is because he emigrated here a long time ago in order to get into a state university. Leonard is in direct-mail marketing now, rapidly making his way to the top because of his gentlemanly English accent—always a great help in the American business world.

Jeane N. Olson (essay date fall 1993)

SOURCE: Olson, Jeane N. "E. M. Forster's Prophetic Vision of the Modern Family in *Howards End*." *Texas Studies in Literature and Language* 35, no. 3 (fall 1993): 347-62.

[*In the following essay, Olson argues that Forster's families in* Howards End *prefigure modern family structure.*]

That contemporaneous reviewers of E. M. Forster's ***Howards End*** [hereafter referred to as ***HE***] failed to recognize his prescient image of a radically new family structure is hardly surprising. In 1910 the institutional, middle-class family in England—static, authoritarian, and based on consanguinity and primogeniture—was still assumed as a given by most readers and novelists. As a result, few readers or novelists at the beginning of this century questioned the accepted institutional model of the family or foresaw the possibility of rejuvenating it to enhance individuality and equality in the family circle.

Thus D. H. Lawrence set the opening chapters of *The Rainbow* at a farm significantly called "The Marsh," but he employed the symbolism of that name narrowly, focusing on women's defiant seizure of sexual freedom rather than remolding the entire family. Expanding on the metaphor, one might say that just as a marsh is a protected nursery richly supplied with the elements necessary for the nurturance and protection of young marine life, so a more expansive and flexible form of the family could provide a richer context for human fulfillment. Forster visualized a more egalitarian, inclusive family that would be a fertile seedbed where all its members, deeply rooted in the past and securely connected with their own emotions, might be equally enriched by energizing currents from the outside.

In his massive study, Lawrence Stone sees that the family was very gradually moving from "distance, deference and patriarchy" to what he calls "affective individualism."[1] Though he finds the seeds of his main features of the modern family in key segments of English society as early as 1750, in the following hundred years, the development of this new family type actually regressed until the end of the Victorian period, when it began to spread slowly into other classes of English society.[2] Peter Gay's *The Tender Passion,* while focusing on examples of true love in marriage, acknowledges "the smoke screens thrown up by purposeful propriety, diligent self-censorship, and tense moral preoccupations"[3] by parents whose power over their children "often enough amounted to little more than a self-indulgent resort to superior legal privileges, emotional resources, or physical strength."[4] Even "the most affectionate and benevolent parents exercised power over their children, husbands over their wives, masters over their servants—always for their good, usually in their name."[5]

Though not a formal student of the family, Forster was a discerning observer of the social scene. More than merely recording what he saw, he pondered the common values of his society and dreamed of a family that would encourage greater fulfillment for the individual, the family, and eventually for all of human society. Gay points out that few men, and even fewer women, aspired in the nineteenth century to "unforced, unmercenary, wholly equal mutual love, of love without power."[6] Forster was one of those yearning for such family relationships; in *Howards End,* through Margaret, he gives passionate voice to his dreams of a new kind of *functional* family, which he considered fundamental to all the other unspoken social contracts of life. In the last chapter of *Howards End,* Forster, a prophet far ahead of his time, projects an impressionistic vision of a radically different, more elastic middle-class family structure that presaged, in 1910, many of the characteristics now common to middle-class families at the end of the twentieth century.

Certainly, Forster was deeply dissatisfied with the conventional family he saw in the first decade of this century. From his first novel, the reader is regaled with the horrors of the institutional family whose children are unmercifully manipulated by a domineering parent to fit his or her preconception of the fortress family protecting itself against the imagined insults of the world. Like Mrs. Herriton in *Where Angels Fear to Tread,* Henry Wilcox in *Howards End* is an unwitting captive of traditional Sawstonite values, epitomizing in numbing detail the conventional paterfamilias of the late Victorian and Edwardian eras. His unexamined adherence to the accepted social mores inexorably leads to his collapse and his son's imprisonment and might have resulted in the destruction of his marriage to Margaret Schlegel but for her determination to nurture new family relationships based on autonomy and trust. Both Mrs. Herriton and Mr. Wilcox stand upon the foundation stones of Property, Propriety, Family Pride, and The Church. Of Mrs. Herriton, Forster says, "Pride was the only solid element in her disposition."[7] Shamefaced

and cautious behind a defensive facade that disguises a fear of emotion, Mr. Wilcox, like Mrs. Herriton, cares too much about apparent success and too little about the lessons of the past, is spiritually dishonest, and engages in oneupsmanship for the sake of controlling every situation. Mrs. Herriton and Mr. Wilcox share with others of Sawston's stolidly conventional middle class an admiration of wealth, cleverness, and barely masked prudery, callous meddling, and a supercilious attitude toward other people. Individual members of all such families in Forster's novels are expected to sublimate their own abilities, wishes, and personalities and to defer to a hazy notion of the "good of the family" defined by the assumed head of the family according to his or her unilateral decisions.

The later years of Victoria's reign saw the beginnings of public awareness of social issues in urgent need of reform. Among those then struggling to effect changes in the social, political, and economic life of England were Beatrice and Sidney Webb; the suffragettes Emmeline Pankhurst and her daughters; Henry Fawcett, M.P., and his wife, Dame Millicent Garrett Fawcett, campaigning for equal educational opportunities for women; and Josephine Butler, whose battle for women's rights was loyally supported by her husband and sons to their professional detriment. At a time when the marital relationship was still defined by the "ancient common law concept of couveture—'the husband and wife are one and the husband is that one,' *Blackstone*"[8]—not one of these reformers proposed restructuring family relationships or changing the organic shape or goals of the family. All implicitly accepted the common view of the family as an immutable institution whose social, economic, and political health far outweighed in importance the personal desires of any individual member. It was the creative writer, not the social reformer, who dared to dream of personal freedom and fulfillment *within* the family.

Forster's authorial eye was clearly on the middle class. The various parliamentary reform acts of the nineteenth century had gradually enlarged the perimeters of the middle class until by the end of the century even a minor clerk such as Leonard Bast could be considered middle class as long as he held a position in a business office.[9] Only with Leonard and Jackie Bast did Forster attempt to describe a family that was not educated, financially secure, and socially stable. He felt the challenge keenly and, with modest pride, thought he had met it successfully.[10] Forster was more certain of his observations of the solid center of middle-class family life as he saw and experienced it. He focused on what he knew and contrasted those observations with his vision that the middle-class family could embody new definitions of such traditional values as work, property, and community.

Descended from both the prominent Thornton family of bankers and the socially and financially precarious Whichelos, Forster acknowledged that much of the freedom he achieved in his adult life was the direct result of his financial security. In the words he gave to Margaret Schlegel in

Howards End, he was one of those who stood "upon money as upon islands,"[11] yet he was ambivalent about money. Knowing well the importance of having enough, he claimed not to like money very much,[12] and later in life ruefully admitted that "money blurs everything now, takes the edge off every character."[13] He absorbed generosity about money at his mother's knee[14] and enjoyed giving monetary gifts, which he believed "should be large so as not to be confused with loans."[15] For the latter, he expected prompt repayment. To give quiet gifts of money, Forster felt, was "an opportunity to perform acts of loving kindness,"[16] exemplifying his philosophy of "athletic love."[17]

Along with money, the institutional family was linked with property in Forster's mind. Having lived in his beloved Rooksnest from before the age of four through pre-puberty and establishing that connectedness with a place, a piece of English soil, that is so important in his writings, the boy of fourteen was traumatized "by his sudden exile from this rural paradise."[18] Years later, reading a paper entitled "Memory" at a meeting of the Bloomsbury Memoir Club, he said, "'If I had been allowed to stop on here I should have become a different person, married, and fought in the war.'"[19] Cast out of his Eden—and paradoxically released from the prison of property—he allowed himself to express his homosexuality, and in creating for himself an extended, nonconsanguineous family with the Buckinghams, he achieved a degree of hard-won personal freedom from the deadly weight of the institutional family. Forster's description of Hannah More—"childless herself, she became the family life that does not die with death"[20]—a critic suggests, can be equally applied to Forster's great-aunt Marianne Thornton and the novelist himself.[21] Margaret Schlegel also fits such a description.

Even though rigid familial boundaries were slowly eroding in his lifetime, Forster was sixty-six years old before he was his own master. As an only child, he had no one to share the Victorian burden of buffering his mother psychologically from her solitary state and the disorderly demands of society. In a judicious summation of his mother's influence, Forster wrote to a friend after her death, "Although my mother has been intermittently tiresome for the last thirty years, cramped and warped my genius, hindered my career, blocked and buggered up my house, and boycotted my beloved, I have to admit that she has provided a sort of rich subsoil where I have been able to rest and grow."[22] Something of the novelist's resignation in the face of intractable societal expectations surfaces in Philip Herriton when he muses that, though he can never escape his mother's demands, he is determined to carve out what limited freedom of movement he can.

Forster's prescience about the modern evolution of the family seems to have escaped his readers and critics, not only when his novels were first published but also later.[23] Neither I. A. Richards, commenting in 1927, nor Lionel Trilling in his 1943 full-scale study of Forster's novels, grapples with the radically different functional family structure that Forster depicts in the last chapter of *Howards End.* While Richards acknowledges Forster's "special preoccupation . . . with the continuance of life,"[24] Trilling is engrossed by parent-child—mainly father-son—relationships. He scarcely mentions the word "family" and perfunctorily notes that "three of the heroines are mothers of sons,"[25] but complains that "they lack maternal warmth" and that "their connections with their sons are tenuous."[26] The warmer, more kindly, mainly female Honeychurch family is simply ignored, as is the male Emerson counterpart. About fathers, Trilling is equally cursory, subsuming his brief mention of male parenthood under the rubric of Forster's attitudes toward authority figures.[27] In Trilling's defense, it must be recognized that the systematic study of the family only attained critical mass in the years after World War II.

Twenty years after Trilling, James Hall is one of the earliest critics to address at length Forster's theme of the family,[28] but it is George H. Thomson, also writing in the 1960s, who first identifies the nongenetic configuration of Forster's new family, observing that Forster assigns to Margaret as ancestors "ancient Danish soldiers who are not her ancestors at all."[29] Thomson also recognizes that the inheritance of Howards End is passing from the consanguineous family to a member of a more flexible and now extended family.[30]

In *Howards End,* Forster breaks with customary family values of the early 1900s and creates, however tersely, his vision of what the family might become. *Howards End* begins with an unconventional family and ends with the outline of a modern one.

The unconventional family consisted of Mr. Schlegel, a widower with three children to raise; Margaret, the eldest, was but thirteen years old. When Aunt Juley Munt, their mother's sister, in accordance with the tradition of the times, offered to run the household and supply maternal affection and guidance to the children, it was Margaret who decided "they could manage much better alone" (*HE,* 11). At Mr. Schlegel's death five years later, the answer was the same.

Mrs. Munt, the quintessential Sawstonite—though not virulent like Mrs. Herriton—gives all the wrong advice about money and would probably do the same regarding marriage, were her wisdom solicited. But the young Schlegels have learned to think for themselves, and Margaret and Helen, if not Tibby, have achieved some degree of self-knowledge and insight into human motivation. Of Mr. Schlegel's ample philosophical legacy to his children, his most important endowment was faith in human nature. If his trust was betrayed, his response was that "'it's better to be fooled than to be suspicious'—that the confidence trick is the work of man, but the want-of-confidence trick is the work of the devil" (*HE,* 39).

In contrast to the Schlegels, the Wilcox family aspires to social orthodoxy—at least Mr. Wilcox does—and vigilantly guards against investing trust in other people. Though Mrs. Wilcox might question the necessity for people with sufficient money to be working so hard to gather more, Mr. Wilcox's world is described by the accumulation of wealth. Mrs. Wilcox's faith that war would end if the mothers of various nations could meet is countermanded by Mr. Wilcox's firm belief in the idea and practice of Empire. As for religion, Mr. Wilcox, reared a Dissenter, turns to the Church of England, but surely not for moral or spiritual guidance. Mrs. Wilcox, of Quaker background, wants "a more inward light" than the rector's sermons provide, "not so much for myself as for baby" (*HE,* 88). Yet she never disputed Mr. Wilcox in anything except whether to pull down the old house and rebuild Howards End, a difference of opinion in which she carried the day. Mr. Wilcox domineers over his family. As a consequence, the children grow up in his image, not their mother's, while her life is "spent in the service of husband and sons" (*HE,* 71).

Though Mrs. Wilcox focuses her centripetal energies on her husband and children, Forster invests her with an important additional and private dimension. What matters to her is not intellection but connection with her own intuition and roots. In describing Mrs. Wilcox's attendance at Margaret's luncheon party, Forster makes clear that what the older woman represents is fragile, imaginative, hard to grasp, and impossible for her to articulate. Her "delicate imaginings" (*HE,* 71)—her experience of her inner intuitive nature at work—are destroyed by rapid-fire clever talk just as surely as Margaret's tentative connection with the countryside—her experience of external Nature—is severed by being driven through it in a motor car at high speed. Mrs. Wilcox lives "nearer the line that divides daily life from a life that may be of greater importance" (*HE,* 74).

Mrs. Wilcox finds in Margaret something lacking in her own offspring, a feeling of connection with the past that can, potentially, lead Margaret to the inner generative power of the human spirit. Mrs. Wilcox also senses in the younger woman what she calls, through her inability to frame a more precise definition, "inexperience" (*HE,* 70), a description of herself that Margaret, at age twenty-nine, finds disconcerting, since she has been the putative head of their family unit for more than ten years. Privately Margaret believes that "if experience is attainable, she had attained it" (*HE,* 71). But intuitively she realizes at the same time that for Mrs. Wilcox experience is a larger interior world of the heart and feelings, not just the superficialities of tea cups and roasts of beef, or even concerts.

Mrs. Wilcox is like a mother to the motherless Margaret, trying to teach her something Mrs. Wilcox's own children are not interested in, something that Margaret's own mother may not have adequately instilled in Margaret before her death. At twenty-nine Margaret is not yet sufficiently attuned to the inner life; she has so far intellectualized her life's experiences; "she mistrust[s] the periods of quiet that are essential to true growth" (*HE,* 77). When

Margaret finally discovers the deeper vein of intuition and feeling that Mrs. Wilcox suggests she needs in order to be truly "experienced" in life, her epiphany lies in the sudden recognition of her love of the spacious land, which surprises the city-bred Margaret. Her newfound appreciation of the land becomes the bridge "connecting on this side with the joys of the flesh, on that with the inconceivable" (*HE,* 202). The novelist makes clear that this epiphany "had certainly come through the house and old Miss Avery" (*HE,* 202), who shared Mrs. Wilcox's deep attachment to the land and its human history.

To her marriage to Henry Wilcox, Margaret brings many of the qualities that Forster valued. Unlike the first Mrs. Wilcox, who is willing "'to leave action and discussion to men'" (*HE,* 74), Margaret never really subordinates her beliefs to her husband's. At first she makes compromises in an effort to humor her husband's ingrained attitudes, so different from hers, yet she never relinquishes her principles, and, in the early days of her marriage, Forster tells us she is undergoing a seminal change, "some closing of the gates . . . inevitable after thirty, if the mind itself is to become a creative power" (*HE,* 259). Thus she is adequate to the crisis when Henry's Victorian values of family privacy and superficial propriety collapse in ruins when his son Charles is charged with the manslaughter of Leonard Bast.

A careful reading of the last chapter of the novel is crucial to an appreciation of Forster's vision of the modern family. Actually he anticipates the novel's destination in the final paragraph of the penultimate chapter when he announces that "a new life began to move" (*HE,* 331) from the moment of Henry's disintegration. In his spiritual collapse, he asked Margaret "to do what she could with him. She did what seemed easiest—she took him down to recruit at Howards End" (*HE,* 332).

That "recruit" in this particular context may suggest a double meaning—a newness of psychological life as well as a renewal of physical strength—seems not unreasonable, particularly as the last chapter of *Howards End* gives the reader a picture of that new life, those new relationships that are springing from the ground so carefully prepared by the novelist in his development of Margaret's character and equally from the collapse of Henry's life-support values: "They were building up a new life, obscure, yet gilded with tranquility. Leonard was dead; Charles had two years more in prison. One usen't always to see clearly before that time. It was different now" (*HE,* 334).

Critics have complained that the last chapter of *Howards End* is too contrived, the characters too overtly manipulated by Forster. There is much justification for such criticism. But if this chapter is approached as a capsulated view of what family relations can be, one sees a succinct summation of Forster's vision of the family to come. Interestingly enough, it was an American reviewer in 1922 who first remarked on Mr. Wilcox's transformation: "It is at Howards End that Henry Wilcox, assured, truculent, successful when he first meets Margaret Schlegel, finally attains to something of her poise and vision."[31]

An overview of the Wilcoxes as an institutional family in the early days of this century shows Henry Wilcox holding his children on a short rein. As thoroughly orthodox as Mrs. Herriton, he too wishes to control his sons and daughter and to use them to advance his own goals, which he thoughtlessly assumes are also theirs. Though Henry desires "no doughtier comrade" (*HE*, 99) when dealing with the emotions and uses his son Charles as a sounding board and coconspirator over the matter of Mrs. Wilcox's will, he can countenance no assumption of equality by Charles in the family business. While carrying out much of his father's "dirty work," Charles is kept psychologically and financially subservient.

With similar lack of consideration, Paul is sent out to Africa to run the family business, only to be unceremoniously summoned back to England to administer affairs there when Charles is sentenced to prison and Henry collapses. Paul's preferences are never asked (*HE*, 330); he is simply expected to accede, though it means giving up the outdoor life that satisfies him. Evie, as a daughter, is to be found a suitable husband and provided with an adequate dowry; meanwhile, to pass the time, she breeds dogs and plays tennis. The Wilcoxes might present a front of impregnable family solidarity to the world, but individually they could not endure close proximity to one another. "They had the colonial spirit, and were always making for some spot where the white man might carry his burden unobserved" (*HE*, 201), the burden being, in Forster's eyes, the failure to achieve family intimacy and trust.

Of the old shibboleths—Property, Propriety, Family Pride, and The Church—the last is of no help to Mr. Wilcox in his agony over Charles's imprisonment. Family Pride lies crushed and, like Propriety, in need of redefinition. As for Property—especially Money—Margaret's and Henry's view are at first widely divergent. Henry is secretive; she is open and frank about what she possesses and how to use it for beneficial purposes. To Margaret money is only "the warp of civilization" (*HE*, 125); the pattern, the enrichment of the tapestry, is created by the woof "'that isn't money'" (*HE*, 127), all those fructifying ends to which money might be usefully applied to enhance the inner, as well as the external, life of humankind, not just of the possessor of money. From the time of their engagement, she urges him to be generous toward his children; she wants nothing monetary from him. But he uses money as a convenient lever of control.

Their ideas about work are equally divergent. While Henry gives his clerks "work that scarcely encouraged them to grow into other men" (*HE*, 179), for himself personally, work is equated with money and power and is a symbol of his selfhood. Margaret looks on work as desirable and liberating, implying a certain harmony between innate ability and its expression in the workplace: "'. . . in the last cen-

tury men have developed the desire for work, and they must not starve it. It's a new desire. It goes with a good deal that's bad, but in itself is good, and I hope that for women, too, "not to work" will soon become as shocking as "not to be married" was a hundred years ago'" (*HE*, 108).

Given Henry Wilcox's rigidity of character, one cannot expect him to manifest major change in the fourteen months between his breakdown and the last chapter of *Howards End.* Yet he does grow. In disposing of much of his accumulated wealth to his children now they have reached maturity, Mr. Wilcox demonstrates he has learned a little bit about being a nurturing father. That he credits Margaret with the idea of sharing his money with his children while he is still alive does not invalidate the fact that he personally made that decision. Nor is he forced by Margaret to leave Howards End to Helen's son; in turn Mr. Wilcox asks each of his children if they want the house; only when they all reject it does he give Margaret the gift the first Mrs. Wilcox had intended her to have.

Over the fourteen months of Henry's "recruitment" since Charles's prison sentence was pronounced, many changes in the Wilcox family are effected by Margaret's influence. "She, who had never expected to conquer anyone, had charged straight through these Wilcoxes and broken up their lives" (*HE*, 339)—broken them up and helped put the pieces back in a more modern shape. Thus the last chapter of *Howards End* reveals the beginnings of a new, blended family: Henry Wilcox and his wife Margaret, his unwed sister-in-law Helen Schlegel (in 1990s parlance, a single parent) and her son. This is also the beginning of an extended family in which genetics is no longer the sole criterion for membership. Tom, the six-year-old farm boy, is a candidate for this extended family. He is not only present nursemaid for Helen's baby but as Helen anticipates to Margaret,

> "They're going to be lifelong friends."
>
> "Starting at the ages of six and one?"
>
> "Of course. It will be a great thing for Tom."
>
> "It may be a greater thing for baby."
>
> (*HE*, 333)

Here is an elliptical suggestion of the importance Forster ascribes to the social cross-fertilization possible between the descendant of yeoman stock (Tom) and the heir (Helen's baby) of an intellectual family consciously making that vital connection with the land as personified by the first Mrs. Wilcox. Here again Forster reiterates the importance he ascribes to the genetic union between Leonard Bast, "grandson to the shepherd or ploughboy whom civilization had sucked into the town" (*HE*, 113), a "noble peasant"[32] who, though removed from his geographic roots, has not forgotten them, and Helen Schlegel, who has never had Leonard's visceral sense of connection with the land but is in her own way, with Margaret, groping intuitively yet deliberately toward that connection. Helen exults in "'such a crop of hay as never!'" (*HE,* 340) just as she exults in her son who unites the genetic strength of the "noble peasant" with the intellectual vigor and sensitivity of educated people like the Schlegel sisters. Forster "cares deeply about the Leonards of England,"[33] just as he does about the urgent necessity for cerebral people to forge their own modern spiritual links with ancient long-forgotten roots in a physical place.

While the definition of the family has been enlarged to include the possibility of nonconsanguineous members, there is no evidence of active exclusion of anyone heretofore considered a family member, as Hall suggests.[34] Mrs. Munt and Tibby may not be the active members of the family group they once were—she is old, and he is launching out on his own autonomous life—but it is impossible to imagine Margaret and Helen ever excluding either of them from their circle; even Henry Wilcox gets along superficially well with both. Paul Wilcox may be estranged from the rest and eager to get away from them all once more by returning to Africa posthaste, but Evie has got over being angry with her father for marrying again. Because of his trial, Charles is loath to live in Howards End after his release from prison and considers going so far as to change his name. But his wife, Dolly, who is not quite so vacuous as Mr. Wilcox likes to think her, defends her family identity, saying, "'Wilcox' just suits Charles and me, and I can't think of any other name" (*HE,* 339).

Not only is the family changing in size and constitution, and its members gaining in individual independence and equality through Henry's sharing out to his children a great deal of his accumulated wealth, but Margaret's attitudes toward the use of money are being implemented practically. Explaining that upon his death his children will receive all the rest of his estate—"'. . . I leave my wife no money. . . . That is her own wish'" (*HE,* 339)—Henry emphasizes Margaret's radical financial decisions. In addition to relinquishing any legal claim she had to Henry Wilcox's money by reason of marriage, she is embarked on giving away to philanthropy half of her own inheritance.

The "breakup and continuance of the family"[35] that Hall sees as a consistent theme in Forster's novels is not capricious; it has a salubrious function. The new Wilcox-Schlegel blended family has already learned how to give texture to the human reconciliation that can grow out of working through life's unexpected challenges. Not only Henry is changing. Margaret's earlier inability to forgive Henry for his treatment of Helen and her intention of leaving him have dissolved as the new life emerges that began to move and germinate during Henry's recruitment. Helen has learned to accept Henry and he, her. Helen has also discovered she has no wish to marry; she has her son. Though Helen's style of life was rare—even outrageous—in 1910, three-quarters of a century later it hardly raises an eyebrow. Margaret does not care for children, but she cares very much for adults and how they get along together in the family. Margaret has become a matriarch without ever being a mother.

Helen gives her all the credit for their "new birth": "'Just think of our lives without you, Meg—I and baby [living on the Continent] . . . he [Henry] handed about from Dolly to Evie. But you picked up the pieces and made us a home'" (*HE,* 336). Margaret acknowledges that "'no doubt I have done a little towards straightening the tangle,'" but, signifying her having learned well Mrs. Wilcox's lesson, she adds, "'. . . things that I can't phrase have helped me'" (*HE,* 337).

Present-day readers of *Howards End* may be excused for faulting the failure of critics of thirty or forty years ago to grasp Forster's brilliant dream of the twentieth-century family. In post-World War II days, and even into the 1960s, working mothers and nurturing fathers were the exception, unmarried mothers still a rarity, and blended families were only becoming more common. The traditional roles for women and men far outnumbered examples of equality between the sexes. From the vantage point of the 1990s, with several additional decades of observing changes in the family, today's readers can better comprehend Forster's prophetic vision of a new and more flexible form of the family; they will discern that contemporary middle-class families have advanced beyond the families of the 1960s toward an expression of Forster's dream of 1910. This palpable advance permits current readers to differ from Hall, who wrote in 1963 (like Trilling in 1943) that "the ending is a *Jane Eyre* one: the offenders are punished severely and the husband is gelded, needing thereafter only a nurse."[36]

Forster makes clear that Margaret's vision is not to be a nurse, serving Henry's wants, but to become an equal partner in the marriage. It can be argued that when Henry collapsed, Margaret responded as would have been expected of the typical nurturing mother and wife of 1910: "She did what seemed easiest—she took him down to recruit at Howards End," giving up her intention of leaving him in order to cleave to her sister Helen and her expected child and exile herself to the Continent to protect the only vital family relationship she had ever had. Instead, following the ineluctable collapse of Henry's values, Margaret seizes the chance to create a new family structure encompassing both Wilcoxes and Schlegels, in which she would be the matriarch—not just a wife, not just an older sister, never a mother, but sharing equally with Henry in heading an extended family. Far from searching for an ideal father figure, as Hall implies,[37] Margaret had needed a mother figure; she found it in Mrs. Wilcox. Margaret had a strong father, one she admired and whose values she had thoroughly assimilated. Mrs. Wilcox was the necessary mother figure whose example of inner strength of intuition helped Margaret to root her views of familial relationships—unorthodox and radical for 1910—in a new experience of intuitive visceral knowledge, not just in intellectual hypotheses.

Likewise, in nurturing a sense of spiritual kinship among very different people, Margaret goes far beyond Hall's 1963 view that "the high barriers to community of spirit remain barriers. Helen and Margaret both try to reach understanding with people of extremely different backgrounds, temperaments, and hopes. The novel yields no ground at all to this possibility."[38] On the contrary, I believe that the novel carefully prepares the ground for exactly this possibility, while recognizing the difficulty of the endeavor. The barriers are truly there, but Forster's sketch of the new structure of the family suggests the possibility of a community of spirit—what Hall earlier calls a "community-in-difference"—among people of widely varying backgrounds.

In **"Pessimism in Literature,"** writing of the modern novelist's search for the truth of the human condition to embody in fiction, Forster tells his audience that separation seems more truly to reflect life than does a happy ending in the form of marriage. Yet, continuing his thesis, he states that since the novelist chooses separation:

> *we conclude, quite unjustly, that he sees in life nothing but separation.* The truth is that modern art has not succeeded in depicting all modern life. It has tried, it would like to, but it cannot . . . a man and an author have different aims. The author looks for what is permanent, even if it is sad; the man looks for what is cheerful, and noble, and gracious, even if it is transitory.[39]

Forster the man may be peeping through in the last chapter of *Howards End.*

Is this newborn family just a passing whimsey of Forster's that is applicable to only one novel? Is it specific to *Howards End*? In the fragments of *Arctic Summer,* we see a reaffirmation of the freer, more individualist family where equality is valued over class, and love between husband and wife includes a strong companionship. The traditional foundation stones of Property, Propriety, and Family Pride—if not The Church—have been redefined.

Martin Whitby feels his wife, Venetia, is "a comrade as well as a wife."[40] She is a working wife and a mother, autonomous, with "clear vision" (*Arctic,* 132), not a conventional woman, but one who, like her husband, hates pseudo-chivalry because "it's against all true intercourse with women, and all progress" (*Arctic,* 141). The son of a manufacturer and a Quaker, Martin attended day school before going up to Cambridge (*Arctic,* 130). He chose a bureaucratic post in the Treasury over a Cambridge fellowship (*Arctic,* 132). Martin and Venetia share outside interests, have a healthy little son named Hugo, and like, as well as love, each other. Theirs is an "orderly love" (*Arctic,* 132), wherein reason and passion work together (*Arctic,* 132), and they have produced wedded love, not wildly exciting perhaps, but comradely and satisfying over the long run (*Arctic,* 133). For their child, they are anxious that he "shouldn't be taught all the rubbish about 'little girls do this' and 'little boys do that'" (*Arctic,* 155). That Hugo should grow up liking people is what is important. And Hugo's parents make no distinction between gentlemen and other men (*Arctic,* 155).

Thus it would seem that the new family so abruptly born in the last chapter of *Howards End* is no aberration. In Forster's new, modern, functional family, equality is basic; the idea of money as power is forsworn; individual autonomy is recognized; and class is being overcome, at least for the next generation. Women have choices regarding marriage and careers, and they work because work fulfills one part of their nature. Men, too, are liberated from the narrow stereotypes of conventional careers. Both parents are nurturers. No longer limited by genetics, families may by choice be nuclear or extended, or even blended. Working wives and mothers are becoming unexceptional. When money is regarded as a means, not an end, people are able to be more generous in spreading its benefits; within or outside the family, philanthropy is not considered extraordinary. The family that emphasizes companionship in its relations strengthens the individuality of each of its members, and this in turn strengthens the sense of community-cum-variety. Communal cohesion springs voluntarily from shared interests and feelings, not just from common bloodlines. People who are very different learn they can coexist and even come to respect and accept each other. Family relationships need no longer be the "white man's burden" (Forster's words) that forces people to flee to the ends of the earth to escape meaningless formality. Education of the young strives to be gender-free. The goal is a classless family of all humanity.

Forster unfailingly emphasized the spirit over the strictly legalistic. "A funeral is not death, any more than baptism is birth or marriage union. All three are the clumsy devices, coming now too late, now too early, by which Society would register the quick motions of man" (*HE,* 100). What was important to the novelist was a new framework for relationships—"love without power," in Peter Gay's graceful phrase—between husband and wife, parents and children, the nuclear family and the extended circle.

Forster was indeed more prescient than he knew. Already in **"Pessimism in Literature,"** dated 1906-07, he had written:

> [T]hough the facts of human nature are constant, the spirit of humanity is not, but alters age by age, perhaps year by year, and, like some restless child, continually groups the facts anew. . . . What new and inspiring combinations it may find, no man can say; that it will find a new combination is surely inevitable, and happy the artist who records it."[41]

As the end of the twentieth century approaches, perhaps readers of Forster's fiction are becoming attuned to the resonance of his visionary ideas about the family. Certainly when he wrote *Howards End* in the first decade of the century, Forster was ahead of his time in identifying and recording a new shape and function for the modern family.

Notes

1. Lawrence Stone, *The Family, Sex and Marriage in England, 1500-1800,* abridged ed. (New York: Harper and Row, 1979), 22.

2. Stone, 22.

3. Peter Gay, *The Tender Passion* (New York: Oxford UP, 1986), 4.

4. Gay, 106.

5. Gay, 106.

6. Gay, 107. For further insight into the nineteenth-century English middle-class family, see also F. M. L. Thompson, *The Rise of Respectable Society* (Cambridge: Harvard UP, 1988). For contemporary personal accounts of parent-child relations, see Linda Pollock, *A Lasting Relationship: Parents and Children over Three Centuries* (Hanover, NH: UP of New England, 1987). For an understanding of the buffering role of servants in isolating children from parents, see Theresa M. McBride, *The Domestic Revolution* (New York: Holmes and Meier, 1976).

7. E. M. Forster, *Where Angels Fear to Tread,* Abinger Edition of E. M. Forster, ed. Oliver Stallybrass, vol. 1 (London: Edward Arnold, 1975), 69.

8. Qtd. in Leonore Davidoff, "Mastered for Life: Servant and Wife in Victorian and Edwardian England," *Journal of Social History* 7 (Summer 1974): 406.

9. For a discussion of the entry of clerks into the lower middle class, see Thompson 68-69.

10. *Paris Review, Writers at Work,* ed. Malcolm Cowley (New York: Viking, 1958), "E. M. Forster," interview by P. N. Furbank and F. J. H. Haskell, 20 June 1952, 23-25.

11. E. M. Forster, *Howards End,* Abinger Edition of E. M. Forster, ed. Oliver Stallybrass, vol. 4 (London: Edward Arnold, 1973), 58.

12. From a 1910 letter to Goldsworthy Lowes Dickinson, qtd. in P. N. Furbank, *E. M. Forster, a Life,* vol. 1 (New York: Harcourt Brace Jovanovich, 1977), 191.

13. E. M. Forster, *Commonplace Book,* ed. Philip Gardner (Stanford: Stanford UP, 1985), 91.

14. Furbank, *Forster, a Life,* 1:24-25.

15. P. N. Furbank, *Encounter* 35 "The Personality of E. M. Forster," (Nov. 1970): 61-68; see esp. 65.

16. Furbank, "Personality of Forster," 64.

17. Furbank, *Forster, a Life,* 2:40.

18. John Colmer, *E. M. Forster: The Personal Voice* (London: Routledge and Kegan Paul, 1975), 3.

19. Qtd. in Colmer, 3.

20. E. M. Forster, *Marianne Thornton, A Domestic Biography, 1797-1887* (New York: Harcourt, Brace, 1956), 41.

21. See Judith Scherer Herz, "Forster's Three Experiments in Autobiographical Biography," *Studies in the Literary Imagination,* 13 (Spring 1980): 64.

22. Quoted in Peter Parker, *Ackerley: A Life of J. R. Ackerley* (New York: Farrar Strauss Giroux, 1989), 157.

23. For contemporaneous reviews, see Philip Gardner, *E. M. Forster, the Critical Heritage* (London: Routledge and Kegan Paul, 1973). See also Frederick P. W. Mc-Dowell, *E. M. Forster, an Annotated Bibliography of Writings about Him* (DeKalb: Northern Illinois UP, 1976), and Helmut E. Gerber, "E. M. Forster: An Annotated Checklist of Writings about Him," *English Fiction in Transition* 2 (Spring 1959): 4-27, bound in *English Literature in Transition,* vols. 1-3 (1957-60). Also see McDowell's articles in *English Literature in Transition,* especially "E. M. Forster: Recent Extended Studies," 9 (Fall 1966): 156-68; "Bibliography, News, and Notes: E. M. Forster," 10 (Spring 1967): 47-64; and "Recent Books on Forster and on Bloomsbury," 12 (Fall 1969): 135-50. Present-day scholars certainly provide subtle insights into specific personal relationships, but no one seems to address the *family* as a major theme. However, Don Austin, in "The Problem of Continuity in Three Novels of E. M. Forster," *Modern Fiction Studies* 7 (Autumn 1961): 219, recognizes the possibility of spiritual, as well as genetic, children.

24. I. A. Richards, "A Passage to Forster: Reflections on a Novelist," *Forum* 78 (Dec. 1927): 918.

25. Trilling designates Mrs. Wilcox, Mrs. Eliott, and Mrs. Moore as his "heroines" (see Lionel Trilling, *E. M. Forster* [New York: Harcourt Brace Jovanovich, 1963], 33-34).

26. Trilling, 33-34.

27. See Trilling, 87.

28. James Hall, *The Tragic Comedians: Seven Modern British Novelists* (Bloomington: Indiana UP, 1963), ch. 2, "Family Reunions."

29. George H. Thomson, *The Fiction of E. M. Forster* (Detroit: Wayne State UP, 1967), 185.

30. Thomson, 185.

31. Gardner, 167, a review by George B. Dutton in the *Springfield Sunday Republican* (Springfield, MA), 1 Jan. 1922. Dutton was a professor of English of Williams College.

32. For a discussion of what this term means and the seminal role of the "noble peasant," see Jeane N. Olson, "The 'Noble Peasant' in E. M. Forster's Fiction," *Studies in the Novel* 20 (Winter 1988): 389-403.

33. I am grateful to the reader of an earlier version of this article for this felicitous phrase, with which I wholeheartedly agree.

34. See Hall, 23-24.

35. Hall, 11.

36. Hall, 22-23.

37. See Hall, 18. Notice also Hall's somewhat different interpretation of Mrs. Wilcox as a mother figure.

38. Hall, 23.

39. E. M. Forster, *Albergo Empedocle and Other Writings of E. M. Forster,* ed. George H. Thomson (New York: Liveright, 1971), "Pessimism in Literature," 137-38; emphasis added.

40. E. M. Forster, *Arctic Summer and Other Fiction,* Abinger Edition of E. M. Forster, ed. Elizabeth Heine and Oliver Stallybrass, vol. 9 (London: Edward Arnold, 1980), 122.

41. Forster, *Albergo Empedocle,* 140.

Burkhard Niederhoff (essay date 1994)

SOURCE: Niederhoff, Burkhard. "E. M. Forster and the Supersession of Plot by Leitmotif: A Reading of *Aspects of the Novel* and *Howards End.*" *Anglia* 112, no. 3-4 (1994): 341-63.

[In the following essay, Niederhoff examines similarities between Forster's discussion of novels in Aspects of the Novel *and* Howards End.*]*

In *Aspects of the Novel,* E. M. Forster writes about Marcel Proust's *A la recherche du temps perdu,* "The book is chaotic, ill-constructed, it has and will have no external shape; and yet it hangs together because it is stitched internally, because it contains rhythms."[1] To illustrate what he means by "rhythms", Forster mentions a leitmotif well known to the readers of the *Recherche.* "There are several examples [. . .], but the most important, from the binding point of view, is his use of the 'little phrase' in the music of Vinteuil. This little phrase does more than anything else [. . .] to make us feel that we are in a homogeneous world" (113 f.). Forster does not tell us in so many words that Proust's novel needs the binding and stitching provided by its rhythms, because it is otherwise lacking in structure and cohesion, but the passage at least implies a relation between the absence of one kind of narrative unity, which he does not specify, and the presence of another, which he does specify: the coherence created by rhythms, or leitmotifs[2]. This implication is spelt out by David Lodge, who seizes on Forster's remarks on rhythm to describe the formal features of modernist fiction:

> To compensate for the diminution of narrative structure and unity, alternative methods of aesthetic ordering become more prominent, such as allusion to or imitation of literary models or mythical archetypes, and the repetition-with-variation of motifs, images, symbols—a technique variously described as "rhythm", "Leitmotif" and "spatial form"[3].

Lodge adds a new aspect to Forster's idea by arguing in historical terms. Whereas Forster does not claim that the

way in which Vinteuil's phrase stitches together the otherwise fragmented *Recherche* is typical of the writing of his contemporaries, Lodge maintains that this structural feature distinguishes the modernist fiction written by novelists like Forster, Lawrence, Woolf, and Joyce from the realist fiction of the 19th century, which dominated the literary scene until World War I and reemerged in the thirties with Orwell, Greene, and the later Isherwood[4].

One of the traditional coherence-creating devices that modernist writers like Woolf and Joyce abandon and replace by leitmotifs is the Aristotelian plot, i. e. an arrangement of incidents that are causally connected and form a unity with a beginning, middle, end and no or relatively few loose ends. *Ulysses* does not have a plot in this traditional sense. From the point of view of the causal logic of such a plot, Joyce's novel is an immense collection of loose ends, and this is one of the reasons why the first-time reader usually experiences it as a sequence of disconnected fragments and details. However, if we reread the novel or use the leitmotif index compiled by William Schutte[5], we will be able to make sense of many phrases or details by relating them to their other occurrences in the novel. Arguably, in *Ulysses* this reading via remembering and anticipation is more important than the ordinary kind of reading, i. e. the linear progression from one word or sentence to the next.

If it is possible to summarize one of the structural features of modernist fiction with the slogan "exit plot—enter leitmotif", it appears that we cannot include Forster's novels in this kind of fiction. Although these novels contain many leitmotifs, they also rely on traditional plot devices, as has been pointed out repeatedly, for instance by Peter Burra[6]. One example from *Howards End* is the way in which the various plot lines and the three different families (the Schlegels, the Wilcoxes, and the Basts) are linked to each other. Henry Wilcox first interferes in Leonard Bast's life when the Schlegel sisters ask him for his opinion on Leonard's situation. Henry's advice that Leonard quit his job leads to the clerk's ending up in constant unemployment. When the enraged Helen Schlegel takes the Basts to Oniton to demand that Henry compensate them for the consequences of his advice, there is an anagnorisis reminiscent of 18th or 19th century novels in that it combines a farfetched coincidence with a moral lesson: Ten years ago Henry had an affair with Jacky Bast. Thus he has not only ruined Leonard's professional prospects but also the moral and social standing of his wife. V. Woolf's novel *Mrs. Dalloway* features a constellation of characters which is similar to that of *Howards End*; Septimus Warren Smith and Mrs. Dalloway are socially at least as remote from each other as Henry Wilcox and Leonard Bast. Woolf, however, does not link her characters by a plot device of the Forsterian kind. She establishes connections between Septimus and Mrs. Dalloway through other means, e. g. by leitmotifs that are associated with both of them, or by abruptly shifting the narrative perspective from him to her (sometimes via an object or sound perceived by both of them, as the ringing of Big Ben).

In spite of these obvious differences between *Howards End* and such modernist novels as *Mrs. Dalloway* and *Ulysses,* I will argue that Forster's novel participates in the modernist project of "exit plot—enter leitmotif". Woolf and Joyce express their discontent with the Aristotelian arrangement of incidents by simply discarding it. Forster expresses a similar discontent by creating a plot and making it fail. *Howards End* is not only a novel about houses, people, views, and values, it is also a novel about the various aspects of the novel, a poetological experiment in which plot is tried and found wanting. A passage which is crucial for this view of the novel occurs at the beginning of the penultimate chapter, when Margaret reflects on Leonard's death and the events and complications that led up to it.

> Events succeeded in a logical, yet senseless, train. People lost their humanity, and took values as arbitrary as those in a pack of playing-cards. It was natural that Henry should do this and cause Helen to do that, and then think her wrong for doing it; natural that she herself should think him wrong; natural that Leonard should want to know how Helen was, and come, and Charles be angry with him for coming—natural, but unreal. In this jangle of causes and effects what had become of their true selves? Here Leonard lay dead in the garden, from natural causes; yet life was a deep, deep river, death a blue sky, life was a house, death a wisp of hay, a flower, a tower, life and death were anything and everything, except this ordered insanity, where the king takes the queen, and the ace the king[7].

The poetological implications of this passage are underlined by its similarities with Forster's remarks on plot in *Aspects*[8]. Margaret thinks of the events she has witnessed as a "jangle of causes and effects"; Forster defines plot as "a narrative of events, the emphasis falling on causality" (60). Furthermore, we find in Margaret's thoughts the king and the queen also used by Forster in his well-known examples of story and plot, which will be quoted below. This is not just a superficial and irrelevant coincidence, but a signal of the deeper underlying similarity between *Aspects* and *Howards End.* Just as Margaret rejects the "jangle of causes and effects" as "senseless" and "unreal", Forster has misgivings about the causal structure of the plot, and just as Margaret feels that there is or should be something beyond the "ordered insanity" of the logical turn of events, Forster looks for other aesthetic aspects that enable the novelist to go beyond fabricating a plot, and the most important of these aspects, as we will see, is the leitmotif. To substantiate and flesh out this comparison between *Howards End* and *Aspects,* I will analyse the remarks on plot and leitmotif contained in the latter work before embarking on a reading of the novel.

In the introductory chapter of *Aspects,* Forster rejects a historical approach to the novel, stating his intention to "exorcise that demon of chronology" (8) and to treat novelists from different periods as if they were all simultaneously at work in one room (9). What may seem like a whimsical metaphorical ornament ("exorcise that demon of chronology") is in fact revealing and crucial, because it reflects one of Forster's basic tenets, his profound aversion to time, an aversion which surfaces in many arguments, metaphors and rhetorical manoeuvres in *Aspects*[9]. Having thus settled on a typological rather than a historical approach, Forster selects seven aspects which will be treated in the subsequent chapters: "The Story; People; The Plot; Fantasy and Prophecy; Pattern and Rhythm" (16). The most relevant for our purposes are of course plot and rhythm, but we will also have to glance at the other aspects, since Forster's book on the novel is, despite his assertion that one cannot approach the "spongy tract" of the novel with "principles and systems" (15), underpinned by a coherent system of ideas and values, and thus the remarks on one aspect often have implications for the others.

According to Forster, the most primitive element of the novel is the story, a mere "narrative of events arranged in their time-sequence" (18), the appropriate audience for a story being a group of "cave-men", whose only response is the question "'And then?'", the curiosity to learn what happens next (60). As the story is governed by the "demon of chronology" so much feared by Forster, his opinion of this aspect is a very low one: "When we isolate the story like this from the nobler aspects through which it moves, and hold it out on the forceps—wriggling and interminable, the naked worm of time—it presents an appearance that is both unlovely and dull" (19). To distinguish the story from other aspects of the novel, Forster opposes a "life in time" to a "life by values". The story is limited to the former, and if the novelist wants to include the latter, he has to do so by "using devices hereafter to be examined" (19), i. e. the other aspects of the novel enumerated above. The distinction between a "life in time" and a "life by values" is a heavily loaded one, as it implies that time is without value and even opposed to it. From a logical point of view, the cogency of the distinction is easily challenged. Values may be atemporal, but so are a host of other abstract notions. Why not oppose time to space, character, stability or eternity? Thus the distinction may not be a very compelling one in logical terms, but it certainly is a revealing rhetorical manoeuvre that reflects Forster's hostility to the "demon of chronology".

According to Forster, a plot differs from a story in that it adds two features to the mere narrative of events in their chronological order: causality and mystery (it does not become quite clear whether the second criterion is an obligatory or an optional one, and this vagueness about the definition of plot is something that we will have to return to later on):

> "The king died and then the queen died" is a story. "The king died, and then the queen died of grief" is a plot. The time-sequence is preserved, but the sense of causality overshadows it. Or again: "The queen died, no one knew why, until it was discovered that it was through grief at the death of the king." This is a plot with a mystery in it, a form capable of high development.
>
> (60)

Plot is superior to story because it requires intelligence and memory on the reader's part. The illustration of why these are required focuses on mystery rather than causality, and we will presently see why. A mystery "occurs through a suspension of the time-sequence", it is "a pocket in time, and it occurs crudely, as in 'Why did the queen die?', and more subtly in half-explained gestures and words, the true meaning of which only dawns pages ahead" (61). As readers of plots with mysteries, we need memory to retain an adequate picture of the "pocket[s] in time", and we need intelligence to recognize the solutions that belong in these pockets when we come across them later on in the novel. I suggest that Forster's appreciation of mystery stems from his dislike of "the naked worm of time" and his esteem for anything that emancipates us, however modestly, from chronology. Forster's first plot criterion, causality, does little to do so; on the contrary, it implies chronology, since causes precede effects. When mystery with its "pocket[s] in time" comes in and makes Tuesday precede Monday and effects precede causes, it has to suspend causality along with chronology.

In his remarks on Meredith, Forster gives us another reason why plot should be appreciated: It can produce surprises like the horse-whipping of Dr. Shrapnel in *Beauchamp's Career.* Here Forster praises plot for something that, once again, does not follow from its first defining criterion. For causality implies predictability; particular causes make us expect particular effects. In order to create surprises, novelists may opt for the easy way out by simply dispensing with causality and introducing a coincidence or a *deus ex machina,* or they may attempt to produce an unexpected effect by contriving a particularly sophisticated arrangement of causes. Thus surprise resembles the two other praiseworthy aspects of plot (the gratification of intelligence and memory) in that it does not follow from its first defining characteristic. It is a triumph over rather than a result of causality.

Forster mentions two further features of plot, both of which, in his eyes, amount to limitations and drawbacks for the novelist. First, the demands of plot clash with those of character. In one of the most delightful passages of *Aspects,* Forster visualizes the plot "as a sort of higher governmental official" who holds forth on the lack of public spirit in the population of the novel (59). Second, plot is planned. The plot-maker "plans his book beforehand; or anyhow he stands above it, his interest in cause and effect gives him an air of predetermination" (67). Forster regards both features as limitations which are inescapable in drama but which the novelist might perhaps replace by something else:

> It [the contribution of a character to the plot] is accorded, and of necessity, by the people in a drama; how necessary is it in a novel? (60) After all, why has a novel to be planned? [. . .] The plot is exciting and may be beautiful, yet is it not a fetish, borrowed from the drama, from the spatial limitations of the stage? Cannot fiction devise a framework that is not so logical yet more suitable to its genius?
>
> (67)[10]

I will argue that the framework envisaged here is provided by the aspect of rhythm or leitmotif, but before we can move on to this aspect, we have to look at an intriguing and rather surprising passage of Forster's chapter on plot. Describing how the reader recognizes clues and establishes chains of cause and effect, Forster introduces a new idea.

> The final sense (if the plot has been a fine one) will not be of clues or chains, but of something aesthetically compact [. . .] We come up against beauty here—for the first time in our enquiry: beauty at which a novelist should never aim, though he fails if he does not achieve it. I will conduct beauty to her proper place later on. Meanwhile please accept her as part of a completed plot. She looks a little surprised at being there.
>
> (61 f.)

As well she might—because Forster does not mention her again in the chapter on plot. And by the time he finally conducts her to her proper place, she may be a little irritated, because he has left her waiting until the final chapter, "Pattern and Rhythm". Beauty also involves Forster in a clear-cut contradiction. Thus, plot is planned and premeditated (67), while beauty should not be aimed at (i. e. planned and premeditated) by the novelist; nevertheless she is part of a completed plot (61 f.). The uncertainty about the proper place of beauty and the ensuing contradictions result from the fact that the term *plot* has to cover a very wide semantic area: all the structural features between the lowest aspect, story, and the highest aspects, pattern and rhythm. Forster uses the term very loosely; sometimes he thinks of plot in broad terms including structural aspects like mystery or surprise and reaching into the realm of pattern, rhythm and beauty[11]. However, sometimes he thinks of it in narrow terms as the planning of a causal chain, as "hammer[ing] away all the time at cause and effect" (22). This second, narrowly defined type of plot occupies a very low rank in the Forsterian value system; it adds nothing to the primitive and time-bound aspect of story but causality and planning, and as we have seen, none of these two features elicits any positive comments from Forster. That the two are related is shown in the statement already quoted above that the plotmaker's "interest in *cause and effect* gives him an air of *predetermination*" (67, my italics).

It is important to be aware of these shifting definitions because otherwise the appreciative remarks on plot in *Aspects* might obscure the close relations between this book and *Howards End,* and furthermore the relations between these works and the project of "exit plot—enter leitmotif" in modernist novels like *Mrs. Dalloway* and *Ulysses.* It is plot in the narrow sense, confined to the features of causality and planning, which is tried and found wanting in *Howards End.* I have already pointed out that causality is the dominant theme in the passage at the end of the novel that reviews the events from Margaret's point of view, and we will see the relevance of the related criterion of planning for an analysis of the novel later on. One might add that even the metaphors of *Aspects* and *Howards End* match up with each other, if one looks at those passages in the theoretical work in which Forster thinks of the plot in its narrow causal sense. If you "hammer away all the time at cause and effect", is not what you produce the "jangle" perceived by Margaret?

Let us proceed to pattern and rhythm. A pattern is a large-scale structure of events, for instance, the "hour-glass" (104) or chiastic one of Henry James's *The Ambassadors.* Whereas the plot appeals to our intelligence, pattern "appeals to our aesthetic sense, it causes us to see the book as a whole" (103). This seeing of the book as a whole is of course a far cry from the cave-dweller's question "And then?"; and the beauty ascribed to pattern is a consequence of its triumph over chronology: "Beauty is sometimes the shape of the book, the book as a whole, the unity" (104). However, patterns have their drawbacks. Like plots, they have to be planned (105), and they take a heavy toll on the characters and on the demands of realism in general (112). After praising James for the beauty of *The Ambassadors,* Forster claims that most readers cannot accept the sacrifices entailed by a pattern, finding it "'beautifully done, but not worth doing'" (112).

After this dismissal of pattern, Forster finally passes on to rhythm: "Still, this is not the end of our quest. We will not give up the hope of beauty yet. Cannot it be introduced into fiction by some other method than the pattern? Let us edge rather nervously towards the idea of 'rhythm'" (112). This is not the language of an impartial narratologist, but that of a writer who has a stake in what he analyses. If Forster has not given up the hope of beauty *yet,* it is implied that the aspects he has looked at so far have been tried and, at least partially, found wanting; and if he is near the end of his "quest", it seems that rhythm is destined to bring about the final fulfillment of his hope for untrammeled beauty. We might also note in passing that the simple fact of the final position has an evaluative function. Stone aptly characterizes the table of contents in *Aspects* as a "hierarchy of value" (110), and Forster generally makes the superior aspect succeed the inferior one: plot comes after story, round character after flat, prophecy after fantasy. Rhythm is indeed the successful end of Forster's quest. By establishing links between various passages of a novel separated in time, it exorcises "the demon of chronology", achieving "the establishment of beauty and the ravishing of the reader's memory" (115) and making "us feel that we are in a homogeneous world" (113 f.). Thus, rhythm is like pattern in liberating us from the tyranny of Forster's archenemy, time, and in the creation of order and beauty; but unlike pattern, rhythm achieves all this without being planned and "without mutilating the characters" (115), i. e. without the sacrifices that make Henry James's hour-glasses "'beautifully done, but not worth doing.'"

It is high time we return to *Howards End,* a novel in which the ideas, values and implications of *Aspects* are embodied in fictional form, and we may as well begin with a quotation from Helen's opening letter to Margaret.

I looked out earlier, and Mrs Wilcox was already in the garden. She evidently loves it. No wonder she sometimes looks tired. She was watching the large red poppies come out. Then she walked off the lawn to the meadow, whose corner to the right I can just see. Trail, trail, went her long dress over the sopping grass, and she came back with her hands full of the hay that was cut yesterday—I suppose for rabbits or something, as she kept on smelling it. The air here is delicious. Later on I heard the noise of croquet balls, and looked out again, and it was Charles Wilcox practising; they are keen on all games. Presently he started sneezing and had to stop. Then I hear more cliqueting, and it is Mr Wilcox practising, and then: "a-tissue, a-tissue": he has to stop too. Then Evie comes out, and does some callisthenic exercises on a machine that is tacked on to a greengage-tree—they put everything to use—and then she says "a-tissue", and in she goes. And finally Mrs Wilcox reappears, trail, trail, still smelling hay and looking at the flowers.

(2)

Before pointing out the relation of this narrative vignette to *Aspects,* plot and leitmotif, I would like to focus on its most noticeable feature, the contrast in characterization. Mrs. Wilcox does not seem to engage in actions that have a purpose extraneous to themselves, whereas the other members of her family "put everything to use", most of all themselves. The males do not play croquet, they "practise" it; and Evie does "exercises". They tack machines on to plants, whereas Mrs. Wilcox prefers to smell and view them. This contrast between useful exercise on the one hand and non-purposive activity on the other derives a paradoxical twist from the fact that Mr. Wilcox and his children engage in games and sports, while Mrs. Wilcox is the only one who actually accomplishes something useful (fetching food for the rabbits). However, even in doing so she does not give her visitor that impression. What strikes Helen is not that Mrs. Wilcox carries the hay somewhere, but that she smells it. This contributes another, seemingly trivial contrastive feature to our interpretation of this passage. The hay Mrs. Wilcox so loves to smell is what makes the rest of her family go "a-tissue". The contrast in characterization is supported by a contrast in structure. Mr. Wilcox's, Charles's and Evie's attempts at useful exercise are single, isolated, and abortive. After they have been driven back into the house, Mrs. Wilcox reappears and repeats what she did before: She looks at the flowers, smells the hay, and her dress trails over the soppy grass. These actions frame and enclose, as it were, those of the rest of her family, and the stability and continuity involved in the repetition of Mrs. Wilcox's actions emphasize the superiority of her non-purposive activity over the others' frustrated attempts at putting themselves to use.

Helen herself indicates that there is something special and significant about the scene described in her letter. "It really does seem not life but a play" (2). This brief "play" is indeed significant because its structure prefigures that of the novel as a whole, with Mrs. Wilcox's reappearance corresponding to the repetition of leitmotifs and to the recurrence of Howards End (which may not, strictly speaking, be a leitmotif itself, but at any rate is composed of leitmotifs[12]), and the Wilcoxes' frustrated attempts at useful exercise corresponding to the major plot lines, by which I mean planned, purposive actions initiated by one or more of the characters. As the Wilcoxes are driven back into the house, so the plot lines tend to end in failure and defeat. Margaret anticipates these failures in one of the first scenes, echoing, on a different level of course, Forster's lack of confidence in planning and premeditation. "'Plans, lines of action—no, Aunt Juley, no'" (7), she opines when she argues with Mrs. Munt about how to react to the news of Helen's engagement to Paul Wilcox. Mrs. Munt's trip to Howards End is one of the many examples of the frustration that typically befalls planned and purposive action in *Howards End.* Mrs. Munt, who argues in favour of a plan (6) and who wants to make sure that Helen's prospective husband is a suitable choice, intends to go about this delicate project very diplomatically. However, by the time of her arrival at Howards End, she has managed to mistake Charles for Paul and get involved in a heated argument with the former about the respective worth of the Schlegel and the Wilcox families, an argument that is all the more pointless and ridiculous since the engagement has already been broken off. Further examples of plots that are thwarted in various ways are Margaret's attempt to prevent a renewed acquaintance with the Wilcoxes, Leonard's endeavour to raise himself through culture, Helen's efforts to help him in doing so, and Henry's elaborate scheme to catch Helen. There appears to be one exception to the rule, Mr. Wilcox's proposal to Margaret, which is both elaborately planned (he manoeuvres her to London on the pretence of offering his flat for rent) and successful. However, we do not experience the proposal as a planned and plotted action, since our point of view in the scenes preceding it is with Margaret. For her and for us, it comes as a surprise, i. e. as the opposite of plans and premeditation.

The prime antagonist to plans and premeditation is Howards End. When it intrudes on the characters' lives, it usually comes as a surprise, and sometimes runs counter to their intentions. The Wilcoxes, for instance, are astonished and far from pleased when they discover Mrs. Wilcox's pencil-written will leaving Howards End to Margaret. When Margaret and Mr. Wilcox have become engaged, they think so little of Howards End as a place to live that they use it as a storage facility for the Schlegels' furniture. On two of the three occasions that see Mr. Wilcox and Margaret at Howards End, they have to go there because of incidents that run counter to their plans: the tenant's leaving the house with the intention to sublet it, and Miss Avery's furnishing the house with the Schlegels' belongings. The third occasion is Henry's scheme to catch Helen, which leads up to the denouement, in which everybody's plans and purposes are defeated. Before this denouement, Henry and Margaret have decided to build a house in Sussex, since Howards End does not suit their needs; Helen wants to go to Munich to move in with an Italian feminist; and Leonard simply wants to apologize to Margaret. Although none of these plans are realized, the stage is not strewn with corpses, and the novel ends on a moderately happy note. Helen, Margaret, and Mr. Wilcox find a refuge at Howards End, and Leonard finds his death (which is more than a defeat, because his son will inherit Howards End, and because death is part of the cyclic order symbolized by Howards End, as I will try to argue below[13]). Although the plot persistently points away from Howards End, the latter keeps on reappearing and finally reemerges as the place and symbol of a sane order which is superior to the "ordered insanity" of plans and premeditation. Thus it encloses and proves superior to the characters' plotted actions in the same way in which Mrs. Wilcox's repeated smelling of the hay frames and supersedes the other Wilcoxes' attempts at putting themselves to use.

The hay does not only recur in the scene from Helen's letter; it also recurs throughout the novel, establishing, with the other leitmotifs, that cohesion and order which the various plot lines fail to achieve. I will conclude this essay by analysing the hay motif and another very important one, the word *connect*. This word is related to what is arguably the most important theme in Forster's writings: the connection between antagonistic and fragmented positions or people[14], in the case of *Howards End* between the aesthetic Schlegels and the utilitarian Wilcoxes, and furthermore between both of these upper middle-class families and the lower middle-class Basts. In addition to its thematic import, the word *connect* indicates its own structural and aesthetic function as a leitmotif. After encountering it for the first time in the epigraph, "'Only connect . . . ,'" we should observe it while reading the novel in the same manner in which a musician observes the composer's *andante* or *allegretto* at the beginning of the score: Only connect the various instances of this and other leitmotifs, and you will perceive something beyond the "jangle of causes and effects", the fragmented realm of the plot. In my analysis of the motif, I cannot treat all its wide-ranging thematic implications in the novel, instead I will attempt a close reading of the motif in some of its contexts, with special emphasis on the question of who it is used by.

In the first occurrence in the epigraph, which I have just quoted, both the quotation marks and the ellipsis are significant. Forster quotes the motif from Margaret's thoughts, thus establishing an alliance between her and himself and making her the most "authoritative" character of the novel. The ellipsis indicates something which is true for most leitmotifs and this one in particular; the motif is not meant to stand in isolation, but to attract and connect various contexts throughout the novel. We next encounter the word when Margaret hesitates to accept Mrs. Wilcox's spontaneous invitation to Howards End. "The nine windows, the vine and the wych-elm had no pleasant connections for her, and she would have preferred to spend the afternoon at a concert" (83). Thus Margaret's first encounter with the motif is not a very enthusiastic one. She is reluctant to connect, because it is risky and difficult, as her sister's disastrous failure to establish a lasting connection with the Wilcoxes has proved. After this first inconclusive instance, however, Margaret uses the motif in an affirmative and emphatic way. In a quarrel with Leonard, she reproaches him because he has not established a connection between his adventurous and romantic nocturnal walk and his everyday life as an insurance clerk (140). In the next instance of the motif she urges Mr. Wilcox in an imaginary plea, "Only connect!" (183). This is the phrasing of the motif that Forster quotes in his epigraph, thus emphasizing Margaret's role as the character closest to the authorial views and values. There are several other instances in which Margaret urges Mr. Wilcox to connect or regrets his inability to do so (206, 246, 329); the most important of these is her demand that he acknowledge the connection between his own affair with Jackie and Helen's affair with Leonard (305).

Although *connect* is Margaret's motif, we also encounter it in the words and thoughts of Helen, Leonard, and Henry, but we will find that these characters have difficulties with the motif. Helen uses it twice, the first instance being somewhat complicated by a doubling of perspectives. On her first visit to Howards End, the solitary and slightly uncanny atmosphere makes Margaret think that she has left the ordinary world behind and entered a new one. "How Helen would revel in such a notion! Charles dead, all people dead, nothing alive but houses and gardens. The obvious dead, the intangible alive, and—no connection at all between them. Margaret smiled. Would that her own fancies were as clear-cut!" (197). Unlike her sister, Helen revels in a lack of connection—if we can trust Margaret's view of her. That we can do so is confirmed by the second instance in which Helen uses this motif, once again failing to connect. When the sisters are reunited at Howards End after their long separation, Helen discovers the greengage tree and asks, "'Why do I connect it with dumb-bells?'" (295). However, she does not remember why and goes on to talk about something else. The answer to her question is that, on her first visit to Howards End, she saw Evie doing callisthenic exercises at the tree, but Helen's lack of memory prevents her from establishing this connection, and memory, our resource against time, is a prime virtue both in *Aspects* and in *Howards End.* The very scene in which Helen asks her questions about the dumbbells shows the two sisters regaining their intimacy by recalling the past and relating it to the present.

Leonard uses the motif twice in a quarrel with Margaret and Helen, which is triggered off by the arrival of Henry and his daughter Evie. Leonard complains that the Schlegels invited him because they want to gather information about the company for which he works. Margaret does not defend herself against this allegation, but starts to talk about his romantic nocturnal walk. Quite understandably, he interrupts her saying that he fails to see the connection (140), a remark which triggers off her speech urging him to connect the romance and adventure of his nocturnal walk with his daily life. During the same quarrel, Leonard appeals to Henry for justice and introduces himself with the words, "'I'm connected with a leading insurance company, sir'" (139). This is almost like a parody of Margaret's use of the motif. The word "connect" is not used in

an attempt to bridge the gulf between business and culture, but in a statement that signals the separation of these worlds and the related separation of the sexes. Talking to a business man, Leonard falls back on his role as an insurance clerk (just as he thought it appropriate to talk culture with the Schlegel sisters in the preceding conversation, while they insisted on discussing work and money). Leonard's appeal to Henry of all people is further undercut by the fact that it is the latter's false advice that will lead to the end of Leonard's connection with the insurance company and his constant unemployment.

Henry uses the phrase once. Plotting with his son Charles how to make Margaret and Helen leave Howards End, where they are spending the night against his will, he says, "'To my mind this question is connected with something far greater, the rights of property itself'" (323). From a purely grammatical point of view, this is an affirmative use of the motif; it does not occur in a question as in Helen's case, nor is it overtly negated as in Leonard's statement that he fails to see the connection. Nevertheless, the phrase itself signals that Henry's use of the motif is a problematic and imperfect one, since it contains a dramatic irony, i.e. a discrepancy between his intention and the interpretation of a reader who knows how to remember and to connect. When Mr. Wilcox talks about "'something far greater, the rights of property itself'", he argues in legalistic terms, but the reader thinks of Mrs. Wilcox's pencil-written will leaving Howards End to Margaret, of Miss Avery's prophecy that Margaret is going to live there, and of the sisters's appreciation for the house. The negative and insufficient way in which Henry, Leonard and Helen use the motif distinguishes them from Margaret, the character who is responsible for connecting the fragments and reconciling the extremes. However, it also distinguishes them from Charles, Tibby, Mrs. Munt and the other characters in whose words and thoughts it does not occur at all. To use it, albeit in a negative or insufficient way, is a privilege, and we might note in passing that the four characters who share the motif with which the novel begins are those that are connected in the final synthesis, that live or die at Howards End.

A second important leitmotif in *Howards End* that we have already encountered twice is the hay[15]. It plays an important part in Mrs. Wilcox's repeated walks across the garden at Howards End in Helen's opening letter, and it also occurs in Margaret's reflections on the "jangle of causes and effects": "Here Leonard lay dead in the garden, from natural causes; yet life was a deep, deep river, death a blue sky, life was a house, *death a wisp of hay,* a flower, a tower, life and death were anything and everything, except this ordered insanity" (327, my italics). The conjunction "yet" separates this passage into two parts. The first belongs to the realm of the plot, in which Leonard's death is nothing but the final link in a causal chain of events; the second part is associated with the realm of the leitmotif, and, significantly, it is not only about death, but includes life as well. The style and the structure of the second part express the contrast between fragmentation and lack of connection on the one hand and the unity and coherence provided by leitmotifs on the other. If we look only at the passage itself and its immediate context, it will remain a jumble of arbitrary and enigmatic metaphors; if we remember the other occurrences of the images, in other words, if we read the passage in terms of its leitmotifs, we shall recognize its meaning and enter a world of order and cohesion, as I will try to show for one of the enigmatic phrases, the "wisp of hay", which is part of the hay motif[16].

If we look at the instances of this motif that occur before the statement that "death [was] a wisp of hay, a flower", we will find none in which hay is overtly associated with death, but in one instance the motif occurs in precisely the same form as in the passage quoted above. Listening to the sophisticated chatter at Margaret's lunch, Mrs. Wilcox feels out of her depth. "Clever talk alarmed her, and withered her delicate imaginings; it was the social counterpart of a motor-car, all jerks, and she was *a wisp of hay, a flower*" (71, my italics). Thus the association of hay with death mostly builds on the associations of the motif with Mrs. Wilcox, as she is the only major character who has died and whose death has played an important part in the novel, when Leonard's sudden end makes Margaret think that death is a wisp of hay. It is Mrs. Wilcox's death that we have to think of in interpreting the motif, and this in turn helps to explain why the passage does not rigidly distinguish death from life ("life and death were anything and everything"). While Mrs. Wilcox was alive, she "cared about her ancestors, and let them help her" (19), and after her death she continues to be a helping and shaping influence on the other characters, especially on Margaret who becomes her successor and heir in several ways and who comes to think that she and Helen "'and Henry are only fragments of that woman's mind'" (311).

The two passages about Leonard's death and Mrs. Wilcox are linked to each other not only by the wisp of hay, but also by the motif of the flower. Leitmotifs are gregarious, the contexts in which they occur are very often other leitmotifs, and the collocation of hay and flowers is not limited to the two passages I have quoted; it also occurs in the passage from Helen's letter in which Mrs. Wilcox smells the hay and looks at flowers at the same time. The association between flowers and death has been prepared for by previous instances of the motif. When Leonard goes to St Paul's to look at an allegorical painting, death is depicted with a "lap of poppies, on which all men sleep" (316), and when he lies dead in the garden of Howards End, Margaret gathers narcissi because to her it seems "wisest that the hands of Leonard should be folded on his breast and be filled with flowers" (328). The most important and intriguing instance of the flower motif occurs in the chapter on the incidents after Mrs. Wilcox's funeral. When it is over, a young man who has been pollarding trees on the cemetery, wrenches a chrysanthemum from the sheaf sent by Margaret, presumably for his girl-friend, because he is thinking about her when he passes by the grave, and when he returns the next morning after "a night of joy", he regrets not having taken all the flowers (87).

The cemetery worker and his "night of joy" disrupt and oppose the contextual association of flowers and death, and there is a similar disruption and opposition of meanings in the hay motif, since we find it associated with young children in several instances. Tom, Miss Avery's grand-nephew, likes to turn somersaults in the straw (266, 296f., 299), and in the final chapter he asks whether Helen's baby is old enough to play with hay (333). Helen takes him and her baby out into the meadow which is being cut, and a little later, holding Tom by one hand and carrying the baby on the other, she rushes into the house to close the novel with her enthusiastic outburst that "'it'll be such a crop of hay as never'". Thomson points out an important passage in the final chapter in which Helen picks up a bunch of grass from the meadow, which has just been mowed, and looks at the different species contained in it. Immediately before, Margaret has reassured her sister that the differences between the two sisters are to be welcomed because they provide "'colour in the daily gray'" of life (336). Thomson is right in pointing out the parallel between these two passages, but the conclusion of his interpretation of them is somewhat cryptic: "Hay represents not just individual man, but man in his individuality" (182). The contrasting meanings of the motif discerned above and the logic of the passage rather suggest that the motif represents a totality that encompasses individual differences. The hay consists of different species, is part of a seasonal cycle that involves different stages of growth, and it moves through a series of different contexts that associate it with such various and opposed meanings as the uproarious somersaults of Tom, the worker's "night of joy", and death. Thus it attempts on a structural and symbolic level what Margaret attempts on a spiritual and personal level: to connect in order to achieve a vital synthesis.

There is one further aspect of the hay motif that needs to be considered, the way in which it creates alliances and oppositions between the characters. While hay, grass, and straw in general are smelt and appreciated by Mrs. Wilcox and the Schlegel sisters, the other Wilcoxes do not appreciate it at all, since they suffer from hay fever. This has been noted by several critics; but to my knowledge it has not been pointed out or sufficiently explained that Margaret's younger brother Tibby is also prone to this allergic complaint. His hay fever is the reason why Margaret cannot accompany Helen on her first visit to Howards End; and when Miss Avery maliciously asserts that "'there's not one Wilcox that can stand up against a field in June'", Margaret reminds us again that her brother also gets it (270). Thus the aesthetic and intellectual Tibby is, surprisingly, grouped with the practical and utilitarian Wilcoxes, although he seems to be at the opposite end of the character spectrum from them; with Charles, for instance, he has "nothing in common but the English language" (306). What is the point of this disruptive grouping of completely opposed characters and contexts? The point is that ***Howards End*** does not favour one world view, family, or group of people over another, but advocates a synthesis of the opposed realms. It condemns extremes like the purely utilitarian Charles Wilcox and the purely intellectual Tibby

Schlegel and underlines their resemblance as extremes that contribute nothing towards bringing about the desired synthesis. Even those who do not heed the epigraph of the novel are connected with each other, if only by their refusal to connect.

Notes

1. *Aspects of the Novel and Related Writings,* ed. Oliver Stallybrass, The Abinger Edition of E. M. Forster, 12 (London, 1972), p. 113. Henceforth cited as *Aspects.*

2. I have decided to use *leitmotif* rather than *rhythm* because it is a more common and accepted term for the repetition of phrases and images throughout a novel. Furthermore, *rhythm* is also used in a different sense by Forster. Besides the "easy rhythm" or leitmotif exemplified by Vinteuil's phrase in the *Recherche* there is a "difficult rhythm" which Forster defines, in a very tentative way, by a musical analogy: "Is there any effect in novels comparable to the effect of the Fifth Symphony as a whole, where, when the orchestra stops, we hear something that has never actually been played?" (115) For an attempt to use the elusive concept of "difficult rhythm", see Audrey A. P. Lavin, *Aspects of the Novelist: E. M. Forster—Rhetoric, Pattern and Rhythm* (Alcala de Henares, 1989). The present paper will only deal with "easy rhythm" or leitmotif; in my view, Forster's "difficult rhythm", the subject of the concluding pages of *Aspects,* is not a concept that can be clearly defined and used in criticism but rather a final rhetorical gesture towards a utopian perfection of the novel.

3. *The Modes of Modern Writing. Metaphor, Metonymy, and the Typology of Modern Literature* (Chicago, 1977), p. 46. The concept of spatial form mentioned by Lodge is a very broad one, including a variety of literary techniques that summarize or compress time. See Joseph Frank, "Spatial Form in Modern Literature", in *The Idea of Spatial Form* (New Brunswick, N.J., 1991), pp. 3-66. Besides the influential article on spatial form, which was first published in the 1945 issue of *Sewanee Review,* this book contains a response to Frank's critics and further reflections on the concept of spatial form.

4. See his chapter "Two Kinds of Modern Fiction", *The Modes of Modern Writing,* pp. 41-52.

5. *Index of Recurrent Elements in James Joyce's* Ulysses (Carbondale, Ill., 1982).

6. "The Novels of E. M. Forster", *Forster. A Collection of Critical Essays,* ed. Malcolm Bradbury (Englewood Cliffs, N.J., 1966), pp. 21-33, 23 f. This important article, which won Forster's approval, is also available in the Penguin edition of *A Passage to India.*

7. *Howards End,* The Abinger Edition, 4, p. 327.

8. Although *Aspects* does not contain a single reference to a novel or short story by Forster, it is by no means an objective and detached treatise on the novel but a plea for and a comment on Forster's own works. This has been recognized by various critics, e. g. by E. K. Brown, *Rhythm in the Novel* (Toronto, 1950), pp. 4 f., but there are further insights to be gained from a close comparison between *Aspects* and the fictional works.

9. Wilfred Stone also points out some of the instances of this antagonism to time in *Aspects (The Cave and the Mountain. A Study of E. M. Forster* (Stanford, Cal., 1966)), pp. 110 and 113. According to Frank, modern literature in general is characterized by an attempt to escape from the change and flux of historical time into a stable world of myth or cyclical repetition (footnote 3, pp. 61-64). Forster, who is not mentioned by Frank, could be cited in support of the latter's idea of "spatial form", because his aversion to time is matched by an appreciation of space. "Very few [novelists] have the sense of space", Forster writes in *Aspects,* "and the possession of it ranks high in Tolstoy's divine equipment. Space is the lord of *War and Peace,* not time" (27). Margaret, the character who is closest to the views and values of the author of *Howards End,* also has this "sense of space" (196, 198, 202).

10. Forster's misgivings about authors who plan are more fully explained elsewhere. In his essay "Anonymity: An Enquiry" (*Two Cheers for Democracy,* The Abinger Edition, 11, pp. 77-86) he argues along Freudian or Jungian lines that there is a lower, anonymous personality in each human mind. According to Forster, this second self contributes much more to a work of art than the upper, individual self. For a fuller exposition and analysis of this belief, see Rukun Advani, *E. M. Forster as Critic* (London, 1984), pp. 94-99. In a way, Forster's misgivings about planning are surprising, since anticipating the future involves an emancipation from the tyranny of time; perhaps one might speculate that Forster's aversion to time is ultimately nostalgic, biased towards memory and the past.

11. At the beginning of the final chapter, for instance, he introduces his definitions of pattern and rhythm by saying, "Now we must consider something which springs mainly out of the plot" (102).

12. Full-blown leitmotifs associated with Howards End are the hay, flowers, the Six Hills, the wych-elm, and the vine. An answer to the question whether Howards End is itself a leitmotif or rather an ensemble of leitmotifs would require a full discussion of the definition of the term. This would take up considerable space and is not essential to the present argument. For a recent attempt to define the term, see the chapter on terminology in Peter te Boekhorst's valuable study, *Das literarische Leitmotiv und seine Funktionen in Romanen von Aldous Huxley, Virginia Woolf und James Joyce* (Frankfurt a.M., 1987), pp. 5-29. To my mind, Boekhorst's definition is a little too

narrow since it requires a verbatim repetition, i. e. a recurrence of the same word or words. However, sometimes leitmotifs are translated (as in the famous French chapter of *Der Zauberberg*) or they are repeated through synonyms.

13. This death and the way it is presented, especially in chapter 41, suggest a purely religious solution for the social and economic problem posed by Leonard. Of course, this is a highly questionable and perhaps an evasive solution, but a full discussion of this question is beyond the scope of the present paper. I am aware that *Howards End* is a problematic and uneven novel, but this paper is an analysis and interpretation rather than a critical evaluation. For a vigorous statement against the evasive tendencies of the novel and its treatment of Leonard Bast, see Stone, pp. 235-66.

14. The following quotation shows that the theme is of paramount importance, and that it also applies to the diverse aspects of one individual. "My defence at any Last Judgment", Forster writes in a letter on *Maurice*, "would be 'I was trying to connect up and use all the fragments I was born with'—well you had it exhaustingly in *Howards End,* and Maurice, though his fragments are more scanty and bizarre than Margaret's, is working at the same job." This letter is printed in P. N. Furbank's introduction to E. M. Forster, *Maurice* (Harmondsworth, 1972), p. 9.

15. Some of the aspects of this motif have been dealt with by previous critics. Brown regards it as an "expanding symbol" that, by the end of the novel, has been "linked with everything that stands out against Wilcoxism" (51); James McConkey analyses how "Margaret's spiritual progression towards Mrs. Wilcox and Howards End is at least partially conveyed by Forster through the association of the hay image with Margaret herself" (*The Novels of E. M. Forster* (Ithaca, N.Y., 1957), p. 126; George H. Thomson interprets hay "as an image for the individual seen under the aspect of death", while the related image of grass "stands as an image for the individual seen under the aspect of life" (*The Fiction of E. M. Forster* (Detroit, Mich., 1967), p. 181).

16. Thomson offers an interpretation of this passage in a short note, "Forster's *Howards End,* Chapter 43", *The Explicator,* 30 (1972), 64. Thomson rephrases the part of the passage that I will focus on as follows: "Life was a house, death a wisp of hay; (life was) a flower, (death) a tower." This neat distribution of images and meanings, which is related to Thomson's interpretation of the motif summarized in the preceding footnote, misses the point of the hay motif which connects, as I will try to show, the meanings of both life and death, as it moves through various contexts. This mistake in interpretation partly results from a shortcoming in the premises of Thomson's and also, to a certain extent, Brown's approach. The latter regards the leitmotif as an expanding symbol, the former as an archetypal object; thus they focus

too exclusively on the meaning of the motif itself and neglect its structural and contextual functions. It is interesting to see what the various contexts of a motif contribute to its meaning, but it is just as important to realize what the motif does to its contexts. James McConkey interprets the passage in question more adequately, he sees that "each of the images of Margaret's moment of horror [. . .] contains its opposite as well" (129), but he does not sufficiently analyse how this implication of the opposite is achieved through repetition in various contexts.

Daniel Born (essay date 1995)

SOURCE: Born, Daniel. "Private Garden, Public Swamps: *Howards End* and the Revaluation of Liberal Guilt." In *The Birth of Liberal Guilt in the English Novel, Charles Dickens to H. G. Wells,* pp. 120-39. Chapel Hill: University of North Carolina Press, 1995.

[*In the following essay, Born considers* Howards End *"the most comprehensive picture of liberal guilt in this century."*]

"I know that personal relations are the real life, for ever and ever."

—Helen Schlegel, in *Howards End*

"We merely want a small house with large rooms, and plenty of them."

—Margaret Schlegel, in *Howards End*

"Reality" and "realty" derive from the same root word, so it is not too surprising that the Schlegel sisters' premium on personal relationships, the "real life" named by Helen, reveals itself to be equally preoccupied with the business of real estate. Of what, after all, does the "real life" consist? Friendships or property?

The question is never put quite that baldly, and Forster endows it with equally serious, equally comic proportions. But such a query goes to the heart of what has been variously called the liberal "dilemma," "paradox," or, as pejoratively denoted by Marxist critics, "the liberal confusion."[1] Through Margaret and Helen, Forster succeeded in delineating the most comprehensive picture of liberal guilt in this century. As an Edwardian, however, Forster was by no means alone in this obsessive desire to reconcile liberalism's commitment to the life of the spirit, if you will, with the competing tugs of power and property. Forster's contemporaries—journalists such as Masterman and Hobson, and novelists such as Gissing and Conrad—share with him the view that social, collective guilt coalesces around the two prime issues of imperial power abroad and growing urban poverty at home. George Gissing's fiction repeatedly examines the plight of the domestic underclass and its effect on intellectuals, while Conrad contemplates most thoroughly the effects of imperialism through the mind of his primary thinker, Marlow. Yet of the Edwardians, it was chiefly Forster who perceived how intimately bound up these two concerns actually were. And it was Forster who wove that sense of interdependence into the fabric of a single literary masterpiece.

The plight of this world's Leonard Basts is connected with the activities of the Henry Wilcoxes: the Schlegels cannot help but see that. Even more importantly, Forster noticed how the privileged vantage point of liberal intellectuals, while it enabled them to see "things whole," still compromised and complicated their disinterestedness: for is the privileged vantage point not dependent on and allied with the very power that liberals mistrust? And corollary to this, is that same power not in part responsible for a socially abhorrent and all too visible poverty? The Schlegel sisters are painfully aware of this condition—at least at the novel's outset.

The unresolved tension of *Howards End* has been stated on many occasions—and, one should note, stated rather gleefully—by critics on both left and right. How can liberal intellectuals reconcile the private activities of aesthetic contemplation, friendships, spiritual formation, with a broader concern for the public and social interest? That is the defining problem for Lionel Trilling's understanding of the "liberal imagination," and, in discussing *Howards End,* he illuminates that question's vital historical importance:

> The 18th century witnessed such a notable breaking up of religious orthodoxies and such a transference of the religious feelings to secular life that it is surely the true seed-time of the intellectual as we now know him. One observes in the social circles of the first generation of English romantic poets the sense of morality, the large feelings of intellectual energy that had once been given to religion.
>
> This moral and pious aspect of the intellectual's tradition is important. Intellectuals as a class do not live by ideas alone but also by ideals. That is, they must desire the good not only for themselves but for all, and we might say that one of the truly new things in human life in the last two centuries is the politics of conscious altruism.[2]

Thus liberal intellectuals, if perceived within this historical tradition, are defined as individuals who seek to integrate their private and public selves. To a degree, this is exactly what the tension between the pursuit of the "real life" and of realty is about in *Howards End.* As numerous critics have noted, the novel is preoccupied with houses, interiors, and real estate;[3] discussion of values in *Howards End* is never rarefied or pursued apart from a material context of physical living space. It is as if Stein's central query in *Lord Jim,* "How to live?" were converted to that of "Where to live?" and Forster succeeds in treating the question with utter seriousness, without banality. Real estate permeates the novel: personal relations never proceed within a material vacuum. Seen this way, a preoccupation with surfaces, houses, and the substance of material living hardly means *lack* of moral penetration—the famous charge Virginia

Woolf brought against the Edwardian writers; instead, that preoccupation, at least in Forster's hands, becomes a *strategy* of moral penetration.

Forster, of course, consciously allied himself with a passing intellectual and literary generation. "I belong," he said, in one of his famous quips, "to the fagend of Victorian liberalism."[4] By calling himself a dinosaur, Forster perhaps thought he could escape the charge of being one. But from our present vantage point it seems he wrote himself off prematurely. For why should such an "old-fashioned" narrative—one seeking, in Forster's words, the channel whereby "private decencies can be transmitted to public affairs"[5]—still maintain its grip on us?

Quite simply, the novel vitally engages present debates about the future of liberalism itself. My approach to the book emphasizes the specific texture of Edwardian liberalism, but ends with reflections on how the novel addresses our situation. Particularly interesting is the way this novel serves as a gloss on the contemporary framing of pragmatic liberalism by philosopher Richard Rorty. Rorty, himself much preoccupied with this question of private and public value, ascribes to imaginative narrative and the activity of reading it the highest rewards possible; yet *Howards End* can itself be read as a criticism of Rorty's influential brand of neoliberal thought.

What is especially ironic is that Rorty, who holds Trilling in the highest regard, should disavow the very endeavor that shapes Trilling's understanding of the liberal intellectual: the attempt to fuse private and public virtue. Rorty argues in *Contingency, Irony, and Solidarity* that "self-creation" and social justice are incommensurate activities. He speaks about the impossibility of ever uniting

> self-creation and justice, private perfection and human solidarity, in a single vision.
>
> There is no way in which philosophy, or any other theoretical discipline, will ever let us do that. The closest we will come to joining these two quests is to see the aim of a just and free society as letting its citizens be as privatistic, "irrationalist," and aestheticist as they please so long as they do it on their own time—causing no harm to others and using no resources needed by those less advantaged. There are practical measures to be taken to accomplish this practical goal. But there is no way to bring self-creation together with justice at the level of theory. The vocabulary of self-creation is necessarily private, unshared, unsuited to argument. The vocabulary of justice is necessarily public and shared, a medium for argumentative exchange.
>
> If we could being ourselves to accept the fact that no theory about the nature of Man or Society or Rationality, or anything else, is going to synthesize Nietzsche with Marx or Heidegger with Habermas, we could begin to think of the relation between writers on autonomy and writers on justice as being like the relation between two kinds of tools—as little in need of synthesis as are paintbrushes and crowbars.[6]

If Rorty is right, then what are we to make of the frequently agonized posture of the Schlegel sisters in

Howards End or the central tension of Forster's authorial voice? If Rorty is right, then all such agonizing is wasted energy. Yet, the activity of reading Rorty through the lens of *Howards End* may prove as informative a task as reading *Howards End* through the lens of Rorty. Especially in his portrayal of Margaret Schlegel, Forster anticipates some of the more privatistic conclusions to which Rorty's theory leads. Margaret, like Rorty, eventually abandons the attempt to articulate a unifying vision for her private and public discourse. And the resulting limitations of her character, I want to argue, have premonitory value in anticipating similar limitations of Rorty's argument.

Forster's novel need not be rescued; it has steadily endured. Yet the tone of much criticism does treat the book, in the spirit of Forster's own wry self-appraisal, as if it were a fossil, an elegiac swan song for an ailing liberal creed. Rorty's pragmatism might be taken to be one more example of this impulse to consign Forster's position to the closet of worn out philosophical postures, for that pragmatism renders any kind of progressivist view of history—crucial for traditional liberalism—naive and any rhetorical articulation of liberalism's philosophical tenets wrongheadedly "foundational." Other, older arguments proposed against the liberalism taking shape in *Howards End* are more familiar. It has become a truism, though one perhaps in need of renewed debate, that World War I effectively shattered for all time liberal humanist conviction. Indeed, the final scene of *Howards End* carries the consciousness of the encroaching "red rust" of suburbia, which also may be read symbolically as the gathering red tide of blood explicitly identified by George Gissing in *The Private Papers of Henry Ryecroft*. Forster himself suggests the tenuousness of his affirmative vision by the novel's end. Other facets of the book, as well, cast doubt on the viability of Forster's liberal affirmation, and we must face these aspects in turn. Liberalism's de facto alliance with imperialism, suggested by Margaret's marriage to Henry Wilcox; liberalism's uncertain response to the plight of the people of the abyss, represented by Leonard and Jackie Bast; and liberalism's less than convincing answer to suburbia, a response couched in nostalgic country-house pastoralism—these features of the Schlegelian outlook do not as a whole impress us with their potency.

So it is that many critics, of practically every ideological persuasion, have perceived the novel as a touching but nonetheless terminal account of flawed liberalism. And yet here it becomes imperative to note: eighty years after the novel's appearance, we find ourselves in a peculiar position relative to a phenomenon usually pictured as enfeebled, ailing, gored by the horns of its own dilemma, or already dead. It seems now that liberalism is not as doddering as either Forster or his critics believed, or at least one can say that liberalism's rivals are all equally bedeviled by disabilities. In fact, the present seems oddly dominated by gloating about liberal democracy's possibilities, although I suspect that this too shall pass.

At any rate, much of the criticism of Forster, in its tacit assumptions about liberalism's decay and death, sounds premature. The time is ripe to take new stock of Forster's novel. The intellectual currents of the moment stand to gain by reconsidering Forster's voice, one which stands implicitly behind Schlegelian liberalism, but often subjects it to scathing interrogation. Maybe this very method suggests Forster's faith in liberalism and its self-correcting potential. Yet part of the problem of reading the book is discovering where Forster's voice separates from Margaret's; the process is much like discerning when Jane Austen's narrator speaks sympathetically through a favorite heroine and when she speaks more critically of her. Certainly it is a game of aesthetic pleasure, but its ethical stakes are never frivolous, for even while giddy in the pleasures of Austen's prose, we feel the bite of her sobriety. Trilling notes, "For all his long commitment to the doctrines of liberalism, Forster is at war with the liberal imagination."[7]

It was partly this moderation in him which led Trilling to comment even more tellingly: "He is sometimes irritating in his refusal to be great."[8] Forster is a writer of cautionary reflection, not Napoleonic intellectual thrusts, and my treatment of the novel may be accused of the same wavering back and forth. Liberalism, as an attempt to find a middle way, is often characterized by its extreme antagonists as shipwrecking not on the shoals of ambition but rather the sandbar of compromise and mediocrity. But in counterpoint to the common assumption that liberal humanism is but a nostalgic whiff to be experienced in books like this, I assume that the milieu within which *Howards End* takes place is not an endpoint or cul-de-sac. The novel represents not a tombstone of liberal crises, but rather a good place to begin sorting them out. As Bakhtin puts it,

> in the ideological horizon of any epoch and any social group there is not one, but several mutually contradictory truths, not one but several diverging ideological paths. When one chooses one of these paths as self-evident, he then writes a scholarly thesis, joins some movement, registers in some party. But even within the limits of a thesis, party, or belief, one is not able to "rest on his laurels." The course of ideological generation will present him with two new paths, two truths, and so on. The ideological horizon is constantly developing—as long as one does not get bogged down in some swamp.[9]

SITUATION COMEDY OR CLASS STRUGGLE?

Sometimes a text can be grasped anew only if ossified assumptions about it are swept away. In this respect, Trilling's analysis of the novel, still preeminent, needs revision on one crucial point. Most distorting is his insistence that the novel's characters all belong to the middle class. This denial of class differences obscures far more than it illuminates, yet few readers have bothered to question it. The flaccid term, "middle class," made here to encompass at one stroke the poverty-line Basts, the independently wealthy Schlegels, and the rapidly rising Wilcoxes, might be an indisputable label as defined by Trilling: everyone who is neither destitute nor blue-blood royalty. Yet the more we consider the term, the less meaningful it becomes.

There seems to be one reason alone for Trilling's use of that tag: that "the class struggle," as he puts it, "is not between the classes but within a single class."[10] Does the finicky distinction matter? It might—but only if one is attempting to combat some narrow strain of Marxist dogma.

There are good reasons to clear away this misleading nomenclature. First, as already suggested, it is descriptively inadequate. When we ponder the enormous differences in cultural outlook, living space, and habits of the Basts, the Schlegels, and the Wilcoxes, the blanket term "middle class" is rendered empty. Second, Trilling's definition, including as it does people of independently wealthy means, alters beyond recognizable form the term "middle class." Imprecise as the term may be, it has usually had associations with working for your living, as opposed to living off interest. Finally, and most importantly, one hardly needs claim a Marxist pedigree to suggest that Trilling's framing of social relations in this way takes the edge off the actual struggle in the book. There is a struggle—Leonard's—demanding recognition. There is economic oppression; there are possessors, and dispossessed. Although Trilling recognizes the pain underlying the humor—"The situation is sad but comic"[11]—his distinctively reassuring, American propensity to see everybody as middle class projects the novel more as living room situation comedy than as economic war. As a rhetorical tag, the term smooths out disjunctions and erases difference. It declaws the cat, makes Forster too benign.

The claws reappear rather sharply when we give even the most cursory nod in the direction of history. For the Edwardians, the spread of the middle-class label was not what it is today. (Of course for the British, it has never been so.) Far more prevalent was a perception of plutocracy on one hand and a growing abyss on the other. Consciousness of the latter pervades ***Howards End*** and raises several questions: how does Forster use that term, what is its specific meaning for the Edwardian audience, and, finally, what is Leonard and Jackie Bast's relationship to it?

The existence and characteristics of the "abyss" were impressed on the Edwardian reading public most repeatedly by the Liberal journalist C. F. G. Masterman. In *From the Abyss: Of Its Inhabitants by One of Them* (1902), Masterman conceived the abyss as a general class marker and associated it with slum dwellers' alleged physical characteristics as well as their living space. Today, perhaps, we too easily lose sight of this initial sociological significance, when understanding of the word "abyss," at least since the modernists, more likely conjures generalized notions of spiritual angst, akin to Helen's experience of the "goblins" in Beethoven's Fifth and conveyed by the Forsterian voice as "Panic and emptiness! Panic and emptiness!"[12] The rich, too, experience the abyss, but as Masterman and Forster remind us, theirs is of a different kind.

Masterman had first detailed the features of the abyss in *The Heart of the Empire: Discussions of Problems of Modern City Life in England. With an Essay on Imperialism* (1901). There he delineated the composite for Forster's Leonard Bast, calling him "the New Town type,"[13] someone

> physically, mentally, and spiritually different from the type characteristic of Englishmen during the past two hundred years. The physical change is the result of the city up-bringing in twice-breathed air in the crowded quarters of the labouring classes. This as a substitute for the spacious places of the old, silent life of England; close to the ground, vibrating to the lengthy, unhurried processes of Nature. The result is the production of a characteristic *physical* type of town dweller: stunted, narrow-chested, easily wearied; yet voluble, excitable, with little ballast, stamina, or endurance. . . . Upon these city generations there has operated the now widely spread influence of thirty years of elementary school teaching. The result is a *mental* change; each individual has been endowed with the power of reading, and a certain dim and cloudy capacity for comprehending what he reads.[14]

The empirical relationship between "stunted" physique and "crowded quarters" is the controlling hypothesis of Masterman's argument. A year later, in *From the Abyss,* Masterman describes that tight space more distinctly:

> The three-roomed tenement forms the staple abode of our people, the characteristic "home" of the dwellers in the Abyss. In some cases a three-storied house cut into layers; in others tenements in a swarming human hive of "artisans' buildings;" in the vast bulk four-roomed cottages, of which one is let off to a lodger. The number in these must run to millions; here is being reared the coming race. Civilization has commenced, though in rudimentary form. The oleographs on the wall, the framed burial-cards of defunct relatives, the cheap white curtains pathetically testify to unconquered human aspiration.[15]

Jack London's *People of the Abyss* (1903), a muckraking, firsthand narrative of the author's experience living in the East End, asserted Masterman's claims even more forcefully. After a lengthy and statistic-ridden account of the cubic feet required to sustain a single human life, London concludes:

> It is incontrovertible that the children grow up into rotten adults, without virility or stamina, a weak-kneed, narrow-chested, listless breed, that crumples up and goes down in the brute struggle for life with the invading hordes from the country. . . .

> So one is forced to conclude that the Abyss is literally a huge man-killing machine, and when I pass along the little out-of-the-way streets with the full-bellied artisans at the doors, I am aware of a greater sorrow for them than for the 450,000 lost and hopeless wretches dying at the bottom of the pit. They, at least, are dying, that is the point; while these have yet to go through the slow and preliminary pangs extending through two and even three generations.[16]

Together, Masterman and London's accounts of the poor city dweller form the prototype in practically every detail for Forster's own Leonard Bast:

> One guessed him as the third generation, grandson to the shepherd or ploughboy whom civilization had sucked into the town; as one of the thousands who have lost the life of the body and failed to reach the life of the spirit. Hints of robustness survived in him, more than a hint of primitive good looks, and Margaret, noting the spine that might have been straight, and the chest that might have been broadened, wondered whether it paid to give up the glory of the animal for a tail coat and a couple of ideas. Culture had worked in her own case, but during the last few weeks she had doubted whether it humanized the majority, so wide and so widening is the gulf that stretches between the natural and the philosophic man, so many the good chaps who are wrecked in trying to cross it. She knew this type very well—the vague aspirations, the mental dishonesty, the familiarity with the outsides of books. She knew the very tones in which he would address her.
>
> (90)

Now for his depiction of the Porphyrion Insurance clerk, Forster has been much castigated. Commentators have called Bast "one of the most interesting and least convincing characters in the book,"[17] "an inspired guess at an unknown class,"[18] and "Forster's one outstanding failure."[19] Peter Widdowson, who accuses Forster of both condescension and ignorance about people like Bast,[20] is especially incensed by Forster's famous disavowal at the beginning of chapter 6: "We are not concerned with the very poor. They are unthinkable, and only to be approached by the statistician or the poet. This story deals with gentlefolk, or with those who are obliged to pretend that they are gentlefolk" (34). Without worrying too much whether Bast has been brought into line with strict standards of literary realism (however those standards may be defined), we can see how carefully Forster relies on contemporary understandings of the abyss to draw his portrait of Bast. Even to the detail of Leonard's death from a weak heart, which we perhaps see too symbolically, Forster's depiction confirms common Edwardian notions about the physical deterioration of the city-dwelling poor. Overlaid on this pattern, there is also much that is reminiscent of Gissing, especially Gissing's proletarian intellectuals who, barely scraping by, manage despite exhaustion to read a little literature in their shortened evenings. Like Gilbert Grail in *Thyrza*, or even Hardy's Jude, Bast has achieved tragic consciousness of his condition. And he is arguably more realistic than many suppose. We might think, in parallel terms, of the university adjunct English instructor. Hopes of finishing the dissertation fade, as he or she signs on to teach one more section of freshman writing. Rent must be paid.

Forster, in his careful description of the Basts' apartment, punctuates both Masterman's and Jack London's observations about the dwellings of the urban poor. The interior of the flat, three rooms railroad style, seems lifted straight out of *From the Abyss* and is fully visualized, down to the kitschy details of "a draped mantelshelf bristling with Cupids" (37). It is "what is known to house agents as a semi-basement, and to other men as a cellar" (36). Forster sums it up as "an amorous and not unpleasant little hole when the curtains were drawn, and the lights were turned on, and the gas-stove unlit" (37).

In the phrase "other men," Forster obviously includes himself. To Widdowson's accusation that Forster is calloused, we can point out that he at least reveals the vantage point from which his observations are made. "Realism" is always an illusion, its effect of objectivity achieved by excluding overt reference to the subjective vantage point and biases of the observer. Therefore, Forster's willingness to reveal his own position vis-à-vis Leonard Bast displays not ignorance of Bast, but in fact necessary recognition that "realism" about Bast is problematic. Forster is undoubtedly guilty of condescension toward Bast; remarks that men of Leonard's "type" show a "familiarity with the outsides of books" seem especially gratuitous and cruel. Yet when Forster comments on Bast's attempts at self-education, he shows not only Leonard's inadequate grasp of Ruskin, but also, and just as pointedly, social critic Ruskin's inability to understand men like Leonard. Forster's implicit criticism of himself seems almost as harsh. In this passage, his identification with Ruskin, verging almost on confession, can be heard:

> Leonard was trying to form his style on Ruskin: he understood him to be the greatest master of English Prose. He read forward steadily, occasionally making a few notes.
>
> "Let us consider a little each of these characters in succession, and first (for of the shafts enough has been said already), what is very peculiar to this church—its luminousness."
>
> Was there anything to be learnt from this fine sentence? . . . Could he introduce it, with modifications, when he next wrote a letter to his brother, the lay reader? For example—
>
> "Let us consider a little each of these characters in succession, and first (for of the absence of ventilation enough has been said already), what is very peculiar to this flat—its obscurity."
>
> Something told him that the modifications would not do; and that something, had he known it, was the Spirit of English Prose. "My flat is dark as well as stuffy." Those were the words for him.
>
> And the voice in the gondola rolled on, piping melodiously of Effort and Self-Sacrifice, full of high purpose, full of beauty, full even of sympathy and the love of men, yet somehow eluding all that was actual and insistent in Leonard's life. For it was the voice of one who had never been dirty or hungry, and had not guessed . . . what dirt and hunger are.
>
> (38)

More cruelties ensue, when Forster goes on to describe Leonard's "half-baked mind" (38), his pathetic belief that he could "come to Culture suddenly, much as the Revivalist hopes to come to Jesus" (39). Yet Forster's satire cuts both ways, especially later on in the dinner party (chapter 15), complete with the reading of a paper in typical Bloomsbury style. Forster's criticism savages those who make a pretense of concern about the plight of people like Leonard, all the while deciding how to dispose of family fortunes. That these women imagine themselves having millions to give away makes scant difference; their leisure time to even speculate about such a thing reveals how comfortable they truly are. (Indeed, Margaret and Helen do have enough of a fortune to allow them independent wealth, and Helen attempts to give hers away, in one of the book's most blatant examples of liberal guilt.) The scene reminds us, uncomfortably, that the book is about rich and poor, and that for all their talk, the Schlegel sisters are firmly allied with the former. A middle-class label such as that proposed by Trilling glosses over the fundamental social problem. Just a year before publication of *Howards End,* Masterman had summarized England's distress this way: "Public penury, private ostentation—that, perhaps, is the heart of the complaint."[21]

THE FAINT SMELL OF THE ABYSS: MARGARET AND MATRIMONY

The rich get richer, and the poor get poorer. This common cry of Edwardian social critics,[22] who lashed out repeatedly against a swollen plutocracy, is thus implicit as well in *Howards End.* Yet, as Jamie Camplin has observed, the focus on the evils of money became largely an excuse for breast beating and righteous indignation. While the social commentators pointed out that inequity of income distribution had become greater than at any other period of history, "the strange result was that radical politicians and conservative critics of contemporary morality engaged in an obsessive and empty concentration on the evils of modern society."[23] In short, indignation does not necessarily spell thoughtfulness or reform. But even more disturbing in *Howards End* is that these very expressions of remorse seem to vitiate, or to substitute, the possibility of meaningful thought or reform. Here Schlegelian liberalism, of both the Helen and Margaret varieties, deserves the sharpest criticism. If Forster satirizes Ruskin's ability to respond to the urban poor, he is just as damning of the Schlegel sisters themselves.

Helen's shortcomings have been frequently noted, usually in counterpoint to the supposed wisdom and perspicacity of Margaret. The novel begins by exposing this younger sister's foolishness; we see her progressive mind-set coopted instantly by the Wilcox élan. Hormones triumph over political convictions with ridiculous ease. Later, Helen repeats an even more destructive cycle of infatuation with Bast. "Leonard seemed," Forster wryly observes, "not a man, but a cause" (246). Here we are reminded of the earlier dinner party, where Leonard's case had been pondered in scholastic and comprehensive fashion. It is after Leonard learns he has been ruined by Wilcox's financial advice—advice conveyed by the Schlegels—that Helen offers both herself and her money to Leonard in a dramatic

gesture, "not in the spirit of instinctive joy," John Colmer observes, "but 'heroically,' as a sacrificial victim from the class responsible for his ruin."[24] The offer of 5,000 pounds further demonstrates the destructive nature of Helen's pity. She confesses: "I wanted to give him money, and feel finished" (247). A few pages later, Forster abandons his usual humorous lilt for this dagger: "She and the victim seemed alone in a world of unreality, and she loved him absolutely, perhaps for half an hour" (250).

If Forster makes Helen an easy target, Margaret's case is more subtle, both because Forster identifies her with the healing earth mother spirituality of the first Mrs. Wilcox, and also because he so often blends his voice with Margaret's own. Yet disturbing conclusions are in store when we consider the eldest Schlegel at length. Chief among the discoveries is this: for all her talk about connection, Margaret seems rather ill equipped, and not at all predisposed, to connect with people. Early on she observes, "The more people one knows, the easier it becomes to replace them. It's one of the curses of London. I quite expect to end my life caring most for a place" (102). This proves to be accurate foretelling. And Forster is explicit about the principal factor related to this distancing process: the marriage to Wilcox, and the subsequent necessity of acting the proper housewife to a man of Henry's position:

> So Ducie Street was her first fate—a pleasant enough fate. The house, being only a little larger than Wickham Place, trained her for the immense establishment that was promised in the spring. They were frequently away, but at home life ran fairly regularly. In the morning Henry went to the business, and his sandwich—a relic this of some prehistoric craving—was always cut by her own hand. . . . When he had gone, there was the house to look after, and the servants to humanize, and several kettles of Helen's to keep on the boil. Her conscience pricked her a little about the Basts; she was not sorry to have lost sight of them. No doubt Leonard was worth helping, but being Henry's wife, she preferred to help someone else. As for theatres and discussion societies, they attracted her less and less. She began to "miss" new movements, and to spend her spare time re-reading or thinking, rather to the concern of her Chelsea friends. They attributed the change to her marriage, and perhaps some deep instinct did warn her not to travel further from her husband than was inevitable. Yet the main cause lay deeper still; she had outgrown stimulants, and was passing from words to things.
>
> (206)

Most particularly, these "things" for Margaret are houses, real houses, and the sense of permanence they impart. Margaret wants a home; from the start she worries incessantly because the flat at Wickham Place is about to be pulled down by a developer in order to make way for smaller, cheaper apartments. The neighborhood is in decline.

Critics have paid too much attention to Margaret's rhetoric about connection and not enough to this primary obsession with realty—the matter largely responsible for her marriage to a man so incompatible as Wilcox. Yet, unless we are clear about her drive for a proper, spacious home, we will be as puzzled as Leavis was about the marriage she chooses. His complaint continues to resound in much of the criticism:

> The Wilcoxes have built the Empire; they represent the "short-haired executive type"—obtuse, egotistic, unscrupulous, cowards spiritually, self-deceiving, successful. They are shown . . . as having hardly a redeeming characteristic, except that they are successful. Yet Margaret, the elder of the Schlegel sisters and the more mature intelligence, marries Mr. Wilcox, the head of the clan; does it coolly, with open eyes, and we are meant to sympathize and approve. . . . Nothing in the exhibition of Margaret's or Henry Wilcox's character makes the marriage credible or acceptable. . . . We are driven to protest.[25]

As Leavis rightly points out, Margaret marries Wilcox with "open eyes." But Leavis, unwilling to follow his own observation to its logical conclusion, finds this marriage inexplicable because he refuses to situate Schlegelian moral values within their threatened urban context.

Forster indicates in the passage above that Margaret knows the distancing between herself and Henry to be "inevitable." Forget the argument about Margaret reforming Henry's views; she knows perfectly well that marrying an imperialist to change him is like marrying an alcoholic to save him. Why, then, does Margaret seek this matrimonial "connection" that she understands will never fulfill the terms of personal connection in any significant sense? Though it may seem harsh to accuse Margaret of making fiscally opportunistic marriage vows, it is just as dangerous to ignore altogether, as Leavis does, the economic shrewdness of her decision to wed. Leavis radically underestimates the allure of Wilcox's "success" for Forster's heroine.

The desire to find a safe, permanent home exists, as well, in direct proportion to Margaret's need to escape contact with the abyss. This is evident long before her marriage to Wilcox. When Jackie initially comes to Wickham Place, under the alias of Mrs. Lanoline, to inquire about Leonard's missing umbrella, Margaret reflects gloomily after her departure: "The flats, their only outlook, hung like an ornate curtain between Margaret and the welter of London. Her thoughts turned sadly to house hunting. Wickham Place had been so safe. She feared, fantastically, that her own little flock might be moving into turmoil and squalor, into nearer contact with such episodes as these" (89). Margaret is depressed, "her thoughts . . . poisoned. Mrs. Lanoline had risen out of the abyss, like a faint smell, a goblin footfall, telling of a life where love and hatred had both decayed" (90). The urban blight of London has begun to invade the privacy of the Schlegel home; Forster dramatizes Masterman's trenchant analysis: "The Abyss has budded."[26] Masterman and London both document the process by which old buildings are knocked down to build suburban houses or cheap apartments, and the subsequent

deterioration in which these slapdash dwellings are further subdivided for a landlord's economic gain—until a slum has been created.[27] Fully conscious of this progressing blight, Margaret does all within her power to escape it. Aware that her income is ample, she also knows it is fixed. Even the "islands" of money (47) upon which she and her siblings stand are finite, and, given the skyrocketing values of London real estate (64), she recognizes the slim likelihood of finding living comparable to Wickham Place. How convenient, then, for a Mr. Wilcox to appear.

Fear that one's neighborhood is decaying, and the desire to escape it, dominates Forster's Londoners. For all their differences, in this respect Margaret and Henry are identical. Shortly after proposing to her, Wilcox comments on the house at Ducie Street—where they plan to reside temporarily while a lavish, new country house is under construction. The awareness of a neighborhood change for the worse resembles the descriptions of deterioration made by Masterman and London, although here there is added irony: the so-called bad element comes from that very artistic class with which Margaret and Helen had previously rubbed shoulders. Henry says, "The house opposite has been taken by operatic people. Ducie Street's going down, it's my private opinion" (143). One can practically imagine the consequences about to ensue: badly sung arias disturbing the tranquillity of the neighborhood, suspicious-looking bohemians trailing fumes of tobacco and red wine. Most interesting about the exchange between Henry and Margaret, within which we find this observation, is Margaret's playing to Henry's business sense, her denigration of Helen's lack of such a sense, and the merging of common pragmatic interests: "she was penetrating to the depths of his soul," Forster observes, "and approving of what she found there" (144). And then follows immediately this most cryptic Forsterism, just preceding their first kiss: "And if insight were sufficient, if the inner life were the whole of life, their happiness has been assured" (144).

Such is the synopsis of a conversation dominated almost entirely by observations about real estate. But this is not contradictory, for the "real" life as Forster shows us, and as Margaret would certainly agree, is in fact grounded in realty. As she tells Helen shortly before this scene with Henry: "He has all those public qualities which you so despise and enable all this—" She waved her hand at the landscape, which confirmed anything. "If Wilcoxes hadn't worked and died in England for thousands of years, you and I couldn't sit here without having our throats cut. There would be no trains, no ships to carry us literary people about in, no fields even. Just savagery. No—perhaps not even that. Without their spirit, life might never have moved out of protoplasm. More and more do I refuse to draw my income and sneer at those who guarantee it" (137-38).

Margaret's thinking is part of what makes Forster's book one of the most insightful and disquieting fictional treatments of the relationship between culture and capital. Moreover, her wish for a grand house providing permanence outside the flux of London's unceasing development unmistakably indicates where the forces of culture and capital can be wed most felicitously. Once inside the house that has been made into a home, all so-called distinctions of inner and outer life fade. "Buildings, and the design of them, the architectural character of a civilization," John Hardy observes, "would seem to be in Forster's mind fundamentally related to its character of manners and morals."[28] Just as the loving description of Howards End is meant to reveal what Schlegel character is about, so a tiny basement apartment conveys the Bast state of mind: dark and cramped. Likewise, the Ducie Street house, when initially let by Wilcox to the Schlegel sisters, is imbued with the imperialist character of its inhabitants on account of the furnishings. Seen through Margaret's eyes, a room can tell us everything we need to know about its owners: "The room suggested men, and Margaret, keen to derive the modern capitalist from the warriors . . . of the past, saw it as an ancient guest-hall, where the lord sat at meat among his thanes. Even the Bible—the Dutch Bible that Charles had brought back from the Boer War—fell into position. Such a room admitted loot" (128). In Margaret's case, the consciousness of rooms of her own means a great deal, means practically everything. Here Woolf's attack on Forster because he dwelt overly much on physical detail ("He has recorded too much and too literally."[29]) can and should be deflected. Take the houses out of **Howards End** and you take the heart out of the novel, for it is this very impulse toward home that puts the liberal conscience to its ultimate test.

This impulse, I would argue, lands Margaret squarely in the arms of Henry Wilcox, whose plenitude of apartments, if not soul, has the potential of refurbishing. Moreover, this same impulse of Margaret's rather neatly coincides with a distancing from the unsavory odors of the abyss. But the joys of establishing one's private garden are not adequate to dispel awareness of the seething, advancing public swamp, and, as so many critics have pointed out, the novel's concluding hymn to pastoral calm does not drown the more disturbing urban sights and sounds.

The Schlegel response to those sounds is far from reassuring. Helen wants to rescue Bast, discovers her own revulsion, and then attempts to assuage the guilt with an offering of money. By contrast, Margaret, very early on, mainly wants to forget he exists; toward him, disengagement and not connection is her actual if unspoken motto. Forster can have him conveniently killed, but it is very hard to make him quiet. Even the pastoral retreat to the green world of the first Mrs. Wilcox's wych-elms cannot quite do the trick.

THE LURE OF THE PRIVATE REFUGE

Must the liberal response to Bast be all heart and no head, or all head and no heart, as Forster suggests in this novel? Perhaps Forster only shows us the wrong roads taken. Perhaps a depiction of other, more successful responses is indeed, as Woolf said, better left to legislators than to novel-ists. Maybe Richard Rorty is right: attempting to integrate private and public value is an abortive enterprise.

Yet a central observation needs to be made about Forster's final resort to the escape-retreat green world of the Howards End estate. Principally, it must be seen as the typical Edwardian gesture to the urban crises of the time: the pastoral escape hatch has exact parallels in Gissing and Masterman. The cry is sounded for the rural virtues. The ideal of the ancient English yeoman is invoked as antidote to modernity, imperialism, and all the attendant crises that made liberals nervous. It almost seems as if these writers, longing for the return of Gabriel Oak, go about composing belated versions of *Far from the Madding Crowd*.[30] Forster's glorification of an organic society is embarrassing stuff: "The feudal ownership of land did bring dignity" (118). And this nostalgic tribute strikingly resembles those of T. S. Eliot and Yeats, who never apologized for linking their ideas of spiritual and aesthetic wholeness with a conservative, authoritarian political order located in a golden past.[31]

What, then, remains at all of Forster's liberal imagination? Commenting on Masterman, from whom Forster seems to derive much of this rosy-hued country gestalt, Samuel Hynes observes:

> The most striking thing about this Liberal's description of the condition of England is its close resemblance to the Tory version. Masterman's account of the loss of national altruism would have pleased Baden-Powell, and his description of suburban idleness and vacuity could have come from any pamphlet of the National Service League. . . . His predictions of increasing lawlessness, his fears of government by violence, and his mood of irresolution and discouragement are all echoed in Tory writings of the time. And so is the note of nostalgia that he struck again and again—nostalgia for a simpler and better past, when life was decent because men were decent, and men were decent because they were in touch with the English earth. This note one expects from Conservatives, but in a Liberal it suggests a facing in the wrong direction. Masterman could write movingly about the things that moved him, and his deep sympathies for the poor sometimes made him sound like a radical reformer; but his emotions were not directed toward action; they were, apparently, sufficient in themselves. If he wrote feelingly about the urban poor, he wrote in the same mood about the decline of the rural peasantry, and in each case the burden of his argument was not reform but decent feelings.[32]

The last phrase is especially telling in the case of Margaret Schlegel. When she towers in righteous fury over Wilcox for his sexual double standard, her intent is that he gain awareness, consciousness of self (perhaps to see, as the Forsterian-Schlegelian voice puts it later in chapter 43, "the inner darkness in high places that comes with a commercial age" [262]); but she hardly proposes any concrete means of reparation to the disenfranchised Basts, whose lives have been sexually and financially destroyed by Henry. On the same note, Jackie Bast's absolute disappearance after Leonard's death is suggestive. She does not come around to spoil the idyll in the hay field; while the child of Leonard and Helen's union seems to trail clouds of glory, the odors of the abyss clinging to her are not allowed to taint this meadow. The feudal past is glorified, the unified culture signified by Helen's son gets deferred to the future, and the ignominies of the present hour are avoided. Margaret fully intends to block the chance of any more of that unpleasantness. As she tells Helen,

> "Then I can't have you worrying about Leonard. Don't drag in the personal when it will not come. Forget him."
>
> "Yes, yes, but what has Leonard got out of life?"
>
> "Perhaps an adventure."
>
> "Is that enough?"
>
> "Not for us. But for him."
>
> (267)

Is Forster aware of the frequent chill he puts into Margaret's voice? I think so. In spite of all his identification with her, Forster depicts her in such a way that our disquiet is bound to increase upon every rereading of the novel. How, we ask, can her rhetoric of connection be reconciled with such coldness?

I would suggest that true connection, to borrow Margaret's term, means at the very least a willingness to ponder, and not forget, the discontinuities between one's private garden and the public swamp, or as the Edwardians named it, the abyss. The connection can be painful, the process of reconciling private pleasures and the public good difficult. Both Schlegel sisters seem perfectly aware of that tension at the outset of this novel, when a man named Leonard Bast walks into their lives. And this tension results in guilt, the painful awareness of the gap, in Trilling's words, between one's "ideas" and one's "ideals." The guilt necessarily forces an examination of personal circumstances, as well as some kind of personal gesture or response to the discontinuity.

The dangers of hasty response become all too clear in Helen's behavior, and conservative critics of liberalism are fond of pointing to the often destructive action generated by liberal pity.[33] For Margaret, though, a movement beyond liberal guilt seems to be the goal early on, and she accomplishes it by removing herself from the place where class disjunction is most obvious: the city. The quality of this detachment finds uncanny expression in Rorty: "My 'poeticized' culture is one which has given up the attempt to unite one's private ways of dealing with one's finitude and one's sense of obligation to other human beings."[34] This is a long way from Arthur Clennam. Elsewhere, Rorty, like Margaret, acknowledges the financial order upon which the life of the mind and culture rests: "We should be more willing than we are to celebrate bourgeois capitalist society as the best polity actualized so far, while regretting that it is irrelevant to most of the problems of

most of the population of the planet."[35] Rorty's argument severs all connection between the private pleasures made possible by bourgeois capitalism—including the luxury to contemplate it from within the academy, as Rorty does—and the public crises engendered by it. Yet Rorty does not want to admit that the sources of one's private pleasures are quite conceivably the sources of other people's pain. Rorty's choice of the word "irrelevant" in the above passage may be most liable to question, as Jeffrey Stout suggests:

> If the concession tagged onto the end of this sentence were intended only to say that bourgeois capitalist society is unlikely to solve most of the problems of most of the population of the planet, Rorty is certainly right. But it is hard to see how bourgeois capitalist society could be deemed irrelevant to most of those problems, at least as a source of dramatically important unintended consequences, many of them bad enough to make celebration seem the wrong tack to take. With no more than asides like this to go on, we are left with what seems a dangerously myopic moral vision, apparently blind to relations of interdependence and dominance within the economic world-system from which we derive our wealth, a vision compatible with gross insensitivity to that system's sorrows, injustices, and corrupting influences.[36]

Rorty's position, like Margaret's, finally is meant to relieve us of the burden of guilt—a guilt engendered by seeing systemic connections. And given the supposedly irreconcilable nature of private pleasures and public crises, it should not take us long to realize which distinct order of being, in Rorty's schema, is more likely to be slighted. For once liberalism abandons its traditional concern to integrate private and public modes of discourse, once liberalism becomes exclusively privatistic, it becomes an intellectual game of diminished energy, and then finally altogether unnecessary. Rorty wants to affirm both private ironists and public ethicists as ongoing, necessary, albeit separate, forms of life. But given the pattern of his thinking, it is almost inevitable that the private ironists—the Tibby Schlegels, perhaps?—will prevail.

That Forster interrupts his final scene with awareness of the encroaching London mass suggests he is not entirely happy with this one-sided vision of serene, private, poeticized culture. The conclusion of the book, which remains stubbornly unsettling, indicates crucial truths about Forster's conception of the liberal imagination: that it cannot relax if it is to remain functional; that any attempt to waft away the odors of the abyss is not only intellectually dishonest, but also damaging to one's liberal ideals; and that the spirit of Bast competes with Mrs. Wilcox for the privilege of hovering over the final scene in the meadow. The suggestion of this novel is a simple one. For Forster, the liberal imagination retains its vitality only so long as we are able to revalue, and not dispense with, liberal guilt.

Notes

1. D. S. Savage, *The Withered Branch: Six Studies in the Modern Novel* (London: Eyre & Spottiswoode, 1950), 46.

2. Lionel Trilling, *E. M. Forster* (Norfolk: New Directions, 1943), 123.

3. Wilfred Stone, in *The Cave and the Mountain: A Study of E. M. Forster* (Stanford: Stanford University Press, 1962), remarks that "houses have the symbolic role in this novel that rooms had in the last" (237). This is true, but we must add that Forster is also concerned with houses in all their literalness and with how those houses, those spaces, impinge on the inner life of values. Especially useful to this examination of the connection between living space and inner values are Malcolm Bradbury, "*Howards End,*" in *Forster: A Collection of Critical Essays,* ed. Bradbury (Englewood Cliffs, N.J.: Prentice Hall, 1966), 134, and Paul B. Armstrong, "E. M. Forster's *Howards End*: The Existential Crisis of the Liberal Imagination," *Mosaic* 8 (1974): 187. Crucial architectural reading that further explains the reverential Edwardian attitude toward the country house includes Clive Aslet's *The Last Country Houses* (New Haven: Yale University Press, 1982), Mark Girouard's *The Victorian Country House* (New Haven: Yale University Press, 1979), and especially Hermann Muthesius's *The English House,* ed. Dennis Sharp, trans. Janet Seligman (1904-5; Oxford Professional Books, 1987).

4. E. M. Forster, "The Challenge of Our Time," in *Two Cheers for Democracy* (New York: Harcourt, 1951), 56.

5. E. M. Forster, "What I Believe," in *Two Cheers for Democracy,* 74.

6. Richard Rorty, *Contingency, Irony, and Solidarity* (New York: Cambridge University Press, 1989), xiv.

7. Trilling, *E. M. Forster,* 13. C. B. Cox notes in *The Free Spirit: A Study of Liberal Humanism in the Novels of George Eliot, Henry James, E. M. Forster, Virginia Woolf, Angus Wilson* (London: Oxford University Press, 1963) that "to make liberalism more aware of its own deficiencies has been the life work of Trilling . . . and he has chosen to write about Arnold and Forster because in them he finds a similar purpose" (5). Proclamations of liberalism's imminent death have become part and parcel of academic discourse and by that constant repetition been rendered less than shocking, or even persuasive. But at the same time, there has been an opposite temptation in the wake of the Cold War to proclaim liberalism as the final triumph over every ideology. Francis Fukuyama's *The End of History and the Last Man* (1992) is the most familiar example of such hubris, and Rorty himself may be accused of the same when he makes utterances such as these: "my hunch is that Western social and political thought may have had the last *conceptual* revolution it needs" (*Contingency, Irony, and Solidarity,* 63).

8. Trilling, *E. M. Forster,* 9.

9. M. M. Bakhtin and P. N. Medvedev, *The Formal Method in Literary Scholarship: A Critical Introduction to Sociological Poetics,* trans. Albert J. Wehrle (Cambridge: Harvard University Press, 1985), 19-20.

10. Trilling, *E. M. Forster,* 118. For a complete discussion of the various elastic uses of the term "middle class," see Raymond Williams, *Keywords: A Vocabulary of Culture and Society* (New York: Oxford University Press, 1976), 51-59.

11. Trilling, *E. M. Forster,* 125.

12. E. M. Forster, *Howards End* (1910; New York: Bantam, 1985), 25. Subsequent quotations from the novel are cited parenthetically in the text and are from this edition.

13. C. F. G. Masterman, *The Heart of the Empire: Discussions of Problems of Modern City Life in England. With an Essay on Imperialism* (T. Fisher Unwin, 1901; Brighton: Harvester Press, 1973), 7.

14. Ibid., 8.

15. C. F. G. Masterman, *From the Abyss: Of Its Inhabitants by One of Them* (London: R. B. Johnson, 1902; reprint, New York: Garland, 1980), 31.

16. Jack London, *The People of the Abyss* (1903; New York: MSS Information Corporation, 1970), 47.

17. Stone, *The Cave and the Mountain,* 247.

18. John Colmer, *E. M. Forster: The Personal Voice* (1975; London: Routledge & Kegan Paul, 1983), 95.

19. H. A. Smith, "Forster's Humanism and the Nineteenth Century," in Bradbury, *Forster: A Collection of Critical Essays,* IIIn.

20. Peter Widdowson, *E. M. Forster's "Howards End": Fiction as History* (London: Sussex University Press, 1977), 90-92.

21. C. F. G. Masterman, *The Condition of England* (London: Methuen, 1909), 25.

22. Jamie Camplin, in *The Rise of the Plutocrats: Wealth and Power in Edwardian England* (London: Constable, 1978), cites a number of Edwardian commentators to this effect, quoting, for instance, L. G. Chiozza Money's *Riches and Poverty* (1905): "more than one-third of the entire income of the United Kingdom is enjoyed by less than one-thirtieth of its people" (147).

23. Ibid., 149.

24. Colmer, *E. M. Forster,* 100.

25. F. R. Leavis, "E. M. Forster," *Scrutiny* 7 (1938): 193.

26. Masterman, *From the Abyss,* 43.

27. Ibid., 41-48; London, *People of the Abyss,* 27-29. In chapter 6 of the novel, Forster provides a rough summary of the same process.

28. John Edward Hardy, *Man in the Modern Novel* (Seattle: University of Washington Press, 1964), 43.

29. Virginia Woolf, "The Novels of E. M. Forster," in *The Death of the Moth and Other Essays* (1942; San Diego: Harcourt, 1970), 169.

30. The most comprehensive study of this pastoralism is Raymond Williams's *The Country and the City* (New York: Oxford University Press, 1973). Among the many other critics who have remarked on the phenomenon specifically in *Howards End,* see John Batchelor, *The Edwardian Novelists* (London: Duckworth, 1982), 9-10, 227; Samuel Hynes, *The Edwardian Turn of Mind* (Princeton: Princeton University Press, 1968), 68; Stone, *The Cave and the Mountain,* 266; and Widdowson, *E. M. Forster's "Howards End,"* 89-90.

31. As C. B. Cox notes in *The Free Spirit,* the misguidedness of this brand of liberalism also becomes evident in the Leavisite version of idealized country living (90).

32. Hynes, "Undecided Prophets," in *Edwardian Turn of Mind,* 68.

33. Thomas A. Spragens, Jr., *The Irony of Liberal Reason* (Chicago: University of Chicago Press, 1981), 190.

34. Rorty, *Contingency, Irony, and Solidarity,* 68.

35. Richard Rorty, "Method, Social Science, Social Hope," in *Consequences of Pragmatism: Essays, 1972-1980* (Minneapolis: University of Minnesota Press, 1982), 210. This observation, by way of a footnote, follows the more explicit defensiveness of Rorty against a socialist perspective: "there seems no particular reason why, after dumping Marx, we have to keep on repeating all the nasty things about bourgeois liberalism which he taught us to say. There is no inferential connection between the transcendental subject—of 'man' as something having a nature which society can repress or understand—and the disappearance of human solidarity. Bourgeois liberalism seems to me the best example of this solidarity we have yet achieved, and Deweyan pragmatism the best articulation of it" (207). Rorty does not explain why the imperative for "human solidarity" should be any more convincing than an argument for common "human nature." Nor does he provide any clue as to how bourgeois liberalism can be translated into solidarity. He simply asserts that to be the case. Frank Lentricchia's criticism of Rorty in *Criticism and Social Change* (Chicago: University of Chicago Press, 1983) is most apt: "Is there culture that is not covert politics?" (14). Rorty's cultural liberalism runs the risk of skirting questions of political commitment, which might give its "solidarity" content. Interestingly, Rorty himself seems aware of this weakness, which explains why so much of his writing since *Contingency, Irony, and Solidarity* has taken on an explicitly political tone.

36. Jeffrey Stout, *Ethics after Babel: The Languages of Morals and Their Discontents* (Boston: Beacon, 1988), 229-30.

Elizabeth Langland (essay date 1995)

SOURCE: Langland, Elizabeth. "Gesturing Towards an Open Space: Gender, Form, and Language in *Howards End.*" In *E. M. Forster,* edited by Jeremy Tambling, pp. 81-99. London: Macmillan, 1995.

[*In the following essay, Langland explores sexual politics in* Howards End, *focusing on Forster's own homosexuality and admitted misogyny.*]

E. M. Forster is a difficult writer to approach because he appears simple. His work presents none of the stylistic resistance and technical virtuosity characteristic of his notable contemporaries like Joyce and Woolf. Further, he seems to have recourse to a nineteenth-century liberal humanism in resolving his novels, an emphasis that sets at naught the complexities of literary modernism.[1] So, at best, Forster claims a precarious stake in the twentieth-century canon. But Forster accomplished something difficult and important in his novel *Howards End* that a gendered politics of reading can uncover. In his personal embattlement with gender and his embattlement with patriarchal culture, Forster exposes the constructed nature of gender and his own ambivalent relationship to traits coded 'masculine' and 'feminine' in his culture.

This gendered politics of reading begins with an acknowledgment of Forster's homosexuality and outspoken misogyny, a textual politics that is tied to a sexual politics. There is substantial evidence that Forster was deeply troubled and preoccupied by his own gender identity during this period. He had spent his own childhood largely in the female company and sheltering presence of his mother and aunt, who no doubt gave him his 'knowledge' of women and female friendship. At the same time, he was uncertain of his own sexual orientation and uncertain of even the basic facts of male-female reproduction, which Forster claimed he never fully grasped until his thirties. The conviction of his homosexuality came shortly after publication of *Howards End* when George Merrill, the working-class homosexual lover of Forster's friend Edward Carpenter, 'touched Forster's backside "gently and just above the buttocks"'. Forster continued: 'The sensation was unusual and I still remember it. . . . It seemed to go straight through the small of my back into my ideas, without involving my thoughts.'[2] That touch conceived *Maurice,* Forster's novel about homosexual love published only posthumously.

It wasn't until 1916 that Forster found 'total sexual fulfilment—or, as he put it, "parted with respectability"'[3]—and not until 1917 that he finally fell in love: with an Egyptian tram conductor, Mohammed-el-Adl. After that fulfilment, Forster wrote to Florence Barger: 'It isn't happiness . . . it's rather—offensive phrase—that I first feel a grown up man.'[4] The offensiveness lies in the implication that a man becomes grown up through sexual mastery.

Thus, in 1910, while composing *Howards End,* Forster was in a great deal of confusion, which we can understand more fully if we consider the Victorian notion of homo-sexuality: *anima mulieris in corpore virile inclusa* or 'a woman's soul trapped in a man's body'.[5] Ironically, that confusion and dissatisfaction precipitated a misogynistic homosexuality, which I suggest we see in light of Forster's fear of the feminine in himself.[6] This understanding also gives us some insight into the process by which the confu-sions that produced this misogyny in Forster also fuelled a desire for something other than the classical opposition be-tween male and female, masculine and feminine, and so initiated his embattled relationship with patriarchy. In *Howards End* we see this relationship played out through the narrator, the leading female characters, certain the-matic oppositions, and the connections between all of these and the dramatic structure of the novel.

At a first glance, Forster appears to offer neither a radical literary practice nor a liberal sexual practice in this story of a younger woman's conventional marriage to an older and successful businessman, who looks upon women as 'recreation'. But textual evidence suggests that this con-ventional image is an anamorphosis reflecting Forster's at-tempt to manage a site of conflict in himself. A close analy-sis of the textual manoeuvres in *Howards End* discloses a radical sexual politics that has been obscured by psycho-biographical approaches and by assumptions about For-ster's literary allegiance to the nineteenth century. We may begin to excavate the layers of the text through its narra-tive stance, which is ambiguous, uneasy, and defensive. The following passage from the middle of the novel first brought me to examine *Howards End* because of the ways it makes problematic the omniscient narrator's voice:

> Pity was at the bottom of her [Margaret's] actions all through this crisis. Pity, if one may generalise, is at the bottom of woman. When men like us, it is for our bet-ter qualities and however tender their liking, we dare not be unworthy of it, or they will quietly let us go. But unworthiness stimulates woman. It brings out her deeper nature, for good or for evil.[7]

The problem emerges from the 'us', which initially ap-pears to refer back to 'woman', used to essentialise all women, with whom the narrator seems to identify.[8] A closer reading suggests that 'us' simply refers to all people, that is, 'when men like people. . . .' The temporary con-fusion arises here because, previously, the events have been focalised through the female protagonist, Margaret Schlegel, and 'us', the first-person-plural pronoun, invokes the feminine perspective.[9]

The 'us' feels problematic, too, because the narrator's pre-vious narrative intrusions have been characterised by an uneasy authority that hovers between irony and sympathy, creating an overall impression of indefiniteness.[10] The nar-rator opens deferentially: 'One may as well begin with Helen's letter to her sister' (p. 3). Shortly thereafter we are told: 'To Margaret—I hope that it will not set the reader against her—the station of King's Cross had always sug-gested Infinity' (p. 12). The special pleading is intrusive here and later: 'That was "how it happened", or, rather,

how Helen described it to her sister, using words even more unsympathetic than my own' (p. 25). Comments on the underprivileged seem to attempt sarcasm but end up sounding defensive: 'We are not concerned with the very poor. They are unthinkable' (p. 45); or, 'take my word for it, that [poor woman's] smile was simply stunning, and it is only you and I who will be fastidious and complain that true joy begins in the eyes' (p. 48). Later addresses to the reader fail to achieve either authority on the one hand or familiarity on the other: 'It is rather a moment when the commentator should step forward. Ought the Wilcoxes have offered their home to Margaret? I think not' (p. 98); and, 'Margaret had expected the disturbance. . . . Good-humour was the dominant note of her relations with Mr Wilcox, or, as I must now call him, Henry' (p. 177).

Forster is more assured when he avoids omniscient com-ment and focuses on Margaret Schlegel, from whose per-spective we see the events of the novel. It is not merely that we share the point of view of a woman here (although that is important to Forster's ends) but also that we tend to take her perspective as representative of the female point of view in general. As the novel develops, Forster compli-cates this identification of Margaret with the 'female' or the 'feminine', but initially it undergirds the binary oppo-sitions informing the novel. The novel is built upon a dia-lectical opposition between male and female, under which several others are subsumed.[11] The most significant opposi-tions for this analysis are those of class—rich and poor; those of philosophy—logic and vision; and those of lan-guage—word and intuition. Under the male side of the equation fall wealth, logic, and the word; under the fe-male, poverty, vision and intuition. These oppositions are worked out on the level of theme and plot.

On the level of theme, that resolution is fairly straightfor-ward, although we should note that those terms subsumed under the aspect of male and female perpetuate a hierar-chical tradition that relegates women to an inferior status. We may want to applaud Forster for attempting to redress the balance by privileging the feminine, but we are still caught in a net of stereotypes that perpetuate hierarchy and binary opposition, ideas that inscribe male perspec-tives in the world, as we shall see in a moment.

Although I have relegated wealth to the male side of the equation and poverty to the female, in fact, the female protagonists of the novel, Margaret and Helen Schlegel, are well-to-do women. Their sympathy with the poor, how-ever, initiates Forster's interrogation of class distinctions. The Schlegels are distinguished from the Wilcoxes, the masculine protagonists, by their recognition of the privi-lege that money confers. Margaret asserts that the rich 'stand upon money as upon islands' in the sea of life (p. 61). As a result of this perception, she and Helen are able to look beneath the social surface of a poor individual like Leonard Bast to the 'real man, who cared for adventure and beauty' (p. 316).

Yet, even as the novel attempts to redress the imbalance between rich and poor, it cannot transcend certain class attitudes which are implicit in Forster's uneven characterisation of the workingman and explicit in Margaret's discovery that Jackie Bast has formerly been Henry Wilcox's mistress. She writes to Helen that 'The Basts are not at all the type we should trouble about' (p. 241), and Helen, 'who is ready enough to sympathise with Leonard Bast, condemns Jackie as 'ready enough to meet' Henry Wilcox and laments that such women 'end in two ways: either they sink till the lunatic asylums and the workhouses are full of them . . . or else they entrap a boy into marriage before it is too late' (p. 253). That Jackie is a victim of patriarchy is understood imperfectly, although Margaret strenuously criticises Henry's double standard. Helen's disclaimer, 'I can't blame her', sounds unconvincing as the novel seeks to deconstruct sexist and class values on the level of theme, which it then reconstructs on the level of plot when Helen has a sexual relationship with Leonard—a woman's classic offering of her body in sympathy—and then arrogantly seeks to compensate him with cash, admitting that 'I want never to see him again, though it sounds appalling. I wanted to give him money and feel finished' (p. 313). Both of these episodes play out basic patriarchal expectations about relationships between men and women, between the rich and the poor. The pattern we see here, where plot reconstructs what the theme interrogates to deconstruct, will be replicated in working out Forster's other binary oppositions.

Thematically, vision is privileged over logic, intuition over word. Of course, logic and the word are related: They are in this novel the logos, the word of the fathers. Forster is committed to an ideology that seeks to defy the phallic mode and, from the novel's opening, logic and the word are made to appear irrational. Charles Wilcox's blustering question to his brother, Paul, about his engagement to Helen Schlegel—'Yes or no, man; plain question, plain answer. Did or didn't Miss Schlegel'—is corrected by his mother's response: 'Charles, dear Charles, one doesn't ask plain questions. There aren't such things' (p. 22). When Henry Wilcox confronts Margaret over Helen's seemingly irrational behaviour at the end of the novel, he echoes his son: 'Answer my question. Plain question, plain answer' (p. 284). Henry's plan to trap Helen like some hunted animal and Margaret's resistance provoke her recognition that the plan 'is impossible, because—. . . it's not the particular language that Helen and I talk' and his counterclaim that 'No education can teach a woman logic' (p. 284). Margaret's later rejoinder—'leave it that you don't see. . . . Call it fancy. But realise that fancy is a scientific fact'—refuses Henry's reductive dichotomies. Margaret is given the final word in the novel as she reflects that, 'Logically, they had no right to be there. One's hope was in the weakness of logic' (p. 339), and she is vindicated in the conclusion as the Wilcox clan gather to hear the word of the father—'And again and again fell the word, like the ebb of a dying sea'—which belatedly, yet inevitably, affirms the intuitive vision of the mother in seeing that Margaret is the 'spiritual heir' she seeks for Howards End.

And yet Margaret's 'final word' is problematic because definitive answers belong to the male-inscribed discourse the novel seeks to deconstruct. We might want to argue that the apparent difficulty is only a matter of semantics. But, in fact, my introduction of a teleology of final word here anticipates the deeper problems we discover on the level of plot.

Forster's central opposition between man and woman would seem, initially, to be played out between Henry Wilcox and Margaret Schlegel. It begins on the level of houses. Margaret recognises that 'ours is a female house. . . . It must be feminine and all we can do is to see that it isn't effeminate. Just as another house that I can mention, but I won't, sounded irrevocably masculine, and all its inmates can do is to see that it isn't brutal' (p. 44). This summary prepares us for the dialectic to follow, but Forster's feminist vision removes Margaret as a single term within the traditional dialectic, replaces her with Helen, and reinterprets Margaret as the principle that will complicate the hierarchical oppositions and provide a new kind of connection. That new connection is not the old androgyny, a merging or blurring of terms and traits;[12] it is a condition that preserves difference.

Whereas Henry Wilcox remains inscribed in a male mode of discourse, set within masculine imagery of dominance and conquest, Forster's descriptions of Margaret transcend the traditionally feminine and reinscribe her within a rhetoric of reconciliation and connection. Through Margaret Schlegel, the traditional terms of masculinity and femininity are scrutinised and subjected to the demands of higher integration. Margaret's point of view, then, is ultimately not representative of a view we might code as essentially female or feminine. Forster is sensitive both to essentialist conceptions of the female and to the social coding of the feminine. He subverts both in his characterisation of Margaret Schlegel, who can calmly state, for example, 'I do not love children. I am thankful to have none' (pp. 337-8), thus debunking ideas of a natural, maternal female.

And Margaret remains constantly alert to social expectations of feminine behaviour, decoding those expectations. She turns the notion of 'reading the feminine' into a lever against the men who are dependent on and limited by its convenient categories. When Henry proposes, Margaret has anticipated his action, but 'she made herself give a little start. She must show surprise if he expected it' (p. 164). Later, when a man hits a cat with his automobile and Margaret jumps out of the car, we learn that 'Charles was absolutely honest. He described what he believed to have happened. . . . Miss Schlegel had lost her nerve, as any woman might.' But the narrator reveals that 'His father accepted this explanation, and neither knew that Margaret had artfully prepared the way for it. It fitted in too well with their view of feminine nature' (p. 215). Later, in response to a question, Margaret 'knew . . . but said that she did not know' (p. 221) because 'comment is unfeminine' (p. 240).

Throughout the novel, Margaret resists being controlled by this dichotomous thinking and instead manipulates the terms with the goal of dismantling and transcending them. From the beginning, she is suspicious of hierarchies, as we discover in her mediation of the English and German claims to superiority. She announces, 'To me one of two things is very clear; either God does not know his own mind about England and Germany, or else these do not know the mind of God' (p. 30). The narrator pronounces her, ironically, 'a hateful girl', acknowledging that 'at thirteen she had grasped a dilemma that most people travel through life without perceiving' (p. 30). That dilemma focuses on the logic of binary thinking. Margaret resists such dichotomous thought and chastises Helen's binary oppositions as 'medieval', telling her 'our business is not to contrast the two, but to reconcile them' (p. 104). Not surprisingly, it is Margaret who is capable of concluding that 'people are far more different than is pretended. All over the world men and women are worrying because they cannot develop as they are supposed to develop' (p. 339).

In his reconceptualisation of Margaret, Forster generates a new integrative principle that is associated with a woman but not ideologically coded as feminine.[13] Part of his success here depends, as I have suggested, on using Helen to re-evaluate the traditionally feminine by associating her with emotion and the inner life.

Helen Schlegel, in contrast to Margaret, is emotional, impulsive, impatient of logic, impatient of all restraint on her generous impulses. She scoffs at moderation and is incapable of balance; she is first seduced by the Wilcox men and then violently rejects them. She extols the 'inner life' and, unlike Margaret, refuses to acknowledge the value of Wilcox energy, which has created a civilised world in which her sensibilities and the inner life can have free play. When Margaret must protect a pregnant and unmarried Helen from the interference of Wilcox men, Margaret herself codes the struggle as a sexual one: 'A new feeling came over her; she was fighting for women against men. She did not care about rights, but if men came into Howards End, it should be over her body' (p. 290). Although Margaret prefers not to be locked into a struggle between opposed faces, under duress she will privilege what Helen represents. Forster has anticipated this moment earlier in the novel when Margaret and Helen disagree over the older sister's impending marriage to Henry Wilcox. Their 'inner life was so safe', we are told, 'that they could bargain over externals. . . . There are moments when the inner life actually "pays", when years of self-scrutiny, conducted for no ulterior motive, are suddenly of practical use' (p. 195). The narrator adds that 'Such moments are still rare in the West; that they can come at all promises a fairer future'. Forster codes the inner life within another set of oppositions—Eastern mysticism versus Western pragmatism—but he reverses the usual hierarchy to privilege the East and the inner life.

In contrast to Helen, Henry is associated with an imagery of war, battle, and self-defence. When Margaret discovers that Jackie Bast was Henry's mistress, the narrator claims that, 'Expelled from his old fortress, Mr Wilcox was build-

ing a new one' (p. 244). Margaret is forced to play 'the girl, until he could rebuild his fortress and hide his soul from the world' (p. 246). Henry believes that 'Man is for war, woman for the recreation of the warrior, but he does not dislike it if she makes a show of fight. She cannot win in a real battle, having no muscles, only nerves' (p. 259). At the end of the novel, in the crisis over Helen, Henry speaks 'straight from his fortress', and Margaret at first fails to recognise that 'to break him was her only hope'. It is only when 'Henry's fortress [gives] way' that Margaret can initiate the process that leads to the integration, the connection, she enacts in the novel's conclusion by bringing Henry and Helen together at Howards End.

It is significant in **Howards End** that the most moving scene occurs between two women, Helen and Margaret.[14] When the sisters meet at Howards End and Margaret discovers Helen is pregnant, she asserts, 'It all turns on affection now' (p. 291). Although at first they feel themselves in antagonism, unconsciously they move toward communion:

> The triviality faded from the faces, though it left something behind—the knowledge that they never could be parted because their love was rooted in common things. Explanations and appeals had failed; they had tried for a common meeting-ground, and had only made each other unhappy. And all the time their salvation was lying round them—the past sanctifying the present; the present, with wild heart-throb, declaring that there would after all be a future, with laughter and the voices of children. Helen, still smiling, came up to her sister. She said: 'It is always Meg'. They looked into each other's eyes. The inner life had paid.
>
> (p. 299)

In stark contrast stands Charles Wilcox's relationship with his father:

> The Wilcoxes were not lacking in affection; they had it royally, but they did not know how to use it. It was the talent in the napkin, and, for a warm-hearted man, Charles had conveyed very little joy. As he watched his father shuffling up the road, he had a vague regret—a wish that something had been different somewhere—a wish (though he did not express it thus) that he had been taught to say 'I' in his youth. He meant to make up for Margaret's defection, but knew that his father had been very happy with her until yesterday. How had she done it? By some dishonest trick, no doubt—but how?
>
> (p. 329)

The traditionally feminine mode is clearly affirmed in these final contrasting scenes that sanction the inner life and 'voiceless sympathy'.

In privileging the inner life, as we have seen, Forster reverses the usual hierarchy in the oppositions of inner/outer, female/male, East/West, intuition/logic. This affirmation is a part of Forster's achievement. More significant, he takes a further step and sets up through Margaret a double reading in which the poles indecidably include each other and the *différance* of this irreducible difference. It is a process made familiar to us by Derrida.[15] We are forced to think or imagine the 'inconceivable', what we have seen as mutually exclusive; we are forced to form conceptions of that for which we have no concepts. The novel's epigraph—'Only connect'—stands at the heart of this difficult process through which Margaret hopes to enable Henry's salvation: 'Only connect! That was the whole of her sermon. Only connect the prose and the passion, and both will be exalted, and human love will be seen at its height. Live in fragments no longer' (pp. 186-7). At Howards End, Margaret senses this connection of comrades between the house and the wych elm tree: 'It was a comrade, bending over the house, strength and adventure in its roots, but in its utmost fingers tenderness. . . . It was a comrade. House and tree transcended any similes of sex' (p. 206). Significantly, Forster has chosen representative terms—a house and a tree—that resist hierarchical placement and the classical oppositional structure of patriarchal thinking. Margaret reflects that, 'to compare either to man, to woman, always dwarfed the vision. Yet they kept within limits of the human. . . . As she stood in the one, gazing at the other, truer relationship had gleamed' (p. 206). Margaret also argues for connection—this discovery of mutual inclusivity—in her conception of proportion: 'truth, being alive, was not halfway between anything. It was only to be found by continuous excursions into either realm, and though proportion is the final secret, to espouse it at the outset is to insure sterility' (p. 195). Finally, in the novel's conclusion, Margaret looks toward an 'ultimate harmony' (p. 330).

To summarise, the connection that Margaret seeks is obviously not born out of an attempt to merge or to blur or reverse oppositions. She fights the 'daily grey' of life, the blending of black and white. Rather, she seeks to dismantle the hierarchical privileging of one term over another. She expresses it as a celebration of 'Differences—eternal differences, planted by God in a single family, so that there may always be colour; sorrow perhaps, but colour in the daily grey' (p. 338).

Ironically, however, although the resolution thematically insists on connections and although the patriarch Wilcox is unmanned, the plot appears to encode the patriarchal structures that the novel seeks to escape. I began this essay with the narrator's ambiguous sexual identification. I then quoted a paragraph which is followed by one that reads,

> Here was the core of the question. Henry must be forgiven, and made better by love; nothing else mattered. . . . To her everything was in proportion now. . . . Margaret fell asleep, tethered by affection, and lulled by the murmurs of the river that descended all the night from Wales. She felt herself at one with her future home, colouring it and coloured by it, and awoke to see, for the second time, Oniton Castle conquering the morning mists.
>
> (p. 243)

We notice the imagery of proportion, of connection, of mutuality monopolising the paragraph which, nonetheless,

concludes with an image of domination, 'Oniton Castle conquering the morning mists'. It is possible Forster is being ironic because Oniton is not to be Margaret's home and she is, perhaps, mistaken in so valuing it. Yet, if this is irony, it is irony of a very subtle sort.

I suggest instead that the pattern is not ironic; rather, it anticipates the resolution of the novel where the value of connection, represented by the presence of Henry and Helen at Howards End, is enacted in the plot by Margaret's conquest of Henry. Henry, in masculine style, has earlier told Margaret, 'fix your price, and then don't budge', and she has responded, 'But I do budge' (p. 155). Nonetheless, on the issue of connection, she, like her masculine counterparts, won't budge: 'He had refused to connect, on the clearest issue that can be laid before a man, and their love must take the consequences' (p. 331). And in the novel's closing paragraphs, Margaret reflects, 'There was something uncanny in her triumph. She, who had never expected to conquer anyone, had charged straight through these Wilcoxes and broken up their lives' (p. 341). Margaret has triumphed, conquered, and broken up their lives. This conclusion to a novel about connection is ironic although not, I would suggest, deliberately so.

The irony arises because Forster inscribes the value of connection within the patriarchal dialectic of conquest and defeat, domination and submission, and within a narrative form that demands a resolution instead of 'continuous excursions into either realm' (p. 195). Although the themes of the novel indicate a desire to deconstruct the patriarchal ideology, ultimately, it seems, Forster is forced to reconstruct that ideology in the structure of the novel, in Margaret's 'victory' over Henry. Plot has demanded a hierarchical ordering of terms for a resolution to conflict even though the novel's themes have argued for replacement of conquest with connection. Forster's often trenchant interrogation of patriarchal language and perspectives appears to give way before the resistless temptation to expropriate the authority available to him in patriarchy. What he *wants* to assert, of course, is the value of the feminine perspective as a first step to dismantling hierarchy, but in the *act* of assertion, he affirms the value of the masculine mode, remaining dependent on patriarchy's hierarchical structures for authority, resolution, and conclusion. Ultimately, Forster recuperates an authority that would thematically seem to be repudiated.

Reaching this point in my argument—where the need to conclude a paper definitively is as imperative as the requirement to resolve a novel—I nonetheless stepped back from my own recuperation of authority, stepped from form to language. Perhaps Forster's critique of patriarchal modes and binary thinking was more trenchant and thoroughgoing than I first perceived. Forster had certainly appropriated the language of conquest, but he had also recontextualised it and, in the process, forestalled expropriation by that masculine terminology. A deep suspicion of conquest in its most notable manifestations—imperialism and war—lies at the very heart of ***Howards End.*** The narrator simply asserts, contrasting the yeoman who is 'England's hope' to the Imperialist who 'hopes to inherit the earth', that 'the Imperialist is not what he thinks or seems. He is a destroyer. He prepares the way for cosmopolitanism, and though his ambitions may be fulfilled, the earth that he inherits will be grey' (p. 323). Strong biblical cadences underline this apocalyptic vision of a world shaped in a masculine mode.

Perhaps, then, Forster is having his joke when Margaret characterises her success as a conquest. 'She, who had never expected to conquer anyone, had charged straight through these Wilcoxes and broken up their lives' (p. 341). In fact, she has not 'charged through'; she has simply done what 'seemed easiest' (p. 334). 'No better plan had occurred to her' (p. 335). She confesses, 'I did the obvious things' (p. 339). 'Conquer', in this context, is not an act of self-assertion and dominance but is redefined as non-assertion, an opening up of space, a refusal to accept the exclusivity of opposition, between Henry and Helen. 'Everyone said [living together at Howards End] was impossible' (p. 338), but Margaret defies this patriarchal logic.

The futility of binary thinking appears in the lives of both Henry and Helen, both of whom declare they are 'ended'. Henry confesses, 'I don't know what to do—what to do. I'm broken—I'm ended' (p. 334).[16] As if in echo, Helen rejoins, 'I'm ended. I used to be so dreamy about a man's love as a girl, and think that, for good or evil, love must be the great thing. But it hasn't been' (p. 337). The man of action and the woman of emotion reach the bankruptcy implicit in their exclusive positions. Margaret's conquest or victory, then, is not the patriarchal one demanding suppression of an other but one that emerges as the traditional oppositions destroy themselves and clear a space for difference.

Forster has anticipated this conclusion, as we have seen earlier, in identifying a warfare mentality with Henry Wilcox. But we may now discover a further step Forster has taken. While Henry Wilcox persistently refers to casualties such as Leonard Bast as 'part of the battle of life' (p. 191) as if such casualties were in the 'nature' of things, Margaret decodes his metaphor: 'We upper classes have ruined him, and I suppose you'll tell me it's part of the battle of life' (p. 224). Margaret herself is a master of words, as we see in her first encounter with Leonard Bast when her speeches 'flutter away from him like birds' (p. 40). But Margaret's strength lies in recognising the way ideologies are encoded in language and in acknowledging the social privilege behind her 'speech'. She early argues 'all our thoughts are the thoughts of six-hundred-pounders, and all our speeches' (p. 61), underlining both the intensity and the futility of Leonard Bast's desire 'to form his style on Ruskin' (p. 49). Ruskin's style cannot 'speak' Leonard Bast's life.

When Margaret rejects Henry's language and metaphor of life as a battle, she rejects his patriarchal ideology and introduces new terms into the novel. She reflects that 'Life is indeed dangerous, but not in the way morality would have us believe. It is indeed unmanageable, but the essence of it is not a battle. It is unmanageable because it is a romance, and its essence is romantic beauty' (p. 107). This passage informs the entire novel and encourages us to reread the metaphors of conquest concluding the novel within a romance topos put into play by the figure of Ruth Wilcox, Henry's first wife.

Margaret's own sense of victory is severely qualified when she learns that Ruth Wilcox had 'willed' Howards End to her, had designated her as its 'spiritual heir', many years earlier: 'Something shook [Margaret's] life in its inmost recesses, and she shivered' (p. 342). Ruth Wilcox is introduced into the novel as one who always 'knew', although no one 'told her a word' (p. 27). Ruth Wilcox is represented as beyond language deployed as power, beyond the words that cripple communication among the other characters, implicated as they are in ideology. Margaret ultimately asserts to Helen: 'I feel that you and I and Henry are only fragments of that woman's mind. She knows everything. She is everything. She is the house, and the tree that leans over it' (p. 313).

Miss Avery, who after Mrs Wilcox's death becomes her representative, prophesies to Margaret: 'You think you won't come back to live here [at Howards End], but you will' (p. 272), and Margaret, who has discounted her words, is disturbed to find them fulfilled when she and Helen sleep in the house: 'It is disquieting to fulfil a prophecy, however superficially' (p. 302). She will, of course, fulfil it much more deeply, making Howards End her permanent home, as, increasingly, Margaret herself recognises the 'power of the house. It kills what is dreadful and makes what is beautiful live' (p. 300).

As Margaret moves toward insight and vision, she, too, moves away from language. The narrator comments, for example, that Margaret's 'mind trembled toward a conclusion which only the unwise will put into words' (p. 205). And later we learn that Margaret 'had outgrown stimulants, and was passing from words to things', an inevitable process 'if the mind itself is to become a creative power' (p. 262). Finally, Margaret admits to Helen, who calls her life 'heroic', 'No doubt I have done a little towards straightening the tangle, but things that I can't phrase have helped me' (p. 339).

At best, because of its ideological character, language can take characters to the brink of understanding as it does when Margaret exposes Henry's hypocrisy in committing adultery himself and refusing to forgive it in Helen. Margaret confronts Henry: 'I think you yourself recommended plain speaking'. And the narrator reveals that 'they looked at each other in amazement. The precipice was at their feet now' (p. 307). Language takes them to the abyss, but it cannot reconstruct their lives on a new basis because they cannot form conceptions of that for which there is no concept. Margaret simply relies on 'the power of the house'.

As we reconsider Forster's resolution in light of Mrs Wilcox and the spiritual heir she seeks for Howards End, we notice that the novel moves toward resolution, but it is a resolution that existed from the beginning as a 'part of Mrs Wilcox's mind' (p. 315). In that respect, the plot subverts its own commitment to hierarchy and sequence, to prior and subsequent events. In addition, the power that has 'defeated' Henry Wilcox, the patriarch, is diffused over the universe. At the end of the novel, Henry Wilcox lies suffering with hay fever, confined to the house, recalling Miss Avery's words with their echoes of battle imagery: 'There's not one Wilcox that can stand up against a field in June' (p. 273). The patriarch is 'shut up in the house', and his wife pronounces, 'It has to be. . . . The hay-fever is his chief objection to living here, but he thinks it worth while' (p. 336).

As previously noted, the novel's last words belong to Helen, who rushes into the house with her child and the neighbour boy accompanied by 'shouts of infectious joy': 'We've seen to the very end', she cries, 'and it'll be such a crop of hay as never' (p. 343). To see 'to the very end', in this scene and in the novel as a whole, is to discover the beginning of possibility: 'such a crop of hay as never'. The last phrase is appropriate, too, concluding with a 'never' that has already been subverted. In its closure, the novel gestures toward an open space, like a field in June, that 'not one Wilcox . . . can stand up against'. It is a 'closure' that echoes Hélène Cixous on *écriture féminine*. Though Cixous is speaking of women writers, she describes what I am arguing that Forster has achieved:

> [Writers] must invent the impregnable language that will wreck partitions, classes, and rhetorics, regulations and codes, they must submerge, cut through, get beyond the ultimate reserve-discourse, including the one that laughs at the very idea of pronouncing the word 'silence', the one that, aiming for the impossible, stops short before the word 'impossible' and writes it as 'the end'.[17]

This reading seems more true to the narrative and linguistic procedures of Forster's *Howards End*. But it raises further questions. Can Forster thus evade the connection between discourse and power by postulating an unspoken knowledge? Indeed, the pressure of resolution may seem inevitably to produce an evasion as Forster gestures toward an alternative to binary thinking, a 'conclusion that only the unwise will put into words'. It is, at best, an uneasy truce. And this final inaccessible metaphysics may leave us frustrated by our own discontinuing embattlement with language, power, and patriarchy.

Notes

[This essay begins with the point that Forster was not part of the literary and cultural movement called 'modernism', associated with Eliot, Woolf, Pound, Joyce, etc. Langland, however, negates the importance of this apparent limitation by suggesting that there is something new in *Howards End*—an attempt to defy patriarchal logic and rationality through writing in a feminine mode, even as though the narrator was a woman. This is a feminist reading of *Howards End* which has begun with the question whether male writers can undo patriarchy in their own writings, and the answer here seems to be positive: the text comes down on the side of the feminine—'deconstructing' the terms which place male above female, and which marginalise the terms which in ideology belong to the feminine—the inner life, intuition, for instance. 'Deconstruction' comes from the theorist Jacques Derrida, whose work aims at showing how structures of thought privilege certain powerful Western myths—including, of course, myths sanctioning imperialism. At one point Langland argues that Forster returns to patriarchal/imperialist ideology, but then concludes by finding in his adherence to and investment in the *mother*, Ruth Wilcox, and his sense of the importance of what cannot be put into language—a commitment to unspoken knowledge—ways in which the text sides with the feminine. The question remains, however. Delany (essay 4) fastens on the text's political limitations: Langland fastens on its strengths with regard to gender politics, about which Delany said nothing. The question of the critical status of *Howards End* remains, depending on which reading is found to be more satisfactory. Can an undoing of patriarchy mean a change in politics? Does an attention to the feminine entail changes that make a difference in public life? Langland leaves the question open. Ed.]

1. After the early, enthusiastic appreciation of Forster's work set in motion by Lionel Trilling, *E. M. Forster* (New York, 1943), and Trilling's identification of *Howards End* as 'undoubtedly Forster's masterpiece', because it develops to their full the themes and attitudes of the early books and connects them 'with a more mature sense of responsibility' (pp. 114-15), other critics have not been content to rest with the thematic coherence of his work and have disagreed with Trilling's assessment. They have located Forster's reliance on nineteenth-century modes as a source of the novel's weakness. See, for example, Frederick Crews, who feels that Margaret's '"connection" with the Wilcoxes is merely diagrammatic' and that Forster's 'plot must finally retreat to an unconvincingly "moral" ending (*E. M. Forster: The Perils of Humanism* [Princeton, NJ, 1962], p. 122). See also Wilfred Stone, who claims that 'The forces of value do not "connect", but pursue each other in a lonely and circular futility. And the circle is especially vicious because Forster seems to see only its "proportion" and not its "emptiness"' (*The Cave and the Mountain: A Study of E. M. Forster* [Stanford, Cal., 1966], p. 266).

I hope my own analysis identifies a new way to see the narrative strengths and challenges of Forster's novel, to perceive those techniques and questions that align him with other literary modernists. At the same time, my goal in this essay is to give another perspective from which to assess the novel's difficulties, which have been too readily grouped under the rubric of Forster's return to a nineteenth-century liberal humanism.

2. Francis King, *E. M. Forster and His World* (New York, 1978), p. 57.

3. Ibid., p. 64

4. P. N. Furbank, *E. M. Forster: A Life,* 2 vols (New York and London, 1977, 1978), II, 40.

5. D. A. Miller, *The Novel and the Police* (Berkeley and Los Angeles, 1988), pp. 154-5.

6. Eve Kosofsky Sedgwick, *Between Men: English Literature and Male Homosocial Desire* (New York, 1985), p. 20, has made an important connection here between misogyny and fear of the feminine. She argues that 'homophobia directed by men against men is misogynistic, and perhaps transhistorically so. (By "misogynistic" I mean not only that it is oppressive of the so-called feminine in men, but that it is oppressive of women).' Sedgwick also notes that, although antihomophobia and feminism are not the same forces, the bonds between them are 'profound and intuitable'.

7. E. M. Forster, *Howards End* (New York, 1921), p. 243. All subsequent references are from this edition, and page numbers are provided in the text.

8. One critic who has observed that the narrator is female is Kinley Roby, 'Irony and Narrative Voice in *Howards End*', *Journal of Narrative Technique,* 2 (May 1972), but his argument differs sharply from mine because he uses the evidence that Forster has created a female narrator to argue for Forster's separation from and *condemnation* of the narrator's narrow and biased attitudes: 'The contrast between the action of the novel and the narrator's view of that action suggests that the narrator and the group for whom she claims to speak see the world neither steadily nor as a whole. . . . Forster seems to be suggesting that the narrator and those like her cannot have their "islands", their illusions and, at the same time, a world worth inhabiting' (p. 123).

9. There is some evidence from contemporaneous reviews that Forster's narrator and the narrative point of view were problematic. Indeed, some reviewers were persuaded that E. M. Forster must be a woman who had adopted a male pseudonym. Elia Pettie of the *Chicago Tribune,* in support of her argument that Forster was female, wrote: 'In feeling the book is feminine' (cited in Philip Gardner [ed.], *E. M. Forster: The Critical Heritage* [London and Boston, 1973], p. 160). Gardner also notes in his introduction that Pettie's conviction had British precedent: 'The idea [that Forster was female] had already been whispered in passing' (p. 5).

10. Philip Gardner, *E. M. Forster* (London, 1977), has also noted of *Howards End,* identifying Forster with his narrator, that 'at times Forster's [comments] to the reader lack his usual authority and aplomb' (p. 25).

11. It is a commonplace to recognise that Forster's novel is built upon oppositions. He himself said about the book's composition: 'I am grinding out my novel into a contrast between money and death' (cited in King, *Forster and His World,* p. 49). Other critics have generally cited the clash between the material and spiritual lives, the seen and the unseen, Bentham and Coleridge, Lloyd George liberalism and classical liberalism. My own interpretation takes the gender conflict as pre-eminent.

12. The subject of androgyny has become a vexed one in contemporary feminist discourse. In early stages of the feminist movement, the argument for equal treatment of women and men seemed to depend on detecting similarities: the masculine in the feminine and the feminine in the masculine. Then androgyny seemed the ideal. Subsequently, women have wanted to argue for the authority of the female perspective and values, and androgyny as a concept has become less attractive. It is interesting, in this light, that Forster doesn't advocate the merging of traits androgyny implies but instead insists on preserving distinctions. He is, in that regard, closer to the spirit of a contemporary discourse that speaks of escaping hierarchies.

13. Glen Caveliero suggests a similar point but does not develop it in *A Reading of E. M. Forster's Novels* (Totowa, NJ, 1979). Caveliero writes: 'Although it is possible to detect an anti-female bias in his work, it is really in the interests of feminine values and fulfilment that he writes, and the kind of wisdom he advocates goes well beyond the contemporary sexual polarisations. Even as a homosexual he was ahead of his time' (pp. 127-8). Also, Anne Wyatt-Brown, in '*Howards End*: Celibacy and Stalemate', *Psychohistory Review,* 12: I (Fall 1983), 29, argues that Forster lends 'his own feelings to Margaret; surely the pressures of virginity that drove her into Henry Wilcox's arms were his own'.

14. Contemporaneous reviewers testify to Forster's success at representing female friendship. An unsigned reviewer in the *Atheneum* wrote: 'the great thing in the book is the sisters' affection for each other . . . personal relationships . . . have never, we venture to say, been made more beautiful or more real' (cited in Gardner, *Critical Heritage,* p. 151). Forster's success here, and I would argue that he does succeed, is the more remarkable if we consider that Virginia Woolf wrote in *A Room of One's Own* (New York, 1929): '"Chloe liked Olivia", I read. And then it struck me how immense a change was there. Chloe liked Olivia perhaps for the first time in literature' (p. 86). Woolf argues that the representation of female friendship depends on female writers and so seems to forget Forster's novel. But his treatment of women must have impressed her at one time. Vanessa Bell invited Forster, after the publication of *Howards End,* to speak at the Friday Club on 'The Feminine Note in Literature'. According to Furbank, 'Virginia told him

[Forster] afterwards it was the best paper the Club had heard so far' (*Forster: A Life,* 1, 193).

It is an interesting, if small, point that critics Wilfred Stone, *Cave and Mountain,* p. 239, and Elizabeth Heine, 'E. M. Forster and the Bloomsbury Group', *Cahiers d'Etudes & de Recherches Victoriennes & Edouardiennes (CVE),* 4-5 (1977), 47-8, have pointed to Virginia and Vanessa Stephen as models for the Schlegel sisters although Forster himself claimed the three sisters of Goldsworthy Lowes Dickinson as his models ('The Art of Fiction', *Paris Review,* 1 [1953], 37).

15. Although I find *différance* a fruitful concept for allowing us to see Forster's achievement in a new light—for allowing us to perceive a radical dimension to his art obscured by previous insistence that he belongs to a nineteenth-century tradition of liberal humanism—I am not doing a Derridean deconstruction on this text. Indeed, the conclusion I postulate—Margaret's ultimate spiritual insight outside language—Derrida would probably see as a metaphysics. I am, however, inevitably led to see the parallels between Forster's conception of connection and Derrida's notion of *différance,* both of which are crucial to the problem of sexual difference.

16. The tendency among critics has been to pose the Schlegel sisters together in opposition to the Wilcoxes. Frederick Crews is one critic who appreciates the distinctions Forster has drawn between Helen and Margaret and the similarities between Helen and Henry: 'Henry and Helen together are people who isolate and simplify rather than allowing their imaginations to play across a broad range of related circumstances. . . . Both the Wilcoxes and Helen are unwilling to come to grips with prosaic reality' (*E. M. Forster,* p. 120).

17. Hélène Cixous, 'The Laugh of the Medusa', in *New French Feminisms: An Anthology,* ed. Elaine Marks and Isabelle de Courtivron (New York, 1981), p. 256.

Kenneth Womack (essay date summer 1997)

SOURCE: Womack, Kenneth. "'Only Connecting' with the Family: Class, Culture, and Narrative Therapy in E. M. Forster's *Howards End.*" *Style* 31, no. 2 (summer 1997): 255-69.

[*In the following essay, Womack examines Forster's social criticism regarding family issues in* Howards End.]

Although David Lodge's *Nice Work* (1988) provides a surprising narrative of reconciliation between the academy and industry, its concluding pages allude to an even more pervasive cultural dilemma that has haunted English life for centuries—the mostly silent war that rages unchecked between the classes. Robyn Penrose, the novel's academic

protagonist, recognizes the acuity of class and cultural distance that separates her students from a young black gardener tending the campus lawn. "The gardener is about the same age as the students," Lodge writes, "but no communication takes place between them—no nods, or smiles, or spoken words, not even a glance. . . . Physically contiguous," Lodge continues, "they inhabit separate worlds. It seems a very British way of handling class and race" (277). Lodge's depiction of the tacit acceptance of England's rigid class structure and the interpersonal distance that it produces in *Nice Work* signal the narrative's place in an historical tradition of British novels that highlight the social and economic discrepancies of life on the sceptered isle and its principalities. From such works as Daniel Defoe's *Moll Flanders* (1722) and Henry Fielding's *Tom Jones* (1749) to Elizabeth Gaskell's *North and South* (1855) and Kazuo Ishiguro's *The Remains of the Day* (1989), British literature echoes with authorial discontent in response to the nation's historical obsessions with rank, social standing, and pedigree. England's dizzying celebration of class and the implicit honor that invariably accompanies it extends to its national folklore as well, from the *anti*-heroic exploits of Empire and colonialism to disaster at sea. Legend has it, for instance, that as the *Titanic* sank during the early morning hours of 15 April 1912, Captain Smith implored first-class male passengers to "be British, boys, be British" and surrender the ship's paucity of lifeboats to women and children. Nevertheless, more first- and second-class male passengers, including the White Star Line's derelict chief executive, J. Bruce Ismay, managed to survive the disaster than children from third-class and steerage combined (Wade 58, 67).[1]

Concern for such a corrosive lack of value for the lives and experiences of the lower or disenfranchised classes underscores the narrative agenda inherent in many of E. M. Forster's fictions, including *Where Angels Fear to Tread* (1905), which problematizes English perceptions of the lifestyles and mores of Italians, and *A Passage to India* (1924), a novel in which Forster surveys the social inequities and atrocities inevitably bred by a class- and race-conscious nation that engages in imperialism. In *Howards End* (1910), Forster assaults the superstructure of the British class system, peels back its many and variegated layers, and argues that only interpersonal connection and compassion will enable England to modify its deafening social distances, the likes of which Lodge depicts in *Nice Work.* The parlance of family systems psychotherapy offers a particularly useful means for explicating Forster's illustrations of class and culture and the roadblocks that they erect in England's pathways to the kind of national morphogenesis necessary for its society to bond and endure.[2] In *Families and Larger Systems: A Family Therapist's Guide through the Labyrinth* (1988), Evan Imber-Black astutely observes that "all families engage with larger systems." Healthy, differentiated families, moreover, "are able to function in an interdependent manner with a variety of larger systems, utilizing information from these systems as material for their own growth and development" (14). Reading the layers of England's class structure as the component parts of a larger, albeit dysfunctional, family system illuminates Forster's critique of class and culture in *Howards End.* By supplying readers with a critical lens that identifies the nature of the feedback loops existing between the novel's characters and the diversity of their class origins, family systems psychotherapy demonstrates the manner in which Forster employs narrative therapy as a means for challenging his nation—with its collection of disparate classes and cultures—to, if nothing else, "only connect."

The family systems paradigm also provides a meaningful critical mechanism with which to examine Forster's philosophical debt to *Principia Ethica* (1902), G. E. Moore's Bloomsbury-era manifesto on the social and ethical rewards of friendship and aesthetic experience.[3] Often acknowledged as one of the central ethical influences upon Edwardian literary sensibilities, Moore's volume endeavors to establish basic principles for considering the notion of goodness and the governance of human behavior in the new century. Moore's moral philosophy argues for the recognition of a variety of ideal states of human existence, especially regarding the quality of the interpersonal connection that human beings share. "The best ideal we can construct will be that state of things which contains the greatest number of things having positive value, and which contains nothing evil or indifferent," Moore writes, "*provided* that the presence of none of these goods, or the absence of things evil or indifferent, seems to diminish the value of the whole" (185). In Moore's postulation, this "value of the whole" signifies as the condition of life in the greater human community: first the family, that human community within which we all begin our interpersonal lives; then the world beyond one's parents and siblings, the larger family system of which Imber-Black speaks. In addition to celebrating the virtues of courage and compassion in human interaction, Moore remarks that "by far the most valuable things, which we know or can imagine, are certain states of consciousness, which may be roughly described as the pleasures of human intercourse and the enjoyment of beautiful objects" (188). In this way, Moore's ethical schema underscores the significance of friendship and human connection as profound avenues toward the consummation of the "value of the whole."

Forster's own narrative interest in highlighting the social inequities of Edwardian life and the aesthetic elevation of the national consciousness demonstrates the ways in which *Howards End* functions as work of narrative therapy.[4] In *Narrative Means to Therapeutic Ends* (1990), Michael White and David Epson augment the tenets of the family systems paradigm to account for the ways in which narrative experiences provide readers with a means for interpersonal development and growth. As White and Epson note, "In order to perceive change in one's life—to experience one's life as progressing—and in order to perceive oneself changing one's life, a person requires mechanisms that assist her to plot the events of her life within the context of coherent sequences across time—through the past, present, and future" (35). These mechanisms—works of narrative

therapy—offer cogent methodologies that assist clients (or readers) in simultaneously identifying with and separating from the dilemmas that plague their lived experiences. Therapists such as White and Epson argue that the externalization of interpersonal problems through narrative therapy enables readers, then, to address their various issues via the liberating auspices of the imagination. Such stories encourage them "to explore possibilities for establishing the conditions that might facilitate performance and circulation of their preferred stories and knowledges" (76). In short, the telling and retelling of story furnishes readers with the capacity for usurping the pleasing equilibrium of homeostasis by effecting a kind of narratological morphogenesis, or the transformation of their lives through the therapeutic interpretation of their textual experiences.[5]

Howards End provides readers with a host of narrative exemplars that underscore Forster's agenda for the reinvigoration of the larger family system depicted in the novel. Populated by characters—and, of course, their families—from across the English class divide, Forster may be seen as offering a work of narrative therapy through his carefully drawn character studies and his insistence that his human creations be distinguished by their capacities for taking pleasure in aesthetic experiences and appreciating the interpersonal qualities of human interaction. As Jerome Bruner deftly observes, "There is widespread agreement that stories are about the vicissitudes of human intention" (18). In *Howards End,* Forster juxtaposes his characters' class standings in relation to their ability to enjoy friendship and recognize culture, as well as their intellectual movement—or, on occasion, their lack of it—toward self-sufficiency and differentiation from the larger family system. Forster suggests, then, that his characters, as they achieve selfhood beyond the homeostasis that the larger family system promises, only serve to rejuvenate that same system by virtue of their personal growth and self-enhancement.[6] The evaluation of the characters and their experiences in *Howards End*—from the powerful, class-conscious Wilcoxes and the leisure-class intellectual Schlegels to the lowly aesthete Leonard Bast and Howards End itself—demonstrates Forster's particular interest in reforming the very heart of England's social conscience.

In the novel, the Wilcoxes' family home essentially functions as yet another component in Forster's indictment of English class and culture. As K. W. Gransden notes, Howards End resides—often, rather ironically, in a state of disuse—in an unusual era in English history, a "high-water-mark of economic and intellectual expansion" (55). A beloved, pastoral nirvana for Ruth Wilcox, the family matriarch, Howards End provides a physical metaphor for Moore's social ontology by challenging readers to consider the intentions—economic, intellectual, or otherwise—of each character who eventually impinges upon its environs. For this reason, Mary Lago perceptively characterizes the residence as a "signifier of the ideal" (49). All of the novel's principal characters invariably reveal the quality of their inner selves as they pass through its abstract social prism. While Ruth Wilcox perceives the house's considerable aesthetic beauty, for example, her husband Henry, a stalwart of the London financial world, only recognizes its material benefits as a parcel of property. He utterly fails to comprehend the benefits of living amidst the house's rustic charm: "Howards End is one of those converted farms," he remarks, "picturesque enough, but not a place to live in" (141-42). In this way, Forster distinguishes each character by his or her capacity to reflect adequately the virtues of Moore's ethical schema, qualities that may yet provide the kind of narrative therapy necessary for the reinvigoration of England's social core in Forster's fictive world.[7]

If Howards End supplies Forster with a locale for testing his characters' ability to shun their class-conscious behaviors through the morphogenesis of social discourse, the character of Margaret Schlegel, *Howards End*'s principal focalizer, exemplifies the family systems paradigm's usefulness in assessing personal growth and development. In many ways, the novel concerns itself with Margaret's social education and her battle with the enduring homeostasis of the class structure of English society. Her intellectual progress through the narrative of *Howards End* brings her into the orbits of a range of characters and social classes, while at the same time furnishing readers with textual examples of her experiences with triangulation, polarization, and differentiation along her path to selfhood. A lover of life and literature, Margaret, like her sister Helen, subsists on an annual income. Yet her considerable social standing hardly mitigates her ability to recognize social injustice and the value of human interaction in the life of a larger family system such as England. Nevertheless, Margaret perceives her internal need for personal growth: "I have everything to learn—absolutely everything," she admits to Ruth Wilcox, to whom she outlines her educational goals "to be humble and kind, to go straight ahead, to love people rather than pity them, to remember the submerged" (75-76).

Margaret encounters the "submerged" or lower classes in the figure of Leonard Bast after Helen—absorbed with passion during a performance of Beethoven's Fifth Symphony—absent-mindedly steals the young clerk's umbrella. Leonard, Forster writes, "stood at the extreme verge of gentility. He was not in the abyss," Forster adds, "but he could see it, and at times people whom he knew had dropped in, and counted no more," (47). Despite his poverty, the tenuous nature of his employment, and his socially problematic relationship with Jacky, a woman of a questionable past from the extreme lower class, Leonard "hoped to come to Culture suddenly, much as the Revivalist hopes to come to Jesus." The clerk spends his spare time engrossed in works by Ruskin and Robert Louis Stevenson or listening "with reverence" to Queen's Hall Concerts (52). Although his family literally disowns him because of his affair with Jacky, Leonard intuitively recognizes the ethics of his romantic commitment to her, as well as the perilous nature of the "fallen woman" in his society's class structure: "I'm not one of your weak knock-kneed chaps," he tells her; "if a woman's in trouble, I

don't leave her in the lurch. That's not my street," he continues. "No, thank you" (55). Like Margaret, Leonard pursues music and literature with the same passion and courtesy with which he regards his interpersonal relationships. Margaret recognizes these qualities in the clerk as well: "While her lips talked culture," Forster writes, "her heart was planning to invite him to tea" (38).

Margaret's interactions with upper-class values in the novel occur when Helen nearly marries into the Wilcox family after visiting Howards End during one of its rare moments of occupancy. At first, Helen responds favorably to the Wilcoxes' aura of social confidence and hospitality. "They are the very happiest, jolliest family that you can imagine," she writes to Margaret. Yet shortly before the demise of her engagement to Paul Wilcox, Helen begins to perceive that "the whole Wilcox family was a fraud, just a wall of newspapers and motor-cars and golf-clubs, and if it fell I should find nothing behind it but panic and emptiness" (26). After Helen departs for an extended, post break-up visit to Germany, Margaret enters into a friendship with Ruth Wilcox, now back in London, where she suffers—unbeknownst to her family, whom, ironically, she would rather not trouble emotionally—from a terminal illness. From Forster's descriptions of Mrs. Wilcox, her friendship with Margaret would seem a foregone conclusion. "There was no bitterness in Mrs. Wilcox; there was not even criticism; she was lovable," Forster writes, "and no ungracious or uncharitable word had passed her lips" (79). Unlike her family, Margaret empathizes with Ruth Wilcox's intense emotional response to her country home's aesthetic attributes. Thus, following her death shortly thereafter, Mrs. Wilcox's will—much to the surprise and consternation of her family—decrees that Margaret shall inherit Howards End.

The disposition of the property precipitates the novel's central crisis: Will the heart of the nation belong to proponents of friendship and culture or to hollow icons of wealth and materialism? Because they correctly assume that Margaret knows nothing of her late friend's sudden generosity, the surviving Wilcoxes choose to ignore Mrs. Wilcox's wishes—she had been "under the spell of a sudden friendship," they reason—and maintain their ownership of Howards End. With their disregard for Mrs. Wilcox's last will and testament, the battle for the future of England had begun within the context of Forster's narrative agenda. To the Wilcoxes, Forster writes, "Howards End was a house: they could not know that to her it had been a spirit, for which she sought a spiritual heir" (103). When Margaret finally visits Howards End during her lengthy courtship with Henry Wilcox, the residence literally reverberates in honor of her arrival—"it was the heart of the house beating, faintly at first, then loudly, martially," Forster writes. Moments later, the caretaker Miss Avery ominously mistakes Margaret for Ruth Wilcox. "In fancy, of course—in fancy," Miss Avery remarks after confusing Margaret's identity. "You had her way of walking" (211). In addition to ushering in Margaret's intense era of personal growth, her later experiences with the class-bound Wilcoxes and the protracted redisposition of Howards End share in the process of differentiation that will ultimately result in Margaret's emergence as a fully realized self.

As Salvador Minuchin and Michael P. Nichols note in *Family Healing: Strategies for Hope and Understanding* (1993), "Almost nowhere in family life are triangles more notorious than in stepfamilies" (195). Margaret's courtship with and later marriage to Henry Wilcox not only initiate the creation of a stepfamily in the novel, but also inaugurate a series of events that result in her painful triangulation between her new husband and Helen. Interestingly, Margaret also finds herself in a triadic relationship between Henry's erotic past and the memory of Ruth Wilcox. In *Systemic Family Therapy: An Integrative Approach* (1986), William C. Nichols and Craig Everett ascribe some manifestations of triangulation between the spouse-spouse dyad and a third party to the notion of "scapegoating," a process that "involves an attempt to dissipate or remove the stress [in the marital relationship] by pushing it away and placing it outside of the subsystem" (136). In each of the aforementioned cases of triangulation, scapegoating provides Margaret with a convenient means for disregarding the actual ethical dilemmas in her marital system in favor of the chimerical issues that she chooses to scapegoat.[8] Metaphorically, Margaret opts to modify, if only temporarily, the higher value system that Forster celebrates throughout *Howards End.* Absorbed with ensuring the success of her marriage and agog over Henry's substantial wealth and property, Margaret simply chooses to ignore her husband's class "type" and his inability to connect.

Margaret initially finds herself triangulated between Henry and Helen, for example, because of her husband's haphazard advice regarding Leonard's vocational fate. Although Henry generally evinces scant concern for the plight of the lower classes, Margaret and Helen seek his advice over Leonard's tenuous employment status at the Porphyrion Fire Insurance Company. It is no surprise that Henry reveals little interest in the lives of the disenfranchised members of his larger human community:

> A word of advice. Don't take that sentimental attitude over the poor. . . . The poor are poor, and one's sorry for them, but there it is. As civilization moves forward, the shoe is bound to pinch in places, and it's absurd to pretend that anyone is responsible personally. . . . There are just rich and poor, as there always have been and always will be. Point me out a time when men have been equal.
>
> (199-200)

In addition to his *laissez-faire* policy on the value of social reform, Henry believes that the lower classes should be kept at a discreet distance, a maneuver that he accomplishes himself through the art of gratuity. During lunch at Simpson's in the Strand with Margaret, for instance, Henry happily remarks to her that "tip everywhere's my motto. . . . Then the fellows know one again. . . . They remember you from year's end to year's end" (159). For Henry, the act of tipping provides a kind of false-friendship—a human relationship, purchased rather than cultivated through genuine social intercourse.

After Henry's careless advice regarding the Porphyrion's financial prospects results in Leonard's unemployment and near-starvation, Helen—already suspicious of the "Great Wilcox Peril" (178)—can no longer fathom her new brother-in-law's mercantile and artificial system of human relations. At one juncture, Helen exclaims, "What a prosperous vulgarian Mr. Wilcox has grown! I have very little use for him in these days" (143). Henry simply has no purpose in Helen's world, a place where poetry matters and "personal relations are the important thing for ever and ever" (181). When Henry refuses to acknowledge his culpability in Leonard's unnecessary state of unemployment, Helen dismisses any notion of tolerating his fractured social views, her triangulation of Margaret and Henry now complete: "I mean to dislike your husband and tell him so," Helen explains to her sister, but "I mean to love you more than ever" (203). Confronted with her beloved sister and her new husband's utter inability to set aside their contradictory mores, Margaret attempts to decrease the stress on their family system by defending Henry's persona as a "type" necessary for advancing the English civilization into its present industrial and intellectual state. Margaret tries to dismiss—or scapegoat, if you will—Henry's social deficiencies as byproducts of what she defends as his essential role in England's ongoing process of nation-building, thereby removing him as a stressor on their triad. "If Wilcoxes hadn't worked and died in England for thousands of years, you and I couldn't sit here without having our throats cut," Margaret pleads with Helen; "there would be no trains, no ships to carry us literary people about in. . . . Just savagery" (183). Even Margaret allows, though, that "some day—in the millennium—there may be no need" for Henry's type (169). Despite Margaret's best efforts to diminish Helen and Henry's differences, their lack of any common ground makes it virtually impossible for them to establish the senses of belonging and acceptance necessary, according to family therapists Mala S. and Roger B. Burt, to develop and grow as members of a functional stepfamily (12).

In addition to the increasing stress on her relationship with Helen, Margaret's marriage to Henry becomes triangulated by virtue of yet another third party, the memory of Ruth Wilcox. In one sense, the ghostly repercussions of Ruth's family's decision to disavow her last will and testament continue to haunt the Wilcoxes' capacity for finding peace in the present. Ruth and Henry's eldest, arrogant son Charles writhes in anxiety, for example, whenever Margaret inquires about the disposition of Howards End. After his father's marriage to Margaret, Charles becomes particularly troubled when Henry suggests that the Schlegels store their belongings in the vacant residence. Charles's hunger for property, rather than any belated sense of guilt over disobeying his mother's final wishes, motivates his disdain. Ruth Wilcox's ghost looms even larger after Leonard and Jacky arrive unexpectedly in the company of Helen at Margaret and Henry's Oniton home. When Jacky recognizes Henry, with whom she had an affair a decade before in Cyprus, he recoils in shame in the presence of Margaret, who quickly forgives him for an indiscretion that occurred long before their union. She finds herself strangely unsettled, however, by his deception of Ruth. Margaret realizes that Henry's "really culpable part—his faithlessness to Mrs. Wilcox—never seemed to strike him" as he begs for her forgiveness (257-58). Yet Margaret, as she ponders the awesome power of the Wilcoxes' wealth and privilege—tacitly participates in the evolution of her stepfamily's dysfunctionality: "She still loved Henry," Forster writes, as she gazes with "deep emotion upon Oniton," the location of her palatial new home (261).

Margaret's later discovery of Helen's secret pregnancy and Leonard's subsequent murder at the hands of Charles Wilcox, however, shatters the novel's series of triangulated relationships and serves as a polarizing mechanism that ultimately results in new frontiers of selfhood for Margaret, Helen, and Henry. Their differentiation provides Forster, then, with fertile terrain for the therapy and would-be transformation of the social values of England's larger family system. As Richard C. Schwartz notes, during polarization "each person in the relationship shifts . . . to a rigid, extreme position that is the opposite of or competitive with that of the other. . . . Because they tend to be self-confirming," Schwartz adds, "these polarizations are likely to escalate in the absence of effective leadership" (20, 59). In *Howards End,* after Margaret's polarization allows her to complete her social education, she provides the kind of interpersonal leadership necessary for Helen and Henry—her partners in triangulation—to achieve selfhood as well. "This process of polarization and escalation is very familiar to systems theorists," Augustus Y. Napier and Carl Whitaker write in *The Family Crucible: The Intense Experience of Family Therapy* (1978), and may result, as with Forster's novel, in the type of "positive feedback [that] tells the system that things are changing, that the system is deviating from homeostasis" (83).

Margaret's polarized relationship with Henry unfolds in dramatic fashion after they cajole Helen into returning to England from Germany—where she awaits the birth of an illegitimate child by Leonard—in order to retrieve her beloved books from Howards End. When Margaret discovers her sister's condition, she agrees to provide a single night's refuge for Helen in the Wilcoxes' family home—now essentially a warehouse for the Schlegels' worldly goods—but Henry seethes with rage at the prospect of a fallen woman sullying Howards End's social grace and upper-class demeanor. "It was the crisis of his life," Forster writes (319). Absorbed with the notion of punishing Helen's as of yet unidentified seducer, Henry fails to understand her desire to be among the soothing presence of her family's books and other sentimental belongings. "I cannot treat her as if nothing has happened," Henry reasons with his wife, and "I should be false to my position in society if I did" (321). Suddenly polarized by Henry's utter inability to perceive the inequity of his stance, Mar-

garet refuses to participate further in her chimerical defense of his socially "muddled" persona:

> You shall see the connection if it kills you, Henry! You have had a mistress—I forgave you. My sister has a lover—you drive her from the house. Do you see the connection? Stupid, hypocritical, cruel—oh, contemptible!—a man who insults his wife when she's alive and cants with her memory when she's dead. A man who ruins a woman for his pleasure, and casts her off to ruin other men. And gives bad financial advice, and then says he is not responsible. These, man, are you. You cannot recognize them, because you cannot connect. . . . No one has ever told you what you are—muddled, criminally muddled.
>
> (322-23)

By finally drawing upon the value systems that marked her pre-marital life with Henry, Margaret begins the process of usurping her pseudo-self and emerging into a new era of selfhood.[9]

Because he still remains unable to recognize the substance of his wife's words, Henry refuses to accede to Margaret's wishes. Yet Margaret, with the powerful seeds of her new-found selfhood already planted, chooses to spend the night with Helen at Howards End, where she witnesses the nature of her sister's own self-transformation. "There is a special complexity, intricacy, and intimacy in sister relationships," Monica McGoldrick writes, because "the desire for and experience of fusion lie at the heart of the difficulty many sisters have in seeing themselves as distinct from each other" (245). The product of remarkably similar value systems based upon the veneration of friendship and culture, Margaret and Helen's relationship understandably began to fissure with Margaret's marriage. Previously unable to reconcile herself with Henry's problematic social mores and his seemingly dysfunctional relationship with her sister, Helen tells Margaret that "I am steady now. I shan't ever *like* your Henry, dearest Meg, or even speak kindly about him," she adds, "but all that blinding hate is over. I shall never rave against Wilcoxes any more" (328). Inexorably altered by her spiritual connection with Leonard and his celebration of nature and poetry, Helen finds herself at peace and enabled, for the first time, to accept her sister's decision to pursue a relationship with anyone beyond the boundaries of their ethical system, even a Wilcox.

Henry's sudden self-differentiation occurs via the tragic activities of his son Charles, who travels on his father's orders to Howards End on the morning after Helen's stay in an effort to learn the identity of her seducer and to expel her from the house's supposedly sacred rooms.[10] When Charles discovers a newly arrived and remorseful Leonard at the residence, he erupts in a fury of class-conscious chivalry and brandishes a sword from amongst the Schlegels' belongings. Thus beknighted with a genuine artifact of aristocratic iconography, Charles startles the unemployed clerk, who collapses from heart failure in, rather appropriately, a shower of books from the Schlegels' substantial library. The morning's sad events furnish Henry with the catalyst for his own self-awakening. Traumatized by his role in Charles's act of manslaughter, Henry's "fortress gave way," Forster writes. "He could bear no one but his wife, he shambled up to Margaret afterwards and asked her to do what she could with him," Forster continues; "she did what seemed easiest—she took him down to recruit at Howards End" (350). Now ensconced in a household that includes his wife, as well as her fallen sister, Henry completes his ethical transformation by composing a will that bequeaths Howards End to Margaret initially, and later, to his newborn nephew, Leonard and Helen's son. "After I am dead let there be no jealousy and no surprise," he informs the other, stunned surviving members of the Wilcox family (357).[11] Even Helen recognizes a change in Henry's demeanor. "I like Henry," she now confesses to Margaret, who laments that, until the recent turn of events, Henry "worked hard all his life, and noticed nothing" (352).[12]

At *Howards End*'s conclusion, Henry seems suddenly able to "notice" much more than his previous human philosophy allowed. Forster depicts him, for example, in the act of smiling at the very sight of Helen's baby, and, perhaps even more amazingly, at the presence of Tom, the son of a local field hand. As Robert Kegan notes, "Development is not a matter of differentiation alone, but differentiation and reintegration" (67). Imbued with faculties that allow him to enjoy the kinds of social and aesthetic experience advocated by Moore and Forster alike, Henry's character now appears to be the "type" of person, who—in the millennium, according to Margaret—will enable England to transcend finally the barriers of class and culture that divide its people. In *The Theory and Technique of Family Therapy* (1979), Charles P. Barnard and Ramon Garrido Corrales discuss the manner in which a family of differentiated selves possesses the transgenerational capacity for producing yet other selves with full senses of identity (36-37). By illustrating the Schlegels and the Wilcoxes in the process of emerging, via their conflicting experiences with Leonard and Jacky Bast, as a functional system from their initially spurious union, Forster's narrative suggests the possibility of a larger family system capable of yielding yet other fully realized selves in the future. While Leonard literally and metaphorically perishes from heart disease in the novel, his brief and intimate connection with Helen signals a sense of resolution between the classes and foreshadows the possible emergence of a new social order, of a world in which poetry and friendship matter. Perhaps even more significantly, Henry's ethical apotheosis at the novel's conclusion also suggests that the Schlegels have won the battle for Howards End—itself a fight for the heart of England, at least in Forster's ethical vision. As Paul Delany observes, Forster's narrative succeeds in one of its principal aims—"to project Schlegel values into a compelling vision of what Britain's destiny might and should be" (69).

In this way, *Howards End* functions as a kind of narrative therapy, as a means for establishing connection and reconciliation between the classes of a larger family system by virtue of Moore's ethical matrix. "How dare Schlegels despise Wilcoxes," Forster presciently asks his readers, "when it takes all sorts to make a world?" (108). By creating a narrative that illustrates the socially debilitating effects of class and cultural inequity upon a larger family system such as English society, Forster effectively postulates a work of narrative therapy, both in the tradition of his literary precursors and also in concert with recent intellectual strides in narrative treatment as theorized and practiced by family therapists. Donald E. Polkinghorne writes that "the recognition that humans use narrative structure as a way to organize the events of their lives and to provide a scheme for their own self-identity is of importance for the practice of psychotherapy and for personal change" (178). The specialized terminology of family systems therapy likewise affords literary critics and therapists alike with a meaningful parlance through which to address story-telling and its propensity for furnishing us with the tools to alter the direction of our lives. "In cultural terms," David Paré argues, narrative therapy operates "much like the global effort for peaceful cohabitation. It suggests a therapy focused on intercultural harmony" (35). In *Howards End,* Forster explicitly constructs his narrative in such a fashion as to establish fertile terrain for an "intercultural harmony" of his own design that may yet dilute the hegemony of class and privilege that problematizes England's larger family system. As Minuchin and Nichols note, "Family therapists recognize the pull of the past and that, to some extent, people live in the shadow of the family that was. But," they add, "family therapy also recognizes the power of the present and so addresses itself to the ongoing influence of the family that is" (35). In his own work of narrative therapy, Forster extends this supposition one step further, arguing that a recognition of the complex, familial interrelations between past and present ultimately influences the course of the future that *will* be.

Notes

1. The *Titanic* and the dramatic conclusion to her maiden voyage essentially function as microcosms of the English class system, from the staggering discrepancies between the ship's first-class and steerage accommodations to the treatment of lower-class passengers during the loading of the liner's lifeboats. Some fortunate steerage survivors later recalled the menacing gates that acted as barriers against their passage to the boat deck. "Undoubtedly, the worst barriers," Wyn Craig Wade adds in *The Titanic: End of a Dream,* "were the ones within the steerage passengers themselves. Years of conditioning as third-class citizens led a great many of them to give up hope as soon as the crisis became evident" (277-78).

2. Family therapists define morphogenesis as the process that allows a given family system "to deviate from its usual relationship among component parts and even to amplify that deviation" (Knapp 67). In *Howards End,* Forster illustrates the dramatic ways in which his characters challenge habitual familial

patterns by contradicting, and ultimately withdrawing from, their respective family systems over such issues as class and culture.

3. Despite what appears to be Forster's obvious affinity for Moore's teachings, the novelist's critics and biographers continue to debate the extent of his knowledge of *Principia Ethica*. While K. W. Gransden attributes the moral philosophies of Forster and other members of the Bloomsbury Group to Moore's influence (4), his biographer P. N. Furbank flatly concludes that Forster "never read Moore" (1: 49). Although Mary Lago also confirms Furbank's assertion, she notes that Forster admitted to aligning himself with Moore's belief "in the possibility of an ideal affection" (58). Claude J. Summers maintains, however, that Forster "imbibed" the Cambridge philosophies of Moore, whose teachings likely justified Forster's own "belief that personal relations and the contemplation of beauty yield life's most valuable states of mind" (6).

4. For additional discussion regarding literature as a means of narrative therapy, as well as a vehicle for the interdisciplinary study of family systems psychotherapy, see Barbara A. Kaufman's "Training Tales in Family Therapy: Exploring *The Alexandria Quartet.*" Kaufman argues that "inclusion of novels in didactic contexts encourages trainees to search their own experiences, thereby maximizing the opportunity for positive therapeutic interaction and highlighting the variety of treatment approaches in the field" (70). See also Janine Roberts's *Tales and Transformations: Stories in Families and Family Therapy* (1994), which features an appendix that enumerates a host of existing "family systems novels."

5. Charles P. Barnard and Ramon Garrido Corrales define homeostasis as a family's tendency—no matter how detrimental it may be—to preserve constancy. "There is no question," they write, "that families devote considerable energy to maintain a certain amount of order and stability. Security," they add, "seems to be tied with a certain amount of stability and predictability" (13). William C. Nichols and Craig E. Everett explain morphogenesis as the process through which families effect radical, meaningful change. Morphogenesis, then, "involves altering the nature of the system itself so that new levels of functioning are achieved" (130).

6. Richard C. Schwartz usefully defines the notion of the self or selfhood as "a state of mind to be achieved—a place of nonjudgmental, clear perspective" (4-5). In *The Stories We Are: An Essay in Self-Creation,* however, William Lowell Randall says that the stories "we tell ourselves [are] not at all neutral" (42). Indeed, he adds, an "interesting sort of feedback loop is at work: what I tell myself about myself affects how I present myself to others; how I present myself to others affects the options they make available to me; and what options they make available to

me reinforce or challenge what I tell myself about myself thereafter" (43). In her valuable essay "Sisters," Monica McGoldrick discusses the peculiar difficulties that sisters encounter while pursuing selfhood outside of their family's systemic boundaries, an issue of obvious significance to any study of the Schlegel sisters and their individual quests for personal growth and development. McGoldrick ascribes such difficulties to "the fact that women have not been raised to have an individual identity; their identity has been seen more as a receptacle for the needs of others. This perhaps influences the special fusion," she adds, "that may exist in the relationship of sisters," as well as in their subsequent quests for selfhood beyond the sibling subsystem (244-45).

7. In *Narrative Knowing and the Human Sciences,* Donald E. Polkinghorne notes that "the reflective awareness of one's personal narrative provides the realization that past events are not meaningful in themselves but are given significance by the configuration of one's narrative. This realization," he continues, "can release people from the control of past interpretations they have attached to events and open up the possibility of renewal and freedom for change" (182-83). Polkinghorne's postulation of storytelling and its value as a means for effecting systemic change underscore the ways in which Forster's novel, with its social and aesthetic vision of England's future, functions as a work of narrative therapy.

8. Napier and Whitaker argue, moreover, that with scapegoating "one of the spouses can agree unconsciously to be 'the problem.'" In this way, "at least one spouse has to be able to cope with the reality world, while the other 'specializes' in contact with the disturbed feelings present in both partners. . . . This decision"—as *Howards End* clearly illustrates through Henry and Margaret's initially dysfunctional marriage—"may have grave consequences for the couple" (149).

9. In poorly functioning systems such as Margaret and Henry's marriage, however, family members develop pseudo-selves—often fostered by fear and anxiety within the system—and thus, such individuals frequently remain unable to maintain any real congruence between their inner feelings and their outward behavior (Barnard and Corrales 85-87). The cathartic qualities of Margaret's dramatic emotional tirade clearly portend that she will subsequently advance into a new, functional era of selfhood.

10. Like Charles, contemporary reviewers of *Howards End* "assumed," according to Lago, "that Leonard is the seducer, for a respectable middle-class girl like Helen could not be actively attracted even briefly to the 'squalid' Leonard" (45). Helen's empathy for and seduction of the clerk, however, allow Forster to establish his narrative of accommodation between the classes. In Forster's ethical schema, Helen truly appreciates Leonard's social and intellectual qualities:

"Such a muddle of a man," Helen remarks to her sister about Leonard, "and yet so worth pulling through. I like him extraordinarily" (155).

11. Notably, while Barbara Rosecrance problematizes Margaret's "almost absolute moral authority" in the novel, she astutely notes that Margaret's "ability to connect seems the moral prerequisite for her guardianship of Howards End" (112, 122).

12. Ironically, Henry's social transformation follows closely on the heels of Leonard's sad recognition of his lower-class fate. Before traveling to Howards End and his untimely death at the hands of Charles, Leonard discusses the social dichotomy between rich and poor in a manner strikingly evocative of Henry's previous social philosophy: "There always will be rich and poor," he tells Margaret; "if rich people fail at one profession, they can try another. . . . I mean if a [poor] man over twenty one loses his own particular job, it's all over with him. I have seen it happen to others," he explains. "Their friends gave them money for a little, but in the end they fall over the edge. It's no good. It's the whole world pulling" (237-38).

Works Cited

Barnard, Charles P., and Ramon Garrido Corrales. *The Theory and Technique of Family Therapy*. Springfield, IL: Thomas, 1979.

Bruner, Jerome. "Life as Narrative." *Social Research* 54.1 (1987): 11-32.

Burt, Mala S., and Roger B. Burt. *Stepfamilies: The Step by Step Model of Brief Therapy*. New York: Brunner/ Mazel, 1996.

Delany, Paul. "'Islands of Money': Rentier Culture in *Howards End*." *E. M. Forster: New Casebooks*. Ed. Jeremy Tambling. London: Macmillan, 1993. 67-80.

Forster, E. M. *Howards End*. 1910. New York: Vintage, 1989.

Furbank, P. N. *E. M. Forster: A Life*. 2 vols. London: Secker and Warburg, 1977-78.

Gransden, K. W. *E. M. Forster*. New York: Grove, 1962.

Imber-Black, Evan. *Families and Larger Systems: A Family Therapist's Guide through the Labyrinth*. New York: Guilford, 1988.

Kaufman, Barbara A. "Training Tales in Family Therapy: Exploring *The Alexandria Quartet*." *Journal of Marital and Family Therapy* 21.1 (1995): 67-75.

Kegan, Robert. *The Evolving Self: Problems and Process in Human Development*. Cambridge: Harvard UP, 1982.

Knapp, John V. *Striking at the Joints: Contemporary Psychology and Literary Criticism*. Lanham, MD: UP of America, 1996.

Lago, Mary. *E. M. Forster: A Literary Life*. New York: St. Martin's, 1995.

Lodge, David. *Nice Work*. 1988. New York: Penguin, 1989.

McGoldrick, Monica. "Sisters." *Women in Families: A Framework for Family Therapy*. Ed. Monica McGoldrick, Carol M. Anderson, and Froma Walsh. New York: Norton, 1989. 244-66.

Minuchin, Salvador, and Michael P. Nichols. *Family Healing: Strategies for Hope and Understanding*. New York: Touchstone, 1993.

Moore, G. E. *Principia Ethica*. 1902. Buffalo, NY: Prometheus, 1988.

Napier, Augustus Y., and Carl Whitaker. *The Family Crucible: The Intense Experience of Family Therapy*. New York: Harper and Row, 1978.

Nichols, William C., and Craig A. Everett. *Systemic Family Therapy: An Integrative Approach*. New York: Guilford, 1986.

Paré, David A. "Culture and Meaning: Expanding the Metaphorical Repertoire of Family Therapy." *Family Process* 35.1 (1996): 21-42.

Polkinghorne, Donald E. *Narrative Knowing and the Human Sciences*. Albany: State U of New York P, 1988.

Randall, William Lowell. *The Stories We Are: An Essay in Self-Creation*. Toronto: U of Toronto P, 1995.

Roberts, Janine. *Tales and Transformations: Stories in Families and Family Therapy*. New York: Norton, 1994.

Rosecrance, Barbara. *Forster's Narrative Vision*. Ithaca, NY: Cornell UP, 1982.

Schwartz, Richard C. *Internal Family Systems Therapy*. New York: Guilford, 1995.

Summers, Claude J. *E. M. Forster*. New York: Ungar, 1983.

Wade, Wyn Craig. *The Titanic: End of a Dream*. New York: Rawson, 1979.

White, Michael, and David Epston. *Narrative Means to Therapeutic Ends*. New York: Norton, 1990.

Michael J. Hoffman and Ann Ter Haar (essay date spring 1999)

SOURCE: Hoffman, Michael J., and Ann Ter Haar. "'Whose Books Once Influenced Mine': The Relationship between E. M. Forster's *Howards End* and Virginia Woolf's *The Waves*." *Twentieth Century Literature* 45, no. 1 (spring 1999): 46-64.

[*In the following essay, Hoffman and Haar explore parallels between* Howards End *and Woolf's* The Waves.]

In a letter to Ethel Smyth on 21 Sept. 1930, Virginia Woolf spoke of her friend Morgan Forster as "E. M. Forster the novelist, whose books once influenced mine, and are very good, I think, though impeded, shrivelled and immature" (*Letters* 4: 218). In earlier letters Woolf had often alluded to Forster's influence, even insisting on one occasion that "I always feel that nobody, except perhaps Morgan Forster, lays hold of the thing I have done" (14 June 1925; *Letters* 3: 188). By 1930 this literary friendship had continued for more than two decades and was characterized by the kind of edginess that often marks the relationships of highly competitive artists. During the same year, Forster recorded his own anxieties about Woolf in a note that we find in his *Commonplace Book:* "Visit to Virginia, prospects of, not wholly pleasurable. I shall watch her curiosity and flattery exhaust themselves in turn. Nor does it do to rally the Pythoness" (54). These comments, written when both writers were well launched as established novelists and public figures, give some indication of the complex literary friendship that goaded and nourished both writers. In this essay we shall explore how that relationship manifests itself in two of their best-known novels, *Howards End* and *The Waves,* through significant parallels in their thematics, narrative voice, and imagery.

Although Forster was himself just three years older than Woolf, he represents an earlier generation, in part because of his extraordinary precocity and also in part because Woolf—not enjoying some of the educational advantages afforded Forster—began her career more slowly, publishing her first novel when she was 33 years old. In contrast, *Howards End,* one of Forster's two most celebrated novels, was published when its author was barely 31, having been preceded by three other novels and followed a year later by a collection of tales. When Woolf's first novel appeared in 1915, Forster had been publishing fiction for ten years, and Woolf considered him a senior peer among British writers.

Woolf and Forster related to one another as practicing novelists, as critics who reviewed each other's work, and as friends within their Bloomsbury connections. In 1910 Forster gave his first talk to the Friday Club on "The Feminine Note in Literature," and before that he had known Leonard Woolf at Cambridge through their membership in the Apostles (Furbank 1: 192). Forster began his practice of reviewing Woolf's novels with *The Voyage Out.* Indeed P. N. Furbank, Forster's biographer, claims that after Forster's "favourable review of *The Voyage Out* in 1915 [Woolf] 'became very dependent on his opinion'" (qtd. in Dowling 85). It is instructive to compare this relationship to the much more vexed one of Woolf and Katherine Mansfield. Viewed within that context, the ties between Forster and Woolf seem extraordinarily positive and long-lasting.

Forster appears to have been most comfortable with Woolf's earlier works, such as *The Voyage Out,* a book similar to his own: in **"The Early Novels of Virginia Woolf"** (1925) he describes it as "a strange, tragic, in-spired book . . . [whose] closing chapters . . . are as poignant as anything in modern fiction . . ." (*Abinger Harvest* 107). (It seems to us that in *A Passage to India* Forster repeats many of the structural and thematic motifs he found in *The Voyage Out.*) But when Woolf began, with *Jacob's Room* (1922), to assume her more distinctive voice, Forster's praise became more ambivalent. Even following the comparative success of *Jacob's Room,* however, Woolf continued to see Forster as her senior in accomplishment until the mid-20s, when her next novel, *Mrs. Dalloway,* established her as the equal of her friend.

But we should not underestimate the element of competition. Both writers were trying to establish the narrative aesthetics of their time, and each resisted definitions developed by the other. In "Mr. Bennett and Mrs. Brown" (1924), Woolf places Forster among the Georgian, or new novelists who are moving away from old-fashioned realism (*Captain's Death Bed* 95); a year later, in **"The Early Novels of Virginia Woolf,"** Forster praises *Jacob's Room* and *Mrs. Dalloway,* particularly as artistic structures, but his reservations peep through when he refers to Woolf's style of "inspired breathlessness" and her "shimmering fabric" (*Abinger Harvest* 109, 111), traits he suggests may be a mask for covering over the lack of real characters in Woolf's books.[1] In *Aspects of the Novel* (1927) Forster also patronizingly lumps Woolf together with Laurence Sterne as a "fantasist," and describes her style as "a rather deliberate bewilderment, an announcement to all and sundry that they do not know where they are going" (19-20).

Woolf's diaries testify to the influence that Forster's critical response had on her self-esteem. Her entries reveal that with each successive novel it is Forster's judgment she awaits and his critique that—other than Leonard's—she values most highly. When he followed his favorable review of *The Voyage Out* with a more measured response to *Night and Day* (1919), a book that almost no one liked, Woolf protests: "I see no reason to be depressed on his account" (*Diaries* 1: 310). After the publication of *Jacob's Room,* the letter containing Forster's simple praise ("I am sure it is good") is the one Woolf "liked best of all" (2: 209). While anticipating reviews of *Mrs. Dalloway,* Woolf writes: "The only judgement on Mrs. D. I await with trepidation (but that's too strong) is Morgan's. He will say something enlightening" (3: 22). When she receives his approbation three days later, her sparse diary entry underscores the significance of the event. "Well, Morgan admires. . . . This is a weight off my mind." She notes, as well, that Forster "kissed my hand" (3: 24).

Two years later, it is not until she receives Forster's letter on *To the Lighthouse* ("It is awfully sad, very beautiful . . . I am inclined to think it your best work") that she feels free to put that novel "behind" her (3: 137). The following year (1929) she is initially concerned that Forster will not review *A Room of One's Own* and is then relieved that he likes it (3: 262). In 1931 she quotes Morgan's response to *The Waves* directly, and at some length, into her diary: "Here I will give myself the pleasure—shall I?—of copying a sentence or two from Morgan's unsolicited letter on *The Waves*." Delighted that Forster declares the novel a "classic," Woolf reports: "I daresay that gives me more substantial pleasure than any letter I've had about any book. Yes, I think it does, coming from Morgan" (4: 52). Later she reflects, "Isn't it odd that I'm really, I believe, ostracized by some of my friends, because of *The Waves,* & lifted to the highest pinnacle by others, because of it? . . . Morgan is the only one, either side, that matters" (4: 54). Woolf dreads Morgan's silence again after the appearance of *Roger Fry: A Biography* (1940), the last book she published before her death. She fears that "Morgan will say—just enough to show he doesn't like, but is kind" (5: 303), then reports that she would "be relieved *if* Morgan approves" (5: 305), and finally records her attempts to cope with Morgan's silence about this book— "No review by Morgan, no review at all. No letter" (5: 308).

For her part, reviewing **Aspects of the Novel** a month after its publication, Woolf contradicts the central tenet of Forster's aesthetics when she criticizes him for his vagueness in defining the novelist's capacity to create "life," the most important of his self-proclaimed evaluative categories. "Life," she writes in fluent condescension,

> it has been agreed by everyone whose opinion is worth consulting, is the only fit subject for novelist or biographer; life, the same authorities have decided, has nothing whatever to do with sitting still in a chair and thinking. Thought and life are poles asunder.
>
> (*Orlando* 267).[2]

Forster apparently responded with a personal letter in which he obliquely expresses both injury and pique.[3] Although each writer was hurt by the other's criticism, Woolf no longer defers to Forster. She is by this time (1927) a well-established, important British writer, and she knows it. When Woolf publishes *The Waves* four years later, Forster the novelist has been silent for seven years, and Woolf clearly feels herself the more prominent literary figure. Thus when Forster compares Woolf to the snake that crushes its prey in his **Commonplace Book** (quoted earlier), he reveals his discomfort with her swelling powers and fame. He may also intuit the shift in her assessment of *his* literary powers; this is the same year, remember, that Woolf tells Ethel Smyth that she finds Forster's works "impeded, shrivelled and immature" (1930).

To illustrate the reversal in their relative positions, we might consider an incident recorded in a series of letters that Woolf wrote to various friends in 1932, a year after publication of *The Waves*. Several of her contemporaries mistook an anonymous book review of Jane Austen's letters, actually written by Forster, to be by Woolf.[4] Woolf responded by disparaging the writing, and disclaiming any similarity to her own, although some anxiety is apparent in the extremity of her reaction. To Ethel Smyth, for instance, she writes:

> Where is your taste, your judgment—I ask in all solemnity (I'm rocking with laughter)—'The Austens are of your very best'—do you really think so? Well, the

article may be a masterpiece—I thought it feeble in the extreme, and said to L. 'heres someone trying my tricks in the Times—' No, of course I didn't write it. Surely—
>
> (13 Nov. 1932, *Letters* 5: 125)

She refers to this matter in two more letters to Smyth (20 Nov. and 29 Nov. 1932), and then again in a letter of 1 Jan. 1933 to W. Colston Leigh, the agent who arranged an American lecture tour by Vita Sackville-West and Harold Nicholson. By the time of her letter to Leigh, Woolf already knows that Forster had written the review. She writes:

> I dislike the expressions separately—in their context, bathed in Morgans very peculiar sensibility they may be all right—I'm not Morgan. Thats one of the puzzles of letters—how an atmosphere—person—taste—pose—can transform the good into the bad.
>
> (5: 143)

What is really going on here? Had Forster swerved stylistically to the extent that he was unconsciously imitating Woolf? Or, in fact, had the two writers, after 20 years of reading each other and measuring themselves thereby, developed similar discursive styles?[5] Given how much earlier Forster started to publish, the issue of Woolf's influence on him does not become strong until she has, with *Mrs. Dalloway* and *To the Lighthouse,* achieved a major reputation, and Forster has published the last novel to appear in his lifetime, **A Passage to India.**

Questions of style and of fame preoccupied both writers and served as a subject of discourse for both. Both were interested not only in developing an individual style and in measuring themselves against their contemporaries and each other, but also, on a grander scale, in trying to imagine their places in a larger literary history, one that extended beyond national boundaries. It is remarkable that in these projections Forster and Woolf often use similar kinds of visual imagery. In his critical assessments, for instance, Forster often employs architectural tropes as images of containment. In **Aspects of the Novel** he envisions the English novelists (regardless of period) "seated together in a room, a circular room, a sort of British Museum reading-room—all writing their novels simultaneously" (21). Similarly, in **"The Early Novels of Virginia Woolf,"** Forster compares English fiction from Fielding to Arnold Bennett to a series of evenly spaced portraits in a picture gallery; the gallery itself is the "one factor that never varies" (**Abinger Harvest** 115). When he describes what Woolf would do to the gallery, Forster expresses both his highest praise and deepest anxiety: "She wants to destroy the gallery . . . and in its place build what? Something more rhythmical. *Jacob's Room* suggests a spiral whirling down to a point, *Mrs. Dalloway* a cathedral" (115). In general, Forster regards the "little mansions" of British fiction as dwarfed by the "colonnades" and "vaults" of such novels as *War and Peace* and *The Brothers Karamazov* (**Aspects** 8). By comparing her works to cathedrals and whirling spirals, Forster was effectively ranking Woolf in the same class as Tolstoy and Dostoyevsky. Similarly, it seems to us that Woolf transmutes Forster's imagery into the sculptural when, while revising *The Waves,* she writes: "What I fear is that the re-writing will have to be so drastic that I may entirely muddle it somehow. It is bound to be very imperfect. But I think it possible that I have got my statues against the sky" (*Diaries* 3: 300).

When Forster asks the question, in **Aspects of the Novel,** "may the writer take the reader into his confidence about his characters?" he answers, "better not" (81). But any reader of **Howards End** soon realizes that Forster's narrative voice never hesitates to tell us about the characters, even though that voice is more explicit in making generalizations about *character* than in giving away secrets about the characters. Here is an area in which the two writers' practices ostensibly clashed, with Woolf attempting either to transmute the narrative voice or do away with it entirely in the Jamesian spirit of dramatizing or rendering. In reality, however, Woolf found other ways to get her comments into the text—for instance, by using one character's voice to describe another character, and by dramatically giving that commenting character a prominence in the narrative that establishes his or her authority (for example, Bernard in *The Waves*).

Literary history has situated Forster and Woolf as part of a community known as "Bloomsbury," often neglecting the nuanced differences in their family backgrounds. Even though most of Forster's contemporaries among the British artists and intelligentsia came from a milieu that resembled that of the Schlegel sisters, his own familial roots were Wilcoxian: property, politics, business. He spent his boyhood (1883-93) on a small country estate called Rooksnest in Stevenage, a home not unlike Howards End. It is no doubt the Wilcox in Forster that seeks to identify an essentially English art, an aesthetics that arises from an English mythology. One can trace a British chauvinism in both his aesthetic and political manifestoes as well as in his desire to compete with such French and Russian masters as Proust and Tolstoy.[6] Forster chose to live in a country town (Weybridge) and a country village (Abinger) consistent with his more rural family roots. Woolf, the consummate city dweller (like the Schlegel sisters whom they resemble, Virginia and Vanessa were natives of London), later took refuge with Leonard in rural Sussex to escape the demands of London literary and political life. Their country home, Monk's House, Rodmell is another dwelling reminiscent of both Howards End and Rooksnest.

There can hardly be two novels that seem more explicitly opposite than **Howards End** and *The Waves.* The first clearly finds its affinities in the long realist tradition of the British social novel, with its concerns about class, marriage, and property. **Howards End** is full of houses; it presents the rich and the poor; it divides the middle class into lovers of property and lovers of the arts; it has three marriages, at least one marriage plot, two infidelities, and an illegitimate birth. These have been conventions of narrative fiction since *Clarissa* and *Tom Jones. The Waves,* on the other hand, is the quintessential "impressionist" novel, meant to be read with the care one brings to a lyric poem full of images, tropes, and archetypes; it moves not on the flow of plot and story line but on accumulated fragments from the lives of a variety of characters, all of whom speak but not all of whom control the discourse; its characters are not created psychologically through action and dialogue but through *aperçus* and juxtaposition. The two books seem as though they were written out of totally different novelistic traditions, as to some extent they were.

Yet their thematic concerns converge. **Howards End** was published during 1910, the year in whose final month human consciousness supposedly changed—as Woolf later suggested in "Mr. Bennett and Mrs. Brown." In its social content **Howards End** sums up a Europe on the brink of a world war that will forever change the fortunes of England. It places in conflict two upper-middle-class families, one descended from English yeomanry (or the folk), the other from cultivated German burghers, bringing them together in a not altogether comfortable marriage and placing both families in conflict with a member of the urban poor, himself descended from yeoman stock. Without focusing on the specifics of international conflict, **Howards End** nonetheless presents a country that is poised between two worlds, those of "culture" (the Wilcoxes) and "civilization" (the Schlegels). In the late nineteenth century, German critics began to make an

> impassioned distinction . . . between *Kultur* and *Zivilisation.* . . . German *Kultur* . . . was said to be concerned with 'inner freedom,' with authenticity, with truth rather than sham, with essence as opposed to appearance, with totality rather than the norm.
>
> (Eksteins 77, 79)

These were binary poles that English critics also contested during the time that **Howards End** was written and during the years preceding the rise of the Third Reich and the war that Woolf prefigures so vividly in her final novel, *Between the Acts* (1941).

If **Howards End** presents an English culture that is ready to disappear in the face of modernity and global conflict, *The Waves* chronicles an England two decades later that emerged from the First World War with the end of its colonial hegemony, the breakdown of traditional relations between the sexes, and the frustrations of individuals who wish in vain for lives like those idealized in **Howards End.** But they now live in an England that is no longer a model that the world can follow or its citizens believe in.

Such thematic elements are as important to *The Waves* as they are to **Howards End,** often in the way they differ from or invert more traditional modes of narrative presentation. For instance, four years after focusing so heavily in *To the Lighthouse* on the Freudian family drama, Woolf presents seven characters in *The Waves,* none of whom appears to have siblings. Similarly, allusions to parents, spouses, or children in *The Waves* tend to be fleeting and mostly insignificant. We hear early in the novel, for instance, that Bernard is engaged, but it is not until his final monologue that he tells us in passing that he has fathered children. In a strange response to Forster's criticism that she did not give "life" to her characters, Woolf denies the characters in *The Waves* almost all forms of "connection," ironically inverting a judgment she makes in her diary that Forster himself was "aloof" (3: 152). Whereas Forster portrays the extraordinary power of family bonds in **Howards End,** Woolf seems intent in *The Waves* upon ignoring the extensive, indeed determinative powers of the family.

In fact, the awareness of separateness and difference—the movement out of a prelapsarian oneness—marks the first apprehensions of the characters in *The Waves* and remains a driving force throughout the narrative: in his final monologue, Bernard remembers that, as children, "We suffered terribly as we became separate bodies" (241). That experience of separateness does not, however, acknowledge separation from the mother, since the family scarcely exists in *The Waves.* And while Woolf avoids certain inscriptions of traditional family elements, she does include, as the first break in the novel, the British compulsion to separate the sexes during adolescence. The characters' destinies are henceforth marked by gender, and the schools they attend are differently endowed. Authority, history, and fellowship compensate for some of the less positive aspects of the boys' boarding-school experience. By contrast, the boarding school of the three girls is like a holding cell: sterile, confining, regimented. One is reminded of the descriptions in *A Room of One's Own* of the differences between male and female Oxbridge colleges, particularly their dinner tables. The boys in *The Waves* are inspired by the speakers at chapel; they become poets on the river banks, lounging in friendship amid the luxury of metaphysical speculations. Woolf clearly envied and idealized the Cambridge experiences of her brothers and their friends, which she felt had been denied to her. Moreover, she grants none of the female characters a destiny she would have desired for herself (although she does write aspects of herself into each): Susan the housemother/earthmother; Rhoda the psychological misfit; Jinny the narcissist. Although Woolf severs her characters from oppressive Victorian/Edwardian family structures, she does not incorporate positive plot options into their adult lives.

This does not mean she treats all characters with strict evenhandedness. Although unhappy, Neville has his poetry, and Louis is one of those powerful men who make the world run. Percival experiences the fate of an athlete dying young, embalmed forever in the amber of Victorian masculinity. And Bernard, whose voice increasingly comes to dominate the novel, completely filling the last 20 percent of it, comes to be a spokesperson for the author. But his ironic, worldly, and somewhat exhausted wisdom seems finally based less on Woolf herself and more on her friend Morgan, in persona, age, and physique, "a rather heavy, elderly man, grey at the temples" (238). (Forster was in his early 50s when *The Waves* was published.[7]) What does this reliance on Bernard's voice suggest? Is

Woolf invoking Forster's voice, consciously or unconsciously, to represent a kind of authority? If so, does she, through this displacement, express envy for the kind of narratorial authority possible only to a male voice of the dominant culture? Or is Woolf trying to show us, through Bernard, the failure of a life lived through the point of view of someone like Forster?

If we are correct in identifying Bernard as a kind of *doppelganger* to Forster, the latter set the precedent for such a gesture by writing characters reminiscent of Virginia Stephen and her sisters into his early novels. Indeed, the Schlegel ménage—two young women independently managing the family resources and directing the education of their younger brother—seems to be directly modeled on the Stephen household after Leslie's death. Clearly the freedoms engendered by the Stephen circle inspired Forster to present them as viable alternatives to more accepted social practices. In fact, Forster proffered a more ironic assessment of the Cambridge experience, as one who had had it himself, in his portrayal of the solipsistic, hedonistic Tibby Schlegel (cf. *Thoby* Stephen, Virginia's older brother who is usually seen as the model for Percival) in **Howards End.**

It is apparent that both Forster and Woolf coveted certain qualities of the other's life, and that they enunciated in their novels many of the social concerns that preoccupied the other. Forster, for example, felt constrained from creating overtly homosexual characters. **Maurice** was, of course, not published until after his death, and the erotic dimensions in the relationships between characters of the same sex (as, for example, between Aziz and Fielding in **A Passage to India**) were veiled. On the other hand, Woolf, through the persona of Neville (usually thought to be based on Lytton Strachey), was able to place a homosexual character into a normal, rather than an exceptional or ostracized life.

In a similar paradox, Forster dealt with a series of feminist issues in **Howards End** long before they became a central subject of Woolf's writing. In that novel Forster obliquely and ironically raises the abiding issue of primogeniture, even though the Englishwoman's right to own and bequeath property had been established by law more than three decades earlier. After exposing the family's collusion in dismissing the first Mrs. Wilcox's deathbed legacy as worthless writing on a piece of disposable paper, Forster delivers his own poetic justice by assuring Margaret's final ownership of the house. He also champions the right of a single mother to bear and raise her (illegitimate) child on English soil in a state of moral impunity. Helen feels guilt not over her sexual impropriety but over the fact that she has taken advantage of someone from another, less protected class. Furthermore, she states at the end that she does not wish to be married to anyone. Forster also exposes the Wilcoxes' sexual double standard, and punishes the family by stripping it of its public powers. In addition, in the character of Margaret Schlegel he heroicizes a woman who is neither young nor strikingly attractive nor likely to bear children (she states her desire *not* to have children), and he aligns his narrative voice and his most perspicacious insights with hers. With the exception of Jacky Bast, Forster's female characters of 1910 fare better than Woolf's of 1931.[8]

Just as the central voice of *Howards End* is that of Margaret Schlegel—whose moral values occupy the book's center and seem most like those of Forster—in *The Waves*, ostensibly written without a narrator in a version of the dramatized poetic novel, the voice of Bernard increasingly dominates, his sections becoming longer and longer, until we overhear the entire final section told in his own voice. By having Margaret Schlegel unaggressively tame the powers of patriarchal capitalism (even as she marries into and accepts its advantages), on the one hand, and by granting her both aesthetic principles and a rational consciousness on the other, Forster hails "feminine" qualities that have nothing to do with fertility, beauty, or youth. Woolf, in creating Bernard, grants him nurturing qualities more often associated with women, as for instance when he comforts Susan in a manner similar to Margaret's comforting of Helen. Both Bernard and Margaret, aside from speaking as the respective moral centers of their novels, also serve a similar, cohesive function in terms of their novels' plots.

Moreover, Bernard's attachment to the public role of the British male in the successful functioning of the British Empire (even at the expense of diminishing his private life) bears an uncanny resemblance to some of Forster's characterizations in *Howards End.* For instance, as an older man Bernard resembles not only Forster but Mr. Wilcox and his son Charles. When he receives a telephone call at breakfast, Bernard entertains the parodic notion that "it might be (one has these fancies) to assume command of the British Empire" (261). He identifies sanity, the entire body functioning properly, with breakfast time:

> Opening, shutting; shutting, opening; eating, drinking; sometimes speaking—the whole mechanism seemed to expand, to contract, like the mainspring of a clock. Toast and butter, coffee and bacon, the *Times* and letters—suddenly the telephone rang with urgency.

> (260-61)

Readers will recall that it is during breakfast at Howards End, following her flirtation with Paul, that Helen Schlegel realizes she does not belong with the Wilcoxes, and it is also at a later breakfast that the Wilcoxes conspire to destroy Mrs. Wilcox's bequest of Howards End to Margaret.

When we examine other images we also find some provocative parallels. Procreation clearly stands in Bernard's consciousness as one's "surrender . . . to the stupidity of nature" (268). For this reason, among others, we find it difficult to believe in Bernard as a father. He is at the book's end a lonely person, unable and unwilling to connect. When he says "Let me be alone" (294), he reminds

us of Mrs. Moore in *A Passage to India,* unable to translate the muddle of life as represented by "ou-boum" and asking to be left alone. In another sense Bernard also resembles Mr. Ramsay, with the Berkeleyan nihilism wherein he questions the existence of the *Ding an sich* and in his attempts to reestablish it as a basis for the continuity of experience. It may well be, however, that in 1910 Forster established the blueprint for all these characters when he has his narrator say of Margaret Schlegel that "she had outgrown stimulants, and was passing from words to things. . . . Some closing of the gate is inevitable after thirty, if the mind itself is to become a creative power" (206).

While Woolf's overall narrative conventions show her independence of Forster's genial prescriptions, Bernard's narrative concerns do echo those of Forster. In *Aspects,* for instance, Forster decried the difficulty of using complex plots without correspondingly intelligent audiences, pointing out that the average reader is interested only in a story that progresses along the lines of a pedestrian, linear chronology, which Forster characterizes with the image of "and then—and then." In the final section of *The Waves,* Bernard more than once uses a similar figure to describe the passage of life, the equivalent of Forster's "story." "Nevertheless," Bernard says, "life is pleasant, life is tolerable. Tuesday follows Monday; then comes Wednesday" (257). "And then—and then," we clearly hear in echo, just as we clearly hear Bernard trying out, though self-consciously, the prophetic voice that Forster attributes to Dostoyevsky (*Aspects* 126).

Not only do these novels have themes that converge, they also share other elements: in particular, their language and tropes show how the friends functioned as almost kindred writing spirits. Houses, to which both Woolf and Forster attach extraordinary significance, seem to represent for each writer a permanence, reflected in Helen Schlegel's remark to her sister that "The house has a surer life than we" (237). The house by the sea that dominates the interludes of *The Waves* recalls the St. Ives holiday home of Virginia's childhood as well as the summer house in *To the Lighthouse,* which serves as the quasiprotagonist of the "Time Passes" section of that novel. And the empty Howards End, bereft of its tenant, remains the monument if not the mausoleum of Ruth Wilcox. Indeed, when Margaret visits it for the first time, the eerie Miss Avery believes that she is the original Mrs. Wilcox come back from the dead to return her maternal spirit to the empty house. But it is in *The Waves* that Woolf raises the house to its fullest archetypal dimensions.

In view of Woolf's overwhelming response to the early death of her mother, many critics have tried to locate the "absent mother" in the substrata of Woolf's novels. Certainly the empty house in *The Waves* broods over the novel in the guise of a departed mother-spirit much as does the house bereft of Mrs. Ramsay in "Time Passes." We should also remember that both Mrs. Ramsay and Mrs. Wilcox die parenthetical, offstage deaths, and the disembodied house of *To the Lighthouse* recalls the fate of Howards End, which remains unoccupied after Mrs. Wilcox's death until another mother (Helen) and another matriarch (Margaret) arrive to regenerate it.[9]

Yet Woolf allows the house in *The Waves* to remain disembodied; she does not intend to create the exemplary house of consciousness. Rather, the house by the sea acts more like a human intervention against a transitory nature that also partakes of the eternal, a kind of *Ding an sich.* The only female character in the novel who distinctly occupies a house is Susan, and the implications of Susan's matriarchy are primarily negative. Her role as house mother destines her to a primitive, almost visceral subsistence, with her emotions suffocated and her personality weighed down by quotidian obligations. Having metonymically associated "house" with "mother" in *To the Lighthouse,* in *The Waves* Woolf neutralizes those charged associations by leaving the mother out of the archetypal house entirely. It is an easier move for Forster to repeople Howards End with the Schlegel angels because he has sentimentalized his own childhood in the English countryside; Woolf, on the other hand, abandons her childhood residence through apostasy, after building a fictional crypt to her parents' consciousness. In *The Waves* Woolf paints the still life of her house in the changing diurnal light as a series of studies not unlike those executed by Monet at Etretat and Rouen.[10]

Both Howards End and the house in *The Waves* are, then, shells of memory, and if Forster insists upon regeneration, Woolf allows her house to remain immaculate, purged of the violent, the visceral, the living. The "house" that signifies for Woolf is the house of the mortal body represented repeatedly (in the interludes) in its vulnerability by the shell of a snail broken open by a bird that spears the soft flesh inside. Bernard himself peoples this microcosmic house when he hears the "tap, tap, tap of the remorseless beaks of the young" (*The Waves* 288), and realizes that the oncoming generations signal his own impending death.

Needless to say, when Bernard finally enters the "dry, uncompromising, inhabited house" near the end of *The Waves,* it does not vibrate with the interaction of the living and the inanimate as do the ultimate furnishings and residents of Howards End (254). Much of Bernard's final soliloquy involves, in fact, a rejection of the domestic in his self-image of the domesticated man: "Was there no sword," he says, "nothing with which to batter down these walls, this protection, this begetting of children and living behind curtains . . . ?" (266) And it is with the flat of the Schlegels' ancestral sword that Charles Wilcox attacks Leonard Bast in an ironic defense of the English moral values that arise from property—including the sexual purity of female family members. The image of the sword, in its flourish, is somewhat reminiscent of the language Forster idealized in a letter to Woolf during their exchange about *Aspects of the Novel*:

> I find the continentals greater than the English not because Flaubert got hung but because Tolstoy etc., could vitalize guillotines etc., as well as tea-tables, could command certain moods or deeds which our domesticity leads us to shun as false.

(qtd. in Furbank 146)

Our final points of comparison touch on what may be the deepest sources of similarity between the two writers: their use of imagery and their attempts to create powerful archetypes for both "life" and England. We shall solidify these points of comparison with evidence of remarkable parallels between the works each writer composed at the end of the 1930s, prefiguring the apparently inevitable approach of another world war. Shakespeare scholars often refer to the "matter of England," meaning by this the material drawn from chronicles of British history that the playwright used in his dramas. Forster and Woolf make their own use of an equivalent "matter of England," demonstrating an abiding concern with English history, landscape, and character. Take, for instance, their contrasting attitudes toward London. If the country house stands as one site of Forster's ode to England, the streets of Bernard's London (and Clarissa Dalloway's, for that matter) represent, for Woolf, the living force of English culture. A central subtext of Bernard's soliloquy is Woolf's own ode to England, expressed through Bernard's wandering in London—a celebration of the urban experience that Woolf attempted in a number of other novels, beginning as early as the opening chapter of *The Voyage Out,* in Mrs. Ambrose's revelation that London consists of more than the West End. If Woolf fails in that passage to capture the Dickensian diversity of the great city, she comes closer to succeeding in Bernard's rendition of London as "the pageant of existence" passing through him (270).[11] Unlike either of the Schlegel sisters, Bernard seems unconcerned by—indeed, even immune to—the complexities of London's real estate; Margaret, in marrying Mr. Wilcox, marries not only a house but property and a landed social class.

Woolf's biographers record that her protectors often considered London to be a source of overstimulation for their ward's fragile emotional state; they often removed her to the country to allow her to recover from the excesses of urban life. While Bernard is clearly exhilarated by the panorama of London life, he also manages to maintain a panoptic distance from it, which allows him to retain mastery over his experience.[12] Moreover, through a classically modernist self-mockery (242, opening paragraph), he avoids losing consciousness completely in the waves of successive impressions that he fashions and that overcome him; in contrast, for instance, to the extremely fragile Rhoda, who in so many ways resembles her creator.

While Woolf executes her contrasts primarily through metaphor, Forster characteristically works more by direct statement. Here are a few examples of his attempts to situate the countryside and London historically and thematically. First is a description of London in relation to the Schlegels, in which Forster presents the city as being "emblematic of their lives." "The literature of the near future," his narrator claims, "will probably ignore the country and seek inspiration from the town." The general public he characterizes as "Victorian, while London is Georgian" (84). In the famous passage on the Purbeck Hills, Forster takes us by panorama from city to country to city again, showing the immense interconnectedness of everything English (131-32).

Later in the chapter, Margaret Schlegel, becoming more and more the novel's central voice, characterizes the Wilcoxes to her sister:

> If Wilcoxes hadn't worked and died in England for thousands of years, you and I couldn't sit here without having our throats cut. There would be no trains, no ships to carry us literary people about in, no fields even. Just savagery.

> (137-38)

The narrator states at the end of chapter 21 that the Wilcoxes will "inherit the earth" (146). We see Forster striving to define a British character worthy of a world-class literature, simultaneously rejecting attributes that might be deemed dainty or domestic (feminine) rather than grand or worldly (masculine):

> Why has not England a great mythology? Our folklore has never advanced beyond daintiness, and the greater melodies about our countryside have all issued through the pipes of Greece. . . . England still waits for the supreme moment of her literature—for the great poet who shall voice her. . . .

> (210-11)

In her most poetic novel Virginia Woolf may well have been responding to that call.

Woolf uses more indirect strategies, particularly after her first two novels. By the time she writes *The Waves* she has submerged any message about England into the dramatization of her characters and, by the end, into the lonely voice of Bernard speaking to an implied listener.[13] Woolf dramatizes her message about the fate of England by presenting characters from middle-class circumstances, each representing a particular personality type rather than a serious cross-section of British society. She makes clear the relative privileges accorded the two sexes, gives a historical panorama of gender relations during the late nineteenth and early twentieth centuries, shows the changing relationship of the colonies to the *patria* in the character of Louis, and almost parodies the imminent decline of England as a colonial power in the death of Percival while riding a horse in India. Bernard speaks in the fatigued voice of a man of rich sensibility who has grown cynical and demoralized about city life and his own failure to "connect," and Woolf lets him end the novel with words that are replete with irony as he echoes "The Charge of the Light Brigade" (a poem Mr. Ramsay and Leslie Stephen both loved).[14]

Only the brief, italicized voice of the interlude follows Bernard's lines, returning us to the eternal recurrence of

the sea, an image that Forster uses in the opening chapter of *Howards End,* as Margaret Schlegel feels the sea's presence even in London: "One had the sense of a backwater, or rather of an estuary, whose waters flowed in from the invisible sea, and ebbed into a profound silence while the waves without were still beating" (4). For Woolf the sea's voice is an objective, unchanging standard against which to measure the passage of time and human lives. Even within the apparently anonymous, transcendent voice of the Interludes, however, Woolf's own preoccupation with the "matter of England" reveals itself when she says that "the sun struck at *English* fields" (149, italics added). Forster also uses images of eternal recurrence, as in the final chapter of *Howards End* when he relies on the eternal round of seasons to lend stability to the odd Schlegel-Wilcox-Bast(ard) menage: "July would follow with the little red poppies among the wheat, August with the cutting of the wheat," and a few lines later, "The noise of the cutter came intermittently, like the *breaking of waves*" (265, italics added).

It is remarkable how even a casual chronological alignment of Woolf's and Forster's thematic concerns reveals their continuing preoccupation with the "matter of England" a decade after publication of *The Waves.* We shall conclude by examining the interplay between two texts—a pageant by Forster called *England's Pleasant Land* (which the Woolfs published in 1940 at the Hogarth Press) and Woolf's final novel, *Between the Acts* (published posthumously the following year). It is our final example of the dialogue that Forster and Woolf conducted for almost three decades. *England's Pleasant Land* is a conventional example of its genre, a celebration over a broad historical panorama of what Forster saw as basic to the English countryside and character.[15] During a series of historical moments he presents the same village characters as if they were timeless and immortal, using the kind of village procession that functions as continuous background in *Between the Acts.* These characters are timeless, but as the historical situations change, they are forced to enact the roles placed upon them by circumstance. Enlivened by Forster's often biting irony, the script portrays the steady rise of the lower classes against the will of the upper, and yet it also demonstrates the eternal domination of the weak by the strong. *England's Pleasant Land* was initially presented on the grounds of a country home, Milton Court, between Dorking and Westcott, with airplanes passing by overhead and, of course, it was interrupted by rain (*England's Pleasant Land* 8).

Does this sound familiar? It is almost descriptive of the setting of *Between the Acts,* including the interruption by rainfall, the setting of an elegant country home, and the village procession. Certainly the irony of Woolf's 1930 claim of Forster's *previous* influence over her work gains resonance when we consider the historical sequence of these two texts. We should also remember that by this time Forster had long since given up writing novels. It is typical of their relationship that Woolf takes matter that Forster has used, perhaps helping to edit it; but then she transmutes the idea, even creating a homosexual, the lesbian Miss LaTrobe, to be in charge of both writing and directing the pageant within the novel. Because he outlived Woolf, Forster had the final word, eulogizing his friend in the Rede Lecture at Cambridge after her death. But in her art Woolf—by transmuting such unlikely stuff into a novel that not only celebrates England but gives us a strong sense of the impending doom that she foresaw in *The Waves*—might well have established mastery over her most enduring literary friend and competitor.

Notes

1. See Gish for a discussion of the gendered nature of Forster's description.

2. Woolf first published "Is Fiction an Art" in the *New York Herald Tribune,* 16 October 1927. In 1928, the year after Forster delivered the Clark Lectures and published them as *Aspects of the Novel,* Woolf published *Orlando,* a novel that is self-consciously vast, spanning several countries and centuries. In one sense *Orlando* may be a response to Forster's comments on the provinciality of the English novel. It is also likely that Woolf could not resist a coded riposte to Forster about the place of "life" in the novel. Discussing such matters in the context of *Orlando* has an obvious double edge, since a "life" is also a biography.

3. According to Furbank, Forster was reacting to the shortened version published in *The Nation/Athenaeum* 12 Nov. 1927. Woolf discusses this exchange at some length in a diary entry:

> An odd incident, psychologically . . . has been Morgan's serious concern about my article on him. Did I care a straw what he said about me? Was it more laudatory? Yet here is this self-possessed, aloof man taking every word to heart, cast down to the depths, apparently, because I do not give him his superlative rank, & writing again & again to ask about it, or suggest about it, anxious that it shall be published in England. . . . Had I been asked, I should have said that of all writers he would be the most indifferent & cool under criticism. And he minds a dozen times more than I do, who have the opposite reputation.

(3: 152)

4. See "Jane Austen: The Letters" in *Abinger Harvest* 155-64.

5. In a prescient early essay published in 1937, Derek Traversi suggested the closeness in "technical devices" of Forster and Woolf.

6. Most of Forster's political essays are collected in *Two Cheers for Democracy.*

7. We are not surprised, then, that Forster cites and commends Bernard in the closing passage of the Rede Lecture, his final statement on Woolf: "The best I can do is quote Bernard again . . . Bernard puts it so well" (*Two Cheers* 258).

8. See Langland for an excellent reading of the sexual politics of *Howards End.*

9. Both houses are prepared for reoccupancy by housekeepers, Miss Avery in *Howards End* and Mrs. McNab in *To the Lighthouse,* the latter of whom is helped by a woman named Mrs. Bast.

10. In Forster's 1941 Rede Lecture on Woolf he compares "Kew Gardens" and "The Mark on the Wall" to impressionist painting: "Lovely little things, but they seemed to lead nowhere, they were all *tiny dots and coloured blobs*" (*Two Cheers* 246, our emphasis). Coupled with the accuracy of his description of Woolf's technique is Forster's failure to appreciate it *as* technique.

11. A variation on this image of "the pageant of existence" is identifiable in Forster's work as early as 1905, in his first novel, *Where Angels Fear to Tread,* when Philip Herriton comments at one of the moral cruxes of the novel: "I seem fated to pass through the world without colliding with it or moving it . . . life to me is just a spectacle" (151).

12. See how Woolf transmutes the idea of spectacle when she has Bernard muse in *The Waves*: "But for a moment I had sat on the turf somewhere high above the flow of the sea and the sounds of the woods, had seen the house, the garden, and the waves break" (287); and "When I look down from this transcendency, how beautiful are even the crumbled relics of bread!" (290). Note the similarity to Philip Herriton's comment quoted in note 11.

13. "Now to sum up," said Bernard. "Now to explain to you the meaning of my life. Since we do not know each other (though I met you once I think on board a ship going to Africa) we can talk freely" (238).

14. "Death is the enemy. It is death against whom I ride with my spear couched and my hair flying back like a young man's, like Percival's, when he galloped in India. I strike spurs into my horse. Against you I will fling myself, unvanquished and unyielding, O Death!" (297).

15. Forster seems to have enjoyed writing in this ephemeral genre. See "The Abinger Pageant" (1934), in *Abinger Harvest,* 347-63. He may also have been influenced by the pageants he observed during his lengthy stays in India.

Works Cited

Clayton, Jay, and Eric Rothstein, eds. *Influence and Intertextuality in Literary History.* Madison: U of Wisconsin P, 1991.

Dowling, David. *Bloomsbury Aesthetics and the Novels of Forster and Woolf.* London: Macmillan, 1985.

Duckworth, Alistair M. *Howards End: E. M. Forster's House of Fiction.* New York: Twayne, 1992.

Eksteins, Modris. *Rites of Spring: The Great War and the Birth of the Modern Age.* Boston: Houghton, 1989.

Forster, Edward Morgan. *Abinger Harvest.* New York: Harcourt, 1953.

————. *Aspects of the Novel.* New York: Harcourt, 1955.

————. *Commonplace Book.* Ed. Philip Gardner. London: Scolar, 1985.

————. *England's Pleasant Land.* London: Hogarth, 1940.

————. *Howards End.* New York: Bantam, 1985.

————. *A Passage to India.* New York: Harcourt, 1952.

————. *Two Cheers for Democracy.* New York: Harcourt, 1951.

————. *Where Angels Fear to Tread.* New York: Vintage, 1920.

Furbank, P. N. *E. M. Forster: A Life.* 2 vols. bound as 1. New York: Harcourt, 1978.

Gilbert, Sandra, and Susan Gubar. *The War of the Words.* New Haven: Yale UP, 1987.

Gish, Robert. "Mr. Forster and Mrs. Woolf: Aspects of the Novelist as Critic." *Virginia Woolf Quarterly* 2 (Summer-Fall 1975): 255-69.

Herz, Judith Scherer, and Robert K. Martin. *E. M. Forster: Centenary Revaluations.* Toronto: U of Toronto P, 1982.

Langland, Elizabeth. "Gesturing toward an Open Space: Gender, Form, and Language in E. M. Forster's *Howards End.*" *Out of Bounds: Male Writers and Gender(ed) Criticism.* Ed. Laura Claridge and Elizabeth Langland. Amherst: U of Massachusetts P, 1990.

Rosecrance, Barbara. "*Howards End.*" *E. M. Forster.* Ed. Harold Bloom. New York: Chelsea, 1987.

Traversi, Derek. "The Novels of E. M. Forster." *Arena* 1 (1937): 28-40.

Trivedi, H. K. "Forster and Virginia Woolf: the Critical Friends." *E. M. Forster: A Human Exploration: Centenary Essays.* Ed. G. K. Das and John Beer. London: Macmillan, 1979.

Woolf, Virginia. *Between the Acts.* New York: Harcourt, 1941.

————. *The Captain's Death Bed and Other Essays.* New York: Harcourt, 1950.

————. *The Diaries of Virginia Woolf.* Ed. Anne Olivier Bell. 5 vols. New York: Harcourt, 1977-84.

————. *The Essays of Virginia Woolf.* Ed. Andrew McNeillie. 3 vols. New York: Harcourt, 1986-88.

————. *The Letters of Virginia Woolf.* Ed. Nigel Nicolson and Joanne Trautman. 6 vols. New York: Harcourt, 1975-80.

————. *Mrs. Dalloway.* New York: Harcourt, 1985.

————. *Orlando.* New York: Harcourt, 1986.

————. *To the Lighthouse.* New York: Harcourt, 1981.

————. *The Waves.* New York: Harcourt, 1978.

Stuart Sillars (essay date 1999)

SOURCE: Sillars, Stuart. "*Howards End* and the Dislocation of Narrative." In *Structure and Dissolution in English Writing, 1910-1920,* pp. 31-61. New York: St. Martin's Press, Inc., 1999.

[*In the following essay, Sillars examines Forster's allusions in* Howards End *to other texts of the Edwardian period in England to gain an understanding of the novel's "duality."*]

In many ways, Forster's **Howards End** is the central text of the Edwardian years. I mean this not in the sense that it demonstrates values that are fundamental to the period—even though, as I shall later show, it addresses many of the age's main concerns—but rather in the sense that it demonstrates that duality of assertion and retreat, continuation and refusal, that I have claimed as the basic mode of so much writing of the time.

To call the structural principle at the heart of the novel a kind of irony would in some measure be valid, but it would also diminish the complexity of the discourse. This complexity has, I think, been the reason for a significant number of misreadings at the hands of otherwise sensitive critics. As Ann Wright has reflected, **Howards End** 'has been condemned for an arbitrary or inadequate motivation of plot or psychology, or for awkward transitions from narrative realism to utopian vision, and embarrassingly obtrusive symbolism' (2). Perhaps we should not be surprised that F. R. Leavis finds the novel a failure: for him, it 'exhibits crudity of a kind to shock and distress the reader as Mr. Forster hasn't shocked or distressed him before' (*The Common Pursuit,* 268-9). Presumably Leavis is referring to plot-events such as the appearance of the Basts at the wedding, and the coincidence of Jacky's having been Mr. Wilcox's mistress. What I find surprising here is not the bourgeois sense of the vulgarity of the characterisation but the apparent rejection of any possibility of the direction of plot to convey any meaning other than literal. Yet similar worries beset a more recent commentator, Norman Page, who asserts that the plot 'often seems extrinsic and almost fortuitous' (78) and advises that the novel 'might have benefited from being a little less heavily plotted'. This suggests that the precise nature of the plot's working has eluded many readers, and that it is this which has led to the misunderstanding of the novel and a failure to acknowledge its true status. This is, of course, true not only of the plot, since structure and discourse are inseparable: the novel's events, narratorial voice, characterisation, use of symbols and its discussion of the fundamental theme of the nature and future of England are all inseparably a part of its fundamental discursive and dialogic strategy.

Writing to A. C. Benson in the year of the book's publication, Forster says, 'I agreed with you that the book is poetical rather than philosophical' (119). This is a key remark, since it identifies the true nature of the novel's oppositional discourse: it is not that between two philosophical extremes, or that between philosophy and the supernatural, but that between an apparently materialist reading and one that is heavily poetic in the sense of being metaphoric, metonymic or—in a larger, structural dimension—mythically distanced from the constraints of a constructed reality. It is this which allows Forster to both continue and reject the mechanisms of the late-Victorian psychological-realist novel; and, paradoxically, his success at combining the two levels has led to the failure of many readers to grasp the novel's fundamental oppositions. How these function in practice can be made clear only by a detailed textual reading: yet before moving to this level of analysis we need first to establish some idea of the horizons of the first readers of this novel which addresses most directly the issues of its contemporaries. By this I do not mean the social and intellectual issues of England in 1910: these have been lengthily explored by several critics including Wiener, Carey and Hynes (1968). Instead, I refer to the allusions to styles and substances of many other texts, known to the novel's first readers but now largely forgotten, to which Forster not only makes reference in the book but which, as I shall hope to prove, are of very considerable importance in guiding our reading of the novel's complex duality.

II

If, as Jonathan Culler claims in *Framing the Sign,* every context is simply an enlargement of the text, in *Howards End* the text spreads outwards to both enrich and be enriched by the compound and complex elements of reference that traditionally might be termed its 'context'. The most significant single dimension of this process is the engagement with other texts which, though either only mentioned in passing or in some cases not explicitly cited at all in the novel, none the less are of major importance in its structure and ideas. Since these texts would have been powerfully apparent to the novel's original readers but are little read today, it makes sense to begin a study of the novel by exploring them and their contribution to key themes and patterns of Forster's book. This network of reference has particular relevance to three ideas which are generally seen as the most important of the novel: the 'only connect' motif of the epigram that signals a need to reconcile mercantile and aesthetic sensibilities; the discussion of the present and future state of England; and the perils and distortions of seeing life not through immediate experience but through the filter of literature in which the style and substance of avowedly artistic writing predetermines the experience that it apparently engenders. These ideas are, of course, inseparable both from each other and from the discursive structure of the novel.

This deliberative assimilation of other texts is part of the simultaneous acceptance and rejection of convention and

formula through which *Howards End* offers us a metafictional stance of a very specific kind. Crucial to this process, as it is to the novel's plot, is the encounter between the Schlegels and Leonard Bast. As representative of the urban, self-educating classes, Bast is presented as being keen to establish his literariness by repeatedly using books as the touchstones of the main events of his life. The Schlegels respond to this with ill-concealed intolerance, preferring to discuss issues of life itself. 'Helen and Tibby groaned gently' (115) at Bast's mention of Meredith and Stevenson, and Helen forestalls a discussion on the latter's *Virginibus Puerisque* by interjecting a nudge towards the actuality of Bast's experience, not its literary basis: 'Yes, but the wood. This 'ere wood' (117). The allegiances set up in this exchange are not only achieved by what the characters say. The narratorial voice, as so often, sides with the Schlegels when it tells us 'But culture closed in again' (116). Nor does the conspiracy against Bast end there: we, the readers, are made accomplices in this process of super-literary dismissal of vicarious journeying, since not only are we denied any other voice in response to Bast's novel-reading zeal but we are also, by this stage in the novel, drawn into the world of the Schlegel family through the common novelistic expedient of having been presented with things from their viewpoint for so long that we quite inevitably adopt their stance. That, however, is not all.

Howards End is a remarkably contemporary book, concerned with issues insistent and immediate when it was written. Since idea, style and literary context are inseparable in the novel, it also addresses the literary tastes of the period, something which may perhaps account for the difficulty that subsequent readers have had with it, and the resultant diminution in depth and quality of their responses. It is not only Bast's habit of seeing life through art that we are led to deplore: it is the kinds of writing that he chooses for the distorting lens. In consequence, the books that Bast takes for the texts of his address—there is a precise homiletic note to it, I think—become very important in our grasp of the novel's ideas and technique.

The first is George Meredith's *The Ordeal of Richard Feverel.* Though banned on its publication in 1859, and never subsequently regarded as amongst the writer's finest works, the novel nevertheless became part of the spectacular, but short-lived, revival in Meredith's fortunes which came about at the end of the century with the publication, by Chapman and Hall, of a collected edition beginning in 1885. By the century's close, Meredith was known to 'the whole number of those who pretended to culture or education':[1] by 1914, when public celebration had reached its peak with the publication of the Memorial Edition of his works in 1909-12, 'his kind of intellectualism had begun to appear facile and academic' (Williams 13). That Bast is reading Meredith's novel, and that the Schlegels are irked by his so doing, convey just this movement: it is a book both well-known to a general readership and considered *passé* by the thinking classes. Forster was at this time read by just such people as the Schlegels: to share the horizon of the original readers we should be aware of the prevailing attitude to *The Ordeal of Richard Feverel* as a novel at best of some worth at its publication but now outdated and read only by the petit-bourgeoisie, and at worst as a *succés de scandale* of which no serious reader would take cognizance. This, of course, drives us further towards the Schlegel camp: however much we may try to sympathise with Bast we become the precursors of Eliot's *hypocrite lecteur* in looking down our critical noses at what he chooses to read. What began as a literary value elides, in an undeniably English way, into a class division.

Yet we should not dismiss the Meredith as solely presented for this reason: there are a number of ways in which its plot, style and structure illuminate those of *Howards End.* Richard Feverel is disowned by his father, Sir Austin, when he marries Lucy Desborough, whom the baronet considers to be of inferior stock. Just the same has happened to Bast, albeit at a lower degree of the social scale: he has married Jacky, and been cast out by his family. Resemblance is countered by divergence: Lucy is, like so many Victorian heroines, poor but honest, whereas Jacky has earlier been seduced and abandoned. A similar pattern of resemblance and opposition is apparent in a further episode. Bast is 'seduced' by Helen Schlegel, an upper-middle-class woman of hitherto spotless reputation whose compassion spills over into physical comfort; Feveral is seduced by Bella Mountfalcon, a *demimondaine* who has been encouraged in the attempt by her estranged husband, who wishes in turn to seduce Lucy, Feverel's wife. At the close of Meredith's novel, Lucy dies, distraught at the wounding of her husband in a duel with Lord Mountfalcon; at the close of Forster's, Bast dies after the assault by Charles Wilcox. In both, the child is left as a figure of mingled renewal and desolation.

For the first readers of *Howards End,* these parallels and divergences would neither go unnoticed nor be wasted: they would set up a series of resonances and intimations about the novel's future course and moral temper. It is what, in Modernist terms, would be termed intertextuality, where allusion provides for us a complex of further layers of signification. Yet at the same time as registering these parallels and divergences a contemporary reader would be aware of the outdated and *déclassé* nature of Meredith in precisely the way expressed by Helen and Tibby: the allusions are there, used at a deep and perhaps subconscious level, but also rejected, in a further dimension of the continuity-refusal pattern that so dominates the text.

Much more apparent than these references is Bast's overt concern to model his own experience of the natural world on that of Richard Feverel: 'I wanted to get back to the Earth, don't you see, like Richard does in the end' (115). Bast is here referring to the passage near the novel's close where Richard is told that he has a son and, leaving his companions, walks through the countryside in a thunderstorm 'at Limburg on the Lahn' (503). Here again there are differences as well as similarities. Bast is actively seeking a oneness with nature itself, whereas Feverel finds,

quite unintentionally, a specific sense of his place in the natural world, as a result of learning that he is a father. Certainly, Feverel's ecstatic feelings towards the natural world—the Rhineland forest 'filling him with an awful rapture' (506), the brook, the glow-worms and the 'tiny leveret' (507) that he holds against him in shelter against the rain—are important; but they are so as a demonstration of his role as father, a kind of extended metaphoric network of paternal love, rather than the 'Earth'—a heavily mystical, literary construction—of which Bast wishes to become part. Getting back to the Earth is Bast's desire, and so he reads this passage as an example of the process: his desire leads him to read the novel in one particular way, not only seeing life through literature but distorting both in the process. It seems unlikely that readers of 1910 who knew Meredith's text would have been unaware of this distortion: certainly, it adds to the rather uncomfortable comedy of the scene, in which Schlegels, narrator and reader ally to look down on Bast's literary and experiential pretensions.

The reference to Meredith is certainly a use of earlier conventions of plot, symbol and allusion to enrich Forster's text, yet it becomes also something very different when we step back and consider the larger effect. Referring to one novel within another has much the same effect as presenting a play within a play: it makes the larger, encasing structure a kind of reality, within and against which the new fiction is presented. This very particular kind of metafiction is remarkable in its effect in *Howards End.* Reading the passage, we both grasp the qualified similarities between Bast and Feverel and look down with the Schlegels' tolerant but exasperated patronage at Bast for attempting to approach 'real life' through literature. Yet the novelistic references within this novel serve to make the encasing text—the fabric of Schlegels, Wilcoxes and Basts—seem more real, since the falsity of seeing life through literature can only be apparent if we discount the circumstance that we are, in fact, reading a novel, and instead attribute the quality of 'real life' to the inhabitants of *Howards End.* So we are drawn into the novel's world just as strongly as in any conventional psychological novel. But at the same time we are kept outside it—not only by the repeated manoeuverings of the narratorial voice, but also by our realisation of the metafictional nature of the 'novel within a novel' frame. Thus we are simultaneously involved in and excluded from a text that both develops and explodes conventions.

A further dimension of this is apparent when the structure of Meredith's novel is considered. A recurrent motif is the use of quotations from *The Pilgrim's Scrip,* a book of aphorisms composed by Sir Austin Feverel as the basis of the 'System' on which he grounds his son's education. He thus lives his own life and governs that of his son through a series of literary perceptions. At the close of the novel, though, when he realises that the System has failed, we learn that the volume also contains the following epigram: 'A maker of Proverbs—what is he but a narrow mind the mouthpiece of narrower?' (521). This is a clear rejection of the literary basis of life that has run throughout the novel, which greatly muddies the waters when we are considering the effect of the allusion in **Howards End.** Bast is basing his view of life on a book that not only itself bases life on literary *aperçus,* but which at its close forcefully rejects this approach. Once again, the pattern is both established and rejected for the reader who can follow through to the full extent of the allusion.

What is the effect of this on us as the novel's readers? Certainly it is to make us feel superior to Bast, who lives his life through a series of literary pre-visions. But just what are we doing while feeling this? Reading a novel. This realisation of our own complicity in the false strategy that we have up to now accepted is a shocking moment: it is almost one of Modernist alienation and exile, from the very text that might be expected to chronicle, rather than induce, such an emotion. That this takes place within and alongside the range of other more traditional techniques and responses of **Howards End** reveals once again the tense symbiosis of tradition and refusal.

The final piece in the jigsaw of allusion is provided by the authorial tone of *The Ordeal of Richard Feveral* and that of **Howards End.** The narrator's deliberative disengagement, quite clearly and at times quite ponderously setting himself apart from the characters' actions and motives, is just as apparent in Meredith as it is in Forster. Though different in mannerisms of style, the two books share the mingling tones of irony, patronage and dismissiveness in the direct address to the reader over the heads of the characters in passages that alternate with those in which a version of the conventional Victorian omniscient narrator speaks with customary unobtrusiveness. A Marxian critic might perhaps see this as an inevitable result of the rapid growth of the process of novel reading that followed social shifts as Forster's Education Act of 1870, and the various items of legislation culminating in the Public Libraries Act of 1892 which greatly extended the literary franchise. Forster's dismissive throw-away is a continuation of this: even in the aspect of the novel which appears most directly to reject tradition, Forster is following it, both by using the tradition of direct, self-ironic address used by other writers and by relying on the tradition of invisible narrator against which it rebels to give it much of its aesthetic shock effect.

This is signalled in another of the references made by Leonard Bast. The self-conscious tone of Forster's narrator can be heard to some degree in the voice used by Stevenson in *Prince Otto* (1885). Bast describes it as 'another beautiful book' (115) and claims 'You get back to the earth in that' (115)—again showing his own brand of nature-mystic reader-response. Yet as well as this reference to event and theme the allusion to narratorial voice is inescapable for those who, like the Schlegels and Forster's original readers, know Stevenson's book. Here, for example, is the first paragraph of the novel, which demonstrates the narrator's tone very well:

> You shall seek in vain upon the map of Europe for the bygone state of Grünewald. An independent principal-

ity, an infinitesimal member of the German Empire, she played, for several centuries, her part in the discord of Europe; and, at last, in the ripeness of time and at the spiriting of several bald diplomatists, vanished like a morning ghost. Less fortunate than Poland, she left not a regret behind her; and the very memory of her boundaries has faded.

(339)

The novel, subtitled *A Romance,* deals with imaginary nations and so cannot be compared too specifically with Forster's concerns, yet the tone is similar in many ways. The references to recent European history and the cynical thrust of the nation's playing her part in its discord; the assumption that the reader will recognise the half-quotation from *The Tempest* in the last sentence; the dismissive reference to 'bald diplomatists'—all these show an awareness of the reader as having both a grasp of the classics of English writing and a world-weary knowledge of international affairs. Similarly, the fall of the prose—in particular the antithesis between 'in the ripeness of time' and 'at the spiriting of several bald diplomatists'—suggests a writer addressing an audience accustomed to the delights of bathos as both a literary convention and a satirical device.

Such prose depends on an awareness of a shared convention between writer and reader that can be both extended and satirised at will, and above this an awareness that the activity being mutually undertaken is the construction of a literary entity. There are, as a later section of this chapter will show, parts of the narratorial voice in **Howards End** that make it uniquely significant, and certainly different in detailed application of techniques from the quoted passage. Yet the closeness to the inflection of the Stevenson, along with hints of a similar detachment in the Meredith, suggest that Forster is once more building on a technique familiar to his original readers and once more demonstrating a rejection that is another form of continuity.

One further instance of what we might call the novel's generative instability in its subversive continuation of convention is shown in the final text mentioned by Leonard Bast and the Schlegels' response to it. When he asks whether they have read E. V. Lucas' *The Open Road,* Helen responds 'No doubt it's another beautiful book, but I'd rather hear about *your* road' (116). Again the literary origin is dismissed in favour of the experience itself. The volume in question is an anthology of poetry and short prose passages concerned with the experience of nature, most particularly in the context of short excursions into the countryside undertaken by city-dwellers. First published in April 1899, it was reprinted that year and at least once each year before the outbreak of the First World War. Its exact intent is stated in the 'EXPLANATION' prefacing the first edition:

> This little book aims at nothing but providing companionship on the road for city-dwellers who make holiday. It has no claims to completeness of any kind: it is just a garland of good or enkindling poetry and prose fitted to urge folk into the open air, and, once there, to

keep them glad they came—to slip easily from the pocket beneath a tree or among the heather, and provide lazy reading for the time of rest, with perhaps a phrase or two for the feet to step to and the mind to brood on when the rest is over.

(Unnumbered prefatory pages)

This is remarkable in stating precisely the aim that the Schlegels so directly dismiss in Bast: to see the countryside through a filter of text, allusion and idea both before and during excursions into a land that, for Bast and the town-dwelling, town-bred clerks of whom he stands representative is relatively unknown and nearly exotic. Not only is Bast representative of this kind of reader: Lucas' anthology is representative of this kind of text. From the 1880s to 1914 large numbers of books were produced which adopt exactly this approach. R. L. Stevenson's *Songs of Travel* (1896) and W. H. Davies' *Autobiography of a Super-Tramp* (1908) are perhaps the most readily thought of, but to them we may add large numbers of literary guide books including the series written by E. V. Lucas himself which seem aimed far more at the armchair traveller than the genuine one. It is also important to remember that Edward Thomas's *The Heart of England* begins with the writer himself leaving the city and walking through the lines of suburban villas on his journey into the country: the first section of Lucas' anthology is headed 'The Farewell to Winter and the Town'. That these books became ends in themselves rather than fulfilling the aims set out by Lucas is evidenced, among other things, by the circumstance that a large quarto edition of *The Open Road,* with elaborately gold-blocked cover and sixteen full-colour tipped-in plates by Claude Shepperson, was produced by Methuen in 1913. It, too, contained the passage quoted above, its absurdity in its new framing only slightly moderated by the embarrassed explanation that the preface is to the 'first, or pocket, edition'.

Bast goes on to refer to another book which should be taken as part of the same convention and outlook, Stevenson's *Virginibus Puerisque* (1881). One of the *Other Papers* referred to in its title is 'Walking Tours', an essay which falls into precisely the same stance as the Lucas and its equivalents, aiming to enhance the pleasures to be found in a walking tour through literary contemplation of them. The volume's dedication asserts 'These papers are like milestones on the wayside of my life' (3), a claim which affirms the complex relation between literature and the country excursion while reversing the usual equation, emblematising literature in a journey instead of a journey in literature.

It is this sort of second-hand, middle-brow relocation of experience within literature that the Schlegels, the narrator and the original, educated reader of *Howards End* combine subtly but superciliously to reject. But not totally: even though the literary dream of oneness with nature and the clerkly longing for a Bank Holiday jaunt are looked down on, we are still made powerfully aware of their importance for Bast—indeed the two stances are interdepen-

dent. As we disengage from the characters and see the novel as a literary entity, we are aware of a further level at which the literary dream of rural idyll is perpetuated: we are ourselves *reading* an account of an experience of the country, even though Bast's walk is disappointing and he ends up cold, hungry and dislocated as the literary dream empties into actual meaning. Continuity and refusal are again fundamental, here in the fabrication of a key stance towards a key site of the novel, the individual's reaction to the countryside and the precise nature of that countryside at a time of rapid urban and commercial expansion. This must, of course, be seen in the novel's larger exploration of the mythic countryside: the more motor-cars, city manners and suburban villas invade, both literally and symbolically, the more we are aware of the ideal that they destroy, given further symbolic currency in the Purbeck Downs, Howards End itself and the quasi-mysticism of its guardian, Miss Avery. Yet here again the antithesis is continually qualified and deconstructed by the way that the symbolism is used.

Forster's use of texts in this fairly early stage of the novel is a supple warning against taking any single view of it, ideologically or structurally. Reading the novel within the frames both of these other texts and of their reading histories gives us some understanding of its subtle web of contradictions and continuities, enriching and confusing its patterns and meanings in a way that, as will become apparent, is typical of the text's identity. We might almost use a symbol that Forster touches on himself, and say that reading the novel resembles being driven in an Edwardian motor-car with the chauffeur's hands alternately on the 'advance' and 'retard' controls on the steering wheel. With this process in mind, and having established a little of the complex tone generated by Bast's references, we may now look in a little more detail at how Forster makes more deliberative, more manipulative, use of the narratorial voice in directing our responses.

III

'One may as well begin with Helen's letters to her sister' (1). Forster's throwaway beginning well demonstrates the specific identity of the narratorial voice of *Howards End.* In one sense, it is representative of a certain kind of English diffidence, a refusal to commit oneself ideologically or personally that conveys an aloofness so often interpreted as dilettante arrogance by the European observer, and perhaps more prevalent at pre-war Cambridge than in many other locales. But to see it simply as this is to misdirect one's reading of the novel towards a feeling that the narratorial voice is merely disengaged, superior, or philosophical in its relation to the characters. Paradoxically, this implies a reading that involves us with the novel's fictive population as real people akin to those inhabiting the pages of H. G. Wells or Arnold Bennett. And, as the book deals with things that are manifestly material—Forster's recurrent references to motor-cars, railways and the material attributes of houses, even though in contradistinction to their moral and affective values—it is easy to see this as an authorial voice that accepts the actuality of its characters even while distancing itself from them.

Clearly this is one dimension of the text—we have already seen how Forster manipulates our involvement with and separation from the characters in the structural and referential exploration of seeing life through literature. Yet if we approach it in a different way, this opening becomes a much stronger part of the novel's discourse. George Eliot's *Daniel Deronda* is important here, since it begins by voicing one of the key problems for the novelist: where to begin? The difference, though, is that Eliot raises this seriously and directly as a problem that must be addressed and shared with the reader before the novel. Forster, on the other hand, assumes that the reader is already aware of that problem, shows that he has his answer, and reveals through his tone the essentially arbitrary nature of all such decisions. He is admitting the reader into the secret that novel-writing is an improvisatory and imperfect business, implying that one might just as easily have begun in any of several other places. This is a novel, the narrator is proclaiming to the reader: we both know the problems involved, and the conventions used to solve them; in the process, I can both use and reject earlier solutions, both involve you with and distance you from the characters, and because you know about these matters you are as much a part of the process as I am.

This is the fundamental tone of the passage: it is as a writer speaking of a literary convention that he both accepts and wryly satirises that we should hear this voice, not as a writer speaking seriously of and to the characters who are his creations and about whom he knows everything, as does George Eliot. Seen thus, this first sentence makes clear one of the novel's key oppositions: between a continuance of tradition and its self-conscious rejection within the form and voice of the novel. That gives the text its characteristic note, but it also establishes its nature as poetical, in the first instance, rather than philosophical: always there is the distance imposed by the knowledge that this is a literary construct. Once we accept this, we can accept too the awareness of fracture that is implicit within it—fracture between the continuance of tradition and its satiric rejection, fracture between characters as 'real' people and embodiments of intellectual and emotional complexes, fracture between events as convincing happenings and moments in the mythic current of fable. Once we become aware of this, the problems with plot and character that have confronted some readers disappear—to be replaced by other, more troubling ones, of course, but at least these are ones proper to the novel's identity, not those foisted on it by literary misattribution.

The fundamental duality of the narratorial voice gives it very considerable freedom and range in its direction both of events and of our responses to them. Implicit within the idea of shared awareness of convention is a further concept of shared awareness of style, and this makes possible one of the most striking and, I think, one of the most neglected overtones of the voice. It needs to be heard as both

serious and as parodic of a number of other voices—in some cases generic, in others specific—and conventions of the contemporary novel. Only by holding in balance this duality will the reader grasp the identity of the discourse and thus understand the oppositional tension of the novel. We have already seen how the texts mentioned by Leonard Bast signal this kind of reading: further sections of this chapter will show other registers to which the voice alludes. For the original reader, the echoes would have been quite clear; for the reader of many decades later, they reveal—but do not simplify—the complexity of attitude and in consequence remove many of the charges of pomposity, obscurity, sentimentality or incomplete social and political awareness that have been laid against the novel.

This complexity is apparent in the voice of the narrator throughout the novel. Forster's comment 'We are not concerned with the very poor' (43) illustrates the paradox well. It is in one sense a direct address about the novel's circumstance, but in its cavalier rejection of a whole social caste it satirises the whole business of authorial selection. To charge it with a lack of social compassion is to overlook its literary self-consciousness and self-irony. For the skilled readers the novel is addressing, this line inevitably recalls another celebrated exclusion clause: 'Let other pens dwell on guilt and misery'. By making such an allusion even by inference, Forster is continuing a tradition while at the same time rejecting it in the self-conscious relation he suggests towards his characters and his readers. Those who see the line as evidence of the novel's narrow canvas and shallow conscience fail to recognise that implicit within it is a questioning of the process of selectivity and exclusion that is basic to the novel as genre: it contains the deconstructive questions, why are we not concerned with the very poor, and who in any case constitutes this apparently very exclusive 'we'?

The complex dualities of the narratorial voice are complemented by the control of the plot, in particular the combination of vagueness and unlikelihood with which the novel is often charged. I read these elements instead as an elaborate mechanism geared to reminding us that we are reading a novel, balancing and offsetting our involvement with the characters at moments when we are beginning to be drawn into the fictive world. This reading allows us to see *Howards End* as a parable: the poetic elements of metaphor and event are revealed in their true identity and we are in consequence forced to consider the larger ideas for which they stand as representatives—the condition of England, the nature of the heart's affections, and the need to 'only connect'. That we do this by being made forcefully aware of the novel's nature as a literary construct is, of course, an embodiment of the novel's other concern with which we have already become acquainted: the need not to see events through a literary filter but as they actually are in the confusion of experience—although, of course, it is still as a literary construct that we see them.

After an account of the removal of Margaret's possessions from her London flat, for example, the narrative voice begins a paragraph with the sentence, 'Shortly before the move, our hero and heroine were married' (254-5). This is disconcerting for the conventional novel reader, and for several reasons. First, the order is reversed so as to be almost comic: the move becomes the important objective, to which the marriage is merely a preface. In a more traditional novel this might well suggest that the real significance of the ceremony is as an alliance of property; but this is unlikely because of the paragraph's subsequent references to Margaret's feelings for her husband. The strange order is contradicted by the use of the terms 'hero and heroine', which suggests a conventional, populist tone of address between author and characters. The result of all of this is a mingled acceptance and rejection, statement and ironic undercutting, of the relationship: we are both offered the couple as the real people of the contemporary materialist novel and distanced from them by the sentence's obtrusiveness as literary language, and once again continuation and refusal of the genre is the dominant note.

Something very similar is seen just after the proposal, where the narrator refers to 'Mr. Wilcox, or, as I must now call him, Henry' (174). Again there is the same self-deprecating tone, suggesting that the speaker is merely playing a part to which he is unused and of which he is self-consciously embarrassed. That it also shows a subtle awareness of the nuances of English social address again simultaneously draws us into the world of the novel and holds us at arm's length from it: continuity and refusal work together again.

This brings us back to Forster's reply to A. C. Benson, and makes clear exactly in what way the book needs to be seen as poetic rather than philosophical. The poetic equation is not between character or setting and metaphoric equivalent; it is between a literary convention self-consciously presented in such a way as to imply its rejection and the events or characters that the convention presents. Forster uses the structural fault-lines of a dying literary convention to explore and exploit ideas about the novel's themes. In this, the novel's structure is metaphoric of a cultural and human malaise, while the novel's characters are metonymic of a similar phenomenon; in consequence, the text offers us both Victorian certainty and a rather later confusion, but it is only the reader who accepts this internal instability who may fully grasp the novel's achievement.

IV

A further dimension of the novel's use of a poetic structure to reveal both literary and social dysfunctions and discontinuities is apparent in its use of symbolism, another area much criticised as clumsy. Forster's symbols are quite deliberate in their crudity, to borrow Leavis's term, for a very specific reason. Only in that way may they draw attention to themselves, reveal themselves as part of a literary artifice, bring that artifice into discussion and doubt, and force us to address the problem of how the social ills they discuss might be better engaged.

One of the most direct forms of this symbolic currency is the naming of the characters. In this, the novel works within a long tradition of giving characters names emblematic of their nature. Dickens' Bradley Headstone suggests the dark, funereal nature of its holder; Brontë's Jane Eyre, lightness and purity; Hardy's Angel Clare, a divine translucency that takes on ironic proportions as the plot continues. *Howards End* both extends and caricatures this tradition. The Schlegel sisters, Helen and Margaret, share the name of one of the more significant German philosophers of the early Romantic movement, and this is made much more explicit when Forster describes their father as 'the countryman of Hegel and Kant, as the idealist, inclined to be dreamy, whose Imperialism was the Imperialism of the air' (26). Thus from very early on the philosophical nature of one half of the novel's human opposition is suggested. Yet, as we learn from the sisters' discussion sessions and their encounters with the Wilcox family, their philosophy is far from clear: indeed, Helen accuses her brother of surrendering too easily to the materialist forces represented by the Wilcoxes. In consequence the reference is made to appear both direct and parodic. The manuscript of the novel (26) has the sisters as direct descendants of the philosopher, and the change from this to something more imprecise seems a fitting index of the text's larger ambivalence—as well, of course, as revealing and reinforcing the complicity between narrator and assumed reader in the silently accepted knowledge of the actual historical figure.

It is the forenames of the two Schlegel sisters that most clearly embody a continuation and an ironic refusal of the tradition. Lionel Trilling was the first to mention that Margaret and Helen are the heroines of the first and second parts of Goethe's *Faust,* 'one the heroine of the practical life, the other of the ideal life' (134). Nicola Beauman points out that 'Margaret means "pearl" and Helen means "the bright one"' (220 n.). Both suggestions need to be taken further. Margaret is a Gretchen who finds, in Henry Wilcox, a severely flawed Faust: since Trilling also points out that Henry was the first name of Goethe's central character. Looked at in this light, both she and her husband reveal new degrees of incompleteness, as Margaret's pearl is flawed and Henry's Faustian energy neither fully realised in the novel's course nor fully defeated at its close. The Greek *helios* from which Helen's name comes is in her case a bringer not of light but of confusion; and the parallel with Helen of Troy is at best severely strained and at worst satirically parodied in her involvement with Bast—no Paris he, nor even Menelaus. Helen launches not a thousand ships but a doomed crusade against Henry Wilcox and what he represents; and she is not so much Leonard's lover as a sisterly comforter whose ministrations take a drastically wrong course. Their brother's name is also important: 'Tibby' suggests something short and ineffectual, almost like Fielding's Blifil: the irony is that the philosophical family has come to such indecisiveness in its male heir, who is attending University.

By contrast, Henry Wilcox bears a name that sounds earthbound and forthright, compounded of a diminutive of William and the Old English *cocca,* suggesting leadership but also aggression or lust. All of these later significances are quite appropriate to the Wilcox who seduces and betrays Jacky, who is authoritarian in his dealings with Margaret and Helen and thoughtless in his advice to Leonard, and who can only 'improvise' his emotions (243). These qualities are offset by his first name Henry, derived from the Germanic *haim ric,* meaning home ruler. This suggests a further degree of arrogance, yet perhaps in a more positive dimension when we recall the use of the name for a line of English kings. Ironically this suggests something of an ancient lineage; yet any sense of antiquity or belonging to country places is explicitly refused later in the novel: 'But the Wilcoxes have no part in the place, nor in any place. It is not their names that recur in the parish register' (246). Henry's son, Charles, takes his name from the Old English *ceorl,* meaning man: but one of its cognates is churl, and we are thus given a sense of the inner contradictions of the character. Taken together, the uses and significances of the Wilcox name constantly contradict and undermine each other, echoing the complexity of plot, character and idea in the novel in a use of a literary convention that goes far beyond the more specifically directed significance it has for the Victorian novelist.

Leonard Bast, too, has a significant name. The short surname is redolent of something terse, incomplete, and of no known root. It is also the first syllable of the word 'bastard', suggesting the rootlessness of the character that is made clear in the discussion of his family with the Schlegel sisters and emphasised in his desire to see everything through books. Yet in his own way he is noble: his treatment of Jacky has about it a note of leonine intensity that is central to the novel's rejection of the hypocrisy of upper-class sexual morality. The forename Leonard, suggesting the bravery and hardiness of a lion, originated in England with the Normans: St. Leonard is the patron saint of peasants and horses. Taken together, these suggest a nobility towards lesser creatures which seems manifestly ironic in the light of Bast's early behaviour, but is in one specific way central to the novel.

This duality becomes clear when we consider the name of Bast's wife, Jacky. At the time of the novel's production, this could only be a diminutive of Jacqueline. In its abbreviation it is an abstract of her history and treatment. After the wedding, when Margaret confronts Henry about how Jacky knows his name, we learn that Jacky was Henry's mistress ten years before, in Cyprus. Earlier, we have been told that she is 'not respectable' (48): now, we are told why. Yet what is most significant is that she has been seduced and rejected by Henry Wilcox, and that Leonard has remained faithful to her despite being cut off by his family. This is indeed a reversal of the usual class-based code of honour, and reveals once again the bankruptcy of the Wilcoxes' moral standards: just as the Imperial and West African Rubber company takes what it wishes from the trees in Cyprus and then departs, so has Henry taken what he wishes of Jacky and then refused any responsibility for her. The name in this context is wholly appropriate: it re-

places the aristocratic completeness of Jacqueline with a diminutive that suggests patronising intimacy in an adult, exactly the kind of treatment she has received from Henry, and an infantile dependency, of the kind she shows towards Leonard, even at one stage sitting childlike on his lap. Her infantilisation and cheapening has been at the hands of the male imperialist establishment, and her name is emblematic of this. That a technique from the high Victorian novel should be used to show the rejection of the values implicit within a good deal of that literary convention shows the subtlety of the novel's subversion of symbolic convention.

The most striking use of names comes with Helen's child. It is historically sound that he is referred to only as 'Baby', but deeply fitting to the inconclusiveness of the novel's ending and the child's ambiguous place in the succession that he should have no name; legally he is illegitimate and will not carry on his father's line, giving another dimension of rootlessness to the Basts and extending the quality forwards in the Schlegels.

Symbolism is important not only in names but also in key points of the novel's unfolding. Here, symbolic discourse functions at a simple and momentary level—that is, it presents us with the kind of metaphoric pairings that we might expect to find in a poem. Perhaps this quality lay behind Forster's own account of the book as primarily poetic: certainly the symbolism has drawn much critical attention in the way that it addresses the issue of the contemporary condition of England, and much adverse comment about its apparent crudity. Here again, such comment overlooks the generic criticism implicit in the text's structures. Symbols are used in a manner that reveals and invites an awareness of their inadequacy and instability: alongside the apparent value that they present in terms of a commentary upon character and issue, there is a counter-thrust revealing their own artifice, a self-consciously ironic use of a key technique of the Victorian materialist novel that reveals its inadequacy for the task it apparently sets itself. This can be seen with particular clarity by looking closely at four symbolic strands: those which make use of motorcars, hay-fever, Teddington Lock and the Schlegel family sword as their signifiers.

Images of motor-cars are important throughout the novel. The intrusive nature of the machine is established early on, in the visit of Aunt Juley to Howards End. When she is driven to the house by Charles Wilcox, a 'cloud of dust' had 'whitened the roses and gooseberries of the wayside gardens' and 'entered the lungs of the villagers' (16): Charles' only response is to ask 'I wonder when they'll learn wisdom and tar the roads' (16). Here the car emblematises the destruction of the countryside by the new order of which the Wilcoxes are part and which, later, is forcefully rejected by the Schlegels, most notably when Margaret jumps from a moving car to go to the aid of a cat that has been run over. These are conventional uses of symbol, but the insistent repetition lends them a force which makes obtrusive their nature as symbols, so that once more the inadequacy of the traditional structure is revealed.

As the novel progresses, this compound use of the motor-car symbol becomes more sophisticated. We are told, for example, that 'the car ran silently like a beast of prey' (286). On the surface this continues the antagonism to motor-cars that is apparent—save in the Wilcox family—throughout the novel: they contain, it implies, something atavistic and destructive. But a moment's thought will reveal the self-conscious absurdity of the metaphor. A beast of prey, whatever else it may be, is natural and instinctive, two things which a motor-car is manifestly not, and two things whose absence Margaret Schlegel much deplores in the world of the Wilcoxes. The image, then, is superficially attractive but intrinsically flawed. Yet the flaw is its essence: it forces us to remember that the mode of discourse that includes easy metaphors of this sort is itself fractured and inadequate. The tradition in which Forster is writing is outrunning itself, and being held up for at least conscious interrogation if not outright rejection.

The same is true of the description of Wilcox's Ducie Street house in the line 'it was as if a motor-car had spawned' (160). Here the absurdity of the metaphor is more obvious: indeed, one might say that the disparity between the tenor and vehicle is so great as to make the image self-consciously ridiculous. Spawning is an activity associated with fish, essentially organic and small; motor-cars are essentially inorganic and large. We can read it as another instance of Forster's dismissive self-irony, the product of the same Cambridge *hauteur* which we may discern in the novel's opening: but it is more serious than that. The image draws attention to itself as a metaphor that does not work: its not working is itself an index of the absurdity of the tradition of literary metaphor, and that is by extension an image of the absurdity of the building.

These short moments of symbolic dysfunction maintain the tone of distance and dislocation in the reader's progress through the journey of the novel, and also work at a deeper structural level in revealing the novel's ideas. The same is true of the images concerning hay-fever which emblematise the relationships between different characters and the land. At the very start of the novel, we learn that Charles Wilcox and his father both suffer from hay-fever, as does Tibby, but that they are 'brave' (2) about it: not only does this suggest that the land is inimical to all the male characters, but it also implies that the businessmen are better able to deal with it, at once stressing the displacement of the Wilcoxes from the land and the feeling of admiration that Helen has for them. By contrast, Ruth Wilcox enjoys the smell of the hay and, when she returns to the house, 'there was actually a wisp of hay in her hands' (19). Near the novel's close, Margaret tells Miss Avery that Henry will not live at Howards End. Her response is 'Oh, indeed. On account of his hay-fever?' (269). A little later, she tells how she has seen Charles Wilcox go out to give precise, pompous instructions to the haymakers but was forced to

return because of 'the tickling', and goes on to claim 'There's not one Wilcox that can stand up against a field in June' (270). That Miss Avery, the custodian of the spirituality of rural England, should say this gives it added force: yet it is, once again, a symbol that is quite deliberately clumsy as a way of stressing the incompatibility of the Wilcoxes and the true identity of the land. This is, I think, in no way undercut when Margaret replies that Tibby, too, suffers from hay-fever. Forster's repeated qualification of the novel's terms of opposition is present here alongside the symbol, and his use of it in both contexts is further evidence of how it functions as a deliberately crude embodiment of a literary technique that is weary and outmoded, inadequate as a way of conveying the complex levels of intellectual and social change that are being approached, and in essence addressed poetically, not philosophically.

A larger symbolic statement that is of equal crudeness has occurred earlier in the book. When the Schlegels emerge from a dinner party that is 'really an informal discussion club' (123) they encounter Henry Wilcox on Chelsea Embankment. After establishing his protective patronage towards the women through his talking down to them about overseas trade, the narrator goes on to establish the Thames as a symbolic entity for both groups of characters:

> The world seemed in his grasp as he listened to the river Thames, which still flowed inland from the sea. So wonderful to the girls, it held no mysteries for him. He had helped shorten its long tidal trough by taking shares in a lock at Teddington, and, if he and other capitalists thought good, some day it could be shortened again.

> (129)

Henry's shortening of the Thames is a symbol of his lack of sympathy with the natural rhythms of the world: instead of the tides, his interest is with trade, and he regulates and enforces the river instead of feeling wonder towards it. The symbol is obvious, and in some measure clumsy: once more it demonstrates the inadequacy of the old literary conventions at the same time as employing them. Yet it takes the process a stage further. Despite Stallybrass's dismissal of the reference as anachronistic (note to 129, 360) Teddington Lock is an actual project, begun in 1890 and opened on 11 June 1904, although it was publicly and not privately funded. An obelisk marking the boundary between the Thames Conservancy and the Port of London Authority was erected in 1909, and it may have been this which, occurring while Forster was working on the novel, caught his attention and led to its inclusion. The absurdity and crassness of Forster's metaphor comes not from an outmoded literary imagination but from an actual event that denies awareness of its own symbolic absurdity. The literary, the literal and the collapse of a symbolic tradition are imploded together in this synecdochic detail of character and action.

The complex ambivalence of symbolism and the careful distancing caused by the direction of the plot come together most significantly in Leonard Bast's death. That he is first beaten by Charles Wilcox with the flat of the sword, and then collapses beneath a shower of Margaret's books, can be read symbolically in many ways. Those who live by the sword shall die by it, and those who live by books shall die, or at least be offered no extenuation of life, by them. The sword is representative of the Wilcoxes' arrogance and imperialist dreams; the books, of Bast's inability to live in daily actuality, but only through literary images, and even then failing to find them satisfying. Those who criticise this symbolic episode for its crassness are missing the point: it must be crass, since the failure of metaphor is by now established as one of the novel's key devices.

A clue to this is given by Charles' words just before he attacks Leonard: 'I now thrash him within an inch of his life' (321). This is the language of Victorian melodrama, not of actuality. An awareness of this different register has been sown in our minds many pages earlier, in Margaret's response to Henry's proposal: '"Oh, sir, this is so sudden"—that prudish phrase exactly expressed her when her time came' (162). In her use of the words of the surprised heroine, Margaret lapses into the language of the popular melodrama. Yet the parallel is ironic: for Margaret the statement completely sums up her surprise, but she is aware of it as not only prudish but a stock phrase or cliché while Charles lacks any similar awareness. The two stand as foils for one another in revealing the characters' awareness, and lack of awareness, of the parodic registers of language, and once again convention in its rejection is used to emblematise the moral polarities of the novel. Charles is unable to grasp the complexities of the personal relationships between Leonard, Jacky, his father and Helen Schlegel, and so resorts to the cliché of popular theatre—incidentally providing another instance of the Wilcoxes' philistinism. In a moment of crisis, he turns to the language of melodrama: this is part of the larger structural pattern of the novel at this point, turning as it does upon symbolic action that is crude and superficial. That the web of relations is outside the grasp of the characters is simultaneously beyond the power of the traditional narrative to handle or control: the action collapses into melodramatic cliché and obvious symbolism. Once more, both reveal the inadequacy of literary tradition through the dialogic relation between symbol and action.

V

The largest evidence of symbolic continuation and refusal is contained in the overall movement of the novel. This can be seen in the two devices employed to direct the plot: the narratorial voice that we have encountered already in the opening of the novel, and the dynamic generated by the chain of events that are presented seemingly without such comment. In a very powerful sense, the novel represents some version of a Shakespearean romance pattern that moves through contradiction and uncertainty, with both potential and actual reversal, towards a closure of resolution and renewal. In the mature Shakespearean struc-

ture, the close involves imagery of the renewal of the natural cycle alongside the birth of an heir or the promise of procreation. Leaving aside the qualified use of this pattern that we have already encountered in *The Ordeal Of Richard Feverel,* such a cycle may be seen, for example, at the end of *Adam Bede,* that most popular of serious Victorian novels, which would have been well known to Forster's readers, and which closes with a sense of renewal in the presence of a new generation within the growing countryside that might be regarded as the novel's largest symbolic dynamic. Overall, in this model of completion, characters are defined and enriched through the self-knowledge obtained by other-knowledge, extremes of immature zeal are countered in experience, and there is hope of continuity in both nature and humanity.

To an extent, the same pattern is present in the final pages of ***Howards End.*** There is the image of the house itself standing firm; the harvest is in progress; Helen's baby, image of the future, is not only playing in the fields (no Wilcox symbolic allergies here) but playing with Tommy, the farmer's child, showing a human bond beyond social class. For a moment we may feel, with Helen, that 'the racket and torture this time last year' (336) are truly gone. Yet so many forces run counter to this resolution that it is not so much a matter of its being deeply qualified but of its being presented as parodic of the kind of ending familiar from *Adam Bede.* The earlier death of Leonard Bast does not necessarily deprive us of a romance closure—it might, indeed, enhance it through offering the idea of renewal in the face of loss. But the usual idea of continuity within ending—the king is dead, long live the king—is severely qualified by the child's illegitimacy. Helen's child is certainly a figure of renewal, but he is heir to Margaret, his aunt, rather than to Leonard, his father, so that any continuity there may be is derived from a wholly unexpected quarter. Furthermore, the child is heir only in the face of the protests of the younger Wilcoxes, and at great cost to Margaret: we are told by Henry Wilcox that she will leave the house 'to her—to her nephew, down in the field' (339). That he cannot find the right word for the child here shows the fracture of any genuine continuity, and the final denial of oneness between the novel's poles. That the house belongs to Margaret, and not Helen, reminds us of Bast's own disinheritance and rootlessness as well as of Helen's unmarried state.

This is balanced by a further parodic irony. It is Paul Wilcox who is presented as the inheritor, and of the Wilcox family business, not of the natural world, a circumstance the symbolic significance of which is revealed in his own words as he rejects with ill grace the idea of his inheriting Howards End: 'As I've given up the outdoor life that suited me, and have come home to look after the business, it's no good my settling down here' (338). The 'outdoor life', of course, is that of the colonies: it is not the nurture of his own land in the true romance sense that Paul sees himself as being forced to relinquish, but the exploitative process of business imperialism that he and his father have championed throughout. Nor is he in truth relinquishing it, merely declaring what was true all along: that his interest is in the 'country' as an economic index rather than as an equation between nature and humanity.

The symbolic limitation is continued in the imagery of the natural world that surrounds the house. The crop, we are told, is not sweetening, but withered: that Margaret's assertion that 'it will sweeten tomorrow' is both symbolic and defiantly optimistic is revealed by Helen's reply 'Oh, Meg, you are a person' (336). But the crop is not wheat or corn but hay—the substance to which all the Wilcoxes and Tibby are allergic, and a crop that is merely sustenance for animals rather than the symbolic staff of life. Even though it is of record proportion, we are left unsatisfied because 'it'll be such a crop of hay as never!' (340). The 'never' suggests that the crop is imaginary, and adds a swinging deconstructive thrust to the idea of the crop's size. Here as throughout the novel, symbols are egregious in their failure: they draw attention to their own inadequacy and that of the literary form of which they constitute a self-conscious, parodic continuation.

VI

All of these examples reveal very clearly the novel's use of conventions, refusals and implosions as its major structural thrust. Their full significance becomes clear only when we address what for many is the main purpose of the novel: its exploration of the current state of the English nation.

Peter Widdowson, who sees the novel as a kind of fictive history, describes it as a 'vision, in 1910, of traditional Liberal England, beset by dangerous, destructive forces, finally prevailing through a realistic, "modern" liberal-humanism, which makes "connections" with other powerful, supportive forces, and leavens them with its values' (86-7). This reading is certainly valid in its references to 'dangerous, destructive forces' but simplistic in its suggestion that liberal-humanism has conquered. The novel's ending is far too ambiguous for that. In any case, such simplicity of closure would argue against the self-deflating complexity of tone and structure seen throughout the book. The account of England is indeed serious, but it is fugitive in vision and inconclusive in argument in ways which considerably enrich the texture of the novel and deepen the reader's engagement in its debate.

To grasp this fully, we need to be aware not only of the peculiarity of tone of the novel's discourse but also of the historical moment of the novel's writing. Just as much as it rests on its readers' knowledge of contemporary literary tastes and their social stratification, it depends on our awareness of the state of the nation. When the novel first appeared, the idea of English identity and the nature of England was the subject of considerable debate. To accuse it of failing adequately to convey its message about the survival of Liberal England is seriously to misunderstand this: it is not a solution to the problem, but a discussion of both the circumstances and dangers that constitute it, and

of the validity of offering such a discussion through a literary medium. As in each of his novels, Forster has no ready, easy answers. Here again the novel's voice, and the other voices to which it makes parodic reference, are crucial, since only when read with an ear to this multivalence of tone does the novel reveal its full complexity as both a contribution to the debate and a wry commentary upon it as a purely literary activity.

Many commentators have drawn parallels between Forster's novel and the most celebrated discussion of the nation, C. F. G. Masterman's *The Condition of England,* which was first published in 1909. Yet, as with the references made by Leonard Bast, a closer look at the text will reveal a much deeper connection between it and the novel. That Forster knew the book is, I think, beyond doubt, even though there are no references to it in his letters: Masterman's text first appeared as a series of essays published in *The Independent Review,* the journal founded and produced by a group of Cambridge academics including G. M. Trevelyan, Forster's tutor Nathaniel Wedd and Masterman himself. Forster contributed to the journal, and it is barely conceivable that he would not have read material on a subject of such close interest to him. Between 1909 and 1911, *The Condition of England* went into four editions: the book had a wide circulation and was clearly well known to contemporary readers.

Reading the novel with an ear attuned to Masterman's prose allows us to hear its resonances within Forster's writing, which significantly alter the novel's final effect. Instead of making the pronouncements on England, suburbia, class or inheritance sound pompous and sentimental, it places them within a kind of buffer: they are offered, parodically, as examples of the kind of solutions that were being presented at the time, rather than being directly advanced. Once again, the novel makes its points in a self-conscious manner, distancing itself and the reader from taking responsibility for them as final judgements. It thus becomes both a contribution to the debate and a statement of its own ineffectiveness and in this way it reveals finally and quite inescapably, through its structure, that the falsity of living through literature applies to the business of making larger socio-political judgements as well as to the more localised affair of experiencing a beautiful sunrise. Bast's expedition through a home counties generated by Lucas and Stevenson fails just as clearly, and for the same reasons, as the narrator's attempt to solve the contemporary problems of England through contributing to a literary debate: the dual inadequacies form a powerful, if paradoxical, statement of the conflicts between life and art.

Masterman's imagery is familiar to anyone who knows the text of **Howards End.** He writes of the annexation of the country by city dwellers, the frenzied activity that this creates and the rural habits that it threatens, in terms that closely mirror Forster's images of despoliation and his tone of distanced despair. The following passage might have come from either text:

> Behind the appearance of a feverish prosperity and adventure—motors along all the main roads, golf-courses,

game-keepers, gardeners, armies of industrious servants, excursionists, hospitable entertainment at country house-parties—we can discern the passing of a race
of men.

(160-1)

That it comes from Masterman's is perhaps discernible
only in the awkwardness of 'hospitable entertainment'.
Close comparison is often revealing. Here is Masterman
on the spread of suburbia:

Villas and country houses establish themselves in the
heart of this departing race: in it, but not of it, as alien
from its ancient ways as if dropped from the clouds
into another world.

(173-4)

And here, *Howards End* on the Wilcoxes:

Day and night the river flows down into England, day
after day the sun retreats into the Welsh mountains, and
the tower chimes 'See the Conquering Hero'. But the
Wilcoxes have no part in the place, nor in any place. It
is not their names that recur in the parish register. It is
not their ghosts that sigh among the alders at evening.
They have swept into the valley and swept out of it,
leaving a little dust and a little money behind.

(246)

In places, the likenesses are even more striking, and go
further to extend the idea of a debate. Masterman frequently quotes the writings of other commentators, most
long-forgotten today but urgent at the time of writing. In
one passage he refers to a sentence from *Towards Social
Reform*, by Canon and Mrs Barnett:

Yet his final conclusion is that 'the working class is the
hope of the nation, and their moral qualities justify the
hope'.

(122)[2]

Compare this with a passage from near the close of
Howards End:

Here men had been up since dawn. Their hours were
ruled, not by a London office, but by the movements of
the crops and the sun. That they were men of the finest
type only the sentimentalist can declare. But they kept
to the life of daylight. They are England's hope.

(320)

What matters here is not so much the specific echo—
'England's hope'—but the longer parallels of tone and
idea, the former measured and distanced, the latter deeply
concerned with what Masterman calls 'the crumbling and
decay of English rural life, and the vanishing of that "yeoman" class' (75). Unless we hear the voice of Forster's
narrator as a contribution to this debate, and one damped
by a note of self-conscious parodic reference, we lose the
peculiar intensity that this distancing contains and see it,
within the movement of the novel's plot and symbolism,
as sentimental or contrived.

This parallelism is apparent in relation to another major
genre of writing of the time. This is the convention of
'country writing' which had developed at the end of the
nineteenth century in response to the sense of displacement from rural roots felt largely by suburb-dwelling English men and women. Yet the exile is more imagined than
real. It is no chance coincidence that the major figures of
this convention—Richard Jefferies, E. V. Lucas, even Edward Thomas—were not born and bred in the country but
were products of the new suburbs or emerging urban
sprawls. Along with the voice of liberal conscience, the
voice of falsely-rooted rural celebration needs to be heard
as part of the dialogic debate implicit within Forster's text.
This opposition, implicit but not stated, silent yet eloquent,
is fundamental to the discussion of England and English-
ness that runs throughout the novel. As with the references
to Meredith, Lucas and Stevenson, the silences of the text
that were audible to its first readers need to be made explicit for later generations, and only by placing ourselves
before the intellectual horizon of a reader of 1910 may we
fully grasp the nature of the novel's sometimes parodic,
sometimes serious use of these other voices.

Seen thus, and with the contemporary volumes of country
writing about England strongly in our minds, the celebrated
discussion of the Purbeck Hills at the opening of Chapter
19 (164-5)—literally as well as figuratively at the very
centre of the book—is one of many passages that adopt a
wholly different conspectus. It is first important to hear the
shift of voice that takes place between the end of the preceding chapter and the start of that discussing the Purbeck
Hills. From the vague, rather fey allusiveness of Mrs Wilcox swaying in and out and observing the proposal scene
we move to something which imposes a far greater rhetorical distance between speaker and reader. The narrator
returns to the impersonal 'one' of the very opening of the
novel, an impersonality that betrays class roots as well as
linguistic ones since it is the idiom used by the English
upper classes to avoid the vulgarity of personal expression. But this is not the main significance, which is to
move us into the register of the country-piece.

In this context it is revealing to look at a contemporary account of substantially the same landscape. Macmillan began publishing its *Highways and Byways* series at the turn
of the century, and by 1914 had twenty-five volumes in
print. *Highways and Byways in Dorset* appeared in 1906:
it was written by Sir Frederick Treves, Bart—not a countryman but instead, as the title-page proclaims, 'Sergeant
Surgeon to H. M. the King; Lord Rector of the University
of Aberdeen'. This is Treves on the Isle of Purbeck:

The Isle of Purbeck is no more an island than is the
Isle of Thanet. . . . A view over the whole of the apoc-
ryphal island can be obtained from the summit of
Creech Barrow. This is a graceful, isolated, cone-shaped
hill near Wareham, so like in shape to a volcano that
when the light hearted tripper sets fire to the gorse and
bracken which cover its sides the belief that there is a
Vesuvius in Purbeck could gain ground. . . . From the
summit of the hill is a view of the Purbeck Downs,

from Ballard Head to Lulworth, while over their broad, smooth backs glitters the blue of the Channel. Southwards too are the Poole estuary, the cliffs and crude villas of Bournemouth, and beyond, drawn in faint grey, the Priory of Christchurch by the sea. To the North, among the generous green of water-meadows, a patch of deep red marks the roofs of Wareham and an unsteady line of silver the River Frome. Far away is the Great Heath, sombre and dull, while on the horizon, like the uplands of a phantom country, loom the heights of Salisbury Plain.

(173-4)

A comparison with the passage from **Howards End** reveals some significant similarities. First is the viewpoint itself, the hilltop stationing which embodies the involved yet distanced stance that is adopted throughout novel and guidebook. Both passages use colour to convey the experience; both describe the movement of river and countryside in clearly anthropomorphic terms. Most significant, perhaps, is the shared, dismissive reference to Bournemouth, the despised suburbia: for Forster, it is an 'ignoble coast' (164); for Treves, it contains 'the cliffs and crude villas'—not the dismissive use of 'villa', found in Forster, Masterman and Treves, to reject the emblem of suburban sprawl.

Once again, the note is not one of simple, specific parody, but the reference is still present: certainly, the reader who does not know this other sort of writing cannot appreciate fully the ironic self-consciousness of Forster's words. This is perhaps most especially evident at the close of the passage, which seems to satirise the failing ecstasy of the country-writer attempting to be inclusive:

> The reason fails, like a wave on the Swanage beach; the imagination swells, spreads and deepens, until it becomes geographic and encircles England.

(164-5)

Once again, the writing parodies the very conventions it continues: the simultaneous development and rejection is, here as elsewhere, the authentic note of Forster's novel. The continuity and rejection of symbolic naming and event, the collapse of plot-event into melodrama, and the parodic reference to contemporary writing on politics and the countryside work together to generate a complex dynamic of self-contradiction that parodies the act that it seems to be performing. For this reason the novel, in its strange cancrizans of advancing and retreating, not only offers us a deeply poetic version of the condition of England: it also presents a model of the linguistic contradiction and complexity that characterises so much of the period's writing.

VII

Where does this supple dance of reference and distancing leave us when we attempt to bring together a reading of the novel? Ann Wright perhaps comes closest to a full definition of how the book works in claiming 'Howards End, then, envisages, and partly defines, a dimension of

crisis beyond that which the narrative has dealt with; but it contains this vision only with some discomfort, and with yet more irony' (61). This is true, but not in the way that Wright has argued. It is not in offering a solution, however flawed, to the problems facing contemporary England, that the novel is most significant, but in revealing the inadequacy of a literary text of a conventional sort in attempting to do so; and the containing discomfort is not so much an irony as a much larger displacement between narrative and idea, in which the shifting between realism and symbolism is part of a deliberative revelation of the inadequacy of the conventions it apparently continues but ultimately rejects.

The most important result of this process is in unveiling a series of distances in the text: between the narratorial voice and the characters, to prevent our becoming involved too closely with their world, as in a materialist fiction; between the narratorial voice and the subject of England, through the use of a series of parodies; and, most importantly, between the text and its ideas, as it constantly and variously destabilises the very techniques it seems to be using to enact them. Emblematic names and elaborate networks of symbolism are revealed as deliberate revelations of the falsity of the literary convention of the novel; parodies of the social enquiry and the country guide warn us against seeing in either a valid solution or a genuine insight, and thrust us again into our own immediate experience by destabilising the medium they appear to enshrine.

That, while presenting us with so many simultaneous dimensions of distance, the novel manages to allow critical readers to become involved with the characters, take the symbols with the degree of seriousness needed to consider them failures, and read it as a genuine contribution to the debate on the condition of England, demonstrates that it is in no small measure continuing the traditions it rejects. In this balance between intimate and distanced, parodic and serious, is the book's identity. That it uses the metaphoric techniques of the Victorian novel to discuss the condition of England reveals it as poetic; that it forces us to recognise them as what they are, with their own limitations, reveals it as philosophical. Its simultaneous extension and denial of form makes it a constantly contradictory, constantly disturbing, book.

For the present-day reader, the text of **Howards End** contains one further contradiction: the last words to appear in the novel are 'WEYBRIDGE, 1908-1910' (340). Though they are no part of the imaginative life of the novel, they are a part of its printed identity. Weybridge is a small town in Surrey that, even in the years mentioned, was moving from rural to suburban or even urban: Forster was himself writing in the strange no-man's-land that much of England had become in the shift he appears to chronicle. The sense of confusion suggested throughout the novel in terms of the identity of England is fittingly emblematised in this strange valedictory imprimatur.

Notes

1. Williams, Ioan, ed. *George Meredith: The Critical Heritage.* London: Routledge, 1971, 9. The writer

goes on to discuss the revival of Meredith's work, and quotes in full (503-18) the influential review of the Collected Works by Percy Lubbock, which appeared in 1910—the year *Howards End* was published.

2. Masterman is quoting from Samuel A. Barnett and Dame Henrietta Barnett, *Towards Social Reform.* London: T. Fisher Unwin, 1909, 7. Barnett was a leading reformer of his age, whose influence encompassed Toynbee Hall and St Jude's Whitechapel. His interest in humanitarian and cultural work in the East End of London led to his making major contributions to the founding of Whitechapel Public Library and Whitechapel Art Gallery.

Henry S. Turner (essay date fall 2000)

SOURCE: Turner, Henry S. "Empires of Objects: Accumulation and Entropy in E. M. Forster's *Howards End.*" *Twentieth Century Literature* 46, no. 3 (fall 2000): 328-45.

[*In the following essay, Turner examines the meaning of money, objects, and accumulation in* Howards End.]

[T]here seems something else in life besides time, something which may conveniently be called "value," something which is measured not by minutes or hours, but by intensity, so that when we look at our past it does not stretch back evenly but piles up into a few notable pinnacles . . .

—E. M. Forster, *Aspects of the Novel* 19

One of the evils of money is that it tempts us to look at it rather than at the things that it buys.

—E. M. Forster, *Two Cheers for Democracy* 6-7

Speaking to a BBC audience in 1946 on the topic of the **"Challenge of Our Time,"** Forster addressed with candor and typical irony a dilemma that he felt keenly and unapologetically: his attempt to reconcile the ubiquity of the "New Economy" with the "Old Morality" that he felt was disappearing and which was to remain so indispensable to him in later years:

But though the education [I received] was humane it was imperfect, inasmuch as we none of us realized our economic position. In came the nice fat dividends, up rose the lofty thoughts, and we did not realize that all the time we were exploiting the poor of our own country and the backward races abroad, and getting bigger profits from our investments than we should. We refused to face this unpalatable truth. . . .

All that has changed in the present century. The dividends have shrunk to decent proportions and have in some cases disappeared. The poor have kicked. The backward races are kicking—and more power to their boots. Which means that life has become less comfortable for the Victorian liberal, and that our outlook,

which seems to me admirable, has lost the basis of golden sovereigns upon which it originally rose, and now hangs over the abyss. . . .

[Y]ou are brought back again to that inescapable arbiter, your own temperament. When there is a collision of principles would you favour the individual at the expense of the community as I would? Or would you prefer economic justice for all at the expense of personal freedom? In a time of upheaval like the present, this collision of principles, this split in one's loyalties, is always occurring.

(*Two Cheers* 56-58)

Faced with the growing disenfranchisement of England's working class and the ugly legacy of Victorian imperialism, the clarity and force with which Forster perceived the demands of ethical responsibility proved difficult to reconcile with his equally profound allegiance to private feeling and individual memory. This very ambivalence was to play a more subdued but nonetheless central role in Forster's later biography of his great-aunt, Marianne Thornton, where it runs throughout his nostalgic account of the Clapham Sect and its distinct blend of philanthropy, sentimentality, and moral conservatism.[1] As a family portrait the work is perfectly balanced, at once generous and deeply sympathetic—even proud—but always shrewd, sharply observed, and conscious of anachronism. Here was the very source of emotions that Forster recognized as most intimately and resolutely his own—the deep attachment to a family home not least among them—and yet the picture jarred with the contemporary world he observed around him, where a friend's farm could be commandeered by the Ministry of Town and Country Planning and appropriated for subdivisions and public housing.[2] His awareness of his own contradictory position could only be made more acute by his fond exercise in family biography: as a young boy Forster had inherited from his great-aunt Marianne the seed capital for a lifetime of investment, dividends, and freedom from conventional wage labor. Although the bequest was to cause him occasional dismay throughout his life, he recognized that it left him free to pursue a career as a professional writer.[3]

Written more than three decades before ***Marianne Thornton, Howards End*** (1910) marks the conversion of a writer's personal ambivalence into a specific formal problem: the work may be read as an extended meditation on the difficulty of representing capital accumulation, in all its elusive and terrifying abstraction, as a total process.[4] Here Forster's negotiation between money and morality takes place through the narrative's persistent attention to the physical objects of everyday life. As concrete objects cluster around the novel's characters to form the fabric of their lives and environments, their accumulation becomes both the narrative's preeminent thematic concern and its primary structuring principle. Forster indicates his discomfort with the modes of capital accumulation made possible in his age by delineating a world in which personal objects and places act as repositories for a sentimental "value" that exceeds the vicissitudes of commerce and commodification. The novel articulates an ambivalent fascination with material substances of all types, as Margaret nostalgically embraces objects for their promise of cultural permanence and stability even as the narrative voice regards them with detached irony, mistrust, or even disgust. In these latter moments Forster is forced to confront the question of how entropy and surplus—the disorder provoked by a super-abundance of objects, people, property, and spaces—fit into the logic of nationalism and imperialism, and how this peculiar, contradictory logic might be accommodated within the formal techniques of the modern novel.

Schlegels and Wilcoxes, family and home, genealogy and real estate: these oppositions form the basic thematic and theoretical structure around which the narrative's total trajectory has been plotted. Nearly every scene charts, in its minute way, the inexorable division of the "house" into these separate conceptual components, and the air of uneasy anticipation that hovers throughout the novel can be traced to the discomfort that Margaret feels as she becomes aware of this growing bifurcation and of the forces that threaten her family's once-solid foundation at Wickham Place. As the Schlegels and Wilcoxes become increasingly intertwined, the separation of family from home can only become more acute, largely because each family's perception of the "house" differs so radically. Each conforms to a distinct, and opposing, model of accumulation: on the one hand, Forster offers the chiffoniers, books, and embedded genealogical memories of the Schlegel household, and on the other the luggage and real estate of the Wilcoxes, with their insistence on the infinite fungibility and latent liquidity of belongings.[5]

Forster's initial description of Schlegel pere, for instance, sketches the faint sense of anachronism ("a type that was more prominent in Germany fifty years ago than now" [26]) updated in his daughters, with its essential characteristics clearly preserved:

> He was not the aggressive German, so dear to the English Journalist, nor the domestic German, so dear to the English wit. If one classed him at all, it would be as the countryman of Hegel and Kant, as the idealist, inclined to be dreamy, whose Imperialism was the Imperialism of the air.
>
> (26)

The reluctant imperialist inveighs against the "clouds of materialism obscuring the Fatherland" (26) and those men who only

> "care about the things that you can use, and therefore arrange them in the following order: Money, supremely useful; intellect, rather useful; imagination, of no use at all. No"—for the other had protested—"your Pan-Germanism is no more imaginative than is our Imperialism over here. It is the vice of a vulgar mind to be thrilled by bigness, to think that a thousand square miles are a thousand times more wonderful than one square mile, and that a million square miles are almost the same as heaven. . . . They collect facts, and facts, and empires of facts. But which of them will rekindle the light within?"
>
> (27)

The Schlegel sisters, however, do not appear as resolute as their father in their condemnation either of imperialism or of the narrow materialism and methodical accumulation on which it rests. Margaret, remarks Forster, will "at times dismiss the whole British Empire with a puzzled, if reverent, sigh" (25), and she retains a vision of the imperialist as hard worker and civilizer (not to mention paragon of productive and knowing masculinity) until the final pages of the novel. As she enjoins Tibby:

> you must work, or else you must pretend to work, which is what I do. Work, work, work if you'd save your soul and your body. It is honestly a necessity my dear boy. Look at the Wilcoxes. . . . With all their defects of temper and understanding, such men give me more pleasure than many who are better equipped, and I think it is because they have worked regularly and honestly.
>
> (109)

Margaret at first playfully adopts a position vis-a-vis work that might describe Forster himself, and she certainly shares his awareness that "lofty thoughts" depend on "nice fat dividends" (Forster, *Two Cheers* 56-57).[6] But later in the novel, as Margaret continues an earnest defense of the great civilizer—and in the name of "us literary people" (171), no less—Forster's gentle irony allows him a polite, but no less firm, distance from the comfortable liberal credo she articulates:

> If the Wilcoxes hadn't worked and died in England for thousands of years, you and I couldn't sit here without having our throats cut. There would be no trains, no ships to carry us literary people about in, no fields even. Just savagery. No—perhaps not even that. Without their spirit, life might never have moved out of protoplasm.
>
> (171-72)

For Forster, it is not only Margaret who "pretends to work" but also the Wilcoxes themselves, as they expend relentless energy doing nothing in particular; aside from Paul (at best a half character, dimly visible over the colonial horizon, clumsy from the saddle, and burnt by the sun) the "work" of the Wilcoxes is distilled into Henry's dictation of a letter (no doubt with great purpose) and his worry over property management.

While the Schlegels gather in a world of cozy "feminine" interiors ("'I suppose that ours is a female house,' said Margaret. . . . 'it must be feminine, and all we can do is to see that it isn't effeminate'" [41]), the Wilcoxes recline in the leather interiors of accumulated imperial spoil:

> The dining room was big, but overfurnished . . . those heavy chairs, that immense sideboard loaded with presentation plate, stood up against [the room's] pressure like men. The room suggested men, and Margaret, keen to derive the modern capitalist from the warriors and hunters of the past, saw it as an ancient guest-hall, where the lord sat at meat among his thanes. Even the Bible—the Dutch Bible that Charles had brought back from the Boer War—fell into position. Such a room admitted loot.
>
> (159-160)

Forster's use of free indirect discourse here again allows him to introduce a critical irony toward the Wilcoxes that cannot be attributed entirely to Margaret herself. Despite her avowed impatience with imperialism—"An Empire bores me, so far, but I can appreciate the heroism that builds it up" (110)—Margaret's complicity lies less in her equivocations than in her willingness to invest psychologically in the materials that empire makes available: she animates these objects with her own visions of masculine grandeur and epic process, just as later, after Henry's proposal, she will exclaim romantically over shares in a currant farm (141). But her swelling concern for the past, both personal and national, and its accumulation in the things of everyday life, is also precisely what separates her and her sister Helen from the Wilcoxes, who care only for the accumulation of profits and the commerce of the future.[7] "You see," says Helen to her cousin,

> the Wilcoxes collect houses as your Victor collects tadpoles. They have, one, Ducie Street; two, Howards End, where my great rumpus was; three, a country seat in Shropshire; four, Charles has a house in Hilton; and five, another near Epsom; and six, Eye will have a house when she marries, and probably a pied-a-terre in the country—which makes seven. Oh yes, and Paul a hut in Africa makes eight.
>
> (167)

The list undergoes perpetual revision as the novel continues: by chapter 31 Henry has both acquired and finally succeeded in jettisoning Oniton (after much implied time and effort), and two pages later we catch a glimpse of Henry and Margaret's plans for the construction of their new home.

It would appear that to represent capital accumulation as an ongoing, abstract process, Forster has adopted a narrative strategy similar to that discerned by Elaine Scarry in the novels of Thomas Hardy, in which "the structure of all narrative action entail[s] (and often even depend[s] on) the physical continuity of man and his materials" ("Participial Acts" 60).[8] But Hardy's problem, according to Scarry, and that of the nineteenth-century realist novel more generally, was to represent the process of work. What are we to make of *Howards End,* in which work-as-process is no longer a question of productive human action—no longer Scarry's humanist vision of the body-at-work—but rather of Margaret's generalized principle of social and personal betterment on the one hand, and an inexorable, silent mechanism on the other, the work not of bodies but of investment, distanced calculation, and profit-making? How much more difficult a problem for representation, when work as the production-of-things—Scarry's vision of work as the personal, intimate transformation of the material environment—has become work-as-accumulation, work as the production not of substance but of possibility, of opportunity, of the further production of abstract representation itself?

Scarry's reading of Hardy suggests two formal possibilities that Forster might adopt for representing the process

of accumulation. He might, for instance, "subdivide the activity of work not into temporal units but into task units . . ." (65-66). But work-as-human-production—work as task—however attractive to the late-nineteenth-century narrative imagination, seems quaintly out of place in the world of early twentieth-century modernism. The division of the "task unit," after all, was crucial to assembly-line mass production and would soon make possible the capital accumulation strategies of Fordism.[9] Representing the process of accumulation—a self-perpetuating process—by dividing it up into "task units" is simply not an option in a novel such as *Howards End,* especially when the body that performs those tasks has been eliminated. "Work" of this type, the "work" of imperialism and the Wilcoxes, busies itself precisely with the effacement of the material body, whether through displacement and repression (the "invisible" colonial margin and its labor), or through the abstract conversion of labor into commodities and profit.

Bodies in *Howards End*—such as they are in a novel whose witty chat, felt confessions, and class-marked characterizations insist repeatedly on the importance of the intellect, the spirit, and the emotions—suffer the onslaught of cheap possessions and obdurate things, innumerable objects that resist Scarry's (and Father Schlegel's) vision of a reciprocal, Hegelian relation with their neighboring human subject. It would be worth pausing, for a moment, to consider the Basts, certainly the most "embodied" characters of the novel: here embodiment is distinctly pathetic, sick, fragile, and bloody (in the case of Leonard), if not monstrous (in the case of Jacky). Do we dare to read their squalid dinner scene, after Scarry, as "part of the resculpting or remaking of the body . . . entailed in work"? ("Participial Acts" 56). The grotesque communion here between the laboring body and its needs—congealed tongue, fat, and dissolving gelatin—could not be further from the ennobling dialectic of self-fulfillment that the nineteenth-century novel would seem to promise.

Nor could the Schlegels be said to participate in this process: they seek spiritual things, an "unseen" that transcends, rather than clinging mercilessly, to the human experience. Helen's sudden (and transgressive) embodiment is the only legacy of a man who does not, after all, "labor" in any familiar sense of the word. Leonard Bast, insurance clerk, produces nothing: he is a condition of possibility for the management of possibility itself, the anticipation of accident and loss, disruption and chaos. He is, moreover, a dispensable condition, as likely a figure for surplus as the throwaway furnishings of his rented flat. These possessions wound: Leonard cuts himself on Jacky's picture, the blood "spilling over onto the exposed photograph" (46), just as Margaret will do 12 pages later, in Mrs. Wilcox's bedroom, although here, as she has just finished uttering to Tibby and Helen, "money pads the edges of things" (58). When Tibby rouses himself to bestow upon the Basts Helen's desperate and utterly inappropriate gift of capital, they have vanished into the pool of surplus populations and underclass space, leaving behind them only a "scurf of books and china ornaments" (253) to mark their disappearance.

This moment, like other discussions of investment and income that appear during the course of the novel—Margaret's personal moral code ("all our thoughts are the thoughts of six-hundred-pounders" (59), or the playful discussions of philanthropy at the women's group, for which Bast is no more than a "conversational hare" (to borrow an expression from Margaret's dinner party)—manifests most clearly the tension between Forster's recognition of capital's indispensability and his profound desire to be rid of it. Like Helen, who "confuses wealth with the technique of wealth" (177), Forster seems fascinated by the power of money to change things and people but at the same time distrustful of its superficiality, of the structures that produce it and that are required to manage it, and of the world of impermanence it ushers in.

Surprisingly few objects circulate in the novel as commodities in the strict sense; in fact, apart from the ubiquitous concern for real estate and investment, other commercial operations make scant appearance. It is as if Forster can bring himself to represent only the most anonymous processes of accumulation and refuses to sully moments of interpersonal, human contact with the stuff of commerce. Only two scenes stand out in which financial exchanges actually occur between two people. At Simpsons, Henry insists on tipping the carver: this is a technique picked up on his Eastern colonial travels ("especially in the East, if you tip, they remember you from year's end to year's end" [149]), a ruse of domestication and humanization ("perhaps it does make life more human," responds Margaret [149]) that passes privilege off as considerate action and civilized manners. A gesture of supreme insignificance enacting the fantasy of largesse, the tip reduces huge processes of economic dependency and structural inequalities to the slip of a coin in the palm and grateful obsequiousness. It is Henry's single attempt to "connect." At an earlier moment in the novel, Margaret accompanies Mrs. Wilcox on her Christmas shopping; here, of course, the scene only emphasizes the impossibility of paying a debt of gratitude with material tokens, since Mrs. Wilcox conspicuously buys nothing for Margaret.

Nor would it be possible to identify in the novel, at least not without some modification, realism's alternative solution to the problem of representing an extended process: "to take the massive fact of work precisely at the moment when there is a tear or lapse in the activity that must be repaired, replaced, or rescued" ("Participial Acts" 66). The interruption of accumulation, unlike work, is not any simple cessation; it is not a periodic moment of leisure, a holiday, a flushed sense of achievement and pride. Accumulation is mute and unnoticed—and its "failure" is nearly inconceivable. And yet if the process of accumulation as a whole appears seamless and self-generating, does it not in some way depend on interruption and rupture after all? It would be worth recalling that rupture and displacement are the very foundations of the accumulation of capital, above all in the production of the commodity and its transformation into a fetish: for an object to become a commodity, it must circulate in physical, spatial terms; it must participate in a foundational break from the site of its production to the site of its exchange and eventual consumption. Forster, I argue, registers one of the crucial conditions of the system of capital accumulation in which he and his characters find themselves and transforms this condition (displacement or rupture from an originary place) into a modernist narrative principle. It would be more accurate here to speak not of commodity fetishism but of what we might call "narratological fetishism," a process whereby objects become charged with symbolic or narratological significance and assume an independent motive force that drives the action of the plot.[10] They are the sites of elaboration for Forster's national and moral philosophical themes and the vehicles for his nostalgic investment; they are the material hinges on which the narrative turns.

The plot of *Howards End* advances primarily through a ceaseless translation of things, a straying of objects across the topography of the novel that draws characters into worlds either desired or feared. Hence Forster devotes long sequences to chance meetings, wanderings from milieu to milieu, and journeys from city to country and back again, all of which finally drive Margaret to insist on a "permanent" place to live ("Don't you believe in having a permanent home, Henry?" [256]). A similar feeling prompts Mrs. Wilcox's lament at the news that Wickham Place will be destroyed (81). Forster's restless, almost cinematic treatment of setting lends to the novel a dislocated sense of time and space: for all the considerable detail with which Forster renders each room, house, or avenue, these remain a series of places, heterogeneous particularities that resist coalescing into a coherent narrative geography or mappable "space."

The narrative reaches what we might call a point of saturation, as, gradually, things (and their owners) begin to spill over into places where they do not belong. Accumulation thus makes its first appearance through its effects, its small disturbances and disruptions in the intersecting personal orders of the novel, which must stretch to accommodate the new intrusion of material. Consider, for example, Leonard Bast's umbrella. Initially the umbrella serves as the perfect conduit for the chance encounters that are the very substance of Howards End, making possible the initial visit between the Schlegels and Leonard Bast. We may perceive, in the rupture of two personal spheres and the subsequent wanderings of objects and people that this rupture provokes, all the latent violence of later events. Nor does the umbrella move only laterally, describing the various social spaces of the narrative, but it is immediately elevated, as a transposed symbol, to the level of ironic social commentary articulated by the narrative voice:

> But in his day the angel of Democracy had arisen, enshadowing the classes with leathern wings, and proclaiming: "All men are equal—all men, that is to say, who possess umbrellas," and so he was obliged to assert gentility, lest he slip into the abyss where nothing counts and the statements of Democracy are inaudible.

(43)

Later Margaret takes recourse to the example of the umbrella to illustrate her feelings toward dividends, inequality, and the poverty of others:

> I stand each year upon six hundred pounds, and Helen upon the same, and Tibby will stand upon eight, and as fast as our pounds crumble away into the sea they are renewed—from the sea, yes, from the sea. And all our thoughts are the thoughts of six-hundred-pounders, and all our speeches; and because we don't want to steal umbrellas ourselves, we forget that below the sea people do want to steal them, and do steal them sometimes, and that what's a joke up here is down there reality—. . . .
>
> (59)

Over the following pages, the umbrella submits to a series of equations or substitutions: its place is taken by the Schlegel's card, which becomes the misplaced, itinerant object: "Months passed, and the card, now as a joke, now as a grievance, was handed about, getting dirtier and dirtier. It followed them when they moved from Camelia Road to Tulse Hill. It was submitted to third parties. A few inches of pasteboard, it became the battlefield on which the souls of Leonard and his wife contended" (120-21). This card, in turn, leads Jacky back to Wickham place, searching, in the words of Helen, "for a husband as if he was an umbrella. She mislaid him Saturday afternoon—and for a long time suffered no inconvenience" (111). When Leonard comes to the Schlegels to explain his wife's visit, he discovers that he has not only been "mislaid" by his wife but also that his original meeting with the Schlegels, the entire event itself, has been forgotten.

The "umbrella," moreover, is increasingly associated not only with the loss of memory but also with theft. First Margaret fears that Leonard suspects her of stealing the umbrella and working a confidence trick; then, after the umbrella has been found and returned, the Schlegel's half-serious discussion turns to the safety of their own property, the "apostle spoons" (39) and the "majolica plate . . . that is so firmly set into the wall" (42). Margaret's attempt to contain loss by appealing to her father's notion of "rent," "to the ideal, to his own faith in human nature" (39), can only take on an uncomfortable irony in light of Leonard and Jacky's threatened eviction and the bailiff who Leonard watches "fingering my Ruskins and Stevensons" (235), calculating their money value.

The interesting aspect of these scenes is the way in which the appearance of the umbrella always implies a certain fragility and darker chaotic underside; it balances at the threshold of two radically incommensurate realities, bridging them even as it holds them apart. For Margaret the encounter with Leonard and his umbrella is more than uncomfortable: it is a murmur from the abyss and the ill portent of a great, impending dislocation: "Her thoughts turned sadly to house-hunting. Wickham Place had been so safe. She feared, fantastically, that her own little flock might be moving into turmoil and squalor, into nearer contact with such episodes as these" (112). The narrative sig-

nificance of the umbrella hinges precisely on this simultaneous, dual value: at the concert, for Helen, the umbrella is absolutely insignificant; she takes no notice of it whatsoever, has no recollection of any accidental contact, and fails to recognize it when she finds it in the hallway. For Leonard, however, the umbrella's value is nearly immeasurable: it exceeds the ordinary uses of an umbrella (protection against the elements) and serves as a crucial mark of social distinction; it is a bulwark against certain despair, if not, within the terms of the novel, nonexistence.

How different is Leonard's umbrella from that other object overlooked at the concert, cousin Frieda's reticule. Its compact utility belies the carelessness of its owner: the address book, a catalogue of personal social order, inscribed social relations, and brilliant itineraries; the map, tool for the tourist and temporarily roofless, an illusion of stable and enduring space that Leonard would hardly recognize; the dictionary, here no doubt an innocent phrase book but bearing within it the tyranny of imperial tongues; and money—agent of all change, the final passe-par-tout. Unlike Leonard's tattered umbrella, the reticule belongs at the concert; it participates seamlessly in its world of leisure and perfectly elaborates the person of Frieda. Mound these belongings, from the smallest accessory to larger places of dwelling and protection, gather intricate cultural narratives of gender, class and national differentiation, wildly divergent value systems, insouciance, and devastating loss.

In choosing to represent accumulation through objects and their circulation, Forster has demonstrated not the failure of accumulation or its temporary rupture but only its persistence, its resourcefulness, even its necessity. And he has, at the same time, made a larger decision not typical of nineteenth-century realism, which is to represent accumulation-as-process by choosing to represent its cost. Immediately (and unwittingly), however, Forster runs up against a quintessentially "modern" problem: how can the full cost of accumulation ever be adequately represented? Jacques Derrida has suggested the difficulties in representing the obverse of accumulation as dissemination, as a radical loss or absence, when the very act of representation is itself firmly inscribed within a metaphysics of recuperation, gain, or preservation—to quote Helen, "Death destroys a man; the idea of Death saves him" (236).[11] In grappling with a process that, however destructive, never disappears or ceases, and, in the face of this relentlessness, turning instead to the cost of the process—somehow trying to see through the process, as if to expose it—Forster forces himself into the position not of representing waste, loss, or absence itself but rather of selecting certain things to be figures for loss and surplus, setting them up to bear the full brunt of the process and thus, as its victims, to reveal its destructive power.

It is here, I think, that we can most clearly register the subtle ambivalence within Forster's social and national vision. In a first movement, his narrative separates the process of accumulation and loss into two seemingly isolated and morally opposed spheres: investment capitalism on the one hand, and on the other, a vision of a sacred national legacy that is both personal and communal and fueled by an ongoing accumulation of sentiment and memory. Forster can thus condemn the work of the Wilcoxes unambiguously ("But the imperialist is not what he thinks or seems. He is a destroyer" [320]), and then immediately humanize the loss by inventing certain characters who stand as figures for surplus and the human cost of capitalism—the Basts—but who are rendered as mere symbols, "flat" characters, placeholders on which to hang, in passing, a certain amount of remorse over the system and its expense. Here Leonard (never a very risky figure) represents the cost, while altogether more probable (not to mention politically charged and historically accurate) representatives for the human cost of capitalism are consigned either to the "abyss" (the underclass who is never represented) or beyond the margins of the novel itself (the colonial subject).[12] Note also that if Forster condemns the imperialist as a destroyer, he does so not on account of the lands he has colonized but rather for the threat he poses to the cultural specificity of England ("he prepares the way for cosmopolitanism" [320]).[13]

Finally, in what I find the most enduring point of interest in the novel, Forster chooses to represent loss as nothing less than a further form of accumulation: an inventive and peculiarly "modern" representation of loss as the accumulation of entropy, the accumulation that results from the decay, rust, and rubble, or "grey" typical of suburbia and London:

> It was the kind of scene that may be observed all over London, whatever the locality—bricks and mortar rising and falling with the restlessness of the water in a fountain. . . .
>
> (44)

> The mask fell off the city, and she saw it for what it really is—a caricature of infinity. The familiar barriers, the streets along which she moved, the houses between which she had made her little journeys for so many years, became negligible suddenly. Helen seemed one with the grimy trees and the traffic and the slowly flowing slabs of mud. . . .
>
> (277)

> "All the same, London's creeping."
>
> She pointed over the meadow—over eight or nine meadows, but at the end of them was a red rust.
>
> (337)

Forster realizes this form of loss most magnificently in the forces that impel the disintegration of the "house": the ubiquitous ebbs and flows, the flux of destruction and reconstruction, the forced vacancies and hemorrhages of superfluous personal belongings:

> The Age of Property holds bitter moments even for a proprietor. When a move is imminent, furniture becomes ridiculous, and Margaret now lay awake at

nights wondering where, where on earth they and all their belongings would be deposited in September next. Chairs, tables, pictures, books, that had rumbled down to them through the generations, must rumble forward again like a slide of rubbish to which she longed to give the final push and send toppling into the sea. But there were all their father's books—they never read them, but they were their father's and they must be kept. There was the marble-topped chiffonier—their mother had set store by it, they could not remember why. Round every knob and cushion in the house sentiment gathered, a sentiment that was at times personal, but more often a faint piety to the dead, a prolongation of rites that might have ended at the grave.

. . . The feudal ownership of land did bring dignity, whereas the modern ownership of movables is reducing us again to a nomadic horde. We are reverting to the civilization of luggage, and historians of the future will note how the middle classes accrete possessions without taking root in the earth, and may find in this the secret of their imaginative poverty.

(146)

Death and chaos lie revealed at the heart of the arranging life. This is not a vision of surplus as profit but of surplus as waste: it marks the vertiginous recognition of the dissolution that new modes of accumulation (both capital and emotional) make possible, and the recasting of this realization in the reassuring metaphors of organicism and dynamic natural forces. Radical loss, itself a structural requirement of capital investment and profit, is here deflected through the strategies of narrative representation into a meditation on emotions, pasts, and families. Even as they threaten to disappear as surplus (the effects of capitalism), the Schlegels' possessions resonate with a personal sentiment that emerges all the more powerfully because of this loss, sentiment later recuperated and poured into the receptacle of Howards End and the national landscape. Likewise, Leonard's umbrella is precious precisely because of its place within a precarious personal order, and its value appears most clearly not in its use but in its absence, when it threatens to carry with it everything else.

In the language of Marx, action has become substance, but action of an entirely different sort from human productive action, human praxis or work; it is rather the restless action of capital accumulation and the waste it produces. Forster grasps that every system has a cost, requires an expenditure, a leftover, an outside. Perhaps in this final recognition Forster momentarily presents, if only to recoil from it, a glimpse of "accumulation" utterly antithetical to the conventional understanding of the term: not a building up, a growth, a saving, a reserve to be tapped and used (whether in terms of capital profit, personal memory, or national past) but simply a ceaseless movement, a restless overturning and change, the acceleration of time and space to the point where, from the motorcar, the scenery before Margaret's eyes "heaved and merged, like porridge," and then "congealed" (195).

The singular importance of Howards End, the house, lies here: as the place "outside" the time and space of modern cosmopolitanism, beyond the bonds of property and finance; the place where Margaret will, in an uncanny moment of alienation and recovery, encounter the Schlegel possessions furnishing the rooms as if they had always belonged there; a place where she will renounce her invested wealth in favor of a house that is both embedded in the national landscape and acts as the metonym of that landscape; a place reappropriated as both the repository of national past and the nursery for the national future.[14]

Forster reaches the profound and unsettling realization that in the modern world (and the world of modernism) accumulation never ceases, can never be interrupted, as work can be: objects multiply and continue to multiply, they slip and jostle against each other, they resist the subject, they kill. Radical, unrecoverable loss, if it can "appear" at all, appears here, adumbrated around the more familiar figures of capital and property: in "scurf" and clutter, or in the mud of the national landscape (pointed out unerringly by the German nationalist cousin: "And the mud of your Poole down there—does it not smell, or may I say stink, ha, ha" [133]). It resonates in Forster's coolly ironic description of West Africa and Henry's office at the Rubber Company ("just the ordinary surface scum of ledgers and polished counters and brass bars that began and stopped for no possible reason" [155]); we glimpse it in the recurring imagery of blurred edges and dim outlines (61, 62) and in Forster's fascination with "the grotesque impact of the unseen upon the seen" (65, 83). It hides behind his casual dismissal of the "unthinkable" poor (43) and by his tendency to contemplate the laboring body—particularly the belabored body of Jacky—as an assemblage of monstrous cliches; it appears in the very disorder of entropy and accident, in shards of glass, the sprinkling of blood on a picture, and a crashing cascade of books.

Notes

1. I am grateful to the anonymous reader for this journal who suggested that I consider *Marianne Thornton* for the light it sheds on Forster's attitudes toward money and property and on my reading of *Howards End.*

2. *Marianne Thornton* is particularly remarkable for its memorializing of Battersea Rise, the Thornton family estate, and for the way it records the Thornton's distinct imaginative and sentimental investment in houses. It was a sensibility that Forster shared, and I am struck by how clearly *Howards End* pre-figures his later exploration of this aspect of his family and of his own earliest memories; he explicitly acknowledges the role that his childhood home in Hertfordshire played in his creation of Howards End, the house (301).

3. Forster received [pound]8,000 when he was eight years old. I am indebted to Delany for the information on Forster's inheritance and what he suggests to be Forster's "lifelong preoccupation with the morality of living on unearned income" (285). Forster himself provides a brief comment on the topic at the

conclusion of his biography of his great-aunt (*Marianne Thornton* 324; see also Furbank, esp. 1: 24 and 2: 317). Forster's dilemma, Delany argues, "is how to uphold the civic and cultural virtues intrinsic to the rentier way of life, yet avoid complicity with commerce or technology" (291). While Delany is chiefly interested in tracing Forster's own attitudes and moral views as they are articulated through the novel's characters, I will be concerned with the way in which these attitudes produced a set of specific formal representational problems, which Forster sought to solve through his treatment of objects and property.

4. My thesis here owes a considerable debt to the work of Scarry, in particular "Participial Acts" but also *The Body in Pain*. I will take up Scarry's argument, and my differences with it, in more detail later. Born makes claims that are similar to Delany's and my own, noting the centrality of real estate to Forster's social and aesthetic vision (142) and claiming that Forster's "preoccupation with surfaces, houses, and the substance of material living . . . becomes a strategy of moral penetration" (142-43). Critical responses to the novel are usefully surveyed in Page; for the purposes of this paper, see in particular ch. 4, "Can a Marxist like Margaret," 37-44. I draw also on Jameson's discussion of the determining power of imperialism on the formal innovations of modernism and on *Howards End,* and on Said 62-80.

5. Bradbury (128-43) observes a similar series of distinctions; Stone also argues that oppositions between the Schlegels and the Wilcoxes are played out primarily in terms of houses (237-38).

6. The virtues and contradictions of the novel's liberalism have been well rehearsed over the years; following Trilling's influential 1943 study, representative examples include virtually every essay in the anthology edited by Bradbury. For more recent reconsiderations of liberalism see Armstrong, who highlights the importance of architecture and horizontal spatial movement in the novel (esp. 187-88), and Levenson. Two articles explore similarities between *Howards End* and the pragmatic philosophy of Richard Rorty: Born, who offers a helpful reevaluation of the central critical claims for the novel's liberalism, and May, who reads Margaret as the premier example of the Rortian "liberal ironist."

7. Born overlooks the real qualitative differences in the investments Margaret and the Wilcoxes make in places and things when he argues that "for all their differences, in this respect [the concern for property and social mobility] Margaret and the Wilcoxes are identical" (154).

8. See also 64-65:

> Although, then, work is extensively represented in the novel . . . it is at the same time . . . a deeply difficult subject to represent. The major

source of this difficulty is that work is action rather than a discrete action: it has no identifiable beginning or end; if it were an exceptional action, or even "an action," it could—like acts in epic, heroic, or military literature—be easily accommodated in narrative. It is the essential nature of work to be perpetual, repetitive, habitual. There is no formal convention in any genre of literature that would make it either possible or desirable to portray it in all its constancy and repetitiveness.

9. See Harvey's discussion (125) of early-twentieth-century economic planners such as F. W. Taylor, whose *The Principles of Scientific Management* was published in 1911, only a year after *Howards End.*

10. The term "narratological fetishism" is indebted, of course, to the classic account of commodity fetishism in Marx and to the wide range of anthropological, historical, and theoretical work that has sought to elaborate the wider cultural meanings embedded in objects and to examine the many social practices they illuminate. In anthropology, see in particular the ground-breaking study by Douglas and Isherwood and the more recent work by Appadurai and the other essays in his collection. See also Mukerji: "here the point is that objects are carriers of ideas and, as such, often act as the social forces that analysts have identified with ideology-as-words" (15). Classic theoretical statements on the semiotics of objects are provided by Barthes and by Baudrillard; after Foucault, Butler has gone furthest in theorizing the body as object.

11. See Derrida's rereading of Georges Bataille's "anti"-Hegelianism and his notion of a "general economy":

> The notion of Aufhebung (the speculative concept par excellence, says Hegel . . .) is laughable in that it signifies the busying of a discourse losing its breath as it reappropriates all negativity for itself, as it works the "putting at stake" into an investment, as it amortizes absolute expenditure, and as it gives meaning to death.
>
> (257)

12. Born (147-50) provides an excellent discussion of possible sources for Bast and the representations of the "abyss" in contemporary social writings such as C. F. G. Masterman's *The Heart of the Empire: Discussions of Problems of Modern City Life in England, with an Essay on Imperialism* (1901) and *From the Abyss: Of Its Inhabitants by One of Them* (1902); and Jack London's *The People of the Abyss* (1903). He argues against the critical censure of Forster on "realist" grounds, and claims that Forster's ironic distance in his treatment of Bast, while cruel, nonetheless suggests his awareness of the impossibility of truly objective realism.

13. As Jameson's comments on the novel suggest, the primary loss endemic to the structure of imperialism is the inability to accurately perceive or articulate loss itself:

> [W]hat the new situation of imperialism looks like from the standpoint of cultural or aesthetic production now needs to be characterized, and it seems best to do so by distinguishing its problems from those of an internal industrialization and commodification in the modernizing metropolis. This last seems most often (paradoxically) to have been lived in terms of a generalized loss of meaning, as though its subject measured the increase in human power negatively, by way of the waning of tradition and religious absolutes. . . . What is determined by the colonial system is now a rather different kind of meaning loss than this one: for colonialism means that a significant structural segment of the economic system as a whole is now located elsewhere, beyond the metropolis, outside of daily life and existential experience of the home country, in colonies over the water whose own life experience and life world—very different from that of the imperial power—remain unknown and unimaginable for the subjects of the imperial power, whatever social class they may belong to. Such spatial disjunction has as its immediate consequence the inability to grasp the way the system functions as a whole.
>
> (50-51) Cf. Said, esp. 63-66

14. Born notes that the novel's country-house close was "the typical Edwardian gesture to the urban crises of the time: the pastoral escape hatch has exact parallels, for instance, in Gissing and Masterman" (156). Social reality was, of course, quite different. Delany, citing C. K. Hobson's *The Export of Capital* (1914), points out that the development of the railways (the very Home Rails invested in by Mrs. Munt, the Schlegels, and Forster himself) was one of the primary forces behind the decline of agriculture and rural depopulation, which in turn made possible the middle-class gentrification of farms such as Howards End (290).

I would like to thank Rob Nixon for his careful reading of this essay in its original form and for many suggestions that made it better than it would have been on its own. I would also like to thank the anonymous readers for the journal, who proposed several helpful additions and avenues of research that I had not considered.

Works Cited

Appadurai, Arjun. "Introduction: Commodities and the Politics of Value." *The Social Life of Things: Commodities in Cultural Perspective.* Ed. Arjun Appadurai. Cambridge: Cambridge UP, 1986. 3-63.

Armstrong, Paul B. "E. M. Forster's *Howards End*: The Existential Crisis of the Liberal Imagination." *Mosaic* 8 (1974): 183-99.

Barthes, Roland. *Elements of Semiology.* Trans. Annette Layers and Colin Smith. New York: Hill, 1967.

Baudrillard, Jean. *Le Systeme des Objets.* Paris: Gallimard, 1968.

Born, Daniel. "Private Gardens, Public Swamps: *Howards End* and the Revaluation of Liberal Guilt." *Novel* 25 (1992): 141-59.

Bradbury, Malcolm. "*Howards End.*" *Forster: A Collection of Critical Essays.* Ed. Malcolm Bradbury. Englewood Cliffs: Prentice, 1966. 128-143.

Butler, Judith. *Bodies that Matter: On the Discursive Limits of "Sex."* New York: Routledge, 1993.

Delany, Paul. "'Islands of Money': Rentier Culture in E. M. Forster's *Howards End.*" *English Literature in Transition* 31 (1988): 285-96.

Derrida, Jacques. "From Restricted to General Economy: A Hegelianism without Reserve." *Writing and Difference.* Trans. Alan Bass. London: Routledge, 1978. 251-77.

Douglas, Mary, and Baron Isherwood. *The World of Goods.* New York: Basic, 1979.

Forster, E. M. *Aspects of the Novel and Related Writings.* The Abinger Edition of E. M. Forster. Vol. 12. Ed. Oliver Stallybrass. London: Edward Arnold, 1974.

———. *Howards End.* The Abinger Edition of E. M. Forster. Vol. 4. Ed. Oliver Stallybrass. London: Edward Arnold, 1973.

———. *Marianne Thornton: A Domestic Biography, 1797-1887.* New York: Harcourt, 1956.

———. *Two Cheers for Democracy.* New York: Harcourt, 1951.

Furbank, P. N. *E. M. Forster: A Life.* 2 vols. in 1. New York: Harcourt, 1978.

Harvey, David. *The Condition of Postmodernity: An Enquiry into the Origins of Cultural Change.* Oxford: Basil Blackwell, 1989.

Jameson, Fredric. "Modernism and Imperialism." *Nationalism, Colonialism, and Literature.* Ed. Terry Eagleton, Fredric Jameson, and Edward Said. Minneapolis: U of Minnesota P, 1990. 43-66.

Levenson, Michael. "Liberalism and Symbolism." *Papers on Language and Literature* 21 (1985): 295-316.

Marx, Karl. *Das Kapital.* Trans. Ben Fowkes. New York: Vintage, 1977.

May, Brian. "Neoliberalism in Rorty and Forster." *Twentieth Century Literature* 39 (1993): 185-207.

Mukerji, Chandra. *From Craven Images: Patterns of Modern Materialism.* New York: Columbia UP, 1983.

Page, Malcolm. *The Critics Debate*: Howards End. London: Macmillan, 1993.

Said, Edward. *Culture and Imperialism.* New York: Knopf, 1993.

Scarry, Elaine. *The Body in Pain.* New York: Oxford UP, 1985.

———. "Participial Acts: Working. Work and the Body in Hardy and Other Nineteenth-Century Novelists." *Resisting Representation.* New York: Oxford UP, 1994. 49-90.

Stone, Wilfred. *The Cave and the Mountain: A Study of E. M. Forster.* Stanford: Stanford UP, 1966.

Trilling, Lionel. *E. M. Forster.* Norfolk: New Directions, 1943.

FURTHER READING

Criticism

Barrett, Elizabeth. "The Advance beyond Daintiness: Voice and Myth in *Howards End.*" In *E. M. Forster: Centenary Revaluations,* edited by Judith Scherer Herz and Robert K. Martin, pp. 155-66. Toronto: University of Toronto Press, 1982.
　　Examines Forster's attempt to create an English mythology in *Howards End.*

Bradbury, Malcolm. "*Howards End.*" In *Forster: A Collection of Critical Essays,* edited by Malcolm Bradbury, pp. 128-43. Englewood Cliffs, N.J.: Prentice-Hall, Inc., 1966.
　　Comments on Forster's ironic tone in *Howards End.*

Mezei, Kathy. "Who Is Speaking Here? Free Indirect Discourse, Gender, and Authority in *Emma, Howards End,* and *Mrs. Dalloway.*" In *Ambiguous Discourse: Feminist Narratology and British Women Writers,* edited by Kathy Mezei, pp. 66-92. Chapel Hill: University of North Carolina Press, 1996.
　　Contends that in *Emma, Howards End,* and *Mrs. Dalloway,* the narrators and characters struggle against one another to depict the heroines.

Park, Clara Claiborne. "Henry Wilcox, Babbitt, and the State of Britain." In *Rejoining the Common Reader. Essays, 1962-1990,* pp. 123-34. Evanston, Ill.: Northwestern University Press, 1991.
　　Examines Forster's depiction in *Howards End* of post-nineteenth-century English industrialism and the rise of the business class.

Parkinson, R. N. "The Inheritors; or A Single Ticket for Howards End." In *E. M. Forster: A Human Exploration. Centenary Essays,* edited by G. K. Das and John Beer, pp. 55-68. New York: New York University Press, 1979.
　　Discusses the role of chance and individual affinity in the inheritance of Howards End.

Rivenberg, Paul A. "The Role of the Essayist-Commentator in *Howards End.*" In *E. M. Forster: Centenary Revaluations,* edited by Judith Scherer Herz and Robert K. Martin, pp. 167-76. Toronto: University of Toronto Press, 1982.

Explains that Forster's use of essayistic narration in *Howards End* mirrors his preference for the essay form throughout his writing career.

Stape, J. H. "Leonard's 'Fatal Forgotten Umbrella': Sex and the Manuscript Revisions to *Howards End.*" *Journal of Modern Literature* 9, no. 1 (1981-82): 123-32.

Analyzes early manuscript versions of *Howards End* to contrast their depictions of sexual and physical encounters with those in the published version of the novel, speculating that Forster may have been uncomfortable presenting sexuality to his readers.

Carlo Levi
1902-1975

Italian novelist, memoirist, journalist, and travel writer.

INTRODUCTION

A medical doctor, artist, and author, Levi was considered one of the most promising writers of post-World War II Italy. His best-known work, *Cristo si è fermato a Eboli* (1945; *Christ Stopped at Eboli*), is a chronicle of Levi's year of exile in Gagliano, one of Italy's poorest regions. The book—considered a travel narrative, memoir, political essay, and anthropological study—catapulted Levi to national prominence in Italy and inspired praise from critics and audiences around the world.

BIOGRAPHICAL INFORMATION

Levi was born November 29, 1902, in Turin, Italy. In 1924 he received his M.D. from the University of Turin. He served in the Italian military in 1925 and founded the Italian Action Party, an anti-Fascist group that opposed Italian dictator Benito Mussolini, in 1930. He also established *Guistizia e Liberta,* an anti-Fascist periodical, in 1931. His political activities resulted in his arrest in 1934; a year later he was exiled to the remote and impoverished village of Gagliano, Lucania. His year in exile provided the material for his study, *Christ Stopped at Eboli,* which garnered much positive critical attention. After his release from exile, he emigrated to France, but returned to Italy during World War II. He continued his subversive activities and was rearrested in Florence on political charges in 1942. After his release he became editor of *Nazione del Popolo* and *Italia Libera,* two anti-Fascist, liberal periodicals. In the 1960s, he served two terms as an independent senator in the Italian senate. An accomplished artist, he had several one-man exhibits of his work in Europe and the United States. Levi died of pneumonia January 4, 1975, in Rome.

tory, psychology, and politics. His novel *L'Orologio* (1948; *The Watch*) chronicles a few days among intellectuals in Rome shortly after the Italian liberation at the end of World War II. Using the symbol of a watch he inherited from his father, Levi explores the themes of time and man's relation to history. In *La doppia notte dei tigli* (1959; *The Linden Trees*), Levi records his impressions from a short trip to postwar Germany. Although the work is categorized as a travel narrative, Levi also strove to analyze the mindset of the German people.

MAJOR WORKS

Christ Stopped at Eboli remains Levi's best known and most highly regarded work. In 1935, exiled for his anti-Fascist activities, Levi spent a year among the peasants in Italy's poorest region. He recorded his experiences, as well as his impressions of the people, their customs, landscape, mythology, and architecture. *Christ Stopped at Eboli* is regarded as a multi-layered study of a region and its people. His other works also emphasized sociology, his-

CRITICAL RECEPTION

Today Levi's critical reputation rests on the worldwide success of *Christ Stopped at Eboli*. When it was published in 1945, it was praised for its compassionate and complex portrayals of the people of the region and their historical, political, and sociological milieu. His ability to provide more than just cursory character sketches earned laudatory reviews in Europe and the United States.

There has been critical debate about the genre of *Christ Stopped at Eboli*; the book has been classified as novel, memoir, diary, sociological essay, anthropological study, and series of sketches. It garnered favorable critical and popular attention, and Levi was viewed as one of Italy's most promising authors in the years after World War II. His subsequent efforts, however, failed to earn such enthusiastic critical reaction.

PRINCIPAL WORKS

Cristo si è fermato a Eboli [*Christ Stopped at Eboli*] (memoirs) 1945

L'Orologio [*The Watch*] (novel) 1948

Paura della libertà [*Of Fear and Freedom*] (essays) 1948

Il futuro ha un cuore antico: Viaggio nell' Unione Sovietica (travel essay) 1956

Le parole sono pietre: Tre giornate in Sicilia [*Words Are Stones: Impressions of Sicily*] (travel essay) 1956

La doppia notte dei tigli [*The Linden Trees*] (travel essay) 1959

Tutto il miele è finito (travel essay) 1964

Coraggio dei miti: Scritti contemporanei, 1922-1947 (memoirs, journalism, novel, and travel essays) 1975

CRITICISM

Lawrence Grant White (review date 19 April 1947)

SOURCE: White, Lawrence Grant. "Beyond Civilization." *Saturday Review of Literature* 30, no. 16 (19 April 1947): 12.

[*In the following positive review of* Christ Stopped at Eboli, *White contends that Levi "has proved his competence by making a readable and interesting book out of grim and forbidding material."*]

[*Christ Stopped at Eboli*] is a well-written account, by a sensitive and cultivated anti-fascist, of a year spent as a political exile at Gagliano, a primitive and remote village in Lucania, which forms the ankle of the Italian peninsula. Here civilization had hardly penetrated. The natives said that "Christ stopped at Eboli," a town in the neighboring province of Campania; and to them, Christ is synonymous with civilization. This explains the obscure meaning of the title.

It was in 1935 that the author, wearing handcuffs, was escorted from the Regina Coeli prison in Rome to Gagliano. With a painter's understanding he describes the stark beauty of the countryside; windswept hills denuded of their once luxuriant forests; white clay pitted with caves in which strange swart people, descendants of some aboriginal Italic race, lived like troglodytes. The intangible characteristics of the locality were hatred, superstition, ignorance, and malaria. There were family feuds dating back to the days of the Bourbons and the Carbonari. The horns of a dragon, slain by a Colonna prince with the timely aid of the local madonna, were venerated in the next village; and the author's housekeeper was a successful witch. The malaria was unchecked by the two incompetent local doctors, who prescribed a harmless white powder sold as quinine by the unlicensed pharmacy.

In such surroundings the author appeared like a visitor from another planet. He had been trained as a physician, and did what he could, without instruments or proper drugs or reference books, to help the sick. They looked upon him as a savior with magical powers, but the provincial government regarded his activities with suspicion, and decreed that he could no longer practise medicine. His patients armed themselves with scythes and wanted to kill the mayor as a gesture of protest.

Local morals were a curious mixture of license and stiff conventionality. Love-making was the principal obsession; the village was swarming with illegitimate children, who were taken as a matter of course. Yet an aged crone could not consult the author professionally unless properly chaperoned; nor could any respectable woman act as his housekeeper. The latter problem was solved in the person of Giulia, the sorceress, whose reputation was already tarnished by the evidence of her sixteen assorted bastards. But even she did not sleep in the house, for she had to live with her current lover, a pink-eyed albino barber.

Levi writes with sympathy and insight about the local "gentry," a word repeatedly used which is probably an unfortunate translation of the Italian word *gente*. As might be expected, they were a queer lot. The queerest was an ancient toothless gravedigger who lay on the cool earth in a newly dug grave to escape the blinding sun. He was also the town crier, and had once been a wolf-tamer, a profession for which sorcery was a necessary qualification—for it was his supernatural powers which enabled him to keep the wolves away from the flocks. Then there was Don Trajella, the sodden and embittered old priest, who consoled himself by writing Latin epigrams against the authorities; the smug mayor, and his powerful sister Donna Caterina, who really ruled the village; and the lieutenant in charge of the local militia, whose ambition was to escape from his own despair and the decay and spiritual poverty around him. The author was deeply influenced by the strange people of Gagliano—so much so that when he returned home to Turin on a short leave of absence he found himself ill at ease amongst his normal surroundings; and when his exile was unexpectedly terminated by the political amnesty at the end of the Abyssinian War, he sought excuses to postpone his departure.

The book is neither a novel nor a diary, but an accurate description of a curious community life. It is also, indirectly, a plea for badly needed political, economic, and social reforms in the hinterland of Southern Italy. His solutions are a more representative form of government, reforestation, more livestock, and the suppression of the middle-class village tyrants.

Mr. Levi has succeeded admirably, with the help of a pleasing literary style, in communicating his own interest. He is said to be a talented painter. If so, a few illustrations of his impressions of Gagliano and its inhabitants would have enhanced the volume. Hailed by Italian critics as one of their most promising contemporary writers, he has proved his competence by making a readable and interesting book out of grim and forbidding material.

C. G. Paulding (review date 2 May 1947)

SOURCE: Paulding, C. G. Review of *Christ Stopped at Eboli*, by Carlos Levi. *Commonweal* 46, no. 3 (2 May 1947): 72-3.

[*In the following favorable review, Paulding applauds the compassionate and evocative portrayal of the peasants of Gagliano found in* Christ Stopped at Eboli.]

When the Italians set forth to conquer the world, starting with Ethiopia, they attended to one little detail by requesting Carlo Levi to live very quietly until further notice within the limits of a village called Gagliano, which is in the province of Lucania, a miserably sad, malarial and abandoned region just north of the Gulf of Taranto. It is just north of Calabria which is abandoned also. Carlo Levi lived in Gagliano for a year or so, and in this book [*Christ Stopped at Eboli*] writes about what he saw, what he heard, what the peasants told him, what he thought.

He thought and the peasants thought that Christ, that Christianity, that any hope, any possibility or reason for hope, had never come nearer to Gagliano than the town of Eboli—a railroad station on the main line, an outpost of Neapolitan civilization, many miles to the north. "We're not Christians," the peasants told him, "we're not human beings, we're not thought of as men but simply as beasts, beasts of burden, or even less than beasts, mere creatures of the wild."

No one ever goes to Lucania—not to stay there. The Romans came with their State and their Religion, but there were more interesting parts to govern, and the peasants looked at them and then were left alone; the Franks came with a feudal society; they failed and departed; the Kingdom of Naples came and left; then the new Italian State, then Fascism. In this war Montgomery came up the coast to join with the Americans below Salerno; the Germans were in Eboli and it was from Eboli that they launched their attack against our beachhead—not from Gagliano or from Lucania; Lucania was still by-passed even by destruction.

So that the peasants have remained always alone, subject, in their poverty, to poverty-stricken land-owners, subject to the delegates of the State, of any state, the tax collectors of all the states that have come one after another.

Carlo Levi is a sensitive man, a doctor and a painter; he has written a beautiful and human book, looking at this immeasurable distress and putting down the reasons for it. Although after his medical studies he had not practiced, it was quite impossible for him to escape the pressing appeal of the Gagliano peasants for help, and so he did what he could until the fascists stopped him—and that too was a way for him to know these people who trusted him. They were open to anyone who would help—but no one had ever helped them, and so habitually they were remote and silent. At dawn the men go down the steep hill from the village to the barren fields; at nightfall they return for short rest and brief oblivion; obstinately they manage to live. For a short moment in their lives the children manage to play—some of them.

You would think that the peasants of Gagliano would be less than men after so many centuries of suffering; eternally in the presence of poverty and death they are what we are all of us—who have forgotten in our safety what it is like to be alone, uncomforted, on earth. Carlo Levi loved these men and women and it is possible in reading his extraordinary and eloquent account to forget the dismal horror of their lives; it is possible to think of them as symbols of man's state, at its simplest, unredeemed. But that they should be living as they live, a long day's motor drive from the capital of Christendom, is surely one of the most flagrant challenges to our trust in Christian solidarity.

David T. Bazelon (review date 24 May 1947)

SOURCE: Bazelon, David T. "Outside of History." *Nation* 164 (24 May 1947): 635-36.

[*In the following review, Bazelon describes* Christ Stopped at Eboli *as a "new kind of modern lyricism."*]

Plot is always the essential—even, or perhaps especially, when it is so subdued as to seem negligible or secondary. When moments are big, it is the context that enlarges them. Overtly, **Christ Stopped at Eboli** is merely sensitive reporting of a year (1935-36) spent in exile by a cultured Italian anti-Fascist. Most of the book consists of description of the daily life and mind of the peasants who live in Gagliano, a village in Lucania, where Christianity—in its ancient or its modern version—has never become an integral form in life. Thus, to some extent outside of history, the peasants are pictured carefully, with interest, in detail. The silent plot of the book, however, resides in the attempt of "history" or "Christian civilization" or "consciousness"—in the person of Mr. Levi—to *see*, or establish continuity with, something that is very much not itself. The product of this attempt is a new kind of modern lyricism: the book is a well-wrought, lyrical vase.

There are two very striking aspects of this new lyricism: one is its great objectivity—the calm, almost total submission to the reality of the Other; the second is the silent, pervading dream quality which is created by this admission of an alien but genuine reality. Considering the material dealt with—the submerged, hopeless lives of peasants whose chief and almost exclusive relation to the civilization of the West (which we so much treasure) has been that of a deadly, even senseless exploitation—considering this, the rather complete lack of tension in the book is surprising. Its primary quality is charm! And Mr. Levi seems to represent, quite adequately, moreover, the highest expression of Western values. Justifiably one might expect an explosion—at least in Mr. Levi, if not in the peasants. But on the contrary the two come together as lovers, with satisfaction. Essentially, I think, Mr. Levi was fulfilled by a thrilling awareness of the peasant sense of timelessness and death (p. 255, read in relation to his failure of will as a doctor). And the peasants were able, in their own way, finally to incorporate Mr. Levi into their pattern of life as a symbol of future good from the Christian civilization which had heretofore always manifested itself as a vile but powerful thief. They made of him a kind of witch-doctor.

I believe Mr. Levi got the best of the bargain, as is clear from the book. He had cleaned out of him enough of the Christian world to be able to perceive the basic meanings that that world attempts—so successfully—to deny. But this denial can never match the eternal *willingness to wait* of the underworld of instinctual reality. The peasants of Lucania have waited more than two thousand years. Mr. Levi seems to be saying that this fact is not to be bewailed too loudly, that it is perhaps just as well that Christ stopped at Eboli. But one likes to think that it would have been good if he had traveled farther, even all the way to Gagliano. One likes to think that he might have learned something from the peasants there.

G. J. Wood (review date August 1947)

SOURCE: Wood, G. J. "Italian Villages." *Canadian Forum* 27, no. 319 (August 1947): 117-18.

[*In the following review, Wood deems* Christ Stopped at Eboli *as a vigorous and colorful account.*]

The South of Italy has long been known to tourists as a land of brigands, poverty, and excessive heat. Although the brigands may have declined somewhat in prestige during this century, lured perhaps to those American centres which felt the need of their peculiar talents, the poverty and the uncompromising climate have remained. Into this stark area, with its forbidding mountains and its wretched villages, came Dr. Carlo Levi of Turin, banished thither in 1935 for his opposition to the Abyssinian Campaign, then about to begin. On Levi, physician, philosopher, and artist, was thus imposed an existence which might well have been the despair of other men of similar parts. However,

determined to make the best of the situation, the exile set out with palette and brush to capture the more interesting features of this land and its people; in addition, he lent a helping hand wherever medical aid was required, although his services in this capacity were somewhat restricted by the petty and officious interference of his village custodians.

[In *Christ Stopped at Eboli*] Levi is as skillful with his pen as with his brush in assisting one to experience with him the atmosphere of this remote community.

Gagliano, a village of the Province of Lucania, lies not far from the Gulf of Taranto, and is situated, needless to say, on a mountain-top. In this forsaken region the life of the peasantry has continued unchanged since the days of the Roman Empire.

The amenities of civilization have never succeeded in penetrating the uninviting mountains in company with the tax-collector. As a result, the peasants have the saying that "Christ stopped at Eboli," that is, all that Christian civilization is supposed to stand for has been denied to them.

Dr. Levi's account of his days among these peasant folk offers a bountiful supply of colorful narrative. In a village alive with flies, goats, and children, but otherwise devoid of incident capable of attracting the average writer, Levi has probed gently but surely beneath the monotonous surface, and has unearthed the feuds, the superstitions, and the idiosyncrasies of the peasants, and has recorded them in a vigorous and fascinating narrative.

Toward the end of the book, Dr. Levi allows himself a short but enlightening commentary on the problem of the relationship between the state and the peasant; the gap between the two, and the sacrifice of the latter to "middle-class tyrants," he holds to be the basic difficulty in finding an efficient system of government today. Where the Communist Silone, in his novel, *Bread and Wine,* urges the achievement of a peasant-sanctioned government, which would mean for the peasantry submission to a new species of centralized control (presumably to include Silone), Levi finds a solution of the problem in a thorough-going autonomy. He shows a respect for the independence of the individual, and it is between the opinions of such men as he, and of those who would demand the submission of that independence to the State in return for whatever benefits the communist system might offer, that Italy vacillates today.

Siegfried Mandel (review date 25 February 1950)

SOURCE: Mandel, Siegfried. "Pre- & Ant-Christian." *Saturday Review of Literature* 33, no. 8 (25 February 1950): 30.

[*In the following review, Mandel outlines the major thematic concerns of* Of Fear and Freedom.]

Carlo Levi is now known in this country for his brilliant *Christ Stopped at Eboli,* a sociological, anthropological, and political diary-novel describing Levi's year of exile in a small Southern Italian town because of political activities against Mussolini in 1935. Toward the close of the book he makes a strong distinction between two civilizations—that of the country and that of the city. The former he regards as pre-Christian, the latter as a civilization no longer Christian.

Of Fear and Freedom explores briefly but profoundly in essay form the question of what is psychologically common to both civilizations and what is materially different. What might be taken for Mr. Levi's main theme is his cogent observation:

> History is nothing but the eternal venture of the human mass in its laborious endeavor to determine itself, to resolve itself into state, poetry, liberty, or to abscond into religion, rite, custom . . .

Each phase of this theme is lucidly developed down to very nearly its last nuance. Along with becoming conscious human beings, there is in the experience of all men the urge to express the inexpressible and to worship and cling to the concrete symbols of that expression—primarily religion and the state.

The author describes this process of expression as an escape from pure anarchy into pure tyranny. Somewhere in between there is the freedom which men fear—a freedom which rejects idols, wars, and concrete symbols that are substitutes for freedom. Until men find that liberty and freedom there remains no choice but "to believe, to obey, to fight," whether it be for God or Caesar.

Mr. Levi's ideas are considerably ingenious, sometimes overly so (but so is the psychology of both the primitive and the sophisticate), and they touch with stylistic finesse on the problems of myth, sin, slavery, symbols, love, art, and politics. These conceptions help explain the "pre-Christian" country civilization with its tendency toward religious expression, and the "no longer Christian" city civilization with its political emphasis. Freedom resides within neither and must still be sought out.

Fond of startling paradoxes, contrasts, and statements whose opposites imply equal, or equally questionable, truths ("There is no rabble without a king, there are no masses without God"), Carlo Levi has the gift of baring psychological motives clearly and of summarizing neatly a wealth of experience. At times Mr. Levi borrows from psychoanalysis and theology but he is indebted more to his personal experiences.

Irwin Edman (review date 3 April 1950)

SOURCE: Edman, Irwin. "Thoughts in the Dark." *New Republic* 122 (3 April 1950): 19-20.

[In the following review, Edman offers a negative assessment of Of Fear and Freedom.*]*

The author of *Christ Stopped at Eboli* commands the interested attention of anyone who read that wise and touching picture of a remote, oppressed peasant community in the hills of southern Italy. One felt in Levi's admirable vignette of eternal humanity the sensibilities of a poet and something of a seer. Now comes a book, written five years earlier, when the author was living in France. It was at the beginning of World War II; Levi was depressed about the future as well as the present and disenchanted with the past. He thought it at least a good moment to make his peace with himself and his estimate of the universe. This volume constitutes a philosophy, the author's philosophy, his confession of faith, his testament of feeling at one of the darkest moments in modern history. Now, in a moment scarcely less dark, he has chosen to issue the book, unrevised.

Of Fear and Freedom is declared by its translator (the exact translation of "Paura della libertà"—"Fear of Freedom"—would have been more meaningful) to be a work of genius, of that special genius in which ideas are merged with the music of their utterance and in which everything is suggestion and intimation, stirring the paths of our subconscious with the depths of wisdom not reducible simply to logical terms. Perhaps in the original Italian, which I have not had the opportunity to see, the effect may be that of poetic magic and moral incantation. In English it reads like a curious special jargon, neither idiomatic English nor language suggesting idiomatic Italian. The book is filled with magisterial aphorisms, or what perhaps in the Italian seem to be aphorisms. I have struggled to understand what is being said. I am confused by what purports to be poetic utterance and manages only to be turgid prose. It is almost impossible, for me at least, to think that the man who wrote the succinct, evocative prose of *Christ Stopped at Eboli* could produce this foggy essay.

Yet a theme somehow does emerge, and a sense of the writer's seriousness and perception. The theme is that of man's fear in the presence of the sacred. Carlo Levi is sound enough in recognizing that religion is not all light, that there is a central core of darkness in it. The sacred is terrifying, and men have always proceeded to try to release themselves from the fear its idols promote. They have converted the sacred, fearsome and terrifying into mystery and ritual. They have worshiped "the divine father and the divine state [which] live eternally and jealously claim throughout eternity the slavery of women and the sacrifice of love." They fear freedom; "a new ambiguity is taking shape, a mechanical and sportive association of power and servitude. . . . The sacred history of the world is a history of willing servitude, of tortures, punishments and mutilations, expulsions and ritual killings, of slaughter and intolerance, of prisons and exiles." The state becomes a substitute god, and its dictatorial laws a surrogate idolatry. "There is the rise of human religion and its liberation." But human nature cannot brook freedom and shudders back to new submission.

This is about what Dr. Levi seems to say, though obscurely. Poetic prophecy is possible to a Blake or a Plotinus; in lesser hands it becomes the rhetoric of impassioned and semi-erudite confusion. *Christ Stopped at Eboli* was a little masterpiece of reflective observation. This book is no masterpiece of philosophy; I am not even sure how much is being said, except platitudes dressed up to sententiousness and tricked out with allusions to recent anthropological studies in religion, and to the current unhappy state of man.

Lawrence Grant White (review date 30 June 1951)

SOURCE: White, Lawrence Grant. "Time and the Man." *Saturday Review of Literature* 34, no. 26 (30 June 1951): 8-9.

[*In the following review, White maintains that* The Watch *is a well-written and worthwhile book.*]

Carlo Levi, the gifted author of *Christ Stopped at Eboli,* has written another book about Italy. Its obscure title, *The Watch,* refers to a graduation present from his father, symbolizing the unity of time and recurring as the subject of a curious dream.

The method used in the two books is similar: the meticulous recording of the author's impressions of scenes and events and the conversations and opinions of the people he meets. But within these similar frames the subject matter differs widely. For *Eboli* is a vivid picture of life in a remote and primitive town, and *The Watch* is a record of a few days among intellectuals in Rome during the confused times immediately following the liberation in the last war. There are a few reminiscences of the author's editorial activities in Florence and a description of his eventful trip to his uncle's deathbed in Naples.

Though not as powerful as the earlier book, *The Watch* is equally well written. The characters are alive, and the scenes are graphically described with the pen of a painter who knows how to write. The result is a glittering mosaic, highly polished but lacking a definite pattern. There is no plot: "*senza storia,*" to use his own words.

On the dust jacket of the Italian edition is a sonnet, reproduced in the author's handwriting, listing the strangely assorted contents of the book. It might be freely translated as follows:

> The sound of lions roaring in the
> night,
> striking at memory from the depths
> of time,
> owls and Madonnas, symbols and
> events
> disrupted and rejoined, without a
> plot;
> jungles of tenements, caves, birds, and
> branches,
> courtyards for rats, and glories over-
> thrown,

> eyes, voices, gestures—gold as well
> as dross,
> a green reburgeoning of evil
> days;
> thieves in the woods, and adders at
> the breast,
> kings true and false, and ministers,
> and beggars,
> peasants at work, while worms are in
> the saddle,
> the timeless wailing and the funeral
> speech;
> courage and famine—patient suffering
> men,
> and Rome, and Italy—such is "The
> Watch."

The reader will find the above items, and many more, in the text. The book opens and closes with the roaring of the lions, a mysterious sound which Mr. Levi seems to hear at night in Rome but inaudible to your reviewer's less receptive ears, which were deafened by the more insistent sound of internal-combustion engines. The owl figures prominently in Mr. Levi's painting on the front of the Italian dust jacket. The Madonnas and rats are plentiful and so are the courtyards of decaying palaces. The author on his way to Naples in a dilapidated truck was nearly shot to death by a brigand ambushed in the woods; but he returned to Rome in style with a cabinet minister.

The snake at the breast is a macabre story of abject poverty in Rome. Although obscenities are not to be found in the text (a pleasant surprise in this day and age), Mr. Levi delights in the horrible and the grotesque. Thus, he describes a man whose nose had been split in two as follows: "The noses were composed of an intricate series of little valleys, cavities, and protuberances, like a mixture of varicose veins and bowels." Strong language, but the reader won't forget it. And here is a telling but less revolting description of an Italian room on a hot day: "The shutters were closed on account of the heat, and only the reflection from the houses opposite filtered through in burning threads."

The true king referred to in the sonnet is Victor Emmanuel III, then still technically on the throne but forgotten and disregarded by his people. The false king is Giuseppe Biscaglia of Poggioreale, who had become king by his wits—a fabulous character, "as rich as the sea," with a throne-room and a real gold throne. Those who have read *San Gennaro Never Says No,* by Giuseppe Marotta, will recall a chapter devoted to him, where his last name is given as Novarra. He probably assumed the name of Biscaglia to further the amusing imposture, described by Mr. Levi, when he successfully masqueraded as the son of a wealthy Neapolitan shop-owner of that name in order to impress his prospective bride's parents. Whatever his name, he would be a scarcely credible character even in an extravagant comic opera.

The anonymous translator has successfully caught the author's mood. There are a few confusing slips, apparently due to what Belloc calls a "deceptive similarity of sound," such as "avocation" for *avvenimento,* "varnish" for *vernice,* a literal translation but an unlikely material for painting political slogans on walls. On the other hand, the formidable paragraphs of the original have been broken up, so that the English version is easier to read than the Italian. And *The Watch* is well worth reading in either language.

Frances Keene (review date 21 July 1951)

SOURCE: Keene, Frances. "One Moment in History." *Nation* 173 (21 July 1951): 54-5.

[*In the following review, Keene provides a laudatory assessment of* The Watch *and views it within the context of Levi's oeuvre.*]

First of all, of course, this isn't a novel, as the jacket and its blurb would have you believe. It would be a mistake to expect Levi to construct, out of historical incident and personal experience, a technically acceptable work of fiction. So let's get the idea out of the way that *The Watch* even pretends to be a novel, complete with plot, sub-plot and, if possible, love interest. Then perhaps we can talk fairly about the book.

It is, instead, a prolonged meditation upon one moment in recent history. Levi's work has always had to do with man in relation to the historical moment, and the present book gives it continuity and cumulative force. He is a writer animated by a clinical interest in his fellow-man, but unlike many clinicians, he has also great love for his fellows. It is not the kind of love which breeds false values or the eternal sentimentalities of men who "mean well." It is the love of a good doctor, which Levi was trained to be, the doctor who knows when merely to advise, when to cut and stitch, even when to prescribe the death draft.

This loving man, this writer who is piling up human and personal documents in his books, has chosen to record—of all the incidents he has witnessed in the event-packed last years—one moment in time which was to some the most searing and shattering, and therefore the most symbolic of all—the fall of the Parri (Resistance) government in Italy in 1946. The importance of this moment was that for so many it spelled the end of hope. Not only for Italy but for Western Europe, the coup d'état sealed a kind of doomed return to the status quo ante and, specifically in Italy, to clericalism and Giolittian impotence.

In the lacerating and beautiful chapters which describe the government crisis and the last press conference of the ousted leader, Levi writes: "The Premier, the fallen Premier whom they wanted either to support or replace, did not fly in the sky [of politics], nor did he even turn to look at it. He walked over a small earth, and did not want to know and see anything but . . . the faces and hands of all those he met on his way. He stopped to talk with them, forgetting everything else, and he wept for their tears."

Opposing this "exotic and courageous" man, Levi aligns not only the other party leaders who maneuvered him out of office but the multitude of inert, malevolent, and sycophantic office-holders who "would no longer have to tremble at the idea of crazy reforms, senseless changes, cruel purges, and ridiculous demands for efficiency, [who] would no longer need to greet superiors who didn't hesitate to humiliate them by rejecting the title 'Your Excellency,' so sweet on the lips." There you have the duality between real and false, between sincere and conventionally bland and faceless, which is the prime element of the book.

This symbolic dichotomy appears again in a notable and intensely credible discussion between two fellow-editors and the author in which one of the former divides all men into producers, *Contadini* ("peasants" in the sense of those who make real things grow), and parasites, *Luigini* ("gentlemen" whose only claim to survival is their genuine passion for a bite, even a small bite, of authority).

Hammering this theme in its various aspects on page after page, Levi yet manages never to make *The Watch* a bitter book. It has the gentle, rolling, and engulfing warmth of mulled wine, as if the author partook a little, despite his Piedmontese origin, of the Neapolitan sense of timelessness, which he describes as a "world that had already lived out its time in its own eternal and unchangeable law and that, in that ancient and sorrowful world, people considered themselves nothing but an ephemeral ornament, a transient expression, and yet were putting all their goodwill into adorning it . . . contemplating their own swift passage through it without illusion."

This acceptance by the author of the inevitability of loss, of disillusion, of political but not moral defeat, never implies fecklessness. Levi calmly mentions at one point his own inertia, which is manifest everywhere in his inability, once started on a descriptive passage or a summoned scene of memory (childhood in Turin, the rout attending the fall of France, a moment in the prison of Le Mantellate when the owls were spied on a nearby roof), to cut it short. But his recorded thought and known anti-totalitarian action attest the fact that his convictions have shaken him loose often enough. He knows whereof he speaks when he describes that army of "men and women [who] went about on the streets of the world, driven into a time which was not their own."

This brings us to the device, arbitrary and baroque but valid, of the watch from which these rambling, meditative memoirs take their name. The writer presents us in his first pages with a Kafkaesque watch, the heirloom given to the son by his father upon his emergence into still-fumbling adolescent sentience and standing clearly for some sort of ordered, upper-middle-class continuity of intellectual and social ideas. Levi's meditations begin with his inherited watch, which is first broken in a dream and then, on his waking, in sober fact.

The symbol is never obtrusive, and it starts us off. We then follow the author in his personal hegira to have the watch fixed, hence to his job as editor of *L'Italia Libera* (the Action Party daily), and on to press conference and printer's, including excursions outside the straight narrative of the political events of those days yet related to them by implication. And everywhere the spiritual and physical climate of Rome in those days follows us. In the end, the watch of Levi's adolescence—broken, we are led to believe, beyond repair—is replaced by another bequest, this time from an uncle, a doctor, a "sage," who transmitted it to him on his deathbed through the hands of a toil-worn peasant woman, representative of the loyalties and stubbornness of the *contadini* at their resistant best.

But there is too much of everything in the book, as if, pouring his hot wine with a steady and generous hand, the author did not, literally, know when to stop. Especially is this true of the overblown Naples passage, in which everything of fact and legend which has meaning for our time comes popping, page on page, before our eyes, until at a certain moment, as if to protect the best of the book against this engulfing flood of scenes, words and more words, we wish to cry stop. But despite such defects of proportion, the book has communicable and convincing greatness.

There are a few lame passages which do not ring or move in English, but on the whole the translation is honest and good. Levi's prose pattern, ornate, swollen with pregnant associative adjectives, with convoluted allegorical and prophetic imagery, is more closely followed in this translation than in any American edition of his other books.

To add spice for the initiate of any nationality, there are the painter's vignettes of De Gasperi, Togliatti, Cianca, Croce (in the dream sequence), and a host of other painters, writers, editors, men of politics, who paraded across the Italian scene in the immediate post-war years.

The Watch is intimately related to Levi's other work. The chronological order of the books, if I recall, places *Fear of Freedom* first (for reasons of prior copyright, this title, the correct translation of the French and Italian title, could not be used in English). Levi's contention that this fear is at the root of man's inability to direct his destiny to a morally more acceptable end is given empirical evidence in his first narrative, *Christ Stopped at Eboli.* Therein the fear and its resultant duality are exemplified in the infinite capacity of man to visit repressive and ignorant cruelty on his fellows. In the present work the author takes us one step farther and confronts man with a moment of choice—in *Christ Stopped at Eboli* there was no choice possible. The recorded moment is that of "the last chance." But even among the *Contadini,* the morally saved or salvageable, there are those who "turn toward peace with such intensity that they refuse to defend it": fear of the responsibilities of freedom engulfs the moment, and it is

gone. This inability to choose, to distinguish with any certainty between the real and the unreal, which Levi saw in his snatched moment of history, when all hopes for a true resurgence of the progressive forces were dashed, is the bleak, tragic pageant *The Watch* records.

At a time when man's concern with himself has shut him progressively away from the other selves who make up his world, it is a healthy experience to come on a subjective and personal work so teeming with awareness of the world about one, an "I" book so human, so honestly thought through, and so vast.

Richard Match (review date 30 July 1951)

SOURCE: Match, Richard. "The Captive Instant." *New Republic* 125 (30 July 1951): 21.

[*In the following review, Match derides the lack of characterization in* The Watch.]

On page 68 of *The Watch,* Carlo Levi (speaking through one of his characters) expresses an opinion about Tolstoy. I quote it here because I think it tells what Levi himself was trying to do in *The Watch.*

"Tolstoy," says Levi, "was not a novelist. The huge machines that he used carried him who knows where, but his true value was a different one. . . . He is the poet of the unique instant, which cannot last nor repeat itself nor change . . . outside of time, outside of every novel . . . fixed and intense . . . beyond story-telling. . . . He's like the great impressionist painters. And like the impressionists, he doesn't need to tell a story or paint historical pictures. All he needs to do is to catch, once and for all, an instant that will never come back, that has no before nor after."

Whether or not the foregoing shoe fits Tolstoy comfortably, it most assuredly fits Carlo Levi, accomplished painter, physician, and perhaps more than any other living writer, "the poet of the unique instant." His new book is neither more nor less than a thousand such instants, magically caught, seen and remembered by a painter's eye in the postwar cities of Rome and Naples. And the sum of those brilliant visual images is the recreation of a unique instant in Italian history: the passing of the postwar Resistance movement, and with it, says Levi sadly, the end of the only peasant revolution Italy ever had.

Levi's blurb writer professes to feel that all these unique instants add up to a novel, in spite of the fact that, collectively, they have no plot, no form, no continuity and no active central character. While the matter of classification is secondary, most readers will disagree with the blurbist. It is my own feeling that no book can be a novel of consequence unless it creates full-scale characters.

This **The Watch** does not do. It is alive, literally teeming, with quick word-pictures of people—waiters, journalists, cabinet ministers, black marketeers, beggars, prostitutes, policemen—but it rarely sees inside anyone. Like a painter looking at his model, Levi sees colors and shapes the rest of us might miss, but he keeps his distance.

Although the "I" of this book appears to be the same man who lived through **Christ Stopped at Eboli** (*i.e.,* Levi himself), he remains this time almost entirely the self-effacing narrator, the passive receiver of impressions. Those impressions of crumbling palazzos and ghastly slums, febrile mob scenes and moonlit colonnades, glitter as vividly as any descriptive writing I have ever read. But they remain just that, brilliant descriptive writing, until the narrator *does* something on his own.

In the last quarter of the book, Levi embarks on a journey to Naples. The sprawling canvas narrows down to nine assorted Italians crammed into an ancient taxicab, the wordy philosophizing and time symbolism of the earlier sections disappear, and the central personality that unified **Eboli** emerges again, wise and strong and tender.

Serge Hughes (review date 10 August 1951)

SOURCE: Hughes, Serge. Review of *The Watch,* by Carlos Levi. *Commonweal* 54 (10 August 1951): 436-37.

[*In the following review, Hughes asserts that* The Watch *"is one of the most beautiful nostalgic works to have come out of Europe recently."*]

Carlo Levi's new book will never vie with his first novel, **Christ Stopped at Eboli,** in popularity. It appeals to a more limited number of readers. Where the first novel was brilliantly successful in conveying a fresh poetical interpretation of Italy's perennial problem, the problem of the South, and all of Levi's vision was focused on one place and one people, this second novel lacks both the intensity and the freshness of theme of the first. And the moods of the two works are so different! Whatever one may think of some of the political reasoning of Levi in **Christ Stopped at Eboli,** it was a hopeful vision he had. It was a very young book which looked to the future and had a warmth and a vitality to it. **The Watch,** instead, is nostalgic, it is mellow, and it does not look to any future but meditates on disillusionment. It is one of the most beautiful nostalgic works to have come out of Europe recently.

It may appear to some that in this instance Levi indulges too much in ideas, that he is flirting with the novel of ideas, but he is not. He uses ideas as he uses his images. His ideas are remarkable for their suggestiveness, their sparkle, but they are more fantastic than cerebral relationships. Perhaps the beauty of Levi's art lies in knowing how to envision fantastic ideas.

The story—no—the incident, for that is what this really is, describes Levi's stay in Rome, where he had gone to take

over a newspaper after the end of the war, and continues up to the time of the fall of the Parri government. It is the tale of the failure, according to Levi, of all those groups who fought Fascism and who were united for one splendid moment in Partisan activities, to remain united for peace and so bring about radical innovations in government.

But Levi does not simply describe that time; he shuttles back and forth from the present, and he does so splendidly. The book is not really at all Proustian, as some have claimed, because the center is always the present and everything always returns to it. Levi's past never becomes an attractive labyrinth in which one may lose oneself but only a place in which occasionally to rest.

The imagery retains those sharp surrealistic touches at which Levi is a master. It is a constantly new imagery, fresh, which takes old experiences and transforms them. Levi's eyes transform the most common market scene, the most habitual café talk, the most routine places and things. That is the beauty of his style, that he always places the object at an unaccustomed angle and makes us see it as something new. The sky of Rome, for instance, unlike the sky of London and Paris, is "rich, dense, crowded with baroque clouds full of changing curves that rest on homes, churches and palaces like a fantastic dome the wind wraps up and turns around."

Delmore Schwartz (review date September-October 1951)

SOURCE: Schwartz, Delmore. "The Miraculous Ayme and Others." *Partisan Review* 18, no. 5 (September-October 1951): 575-81.

[*In the following review, Schwartz notes the lack of thematic unity in* The Watch.]

Many passages in Carlo Levi's **The Watch** have a wonderful eloquence, vividness, and vigor. Yet the book does not make a whole, and the reader finds himself in the middle of it making a fresh start again and again. This is partly due to the subject, which is panoramic and includes all of Italy soon after the second World War; and it is partly due to Levi's attitude toward his subject. He writes in the first person and in his own literal being as an Italian, a painter, and an author. But he holds back and refuses to involve himself in the subjectivity of personal revelation: at one point, he actually says of a relationship which he deliberately keeps hidden: "It is a true story, too true for me to want to talk about it, or to be able to talk about it; at least until I am so old that the words will come out of my mouth like stones." And this refusal is matched by an equal unwillingness to commit his perceptions to the process and the order of a genuine narrative, an unwillingness which may be an aspect of Levi's complete fidelity and exactitude, but with the result that much of his book occupies some undefined middle ground. At times, it is the journal or diary of a human being of the greatest sensitivity and awareness; and at other times, the experience which is being reported transforms itself, such is its intensity and meaningfulness, into scenes which have the inexhaustible implications of true fiction.

Levi does make an effort to impose a unity upon his heterogeneous material in the figure of the uncle, Luca, and in the symbol of the watch. Luca is the wise man who has given the protagonist a vision of existence which arrives at affirmation through and after knowledge, and which leads to a sense that old age may bring with it increasing joy and truth. But convincing though he is in himself, Luca does not pull together the other episodes, characters, and events in a dramatic generalization. He remains like the others an intermittent figure who appears, is forgotten, reappears and is forgotten again. Levi's essential point of view is that of a bemused and helpless spectator who loves and suffers with the beings he looks upon, and yet cannot come very close to them. Sometimes he feels he is moving about Italy like Jonah in the belly of the whale; sometimes "I sat on the iron seat like a spectator who happens to be in a theater by pure chance," and at such times he regards the Premier making a speech and this shy man looks to him like a chrysanthemum on a dung heap; and frequently at other times, he moves in a setting in which "the streets were deserted and my footsteps resounded from the façades and the courtyards like blows hitting a hollow body," an image evoking the early Chirico. This very ambiguity and shifting and uncertainty of the narrator's role makes for the sharpness and genuineness of a good many passages, but it also makes the book not a single experience mounting in meaning, but a set of experiences superficially connected and actually separate and disparate and without a truly illuminating relationship to each other. Nevertheless the power and the beauty of certain pages are so great, and the capacity for the assimilation of experience so comprehensive that one concludes with the feeling that this may be the kind of a book which, knowingly or unknowingly, has been written as the preparation for a masterpiece.

Harvey Swados (review date autumn 1951)

SOURCE: Swados, Harvey. "Fiction of Three Countries." *Hudson Review* 4, no. 3 (autumn 1951): 467-70.

[*In the following excerpt, Swados offers a negative review of* The Watch.]

The dust jacket of the new Carlo Levi volume describes it as "a new novel", which is stretching the term out of recognition, for *The Watch* is a highly personal memoir of Levi's experiences over a brief period in the early days after the Liberation. If names have been changed, even if incidents have been rearranged and invented in order to dramatize the author's emotional reaction to the time when it looked as though Italy might really be reborn, that is hardly

sufficient reason to charge Levi with having committed a novel. There are other criticisms that should be made of the manner in which *The Watch* has been presented. The anonymous translation, although occasionally rising to lyrical heights, seems to have been done in haste: "'And why did you come back?' asked Matteo with interest, who, as an old immigrant, looked on America as his second fatherland." And while the publishers have mercifully spared us the fantastic collection of footnotes citing Stalin, Hemingway, Veblen, and 123 others which appeared in the Italian edition, they have not attempted to cut the text itself, which in this case is a pity; for *The Watch* is as undisciplined as a writer's private journal. Description after minute description of the noses, chins, eyes, and ears of passersby who have no connection with the narrative other than their momentary impingement on Levi's consciousness are excellent as practice notations but almost disastrous in an ambitious work like *The Watch*.

Levi's intoxication with his own prose does more than slow the pace of his narrative. It obscures his major design, a philosophic and poetic conception of the passage of time as illustrated by his own symbolic experiences in 1946; and most important, it conceals those really beautiful passages which disclose with charm and vivacity not only the author, but Italy as well. If it were possible to compress this volume to such scenes as the midnight discussions of the young journalist-intellectuals, the frantic bus ride from Rome to Naples with a brigand firing wildly through the windows, the encounter with a corpse in the corridor of a palace-roominghouse, the tour through a hideous rat-conquered Roman slum with a brilliantly sketched lovesick composer in search of his lost mistress—then we might have a work of permanence and stature. As it is, *The Watch* is by turns thrilling and exasperating, graceful and tedious. It makes one wonder whether Levi, whose gifts are equal to those of almost any other European, will ever succeed in harnessing his furious talents to the precise demands of an art form with architectural as well as pictorial elements.

John H. Secondari (review date 6 September 1958)

SOURCE: Secondari, John H. "Golden Coast and Barren Interior." *Saturday Review* 41, no. 36 (6 September 1958): 35.

[*In the following review, Secondari comments on Levi's distance from his subject matter and the lack of facts in* Words Are Stones.]

As a prophet is least attended in his own home, Carlo Levi is less thought of in Italy than abroad. Certainly much less in Italy than in the United States, where his reputation rests solidly on the impact and success of his wartime *Christ Stopped at Eboli.* That was possibly the first book to pull back the curtain from the tragic, desert-like, dusty world of the Southern Italian peasant, and allow a foreign audience to peek. It was only after the war that the Italian Communists made the conditions of the Southern Italian peasant and land reform twin subjects generally familiar to the world at large.

Words Are Stones deals with that same world. It is about Sicily, and the fantastically beautiful sea which now is almost completely empty of fish. It describes that ancient life, a mixture of Arab and Greek, Spanish and Norman, and a little bit of Italian. It pictures the golden coast and the barren interior, where peasants live and die where they are born, never even finding out what lies on the other side of the mountain. It tells of the slowly changing world which is—in one of its aspects—substituting trucks for the painted Sicilian carts. All this Mr. Levi does.

He deals with the social aspects of this tragic land, and the hopeless lives of the peasants. He writes of the feudal estates and the Mafia (which, he says, enforces the law of the estate) and of the Italian police who look on and allow the terror and the murders which are the Mafia's tools. He does this at length in the third part of the book, which reports the murder of a peasant Communist organizer in a village in Sicily.

To an extent, Mr. Levi also considers the social value of things Sicilian when, in another part of the book, he reports the visit of then mayor of New York, Vincent Impellitteri, to his native village in Sicily. The comment lies in a note of wonder at the almost divine value which the villagers placed on this son of theirs who had traveled so far and risen so high. But Mr. Levi's wonder is counterpointed by the vein of his personal contempt that people should believe that there was anything extraordinary in what Mr. Impellitteri had been industrious enough, smart enough, lucky enough to achieve in his life. Above all, the contempt that the people who believe this should be these tragic people of Sicily, whose backward lives he has chosen to champion for a change to the better.

To this reader, it is a note which, once discerned in this first part of the three-part book, cannot but be noticed elsewhere in the pages. Mr. Levi does not feel himself one of the peasants; he says so quite frankly. He merely observes them, and writes about them. One has the impression he does not understand them. And Mr. Levi's observations are brief indeed, for he tells in the introduction that each of his visits preceding the writing of the book lasted no more than two days.

Which raises the point of how this book should be judged. Certainly not as a report, since it is admittedly too shallow in research for a report. Essentially it is not a political pamphlet, though there are overtones of politics, as there are in everything Mr. Levi writes. Then perhaps as a travelogue, written in a language somewhat more readable than Baedeker.

From the title one imagines that Mr. Levi intended every word to be a stone cast against the complacent lack of in-terest of the Italian government in Rome. In English the words are more bread crumbs than stones. In Italian they could hardly carry any more weight, because it is not words that are stones, but facts, and this book lacks facts.

And there may lie the explanation of why Mr. Levi is more highly regarded here than in his own country—because in Italy the people who read his books are also acquainted with the facts.

Milton Rugoff (review date 7 September 1958)

SOURCE: Rugoff, Milton. "Powerful Pictures of Sicily's Peasants." *New York Herald Tribune Book Review* (7 September 1958): 3.

[*In the following review, Rugoff commends Levi's portrayal of the Sicilian people in* Words Are Stones.]

Having interpreted southern Italy with extraordinary understanding in *Christ Stopped at Eboli*, it is not surprising that Carlo Levi should now turn to Sicily. Not that this small collection of reports and impressions is comparable to the earlier book. And yet at its best it displays the same remarkable capacity to see a people with all their past upon them—from the eras of Greek and Saracen, through generations of feudal lords, down to the Mafia-and-landowner rule of today—victim of a hundred wilful masters.

Perhaps that is why he opens his book with a piece about the return of Vincent Impellitteri—onetime Mayor of New York—to his native town of Isnello. Impellitteri embodied for the Sicilians who welcomed him the legend of an earthly Paradise where a poor shoemaker's son could become the head of a great city; and at the same time he pointed up the hopelessness of life in Sicily itself. The fact that Impellitteri never himself knew Isnello, having left it at the unripe age of one, or that he was a less than memorable public figure, only underscores the point, which is that as far as the average Sicilian was concerned he was a dream come true.

A second group of episodes revolves around Levi's visit to the sulphur mines in the Lercara district. On the one side he found the miners on strike for the first time in history, full of wonder at the feeling they had that they were human beings, and on the other side the mine owner, Signor N., like a baron in an old woodcut. As outworn a phenomenon as the mine owner, and an even more bizarre instance of Sicily's isolation, was the cemetery in a Capuchin monastery where, from 1559 to 1881, the bodies of thousands of Palermo's dead were embalmed and dressed in their finery, ranged along the walls of a labyrinthine catacomb.

Part II, devoted to the Catania, Taormina and Mt. Etna area, reminds us that Levi is a painter as well as a writer, for it creates with powerful strokes visions of an ancient

Greek world dominated by a black volcanic god, of broad-faced peasant women "with large, long eyes like archaic statues," of the "curved beach of Aci Trezza covered with painted boats," of puppet plays in Catania that run in serial form for seventy-five evenings, of the luxuriant country-side around Bronte and the nightmarish poverty in the town itself.

But the most affecting section of the book is the last, which begins by explaining the Mafia as the inevitable result of a land of feudal estates and government from abroad, and then goes on to the story of a young peasant, Salvatore Carnevale, who became a trade unionist and led the peasants of Sciara to challenge the feudal system and the Mafia terror. When he ignored both bribes and threats, the Mafia murdered him, ritualistically mutilated his face and held a banquet to celebrate the deed. Nominally the episode would have ended there. But Carnevale's mother refused to remain silent and, speaking out, broke, as it were an ancient spell, releasing the peasants from their captivity. Levi's account of how she first heard of the murder, ran to see if it was her son, and identified the body from the way the feet lay, is bare and terrible, full of antique Greek figures and gestures. In a single moment, as Levi describes it, the mother is transformed from a helpless peasant woman into an articulate, aware and implacable foe of the Mafia and the system, a woman for whom "tears are no longer tears but words, and words are stones."

Joseph G. Harrison (review date 10 November 1958)

SOURCE: Harrison, Joseph G. "Island with Individuality." *Christian Science Monitor* 50, no. 294 (10 November 1958): 9.

[*In the following review, Harrison calls* Words Are Stones *"a perceptive and ably written book, which confers a deep insight into a storied but tortured part of the Western world."*]

Each morning I ride to work with a friend who, during and after World War II, traveled widely in a number of African and European countries. In discussing these lands we have found only one point of deep disagreement—our respective views of the island of Sicily. To him, having tramped and ridden the parched roads of the island during the Allied advance, having seen the poverty of the villages and the distress of the villagers, Sicily is a region to be avoided, an area without charm or attraction, sad and pitiful.

There is, of course, no denying the validity of this view, for Sicily is one of the most impoverished, neglected and, in many ways, unhappy corners of the Mediterranean world. Yet, to this reviewer, it has long been an island with a particular fascination. Its immense antiquity and turbulent history, its many unique customs, the fiery pride and dignity of its inhabitants, the wonderful clarity of its

air, sea, and mountains, all these confer upon it an unusual and powerful individuality.

It is this individuality which created this short volume of reporting and comment by the author of the worldwide postwar best seller *Christ Stopped at Eboli,* in which Carlo Levi wrote of his life as Mussolini's prisoner among a folk not dissimilar to the Sicilians, the forgotten Lucanians of southern Italy. For the present book is primarily an account of certain major ways in which Sicily differs, not merely from Europe, but from that Italy of which it is so tenuous a part.

Essentially it is a sad book, interwoven with the feeling of tragedy which hangs over the lives of so many Sicilians, a tragedy in which the Mafia flourishes, in which men labor for a pittance in the sulphur mines, in which a seething sense of rebellion bursts forth in the banditry of Salvatore Giuliano, and in which the visit of a former Mayor of New York City assumes almost apocalyptic proportions.

Indeed, it is when describing the visit of Vincent Impelliteri to his natal village of Isnello that *Words Are Stones* reaches its highest pitch. Present at this occasion, Mr. Levi describes it in terms which, were they not kindly meant, might almost appear blasphemous, for, in his eyes, the citizens of Isnello looked upon "Impy's" success and return as little short of divine, leaving behind a permanent myth in island folk lore.

A perceptive and ably written book, which confers a deep insight into a storied but tortured part of the Western world.

Seymour Freidin (review date 11 March 1962)

SOURCE: Freidin, Seymour. "An Italian on His First Visit to Germany." *New York Herald Tribune Book Review* (11 March 1962): 6.

[*In the following review, Freidin is dismayed by Levi's negative portrayal of Germany and its citizens in* The Linden Trees.]

Germany has many scars that go more than skin deep. Gifted, highly sensitive Carlo Levi seems to have run his delicate fingers over them like an expert surgeon. He made his diagnosis before he set out from his homeland, Italy. It was based on what Mr. Levi calls pre-judgment. Some would call it prejudice. The talented Italian writer probably would not disagree if it were put to him that way. He admits he has prejudices especially when Germany and its Germans are up for analysis and assessment.

This slender book is more than just a travel narrative. It is the compulsive attempt of an artist to sift through the sights, sounds and smells of a divided Germany. Mr. Levi tries to tell, from his point of view, why Germans—East and West—behave today as they do. *The Linden Trees* is an apolitical book in the sense that other contemporary efforts are consciously, and often ponderously, political.

Mr. Levi has found, in his travels and encounters in Germany, deeply-rooted senses of guilt, a haunting desire to belong to someone or something and a search for the future in today. He does not attempt, as he writes, to compare gross national products or assess the sordid by-play of ambitious men who make political deals. The German, Mr. Levi believes, is today in a great squeeze. He may have a lot but his life is empty. Or, his may be the plight of misery and poverty. His life is still empty.

In a stream of consciousness approach, Mr. Levi reviews Germans he met and to whom he talked on this rather unsentimental journey. On the whole, he finds too many distasteful. But, as he contends, they are looking for something and this emptiness in their lives cannot long endure without explosion. His prose is often marmoreal; his political conclusions are frequently naive.

For example, in his wanderings, Mr. Levi found saber-scarred students. Duelling for scars goes on in the universities today. But in the years since World War II, I think that I found only four thin-lipped, devoted young duellists with scars creasing their cheeks. It could be that I didn't look hard enough as Mr. Levi obviously did. The practice is abhorrent even to those not so keenly sensitive as Mr. Levi. I daresay that German students play more "chicken" with motorcycles than they slash at each other with sabers.

German eating habits, the gorging kind, didn't please Mr. Levi. You can find that habit a daily routine at many restaurants and cafes. The annual gargantuan eating-and-drinking Oktoberfest in Munich would make an outsider quail and swear eternal fidelity to a strict diet. You can look for—and find—George Grosz tintypes in Germany. Yet you also can find others—alert, keenly aware, difficult and diffident. Mr. Levi didn't seem to find many of these.

In Berlin, Mr. Levi did the tours all newcomers make. He trod the glittering main streets of West Berlin and went across, past the Brandenburg Gate, to the shoddy exteriors of East Berlin. There aren't any more linden trees, by the way, on Unter den Linden. The sight and atmosphere of East Berlin depressed Mr. Levi as much as the out-thrust opulence bemused him on the other side of the line. Mr. Levi finished his trip some time before the wall was erected by the Communist Germans. Sight of the wall, an offense to human dignity, would certainly have moved him. One can only hope he will complete some sort of sequel to his present travel narrative, even for his own satisfaction, by making another trip some time soon to Berlin.

Elias Cooper (review date 2 June 1962)

SOURCE: Cooper, Elias. "The Eye of a Cyclone." *Nation* 194 (2 June 1962): 499-500.

[*In the following review of* The Linden Trees, *Cooper praises Levi's poignant and insightful observations on post-World War II Germany.*]

The poet Umberto Saba has said, "After Maidenek all men have in some way been diminished. All of us—executioners and victims—are, and for many more centuries to come will be, much less than we were before." In *The Linden Trees,* his narrative of travel in Germany, Carlo Levi agrees with that judgment, but postulates that "even at the extreme edge of the dehumanized a new human moment can come to birth." It is for that "human moment" that Levi searched in Germany. He is not sure that the absurd violence of the past may not be "in some mysterious and necessary fashion also in ourselves." The Germany of today represents to him the most important mystery of our time. Is the new Germany different? "Our very life," he says, "depends on this."

Carlo Levi did not go to Germany as a hunter of facts, incidents, or news items. He spent only two short weeks there. It was his first visit to the country and he admits that what he offers are the hurried impressions of a humanist. He has none the less written with greater insight on the German reality than have most experts or experienced travelers since the end of the war. He does not attempt to answer all questions, nor pretend to be able to do so. The German reality, he admits, does not allow an easy definition, but he was struck by the contradictions of Germany and by her ambivalence. The difficulty he encountered in attempting to analyze the German reality he attributes to the fact that "Germany is hiding." She is not hiding from Carlo Levi or from others, but from herself, from Nazism, which the author terms a "trauma of immeasurable magnitude." He sees the Germans undergoing a natural process of repression which enables them to go on living while hiding the Nazi past. There is, he says, "a deep inner censorship at work throughout the entire country." He likens this Germany in the center of Europe to "the eye of a cyclone, the calm center in which the air is unnaturally still." Levi persistently speaks of Germany as "sleeping" with eyes "stubbornly shut." Just as sick people try to get well by sleeping, so Germany is trying to recover by refusing to face reality.

Levi's impressions are drawn from hurried visits to several Bavarian cities and the two Berlins. In Munich he stayed at the Hotel Vierjahreszeiten (the Four Seasons Hotel), where twenty-five years ago the Munich Pact was signed. Now all that is noteworthy about the place is the massed presence of gluttonous women and fat gentlemen consuming the "intestinal" wealth that blankets Germany. Several blocks away, at a beer hall, a bereaved father poured out his soul to Carlo Levi. "Whose fault is it?" the old man asked, and answering his own question he said, "It's God's fault—because God is Jewish." At another place a young architect told the author, "My brother is a doctor. I design houses for small families—and let's not talk about wars." Are such chance encounters enough, one may ask, to form an impression of so vast a country as Germany? They do not suffice if one is looking for statistical verification of a proposed phenomenon. But an impression is valid when one encounters the same readiness to defend the new Germany and the same reluctance to speak of the past on the part of derelicts, refugees, anti-Nazi exiles returned home, prosperous businessmen, waiters, farmers, engineers and university professors.

Levi found Germany a land of contradictions. There is Dachau, filled with new inhabitants—disconcerted refugees from East Germany—and there is the medieval harmony in the workers' homes that belong to the ancient Fugger company complex in Augsburg. There is modern, shiny, industrial Stuttgart ("This desert of busy, hardworking, painstaking, persistent men, their eyes so firmly riveted on the object of their labor, or on money, its equivalent and symbol, that they cannot look either to right or to left"), and serene Tübigen where Hegel, Schelling and Hölderin were students together.

Most visitors to Berlin are quick to notice the contrasts between the two halves of the city. The familiar story tells of brightness, wealth, the absence of ruins as reminders of the past death and inhumanity, and the freedom of thought and economic opportunity in West Berlin; as opposed to the drabness, poverty, the numerous bombed-out dwellings, the suppression of the spirit and the egalitarianism in East Berlin. To Carlo Levi, the humanist, these are only first impressions. They did not escape him, but he writes: ". . . I felt that the contrasting things I had seen in my first look at the two Germanys sprang, albeit in contrary fashion, from the same entity—as though they were but two faces of the same coin, on one side a human face, on the other an eagle, both stamped by the same die." To Levi, the two Berlins, and the two Germanys, are identified in their opposition. Each half carries to extremes the principles of the world that governs it. But the Berliners, despite the tenacity they display for these opposing ideals, do not really believe or hold to them. It seems "as if in both camps the two roads now being traveled—moving farther apart with each passing day until the distance between them might seem unbridgeable—were nothing but a means of action." Champions of separate causes, they are none the less champions of the same mold. They are like one flock of sheep arbitrarily divided, and distant trumpets can cause them to stampede in an unpredictable direction.

Whether the new Germany is different or not is a question that Levi never answers. What he has done more poignantly than any other observer is to portray a unique historical process at work in Germany—a mass repression of the recent national past. This refusal to thrash out the Nazi past on all levels of society, including the intelligentsia, is certainly dangerous. It facilitates the cry of *"Deutschland erwache!"* to be started up again, and "like a sleep-walker abruptly aroused [Germany] will open its eyes with a mortal shriek of violent madness." This central theme is captured more vividly in the original Italian title of the book, *La Doppia Notte Dei Tigli,* which is taken from two lines in Goethe's *Faust* ("Fiery glances see I flashing through the lindens' double night."). Joseph M. Bernstein's translation is otherwise excellent.

R. D. Catani (essay date summer 1979)

SOURCE: Catani, R. D. "Structure and Style as Fundamental Expression: The Works of Carlo Levi and Their Poetic Ideology." *Italica* 56, no. 2 (summer 1979): 213-29.

[*In the following essay, Catani provides a stylistic analysis of Levi's prose works.*]

The resurgence over the last decade in critical studies on Levi has largely been based on a recognition that convictions first expressed theoretically in *Paura della libertà* (1939) offer a key to a deeper comprehension of his work. As a result, a daunting task of interpretation has been set and undertaken.[1] This article will attempt to define and analyze certain processes in the author's prose writings as illustrating the interrelated concepts of *differenziazione* and *contemporaneità* which are central to his fundamental convictions. The first part of the article will deal with the conscious application of these concepts to literature in structural processes directed towards the intentional breaking down of conventional narrative sequence: especially in Levi's own peculiar methods of character presentation, best illustrated by a close analysis of *L'orologio* (1950), but also in his various memorial devices and cumbersome factual insertions. The second part of the article will try to show how certain stylistic processes, in particular well known recurring symbols and the prominent use of color, carry the same significance as the structural ones by being functions of the same fundamental poetic beliefs.

In the solemnly enigmatic language of *Paura della libertà,* Levi postulates the ideological premises of his poetic world:

> Esiste un indistinto originario, comune agli uomini tutti, fluente nell'eternità, natura di ogni aspetto del mondo, memoria di ogni tempo del mondo. Da questo indistinto partono gli individui, mossi da una oscura libertà a staccarsene per prender forma, per individuarsi—e continuamente riportati da una oscura necessità a riattaccarsi e fondersi in lui.

The moment of poetic creation comes when man can simultaneously avoid the two poles of oblivion (the egoistic abstraction of total separation from the indistinct mass, and the mute servility of total immersion in that mass): when

> i due opposti processi di differenziazione e di indifferenziazione trovano un punto di mediazione, e coesistono nell'atto creatore.

(p. 23)

In the civilized world of reason and history, however, this poetic moment is, he asserts, elsewhere, like the memory of a previous existence, like an underground river that surfaces unexpectedly because

> la sicurezza della ragione, la sicurezza del tempo, copre questo fiume sotterraneo sotto il ritmo matematico dell'orologio.[2]

Levi's Jungian vision in fact asserts the existence of a boundless temporal dimension, "la compresenza dei tempi" or *contemporaneità,* which constitutes the strongest single bond linking his volumes together. The origins of modern civilization, in ancient myth and before that in an initial, chaotic darkness, are present in any single moment and can reappear suddenly:

> quello che è stato può tornare, quello che è celato raffiorare alla coscienza, come riappaiono le spiagge al ritirarsi della marea.
>
> (*Paura,* p. 28)

A sense of contemporaneity, of course, permeates Levi's Lucania where, as he tells us in the opening of *Cristo si è fermato a Eboli* (1945), "nessuno degli arditi uomini di occidente ha portato . . . il suo senso del tempo che si muove," but he felt it intuitively within him long before he conceived or wrote the work,[3] and it is unswervingly maintained throughout his writings. Contemporaneity is one of the twin themes of *L'orologio* (1950) and predominates in his subsequent books.[4] In all of them, Levi emerges as "il testimone della presenza di un altro tempo all'interno del nostro tempo," to use Italo Calvino's phrase,[5] and in the last of them, *Tutto il miele è finito* (1964), he still communicates this conviction as forcefully as ever:

> Come la realtà è molteplice; come, in ogni cosa, co-esistono tempi diversi e lontanissimi! E quanto più viva, reale e complessa è una persona, quando in lei questa contemporaneità di condizioni e di situazioni diverse, come strati geologici, questa eternità della storia e della preistoria, è presente: e quando gli elementi arcaici non sono relegati o totalmente nascosti in un oscuro subcosciente dove possono parere dimenticati e del tutto inoperanti, ma affiorano alla superficie, e diventano contenuti di poesia, energia vitale, capacità di comprensione universale, fuori della meccanica limitazione degli schemi sociali e psicologici della vita quotidiana.
>
> (p. 75)

Levi admires those writers who share his conception of time and the individual: Tolstoy because he gives expression to "momenti fuori del tempo, fuori di ogni romanzo e di ogni storia, fermi ed eterni"; Chekhov because in his works "non vi è mai un taglio, un isolamento, né principio o fine, astratto tempo"; and the Stendhal of *Rome, Naples et Florence* because "ha capito, forse per primo, il valore poetico del casuale, del particolare, dell'interrotto e parziale e istantaneo, nella contemporanea totalità di una immagine."[6] He is fascinated by narrative technique in certain works which are difficult to define, such as Paustovski's: which consists, he tells us in *Il futuro ha un cuore antico* (1964, pp. 162-3), of "un racconto sul modo di fare un racconto" where disparate elements are united, not by form, but by the personality of the author ("il modo più legittimo di scrivere"). But the strongest fascination is exerted by *Tristram Shandy.* He names it explicitly as the model for *L'orologio* and indicates clearly how the concept of contemporaneity can be reflected in narrative and structural manipulations:

> L'invenzione dell'Io come motivo essenziale e forma della realtà crea una nuova dimensione. Per questo Sterne è un grande maestro di stile, e un precursore del futuro. Si creano nuove forme, e nuovi contenuti: si introducono nelle cose i sentimenti e l'ironia, e il senso della infinita mutevolezza della realtà, del suo essere fatta di rapporti inesauribili, della contemporaneità dei tempi . . . È l'invenzione della durata, che si sostituisce al tempo, e costringe a una vaga corsa dietro alla sfuggente realtà, e scioglie e distrugge la struttura e il tempo del romanzo, i limiti dei personaggi e la loro psicologia, con quasi due secoli di anticipo.[7]

Levi extols and adopts the processes whereby Sterne, through the rejection of a pre-established scale of values, restores significance to the seemingly insignificant and, through his narrative disgressions, attains the eternal reality of contemporaneity by transforming the transiency of conventional time into the eternal time of the imagination.

Certain methods of narration and character presentation which have come to be regarded as established hall marks of Levi's works are no more or less than practical demonstrations of the views on literature which he shares with Sterne. The most strikingly recurrent device is his *bozzettismo,* his repeated indulgence in elaborately executed portraits and more frequent vignettes. Its functions are clear in *Cristo si è fermato a Eboli*: to serve an expository plan, to lead naturally into pertinent stories and episodes, or to give tangible expression to a magical existence. In other works, especially *Il futuro ha un cuore antico* (1956) and *La doppia notte dei tigli* (1959), it is often emblematic, or instrumental in the presentation and investigation of a society. It is more significantly to the fore in *L'orologio* where it has received sharp criticism which, however, fails to grasp its essential function.[8] Here, character sketches, in the way in which figures abruptly emerge from and are re-immersed into the mass of humanity, reflect a primary concept by balancing the work on the all-important point of differentiation or individuation, and by maintaining the focus on the ambiguous moment of creation. By refusing to round off characters, following Sterne's guidelines, Levi expresses the limitlessness of individuals and, by expressly truncating and interrupting character development, rejects the over-schematic abstraction of the traditional narrative.

He does this with particular insistence in two carefully arranged and constructed sections. The first, towards the end of chapter IV, describes a meal in a Roman restaurant (pp. 90-111). Thumbnail sketches fall fast and furious on the page. We are presented with Elena the one-legged prostitute with her "sorriso interrogativo," then with intertwining glimpses, which alternate with bewildering abruptness, into the lives of Giacinto the effeminate, talkative waiter and the sullen, bearded Marco. Bracco the painter suddenly interrupts only to be cut short in his turn by the arrival of Ferrari and his sister. He acts as a mouthpiece for a long digression on government ministries. It gives way unexpectedly to the songs of the guitarist Fortunato which finally precipitate a frenetic dance by a group of Polish soldiers. Likewise in chapter IX half-way between this episode and the end of the novel (pp. 214-26), he describes an interlude in a bar with some of his newspaper workers during a power-cut. A similar succession of *bozzetti* (of the printers, the hypocritically obsequious beggar-woman, "la nonnina," a blind musician and woman singer, the landlord, a drunken Sardinian peasant, a tattooed man, a beautiful mother) ends in the ever quickening rhythm of singing and dancing broken off when the lights come on again. Particularly enlightening are the identical techniques used in both passages. In each he pauses to dwell on the enigmatic, unfathomable aspect of a particular figure: in the first, it is Ferrari's younger sister Elda ("nessuno avrebbe mai conosciuto i suoi semplici segreti"), in the second, the mysteriously regal young mother ("Di dove veniva quella donna, qual era la sua storia?"). This is a recurring device in Levi's works, intended to protect the boundless possibilities of the individual from schematic treatment. Each episode also builds up to an almost frenzied final crescendo which is abruptly halted to focus our attention on a contrasting symbolic image: in the first, it is the silent gaze of Elena, "sorridendo, come una bambola"; in the second, it is the blind man, alone and sadly out of tune, prolonging his accompaniment, "come la coda di un disco che continui a girare sul grammofono, a vuoto." Both images are designed to emphasize the futility of attempting to encompass and entirely individuate the persons that have been fleetingly paraded before us, of trying to stem an irrepressible flow in the "vaga corsa dietro alla sfuggente realtà." The reader who expects the continuity of traditional narrative or neatly rounded character sketches is purposely frustrated and disorientated.

This is also the author's intention in dealing with recurring characters who are considered in greater depth, such as the pretentious maid signora Jolanda and her eccentric cousin Giovanni. Their presentation in chapter VI, when Levi first visits his new lodgings (pp. 142-5), seems to be intended, not simply to satisfy the whim of a self-conscious *ritrattista*, but to prepare for a fully rounded treatment to follow. When in chapter X he describes his first meal with them (pp. 241-52), he starts off by showing something of a captivating narrative flair and relaxed handling in depth of character study, only to lapse into a long exposé of his own views on popular literature and abandon Jolanda and Giovanni with a detached ironic aside. Once again, the reader who applies a false yardstick is dismayed to see them recede from view, their "story" and "characterization" incomplete, their lives unbounded by a beginning and an end. In fact, they are representatives of the infinite possibilities of the individual and of the existence of duration rather than time.

Our analysis of these passages is amply corroborated by Levi's explicit assertions in the novel that the differentiated individual cannot be restricted within the limits of abstraction and arbitrary time. These assertions occur in the section (pp. 50-74) where he expertly portrays and individualizes his young comrades in the Partito d'Azione. Having described at some length the contrasting characteristics of Casorin and Moneta, he is at pains to point out that he has shown only one tiny facet of their existence, and laments the fact that "tagliamo una piccola fetta di questa infinita realtà, . . . la facciamo entrare a forza nella nostra vicenda, nel nostro tempo, nelle nostre misure," so that, "senza volere, facciamo dell'onda sconfinata del reale, di una persona che, come noi stessi, e identica a noi, non ha limiti, un soggetto di novella, una tessera colorata di un mosaico disegnato prima, un elemento di un astratto giuoco" (p. 56). This and similar statements (see for example pp. 64-5) indicate a potentially fruitful grid of interpretation for the structure of the novel.

While the passages so far examined would amply suffice as practical rebuttals of abstraction, the author makes it clear that they are more than marginal exercises by providing us with a complete and detailed structural model. The entire penultimate chapter constitutes no less than Levi's "anti-novel" *in parvo*, an exemplar in which he uses not only the devices peculiar to **L'orologio** but others which we will shortly see repeated. It is in fact evident that chapter XI (pp. 264-309), where he narrates his car journey from Rome to Naples, a chapter which is thematically coherent in conception and eventful in itself, might easily have enjoyed the traditional unity of the successful *novella*. But it is equally evident that it has been intentionally transformed by the process of fragmentation and the concomitant interfusion of the narrative ego. The first few pages include digressions in which dead bodies seen by the author in wartime and preparations for journeys made in his youth are recalled. When the car is eventually moving, the sound of a tire bursting reminds him of an adventure from his days as an anti-Fascist activist. While the tire is being repaired, he indulges in a typical series of sketches of his fellow travellers: the two women, the country priest, with his mysterious suitcase whose contents are never revealed, the tattooed sailor, the Neapolitan student, and the Calabrese farmer. Cars abandoned by the roadside spark off an extremely long succession of flashbacks to journeys and escapes made in France and Italy (pp. 278-82), ending in a series of disconnected, lightning images which he calls "le infinite apparenze delle sorti infinite, fuori di noi e in noi, senza termini conoscibili, fuor di una immagine che fugge, fragile, nel vento della corsa" (p. 282). Later, the ruins at Itri provoke a memory of his imprisonment in the Carcere delle Mantellate. Then, the narrative highlight is reached with the quick moving account of the hold-up, its ensuing dangers and the lively reactions of the frightened passengers, which afford a tantalizing insight into their make-up. But the flow is quickly and definitively stemmed by three desultory sections which the author paratactically juxtaposes as a final renunciation of abstract literary notions of character and time. In the first, he clumsily imparts information on southern folklore through a lengthy, unconvincing monologue in which the Calabrese peasant recounts the legendary stories of Sant'Antuono. In the second, he imagines the brigand hiding in the undergrowth, existing in an animalistic, arboreal world "dove il bene e il male si annullano e si confondono, alternandosi in una vicenda di giorni e di notti, e di stagioni senza fine" (p. 303). This thought draws Levi's memory back to the contemporaneous world of Lucania and the principle of "doppia natura." The third and closing section deals at length with the popular, picaresque legends of the Nea-politan poor, which monopolizes the reader's attention and obliterates any trace that might remain of concern with narrative incident or characterization.

Such passages are painstakingly orchestrated. Although Dominique Fernandez is one of the first critics to point out that Levi's manner of story-telling "gli permette di negare . . . ciò che costituisce, da sempre, la letteratura," he is wrong to assert that the book is no more consciously con-structed than his other works, and is not entirely accurate in comparing his narrative technique, "più o meno delib-erata," to that of a child, in its wanderings and discon-nected juxtapositions.[9] Nor is it sufficient to call it simply, as Gigliola De Donato does, a technique "ad incastro" which is essentially dependent on the memorial factor and an interplay between temporal levels.[10] Italo Calvino is right to insist that *L'orologio* "è il suo libro più costruito, più *scritto*."[11] Although it is true to say that it is mainly concerned with the fundamental concepts of individuation and contemporaneity, they are not solely communicated through direct statement, intricate symbolism or intuitive expression. Almost a third of the work is devoted to their planned illustration in structural terms.

While, at its simplest, the memorial device of interposing autobiographical reminiscences sets up correspondences between separate temporal spheres, it is also both ancillary to the technique of structural fragmentation, and its con-verse in so far as it establishes the author's *persona* rather than formal unity as a cohesive factor. Moreover, it often permits more direct expression of the ideology under con-sideration by forming its correspondences with specific moments that are in themselves representative of that ide-ology. This explains the predominance of his childhood and Lucania in Levi's recollections. His memory poeti-cally regresses, not to the chaos of "l'indistinto originario" which is as abhorrent to him as the conventional present, but to the exceptional moments of initial differentiation. His childhood is clearly one of those moments,[12] and Lu-cania is important as "una realtà nel suo farsi originale" which contains "un momento essenziale e necessario per la poesia."[13] In *Il futuro ha un cuore antico* both are re-called with particular frequency because they represent honest virtues which he recognizes in Russia, whereas *L'orologio* is characterized by *souvenirs volontaires* of the Resistance which expertly link the twin themes of the novel. In *Tutto il miele è finito* he chooses to adopt a sub-tler memorial device: by superimposing the differing im-ages of places visited more than once, he creates "una di-versa, quasi stereoscopica, qualità intrinseca della visione" which becomes an escape from the changes of time, the establishment of an "identità che . . . prevale sul tempo" (pp. 7 and 57-8).

Another constant feature which leads to morphological ir-regularity is the undisguised, obtrusive insertion of factual information on customs, folklore and politics into the nar-rative, which constitutes the contribution of the *saggista*. We have already noted the Calabrese's monologue in *L'orologio*. Similarly, in *Tutto il miele è finito,* when de-scribing a convivial evening in Orune, the author is preoc-cupied with recording the traditional songs and magic for-mulae of Sardinia (pp. 50-54). On other occasions, just as in *Cristo si è fermato a Eboli* he explores the significance of *il brigantaggio* (pp. 21-4) and other phenomena, he candidly assumes the mantle of the essayist. Such is his treatment in *Le parole sono pietre* (1955) of the secrets of the Mafia (pp. 141-4), and in *Tutto il miele è finito* of the laws of vendetta (pp. 76-7). Often, the documentation is almost reluctantly presented in the guise of a direct or re-ported conversation, as when he deals with the age-old Sardinian conflict between farmers and shepherds in *Tutto il miele è finito* (pp. 105-8), or in the seemingly intermi-nable monologue by Valenti in *L'orologio* (pp. 175-87) which defines the essential political opposition between "Luigini" and "Contadini" but which is totally lacking in verisimilitude.[14] Typical of Levi's handling of such mate-rial is his long consideration in *L'orologio* of Rome's po-sition as a symbol of unity and authority in the state: he opens with some measure of concession to the narrative by presenting it through the mouths of four emblematic *settentrionali* (pp. 202-4), but soon abandons this clearly unsatisfactory device and continues by directly expressing his own comments and experiences on the question (pp. 205-9). For many readers, such passages are understand-ably the most discordant since they create an irreconcil-able duality of expression. Levi in fact always strives to highlight the much discussed ambivalence of his writings. Such informative digressions, however important they might in themselves be to the author, remain firmly on a cerebral, analytical level: they are essentially centrifugal in so far as they divert attention from the all-important "Io come motivo essenziale e forma della realtà," unlike the centripetal, memorial digressions, and constitute the weightiest of all impediments to conventional narrative se-quence.

Since for Levi artistic creation lies, as we have seen, in an equilibrium between the undifferentiated and the differen-tiated, his works share a timeless, static quality that is alien to the narrative and to categorization. They are sub-ject, in other terms, to the "inerzia del mondo" and the un-changing continuity of things (see *L'orologio,* pp. 212-3), to the crushing weight of an omnipresent "oscurità illimi-tata," of the "zona nera di eterna passività" that is in the hearts of everyone (see *Paura*, p. 105). At the same time, the focal point is the writer's ego in the act of individua-tion and self-assertion, which is not, as has mistakenly been supposed, egotism, but a humanistic individualism which concentrates on the spheres of nascent differentia-tion and contemporaneity that are common to all men.[15]

Carlo Levi is also renowned for certain techniques which are more properly stylistic than concerned with narrative structure or characterization. They are usually superficially associated with his role as an accomplished painter: his detailed descriptions of sunsets or moonlit scenes, for example, or the intense and meticulous attention which he pays to color in general. But these techniques, in a subtler way, are also an expression of the author's basic convictions. Painting, for Carlo Levi, operates in the same creative province as literature, and derives ideally from "il senso dell'esistenza come creazione, dell'identità dell'uomo col mondo, di ogni relazione come atto d'amore" (*Paura,* p. 129). Just as he admires authors like Sterne, he is drawn to painters who share his temporal vision.[16] But his much mentioned *bilinguismo* does not lie in the balanced co-existence of two equally effectual expressive channels. Falaschi has drawn attention to Levi's belief in the superiority of painting which for him possesses the particular technical potential of direct communication with the archaic and arcane.[17] This is why he draws on the prominent chromatic component of his stylistic armory when it comes to a direct perception of basic truths. Color is much more than an accidental embellishment of his prose: it constitutes his most significant instrument of stylistic expression, and has, in specific associations, a deep-rooted symbolic importance.

These associations are with the sunsets and moonlit scenes that figure conspicuously in his work. The poem "Passano i giorni in fretta" (August 1942) already hints at their temporal significance ("o interminabili tramonti d'infanzia rossi . . . !").[18] This is confirmed in a key passage in the opening section of *L'orologio* where he recalls the "senso terribile nel rapporto, col tempo, delle cose nascenti" (p. 16) of his infancy:

> Come'erano lunghi, senza fine, i giorni dell'infanzia! Un ora era un universo, un'epoca intera, che un semplice gioco riempiva, come dieci dinastie. La storia era ferma, stagnava in quel gioco eterno. . . . I tramonti duravano ore e ore, come se la giornata si rifiutasse di terminare, e quel sole infantile, già mezzo nascosto tra le montagne azzurre, stesse troppo bene in cielo. Erano tramonti lentissimi, pieni di tutti i colori più meravigliosi; dove il rosso del fuoco passava all'arancione, ed al giallo, e a uno strano verde marino pieno d'incanto, e al viola dei fiori, chiaro come le prime violette di primavera, e poi sempre più cupo e notturno.
>
> (pp. 18-19)

These lines establish both the emblematic function of the sunset and the pattern of its ever-darkening chromatic gradations. It often coincides with the numerous departures and returns described in the opening and closing pages of his books or their sub-sections, which are intended to mark the transition to or from a new temporal world. The few examples appearing in *Cristo si è fermato a Eboli* are stylistically embryonic because here Levi found himself involuntarily immersed in a different time-sphere (see pp. 10, 18, 52). Subsequent volumes strive to recreate, nostalgically and arbitrarily, his exceptional Lucanian discovery. This explains the carefully tinted sunsets that mark a temporal transition on the first page of *Il futuro ha un cuore antico* and the last page of *La doppia notte dei tigli.*

Their most intense and significant use, however, occurs in certain contemplative, lyrical pauses centered on an intimate communication with unfathomable forces of the universe. One such pause falls midway through *L'orologio* when Levi wanders aimlessly in the district surrounding his new lodgings. Bathed in the dying sun's light, buildings speak to him in "un linguaggio sensibile della contemporaneità dei tempi," and assume a human aspect:

> L'ultimo sole batteva sulla cima delle facciate, e le tingeva di un color di rosa, umano come quello delle nuvole, contro il verde e il violetto del cielo.
>
> (p. 155)

This merging of houses and people in a luminous, vital force fills him with sudden joy as he is immersed in the happy crowd watching a puppet show. All things, persons and objects, reveal themselves openly and unashamedly:

> ma sentiamo che ce ne sono altre infinite che non si dicono, che stanno nascoste, sentimenti vaghi, e forse sono esse che dànno al cielo questo incanto rosato, al cuore questa pienezza solitaria.
>
> (p. 155)

The color of the setting sun is a clear symbol of communion with a boundless, eternal reality, as it is in the meditative section of *La doppia notte dei tigli* which describes his visit to Tübingen with its ancient streets "piene di tempo e di memoria" (p. 90). He ends his visit at sunset by going down alone to the banks of the Neckar to enjoy "un momento assoluto di meraviglia" created by the subtle coloring of the houses in the rays of the dying sun (pp. 92-3).

A similarly intimate description of the Georgian countryside in *Il futuro ha un cuore antico* introduces the symbolism of the second luminary:

> e, subitaneo, arriva il tramonto, sfavillante di luce rossa, purpurea, gialla tra quelle montagne solitarie, e già in cielo, bianca e rotonda, naviga la luna piena. Scende improvvisa la notte violetta; la luna si accende, a mano a mano, e splende, e si fa più grande sulla spettrale distesa dei monti; . . . mi pare che potrei parlare con la luna, che siamo soli, io e lei, in quel grande mondo silenzioso.
>
> (p. 175)

In the closing sentence of the same book, the moon is explicitly associated with the passage from internal to external time:

> Soli con la luna, gialla all'orizzonte, navighiamo sul nero del mare, verso Roma, il ritorno, la casa, i cuori fedeli, e la semplice grazia delle ore di ogni giorno.
>
> (p. 306)

The temporal connection is made unmistakably clear in the ending to Levi's unpublished *Viaggio in India* (1958):

La luna coricata è alta in cielo, perduta la sua cupola, a poco a poco sfrangiandosi in alto, e calando. Non mi pare di tornare da un altro mondo, ma da un mondo interno, arcanamente esistente fuori di noi. Il mondo da cui parte il tempo e a cui ritorna, fermate in infinita molteplice contemporaneità le sue onde, su cui naviga la luna.[19]

As with the sunsets, the moon's role as an emblem of unchanging time is directly conveyed in lyrical moments of intense intimacy through pallid landscapes. The emotionally climactic moment of **Cristo si è fermato a Eboli** is during Levi's visit to Il Pantano in a vain attempt to save a dying peasant, when he is overcome by "il senso fluente di una infinita pienezza" (p. 199). The experience is prepared for by the enchantment of his journey there:

La luna riempiva il cielo e pareva si versasse sulla terra. Su una terra remota come la luna, bianca in quella luce silenziosa. . . . Su quel paesaggio spettrale mi pareva di volare, senza peso, come un uccello.

(p. 197)

In **Tutto il miele è finito** his description of nightfall at Orgosolo, after he has attended the bricklayer's funeral, conveys a similarly contemplative moment of involvement with a timeless force, expressed in a landscape where "le rocce biancheggiano di quel chiarore notturno che è come l'ombra trasparente della luna" (p. 85). In the closing pages of the same work, the abrupt transition from the eternal world of the shepherds to a contrasting time-sphere is again represented by a darkening sky, the appearance of a countryside with a distinctive coloring, "quello delle cose sempre esistite, dello stingersi del sole sulla terra" (p. 118), and finally the timeless spell cast by moonlight:

In quell'aria ormai bruna sempre più eravamo penetrati dall'incanto lunare e pastorale della presenza dolente di una vita che ripete le sue domande e il suo lamento fuori dalla storia.

(pp. 118-9)

Levi in fact ends his last book by reiterating the contrast between temporal rhythms: "quello ondulante del gregge e della luna, quello matematico dell'orologio" (p. 120).

Less evident than the symbolic importance of sunsets and moonlight, is the significance of the detailed attention which he pays to color in certain consciously studied descriptions. Sometimes the proximity of such descriptions to intimate lyrical moments shows them to be a foretaste or afterglow of these moments on a secondary expressive level. In **L'orologio** when he is left on his own in his new room for the first time, a switch of pace and quality of perception is created by the subtle chromatic harmony of a view from the window:

Tutta la città si apriva davanti a me, in una successione infinita di tetti, di terrazze, di finestre, di cupole, in una distesa chiara di grigi aerei, di gialli leggeri, di rosa dorati, di intonaci trasparenti di vecchiaia, appena un po

viola nelle ombre. Ogni cosa era nitida e lontana, immersa in un'aria visibile e colorata, dove pareva circolassero miriadi di impalpabili corpuscoli d'oro.

(p. 147)

The view is exhaustively depicted, gradually assuming the first pink hues of the same sunset that a few pages further on is to produce the ineffable feeling that overwhelms him when watching the puppet show. Likewise, his trip to Tübingen in **La doppia notte dei tigli,** which is to become a voyage on "il mare del tempo" and culminate, as we have seen, in "un divino respiro," begins with the preparatory representation in a minor chromatic key of an ancient monastery and its surrounding village (p. 89). The temporally symbolic colors seen at daybreak from the train approaching the Straits of Messina at the start of his second Sicilian visit, are in similar fashion immediately echoed in a polychromatic depiction of his fellow passengers on the ferry (**Le parole,** pp. 95-6). On other occasions, such descriptions are ancillary to the expression of intimate experiences that are not themselves represented by chromatic techniques. In **La doppia notte dei tigli** his momentary view of the old streets of Augsburg which impart "il senso fisico della stratificazione di sentimenti non modificati profondamente dal tempo" (p. 70) is followed by a rapid burst of color in his description of the market. Shortly afterwards, as he is nearing Ulm, we are presented with the greens, greys and blacks of the landscape and the green of the river, just before a silent meditative pause as he and Mina contemplate the waters of the Danube (p. 73). In **Il futuro ha un cuore antico,** the splash of color in the bustling scene from the window of his Moscow hotel comes immediately after the feeling of utter contentment, unqualified by time and place, experienced the previous night (pp. 30-31). What is more, color on one or two rare occasions seems to form an integral part of his poetic perception, as in the sudden appearance of a Doric temple during his journey to Calatafimi:

ecco, nel centro di una grande conca di monti gialli, chiusa da ogni parte dell'orizzonte sotto un mantello dorato di stoppie . . . rizzarsi il tempio di Segesta, dello stesso colore d'oro e di grano e di solitudine arcana di quella terra, e insieme rosato come un corpo umano o divino, come la traduzione armonica, eternamente serena, di quella tragica natura, semplice in modo da trasformare una storia infinita e la stessa presenza degli Dèi in un modulo.

(**Le parole,** p. 147)

This expressive mode is even more striking in a subsection towards the end of **L'orologio** (pp. 317-22) which depicts the flow of the Neapolitan masses and the ever-changing flux of objective reality. The climax is reached in a description of the market at Porta Capuana and in particular of the array of fish which clearly symbolizes the creative act of differentiation of individual entities from an eternal, indistinct mass. Far from being a superficial adornment, the chromatic component emerges as a stylistic instrument essential to the expression of a poetic ideology:

polipi bianchi e violetti si intrecciavano in viluppi: ceste di cozze nere e di vongole grige splendevano a contrasto del giallo dei limoni e del lucente verde delle alghe; le triglie rosseggiavano come fiori . . . più in là, in un altro cesto, un mucchio di pesci dorati, o un groviglio serpentino di murene gialle e nere attirava il mio sguardo e più lontano, verdure e frutte e erbe splendidissime rilucevano al sole.

(p. 319)

At times, however, whether he is describing the spectacular dress of Kurdish women or a studied landscape near Cagliari, like a picture by Bosch, or the leitmotif of yellow and black in his journey from Stuttgart to Berlin,[20] colors reveal no more than Levi's technical expertise and have no extraordinary expressive function. Moreover, it is often difficult to forget that sunsets and moonlight are hackneyed literary symbols of harmony and fulfilment, and indeed a slight tendency towards pseudo-lyricism and strained *tours de force* can be detected in his writings. These factors have combined to obfuscate Levi's otherwise clear use of color as meaning which, far from being a stylistic vener, is an intrinsic, poetic translation of the same basic persuasions on time and the individual that dictate his structural patterns.

Carlo Levi's creative writings suffered too long from being designated, whether in derision or admiration, in terms such as *bozzettismo* and *pagine d'antologia*. On a very shallow level, of course, much of his prose answers to both of these descriptions. Herein lies the danger. For, on a deeper level, the same prose serves as the expressive vehicle of his poetic ideology.

Notes

1. Following the intense critical activity surrounding *Cristo si è fermato a Eboli* (1945) and *L'orologio* (1950), with enthusiastic approbation to the former and generally a negative judgement on the latter, interest in Levi declined till the revival marked by the studies in *Galleria*, XVII, 3-6 (May-December 1967). Important steps in subsequent advances are the volumes by G. Falaschi (*Carlo Levi*, Florence, 1971) and G. De Donato (*Saggio su Carlo Levi*, Bari, 1974), as well as the posthumous publication of anthologies of Levi's less accessible writings in *Coraggio dei miti: Scritti contemporanei 1922-1974*, edited by G. De Donato, Bari, 1975 and *Contadini e Luigini: Testi e disegni di Carlo Levi*, edited by L. Sacco, Rome-Matera, 1975. For an assessment of these more recent contributions, see E. Catemario, "La nuova stagione di Carlo Levi," *Annali dell'Istituto universitario orientale di Napoli* (sezione romanza), XIX, 1 (January 1977), 109-25. References to Levi's works in this article are to the following editions, all published in Turin: *Cristo si è fermato a Eboli*, 1963, *L'orologio*, 1963, *Paura della libertà*, 1964, *Le parole sono pietre*, 1956, *Il futuro ha un cuore antico*, 1964, *La doppia notte dei tigli*, 1962, *Un volto che ci somiglia*, 1960, *Tutto il miele è finito*, 1964. Abbreviated titles will be used in the notes.

2. *Coraggio dei miti*, p. 58 (from a lecture delivered in Turin, March 1950).

3. A. Marcovecchio has shown that it is paradigmatically present in Levi's unpublished *Quaderno di prigione* (1935) in "Il periplo del mondo," *Galleria*, pp. 99-109 (pp. 103-5). See also the poem "Strega con filtri veri" (1941), *Galleria*, pp. 118-9.

4. It is explicitly reiterated in the prefaces to *La doppia notte* (pp. 16-17) and *Tutto il miele* (p. 7), and throughout *Un volto* where he defines it as "il processo stesso del progredire di un mondo differenziato" (p. ix).

5. "La compresenza dei tempi," *Galleria*, pp. 237-40 (p. 238).

6. See respectively *L'orologio*, p. 63, "Anton Checov," *Literaturnaia gazeta*, XII (January 1960) now in *Coraggio dei miti*, pp. 273-4 and the preface to *Roma, Napoli e Firenze* (Rome 1960) now in *Coraggio dei miti*, pp. 275-86 (p. 275).

7. Preface to an Italian translation (Turin 1958) now in *Coraggio dei miti*, pp. 264-72 (pp. 267-8).

8. See especially L. Russo, *I narratori (1850-1957)*, third edition (Milan-Messina 1958), pp. 356-60.

9. "Uomini-dei o uomini-piante," *Galleria* pp. 161-2 and 172. His article is still significant in that it broke new ground on several fronts.

10. See De Donato, pp. 122-3. Her analysis of the novel's structure nevertheless remains the most complete and perceptive to date: especially p. 127.

11. Article cit., p. 238.

12. See *L'orologio*, pp. 15-20 and *Coraggio dei miti*, p. 69 and p. 122.

13. *Coraggio dei miti*, p. 306 (from a speech delivered in July 1969).

14. It is significant that Levi admitted that Valenti is a mere mouthpiece in a lecture given in April 1951: see *Coraggio dei miti*, p. 66.

15. For a defense of Levi against the charge of egotism in *Cristo*, see R. D. Catani, "Detachment and Compassion in Carlo Levi's *Cristo*," *Journal of the Association of Teachers of Italian*, XVII, (Autumn/Winter 1975-6, pp. 3-7.

16. Such as Rembrandt (see *Il futuro*, pp. 122-3) and Casorati (see *Coraggio dei miti*, p. 344).

17. See Falaschi, pp. 97-100.

18. See *Galleria*, p. 121.

19. *Galleria*, p. 158. See also the opening to the second part of *Le parole* (p. 95).

20. See, respectively, *Il futuro*, p. 182, *Tutto il miele*, p. 27 and *La doppia notte*, pp. 102-3.

Lawrence Baldassaro (essay date summer 1995)

SOURCE: Baldassaro, Lawrence. "*Paura della libertà*: Carlo Levi's Unfinished Preface." *Italica* 72, no. 2 (summer 1995): 143-54.

[*In the following essay, Baldassaro offers an overview of* Paura della libertà, *perceiving it as "a watershed moment" in his literary development.*]

Long before the Resistance movement evolved into the armed rebellion depicted in neorealist films, Carlo Levi was one of that handful of Italians who challenged the fascist regime armed only with the words they printed in clandestine newspapers and magazines. Levi was only twenty years old when, in 1922, he began his anti-fascist activities by contributing to Piero Gobetti's weekly review, *La Rivoluzione liberale*. Later he played a key role in *Giustizia e Libertà*, the underground political movement that was a major force in the struggle against fascism in the thirties.[1] Levi was twice imprisoned for his anti-fascist activities, first in 1934, then again in 1935. It was this second arrest that resulted in his year-long confinement in Lucania, the experience that was to become the subject of *Cristo si è fermato a Eboli*.

Following his release from confinement, Levi, as he had so often done since completing medical school in 1924, went to France. In 1939, after so many years of political struggle, he found himself witnessing the total domination of Italy by fascism, the beginning of Hitler's assault on Europe, and the apparent demise of European civilization. It was then, as British troops were disembarking near his house in the coastal town of La Baule, that he wrote his first book, *Paura della libertà,* an anti-fascist tract *sui generis*. Because of the war, the book was not published until 1946, one year after the publication of *Cristo si è fermato a Eboli*. The book received little attention from critics, and the attention it did receive was due, no doubt, to the astounding success of *Cristo*.[2] The general response to *Paura* was one of surprise, and disappointment, that this work had been produced by the same man who had written *the* literary sensation of post-war Italy.

Paura della libertà remains a relatively obscure work, primarily because of its reputation as a difficult book. Unlike the detailed depiction of life in a remote Lucanian village found in *Cristo, Paura* is a dense, rambling philosophical rumination on the human condition on the eve of World War II. Yet, it is a book that deserves reconsideration, both as the work that defines the world view that would guide Levi in all his subsequent writings, including *Cristo,* and as a testament of its time, a diary of an intellectual's confrontation with the moral crisis of interwar Europe.[3]

Paura della libertà is an unfinished work. Levi's original intention was to write a lengthy opus, a sort of twentieth-century *Summa*, with chapters dedicated to analyses of such topics as politics, art, philosophy, religion, science, and social life. The progress of the war interrupted Levi's work on *Paura* when he had completed eight chapters, which, he writes in his preface, would have been only the introductory part of the projected whole. Levi, however, chose not to return to the work, not only because of the war but also because he felt that "tutti gli svolgimenti particolari che avevo avuto in animo di fare vi erano impliciti" (11). In spite of its brevity (126 pages in the edition I cite), *Paura* is too abstract and, at times, too abstruse a work to lend itself to a brief synopsis. The chapter titles suggest the abstract and somewhat disjointed nature of the work: "Ab Jove principium"; "Sacrificio"; "Amor sacro e profano"; "Schiavitú"; "Le muse"; "Sangue"; "Massa"; "Storia sacra." Like *Cristo si è fermato a Eboli,* and like Levi himself, *Paura* defies categorization. Suffice it to say that *Paura* is Levi's attempt to understand why the world around him was falling apart.

In his preface, Levi recalls that moment of apocalyptic desperation in the Europe of 1939:

> Tutte le vecchie ideologie parevano crollare; . . . un vento di morte e di oscura religione sconvolgeva gli antichi stati d'Europa. . . .
>
> La vita normale, la continuità delle generazioni e degli istituti era finita. I nuovi dèl dello Stato soffiavano via dal mondo i valori umani, il senso stesso del tempo: e per difendersi gli uomini dovevano accettare questa aridità della strage, abbandonare le case e le famiglie, buttarsi dietro le spalle tutto quello che erano stati, e perfino il ricordo dei legami infantili.
>
> (10)

In *Paura* we hear the voice of a middle class intellectual pondering the disintegration of western civilization, struggling to comprehend the fragility of the culture that had nourished him. Though Levi indicates in his preface that when he wrote *Paura* "[n]on avevo con me alcun libro" (11), the extensive references and citations throughout the book clearly demonstrate the breadth of his knowledge of European literature and philosophy. And while critics have noted the imprint of such influential thinkers as Freud, Jung, and Vico in Levi's ruminations, *Paura* is decidedly Levi's personal vision of the world in which he finds himself.[4] It is a world gone wrong, but Levi wants to understand his age as something more than the sum of its nasty little parts; he tries to see the forest while trapped among the tangled trees, and it turns out that the forest he sees is primeval. Rationality alone cannot explain the chaos he sees around him.

Unable to understand the collapse of western civilization in purely rational terms, Levi turns instead to the dark recesses of the human soul, to "quel punto inesistente da cui nasce ogni cosa . . . nei luoghi piú terrestri e oscuri, negli abissi umidi e materni" (21). He seeks "le cause comuni e profonde della crisi," which are to be found "piú che in questo o quell'avvenimento particolare, nell'animo stesso dell'uomo" (11). What he finds in the human mind is a profound fear of the primitive, threatening force that he terms "il sacro," which he defines as: "[i]l senso, e il terrore, della trascendenza dell'indistinto, lo spavento dell'indeterminato in chi è nello sforzo di autocrearsi e di seperarsi" (24). In other words, the "sacro" is an instinctive awareness, inherent in all humans, of our connection with the mysterious totality of creation, an innate religious impulse that inspires at once a sense of connectedness and a sense of terror. The sacred engenders terror in humans, according to Levi, precisely because it puts us in touch with the "indistinto originario," the primordial chaos that preexists human consciousness and out of which we are all born.

Innate in every human, argues Levi, are two contradictory instincts. On the one hand, there is the instinct to emerge from the "indistinto originario," to establish an individual identity and thus become distinct from the masses. At the same time, we are constantly driven by an obscure need to be absorbed back into the "indistinto originario," which, given its premise of a universal and impersonal preconscious human experience, is not unlike Jung's collective unconscious:

> Esiste un indistinto originario, comune agli uomini tutti, fluente nell'eternità, natura di ogni aspetto del mondo, memoria di ogni tempo del mondo. Da questo indistinto partono gli individui, mossi da una oscura libertà a staccarsene per prender forma, per individuarsi—e continuamente riportati da una oscura necessità a riattaccarsi e fondersi in lui.
>
> (23)

Both instincts are imbued by Levi with positive and negative aspects. To remain submerged within the indifferentiated masses is to remain without a voice or individual identity, trapped in a "mistica oscurità bestiale" (23). Yet the individual who is cut off completely from the primordial spirit of the "indifferenziato," who does not maintain a bond with the roots common to all humanity and to all existence, finds himself lost in a "vuota ragione egoistica" (23), alienated in a vain and abstract freedom, isolated from humanity. He is, in other words, one who feels no connection with the myths of his own ancestral past, a connection which, for Levi, is a fundamental aspect of the human experience.

This dichtomy between the indifferentiated masses and the differentiated individual is fundamental to the structure of *Paura della libertà*. It is a dichotomy that is relevant both in historical terms, in the evolution of the species, and in existential terms, in the evolution of the individual. What hinders the evolution from "massa" to "individuo" is fear of the sacred, which impinges on the manner in which humans relate to each other, both on the interpersonal and societal levels. Paradoxically, every human relationship is "sacro e religioso" (24), requiring an identity of the "I" with the other. That identity with the other is possible only when our common humanity is acknowledged, which means a return to the mysterious and intimidating territory of the "indistinto originario." Thus the sense of fear that hinders human rapport. Fear of freedom, then, is the fear of confronting our own humanity, which can be known

only through the process of self-awareness that distinguishes the individual from the anonymity of the "indistinto originario." To avoid the terrifying freedom and responsibility of individual consciousness, we revert to the distancing strategy of symbols and icons.

Among other things, *Paura* is about what humans do to avoid their fear of "il sacro." One way to combat the fear of the unknown that threatens to engulf us, Levi concludes, is to give it a name, give it a structure, and deify it. In other words, turn the sacred into the sacrificial, transforming the ineffable into words, and myths into rituals. The concepts and rites of organized religion are, in effect, a defense against the mystery and terror of direct religious experience: "*Religione* è la sostituzione all'inesprimibile indifferenziato di simboli, di immagini reali e concrete, in modo da relegare il sacro fuori della coscienza . . ." (24). But the gods that are thus created out of fear impose their own demands on us, so that sacrifice is ultimately a blood sacrifice, both of the god, which must be killed to be safe for worship, and of the worshipper.

Though Levi's point of departure is his analysis of the process, common to all religions, of transforming the sacred into the sacrificial, his primary concern in *Paura* is with the analogous process adopted by the State, or more specifically by the totalitarian State. (In his preface, Levi specifies that *Paura* contains "una teoria del nazismo, anche se il nazismo non è una sola volta chiamato per nome" [12].) Within *Paura*, Levi's political analysis evolves organically from his thoughts on religion and the human condition in general. For Levi, the religion of blood is all-encompassing; it is political as well as religious. Like religious and social institutions, the State also creates divinities which demand human sacrifice:

> Come la tribú e la famiglia e il patriziato divinizzati, cosí lo stato, in ogni sua forma piú complessa, quando non sia fatto di libertà o sottomesso ad altri ideali, ma sia esso stesso una divinità, un idolo che richiede l'adorazione, non può vivere che di sacrifici umani.
>
> (36)

The requisite sacrifice is individual and collective, both requiring the loss of freedom and identity:

> Sul piano individuale, il sacrificio necessario è la rinuncia all'autonomia, e una serie infinita di divieti e di rispetti, e il senso della giusta inaccessibilità delle funzioni statali. . . . Il *segreto di Stato* è allora veramente il segreto di un tempio: non si avvicinino i profani. Perché la facoltà di governarsi dell'uomo diventi idolo, la sua stessa umanità deve essere, a ogni momento, rifiutata ed espulsa, come cosa sacra, innominabile e vergognosa.
>
> Sul piano sociale, il sacrificio necessario sarà una mutilazione di una parte della società. Un gruppo, una classe, una nazione dovranno forzatamente essere espulsi, essere considerati nemici, diventare stranieri per poter essere testimoni del dio, e vittime.
>
> (36-37)[5]

The individual, then, must sacrifice part of himself in order to deify the State. Essentially, Levi equates fascism, or more specifically its control over the masses, with the instinctive human fear of freedom. What is true of relations between individuals is also true of relations between the individual and the State. The allegiance of the masses to the totalitarian state is nothing less than a flight from the self, a means of avoiding the fear of confrontation with the self, without which there can be no sense of identity or freedom. The apparently contradictory title, *Paura della libertà,* says a great deal about the substance of the book. Freedom, one of the most cherished of human ideals, ironically engenders fear because the individualization that goes with that freedom requires a confrontation with the frightening reality of "il sacro." That is why the State, by providing the idols that replace the awesome responsibility of choice and individuality, can placate the masses who, by subjecting themselves to that control, abdicate their potentiality to be free. Just as the individual ceases to idolize the father only when he achieves his own equal status as an adult, so too with the individual's rapport with the State:

La divinizzazione dello Stato (e la servitú che ne risulta) durerà finché non sarà finita l'infanzia sociale, finché ogni uomo, guardando in se stesso, non ritroverà, nella propria complessità, tutto lo Stato, e, nella propria libertà, la sua necessità.

(26)

For Levi fascism was not, as Croce had called it, a temporary abberation, a brief, violent interruption of the otherwise positive evolution of Italian society. Instead, he saw it as the logical outcome of a post-unification political and economic system whose values and ideals had atrophied over time, the consequence of a half-century of compromise and accommodation among Italy's ruling class. In a society which had lost faith in the promises of rationality and progress, fascism represented the other side of the coin, the emergence and exploitation of the irrational, infantile side of human nature. Levi's psychoanalytic interpretation of fascism—as the monster that emerges from the collective unconscious and rebels against the aridity of a moribund rationalism—while suggested in metaphoric terms in *Paura,* would be spelled out more explicitly in "**Crisi di civiltà,**" an article Levi wrote for the September 2, 1944 issue of *La Nazione del popolo,* the newspaper he was then editing:

La società che era sorta, ricca di un vigoroso individualismo, con i Diritti dell'Uomo, aveva perduto, dopo un secolo di straordinaria vitalità, le sue capacità creative. . . .

Il nazismo, e il fascismo . . . furono una rivolta interna delle forze irrazionali compresse in questo mondo sclerosato: il sussulto barbarico e infantile di una società moribonda. . . . Di fronte a un mondo inaridito di sola ragione essi suscitarono dal profondo dell'inconsciente collettivo[6] gli antichi mostri, gli spaventosi idoli del sangue e della razza. Era il rovescio della medaglia: il mondo sotterraneo degli istinti ca-

otici e della disperazione senza forma che si agitava sotto quell'altro mondo tutto determinato, ottimista e progressivo.

(*Coraggio dei miti* 53-54)

History, for Levi, is ultimately incomprehensible without an awareness of an "oscura necessità" (37) which renders all servitude voluntary, all victims sacred. At the root of what we call history is an obscure, irrational motivation that, because of our terror of the unknown, necessitates the creation of idols and gods, which in turn necessitate human sacrifice:[7]

Vagavano, secondo il mito, i primi uomini nella selva senza forma, finché si fermarono in *certi* luoghi, amarono *certe* donne, e adorarono *certi* dei. Vagano tuttora gli uomini nella eterna selva, e cercano una esterna certezza: una certezza che si paga con servitú e con morte.

(38)

Levi's vision of his world is predictably stark. The state-idol demands uniformity instead of spontaneity, obedience instead of creativity. Under the deadening effects of the "stato-idolo," culture disintegrates. Creativity, the true sign of freedom for Levi, is possible only at the moment the individual distinguishes himself from the "massa." The fascist state, with its insistence on the acceptance by the masses of its own idolatry, extinguishes that creativity and denigrates art to the level of propaganda:

Il linguaggio poetico è impossibile, e con esso l'arte e la cultura: esso deve essere sostituito dal linguaggio religioso, dal ritmo delle armi, dalla ripetibile certezza. L'architettura delle città diventa uniforme: . . . L'arte diventa monotona ripetizione, litania, quando non è sforzo disperato di impossibile libertà, nostalgia o speranza. Si perde il senso dei rapporti vivi, poiché essi sono tutti sostituiti da un solo rapporto simbolico e arbitrario. . . . La cultura . . . non ha piú senso, nella indistinzione della massa. Al suo posto sta il suo equivalente religioso, una totalitaria, arbitraria volontà di confondere, che si espande, come una materia, per propagazione, e che vale non per un valore, ma per un peso: la *propaganda,* la cultura della massa.

(111-12)

Yet, for all its starkness, *Paura* is ultimately not a chronicle of doom, but a prophecy of renewal. Though Levi looks into the abyss, he does not despair. On the eve of World War II, standing, as it were, on the border of hell, Carlo Levi does not see evil, nor does he believe in sin. What he sees is the psychology of fear as an instrument of oppression, both of the self and of others. What he writes in *Paura* is born of a skepticism of all established creeds, political and religious. In his opinion, the goal of sacrificial institutions, both Church and State, to dictate and subjugate is achieved to the extent people are willing to submit to that subjugation because of their innate fear of freedom. Ultimately, Levi's optimism will not allow him to give up hope that the cycle will end and the human spirit will emerge from the quiet servitude of indifferentiation. Convinced of the failure of the modern European myths of positivism and endless progress, Levi invokes ancient myths (including the Old Testament of his Hebraic heritage) as a counterbalance to the spiritual vacuum of his own age. In the prophetic Biblical tone that is characteristic of Levi's style throughout *Paura,* he writes: "Finché vi sono dieci uomini giusti, la città non viene distrutta" (114), and:

> Babilonia la grande sarà distrutta, la città delle uccisioni e della schiavitú, del mistero e della religione. Il nuovo paradiso, il Gerusalemme celeste, è la riacquistata libertà.
>
> (125)

And it is precisely in that dark realm of fear, in the terrifying realm of the sacred, that Levi finds hope for renewal and for limitless possibilities:

> Una foresta, al principio dei tempi, era, secondo il racconto, sulla faccia della terra. Quella stessa prima foresta informe e piena di germi e di terrore, nera nasconditrice di ogni volto, portiamo in noi; . . . selva giovanile di possibilità illimitate.
>
> (37-38)

In the "indifferentiated" zone of human existence, where the individual has neither been born nor sacrificed to the idols of the State, lies the potential for regeneration:

> Nel profondo dell'uomo sta la buia notte; il sole splende sulle sue opere; e quando è tramontato, qualche stella o qualche barlume notturno testimoniano del domani. . . . Il terrore dei rapporti umani non può essere mai assoluto; la parola non mai del tutto ammutolita, la preghiera non mai l'unica espressione; la servitú non mai completa, la guerra non mai senza paci, lo Stato non mai completamente totalitario.
>
> (114-15)

As has happened before, the chaos that seems to engulf the world may bear the seeds of new beginnings. Levi draws an implicit parallel between the "stato-idolo" of his time and that of the Roman Empire, which "toglieva ormai ai rapporti umani ogni carattere di libertà" (67). The dissolution of the Empire meant the death of the Latin language—"lingua sacra di una morta divinità imperiale" (68)—but also, in time, the gradual rebirth of freedom and of new poetic languages: "con l'incerto nascere della libertà, si venivano creando le nuove lingue poetiche" (68). The same pattern of death and rebirth may occur in the work of the individual artist, for whom a change in style reflects a need to cast off old, dead symbols in order to achieve a sense of freedom and creativity:

> La maggior parte dei mutamenti di stile o di periodo di un artista, sono crisi religiose nei riguardi di una propria religione artistica privata: necessità di sbarazzarsi di vecchi simboli morti per creare nuovi miti, di uscire da una fissazione.
>
> (71-72)

But freedom demands a confrontation with the terror of the sacred, which Levi identifies as both the continual negation of freedom and of art and, at the same time, the "generatore continuo della libertà e dell'arte" (21). The most creative moments, in both collective and individual history, occur when the individual emerges from the mass, yet retains contact with the fearful sense of the sacred:

> . . . i soli momenti vivi nei singoli uomini, i soli periodi di alta civiltà nella storia, sono quelli in cui i due opposti processi di differenziazione e indifferenziazione trovano un punto di mediazione, e coesistono nell'atto creatore.
>
> (23)

What is evident throughout *Paura,* and would prove to be a hallmark of Levi's future work, was an independence of spirit, a distrust of all authoritarian structures and symbols, and a freedom from any strict ideological posture. That refusal to adhere to any political dogma reflects one of the primary motifs of *Paura*: Levi's insistence on the primacy of autonomy and spontaneity over bureaucracy and conformity. Obvious in Levi's aversion to the monolithic power of the State is his passionate devotion to the freedom of the individual and the autonomy of local communities, both of which were to be recurring themes in his subsequent work: "Ogni autonomia, ogni atto creatore, è, per sua natura . . . nemico dello Stato, sacrilegio" (112).

Though Levi's political education was well-formulated before his exile—as I indicated at the outset of this essay—it is unlikely that *Paura* could have been written before, or without, his experience in Lucania. What he found in the peasant civilization of the South was an alternative to the ideology and practices of the fascist state, an alternative that lent itself to poetic expression. Against what he considered to be the deadening forces of fascist rhetoric and idolatry stood the discovery of a world which was not yet born, a world filled with unrealized potential for humanity. Against the bankruptcy of a civilization gone sour, Levi found the metaphor of a nascent civilization, uncorrupt and waiting to blossom, the "selva giovanile di possibilità illimitate" (38). *Paura* is the meeting ground of Levi's prior intellectual formation and his personal discovery of that other world, a merger of theory and experience that enabled him to crystallize his thinking in the book that would serve as the touchstone for everything he would write thereafter.

. . . . .

Paura della libertà both is and is not vintage Carlo Levi. It is in the sense that it reveals the breadth of his precocious intellectual interests, as well as certain characteristic concepts that Levi would adopt in *Cristo si è fermato a Eboli* and subsequent works: tension between rational and irrational, between civilization and history, on the one hand, and the prehistoric humanity of the "indifferenziato" and the "sacro" on the other. *Paura* anticipates *Cristo* in its struggle to comprehend the causes of a current reality. And, in both works, the image of the individual who has not yet been suffocated by history and the State represents the symbol of opposition to the rigid authority of the regime, as well as the hope of rebirth in the midst of what is, for Levi, the spent energy of European rationalism.

Paura, however, is unique among Levi's works for its abstractions, both in content and style.[8] In his reflective effort to ponder the apparent chaos around him, Levi abandons himself to abstract language and to theoretical musings about the human condition. Notwithstanding its anti-fascist premise, *Paura* is a book written "dall'alto," in an authoritative, almost aristocratic voice that is uncharacteristic of his subsequent works. One has to wonder why he did not write *Cristo* instead of *Paura* after his release from exile in Lucania. It is as if, following his return to relative freedom, he becomes again the intellectual, the man who is thoroughly familiar with French, German, and English culture, who is interested in film and occasionally writes screenplays. He seems to forget about his experience in Lucania and even stops painting pictures of Aliano and its residents.

Instead, he decides to write *Paura,* a long essay. What Levi would later couch in the concrete narrative of *Cristo*—the latent hope of renewal embodied by the timeless civilization of Lucania—is, in *Paura,* expressed in the abstract language of philosophical speculation. But Levi's strength is not in the systematic ordering of ideas required by the essay form. He is at his best in telling a story through images, color, and intuition, and when his point of departure is the concrete fact, such as his personal encounter with the world of Lucania. Though inspired by external circumstances, *Paura* is a book born in Levi's mind, the fruit of his political, intellectual, and artistic formation. In *Cristo,* Levi moves from abstract reflection to concrete description. In place of the dense conventionality of the aulic language of *Paura,* there emerges in *Cristo* the concrete language of narrative. But what makes *Cristo* distinctive is its sense of discovery, which could only come out of Levi's reflection on, and analysis of, his experience in that other world. The theoretical groundwork that made possible his awareness of the meaning of that other world is laid in *Paura della libertà.*

With the affection that writers often express for their minor works, in his later years Carlo Levi would refer to *Paura* as his most important book. His self-assessment is accurate, I think, in that *Paura* contains the nucleus of the world vision that would guide him throughout his subsequent works. As difficult a book as it may be, *Paura* is an important work to read if one cares to understand Levi's perception of the State, and of the human condition in general. In *Paura,* which provides insight into the philosophical framework that Levi had developed in his formative years, he synthesizes his thought into a more or less coherent whole. This consolidation of his intellectual background provided the theoretical framework that made it possible, eight years after his experience in Lucania, first to discover, through his memory, the meaning of that experience, and then to forge, *from* his memory, the narrative

that brought order to that experience in *Cristo si è fermato a Eboli. Paura* clearly represents a watershed moment in Carlo Levi's development, a moment of synthesis in which he brings together the various elements of his cultural formation and fuses them with his own perceptions to formulate the personal vision that would serve as preface for all his subsequent work, as writer and as political activist.

Notes

1. For a history of the anti-fascist press in Italy, see Rosengarten. The articles by Tedeschi and Contarino in *L'età presente* provide an overview of Italian anti-fascist essays and narrative. The segment devoted to Carlo Levi includes a brief discussion of *Paura della libertà* (144-45).

2. Among the early reviews are those of Alatri, Bizzarri, and Bortone. More extensive analyses appeared later in Giammanco's essay, in the monographs by Falaschi (7-14) and Miccinesi (41-54), and in De Donato's *Saggio* (52-73), which provides the most extensive and insightful examination of *Paura* to date.

3. In his preface to the first edition, Levi indicates that he wrote *Paura della libertà* "per me solo e senza progetti di pubblicazione" (11). All citations are from the 1975 reprint edition.

4. Giammanco (245) identifies several thinkers whose influence is evident in *Paura* (including Vico, Freud, Jung, Bergson, Spengler, Jaspers, and Ortega y Gasset) and De Donato (52-60) provides a general analysis of Levi's intellectual formation relative to *Paura.* Both Falaschi and De Donato compare *Paura* to earlier works concerned with the crisis of western civilization, especially Huizinga's *Crisi di civiltà* (Falaschi 8, De Donato 54) and Jung's *Il problema psichico dell'uomo moderno* (De Donato 55). Giammanco further notes that Levi's familiarity with a broad range of European intellectuals reveals "un'esperienza culturale che, in quei tempi in cui in Italia regnava un provincialismo più spaventoso di quello di sempre, dava a Carlo Levi prospettive e termini di confronto assai più ampi" (245).

5. This second paragraph, with its allusions to discrimination and expulsion, has a particular relevance to Levi himself, both as a Jew and a political exile.

6. De Donato (374) points out that the Jungian term "l'incosciente collettivo" had previously been used by Levi in his unpublished *Quaderno di prigione,* written in 1935.

7. In his discussion of *Paura,* Falaschi derides Levi for "la forte vena irrazionalistica che ne pervade il pensiero" (10). He is also critical of what he considers Levi's apolitical analysis of fascism, particularly Levi's contrast between "massa" and "individuo differenziato," which he considers "una strana, immobile dialettica" (9). Levi's ethical-social methodology

is, Falaschi concludes, "l'unica forma possibile di intendere il meccanismo politico dei fatti per una *forma mentis* letterario" (12). De Donato, on the other hand, likens Levi's analysis of the totalitarian state to those of Croce, Mann, and Huizinga, "che vollero vedere nelle dittature borghesi un fenomeno che sfugge all'analisi delle categorie storiografiche, non spiegabili, o quanto meno non totalmente, come manifestazioni delle lotte di classe, nella fase dell'imperialismo, ma, per la loro stessa natura antitetica alla ragione in generale" (54). Nicola Carducci also argues convincingly against the criticism that Levi considered fascism strictly as a psychological phenomenon, citing in particular his social and political-economic analyses of the forties.

8. It may be argued that the elusive style is due to the need to evade Fascist censorship, but that conclusion is contradicted by Levi's prefatory declaration that he wrote the book "per me solo e senza progetti di pubblicazione" (11).

Works Cited

Alatri, Paolo. "Carlo Levi: *Paura della libertà.*" *La Repubblica* 16 marzo 1947: 3.

Bortone, Leone. "Carlo Levi: *Paura della libertà.*" *Il Ponte* (giugno 1947): 5, 92-93.

Bizzarri, Aldo. "Un saggio di Carlo Levi." *La fiera letteraria* (13 feb. 1947): 6-7.

Carducci, Nicola. "Tra rivoluzione e restaurazione: per una biografia intellettuale di Carlo Levi (1942-1948)." *Misure critiche* 43 (1982): 25-52.

De Donato, Gigliola. *Saggio su Carlo Levi.* Bari: De Donato, 1974.

Falaschi, Giovanni. *Carlo Levi.* Il Castoro 52. 1971. Firenze: La Nuova Italia, 1978.

Giammanco, Roberto. "*Paura della libertà.*" *Galleria* 17 (1967): 243-49.

Levi, Carlo. *Coraggio dei miti: Scritti contemporanei, 1922-1974.* Ed. Gigliola De Donato. Bari: De Donato, 1975.

———. *Paura della libertà.* 1946. Reprint ed. Torino: Einaudi, 1975.

Miccinesi, Mario. *Carlo Levi.* Invito alla lettura 14. 3rd ed. Milano: Mursia, 1977.

Rosengarten, Frank. *The Italian Anti-Fascist Press (1919-1945).* Cleveland: Case Western Reserve UP, 1968.

Tedeschi, Marcella and Rosario Contarino, "Pubblicisti, saggisti e narratori dell'anti-fascismo." Chapter 2 of *L'età presente: Dal fascismo agli anni sessanta.* Bari: Laterza, 1980. Vol. X, Part 1 of *La letteratura italiana: Storia e testi.*

David Ward (essay date 1996)

SOURCE: Ward, David. "Carlo Levi: From Croce to Vico." In *Antifascisms: Cultural Politics in Italy, 1943-46,* pp. 157-91. Cranbury, N.J.: Associated University Presses, 1996.

[*In the following essay, Ward examines Levi's journalistic and political writings and traces the development of his work.*]

PAURA DELLA LIBERTÀ: CARLO LEVI, RESISTANCE, AND CREATIVITY

Succeeding Alberto Cianca, Carlo Levi was editor of *L'Italia Libera* (*IL*) from August 1945 until his resignation in February 1946 in the wake of the split that took place in the Action Party during its first postwar congress in Rome. Previously, while participating in the Tuscan CLN, Levi had written a number of leading articles for the Florence-based Resistance newspaper *Nazione del popolo* (*NdP*). Over a span of eighteen months, Levi contributed at least seventy-five articles, signed and unsigned, to both newspapers, relatively few of which have been republished elsewhere.[1]

Many of his articles rehearse Action Party themes and analyses that we have already had occasion to observe: that the party was a newcomer to the political scene, free from the pre-Fascist legacy that still trammeled other parties; that Fascism itself was the inevitable result of the inadequacies of pre-Fascist Liberal Italy; that the seeds of a new form of fascism lay in the Liberal Party's insistent harking back to pre-Fascist Italy as the model on which to build the post-Fascist nation; and that the Resistance experience signaled the possible beginning of a new historical course that owed nothing to and effected a deep rupture with Italy's past. For example, in greeting the participants at the congress that was to result in its downfall, Levi writes that the Action Party, unlike others, "whose mental laziness keeps them attached to traditional schemes and inherited mythologies," takes up radically new positions that have not yet been "exhausted by time." Nor, Levi goes on, does the Action Party limit itself to repeating formulas "rubbed smooth by overuse, like pebbles made round by flowing water."[2] As to fascism, Levi wrote in an article entitled, significantly, **"Rompere con il passato"** (**"Break with the past"**), published in January 1946, a month or so after the fall of the Parri government, it "did not fall from the sky like a sudden meteor, but was the fruit of half a century of compromises and shortcomings." Italy's great problem, he goes on, was that it had never had a "modern, active bourgeoisie." The bourgeoisie the country did have had been born out of compromise with the forces of the old regime and under the aegis of the monarchy. Developed through protectionism and the rifling of the state's coffers, the bourgeoisie had produced a state in which the lower classes were excluded and absent from its formation and life. This was a state that did not come of popular conquest, and it had established so antidemocratic a political culture that it became the perfect instrument with which to welcome the totalitarian experience of fascism.[3]

Against the Crocean notion of both fascism and, as we shall see shortly, Resistance as parenthetical phenomena, Levi writes of those Partisans for whom "fascism was not an episode to be shrugged off, as a dog does with water after a bath, to take up once again the vices and errors of before. Rather, it was a fundamental experience that brought to light and changed the terms of our country's deep problems, staking a claim like never before for the need of a new liberty."[4]

Also emerging from the pages of Levi's journalistic writings, however, is an analysis of the origins of fascism that goes well beyond that put forward by any other Action Party intellectual. Of particular importance in this regard is Levi's cutting critique of not only Italy's but also the entire Western world's past and history. So deep does this critique cut that one critic, Dominique Fernandez, has spoken of Levi's quest "against Western man."[5] We find a clear example of this tendency in **"Firenze libera!" ("Free Florence!")**, the final article Levi wrote for *NdP* to mark the first anniversary of the liberation of Florence in August 1945. In the article, it becomes clear that, for Levi, the unprecedented experience of the Florentine Resistance is largely unconnected with the city's past. In Florence, something new and unique had happened, a new type of political subject had been created, amid, and even perhaps driven by, the city's isolation under Nazi occupation from the rest of Italy. This interstice had created a unique opportunity. Instead of relying on inherited forms of self-government, the Florentine Partisans had created their own to meet their specific needs. The resources on which the city drew, what Levi calls the universal spirit with which the city had resisted the Nazis, did not come from the inspiration given them by Florence's past. "This Ducal city," he writes, "which had fallen asleep in the lazy shadows of its glorious buildings," had been awoken by a real sense of "lived history" that "one could feel in the air, and that did not come, this time, from memories. Nor did it come from towers or palaces, but from living men, and from those who died for their cause." The Florentine Resistance experience, then, was not, as Levi saw it, the continuation of the city's past history, nor were the new forms of self-government the city gave itself based on old models. Rather, the Florentine Resistance experience had broken with the past and had *created* something entirely new, unique, and without precedent:

> Florence had to *invent* the Partisan war, the war in the city, the Liberation Committees as organs of government. These were discoveries born out of necessity, because they did not come from the plans of a few enlightened men, but from the common will of a people freeing itself. In its new born liberty, paid for with blood, the people wanted to express themselves and did so for the first time with self-government.[6]

Levi's reservations about the ability of the past to provide the present with viable models also animate his critique of

Italy's, particularly Liberal Italy's, *Risorgimento* legacy. In one of his early essays, published in *Rivoluzione liberale* (Liberal revolution) in 1922, he condemns Liberal Antonio Salandro's reliance on a *Risorgimento* model that had become "the predetermined form on which we should fashion not only our present, but also our future state life, as if that were the sacred tablets of the law from which everything and everyone must take form."[7] As the quotation suggests, Levi's reading of the *Risorgimento* period was very much in step with that of Antonio Gramsci. For both, the *Risorgimento* had resulted not so much in the unification of Italy as a single state, as in the attempt to extend Piedmont's hegemony over the whole country, even to those regions where the Piedmont model was plainly inapplicable.[8] Among Levi's personal papers, now held at the *Archivio nazionale dello Stato* (Italian National State Archive) in Rome, there is lodged a series of notes and pamphlets that bear on the Piedmont occupation of Sicily. One of the pamphlets bears the title *Un buco nell'acqua: ovvero Le debolezze, le malizie, gl' imbrogli, li errori, e le camorre in varie amministrazioni della Sicilia. Frammenti di scandalosa cronaca contemporanea* (A hole in the water, or, the weaknesses, the maliciousness, the tricks, the mistakes and the mafias in various Sicilian administrations. Fragments of a scandalous contemporary chronicle), written by Gaetano Marini.[9] Marini was a Piedmont official who had the unenviable task of introducing the metric system of weights and measures to Sicily. This, evidently, was no easy task. His pamphlet, which turns into a vicious attack on all things Sicilian, chronicles the resistance to his attempts and stands as testimony to the huge cultural gap that existed between the Piedmontese aim to standardize Italy on the basis of its own system and the reception that project met. I have no knowledge of what intentions Levi had for this material, which also includes a pamphlet entitled *La Madonna di Saletta. Invocazione Siciliana contro i Garibaldini* (The Saletta madonna. Sicilian invocation against the Garibaldini) by Nicolosi di Sciacca and contains material on Sicilian resistance to the *Risorgimento* forces. It seems likely, however, that Levi's interest in the matter lay in the same incompatibility between cultures he had denounced in his first novel, *Cristo si è fermato a Eboli* (*Christ stopped at Eboli*), apropos of Fascist attempts to standardize across the whole country, among other things, agricultural policy.[10]

But Levi does not limit his critique of history to the *Risorgimento* or Fascist periods in Italy's recent past. In fact, it is hard to find any historical period at all which he treats with any admiration. The only strong enthusiasm I have found expressed for any periods is for that of the Provençal courts and their troubadours and that of the Sweet New Style expressed parenthetically in his *Paura della libertà* (*Fear of liberty*).[11] It is, in fact, with this short, obscure, and repetitive text, written while Levi was in exile in France as WWII was breaking out, that he offers his diagnosis of fascism as the inherent disease of all Western civilization.[12]

Informed by his readings and the language of Vico and the Old Testament, Levi's book is a very ambitious attempt to locate the origins of the flaw in humankind that has led it, in the case of Western Europe, to accept and welcome a phenomenon like fascism. As the title of the book suggests, it is in humankind's generalized fear of its own liberty that the key to the question lies. Unlike many theories that seek to explain fascism, Levi's pays no attention at all to economic factors.[13] Rather, the cornerstone of Levi's theories lies in humankind's fear of its inherently creative powers. Yet, it is in those powers that humankind's potential for happiness and liberty lie. By marshaling our creative forces, we can forge for ourselves a unique identity that allows us to differentiate ourselves from the other equally unique identities forged by our fellow human beings. To argue this, Levi goes back to a state, which he calls the originary indeterminate state (*indistinto originario*): "There exists, common to all men, an originary indeterminate state flowing in eternity, the nature of every aspect of the world, spirit of every being in the world, memory of all time in the world" (23). Levi also illustrates the concept by way of reference to Vico's forest: "A Forest, in the beginning, according to the story, covered the face of the earth. We carry that very first Forest, formless and full of buds and terror, the black hiding-place of all time within us. From it the journey begins" (138).

The journey, then, is away from the state of indeterminate formlessness in the primitive magma of the forest, and toward form. This, however, is not a process which takes place once-and-for-all at the beginning of a life, nor does it set the self up for what it will eternally be. Rather, for Levi, the process of self-differentiation is an endlessly renewed and self-renewing creative experience: "All men are born out of chaos, and they can regenerate themselves in that chaos" (23). Humankind's initial desire to seek form out of the formless chaos into which it is born is its first inkling of its possible liberty: "Individuals begin their journey from this indistinct state, moved by a dark desire to detach themselves from it in order to take on form, to become individuals." But once individuals have differentiated themselves from the indeterminate magma, they are always drawn back to the state from whence they came to regenerate and recreate themselves in an ongoing process of birth and rebirth. Individuals are, then, "continually pulled back by a dark need to reattach themselves and dissolve themselves in it" (23). The creative self's authentic mode of being lies, therefore, in a state that includes both differentiation and nondifferentiation in the same creative act: "The only living moments in humankind, the only periods of high civilization in history are those in which the two opposing processes of differentiation and nondifferentiation coexist in the creative act" (23). To effect sheer transcendence of the indeterminate magma is to bring the self to a realm of pure and abstract reason; not to effect any transcendence at all is to give oneself over to the beast. The process of birth and rebirth is, writes Levi, not to be thought of in terms of death. Quite the opposite. It is the essence of life. Death is when one ignores the process of regeneration that is inherent to authentic living: "This effort stands between two deaths: the prenatal chaotic one, and the natural definitive one. But the only true

death is the complete separation from the flux of non-differentiation. That is, empty egotistical reason, abstract liberty. And, at the other extreme, the complete inability to differentiate oneself. The mystical, beast-like obscurity, slavery to the inexpressible" (23).

For Levi, then, both extremes of the polarity serve a purpose: on the one hand, creative differentiation in order to affirm ourselves as individuals, and on the other, a beneficial and necessary return to the magma as an antidote to reason's dangerous excesses. Underlying Levi's thought on these pages are two considerations that go to the heart of his critique of Western civilization: first, his conviction of the inauthenticity of life when it is governed by inherited codes and practices, and second, his polemic with the modernist conception of history as a linear narrative of ongoing emancipation and progress. For Levi, the creative acts with which individuals extricate themselves from the indeterminate state can be deemed authentic only when they are unique and fit the needs of the contingencies of individuals or groups of individuals. Whether in the fields of art, language, politics or religion, Levi is always convinced that the creative actions of individuals must be determined by the specific circumstances in which individuals find themselves. When, on the other hand, individuals seek solutions to given problems by recourse to preexisting codes or models imposed from above by schools or authorities, or inherited from tradition, then, humankind renounces the creative gift inherent to it and chooses to limit its own liberty.

Levi sees one of the greatest threats to liberty in religion, which he considers a retreat into a safe, reassuring haven made of "rituals . . . formulas, evocations, and prayers" (68). Worse still, humankind's fear of its creative faculties pushes it into accepting the limits imposed on its freedom by the codes of this or that cult. Religion is, then, "an act of faith in certain forms that have become symbolic and divine: a renunciation of free, dangerous creativity in order to reach certainty through sacrifice." Against the unlimited possibilities of human creativity,

> religion is the individualizing limitation of that which has no form, symbolic fixation of that which is indeterminate. . . . Religious language is born of the need for stability and certainty. The religious image or word, in its limits, replace an awesome reality. . . . Religious expression is then the opposite of poetic expression. The one is the symbolic limitation of the universal, the other its concrete expression; the one is the certain manifestation of a liberating and divine slavery, the other the very voice of human liberty; the one is fixed ritual, the other mythology.
>
> (68-69)

In politics, the same thinking leads Levi to distrust any course of political action that is tied to the dictates of a given ideology. As Dominique Fernandez has pointed out, Levi is not interested in the applicability of formulas to a variety of situations but in the unicity of experience and how life can be constituted by a series of first times, each one unique and contingent on the specifics of given circumstances and needs. What interests him, then, is "that precarious moment of the discovery of self by men and women . . . the point of balance between primitive confusion and the timid and proud awakening of consciousness, the mystery of birth and the coming of a new world."[14] Although Levi himself is not always consistent in his own choice of terminology, the master metaphor of artistic activity is not that of finding but that of inventing, creating: "Poetry is the invention of truth, invention or the creation for the first time. It is neither repeatable nor repeated: it is the moment in which expression coincides with reality for the first time. I prefer to say invention, rather than discovery, because discovery implies something external that is prior to its uncovering. Invention puts emphasis on the creative character of the relationship with things."[15]

Creativity also spills over into cultural politics. In his involvement with the political organization of the peasant movement in Italy's backward agricultural South, Levi is, on the one hand, ready to admit the crucial importance of the writings of Antonio Gramsci, the great theorist of an alliance between Northern workers and Southern peasants. On the other, however, he is at pains to point out that Gramsci's thought should not be taken as an orthodoxy good for all times and places. Indeed, to treat Gramsci in this manner is to misunderstand the lesson of liberty his example has left us:

> Gramsci [was] a great creator of thought . . . a great creator of culture and, above all, . . . a great creator, discoverer, inventor and champion of liberty. . . . But one cannot be, by definition, orthodox Gramscians, because orthodoxy is in contradiction with the very quality of Gramsci's thought. One cannot be an orthodox Gramscian, one cannot adopt his formulas. What we can do is follow his method of liberty and historical investigation.[16]

The crucial importance of recognizing the unicity of local circumstances, and tailoring one's creative responses to match those circumstances, also explains Levi's reluctance to embrace the modernist idea of history as ongoing narrative of progress. Anticipating elements of the postmodernist critique of history as emancipatory narrative, Levi develops a pluralized notion of history as histories, each one belonging to and reflective of different social realities.[17] Spearheaded by what has often been considered to be civilization's center and most advanced point of progress—Western European man—the idea of history as master narrative of the world, as a unitary process toward ever greater liberty, has been fundamental to modernist thinking, into which systems of thought and belief as disparate as Marxism and Christianity have bought.

Levi is a forthright critic of the Western notion of history and is quick to denounce the damage its colonization has done to cultures on its margins. The peasant culture of Lucania, where Levi was exiled in the 1930s on account of his anti-Fascist activities in Turin, was of interest to him precisely because it had remained immune to history. Indeed, it was the peasants' immunity from the codes of conduct and figures of thought mandated by history that had preserved in them the creativity to solve the contingent problems they came across in the course of their daily lives:

> Since peasant civilization is placed at the limits of the indeterminate state it continues to live in that ambiguous region in which for the first time the individual separated himself, took form and consciousness of himself. All around there is always present and impending the sense of sacrality, of the original indistinct state where every action, word and image have the character of things thought for the first time . . . an affirmation of liberty.[18]

The absence of history from peasant life is also underscored in the wonderful lines we read on the opening page of *Christ*: "Christ never arrived here, nor have time, nor the sense of an individual soul, nor hope, nor the connection between cause and effect, reason and history. Christ never arrived here, just as the Romans never arrived . . . nor the Greeks."[19]

Against a view that sees, as he puts it in the novel's opening lines, "what we are used to calling History" as a linear narrative of progress, Levi goes back to an older view based on repeated cycles of birth, death, and rebirth.[20] His reservations about history as master narrative are not only provoked by his apprehension of the inapplicability of totalizing models to marginal communities, but also by something more. In the cyclical view of time he finds a beneficial and humbling contact with death that is entirely absent from the progressive view. In an anonymous newspaper article he wrote for *NdP* in 1944, he speaks of the time "when human progress seemed necessary and endless, and when we had forgotten about death."[21] For Levi, one of the most beneficial aspects of the Resistance was that, in making plain the risk of losing their own life and in the actual deaths of their comrades, men and women were brought face-to-face with the experience of death. The experience is beneficial because it acts as a timely reminder that all things human are precarious, and that nothing lasts for ever, even that which appears to be built on the most robust of foundations. At the same time, the experience also clears the way for men and women to question those structures that had until then governed their lives. Referring to the Resistance in an anonymous article dated December 1945, Levi writes: "Since then the world has seen a revolution that has changed every value, created new forces, and put before the eyes of everyone the experience of death, which had been forgotten for such a long time. It has placed everyone before the need to revise everything that had traditionally been accepted."[22]

Life, then, for Levi is not to be led according to a single overarching narrative that stretches out from the beginning of a life until its end, but according to a series of phases, each one of which begins and ends within a life to give rise to a new phase. Writing in the 25 December 1944 edition of *NdP*, Levi speaks of Christmas as the emblem of the rebirth "that happens eternally in time and in each man if, stopping in the night of his journey, under a new star, he is able to throw away from himself the old man."[23] In *Christ,* we find a beautiful passage offering a perfect illustration of the liberating effect authentic contact with death produces. Here, called to cure an old man dying of a perforated appendix, Carlo finds he can do nothing except offer comfort. As the man lays dying in an adjoining room Carlo listens to his cries:

> From the door the continuous lament of the dying man reached me: "Jesus, help me, Jesus, help me, Doctor, help me," like a litany of uninterrupted anguish, with the whisper of the women's prayers. . . . Death was in the house: I loved those peasants, I felt their pain and the humiliation of my inadequacy. Why then did such a great peace descend on me? I felt as if I was separate from every thing, from every place, remote from any determination, lost, outside time, in an infinite elsewhere. I felt concealed, unknown to men, hidden like a bud under the bark of a tree. I turned my ear to the night and I felt as if I had suddenly entered the very heart of the world. An immense happiness that I had never before experienced was in me, and filled me completely, the flowing sense of an infinite plenitude.[24]

The original indeterminate state, to which Carlo here returns, is not an absolute beginning. Rather, it is a cyclical phenomenon, a repeated moment that takes place both in history and in an individual's life. Through his proximity to the experience of death, Levi is returned to a condition akin to that of the originary indeterminate state of which he had written in *Fear.* His return to this state is the enabling condition for a new birth and new creative activity, as he feels an immense plenitude welling up within him—a bud under the bark of a tree waiting to burst through and blossom. In the fusion of love making, the self can also be returned to the "black wood, full of convulsions and indistinct noises. . . . Only in the eternal, endless night is there the sacred formlessness of love. And the face of the beloved has the color of the night. Complete fusion does not know liberty, nor will, nor gods, only the dark necessity of the blind originary abyss."[25] For Levi, such returns are part of the fabric of authentic living. Indeed, in his own life we can identify such moments: his time spent in prison, for example, which, he writes in a letter, "can perhaps represent a beneficial return to the originary indeterminate state" out of which his own creativity will lift him: "If nothing is given to me I will have to give everything, reconstruct, extracting the terms and the distinctions from within myself and, without bricks and mortar rebuild the city, and once it is built, inhabit it actively."[26] A second return might be represented by his exile in France in the 1930s, when he wrote *Fear*; a third by his experience with the peasants in Lucania; and a fourth, perhaps, by his period of blindness in the final years of his life, to which the posthumous volume of notes entitled *Quaderno a cancelli (Gated notebook)* testifies.[27]

Yet, returns to the originary indeterminate state are not only personal but also historical. There come times in history when a given period runs its course, and the society,

customs, and culture it had founded collapse. The years around the fall of Fascism, Italy's double occupation, the Resistance, and the chance to rebuild from new foundations represent, for Levi, one of these moments. The historical course that had led to pre-Fascist Italy and Fascism "had lost its creative abilities after a century of extraordinary vitality. The idea of the individual, which had been its base, had become purely rationalistic; the idea of liberty purely formal. The sense of a living connection between individual and State, entities which were schematic and allowed for no mediation, had been lost."[28]

The terrible chaos and confusion that had rocked Italy in this transition phase were, paradoxically, propitious to a new beginning. The fall of Fascism, the war, and the dislocation experienced in all fields of life had swept away the ingrained habits of an entire society. If ever history had presented Italy with a blank page on which to recreate itself, this was it. There had been a

> complete turnaround in the habits, customs, inherited ideals, relationships between classes, different parts of Italy, and between city and country; the economic and moral bases of life. All the old problems of our national life are now posited on a different basis. They need to be taken up from the beginning, and can at last find a solution, unless we allow ourselves to be suffocated by the residues of a dead past.[29]

Or, as he put it in September 1944:

> Families have been dispersed, houses devastated, property destroyed, states overturned. If these ruins were only material the world would quickly go back to what it was. But the old sense of the family has been lost, the old sense of home has changed, the old sense of property no longer has the validity it once had, the old sense of the State has lost all power. And something deeper has changed in men's souls, something which is difficult to define, but which is expressed unconsciously in every act, every word, every gesture: the very vision of the world, the sense of the relationship of people with each other, with things and with destiny.[30]

Yet, a question remained. Since only those parts of Italy that had experienced vast dislocation presented propitious conditions for a new start, what of those other areas, Rome and the entire South, where daily life had been far less disrupted? This, indeed, was to be one of the challenges that the Action Party, once ensconced in the Roman corridors of power after the heady atmosphere of Resistance life, was asked to face and was unable to meet. Those areas of Italy that had not experienced the new climate created by the Resistance were cause for great concern. There, no new Northern wind, as the Resistance came to be known, had blown away the structures of the pre-Fascist state. In his article commemorating the liberation of Florence, Levi writes, "The peasants in the South had not been able to become Partisans, nor become aware of their own civil worth through the war. The political and social problem of the South came from this continued and aggravated lack of participation." The same obtained for the capital: "Rome had been liberated without a struggle, and remained, despite the efforts of the few, the eternal bureaucratic ruin." Indeed, it was to be the Action Party's traumatic impact upon the Roman corridors of power, and its own inability to replace old modes of government with new ones that was to contribute to its demise.[31]

These reservations were very much to the fore in the Actionists' thoughts, especially Levi's. He was mindful of the decrepit bourgeois class he had occasion to experience in the South during his exile. Nevertheless, the overwhelming feeling was of great optimism. For Levi especially, this was a time when the creative gift that is the patrimony of all humankind to forge form out of nothingness could be given full rein. Creativity could now act as an antidote to a world which had become "too mechanized" and separated from its inherent inventive capacities. We have already noted how the Tuscan Partisans in Florence had invented governing institutions to meet their specific needs. For Levi, in the Italy of 1944 and 1945, creativity was the order of the day and was to inform the entire work of reconstruction. Liberty, he writes in *NdP,* is a "continually creative activity"; the CLNs were the fruit of "creative spontaneity"; the Resistance itself was "a young and creative popular force"; the Constituent Assembly, which was to write Italy's postwar constitution, was a "work of spontaneous creation . . . in a period which breaks its links with previous law." It was in this sense that the Assembly was also a poetic moment which could rightly be compared to the "work of the grammarians who elaborate into precise laws the as yet uncertain forms of a new language. Or better: that of a great writer who first chooses and then puts into place with the authority of his poetry, in the still changing language of the people, what will remain its definitive forms."[32]

For Levi, as indeed for the Actionists in general, this was a period of radical change, a literal rewriting of the laws which had governed pre-Fascist and Fascist Italy. For this reason, they were very aware of the need to underline the qualitative break with present and past they wanted to make, as well as to guard against the reemergence on the political scene of personalities who had been most involved with Fascism. As we saw in the previous chapter, the Action Party's conviction of the need for a political purge of these elements was motivated by its desire to effect a break with Italy's past. It was for this same reason that many Actionists objected to the claims made in Liberal circles that once the Fascist regime had fallen the anti-Fascist movement no longer had a reason to exist.[33] Echoing Rosselli's contention that the anti-Fascist movement was not merely negative and reactive to fascism, many Actionists insisted on its positive connotations as a movement going well beyond opposition to Fascism as a regime (or as a parenthesis) and digging deep into the fabric and hidden recesses of Italian and European society, where the seeds of Fascist culture lay dormant: "We are anti-Fascists not only because we are *against* that series of phenomena that we call Fascism, but because we are *for* something that Fascism denies and offends, and violently

prevents us from pursuing. . . . [O]ur anti-Fascism implies therefore a positive faith, the positing of a new world against an old world that generated Fascism."[34]

Following Rosselli, Levi wrote in December 1944 of the need to guard against conservative tendencies within the anti-Fascist political parties themselves. He underlines that through the war not only must Nazism and fascism disappear, but also "the entire old European world and its insoluble antitheses, its schemes which have been emptied in the course of history, its state and national idols, its ancient ruling classes incapable of renewal, its contradictory political, economic, moral and aesthetic concepts, its impotent thirst for religion, its inability to reach full human unity." Drawing on one of the founding notions of *Fear,* he goes on to say that a limited notion of antifascism must also die with the old world that is dying. "Fascism and anti-Fascism are still two sides of the same world," he writes, and to complete the work of renewal being done by the traditional parties, the victors of the struggle must go beyond the antithetical vision that has animated the struggle thus far. "The victors know that they can only really win if they are able to renew themselves radically, if they can abandon the old man that lasts and resists in them, if they can found with truly self-liberating work the Europe of tomorrow." If Italian antifascism proved unable to take this step of reneging its purely negative connotations, the consequences would be not radical revolution but "a simple, anti-historic restoration. Once the field was cleared of Fascism, conservative anti-Fascism would reconstitute the exact same world from which Fascism took origin. And Fascism would be reborn in a new form, in an endless series of wars and barbaric convulsions."[35]

Although never stated in explicit terms, the referent of Levi's remarks is the Italian Liberal Party, one of the Action Party's allies in the anti-Fascist coalition. Many Actionists feared that the continued survival of the Liberal Party in the same form as it had existed in the pre-Fascist period preserved the cultural and political conditions that were propitious to the coming of fascism in another form. In his *Le parole sono pietre* (*Words are stones*), a book based on three journeys he made to Sicily, Levi reports an epigrammatic pun that circulated in anti-Fascist circles around 1944:

DANS LE PLI DE L'ÉTENDARD
ATTENTION: LES CAGOULARDS![36]

(In the fold of the flag
Beware: Fascists!)

The play is on the French word *pli,* which means "fold," but is also the acronym of the *Partito liberale italiano,* PLI. Indeed, the firmest opposition to the Action Party's ambitious plans and, in particular, to the government headed by party leader Parri, came from Liberal circles. The opposition culminated in the delegitimatization and ultimately the forced resignation of Parri, an act that for many Actionists, Levi included, signaled the end of any chance of radical postwar renewal in Italy. The events leading up to, around, and beyond Parri's resignation are the subject of Levi's second novel, *The Watch,* to which I now turn.

CRISTO SI È FERMATO A EBOLI AND *L'OROLOGIO*:
LEVI AND THE CIVIL WAR

The government headed by Parri held office from June until November 1945. Its failure to deliver on its promises of innovative reform can be attributed in part to the inability of Parri himself to provide effective leadership and guidance. As a Partisan leader, Parri, under the battle name Maurizio, had had a distinguished career, but his effective leadership in the field did not translate into effective leadership in the corridors of power. Greater responsibility for his government's demise, however, lay with the Liberal Party, which in November 1945 withdrew its support and, with the backing of the Christian Democrat leader Alcide De Gasperi, forced Parri's resignation. De Gasperi, in fact, was to be prime minister of the government that succeeded Parri's, inaugurating the long succession of Christian Democrat-led administrations, which has been the source of a great many of postwar Italy's political problems. In one of the intricate tactical moves that have always characterized, and even today continue to characterize, Italian politics, Parri received no support at all in his hour of need from his natural allies, the PCI and the Socialist Party. Both had already identified the intransigence of Parri and the Action Party as an obstacle to their project of forging alliances with the moderate forces of the bourgeoisie gathered around the Christian Democrat camp.[37]

If, as Foa has suggested, this PCI and Socialist alliance rang the death knell for Parri, it is the long and bitter polemic with the Liberal Party that emerges more forcibly from the Action Party press of the period. Many of the articles Levi wrote as editor of *IL* locate the principal ideological enemy fairly and squarely in the Liberal Party's attempts to delegitimate and limit the scope of action of Parri's government. Providing confirmation for the Actionists' thesis that they were the agents for the restoration of the pre-Fascist state, the Liberal strategy aimed to limit the political powers of the newly created bodies that were to be the institutional basis for post-Fascist society: first, the CLNs themselves, of which the Parri government was a direct emanation, and from which the Liberals sought to transfer political power back into the hands of the lieutenant, the stand-in for the disgraced monarch; and second, the *Consulta,* the body that was to prepare the way for Italy's new constitution, which the Liberals sought to deprive of operative powers, limiting it to the production of consultative documents.

The majority of Levi's articles for *IL* during the final months of 1945 take the form of attacks on Liberal Party policy. Focusing on the shift in the Liberals' internal balance of power, which resulted in greater influence for the party's Southern land-owning component, Levi underlines how Parri's government posed a threat to this constituency's vested interests. It was, he suggests, for this reason

that the government's resignation had been forced.[38] The newly created political situation also brought about a change in Levi's journalistic writings. There is, in fact, a distinct difference in tone between his articles for the *NdP* and those for *IL.* While the first had been optimistic, positive, in their celebration of how Resistance Italy had seemed to overcome the fear of liberty that had dogged Western civilization, the latter were defensive and, as the political crisis deepened, pessimistic about the chances of effecting any genuine renewal. Although Levi certainly does not ignore the importance of the Southern land owners' threatened vested interests, at the same time he suggests on more than one occasion that underlying their hostility to Parri was a more basic fear, the fear of liberty and humankind's ability to create new forms of government and self-regulation that his Resistance experience had led him to believe had been overcome. But what is precisely this fear of liberty? To answer this question we need to go back to his earlier *Fear.*

Although *Fear* is, on the one hand, a celebration of human creative powers, on the other, it is a tract on humankind's renunciation of those powers. Our creative powers and ability to invent new forms out of formlessness are, to human eyes, literally awesome. The history of Western civilization has been marked by a tendency to recoil away from these powers, from what Roberto Giammanco has called "the terror of man before his immense resources, the irresistible power of his own creations." Turning away from this immense power, and intimidated at the rate at which the world continually creates and recreates itself, men and women have sought refuge in prepackaged solutions, in codified, inherited responses, "in old explanations, pathetic myths."[39]

For Levi, this means, as we saw earlier, a shift from a sacred vision of things to a religious vision, and a religious vision always implies relegation, the substitution of preexisting symbols, images, and idols to fill the void left by the inability, unwillingness, or fear of the individual to create one's own world. "Religion is relegation. Relegation of the god into the realm of formulas, evocations, prayers to make sure that it doesn't follow its ungraspable nature and escape. The sacred, which is the very aspect of terror, becomes the law in order to save it from itself."[40] The same process of relegation also takes place in other fields. The greatest idol humankind has built for itself is the state. Levi saw the most tragic abdication of human responsibility in the Fascist state and the unquestioning adulation it demanded of its followers, which they willingly and freely repaid. Most damaging of all, and returning to one of the pillars of GL's political thought, Levi underlines how humankind's fear of liberty turned the potentially individual and unique *person* into a component of an anonymous, amorphous, indeterminate *mass* that had become easy prey for fascism. The valorization of the individual is a key concept for Levi. He was always reluctant to relinquish it and, even for contingent political reasons, he was unwilling to countenance any notion of mass. His ideological difficulties with the so-called mass political parties—the PCI, the Socialists, and the Christian Democrats—come from this reluctance.

The problem with mass parties was that they had developed a monolithic mode of thinking that did not allow them to see the subtleties and nuances that contributed to the formation of political and social reality. This monolithic mode of thinking had led them to theorize the rise of fascism as the result of the gargantuan clash between two opposing but innerly homogeneous groups. In January 1946, after the fall of Parri's government, and with the Action Party in disarray looking for new allies to its Left, Levi took his distance from the Communist proposal of a vast democratic unity among like-thinking parties. Arguing that if the anti-Fascist parties were to elaborate an effective mass strategy, it must not replicate the limits of earlier monolithic thinking and be based on an idea of "differentiated mass," Levi criticized the analysis of fascism advanced by Mauro Scoccimarro, a leading exponent of the PCI. Although he paid close attention to the role of the industrial and agrarian groups, Scoccimarro's analysis paid no attention at all to the smaller, more variegated group of the petite bourgeoisie. To see fascism only as a capitalist conspiracy, Levi goes on, is to misunderstand

> that sense of multiplicity and complexity of the forces in play, the variety of interests that formed the knot from which totalitarianism was born. . . . What is lacking in his study is a consideration of the petite bourgeoisie whose attempt to conquer the state, together with the new mythologies which came from their inferiority complex, gave rise to the Right-wing revolution, the "petite bourgeois palingenesis," Fascism and its state.[41]

These last remarks bear on Levi's conviction that the Fascist state, far from being the single effect of a conspiracy led by economic groups anxious to protect their own interests, is the logical outcome of a mass society gone mad. The masses' "most powerful of idols," the state, has not only been imposed from above but has also come as a welcome relief to those individuals, "children of fear," who are drawn to it in order to "forget themselves, to free themselves from themselves and from their fear." Beneath the physical fear of the bombs and massacres of WWII, Levi locates a more deeply rooted fear: "The elementary fear of existence, of being free, the fear of the man that is in man. To those who are incapable of contact, incapable of liberty . . . their only recourse was the sterile solitude and the need to lose themselves in an amorphous collectivity."[42]

Levi traces a direct line of continuity linking the ingrained fear of liberty with a mass culture and its culmination in fascism. He could not have stated this point in clearer terms. In an article bearing the same title as the book he had written a few years earlier, **"Paura della libertà,"** published in November 1944, he writes:

> The fear of liberty is the sentiment that has generated fascism. For those who have the soul of a slave, the only peace, the only happiness is to have a master. And

nothing is more difficult, and truly frightening, than the exercise of liberty. This explains the love of so many slaves for Mussolini, this mediocrity become god, made necessary to fill the void in the soul, and settle its sense of unease with a sense of restful certainty. For those who are born slaves, abdication from oneself is a beatific necessity.[43]

Levi goes on to offer a theory to explain the process by which fascism can appear to the masses as a beneficial, providential antidote to their own sense of loss and confusion. He calls this a process of "artificial crystallization," which takes place not at the rational level but in the hidden recesses of the "uterine politics of the unformed masses, their uncertain terrors, unexpressed needs . . . ambitions and inferiority complexes that have found in fascism and Nazism their most recent and clamorous expression." The process itself is very simple. In seeking a sense of certainty and stability with which to fill the void that their fear of liberty has left in them, the masses are drawn to the "man, name, formula" who has been most able to present himself to them in what seem to be the most convincing terms. Once this Mussolini or Hitler figure has conquered the confidence of the masses as the providential answer to their woes, the crystallization takes place. This process is not limited to right-wing dictators. Indeed, Levi sees some of the events of postwar Italy as attempts to crystallize public opinion around figures and bodies other than the CLNs and representatives of the Partisan movement: first, the formation of a "Lega per la difesa delle libertà democratiche" (League for the defense of democratic liberties) by the Liberal Party, in which their most presentable exponents were involved; and second, the appearance of the right-wing political movement "L'uomo qualunque" (The ordinary man), headed by Guglielmo Giannini.[44] In this case, however, his lack of real political charisma, wrote Levi, would ensure that no long-lasting crystallization took place.[45]

It was to replace the monolithic national state, which had reached its apotheosis with fascism, that the Action Party elaborated its policy on local government. The policy envisaged the creation of a series of local, autonomous regions or provinces, each of which would make provision for the region's specific needs and demands. In other words, a state built from the bottom up, and not imposed from above, a state whose structures would have to be created by its citizens, and not inherited from past practices.

Levi speaks most vociferously of this project, which he held dear, in the final pages of *Christ,* where he expounds the question in terms of two irreconcilable cultures: the industrial, advanced culture of the North and Center, on the one hand, and the agricultural, backward culture of the South, on the other. The fruit of his time spent in exile was the firm conviction that an unbridgeable abyss separated North and Central Italy from the South. The negative consequences of this abyss had been exacerbated by two factors: first, the inability of the North to understand that the two cultures could not be assimilated,[46] and second, the role of the degraded petite bourgeoisie of Southern villages. Fascism had only been the latest of a series of centralized, state-run attempts to arrogate the South to its methods and practices. For Levi, these colonial-like attempts to impose a foreign culture on the South are not only destined to fail but also have the effect of deepening the acrimony felt by the peasants toward the state and widening the gap that separates them from central government.

The situation is made even worse by the representatives of central government, the members of the degraded petite bourgeoisie of Southern society, who receive by far the worst treatment in *Christ.* In the 1930s, the petite bourgeoisie had declared its allegiance to Fascism, but the practice of their Fascism was nothing new, writes Levi. In their hands, Fascism was simply the contemporary form taken by a power struggle between bourgeoisie and peasants that had a long and deeply embedded history. Their antecedents had been allies of whichever political faction, Left, Right, or Center, held power at a given moment (30-31). It is this class that constitutes the real problem in the South. Any political solution elaborated to address the economic and social issues of the South that failed to dislodge this class from its position of power as local agents of a central government that has never understood the complexities of local situations is destined to result in the continuation, in amended form, of the "eternal Italian Fascism" (210).

Underlying Levi's attack on the inadequacies and nefarious effects of centralized forms of government is his refusal to accept the idea that historical development takes place according to the logic of the master/slave dialectic. As his remarks about "internal colonization" suggest, Levi sees the present relationship between city and country, center and margin, in terms analogous to that between first and third worlds (202; 209). The proposal which Levi launches from the pages of *Christ* for the creation of a new state of, by and for the peasants, based not on a single and totalizing centralized body, but on an "infinite number of autonomous units, an organic federation" is an implicit rejection of the first world's claim to be historically more advanced than the third (211). Levi's proposal, in fact, cuts to the heart of the logic by which colonization offers a justification of itself insofar as it is ultimately beneficial to the historically backward colonized, who are thus brought into the "evolutionary narrative of Western history."[47] Having seen how in Italy and Western Europe historically advanced countries had progressed only insofar as they had prepared the way for fascism, Levi elaborates an early theory of separate development. The new state these pages adumbrate must "allow the coexistence of two different cultures. The one must not oppress the other; the other must not be a weight on the one" (211).

To a great extent, however, this proposal, which was also part of the Action Party manifesto, remained a dead letter. As Levi also tells us in *Christ,* on a short trip back to Turin on the occasion of the death of a close relative, from conversations with his friends he discovered that the idea

of a centralized state as "something transcendent . . . tyrannical or paternalistically provident, dictatorial or democratic, but always unitary, centralized and distant," hovering over the infinite multiplicity of the country, was shared by representatives of all sectors, Left, Right and Center, of the political spectrum (207-8). All of them, in fact, whether they knew it or not, were "worshippers, idolizers of the State" (207).

The inability of even the most enlightened members of the Turin intelligentsia, probably the most advanced and creative laboratory of political culture Italy has ever known, to imagine a future country governed by a state in any fundamental way different from the present or previous ones, was a sign to Levi of the extent to which fear of the radically new had penetrated the highest and most sophisticated echelons of society. For a while, the heady atmosphere of the Resistance had led Levi to believe that this fear had been overcome. But as the dust settled and the task of governing postwar Italy got underway, Levi was to make some bitter discoveries. Elaboration of new forms of self-government was hindered not only by the structures of Rome's eternal bureaucratic ruin, deeply rooted in pre- and post-Fascist practices and codes, but also by less expected resistances and fears from within the Parri government, the Action Party, and even Levi himself.

Written between 1947 and 1949, in the months and years that followed the fall of Parri, *The Watch* is often cited as the novel that recounts the end of the Action Party's hopes for a post-Fascist Italy different from its pre-Fascist precursor. Indeed, one of the key scenes in the text is the press conference called by Parri to announce his resignation, in which he describes the toppling of his government as a "coup d'état." Yet, to reduce *The Watch* to a chronicle of those events is to do an injustice to a text which goes far beyond the bounds of mere historical reconstruction. For one thing, the novel is structured in such a way as to be hardly recognizable as a conventional historical novel. Although it has a beginning and an end, and includes the figures who were making history at that time—Parri, De Gasperi, Togliatti, though they are never named as such— Levi also includes in his novel, and gives equal space to, a cast of characters normally found on the edges of history. In the course of its more than 300 pages, *The Watch* plots a meandering course that follows Levi's political and personal adventures in Rome and Naples over a three-day period in November 1945. Often interrupted by reminiscences of exile, childhood memories, and philosophizing along the lines of Levi's earlier *Fear,* the book contains an impossible number of characters and events by any conventional realistic literary canon. In the course of day 1, for example, we are introduced not only to the journalists who worked for *IL* but also to characters like Teresa the cigarette seller, groups of Partisans, Levi's friend Marco, his new neighbors Jolanda and Giovanni, Teo the porter, Palmira the alcoholic waitress, and many others. In addition to Parri's press conference in the *Viminale* and Carlo's long walk through the *Traforo* traffic tunnel in the company of two party comrades, the text tells of Carlo's dream of losing his watch; how the next day he actually broke his watch and attempted to have it fixed; the death of a young woman killed by an American jeep; lunch in the same small restaurant as a group of Polish soldiers; his trip to the poor and squalid Garbatella quarter to look for a certain Fanny, Marco's girlfriend, but of whose existence we have strong reason to doubt; an evening in an *osteria* with journalists and printers waiting for the electrical current to be restored; and Carlo's finding of a dead man and his barking dog on the steps leading to the apartment where he was going to sleep. Days 2 and 3 contain a trip to Naples, where Carlo visits his dying uncle; an attack by bandits; his return to Rome in the company of two of the ministers who had just resigned from Parri's government; and his temptation to pay a visit on Benedetto Croce, which he resists.

Many of the characters who people the text are recognizable as the protagonists of the political crisis of those final months of 1945. None of them, however, is identified by his or her real name. About the only characters to retain their real names are Croce and Vico, to whom I will return shortly. To help readers follow a text that is deeply imbued in the atmosphere and events of fifty years ago, Manlio Rossi Doria has furnished a who's who of some of the characters: Casorin and Moneta, two *IL* journalists, are Manlio Cancogni and Carlo Muscetta; Fede and Roselli, two leading exponents of the Action Party, are Vittorio Foa and Altiero Spinelli; Andrea Valente and Carmine Bianco, Carlo's companions on his walk through the *Traforo*, are Leo Valiani and Manlio Rossi Doria; Nardelli is Mario Alicata; Tempesti is Emilio Sereni, father of Clara, the contemporary novelist; La Torre is Ugo La Malfa; Rinaldi and Rattani are Orlando and Cattani, two of the Liberals responsible for bringing down the Parri government; and the "great poet" who pays a visit to the typography is Umberto Saba, whose daughter, who also appears briefly in *The Watch,* was to become Levi's companion in the final years of his life.[48]

In truth, none of the portraits is very flattering. Levi does not let his friendship with many of the above prevent him from pinpointing in their intellectual and political limits responsibility for failing to deliver on their promises. Levi, however, is on record as saying that these characters were not to be understood as exact replicas of the actual figures of that period. Rather, he has said, they are mixed and even counterfeited versions of those figures.[49] Indeed, Levi uses many of the characters in the novel as a ventriloquist's dummy, expressing thoughts and reflections that are his. In providing a mixed panoply of the various characters and types in the political life of that period, Levi is suggesting less that the demise of the movement's hopes be ascribed to the limits of a given team of political personnel than that it be ascribed to the failure of a whole generation, himself included, to translate their aspirations into political reality. The reasons for this are the major thematic and philosophical thread of the entire novel.

Rather than with individual shortcomings, *The Watch* is concerned with a general question that Levi had already discussed in *Fear*: namely, the massive extent to which all aspects of daily life, be they political, personal, cultural, artistic, or social, are determined by adherence to preexisting, inherited codes and practices. Levi's apprehension that literature is largely dependent on adherence to such codes, and how that adherence leads to a representation of a partial, reduced version of reality, is a concern that invests the entire text. Furthermore, Levi also suggests that such codes determine not only literary activity but also the perceptions of the people and events we come across in our daily life, and so take on the form of agency. Commenting on the characters Casorin and Moneta, for example, Levi is at pains to point out the inadequacy of the portraits he has supplied of them. These, he says, represent only the one-thousandth part of what he knows and could say about them. In giving names to people, and in attempting to draw for ourselves concrete, stable, and recognizable images of them out of the "infinite reality" each human being is, we are forced to "cut out a small slice of that reality, we make a partial image . . . which we then force into our affairs, our time, our measure."[50] Knowing that the image we have created is partial and ignores "all the rest, all that we haven't said and must overlook, but which exists," we are left with a feeling of loss about our ability to represent and apprehend reality (48). In this way, not only characters in literature but also the perception we have of people in our daily lives are like the images we see from the window of a passing train. These frozen instants belonging to a contingent moment of a life become the images with which we associate and summarize that person's entire being: "So, unintentionally, we make a character in a short story, a coloured fragment of a previously drawn mosaic, an element in an abstract game out of the boundless wave that is the real, out of a person who like us, identical to us, has no limits" (49).

Casorin makes a similar point in the literary discussion he has with Moneta in the newspaper office. His beef is with the form of the modern novel, in which he sees the dangerous abstraction that has blighted modernist culture: "The abstract novel was written and drawn in an abstract time. It begins and it ends, cut arbitrarily out of the world" (57). His argument then goes on to consider Levi's fundamental theme of mass: in the modern novel, "we have the individual and we have the masses, but there are no human relationships. Take this single, arid man, split him up into various schemes, make an object of him, make him more complicated with events, lock him up in a before and after and tell his story, if you can: but you'll always be a prisoner of abstraction" (57). This abstraction, he goes on, echoing the same line of thought which sees Nazi and Stalinist death camps as the inevitable result of reason gone mad, has led to the same dehumanization that made Auschwitz and Buchenwald possible: "This is the conclusion, the end of your novels, of your abstract reason . . . a piece of soap" (57). His final image is one that recurs throughout the text, that of the forest:

> There is not only one blade of grass in a field. Not a tree, but a forest, where all the trees stand together. Not before and after, but together. Big and small, with the

mushrooms and the bushes and the rocks and the dry leaves and the strawberries and the blackberries and the birds and the wild animals, and perhaps even the fairies and the nymphs and the wild boar and the poachers and the lost travellers, and who knows how many other things. The forest.

(58)

How adherence to such life-denying codes leads to the excessive disciplining of our apprehension of the total experience that is reality is illustrated in some of the many encounters Carlo has in the course of the novel. On moving to his new apartment, he meets Jolanda and Giovanni, the previous tenants' maid and her mysterious cousin. Jolanda has invented for herself an identity as the abandoned noble child born of a beautiful Spanish princess's illicit love affair. The identity she fabricates for herself owes nothing to anything she is or might be, but corresponds perfectly to the codes of noble living which she assumes have been accepted by all. A present-day version of Jolanda would perhaps live life according to the pseudo codes of high living transmitted by American afternoon television: "The starting point of her life was an invention made of imitations of invented and inexistent things, of unsupported appearances. She knew the world to which she claimed to belong only insofar as she had seen it from the bottom up, or through the key-hole, or on the basis of the laundry she washed" (225).

Her cousin Giovanni, who wears a blond wig and never takes off his dark glasses, is a functionary at the Ministry for Italian Africa, a unit set up under fascism to administer Italy's colonies. Because he only needs to go to work once a month, his hobbies of writing, composing, and drawing have become his main activities. Yet, like Jolanda, Giovanni too has constructed his creative activities around what he assumes to be unquestionable codes: "What was the world of the aristocracy for Jolanda was the world of art for Giovanni" (229).

In the world of politics, the same adherence to inherited and barely questioned practices has opened the door for the restoration of pre-Fascist Italy that many Actionists feared but were unable to prevent. In Levi's eyes, the main reason why the Action Party failed, once it had come to a position of executive power with the Parri government, was that, unable to elaborate new political codes and practices, it fell back on the old ones shared by more traditional parties. Thus, from a political organism that was potentially innovative, it was transformed into a replica of existing parties. In his autobiography, Vittorio Foa, who as Fede is pinpointed in the novel as one of the guiltier parties in embracing the ways of traditional politics, agrees with Levi's analysis. He writes: "Many of us fell in love with the techniques of politics. We got revenge on defeated Fascism by avidly rediscovering all the instruments that it had taken from us. We used them to the full: Parties, free press, congresses, meetings, contacts, conversations, tactics that were so refined as to exasperate us. We deluded ourselves into thinking we could defeat the restoration with its own arms."[51]

For Levi, though, the conditions for the Action Party's defeat were already in place before the fall of Parri in November 1945. Already six months had passed since Liberation in April and the window of opportunity that the chaos of the war and the occupations had opened up had now been all but closed as old practices reestablished their hegemony and had the effect of blunting the ever-decreasing instances for radical renewal. After meeting his staff on his first day as editor of IL, the feigned interest shown by his colleagues as he expounds his plans for the newspaper reminds Carlo not so much of a political avant garde as a group of the *signori* he had met in Lucania. Far from the vital revolutionary context he had enjoyed in Tuscany, Carlo finds himself in a stagnant world of intrigue, petty jealousy, and infighting, especially so when he realizes that his appointment as editor is based less on his individual merits than on a compromise solution negotiated by the two warring factions within the party: "I felt that once again I had fallen into a stagnant pond of interests and intrigue the logic of which would always escape me. An impenetrable and closed world. . . . And it seemed to me as if I had gone back to a village in Lucania and to listen to the *signori* speak of thier eternal hatreds, their eternal boredom" (41-42).

Actually, Carlo's discovery of the stagnant reality of Rome politics is a replay of an experience he had had earlier while involved with the Tuscan Resistance. As one of the members of a CLN delegation representing all the parties that had fought together in Florence, Carlo had come to Rome to speak with the representatives of those same parties, which then made up liberated Italy's provisional government. As we have already had occasion to see in Levi's article **"Firenze libera!,"** the delegates brought to the meeting the optimism and creative spirit that had enabled the occupied city to resist and reconstitute its governmental and institutional life. In *The Watch,* Levi recalls those days when there seemed to be no gap between politicians and the needs and aspirations of the common people. Speaking of his arrival in Rome in late August 1945, Levi writes in *The Watch*: "I came directly from Florence. . . . A few hours earlier I had left that city where everyone seemed still to be living in the vivifying atmosphere of the Resistance, and where there was thought to be no difference between politicians and the common people" (31). But Levi's fear that the "active and creative freedom" (31) that pervaded Florence would not last long finds confirmation in the meeting between the local CLN and its national counterpart. The Tuscan delegation had brought with it a series of proposals, based on its own concrete experience of self-government, which it hoped the national CLN would find interesting and incorporate into its policy. The innovative aspect of its proposals was that it aimed to take the power to nominate prefects out of the hands of central government and give it to local organizations in such a way as to have prefects who would be sensitive to the grass-root needs of citizens. Although they were received by the national leaders of the parties in which the delegation's members militated, the members of the Tuscan delegation met nonetheless with a lukewarm response. Faced with proposals that would take power away from central government, even those ministers who owed their present status to their role in the Resistance struggle either turned them down immediately or assented in only the vaguest of terms. The episode took on the contours of an emblematic event for Levi, the clash between a living, creative marginal constituency and dull, arid power structures intent only on the cultivation of their own power base: "a different world, different interests, a different language in which everything was changed" (189). More disturbingly, some of the members of the Tuscan CLN delegation were to meet the same fate. On being transferred to Rome, "they gained greater experience and power, and forgot their earlier juvenile furor" (191).

In geographical terms, the optimism of the early CLN experience becomes pessimism with the shift from the series of local struggles that made up the Resistance, like Levi's Tuscan experience, to the centralized stalemate of national government in Rome. ***The Watch*** attempts to explain the failure of the Action Party project as the consequence of what happens when a movement clashes with the rigidity of centralized political structures. To have an idea of how Levi sees this process, we need to turn to chapter 8 of the text and the important conversation between Carlo, Andrea Valente (based on Leo Valiani), and Carmine Bianco (based on Manlio Rossi Doria). It takes place in the *Traforo* traffic tunnel immediately after Parri's announcement of his resignation.

Even if it may seem paradoxical to those who know the place, Levi describes the *Traforo* as if it were a modern-day version of Plato's cave: "an anonymous cave" (158), "like a grotto" (159), "that cave" (161)—in other words, a place of imprisonment where chained slaves, forced to look in a single direction, see only a series of shadows, half truths, which they mistake for truth itself. Like the cave, Levi's *Traforo* is also a place of reduced vision where "the rare lights . . . caused the white tiles to sparkle" (158), and of echoes where the three friends' "voices reverberated as they were thrown back into the vault and dissolved into a deafening hubbub" (158). It is also a place of diminished truthfulness. The closed spaces of the *Traforo* contrast with the open spaces of the "interminable streets" of Turin which, Carlo tells us as the conversation is about to begin, "seem made especially for peripatetic growth . . . which was full of an unconfined, endless power" (157). Against the open spaces of Turin, Carlo is now plunged into the dark Roman tunnel.

It is in this confined space, this "nowhere . . . outside of time" (158), that Andrea, to whom Levi entrusts many of his own thoughts, explains the Action Party's demise. Once arrived in Rome, following the creative freedom they enjoyed in Tuscany and elsewhere, the Actionists became, as it were, slaves to Rome-style politics, codes, and practices. This is without question the sense of Andrea's long and much-quoted speech in which he poses the question in linguistic terms: politics, he says, is made up of a conventional language that "rests on nothing" and is com-

prehensible only to those like Carlo, Andrea, and Carmine, who "one day decided to accept it once and for all" (159). This language, and here we find the most explicit reference to Plato's cave, forces us to "run after shadows" to touch something "which escapes us and runs away from us" (159). It is in this context that Andrea elaborates the theory of two modes of being represented by, on the one hand, the *Contadini* (peasants) and, on the other, the *Luigini* (petite bourgeoisie). The former are a loose, unorganized coalition that includes the real peasants who maintain an "adherence to things, a contact with animals. . . . [They are] the dark vital origin that is in each of us" (165). In addition to the peasants, also included are the enlightened factory and land owners, as well as the workers. Their distinguishing characteristic is their contact with things and their productivity. They are, in other words, the creative elements—poets who do not speak a conventional, worn-out language. On the other hand, the speakers of a worn-out language, the *Luigini,* are those who have a vested interest in continuing the present state of affairs, be they political, economic, or social. They are, and here Levi gives Andrea some lines that could have come out of ***Fear***, "the great majority of the endless, unformed amoeba-like petite bourgeoisie, and all its species, sub-species and variations. They have their miseries, their inferiority complexes, their moralism and immoralism, wrong ambitions, their idolatrous fear. . . . They are the crowd of bureaucrats, the State workers, the banker clerks, the administrators etc." (166-67). The militants in the Action Party, of course, were peasants. Their problem was, however, that the *Luigini,* in Andrea's words, "have the numbers, have the State, the Church, they have the political language" (167). If, then, the forms of politics are made in the image of the *Luigini,* in order that their voice be heard in a political context, the peasants are forced either into silence or to speak a language which is not theirs and which belongs to their ideological enemy. In this way, concludes Andrea, the *Luigini* have had an easy time co-opting the peasants to their way of thinking.

Andrea himself, as he freely admits, speaks the language of the *Luigini* perfectly (171), as his long exposition on the evils of the political situation testifies. The lucidity, the mathematical precision, the virile sense of certainty, the neat division of things into two opposing camps that informs his analysis has very little in common with "peasant" creativity. Andrea, in fact, may be considered an emblem of the failure of the Action Party project as it ran aground against the sandbars of Rome. Like those slaves who succeed in liberating themselves, Andrea believes he has seen not shadows but the forms themselves, and like the philosopher, he goes back into the cave to inform the less fortunate slaves and to show them the path toward liberty. But with the language he has Andrea use, Levi complicates the Platonic allegory and rereads it in a more pessimistic mode. Levi gives us reason enough to suspect that Andrea, far from being the free-thinking philosopher he believes himself to be, is in fact the worst of all slaves—that is, the slave who is convinced he is free, but who in reality is still prisoner to the same slave owner who seems to have given him his freedom. Although Andrea is well aware of how politicians, severed from contact with real things, chase shadows, he is perhaps less aware of the extent to which he too, as well as his party comrades, has fallen into the same insidious trap. If Andrea is indeed chasing shadows, then the value of the prophecies he makes in the *Traforo* also comes into question. Presented in such terms as a kind of Delphic oracle, "a sibyl's lair" (158), a place "suitable for prophetic words" (158), where Andrea is "animated by prophetic spirits" (166), the *Traforo* takes on once again the connotations of Greek myth. But the prophetic truths both Andrea and Carmine express are, in fact, little more than half truths. Andrea, for example, predicts that the recently created political situation would soon change, that the resuscitated old-style political parties would be destined to be replaced by an "infinity of autonomous organizations" (169), while Carmine is convinced that the new government led by Christian Democrat De Gasperi, which he disparagingly refers to as the "government of priests," would only last a short while: "Events change quickly. If we were now in a phase of stasis we would soon start moving again. Even if we did have a government of priests it wouldn't last long. A month or two, maybe a year" (160).

With the benefit of hindsight, we know that neither of these prophecies even came close to predicting Italy's future. The traditional political parties certainly did not disappear and, as time passed, they exercised an ever stronger grip on all aspects of Italian society. Neither were they replaced by "autonomous organizations," and De Gasperi's government of priests, far from being an interlude, heralded nearly fifty years of uninterrupted Christian Democrat involvement in single-party or coalition rule.

At the time of writing **The Watch,** however, Levi, who remains largely silent during the walk through the *Traforo,* also knew that these prophecies were far from the mark, especially after the elections of 1948, which consolidated the power of the center-right parties. Levi does not remain silent because he is not privy to the prophecies made by Andrea and Carmine. Let us recall that the terms of the analysis expressed by Andrea—peasants and *Luigini*—and his proposal for the creation of "an infinity of autonomous organizations" are identical to those Levi himself had elaborated in **Christ** and elsewhere. In Andrea, then, we can glimpse, if not exactly a self-portrait, then at least an ironic, belated representation of the risk that Levi knew he was running with his political activity in and around the Roman *palazzi*. Just as, in Andrea's words, the Action Party will inevitably become more and more like the *Luigini* ("si illuiginerà" [168]), the danger for Levi is that the same destiny will await him—or, that his own picture of a future Italy based on the Florence experience during the Resistance and on self-government from below was as deluded as Andrea and Carmine's, and that his own prophecies prove just as empty.

It would be wrong, however, to imagine that **The Watch** is a novel which limits itself to placing blame for Italy's postwar ills on Rome and Roman society. To be sure, Levi portrays Roman political society in the harshest of terms. On the other hand, the city itself, especially its popular quarters, is portrayed as a marvelous source of energy, creativity, and regeneration. The major contrast on which the whole novel is structured is between the vitality of the city streets as people attempted to construct a new life for themselves out of the ruins of the old world, and the sedimented, codified regime of political society, intent on reestablishing that old world.

The streets of Rome are a hive of endless, variegated, creative activities, and their descriptions make for some of the text's highest moments:

> The street was full of people, elbow to elbow, summer shirts, heavy overcoats, shawls, handkerchiefs, hats, rags, Allied military jackets, sandals, heavy shoes; big-chested women rolling their hips and giving you the look, old women standing guard over the shop windows, dirty excited kids playing who knows what game or barter, British, American, Italian, black soldiers; workers in their overalls, clerks who had just stepped out of their banks or Ministries, ready to jump on ramshackle trucks. Everyone was moving, gesticulating, looking with their dark shiny eyes, they were thinking, speaking, screaming, their intent faces, full of intensity and character, following or contemplating their daily adventure. And all of them themselves *were* an adventure, an uncharted river made of a thousand ever new waves flowing through rocky banks and flowering islands.

> (71)

On arriving in the capitol, Levi shared the same sense of adventure, discovery, and creativity he had sensed in Tuscany in the Roman streets. Rome, he conjectures, was the place from which the beginning of a new postwar course could be made. The novel's very first lines, in fact, recall the notion of the original indeterminate state we previously encountered in **Fear,** and which also plays an important role in **The Watch**:

> At night in Rome you can almost hear the roar of lions. An indistinct murmur that is the city's breath, between its black cupolas and distant hills, here and there in the sparkling shadow. And at times you can hear the deep sound of sirens, as if the sea were nearby, and ships were leaving from the port towards who knows what horizons. And that vague yet wild sound, cruel yet strangely sweet, the roar of lions, in the nocturnal desert of the houses.

> (3)

The sounds return Levi to a childhood state—"the sound penetrated me like a frightening, moving, strange childhood image, from another time" (3)—that is in every way comparable to the new beginning his initial impact with Rome presages. In this new beginning, Levi finds himself at the point where the personal and the historical intersect. It is historical because he is bound up in the new course that the recent events have ushered in: "a stormy wind had begun to blow over Europe's bitter soil and carried men like leaves plucked from a tree on white unknown roads. After seven years of massacres and troubles the wind had fallen, but the old leaves could not return to their branches, and the cities seemed like stripped woods awaiting, under a modest sun, the disordered blossoming of new buds" (4). At the same time, Levi's arrival in Rome also signals a new personal beginning. After years in either exile or hiding, Levi has lost all contact with the habits and practices that had constructed his earlier life. Now a man whose personal history has been pushed back far into time, listening to the indistinct roar of the lions, "it seemed to me that I had nothing to the back of me if not the void, and that before me I had an enormous, mysterious forest" (7).

The forest, perhaps the key image of the entire text, recurs at important junctures. One such is in Carlo's final telephone conversation with his Uncle Luca. Called to Naples to visit his sick uncle, and arriving too late to pay a visit that night after an adventurous journey from Rome, Carlo speaks to him on the phone. Luca had been a fundamental figure in Carlo's life. It had been Luca, in fact, who had first introduced Carlo to the joys of painting, and as a fellow doctor there had always been a strong bond between them. Luca is very much Carlo's father figure. In fact, we hear more about Luca than about Carlo's biological father, except that Carlo had been absent from his funeral, presumably because he was in exile, and felt a "bitter sense of liberty . . . the liberty made of things lost, bonds broken, loneliness" at his death (303). Luca, however, had a role in Carlo's life which seems just as central. Luca, in fact, had become "more than an uncle, a friend, master and father" (239).

But when Carlo arrives the next day at his house, he discovers that his uncle has died in the night. Carlo's visit to Naples is very much an encounter with death. Yet, death here loses many of its purely negative and destructive connotations to become the essence of life, the enabling condition for life itself to carry on. Luca's reference to the forest of the world—"il bosco del mondo" (287)—comes, paradoxically perhaps, as he sings the praises of death. As a scientist, Luca had been engaged for many years in a private research project which he called the *Teorica*. Never publishing any results, Luca so immersed himself in his research that he gave over his whole life to it. The project, which for Luca revealed the "secret key of the biological world," bore on the "continuous and continuously broken and reconstituted unity of two principles, which are eternally distinct and eternally the same in an eternally endless circulation" (238). Levi makes no judgment on the value of his uncle's project, but he hints at its limited scientific value. What is important for him, though, is not so much its status as hard scientific fact as the "intensity, the infinite energy" his uncle dedicated to it and which proved that this was "the true life of a true man" (239).

In his phone conversation with Carlo, Luca explains how his approaching death has enabled him to appreciate and better understand life. The coming of death has the effect of illuminating life's dark mysteries. But what is the dark mystery that Luca has now glimpsed? It is that life consists of "infinite truths" that stretch out into the future beyond the span of a single person, each one as true as the next, but none more so than any of the others: "You can wear yourself out in vain trying to catch them all, one after the other, like a many-coloured crowd, but whose common language and common human nature you don't know." But as one comes closer to death, "you learn to distinguish in the copresence of time, in the forest of the world, that common nature" which is open-ended: "Instead of focusing on a point or on a single object, your thought takes that object as its starting point and expands in a limitless wave-like motion. It's as if you climbed a mountain and at every step the horizon spread itself wider beneath you. Perhaps, when you reach the top the horizon will be so vast and distant that it will join up with the sky: this, perhaps, is death. If so, we live in order to die" (287-88).

Carlo experiences the same fusion of death and life in the streets of Naples. Observing the frenetic daily activity of the Neapolitans, he notes in the faces of the heterogeneous crowd an awareness of their own finitude and fragility, their own impermanence on this earth, but which nevertheless does not prevent them from fully investing their creativity in life:

> It was as if behind each of those men and women . . . there were another world which had already been fully lived according to an eternal and unchanging law of simple pain. It was as if they thought they were nothing other than an ephemeral object, a transitory expression of that ancient and painful world. Yet, they spared nothing to adorn it with passion and grace as without illusion they contemplated their own fleeting passage, like the splendid, tender light of the morning.
>
> (295)

In a scene that is reminiscent of *Christ,* walking between the market stalls selling fish and meat with their innards exposed, and comparing himself to Jonah in the whale's belly, the close contact with images of death and with the "men who lived in these intestinal walls . . . and had been, who knows how many times, destroyed and resuscitated," brings Carlo to feel that "I was in a true place, in one of the true places of the world" (301). These are strong words, as strong as Levi's sense that he was in the heart of the world when he heard the cries of the dying man in *Christ.* But what is it that Levi discovers in the concatenation of life and death in the Neapolitan streets? We get a strong clue in the text's very next paragraph, with Levi's reference to Giambattista Vico.

In his wandering through the city, Levi comes across the house where Vico used to act as tutor to the young son of a Neapolitan noble. The reference to Vico is timely because his philosophy of history as an ongoing series of rises and falls, or as he puts it, courses and recourses, approximates most closely the thoughts that Levi himself was developing in *The Watch.* Vico, as we have seen earlier, had also been a great influence on **Fear.** What Levi sees in the streets of Naples, we can imply, is the same or similar scene as that which presented itself to Vico 250 years earlier, and which perhaps molded his thought.

Levi sees in the Neapolitan streets a willingness to embrace human existence as a dialectic between life and death in which both are inextricably bound up, feed off one another, the one creating the conditions for the other. To be aware of the finitude of one's own self means having learned the simple lesson of humility that comes with having an awareness of the fragility of all things human and the achievements one can accomplish within a life. To be aware of one's own finitude also means that we are less tempted to inhabit the abstract sphere of pure thought and form, but remain, rather, in close contact with the physical and material things of the world and the experience of death that inheres in them. From this standpoint, finitude takes the form not so much of an existential defect as of the necessarily limited parameters within which we live our lives. Furthermore, finitude reminds us that no human life can ever be complete and that the creative activity of one course prepares the way for another. This means that life lived at its fullest and most authentic takes the form of an ongoing project, itself taking the form of a series of individual courses. Each one of these courses is vitally important to the needs and demands of an individual or a whole society at a given moment, and each one contributes uniquely to the creation and growth of that self or society. At the same time, however, each course has its limits, as well as its strengths, and when its time comes, as it must as circumstances change, or as the world turns and new creative tools are required, individuals and societies as a whole must know when to abandon one course and start a new one.

What might have drawn Levi to Vico is the kind of metaphysics the Neapolitan philosopher outlined in his "Conclusion" to *De Antiquissima Italorum Sapientia* (On the most ancient wisdom of the Italians): "Here then . . . for your greater wisdom you have a metaphysics compatible with human frailty, which neither allows all truths to men, nor yet denies him all, but only some."[52] Furthermore, the notion of error, both in its sense of "trial and error" and "wandering," which Vittorio Mathieu has noted and which underpins Levi's thought, finds in Vico an illustrious precursor. If error is at the basis of truth, then each attempt at locating it is delimited by knowledge of the inadequacy of any and all modes of critical inquiry. History, then, argues Mathieu,

> becomes a *sequence of inadequacies* through which providence shines . . . *abscondita sub contrario.* . . . Vico's cycle is therefore a process by which man's ability to manifest truth is gradually transformed in qualitatively different ways but never ceases to be intrinsically inadequate. The courses and recourses are the periodic succession of inadequate forms of participation in truth, passing continuously from one phase to the next because in none of these does truth find a completely satisfactory ground.[53]

Translated into political terms, this means that the course of history that had brought Italy up to its pre-Fascist Liberal governments had run its course and must be replaced by a new one, this time born out of the Resistance experience, with the Action Party as its figurehead. As we have seen, however, the greatest objections to beginning such a new course came from within the Liberal Party, unwilling to relinquish its position of power, reluctant to contemplate a postwar Italy organized along anything other than familiar pre-Fascist lines. In the very same paragraph of **The Watch** where we find the reference to Vico, we also find a reference to Croce, the president and leading figure within the Liberal Party. The house where Vico used to tutor the noble's son has now been taken over by Croce as his residence. This is Croce's second appearance in the novel. Earlier, in a dream, Croce had appeared to Carlo as a judge called on to decide who was the rightful owner of a watch he had previously lost. Seeing Croce in the courtroom, Levi describes him thus: "The Neapolitan Virgil, honor, light, Duke, Lord and master of my contemporaries" (19).

On this second occasion, Levi does not mention Croce by name but notes simply that "Vico . . . used to climb these stone steps and the floors of the huge unadorned rooms" where now "the master of our wise men, the sharp old philosopher" lived (301). Carlo's brief sojourn outside Croce's house, and his decision not to act on his earlier idea of paying him a visit, amount to a refusal on his part to be seduced by the great philosopher in the way that so many of his contemporaries had. Initially attracted by a bas-relief of the mythological sailor *Cola Pesce* on Croce's door—"the male mermaid who calls other sailors into the abyss and devours them"—Levi suggests that this is the perfect image for Croce: "Perhaps for good reason the *signore* of that place kept it on the door in place of a name plate. The *signore* who knew how to seduce the young men and women who adventured on the sea of dialectic with his sweet song, who sank the ships bedecked with pseudo-concepts down into the vortex of distinctions, and grabbed with his scaly hands the unprepared sailors, captains and crewmen to devour them" (301-2).

This is hardly the most flattering of portraits, and overcome by a sense of uneasiness, Carlo hurries on to his uncle's house. In this section of the novel, one is left with the impression, even if it is only hinted at, that Croce has occupied a space that once, if only temporarily, had or could have been occupied by Vico, perhaps the most misunderstood and underestimated figure in Italian thought. Although this might seem excessively speculative, we find elsewhere in Levi's writings evidence that lends support to this view: first, in Levi's journalistic writings on Croce, and second, in the conclusion to **The Watch,** which takes the form of a Vichian new course.

The similarities between Levi and Croce are deceiving. We should not let the crucial importance that Levi gives to the same concept of creativity that figures so prominently in Croce's thought blind us to the deep divisions that separated the two, and which are illustrated by the *Cola Pesce* vignette. As we shall see, the creativity of the one is not the creativity of the other. Furthermore, Levi certainly does not share Croce's attachment to the *Risorgimento* tradition. Indeed, he sees in its limits the source of Italy's turn to Fascism. At the height of the political crisis of the final months of 1945, with the Liberal Party making great efforts to delegitimate and bring down Parri, Levi wrote an article for *IL* entitled **"Giolittismo ideale"** (**"Ideal Giolittism"**), a reference to the Liberal prime minister in whose cabinet Croce had served. In this article, Levi accuses Croce, the philosopher of liberty, of the fear of liberty he had theorized in his earlier book. In other words, for Levi, Croce is afraid of the concepts of liberty and creativity the philosopher himself had elaborated.

Opening with "Nothing is more unpleasant than to have to open a polemic with the most venerated of Masters," the article, as well as singing the praises of Croce the philosopher in its *captatio benevolentiae,* also makes pointed remarks about the inconsistency of his practical behavior vis-à-vis his thought, and his political errors of judgment in the early years of Fascism. Yet, the thrust of the article is to level a crucial charge: that Croce's theory of history as permanent creation has been betrayed by the stagnation that has resulted from his actual political practice. Specifically, Levi accuses Croce of failing to understand a crucial Vichian lesson: that no given historical course, as successful as it may have been for a more or less limited period of time, is or can be coterminous with history itself. For Levi, Croce had invested so much of his intellectual and political self into the ideology and forms of government developed in the period of Liberal government under Giolitti that he has "confused his own individual experience and preference with the very reason of history." For Croce, he goes on, "that experience became the eternal paradigm of politics, the very form of the dialectic of liberty, which for him is nothing if not an ideal Giolittism [*giolittismo ideale*]."

If now in post-Resistance Italy a new social and historical reality had been created, exposing the limits and present inapplicability of the previous historical course, Croce, writes Levi, is still attached to the worn-out schemes of the past: "Since then the world has had a revolution that has changed all our values, has created new forces, has placed each one of us face to face with the experience of death, which for so long had been forgotten, and has placed each man before the need to revise everything that had been traditionally accepted. But Croce has noticed none of this."[54]

As the reference to death suggests, Levi is here doing to Croce what Croce had done to Hegel: that is, distinguishing between what is alive in his thought and what is dead. As it turns out, very little is alive. Levi's charge to Croce is essentially that he was afraid of the opportunity for creative liberty that the present historical moment offered up, and faced with this new challenge sought refuge in the codes and practices that had governed a previous era. In-

stead of welcoming the present moment and embracing the chance to create new forms, Croce had allowed his thought to crystallize around the institutions and modes of government of the Giolitti era. Croce, then, commits what for Levi is the worst and most dangerous of sins. His insistence on extending the applicability of the paradigms that had underlaid the Giolitti government to the newly created present situation was tantamount to turning those paradigms into idols whose effect, indeed purpose, was to stifle creative activity and channel it into the adoration of fixed and codified norms: "Croce . . . has stayed faithful to his 'giolittismo ideale' . . . the parliamentary institutions, traditional constitutional and administrative forms which are the negation of real liberty, of the autonomy of the forces in play, of the real value of liberty."[55]

Croce, in fact, had allowed himself to be left in that phase of human development that Vico called the "barbarism of reflection," that R. G. Collingwood describes in his *The Idea of History* as being "where thought still rules, but a thought which has exhausted its creative power and only constructs meaningless networks of artificial and pedantic distinctions."[56] For Levi, this is a dangerous phase in human development because, as he had outlined in *Fear,* the mechanical application of worn-out schemes and formulas is not only the death of creativity but also prepares the kind of cultural terrain on which a Fascist-like phenomenon can prosper. Levi is perfectly serious when he constructs a line of direct continuity between a historical age like the one Vico identified as the "barbarism of reflection" and a phenomenon like fascism. But how to prevent an era from degenerating into the barbarism of reflection? How to prevent institutions and forms of thought created for a specific age and circumstances from sedimenting into a series of codes and formulas? Levi's answer is to suggest that we endorse the side of Vico's thought that Croce had been reluctant to endorse: namely, his cyclical theory of history. If we accept that our lives are not structured as a single, unilinear narrative stretching homogeneously from birth to death, but on a series of narratives, or phases, a succession of rises and falls, similar to Vico's courses and recourses, we might be able, first, to avoid the stagnation and regenerate our creativity as we enter each new and different phase; and second, in so doing, construct a bulwark against the dangerous sedimentation of thought that had, for example, taken over Italian liberalism, and could, in the worst of hypotheses pave the way for a new form of fascism.

One young Crocean who had realized at an early stage the limits of Italian liberalism was Piero Gobetti. A great friend and influence on Levi, he is quoted twice in the article on Giolitti. On the first occasion, Levi quotes him to underline Croce's status as Italy's least-provincial thinker, something Gobetti thinks will never be forgiven him by a thoroughly provincial Italy. Indeed, Levi's article gives us a picture of a Croce hostage to the parochial interests of the Liberal land-owning classes. On the second occasion, Gobetti is quoted to point out the ideological duplicity of Croce's proposal for an "apolitical" government to replace

Parri. In Gobetti's words, the claim to occupy an apolitical center is nothing other than a recipe for restoration in the guise of moderation: "Those who claim to be apolitical are always wrong: their apolitical stance is always biased, they are an inert force which plays to the advantage of conservative and reactionary interests."[57]

Although holding fast to the fundamental Liberal tenet of history as perpetual creation, Gobetti also saw how liberalism, once it occupied positions of government power, in practice tended toward stagnation and complacency. Indeed, one of Gobetti's most memorable remarks is that, rather than as a social class, the bourgeoisie stands for "the moment of inertia" which inevitably invests all courses of history.[58] Differently from Croce, who tended to limit creativity to the efforts of single individuals, Gobetti found a guarantee of ongoing creativity in the political activity of the working class. In Turin, Gobetti had been able to observe the factory council movement, which sprang up during one of the most potentially revolutionary periods in twentieth-century Italian history, the so-called "red biennium" of 1919-20. Importantly for Gobetti, the factory councils were not set up according to the dictates of a prior revolutionary program but were born out of the workers' needs and demands from below. Gradually acquiring greater power, the councils became training grounds where a new working class could acquire the skills it would need if its members were to sit on committees and comanage the factories. The movement gained most momentum between April and September 1920 when, during a management-initiated lock-out, the workers effectively took over the running of the factories and continued production. Although the workers' demands were not met by the compromise settlement which brought the lockouts to an end, Gobetti was deeply impressed by what he had seen.

Gobetti's positive response to the creativity from below which had characterized the Turin factory council movement is identical to Levi's response to the same creative activity in Florence during the Resistance: in both cases, those involved worked autonomously, with no guidelines except the ones they fashioned for themselves as the need arose. Furthermore, both Turin workers and Florentine Partisans operated outside traditional institutions and created new ones. For both Gobetti and Levi the creative activity they had been fortunate to witness in Turin and Florence was infinitely renewed and self-renewing, as each new phase presented society and individuals with new, concrete problems to be solved, each of which required new creative efforts. For Gobetti, this meant rejecting the Marxist interpretation of history as the road towards the classless society, and developing a theory of ongoing social antagonism between the classes as a way of guaranteeing the perpetual creativity that propels history.[59] For Levi, it meant turning to Vico and his theory of history as course and recourse.

The Watch concludes with a number of Vichian resonances and with the promise of a new course. After his journey back to Rome from Naples in the company of two ministers, both of whom, despite their differing ideological positions, were supremely confident that they were in the forefront of history, Carlo's political phase as a militant and intellectual in the Action Party comes to an end. In Naples, Carlo had been given his Uncle Leo's watch, to which presumably the novel's title refers. This watch replaces the one Carlo had broken at the beginning of the novel, which had been given to him by his father. Although Carlo takes this first watch to be repaired, the text itself gives us no further information about it.

Watches in general receive bad press in the novel. The time that watches and clocks beat, he tells us on one of the text's opening pages, is "the opposite of that real time that was in and around [him]" (12) during his childhood days, when the "long days seemed endless" (11). Clock time, the opposite of the authentic experience of time enjoyed by peasants, and which still exists at a subterranean level in all of us, as he writes in his 1950 essay **"Il contadino e l'orologio" ("The peasant and the watch")**,[60] knows no "hesitations, [is] a mathematical time, a continual material movement that is both restless and devoid of anxiety" (11). Like the splendid gold Omega model his father had given him on graduation, watches mark the adolescent's passage into adulthood. This represents one of the early phases in which the young self extricates itself from the "past, from the indistinct security of the tepid family clan and you begin to follow your own personal time" (12). As we know from ***Fear,*** for Levi, the moment of differentiation must be complemented and completed by beneficial returns to the undifferentiated state, where the self can reinvigorate itself and embark on a new course. Should this not happen, the self remains a prisoner of its initial course.

This is what happens with the watch. The self's personal time, in fact, turns out to be more a mirage than an index of newfound freedom. After a while, the codes and rhythms of adult life exert their influence over the young self, as the watch "beats time like a bodiless intellectual essence which like a tyrant attempts to carry our heart off for itself" (12). If the self does not put up resistance to this process, it falls into a military-style pattern of life which is completely determined by externally imposed clock time: "One! Two! One! Two! Our feet seem to move on their own and without realizing it we have already followed them" (12). For Levi, then, to break and then effectively lose the watch also means that he frees himself from a phase in his life in which his creative energies had been exhausted, and opens him to the possibility of a new phase, whose starting point is emblematically represented by his descent into and rise from the original indeterminate state inside the whale's belly in the streets of Naples.

But what of the second watch, which Carlo receives after leaving the whale? It is in every way the equal of the first one. This time, however, it is not inherited from his father but from his uncle, who while not being his biological father, is certainly his metaphoric one, a father figure who in the economy of the novel seems to have greater importance for Carlo than does than his real one. Both the new watch and Leo can be seen as emblems of the new phase that Carlo is about to embark on. After Parri's resignation and the trip back from Naples with the two politicians, Carlo is convinced that the phase of life and history driven by the creative energy of the Resistance has come to an end. Indeed, the novel is often read, rightly I believe, as the Resistance's epitaph. Yet the novel does not limit itself to mourning what might have been. The line of continuity between uncle and nephew signaled by the watch suggests that for Carlo the next phase will be marked not so much by activity in the public sphere of politics as in the intense, but nonetheless gratifying, private sphere in which Leo carried out the research that brought him into contact with first things. At the same time, what we have learnt about watches reminds us that all phases, even the new one on which Carlo embarks, tend ultimately to exhaust themselves and become constricting. As the novel concludes, however, Carlo finds himself at the beginning of his new course.

As he returns home to Rome, he looks out over the city from his balcony and hears once again the lion's roar he had heard at the beginning of the novel. In its concluding paragraph, the text returns us to the original indistinct state, to Vico's primordial forest—"the indistinct hum of a forest of ancient trees"—where the novel began. Carlo is taken back to the "depths of memory" by "the murmuring silence . . . the strange noise of the night, the lions' roar, like the echo of the sea in an abandoned shell" (312), where his new journey out of the ancient forest will begin anew.

For Levi, liberty meant something more than the formal democratic structures that enable us to change our governments. Liberty was also the courage to examine ourselves and the assumptions on which we have based our own lives, the courage to change ourselves. He saw that the fear of liberty was deeply ingrained in the European consciousness, even in those who proclaimed themselves revolutionaries, and had culminated in Europe's many fascist regimes. Overcoming the fear of liberty constituted the personal battle that had to be won if a genuinely new anti-Fascist culture was to be created. Liberty, wrote Levi in *Fear,* is like a war one fights within oneself against oneself, "an inner war, an enrichment, an increase in peace, a civil war: that civil war that has neither beginning nor end," the only war worth fighting.[61] Acknowledging the question of civil war that neither Communist nor Liberal cultures had been, in his terms, willing to raise, Levi elevates the question to the level of metaphor for the introspective and self-critical mode of being that is necessary if we are to understand the phenomenon that is fascism, the deeper recesses within history from which it comes, and the personal and collective needs to which it responds. This was an ambitious project, a project of its time, inspired by the optimism that pervaded Italy in the months which followed the fall of fascism in September 1943, as the example of the Resistance seemed to provide Italian

society with a foundation on which to construct itself anew. It was also a project that largely failed, yet it may have been a project of this kind, without equal in post-Fascist Italy or Europe, requiring a sea-change in attitudes, expectations, and culture, and to which post-Fascist Europe attended only minimally, that Levi's friend Piero Gobetti had in mind when he wrote that antifascism was a question of style.

Notes

1. For the authenticity of the unsigned articles, I have relied on the *Fondazione Carlo Levi,* Via del Vantaggio, Rome, Italy. Some of Levi's articles have been republished in the exhibition catalogue *Carlo Levi: Disegni politici, 1947-1948* (Rome: np, 1993) and in Leonardo Sacco, ed., *Contadini e luigini: testi e disegni di Carlo Levi* (Rome-Matera: Basilicata Editrice, 1975). For a complete list of the titles of his articles, see appendix 1.

2. Carlo Levi, "Saluto ai congressisti," IL, 3 February 1946, series 4, issue 29. For critical studies dedicated to Levi's politics, see Ghislana Sirovich, *L'azione politica di Carlo Levi* (Rome: Il Ventaglio, 1988), and Vincenzo Napolillo, *Carlo Levi: dall' antifascismo al mito contadino* (Cosenza: Brenner, 1984).

3. Carlo Levi, "Rompere con il passato," IL, 3 January 1946, series 4, issue 2.

4. Levi, "Saluto ai congressisti."

5. Dominique Fernandez, "Uomini-dei o uomini-piante," in *Galleria,* fascicolo dedicato a Carlo Levi, ed. Aldo Marcovecchio 17, no. 3-6 (May-December 1967): 160.

6. Carlo Levi, "Firenze libera!" NdP, 15 August 1945, series 2, special issue.

7. Carlo Levi, "Antonio Salandra," in *La rivoluzione liberale,* 27 August 1922; in *Il coraggio dei miti: Scritti contemporanei 1922-1974,* ed. Gigliola De Donato (Bari: De Donato, 1975), 11.

8. See Antonio Gramsci, *Il Risorgimento* (Turin: Einaudi, 1949).

9. See Archivio Carlo Levi, Archivio nazionale dello Stato, B. 69 Doc, Fasc. "Garibaldi" 145. Gaetano Marini, *Un buco nell' acqua: ovvero Le debolezze, le malizie, gl' imbrogli, li errori, e le camorre in varie amministrazioni della Sicilia. Frammenti di scandalosa cronaca contemporanea* (Sciacca: Tipografia Guttemburg, 1864). In the same folder, see also Nicolosi di Sciacca, *La Madonna di Saletta. Invocazione Siciliana contro i Garibaldini,* circa 1871.

10. Carlo Levi, *Cristo si è fermato a Eboli* (Turin: Einaudi, 1945), 48. Translated by Frances Frenaye as *Christ Stopped at Eboli* (New York: Farrar and Strauss, 1963).

11. Carlo Levi, *Paura della libertà,* 3rd ed. (Turin: Einaudi, 1964), 41. Translated by Adolphe Gourevitch

as *Of Fear and Freedom* (New York: Farrar and Strauss, 1950). In this chapter, further references to this work will appear parenthetically within the main body of the text.

12. See Giammanco, "Paura della libertà," 244. See also Lawrence Baldassaro, "*Paura della libertà*: Carlo Levi's Unfinished Preface," *Italica* 72:2 (Summer 1995): 143-54.

13. See Gigliola De Donato, *Saggio su Carlo Levi* (Bari: De Donato, 1974), 36.

14. Fernandez, "Uomini-dei o uomini-piante," 170.

15. Carlo Levi, "L'invenzione della verità," in *Coraggio dei Miti,* ed. Gigliola De Donato (Bari: Laterza, 1975), 121-22.

16. Carlo Levi, "Gramsci e il mezzogiorno, oggi," *Basilicata,* 11, no. 5-6 (1967): 47.

17. See Gianni Vattimo, *The End of Modernity,* trans. and intro. Jon R. Snyder (Baltimore: Johns Hopkins University Press, 1988), and, by the same author, *The Transparent Society.*

18. In Gigliola De Donato, *Saggio su Carlo Levi* (Bari: De Donato, 1974), 71, citing Carlo Levi, *Quaderno ACI,* vol. 2 (Turin: n.p., 1953).

19. Levi, *Cristo si è fermato a Eboli,* 15.

20. Ibid.

21. Carlo Levi, "Crisi di civiltà," *NdP,* 12/13 September 1944, series 1, issue 14.

22. Carlo Levi, "Giolittismo ideale," IL, 1 December 1945, series 3, issue 287.

23. Carlo Levi, "La speranza," *NdP,* 25 December 1944, series 1, issue 103.

24. Levi, *Cristo si è fermato a Eboli,* 188-89.

25. Levi, *Paura della libertà,* 41.

26. Carlo Levi, *Quaderno di prigione,* 14 July 1935, quoted in Aldo Marcovecchio, "Il periplo del mondo," in *Galleria* 17:3-6 (May-December 1967): 103.

27. Carlo Levi, *Quaderno a cancelli* (Turin: Einaudi, 1979). See also Levi's writing on India, in *Viaggio in India* (Journey to India), written in 1957 and now in Marcovecchio, *Galleria.*

28. Levi, "Crisi di civiltà."

29. Carlo Levi, "Rivoluzione democratica," IL, 27 October 1945, series 3, issue 257.

30. Levi, "Crisi di civiltà." See also in the same article: "The crisis of civilization which has long been manifest in all fields, in art, in religion, in economy, in social life, in philosophy."

31. See Foa, *Il cavallo e la torre,* 171-72.

32. Carlo Levi, "La costituente," *NdP,* 6 October 1944, series 1, issue 35.

33. See Erasmus [pseud.], "Fascismo e antifascismo," RL, 15 December 1945, series 3, issue 270.

34. Rosselli, "Fronte verso l'Italia," GL, 18 May 1934; in *Scritti dell' esilio,* 2:4. See also Foa, *Il cavallo e la torre,* 167, for the broader agenda that many Actionists gave to their antifascism.

35. Carlo Levi, "Al di là dell'antifascismo," *NdP,* 4 December 1944, series 1, issue 85.

36. Carlo Levi, *Le parole sono pietre* (Turin: Einaudi, 1955), 132.

37. For more detailed information about the political climate of 1945-46, see Paul Ginsborg, *Storia d'Italia dal dopoguerra a oggi: Società e politica, 1943-1988* (Turin: Einaudi, 1989), especially 116-19. See also Foa, *Il cavallo e la torre,* 169.

38. Among the articles Levi wrote in IL attacking Liberal party policy, see "La consulta," 25 September 1945, series 3, issue 229; "Dubbi liberali," 2 October 1945, series 3, issue 235; "La vendetta del Presidente," 4 October 1945, series 3, issue 237; "Favole e realtà," 18 October 1945, series 3, issue 249; "La crisi dei 'galantuomini,'" 6 November 1945, series 3, issue 265; "La crisi dei morti," 17 December 1945, series 3, issue 275; "L'ombra di Facta," 20 November 1945, series 3, issue 277; "Responsabilità," 23 November 1945, series 3, issue 280; the unsigned article "Giolittismo ideale"; and "Le ambizioni sbagliate," 6 December 1945, series 3, issue 291.

39. Giammanco, "Paura della libertà," 248.

40. Levi, *Paura della libertà,* 21-22.

41. Levi, "Rompere con il passato."

42. Carlo Levi, "Liberazione dal terrore," *NdP,* 9 October 1944, series 1, issue 37.

43. Levi, "Paura della libertà," *NdP,* 2 November 1944, series 1, issue 58.

44. For more on this short-lived political movement, see Sandro Setta, *L'Uomo qualunque* (Bari: Laterza, 1975).

45. Carlo Levi, "Cristallizzazione artificiale," IL, 6 October 1945, series 3, issue 239, and "Favole e realtà."

46. Levi, *Cristo si è fermato a Eboli,* 209. In this chapter, further references to this work will appear in parentheses.

47. See Robert Young, *White Mythologies,* 2, for how Marx also came to welcome British colonialism in India as a means of bringing this extrahistorical country into the mainstream of history.

48. Manlio Rossi Doria, "La crisi del governo Parri nel racconto di Carlo Levi," in *Carlo Levi nella storia e*

nella cultura, ed. Gigliola De Donato (Manduria, Bari and Rome: Piero Lacaita, 1993), 181-91.

49. Ibid., 187.

50. Levi, *L'orologio,* 48. In this chapter, further references to this work appear in parentheses.

51. Foa, *Il cavallo e la torre,* 171-72.

52. Giambattista Vico, *On the Most Ancient Wisdom of the Italians,* trans. and with an introduction by L. M. Palmer (Ithaca: Cornell University Press, 1988), 109.

53. Vittorio Mathieu, "Truth as the Mother of History," in *Giambattista Vico's Science of Humanity,* ed. Giorgio Tagliacozzo and Donald Philip Verene (Baltimore: The Johns Hopkins University Press, 1970), 118-19. Mathieu continues: "When the thought of truth should wish to cease its wanderings, this illusory disappearance of error, and of the relevant myths, would in fact be the most radical obnubilation of truth" (119). See also Sir Isaiah Berlin, "Vico and the Ideal of the Enlightenment," in *Vico and Contemporary Thought,* ed. Tagliacozzo, Mooney, Michael, and Verene (London: MacMillan, 1980), 250-63.

54. Levi, "Giolittismo ideale."

55. Ibid.

56. R. G. Collingwood, *The Idea of History,* rev. ed., ed. and with an introducton by Jan Van Der Dussen (Oxford: Clarendon Press, 1993), 67.

57. Ibid.

58. Gobetti, *La rivoluzione liberale,* 135.

59. See Piero Gobetti, *Opere complete,* vol. 1 of *Scritti politici,* ed. Paolo Spriano (Turin: Einaudi, 1969), 515: "Our Liberalism . . . sees in reality a conflict of forces, capable of producing ever new leading aristocracies provided that the popular classes revitalize the struggle with their desperate will to elevation." Cited in Roberts, *Benedetto Croce.* My argument here draws on pages 241-48 of the above volume.

60. Carlo Levi, "Il contadino e l'orologio," in *Coraggio dei miti,* ed. Gigliola De Donato (Bari: De Donato, 1975), 55-60.

61. Levi, *Paura della libertà,* 100.

Mark Friguglietti (essay date 1997)

SOURCE: Friguglietti, Mark. "Carlo Levi's *Cristo si è fermato a Eboli*: An Anthropological Assessment of Lucania." *Annali d'Italianistica* 15 (1997): 221-36.

[*In the following essay, Friguglietti reads* Christ Stopped at Eboli *as an anthropological study and focuses on the descriptions and role of architecture in the southern Italian village.*]

Lucania, the mountainous region wedged between Campania, Calabria and Apulia, comprises a large percentage of the hinterland of Southern Italy. Insular and remote, Lucania has infrequently attracted the interest of historians and anthropologists. The culture of the people who have inhabited this desolate land for millennia has been too neglected in historical accounts, which have focused primarily on the politico-economic forces that have struggled to dominate Southern Italy. For its own part, the indigenous population of Lucania was largely nonliterate and incapable of leaving its own written testimony of its unique culture. Today, as modern society rapidly encroaches upon older cultures throughout the world, evidence of this unknown Lucania is rapidly vanishing and it has become imperative to establish a valid account of this past before it disappears altogether.

One of the few written texts offering cultural evidence of Lucania is not an anthropological treatise, but the novel *Cristo si è fermato a Eboli* by Carlo Levi. Despite the personal nature of Levi's account of his nine-month confinement in Aliano during 1935-36, the narrative focuses attention primarily on the world of the peasants, what the author refers to as "quell'altro mondo" (15) and "la civiltà contadina" (121). In the opening two paragraphs which frame the entire work, Levi draws attention to the cultural and historical neglect that the world of the peasants has endured. He poetically renders it as outright negation by emphasizing that their world is

> serrato nel dolore e negli usi, negato alla Storia e allo Stato, . . . terra senza conforto e dolcezza. . . . Cristo non è mai arrivato qui, né vi è arrivato il tempo, né l'anima individuale, né la speranza, né il legame tra le cause e gli effetti, la ragione, e la Storia. . . . Parliamo un diverso linguaggio: la nostra lingua è qui incompresibile.
>
> (15-16)

Levi indicates that we readers, the literates of the modern world, speak a different language than the peasants of that remote land. Both our language and our culture are not valid standards for assessing the civilization of that the peasant world. Rather, an accurate measurement of that civilization requires diverse cultural parameters.

By recognizing the peasants, Levi counters the negation of their culture and affirms their place in history. His text offers present day scholars one of the only written accounts of a world being forgotten at the end of the twentieth century. The purpose of this paper is to demonstrate how Levi's narrative serves as an indispensable document for reconstructing an authentic history of the culture of the peasants of Lucania. In order to construct a cultural portrait from the written text, I will consider less Levi's subjective analysis and focus attention more on his circumstantial descriptions of the material world, in particular, the vernacular architecture. Supported by a theoretical approach to material culture which considers architecture to be a direct expression of the culture of a nonliterate society, I will suggest that Levi's descriptions of the peasants' houses are a valid means for defining their "civiltà conta-dina." Noting that Levi's examples of vernacular architecture are some of the most significant to have been passed down to the present day, I will extend the examination of the architectural house types so that the structure of the peasant house can be viewed as an explicit expression of the peasant way of life, specifically the peasants' affinity with nature and their strong sense of community. Those aspects of Levi's narrative that center in or around the houses will be read as direct reflections of the most meaningful and basic social interactions of the community and its relationship with the surrounding natural environment.

Artifactual Evidence as an Expression of Culture

The accurate reconstruction of the history of a nonliterate people from written sources is a difficult task. Written documents collected from writers and scribes external to the group are prone to inaccuracy and bias at many levels.[1] Even unbiased documents and observations that are accurate are frequently incomplete representations of the people they attempt to describe.

In order to compensate for the lack of satisfactory written records, contemporary scholars from a variety of disciplines have been increasingly turning to material culture.[2] One of the most direct methods of uncovering information about a society that left little or no written documentation is to study the material it produced. Archaeologists, anthropologists, folklorists and cultural geographers painstakingly examine artifactual remains as evidence of human culture. Artifacts are evidence that can be viewed as a corpus, what James Deetz points to as "culturally sensitive data" (*Historical Archaeology* 10). Artifacts are not merely studied as things in themselves, but as a means to expose the culture inherent in their production.

One dominant course of study takes a cognitive approach. This study of artifacts goes beyond the superficial analysis of objects and passes to the study of the human mind. Henry Glassie proposes that an analysis of historic artifacts is the attempt to understand how objects relate to human thought.[3] He is primarily interested in the artifact as "an expression of cognitive pattern." In prefacing his treatise, *Invitation to Archaeology,* Deetz suggests that the patterning discovered in the artifact is a direct reflection of the culture which produced it (7). An analysis of the structure inherent in an object is an indication of the mind that thought it, made it, and eventually used it.

The house can be considered one of a community's largest and most significant artifacts. It follows that the objects which humans construct as habitats can be read as an expression of their culture. In a detailed study of Native American architecture, Peter Nabokov and Robert Easton affirm that it is "only natural to consider houses and human spaces as the most immediate evidence of culture" because patterns of social life occur in and around houses (411). They suggest that Native Americans leave some ex-

pression of their existence in the buildings and homes they create. This statement of material culture can be extended to vernacular architecture around the world. In particular, houses are artifacts which reflect the culture of nonliterate populations. By examining the houses of Lucanian peasants as reflections of cognitive pattern, it is possible to shape an understanding of the culture and history of the peasants.

With regard to vernacular architecture in Lucania, an historical study is not a simple matter of counting houses. Difficulties lie in acquiring first-hand material evidence for basic reasons. Examples are insufficient, and data collection is hampered because peasant houses have not survived for centuries. In Lucania, homes were periodically lost to both the landslides and the earthquakes that periodically strike the area. Despite construction and reconstruction, peasant houses were not generally well made. Levi refers to both of these facts in **Cristo.** Immediately upon arrival in Gagliano he says that the houses appear poorly constructed and "piene di fenditure" (18). Don Trajella, the parish priest, points out to Levi that there are re-occuring landslides: "Qui ci sono continuamente le frane. Quando piove, la terra cede e scivola, e le case precipitano" (44). Enrico Pani Rossi indicates that the area as a whole has been destroyed with regular frequency by earthquakes (72). As a result, vernacular architecture in Lucania must be studied from a dual perspective, combining both written and artifactual sources. Material culture can be used not only to corroborate historical documentation, but to widen the understanding of history and to add new perspectives which emphasize the culture of the peasants.[4]

Early Documentation of Lucanian Vernacular Architecture

By the end of the nineteenth century, anthropologists and historians had developed only limited interest in Lucania. Some of the more prominent names from both disciplines include Michele Pasquarelli, Giacomo Racioppi, Enrico Pani Rossi, Decio Albini and Michele Lacava. The concern among the historians was to celebrate important historical figures and document major political events. On the other hand, the tendency among the anthropologists was to observe and record limited details of peasant life, in particular, proverbial expressions and brigand tales. Neither of two groups of scholars devoted ample attention to a study of the daily lives of the common folk and their diverse culture.

Few studies had been made of the peasants' living conditions and they are by and large scarce and inadequate. Luchino Franciosa wrote the first major study on Lucanian rural architecture in 1942. In *La casa rurale nella Lucania,* he reports the scarcity of prior studies of vernacular architecture: "Pochissimi sono le opere contenenti notizie sulla casa rurale nella Lucania" (11). Franciosa's examination of external factors that affect rural housing in Lucania represents a major contribution to the study of Lucania architecture. He divides the region into geographic areas, categorizing farm houses according to characteristics related to the topographic and climatic conditions. His analysis focuses specifically on the rural houses found on agricultural land, intentionally excluding the houses in the villages. Unreported are the dwellings used by the majority of peasants who lived in town and commuted daily to the fields.

One of the few studies made prior to Franciosa's 1942 work is found in *Atti della Giunta per l'Inchiesta Parlamentare Agraria e sulle condizioni della classe agricola*. Franciosa refers to this study, which incorporates brief descriptions. Dated 1884, *Atti della Giunta* presents the Lucanian housing in the following terms:

> le abitazioni dei contadini sono meschine, disagiate e composte di uno o due ambienti. In uno c'è la cucina con un mal costrutto fumaiolo, nell'altro la stanza da letto con la mobilia stipata. Moltissime volte si vede una sola camera, dove si cucina e si dorme e spesso ha ricetto anche il maiale e il somaro.
>
> (12)

Some of the basic components that constitute the peasant house are illustrated in this observation (one or two rooms divided into the kitchen with singular fire and sleeping area with animals). Although the account presents significant characteristics, it depicts living conditions as inferior. The house is economically insufficient. The flue pipe is poorly made. The furniture is crammed into the space. Frequently animals, a pig and a donkey, share the living space with humans.

Franciosa associates the reports with a second, similar description by E. Anzimonte in *Inchiesta parlamentare sulle condizioni dei contadini nel mezzogiorno,* dated 1908. Anzimonti writes:

> La casa a un sol piano è generalmente anche a un sol vano, piuttosto grande. . . . In queste case l'aria e la luce, quando non entrino dalle connessure del tetto, non abbondano mai; mancano sciacquatoi, mancano latrine; mancano stalle. Gli animali stanno nel medesimo ambiente. . . . Il focolare non manca in ogni casa, ma il camino non è sempre tale da assicurare la perfetta fuoruscita dei prodotti della combustione . . .
>
> (12)

The latter description's basic house plan is almost identical to that of the previous account. Anzimonti's description also implies a substandard living environment. He cites the components that are lacking or nonexistent: lighting, sink and toilet. He also notes that the animals share space with humans and that the air is filled with smoke. Enrico Pani Rossi, in a study published in 1868, observed similar conditions, saying that the houses were often cellars in which "viene poi l'aura o la luce dal foro . . . donde oscurità o tenebre quasi perfette. Colà fucina per domestiche bisogne e senza comignolo onde il fumo vi s'accoglie" (69).

The illustrations discussed above describe the same basic image of the peasant house, although these representations are cursory and incomplete. Specifically, the data are insufficient and the method is unscientific. In particular, no true figures or measurements are given. Moreover, each account suggests a bias that the peasant accommodations are inferior in relation to standards that exist for the outsider. The houses appear deficient primarily because they lack the characteristic priorities considered requisite by the observer: running water, ample lighting, sterile air and abundant space. These observations offer only a partial understanding of the relationship of the houses to the peasants' particular world.

Within the context of a literary narrative, Levi's description of Lucanian vernacular architecture confirms the information summarized years earlier by anthropologists. Although his purpose was not primarily anthropological, he presents a similar portrait of the peasant house. Trained as a physician and practiced as a painter, he was capable of detailed observation. His term of confinement gave him unique access to the otherwise infrequently noted world. He states that, as physician to many of the peasants, he had the opportunity to enter their houses and observe interior in detail. He notes that almost all the houses were comprised of one room which had no window and which received its light from the door (45). When he attends to a sick peasant, he describes the room as dark: "La stanza era buia, a malapena potevo discernere, nella penombra, delle contadine" (20). The main features of the houses are identical to those elements in the descriptions noted by Franciosa above:

> Le case dei contadini sono tutte uguali, fatte di una sola stanza che serve da cucina, da camera da letto e quasi sempre anche da stalla per le bestie piccole. . . . Da una parte c'è il camino, su cui si fa da mangiare con pochi stecchi portati ogni giorno dai campi: i muri e il soffitto sono scuri pel fumo. La luce viene dalla porta.
>
> (106-07)

Levi describes a simple one room house with a single door. In one area there is a fireplace. It is used for cooking and darkens the walls and ceiling with smoke. Animals and humans share the limited space. Levi describes how it is apportioned:

> La stanza è quasi interamente riempita dall'enorme letto, assai piú grande di un comune letto matrimoniale: nel letto deve dormire tutta la famiglia, il padre, la madre, e tutti i figlioli. . . . Sotto il letto stanno gli animali.
>
> (107)

In addition, he states that infants are placed above the bed in baskets so that their mothers might easily gain access to them for feeding during the night. In this manner the space was divided into three levels, with the animals on the ground, the humans in the bed and the infants in the baskets.

Don Trajella, the impoverished priest, lives with his mother in a large, cavernous, one room house, like that of the peasants: "Nel fondo della spelonca, separati da una tenda verde sbrindellata, c'erano due lettini gemelli. . . . galline correvano e svolazzavano qua e là per la stanza" (83). Levi notes that because of the chickens, the house smells like a chicken coop.

It is apparent from Levi's interaction with the mayor and the doctors that the gentry as a whole consider the peasant houses crude structures, inferior in quality to their own houses. The distinction is pointed out to Levi by the mayor when Levi seeks accommodations: "Per un uomo come lei non ci vuole una casa di contadini. Ma le troveremo meglio, dottore!" (47). The mayor suggests that Levi, an intellectual from a different social environment, should require more sophisticated living quarters than those that suffice for the peasants.

The distinction posed by the mayor reflects the general bias noted in the brief descriptions by anthropologists above. Levi's general tone in the narrative does not emphasize the disparagement in lifestyle; however, at certain moments he refers to the peasant houses in a slightly derogatory language. He identifies them as "catapecchie contadine" (45), "tuguri" (67), "capanne" (131) and the house of the impoverish priest as "uno stanzone, una specie di spelonca" (83). He frames his arrival in the village with a negative note about the houses: "le case stavano come librate nell'aria . . . parevano in bilico sull'abisso, pronte a crollare e piene di fenditure" (18). He suggests that the peasant houses are shacks, unclean and substandard. General characterizations imply that the world of the Lucanian peasant is inferior to the standards of the world from which he came. Initially, Levi was prone to some of the bias of the outsider. Born and raised in Turin, he was slowly accepted into the peasant world and his eventual association with the peasants reflects that acceptance.

EVIDENCE OF PEASANT HOUSES IN LUCANIA TODAY

In a study of material culture, one particular question continually resurfaces: Why should one study objects when studying the people directly would seem less complicated? Would it not be simpler to observe the peasants themselves than analyze their houses? The answer might be affirmative if there existed a clear image of the peasant world in Lucania. However, with the invasion of the modern technological world into this insular society, it is more difficult today to recognize signs of original peasant culture. Furthermore, recent studies of the people of Lucania continue to reflect the bias noted in the descriptions above. In 1976, Ann Cornelisen published a portrait of Lucania based on twenty years of personal experience there. She highlights the vernacular architecture with the same bias as the anthropologists a century earlier. Her interpretations are colored by a standard of living which she brings from the modern world. Cornelisen's point of reference in describing the peasant houses is fashioned by her own sense

of comfort: "Money could not buy comfort, much less delicacies or amusements" (4). She adds: "Delicacies were out of the question" (5). Based on research conducted in a Lucanian village during 1954-55, Edward Banfield concludes that the peasants economic well-being is thwarted by their flagrant disregard for community welfare, a condition that he labels "amoral familism" (163).

Seeking an understanding of Lucania through direct contact with the material culture as it remains nowadays, I studied several houses in the village of Montemurro during the summer of 1991.[5] Hidden underneath the paint of both new and old walls, I identified two structurally different house types. One house type was based on a design that opened directly from the street into the main room. From the street, this type presented a single door set asymmetrically in the façade. There was a single window placed to one side of the door. The door was the "Dutch" type, divided into three panels: one full vertical panel on the left side and two half-panels of the right side, the upper panel of which opened like a second window into the kitchen. In the kitchen was the fireplace and near the fireplace, a large table with chairs. The fireplace was located in one of the two side walls, close to a front corner and on the same side as the single window in the façade. Because it was the only window in the entire house, the natural light fell primarily over the fireplace. In addition to the main room in which the fireplace was located, there was usually a smaller, unheated, back room.

The second house type was based on a design that presented a hallway in the center of the house. In comparison to the first type, the hallway had a significant effect on the plan. In these houses, the main room with the fireplace was separated from the entrance door. The room tended to be smaller, because the hallway required some of the floor space that might otherwise have been given to the main room. Also, this design separated the main room from the street at more than one location. First, at the street, a short gate limited access to the front door. Then the front door opened to a hallway delaying access to the main room. Finally, a door to the main room further discouraged access to the fire. The hallway, leading not only to the main room, but also to all the various rooms, caused confusion as to which door opened to the main room, with its fireplace. Further confusion was created by the façade which presented several windows, not necessarily symmetrical, but appearing on both sides of the door, offering a less than clear image of the direction to the fireplace.

The first house style, which offered direct access to the main room and fireplace, appeared in houses that showed signs of physical age and seemed to be older. The second house type, with the gate and the hallway, appeared in houses that were recently renovated and seemed to be more contemporary. Determining the history and the age of a house in Montemurro can be complicated, however, for two interrelated reasons. First, because the area is on a geological fault, houses are periodically destroyed. As noted above, Pani Rossi indicates the ruin caused by earthquakes. Schiavone also writes: "Data la natura del terreno soggetta a terremoti e frane, la maggior parte delle costruzioni risalgono alla seconda metà del XIX secolo" (14).[6] In 1980, much of Montemurro was again destroyed by an earthquake that struck Southern Itay on November 23 of that year and caused much destruction in Campania and Basilicata. Since houses are rebuilt on the existing sites, it is difficult to assess a date.

To interpret the distinction between the two types of houses, I documented two older houses, each structurally different. One, the Infantino house, had been built in the nineteenth century and was long since uninhabited.[7] It had a modest façade with no ornamentation. There was a large Dutch door and an arched window above the door. There was also a small shuttered window to the right of the door. The door opened directly into the one dark, cavernous room. The only feature in the room was a small fireplace set into the right wall, near the front corner. All light entered from the front, either from the door, the arched window, or the small window. The small window, set near the corner, cast light directly over the fireplace. The back of the room was dark and the far corner had an old bed. Margherita Infantino recalled how in her childhood everyone ate and slept in the single space. She identified the old tripods and hooks in the fireplace, reminiscent of a time when her family cooked there. She also recalled that neighbors stuck their heads in through the open upper panels of the door and conversed with her family. In a description almost identical to Levi's, she remembered that the air was thick with smoke and that chickens, dogs and a donkey also inhabited the house. The structure of the Infantino house bears a close resemblance to the one-room house noted above in the descriptions by Levi and by the historians.

The second house, that of Francesco Labattaglia, was also built before 1900, although the exact date of construction was not known. The façade of the Labattaglia house presented a front door that was set directly below a lunette-shaped window. The entire unit was framed by decorative moulding. The door opened into a hallway lit only by light from the windowed arch and the door. The hallway, in turn, led to three rooms. Immediately on the left was a kitchen with a fireplace. At the end of the hall on the right was a second room, also with a fireplace, and a toilet which was enclosed in a small adjoining room. Directly to the rear of the hallway was the third room. It was without a fireplace. From the street, the front door was separated by a tall, solid gate and a stone wall. The house had a classically symmetrical façade, with one large window on each side of the door. While the Infantino house may be associated structurally with the simple one room house, the Labattaglia house, with its classical symmetry and partitioned rooms, is further removed from the peasant style.

The ground floor plan of vernacular architecture is a central aspect of house design. R. W. Brunskill states that major differences in design "depend on the inter-relationships between the positions of the main hearth, the main stair-case, the main entrance, and the overall plan shape" (94-95). Addressing discrepancies in house design similar to those I found in Montemurro, Glassie identified and analyzed two different house types in Northern Ireland. He explains that when he thought about the various houses as "spaces to use," he discovered that one type was open and one step led from outside directly into the main room. With the upper panel of the door left open, nothing stood in the way of the visitor and the fire. The second house type was more closed and one step led not to the main room, but into an unheated, unlit corridor. In order to find an inhabited room the visitor had to pass first through the corridor. With the open house type, the design unfolded from the interior concealing nothing from the approaching visitor. The façade projected the logic of the interior onto the exterior. With the other type of house, a symmetrical façade suggested order while at the same time concealing the interior. The visitor was uncertain what lay behind the front door. Furthermore, because of the corridor, the visitor was no longer able to enter directly into the house's main room. The most public room was only as accessible as the most private room was in earlier buildings. Generally, the house with the hallway closes, creating an atmosphere which Glassie describes as a "social lock between the people of the house and others" (*Ballymenone* 398). The result was that the hallway respresented an increase in privacy, or a shift from the community's concerns toward the private concerns of the individual. This house type was newer in style, rational and symmetrical. The design and plan were directly linked to the man-centered universe of the Renaissance and the beginnings of the modern Western world. In contrast, the open style was older, suggestive of an ancient and premodern era of human existence (note 3).

This interpretation of the hallway and façade as reflections of the qualitative concerns for community and privacy is directly applicable to the two designs of Montemurro houses. The Infantino house, a more ancient style, would have welcomed the visitor to the fire. Both the entrance and the façade offered a passerby access to the family's place at the fire. As in the recollections of Margherita Infantino, neighbors often stuck their heads into the house to greet the family. The architectural arrangement led to human interaction, which in turn would create a broader sense of community. In contrast, the Labattaglia house, in part as a result of the values of the modern world, excluded the passerby from any interaction with the family. The message presented by the architecture would have been apparent to the approaching visitor. The balanced façade of the house, characterized by multiple windows, protected the interior behind an ordered, unreadable external aspect. It offered the passerby no indication of the direction to the fire. Unwelcoming, the gate was an obvious statement of privacy. The visitor who negotiated that first obstacle, arrived at the door and came into contact not with a warm hospitable fire, but only with a cold corridor. The removal of the fire to a hidden room further signified a desire for privacy and separation.

If this interpretation of two very different styles of architecture is extended to the peasant houses Levi observed in

Aliano, the peasant house can be viewed as reflection of a way of life that embodies more a desire for community and less a need for privacy. In *Cristo* there exists an underlying sense of community present in the representation of the peasant world. The form of the houses confirms this peasant value. Moreover, the narrative also features other characteristics valued by the peasants which can be substantiated by a faithful interpretation of the structure of the house.

LEVI'S PORTRAIT OF THE PEASANT WORLD

In *Cristo* Levi presents a unique report of the peasant world by virtue of his characterization of the peasants' daily lives. Within the framework of the narrative, he describes the peasants as they face the immediate environment of Lucania and contend with the difficulties posed by that particular environment. Levi repeatedly documents, even if circumstantially, the role the house plays within the peasant world. Although not specifically an examination of the living conditions, Levi's descriptions show how the peasants lived in their surroundings, and thus their houses emerge as a central point of reference.

Levi characterizes a peasant sense of community throughout the novel. From the first pages he describes groups of peasants entering freely into their neighbors' houses. He writes: "una piccola folla di uomini, di donne e di bambini erano sulla strada, e tutti entrarono in casa" (20). He even presents himself stepping easily through doorways into kitchens: "entrai dalla vedova, . . . e mi sedetti in cucina" (19). He writes the same of the peasants: "Ero da poco nella cucina della vedova . . . quando si batté alla porta, e alcuni contadini chiesero timidamente di entrare. Erano sette o otto . . ." (19). Levi depicts the peasants interacting in their doorways or offering a friendly greeting. The open design of the houses invites entrance into the main room, enhancing social activity.

In contrast, the world of the *signori* is less integrated and is divided within itself. Many of the gentry are at odds with one another for petty reasons, and the village is a world "chiuso" and "gli odî e le guerre dei signori sono il solo avvenimento quotidiano" (28). Their houses do not reflect an open community, but rather a separated individuality. When Levi goes to meet the mayor's sister, he must be accompanied by the mayor to her door, where he is greeted formally: "Mi accolse con grande cordialità sull'uscio" (53). Unable to step directly into the heart of the house, he is led into an insular sitting room: "mi condusse in salotto" (53). Entering into the houses of the gentry does not happen with the same ease as entering into those of the peasants.

For the peasants, the house is a whole, undivided unit. The division occurs between the house itself and the out-of-doors, which corresponds to the division of labor that exists between the sexes. During the day women work in the house and men work in the fields. Levi refers to this separation repeatedly. During the day the men are out of the village: "Il paese pareva deserto di uomini" (62); in the daytime: "i contadini sono lontani" (92). He points out that the reason is because the peasants go to work in the fields and he describes the daily departure of the men as "l'emigrazione quotidiana" (41). He describes this trip as long: "i contadini si levano a buio, perché devono fare chi due, chi tre, chi quattro ore di strada per raggiungere il loro campo" (41). This exodus lasts all day and the peasants only return as the sun is setting: "I contadini non si vedevano che all'alba e al tramonto" (142). Levi often observes the peasants returning home after a day's work: "i contadini, piccoli nella distanza, si affrettavano per i sentieri lontani nelle argille, verso le loro case" (21). Even when the men are in the village, they are infrequently inside the house. Their customary place, rather, is outside in the square: "Dall'altra parte, addossati alle case, stanno i contadini, tornati dai campi, e non si sentono le loro voci" (21). Levi notices that they play cards in their humble taverns "s'incontravano nelle grotte del vino, a giocare interminabili passatelle" (163). Only during bad weather do they stay at home, and in this case they sit near the door.

With the men away at the fields, the domain of the house belongs to the women: "le donne si celavano dietro le porte semi-chiuse" (62). They attend to all household duties, which are easily performed in the singular space of one room. In that space they watch over the family: "il paese è abbandonato alle donne, queste regine-uccelli, che regnano sulla turba brulicante dei figli" (92). With no men about, women and children are protected in their one-room houses with the doors secured: "Le porte erano sbarrate, poiché i contadini erano nei campi: a qualche soglia stavano sedute delle donne con i bambini in grembo" (45). Attending to their primary household duties, they maintain the fire and upon the fire they prepare the meals. For example, Levi's housekeeper, Giulia, "preparava il fuoco e il pranzo" (95) and at the fireplace she cooked dishes that were "saporiti" (95). He explains that like most peasant women, Giulia knew how to be economical by making a fire with only a few pieces of wood.

Custom demands community among the peasants. Levi explains that when the women leave the house, they must not do so alone: "Nessuna donna può frequentare un uomo se non in presenza d'altri, soprattutto se l'uomo non ha moglie: e il divieto è rigidissimo" (89). The mores exist to protect the peasants' sense of family from the devious force of human sexuality. It pertains to all women, regardless of age. Even the women who came to Levi for medical treatment came with a companion so as not to break this unwritten law. If the women go out to visit neighbors or perform chores, they do so in groups: "stavano l'una vicino l'altra" (36). Such behavior goes hand in hand with community interaction. Levi noticed while he was staying at the widow's house: "La porta di strada ogni tanto si apriva, ed entravano delle donne, le vicine, le conoscenti, le comari della vedova" (36). These neighbors meet in groups continuously when they fetch their daily supply of water. The fountain area was affollata di donne, come la vidi poi sempre, in tutte le ore del giorno. Stavano in gruppo, attorno alla fontana. . . . Stavano immobili nel sole, come un gregge alla pastura.

(50)

Levi explains that the main fountain "dava l'acqua per tutta Gagliano di Sotto e per una buona metà di Gagliano di Sopra" (50) and that the women carry the water "con una botticella di legno sul capo, e la brocca di terra di Ferrandina" (50). Performing this arduous task offered the peasant women the opportunity to interact on a daily basis.

Not only does Levi confirm that the peasants' humble homes are without running water, but also that the houses serve as a shelter for animals, especially when no secondary building is available. He remarks that chickens and pigs run between his feet when he attends sick patients at their beds and that chickens run about the room during his visit to Don Trajella. The peasants are accustomed to living with animals. As noted above, Levi observes that the peasant houses are divided into three horizontal planes, with the humans sleeping on the level of the bed, babies hanging in baskets above the bed and the animals sleeping under the bed on the ground.

Furthermore, this organization of space, a practical response to the basic needs of the peasants, can be seen as evidence of the fundamental structure inherent in the peasant world. Levi learns that the values of modern civilization have no meaning in a land where "[nessun] muro separa il mondo degli uomini da quello degli animali" (72). He says that "non vi è alcun limite sicuro" between what is human and what is animal (99). It is not unusual for the peasants to live together with their animals when humans are seen to have animal characteristics and animals are seen to have human qualities. Animals are more than mere biological creatures. For the peasants, animals are part of a deeper reality, a mysterious world. The peasants teach Levi that in their world all animals have a double significance: "un doppio senso." One woman, a peasant married with children, is the "figlia di una vacca" (99). The peasant men sometimes change into wolves at night and their human nature is totally transformed (100). Goats have a satanic power and even Levi's dog, Barone, has the traits of a human of noble quality. Thus, in "quell'altro mondo" of the peasants, the relationship with animals goes beyond the simple sharing of physical space.

Levi comes to understand that the peasants are deeply tied to all of nature. He describes the connection as a "legame non religoso, ma naturale" (72). The peasant world is a natural world, where the human being is not separated from nature. Rather the peasants are immersed in nature, part of nature. The peasant house, for all its simplicity and poverty, reflects this closeness to the natural world. Poetically stated, "no wall separates the peasant from nature." The peasant society's respect for nature parallels that of other groups who revere relationships with animals and nature, like the Native American or the Aboriginal Australian.

The home is as much a tribute to the proximity to nature as it is a result of economic hardship. The space is above all practical. The one or two room house is open to nature. One door leads outside and people and animals easily come and go. In the practical world of the peasant, ther was little room for comfort. By day, the singular main room is kitchen space and work space, serving only one gender. Men are in the fields, working in nature. Women work in the main room, preparing food and watching over children. When the women need to go out, it is one step that leads them there. No hallways or gates obstruct the path to the fountains. By night, the main room is first dining area and then bedroom. During the day, leisure space is not required, and at night the entire family, including the animals, share the same space as one unit.

Comfort, sought-after and fashionable in the civilized cities of the modern world, was not a primary concern in the peasants' ancient world. Weather was more easily accepted because the houses were open and nature was close. The cold was part of the house. The fire heated a part of the space and the family managed to survive. In addition, the animals contributed to the heating of the room. By contrast, comfort was seen as a priority in the style of house that was adapted by the gentry. They further separated the inhabitants from the environment. The hallway helped block out the cold, securing the warm inner room with its fireplace from the cold of nature. Animals were kept from the house. The internally partitioned house, with hallways and multiple rooms, also divided life within the house itself. Living and sleeping spaces were divided, separated and private. Comfort is opposed to both a proximity to nature and a desire for community, the latter being contrasted to a desire for comfort and privacy. The contextual evidence that Levi presents suggests that the peasant house is representative of a world that promotes a sense of community but also reflects an affinity with the natural and animal world.

CONCLUSION

From an historical perspective, the peasant civilization of Lucania was a largely nonliterate world. That world was defined by a distinct language and peasant logic, both of which were traditionally structured according to an ancient sense of community and a fundamental closeness to nature. Understanding the nonliterate peasant world as it existed during Levi's time requires an ability to read and decode the language and mind of the peasants in the context of their daily lives. The simple houses that the peasants produced are texts in themselves. They are indications of the peasants' logical processes in an effort to manage their environment. Thus they represent important artifactual evidence of their peasant civilization. The sense of community and association with nature can be seen in the structure of the houses, both in relation to the daily lives of the peasants and also in contrast with the houses of those who were not part of the peasant society.

If the Western world attempts to define the peasants of Lucania by its own established standards, it will most likely fail to understand these people as members of a distinct civilization. It is convenient to form conclusions based on external standards which would suggest that ignorance and poverty are the primary factors contributing to what could be interpreted as a substandard quality of life. Understanding the peasant world is a complex task. Furthermore, accustomed to searching for answers in written texts, the scholar is often incapable of reading the artifacts created by nonliterate people. For Levi the problem was identified as one of fundamental difference: "Siamo anzitutto di fronte al coesitere di due civiltà diversissime" (209). *Cristo si è fermato a Eboli*; a narrative statement, affirms the peasant civilization through material culture. Levi's recollection of the peasants fosters an essential anthropological understanding of their "other world" by connecting the written text with material culture.

Notes

1. Historians traditionally regard the written record as the key to the past. These scholars sort through old documents in an attempt to synthesize a chronicle of earlier times. One of the pitfalls of an approach to history which bases conclusions solely on documentation is that it is representative of only a very small minority of people. In the past, the majority of people were illiterate and thus incapable of leaving firsthand records describing their thoughts and actions. In response, historians seek to develop "micro" histories of the undocumented, illiterate populations by examining supplemental and secondary sources. Sources such as court records, however, are prone to bias. They are again written by the literate minority and do not present a complete picture of the vast majority of people who were not part of the legal proceedings of the courts.

2. It is not my intention to evaluate the arguments in the ongoing debate between those scholars who value the written texts as singularly fundamental and those scholars who esteem artifacts and material culture.

3. Glassie's study examines material culture in several parts of the world. For details of Glassie's theory on houses, I refer in particular to the chapter "Home" in *Passing the Time in Ballymenone*. He states in the notes to that chapter that his approach to architectural analysis runs through *Folk Housing in Middle Virginia*. His most recent work is *Turkish Traditional Art Today*.

4. In the introductory section of *History of Things: Essays on Material Culture,* Steven Lubar and W. David Kingery indicate that artifacts are valid texts from which historians may support their arguments and that by neglecting artifacts, historians limit the potential for a wider interpretation of history (ix).

5. Montemurro is in the Province of Potenza. It is a small community of less than 2000 inhabitants (1746 according to the town register on June 30, 1991). It is located in the Agri Valley approximately 20 miles to the west of Levi's Aliano. Levi refers to Monte-

murro several times during the course of his narrative: Montemurro being the home of his guard, De Luca (206), the home of Don Luigi's maid (218) and the home of the pyrotechnicians (105).

6. Schiavone recounts that powerful earthquakes struck Montemurro in 1343, 1561, 1659, 1807, 1826 and 1857. Although he writes that census records are nonexistent for the period of 1857, his research indicates that 2502 people out of a total of 7000 were killed and approximately three quarters of the village was destroyed by the earthquake that struck that year. He notes that popular belief, however, suggests that 4000 people out of a total of more than 8000 were killed (53-54).

7. In an interview in 1991, Margherita Infantino, then over ninety years old, told me that the house dated to before the earthquake of 1857.

Works Cited

Albini, Decio. *Montemurro per la rivoluzione Lucana.* Roma: Mundus, 1912.

Banfield, Edward C. *The Moral Basis of a Backward Society.* Chicago: Free Press, 1958.

Brunskill, R. W. *Illustrated Handbook of Vernacular Architecture.* New York: Universe Books, 1970.

Cornelisen, Ann. *Women of the Shadows.* Boston: Little, 1976.

Deetz, James. *Invitation to Archaeology.* Garden City: Natural History Press, 1967.

Ferguson, Leland, ed. *Historical Archaeology and the Importance of Material Things.* Papers of the Thematic Symposium, Eighth Annual Meeting of the Society for Historical Archaeology, Charleston, South Carolina, January 7-11, 1975. Columbia: Soc. for Historical Archaeology, 1977.

Franciosa, Luchino. *La casa rurale nella Lucania.* Firenze: Olschki, 1942.

Glassie, Henry. *Folk Housing in Middle Virginia: A Structural Analysis of Historic Artifacts.* Knoxville: U of Tennessee P, 1975.

——. *Passing the Time in Ballymenone: Culture and History of an Ulster Community.* Philadelphia: U of Penn P, 1982.

——. *Turkish Traditional Art Today.* Bloomington: Indiana U P, 1993.

Lacava, Michele. *La Lucania.* Potenza, 1874.

Levi, Carlo. *Cristo si è fermato a Eboli.* 17th ed. Milano: Mondadori, 1980.

Lubar, Steven, and W. David Kingery, eds. *History from Things: Essays on Material Culture.* Washington: Smithsonian Institution P, 1993.

Nabokov, Peter, and Robert Easton. *Native American Architecture.* Oxford: Oxford U P, 1989.

Pani Rossi, Enrico. *La Basilicata.* Verona, 1868.

Pasquarelli, Michele Gerardo. *Medicina magia e classi sociali nella Basilicata degli anni venti: scritti di un medico antropologo.* Ed. Giovanni Battista Bronzini. 2 vols. Lecce: Congedo, 1987.

Racioppi, Giacomo. *Storia dei popoli della Lucania e della Basilicata.* 1902. 2 vols. Roma: Deputazione di Storia per la Lucania. 1970.

Schiavone, Enrico. *Montemurro: Perla dell'Alta Val d'Agri.* Roma:Pubbliprint, 1990.

Guy P. Raffa (essay date 1997)

SOURCE: Raffa, Guy P. "Carlo Levi's Sacred Art of Healing." *Annali d'Italianistica* 15 (1997): 203-20.

[*In the following essay, Raffa explores Levi's anthropological vision in light of the theories of Victor Turner and René Girard.*]

Written in 1935[1], the year of Carlo Levi's exile in Lucania, Charlotte Gower Chapman's *Milocca: A Sicilian Village* is an anthropological study of a Sicilian village based on the author's fieldwork in 1928-29.[2] Modeled on Robert Redfield's *Tepoztlan, a Mexican Village* (1930), Chapman's *Milocca* is the "only full-scale Italian village study in existence which was carried out before World War II" (Cronin 18). While Levi's *Cristo si è fermato a Eboli* (1945), despite its resistance to generic classification, was unquestionably the product of—among other things—its author's literary-artistic imagination, it also inaugurated a new direction in Italian anthropological research along the lines of Chapman's study as the nation sought to rediscover itself after the years of Fascism and the war. Levi's first novel, in fact, provided the "stimolo determinante" for Ernesto de Martino's expedition to Lucania in the early 1950s (Lanternari 213), fieldwork that represented the initial stage of the ethnologist's important trilogy treating religion and magic in the Mezzogiorno: *Sud e magia* (1959), *Morto e pianto rituale nel mondo antico* (1959), and *La terra del rimorso* (1961). From de Martino's field notes documenting his reliance on Levi's novel as a sort of vademecum for his Lucanian research, Carpitella concludes that *Cristo* "rappresentava un testo di riferimento che oggi diremmo squisitamente antropologico" (206). Lanternari elegantly describes the complementary roles of de Martino and Levi in the development of "una nuova coscienza di umanesimo antropologico" (213); if de Martino was the practicing anthropologist, scientifically and historically oriented, then Levi was the

> annunciatore e profeta d'una antropologia meridionalista assolutamente nuova, carica di passione civile e sociale, permeata da un visionarismo poetico e mossa da una vibrante sensibilità e attenzione per l'intero mondo culturale, il vissuto immediato dei contadini del Sud, scoperti da lui del tutto occasionalmente in rapporto alla sua condizione di confinato politico antifascista.
>
> (213)

Although Levi has been rightly criticized, from an ethnological perspective, for his mythologizing, a-historical conception of the *contadini* (Carpitella 207; Lanternari 215), his "antropologia meridionalista" nevertheless inspired—in part, no doubt, *because* of his mythic imagination—unprecedented attention to the "other" Italy.

Levi's anthropological vision, however, is not limited to an ethnological interest in the rural communities of Southern Italy, those of Lucania in particular. Nor is it merely the result of his presence in Grassano and Aliano (Gagliano in the novel) as a political exile. On the contrary, I shall argue in this essay that a crucial if understudied aspect of Levi's anthropology is precisely its mythic-philosophical dimension and the consequences of this anthropological theory for Levi's socio-political program. Specifically, I shall show that Levi's intense interest in the relationship of the individual to social structures, theorized in **Paura della libertà** and dramatized in **Cristo si è fermato a Eboli**, makes him a worthy contributor to discussions of the sacred and the dialectic of differentiation and undifferentiation put forth by such influential thinkers as Victor Turner and René Girard. I view Levi's figuration of medicine in **Cristo**—raised, under the sign of magic, to an art of healing—as emblematic of both the creative energy generated by contact with the sacred and the limitations of such contact. Locating Levi at the intersection, so to speak, of Turner and Girard, I consider, finally, how Levi's call for political autonomy as an ideal "punto di mediazione" between the individual and the state has recently evolved in ways he could hardly have imagined.

In *Violence and the Sacred,* Girard seeks to account for the violence unleashed in communities still immersed in the sacred and, conversely, to explain (in at times apologetic tones) the role of Western institutions, especially religion, in curbing such violence.[3] To be sure, there is a sense of urgency to Girard's argument insofar as he thinks we are on the brink of a sacrificial crisis, a moment which "coincides with the disappearance of the difference between impure violence and purifying violence"; he warns that "[w]hen this difference has been effaced, purification are no longer possible and impure, contagious, reciprocal violence spreads throughout the community" (49). Anticipating the more overt theological and religious framework of *Things Hidden since the Foundation of the World* and *The Scapegoat,* Girard chides modern thinkers who, through "willful blindness . . . continue to see religion as an isolated, wholly fictitious phenomenon cherished only by a few backward peoples or milieus" (317). Writing at a time of considerable social and intellectual upheaval, under the shadow of the cold war and the arms race, he concludes *Violence and the Sacred* with an apocalyptic flourish: "We have managed to extricate ourselves from the sacred somewhat more successfully than other societies have done, to the point of losing all memory of the generative violence; but we are now about to rediscover it. The essential violence returns to us in a spectacular manner—not only in the form of a violent history but also in the form of subversive knowledge" (318).

Aptly called a "christianisation des sciences humaines" (Lagarde), Girard's project "pivots upon nothing less than a claim about the impact that a truly divine revelation has had on the human social order" (Livingston xvii). Thus, when Girard asserts that the function of ritual is "to keep violence *outside* the community" (*Violence* 92), he generally means that the purpose of the sacrificial rites of religion is to contain the violence "at the heart and secret soul of the sacred" (31). For Girard, then, the sacred is primarily figured as a danger, the embodiment of "all those forces that threaten to harm man or trouble his peace" (58).[4] More important, Girard's linkage of violence and the sacred hinges on the loss of differences, "the disintegration of distinctions within the community" (114). The sacrificial crisis, in other words, occurs when the "differences disappear in the domain of the sacred only because they are indiscriminately mixed together and become indistinguishable in the confusion" (282). The community, by contrast, is defined by its separation from the undifferentiated world of the sacred since its "[o]rder, peace, and fecundity depend on cultural distinctions" (49). For this reason, the ritual victims needed to restore societal order are found outside the community, "from creatures (like animals and strangers) that normally dwell amidst sacred things and are themselves imbued with sacredness" (270). Against Lévi-Strauss, Girard views ritual as the means to eliminate the "evil mixture" of the undifferentiated sacred and thereby "make culture safe for differentiation" (*"To Double Business Bound"* 169).

Victor Turner, on the other hand, carves out a more positive space for the interrelated concepts of undifferentiation and the sacred. In *The Ritual Process* he considers groups as diverse as tribal societies, medieval religious communities, millenarian movements, and hippies to show how individuals satisfy their need to participate in both "structure" and "communitas," two models of "human interrelatedness, juxtaposed and alternating" (96). Turner's own juxtaposition of his definitions of structure and communitas immediately discloses a significant reversal in emphasis from Girard's privileging of differentiation over undifferentiation:

> One . . . is of society as a structure of jural, political, and economic positions, offices, statuses, and roles, in which the individual is only ambiguously grasped behind the social persona. The other is of society as a communitas of concrete idiosyncratic individuals, who, though differing in physical and mental endowment, are nonetheless regarded as equal in terms of shared humanity. The first model is of a differentiated, culturally structured, segmented, and often hierarchical system of institutionalized positions. The second presents society as an undifferentiated, homogeneous whole, in

which individuals confront one another integrally, and not as 'segmentalized' into statuses and roles.

(177)

Through a detailed discussion of rites of passage, rituals of status elevation or reversal, and the rise of ideological communities, Turner examines the experience of those who pass through or embody communitas in terms of liminality, marginality, and "structural inferiority" (128). He further observes that, in each of its three manifestations, communitas "is almost everywhere held to be sacred or 'holy,' possibly because it transgresses or dissolves the norms that govern structured and institutionalized relationships and is accompanied by experiences of unprecedented potency" (128).

Whereas Girard views the sacred as the harbinger of violence precisely because it is predicated on undifferentiation, for Turner it is only from the perspective of those invested in maintaining structure that "all sustained manifestations of communitas must appear as dangerous and anarchical, and have to be hedged around with prescriptions, prohibitions, and conditions" (109). The real threat, according to Turner, arises from the cultural distinctions privileged by Girard as the necessary condition for order and stability. Thus, in a passage cited by Girard as an example of "an 'antidifferential' prejudice" in ethnological studies (*Violence* 50), Turner writes: "Structural differentiation, both vertical and horizontal, is the foundation of strife and factionalism, and of struggles in dyadic relations between incumbents of positions or rivals for positions" (*Ritual* 179).[5] For Turner, then, differentiation itself, even more so than the dissolution of differences in communitas, is a variable that must be closely monitored to prevent outbreaks of conflict and violence.

In practice, of course, both Turner and Girard recognize the interdependence of undifferentiation and differentiation—the sacred and the sacrificial, communitas and social structure—as an intrinsic feature of individual and group life. Girard, noting the "complex and delicate nature of the community's dealings with the sacred," advocates an "optimum *distance*": "If the community comes too near the sacred it risks being devoured by it; if, on the other hand, the community drifts too far away, out of range of the sacred's therapeutic threats and warnings, the effects of its fecund presence are lost" (*Violence* 268). And Turner, who warns that exaggerated structure or communitas could trigger a dangerous backlash effect (*Ritual* 129), elsewhere opines that "much of the misery of the world has been due to the principled activities of fanatics of both persuasions" ("Passages" 268). While "spontaneous communitas" may be inattentive to the material and organizational needs of society, "structural action swiftly becomes arid and mechanical if those involved in it are not periodically immersed in the regenerative abyss of communitas" (*Ritual* 139). "Wisdom," Turner therefore suggests, "is always to find the appropriate relationship between structure and communitas under the *given* circumstances of time and place, to accept each modality when it is paramount without rejecting the other, and not to cling to one when its present impetus is spent" (139).

A similarly dialectical, contextual treatment of differentiation and undifferentiation is, in fact, the hallmark of Carlo Levi's argument in **Paura della libertà**. This short but substantive amalgam of, *inter alia,* religious myth, Jungian psychoanalysis, and Vico's philosophical thought is nothing less than Levi's ardent attempt to probe the underlying reasons for the huge historical crisis of Western civilization while "un vento di morte e di oscura religione sconvolgeva gli antichi stati d'Europa" (10). Written during a period of exile in France as German tanks began to overrun Poland in 1939, Levi initially conceived of the work as a massive cultural assessment of the mythic and historical underpinnings of such institutions of collective human existence as religion, politics, art, science, and technology. He felt compelled to take on this encyclopedic project to account for the dissolution of values and ideologies occasioned by the triumph of Nazifascism. Like Girard writing three decades later, though undoubtedly confronted with a more imminent, tangible crisis, Levi sought to explain, if only for himself, the underlying reasons—philosophical, psychological, and anthropological—of the human capacity for violence. The outbreak of war, combined with the death of his father, proved decisive: "Se il passato era morto, il presente incerto e terribile, il futuro misterioso, si sentiva il bisogno di fare il punto; di fermarsi a considerare le ragioni di quella cruenta rivoluzione che incominciava" (11). Although Levi abandoned his encyclopedic enterprise when the Nazis occupied France, he later realized that the eight introductory chapters he had already written contained *in nuce* his argument. He eventually published them as **Paura della libertà** in 1946, a year after the appearance of **Cristo.**

Long recognized as the foundation for Levi's subsequent creative and intellectual work, **Paura** has recently received insightful critical attention, both as an expression of Levi's views of the State, history, and the human condition (Baldassaro) and as the diagnosis of Nazifascism subtending Levi's antifascist politics (Ward 157-68).[6] **Paura** is also Levi's *ante litteram* response to Girard and Turner articulated at a moment when understanding the role of the sacred and its relationship to the individual and society was essential for rethinking the values, and imagining the renewal, of Western civilization. Indeed, the sacred is a powerful concept for Levi that figures, paradoxically, as both the exterminator and generator of freedom and art, the creative impulses of the human spirit in individual, social, and historical contexts. "Sacro," Levi writes, is "l'oscura continua negazione della libertà e dell'arte, e, insieme, per contrasto, il generatore continuo della libertà e dell'arte" (17). This double-edged conception captures Girard's alignment of the sacred with "all those forces that threaten to harm man or trouble his peace" (*Violence* 58) as well as Turner's view that the sacred is experienced through periodic immersion "in the regenerative abyss of communitas" (*Ritual* 139).

Levi appropriately defines the sacred in relationship to the dialectic of differentiation and undifferentiation. "Sacro" is precisely "lo spavento dell'indeterminato in chi è nello sforzo di autocrearsi e di separarsi" (20). He uses the images of "caos" and "massa" to figure the primordial undifferentiated state, also called the "indistinto originario" (19), out of which differentiation occurs: "ogni uomo nasce del caos, e può riperdersi nel caos: viene dalla massa per differenziarsi, e può perder forma e nella massa riassorbirsi" (19). Individuals are moved by an "oscura libertà" to separate from this undifferentiated condition and acquire distinct characteristics ("individuarsi") at the same time that they are driven by an "oscura necessità" to rejoin the universal, formless mass (19). Oscillations between these competing impulses begin with the individual's first, "prenatal" death (separation from the chaotic mass) and continue to its natural death. However, "true death," like the misery wrought by the fanatics of structure and communitas in Turner's account, occurs only when either side of this dialectic is taken to an extreme: "il distacco totale dal flusso dell'indifferenziato, vuota ragione egoistica, astratta libertà—e, all'opposto, l'incapacità totale a differenziarsi, mistica oscurità bestiale, servitú dell'inesprimibile" (19).

History itself, according to Levi, is nothing less than alternating periods of separation from, and regeneration in, the "indistinto originario" (106). Differentiation can release the creative potential of individuals and the community, but contact with the undifferentiated mass is equally necessary for re-creation when the state and religion are reduced to the arid determinations of reason, law, and ritual. Ultimately, what really matters, the true moment of civilization and creativity, is some ideal point of equilibrium between the two extremes:

> Ma i soli momenti vivi nei singoli uomini, i soli periodi di alta civiltà nella storia, sono quelli in cui i due opposti processi di differenziazione e di indifferenziazione trovano un punto di mediazione, e coesistono nell'atto creatore.
>
> (19)

This "punto di mediazione," in which differentiation and undifferentiation coexist in a creative act, takes various forms in Levi's thought. Mythically, he figures prelapsarian Eden as the place where "indeterminatezza era insieme determinazione," a time when "Ogni atto era atto di libertà . . . ogni opera era creativa" (120). In the world of time and history, Levi likewise asserts that peace and freedom can coexist for humankind only when "la sua libertà gli consente di essere insieme individuazione personale e universalità illimitata" (88-89). While large, sprawling cities, as well as wars, reduce humanity to an undifferentiated mass, smaller social units—from the family to the mid-sized town—present possibilities for "punti di mediazione" insofar as "[t]utti si conoscono, e devono perciò differenziarsi" (108). Levi therefore celebrates life and creativity—in individual, artistic, social, and historical contexts—at the point of equilibrium between the opposing impulses of separation and immersion, sacrifice and the sacred.

In the chapter of *Paura* titled "Schiavitú," Levi describes the anthropological and historical dilemma of Italy in terms of an incomplete fusion of two very different civilizations, "l'originale innesto di una civiltà militare, statolatra, religiosa, giuridica, su una civiltà contadina, anarchica, irreligiosa, poetica" (55). This is the problem that Levi, far from resolving, revisits in dramatic fashion in *Cristo si è fermato a Eboli,* his major work composed some five years after *Paura della libertà* but similarly based on his experience as an antifascist "confinato" in the Lucanian towns of Grassano and Aliano (Gagliano) in 1935-36. Levi immediately establishes the "desolate terre" of Lucania as an undifferentiated realm, a place untouched by the "civilizing," differentiating forces of time, religion, reason, and history (15).[7] To say that Christ stopped at Eboli means, for Levi, that the Western tradition, characterized by historical progress and the theocratic state, has never entered the mountains and forests of Lucania "se non come un conquistatore o un nemico o un visitatore incomprensivo" (15-16). Levi figures the encroachment of the rituals of Western civilization not as Girard's therapeutic curb on, but as the very origin of, violence and blood sacrifice. Based no doubt on his virulent opposition to Fascism and the mythic structures used to support it, Levi praises Virgil as a "grande storico" for describing the religion of the Trojans, ancestors of the Romans, as "feroce" since it required human sacrifices: "sulla pira di Pallante, il pio Enea sgozza i prigionieri, come sacrificio ai suoi dèi dello Stato" (122).

However, insofar as Carlo Levi is himself a product of this Western tradition the problem he faces is how to represent, through the faculty of memory, his contact as an "intellettuale differenziato" with the "massa indifferenziata" of the Lucanian *contadini* (Falaschi 64). This contact occurs primarily through the protagonist's medical and artistic activities. These two roles, in addition to representing "l'incarnazione della volontà di liberazione e d'autodeterminazione dell'uomo" (Bassani 37), provide the key that allows the differentiated subject to penetrate the closed world of the *contadini* and renew himself in the creative chaos of undifferentiated humanity. Levi himself figures his contact with Lucanian culture through the metaphor of "penetration" by means of a "key" when he recounts how, against the advice of Dr. Milillo, he exposed himself to the magical "filtri" of the peasant women by accepting their invitations for coffee or wine:

> Se c'erano dei filtri, forse si sono vicendevolmente neutralizzati. Certo non mi hanno fatto male; forse mi hanno, in qualche modo misterioso, aiutato a penetrare in quel mondo chiuso, velato di veli neri, sanguigno e terrestre, nell'altro mondo dei contadini, dove non si entra senza una chiave di magía.

(23-24)

This reflection ironically counters Dr. Milillo's misogyny and hostility toward the *contadini* by respecting the magical powers of this "closed world," those of the "filtri" in particular. Seeking a key to penetrate the mysterious world of the *contadini,* Levi thus adopts the authenticating strategy that Clifford Geertz ascribes to anthropologists when they write up their fieldwork:

> The ability of anthropologists to get us to take what they say seriously has less to do with either a factual look or an air of conceptual elegance than it has with their capacity to convince us that what they say is a result of having actually penetrated (or, if your prefer, been penetrated by) another form of life, of having, one way or another, truly 'been there.' And that, persuading us that this offstage miracle has occurred, is where the writing comes in.

(4-5)

Levi's legitimating claim in *Cristo* to having "actually penetrated" or "been penetrated by" the culture of the Lucanian *contadini* hinges on the mutually reinforcing activities of magic and medicine.[8]

Since most of Carlo's acquaintances among the *contadini* of Gagliano result from their need for medical attention (73), it is natural that he would both "penetrate" and "be penetrated by" their undifferentiated world through his healing art, referred to in a letter from his sister Luisa, herself a "medico valentissimo" (*Cristo* 73), as his "nobile e utile missione."[9] Yet, this reciprocal influence is neither immediate nor automatic. Rather, the development of this reciprocity itself constitutes a major theme of the novel, as the distance traveled between the two principle medical episodes vividly illustrates. In the first case, shortly after his arrival in Gagliano, Carlo, who has medical training but little practical experience, is asked to visit a sick peasant. A group of men dressed in black eventually convince him to see the moribund patient, and they introduce him to a veritable ritual of death: in a dark room the sick man, fully dressed, including hat and shoes, lies on a makeshift stretcher, with women wailing and crying in the shadows. The narrative description of the doctor's visit is cold and to the point. He has been asked to try to save the man:

> Ma non c'era piú nulla da fare: l'uomo stava morendo. Inutili le fiale trovate a casa della vedova, con cui, per solo scrupolo di coscienza, ma senza nessuna speranza, cercai di rianimarlo. Era un attacco di malaria perniciosa, la frebbre passava i limiti delle febbri piú alte, l'organismo non reagiva piú. Terreo, stava supino sulla barella, respirando a fatica, senza parlare, circondato dai lamenti dei compagni. Poco dopo era morto.

(20)

The physician's emotional involvement remains restrained—virtually non-existent—as he leaves the house of death. He walks out onto the piazza and, as the sun sets over the Calabrian hills to the west, observes the *contadini* returning home from their fields (20-21). In the terms of *Paura,* the patient may have died but it is the doctor here who dies the "morte vera" that results from "il distacco totale dal flusso dell'indifferenziato" (19). Burdened with the "vuota ragione egoistica" and "astratta libertà" concomitant with this state of extreme differentiation (*Paura* 19), Carlo begins his stay in Gagliano completely detached from the source of creative regeneration and true freedom.

Given this inauspicious start, it is no surprise that Carlo at first tries to shirk his medical responsibilities, not only because of insufficient preparation and a subsequent lack of confidence in his abilities, but also because of fear of getting involved in the town's factional politics (41-42). Yet, despite Carlo's detached, almost clinical response to the death of his patient, the Gaglianesi see that he is not like the "medicaciucci" of the town, and the women insist on bringing their sick children to him for medical treatment. Amazed and embarrassed, he attributes this display of trust either to the fact that he at least tried—albeit unsuccessfully—to save the malaria victim, or to the power with which the "outsider" is often invested in traditional cultures: "Era forse il prestigio naturale del forestiero che viene da lontano, e che è perciò come un dio" (42). Indeed, as this *forestiero-dio*, a political exile with healing powers, Carlo possesses the status of "outsiderhood" as described by Victor Turner in "Passages, Margins, and Poverty." Expanding on his distinction between communitas and social structure from *The Ritual Process,* Turner argues that "outsiderhood," along with "liminality" and "structural inferiority," entails at least provisional contact with the undifferentiated whole often associated with the sacred. Outside of both the dominant Fascist culture and the a-historical world of the Lucanian *contadini,* Carlo is like the shamans, diviners, mediums, and priests included in Turner's list of individuals who experience the condition of "outsiderhood" by "being either permanently and by ascription set outside the structural arrangements of a given social system, or being situationally or temporarily set apart, or voluntarily setting oneself apart from the behavior of status-occupying, role-playing members of that system" (233).

Similarly, "structural inferiority," Turner's designation for the lowest level of social stratification, accurately describes Levi's perception of Lucania's *contadini* as the oppressed, indigenous people who are thought to possess "a mystical power over the fertility of the earth and of all upon it" (234).[10] Outside of time and history, the poorest inhabitants of Italy's rural Mezzogiorno take on "the symbolic function of representing humanity, without status qualifications or characteristics" (234). In contrast to the highly differentiated system that Turner aligns with social structure, this "undifferentiated whole whose units are total human beings" (234)—the basis of his communitas—"often appears culturally in the guise of an Edenic, paradisiacal, utopian, or millennial state of affairs, to the attainment of which religious or political action, personal or collective, should be directed" (237-38). While Turner's description of communitas here is far more optimistic than Levi's ambivalent view of the *contadini* as well as his conception of the sacred and undifferentiation in general, it also qualifies Girard's univocal figuration of the undifferentiated realm of the sacred as a dangerous power that must be contained through sacrificial rites.

As both the "oscura continua negazione della libertà e dell'arte" and the "generatore continuo della libertà e dell'arte" (*Paura* 17), Levi's figuration of the sacred is inherently dialectical. He is faithful to this ambiguity in *Cristo.* Like Plato's *Pharmakon,* a related term that can mean either "poison" or "remedy," the meaning of Levi's *sacro* changes with the context or depends on the perspective from which it is considered. Thus he describes the world of the *contadini* as, on the one hand, a place "senza

determinazioni" that precludes hope and happiness, allowing only "la cupa passività di una natura dolorosa" (72); on the other hand, alive in this same world is "il senso umano di un comune destino" (72), the capacity to establish human bonds according to "il senso sacro, arcano e magico di una comunanza" (81).[11] It is this "comunanza"— the communitas imagined by Turner as a place for individuals to meet "not as role players but as 'human totals'" ("Passages" 269)—that Carlo must enter to experience the creative freedom generated by the undifferentiated world of the sacred.

By the time the second major medical episode occurs Carlo has spent the better part of a year in Gagliano, much of that time in the company of his household servant, Giulia La Santarcangelese, a "strega contadina" familiar with "le erbe e il potere degli oggetti magici" (95). Possessing her own medical powers, *in bono* and *in malo,* Giulia "[s]apeva curare le malattie con gli incantesimi, e perfino poteva far morire chi volesse, con la sola virtú di terribili formule" (95). After the petty town politics have resulted in an order prohibiting Carlo from practicing medicine, Giulia tells him that the authorities will not be able to prevent him from continuing to treat the *contadini*: "se non ti lasciano fare il medico, tu curerai lo stesso. Dovresti fare lo stregone. Ora hai imparato tutto, sai tutto. E quello non te lo possono impedire" (197). In fact, he admits to having become "maestro in tutto quello che concerne la magia popolare, e le sue applicazioni alla medicina" (198), and this knowledge, combined with his beautiful "voce da prete," makes him appear to Giulia as the embodiment of "tutte le virtú del Rofé orientale, del guaritore sacro" (198). This power as "sacred healer" derives from Carlo's tolerance—if not outright endorsement—of the peasant superstitions, including the traditional "abracadabra" that many of his patients wear as protection against illness. Where other doctors would scorn these popular beliefs, Carlo respects them: "ne onoravo l'antichità e la oscura, misteriosa semplicità, preferivo essere loro alleato che loro nemico, e i contadini me ne erano grati, e forse ne traevano davvero vantaggio" (199). Besides, he continues, even the "legittimate" medical practice of writing a prescription for every patient, especially when such prescriptions were written in Latin in indecipherable handwriting, could rightly be considered "una abitudine magica" (199).

Michael Taussig, a physician and anthropologist, argues that the doctor-patient relationship, more than merely technical, "is very much a social interaction which can reinforce the culture's basic premises in a most powerful manner" (86). Carlo shows exceptional awareness of this conception of medical practice as a set of social relations by valorizing the magical beliefs of his "primitive" patients while at the same time calling into question the positivist assumptions of "modern" science and medicine. In a culture where "anche la medicina ha potere soltanto per il suo contenuto magico" (201), Carlo wisely adapts his medical practice to the attitudes and behavior of the *contadini*. Thus, at one point in his heroic attempt to combat malaria, he replaces quinine, a medicine whose efficacy is limited because the peasants do not believe in it, with two newer medicines that work "meravigliosamente" because they function as both "sostanze chimiche" and "influenze magiche" (202). Whereas Chapman, whose Milocca was another village "forgotten by God and by man" (2), offers the "scientific" interpretation of curative magic as "probably a valuable device in the healing of maladies of purely nervous origin" (208), Levi's physician-protagonist refuses to delegitimize the power of magic and witchcraft to affect even the physical well-being of his patients.

Having thus reconciled his medical practice with the magical forces of his environment, Carlo is finally able to "return" to the sacred "comunanza" of the undifferentiated mass and thereby experience the liberating effects of a creative rebirth. In the second major medical episode, toward the end of his stay in Gagliano, the narrating subject's emotional involvement is strong and personal, even though this case, like the first, is hopeless from the start. Paradoxically, his participation is so extreme that the presence of death elicits neither horror nor indifference but an intuition of transcendent happiness and completeness:

> La morte era nella casa: amavo quei contadini, sentivo il dolore e l'umiliazione della mia impotenza. Perché allora una cosí grande pace scendeva in me? Mi pareva di essere staccato da ogni cosa, da ogni luogo, remotissimo da ogni determinazione, perduto fuori del tempo, in un infinito altrove. Mi sentivo celato, ignoto agli uomini, nascosto come un germiglio sotto la scorza dell'albero: tendevo l'orecchio alla notte e mi pareva di essere entrato, d'un tratto, nel cuore stesso del mondo. Una felicità immensa, non mai provata, era in me, e mi riempiva intero, e il senso fluente di una infinita pienezza.

(189)

The doctor's perceived detachment from the world, his feeling of being "remotissimo da ogni determinazione," attests to a complete immersion in the undifferentiated world of the sacred as it is described in *Paura della libertà* (Ward 164), a return to the "indistinto originario" needed for regeneration and renewed creative energy. Through the key of his healing art, as ineffectual—technically speaking—in this case as in the first, Carlo has not only succeeded in unlocking the closed door of this world outside of time and history, but he has even experienced the sensation of having entered the very heart of the universe.

However, the beneficent effects of this sacred immersion are short-lived as Carlo soon begins to feel the oppressive weight of resignation, frustration, and indifference that will ultimately make him glad to be released from his confinement two years earlier than expected. Returning to Lucania after a brief visit to Torino occasioned by the death of a close relative, he feels the mountains shut him in as if they were gates to a prison (212). Just before receiving notice of his freedom, Carlo reaches a "punto estremo di indifferenza":

> Mi pareva di essere un verme chiuso dentro una noce secca. Lontano dagli effetti, nel guscio religioso della monotonia, aspettavo gli anni venturi, e mi pareva di essere senza base, librato in un'aria assurda, dove era strano anche il suono della mia voce.

(220)

Yet, it is unlikely that Carlo's release from confinement in Gagliano and return to Torino will bring him the sense of joy and completeness he experienced, if only for a moment, in the Lucanian village. Reflecting on his recent trip to Torino, he realizes that the lives of his family and friends in the Northern metropolis, with their interests, ambitions, and hopes, are no longer his life (206). The large, modern city, after all, is another manifestation of the undifferentiated mass imbued with the sacred and hence capable of suffocating individual freedom and creativity in addition to generating it (*Paura* 108).[12]

Fittingly, the true "punto di mediazione" in Levi's novel, the moment where the processes of separation from, and immersion in, the sacred interact to produce creative energy occurs in Grassano, the town in which Levi was confined prior to his transfer to Gagliano. Whereas Gagliano is a small village "lontano dalle strade e dagli uomini," Grassano is considerably larger and located on a major thoroughfare not far from the provincial capital (29). And while Gagliano consists only of a few *Signori* and many *contadini,* Grassano has a significant middle class composed of artisans, carpenters in particular (142). Carlo recalls this town, in which he had arrived following months of solitary confinement, as a "terra di libertà" (137). He is therefore overjoyed when he is permitted to return to Grassano for a short period in order to finish some paintings, and once reunited with some old friends it does not take him long to become again "un uomo libero" (145). Described as an "insperata vacanza" (135), this interlude in a community considerably larger and differentiated than Gagliano, yet smaller and less impersonal than Torino, provides an opportunity for a flourish of creative activity, from Carlo's paintings and the lively stories told by travelling merchants to the preventive medicine practiced by the town's two valid doctors and the theatrical production of d'Annunzio's *La Fiaccola sotto il Moggio,* amazingly brought to life—despite the aestheticism of the playwright—by a troupe of Sicilian actors and a lively audience.

Levi's celebration of creativity in Grassano is analogous, in political terms, to his promotion of the "nuovi valori di libertà" that he hoped would emerge from the Resistance (**"Crisi di civiltà"** 54).[13] For Levi, the Resistance, like the thriving artisan class of Grassano, represented a creative "punto di mediazione" between undifferentiation and differentiation capable of releasing "le nuove energie liberatrici" (De Donato, Introduction xxxvi). However, Levi and his political allies soon came to realize that, because the *contadini* in the Mezzogiorno had been largely left out of the Partisan struggle, they were virtually unaffected by the liberating climate of the Resistance (Ward 166). Similarly, even as the relatively large middle class of Grassano serves as a conduit for the creative energy of such activities as painting, story-telling, and theater, Levi must acknowledge that the lives of the *contadini* here are no less wretched than those of their counterparts at Gagliano (*Cristo* 142). In fact, the *contadini* of Grassano are in some ways worse off precisely because they have more contact with the outside world—and therefore greater desire to escape—while the likelihood of actually improving their circumstances remains small (143). It is against this bleak backdrop that Levi analyzes the "problema meridionale" not only as an economic and social problem, but first and foremost as the problem of reconciling "[c]ampagna e città, civiltà precristiana e civiltà non piú cristiana" (209)—that is, as an anthropological problem.

In the final pages of **Cristo,** Levi proposes social and political autonomy as the way out of the vicious circle of fascism and anti-fascism in Italy. The *contadini,* for instance, would have greater control over their lives by belonging to a "comune rurale autonomo" (211). Levi envisions the nation as a network of such autonomous units: "Ma l'autonomia del comune rurale non potrà esistere senza l'autonomia delle fabbriche, delle scuole, delle città, di tutte le forme della vita sociale. Questo è quello che ho appreso in un anno di vita sotterranea" (211). David Ward delineates the autonomous approach theorized by Levi and initially adopted by the *Partito d'azione* after the war:

> It was to replace the monolithic national state, which had reached its apotheosis with fascism, that the Action Party elaborated its policy on local government. The policy envisaged the creation of a series of local, autonomous regions or provinces, each of which would make provision for the region's specific needs and demands. In other words, a state built from the bottom up, and not imposed from above, a state whose structures would have to be created by its citizens, and not inherited from past practices.
>
> (172)

In philosophical terms, Levi's local, culture-specific approach to the twin perils of oppression and indifference accords with his imagining of optimum creativity at the intersection of the processes of differentiation and undifferentiation. Like the artisan class of Grassano, Levi's autonomous groups would possess distinct identities without losing contact with the sacred bonds of shared humanity, an ideal configuration of "societas" as described by Turner: "a process involving both social structure and communitas, separately and united in varying proportions" ("Passages" 238). Politically, however, Levi's conception of the State as an "insieme di infinite autonomie, una organica federazione" (**Cristo** 211) stood little chance of becoming policy. Included in the manifesto of the *Partito d'azione,* it nonetheless "remained a dead letter" (Ward 173), to a large extent because all the politicians with whom Levi discussed the "problema meridionale" were "degli adoratori, piú o meno inconsapevoli dello Stato" (**Cristo** 207).

Some fifty years later, the reappearance of some of Levi's ideas in Italian public discourse creates a striking incongruity, thereby illustrating once again his fundamental lesson that cultural and historical contexts determine the ethical value of specific socio-political agendas. Whereas Levi championed the principle of greater regional and cultural autonomy to free the economically disadvantaged Mezzogiorno from the tyranny of centralized state control, Umberto Bossi, the leader of the Northern League, has recently espoused similar ideas to the opposite effect: his call for "federalismo" aims to extricate the more prosperous North (Padania) from its putative burden of supporting the poorer South.[14] In fact, with the victory of the center-left coalition in the national elections (21 April 1996) and the formation of the Prodi government, Bossi's rhetoric has intensified to the point where he defiantly speaks of "secessionismo" as often as "federalismo"—a politics of divisiveness in words if not in fact.[15]

Bossi's blatant recourse to scapegoating, clearly intended to exploit the lowest common denominator of a heterogenous society, stands in marked contrast to the example of Carlo Levi, an Italian from Torino who asked to be buried in Aliano. Although Levi's socio-economic analysis was ultimately impractical,[16] limited perhaps by his anthropological and philosophical vision, his humanistic impulses—best seen in **Cristo** through his work as an artist and a physician—remain a powerful testament to the commitment of inspired individuals to work toward positive social change even and especially under difficult conditions. Christ may have stopped at Eboli, but Carlo Levi and those like him courageously resist oppression and injustice precisely where others give in to resignation and indifference.

Notes

1. I am grateful to the South Central Modern Language Association for a travel grant that enabled me to conduct research for this article in Rome in May, 1996. I also thank Dott. Gigliola De Donato, member of the administrative council of the Fondazione Carlo Levi, and Dott. Margherita Martelli, archivist for the foundation at the Archivio centrale dello Stato, for making Levi's papers available to me on short notice. And I am indebted to Maria Wells, Italian curator for the Harry Ransom Humanities Research Center, for generously sharing with me her extensive knowledge of the manuscript of Levi's *Cristo si è fermato a Eboli.*

2. The book was published in 1971 when the manuscript was found in the files of the Department of Anthropology at the University of Chicago.

3. Girard develops his argument with examples drawn from literary tragedies, both Greek and Shakespearean, and anthropological studies of traditional societies in Latin America, Africa, and Southeast Asia. He views other writers, from Dante to Camus, through the lens of "the mimetic cycle and unanimous victimage mechanism" in "*To Double Business Bound.*"

4. Although Girard elsewhere writes of the "dual nature" of the sacred ("it is both harmful and beneficial," *The Scapegoat* 199), he clearly privileges its threatening and "harmful" effects in his work.

5. Adducing evidence from Greek tragedy and primitive religion, Girard counters that "it is not the differences but the loss of them that gives rise to violence and chaos. . . . This loss forces men into a perpetual confrontation, one that strips them of all their dis-

6. Two other important discussions of *Paura* are Falaschi (59-64) and De Donato (*Saggio* 53-73).

7. Levi later frames this discussion in terms of univocal meaning and multiplicity: "La ragione soltanto ha un senso univoco, e, come lei, la religione e la storia. Ma il senso dell'esistenza, come quello dell'arte e del linguaggio e dell'amore, è molteplice, all'infinito" (103). In the manuscript Levi adds "storia" and "linguaggio" to an earlier draft of the passage on the back of fol. 125, the only time two versions of the same passage appear in the manuscript.

tinctive characteristics—in short, of their 'identities'" (*Violence* 51).

8. Levi similarly seeks a key to penetrate the politics and passions that animate the "Luigini," the corrupt middle class of Gagliano (28-29).

9. Medical issues, ranging from the treatment of malaria and the measles to the payment of annual dues to the "sindacato Medici," are a frequent topic of Luisa's many letters to Carlo during his confinement. Moss observes that it is primarily through the doctor's access to the peasants that Levi "builds up a fascinating anthropology of peasant life and culture" (27).

10. Thus Levi describes Giulia, his mythical *strega-domestica,* as a powerful woman "legata alla zolla e alle eterne divinità animali" (*Cristo* 94).

11. Inspection of the manuscript of *Cristo* reveals that Levi inserted the phrase "nel loro terrore del sacro" to another important passage (103; fol. 126), a revision that reinforces the author's identification not only with Barone, his beloved dog who was "mezzo barone e mezzo leone," but also with the undifferentiated world of the *contadini* with whom he lived.

12. In *L'orologio* Levi imagines a more positive—or at least ambiguous—association of a large city, Naples, with the "indistinto originario" (Ward 190), thereby providing an urban analogue to the sacred world of the *contadini* in *Cristo.*

13. In his "Ricordo di Leone Ginzburg," whose death is commemorated in the manuscript of *Cristo* with "Leone" and a small red cross next to the date "7/2/44" (fol. 159), Levi writes: "Se la Resistenza fu insieme il primo momento rivoluzionario e popolare della nostra storia e un grande fatto di cultura, lo si deve agli uomini come Leone Ginzburg che per elevatezza d'ingegno e rigore di vita morale avevano intransigentemente precorso in se stessi quella nuova unità umana, quella solidarietà operante e creativa" (167-68).

14. Ward describes the *Lega nord* as a movement "which is intensely critical of the unified Italian state that was born out of the *Risorgimento,* and whose main political proposal is the creation of a tripartite federal Italy divided into semiautonomous republics . . ." (26).

15. Claiming that "federalismo non serve più a niente," Bossi threatened secession, the League's next phase, as "quella decisiva contro Roma ladrona" (Buzzanca 7). He and a group of twenty-seven senators walked out of Parliament when the Senate leader refused to recognize the group's request to be named "Lega-Parlamento della Padania" (Buzzanca), a day after the leader of the Camera dei Deputati similarly rejected "Lega Padania indipendente" (Stanganelli).

16. Levi, according to Moss, was right in asserting the impossibility for the peasant traditions to remain intact under a centralized state, but "he was wrong in thinking that, in human development, the two areas of consciousness and material conditions can be kept separate" (32). That is, as the socio-economic landscape changed (slightly for the better) in Southern Italy, the peasants themselves began to adopt some of the qualities of the "piccola borghesia" so despised and maligned by Levi in the novel. See Napolillo for a sustained, occasionally harsh, critique of Levi's *meridionalismo.*

Works Cited

Baldassaro, Lawrence. "*Paura della libertà*: Carlo Levi's Unfinished Preface." *Italica* 72.2 (1995): 143-54.

Bassani, Giorgio. "Levi e la crisi." *Paragone* (Aug. 1950): 32-40.

Buzzanca, Silvio. "Bossi lascia il Senato: 'Salgo sull'Aventino.'" *La Repubblica* (17 May 1996): 7.

Carpitella, Diego. "L'itinerario di Carlo Levi e la ricerca interdisciplinare di Ernesto de Martino." De Donato, *Carlo Levi nella storia* 203-12.

Chapman, Charlotte Gower. *Milocca: A Sicilian Village.* Cambridge: Shenkman, 1971.

Cronin, Constance. *The Sting of Change: Sicilians in Sicily and Australia.* Chicago: U of Chicago P, 1970.

De Donato, Gigliola, ed. *Carlo Levi nella storia e nella cultura italiana.* Manduria: Piero Lacaita, 1993.

———. Introduction. Levi, *Coraggio dei miti* vii-lxii.

———. *Saggio su Carlo Levi.* Roma-Bari: De Donato, 1974.

Falaschi, Giovanni. "Carlo Levi." *Belfagor* 26 (1971): 56-82.

Geertz, Clifford. *Works and Lives: The Anthropologist as Author.* Stanford: Stanford UP, 1988.

Girard, René. *The Scapegoat.* Trans. Yvonne Freccero. Baltimore: Johns Hopkins UP, 1986.

———. *"To Double Business Bound": Essays on Literature, Mimesis, and Anthropology.* Baltimore: Johns Hopkins UP, 1978.

———. *Violence and the Sacred.* Trans. Patrick Gregory. Baltimore: Johns Hopkins UP, 1977.

Lagarde, François. *René Girard ou la christianisation des sciences humaines.* New York: Peter Lang, 1994.

Lanternari, Vittorio. "Da Carlo Levi a Ernesto de Martino: verso la nuova antropologia." De Donato, *Carlo Levi nella storia* 213-25.

Levi, Carlo. *Coraggio dei miti: scritti contemporanei, 1922-1974.* Ed. Gigliola De Donato. Roma-Bari: De Donato, 1975.

————. "Crisi di civiltà." Levi. *Coraggio dei miti* 52-54.

————. *Cristo si è fermato a Eboli.* 1945. 21st paperback ed. Milano: Mondadori, 1985.

————. *Cristo si è fermato a Eboli.* Autograph ms. Harry Ransom Humanities Research Center. U of Texas, Austin.

————. *Paura della libertà.* 1946. 2nd ed. Torino: Einaudi, 1948.

————. "Ricordo di Leone Ginzburg." Levi. *Coraggio dei miti* 166-68.

Levi, Luisa. Letter to Carlo Levi. 20 Feb. 1936. Busta 1, fasc. 1. Archivio Carlo Levi. Archivio centrale dello Stato. Rome, Italy.

Livingston, Paisley. *Models of Desire: René Girard and the Psychology of Mimesis.* Baltimore: Johns Hopkins UP, 1992.

Moss, Howard. "The Politics of *Cristo si è fermato a Eboli.*" *Association of Teachers of Italian Journal* 52 (1988): 27-36.

Napolillo, Vincenzo. *Carlo Levi dall'antifascismo al mito contadino.* Cosenza: Brenner, 1984.

Stanganelli, Mario. "Violante boccia la 'Padania indipendente.'" *Il Messaggero* (16 May 1996): 5.

Taussig, Michael. "Reification and the Consciousness of the Patient." *The Nervous System.* New York: Routledge, 1992. 83-111.

Turner, Victor. "Passages, Margins, and Poverty: Religious Symbols of Communitas." *Dramas, Fields, and Metaphors: Symbolic Action in Human Society.* Ithaca: Cornell UP, 1974. 231-71.

————. *The Ritual Process: Structure and Anti-Structure.* Chicago: Aldine, 1969.

Ward, David. *Antifascisms: Cultural Politics in Italy, 1943-46.* Madison: Fairleigh Dickinson UP; London: Associated U Presses, 1996.

FURTHER READING

Criticism

Arndt, Mari. "Sean O'Faolain and Carlo Levi: Travelling on Different Passports in Southern Italy." In *The Classical World and the Mediterranean,* edited by Giuseppe Serpillo and Donatella Badin, pp. 147-51. Cagliari, Italy: Tema, 1996.
　　Contrasts the descriptions of southern Italy of Levi and the Irish writer Sean O'Faolain.

Basso, Hamilton. "Carlo Levi's Memorable Year." *New Yorker* 23, no. 10 (26 April 1947): 91-3.
　　Positive review of *Christ Stopped at Eboli,* Basso asserts that "the best thing about Mr. Levi's book, and the thing that gives it enduring value, is the story it has to tell of peasant culture."

Coleman, John. "Two Italies." *New Statesman* 103 (30 April 1982): 28.
　　Positive review of the cinematic version of *Christ Stopped at Eboli.*

Guerard, Albert. "Carlo Levi's 'Theology'." *Nation* 170, no. 7 (18 February 1950): 158.
　　Guerard provides a personal reaction to *Of Fear and Freedom,* contending that the book "is not communication but communion."

Pauker, John. Review of *Christ Stopped at Eboli,* by Carlo Levi. *Furioso* 3, no. 1 (fall 1947): 79-81.
　　Favorable review of *Christ Stopped at Eboli,* Pauker discusses Levi and his work as part of the European tradition.

Simon, John. "Interior Exiles." *National Review* 32 (30 May 1980): 672-73.
　　Favorable assessment of the cinematic adaptation of *Christ Stopped at Eboli.*

Carl Rogers
1902-1987

(Full name Carl Ransom Rogers) American psychologist.

INTRODUCTION

Rogers was among the most influential figures of humanistic psychology, a school of psychotherapy that rejected medical and psychoanalytic models of treatment and instead put forth a theory of personality and behavior that presumed the source of psychological health ultimately resides in the individual person rather than in a program based on the expert knowledge and authority of a psychiatric professional. Rogers's specific form of humanistic psychology is broadly based on his view of human personality, which he believed naturally tended to develop in what he considered a healthy manner unless it is adversely influenced by life experiences. From this theoretical basis, Rogers created a form of therapy that he called "client-centered," as opposed to forms of treatment that are directed by the expertise of the therapist.

BIOGRAPHICAL INFORMATION

Rogers was born on January 8, 1902, in Oak Park, Illinois. One of six children born into the family of a contractor/engineer and his wife, he characterized his childhood environment as "anti-intellectual" and dominated by a religiosity of the fundamentalist type. Raised on a farm from the age of twelve, Rogers entered the Agricultural College of the University of Wisconsin in 1919, although he ultimately graduated with a degree in history. While in college he felt a religious calling and eventually began training to become a Protestant minister, and after graduating in 1924 he enrolled at the Union Theological Seminary in New York City. From there he transferred to Teachers College at Columbia University in order to pursue counseling rather than the strictly religious aspect of his ministerial profession. He subsequently focused on clinical and educational psychology, writing his doctoral dissertation on personality adjustment in children. Throughout the 1930s, Rogers worked in the field of child psychology, and in 1940 he accepted a position as a professor of psychology at Ohio State University. It was at this time that he began to develop the theories and methodology for which he would later become renowned. The incipient concepts of Rogers's therapeutic approach appeared in his 1942 book *Counseling and Psychotherapy,* and within the next few years he developed his concept of the self as the organizing element in human personality and the principles of the "nondirective," or client-centered, style of therapy. In 1945 he took a position as professor of psychology and head of the counseling center at the University of Chicago, where,

over the next twelve years, he further refined and articulated his ideas, publishing *Client-Centered Therapy* (1951) during this time. A charismatic figure, Rogers's influence over students, colleagues, and various collaborators, as well as his publication of best-selling books such as *On Becoming a Person* (1961) and *Person to Person* (1967), made him the central figure in American humanistic psychology throughout his lifetime. In addition, with the establishment of the Center for the Study of Persons in 1968, the principles of the client-centered version of therapy came to be applied in other contexts and institutional settings, including marriage relationships, school systems, larger-scale community groups, and corporations. Until his death in 1987, Rogers remained active in promulgating his view of the nature of human personality and procedures for correcting psychological disorders.

MAJOR WORKS

Rogers's therapeutic scheme as outlined in his books and practiced in therapy is premised on the existence within each individual of what he termed the "organismic valuing process," sometimes described as an internal monitor of a person's experiences in life that, under favorable circumstances, allows the development of healthy men or women possessing optimum self-esteem and an accurate sense of who they "really are" as well as who they would ideally like to become. The obstacle to this development, according to Rogers, are conditions, primarily those inflicted by a child's parents, in which the individual is denied "unconditional positive regard" and is thereby influenced by either positive or negative "conditions of worth" which instill values and elicit behaviors that are at odds with a person's inborn organismic valuing process. The result of exposure to these conditions of worth is the development of individuals who look to the approval of others for their sense of identity rather than finding it within themselves. Consequently serious conflicts arise within the personality between its natural organismic valuing process and its perception of conditions of worth that are alien to it. Such conflicts are the source of the vast array of neurotic symptoms and disorders that have been catalogued since the inception of psychology as a professional discipline. In order to cure his patients, whom he called "clients" so as to relate to them in a more equitable manner than did doctors or traditional psychoanalysts, Rogers provided them with the unconditional positive regard they were denied previously by practicing "nondirective" techniques of therapy that avoided communicating to the client the judgmental or interpretive conditions to which they had already been subjected in life and which were only perpetuated in other therapeutic methods, especially psychoanalysis. A principal, perhaps inevitable, technique of nondirective therapy is that of "reflection," whereby the therapist literally restates, or reflects back, whatever clients say so that they themselves may serve as the instrument of their own rehabilitation, gaining insight by their own direction into who they are and the type of person they would have become without the judgmental interference of others. In *On Becoming a Person* Rogers expressed his realization of the superior effectiveness of this technique as opposed to those of psychoanalytic or behaviorist schools of psychology. "Unless I had a need to demonstrate my own cleverness and learning," he wrote, "I would do better to rely upon the client for the direction of movement." By this means, clients were able to attain the highest goal of his client-centered, later renamed "person-centered" approach—that of "getting in touch with themselves."

CRITICAL RECEPTION

Critiques of Rogers's person-centered therapy begin with his basic conception of human nature as tending toward the good and the healthy, not to mention his assumption of the very existence of a personal self toward which one might strive. Furthermore, critics of Rogers's theories maintain serious doubts that therapists can, or should, establish a relationship of unconditional positive regard in the case of dangerously violent persons. They also fail to understand how parents might put into practice his ideas when raising children whose behavior may sometimes be difficult to countenance with wholehearted approval. At best, Rogers's detractors claim, his ideas may be applied only among a limited range of clients, specifically those suffering from the milder forms of neurosis, acknowledging that while person-centered therapy may prove no more effective than any other method, it has yet to demonstrate that it is harmful in any way. Despite such criticisms, Rogers's theory of personality and his therapeutic methodology continue to gain adherents and have become among the most widely influential trends in the history of psychology.

PRINCIPAL WORKS

Measuring Personality Adjustment in Children Nine to Thirteen Years of Age (nonfiction) 1931

The Clinical Treatment of the Problem Child (nonfiction) 1939

Counseling and Psychotherapy (nonfiction) 1942

Client-Centered Therapy: Its Current Practice, Implications, and Theory (nonfiction) 1951

On Becoming a Person (nonfiction) 1961

Person to Person: The Problem of Being Human (nonfiction) 1967

Freedom to Learn: A View of What Education Might Become (nonfiction) 1969

Becoming Partners: Marriage and Its Alternatives (nonfiction) 1972

Carl Rogers on Personal Power (nonfiction) 1977

A Way of Being (nonfiction) 1980

Freedom to Learn for the 80s (nonfiction) 1983

Carl Rogers: Dialogues (nonfiction) 1989

CRITICISM

Carl Rogers and Mary Harrington Hall (interview date December 1967)

SOURCE: Rogers, Carl, and Mary Harrington Hall. "Carl Rogers Speaks Out on Groups and the Lack of a Human Science." *Psychology Today* 1, no. 7 (December 1967): 19-21, 62-66.

[*In the following interview, Rogers and Harrington discuss group therapy methods, and Rogers criticizes modern psychology for ignoring patients' personal needs.*]

[*Hall*]: *Shall we talk about groups—encounter groups, T-groups, sensitivity-training groups, group therapy? The group phenomenon demands exploration and explanation. And I've wondered . . . are people drawn toward this intense group experience because they feel loneliness and alienation in our strange society?*

[Rogers]: Of course that's a major reason. Out of the increasing loneliness of modern culture, we have in some social sense been forced to develop a way of getting closer to one another. I think encounter groups probably bring people closer together than has ever been true in history except with groups of people together during crisis. You put men together during war, for instance, and they really know each other to the depths, and so it is in groups. So often someone will say at the end of a group experience: "I just can't believe that I have known you people here better than I know members of my own family, and you know me better than my family knows me."

We have found a way for closeness to develop with amazing rapidity. I think that group work is a far more important social phenomenon than most people realize. Group encounters, by whatever name you call them, are becoming a major force.

A lot of people in and out of psychology question the useful purpose of such closeness with groups of people who have an experience together for a week or for a weekend, get to know each other's problems and dreams, and then may never see each other again, Carl. Perhaps you're one of the best people in the country to answer this argument. You developed the form of therapy in which the therapist permits himself to become involved with his patient, in a frankly caring relationship with the therapist both permissive and involved. And Rogerian therapy certainly is based on interaction.

You're actually putting two questions in a polite way, Mary. What you're questioning is the *usefulness* and the *legitimacy* of the group experience. There is a good deal of argument and furor about the intensive group experience. There have been vituperative articles about how terrible group encounters are, how they take on the Communist brainwashing technique, and such nonsense. You get even more people who think the group experience is simply great. This is a very potent phenomenon. One can't just take it or leave it alone. You either become involved, in which case group encounter does bring about changes in you, or you can resist it completely. The group experience is not something people remain neutral about.

Let's differentiate between group therapy and encounter groups.

They are really two rather different dimensions. Group therapy is for the person who is already hurting, who has problems, and needs help. Encounter groups are for those who are functioning normally but want to improve their capacity for living within their own sets of relationships. And the leader role is, of course, quite different. One leader must be therapeutic, the other more of a facilitator. Tradi-

tional group therapy, with its weekly meetings over a long period, well may be replaced one day by an intensive week or month, or even weekend experience. The intense encounter seems to work wonders in therapy, too.

You know that I always have been somewhat of a skeptic, or possibly afraid, about the group experience, and thus a questioner of the purpose for people getting together to talk a lot—and cry a lot. But I really want to know: what do people bring home to their daily lives from group encounters?

There are so many hundreds and thousands of examples to give. The most common report is that people behave differently with their families and with their colleagues. A school administrator (in a workshop we ran for a California school system not long ago) is typical. She said she *felt* different but was unprepared for how quick her family's response would be. She wrote that her daughters sensed a change in her immediately. Before she had been home a day, she and her daughters had talked over a whole list of things—God, death and hell, menstruation, nightmares, a whole range of things.

Both her 14-year-old and her ten-year-old daughter wanted to be bathed by her, the first time in years they had been so intimate. Finally, the young one said: "What did they teach you at that meeting—how to be nice to kids?" The woman wrote that she replied: "No, I learned how to be myself and found out that was pretty nice." Now, this woman is a teacher. I think she is going to be different with her students, too.

What about the argument that encounter groups are fine for those who are emotionally stable but may be very upsetting indeed for those with problems—and our number is legion?

The possibility of damage concerns me, too, but I think the risk is much, much less than is ordinarily presumed. I did a questionnaire study, a six months' follow-up, of more than 500 people involved in groups which I either led or in which I was responsible. Out of 481 people who responded, only two felt the experience had been more hurtful than helpful. You know, a deep relationship is a very rare experience for anyone, and it always means change.

How much change and what kind?

I think encounter groups help make people more open to experiences that are going on within them, more expressive of their feelings, more spontaneous in their reactions, more flexible, more vulnerable, and probably more genuinely intimate in their interpersonal relationships. Now, I value this type of person, don't you?

That sounds like the ideal man.

Well, there are whole cultures built on exactly the opposite ideal. And many people in our own culture feel also that a person should be contained, disciplined, preferably unaware of his feelings, and should live in terms of a firm set of disciplines that are handed down by someone—God, or someone up there—whomever he looks to as an authority. The person who emerges from encounter groups is likely to be more self-directed and not so easily persuaded by others. I think the absence of open debate about what is the desirable sort of personal development has stirred up misunderstanding and public reaction against the intense-encounter technique.

But, Carl, you can measure attitude change and you can do empirical studies of behavior change, yet you can't measure the essential experience in groups that brings those changes, can you? How can you explain the phenomenon so people will understand?

It troubles me, and troubles me deeply, whether we really do know how to have a human science, Mary. Groups are potent, and something very significant is going on. I have gotten increasingly restive about the point you raise, that we can't measure the essential experience that brings about those changes. I feel very perplexed. A lot of my life has been devoted to measuring; I keep being sure it can be done with the group experience, and then failing.

Last year Michael Polanyi, the British philosopher of science, said something I really didn't like at the time, but he may be right. He said we should lay aside the word *science* for the next decade or two and give people the freedom to find out that we need more *knowledge*. He said the word *science* is so wrapped up with the machinery of science that it was stifling rather than helping us at this point, at least in the behavioral sciences. I know that many of us in psychology have gotten so wound up with methodology that we forget to be curious, really. With today's knowledge, we don't know how to study what happened to a businessman for whom the encounter experience had an on-going effect for sixteen years. I don't know how to study that. Or why was an intense-encounter experience something a high-school girl told me she had found to be the most important and beautiful experience in her relatively short life?

You seem to be saying that psychology is groping now toward being a more human science. If that is so, what will happen when you break through?

I don't know. The closer one gets to trying to assess the intangible things which probably are most important in personality change, the less are customary instruments being used, and the more suspect are the only instruments that seem to me to make any sense. I think that in those intangibles the only person who can help us out is the person to whom something has happened. We need to get more pictures of what it seems like to the person *inside,* who has experienced the change.

If we adapted Polanyi's suggestion and just said: "Well, science or no science I'm trying to find out something

about this," we might have taken a valuable and freeing step. One of the unfortunate things about psychology is that it has tried to make one great leap and become a science like physics. I think we will have to recognize the fact that people observed things, and thought about things, and fiddle around with things a long time before they came up with any of the precise observations which made a science out of physics.

We may have to go back and do much more naturalistic observation, make more of an attempt to understand people, behavior, and the dynamics of things.

Then, perhaps someday, out of that might grow a real psychological science, not an imitation of physics, a human science that should have as its appropriate subject, man. I think the reason so much psychological experimentation is done on rats and cats, and such, is that we realize perfectly well that we don't have the tools for understanding human beings.

But, after all, we do learn about humans by animal study. Do you think psychologists have been defensive because psychology is sometimes seen as a stepchild of science?

I guess psychologists are about the most defensive professional people around today. We have this terrific fear of looking unscientific. A terrific fear of spinning out wild theories to see how they sound, and a fear of trying them out. We think we must do everything from a *known* base with *known* instruments. Actually, this is *not* the way in which creative scientists, even in the hard sciences, operate. For instance, I think one of the real tragedies of graduate education in psychology is that graduate students in many, many institutions become less and less willing to spout original ideas for fear they will be shot down by their colleagues, and by their professors. This is *not* the way to do things.

The great intuitive chemists and physicists certainly aren't afraid. They spend a lifetime on hunches, don't they? I'm thinking particularly of one of our mutual close friends, Harold Urey.

That's it! They aren't afraid. What psychology needs are ideas that someone dreams up on the basis of hunches and intuition, from experience, or to try to make sense out of some complex set of phenomena. It may take a lifetime to find out if it was a worthless dream or a really significant pattern of thought. We need that kind of dreaming in psychology, and graduate departments of psychology have no time for dreams. I think they are definitely fearful.

And maybe it takes someone like you—a former president of the American Psychological Association, a man with every honor his profession and the academic world can bestow—to be so fearlessly critical of his own profession. Or maybe you're impatient to have psychology take that major leap forward to answer your own questions about why group encounters do seem to affect people so deeply?

Or maybe I'm just used to being involved in controversy? Perhaps all three, Mary. But still, psychology is a defensive profession. I'll give you an example. At a conference last year on "Man and the Science of Man," all the discussions were taped. These were all top scholars. Only three participants refused permission to trust editors to put their taped remarks in shape for future listeners. Two of those three were psychologists. Another example was the dialogue I had in Duluth with B. F. Skinner, the father of operant conditioning, the creator of the modern study of behaviorism. He was unwilling to have the tape of our dialogue transcribed. I thought it was understood in advance that it *would* be transcribed. I call that needlessly fearful.

By the way, Fred told on interesting anecdote about you in his interview with us in September, Carl.

Yes, the ducks. Funny story, but he knows that it's not true. He said I was duck hunting and used the art of gentle agreement to get for myself the duck another man shot. Actually, my brother and I were hunting, we shot at the same time, and tossed a coin to see who got the duck. And I've told Fred I lost the toss. Fred and I actually are friends, you know. He's a marvelous mind. Another friend, Rollo May, whom you rightly labeled in your wonderful interview as "Mr. Humanist," told the story that I once questioned the existence of tragedy by saying that Romeo and Juliet might have been all right with just a little counseling. I probably did say that. I'm more optimistic than Rollo. He is an existentialist—so am I, but my philosophy has more room for hope.

Your background and Rollo May's are quite similar, though, aren't they?

We're both from the rural Midwest. I was a farm boy, he from a small town. This is a good, strong background, you know. He graduated from the Union Theological Seminary. After I graduated in history from the University of Wisconsin, I studied there, and then I went across the street to get my Ph.D. in psychology from Columbia. In 1926, the Seminary was a freewheeling, stimulating place to be. Arthur McGifford, a real scholar, was president. A group of us students decided we didn't have enough chance to talk about issues that really concerned us, so we asked for a seminar which we would run ourselves and for which we would receive credit. Any institution today would drop dead if you made such a suggestion. The Seminary agreed and in many ways it well may have been the very first encounter group, although it was a little more intellectual than most encounter groups as we know them today. Many of us left the Seminary and went into allied fields. I still was very much interested in working with people but I didn't want to tie myself to some particular creed.

I worked for the New York Institute for Child Guidance, and for the Rochester Society for the Prevention of Cruelty to Children before getting into the University life, you know. I earned the glorious sum of $2,900 a year on my first job, with a wife and child to support.

Then, of course, I went to Ohio, to the University of Chicago and to Wisconsin, before I got fed up finally with the restrictions of the academic life, particularly with the frustrations for graduate students, and became a fellow of the Western Behavioral Sciences Institute in Southern California.

*Your book, **Counseling and Psychotherapy,** was published in 1942, Carl, but didn't your major impact come about after **Client-Centered Therapy** was published in 1951?*

I think so, really. Acceptance came very slowly.

When did you become interested in groups?

My first groping toward using the intensive-group experience in a constructive way came in 1946, when I was in charge of the University of Chicago's Counseling Center. We had a Veterans Administration contract for training all personal counsellors for returning servicemen and we had to make them into effective counsellors within six-week training programs. They all had Master's degrees, but none of them had done much counseling. We couldn't give them individual counseling, which we thought would be the best way for them to learn, so we put them together in small groups. It worked very well.

There was no such thing as encounter groups then, but was there any group therapy?

There was some group therapy just beginning. I remember that in about 1945 I told a group of my students that I would be glad to try to conduct a group-therapy program for them, but it would be my first experience. Now, the National Training Laboratories in Bethel, Maine, started at about this time, but I was unaware of that.

My groups of personal counsellors and students at Chicago became more and more personal in their discussions and revealed more and more of what was going on within them. It was similar to what goes on in an encounter group today. However, I didn't carry on in this field, partly because I didn't think that group work was a good field for research. I thought that there were enough complexities with the one-to-one-relationship so that we couldn't possibly study a group situation.

You certainly have changed your mind since that time.

Oh, yes, I have certainly revised my opinion. The next time I was closely involved in a group experience was in the autumn of 1950 when I conducted a postgraduate seminar type of therapy held just before the A.P.A. meetings. I remember that for one hour each day I counseled a client in front of a group of twelve. It started off on a somewhat academic basis, but as we got into it, sharing more and more deeply of our personal experiences, our failures, and our difficulties, it became a moving personal experience. All of us left there feeling we had gained deeply. What amazed me was the long, lasting effect from the experience. It was then that I began to realize the potency of group experience.

Didn't the National Training Laboratories, in Bethel, Maine, begin the sensitivity-training programs for executives, the famous T-Groups, at about the same time you did your first group work at Chicago?

At just the time I began putting on summer workshops organized by the Counseling Service Center, I heard that something was going on in the East. Then, one of our members took part in one of the N.T.L. groups, and came back rather unimpressed. We were following different patterns; our groups focused more on the interpersonal relationship and on building a climate where people could express or withhold as much as they wished.

Over the years there has been cross-fertilization, and it is no longer accurate to say we are working two different ways. I conduct N.T.L. workshops every year—the Presidents' Lab program for top executives.

Where does the term T-Group come from, Carl?

T-Groups originally were thought of as *Training* groups. I don't think we are in the business of *training*. The term is misleading. I think there still is a different flavor between N.T.L. workshops—and all Eastern approaches—and what is going on in the West.

N.T.L. did the real pioneering in the encounter-group movement, and really have been the prime moving force in the whole thing. They have put on thousands of groups, and they are responsible for getting the business community involved to the point where the top men in the country attend N.T.L. Presidents' Labs. All groups start from there. What a great thing they did, and yet the West Coast is far more active than is the East, the home of groups.

Someone once said—me, I think—that the West is on a great group binge. Why is it that groups are more popular on the West Coast? Do you agree with May, who says it's because the West is anti-intellectual?

Actually, I think the East Coast shows signs of being an older culture. Their procedures are more rigid, with too much stress on paper credentials. On the West Coast, partly because it is a newer part of the country, partly because the California psychological climate, in particular, is freer, there is more regard for essentials of the work. We've used nonprofessional leaders in groups. N.T.L. would frown on anyone without the proper paper credentials.

Do you find the West more experimental in its approach to psychology?

I certainly do, and I approve. It will be sad if the West settles into a fixed mold. I believe every organization and every profession ought to be upset—put through the mixer—every decade or so, and start again fresh and flexible.

What makes California especially so different? Is it the fluid population?

I cannot account for it. What gives the particularly loose, freewheeling character to the California psychological climate, I don't know. I just know that you can *feel* it.

Ann Roe, a research psychologist, did an extensive study some years ago on 100 creative physical and social scientists who were most highly regarded. Fifteen years later she said that out of the 100, some 70 now live in California—and they aren't retired for the most part—they're still swingers. The great universities are only part of the answer, I think, but an important part.

Tell me about your Honker group at Cal Tech, Carl. I know that elimination of the grading system for Cal Tech freshmen and sophomores came out of those sessions.

I was surprised to be asked by Cal Tech to serve as a consultant on human and educational problems, and I decided that if I worked with students, it might cause a student rebellion—so I chose faculty.

We weren't a committee or a group with any legal authority. I didn't want that. We put together top faculty and administration people and I think I was able to develop a freer discussion climate than they ever had. We began to take up issues of deep concern, and since they didn't have to arrive at any motions and pass them, they discussed frankly.

Did the name Honker come from the gabbling of the group?

We met first at the Honker Restaurant. The original group met for two years, and finally we had faculty-student groups, and new faculty groups.

We had to break up the original Honkers because the faculty began to fear them as an elite power group. And the new groups were just as effective.

The grading system and a number of good new things just naturally evolved. Most faculty members, incidentally, have never been willing to get off the intellectual level and into the intensive experimental encounter. But there is quite an encounter program now among students.

You have a grant to do research in the effect of encounter experiences in an educational system, haven't you?

We have a two-year Babcock Foundation Grant of $80,000 a year, with an additional $30,000 personal gift from Charles Kettering to see whether the basic encounter group can be an instrument for self-directed change in school systems. Many school systems were interested but I selected the Immaculate Heart College in Los Angeles. It's a marvelous school, and it also certifies about 70 teachers a year, and staffs and supervises eight high schools and 50 elementary schools.

Carl, I was terribly excited when you told me a year ago that you hoped to do a vertical thing in a school system, starting with administrators in groups, then teachers, parents, and students—and then putting them together. This might end the crashing boredom of most school systems.

Well, we've begun now. We've held six weekend workshops, for college faculty, for high-school faculty and student leaders, and for elementary-school principals and teachers. I am hopeful. We'll know in three years.

What has happened? Are people getting involved?

The student councils have asked if our program leaders can meet on a weekly basis to help them iron out interpersonal problems. Lay faculty members have asked for a weekend encounter group for themselves and their spouses. Various departments are asking for encounter groups. Everyone is excited. (Sister Mary Corita, the artist and the most joyous soul anywhere, is in the Immaculate Heart Art Department, you know. So you can imagine what a grand place this college is.)

And just as in all school systems, faculty members resisted group encounters with students, but that is working out.

We meet for solid weekends. Groups may meet Friday evening and all day Saturday, then again until Sunday noon. Or perhaps for a very long Saturday till midnight, and then again for a long Sunday.

All right, let's say I'm a school principal in an encounter group. What is this going to do for the school system?

It will affect the system because you are going to be more democratic and more willing to take feedback from your staff, Mary. The teacher I told you about who suddenly was closer to her own daughters had attended one of our Immaculate Heart workshops.

Some people say, "Well, this approach can't change a system." I say it will make systems more open to innovations.

What do you think frightens people about intense encounter groups?

I think many of us live in kind of a precarious balance. We have learned to get along with ourselves and our world in some way, and the possibility that this balance might be upset is always a frightening one. Almost invariably in groups, every person finds the balance is disturbed, or possibly upset, but finds that in a climate of trust he is enormously supported in being *more* himself.

As you were talking, I thought of the last lines of Cyrano de Bergerac. *Dying, he reaches for his gaudy hat and says: "My plume, my sacred plume. My pride, my pose, my lifelong masquerade."*

That moves me. In an encounter group, people learn they really do not need to keep that masquerade. In our last workshop, there was a man who came across as being very competent, very efficient, very self-sufficient. You just felt, here's a guy who really has it made. He has an important job and everything is rosy. It turned out that he is *so* hungry for appreciation and love; he feels he lets other people know that he appreciates them but who in the hell listens to him, or cares about him—nobody. I am thinking of one Navy commander, who appeared to be a complete martinet. We weren't very many days into the workshop before he was telling us some of the personal tragedies that he had in his life, particularly of his son—he felt terrible about what he had helped to do to his son. Then he got to telling about how he was known as a disciplinarian, but that when he was the commander of a ship during the war he got himself in trouble with his officers because of one enlisted man who was always in trouble. This officer felt he was really so much like the bad guy that he couldn't punish him. Others would come up with minor offenses and they got so much time in the brig, and this guy would do horrible things and the officer couldn't bear to punish him because the sailor did things he himself never dared to do. Among the many things that happened during his group experience, he decided to go back and try to rebuild his marriage—I don't know how much success he had in that. When he got back he was going to tell his top staff about the real softy he was inside, and try to loosen up his organization. This is the sort of thing where you see that people *can* change and *do* change and *do* become more human.

This interview with you leads off a special section on the group phenomenon, Carl. The article following this interview is by a very bright young Harvard psychologist, Tom Cottle, who has experimented with self-analytic groups of Negro and white high-school students just before their school integration. He thinks such encounters can greatly ease racial tensions.

I'm sure he's right. Group encounters can help end the tragedy of two races which meet fearfully and don't know what to do.

What we need is an enormous effort of the scope of the Manhattan Project. We should call in everyone who has any theoretical contribution to make, everyone who has tried out practical things such as you are describing and such as I have done. We should round up interdisciplinary knowledge that would focus on how tensions can be reduced. Such a project could contribute enormously in the resolving of racial tensions. This approach also could contribute to the resolution of labor and management tensions. I believe it could contribute to the terrifying problems of international tensions, too.

I would not be in the least afraid to be a facilitator for a massive group program in Watts. I know the tensions and bitterness would be terrific, but the people would be speaking for themselves. And I'm sure we could come to a more harmonious understanding than is possible any other way.

Fred Stoller, who with George Boch invented the marathon group you have said is effective, has an article in this group section. So does Mike Murphy, president of Esalen Institute. I know you've led workshops there. What do you think of Esalen, Carl? Murphy says he doesn't think you're sold on it.

I admire the nerve Mike has. His basic idea is very good. Living in California has made me realize that there is no sharp dividing line between the cutting edge in psychology and the too-far-out hogwash.

Mike is covering the whole spectrum in his Esalen seminars and workshops. We'll look back in ten years and find that some of the things he has sponsored helped start an important trend.

I'm pleased that he has set up a San Francisco headquarters, because I think that his Big Sur place is a little too involved with the sort of hippie culture that has tended to limit the kind of people who participate in seminars there.

How do you assess your own contributions to psychology?

If I have made a contribution it is around the central theme that the potential of the individual—and I would even add, the potential of the group—can be released providing a proper psychological climate is created. And that is an optimistic point of view!

If I, the therapist, can come through to my client as a person who cares about him and understands what he is struggling to express, he gradually will begin to choose healthier directions for himself.

Your work certainly has emphasized the importance of interpersonal relationships.

That is another aspect of whatever contribution I have made. Instead of focusing on the diagnostic or causative elements of behavior. I always have been more concerned with the dynamics of interaction. Not about how a person became what he is, but about how does he change from what he is.

I always have felt psychologically nourished by deep communication with people with whom I was working. I think sometimes people in clinical work apologize if they feel they are getting something out of it. I believe that if a therapist doesn't find particularly deep relationships with people he works with, he shouldn't be either a therapist or working with groups.

This involvement was very true for me when I was doing individual therapy. When I had to give that up because my life was just too hectic, I wondered what would take its place. And soon I found that working intensively with groups—and with individuals in those groups—provided me with the same kind of psychological nourishment.

For people who criticize the permissiveness of your approach, the way your son and daughter turned out is an answer which must make you and Helen very proud.

Well, they have nice families of their own now. Our son, David, is chairman of the Department of Medicine at Vanderbilt University. He was chosen one of the ten outstanding young men in the country for *Life* magazine's issue on the "take-over" generation. He has two daughters and a son.

Our daughter is Mrs. Lawrence Fuchs. Her husband is Professor of American Civilization at Brandeis University and they have three daughters. He organized the Peace Corps in the Philippines. Natalie took her M.A. in psychology with Abe Maslow (present APA president). She's very interested in counseling work. She's *good,* too.

You said you were used to being somewhat controversial, Carl. Where have your battles been?

Of course I was very much involved in the battles during the 1930's and 40's in which there were many attempts to stop psychologists from practicing psychotherapy. The last go-around on that was during the 1950's. It's a dead issue now.

Another controversy that somehow hit the clinicians' value system—and threatened many therapists—was my confidence in the potentiality of the individual.

It was my publications, based on my conviction and research, which upset many psychologists and psychiatrists. I said the individual can discover his own patterns of capabilities and his maladjustments, and that he can find insight *on his own* and take action to help solve his own problems.

The point of view threatens people who like to be experts. It is far more satisfying to be the man pulling the strings than to be the man who provides a climate in which another person can *do* something. So, there were attacks—there were famous jokes that about how all I did was agree with people.

That brings up a question. There is a classic Rogers joke . . . a man in therapy with you is depressed. He says so. You say: "You're depressed, aren't you?" He says he feels like jumping out the window in your office, and you say—

I *know* the story. My answer, for once and for all time, is that I would not have let him jump out the window.

Diane C. Mader (essay date winter 1980)

SOURCE: Mader, Diane C. "What Are They Doing to Carl Rogers?" *ETC: A Review of General Semantics* 37, no. 4 (winter 1980): 314-20.

[*In the following essay, Mader argues against the trend in rhetoric study that positioned Rogers as an Aristotelian rhetorician while ignoring the real goals of his methodology.*]

Recent college composition texts seem to imply that there is a new rhetoric, or, at the least, an alternative to classical persuasion strategy. In *Rhetoric: Discovery and Change* the authors advocate Rogerian argument as an alternative to the traditional Aristotelian framework; similarly, the author of *A Contemporary Rhetoric* has a section that points to "A New Kind of Argument . . . the Rogerian Approach."[1] Although it seems questionable whether the Rogerian approach can be viewed as a form of "argument" (if only because the rationale for the Rogerian method is to minimize both argument and strategy), the only serious challenge to this "new persuasion" does not question that Rogerian methods are, indeed, argument. Instead, Professor Andrea Lunsford contends that Carl Rogers the therapist and Aristotle the rhetorician are no more than variations on the same theme, so much so that if one looks hard enough, he will find what Rogers says in Aristotle's *Rhetoric*.[2] The burden of the present article is to demonstrate that to portray Rogers' method as a form of argument is to seriously misunderstand his intent and that, while Rogers and Aristotle are superficially similar, their differences are profound.

The differences between the Rogerian and Aristotelian approaches tell us something about a speaker's motivation and purpose, his attitude towards an audience, and how motivation and attitude shape discourse. In examining the differences between Rogers and Aristotle, we need not choose up sides (although Aristotle would prefer that we do so), but simply listen to both (a Rogerian type suggestion) and take from either what is appropriate in a given situation. Let me be more specific.

According to the authors of the "new" *Rhetorics,* the first step in using Rogerian argument is to convey to the other that he is understood. The purpose of this task is to induce the opponent to consider the persuader's position and become open to change so that the persuader may win the argument.[3] Is this Rogers' purpose? In *On Becoming a Person,* Rogers says that empathic understanding is possible provided that one avoids making evaluative statements or judgments, which avoidance allows the other person to accept responsibility and work out his own solutions.[4] Communication along these lines must thus convey that the speaker trusts the listener to make the right decision, that he recognizes that the listener is capable of making choices that make sense. Rogers asks, "Can I permit [the other person] to be what he is . . . or do I feel that he should follow my advice?"[5] Rogers answers "yes" to the first question because his goal is not to argue with the other person, but to maintain a continuing relationship through an unconditional acceptance of the other which will "promote the growth, development, maturity, improved functioning, [and] improved coping with life of the other."[6] In sum, the process which Rogers describes is not argument; Rogers does not speak of opponents or victory. The change is not some pre-determined position to which Rogers seeks assent; it is the removal of threat so that the other may grow and become capable of autonomously accepting responsibility and working out his own solutions.

Let us now consider whether the Rogerian goal of conveying to the other person that he is understood is "related closely to Aristotle's insistence that the rhetor must be able to argue on both sides of the question."[7] On the contrary, Aristotle's admonition to master either side of a question does not seem aimed at understanding. In fact, Aristotle makes it clear that the "other side" is "evil," so that the primary reason for mastering the wrong side is to know how to refute it:

> We must be able to employ persuasion, just as correct reasoning can be employed, on opposite sides of a question, not in order that we may in practice employ it in both ways (for we must not make people believe what is wrong), but in order that we may see clearly what the facts are . . . Nevertheless, the underlying facts do not lend themselves equally well to the contrary views.[8]

Aristotle's approach to "understanding," therefore, is that of a partisan anxious to achieve victory; the persuader characteristically seeks to influence belief or to have the audience adopt a specific course of action. What the persuader has to understand, then, is the nature of the competition: "For where there is competition, there is victory. That is why forensic pleading and debating contests are pleasant to those who are accustomed to them and have the capacity for them."[9] And this is the approach to victory:

> You should . . . make room in the minds of the audience for your coming speech; and this will be done by getting your opponent's speech out of the way. So attack that first—either the whole of it, or the most important, successful, or vulnerable points in it, and thus inspire confidence in what you have to say yourself.[10]

In short, the person who is to be "unconditionally accepted" is the speaker, *not* the adversary or the audience. And this "unconditional acceptance" must come about by the speaker's stifling criticism as quickly as possible. True, to achieve this end the Aristotelian speaker will make use of an audience's attitudes, prejudices, and premises. But Rogers very clearly rejects this strategic use of understanding when he deplores confirming the other in order to "reinforce certain types of words in the other . . . [If I do this] I tend to confirm him as an object—a basically mechanical, manipulable object."[11] Rogers opts for *understanding with* a person, an empathy that enables the speaker "to see the other's point of view," but which also places emphasis on "solving a problem rather than . . . attacking a person or group."[12] *Understanding with* a person avoids thoughts of competition and victory and manipulation of the other, whereas *understanding about* (Rogers' term) implies an attempt by the speaker to control the other person, to bring the other person to approve of what the speaker advocates. This objective Rogers explicitly eschews when he states, "I become less and less inclined to hurry in to fix things, to set goals, to mold people . . . I am much more content simply to be myself and to let another person be himself."[13] In sum, the Rogerian approach is tentative and cooperative and non-argumentative. By contrast, Aristotle is advising speakers who "know" the truth and who must struggle against adversaries who advocate the opposite of that truth.

The second step in the "Rogerian approach to argument" is to delineate the area within which the listener's position is valid.[14] Does Rogers suggest this strategy? Significantly, Rogers admonishes against any kind of evaluation, positive as well as negative. The purpose of listening to understand is to remove the threat of judgment.[15] However, ". . . a positive evaluation is as threatening . . . as a negative one, since to inform someone that he is good implies that you also have the right to tell him that he is bad."[16] This position would seem to preclude the delineation of the area within which a listener's position is valid because such delineation implies an evaluation.

Now let us turn to the critique of this step in Rogerian "argument." It does not deny that such delineation is valid Rogerian technique; rather, it affirms that such technique is "closely related to Aristotle's discussion of the enthymeme."[17] However, Rogers contends that if the speaker genuinely relates to the other's position, if the speaker can get within the listener's frame of reference, the speaker's "own comments will have to be drastically revised."[18] It is as though the speaker tries on someone else's shoes and discovers that they fit better than his own.

This kind of role-playing, however, is far from what Aristotle sees as the usefulness of the enthymeme. Rather than suggest to the Greek orator that he stand in someone else's sandals to test the fit, Aristotle encourages the orator to seek ways of *invalidating* the adversary's conclusions and to do so by employing premises acceptable to the audience, (not the adversary) that lead to opposite conclusions. Aristotle's interest is not in "delineating the area within which the listener's position is valid" but rather in choosing premises acceptable to the audience that make the speaker's *conclusions* valid. For example, were a speaker to argue with someone on whether all citizens should have an equal share of the nation's wealth, his position on the issue would determine which of two premises, both of which are acceptable to the audience, he would use: "[S]ometimes it may be argued that what all share is the better thing, since it is a dishonor not to share in it; at other times, that what none or few share is better, since it is rarer."[19] Aristotle urges, in other words, that the "validity" of a premise is correlated with whatever position the speaker is advocating. Unlike the Rogerian approach, the Aristotelian strategy is to understand what the audience is willing to accept rather than measure the validity of the audience's position. In fact, in the best of all worlds, the Aristotelian audience would have no "position"; rather, the audience would listen to the speaker and his adversary and then come to a decision. In such case, the speaker does not regard his adversary as a listener or the "other"; the adversary must be defeated and his case invalidated. This is simply not Rogerian.

A third area of imprecision in the "new" *Rhetorics* is that which presents the Rogerian method as an argumentative strategy appropriate to dyadic situations. Although Rogers' method was generated in two-person communication, the "new" *Rhetorics* stray far from Rogers' intent when they portray it as dyadic argument. This misapprehension can best be demonstrated by contrasting the way Aristotle, the "new" *Rhetorics,* and Rogers view the audience.

In the traditional framework the persuader sees those whom he seeks to influence as judges. "We may say, without qualification, that anyone is your judge whom you have to persuade."[20] Persuasion, then, demands that the listener assume *two* roles, that of listener and that of judge. This imposes on both speaker and listener the necessity of maintaining a distance between them. On the part of the speaker, the distance is maintained by means of concealment: "Rhetoric is perfect only when it perfectly conceals its own use. To be assured of effectiveness, a speaker must operate unilaterally upon his audience, and at the same time prevent it from seeing that he is acting unilaterally."[21] In other words, the speaker cannot be what Rogers calls "transparently real."[22] The speaker must control the situation, which means that he must keep a sufficient psychological distance from the listener so that the listener does not divert him from the position he is advocating.

At the same time, persuasion that is not resisted by the listener-judge simply is *not* persuasion. As Aristotle points out, one does not debate about the obvious, since the obvious is irresistible, and then persuasion is superfluous.[23] This implies that the distance the listener maintains from the speaker is based on the listner's resisting what the speaker is saying, both because the listener serves as opponent and judge of the speaker. Kenneth Burke calls this kind of distance "standoffishness," and he explains it this way: "Since the ultimate form of persuasion is composed of three elements (speaker, speech, and spoken-to), as regards the act of persuasion alone obviously you could not maintain this form except insofar as the plea remained unanswered. When the plea is answered, you have gone from persuasion to something else."[24] Granting that Burke is indulging in a certain amount of word-play, there is a significance to this semantic exercise. For an audience to judge a speaker's argument properly, it must not be "taken in" by the speaker lest a judgment be grounded in nonrelevant considerations. To the extent that the listener "stands apart" from the speaker, there is a better chance that the listener's evaluation of the speaker's position will be in line with objectively acceptable criteria.

This perspective is congruent with the advice in *Rhetoric: Discovery and Change* which states, "The writer induces his opponent to listen to his position, to understand it, and to see the truth in it, by demonstrating that he has done the same with the opponent's position."[25] What is here described is a persuasive stratagem by which the persuader paraphrases the other's argument for the purpose of inducing the listener to modify his position. He does not himself intend such modification, and this he must conceal. Thus, the attitude toward the audience found in the "new" *Rhetorics* coincides nicely with that found in Aristotle. However, is either viewpoint congruent with Rogers'?

By contrast, Rogers objects to maintaining a distance between speaker and listener, as he indicates in his comment on the relationship between therapist and patient: "We are afraid that if we let ourselves freely experience . . . positive feelings toward another we may be trapped by them. This may lead to demands on us, or we may be disappointed in our trust, and these outcomes we fear. So as a reaction we tend to build up distance between ourselves and others—aloofness, a 'professional' attitude, an impersonal relationship."[26] In other words, Rogers sees no justification for distance between speaker and listener because judgment regarding what one or the other is doing is not conducive to the understanding both should be seeking from each other.

A final attempt to reconcile Aristotle and Rogers is the claim that both are congruent in regard to the search for understanding and truth.[27] Rogers' emphasis is on understanding, cooperation, and truth-seeking, and it is intended to strengthen and maintain ongoing relationships—relationships that are subject to the danger of *mis*understanding. Rogers believes that misunderstanding is eliminated by minimizing threats, by avoiding opposition and controversy.

By contrast, Aristotle maximizes opposition as the ground for stimulating judges to make decisions. Moreover, the Aristotelian concept of "understanding" implies a consensus, based on the conflicting information available, that doubt exists as to the best course of action to take. The way to resolve this doubt is to have two antagonists fight it out before a group of judges, such struggle ideally providing the clearest and best case for either side of the question. Admittedly, Aristotle does not envision a verbal carnage, but his emphasis is on persuading judges, and communication must be shaped in light of that emphasis. At the end of the *Rhetoric*, in fact, Aristotle says, "I have done. You have heard me. The facts are before you. I ask for your judgment."[28] That last sentence would make Rogers unhappy.

What an exploration of Aristotle and Rogers will establish is that two perceptive and well-intentioned minds may see the same situation from different perspectives, with the result that each will formulate discourse based on his perspective. Rogers' perspective is grounded in trust and long-range goals. Aristotle's perspective accepts the human being as he is, acknowledging his strengths as well as his limitations; if there is any doubt about this, Aristotle's incisive and affecting passage on the various ages of man should be read.[29] But Aristotle's focus is on short-term goals, getting an audience to make a decision as quickly as possible in the awareness that to argue exhaustively may postpone the adoption of needed policies. The speaker's relationship to the audience, therefore, is ephemeral. In short, Rogers sees solutions to problems in terms of healthy relationships, and Aristotle solves problems with sharp arguments. Given the inherently ecumenical character of the reasonable mind, the best approach in any given situation is probably somewhere in between, and it is worth talking—or arguing—about.

Notes

1. See Richard E. Young, Alton L. Becker, Kenneth L. Pike, *Rhetoric: Discovery and Change* (New York: Harcourt, Brace, and World, 1970), pp. 274-282; Maxine Hairston, *A Contemporary Rhetoric* (Boston: Houghton Mifflin, 1974), p. 207. See also Maxine Hairston, "Carl Rogers's Alternative to Traditional Rhetoric," *College Composition and Communication* (December 1976), pp. 373-377.

2. "Aristotelian vs. Rogerian Argument: A Reassessment," *College Composition and Communication* (May 1979), pp. 146-151. Lunsford refers to Carl Rogers' *On Becoming a Person* (Boston: Houghton Mifflin, 1961). Rogers makes no mention of Aristotle in that book, but on page 333 he says: "I am indebted to Dr. S. I. Hayakawa, the semanticist, for pointing out that to carry on psychotherapy [by trying to see the other person's point of view] is to take a very real risk, and that courage is required." Since the number of references to Hayakawa are infinitely greater than the references to Aristotle, perhaps further research is needed to determine whether Rogers is a general semanticist.

3. Young, Becker, and Pike, op. cit., pp. 274-275.

4. Rogers, op. cit., pp. 54-55.

5. Ibid., p. 53.

6. Ibid., p. 40.

7. Lunsford, op. cit., p. 148.

8. *The Rhetoric of Aristotle,* trans. W. Rhys Roberts (New York: Random House, The Modern Library, 1954), pp. 1355a, 30.

9. Ibid., pp. 1371a, 5.

10. Ibid., pp. 1418b, 15.

11. Rogers, op. cit., pp. 55-56.

12. Ibid., p. 336.

13. Ibid., p. 21.

14. Young, Becker, and Pike, op. cit., p. 276; Hairston, op. cit., p. 210.

15. Rogers, op. cit., pp. 231-232.

16. Ibid., p. 55.

17. Lunsford, op. cit., p. 149.

18. Rogers, op. cit., p. 33.

19. Aristotle, op. cit., pp. 1365a, 5.

20. Ibid., pp. 1391a, 10.

21. Henry W. Johnstone, Jr., *Philosophy and Argument* (The Pennsylvania State University Press, 1959), p. 47.

22. Rogers, op. cit., p. 51.

23. Aristotle, *Nicomachean Ethics,* trans. Martin Ostwald (Indianapolis: Bobbs-Merrill Company, 1966), III, 3, line 20.

24. Kenneth Burke, *A Grammar of Motives and A Rhetoric of Motives* (New York: Meridian, 1962), p. 798.

25. Young, Becker, and Pike, op. cit., p. 283.

26. Rogers, op. cit., p. 52.

27. Lunsford, op. cit., p. 150.

28. Aristotle, op. cit., pp. 1420b, 35.

29. Ibid., pp. 1389b, 10.

James S. Baumlin (essay date winter 1987)

SOURCE: Baumlin, James S. "Persuasion, Rogerian Rhetoric, and Imaginative Play." *Rhetoric Society Quarterly* 17, no. 1 (winter 1987): 33-43.

[In the following essay, Baumlin explores the role of Rogerian group therapy in persuasive argument.]

Ideas can shape us, change us, and a change in beliefs enacts a change in self: witness, in an extreme literary case, Ebenezer Scrooge, or the man who admits, after years of self-deception, that he is an alcoholic. Yet teachers, preachers, politicians alike know that real change is rare and slow; we are, as a species, resistant to changes in our belief-structures. Reasons for this resistance are easy to find. When beliefs become reflexes, habits of thought engrained through a lifetime of unquestioned repetition, they become—as habits—hard indeed to change: so often we cling to a value or belief like the alcoholic to his bottle, afraid to question its effect on us, afraid of facing life without it. And logical appeal alone can never overcome such habit. There is yet another reason for this resistance, more subtle and more compelling: if we change with our beliefs, then surely our very identity, our sense of self, becomes threatened along with our belief-structures. For whatever security and certainty and stability we perceive in ourselves and in the world rests on the stability of our network or web of beliefs. Right or wrong, our beliefs give us our comforting sense of security in a stable, predictable, understandable world; they also contribute to our sense of a fixed, stable self.

We choose, therefore, to live in a Newtonian, indeed Platonic universe of fixed laws and stable phenomena—a universe of fixed identities. Need we wonder why? The alternative ontology, the universe described by the modern physicist Werner Heisenberg—or, for that matter, the ancient Sophist Gorgias—denies certainty and fixture: things change. And people change. And there is, for most of us, anxiety in such a recognition, a threat to our identities. Yet we have experienced the sad results when beliefs clash in their attempt to dominate, indeed define a "singular" reality: the more powerful ideology tyrannizes over the rest,

treating them all rather as competitors for defining a single and stable reality than as collaborators in fashioning a world of greater complexity and potentiality. We fight for our beliefs as if our lives were at stake (and, since we define ourselves in accordance with our beliefs, in this real sense they are). We fight because in this arena we have not yet learned to play—I will explain this in later paragraphs—and we fight because we have forgotten that we *can* change ourselves, change each other, grow towards each other rather than apart. In this arena of beliefs and values, we can and should enjoy the capacity, at least, of persuading and being persuaded.

1

Speakers and audience alike rarely exercise their capacity for persuasion. Most speakers accept the resistance of an opposing audience as given, and changing the beliefs of such an audience is, in fact, rarely their goal. Many arguments do not even *attempt* to persuade but seek only to *confirm* an audience's adherence to beliefs they already hold. The strongest pleas often serve only to strengthen the believers—or alienate and anger more fully those who oppose. The strongest pleas may move our emotions and our wills to action (or reaction, if opposed); but rarely do they change us, converting those of no prior belief. This process of confirming an audience is not useless, of course. Most of us, on most issues, show a bored lack of concern, or show a bland, "intellectual" sort of adherence to a value or issue; we may agree "in principle" with philanthropy, but ignore the poverty in our midst, oppose apartheid "in principle" but not work toward its dismantling. Most of us, on most issues, at most times, live our lives in a passive state of disinterest toward issues, giving a numb sort of "yea" or "nay"—for we do not see our identities fully engaged and committed (or, conversely, threatened). And passive adherence must be turned to *acts,* involve our emotions and will—our whole self—in our beliefs. Catholicism provides an analogy: once one is baptized, one must be comfirmed in the faith. Confirmation, then, serves an important purpose for the speaker: to move a convinced audience toward action. But how can a speaker succeed when his goal is to change minds?

If there is *confirmatio,* where, in our discourse, can there be *conversio*—literally, the change in belief, change in self? Certainly it cannot occur in a model for discourse that envisions only the three audience responses of opposition, disinterest, and identification. Note, however, the continuum these responses form. Separating opposition from identification is disinterest, the refusal to engage or identify with an issue; one might not disagree with a belief or value here as much as simply ignore it. If one does disagree, it is a disagreement of words—and not of the heart; a person reacting in disinterest typically says "No; but I don't care." Conversely, a person may agree with an argument, but not translate this agreement into a personal commitment or action. In either case, an emotional involvement is lacking. Emotional involvement occurs, rather, on the extreme ends of this continuum, in opposition and in identification. Here the whole man—mind, emotions, and will—is engaged in the argument and indeed *identifies itself* with the issue at hand. The world-views of speaker and audience become one: Kenneth Burke is right in equating persuasion with identification. Opposition, on the other hand, defines the self of the audience in its difference from the speaker's values and world-view. The audience's distinctive identity is asserted and preserved in its rejection of the speaker's argument.

The above model, though simplistic to the point of brashness, is a fairly traditional version of audience response. Its strength, if it has any, is that it observes two distinct features of this response: the extent of emotional engagement, and the way that the self is defined, either by identification with or in opposition to another's worldview. In each case, however, the self described by this model is fixed and singular, either this or that, and there seems to be no mechanism by which the self of the audience can be transformed from one of difference (or opposition) to one of identification with the speaker's world-view. Confirmation of belief remains possible—for the direction of movement in this traditional model is toward strengthened belief or opposition (and therefore towards an equal strengthening of one's self-identity). But in such a model the *direction* of one's belief appears unchangeable. Disinterest cannot mediate between the two poles of opposition and identification: it forms a chasm against rather than a bridge for change. True persuasion, in this particular model of audience response, is an impossibility.

There is another possible response, however, one in which the audience says—not "I agree" or "I disagree" (or "I don't care"), but, rather, "I understand." Understanding (or imaginative play, as I shall soon call it) turns this trinity into a quaternity of responses, offering an alternative that can in fact *mediate* between opposition and identification—that can become a mechanism, in other words, for change or true persuasion. Psychologist Carl Rogers, who was the first to explore the role of sympathetic understanding in persuasion, suggests that "the major barrier to mutual interpersonal communication is our very natural tendency to judge, to evaluate, to approve or disapprove, the statement of the other person" (284). Of course we evaluate and approve (or reject) another's discourse in comparison with our own world-view. But if we foster in ourselves an attitude of understanding, we will, according to Rogers, "see the expressed idea and attitude from the other person's point of view . . . sense how it feels to him . . . achieve his frame of reference in regard to the thing he is talking about" (285). As a result of such an attitude we "will find the emotion going out of the discussion, the differences being reduced, and those differences which remain being of a rational and understandable sort" (286). Paul Bator elaborates: "a necessary correlate of acceptance (of another's view) is understanding, an understanding which implies that the listener accepts the views of the speaker without knowing cognitively what will result."

> Such understanding, in turn, encourages the speaker to explore untried avenues of exchange. Rogers explains: "Acceptance does not mean much until it involves un-

derstanding. It is only as I *understand* the feelings and thoughts which seem so horrible to you, or so weak, or so sentimental, or so bizarre—it is only as I see them as you see them, and accept them and you, that you feel really free to explore all the hidden nooks and frightening crannies of your inner and often buried experience."

(428-29)

The Rogerian strategy, in which participants in a discussion collaborate to find areas of shared experience, thus allows speaker and audience to open up their worlds to each other; and in this attempt at mutual understanding there is the *possibility*, at least, of persuasion. For in this state of sympathetic understanding we recognize both the *multiplicity* of world-views and our *freedom* to choose among them—either to retain our old or take a new.

To complete the model, then, and allow for the possibility of change in an audience, we must place as an alternative to disinterest and opposition the Rogerian attitude of receptive, sympathetic understanding. Given recent interest in Rogerian rhetoric, it should not be surprising to find understanding at the heart of any modern description of persuasion; through the rest of this essay, though, I shall explore some epistemological implications of Rogerian argument that have gone largely unnoticed by rhetorical theorists. For understanding, as I shall argue, can be achieved only in a world-view that conceives of self and reality as fluid and potentially multiple. And understanding demands not only a collaborative, as opposed to a combative or manipulative, rhetoric: it demands a rhetoric that is essentially playful or ludic in nature. Understanding, then, is possible only in a world of indeterminacy (and therefore of infinite potentiality), where the true *homo rhetoricus* is recognized as *homo ludens*. Thus, I would call understanding a realm of plural selves or identities. For we achieve this attitude when we sympathize with another's beliefs and world-view—when we role-play, in a sense, the life and values of another person. In a spirit of play and with suspended emotions we become that other person, taking on his value-system and trying out his world. Understanding requires, therefore, a temporary negation or effacement of self: we cease being only ourselves, cease reacting and thinking in ways we have become habituated to, and give ourselves over to an alien, often chaotic, inevitably unstable mixture of interests, values, desires. We mix another's values—we mix another's world—with our own. And out of the chaos we may see patterns of behavior and belief emerge that we can give fresh and perhaps full assent to. These beliefs were not originally our own; the self that emerges within these new patterns was not originally us—self invents itself anew in the free play of worlds.

Two of the above propositions—that rhetoric is a form of imaginative play, and that human personality consists of a dynamic multiplicity of selves—received not their first but surely their strongest formulation by Richard Lanham:

> Rhetorical man is an actor; his reality public, dramatic. His sense of identity, his self, depends on the reassurance of daily histrionic reenactment. He is thus cen-

tered in time and concrete local event. The lowest common denominator of his life is a social situation. And his motivations must be characteristically ludic, agonistic. He thinks first of winning, of mastering the rules the current game enforces. He assumes a natural agility in changing orientations. . . . he has dwelt not in a single value-structure but in several. He is thus committed to no single construction of the world; much rather, to prevailing at the game at hand.

(4)

The multiplicity of value-structures and indeed of worlds is the *sine qua non* of persuasion, and indeed of rhetoric as a mode-of-thinking and a way-of-living. Human values, and human roles, change—and rhetoric itself is the effecting of change through language. This multiplicity of perspectives, and the ludic nature of rhetoric, are aspects of Lanham's thesis which I wholeheartedly espouse. But I hope to extend his thesis in a few significant ways. Lanham focuses almost exclusively on the speaker's ludic activity, ignoring the full impact of rhetorical play on audience. In addition, he emphasizes the antagonism and combativeness of rhetoric—elements that work, as I have argued, to *confirm* audience beliefs, but which cannot cause change. Actual persuasion occurs not through combat with an audience but through *collaboration* (though *collusion,* foregrounding *lusus* or play, is perhaps the more accurate term); as such, the notion of imaginative play can explain the workings of both Rogerian therapy and rhetorical persuasion. Finally, I would like to suggest an alternative to Lanham's model of human personality, which posits a number of dramatic, "rhetorical" selves arrayed around a serious, "central" self. I would argue (and I suspect Lanham would ultimately agree) that the central self, which each of us looks toward as the stable, unchanging core of our personality, is as much a "rhetorical" invention as the social roles/selves arrayed around it. The perceived stability and fixture of our central self becomes, in other words, an act of will, and not a part or an expression of our essence. A sense of fixed self provides us with a secure identity and with our sense of continuity, but this fixture and stability is nevertheless willed into existence—invented and maintained through patterns of language-use and general behavior. As such the central self, our sense of a fixed identity, becomes susceptible to rhetoric, capable of change. The following paragraphs will show debts to others besides Lanham, to literary theorists (particularly in reader-response criticism) and contemporary hermeneuticians. This is itself worth noting: in past decades, the most exciting research into audience-response has come not from students of rhetoric but from students of literature, philosophy, psychology. Rhetoric—traditionally the study of response and change—needs still to catch up with these disciplines.

2

In a recent *PMLA* article Marshall W. Alcorn and Mark Bracher survey critics "who argue that reading literature can influence if not actually mold the structure of the reader's self." They cite Georges Poulet on the idea that when one reads a text, "one's own identity is set aside and the text constitutes a new subjectivity within oneself." They quote Wolfgang Iser: "if reading removes the subject-object division that constitutes all perception, it follows that the reader will be 'occupied' by the thoughts of the author, and these in turn will cause the drawing of new 'boundaries.' . . . Every text we read draws a different boundary within our personality, so that the virtual background (the real 'me') will take on a different form, according to the theme of the text concerned" (342). We need simply add that this re-drawing of psychic boundaries can result from an interaction with any kind of discourse—surely with persuasive discourse—and that hearing, as well as reading, can have this effect. But we must still ask ourselves: what allows for this re-experiencing, this re-creating of self—this meeting and intermixture of two worlds? Doesn't the very admission of alternative worlds confirm Heisenberg's principle of indeterminacy—and wouldn't this, in turn, foster the anxiety and insecurity that we all, very humanly, try at all costs to avoid in our lives? The realm of understanding is, after all, a realm of *potentiality,* and therefore of *uncertainty*: more than one course of action is admitted in understanding, more than one set of values—and this necessarily introduces contradiction, confusion. Indeed the realm of understanding (that is, of freely imagining and "trying on" another's beliefs) fosters at the same time a state of doubt (that is, of questioning the invincibility or even validity of one's own previously-held world-view). Put otherwise, to understand—to imagine freely another's experience and to admit its validity and truth and goodness—is, in some degree, to doubt the self and its seemingly secure world-view. So if understanding breeds, at the same time, uncertainty, why do we not simultaneously feel threat and insecurity?—and why shouldn't an audience's opposition follow, therefore, from such a threat to identity?

A possible answer to such questions, one developed progressively by J. Huizinga, Hans-Georg Gadamer, and Richard Lanham, is that sympathetic understanding and persuasion result from imaginative play, and that by appealing vividly and directly to the imagination—by making one's case within the playground of the audience's mind—a speaker can control, even reduce the perception of threat. Perhaps rhetoric is best explained as a mental activity of "playing man" or *homo ludens,* as J. Huizinga describes our species. "Play," Huizinga notes, "creates order, *is* order. Into an imperfect world and into the confusion of life it brings a temporary, a limited perfection" (10). Play, in other words, is world-building, and allows for imaginative transport out of one's self "without, however, wholly losing consciousness of 'ordinary reality.'" Thus the playing child's—and I would add the rhetorician's—representation of a game-world "is not so much a sham-reality as a realization in appearance: 'imagination' in the original sense of the word" (14). Most significant, Huizinga observes that playing together fosters *identification*:

> A play-community generally tends to become permanent even after the game is over. . . . the feeling of being "apart together" in an exceptional situation, of shar-

ing something important, of mutually withdrawing from the rest of the world and rejecting the usual norms, retains its magic beyond the duration of the individual game.

(12)

Isn't this description of imaginative play—of voluntary imaginative activity taking place within prescribed limits of time and place, apart from the world but genuinely affecting the spirit of the participants—a description also of Rogerian and indeed of most methods of psychotherapy? Doesn't therapy allow one to "play out" otherwise threatening conflicts within the secure confines of a "game situation" (i.e., the analytic session)? Alcorn and Bracher have made this very claim for literature, which—like psychotherapy—can "promote greater tolerance of unfamiliar and potentially traumatic experiences. Meissner observes that experiencing potentially overwhelming emotions in a safe and supportive context 'can have an effect similar to desensitization, so that the patient is much better able to tolerate these affective experiences and to integrate them with the rest of his experiential life'" (344-45). Though their evidence comes from W. W. Meissner rather than Carl Rogers, the implication is the same: the controlled, game situation of therapy, like other forms of imaginative play, offers a "safe and supportive context" for exploring the "unfamiliar and potentially traumatic." And by freeing the patient from fear and habitual patterns of response, such play gives the patient freedom to accept what was once unfamiliar and perhaps even threatening, and to integrate it into the self.

Whether it occurs from our interaction with literature or with other forms of discourse—including the dialogue of psychotherapy—imaginative play reduces the threat we feel when facing alternatives; it does not, however, reduce the seriousness or the risk involved in the choices themselves. Paradoxically, play emphasizes the necessity of choice even as it affirms our freedom to choose among alternatives. As Hans-Georg Gadamer writes, a person engaged in the play of imagination

> still has the freedom to decide one way or the other, for one or the other possibility. On the other hand this freedom is not without danger. Rather the game itself is a risk for the player. One can only play with serious possibilities. This means obviously that one may become so engrossed in them that they, as it were, outplay one and prevail over one. The attraction of the game, which it exercises on the player, lies in this risk.

(95)

The risk Gadamer speaks of is that game can become actuality, that choices made in play can become choices of life. The game can outplay us. In fact we do not play the game: the game plays us, taking over our world, making its rules of decision and conduct our own. And as Gadamer suggests, reading and response to literature enacts just such a serious game: "the work of art has its true being in the fact that it becomes an experience changing the person experiencing it" (92).

Once again, isn't this description of imaginative play also a description of rhetoric's impact upon an audience? Surely the first great rhetoricians of antiquity, Gorgias and the Sophists who followed him, recognized both the existence of a manifold reality and the ludic nature of persuasive speech. As Gorgias asserts in his "Encomium to Helen," speech "has the power to put an end to fear, to remove grief, to instill joy and increase pity" (8); what gives speech such power over an audience is its ability to create mental images—to substitute images in the mind for palpable phenomena—and in this way give imaginative reality to that which is as yet only possible. Play, being nonthreatening, allows the potential and hypothetical to come to temporary imaginative life in the mind of the audience. That which is imagined *is* only potential; it is up to the audience to give life to a thought—to embody a belief or adopt a course of action, ultimately, as its own. That which is "unthinkable" or perhaps even threatening to the rigidly-defined, single self poses no danger to a fluid self engaged in imaginative play; that which one imagines *is,* once again, only *potential*—a vain bubble if rejected, an exciting prospect if we give it our assent. And we can explore issues more courageously in our imaginations than we are willing to do in the actions and thoughts of our daily lives. Thoughts freely and imaginatively pursued involve little threat, then, to the thinker—much less, at any rate, than the muzzle of a gun or a picket line, other more palpable, though generally failed means of persuasion. The classical rhetorical concept of *enargeia,* which Chaim Perelman resuscitated in the notion of "presence," is thus instrumental in establishing an attitude of understanding: potentially new worlds, potentially new roles—potentially new selves—are given imaginative presence in the mind of the audience, revealing for examination and choice a new realm of experience. Again, the logic of discourse may *convince;* yet the extent to which discourse *invites such imaginative participation* and mixing of worlds will determine its success or failure as *persuasion.*

Like poetry, persuasive discourse can rely heavily on the compelling image to draw our imaginations into new worlds and new roles. It does not surprise, then, that the histories of rhetoric and poetry have been intertwined since antiquity. Gorgias, for example, looked upon his speeches as prose-poems, and both Isocrates and Cicero claimed a close kinship between the orator and poet. Undoubtedly, that kinship tie is their mutual grounding in imaginative play. For *poesis,* as Huizinga suggests, "is a play-function. It proceeds within the playground of the mind, in a world of its own which the mind creates for it. There things have a very different physiognomy from the one they wear in 'ordinary life,' and are bound by ties other than those of logic and causality" (119). Poetry, therefore, and fiction are among the most powerful tools in creating new worlds, and inviting understanding; so much so that there are, quite possibly, elements of *poesis* (and certainly of *enargeia*) in all truly persuasive discourse. Indeed the distinctions made throughout this essay between "literature" and "persuasive discourse" prove more apparent than real: the literary response, like the response to persuasion, rests squarely on imaginative play.

3

Finally, we exercise our freedom when participating in another's discourse—for otherwise we respond with disinterest or opposition, boredom or indignation. The realm of imaginative play, then, allows us to maintain our freedom while we explore new roles. More importantly, it is only in the realm of imaginative play, of understanding, that we actually make choices about who we shall be. In a state either of opposition or of identification the self is single and fully, indeed rigidly, defined. Only in a state of play, of unlimited potentiality, is the self equally fluid and changeable. In addition habit, emotion, and previous structures of belief—those elements of personality that sustain our illusion of a single, fixed self—become constraints upon our freedom, constraints upon our ability to create a new self and a new world to live in. Only in a world of play can such constraints be thrown off. Paradoxically, then, in our recognition of and sympathy toward the other we realize our own freedom to change—that is, to re-create our selves along new lines. The value of discourse itself lies ultimately in this ability to lead us into a realm of potentiality and of fluid, changeable identity, where we can actualize the limitless potential that man has for self-creation. I am arguing, in fine, that persuasion is impossible in any model of discourse that views the self as a single, fixed entity. This, rather, is persuasion: to open up a new world to the imagination of an audience and to free the audience from rigid structures of habit and belief. And while persuasion has often been connected with manipulation and coersion, it should in fact *return freedom* to an audience; it should return to them the ability to invent themselves and assume responsibility for creating their selves and their world.

Reference

Alcorn, Marshall W., and Mark Bracher, "Literature, Psychoanalysis, and the Re-Formation of the Self: A New Direction for Reader-Response Theory." *PMLA* 100 (1985), 342-54.

Bator, Paul. "Aristotelian and Rogerian Rhetoric." *College Composition and Communication* 31 (1980), 427-32.

Burke, Kenneth. *A Rhetoric of Motives.* Englewood Cliffs, NJ: Prentice-Hall, 1950.

Gadamer, Hans-Georg. *Truth and Method.* New York: Seabury Press, 1975.

Gorgias. "Encomium of Helen." In *The Older Sophists.* Ed. Rosamund Kent Sprague. Columbia: University of South Carolina Press, 1972.

Heisenberg, Werner. *Physics and Philosophy: The Revolution in Modern Science.* New York: Harper and Brothers, 1958.

Huizinga, J. *Homo Ludens: A Study of the Play-Element in Culture.* Boston: The Beacon Press, 1950.

Lanham, Richard. *The Motives of Eloquence: Literary Rhetoric in the Renaissance.* New Haven: Yale University Press, 1976.

Perelman, Chaim, and L. Olbrechts-Tyteca. *The New Rhetoric.* Notre Dame: University of Notre Dame Press, 1971.

Rogers, Carl. "Communication: Its Blocking and Facilitation." In Richard E. Young, Alton L. Becker, and Kenneth L. Pike, *Rhetoric: Discovery and Change.* New York: Harcourt, Brace, and World, 1970, pp. 284-89.

Wayne Pounds (essay date winter 1987)

SOURCE: Pounds, Wayne. "The Context of No Context: A Burkean Critique of Rogerian Argument." *Rhetoric Society Quarterly* 17, no. 1 (winter 1987): 45-59.

[*In the following essay, Pounds presents a critique of the Rogerian rhetoric of love using Kenneth Burke's rhetoric of killing.*]

> But there is one aspect of the rhetorical tradition that so far as I can tell remains quite dead—its focus on public discourse. . . . a rhetoric is defined not just by its theory, but by the sorts of rhetorical problems it gives most emphasis to.[1]
>
> —S. M. Halloran

My title refers to the problem of idealism in contemporary rhetoric, and by "idealism" I mean ideas abstracted from the social matrix, which is always conflictive. This lack of social-historical context is what George Trow, in his critique of the vacuous human image created by corporate advertising, calls "the context of no context."[2] Idealism of this sort reduces student and teacher alike to autonomous subjectivities operating in seeming omnipotence in personal dimensions but rendered impotent to deal with objectivity, the socio-economic dimensions of conflict. The problem is posed most accessibly by Rogerian argument and student-centered teaching approaches, which are all the more insidious in that they appeal to the naive good will of the liberal teacher. For evidence, I take the last of a series of seven essays on Rogerian argument which appeared between 1976 and 1985.[3] I choose this essay because it culminates the series, summing up the previous work and asserting the limits of Rogerian strategies with the hope of transcending them. It tries to escape the gravitational field of argument by igniting the booster rocket of an intensified subjectivity, but it engineers only a flight into an ahistorical inane. The failure speaks more loudly than anything the essay says and reveals the inherent flaws of its philosophical basis.

To begin with, let the reader contrast two examples of rhetorical practice, one which appears to be a rhetoric of killing, the other which calls itself a rhetoric of love. Rhetor 1 takes up the case of "an old poet, libertarian and regicide, blind fallen on evil days," who "in sullen warlike verse celebrates Samson." Rhetor 1 considers, among the "uses to which *Samson Agonistes* was put, the poet's identification with a blind giant who slew himself in slaying enemies of the Lord. Identification . . . allows the poet a ritualistic kind of historiography in which, by allusion to a Biblical story, he can foretell the triumph of his vanquished faction. . . . Seen from this point of view, then," says Rhetor 1, "an imagery of slaying . . . is to be considered merely as a special case of identification. Or otherwise put: the imagery of slaying is a special case of transformation, and transformation involves the ideas and imagery of *identification*" (RM 3, 19-20).[4]

Rhetor 2 has written an essay whose title I shorten to "Rhetoric as Love." He takes up the case of "two nations" who "confront each other in . . . a shocked and total inability to understand or even to recognize each other, as in continuing conflicts between the United States and Russia," and he suggests as a possible resolution that "we change the way we talk about argument." "Argument," says Rhetor 2, "is emergence toward the other . . . , an untiring stretch toward the other, a reach toward enfolding the other. . . . How does this happen? Better, how can it happen? It can happen if we learn to love before we disagree."[5]

You will have observed that Rhetor 1, who is obviously Kenneth Burke, takes a case of conflict, killing, and finds that through a process of persuasion, which he calls identification, it works through to a resolution. Burke's concept is dialectical, involving an interplay of the opposites "identification" and "division." He writes, "one need not scrutinize the concept of 'identification' very sharply to see, implied in it at every turn, its ironic counterpart: division. Rhetoric is concerned with the state of Babel after the Fall" (RM 23). Rhetor 2, whom I take as the figure of the Rogerian rhetorician and therefore denominate Professor Fog, takes an even more extreme example of conflict, the threat of war, and in effect denies all conflict by asserting the priority of love. "Love," which according to Burke should be a dialectical term, since it has a clear opposite, is treated instead as a positive term, a simple concrete noun like "apple" (PLF 93-95n.7). In Professor Fog's blanket usage the word "love" functions to conceal the existence of its opposite.

Frank Lentricchia has recently argued that Burke's contribution has been to rescue the vexed notion of ideology for use in "rhetoric, the literary, and the media," or what Burke calls "adult education in America."[6] Though the diffuseness of Burke's arguments and his baroque terminology have made him famous for unwieldiness, in the three books I am primarily using here, chiefly *A Rhetoric of Motives* and to a lesser extent *A Grammar of Motives* and *The Philosophy of Literary Form,* functional, well-shaped tools lie at hand. In employing them to analyze the social meaning of Rogerian rhetoric, my interest includes not only Professor Fog but the uses of Burke for ideological analysis.

Though the focus here is on Rogerian rhetoric and limited to an examination of one representative text, I mean the

argument to have wider implications. The reader should remember Richard Ohmann's 1976 critique of the reduced figure of the student in our standard rhetoric textbooks. In *English in America* Ohmann showed that with few exceptions the student of our textbooks was a figure without history, society, or limiting context. There is no difference between the forlorn vapor Ohmann describes and the figure of the student in Rogerian treatment. From the standpoint of theory, the model of this idealism is the commodity structure, as Lukacs pointed out sixty years ago:

> It is no accident that Marx should have begun with an analysis of commodities when, in the two great works of his mature period, he set out to portray capitalist society in its totality and to lay bare its fundamental nature. . . . the structure of commodity-relations [can] be made to yield a model of all the objective forms of bourgeois society together with all the subjective forms corresponding to them. . . .
>
> The essence of commodity-structure has often been pointed out. Its basis is that a relation between people takes on the character of a thing and thus acquires a "phantom objectivity," an autonomy that seems so strictly rational and all-embracing as to conceal every trace of its fundamental nature: the relation between people.[7]

The fundamental problem of idealism, Lukacs argues, the dualistic separation of subject and object, has its prototype in the structure of commodities, in which products appear as objects divorced from the workers who produce them. In current composition pedagogy in the United States, the rhetoric textbook and Rogerian argument join with modern advertising in the commodification of the student, proliferating an idealized image devoid of content and context.[8]

In using Burke to talk about Rogerian rhetoric, three terms suffice: *transformation, identification,* and *representation.* These terms are a subset of a fourth term, *symbolic action,* which is introduced in *The Philosophy of Literary Form* in a familiar passage: "poetry, or any verbal act, is to be considered as 'symbolic action.'" In introducing the phrase Burke emphasizes "action" over "symbolic" and is careful to disassociate his concept from any sense of "symbolic" which would imply the ineffectiveness of symbolic action. Before proceeding, it may help to explain the three terms and link them together syntactically. The formula produced may lose a degree of Burke's complexity, but it should gain a corresponding degree of utility, demonstrating that this section of Burke's terminology may readily be appropriated for practical criticism.

Transformation, the first term, is simply a way of talking about the effect of the text on the reader. Transformation does its work through *identification.* The latter term is frequently taken to mean "persuasion" but Burke is clear that he means "identification" as a complement to (not a substitute for) "persuasion" in order to "develop [his] subject beyond the traditional bounds of rhetoric" into the contested "area of expression that is not wholly deliberate, yet not wholly unconscious" (RM xiii), the contested terrain otherwise known as ideology. Burke mentions specifically his reading of Marx's *The German Ideology* as the source of his dissatisfaction with the limits of the older term "persuasion."[9]

Transformation works through identification, and it also works through *representation*. This last term is most easily understandable as the figure of synecdoche, a trope for the part-whole relationship. The coercive power of representation is that any representation makes a claim that some part stands for the whole. Frank Lentricchia has traced the problematic nature of representation back to the *Poetics* of Aristotle, in which "the proper representation of character, its 'necessary' and 'probable' mimesis according to the dictates of human nature, is stipulated by bringing forth the examples of women and slaves," the one said to be inferior by nature and the other, by the same standard, said to be shiftless. "Aristotle is saying that if you would represent women and slaves in a fashion that would satisfy the conditions of human nature, if you want to persuade reason's tribunal, philosophy itself, then you must not give them the qualities appropriate only to a free male."[10] Conversely, if you want to represent free males you must ignore the qualities of women and slaves. For Burke, "representation" is a sign of the inseparability of the aesthetic and the political; the aesthetic is always involved with political power. Burke says, it is "no mere accident of language that we use the same word for sensory, artistic, and political representation" (PLF 23).

Here then, in capsule, is the simplified Burkean formula I propose: Transformation works ultimately through identification. It works to produce, among other things, representations. The process of this work, or production, is symbolic action.

Transformation works ultimately through identification, but it works mediately through ambiguity or ambiguous terms. "It is in the areas of ambiguity that transformations take place," says Burke; "in fact, without such areas, transformation would be impossible" (GM xix). Ambiguity may function constructively or viciously. "What we want," says Burke, "is not terms that avoid ambiguity, but terms that clearly reveal the strategic spots at which ambiguities necessarily arise" (GM xviii). Such, it seems reasonable to assume, are Burke's own terms, including those I am employing here. The vicious use of ambiguity is for a mystifying or ideological persuasion, which operates by occluding the opposite of any dialectical term so that the term is no longer dialectical but positive or monological.

Two such terms, "love" and "history," call attention to themselves in Prof. Fog's essay. Taken as a pair, the terms pose the contrasting pairs "subject" and "object," or, as Burke formulates it, "psychology" and "economics" (PLF 263). Each of Fog's terms is in itself dialectical. Love is the simplest kind of dialectical term, defined by its opposite, but it has already been noticed that in Prof. Fog's essay the dialectical playing field of love-hate is covered over by the monolithic use of the term "love." This is not

to say that there is no notion of conflict in his essay. It is there—indeed it provides the basis for his assertion of the limits of Rogerian argument—but it is stripped of all public, social reference and reduced to purely personal dimensions.

Fog, arguing for the limits of Rogerian argument, says that it cannot deal with conflict, and he quotes an earlier writer in the series of essays on Rogerian argument who says that Rogerian strategy is effective when students "encounter non-adversary writing situations" (22).[11] Another writer in the series included racial and sexual conflict in her 1976 formulation of the fields of Rogerian effectiveness, but, as if in recognition of similar limits, she has dropped the reference to "racial and sexual matters" from the latest edition of her textbook.[12] Fog sees his own contribution as going beyond Rogerian limits to tell the arguer how to deal with situations that are adversarial or conflictive.

As examples of conflict, Fog mentions the pro-life movement, farm subsidy issues, and war between Middle Eastern "tribes." But the meaning of these issues is determined by the way he defines conflict: "I mean . . . the kind of setting in which contention generates that flushed, feverish, quaky, shaky, angry, scared, hurt, shocked, disappointed, alarmed, outraged, even terrified condition I have mentioned" (25). The socio-economic dimensions of the conflicts have disappeared; conflict is confined within the individual organism and is perceived as psychosomatic reactions.

Rogers, to whom Fog confesses himself "much indebted" (Fog 23), makes his presence felt here, for these hypothalmic responses are reactions to what Rogers calls "threat"—that which calls individual identity into question. Thus, in the context of no context, public, social conflict is immediately reduced to two red-faced people each absorbed in his or her psychosomatic reactions.

If "love," rightly considered, is a simple dialectical term, "history" is a complex one, not defined by a simple opposite but containing within it a multitude of oppositions: past and present, present and future, subject and object, personal and public. Here a supplementary definition from Burke is helpful: dialectical terms "refer to *ideas* rather than to *things*. Hence they are more concerned with *action* and *attitude* than with *perception* . . ." (RM 185). Burke connects ideas to actions, a move directly counter to Fog's formula: "argument is not something *to present* or *to display*. It is something *to be*. It is what we *are* . . ." (Fog 26). What happens to history in Rogerian argument? It becomes personal history, and objective or public history becomes impossible. Fog begins his essay by asserting that we are "All authors, to be sure, we are more particularly narrators, historians, tale-tellers. . . . None of us lives without a history; each of us is a narrative" (16). History is personal history, the narrative of a person's life, and each of us has one. As to "an objective, externally verifiable history," it "is not possible anywhere" (17).

The critical reader may well wonder what this last sentence means. On the one hand, and perhaps this is Fog's intention, it might seem to be the familiar hermeneutical assertion that we are always involved in interpretation. But in the context of no context, where we autonomous agent-subjects are always, as Fog says, "inventing the narratives that are our lives" (17), there is no subject-object dialectic and thus no constraints to prevent subjectivity from taking over the whole discursive field. He cites the following passage, supposedly from the historian Gertrude Himmelfarb:

> Whatever "truth or validity" adheres to history . . . does not derive, as the conventional historian might assume, from an "objective" world, a world of past events waiting to be discovered and reconstructed by the historian. For there is no objective world, no historical events independent of the experience of the historian, no events or facts which are not also ideas.

(28)

According to Fog, he is quoting Himmelfarb from her essay "Supposing History Is a Woman—What Then?" But this quotation, asserting the impossibility of history, does not represent Himmelfarb at all; rather, it is her paraphrase of the philosopher-historian Michael Oakeshott, whose view of history she is attacking. The thesis that "whatever 'truth or validity' adheres to history . . . does not derive . . . from an 'objective' world" is Oakeshott's, and Himmelfarb criticizes it for its "inhibiting effect" on the practice of writing history.[13] If Oakeshott's thesis makes history writing impossible, as Himmelfarb argues, the rhetoric of Fog blankets the abyss with an impenetrable euphoria in which each person becomes the unconstrained historian. "We are always," Fog says, "inventing the narratives that are our lives" (Fog 17), but he does not recognize at what cost. Lukacs argues that when the values of the self "draw their justification only from the fact of having been subjectively experienced," the price of "this immoderate elevation of the subject" is the "abandonment of any claim to participation in the shaping of the outside world."[14]

"We are always . . . inventing the narratives that are our lives," says Fog. He means the word "invention" first of all in its rhetorical sense, but in the context of no context invention becomes a solipsistic omnipotence. Invention, says Fog, first opens us to the other. In the Rogerian scenario, however, the other is the empathetic "congruent" listener—not an adversary or opponent. Invention is thus free to expand outward like a released gas and envelops the world of the other. Fog pursues, "Beyond any speaker's bound inventive world lies another: there lie the riches of creation, the great, unbounded possible universe of invention. All time is there, past, present, and future" (29). The language images the bourgeois subject as the original cornucopia, an unbounded plentitude whose omnipotence encompasses "past, present, and future," collapsing them into an eternally present now. This fantasy of the omnipotent ego is the extreme of idealism. To get a fix on our position in this weird space it may be sufficient to recall a famous text from the opposed tradition: "Men make their own history, but they do not make it just as they please; they do not make it under circumstances chosen by themselves, but under circumstances directly encountered, given, and transmitted from the past."[15]

To return to Burke's term "transformation," in Fog's essay we the readers are transformed or acted upon by means of the ambiguous terms "love" and "history." In the familiar pattern of our cultural schizophrenia, we are moved to accept an illusory subjective omnipotence, which has the effect of reconciling us to our real objective impotence. Transformations, I said, work mediately through ambiguity and ultimately through—the second term to be highlighted here—identification. In Fog's essay both the reader and the author are identified with an undifferentiated "we." How do we, the actual readers of Fog, identify this "we"? (Note the useful ambiguity of the word "identify": as unresisting readers, we are likely to make an identification *with*; as resisting or critical readers we may make an identification *of*. That is, we may identify—in the sense of find out—the hidden persuasion of identification.)[16]

The "we" in Fog, I have already implied, is unitary and homogeneous. It has two variant terms, "I" and "the arguer," neither of which leaves any streak in the uniform vanilla of "we." "I" is the voice of sentimental reason—reason in the empathetic mode, ready to love first so that the reader cannot disagree without making himself seem a surly dog such as I may appear to be. The arguer is of course the unconstrained agent-subject at whose will the cornucopia of invention spills forth. Consider these three sentences or sentence groups with "we" as the subject. The first is one cited earlier: "All authors, to be sure, we are more particularly narrators, historians, tale-tellers" (16). The second: "Each of us is a narrative. A good part of the time we can live comfortably adjacent to or across the way from other narratives" (18). The third: "We have not learned how to let competing normalities live together in the same time and space. We're not sure, we frail humans, that it is possible" (30).

In these sentences "we" are autonomous agent-subjects, unconstrained in our invention of personal history. These personal histories, as adjacent but separate units, provide an area in which "we live comfortably," a sort of segregated suburb of personal stories in which the neighbors all keep quiet and mow their lawns once a week. This suburb—which may remind us of the rings of armed white suburbs that encircle our major ghettos—is segregated not because of any specifiable act or system of injustice but because "we" have not yet learned some moral wisdom which would make us more tolerant of differences. But this lack on our part reflects no objective social fault capable of amelioration; it reflects, rather, the human condition, something which "we frail humans" are unable to do anything about.

Fog's "we" is an example of what Burke calls a "unitary term" or "merger term." In the section of *A Rhetoric of Motives* called "Marx on 'Mystification,'" Burke writes, "as regards the purposes of rhetoric, [a Marxist analysis] admonishes us to look for 'mystification' at any point where the social divisiveness caused by property and the division of labor is obscured by unitary terms (as with terms whereby a state, designed to protect a certain structure of ownership, is made to seem equally representative of both propertied and propertyless classes.)" We do not have to accept all Marxist claims, says Burke, in order "to apply the Marxist diagnosis for rhetorical purposes. . . . It is enough for our purposes to note the value of the admonition that private property makes for a rhetoric of mystification, as the 'ideological' approach to social relations sets up a fog of merger-terms where the clarity of division-terms is needed" (RM 108-09). From this last phrase, "a fog of merger-terms," I have drawn the name I have given to the figure of the Rogerian rhetorician.

If in the quotations of Fog's unitary "we" a moment ago, you as the reader felt yourself resisting inclusion, what you were conscious of was the force of *representation,* which troublesome term may now be considered. Fog's use of the term "we" is a good example of how representation works by fusing social difference into uniformity; or, to recall the example from Aristotle again, in representing free males Fog prudently excludes the condition of women and slaves. How then do the oppressed fare in Rogerian argument? We have already had occasion to notice one representation of woman in Fog's text; the reference, in fact, is three-fold. The woman is present in Gertrude Himmelfarb; she is suggested in Himmelfarb's title "Supposing History Is a Woman—What Then?"; and as the muse Clio she is represented by History herself. I have mentioned already the violence Fog does to both Clio and Himmelfarb. Clio is deprived of existence in the public sphere, reduced to a subjective vapor; Himmelfarb is deprived of her own voice, of her assertion of the possibility of history, and in its place appear the words of Michael Oakeshott, attributed to her, declaring the impossibility of history.

So that I don't seem to exaggerate what may have been only a simple error of ascription, notice the other representation of woman in Fog's text. I have already cited the passage where Fog gives examples of "seemingly hopeless" adversarial situations, including pro-life and farm subsidy issues and Middle Eastern conflict. I didn't point out, however, that these items of public import are given in the form of a *gradatio* whose climactic term is "a beautiful Jewish woman encounter[ing] an aged captain of guards for Dachau" (Fog 25).[17] That is, the series of struggles in the public sphere culminates as a "conflict inside the head of a single lonely man or woman"—a single lonely man who can only be Fog himself—and the psychological conflict determines the meaning of the series. The *gradatio* thus serves to shrink the public and collective to the personal and individual, and it shrivels the century's greatest conflict and holocaust to a private psychomachia.

Himmelfarb's title, "Supposing History Is a Woman—What Then?" directs the reader to search for the woman in Fog's text, and the "beautiful Jewess" is her most striking representation. As a holocaust survivor, she combines the condition of both of Aristotle's figures, woman and slave. In Rogerian rhetoric, however, she is reduced to a personal

history, which she like each of us possesses, and she thus becomes another indistinguishable integer in the uniform mass. It is impossible to conceive a greater violation of the woman than this reduction which strips her of the context which alone gave meaning to her brutalization. She is left possessing only the one attribute the male was willing to allow her to keep—her looks, which qualify her to be a commodity for male consumption. And if we understand the Jewess as violated history, how do we understand the captain of the guards except as a demonic type of the Rogerian rhetorician, the violator of history, the imperial ego whose violence in Fog's text has been precisely to strip the Jewess of culture and history?

Finally, it should be noted that in the *Philosophy of Literary Form* representation is but one of a series of metonymic substitutions for symbolic action. Among this series are such terms as "strategy," "magical decree," "fetish," and "medicine" (PLF 3, 5, 23, 264). In the present context, the last term must give us pause. Rhetoric as medicine has two uses, prophylactic and therapeutic, with the common element underlying each being the consolation of philosophy.[18] "Consolation," dialectically considered, implies a pre-existing disconsolation which, following Freud, may be taken as the personal malaise produced by collective repression. Russell Jacoby, in his critique of conformist psychology, shows that the Rogerian therapist sees this malaise as a psychological need left over after material needs are filled:

> The clear distinction between material and psychic needs is already the mystification; it capitulates to the ideology of the affluent society which affirms the material structure is sound, conceding only that some psychic and spiritual values might be lacking. Exactly this distinction sets up "authenticity" and "fulfillment" as so many more commodities for the shopper. . . . Rogers accepts the fissure and prescribes a double dose as the cure: after a hard day on the job, the weary are to unwind with a little "authenticity." This is the same message forced in through every pore by media; the attention of the discontented is diverted from the source to the surface.[19]

The question of therapy, broadly stated, is the question of the construction of subjectivity, in which process schools are a major site.[20] In the idealist context of no context, in the absence of any consciousness of social conflict and the constraints of social structure, the individual—the student or teacher—learns to personalize problems and thus is prepared for the role of Rogerian client.[21] Essentially, the student learns to blame herself because she accepts the ideology which locates the source of all action and value in the individual self. The subjectivism of Rogerian argument posits the human subject without objective history, without a world. History is only personal history, which exists without any capacity to bring about change in the objective world. Public or social history is impossible. Both students from the oppressed and those from the oppressing classes are thus co-opted into a passive view of history as a force outside human control.

Only a view of history as conflict can show how human beings create history; only such a view makes social change possible. The necessary corrective is supplied by the later Sartre, who is one of the sources of the existentialism, however shrunken from the Sartrean original, that undergirds Rogerian argument. "We were convinced," says Sartre of his generation," *at one and the same time* that historical materialism furnished the only valid interpretation of history, and that existentialism remained the only concrete approach to reality."[22] The subjectivity we cultivate in our students must be complemented with history; otherwise, we will never get beyond the ephemeral compulsory communities based on ego massage and never create real communities based on genuine social purpose.

I hope I am not misunderstood. I don't recommend we ignore individual psychology where its use is to empower the student for action, as in the work of Kenneth Bruffee and Ira Shor.[23] What I object to is a psychological practice which enfeebles students by adjusting them to collective repression. For a critical rhetorical theory, the notion of love is a fragment of a social theory and a misconception of argument. As a social theory, Rogerian idealism darkens the objective social relationship of love into an impenetrable fog of subjectivity. A proper understanding of subjectivity must recognize its objective basis, as Volosinov (Bakhtin) asserts: "Individualistic confidence in oneself, one's sense of personal value, is drawn not from within, not from the depths of one's personality, but from the outside world. It is the . . . interpretation of one's social recognizance . . . and of the objective security and tenability provided by the whole social order, of one's individual livelihood."[24] Or, as Jacoby restates the necessity, emphasizing the dialectic: For subjectivity to attain itself, to become subjective, it must achieve self-consciousness: insight into the objective reality that falsifies the subject."[25] As a theory of argument, "Rhetoric as Love" not only contradicts the adversarial tradition of argument (a point made by other writers on Rogerian rhetoric[26]); it ignores that the traditional Western understanding of argument as conflict is based on a fundamental social dynamic. George Lakoff and Mark Johnson demonstrate that "the ARGUMENT IS WAR metaphor is one that we live by in this culture; it structures the actions we perform in arguing." Metaphor, in their understanding, is not a simple linguistic epiphenomenon; rather, our conceptual system "is fundamentally metaphorical in nature," governing "how we perceive, how we get around in the world, and how we relate to other people."[27]

To conclude by returning to the rhetorics of killing and love, the Rogerian rhetoric of love turns out to be a rhetoric of collective repression because it precludes the social, the principle of which is a dialectic of division and unity. What Rogerian rhetoric offers as love is a co-opted subjectivity incapable of insight into the objective reality that falsifies the subject. Burke's rhetoric of killing, on the other hand, includes a rhetoric of love, because it implies a social context in which love is possible. "We need never deny the presence of strife, enmity, faction as a character-istic motive of rhetorical expression. We need not close our eyes to their almost tyrannous ubiquity in human relations;" yet "identifications in the order of love are also characteristic of rhetorical expression" (RM 20).

Notes

1. Michael Halloran, "Rhetoric in the American College Curriculum: The Decline of Public Discourse," *PRE/TEXT* 3 (1982): 263.

2. George Trow, *Within the Context of No Context* (Boston: Little and Brown, 1981), passim. I have profited from Ann Clark's application of Trow in "Resisting False Consciousness in the 80's: The Girl," unpublished paper, 1986.

3. Maxine Hairston, "Carl Rogers' Alternative to Traditional Rhetoric," *College Composition and Communication* 27 (1976): 373-77; Andrea Lunsford, "Aristotelian vs. Rogerian Argument: A Reassessment," *College Composition and Communication* 30 (1979): 146-51; Paul Bator, "Aristotelian and Rogerian Rhetoric," *College Composition and Communication* 31 (1980): 427-32; Diane C. Mader, "What Are They Doing to Carl Rogers?" *ETC* 37 (1980): 314-20; Maxine Hairston, "Using Carl Rogers' Theories in the Composition Classroom," *Rhetoric Review* 1 (1982): 50-55; Lisa Ede, "Is Rogerian Rhetoric Really Rogerian?" *Rhetoric Review* 3 (1984): 41-48; and Jim W. Corder, "Argument as Emergence, Rhetoric as Love," *Rhetoric Review* 4 (1985): 16-32.

Not all of these writers are advocates of Rogerian argument. Mader questions whether the Rogerian approach can be viewed as a form of argument (314), and Ede goes as far as to suggest something (undefined) "potentially harmful" in a Rogerian pedagogy (41).

4. Citations from Burke are made in the text as follows: GM: *A Grammar of Motives* (Berkeley: U. California P., 1969); GR: *A Rhetoric of Motives* (Berkeley: U. California P., 1969); and PLF: *The Philosophy of Literary Form,* rev. ed. (New York: Vintage, 1957).

5. Corder, 25-26. Hereafter cited parenthetically in the text as Fog.

6. Frank Lentricchia, *Criticism and Social Change* (Chicago: U. Chicago P., 1983), p. 23. Like Lentricchia's, my evaluation of Burke's uses for ideological analysis is more positive than that of Frederic Jameson. See his "The Symbolic Inference; or, Kenneth Burke and Ideological Analysis," *Critical Inquiry* 4 (1978): 507-23.

7. George Lukacs, *History and Class Consciousness,* tr. Rodney Livingstone (Cambridge, MA: MIT Press, 1971), p. 83.

8. Susan Buck-Morss, *The Origin of Negative Dialectics: Theodor W. Adorno, Walter Benjamin, and the Frankfurt Institute* (New York: The Free Press, 1977), p. 151; Trow, passim; and Crane, passim.

9. Kenneth Burke, "Methodological Repression and/or Strategies of Containment," *Critical Inquiry* 5 (1978): 403.

10. Lentricchia, pp. 153-54.

11. Bator, p. 430.

12. Hairston, "Carl Rogers," p. 373; and *A Contemporary Rhetoric,* 4th ed. (Boston: Houghton Mifflin, 1986), p. 346.

13. Gertrude Himmelfarb, "Supposing History Is a Woman—What Then?" *The American Scholar* 53 (1984): 502.

14. George Lukacs, *Theory of the Novel,* tr. Anna Bostock (Cambridge, MA: MIT Press, 1971), p. 117. For a more systematic treatment, see Michael Ryan, *Marxism and Deconstruction: A Critical Articulation* (Baltimore: Johns Hopkins U. P., 1982), pp. 123ff.

15. Karl Marx, *Basic Writings on Politics and Philosophy,* ed. Lewis S. Feuer (New York: Doubleday, 1959), p. 320.

16. Lentricchia, p. 149.

17. Could Fog have found this encounter in E. L. Doctorow's "False Documents," *The American Review* 26 (1977): 229? Fog cites Doctorow's essay but to the same effect he cites Himmelfarb's: to reverse the meaning of a writer committed to the possibility of history.

18. Lentricchia, p. 155.

19. Russell Jacoby, *Social Amnesia: A Critique of Conformist Psychology from Adler to Laing* (Boston: Beacon Press, 1975), pp. 48-49.

20. Henry A. Giroux, *Theory and Resistance in Education: A Pedagogy for the Opposition* (South Hadley, MA: Bergin and Garvey, 1983), p. 78.

21. "Often, [Paolo] Freire says, students unaware of the connections between their own lives and society personalize their problems." Kyle Fiore and Nan Elsasser, "'Strangers No More': A Liberatory Literacy Curriculum," *CE* 44 (1982): 116. Freire's insight recurs in a different context in Richard Ohmann, "The Shaping of a Canon: U.S. Fiction, 1960-75," *Critical Inquiry* 10 (1983): 212.

22. Jean-Paul Sartre, *Search for a Method,* tr. Hazel E. Barnes (New York: Random House, 1968), p. 21. Jameson notes an emphasis on the act links "Sartrean praxis philosophy" with Burke's dramatism and "explains the affinities of both for a certain Marxism" (513).

23. Kenneth Bruffee, "Collaborative Learning and the 'Conversation of Mankind,'" *CE* 46 (1984): 635-52; and Ira Shor *Critical Teaching and Everday Life* (Boston: South End Press, 1980). I have also admired Mary C. Savage's "The Material Conditions of Writing in the College Classroom," unpublished paper, 1985.

24. V. N. Volosinov [M. M. Bakhtin], *Marxism and the Philosophy of Language,* tr. L. Matejka and I. R. Titunik (New York: Seminar Press, 1973), p. 89.

25. Jacoby, p. 128. This is also Paolo Freire's argument in *Pedagogy of the Oppressed* (New York: Seabury, 1970), pp. 35-36.

26. Mader and Ede. See note 3 above.

27. George Lakoff and Mark Johnson, *Metaphors We Live By* (Chicago: U. of Chicago P., 1980), p. 5.

Phyllis Lassner (essay date spring 1990)

SOURCE: Lassner, Phyllis. "Feminist Responses to Rogerian Argument." *Rhetoric Review* 8, no. 2 (spring 1990): 220-32.

[*In the following essay, Lassner examines the responses of female writing students to Rogerian persuasive techniques.*]

When Rogerian argument was introduced in the 1970s, it was hailed as a heuristic which would "break the stalemate" that occurs when writers close themselves off from feeling the validity of an opposing argument (Hairston, "Carl Rogers' Alternative to Traditional Rhetoric" 373). Young, Becker, and Pike presented Rogerian argument as an alternative to traditional argument on the grounds that instead of using logic to destroy the opponent's case and legitimize your own, "Rogerian argument . . . serves an exploratory function, helping you to analyze the conditions under which the position of either side is valid" (*Rhetoric: Discovery and Change* 282). In more recent years, the bloom has been fading from those enthusiastic claims, and yet Rogerian argument is still very appealing to those who want to teach writing as "real communication with people, especially about sensitive or controversial issues" (Hairston, "Using Carl Rogers" 50). Particularly because there are contradictions in teaching academic literacy while showing sensitivity to students' various cultural backgrounds, Carl Rogers' "humane rhetoric" is attractive (Hairston, "Alternative" 373). Rogers encourages empathy instead of opposition, dialogue instead of argument. These are views that reflect the experiences of teachers who have found that traditional argumentation only inhibits self-reflection and the willingness to engage with the critical argument of another.[1] Likewise, the criticisms of Rogerian Rhetoric have come from teachers.

Any attempt to translate Carl Rogers' theories into practice must base its claims on his assumptions. To use his "person-centered approach," based on "empathic understanding" of another's feelings and experience, teachers would have to consider how the assignment affected, not only themselves, but the students who write Rogerian argument.[2] While we teachers can wax poetic over Rogers' humanistic escape from more authoritarian models of discourse, we return to our position on high so long as we prescribe what is good for our students without challenging our own assumptions and his.

My purpose here is to attempt such a challenge by exploring the responses of students in my "Women and Writing" course to writing Rogerian argument. I don't claim that their responses can be universalized. But in the very specific nature of what they have to say, these students present an authentic individual response to the affective claims made on behalf of Rogers' empathetic theories of communication.[3] In no way is this an objective, scientific study, but rather an effort to understand the conditions and contexts which shaped an almost entirely negative response.

When I asked this group of sixteen women students how they liked writing a Rogerian argument, I was greeted with jeers, boos, and this statement:

> I hated it. The Rogerian model is male, masculinist, and denialist. It leaves no space to be persuasive with anger. It denies that women have a right to be angry at being left out of most methods of persuasion and that anger is worthwhile listening to, even if it's threatening, because for women to be recognized, everyone needs to know how they feel.

I reeled with disappointment. I had viewed this assignment as a perfect opportunity to bring together the student-centered values of Composition and Women's Studies in a course which fulfills a University-of-Michigan graduation requirement for upper-level writing. Readings and discussions of composition and feminist theory would become more "real," I felt, in the experience of arguing about issues that were central in these students' lives. In turn, I assumed that arguing on behalf of both sides of an issue would test their own assumptions and claims and "humanize" their opponents'. Turning my dismay into a call for inquiry and action, I responded with a challenge: "OK, your next writing assignment is to tell my why."

As I try to understand both the substance and the passion of my students' denouncement, I look at the assumptions of those who promoted the application of Rogers' theories to composition, some critiques of his theories and their application, and then weave together my students' statements with my analysis of their implication for teaching writing.

Maxine Hairston and Young, Becker, and Pike introduced Carl Rogers' theories to composition studies.[4] Hairston extrapolated guidelines from Rogers' thought to develop a self-reflective method of argumentation which encourages writers to be as self-critical as they would become empathetic with the positions of the other. Rogerian argument would thus provide a heuristic by which students come to understand the assumptions and biases on which their positions are based, as well as the positions, attitudes, and values of those who differ from them. Paul Bator summarizes Young, Becker, and Pike's goal as learning to sense "when it is appropriate to confront 'opponents' and when it is more advantageous to strive for change through mu-

tual acceptance and understanding by each party of the other's view" ("Aristotelian and Rogerian Rhetoric" 427).

The assumptions of Rogerian argument have been challenged by a growing awareness of the political implications of all rhetorics. In "Rhetoric and Ideology in the Writing Class," James Berlin observes that the structure of a rhetoric will "favor one version of economic, social, and political arrangements over other versions" and is therefore never "a disinterested arbiter of the ideological claims of others because it is always already serving certain ideological claims" (477). As Michael Awkward reminds us, no writing can be empathetic unless it considers the reader's ideological assumptions as "a politics of interpretation that is determined by race . . . and gender" ("Race, Gender, and the Politics of Reading" 5). For what constitutes understanding and communication is shaped by the ways we experience our cultural identities as we relate to each other and formulate "sensitive or controversial issues."

Rogers' person-centered communication is designed to enable us to learn to live with new knowledge about others, but as James P. Zappen points out, this can lead to manipulation ("Carl Rogers and Political Rhetoric" 107). For even though Rogers' psychology validates both the "independence and integration of the individual" and questions "any presupposition of social cohesion," it also presumes a definition of "the unity and integrity of the individual" (Zappen 102, 106, 105).[5] This definition in turn is socially constructed on a foundation of cultural hegemony and one towards which the client or reader is being guided to accept. In order to avoid manipulation, the "politics of interpretation" deeply embedded in the ideology of humanist therapy must be considered. Only then can we begin to understand, much less accept, the goal "of facilitating change by striving for mutual understanding and cooperation with the audience" (Bator 429).

If the threat of manipulation is present in nondirective therapy, where clients are encouraged to shape the terms and structure of their treatment, it becomes highlighted in writing. Lisa Ede points out that Rogers' wish to have the therapist's empathy replace judgment and guidance requires active dialogue; this is impossible in writing.[6] In Rogerian argument the writer's stance looks nondirective and active because it states the opposition's position, but in fact guides the reader to accept the writer's arguments as fair and empathetic. As Ede and Nathaniel Teich observe, to translate Rogers' humanistic therapy into a "formula" or "rhetoric" may be a contradiction in terms, since written argumentation still assumes that one side will win (Teich, "Rogerian Problem-Solving and the Rhetoric of Argumentation" 53). Ede notes that "Young, Becker, and Pike consistently call the reader 'the opponent'" and constantly refer to "winning as a strategy to gain the reader's attention" ("Is Rogerian Argument Really Rogerian?" 45). If writers of Rogerian argument are out to win, they are clearly very different from the therapist who submerges her own needs and adapts to the client's ego by changing her style of discourse in response to the client's needs.

For those who do not recognize themselves as worthy opponents with a fair chance of winning, Rogerian rhetoric can be as inhibiting and as constraining as any other form of argumentation. As Jim Corder shows, before we can build bridges between opponents, we must "face the flushed, feverish, quakey, shakey, angry, scared, hurt, shocked, disappointed, alarmed, outraged . . . condition that a person comes to when his or her narrative is opposed by a genuinely contending narrative" ("Argument as Emergence" 21). Feminist scholars have shown how far women have to go before they can even face that contending narrative. This is because women feel they must capitulate to the the values of the majority culture in which they live. Engaging in a person-centered dialogue fails to acknowledge women's ambivalent relations to culture, the fact that although the language of the majority culture does not always fit their experiences, they often behave as though it does. Because women and other marginalized people don't always see themselves represented either at all or accurately in their culture, they often find language to be inhibiting rather than expressive. Hairston's claim that neutral language improves communication is therefore problematic because in the experience of many no language is neutral, nondirective, or nonjudgmental.

Historically, some women writers have resisted being coerced into accepting the claims of traditional rhetorical forms by concealing their feelings. In order to even find an audience, they expressed their experiences in a rhetoric of disguise.[7] Women's writing has been suppressed, according to Joanna Russ, because their concerns are judged as too limited because too personal, and their emotions as interfering with rational discourse.[8] This is as true today as it was in the writing of Mary Wollstonecraft and Charlotte Brontë. Pamela Annas observes that when her women students internalize "a sense of audience—the academic establishment," there is a struggle in "sensing that their truth, because it is new, because it challenges old beliefs, can't be contained inside the bounds of traditionally defined objectivity" ("Style as Politics" 364).

We now understand that argumentative forms are governed by different historical and psychological experiences. In academic writing women students have said that they feel assumptions about objectivity, evidence, even subject matter, do not address their experiences and in fact present them with a double bind. They must write about subjects in which women are invisible. They must use linguistic and rhetorical conventions which invalidate the logic of their experiences. And all this turns out to be for the purpose of educating women to identify with those who ignore or dismiss their concerns.

In their studies of women's responses to classroom activity and women's "ways of knowing," feminist teachers show that women do not respond to language as though it generically represents their experience.[9] Radical feminists have argued that as long as language represents white, middle-class, patriarchal culture as the norm, women will have to create a language of their own in order to express their experiences as they feel them. If the feelings and experiences of women neither translate readily into conventional academic language nor can be expected to be received with "unconditional acceptance" (Ede 44), then what is the experience of women students writing Rogerian argument? In "Women and Writing," students read and write about feminist and composition theories while questioning old and new assumptions about the ways women think. In this course as in many Women's Studies courses, gender and race become categories of analysis as students explore the social construction of gender and the differing sense of self which grows out of the experiences of women of different cultures. Students are encouraged to question ideological assumptions in their readings and assignments in order to understand how learning itself is politically charged. Having read Carol Gilligan's study of women's moral choices, *In a Different Voice,* the class of winter 1987 wrote a Rogerian argument on a moral dilemma to which they felt particularly committed.

These students also kept journals in which they recorded how they felt about presenting both sides of the dilemma fairly, empathetically, and yet as objectively as they could, and finally about how they experienced their composing processes as liberated or constrained by this exercise. The results showed that the whole notion of communication is highly charged, that what we see ordinarily as negative, that is "communication breakdown" (Hairston, "Alternative" 374), may imply a positive move for some writers and that "acceptance and understanding" may sometimes be constraining. Of fourteen students in the class, ten felt in varying degree that Hairston's form was "easy to follow" and easy to revise once they had figured out how to "quell emotions" in order to produce the "detached writing" Hairston interprets Rogerian argument as demanding.

The steps these women writers felt it necessary to take in order to be "fair and present both sides impartially" were experienced by everyone as "unnatural." Although the writers admitted it was a worthwhile effort to try to understand the values of their opposition, they also felt that "fair" was a judgment already biased in its suppositions. It impelled them to present the other side as equally valid in its need for recognition and protection as their own, and in a sincere voice. They said they felt out of sync with their adopted voice. Several students reported that as a result of disguising their feelings they felt powerless and isolated from those who stood on different sides of the issues they chose for argument. Hairston identifies this problem as "rhetorical stance," and suggests projecting "a personal voice that inspires trust and acceptance" ("Alternative" 376). For these students, the rhetorical problem expressed, but also concealed and disguised an underlying one. They needed to figure out how to be comfortable in the role of "an equal" in relation to those on the other side of the issues who had failed to regard them as such. They wondered how they could be "impartial," a frame of mind which assumes one is partial to, that is, comfortable in the style and form of the debate.

The students' papers showed attempts in every step to recognize and understand the positions of those who oppose abortion on demand, who vote against the right to private consent of homosexuals, who will not include language expressing women's experience in prayer, who will not consider pornography a civil offense, and several other positions of concern to women today. The statements made by these students in discussion and in their journals show a conjunction between their experiences and the problems studied by Ede and Zappen.

One writer turns an assumption of Rogerian argument into a question that can be applied to all the moral dilemmas the students chose to explore: "How can you really know what others feel?" Those whose experiences are marginal or run counter to the assumptions of cultural norms understand how difficult it is to recognize another when her own needs have been misunderstood, ignored, and sometimes even condemned. For a gay couple who wishes to adopt a child or for women who feel alienated from the language and ritual of religious service, the values in question on both sides of the issue legitimate the sense of self at such a basic level that each side is experienced as a threat to the other's sense of wholeness and integrity. Hairston's interlocking claims about the ability of Rogerian communication to diminish threat disregards the depth of this sense.[10]

How can those who feel marginalized by the social, legal, and educational institutions that structure their lives be expected to "establish an atmosphere of trust and suspend judgment" (Hairston, "Using" 51-52)? Not only do they not trust, but they feel they are not trusted. Moreover, they feel oppressed by their own experience—where they have had to trust and suspend judgment in an adversarial situation and have found their trust betrayed. As one student argued on the issue of gay couple adoption, "Even to express the 'natural' joy of parenthood is threatened when you know the social worker is, with the best intentions, holding back feelings of revulsion in order to be fair." Even if one consciously chooses nonemotional language for the discussion, emotions crop up in the tone of the empathetic voice the writer tries to assume. For anyone who has prior experience of total rejection, who feels, in the words of one student, "as if my very identity is going to push me over the edge . . . to be empathetic means I'm also going to be pretty defensive." Defensiveness will not be masked; it will show through an unconsciously deployed irony or unexpected humor, the choice of metaphor, or in ambiguous language.

As the writer feels the feelings of the other, her own position is threatened by knowing she is using language that both disguises and exposes her vulnerability. For neutral language is really the provenance of those social institutions, such as education and social welfare, in which she feels marginalized. What these students experienced as "detached writing" implies once again detaching women's needs from the concerns of a dominant culture. As one student wrote:

> Because I feel it's so necessary to eliminate violence against women from our society, it is very easy to over-

state my point through sheer emotion. Although the con side may be covered clearly and factually, it is overpowered by the overwhelming emotion coming through from me. I guess the trick is to try to find and represent the emotion of those on the con side. The choices are: divorce all emotion or charge both sides with equal emotion.

The ironic result of either choice is that the woman writer loses her voice.

To detach her emotion means, in effect, to deny her sense of herself. While this detachment, in one writer's words, "is more civilized," it relies on a notion of rationality which dismisses emotion as nonrational and disruptive and insists on distinctions between feeling and thinking. As Ann Berthoff has shown repeatedly, this dichotomy derives from reliance on positivist assumptions. Despite the claim of positivists that their assumptions are scientific because they observe categories of difference, philosophers such as Suzanne K. Langer have shown how these assumptions are unscientific because they create categories which discriminate against kinds of knowing which include emotion. To continue to insist that rationality can be exercised without emotion is to protect a system of thought which is exclusionary, despite the imperative from Rogerian argument that under all circumstances the other side has to be recognized on the part of both sides. For as Susan McLeod observes, we have "ignored the affective domain in our research on and speculation about the writing process. This is partly due to our deep Western suspicion of the irrational, the related scientific suspicion [of] anything which cannot be observed and quantified . . . and the simple fact that we lack a complete theoretical perspective and common vocabulary with which to carry on a cogent academic discussion of affect" ("Feelings" 426). The impact on women writers of dismissing the affective domain is revealed by another student:

> Rogerian argument feels like a model of mock democracy—too sweet, pretending to accept the minority view but writing in a way that makes women ignore how they feel. If they ignore how they feel no one else has to pay attention to them.

For this writer, Rogerian rhetoric manipulates women into feeling that they must change their way of thinking in order to be part of the majority culture. Zappen observes that it is not Rogers' "intention to change people but to assist them in changing themselves, with a full understanding of the process" (107). For the student quoted above, that would simply mean that women will repress their authentic feeling and comply with values and expectations of what others wish them to be, not with what they feel themselves to be. Such manipulation reflects the way our cultural institutions also pressure women into complying with their own exclusion. To understand the process simply legitimizes the process of suppression in the woman writer's mind. One student wrote how her insecurity about arguing for female inclusive language in the Bible and in Christian liturgy was exacerbated by her "fear of those in the powerful positions of deciding what was the language of God and gospel":

Presenting the position of church leaders and traditional congregations meant a confrontation for me that
made me feel fearful because I was ambivalent. I still
wanted to be part of the church while I realized I had
been excluded and I was afraid if I challenged their
language and rituals they would find reasons for excluding me. The reason I felt ambivalent and fearful of
my opposition was that not long before I wrote my paper, I had actually sided with my opposition.

To present the position of those in authority created a situation for this writer which did not allow her to feel safe in
self-reflection, a primary goal of Rogerian argument. To
be convinced by the opposition would mean giving up her
insights about experiences which put her in opposition to
authority in the first place. Her newly discovered, still
fragile views were threatened by the certainty of beliefs
legitimized by deeply entrenched tradition. The very act of
presenting the views of those she opposed reinstated their
validity in her experience. Her ability to fulfill the Rogerian contract was affected by her anxieties and lack of
confidence. She overstated the cause of the Church. She
knew its terms so well, in their logical system, in their
rhetoric, and perhaps most significantly, in the history of
the church's need to consolidate an otherwise pluralistic
and secular community. Having won its struggle, the
church could rely on a united, unchallenged voice. Indeed,
its language joined a community together with words
whose familiarity and certitude overwhelmed their individual differences. To question the language of prayer, sermon, and liturgy was to underline uncertainties in the student's own argument. If there was no historical evidence
or even question that God was man or woman, if many
women who served the church out of their belief in its importance to their lives accepted and even enjoyed identification with patriarchal power, on what basis could the religious needs of this woman challenge her own community
to integrate her experience into theirs?

What is the rhetorical solution to the experience of feeling
anxious and threatened by a neutralized presentation of a
message which denies otherness? As these students discovered, neutralizing an inherently threatening position ex-
acerbates the danger because they felt it as disguised and
concealed and therefore manipulative and disingenuous.
Empathy requires acceptance of the other. For many, there
are no social, religious, or legal structures that even recognize their needs, much less affirm them as legitimate. The
presentation of women's needs, even in nonevaluative language, cannot conceal the threat to self and community
experienced by those opposing abortion on demand or the
decriminalization of prostitution. In one small group discussion of a paper, a student reader made the point that
"even if I sympathize with the economic plight of prostitutes, and feel empathy for their situation, I understand,
from the point of view of being a woman, that others
would not want their daughters to know that prostitution
was in any way legitimate, even if the women on the street
were protected. I would be afraid of prostitution becoming
an attractive profession." Here, precisely because empathy
was real, not an assumed voice, the writer felt the strength

of her own position eroding. Hairston argues that people
"stop listening [to a threatening message] in order to reduce anxiety and protect the ego" ("Using" 52). The writing experiences of my students testify that they might stop
listening to their own messages because they are a threat
to themselves and to their opponents. For them, writing to
achieve mutual understanding would have to begin with a
plea for recognition, knowing that mutual empathy was
many writing tasks away.

In the third step Hairston directs the write as follows:

> The writer must present his own side of the issue with
> such restraint and tact that the person reading the argu-
> ment will not feel threatened by either the information
> or the language. Doing this requires using descriptive
> rather than evaluative language and stating one's points
> as hypotheses or opinions rather than as assertions.
> Young, Becker, and Pike suggest 'provisonal writing,'
> using a tentative, unassertive tone.
>
> ("Alternative" 376)

If we substitute *her* for "his," we must consider that for
women using a "tentative, unassertive tone," is, in effect,
self-effacing; to validate the position of the other replicates
a history of suppression.[11] According to Carol Gilligan, as
caretaker of patriarchal worlds, women have acted out a
morality of concern for others to the point of neglecting
their own needs. The insecurities and anger of the students
in "Women and Writing" expressed the fear that they were
reinscribing, indeed underwriting, their own neglect.

Because we are so concerned with students' ability to
learn the conventions of writing academic prose, it may
seem counterproductive to question and perhaps undermine heuristics that facilitate the teaching and learning of
argumentation. No matter how much we urge freewriting
and create assignments which sequence the process of
self-discovery in the social contexts in which students live
and work, no matter how much we work against the production of "theme-writing," we are all aware, as David
Bartholomae and others have observed, that students must
adjust their self-expression to the requirements of academic coursework. How do the critical assumptions of a
Woman's Studies curriculum accord with these purposes?

Hairston claims that Rogerian argument makes students
more aware of what and how they are achieving by challenging students to replace "conventional pieties" with
careful reflection about the values embedded in their writing ("Alternative" 377). A principal method in Women's
Studies is the examination of ideological assumptions behind the language of men and women, and of the institutions which govern their lives. In their own writing, therefore, Women's Studies students are encouraged to explore
their own biases in order to see themselves in relation to
others. What is felt to be natural or unnatural comes to be
seen as a cultural construct and not a matter of one's essential nature. By the same token, we discuss what it
means to be a member of a community and how we must
recognize the social and psychological forces that margin-

alize people and how we become complicit in our own oppression by internalizing social and cultural pressures.

Through this process of recognition, we try to figure out what values we share with our home communities and about which so much anger has been generated. Instead of presenting a persona that is trustworthy because it expresses empathy, a student might present a self that is ambivalent about the position of the other and is uncomfortable presenting her own position. There are no conventional pieties here, but rather an honest attempt to see what keeps self and other apart, but mutually respectful. As Geoffrey Chase reminds us, "writing needs to be seen as an ideological process whose aims should include teaching students to write as a part of a larger project in which they can affirm their own voices, learn how to exercise the skills of critical interrogation, and, finally, exercise the courage to act in the interests of improving the quality of human life" ("Accommodation" 22).

From the writing experiences of these women students, it is possible to imagine a form of argumentation that also works as inquiry into the ideological constructs of self in relation to other. Exploring the anxieties that writer and reader might bring to an issue would be a first step towards demystifying a subject whose object remains unknowable until looked at as real human beings living in a culture of its own and with its own values, and yet very much a part of the more dominant culture with which it is at logerheads. No matter how alien, how repugnant those values might be to the writer or reader, recognition that they share the same world might very well be the bridge on which argumentation can begin.

Notes

1. See, for example, Patricia Bizzell. Andrea Lunsford points out that Aristotelian rhetoric does presuppose difficulties in communication and begins at the point where communication becomes possible.

2. Nathaniel Teich discusses the evolution and purpose of Rogers' term ("Rogerian Problem-Solving and the Rhetoric of Argumentation" 52-3).

3. For example, see Zappen (104-05), Young, Becker, and Pike (275), and Jim W. Corder for discussion of the affective components of Rogers' theory of empathy.

4. See Maxine Hairston and Richard Young, Alton Becker, and Kenneth Pike.

5. Paul Bator observes that Rogers' psychological model "questions the classical ideology of man as a rational animal living in a relatively homogeneous society" (428).

6. Teich notes that Rogers never saw his communication theory applicable to writing (52).

7. See Sandra M. Gilbert and Susan Gubar.

8. Cora Kaplan shows how women's written arguments which express their "need, demand and desire . . .

exceed social possibility and challenge social prejudice: (Pandora's Box 169).

9. See *Women's Ways of Knowing,* ed. Mary Field Belenky et al.

10. For this group of women writers, Teich's recommendation to draw topics from students' "own experiences," but to avoid "potentially loaded topics as abortion" is contradictory (57).

11. For James S. Baumlin, "understanding requires . . . a temporary negation or effacement of self" (37). For these students, this would be a double bind. In the same vein, Helen Rothschild Ewald warns against Rogers' mission to change as "adversarial" (174). To change is to yield one's sense of self to another's.

Works Cited

Annas, Pamela J. "Style as Politics: A Feminist Approach to the Teaching of Writing." *College English* 47 (April 1985): 360-70.

Awkward, Michael. "Race, Gender, and the Politics of Reading." *Black American Literature Forum* 22 (Spring 1988): 6-27.

Bator, Paul. "Aristotelian and Rogerian Rhetoric." *College Composition and Communication* 31 (1980): 427-32.

Baumlin, James S. "Persuasion, Rogerian Rhetoric, and Imaginative Play." *Rhetoric Society Quarterly* 7 (1987): 33-44.

Belenky, Mary Field, et al. *Women's Ways of Knowing.* NY: Basic Books, 1986.

Berlin, James. "Rhetoric and Ideology in the Writing Class." *College English* 50 (September 1988): 477-94.

Bizzell, Patricia L. "The Ethos of Academic Discourse." *College Composition and Communication* 29 (1978): 351-55.

Chase, Geoffrey. "Accommodation, Resistance and the Politics of Student Writing." *College Composition and Communication* 39: 13-22.

Corder, Jim W. "Argument as Emergence, Rhetoric as Love." *Rhetoric Review* 4 (September 1985): 16-32.

Ede, Lisa. "Is Rogerian Rhetoric Really Rogerian?" *Rhetoric Review* 3 (September 1984): 40-47.

Ewald, Helen Rothschild. "The Implied Reader in Persuasive Discourse." *Journal of Advanced Composition* 8 (1988): 167-78.

Gilbert, Sandra M., and Susan Gubar. *The Madwoman in the Attic: The Woman Writer and the Nineteenth-Century Literary Imagination.* New Haven: Yale UP, 1979.

Hairston, Maxine. "Carl Rogers's Alternative to Traditional Rhetoric." *College Composition and Communication* 27 (December, 1977): 373-77.

———. "Using Carl Rogers' Communication Theories in the Classroom." *Rhetoric Review* 1 (September 1982): 50-55.

———. *A Contemporary Rhetoric.* 3rd ed. Boston: Houghton Mifflin, 1982.

Kaplan, Cora. "Pandora's Box: Subjectivity, Class and Sexuality in Socialist Feminist Criticism." *Making a Difference.* Ed. Gayle Greene and Coppelia Kahn. London: Methuen, 1985. 146-76.

Lunsford, Andrea. "Aristotelian vs. Rogerian Argument: A Reassessment." *College Composition and Communication* 30 (May 1979): 146-51.

McLeod, Susan. "Some Thoughts about Feelings." *College Composition and Communication* 38 (December 1987): 426-34.

Rogers, Carl R. *On Becoming a Person.* Boston: Houghton, 1961.

———. *Client-Centered Therapy.* Boston: Houghton, 1951.

Russ, Joanna. *How To Suppress Women's Writing.* Austin: U of Texas P, 1983.

Teich, Nathaniel. "Rogerian Problem-Solving and the Rhetoric of Argumentation." *Journal of Advanced Composition* 7 (1987): 52-61.

Young, Richard E., Alton L. Becker and Kenneth L. Pike. *Rhetoric: Discovery and Change.* NY: Harcourt, 1970.

Zappen, James P. "Carl R. Rogers and Political Rhetoric." *PRE/TEXT* 1 (Spring-Fall 1980): 95-113.

Brian Thorne (essay date 1992)

SOURCE: Thorne, Brian. "Criticisms and Rebuttals." In *Carl Rogers,* pp. 64-89. London: SAGE Publications, 1992.

[*In the following essay, Thorne outlines major arguments against Rogers's methodology.*]

CRITICISMS

Rogers had his critics from the very beginning and they have not grown less vociferous with the passage of the years. At the present time the standing of person-centred scholars and therapists within the world of academic psychology is not high: they tend to be patronized as naive enthusiasts from a former age or to suffer the greatest indignity of all—indifference. Certainly the person-centred viewpoint does not align itself easily with the spirit of the age. We live at a time when the pressure of life encourages swift answers to problems, the application of slick techniques and, above all, procedures which are demonstrably cost effective. In such a climate experts are sought after who can provide authoritative guidance and effect

rapid change. Rogers, with his insistence on the uniqueness of individuals and with his unshakeable faith in the capacity of persons to find their own answers, is not a natural hero for the age. His profound distrust of the power-hungry ambitions of many in the helping professions makes him the natural enemy of those who would ply their therapeutic wares in the competitive market-place in order to convince prospective clients that the wonder cure has arrived and that they possess it.

If Rogers' standing in academia is currently at a low ebb, his influence on therapists throughout the world seems to be curiously persistent. Practitioners from many different therapeutic traditions acknowledge their indebtedness and in 1982 a survey of American therapists revealed him as, for them, the most influential figure in twentieth-century psychotherapy, surpassing even Freud (Kirschenbaum and Henderson, 1990a: xiii). In some sense it seems that he has become an idealized figure symbolizing a 'purity' of approach and a hopefulness about both people and therapy which somehow continues to inspire other practitioners even if they openly disagree with his theories and denigrate client-centred practice as altogether too utopian or too demanding in its claims on the therapist's commitment. It is a strange and confusing picture which has its origins in the criticisms thrown at the early pioneers, who were accused at one and the same time of 'doing nothing' in their 'nondirective' therapy and of encouraging a narcissistic ego inflation in their clients. Rogers was castigated throughout his career for being both ineffective and too effective.

POWER ISSUES

Rogers' ideas threaten those whose professional identity resides chiefly in their psychological knowledge and in their capacity to embody the role of 'expert'. He consistently maintained that the therapist's competence derives not from his or her level of knowledge but from the ability to offer a particular kind of relationship in which the client can gradually move to a new self-concept and way of being. Rogers' persistent battles with the medical and psychiatric professions and the ambivalence he experienced from his fellow psychologists are powerful evidence of the fear he instilled in those who sensed that his theories and practice might undermine their authority and credibility. It is small wonder that they sought to discredit him and even to suggest that he was behaving irresponsibly in encouraging his clients to determine their own way forward. Profound issues of power are at stake in these conflicts and the accusations of superficiality or of irresponsibility are a scarcely veiled attempt to silence someone who calls into question the authority of psychological knowledge and the right of any therapist to diagnose mental conditions—let alone to prescribe courses of treatment. The radical belief that it is the client who knows what hurts and how to find healing throws a mighty spanner in the works for those who see it as their task to evaluate 'conditions' and to set up programmes to remedy problems and to alleviate pain. The tendency of those who feel threatened in this way is to accuse Rogers of misguided naivety and to ridicule him for daring to suppose (for example) that therapeutic relationships can be offered by those with no formal psychological education.

It would be utterly wrong, of course, to maintain that Rogers in reality saw the therapist as a non-expert. On the contrary, he believed that the highest level of expertise was required by anyone who was bold enough to offer psychological assistance to another human being. It was the precise nature of this expertise, however, which concerned him deeply; he saw it as residing not in the therapist's cognitive or even experiential knowledge but in his or her capacity to offer clients a relationship where growth could take place. He believed that such a capacity demanded dedicated commitment on the part of the therapist together with a willingness to develop a rigorous discipline of self-exploration which would ensure a high level of congruence, empathy and acceptance. To those critics who accuse Rogers of selling psychotherapy short and reducing it to the level of a mere loving relationship it should be pointed out that such a relationship, marked as it is by the involvement of the therapist's total responsiveness, is rare in the extreme and constitutes not a cheapening but an elevation of psychotherapy to an altogether different plane of experience.

HUMAN NATURE: CRITICISMS OF ROGERS' VIEWPOINT

Rogers' trust in the client is buttressed by and indeed dependent upon his beliefs about the essential nature of the human being and these beliefs have often come in for the severest criticism from the same people who feel their own power base threatened by the person-centred philosophy. Depending on your viewpoint, it is clearly naive to trust persons if you believe that they are by definition untrustworthy or behaviourally conditioned or corrupt or a mass of potentially destructive instinctual drives. Such beliefs and others equally denigratory of human personality are held by many of Rogers' critics in both the psychological and theological domains.

Rogers, as we have seen, makes clear assumptions about human nature and emphasizes that humans are growth oriented and will naturally progress towards the fulfillment of their innate potential if psychological conditions are favourable. By contrast, Freud in *Civilization and Its Discontents* (1930) portrays men and women as essentially 'savage beasts' whose aggressive tendencies and unpredictable sexuality can only be domesticated by the processes and structures of civilization. Freud was pessimistic about human nature and saw the instinctual drives as pushing individuals towards the selfish satisfaction of primitive needs or the relief of powerful tensions. This gloomy view is supported and reinforced by the strong emphasis which Freud placed on the unconscious with its powerfully destructive elements. The primary significance of the unconscious sources of human disturbance and unhappiness characterizes the analytical point of view in its many varieties—neo-Freudian and otherwise—and even when

the unconscious is seen as the repository of many positive forces (as, for instance, in the work of Carl Jung) there often remains the predominant sense of a human nature which is essentially unpredictable, untrustworthy and in continual need of careful monitoring and control. Not surprisingly, therefore, many analytical theorists regard Rogers' view of human nature not only as naive but also as seriously misguided because it fails to do justice to the unconscious which, for the analytical practitioner, largely determines an individual's behaviour and perception of reality.

The behavioural tradition tends to regard all hypotheses about the inner workings of the human being as largely irrelevant. For the convinced behaviourist they must for ever remain hypotheses in so far as they can never be adequately researched and tested. Quite simply it is not possible to prove the existence of the Freudian unconscious or of Rogers' internal locus of evaluation any more than it is possible to prove the existence of God. In the circumstances the behaviourist opts to understand human beings in terms of genetic structure and, more significantly, of environmental variables. He rejects the notion that behaviour arises from some source within the human being and prefers instead to see an individual's behaviour, including his or her thoughts and feelings, as primarily determined by environmental history and the present circumstances of the person's life. In some ways the behaviourist can appreciate the force of Rogers' emphasis on the central importance for human development of the core conditions because this is to speak in terms of a reinforcing environment which determines the individual's behavioural direction. The behaviourist parts company with Rogers, however, once the emphasis changes to an endorsement of the subjective life of the individual and to the fundamental significance of the internal locus of evaluation. This essential conflict is revealed in the famous dialogue between Rogers and the doyen of behaviourists, B. F. Skinner, which took place in 1962 and which has only recently seen publication in *Carl Rogers: Dialogues* (Kirschenbaum and Henderson, 1990b). At one point in this dialogue Skinner remarks:

> I always come back to the discovery that when I give up trying to account for something with an inner entity of some sort and try, very awkwardly at first, to deal with external entities which might be responsible for it, in the long run it comes out.

A few minutes later Rogers responds:

> In your talking about the external causes of behaviour, you spoke as though for every external cause we can find, then you can drop a previous erroneous internal cause which you formerly posited. . . . Yet one lives a subjective life as well as being a sequence of cause and effect. It seems to me this has an importance which you don't always acknowledge.

> (Kirschenbaum and Henderson, 1990b: 97-9)

The difference in theoretical standpoint could scarcely be clearer and the implications for therapeutic practice are enormous. For the behaviourist, Rogers' confidence in the individual's capacity to discover his or her own internal resources and wisdom is to fly in the face of the fact that we are all subject to external forces and conditions which must be controlled and manipulated so that we can be provided with opportunities for acquiring alternative behaviour to replace and extinguish the maladaptive patterns that spoil our lives.

Rogers' religious and theological critics are numerous, even if they are seldom united in their objections to his theories and practice. Most are agreed, however, that his understanding of human nature is at best defective and at worst erroneous. If, for the behaviourist, the notion of the internal locus of evaluation is an untestable hypothesis, for some theologians it smacks of a godless universe where the isolated conscious self becomes the sole judge of what the self should value and how it should behave. Rogers' human being is a creature without a sense of his or her creator and, as such, is woefully ill equipped for the challenges of life and for the encounter with death. Rogers' view of the individual is seen as selling human beings short by divorcing them from higher sources of wisdom and energy and from the religious and spiritual traditions that seek to give access to those sources. Critics of this persuasion see in Rogers' understanding of human nature a profoundly narcissistic tendency whereby the individual becomes the only arbiter and evaluator of his or her own conduct and experience. Without the concept of God or of a higher spiritual authority the individual is totally at the mercy of self-delusion and is likely to succumb to the cult of self-worship. One of the most virulent attacks on Rogers' view of human nature is contained in Paul Vitz's *Psychology as Religion* which has as its subtitle the very words 'the cult of self-worship' (Vitz, 1977). Vitz, a Christian professor of psychology, argues with great passion that humanistic psychologists in general and Rogers in particular have evolved a theory of human nature which inevitably leads to psychology itself becoming a religion in the form of a secular humanism based on worship of the self.

For many Christian apologists the inadequacy of Rogers' view of human nature resides not so much in its rejection of God as the source of all being but in its refusal to acknowledge the ravages of Original Sin. For these critics such blindness is as baffling as Rogers' apparent neglect of the unconscious is for the analyst. To the Christian, reared on the doctrinal tradition of the Fall—Redemption theology originating in St Augustine and alive and well today, it is inconceivable that anyone could be so wilfully obtuse as to regard human nature as essentially good and forward moving; such a perception of humanity is dangerous for it suggests that men and women have no need of redemption, that they do not require a saviour and that the death and resurrection of Christ are without meaning or significance. For such Christian critics Rogers' view of human nature strikes at the very heart of their understanding of the Christian gospel and, as such, ranks as a major heresy to be eradicated at the earliest opportunity. It is not only the understanding of human nature which is at stake, for Rogers' reluctance to acknowledge the fundamental defect in human beings and their built-in tendency to corruption brings into question the whole issue of evil in the world and in the cosmos. Nothing pleases the devil so much, such critics would argue, as the assumption that he does not exist.

CRITICISMS OF THERAPEUTIC PRACTICE

In 1957 Carl Rogers met in public dialogue with the famous Jewish scholar and philosopher, Martin Buber. Buber's great contribution to the understanding of human development lies in his conviction that men and women are essentially relational creatures. In his celebrated *I and Thou* (1937) he enshrined his major thesis that 'life is meeting' and that salvation lies in glorifying neither the individual nor the collective but in the open dialogue of relationship. That Buber should debate with Rogers was wholly appropriate, for Rogers is often portrayed as the therapist who more than any other stresses the quality of relating between therapist and client as the primary source of healing. The dialogue that took place between the two men is notable on many scores and is of particular relevance for our present purposes because it ended with Buber clearly unconvinced about the nature of the relationship which Rogers experienced with his clients (Kirschenbaum and Henderson, 1990b: 63). Indeed, in the closing minutes of the dialogue, Buber implies that the therapeutic relationship resulting from client-centred therapy may produce individuals rather than persons, and he roundly declares himself to be against individuals and for persons. An individual, he explains, 'may become more and more an individual without making him more and more human. I have a lot of examples of man having become very very individual, very distinct of others, very developed in their such-and-such-ness without being at all what I would like to call a man.' Buber arrives at this disturbing reservation about the therapeutic practice which Rogers has sought to explain and explore in their conversation because he is unconvinced about the reciprocity of the therapeutic relationship. 'You are not equals and cannot be,' he says at one point and in these concise words he throws doubt on two issues central to Rogers' viewpoint. In the first place, he questions the power base of the therapeutic relationship and secondly he raises grave reservations about the individual's process of becoming if that process is not firmly anchored in what he calls 'real reciprocity' (Kirschenbaum and Henderson, 1990b: 50-63).

Many of the criticisms which have been directed at Rogers' way of 'doing therapy' can be traced back to one or other of these central issues. The behaviour of the therapist, it is suggested, can create a situation where the client experiences confusion rather than empowerment, which then leads not to increasing autonomy but to a dependency on the therapist whose very acceptance and empathy leave the client without reference points of any kind. Furthermore, as the client becomes more in touch with powerful but repressed feelings he or she may develop a concept of self which, as it grows in strength and uniqueness, may feed a sense of alienation rather than of belongingness if the therapist is unable to safeguard the client's experience of connectedness.

The trust that the therapist places in the client leads to the attentive empathic listening which frequently characterizes much of client-centred therapy. When this is allied to a deep acceptance of the client there can be little doubt that for the vast majority of clients the therapist becomes unique in his or her experience. Nobody else in the client's life, it can safely be assumed, listens and accepts with such dedicated commitment and intensity. For the client this may be liberating and validating but it is also possible for the experience to be unnerving. The client is placed in a position where his or her words are accepted at face value and where the therapist apparently does not believe it necessary or even relevant to express an opinion about the rightness or wrongness of what is expressed. Harry Van Belle has suggested that for many clients this response may well seem mystifying in the extreme—precisely because it is so unlike their experience with other people in their lives (Van Belle, 1980: 148). They may conclude that the therapist sees them in a way that they cannot fathom and that, in this sense, the therapist is 'up to something' which is unknown to them. Van Belle comments that in such a situation the client may have no option but to trust the therapist totally on the assumption that the therapist at least knows what he or she is doing even if the client knows neither who he is nor what he should be doing! In an ironical way the therapist's trust in the client which finds expression in attentive listening, empathic understanding and deep acceptance leads not to the client trusting himself but to a total trust in the therapist. Far from empowering the client, Van Belle is suggesting that the therapist's response may induce a massive dependency which springs from the confusion at being received in so singular a fashion. This is another sign of the lack of reciprocity to which Buber draws attention in the dialogue and about which he clearly felt so uneasy. For Buber there is an imbalance in the relationship which deprives it of the creativity that is the hallmark of the true I—Thou dialogue, whereas for Van Belle it is the very operation of empathy and acceptance that can leave all the power with the therapist despite, perhaps, his sincere intention to empower the client.

These are serious criticisms for they strike at the heart of Rogers' beliefs. He attaches great importance to not interfering in the life of the client and to facilitating the process of the client's growth rather than directing it. He refrains from diagnosis and from interpretation in any traditional sense. Indeed, as Van Belle points out, such behaviours are regarded as antitherapeutic (Van Belle, 1980: 146). And yet the very absence of such feedback may serve to prolong and even exacerbate the power imbalance which it is Rogers' avowed aim to eradicate.

More serious still, perhaps, is the implication of Rogers' acceptance at face value of what clients say. Nye, amongst others, has questioned the adequacy of a therapeutic method that relies on data obtained simply by listening empathically to those who seek help (Nye, 1986: 150). He refers to the large body of psychological evidence which indicates that it is often very difficult for a person to be understood let alone to express adequately 'real' feelings or thoughts. When to this difficulty is added the possibility that conscious, let alone unconscious, distortions may be present in client statements then it becomes even more questionable whether a satisfactorily complete picture of individuals can be obtained simply by listening to them. The accusation can readily be levelled that Rogers' methodology is the inevitable outcome of his phenomenology and that both are equally naive.

Buber's uncomfortableness about the evolution of individuals rather than persons points to the most serious criticism of all as far as Rogers' view of therapeutic process is concerned for, if it has substance, the whole theoretical edifice of Rogers' work is endangered. Buber implies that it is possible for an individual to achieve an increasingly strong sense of his or her own unique identity without a corresponding awareness of others and without the development of the responsiveness which makes for social responsibility. Rogers, on the other hand, repeatedly affirmed his belief that men and women are essentially social creatures and that, given the opportunity to experience their own value, they will inevitably develop in a way which is socially constructive. Buber's scepticism about this optimistic viewpoint closely mirrors the Christian objection that Rogers fails to acknowledge humanity's basic tendency to evil. In terms of therapeutic process this theme is strongly revisited in an 'Open Letter' which Rollo May addressed to Rogers in 1982 through the pages of the *Journal of Humanistic Psychology*. In this letter May refers to the Wisconsin experiment, which Rogers and his colleagues had conducted with schizophrenic patients twenty years earlier, and to his own experience of listening to tapes of the therapy conducted at that time. He comments:

> After listening to the tapes you sent me, I reported that, while I felt the therapy was good on the whole, there was one glaring omission. This was that the client-centered therapists did not (or could not) deal with the angry, hostile, negative—that is, evil—feelings of the client.

Later in the same letter, he goes on to say:

> The issue of evil—or rather the issue of not confronting evil—has profound, and to my mind, adverse effects on humanistic psychology. I believe it is the most important error in the humanistic movement.

(May, 1982: 10-21)

The combined criticisms of Buber and May cast doubt on the 'realness' of the therapeutic relationship in client-centred therapy in so far as it may lack genuine reciprocity, and on the capacity of client-centred therapists, because of their belief system, to acknowledge and confront the evil and destructive tendencies in their clients. The very mode of therapy, it is suggested, can encourage the development of a narcissistic individualism based on a misplaced self-love which evades the confrontation with the negative. In short, the process induced by client-centred therapy is not trustworthy. Van Belle, in his mainly sympathetic book on Rogers (Van Belle, 1980), adds further fuel to the critical fire by calling into question not only the validity of the therapeutic process as Rogers describes it but also the emphasis in Rogers' work as a whole on process and changingness.

Van Belle notes that in Rogers' concept of the fully functioning person it is the quality of changingness which merits the highest accolade; indeed for Rogers the fully functioning person is the 'epitome of man as a process'. Van Belle is troubled by this notion and sees in it the danger that men and women could be tied to a life of excessive change and could thereby lose all sense of a solid identity. Once more there seems to be the lurking danger of confusion, disorientation and a lack of anchorage. Van Belle is equally unhappy about Rogers' conviction that the process of therapy itself will follow an inevitable path. He questions whether the client's open expression of feelings and their empathic and acceptant reception by the therapist will automatically be followed by insight and cognitive clarification and he is equally uncertain whether this phase will be followed by the client's capacity to act upon his insights. Van Belle's doubt about the inevitability of the therapeutic process is great enough for him to question Rogers' fundamental belief that the therapist has only to be the facilitator, the companion of the client, for the process to occur. In the closing pages of his book Van Belle goes so far as to reject the notion of therapy as a facilitative event and with it the belief that the therapeutic process can occur spontaneously in the client once the core conditions have been established. He argues that the process, if it is to occur, needs the aid of the therapist's intervention every step of the way and that therapy must be a *co-operative* activity. Indeed, it is difficult to avoid the conclusion that Van Belle, after painstakingly exploring Rogers' theoretical beliefs and clinical practice with consummate accuracy and sensitivity, proceeds in the final quarter of his book partially to demolish the elegant edifice which he has illuminated (Van Belle, 1980: 145-55).

It would be impossible to consider criticisms of Rogers' therapeutic practice without drawing attention to one issue that has continually attracted debate and not infrequently led to heated differences of opinion. For analytical practitioners the concept of the transference is central to the understanding of therapeutic process and the 'working through' of the transference is often seen as fundamental to the successful outcome of therapy. In such 'working through' clients have the chance to re-experience earlier relationships as they 'transfer' past emotions on to the therapist. In doing this they may experience the therapist by turn as positive, demanding, even rejecting and, as the process develops, the therapist must take great care to guard against countertransference, which is an inappropri-

ate emotional reaction to the client, and to remain objective in the face of what can at times be a bewildering array of emotions. Because of Rogers' inadequate attention to unconscious forces, as the analyst sees it, the whole transference—countertransference dynamic is missing from client-centred therapy, at least in any overt way. The analytical criticism, however, revolves around the belief that transference takes place *whether the therapist acknowledges this or not* and that Rogers, by his failure to give due respect to this unconscious dimension, is in danger of attributing to the relationship which he forms with his clients a quality of present reality that cannot be sustained. Rogers himself was never tempted into lengthy dispute about this contentious issue but because the concept of transference is so widespread and still seems to have such a powerful grip on the therapeutic professions and even on many members of the public, it cannot be ignored in a survey of critical responses to Rogers' way of 'doing therapy'.

THE CASE OF JEFFREY MASSON

In 1989, in his book *Against Therapy,* Jeffrey Masson, former analyst and projects director of the Sigmund Freud archives, launched an extraordinary attack on the very foundations of modern psychotherapy. His disenchantment with psychoanalysis had set in much earlier with his attack in *The Assault on Truth* (1984) on Freud's suppression of the seduction theory but the 1989 book casts its net of condemnation much wider. Masson's thesis is that abuse of one kind or another is built into the very fabric of psychotherapy because it is of the nature of psychotherapy to distort another person's reality. Much of Masson's book is taken up with a devastating exploration of various figures in the history of analysis and he reserves his most violent attack for the discredited John Rosen, the initiator of so-called 'direct psychoanalysis'. There is a chapter on sex and battering in psychotherapy where Masson assembles overwhelming evidence of physical and sexual abuse of a most extreme kind. Immediately following this chapter Masson turns his attention to a therapist who, by universal recognition, he acknowledges to be 'kind, compassionate, helpful'. This is Carl Rogers, who comes under Masson's condemnatory searchlight to be shown as a benevolent despot whose practice is built on the same bedrock as that of the manifest abusers Masson has already exposed so ruthlessly.

Masson seeks to demonstrate that there can be no real genuineness in the relationships offered by a client-centred therapist because it is only the artificiality of the therapy situation which enables the therapist to 'play out' the core conditions for brief periods of time. Nobody, Masson argues, could ever in 'real life' do the things Rogers prescribes that the therapist should do. 'If the therapist manages to do so in a session, if he appears to be all-accepting and all-understanding, this is merely artifice; it is not reality.' Masson goes on to accuse Rogers of complete indifference to the glaring injustices suffered by many clients as a result of societal and other forces. In a powerful analysis of Rogers' Wisconsin research project on hospitalized schizophrenics he shows Rogers to have been callously indifferent to the abusive practices of psychiatry and condemns him for having closed his eyes to the evident injustices and humiliations which many of the patients endured. Indeed, he berates Rogers for having colluded with the hospital administration in order to further his own professional interests and that of the research project. In a final section, Masson turns his attention to the practice of empathic responsiveness and to Rogers' determination not to make interpretations of his clients' statements. He praises Rogers for his genuine desire not to intrude on the thought processes of his clients but concludes that this is simply not possible: 'There is no way out of this dilemma. It is in the nature of therapy to distort another person's reality' (Masson, 1989: 229-47).

Masson's attack on Rogers must be seen in the context of his impassioned onslaught on the whole practice and profession of psychotherapy but in its specific criticisms it reverberates with other opinions rehearsed in this chapter. His cynical view of the artificial nature of the therapeutic relationship is a much more extreme expression of the doubts expressed by Buber. The lack of attention to the realities of social injustice and the abuse of medical power is further ammunition for the behaviourist point of view which sees Rogers as seriously deficient in his evaluation of external forces. The impossibility of offering an empathic understanding which does not distort the client's reality belongs to the same category of criticism as Van Belle's questioning of the empowerment of clients through empathy and acceptance. The force of Masson's attack lies, however, in his acknowledgement of Rogers' benevolence. The benevolent despot is seen as a figure who is just as sinister as his malevolent counterpart, for he exercises power covertly. In Rogers' case, Masson would argue that the abuse of power is concealed by the claim that the very reverse is happening. The therapist who professes to be relinquishing power so that his client may be empowered is, in reality, intervening in the life of another person with powerful and manipulative intent.

RESEARCH CRITIQUE

In their introduction to *Client-Centered Therapy and the Person-Centered Approach* (Levant and Shlien, 1984), the editors point to the troubling situation in the area of research into client-centred therapy. They show that until the mid-1970s there was considerable support for Rogers' hypotheses regarding the necessary and sufficient conditions for psychotherapy or at least for the clear connection of the facilitative conditions with therapeutic outcome. This favourable conclusion was, however, much in dispute by the end of the 1970s as researchers from traditions other than the client-centred conducted studies and as other workers exposed faulty research design in previous studies. Levant and Shlien conclude that as far as client-centred therapy is concerned neither research methodology nor outcome evaluation have much to be proud of. This gloomy summary somewhat undermines the previous security expressed by many client-centred therapists as a re-

sult of the knowledge that their approach was one of the best researched in the whole field of psychotherapy.

Later in the book, however, Neill Watson in a detailed review of a large number of research studies presents a further reflection. He concludes that in his review he located no studies that adequately tested Rogers' hypotheses. Most particularly, he draws attention to the fact that a large number of studies have used judge ratings of the therapist-provided conditions to the total neglect of client perceptions of the relationship, which are essential to a test of the hypotheses. Where studies *have* explored client perceptions of the relationship they have typically not included all the hypothesized conditions and have therefore failed to take account of the fact that Rogers' propositions address a *set* of necessary and sufficient conditions. Watson ends his review: 'After twenty-five years of research on Rogers' hypotheses, there is not yet research of the rigor required for drawing conclusions about the validity of this important theory' (Watson, 1984: 40).

It is intriguing, to say the least, that Watson's review reveals the difficulty that researchers have apparently experienced in giving the primary to the client's perception of what is going on in the therapeutic process. The reliance on 'expert' external judges makes nonsense of Rogers' hypotheses and yet it appears that such research has been carried out in good faith, sometimes at Rogers' own instigation, without awareness of its irrelevance to the testing of the hypotheses. Those who criticize the research on client-centred therapy for its inadequacy or inconclusiveness are justified, but it is worth recalling again that towards the end of his life Rogers was increasingly aware of the need for new research paradigms if the phenomenological world of the client was to become the cornerstone of research in the same way that it is central to the therapeutic endeavour of the client-centred therapist.

SUMMARY OF CRITICISMS

Many of the criticisms which have been levelled against Rogers and his work have their origin in what his critics see as his grossly inflated trust in and regard for the individual. Such a view threatens those whose professional identity is closely bound up with the importance of their psychological expertise and knowledge in the healing of others: Rogers reinforced such anxiety by his deep ambivalence towards institutions of all kinds, by his own distrust of authority and by his conviction that nothing of significance could ever be taught. The only learning that significantly influences behaviour, he believed, is self-discovered learning.

His view of human nature has proved unacceptable to a wide variety of critics. For the analysts and for many Christian commentators he not only has too optimistic a perception of human potential but also greatly underrates the forces of the unconscious and of evil. For the behaviourists his belief in the subjective core of the human personality is an unprovable hypothesis which blinds him to the overriding influence of environmental conditions and behavioural reinforcements. For all these critics, Rogers' notion of the internalized locus of evaluation as a kind of innate mechanism which is trustworthy remains unconvincing and unpersuasive.

Rogers' therapeutic practice has been criticized on many scores but among the more serious criticisms is the doubt cast on the effectiveness of the relationships created by client-centred therapists to develop a socially responsive attitude in clients. It has also been argued, by Van Belle, that the belief in the core conditions as facilitating client autonomy may be misplaced and that the experience of intensive empathy and acceptance may actually engender a deep dependency on the therapist. Van Belle has cast doubt, too, on the notion of therapy as simply facilitative and has questioned the inevitability of the therapeutic process as Rogers describes it. The validity of the therapeutic relationship in client-centred therapy is deeply suspect in the eyes of many analytical practitioners, who see Rogers' neglect of transference processes as an omission with far-reaching consequences.

Jeffrey Masson's ferocious attack on psychotherapy in general and on Rogers as the seductive example of the benevolent despot draws together in accentuated and radical form many of the threads of opposition discernible in other writers. The force of Masson's critique lies in its contention that Rogers' very benevolence obscures the essential abuse of power which characterizes his therapeutic practice.

The considerable body of research into client-centred therapy has been shown by recent reviews to be seriously flawed in many respects. The proud boast that Rogers was wont to make that client-centred therapy was well supported by empirical research (much of it instigated by himself and his associates) is now shown to be less than convincing. Indeed, it would seem that, as yet, Rogers' own hypotheses as he originally formulated them, remain untested.

REBUTTALS

CONTEMPORARY RELEVANCE

The market-place mentality and the desire for quick solutions at financially affordable prices are aspects of only one dimension of contemporary western society, albeit an overtly dominant one. Nor does the search for experts and instant gurus reflect the whole picture. There is plenty of evidence to suggest that we are living at a time when disenchantment with political systems of all kinds is widespread and where materialism, both economically and philosophically, is showing signs of incipient collapse. The re-emergence of political conservatism and even of pockets of fundamentalist Christianity both in America and Europe are a somewhat desperate if determined attempt to put the clock back to an era where authority structures were for the most part unquestioned and unchallenged. It is not necessary to be a social analyst to observe that in

most western cultures the movement towards greater personal consciousness is well-nigh universal.

Recent events in the former Soviet Union mark an increasing acceleration of this astonishing process. In Britain the development of counselling and therapy during the past decade indicates an important sea-change: it is now culturally acceptable to seek help for emotional and psychological concerns. In such a changing context Rogers and his ideas find a ready audience: his validation of subjective experience and his emphasis on the facilitative relationship appeal greatly to a generation which has little faith in dogmatic rigidity of any kind and which often pines for intimacy and meaning in personal relationships. It may be that Rogers and client-centred therapy are looked at askance in academia and in some professional circles but in countless self-help groups, in counselling skills courses in colleges, churches and evening institutes, in human relations programmes within educational and institutional settings, it will more often than not be the work of Rogers which underpins the enterprise. Rogers' confidence in the individual person and his commitment to the development of personal power draw a ready response from those innumerable individuals who find in his work a path to greater self-awareness and deeper relationship. Rogers may be out of tune with the technological market-place and its frenetic search for psychological magic but he is assuredly a principal source of inspiration for those who are already disenchanted with mechanistic views of reality and sense that new paradigms must soon be embraced if society is to move away from the brink of disaster.

HUMAN NATURE

To those critics who accused him of having too optimistic a view of human nature, Rogers always gave essentially the same answer. He pointed to his own experience as a therapist and called upon the evidence. Thus it is that in an article in 1957 he writes:

> My views of man's most basic characteristics have been formed by my experience in psychotherapy. They include certain observations as to what man is *not*, as well as some description of what, in my experience, he *is*. Let me state these very briefly. . . .
>
> I do not discover man to be well characterized in his basic nature by such terms as *fundamentally hostile, antisocial, destructive, evil.*
>
> I do not discover man to be, in his basic nature, completely without a nature, a tabula rasa on which anything may be written, nor malleable putty which can be shaped in any form.
>
> I do not discover man to be essentially a perfect being, sadly warped and corrupted by society.
>
> In my experience I have discovered man to have characteristics which seem inherent in his species, and the terms which have at different times seemed to me descriptive of these characteristics are such terms as *positive, forward-moving, constructive, realistic, trustworthy.*
>
> (Rogers, 1957b: 200)

In 1982 in a response to Rollo May's 'Open Letter'—and equally pertinent to the attack by the Christian critic, Paul Vitz—he wrote:

> When you speak of the narcissism that has been fostered by humanistic psychology and how many individuals are 'lost in self love', I feel like speaking up and saying 'That's not true!' . . . In the groups with which I've had contact, the truth is quite the contrary. Such groups lead to social action of a realistic nature. Individuals who come in as social fanatics become much more socially realistic, but they still want to take action. People who have not been very aware of social issues become more aware and, again, opt for realistic actions on those issues. We have had plenty of evidence of this in our encounter groups and workshops. Irrational anger and violence are sometimes defused, but action of a more realistic sort increases.
>
> (Rogers, 1982: 85)

The issue of self-love is addressed again in Rogers' review of the book *The Self and the Dramas of History* by the theologian, Reinhold Niebuhr which appeared in 1956. Once more Rogers draws on his therapeutic experience, this time to refute Niebuhr's notion of Original Sin.

> It is in his [Niebuhr's] conception of the basic deficiency of the individual self that I find my experience utterly at variance. He is quite clear that the 'original sin' is self love, pretension, claiming too much, grasping after self-realization. I read such words and try to imagine the experience out of which they have grown. I have dealt with maladjusted and troubled individuals, in the intimate personal relationship of psychotherapy, for more than a quarter of a century. This has not been perhaps a group fully representative of the whole community, but neither has it been unrepresentative. And, if I were to search for the central core of difficulty in people as I have come to know them, it is that in the great majority of cases they despise themselves, regard themselves as worthless and unlovable. . . . I could not differ more deeply from the notion that self love is the fundamental and pervasive 'sin'.
>
> (Rogers, 1956: 4)

Rogers' own experience of human beings constantly leaves him baffled by the propositions of theologians and psychologists alike. In the 1957 article referred to above he confesses himself bewildered by the statement of the Freudian, Karl Menninger, that he perceives man as 'innately evil' or 'innately destructive'. Rogers asks himself how it could be that Menninger and he, working with such similar purposes in intimate therapeutic relationships, could come to view people so differently. He even goes so far as to advance hypotheses as to the reasons for the wide discrepancy between the Freudian view of man's nature and his own. Interestingly, he suggests that because Freud relied on self-analysis he was deprived of the warmly acceptant relationship which is necessary if apparently destructive and negative aspects of the self are ever to be accepted fully as having meaning and a constructive part to play.

Rogers' deep and lasting trust in human nature did not blind him to the reality of evil *behaviour*. In his discussion of Niebuhr's book he refutes the notion that he is an optimist. 'It disturbs me,' he writes, 'to be thought of as an optimist. My whole professional experience has been with the dark and often sordid side of life, and I know, better than most, the incredibly destructive behaviour of which man is capable. Yet that same professional experience has forced upon me the realization that man, when you know him deeply, in his worst and most troubled states, is not evil or demonic' (Rogers, 1958: 17). In his reply to Rollo May he writes in similar vein:

> In my experience, every person has the capacity for evil behaviour. I, and others, have had murderous and cruel impulses, desires to hurt, feelings of anger and rage, desires to impose our wills on others. . . . Whether I, or any one, will translate these impulses into behaviour depends, it seems to me, on two elements: social conditioning and voluntary choice. . . . I believe that, theoretically at least, every evil behaviour is brought about by varying degrees of these elements.
>
> (Rogers, 1982: 88)

There is evidence that Rogers was not wholly satisfied with his own arguments in favour of man's essential trustworthiness despite the almost overwhelmingly positive data from his therapeutic experience. In the response to Rollo May he admits that he finds 'a shocking puzzle' in the famous experiments by Stanley Milgram and Philip Zimbardo which demonstrated, in the first case, that 60 per cent of people were willing to turn up electric current to a voltage which they knew would kill others and, in the second, that randomly assigned 'guards' and 'prisoners' were rapidly caught up in violent destructiveness which became life threatening. Furthermore, in 1981 he contributed a leading article to the first number of the short-lived 'international notebook', *Journey,* in which he wrote:

> We are often asked, how do we account for evil or the dark side of human nature, the shadow side? How do we explain irrational violence and the rising crime rate etc? My own feeling is that we have an answer to this question, but I am not sure that it is an adequate answer.
>
> (Rogers, 1981: 1)

Adequate answer or not, Rogers did not deviate from his belief in the positive and trustworthy basis of human nature and continued through the years to give the primacy to his own experience as a therapist. He seems to have been ignorant of theological traditions that might well have buttressed his own deeply held convictions. His family background together with the attacks made upon him by Christian writers steeped in the Augustinian notion of Original Sin meant that to the end of his life he saw Christianity as essentially hostile to human nature and caught up in guilt-inducing judgementalism. In recent years, however, the more ancient spiritual tradition of original righteousness and original blessing is being rediscovered in the Christian church and with it the hopefulness for human evolution which is characteristic of Rogers' viewpoint. Such hopefulness is not to be confused with optimism for, like Rogers, theologians of this tradition are too much in touch with the pain and tragedy of human existence for that (for example Allchin, 1988). Nonetheless the doctrines of original righteousness and deification proclaim a humanity that is made in God's image and that men and women are partakers of the divine nature and are made for union with God. Such doctrines have inspired those Christians down the ages who have seen the glory of men and women as lying in their capacity to realize their divine potential through their relationship both with God and with each other. Theologians of this school of thought would agree with Rogers that, far from being caught up in the grandiosity of self-love, most human beings are trapped by feelings of worthlessness and self-contempt. It is only by recognizing and escaping from the deeply damaging effects of such self-denigration that they come into their divine inheritance. In brief, such a theology enshrines belief in a God who is unconditionally accepting and bears no resemblance to the judgmental figure of Rogers' youth and the theological tradition which he came so much to detest. The 'creation-centred' tradition, as it is often known, offers a view of the divine nature and of the evolving cosmos which is wholly supportive of Rogers' understanding of human beings and of their capacity for growth once they have internalized the liberating truth that they are unconditionally accepted.

Rogers' admission that he was not convinced that his answer to the problem of evil was an adequate one together with his response to Rollo May that evil behaviour springs from varying degrees of 'social conditioning and voluntary choice' together constitute a humble but powerful response to both the behavioural and analytical viewpoints. It is the essence of the phenomenological position, when carried to its logical conclusion, that the human organism is unknowable in scientific terms. Because of the primacy given to subjectivity, each individual, according to Rogers, lives in a private world of experience which he or she alone has the capacity to understand. Not even the most empathic and sensitive therapist can fully understand another person. Rogers' tentativeness and deep respect for mystery makes it impossible for him to accept either the determinism of behaviouristic psychology or the complex theories of the unconscious advanced by the analytical schools. In response to the behaviourists he acknowledges the power of social conditioning and indeed much of his own understanding of human development is based on the adverse effects of the conditions of worth imposed by others. At the same time, however, it is impossible for him to deny the reality and the importance of human choice. From his experience in therapy he has observed individuals struggling to develop and wrestling with decisions which ultimately they have made. To this extent he has seen people being the architects of their own lives. Once more it is his *experience* of intimate relating to others which compels him to reject the absolutism of the behavioural position.

The same experience prevents him from embracing any of the maps of the unconscious, for it is clear that we are all to some extent influenced by forces outside our awareness. Far from pleading guilty to the charge that he ignores the unconscious, Rogers would assuredly claim that his respect for the unconscious compels him to refrain from adopting any map of this essentially unknowable terrain which might lead him to impose his view or interpretation upon his client. In short, Rogers accepts both the reality of social conditioning and of the unconscious but refrains from elevating either to a position where they threaten to deprive individuals of the freedom to trust their own subjective experience and the mystery of their own natures.

THERAPEUTIC PRACTICE

Many of the criticisms of Rogers' therapeutic practice, as we have seen, revolve around the unreality of the relationship which is created between therapist and client. Buber complained about the lack of true reciprocity and was unconvinced by Rogers' contention that a meeting or dialogue can take place purely within the experiential world of the client. For Buber the life-giving 'I-Thou' relationship is only possible when both frames of reference are experienced simultaneously. Egocentricity is thereby transcended as both partners in a relationship experience themselves in the other person's skin without losing contact with their own realities. May accuses Rogers and his colleagues of failing to cope effectively with negative feelings in their clients, Van Belle questions the efficacy of empathy and acceptance in encouraging client autonomy while Masson dismisses the whole therapeutic enterprise as grotesquely inauthentic and inevitably manipulative.

Rogers in his reply to May makes an admission which has considerable relevance to this discussion. Commenting on May's judgement that client-centred therapists fail to accept and respond to negative feelings in general he says: 'I think that to some extent this was definitely true of me in the distant past.' He goes on to describe the changes in himself over the years and refers to both films and published transcripts which demonstrate his growing ability to handle negative and hostile reactions. He concludes: 'I believe I have learned to be acceptant of anger toward me and toward others' (Rogers, 1982: 86).

It can be seen from these brief comments that Rogers himself believed that his therapeutic style had changed over time, and this is supported by researchers who have studied his work in the years since his death (for example Van Balen, 1990; Temaner Broadley, 1991). Although these studies show no change in Rogers' dedication to discovering the perceptual world of the client, they do indicate a shift in his willingness to give a more personal expression of himself in his interaction with his clients.

Van Balen in his study sees the dialogue with Buber as having a decisive influence on Rogers' practice and quotes Rogers himself, writing in 1974, in support of this thesis:

> This recognition of the significance of what Buber terms the I-Thou relationship is the reason why, in client-centred therapy, there has come to be a greater

use of the self of the therapist, of the therapist's feelings, a greater stress on genuineness, but all of this without imposing the views, values or interpretations of the therapist on the client.

(Rogers, 1974b: 11)

Van Balen and others are also agreed that the 'Wisconsin project' with schizophrenic patients, despite May's reservations, actually gave rise to an increased emphasis on the therapist's use of his own thoughts and feelings in order to establish contact with persons who might themselves be very uncommunicative or even completely silent. It seems that this project together with the intensive group experiences in which Rogers was later to participate gradually led him to the point where he could state unequivocally that genuineness or congruence was the most basic of the conditions that foster therapeutic growth.

This movement towards greater authenticity and appropriate self-revelation is, I believe, the most powerful reply to those who accuse Rogers of creating one-sided relationships which are essentially manipulative or which encourage an unanchored narcissism. Through his increasing emphasis on the congruence of the therapist Rogers acknowledges that self-revelation, without imposition, can help to bring about the reciprocity of relationship which engenders mutual respect and avoids the dangers of confused dependence which Van Belle sees as a possible outcome of undiluted acceptance and empathy. There is a particular irony in the notion that the Wisconsin project played a crucial part in this move towards what Van Balen has called 'authenticity as an independent pole of interaction', for one of the other commonly held criticisms of client-centred therapy is that it is useful for articulate neurotics but of little value in the treatment of mentally ill individuals. It would seem that Rogers in his work with the Wisconsin patients not only demonstrated the validity of client-centred therapy with those suffering from so-called psychosis but also gave a new impetus to the practice of his approach. Increasingly 'being open to the other' became a significant goal for both therapist and client and was seen to be related to the client's achievement of self-acceptance as a consequence of feeling accepted. Perhaps acceptance of this life-transforming kind can only be experienced at the hands of a person whose own reality and vulnerability are readily accessible: an acceptant, empathic mirror or *alter ego* is not enough.

Jeffrey Masson's depiction of Rogers as a man indifferent to the abuses of the psychiatric system and blind to political realities scarcely seems just in the light of Rogers' lifelong struggle with the psychiatric 'establishment' and his deep and energetic commitment to world peace in his final years. Most people, after all, would have been content to relax into a well-merited retirement. Masson's basic premiss that it is the nature of therapy to distort another person's reality is more difficult to refute for unless a therapist is a perfect mirror—and hence a frustrating bore for his or her clients—there must be a sense in which the therapist interacts with the client's reality and to that ex-

tent changes or modifies it. Masson's argument is that this is what we do all the time in our social relationships and that it is therefore dishonest and deceitful for Rogers to suggest that he does not. I am not sure that Rogers ever claims to be so totally non-intrusive but it is certainly the case that in many of his writings he presents the therapist as solely the facilitator of the client's process which, once the core conditions have been established, unfolds spontaneously and inevitably. When Van Belle argues that this concept of facilitation is an erroneous analysis of the therapist's role he seems to be joining with Masson in accusing Rogers of a certain level of self-deception. Such criticism loses some of its force, however, if we believe all human life to be essentially relational. In this sense—and here again Buber's position is relevant—we need the other for our own completion. My reality needs the other's response if it is to be complete, and distortion comes not through the response in itself which is essential to the integrity of my reality but through a lack of respect for and understanding of my inner world. To accept Masson's critique of therapy as a distorting activity is tantamount to writing off all human relationships as destructive of the individual's subjective reality. Masson, it seems, would prefer us to be isolated creatures who steer clear of human interaction in the interests of preserving our perceptual purity. This seems conducive to madness because it is a denial of our need for relationship if we are to establish a sense of self.

Van Belle's rejection of facilitation in favour of co-operation as the essential task of the therapist is one with which I have considerable sympathy. I also believe it to be in keeping with the behaviour of the later Rogers for whom the capacity to be congruent assumes increasing importance. Barbara Temaner Brodley, in her recent study of Rogers' verbal behaviour in therapy sessions, states of his latest period (1977-86) that Rogers' responses from his own point of view increased from 4 to 16 per cent over the previous period (1944-64). Interestingly most of the increase appears in the categories of therapist's comments, interpretations and explanations. She notes, too, that Rogers in these closing years was slightly more inclined to voice agreement with his clients and to pose leading questions (Temaner Brodley, 1991: 13). It appears that Rogers through his manifest behaviour had come close to accepting the validity of Van Belle's point of view that the therapeutic process requires the active participation of the therapist all the way. Therapy is a co-operative event achieved by the client and the therapist working together (Van Belle, 1980: 150).

In 1984 John Shlien, one of Rogers' earliest students and an Emeritus Professor at Harvard, published a startling paper entitled 'A countertheory of transference'. It begins with the provocative statement: 'Transference is a fiction, invented and maintained by the therapist to protect himself from the consequences of his own behaviour' (Shlien, 1984: 153). The paper caused considerable debate and some three years later an edition of the *Person-Centered Review* was largely devoted to responses and reactions to

Shlien's ideas from a number of eminent therapists of different therapeutic traditions. Rogers contributed to this symposium but by the time it was published in May 1987 he had died, at the age of 85. There is something poignant about the fact that the issue of transference should have been the subject of Rogers' last theoretical paper for, despite the controversial nature of the subject, he had not previously chosen to enter into combat on the issue.

In the *Review* article, Rogers begins by welcoming Shlien's paper as competent, timely and important. He also declares himself to be in agreement with its major thesis and is particularly delighted that it should have come from the pen of a man who was 'an enthusiastic student of Freudian analysis' before he became a client-centred practitioner. Here Rogers is relishing the opportunity to express his support for Shlien and it is not surprising that what follows contains much scarcely concealed hostility towards analytical orthodoxy. After first discussing client feelings that are an understandable response to the therapist's attitudes and behaviour, Rogers embarks upon his discussion of client reactions which are 'the emotions that have little or no relationship to the therapist's behaviour'. Such emotions he describes as truly 'transferred' from their real origin to the therapist and he labels them projections which may be positive feelings of love, sexual desire and the like or negative feelings of hatred, contempt, fear, distrust. He continues: 'Their true object may be a parent or other significant person in the client's life. Or, and this is less often recognised, they may be negative attitudes towards the self, which the client cannot bear to face.' The paragraph which follows is a clear expression of Rogers' view on how such feelings should be handled in a therapeutic relationship, and merits quoting in full:

> From a client-centered point of view, it is not necessary in responding to and dealing with these feelings, to determine whether they are therapist caused or are projections. The distinction is of theoretical interest, but is not a practical problem. In the therapeutic interaction all of these attitudes—positive or negative, 'transference' feelings, or therapist-caused reactions—are best dealt with in the same way. If the therapist is sensitively understanding and genuinely acceptant and nonjudgmental, therapy will move forward through these feelings. There is absolutely no need to make a special case of attitudes that are transferred to the therapist and no need for the therapist to permit the dependence that is so often a part of other forms of therapy, particularly psychoanalysis. It is entirely possible to accept dependent feelings without permitting the client to change the therapist's role.

(Rogers, 1987: 183-4)

There then follows a case example previously published in **Client-Centered Therapy** in 1951 and the article concludes with some observations about psychoanalysis which show Rogers at his most militant and aggressive. Having once more made the point that *all* feelings directed towards the therapist should be dealt with by the creation of a therapeutic relationship characterized by the core conditions, he continues:

To deal with transference feelings as a very special part of therapy, making their handling the very core of therapy, is to my mind a grave mistake. Such an approach fosters dependence and lengthens therapy. It creates a whole new problem, the only purpose of which appears to be the intellectual satisfaction of the therapist—showing the elaborateness of his or her expertise. I deplore it.

Even then Rogers has not finished and it seems as if his anger must find further expression. He challenges the analysts to present their data and provide evidence for their belief that the 'transference neurosis' is so important to successful therapy. Where, he asks, are the recorded interviews which would prove the point? The article ends with a challenge which, one suspects, Rogers knew was unlikely to be accepted. 'Why the reluctance to make known what actually happens in the therapist's dealings with this core of the analytic process? . . . The questions cannot be finally answered until psychoanalysts are willing to open their work to professional scrutiny' (Rogers, 1987: 187-8).

RESEARCH

It is difficult to accept that the formidable amount of research undertaken on client-centred therapy has been utterly in vain. Whilst it appears true that Rogers' original hypotheses remain untested because of faulty research design and a failure to explore the hypotheses as a complete package, there remains considerable support for the more modest assertion that the qualities of acceptance, empathy and congruence are at least connected with therapeutic effectiveness. Evidence for the potency of the facilitative conditions also comes from research in hundreds of classrooms both in the USA (Aspy and Roebuck, 1983) and in Germany (Tausch, 1978). Clearly, we still await the necessary conditions for evaluating client-centred therapy and it remains to be seen whether the eventual breakthrough will come through the more rigorous application of the 'objective' methods of yesteryear or through the development of new research paradigms more in harmony with the spirit of the phenomenological view of reality (Mearns and McLeod, 1984). What is certain is that researchers are once more wrestling with the complexity of the task in an attempt to revive Rogers' earlier commitment to a coherent integration of theory, practice and research.

CONCLUSION

Many people find in Rogers' writings a clear articulation of what they themselves have felt and thought confusedly for many years. Such people—and I count myself among them—respond instantly to a person who conveys powerfully what it involves to struggle towards self-acceptance and to discover a respect for one's own experience. Rogers' theoretical formulations also offer a way of relating to oneself and to others which is compelling in so far as it encourages honesty, openness, understanding and acceptant responsiveness. Rogers offers a way of being which is attractive and even seductive, for it gives absolute primacy to subjective reality and yet places this supreme value within the context of a mode of relating which promises a high level of intimacy.

Rogers' critics are for the most part resistant to such seduction. They are less inclined to attribute such overriding importance to subjective reality and doubt the capacity of human beings—even well-intentioned therapists—to embody the core conditions to the extent that Rogers advocates. They detect within Rogers' concern for the autonomy of the individual an ambiguity about the nature of the relationship which is being offered in therapy. At times the apparently self-effacing behaviour of the therapist suggests that, once the core conditions have been established, he or she only has to provide a particular psychological environment and the therapeutic process in the client will unfold spontaneously and inevitably. At other times Rogers appears to acknowledge the centrality of the therapist's own congruence and his or her willingness to be involved in a reciprocal exchange as long as there is no intention of imposing on the client's reality.

There was initially, I believe, a genuine confusion at the heart of Rogers' thinking and his critics in one way or another tend to sniff this out. Rogers never seemed to be absolutely sure whether men and women are essentially relational beings or not. His tendency to employ images culled from agriculture and his emphasis on the actualizing tendency and the wisdom of the organism can lead to a highly positive view of the human being but one which is strangely non-relational except that the evolution of the species is seen to be part of a universal formative tendency. Because of this central confusion Rogers' critics—rightly in my view—question the nature of the relationship between therapist and client and raise doubts about Rogers' view of therapy as essentially the facilitation of inherent growth processes. Rogers' constant emphasis upon process and changingness and his apparent preference for affective as opposed to cognitive experience have led some of his critics to accuse him of, at one and the same time, affirming the uniqueness of persons and denying them any continuing or stable identity.

For my own part, I acknowledge the inconsistencies and, at times, the logical contradictions in Rogers' point of view. I am reassured, however, by my powerful memories of the man himself. In my own relationship with him, I never for one moment feared that we would be lost in an infinite process of becoming. On the contrary, I recall many an encounter from which I gained a heightened sense of my own identity and a powerful impression of Rogers' complex but integrated personality. In practice, there was never for one moment any doubt that we were both unique and that our uniqueness was characterized by the fact that we were relational beings. Rogers' keen interest in everything around him and his capacity for drawing pleasure from his social environment provided ample evidence that he was well aware of the ways in which our social context can support personal development as well as impede it. For a man dedicated to the understanding of the subjective world of others he was wonderfully at home in the mundane world of eating, drinking and catching the next post.

Samuel J. Sackett (essay date fall 1995)

SOURCE: Sackett, Samuel J. "The Application of Rogerian Theory to Literary Study." *Journal of Humanistic Psychology* 35, no. 4 (fall 1995): 140-57.

[*In the following essay, Sackett argues that the focus of Rogerian theory on empathetic understanding of the other can be successfully applied to the study of literature.*]

The Genesis of Literary Works

Literary critics have long wrestled with the questions of why authors write at all and why a certain author wrote a certain work. The answers to these questions usually given by Freudian critics, not wholly in keeping with Freud's own attitudes, have tended to postulate that writers write because they feel tensions that they cannot resolve in the real world and hence need to resolve in fantasy. The work, then, can be seen as the fantasy in which the conflict is worked out, and its content is determined by the needs of its author. A theory of literary creation emerging from the writings of Rogers would be far different.

Rogers's paper **"Toward a Theory of Creativity"** (1961) can provide us with a basis from which we may view literary creation (pp. 347-359). Rogers defines the creative process as "the emergence in action of a novel relational product, growing out of the uniqueness of the individual on the one hand, and the materials, events, people, or circumstances of his life on the other" (p. 350). It is motivated, he says, by "man's tendency to actualize himself, to become his potentialities" (p. 351). It is, moreover, based on certain conditions that Rogers enumerates: (a) openness to the creator's own experience, (b) an internal locus of evaluation, and (c) the ability to toy with elements and concepts. Of these conditions, Rogers considers the last as the least significant, though without it the other two alone cannot lead to creativity.

Let us begin by seeing how the first condition applies to the literary artist—the poet, novelist, or dramatist. Rogers (1961) explains:

> In a person who is open to experience each stimulus is freely relayed through the nervous system, without being distorted by any process of defensiveness. Whether the stimulus originates in the environment . . . or . . . in the viscera, . . . it is available to awareness. This means that instead of perceiving in predetermined categories . . . the individual is aware of this existential moment as *it* is, thus being alive to many experiences which fall outside the usual categories.
>
> (p. 353)

Thus, for example, we may postulate that a poem arises in the mind of the poet, a novel in the mind of the novelist, or a play in the mind of the playwright as a deeply personal, experiential insight into the nature of reality. Such insights may be as various as a vivid perception of what snow really looks like, of what another person's motivations really are, or of what the value of an action really is. This element of Rogers's theory of creativity is applicable chiefly to the content of the literary work.

Keats's "Ode to a Nightingale," therefore, may be hypothesized as resulting from the poet's hearing a birdsong and realizing that generations before his birth had heard the same song and that generations after his death would also hear it. Melville's *Moby Dick,* similarly, may have resulted from its author's musing back on his own whaling experiences and understanding how a man wounded in an encounter with a whale might come to the anthropomorphic belief that the damage had been done by the animal out of deliberate malevolence. Or Shakespeare's *Macbeth* was perhaps generated by its author's experience or observation suggesting to him that guilt has a way of betraying a perpetrator, sometimes in ways that are unexpected and dismaying. Although as Lesser (1957) points out, it would be reductive to maintain that such observations account for the whole of these works, their origins may have lain in a desire to communicate these perceptions to others (pp. 62-67).

It can readily be seen that, in contrast to the Freudian interpretation, a Rogerian literary theory would assume that literature arises from the health, not from the pathology, of the artist. At this point, one must confront the fact that many creative writers have had demonstrable pathologies. The depression of Mark Twain is well known, for instance, and recent studies of Robert Frost have emphasized the elements in his poems that show him to have been, as he himself wrote, "one acquainted with the night" (Latham, 1969). On the other hand, there is certainly no reason to doubt the essential psychological healthiness of some of the greatest writers in English, such as Shakespeare, Chaucer, and Fielding, and the vitality of their works suggests that healthy minds produced them. The apparent dilemma may be resolved by postulating that literary creativity is a healthy tendency, though the creations may express painful experiences. The expression of a painful experience may indeed be therapeutic for a writer, providing him or her with new insight into the experience.

In the absence of any experimental verification as to the validity of either Freud's or Rogers's view, one may at least say that the Rogerian conception of literary genesis is likely to be more easily accepted than the Freudian by those who value literature highly and who honor those who produce it. The Rogerian conception also seems on the face of it more congruent with everyday experience, as well as with clinical observation, because so much of the energy of the neurotic or psychotic goes into maintaining his defenses that he has little left for productive work; hence there is an essential implausibility in Freudian theory that Rogers, as well as his predecessor Rank (1932/1989, p. 27), avoid.

Freudian literary critics have focused almost entirely on the content of literary works, treating it as symbolic in the same fashion that Freud treated the content of dreams. The theory of Rogers (1961), on the other hand, gives an explanation also for literary form:

> Perhaps the most fundamental condition of creativity is that the source or locus of evaluative judgment is internal. The value of his product is, for the creative person, established not by the praise or criticism of others, but by himself. . . . If to the person [the product] has the "feel" of being "me in action," . . . then it is satisfying and creative, and no outside evaluation can change that fundamental fact.
>
> (pp. 354-355)

The third element that Rogers postulates as essential to artistic creation is "the ability . . . to juggle elements into impossible juxtaposition, . . . [a] spontaneous toying and exploration" (p. 355).

From these conditions, we may draw a picture of the literary artist playing with his or her production, trying this word and that, this character and that, this episode and that, until finally it jells into a form that "feels right." Then the creator maintains this form as appropriate in the face of criticism. This view emphasizes the originality of great writers as creators of new forms, or as the creators of new applications of old ones.

The three writers I have already cited, Keats, Melville, and Shakespeare, will serve us also here. The brief career of Keats may be seen as a continual search for forms that "felt right" to him. Rather than introject the values of the poetic school that still predominated in England when he began to write, a school that was devoted to imitations of Dryden and Pope, Keats began a restless rummaging through previous poets, seeking models with whom he could feel more comfortable. He "tried on" Milton at various times, with varying degrees of success in his longer poems but with much success in his sonnets; he tried on Spenser for "The Eve of St. Agnes"; and for his odes, despite the claims of the so-called "Neoclassical" poets that they used models from Latin literature, he found unused as models the stanzaic odes of Horace. Unfortunately, Keats died before he could go beyond the use of prior models and develop a fully personal and individual form. But his formalistic experiments were already so unlike the Popean poems of his immediate predecessors that his works, when noticed at all, received extremely hostile reviews. These reviews were so devastating, in fact, that his colleagues Shelley and Byron somewhat sentimentally laid his death to them rather than to the tuberculosis bacilli that infested Keats's lungs. Yet if Keats had been hurt by the unfavorable reviews, all he had to do to avoid the pain was conform his poetic output more acceptably to the standards of the influential reviewers of his day; instead of doing so, he maintained his idiosyncrasies in the face of them.

Melville, too, maintained his individual vision in the face of public misunderstanding and rejection. When *Moby Dick* was originally published, it was perceived by the reviewers as a falling off from his earlier, more straightforward adventure books, *Typee* and *Omoo,* with which he had at first established his reputation. From the formal standpoint, Melville began to use ambiguity as a structural device, forcing more attention and thought on the reader's part than had been necessary in his simpler books. Seeing *Moby Dick* scorned by contemporary reviewers, Melville had the option of returning to the kind of writing that had been successful for him in gaining popular acceptance; instead, however, he defiantly maintained the trend he was on, expanding the form of the novel to include more and more ambiguity and reducing the significance of story, through *Pierre* and *The Confidence Man*. The inability of contemporary readers to respond to this formal quality of his work was difficult for Melville to accept; after *The Confidence Man* (1857) he did not attempt to publish another novel for the rest of his life (he died in 1891). Yet although he did not publish it, he wrote one: *Billy Budd*, now perceived as a minor masterpiece, which was not put into print until 1924. His personal satisfaction with what he was doing in developing the novel's form was so intense that he put the labor that might have gone into another *Typee* into creating a work that during his lifetime served only for his own enjoyment.

Less is known about Shakespeare's life—so little, indeed, that it has become for some people a kind of academic game to try to decide who "really" wrote his plays. Yet there are indications that Shakespeare had some criticism to overcome from his contemporaries. Although the formal pattern had by no means been set in Shakespeare's England, and although his professional contemporaries such as Kyd and Marlowe were obviously liberated from it, on the level of the academic critics (such as Sir Philip Sidney), the theory of Aristotle, as interpreted by Castelvetro, and the practice of Seneca formed the approved model for tragedy. Shakespeare's early effort to conform to this model, *Titus Andronicus,* may be characterized as either dismal or absurd, but it can hardly be considered a success. It was only when Shakespeare had broken away from the Aristotelian-Senecan pattern and begun writing plays that in their freedom from dramatic convention were more like a 20th-century film script than like a Senecan tragedy that he produced his early successes—*Romeo and Juliet, Antony and Cleopatra,* and the great series of tragedies that crowned his career—*Hamlet, Othello, King Lear,* and *Macbeth.*

Although Shakespeare was apparently always a great box-office draw, the denigrations of such contemporaries as Robert Greene indicate that the university-educated writers of his day considered the butcher's son from Stratford as an "upstart," to use Greene's term; whereas part of their attitude may have stemmed from jealousy, part may also have resulted from Shakespeare's tendency to scrap the rules of academicians and present his story in the form he felt most appropriate. There may be significance in an anecdote recounted by his contemporary Ben Jonson. When it was reported to Jonson that Shakespeare boasted that he never blotted (revised) a line, Jonson, whose tragedies followed the strict Aristotelian pattern but were not as popular as Shakespeare's, exclaimed, "Would he had blotted a thousand" (Jonson, 1951, p. 156)! In recounting this incident, Jonson explained that he did not intend to express a desire that Shakespeare had not written at all, or even written less, but instead a desire that Shakespeare had not committed the many solecisms that in Jonson's view marred his work.

The examples of Keats, Melville, and Shakespeare, therefore, suggest that Rogerian theory may be fruitful for the study of literary genesis. Rogers's concept of "openness to experience" gives us a theory of creativity that, when applied to the literary artist, indicates that the artist's healthy condition of awareness leaves him or her receptive to insights about his or her own experience and about circumambient objects, people, and incidents, and that these insights serve to precipitate the content of the work. The literary work, then, is seen as a desire to communicate these insights to other people. The ideas of "internal locus of evaluation" and "ability to toy with elements and concepts" give us a theory that depicts the literary artist playing with the form of his or her communication until it provides the experience of satisfaction that it "feels right," the artist then maintaining this personal and unique experience in the face of the opinions of others that the form "ought to be" something more conventional.

The Interpretation of Literature

As the Freudian critic approaches the problem of interpreting the meaning of a literary work, he or she tends to see the literary production as a network of symbols and interprets the work much as a psychoanalyst interprets a dream: a gun or a tree is a penis, a bowl or a cave is a vagina, and so forth. There is an important methodological inconsistency in this practice that has never been thoroughly explored, in that a dream is a production of the unconscious, whereas a literary work is in larger measure a production of the conscious mind.

Moreover, because the focus in Freudian literary interpretation is on the individual detail, there is some difficulty in moving from a welter of details to an interpretation that integrates all these details into a single, unified impression of the work as a whole. Frequently, indeed, Freudian critics must resort to the hypothesis that a work has many "levels," and a symbol may mean one thing on one level and its opposite on another. In addition, as the many contradictions between Freudian critics show, the interpretation of symbols may be affected by the psychology of the interpreter.

The application of Rogerian theory to literary criticism would proceed far differently. It would conceive of the literary work as an artifact that contained, among its other elements, a system of values; the values would reveal themselves by a number of means (selection of emotion-charged words, sympathetic vs. unsympathetic characterization, treatment of incidents, etc.), but they would be apprehended by readers through their responses to the work, which would lead them empathically to an intuitive apprehension of the author's emotional attitudes.

Following Morris (1956), Rogers's (1969) view of operative value is that it may be defined as "the tendency of any living beings to show preference, in their actions, for one kind of object or objective rather than others" (p. 241). In the infant, Rogers says, the valuing process is organismic:

> Each element, each moment of what he is experiencing is somehow weighed, and selected or rejected, depending on whether, at that moment, it tends to actualize the organism or not. . . . Another aspect of the infant's approach to value is that the source or locus of the evaluating process is clearly within himself. Unlike many of us, he *knows* what he likes and dislikes, and the origin of these value choices lies strictly within himself.

(pp. 242-243)

Here it will be enough simply to state that in Rogers's view the organismic source of value and its internal locus become distorted through conceptualizations introduced from the child's environment as he or she grows up. The important element in Rogers's thinking from the standpoint of interpreting literature is that operative value is a matter of what a person likes and dislikes; an individual values what he likes and disvalues what he dislikes.

A literary work may be regarded as a device by which the author reproduces in his readers the emotions he feels toward incidents, characters, and theme. The emotions generated may be regarded as either positive ("likes") or negative ("dislikes"). Some of the emotions produced may indeed be irrelevant to the experience of the work, arising from the prior experience of the reader rather than from the reading at hand; other emotions will inhere in the work.

This could be experimentally verified by the process of inviting students to record their emotional responses to a literary work, much as I. A. Richards (1929) did with his students at Cambridge, but restricting the students, as Richards did not, to emotional responses. The results would fall into two categories: (a) those emotional responses that appeared in only one or, at most, a few papers, and (b) those that appeared in several, most, or all.

Those in the first category could be considered idiosyncratic, arising from what Richards called "irrelevant associations," as well as from doctrinal prejudice, which Richards identified as the two causes of idiosyncratic readings. Those in the second category could be considered as inhering in the work itself and hence would be felt by readers who were empathic with the author.

This is not to recommend that so mechanical a procedure should replace other, more personal and more subjective, methods of literary criticism; or, indeed, that it should actually be applied at all. For one thing, reducing the interpretation of literature to an analysis of what Richards called "protocols" would eliminate the enjoyment of criticism and any scope for the exercise of the critic's personal flair. The experiment was proposed merely to point out that certain emotional responses do in fact inhere in the work itself.

And it would not be reductive of the role of literary critics to challenge readers to approach a work with the goal of using their own sensitivities to determine the extent to which emotional responses inherent in a work constitute a value system. One function of critics in a Rogerian approach to literary study would be to respond empathically to the work, to examine their own reactions carefully, to use those reactions to discover the values of the author (to the extent that they were revealed in the single work under consideration), and to present those values fairly from the author's point of view.

An example of how such a critic might function can best be provided through an examination of a short work. For this purpose, I have chosen Keats's sonnet "On First Looking into Chapman's Homer." The poem can be divided into two sections, according to the emotional responses it arouses; these two sections correspond to those in which it is arranged on the page typographically. During the first eight lines, the emotion is positive, but muted, so that it is hard to identify; it might be labeled as "interest," the emotion that one would feel toward a traveler who had returned from strange lands and was telling the wonders that he saw. But then, in the last six lines, the emotional charge increases; it remains positive but the interest quickens into excitement, so that the reader no longer is the passive listener to the discoveries of others but shares empathically the emotions of the discoverer himself. Judging simply from the emotional responses of the reader, therefore, it would be reasonable to say that Keats valued both second- and firsthand experience, but that he valued firsthand experience more highly.

The cognitive content of the poem validates this reading, because the poem describes how, previous to reading the translation by George Chapman, Keats felt that his experience of Homer had been only secondhand; but when he read Chapman's translation, his experience was so direct that it was as if he were experiencing the Greek poet's "pure serene" firsthand. In this illustration, therefore, a critic, simply by examining his or her emotions, could arrive at the same conclusion that another critic might reach by the more conventional methods of interpreting the cognitive content of the poem.

This discussion leaves unanswered the question of the author's intention. From this standpoint, that question is irrelevant. Whatever appears in a literary work was put there by its author. Whether the author was conscious of his or her reasons for putting it there can rarely be determined, and, accordingly, that question is unanswerable as well as unimportant. An empathic understanding of the work will reach, interpret, and express the author's feelings, whether he or she was conscious of them or not.

Whereas this discussion of the role of critics in literature has focused solely on their potential use of a Rogerian approach to derive interpretations of the works, another possibility, which will not be explored fully here, can be mentioned. Basic to the type of criticism that has been suggested above is the critic's analysis of his or her own emotional response to the work. The reader of the criticism will have his or her own response, as well; and as he or she reads the critic's responses to the work they both have read, the reader will in a sense come into a confrontation with the critic. The reader may agree with the critic's emotional response, or disagree. In the latter event, the reader has gained from the reading of criticism some information about himself or herself that may lead to deeper insight. Consideration of this information might lead the reader to conclude either that he or she responded to the item in question more sensitively than the critic, or less sensitively. In the former instance, the reader may gain confidence in his or her ability to rely on his or her own organismic experiences; in the latter, the very recognition that sensitivity is lacking may aid in the development of it.

The example of Keats's sonnet supports the contention that the reader's affective responses to a literary work can lead to a comprehension of its value system and hence the contention that a Rogerian approach to literary analysis will yield an interpretation that will meet criteria of internal consistency, completeness, and centerdness in the work itself.

The Analysis of Character

The Freudian approach to character analysis has led principally to psychodiagnosis. Most famous among such studies is probably Ernest Jones's (1949/1976) theory that Hamlet's tragic flaw is an Oedipus complex. A Rogerian approach to character analysis would be substantially different, being in one way simpler and in another more complicated.

Whereas there are abundant expressions throughout Rogers's work of his ideas in general (e.g., 1961), the paper in which he most thoroughly explores the etiology of behavior in an individual is **"Ellen West—and Loneliness"** (1980, chap. 8). In his examination of this case, Rogers finds the source of West's problem in an incongruence between the experiencing of her own autonomous organism and those feelings that she feels obligated to have because of pressure from her family. For example, her own experiencing tells her that she is in love; but her family tells her that she is mistaken. She comes, therefore, to distrust her own experiencing, to believe that it is an untrustworthy guide, and, consequently, to believe that she is an inadequate person who is seriously unequipped to reach her own decisions about life's problems. In the end, Ellen West committed suicide.

Rogerian character analysis would be simpler than Freudian because ultimately for Rogers, all characterological problems spring from a single source: incongruence between the internally experienced reactions of the person and the reactions he or she considers him- or herself obligated to have because of pressures from the environment, usually parents or other significant adults, while he or she

is a child; and usually the incongruence arises because the individual must, or believes he or she must, modify his or her reactions to receive love from these adults.

But Rogerian character analysis would also be more complicated than Freudian because the number of ways in which this fundamental incongruence can manifest itself is not, for Rogers, limited to the number of psychoses, neuroses, and personality disorders in the psychiatric system; it is, rather, infinite. The number of ways in which a person's behavior may manifest the incongruences in his or her values is greater than the number of persons, because the same person may have more than one incongruence and may manifest each of them in more than one way.

Because a famous Freudian analysis of Hamlet has already been mentioned, it would be interesting to contrast that with what a Rogerian analysis of the same character would reveal. Rather than an Oedipus complex, a Rogerian critic would seek an incongruence; and he would not need to seek far. One of the most striking things about Hamlet is the incongruence between the prince we see in action—charming, capable of deep affection, courageous, able to seize control of the most difficult situations and master them—and the prince who is revealed to us in the famous soliloquies ("Oh, what a rogue and peasant slave am I!"). Hamlet has an extremely low self-image, indeed has so little sense of his own worth that he meditates suicide ("To be, or not to be"); yet this low opinion of himself seems totally unwarranted.

As the play proceeds, we observe that much of Hamlet's planning is counterproductive: he feigns insanity (an "antic disposition") to become inconspicuous and succeeds only in calling attention to himself; he produces a play mimicking the real murder of his father by Claudius to verify what he already knows and succeeds only in putting Claudius on guard against him; and so on. One explanation for such behavior is that he is afraid of success; he has an image of himself as a failure, and so he mismanages his revenge to fulfill his own image of himself.

This leads us to wonder whether the significant adults in Hamlet's life have created this low self-image. And the scenes between Hamlet and his father's spirit support that conjecture. Hamlet already knows from his "prophetic soul"—Shakespeare's name for what Rogers calls the autonomous organism—that Claudius has killed his father; but he has been so accustomed to using inactivity as a way of gaining his busy father's attention that he takes no action until finally the elder Hamlet must literally return from the grave to tell the prince what he knows already. Ineptitude is another way in which the prince has been able to get King Hamlet to notice him; he had learned bumbling as a habitual behavior because bumbling always brought Daddy to straighten things out, and so he bumbles his vengeance until finally the ghost must make his second appearance to bring Hamlet back to the accomplishment of his "almost blunted purpose."

Like Ellen West, Hamlet is afraid to rely on his own internal experiencing, because he feels obligated to have the low opinion of himself that he has learned from his father. This is rather different from saying, as Ernest Jones does, that Hamlet is a rival of his father for Gertrude's affection; the point is rather that Hamlet is an unsuccessful suitor for his father's attention.

This example demonstrates that Rogerian psychology provides the literary critic with a tool for analysis of character: the concept of incongruence between the experiences of the individual's autonomous organism and the values that the individual accepts because he must, or feels he must, to gain the love of significant adults in his childhood environment. Such analysis may be applied not only to characters in dramatic or narrative works but also to the authors who reveal themselves in lyric poems, in which they function as characters much as the speakers of speeches in plays, or dramatic monologues, do.

THE VALUE THEORY OF LITERATURE

One of the basic issues that has concerned literary critics and aestheticians since the time of Aristotle is the purpose or function of literature. Many proposals have been made, and many literary movements have crystallized around these proposals, but no widespread agreement has been reached. The substantial discussion of this matter in Wellek and Warren (1956) indicates both the importance of the problem and the difficulty of its solution. It would be too much to expect that an application of Rogerian psychology to literature would resolve the question of what value it has as a human activity where so many previous attempts have failed. But that Rogerian psychology provides an answer to the question that has not previously been suggested indicates at least that it can offer literary study a positive contribution to the continuing debate, a contribution that will stimulate consideration of new possibilities.

In Rogers's system, what he calls "the experiencing of feeling" is extremely important. "In our daily lives," he writes, "there are a thousand and one reasons for not letting ourselves experience our attitudes fully, reasons from our past and from the present, reasons that reside within the social situation" (Rogers, 1961, p. 111). The suppression of this experiencing becomes one of the reasons why a therapeutic relationship becomes necessary; its expression therefore becomes an important goal of such a relationship. "When a person has, throughout therapy, experienced in this fashion all the emotions which organismically arise in him, and has experienced them in [a] knowing and open manner, then he has experienced *himself*, in all the richness that exists within himself" (p. 113).

Earlier I stated that one way of looking at a work of literature is that it is a device for creating emotional responses in a reader. As the reader proceeds through the work, he or she is pulled now into apprehension, now into indignation, now into contempt, now into affection—if one reads long enough, indeed, all the emotions that are capable of organismically arising in a reader will be stimulated into existence. To read a work of literature, then, is in Rogers's

sense of the word a "facilitative" experience, because it increases the degree of access that the reader has to his or her organismic experience.

Such a concept of literature may be tested by examining some specific works of literature. It will be convenient to use Herman Melville's requiem "Shiloh: A Requiem" (April 1862) as an illustration of how reading a poem might hypothetically function as a facilitative experience for readers. The text is as follows:

> Skimming lightly, wheeling still,
> The swallows fly low
> Over the field in clouded days,
> The forest-field of Shiloh—
> Over the field where April rain
> Solaced the parched ones stretched in pain
> Through the pause of night
> That followed the Sunday fight
> Around the church of Shiloh—
> The church so lone, the log-built one,
> That echoed to many a parting groan
> And natural prayer
> Of dying foemen mingled there—
> Foemen at morn, but friends at eve—
> Fame or country least their care:
> (What like a bullet can undeceive!)
> But now they lie low,
> While over them the swallows skim,
> And all is hushed at Shiloh.

The poem begins with an image of swallows flying over a field, an image that gives the reader a peaceful emotion. One by one Melville introduces details that disrupt the peacefulness because of their associations: first the name Shiloh itself, celebrated as the name of a Civil War battlefield; then the negative emotions associated with "parched" (water deprivation) and "pain" (wounds); then the ironic detail (and from this standpoint irony can be identified as an exception) that the soldiers were fighting around a church on Sunday; then the sadness associated with the groans and prayers of the "dying foemen." This movement is suddenly interrupted by surprise as Melville calls them "friends at eve." Why were the foemen friends at evening? He answers that question in the following line: In death or even only in agony, they were no longer concerned about their personal competition for fame or about the success or failure of their contending governments. And in the following line ("What like a bullet can undeceive!"), his use of the word "undeceive" indicates that he believes that concern with fame and country is a deception, indicating false values. The poem ends with a return to the image of the swallows, restoring the peace of the opening but this time with a tinge of sadness for the dead who died as a result of being deceived about what was important.

Reading the poem empathically in this way results in a conclusion that the cognitive content validates: Melville values nature, as the positive emotions associated with the swallows demonstrate, and he disvalues war, as the negative emotions associated with his description of the wounded and dying men demonstrate equally well. But there is also another dimension of the poem revealed by this analysis of the affective content. The positive emotions associated with nature and the negative ones associated with warfare work against each other to provide an implication that war is unnatural, a violation of nature.

Moreover, the analysis shows a sudden interruption of the emotional flow of the poem, occasioned by the surprise generated by the expression "friends at eve." This surprise arouses curiosity, which Melville proceeds to satisfy in purely cognitive terms through the line "Fame or country least their care," which is explanatory rather than evocative—a line that has very nearly no affective content at all. It is puzzling to determine why Melville felt the need for a sudden shift from affect to cognition, because he had already made his point adequately by working on the emotions of his reader. It is tempting to conjecture that he distrusted the ability of the emotions to communicate the point he wanted to make about war and felt the need to turn to a relatively plain statement, editorializing by presenting an abstract idea to the reader's mind rather than relying wholly on an appeal to the reader's emotion. And it is hard not to feel that this intrusion of the abstract into the poem is not, from the standpoint we have been taking, a blemish.

The contrast between the emotions at the beginning and ending of the poem might well be facilitative. The experience of psychotherapists will endorse the assertion that there are people who have no trouble at all in recognizing single, uncomplicated emotions but who do have trouble when their emotions are mingled or mixed. Such persons reading "Shiloh" would have the experience of feeling peacefulness twice within a very few lines, once as a simple emotion and then once mixed with sadness. They would therefore be led to experience their emotions in a more knowing manner.

Rogers (1961) speaks of "the safety and freedom of the therapeutic relationship," which allows emotions to be experienced fully (p. 111). The literary relationship between the reader and the work allows the reader as much safety and freedom as the therapeutic relationship between the client and the therapist. In the privacy of his own chair, the reader is free to feel whatever emotions he or she may and is safe from any adverse consequences.

No single work will suddenly open a reader to his or her own experience; some people may spend a lifetime reading without being fully opened to their own experiences. But the general tendency of the literary relationship is in the direction of providing readers with the same kind of situation as the therapeutic relationship—a safe environment where they are free to feel whatever they feel and accordingly are more open to their own attitudes and more aware of what those attitudes are.

No claim is here made that all readers will be facilitated by literature in the same way. The purpose of this discussion is only to demonstrate that literature has the potentiality of functioning facilitative and thus to suggest that one value of literature is that the reader will be helped to become more aware of his or her organismic emotions through having these emotions aroused in literary situations and hence made accessible.

This contribution to the continuing discussion among literary critics and aestheticians as to the value of literature is yet another way in which Rogerian psychology can be fruitful for literary study.

CONCLUSION

Freudian psychology has provided literary study with enough in the way of useful applications that it has won its right to be considered a fruitful theory, one which yields insights beyond the limits of the discipline in which it was originally developed. Rogerian psychology also passes this test of fruitfulness, because it can be used to provide literary study with a theory of literary genesis, a procedure for literary interpretation, a conceptual framework for the analysis of characters, and an explanation of why literature has value.

It is, indeed, superior to Freudian psychology in this regard. The theory of literary genesis used by Freudian critics suggests that creativity is pathological, which is difficult to accept because the amount of libido that is cathected by pathological conditions would leave the artist little energy for his work; Rogers more plausibly sees creativity as a sign of healthy self-fulfillment and in addition provides an explanation for the importance of literary form that is generally omitted from consideration by Freudian critics.

Whereas Freudian interpretations of works tend to seek symbols and to interpret them as a psychoanalyst would interpret dreams, Rogerian interpretation would focus on the emotions aroused by the work and use those emotions to analyze the value system of the work—a simpler procedure and one that would lead a critic to concentrate on the total effect of the work rather than on the details.

Rogerian character analysis would be at the outset simpler than Freudian, because it would begin by seeking an incongruence in the character; but then in its outcome, it would be richer, because it would not be limited by the categories of psychodiagnosis but could deal with the infinite variety of humanity.

And, finally, Rogerian psychology suggests a reason why literature is valuable to a reader, whereas most Freudian critics have been reluctant even to propose solutions to this problem. One of the more persuasive Freudian critics, it is true, argues that the value of literature is that it relieves anxiety (Lesser, 1957); but compared to this, the value that one finds proposed by Rogers, that literature functions facilitatively for the reader, is much broader.

References

Jones, E. (1976). *Hamlet and Oedipus*. New York: Norton. (Original work published 1949)

Jonson, B. (1951). Ben Jonson. In H. C. White, R. C. Wallerstein, & R. Quintana (Eds.), *17th-century verse and prose* (pp. 154-156). New York: MacMillan.

Letham, E. C. (1969). *The poetry of Robert Frost*. New York: Henry Holt.

Lesser, S. O. (1957). *Fiction and the unconscious*. Boston: Beacon.

Morris, C. (1956). *Varieties of human value*. Chicago: University of Chicago Press.

Rank, O. (1989). *Art and artist: Creative urge and personality development*. New York: Norton. (Original work published 1932)

Richards, I. A. (1929). *Practical criticism*. London: Kegan Paul.

Rogers, C. R. (1961). *On becoming a person*. Boston: Houghton Mifflin.

Rogers, C. R. (1969). *Freedom to learn*. Columbus, OH: Charles E. Merrill.

Rogers, C. R. (1980). *A way of being*. Boston: Houghton Mifflin.

Wellek, R., & Warren, A. (1956). *The theory of literature* (3rd ed.). New York: Harcourt Brace.

FURTHER READING

Biography

Kirschenbaum, Howard. *On Becoming Carl Rogers*. New York: Delacorte Press, 1979, 444 p.
  Comprehensive biography.

Criticism

Evans, Richard I. *Carl Rogers: The Man and His Ideas*. New York: E. P. Dutton, 1975, 195 p.
  Surveys Rogers's psychological theories and considers their social and philosophical implications.

Hart, J. T., and T. M. Tomlinson, eds. *New Directions in Client-Centered Therapy*. New York: Houghton Mifflin, 1970, 619 p.
  Collection of essays that consider various aspects and implications of Rogers's client-centered therapy.

Ida B. Wells-Barnett
1862-1931

American social activist and writer.

INTRODUCTION

Wells-Barnett was one of the most important African-American women reformers of her day. Her anti-lynching campaigns, as well as her efforts on behalf of women's suffrage and issues of justice for black Americans, have given her an important place in American reform history.

BIOGRAPHICAL INFORMATION

Wells-Barnett was born in Holly Springs, Missouri, on July 16, 1862, the oldest of eight children in the Wells family. She attended Shaw University (later renamed Rust College), a school established for freedmen after the Civil War. She assumed the care of her younger siblings following the death of her parents, taught school for a time in Holly Springs, and later moved to Memphis, Tennessee. In 1884, she sued the Chesapeake, Ohio, and Southwestern Railroad for removing her from an all-white railroad car. Although she eventually lost the suit, this event marked the beginning of her lifelong pursuit of social justice for African Americans. Wells-Barnett worked for a number of African-American newspapers and magazines in Memphis, writing about such issues as the deplorable conditions in local black schools. After the office of her employer, *Free Speech,* was destroyed following her stories on the evils of lynching, she decided to moved to New York City to work for the *New York Age.* There she launched an anti-lynching campaign, publishing two booklets on the subject drawn from her feature stories. As her fame spread, she began a lecture tour of England, Wales, and Scotland, bringing to the world a new awareness of lynching practices in the American South. Wells-Barnett continued her search for justice by protesting the lack of a black presence at the Chicago World's Fair of 1893 and also earned the unofficial title "Mother of Clubs" when she encouraged the growth of many black women's clubs. After her marriage in 1895 to Ferdinand L. Barnett, an African-American attorney and another social activist, she devoted several years to motherhood. Later she continued her campaign for equal rights for blacks and also founded the first women's suffrage club for black women. Her crusades against violence and injustice continued well into the 1920s. She died on March 25, 1931, in Chicago.

MAJOR WORKS

Wells-Barnett's best-known works were her accounts of lynching practices, *Southern Horrors: Lynch Law in All Its Phases* (1892) and *A Red Record: Tabulated Statistics and Alleged Causes of Lynching in the United States, 1892-1893-1894* (1895). In these works she indicts, in strong, readable prose, the hypocrisy of American whites who used any pretext, such as trumped-up rape charges and miscegenation laws, to justify the murder of blacks. With Frederick Douglass, I. Garland Penn, and her future husband, Ferdinand L. Barnett, Wells-Barnett issued a pamphlet, *The Reason Why the Colored American Is Not in the World's Columbian Exposition,* in 1893. Her *Mob Rule in New Orleans: Robert Charles and His Fight to the Death* (1900) was another account of a real-life example of gross injustice toward blacks. As she continued her newspaper crusade against violence, she visited Arkansas in the early 1920s, where she investigated the murder of twelve innocent African-American farmers, publishing her report in 1922 as *The Arkansas Race Riot.* Toward the end of that decade Wells-Barnett began her autobiography, which her daughter, Alfreda Duster, published posthumously in 1970 as *Crusade for Justice: The Autobiography of Ida B. Wells*. An edited version of *The Memphis Diary of Ida B. Wells* was also published posthumously in 1995.

CRITICAL RECEPTION

Very early critical reaction to Wells-Barnett's work in the newspapers of the day was generally confined to negative or favorable reviews of her anti-lynching speeches and editorials. Although Wells-Barnett's name appeared in a number of reference books devoted to African-American notables during the early and mid-twentieth century, interest in her life and writings was not strong until the publication of her autobiography, edited by her daughter, in 1970. Coming as it did at the height of the American civil rights movement and at the beginning of the feminist movement, the autobiography kindled a new interest in Wells-Barnett as a radical speaker and writer. During the 1980s and 1990s a number of journal articles on Wells-Barnett appeared which dealt with her rhetorical style, her importance to the field of black female autobiographical narrative, and the social, moral, and historical contexts for her work. Two critical biographies of Wells-Barnett in 1990 and 1998, along with the publication of a collection of her selected works in 1991 and the edited version of her Memphis diary in 1995, have brought even more critical attention to this important American crusader, whose stated ideals of equality and justice resonate to this day.

PRINCIPAL WORKS

Southern Horrors: Lynch Law in All Its Phases (booklet) 1892

The Reason Why the Colored American Is Not in the World's Columbian Exposition—the Afro-American's Contribution to Columbian Literature [with Frederick Douglass, I. Garland Penn, and Ferdinand L. Barnett] (pamphlet) 1893

A Red Record: Tabulated Statistics and Alleged Causes of Lynching in the United States, 1892-1893-1894 (booklet) 1895

Mob Rule in New Orleans: Robert Charles and His Fight to the Death (pamphlet) 1900

The Arkansas Race Riot (pamphlet) 1922

Crusade for Justice: The Autobiography of Ida B. Wells (autobiography) 1970

Selected Works of Ida B. Wells-Barnett (collected prose) 1991

The Memphis Diary of Ida B. Wells: An Intimate Portrait of the Activist as a Young Woman (diaries) 1995

CRITICISM

Karlyn Kohrs Campbell (essay date November 1986)

SOURCE: Campbell, Karlyn Kohrs. "Style and Content in the Rhetoric of Early Afro-American Feminists." *Quarterly Journal of Speech* 72 (November 1986): 434-45.

[*In the following excerpt from a rhetorical analysis of the speeches of Sojourner Truth, Wells-Barnett, and Mary Church Terrell, Campbell points out that Wells-Barnett's style shares many aspects of similar speeches by other reformers but that she disdained traditional "feminine" modes of rhetoric.*]

Afro-American women, in addition to the special problems arising out of slavery, historically faced the same problems as all other women. Married, they were dead civilly; unmarried, they were dependents with few possibilities for self support; regardless of marital and socio-economic status, they were oppressed by the cult of true womanhood, which declared that true women were pure, pious, domestic, and submissive.[1] As a result, even free Afro-Americans in the North prior to the Civil War confronted the same proscriptions against speaking in public as their middle-class white counterparts, and when they spoke, they were censured.[2]

It is not surprising, then, that Afro-American women's rhetoric from the 1830s to 1925, the period usually accepted as that of the earlier United States feminist movement, should present problems for the rhetorical critic. Sometimes these Afro-American women rhetors can be viewed as part of the tradition of early women's rhetoric, sometimes they differ from that tradition in style, sometimes in content.[3] I shall argue that a simultaneous analysis and synthesis is thus necessary in order to understand these similarities and differences, and I shall illustrate convergences and divergences through speeches made by Sojourner Truth, by Ida B. Wells, and by Mary Church Terrell. . . .

IDA B. WELLS

Many Afro-American women were involved in efforts for woman suffrage, because they saw the vote as a means to fight for their own cause, particularly against segregationist legislation that denied Afro-Americans continued participation in or entry into American life. Ida B. Wells and Mary Church Terrell were part of this group. Wells, for example, founded the first Afro-American woman suffrage club, and Church Terrell spoke at National American Woman Suffrage Association Conventions and at the International Council of Women in Berlin between 1898 and 1905.[4] However, their primary concerns were the problems of Afro-Americans, especially the practice of lynching. The conjunction between the concerns of Afro-American and white women is clearest in their common cause on the issue of lynching.

Ida B. Wells's speech, **"Southern Horrors: Lynch Law in All Its Phases,"** delivered in 1892, stands as a counterpoint to two more frequently studied rhetorical events.[5] On December 22, 1886, Henry Grady, a prominent white southern journalist delivered a speech on "The New South" to the New England Society of New York City at its annual banquet.[6] Wells referred to Grady's speech and made explicit the fact that her speech was intended to be a dramatic refutation of the picture of the South that Grady had painted. Three years after Wells began her anti-lynching campaign, Booker T. Washington was invited to address the opening of the Cotton States' Exposition at Atlanta, Georgia, on September 18, 1895.[7] Washington addressed a mixed audience of white and Afro-Americans and articulated the view that southerners of both races could cooperate in all things economic while remaining socially separated. His gradualist views were in contrast to those of W. E. B. Du Bois, who demanded full legal equality and economic opportunity. Wells's speech makes clear that she sided with Du Bois and, like him, she was one of the founders of the National Association for the Advancement of Colored People. In fact, Wells's calls for economic boycotts and armed self-defense would have been congenial to Black Power advocates of the 1960s.

Wells's speech is important as a historical document and as the initiating event in what became a social movement; as a rhetorical work, it is noteworthy in three respects. First, as in her writings, she used evidence and argument in highly sophisticated ways, ways that prevented members of the audience from dismissing her claims as biased or untrue. Second, the speech was an insightful and sophisticated analysis of the interrelationship of sex, race, and class. Third, in contrast to the rhetorical acts of other women, this speech contained no stylistic markers indicating attempts by a woman speaker to appear "womanly" in what is perceived as a male role—that of rhetor.

Wells's use of evidence and argument had to overcome severe obstacles. She had to refute the cultural history of sexism that made the cry of rape (of a white woman) adequate justification for violence against Afro-Americans.[8] She had to show that lynchings were frequent and that rape was not even alleged in a majority of cases. She had to draw this evidence from unimpeachable sources, and she had to use the statements of whites to reveal the real motives behind these acts.

The evidence Wells presented was part of a carefully constructed case. Initially, she argued: "White men lynch the offending Afro-American, not because he is a despoiler of virtue, but because he succumbs to the smiles of white women." Some seventeen relatively detailed examples were presented in support of this claim. The detailed examples allowed her audience to weigh the evidence and consider its plausibility, and the fact that much of it came from the public press, in some cases from white southern newspapers, added to the credibility of her accounts. She left her audience in no doubt that real human beings were caught in lethal dilemmas again and again throughout the South, and emotional response was prompted by the argument of these details rather than by exhortation.

Her argument revealed the terrible double standard: "[I]t is not the crime but the class," she said, referring to the fact that when the victims were Afro-American women, no protection was afforded, no avenging was needed. Once again, her proof was a series of six dramatic examples intended to show that there was no concern to protect Afro-American women or female children or to punish those who assaulted them. Hence, if the reason for lynching was not the protection of white womanhood, some other motive was at work. Wells argued that lynching was done to control Afro-Americans—lynching was political, with the allegation of rape used as justification. She first pointed to the other forms of control that were then widespread throughout the South, the "Jim Crow" laws that had been passed since the 1875 Civil Rights Act had been declared unconstitutional in 1883.[9] Wells noted that, despite these other forms of control, lynching had increased. Here she used evidence gathered by a northern white newspaper, the Chicago *Tribune,* to document with statistics the extent of the problem and the fact that, in only one-third of the cases, was rape even alleged.

She then cited two editorials from white newspapers in Memphis. The first quotation embodied the mythology of the bestial Afro-American rapist, despite the fact that no incidents supporting that mythology had occurred in the city of Memphis, the source of the editorial. The second editorial made explicit the intent to coerce submission through violence. It was a classic statement of the view that "uppity Negroes" should be punished violently.

Wells went on to describe the 1892 lynching in Memphis about which she had written and for which her life had been threatened. This particular lynching, occasioned by economic competition, became a paradigmatic case of lynching throughout the South. Wells concluded by stating that all who disapproved of lynching and remained silent became accessories, because lynch mobs would not persist if their members knew that the forces of law and order would be used against them. Throughout this argument there was a strong appeal to fundamental values of fairness, to the right to trial by jury, and to the right to full and careful investigation of crimes, appeals that added weight to her accusation that silent bystanders were guilty of complicity.

Wells concluded that, given the legal protection or redress, Afro-Americans had to turn to self-help. They had to learn the facts of such cases for themselves in order to judge what the truth was. Such cases called for investigative reporting such as her own. They had to use economic boycotts to demand appropriate legal action against lynchers, and they needed to arm themselves to act in self-defense to prevent mob violence. Here, too, examples were used, including that of Memphis where a boycott in response to the 1892 lynching had had some effect, although not enough to force action against the lynchers, all of whose names were known. Two examples where lynchings were prevented by armed self-defense were noted but not detailed. Wells ended by proposing that these three solutions in concert could solve the problem, that is, stamp out lynch law.

Wells made a carefully constructed case that rested on kinds of evidence that made the problem vivid, demonstrated its scope, supported the speaker's analysis of its causes, and suggested the futility of alternative solutions. Wells understood the kind of problem she faced. Given the general acceptance of the mythology that lynching was caused by sexual assaults on white women, Wells knew that her audience would find it hard to believe her. The evidence was carefully selected to prevent such a response. Hearers and readers encountered case after case that challenged that casual assumption. They learned the statistical facts from a white northern newspaper. They heard the mythology and the political coercion out of the mouths of the editors of newspapers in the very town from which Wells had been driven. Wells was calling into question her audience's prior beliefs and opening their minds to future evidence.

The soundness, indeed the power of Wells's analysis of the relationship of sex, race, and class in the phenomenon of lynching, is attested to by the fact that her conclusions recurred in the resolutions, declarations, and speeches of southern white women. What follows is not a story of interracial cooperation, but of the convergence of the concerns of Afro-American and white women.

In response to the lynching of an Afro-American farm laborer named George Hughes, a Texas suffragist named Jessie Daniel Ames founded the Association of Southern Women for the Prevention of Lynching (ASWPL) in 1930.[10] The goals of this all-white group were to find practical ways to prevent lynchings, to convince southern white women that lynching posed a threat to their own interests, and to use the women so persuaded to arouse public opinion against this crime. Regarding the ASWPL's beginnings, Ames wrote:

> We began our work under adverse conditions. The year 1930 was not a propitious one in which to open an attack on this problem of lynching. Fear of the future and a definite hopelessness in the present prevailed throughout the country. In the South nerves were especially on edge in regard to the race question. Politicians, avid for votes, were stirring up racial antagonisms which had lain more or less dormant since the high year of the Ku Klux Klan. Fear of "social equality" and demands for "jobs for white men before Negroes" were breeding secret organizations to uphold white supremacy. Lynchings had reached a new high level by that November of 1930. Publicity given to the crimes out of which so many lynchings are alleged to grow confirmed lynchers and their sympathizers that the mob provided white women the only protection of which they could be sure.[11]

The approach of the ASWPL was obviously rhetorical; indeed, they did not support federal anti-lynching legisla-tion. After one year's work, the leaders decided that, given public opinion, more information on the causes of lynching was needed, and they directed their research efforts toward responding to the typical questions and objections raised by their audiences. Like their earlier counterparts, these women rhetors aroused hostility. Ames reported that in some states, keen resentment was expressed "against women assuming leadership in an open educational program to eradicate lynching, on the grounds that it reflected upon the judgment and the gallantry of the Southern men who had fought and survived the War Between the States. The best way to take care of this, the women believed, was not to argue, but to increase the number of women willing to undertake to speak against lynching."[12] Women like Ames gathered information, but still faced obstacles. In Ames's words, "We were confronted by the delicate problem of how to use them [the facts] to convince our audiences instead of alienating them," since women who lived where lynching had been committed would be in the audience and since some of the men affiliated with those women might have been members of a lynch mob. Moreover, she wrote, "We knew that they believed the stories which had appeared in the press. Yet, we must ask them to accept for truth what we said even though we contradicted the stories of men whom they loved and trusted."[13]

The ASWPL developed three claims. The first, and the most important, rejected the major justification for lynching: that only the threat of immediate retribution stood between the white women of the South and the lust of the Afro-American rapist. Like Wells and the NAACP, the ASWPL attacked this false claim with facts: Rape was overwhelmingly an intraracial event; in only a small percentage of lynchings was the victim even alleged to have made a sexual assault.[14] The claim that lynching was necessary to protect white women, they argued, was used to mask the economic exploitation and sadism out of which mob violence really sprang.

The second claim was that publicity about lynching throughout the world brought contempt upon the United States and upon the Christian religion. From the outset of Wells's campaign against lynching, Americans were sensitive to criticism from abroad, and the ASWPL warned that the reputation gained from lynching created "a fertile field for . . . communistic doctrines subversive of American democracy at home" and frustrated missionary efforts abroad.

The third claim insisted that lynching discredited legal processes and undermined respect for officers of the law, lessening the ability of established authority to maintain law and order. According to the original ASWPL anti-lynching resolution: "Instead of deterring irresponsible and criminal classes from further crime, as it is argued, lynching tends inevitably to destroy all respect for law and order."[15]

The ASWPL recognized that lynching had its roots in the very nature of white supremacy. At the annual meeting in 1934, the members adopted this resolution:

We declare as our deliberate conclusion that the crime of lynching is a logical result in every community that pursued the policy of humiliation and degradation of a part of its citizenship because of accident of birth; that exploits and intimidates the weaker element . . . for economic gain; that refuses equal educational opportunity to one portion of its children; that segregates arbitrarily a whole race in unsanitary, ugly sections; . . . and finally that denies a voice in the control of government to any fit and proper citizen because of race.[16]

The information gathered and the arguments made by the ASWPL were not new, but their speeches and literature simplified and reiterated the work of other reformers and made it comprehensible to the relatively uneducated and palatable to the people of the rural South. However, Jacquelyn Dowd Hall concluded:

Most significantly it shaped its rhetoric in accord with specifically feminine interests and assumptions. . . . Lynching, they maintained, far from offering white women an indispensable shield against sexual assault, in fact made them pawns in a deadly masculine conflict and hedged them about with an exaggerated myth of female vulnerability and dependence. . . . In the context of a period and a region profoundly inhospitable to feminist protest, they articulated and acted upon a sense of group identity, registering a significant, if muted, protest against the cultural shibboleths of their time. In all these endeavors, ASWPL members held proudly to the image of the southern lady, while at the same time seeking to remake that image according to their own definition of responsible womanhood. In this sense, Jessie Daniel Ames led a revolt against chivalry that was part of a long process of both sexual and racial emancipation.[17]

The ASWPL was not, as I have noted, a case of interracial cooperation, but of an issue over which the concerns of Afro-Americans and white women converged. As Dowd Hall recognized in the title of her book, the women of the ASWPL were revolting against chivalry, against the constraints placed on southern white women by the "womanbelle ideal." They were also horrified by mob violence and refused to allow conceptions of white womanhood to be used to rationalize such conduct. That their analysis coincided with that made earlier by Wells testifies to Wells's understanding of the dynamics of sexism and racism.

Wells's speech was a well-made case. It was also a cogent analysis of the interrelationship of sex and race. However, in striking contrast to most other early feminist rhetoric, Wells's speech contains few indicators or markers of "femininity" or "womanliness." There was and is a "feminine style" or a mode of address that is consistent with traditional norms of femininity. Such a style has certain characteristics. They include modes of accommodation used by oppressed groups to adapt to their oppressors and means of persuasion responsive to the special conditions and experiences of the oppressed. The most elegant example of this mode of discourse is found in Virginia Woolf's *A Room of One's Own*.[18]

Structurally, "feminine" rhetoric is inductive, even circuitous, moving from example to example, and is usually grounded in personal experience. In most instances, personal experience is tested against the pronouncements of male authorities (who can be used for making accusations and indictments that would be impermissible from a woman) and buttressed by limited amounts of statistical evidence demonstrating that personal experience is not atypical. Because of their "natural piety," women may appeal to biblical authority. Metaphors and figurative analogies are frequent, as these prompt participation from the audience, which generates self-persuasion. Rhetorical questions, seeking audience assent to what is shared or obvious, are frequently used. Consistent with their allegedly poetic and emotional natures, women tend to adopt associative, dramatic, and narrative modes of development, as opposed to deductive forms of organization. The tone tends to be personal and somewhat tentative, rather than objective or authoritative. The persona tends to be traditionally feminine, like that of teacher, mediator, or layperson, rather than that of expert, leader, preacher, or judge. Strategically, women who use this style will seek ways to reconcile femininity with the traditional "masculinity" of public discourse. A "womanly" speaker tends to plead, to appeal to the sentiments of the audience, to "court" the audience by being "seductive."

While peculiarly adapted to the conditions of women, this mode of discourse is suitable for both male and female audiences.[19] The style that is "feminine" has many of the characteristics of the "consciousness raising" that has been a central part of the contemporary feminism.[20] Generally, women have perceived themselves in ways that precluded them from functioning as audiences or agents of change.[21] At its best, "feminine" style can be empowering, a way of speaking to those who work in crafts taught largely through personal experience, who are usually separated from one another, and whose concerns are excluded from the channels of public discourse. In other words, it can be a way to address women consistent with traditional female experience and modes of learning. It is also a style that invites female audiences to act, to draw their own conclusions and make their own decisions, in contrast to a traditionally "masculine" style that approaches the audience as inferiors to be told what is right or to be led.[22]

What is astonishing about Wells's speech is that, with the exception of her reliance on the example, almost none of these stylistic markers appear. The language of the speech was blunt, as for example, when she quoted what she had written: "Nobody in this section of the country believes the old threadbare lie that Negro men rape white women." As indicated above, the structure was deductive. The tone is authoritative, at times, even sarcastic. Her claims were clearly stated, and although the Memphis example came from her personal experience, she did not present it as her personal experience—it was a paradigmatic case to be examined objectively. The analogies were literal, and metaphors were not used. The single exception was a comparison of Afro-American men to Samsons tempted by white Delilahs! Wells spoke as an authority and as a leader who could determine the right courses of action, as illustrated by her conclusion. She spoke impersonally; the pronoun "I" appeared only when she asserted her claims. She used white male newspaper editors as authorities, but only in ways that were damaging to them. She was willing to speak the accusations, to make the indictments, in her own voice. The speech is replete with such assertions as, "There is little difference between the Ante-bellum and the New South." Quite simply, there is nothing in this speech to indicate that it was given by a woman, and as such, it is an astonishing rhetorical work, for this period or for any other.[23]

Notes

1. Barbara Welter, *Dimity Convictions: The American Woman in the Nineteenth Century* (Athens, OH: Ohio University Press, 1976).

2. The similarity of the conditions faced by white and Afro-American women at the outset of U.S. women's rhetorical history is illustrated by the case of Maria W. Stewart, an Afro-American, who was the first U.S. woman to give a public lecture. See Maria W. [Miller] Stewart, "Why Sit Ye Here and Die," in *Provisions: A Reader from 19th-Century American Woman* ed. Judith Fetterley (Bloomington: Indiana University Press, 1985), pp. 65-9. That speech, as well as her farewell address of 1833, give strong indications of the hostility she faced. Material from her farewell can be found in Dorothy Sterling, ed., *We Are Your Sisters: Black Women in the Nineteenth Century* (New York: W.W. Norton, 1984), pp. 157-58. The text of another speech, "African Rights and Liberty," delivered on February 27, 1833, in the African Masonic Hall of Boston, is found in *Outspoken Women* ed. Judith Anderson (Dubuque, IA: Kendall/Hunt, 1984), pp. 169-73.

3. The relationship between the early and contemporary feminist movements and Afro-American women is the subject of a number of important works, including Angela Y. Davis, *Women, Race & Class,* (New York: Random House, 1981); Tracey A. Fitzgerald, *The National Council of Negro Women and the Feminist Movement, 1935-1975,* The Georgetown Monograph in American Studies (Washington, D.C.: Georgetown University Press, 1985); Paula Giddings, *When and Where I Enter: The Impact of Black Women on Race and Sex in America* (New York: William Morrow, 1984); Bell Hooks, *Ain't I A Woman: Black Women and Feminism* (Boston: South End Press, 1981); Rosalyn Terborg-Penn, "Afro-Americans in the Struggle for Woman Suffrage," unpublished Ph.D. dissertation, Howard University, 1977.

4. Church Terrell's views of woman suffrage are summarized in "The Justice of Woman Suffrage," *The Crisis,* 22 (September 1912); reprinted in *The Crisis,* 90 (June/July 1983), p. 6. The story of Wells's life is told in Alfreda M. Duster, ed., *Crusade for Justice: The Autobiography of Ida B. Wells* (Chicago: Univer-

sity of Chicago Press, 1970). See also Dorothy Sterling, *Black Foremothers: Three Lives* (Old Westbury, New York: The Feminist Press, 1979) for brief biographies of Wells and Church Terrell, and Giddings, pp. 17-31, who recounts the stories of the early efforts of Wells and Church Terrell and links the events in their lives. Church Terrell's autobiography is cited below.

5. "Southern Horrors: Lynch Law in All Its Phases," in Ida B. Wells-Barnett, *On Lynchings: Southern Horrors, A Red Record, Mob Rule in New Orleans* (1892; rpt. New York: Arno Press, 1969), pp. 4-19.

6. The text of the speech comes from *Proceedings of the New England Society (Year Book)* 1886 as reprinted in *Henry W. Grady, His Life, Writings and Speeches* ed. Joel Chandler Harris (Cassell Company, 1890), pp. 83-93.

7. Booker T. Washington, "Atlanta Exposition Address," in *Up From Slavery* (New York: Doubleday Page, 1901), pp. 217-25.

8. See, particularly, "The Function and Mythology of Lynching" in Donald L. Grant, *The Anti-Lynching Movement: 1883-1932* (San Francisco: R and E Associates, 1975), pp. 1-19. See also the 1901 exchange between Jane Addams and Ida B. Wells *Lynching and Rape: An Exchange of Views,* ed. Bettina Aptheker (New York: American Institute for Marxist Studies, 1977).

9. For a history of Civil Rights legislation and decisions, including the history of segregation, see Constance Baker Motley, "The Legal Status of the Negro in the United States," in *The American Negro Reference Book* ed. John P. Davis (Englewood Cliffs, NJ: Prentice-Hall, 1966), pp. 484-521.

10. The Story of the ASWPL and of the life of its leader, Jessie Daniel Ames, is told by Jacquelyn Dowd Hall, *Revolt Against Chivalry: Jessie Daniel Ames and the Women's Campaign Against Lynching* (New York: Columbia University Press, 1979). I am indebted to Dowd Hall's work for the material presented here on the ASWPL.

11. Jessie Daniel Ames, "Southern Women Look at Lynching," pamphlet printed by the ASWPL, Atlanta, Georgia, February 1937, p. 4.

12. Ames, p. 6.

13. Ames, p. 8.

14. According to the information gathered by the ASWPL, only 16.7% of those lynched between 1889 and 1930 and only 16.1% of those lynched between 1931 and 1941 were accused of rape. See Jessie Daniel Ames, *The Changing Character of Lynching,* Commission on Interracial Cooperation, Atlanta, July 1942, p. 6. Cited by Jacquelyn Dowd Hall, "'A Truly Subversive Affair': Women Against Lynching in the

Twentieth-Century South," in *Women of America: A History* ed. Carol Ruth Berkin and Mary Beth Norton (Boston: Houghton-Mifflin, 1978), p. 388. See also Ida B. Wells, "A Red Record," originally published in 1895, in *On Lynchings*. My analysis of the major ASWPL arguments is drawn from Dowd Hall, "'A Truly Subversive Affair,'" pp. 370-74.

15. Ames, cited by Dowd Hall, "'A Truly Subversive Affair,'" p. 373.

16. Ames, cited by Dowd Hall, "'A Truly Subversive Affair,'" p. 380.

17. Dowd Hall, "'A Truly Subversive Affair,'" p. 382-83.

18. Virginia Woolf, *A Room of One's Own,* (New York: Harbinger, 1929).

19. For a rhetorical analysis showing how "feminine" style can be used effectively for male audiences, see Karlyn Kohrs Campbell, "Stanton's 'The Solitude of Self' A Rationale for Feminism," *Quarterly Journal of Speech,* 66 (1980), 304-12.

20. Consciousness-raising has played a significant role in a variety of protest movements, ranging from the use of testimony in the U.S. civil rights movement to "speaking pain" in the Maoist revolution in China. For the characteristics of consciousness-raising as a rhetorical style, see Karlyn Kohrs Campbell, "Femininity and Feminism: To Be or Not To Be A Woman," *Communication Quarterly,* 31 (1983), 105-07.

21. Jo Freeman, "The Building of the Gilded Cage," in K. K. Campbell, *Critiques of Contemporary Rhetoric* (Belmont, CA: Wadworth, 1972), pp. 165-66, cites studies of women's self-perceptions done in the 1950s that demonstrate extremely negative self-images, including notions of passivity. Presumably contemporary feminism has begun to alter such self-perceptions.

22. Richard Nixon's first inaugural address is a cogent example of self-absorbed, masculinist rhetoric. Robert L. Scott calls attention to Nixon's excessive and inappropriate use of the pronoun "I" in "Rhetoric That Postures: An Intrinsic Reading of Richard M. Nixon's Inaugural Address," *Western Speech,* 34 (1970), 47.

23. There are other examples of early women's rhetoric that contain almost no marks of "feminine" style; for example, Susan B. Anthony, "Is It a Crime for a U.S. Citizen to Vote?" in *An Account of the Proceedings on the Trial of Susan B. Anthony* (Rochester, NY: Daily Democrat and Chronicle Book Print, 1874), pp. 151-78.

Joanne M. Braxton (essay date 1989)

SOURCE: Braxton, Joanne M. "Crusader for Justice: Ida B. Wells." In *Black Women Writing Autobiography: A Tradition within a Tradition,* pp. 102-138. Philadelphia: Temple University Press, 1989.

[*In the following chapter from her full-length study of a number of autobiographical narratives written by African-American women, Braxton analyzes Wells-Barnett's Crusade for Justice both as an historical memoir and a confessional.*]

> *Who shall say that such a work accomplished by one woman exiled and maligned by that community among whom she had so long and so valiantly labored, bending every effort to the upbuilding of the manhood and womanhood of all races, shall not place her in the front rank of philanthropists, not only of the womanhood of this race, but among those laborers of all ages and all climes?*
>
> *—G. B. Mossell (1894)*

The importance of black autobiography as literature and history is well documented. The historian John Blassingame views black autobiography as "a counterweight to the white historian's caricature of black life," possessing a "therapeutic value" for both authors and readers, "a vehicle blacks used to express their true feelings without having them distorted by whites." One of the "mainsprings of the black novel," autobiography has also been "one of the major forums of black protest, a chief source of adequate historical information, and a link in the black literary tradition."[1] In *The American Autobiography,* the literary critic Albert E. Stone suggests that "the best place to start to understand autobiography as a cultural act is with history," that is to say, "historical consciousness speaks *out* of a singular experience, for some particular social group, to a wider audience. This . . . articulation is at once an act of perception and creation. Autobiography is, simply and profoundly, personal history."[2]

Like *The Education of Henry Adams* (1907) or *The Autobiography of W. E. B. Du Bois* (1968), Ida B. Wells's **Crusade for Justice** represents a posthumously published autobiography by a well-known public figure. Wells employs the medium of the historical memoir, a subgenre of autobiography dominated almost entirely by men, to create her lasting version of the self.

"The memoir," James Cox asserts, "is a category of autobiography that needs attention," part of the "lost ground" of American literature. "There is a distinct tiresomeness about the ease with which literary critics assure themselves that 'mere' fact has nothing to do with the art of autobiography. The truth or falsity of autobiography is thereby subordinated to the creativity, the design, 'the inner' truth of the narrative." Cox observes, moreover, that "autobiographies devoted to the emotional consciousness of the writer have been much more subject to investigation than the memoir, particularly the memoir of a well-known public figure."[3] Thus, Wells's **Crusade for Justice,** as the memoir of a well-known public figure who is also a black woman, constitutes part of the "lost ground" of Afro-American literary tradition. It does much to establish continuity within black female autobiographical tradition, for this text has distinct characteristics common to both nineteenth- and twentieth-century autobiographies by black American women. The title **Crusade for Justice** refers primarily to Wells's recollections of her public life, but it also borrows from the confessional mode of autobiography to allow Wells the latitude to discuss her experience of marriage and family as it influenced her work and public life. Therefore, the "confessional" aspect is more fully developed in *Crusade* than in most historical memoirs.

In at least one respect, Wells departs from the traditional autobiographical stance of an older person looking back and settling accounts;[4] she is not a wise and paternal elder, some "articulate hero" looking back at the end of a quest fulfilled. In *Crusade,* the outraged mother of the slave narrative emerges in the personal myth of a "fiery reformer, feminist, and race leader."[5] Speaking as the outraged mother who carries her nursing son on an antilynching speaking tour, Wells's autobiographical posture is that of a protector of black manhood and a nurturer and defender of black womanhood. Marked by unpredictable shifts in narrative movement similar to those found in earlier autobiographies by black American women, *Crusade* emphasizes the public sphere more in the first half of the narrative, and home and family life more in the second, with a perceptible break at Chapter 30, "A Divided Duty." Although Stephen Butterfield argues that *Crusade* represents "the slave narrative in its purest and truest light," this autobiography is organized according to more sophisticated principles than the slave narrative, and the sensibility is a broadened one.[6] Although Wells deemphasizes her personal life in order to focus on her public career and achievements, *Crusade for Justice* qualifies as what James Olney calls a "duplex" autobiography in that Wells gives the reader enough of a view of her domestic sphere to round out what she presents of herself as a public person.

The structure of *Crusade for Justice,* like that of many autobiographies, is chronological rather than thematic or topical. Organized into forty-six short chapters, the memoir has the same "disconnected" quality of many women's narratives.[7] Although it begins with Wells's recounting of her painful adolescence, the autobiographical "I" shifts to the viewpoint of the mature young woman fighting against lynching, then to that of an older woman wise in many ways, looking back on her life, ordering her experience in the recreation of the self.

Part of its intrinsic cultural value is that *Crusade for Justice* presents prime source material for speculation on the role of race and sex in the development of Wells's psychosocial identity and her autobiographical point of view. In his *Life History and the Historic Movement,* Erik Erikson defines the autobiographer's psychosocial identity primarily in relation to "the personal coherence of the individual and the group." Erikson postulates that "one must first ask oneself under what circumstances the memoirs were written, what their intended purpose was, and what form *they assumed.* Only then can one proceed to judge the less conscious motivations, which may have led the autobiographer to emphasize selectively some experiences and omit other equally decisive ones . . . to correct what might spoil the kind of immortality he has chosen for himself."[8] Certainly such questions must be asked of Wells's autobiography, which was written toward the end of her career and her life, when she might have been susceptible to such "less conscious motivations." And if Erikson had read *Crusade for Justice,* he might have criticized it as one of those "autobiographies . . . written at certain late stages of life for the purpose of recreating oneself in the image of one's method."[9]

Wells began her autobiography in 1928; she died in 1934, leaving her work in midsentence. According to Alfreda M. Duster, her youngest child and editor of the posthumously published autobiography:

> Ida B. Wells really wrote her own autobiography beginning in 1928. Our home had a large dining room with a huge dining table that could be expanded by putting "leaves" where the halves were pulled apart. That table was extended to its fullest length and was covered with papers, notes, books, etc.
>
> She spent most of her days there, except when she was attending meetings, giving lectures, or answering requests for help from people in trouble, which were many.
>
> She wrote the preface and the first three chapters by hand, writing and re-writing, then she secured the services of my brother's secretary, Miss Sinclair, for the rest of the chapters or re-typed at the next session.[10]

Although the editors at the University of Chicago Press supplied the book and chapter titles (since Wells did not), the manuscript was otherwise printed "just as she wrote it," partly because the editor was aware that as Wells's daughter, anything she wrote would be suspect. Thus the text may be regarded as essentially Wells's own, although the published work represents an impressive feat of mother-daughter bonding and personal and political commitment spanning two generations. *Crusade for Justice* is a family and community document as well as the celebration of an individual triumph.

In Duster's words, "My role was a determination to see that this book was published. I knew it was a valuable story—one that should be published by a press which had nation-wide and even international distribution facilities, and I would not settle for less. So I just kept seeking and sending, and when the manuscript was returned, I just kept looking for another publisher." According to Duster, the cycle of rejection started shortly after her mother's death and went on for about thirty-five years. "I knew the story should be told," she wrote in answer to my query. "I knew it had significance, and I wanted it published . . . if I'd given up and put the manuscript somewhere and never tried, it would never have been available." But Duster's true role extended beyond a determination to see her mother's autobiography published. For three years after the book was accepted, she worked under the supervision of the historian John Hope Franklin, "reading, travelling all over the country, verifying what mother had written from memory by facts and figures, articles, books, newspapers, correspondence, etc."[11] In his foreword, Franklin attests to Duster's scrupulous editing:

Although her interest in the subject is understandably deep and her knowledge of the things about which her mother writes is great, Mrs. Duster has not intruded herself into the story that is, after all, the story of Ida B. Wells. She has accurately perceived her role as an understanding and sympathetic editor, scrupulously avoiding the pitfalls of filial subjectivity.[12]

Where an error or discrepancy occurs, Duster includes a note of correction, but her concern with historical accuracy does not intrude; the reader can almost hear Ida B. Wells through the immediacy of the text. This sense of presence represents one of the central paradoxes of *Crusade for Justice,* the dependence of the deceased mother on the living daughter for the revelation and publication of her autobiography.

Presumably, therefore, Duster had some voice in the selection of the title and subtitle, which were not supplied by the autobiographer. The title, *Crusade for Justice,* signals the central concerns and forecasts the dominant metaphors and "necessary fictions" of the text; it also suggests a holy war, a figure of thought that runs throughout Wells's narrative. The subtitle, *The Autobiography of Ida B. Wells,* indicates the intention to minimize the autobiographer's personal life in order to portray her participation in a vast historical drama; *Crusade for Justice* is clearly presented as the story not only of Ida B. Wells but also of her times.

Duster's introduction occupies a crucial position, following the foreword by John Hope Franklin and preceding Wells's own preface. Unlike the authenticating subtexts of nineteenth-century slave narratives, which seem to challenge or undermine the narrator's authorial control, the Duster introduction engages in a kind of literary call and response with Wells's preface and the larger text, resulting in a remarkable resonance between *Crusade for Justice* and its authenticating subtexts. Duster begins her introduction by quoting Norman B. Wood's *The White Side of a Black Subject*:

> God has raised up a modern Deborah in the person of Miss Ida B. Wells, whose voice has been heard throughout England and the United States . . . pleading as only she can plead for justice and fair treatment for her people. . . . we believe God delivered her from being lynched at Memphis, that by her portrayal of the burnings at Paris, Texas, Texarkana, Arkansas and elsewhere she might light a flame of righteous indignation, in England and America which by God's grace, will never be extinguished until a Negro's life is as safe in Mississippi and Tennessee as in Massachusetts or Rhode Island.[13]

Duster asserts that Wood's "was not an unusual description" of Wells, "who was described over and over again as militant, courageous, determined, impassioned, and aggressive."[14] In the remainder of the first paragraph, Duster authenticates her mother's slave birth, her uncommon parentage and upbringing, and much of the factual content of the early chapters of *Crusade.*

But Duster does more than attest to the truth value of her mother's narrative; by quoting a white author who likens her mother to Deborah, a prophetess and judge among the Hebrews of the Old Testament, she participates in the mythmaking process. Like the Old Testament heroine, who "arose a mother in Israel" to lead an army against the enemies of her people, Ida B. Wells led the crusade against lynching, full of outrage and indignation, going where men feared to tread. Thus Duster's rhetorical strategy works partly because she directs the reader's attention away from herself as authenticator, and because she contributes to the development of Wells's myth. Near the end of her introduction, Duster forecasts and softens the "strained analogy" that opens her mother's preface, as she supports Wells's personal identification with Joan of Arc:

> In the preface to her autobiography she mentions that a young lady compared her to Joan of Arc. The analogy is, at best, strained, but the odds against [Wells] were in many ways greater. True enough, Joan was a peasant girl in a time when peasants and girls had nothing to say to the ruling class in France. But Ida B. Wells was a black woman born into slavery who began carrying the torch against lynching in the very South bent upon the degradation of the blacks.[15]

The torch of righteous indignation carried in the crusade against the barbaric practice of lynching becomes one of the central metaphors of Wells's text.

Wells's own preface affirms the "holy war" motif as she begins with the reference to Joan of Arc in an indirect advancement of a statement of her autobiographical purpose and intention:

> A young woman recently asked me to tell her of my connection with the lynching agitation which was started in 1892. She said she was at a YWCA vesper service when the subject for discussion was Joan of Arc, and each person was asked to tell of someone they knew who had traits of character resembling this French heroine and martyr. She was the only colored girl present, and not wishing to lag behind the others, she named me. She was then asked to tell why she thought I deserved such mention. She said, "Mrs. Barnett, I couldn't tell why I thought so."[16]

Wells's identification with Joan of Arc recalls the preface to Sojourner Truth's *Narrative* where Truth evokes the same image; thus Wells revises and recasts Truth's chosen historical metaphor. Wells underscores her historical intention as she builds her personal myth of self:

> When she told me she was twenty-five years old, I realized that one reason she did not know was because the happenings about which she inquired took place before she was born. It is therefore for the young who have so little of our history recorded that I am for the first time in my life writing about myself. I am all the more constrained to do this because there is such a lack of authentic race history of Reconstruction times written by a Negro himself.

> (*Crusade,* 3-4)

Moreover, Wells's preface advances a historical association with Frederick Douglass, an association often reinforced in the text. Wells writes:

We have Frederick Douglass's history of slavery as he knew and experienced it. But of the storm and stress immediately after the Civil War, of the Ku Klux Klan, of ballot stuffing, wholesale murders of Negroes who tried to exercise their newfound rights as free men and citizens, the carpetbag invasion about which the South published much that is false, and the Negroes' political life in that era—our race has little of its own that is definite or authentic.

(*Crusade,* 4)

The autobiographer's goal is clearly one of definition, documentation, and authentication; her story is intended not only as her own but as the story of her people and her times. She presents her life as a representative and symbolic one.

Wells's documentary mode is signaled by the form of the "linear narrative," which is heavily influenced by journalism and reportage, and authenticated by quotes from newspapers, letters, and "other verifiable, external records." Yet another clue concerns the autobiographer's "attention to chronology and causes," and her brooding historical consciousness, which seems to pervade every word.[17] In *Crusade for Justice,* Wells attempts to compensate for a public image frequently maligned in the white press. Like the fugitive slaves, Wells feels compelled to tell her story from her own point of view. She wants to set the record straight.

The development of Wells's consciousness resembles the growth of Harriet "Linda Brent" Jacobs's as it unfolds in a series of autobiographical turning points, which might also be viewed as autobiographical "cover memories." A cover memory, according to Erik Erikson, is "a roughly factual event that has come to symbolize in condensed form a complex of ideas, affects and memories . . . living on in adulthood" as an "account to be settled."[18] The narrative movement of *Crusade for Justice* proceeds from one cover memory to the next; thus, "settling accounts" becomes an important figure of thought and a locus of thematic meaning in the text.

As in many other autobiographies by black women, childhood receives scant treatment; Wells treats her childhood in fewer than fifteen pages. While these memories seem dim, what Wells recalls from childhood prefigures a motif of central importance in the later text: the division between public and private duty. Born into slavery, Wells's "earliest recollections" are of reading the newspaper to her father and "an admiring group of his friends." Of her father, she writes, "He was interested in politics and I heard the words of the Ku Klux Klan long before I knew what they meant. I dimly knew that it meant something fearful, by the way my mother walked the floor at night when my father was at a political meeting." Wells portrays her mother as a "deeply religious woman" who "won the prize for regular attendance at Sunday school" and taught her children "the work of the home" as well as the virtue of literacy as a tool of liberation. "She was not forty when she died, but she had borne eight children and brought us

up with a strict discipline that many mothers who had had educational advantages have not exceeded. She used to tell us how she had been beaten by slave owners and the hard times she had as a slave" (*Crusade,* 9). Jim and Lizzie Wells provide for Ida a direct contact with an oppressive slave past. Jim reinforces the connection of freedom, literacy, and struggle, while Lizzie triumphs as nurturer, protector, and defender of her family.

The young Ida B. Wells does not understand the implications of everything that she sees and experiences. The narration in the early pages of the autobiography by the mature Ida B. Wells profits from the child's point of view; although incidents narrated seem randomly chosen, Wells endows each "cover memory" with symbolic significance. The feminist critic Patricia Spacks argues that attitudes of many women autobiographers toward adolescence differ from those of men in that women tend to remember adolescence with a kind of "nostalgic pleasure," but that black women writing autobiography do not fit this model: They typically have tragically short childhoods. The black woman autobiographer typically substitutes a concern for survival for the flirtations and diversions of traditional "white" adolescence.[19]

The death of Wells's parents during a yellow fever epidemic propels the teenage girl into a world of adult reality. Reborn into a world of "Hard Beginnings," Wells is suddenly charged with the responsibilities of an adult. In presenting this experience, the autobiographer employs both the inquiring mind of the historian and the selectivity of the artist. Wells's narration of her conversation with the conductor of the train that took her home develops the myth of the stalwart "Christian soldier," who serves family and community under the most adverse circumstances. She finds ample opportunities for heroism in her everyday life and possesses the courage necessary to fulfill a heroic role:

It was a freight train. No passenger trains were running or needed. And the caboose in which I rode was draped in black for two previous conductors who had fallen victim to this dreaded disease. The conductor who told me this was sure that I had made a mistake to go home. I asked him why he was running the train when he knew he was likely to get the fever as had those others for whom the car was draped. He shrugged his shoulders and said that somebody had to do it. "That is exactly why I am going home. I am the oldest of seven living children. There's nobody but me to look after them now. Don't you think I should do my duty, too?"

(*Crusade,* 12)

In choosing these images and metaphors, Wells, like many other twentieth-century autobiographers, accentuates her adolescent performance. She also conforms to this pattern by diminishing the importance of the actions of her siblings in this crisis. "There were six of us left, and I the oldest, was only fourteen years old. After being a happy, light-hearted school-girl, I suddenly found myself at the head of a family" (*Crusade,* 12). Wells's recognition that she will have to rely on personal resources parallels that of Harriet Jacobs. Like the fugitive slaves, Wells achieves self-reliance by facing hardship. Reflecting the values of the slave narrative, Ida struggles to keep her family together, even after well-meaning friends and neighbors offer to take the children in:

> I said that it would make my mother and father turn over in their graves to know their children had been scattered like that and that we owned the house and if the Masons would help find work, I would take care of them. Of course they scoffed at the idea of a butterfly fourteen-year-old schoolgirl trying to do what it had taken the combined effort of mother and father to do. . . .
>
> I took the examination for a country schoolteacher and had my dress lengthened, and I got a school six miles out in the country.
>
> (*Crusade,* 16)

In striving for self-sufficiency, the young woman unconsciously oversteps the boundaries of community-sanctioned propriety. The death of Wells's parents and her efforts to keep the family together precipitate an adolescent identity crisis, for Ida rebels against her perceived lack of power and an unwritten code of social etiquette designed to protect young black women from the sexual advances of white men.

For example, after Wells's father had died, the family physician, a friendly white man, had locked up $300 of Jim Wells's money for safekeeping, and sent for Ida, the oldest child. When Ida returned to Holly Springs, the doctor made arrangements to have the money transferred to her. This conscientious act of decency leads to a confrontation:

> But someone said that I had been downtown inquiring for Dr. Gray shortly after I had come from the country. They heard him tell my sister he would get the money, meaning my father's money, and bring it to us that night. It was easy for that type of mind to deduce and spread that already, as young as I was, I had been heard asking white men for money and that was the reason I wanted to live there by myself with the children.
>
> As I look back at it now I can perhaps understand the type of mind which drew such conclusions. And no one suggested that I was laying myself open to gossiping tongues.
>
> (*Crusade,* 17)

This negative interaction impresses the young Ida B. Wells with an awareness of her sexual identity as well as her social powerlessness. Here Wells's ingrained concept of duty to family conflicts with the conventional notions of ideal womanhood espoused by her community. By demanding to be allowed to stand as the head of her family, Wells had unintentionally violated the racial and sexual etiquette of her community, which dictated that respectable young black women, white men, and money did not mix. Generally, the community did what it could do to discourage its women from having anything to do with white men; this conservative behavior served to minimize the potential for violence to some degree. Reinforcing the "hometraining" she had received from gentler hands, this incident helped both to form and to transform Ida's identity.

Outraged at the unjust accusation, Wells becomes even more set in her ways. In relating this experience in the pages of her autobiography, Wells introduces the idea of identity formation through conflict, a motif that can be linked to the literary strategy of settling accounts, as the autobiographer moves from one psychological turning point to the next.

The early narrative treatment of another incident, which occurred in 1884, clearly demonstrates the growth of what Erikson might view as a "pattern of analogous events . . . that combine to suggest a plausible direction."[20] Here a defiant Wells confronts the Chesapeake and Ohio Railroad with regard to its "color policy":

> But ever since the repeal of the Civil Rights Bill by the United States Supreme Court . . . there had been efforts all over the South to draw the color line on the railroads.
>
> When the train started and the conductor came along to collect tickets, he took my ticket, then handed it back to me and told me that he could not take my ticket there. I thought that if he didn't want the ticket that I wouldn't bother about it and so went on reading. In a little while when he finished taking tickets, he came back and told me that I would have to go into another car. I refused, saying that the forward car was a smoker, and as I was in the ladies car, I proposed to stay. He tried to drag me out of the seat, but the moment he caught hold of my arm I fastened my teeth into the back of his hand.
>
> I had braced my feet against the seat in front and was holding to the back, and as he already had been badly bitten, he didn't try it again by himself. He went forward and got the baggageman and another man to help him and of course they succeeded in dragging me out.
>
> (*Crusade,* 18-19)

This "cover memory" contributes to a pattern in the development of Wells's consciousness. The outraged young school-teacher with her teeth in the back of the conductor's hand is one of the selves of the autobiographer. In *Crusade for Justice* Wells performs on a historical stage, seeking a larger audience than that of the white "ladies and gentlemen" in the train car. She authenticates her narrative elaborately, quoting one of her many subtexts, a headline from the *Memphis Commercial Appeal* that read: "Darky Damsel Obtains a Verdict for Damages against the Chesapeake and Ohio Railroad—What it Cost to Put a Colored School Teacher in a Smoking Car—Verdict for $500." Eventually, the railroad appealed the case to the state supreme court, which reversed the findings of the lower court, and ordered Wells to pay court costs. Even so, Wells's strategic inclusion of this incident in her "authenticating narrative" strengthened her posture as a crusader for justice.

Never enthusiastic about teaching, Wells found the profession too confining; she felt stifled and isolated. In the chapter titled "Iola," she writes: "The confinement and monotony began to grow distasteful. The correspondence I had built up in newspaper work gave me an outlet through which to express the real 'me'" (*Crusade,* 31). Journalism propels Wells out of teaching, as her outrage flares into another, more public conflict with community leaders. As a writer and editor for the *Memphis Free Speech,* Wells writes an editorial that attacks the morals of Memphis teachers. This sparks a dispute that embarrasses her employers on the Memphis School Board and contributes to the suicide of a black female teacher who had allegedly been involved in an affair with a white lawyer employed by the same board. Wells's public revelations were not news to the rest of the community, but she had disrupted a delicate balance of race relations by revealing a situation about which community leaders had agreed to keep quiet.

Losing her job as a result of the controversy, Wells becomes totally involved in publishing. As an investigative reporter, she continues to define her identity through the adversary relationship. Publishing provides Wells with a wider audience and greater opportunities for identity-defining experiences. Thus, early in *Crusade,* Wells reveals her established pattern of forming her identity through public conflict.

In 1892, the lynching of three black Memphis citizens stirs Wells's moral indignation, and her reaction places her in a position of national prominence. Wells's autobiographical response to the "Lynching at the Curve" proves Robert Stepto's assertion that "personal history may be created through immersion in an elaborately authenticated historical event." By re-creating this historical event as an "act of language," Wells elevates it to the equivalent of metaphor in what Stepto calls "rhetorical usefulness."[21] As an event, the "Lynching at the Curve" lives on in Wells's autobiographical consciousness as a "supreme account to be settled."

> One day some colored and white boys quarreled over a game of marbles and the colored boys got the better of the fight which followed. The father of the white boys whipped the victorious colored boy, whose father and friends pitched in to avenge the grown man's flogging of a colored boy. The colored men won the fight, whereupon the white father and grocery keeper swore out a warrant for the arrest of the colored victors.
>
> Sunday morning's paper came out with lurid headlines telling how officers of the law had been wounded while in the discharge of their duties, hunting up criminals whom they had been told were harbored in the People's Grocery Company, this being "a low dive in which drinking and gambling were carried on: a resort of thieves and thugs." So ran the description in the leading white journals of Memphis of this successful effort of decent black men to carry on a legitimate business.
>
> (*Crusade,* 48-49)

Wells used this case as a prime example of the economic motivation behind some lynchings. According to Wells's analysis, the quarrel over the game of marbles was designed to involve black men in a dispute that would cost them their business.

The "Tennessee Rifles," a black militia group, guarded the jail where the black men were held as long as they felt the white "officers" were in danger of dying. When they left their post, after deciding that tensions were easing, a group of white men crept into the jail at night, carried the black prisoners a mile outside the city, and "horribly shot them to death" (*Crusade,* 50). The lynching had a profound effect on Wells. Although she was in Natchez when the incident occurred, she knew all three men personally. That week, in the newspaper *Free Speech,* Wells carried words of advice for Memphis blacks:

> The city of Memphis has demonstrated that neither character nor standing avails the Negro if he dares to protect himself against the white man or become his rival. There is nothing we can do about the lynching now, as we are out-numbered and without arms. There is therefore only one thing left that we can do; save our money and leave a town which will neither protect our lives and property, nor give us fair trial in the courts, but takes us out and murders us in cold blood when accused by white persons.
>
> (*Crusade,* 52)

This editorial, which Wells excerpted in her autobiography, precipitated a series of events that led to the smashing of Wells's press and her forced exile. Following Wells's advice, blacks disposed of their property and left Memphis, bringing business to a virtual standstill:

> Music houses had more musical instruments, sold on the installment plan, thrown back on their own hands than they could find storage for. Housewives found a hitherto unknown shortage of help and resorted to the expedient of paying their servants only half the wages due them at the end of the week.
>
> (*Crusade,* 53)

The article that led to the final destruction of Wells's press pointed to the root cause of many lynchings. Some few months after the lynching at "the curve," Wells wrote the following in a May 1892 editorial in *Free Speech*:

> Eight Negroes lynched since the last issue of the *Free Speech.* Three were charged with killing white men and five with raping white women. If Southern white men are not careful . . . a conclusion will be reached which will be very dangerous to the moral reputation of their women.

In response to this editorial, a white rival paper, the *Memphis Commercial Appeal,* called on "chivalrous" white men to avenge this insult to the honor of white womanhood. As a result, the type and furnishings of Wells's *Free Press* were demolished, and a note was left behind saying that anyone attempting to publish the paper again would be killed. Wells received the information while attending a series of conferences in the Northeast. She had lost her paper, and been threatened and exiled from her home, for telling the truth as she saw it.

This experience, perhaps more than any other, contributed to Ida B. Wells's self-image; it reinforced her sense of self as a black woman who did her Christian duty by decrying the evils of lynching and the moral decay at its root. According to Erikson, "Leadership is prominently characterized by the choice of the proper place, the exact moment, and the specific issues that help" to make a point "momentously."[22] Wells liberated her power to effect change and became a woman of action in response to a given historical moment and a specific issue, lynching. In psychosocial terms, her lifelong struggle against lynching became what Erikson would have called a defense against "identity confusion."

As an investigative reporter, Wells published several booklets on lynching. The first of these, *Southern Horrors, Lynch Law in All Its Phases,* originally appeared as an article in the June 25, 1892, issue of T. Thomas Fortune's *New York Age,* the paper on which Wells worked after her forced departure from Memphis. In *Southern Horrors,* Wells established the falseness of the rape charge as an alleged cause of lynching and exposed many of these "rapes" as mere cover-ups for interracial love affairs between black men and white women. She also pointed to a deeper irony:

> The miscegenation laws of the South only operate against the legitimate union of the races; they leave the white man free to seduce all the colored girls he can, but it is death to the colored man who yields to the force and advances of a similar attraction in white women. White men lynch the offending Afro-American, not because he is a despoiler of virtue, but because he succumbs to the smiles of white women.[23]

Decrying the sexual double standard at the root of America's race war, Wells recognized the issue as one embedded in cultural and sexual stereotypes of black men, as well as conventional (and often false) notions of white womanhood. Although lynching proved an effective sanction against sex between black men and white women, white men were rarely punished for their sexual exploitation of black women. Such interracial liaisons degraded not only black women but white women, who perceived the features of a husband or a brother in a young mulatto face.

It was during this early part of her public career that the "Sage of Anacostia" became interested in Wells's work:

> Frederick Douglass came from his home in Washington to tell me what a revelation of existing conditions this article had been to him. He had been troubled by the increasing number of lynchings, and had begun to believe that there was an increasing lasciviousness on the part of Negroes. He wrote a strong preface to the pamphlet which I afterward published embodying these facts. This was the beginning of a friendship with the "Sage of Anacostia" which lasted until the day of his death, three years later. I have never ceased to be thankful for this contact with him.
>
> *(Crusade,* 72-73)

Despite Wells's assertion and Douglass's authentication of her life and work, there is no known evidence to suggest that he ever believed "there was an increasing lasciviousness on the part of Negroes." The above passage illustrates a certain self-serving behavior that is characteristic of Wells's autobiographical persona, a form of posing that, when manifested in life, did not endear her to the leadership that moved forward to fill the void left by Douglass's passing. Even though the Wells assertion may be true, a more modest estimation of her contribution to Douglass's ideas would have been more persuasive to the cautious reader.

Douglass's preface to *Southern Horrors,* written at Wells's request, emerges as yet another key subtext in the interpretation of Wells's authenticating strategy. On October 17, 1892, Wells queried Douglass on stationery from the *New York Age.* "Dear Mr. Douglass," she wrote, "I take the liberty of addressing you to ask if you will be so kind as to put in writing the encomiums you were pleased to lavish on my article on Lynch Law published in the June 25 issue of the *Age.*"[24] Wells wrote that she was "revising the matter for a pamphlet" and asked for a letter she could use as an introduction; the pamphlet later appeared as *Southern Horrors.* In 1895, Wells recycled Douglass's letter as an introduction to *A Red Record: Tabulated Statistics and Alleged Causes of Lynching in the United States, 1892-1893-1894.*

Douglass's letter authenticated Wells's "moral sensibility" and the bravery of her response to the "persistent infliction of outrage and crime against colored people." He also affirmed the significance of Wells's investigative reporting when he wrote, "There has been no word equal to it in convincing power. I have spoken, but my word is feeble in comparison. You give us what you know and testify from actual knowledge. You have dealt with the fact, and cool, painstaking fidelity and left those naked and uncontradicted facts to speak for themselves."[25] In the view of many veterans of the antislavery movement, the struggle against lynching was a continuation of the fight for a freedom that would never be secure until blacks were able to exercise full civil rights without fear of reprisal. A spirit of black resistance metamorphosed into a budding nationalist consciousness, uniquely Afro-American in character. A contemporary of Booker T. Washington, W. E. B. Du Bois, Francis E. W. Harper, Anna Julia Cooper, and Mary Church Terrell, Ida B. Wells contributed to the development of this black political awareness. In this endeavor, race, not sex, served as Wells's point of departure, for she knew that black women were oppressed primarily because they were black and not because they were women.

Continuing in her role as outraged mother and defender of the race, Wells produced *A Red Record,* her most substantial and best-known antilynching book. For this work, Wells collated only undisputed reports of lynching previously published in the reputable *Chicago Tribune.* Her analysis showed that a large percentage of the men and women lynched were innocent of any crime. She reported that blacks were lynched for wife beating, hog stealing, quarreling, "sassiness," and even for no offense.

In her autobiography, Wells returns to the rape myth and gives the history of several cases that discredit it. One of the cases Wells cites is that of Edward McCoy, who was burned alive in Texarkana, Arkansas, after being accused of assaulting a white woman. "He was tied to a tree, the flesh cut from his body by men and boys, and after coal oil was poured over him, the woman he assaulted gladly set fire to him, and 15,000 persons saw him burn to death." In this case, the woman involved was known to have been intimate with the man for "more than a year previous." As she lit the pyre, McCoy "asked her if she would burn him after they had 'been sweethearting' so long." Ironically, Wells writes, a "large majority of the 'superior' white men" responsible for the lynching were "reputed fathers of mulatto children" (*Crusade,* 93). Thus the McCoy case is paradigmatic of the lynching phenomenon and the sexual double standard at its root.

Often instigated by the alleged rape of a white woman, lynching assumed cruel and atrocious forms of murder and "slow death," including mutilation, castration, and burning alive. As Wells systematically demonstrated, many of the men lynched were innocent of any crime. Conscious recognition of this fact and its culturally symbolic significance led Wells to a course of action that assured her rise to national and international prominence. She had seized upon the issue, time, and place.

Although the *New York Age* was on an exchange list with many white periodicals, Wells maintained that none of them commented on her investigative reporting. Initially, it seems, very little attention was paid to Wells in the white press; her support came from the black community. In 1892, the black women of Brooklyn and New York City gave Wells a testimonial that called immediate national attention to her antilynching activities. This event marked the beginning of Wells's public speaking career. Nowhere is Wells more modest in her autobiography than she appears in the chapter entitled "The Homesick Exile," as she looks back on her first public speech:

> When the committee told me that I had to speak I was frightened. I had been a writer, both as a correspondent and editor for several years. I had some little reputation as an essayist from schoolgirl days. . . . But this was the first time I had ever been called on to deliver an honest-to-goodness address.
>
> After every detail of that horrible lynching affair was imprinted on my memory, I had to commit it all to paper, and so got up to read my story on that memorable occasion. As I described the cause of trouble at home my mind went back to the scenes of the struggle, to the thought of the friends who were scattered throughout the country, a feeling of loneliness and homesickness for the days and the friends that were gone came over me and I felt the tears coming.
>
> (*Crusade,* 79)

Wells dates this 1892 testimonial as the beginning of the black women's club movement, thus asserting a founding role. She describes her early work in establishing clubs in New York, Boston, Providence, Newport, and New Haven. Following addresses by Wells in these cities, black women met to organize clubs such as the Women's Era Club of Boston and the Twentieth Century Club of New Haven. Wells's involvement in the black women's club movement should not be diminished, for it involved the active fusion of powerful influences: black feminism and black nationalism. The result of this fusion was the development of a race-centered, self-conscious womanhood in the form of the black women's club movement. Whereas the white woman's movement reflected her commitment to temperance and suffrage, the black woman's movement was born in the outrage of the slave mother and the struggle against lynching. Racial oppression, not sexism, was the primary issue. For an Ida B. Wells or a Frances E. W. Harper, a blow at lynching was a blow at racism and at the brutally enforced sexual double standard that pervaded the South. It was a defense of the entire race.

Through her antilynching activities, Wells made a unique contribution. The historian Gerda Lerner assesses Wells's leadership role in this way:

> In the 1890's, under the leadership of Ida B. Wells, who initiated an international crusade against lynching, Negro women's clubs launched a national campaign against this evil, and challenged white club women to support them. An early example of the now familiar pattern of the white liberal, accused of racism by black friends, grew out of this antilynching campaign and involved Frances Willard, the president of the Women's Christian Temperance Union, whose earlier abolitionist convictions and interracial work were a matter of record. Mrs. Willard was hesitant and equivocal on the issue of lynching and defended the Southern record against accusations made by Ida B. Wells on her English speaking-tour. Severe attacks on her in the women's press and a protracted public controversy helped to move Mrs. Willard to a cautious stand in opposition to lynching. Black women continued to agitate this issue and to confront white women with a moral challenge of their confessed Christianity.[26]

The conflict between Wells and Frances Willard recalls an earlier confrontation between Frederick Douglass and Susan B. Anthony over the passage of the Fifteenth Amendment, which (theoretically) guaranteed black men the right to vote with white men, but which, in effect, continued to deny the vote to women of any color. Douglass had been elected one of three vice-presidents of the American Equal Rights Association, founded with the aim of gaining suffrage for black men and for all women. When it became apparent what the ultimate outcome of the Fifteenth Amendment would be, Anthony led white women in withdrawing their support for the organization.

At the 1866 Albany convention of the association, Douglass had a serious clash with Anthony and Elizabeth Cady Stanton, who accused him of "pushing one reform at the expense of another," and the women began to talk of actively opposing any amendment that did not grant suffrage to women. With the enfranchisement of black men, the tentative alliance between profeminist black abolitionists and proabolition feminists dissolved into confusion. Douglass saw a need for continuing equal rights agitation and sought to extend the life of both the American Anti-Slavery Society and the American Equal Rights Association until all blacks and women were granted full suffrage. Nevertheless, the 1866 convention ended in the dissolution of the American Equal Rights Association and in the formation of the National American Women's Suffrage Association (NAWSA), which did not address itself to black rights.

In the chapter of *Crusade* titled "Susan B. Anthony," Wells takes up some of her arguments with NAWSA and the Women's Christian Temperance Union (WCTU). Although a member of NAWSA, Wells believed that the vote would change neither "women's nature nor the political situation" of the South (*Crusade*, 230). She also believed that white women would continue to vote the way their husbands did. Wells viewed a feminism that confirmed white women's racist attitudes as not only invalid for black women but as a dangerous threat to the entire race. Through the women's club movement and its antilynching campaign, Wells began to renew an old alliance with white women and to clarify the terms under which such cooperation would be acceptable to black women.

During this year, 1892, Wells began to receive what she interpreted as the "loyal endorsement and support" of the black press, but she was disappointed that the white press remained virtually untouched by her campaign. Through Peter Still, the black former Underground Railroad agent, she met Catherine Impey, editor of the *Anti-Caste* of Somerset, England, who was visiting with Quaker relatives in Philadelphia. Their meeting, Wells writes, "resulted in an invitation to England and the beginning of a worldwide campaign against lynching" (*Crusade*, 82). As Wells relates in her autobiography, she was visiting in the Washington home of Frederick Douglass when the invitation to go to England arrived. Her metaphor for this opportunity reaffirms her relationship to the narrative tradition of the fugitive slaves:

> It seemed like an open door in a stone wall. For nearly a year I had been in the North, hoping to spread the truth and get moral support for a demand that those accused of crimes be given a fair trial and punished by law instead of by mob. Only in one city—Boston—had I been given a meager hearing, and the press was dumb. I refer, of course, to the white press, since it was the medium through which I hoped to reach the white people of the country, who alone could mold public sentiment.

> (*Crusade*, 86)

Wells made two trips to England, one in 1893 and one in 1894, on both occasions seeking a larger, more receptive audience. She lectured throughout England and Scotland, and during the 1894 trip she served as overseas correspondent for the *Inter-Ocean* newspaper. Her lectures were well attended, and she generally received good coverage in the English press. Thus Wells internationalized her movement.

Employing the strategy of authentication used throughout the text, Wells quotes the *Birmingham Daily Gazette* of May 18, 1893, to describe a meeting of that same date:

> Having given some particulars showing flimsy evidence on which people who afterwards were proven innocent were lynched, Miss Wells said that when the woman was black and the man who assaulted her was white the offender was not even punished by law. The white men of the South had forgotten entirely that in the war when their fathers and brothers were away the white women of the South had been in charge of the black men, against whose freedom their masters were fighting and not one black man was accused of betraying his trust.

> (quoted in *Crusade*, 97)

Conscious of her historical connection with the abolition movement, "Miss Wells argued from the result of the antislavery agitation that British public opinion if properly aroused would have good effect on the people of the United States, and strengthen the hand of those in America who were desirous of putting an end to these cruel proceedings" (quoted in *Crusade*, 97-98). Wells knew that one way to get American papers to comment on lynching was to arouse public opinion abroad. Black abolitionists and former slaves had provided early models for this strategy. Wells simply followed the route of fugitive slaves, who used English public opinion to bring about an end to the cruelty and brutality of slavery. In fact, she was even received as the "honored guest" of Ellen Richards, the woman who had previously purchased the freedom of Frederick Douglass and William Wells Brown.[27]

In her public speeches and lectures in England, Wells continued to attack the racial and sexual myths believed by many Americans who condoned lynching, and she articulated the roots of the American race war. Additionally, she pointed out that women as well as men were lynched, often for violating the unspoken code of racial etiquette:

> It is true they had read of lynchings and while they thought them dreadful had accepted the general belief that it was for terrible crimes perpetrated by Negro men upon white women. I read the account of that poor woman who was boxed up in a barrel and rolled down a hill in Texas, and asked if that lynching could be excused on the same ground.

> (*Crusade*, 154)

Through this and similar examples, Wells demonstrated the cruelty and brutality of lynching and defeated the "threadbare notion" that whites lynch blacks because they rape white women. Moreover, Wells attested, some white women were "willing victims":

> I found that white men who had created a race of mulattoes by raping and consorting with Negro women were still doing so whenever they could; these same

white men lynched, burned, and tortured Negro men for doing the same thing with white women; even when the white women were willing victims.

(Crusade, 71)

It took courage for Wells to publish these radical statements, for here she attacked the heart of southern racial mythology. Wells's attitude toward interracial sexual relationships was determined by her belief that these relationships could not exist on a basis of social parity with same-race relationships. Rightly or wrongly, she viewed black men who accepted sexual favors from white women as "weak." Relationships between black women and white men she viewed as one-way exploitation.

In Europe, Wells continued her established pattern of seeking and defining her identity through public conflict. In a chapter titled "An Indiscreet Letter" Wells treated the controversy surrounding her 1893 trip; she continued to settle "accounts outstanding." Catherine Impey, one of Wells's English sponsors, made the mistake of sending an unsolicited love letter to an East Indian physician working in the anticaste movement in England. The horrified doctor gave the letter to Fyvie Mayo, who edited the *Anti-Caste* newspaper with Impey. Mayo reacted strongly, banishing Impey from the movement. Wells writes that her dismay increased when Mayo "insisted on the destruction of the entire issue of *AntiCaste* which had their names jointly as editors and demanded that I quit Miss Impey and go with her in an effort to carry on the work" (*Crusade,* 104). Although Wells agreed that Impey had been indiscreet, she saw no need to publicize the incident. She could not agree with Mayo's assessment "that Miss Impey was the type of maiden lady who used such work as an opportunity to meet and make advances to men" (*Crusade,* 104). The final blow came when "Dr. Ferdinands himself wrote and strongly condemned Wells for staying with Miss Impey" (*Crusade,* 105). Settling her account with Ferdinands, Wells notes, "Although I did not answer his letter I often wonder if he realized his mistake in passing on the offending letter instead of destroying it" (*Crusade,* 104). Had Ferdinands simply destroyed the letter, Wells asserted, the controversy could have been avoided.

In a chapter titled "A Regrettable Interview," Wells treats the controversy that disrupted her second trip to Europe. Because she continued to assail the indifference of the WCTU and other "Christian and moral influences" in the United States toward lynching, Wells became very unpopular with some of Frances Willard's English friends. When Wells reprinted an interview from the *New York Voice* in which Willard condoned lynching in the influential British magazine *Fraternity,* Lady Henry Somerset countered with a new interview with Willard intended to cast doubt on Wells and her mission. In this interview, Willard, for the first time, expressed a cautious stand against lynching.

Still showing her concern for setting the record straight, Wells documents this chapter with quotes from both the Somerset interview and her editorial response to it, which appeared the next day in the same publication, the *Westminster Gazette.* Wells's editorial represents a written equivalent of Harriet Brent Jacobs's "sass":

Sir:

The interview published in your columns today hardly merits a reply, because of the indifference to suffering manifested. Two ladies are represented sitting under a tree at Reigate, and, after some preliminary remarks on the terrible subject of lynching, Miss Willard laughingly replies by cracking a joke. And the concluding sentence of her interview shows the object is not to determine best how they may help the Negro who is being hanged, shot and burned, but "to guard Miss Willard's reputation."

With me, it is not myself nor my reputation, but the life of my people which is at stake, and I affirm that this is the first time to my knowledge that Miss Willard has said one single word in denouncing lynching or demand for law. The year 1890, the one in which her interview in *The Voice* appears, had a larger lynching record than in any previous year, and the number and territory of lynching have increased, to say nothing of the number of human beings burned alive.

Here Wells asserts her relation to the unifying symbol of her autobiography and her life, and to a personal myth of self that reflects the outraged mother defending the life of her people. This is accomplished through the "crusade" motif that provides the central metaphor for Wells's experience in the same way that "education" serves for Henry Adams. The extensive use of quotes in the chapter on Wells's experiences in England serve as part of the text's "historicizing paraphernalia." The quotes authenticate both the text and the author's image of self, as they signal the historical intention in Wells's autobiographical impulse. Unfortunately, they also contribute to the eclectic quality and choppiness of form that characterize the text as a whole, especially the fourteen chapters on Wells's experiences as an antilynching lecturer abroad.

White newspapers in the United States, receiving marked copies of the articles from the British press, attempted to defame the crusader, providing another account to be settled. Wells's old enemy, the *Memphis Daily Commercial,* referred to her as a "Negro Adventuress." Defending her autobiographical stance in the chapter "You Can't Change the Record," Wells quotes an article from the June 13, 1894, *Liverpool Daily Post* that showed British reaction to the article published in the *Memphis Daily Commercial*: "If we were to convey an idea of the things said we should not only infringe upon the libel law, but have every reason to believe that we would do a gross and grotesque injustice." In the "Ungentlemanly and Unchristian" chapter, Wells writes about how she met the editor of the *St. Louis Republic* while speaking against lynching in that city in 1894: "He remarked that he had been to great pains in sending persons throughout the south where I had lived in an effort to get something that he could publish against me. 'Well,' he answered, 'you were over there giving us hail columbia, and if I could have found anything to your discredit I would have been free to use it on the ground that all is fair in war'" (*Crusade,* 234). The effect of these attacks, the autobiographer argues, was to increase public interest in her cause: "The *Brooklyn Daily Eagle* said it would pay Memphis to send for me and a salary to keep me silent; that as long as I was living in Memphis and publishing only a 'one horse' newspaper few people outside my district knew about me" (*Crusade,* 221).

"With help from her detractors," writes the cultural historian Paula Giddings, "Wells' British tour was a personal triumph, and in the end had a great impact on the anti-lynching campaign. . . . English opinion had also broken the silence of many prominent American leaders. No longer could they afford to ignore 'the talented schoolmarm,' and such influential people as Richard Gilder, editor of *Century* magazine, Samuel Gompers, the labor leader, and yes, Frances Willard eventually lent their names in support of the campaign."[28] In some sense, Wells seems to have understood and appreciated the dynamics of confrontation and identity formation as it functioned in her life and work, as well as the importance of choosing the proper time, public place, and issue for speaking out and assuming leadership. Never before had a black woman so publicly articulated the roots of the immediate oppression of her people or mounted an international campaign against the horror that oppression implied. Ironically, Wells's exile from Memphis gave her the opportunity to have an impact of greater magnitude. Yet this impact would be felt in Memphis as much as elsewhere. Giddings argues that the decrease in lynchings in 1893 and each year thereafter "can be directly attributed to the efforts of Ida B. Wells" and that "the effect of Wells' campaign was aptly demonstrated" in her "home city" of Memphis. "Memphis exported more cotton than any other city in the world, and Wells' assertions had been especially damaging to its image. So, as a direct result of her efforts, the city fathers were pressed to take an official stand against lynching—and for the next twenty years there was not another incident of vigilante violence there."[29]

After her first trip to England in 1893, Ida B. Wells returned to Chicago and a position on the *Chicago Conservator.* On June 27, 1895, she married Ferdinand L. Barnett, one of the founders of the *Conservator.* Wells's courtship coincides with a noticeable gap in her narrative; yet this is not surprising when one considers that *Crusade for Justice* is primarily a story of Wells's public life. She says only that Barnett proposed before she went to England the second time and that, when she returned, they married. Some of the details of their courtship are available from Alfreda Duster, who reports that her parents met "in the work." After the death of his first wife, Barnett, the father of two small sons, was often asked if he would marry again: "He wasn't interested in just anybody, he was looking for a certain type of woman who would mean something to his life and career. And evidently Mama fit that pattern. He pursued and married her."[30]

When Wells "came back the second time, she went across the country, trying to organize anti-lynching leagues . . . and while she was touring the country, her itinerary was known and wherever she stopped there would be a letter from my father. And so they had a long distance correspondence courtship and I understand—I never saw one—but I understand my father could write a beautiful love letter."[31] According to her daughter, Wells was delighted to have found a man who believed in, and would agitate for, the same principles. At the time of their marriage, Wells began using the hyphenated surname Wells-Barnett. She was then thirty years old. "So far as her perception was concerned," says Duster, "she was continuing her work. She was continuing in journalism because she took over the editorship of the *Conservator* within a week after they married. She wrote and she didn't want to lose the identity of Ida B. Wells."[32]

A perceptible change in Wells's autobiographical focus and the direction of her narrative occurs in the chapter entitled "A Divided Duty." Thereafter, the text concentrates more on local affairs and on Wells's private life, the "rounding-out possibility" of the domestic sphere. Wells's treatment of the early years of her marriage explores the tension between the roles of public crusader and private woman—a theme introduced early in the autobiography and further developed in the written re-creation of her first speaking engagement in New York. Having returned from Europe and married Barnett, Wells purchased the *Conservator* from her husband "and others who owned it," embarking on "A Divided Duty": "I decided to continue my work as a journalist, for this was my first, and might be said, my only love" (*Crusade,* 242). Immediately following her marriage, Wells "took charge of the *Conservator* office." "My duties as editor, as president of the Ida B. Wells Woman's Club, and speaker in many white women's clubs in and around Chicago kept me pretty busy. But I was not too busy to give birth to a male child the following 25 March 1896" (*Crusade,* 244-245).

Ida Wells-Barnett remained active. She named her firstborn Charles Aked Barnett, after the Reverend C. F. Aked of Liverpool, one of her English antilynching allies. Shortly after the child's birth, she undertook an antilynching speaking tour: "And so I started out with a six month old nursing baby and made trips to Decatur, Quincy, Springfield, Bloomington, and many other towns. I honestly believe that I am the only woman in the United States who ever travelled with a nursing baby to make political speeches" (*Crusade,* 244). Perhaps one of the greatest moments of her life came at the founding meeting of the National Association of Colored Women (NACW). Present were Rosetta Sprague, daughter of Frederick Douglass, Ellen Craft, daughter and namesake of another famous slave narrator, Frances Ellen Watkins Harper, and "General" Harriet Tubman, the "Moses" who had led hundreds of fugitive slaves to freedom. Harriet Tubman, "the grand old woman" of the convention and the oldest member in attendance, "arrived to a standing ovation." Charles Aked Barnett, the youngest in attendance, was named "Baby of the Association." Thus, with the founding of the NACW, a symbolic torch was passed to a new generation, proclaiming both the emergence of "Black women into the forefront of the struggle for Black and women's rights" and the launching of "the modern civil rights movement."[33]

The latter portion of *Crusade for Justice* alternates between the activities of the political organizer and the life of hearth and home. The following anecdote symbolizes Wells's life of "divided duty" and demonstrates the complex practical problems facing a public figure who is also a mother:

> When the time came for me to speak I rose and went forward. The baby, who was wide awake, looked around, and failing to see me but hearing my voice, raised his voice in angry protest. Almost unconsciously I turned to go to him, whereupon the chairman, who instantly realized the trouble, put someone else in the chair, went back to the back of the platform, and took the baby out into the hall where he could not hear my voice and kept him there until I had finished my task.
>
> (*Crusade,* 245)

Ida Wells-Barnett soon discovers the demands of motherhood: "I found that motherhood was a profession by itself, just like schoolteaching and lecturing, and that once one is launched on such a career, she owed it to herself to become as expert as possible in the practice of her profession" (*Crusade,* 255). Even though she writes that she had not "entered into the bonds of holy matrimony with the same longing for children that so many other women have," she believes that the creator has given woman "a wonderful place in the scheme of things" and revels in "having made this discovery" for herself. She writes that she is happy to have rejected birth-control information on her wedding night (*Crusade,* 241).

On the birth of her second son, Herman K. Barnett, in 1897, Wells-Barnett resigned the editorship of the *Conservator* and gave up the presidency of the Ida B. Wells Woman's Club in order to give full attention to raising her children. For the next fifteen years, motherhood was her primary occupation. Wells's autobiographical reticence about her private experiences in marriage reinforces the public nature of her narrative, as well as its authenticating structure. Apparently, many in the antilynching movement felt that Wells had "deserted the cause" by taking up her new "profession of motherhood." In "Divided Duty," Wells narrates an encounter with Susan B. Anthony:

> She said, "I know of no one in all this country better fitted to do the work you had in hand than yourself. Since you have gotten married, agitation seems practically to have ceased. Besides, you have a divided duty. You are here trying to help in the formation of this league and your eleven-month-old baby needs your attention at home. You are distracted over the thought that maybe he is not being looked after as he would be if you were there, and that makes for a divided duty."

Although it was a well-merited rebuke from her point of view, I could not tell Miss Anthony that it was be-

cause I had been unable, like herself, to get the support which was necessary to carry on my work that I had become discouraged in the effort to carry on alone.

(*Crusade,* 255)

So "carry on alone" becomes a central motif of the autobiography. When Wells married Barnett, she felt her own people censured her for having "abandoned the struggle." From her point of view, "they were more outspoken because of the loss to the cause than they had been in holding up my hands when I was trying to carry a banner" (*Crusade,* 241). The passage cited above reflects a tone of conciliation affected by Wells's autobiographical persona from time to time. By telling the reader that some feminist leaders criticized her for diverting her energy away from her active public role into the private maternal sphere, and by registering her disappointment in not receiving more support from the black community for her crusade, Wells wins our sympathy for her difficult role of "carrying on alone." Through the use of the earlier quotation attributed to Susan B. Anthony, Wells suggests that the overall success or failure of the antilynching campaign depended, at this time, largely on her individual effort. There is considerable validity to her claim. In the estimation of the historian August Meier, "Later on, after World War I, the NAACP entered upon the anti-lynching campaign, but at the turn of the century opposition to this vicious practice was essentially one and the same with the activities of Ida Wells-Barnett."[34] Dedicated to both motherhood and activism, Wells refused to sacrifice either the public or the private role, but motherhood increased the enormity and complexity of her task.

In a later chapter, "Illinois Lynchings," Wells relates her reluctance to continue the antilynching work after the birth of her children. In addition to the charge that she has "deserted the cause," she also has been "accused by some of our men of jumping ahead of them and doing work without giving them a chance" (*Crusade,* 311). For these and other reasons, she writes, she has become less willing to do the hard and "thankless" work of investigating lynchings. But she *did* go, with the encouragement and blessing of her husband and family. Wells's "duty" absolves the "true woman" of the need to be politically quiescent:

> I thought of that passage of Scripture which tells of wisdom from the mouth of babes and sucklings. I thought if my child wanted me to go I ought not to fall by the wayside. . . .
>
> Next morning all four of my children accompanied my husband and me to the station and saw me start on the journey.
>
> (*Crusade,* 311-312)

As a result of her efforts, Wells contends, the governor issued a statement that outlawed lynching in Illinois. And he refused to reinstate the Cairo sheriff who had cooperated with the mob that took the life of "Frog" James. Wells writes: "That was in 1909, and from that day until the present there has been no lynching in the state. Every sheriff, whenever there seem to be any signs of the kind, immediately telegraphs the governor for troops" (*Crusade,* 346). Of course, many lynchings went unreported. Despite the lack of a clear causal relationship between the actions of Wells-Barnett and those of the governor, her investigation did exercise a significant influence on public opinion.

In her role as wife and mother, Ida B. Wells fulfills the dream of Harriet Brent Jacobs—the dream of having a legitimate relationship with a man who will cherish and protect her. Ferdinand L. Barnett offered Wells this security, as well as a degree of financial independence and unlimited "moral" support for her mission. In the pages of her autobiography, Wells diminishes her personal importance to emphasize the importance of "the work," the crusade of the outraged mother. On the other hand, she highlights the relationships she shared with her dependent children, for they help illustrate her life of "divided duty." With the support of her dynamic mate, Wells-Barnett was able both to raise a family and to carry on her struggle against lynching. Barnett pushed her ahead, and in the folk idiom of Zora Neale Hurston, he propped her up on "every leanin' side."

A look at the interview with Alfreda Duster on record at the Black Women's Oral History Project at Harvard University yields some of the personal information missing from the text. To the young Alfreda, Ida B. Wells-Barnett was "just mother," a homemaker active in civic life. Duster remembers that her father did most of the cooking and that it was her job to have the potatoes cooked and ready for dinner when her father came home; she also remembers that her mother took an active part in the educational life of her children, often visiting teachers at school.[35] Like her own dear parents, Wells-Barnett stimulated in her children a love of reading and an appreciation for the importance of a good education. The archetypal outraged mother, Wells-Barnett was both protective and strict with her children. When her daughters were young, she established a rule that they must play in plain sight of the front door at all times. Discovered out of view in a friend's house, young Alfreda received a spanking.[36]

Wells never grew quiescent. Despite the responsibilities of motherhood, she remained active in the struggle against lynching, the women's club movement, and the formation of the NAACP. Even when she had given up her work at the *Conservator* and the presidency of the Ida B. Wells Club, she remained active in the city where she founded the Negro Fellowship League and the Alpha Suffrage Association. She was also a charter member of the National Negro Committee, a forerunner of the NAACP. In her work with the Alpha Suffrage Association in Chicago in 1914, Wells organized black women to canvass their neighborhoods and report their progress:

The women at first were very much disappointed.

They said that the men jeered at them and told them that they ought to be home taking care of the babies. Others insisted that the women were trying to take the

place of men and wear the trousers. I urged each one of the workers to go back and tell the women that we wanted them to register so that they could help put a colored man in the city council.

(*Crusade,* 346)

Black men's reluctance to support female suffrage was understandable in the light of the racist attitudes of some white suffrage leaders and segregation within the suffrage movement. In fact, some southern white women hoped suffrage would offer "a means to the end of securing white supremacy."[37] But Wells continued to attack racism within the movement as she organized the black community. In the end, her appeal to the black men of Chicago was successful.

Overall, Wells's work with the Alpha Suffrage Association would seem to indicate that black men who were reluctant to support women politically overcame that reluctance when presented with sound arguments about black women's suffrage. Many black men agreed with the analysis of W. E. B. Du Bois: "Votes for women means votes for Black women." The consensus of masculine opinion, in the words of Paula Giddings, was that "political empowerment of the race required the participation of Black women."[38] Thus Wells advanced the cause of the race through advancing the cause of black women and challenging publicly, at every opportunity, the racism of white suffragists. But always, even in this endeavor on behalf of women, the interests of the race came first.

If Du Bois was correct when he asserted that the Afro-American is a kind of seventh son gifted with double consciousness of himself as a black and an American, then Wells acquired a triple consciousness of herself—as an American, a black, and a woman. For Wells, existence was a phenomenon in which belief and action could not be separated. She believed, and therefore she acted, attaining an escape from the South that liberated her for an even greater potential. Her autobiography reflects a model of "antislavery" expression. Because lynching was one of the tools by which whites hoped to reduce blacks to their previous condition of servitude, antilynching agitation was truly antislavery agitation in the hearts and minds of its supporters. Despite the enormity of her task, Wells forged a legitimate black feminism through the synthesis of black nationalism and the suffrage movement, providing a useful model with race, not sex, as a point of departure. Her work established not only the ideological basis for later antilynching work by the NAACP but also for similar work done by the Association of Southern Women for the Prevention of Lynching, a white group headed by the Texas feminist Jessie Daniel Ames. This Wells accomplished either because of, or in spite of, her racial and sexual identity.

In *Crusade for Justice: The Autobiography of Ida B. Wells,* the intelligence and sensibility of the narrator far exceed that of the unlettered slave. Here an aging author "confront[s] and connect[s] nineteenth and twentieth century experience" by placing herself at the center of a "repossessed past."[39] Yet this twentieth-century autobiography possesses distinct formal attributes that help to identify its place in a tradition of black women writing autobiography. Wells's autobiographical consciousness alternates between the confession and the historical memoir, allowing the autobiographer the necessary latitude to discuss both her public and her private duty. This Wells required in order to demonstrate her development, not only as a political activist, but as a wife and mother. Throughout the autobiography, the concept of extended family reaches out to others in "the work." In this way, **Crusade for Justice,** Wells's historical memoir, looks forward to the modern political autobiographies of Ann Moody, Shirley Chisholm, and Angela Davis. It represents an important link between the old and the new, part of the "lost ground" of Afro-American literary tradition.

Notes

1. John W. Blassingame, "Black Autobiographies as Histories and Literature," *Black Scholar* 5, no. 4 (1973-1974): 7.

2. Albert E. Stone, *The American Autobiography* (Englewood Cliffs, N.J.: Prentice-Hall, 1981), 2-3.

3. James Cox, "Recovering Literature's Lost Ground through Autobiography," in *Autobiography: Essays Theoretical and Critical,* ed. James Olney (Princeton: Princeton University Press, 1980), 124-125.

4. See Patricia Meyers Spacks, "Stages of Self: Notes on Autobiography," in Stone, *American Autobiography,* 44-45.

5. Alfreda M. Duster, Introduction, *Crusade for Justice: The Autobiography of Ida B. Wells* (Chicago: University of Chicago Press, 1970), xiii-xiv.

6. Stephen Butterfield, *Black Autobiography* (Amherst: University of Massachusetts Press, 1974), 200.

7. See Estelle C. Jelinek, Introduction, *Women's Autobiography* (Bloomington: Indiana University Press, 1980), 1-20.

8. Erik Erikson, *Life History and the Historical Moment* (New York: Norton, 1975), 135.

9. Ibid., 125.

10. Alfreda M. Duster, letter to Joanne M. Braxton, January 30, 1983.

11. Ibid.

12. John Hope Franklin, Foreword, *Crusade,* x-xii.

13. Duster, *Crusade,* xiii. See also Norman B. Wood, *The White Side of a Black Subject* (Chicago: American Publishing House, 1897), 381-382.

14. Duster, *Crusade,* xiv.

15. Ibid., xxxi.

16. Ida B. Wells, *Crusade,* xiii-xiv. Hereafter cited in the text as *Crusade,* followed by page number.

17. Albert E. Stone, *Autobiographical Occasions and Original Acts* (Philadelphia: University of Pennsylvania Press, 1982), 29.

18. Erikson, *Life History,* 161.

19. See Spacks, "Stages of Self," 48.

20. Erikson, *Life History,* 141.

21. Robert Stepto, *From Behind the Veil: A Study of Afro-American Narrative* (Urbana: University of Illinois Press, 1979), 26.

22. Erikson, *Life History,* 55.

23. Ida B. Wells, *Southern Horrors, Lynch Law in All Its Phases* (New York: Arno Press, 1969; originally published 1892), 2.

24. Ida B. Wells, letter to Frederick Douglass, October 17, 1892. Frederick Douglass Collection, Library of Congress, Washington, D.C.

25. Frederick Douglass, letter to Ida B. Wells, October 25, 1892. Frederick Douglass Collection, Library of Congress.

26. Gerda Lerner, *The Majority Finds Its Past* (New York: Oxford University Press, 1979), 109.

27. Gertrude B. Mossell, *The Work of the Afro-American Woman* (New York: Oxford University Press, 1988; originally published 1894), 38.

28. Paula Giddings, *When and Where I Enter: The Impact of Black Women on Race and Sex in America* (New York: Morrow, 1984), 92.

29. Ibid.

30. Interview conducted by Marcia Greenlee with Alfreda M. Duster on March 8-9, 1978, for the Black Women's Oral History Project at the Schlesinger Library, Radcliffe Collection, Harvard University, 62. Quotes are used with the written permission of Alfreda Duster, August 6, 1981.

31. Ibid., 11.

32. Ibid., 16.

33. Giddings, *When and Where I Enter,* 94.

34. August Meier, Introduction to *On Lynchings,* by Ida B. Wells-Barnett (New York: Arno Press, 1969), i.

35. Duster-Greenlee interview, 4.

36. Ibid.

37. Giddings, *When and Where I Enter,* 126.

38. Ibid., 121.

39. Stone, *Autobiographical Occasions,* 29.

Emilie Maureen Townes (essay date 1993)

SOURCE: Townes, Emilie Maureen. "Ida B. Wells-Barnett: Her Social and Moral Perspectives." In *Womanist Justice, Womanist Hope,* pp. 107-30. Atlanta, Ga.: Scholars Press, 1993.

[*In the following full-length study of the ways Wells-Barnett's life typified the experience of African-American women reformers of her day, Townes examines the social and moral content of Wells-Barnett's writings.*]

Ida B. Wells-Barnett was an active participant in the women's club movement and other programs for social changes of her time. Her deep and abiding spirituality was forged in the Black Church of the South. Her rebellion against the traditional roles assigned to women emerged in her career as activist and newspaper journalist. She bowed to societal conventions surrounding domesticity and took time away from the socio-political world to raise her children, returning to her work as quickly as time and circumstance allowed. Her concern for decent jobs and wages for African-Americans found voice and action in the Negro Fellowship League.

Wells-Barnett responded to and helped shape her era. The greatest contribution she made to United States society as a whole was her untiring work in the anti-lynching movement. Her work in this movement was shaped by the political, social, cultural, and economic movements of her day. She attempted an integrated analysis of discrimination and violence, and sought to call the nation to task for violating its social principles regarding race.

EARLY YEARS: RELIGIOUS COMMITMENT AND SOCIAL CRITICISM

Wells created a standard for herself, her people, and United States society. Her earliest writings reflect a woman with a strong sense of Christian duty. The first of her two surviving diaries was written between 1885 and 1887. This early diary illustrates a young woman in her early twenties wrestling with her faith and her culture. It reveals some of the intensity of her internal struggle for moral rectitude and agency. The early diary also contains reflections on some of the later issues with which Wells would wrestle: clerical leadership, the mission of the church, lynching, Black unity, interracial marriage and sexuality, and Black womanhood.

CHRISTIAN DUTY

Wells' understanding of Christian duty was rooted in her belief in an immanent God in Christ. The mission of her Jesus was to offer salvation for sinners. She revealed much of her personal theology in commenting on Dwight Moody's preaching at a revival held in Memphis.

> His style is so simple, plain and natural. He told the old, old story in an easy conversational way that charms the listener ere he is aware and the secret of his success is, I think—that he does not preach a far-away God—a

hard to be reconciled Savior but uses a natural earnest tone and tells in a natural way without long drawn doctrine or finely spun theology or rhetoric the simple truth that Christ Jesus came on earth to seek and save that which was lost.[1]

Wells' understanding of God and Christ was typical of both slave and free Blacks of her day who saw God as personal and just. Writing after a watch meeting at one o'clock in the morning, she gave the reader a lucid picture of her intensely personal experience of God and its importance for her integrity:

> . . . and I felt lifted up and I thank God I opened my mouth and told of His wonderful mercies to me and my heart overflowed with thankfulness. . . . and tonight I came away after greeting them all and finding their hearts warm and inclined to me—with a lighter and more peaceful forgiveness with all mankind and I thank God for it. . . .[2]

Wells' words echo the rhythm and motion of slave worship and its evolution into the Black evangelical Christianity of the late nineteenth century. The slave tale told by Simon Brown also reveals an immanent God:

> The folks would sing and pray and testify and clap their hands, just as if God was right there in the midst of them. He wasn't way off up in the sky. He was a-seeing everybody and a-listening to every word and a-promising to let His love come down.[3]

A strong sense of God's judgment and the necessity of right action in relation to God's will also pervades Wells' writing. Her commitment to Christian duty and responsibility is evident in her early years. In the midst of deciding whether she would remain in California with her aunt and sisters, Wells writes:

> I know not if I will ever have another chance yet I try not to be rebellious but extract consolation out of the thought that my Heavenly Father will reward and bless me for doing what is right and just. And if I did nothing, sacrificed nothing in return for all that has been done for me, I could not expect his blessing and sanction. Help me and bring success to my efforts I pray.[4]

Her diary entries of January, 1887, reveal a fully developed and unequivocal understanding of moral action and Christian duty. Wells decided to teach a Sunday school class as a way to begin to work for God who had done much for her. She was disappointed with the way the Bible was taught and preached and hoped to influence her charges "in a small degree to think of better things." She concluded her entry with a covenant plea and commitment.

> God help me to try. I shall begin this year with that determination, so that another year may find me with more to offer the master in the way of good works. God help me to be a Christian! To so conduct myself in my intercourse with the unconverted. Let it be an ever present theme with me, and O help me to better control my temper! Bless me for the ensuing year; let me feel that Thou art with me in all my struggles.[5]

By January 18, she had organized a class of young men who promised to come regularly on Sundays. However, her relationship with her brother who was in the class was strained. Some of the difficulties she would encounter in later life, as she tried to work with others toward her understanding of justice and moral rectitude, were revealed in her analysis of her relationship with her brother. Wells understood that she alternated between harshness, indifference, and repulsion in his regard. She asks, "God help me to be more careful and watchful over my manners and bearing toward him. Let not my own brother perish while I am laboring to save others!"[6]

In another set of entries during February, Wells encountered her humanity and her responsibility in a direct manner. After asking God to bless her in her undertakings and guard her against evil,[7] she was brought up short by Mr. Dardis (apparently an authority figure to the young Ida Wells) who gave her a severe lecture on going to the theater. In reflecting on herself as both leader and role model, Wells revealed her humility as well as her resolve to put teaching and deed in harmony:

> I had not placed so high an estimate on myself. He [Dardis] certainly gave me food for thought and hereafter when I grow weary or despondent and think my life useless and unprofitable, may I remember this episode, and may it strengthen me to the performance of my duty, for I would not willingly be the cause of one soul's being led astray. O thou, Help of the weak and helpless! Help me be firm and strong for the right and watchful for my own conduct.[8]

Later, as Easter neared and she heard a sermon on the cost of religion, she resolved to put away her plans for fun and pleasure during the Easter season. She would fast for her "many sins of dereliction and remain home to work, watch and pray, and praise for the wonderful goodness of my Father to an unworthy servant."[9]

In an entry near the end of this diary, Wells reflected on her life and her future as she celebrated her twenty-fifth birthday. She found herself falling short of the mark, particularly where her education was concerned. She noted her "hunger and thirst after righteousness and knowledge" but felt that she was not as persistent as she should be in her pursuit of both. She asked God for the "steadiness of purpose" to acquire both and hoped that in ten years hence she would be "increased in honesty and purity of purpose and motive!"[10]

Wells was clear about the correct behavior God expected from a faithful Christian. She had a strong sense of personal sin and personal salvation. However, she did not remain individualistic in her approach to religion. Rather, she blended this forceful sense of personal responsibility for moral agency with a larger critique of worship and the role of clergy. She held her personal standard as the model of authentic moral action and Christian witness.

ROLE OF INSTITUTIONAL RELIGION

Wells could not accept segregated worship. After listening to Dwight Moody[11] preach in 1885, she was moved by his simple, yet eloquent message, and wrote:

> I intended writing Mr. Moody a letter asking him why ministers never touched on that phase of sin—the caste distinction—practiced even in the churches and among christianity (?) but rather, tacitly conniving at it by assenting to their caste arrangements, and accepting it as a matter of course, instead of rectifying it—but I had no chance, and he left the city yesterday; so I know not where to address him.[12]

Wells echoed the words of Simon Brown again when he saw "so much pretending in the white man's religion that I felt better off being an honest sinner."[13] For Wells, even though she admitted to hearing a good sermon, she also "witnessed practical evidence of 'white folks' Christianity,'" in the haste with which they passed us by when choosing a seat."[14] The reference to being "passed by" is an allusion to the fact that Blacks, both slave and free, were relegated to the back of the church or into the balcony in churches where whites and Blacks worshipped.

Like other African-Americans of her day, Wells could not understand or accept a Christianity which separated the people of God from one another on the basis of race. Wells held a high view of religion. For her, religion and the church constituted a *living* faith in a just God, faith in which the believer's action must conform to the teachings of the Bible. She did not suppose that the true believer made exceptions to the demands of the word of God. Rather, he or she lived the word and sought to embody God's presence in the world.

Her strong sense of moral agency extended to the clergy as well. She was biting and uncompromising in her estimate of a young preacher she encountered:

> Went to service yesterday morning and found a very slender, puerile-looking, small specimen of humanity occupying the pulpit. His "talk" was premature somewhat, and yet applicable; his peculiarities and oddities certainly have the spice of novelty and daring which surprises too much for demur and carries one by storm almost against the judgment. . . .[15]

She returned that evening to hear him *preach* (her emphasis) and reached a conclusion about his fitness for ministry. Her evaluation was negative and to the point. She found his discourse to be:

> A constant arraignment of the negro as compared to the whites, a burlesque of Negro worship, a repetition of what he did not believe in, and the telling of jokes together with a reiteration of his text "ye must be born again" made up his "sermon."[16]

Further,

> . . . he lacks some of the essential elements that compose a preacher; he *seems* to be wanting in stability, and there seems also, to my mind, to be a lack of rev-

erence in touching and dealing with holy things; a disregard of the Father's command to "take off thy shoes; for the ground on which thou standest is holy."[17]

In Wells' estimation, for a person to become an ordained minister demanded a serious commitment to adhere to the word of God and to be a model for the worshipper. She extended her personal high standards of moral rectitude further for the preacher than for the layperson.

As biting as she could be in her condemnation, she also could be magnanimous in her praise. Writing over a year later, she wrote with delight about the preacher of her church. She found him to be "the most energetic man I know. He has made the waste places blossom as a rose and the church is beginning to look up." Wells marveled at his ability to handle difficult congregants and keep them involved in the life of the church. She ends this entry with the observation that "he is certainly a splendid judge of human nature."[18]

Wells' words reveal her standards for leadership. Ultimately, the preacher needed to be a good judge of human nature who could lead the church in its mission. The preacher must show stability to provide the members of the church with a firm model of moral agency. The preacher could not shy away from belligerent behavior. He must address it directly while bringing the difficult person or persons into fellowship with the whole church. Wells held the ordained minister in high regard. Her personal code of moral conduct demanded much of herself and others.

LYNCHING

Wells' early diary also reveals her growing concern against lynching and the brutalization of Blacks by whites. Writing in March of 1885, she reflected on the shooting of thirteen Black men in Carroll County, Mississippi:

> O, God when will these massacres cease—it was only because they had attempted to assassinate a white man (and for just cause I suppose). Colored men rarely attempt to wreak vengeance on a white one unless he has provoked it unduly.[19]

A year and one half later, Wells expressed her outrage in print when she learned of a Black woman who was accused of poisoning a white one. The Black woman was:

> taken from the county jail and stripped naked and hung up in the courthouse yard and her body riddled with bullets and left exposed to view! O my God! can such things be and no justice for it? The only evidence being that the stomach of the dead woman contained arsenic and a box of "Rough on Rats" was found in this woman's house, who was a cook for the white woman. It may be unwise to express myself so strongly but I cannot help it and I know not if capital may not be made of it against me but I trust in God.[20]

In the face of this growing onslaught against the humanity of African-Americans, Wells rejoiced at the growing unity she perceived forming among Blacks of that period. In 1887, she wrote that Blacks were beginning to think and realize that only in unity can there be strength. She also revealed her penchant for action, noting that "the men of the race who do think are endeavoring to put their thoughts in action to inspire those who do not think."[21] For her, Black people had to unite if they were to survive. The most effective spokespersons for Black people were those Blacks who evaluated what needed to be done and then drew a blueprint for action.

WOMANHOOD

Wells was a true spokesperson of the women of her period. She adhered to the ideal of the cult of true womanhood and its emphasis on virtue for women. She recorded a defense made by the editor of one of the local Memphis papers, *The Scimitar,* on behalf of "respectable" Black people and added that his defense included Black womanhood:

> it was not now as it had been that colored women were harlots etc., whose virtue could be bought, that there were as decent among them as among their own race; that there were some who were disgraces to their race, but that the white race had no room to talk, the same was true of them.[22]

Although she was intolerant of immorality, Wells defended the reputation of a "silly woman" who engaged in an extramarital affair with an "equally scatterbrained boy" who boasted about their relationship. The young man was killed by the brother of the woman and Wells wrote:

> It seems awful to take human life but hardly more so than to take a woman's reputation and make it the jest and byword of the street; in view of these things, if he really did them, one is strongly tempted to say his killing was justified.[23]

Wells equated murder with the sullying of a woman's reputation. She hedged somewhat on vindicating the actions of the outraged brother. Her general tone was sympathetic toward the woman, but less so for her unfortunate lover.

Like many women of her day, Wells utilized her strong sense of Christian duty in the public realm. She did so from the understanding that women must be in the world of thought and action. When she was called to respond to the theme of women and journalism at a newspaper convention, she lamented over what she did not say because she was surprised at the request.

> I offered no word of thanks on behalf of my sex for the flattering encomiums bestowed on them by our editors and the hearty welcome accorded our entrance into this field. I wished and may never have a more favorable opportunity to urge the young women to study and think with a view to taking place in the world of thought and action. The suddenness of the thing drove everything out of my head but I will remember next time.[24]

Wells developed and expanded these themes found in her early diary in her later adult professional public and private writings. These early concerns and attitudes matured and set the tone for her perceptions of the growing industrial order surrounding her. This emerging order with its understanding of religion, work, class, and roles was complex. However, Wells held to her early ideals. They became her guides as she faced change and resistance to change. Her perception of justice and duty, evidenced so early in her diary, never wavered in adulthood. Throughout her life, she responded to lynching and violence, Christian duty and responsibility, leadership, and the role of religion out of the stance of her early years.

MATURE YEARS: SOCIAL CRITIC AND ACTIVIST

In her mature writings, Wells amplified the themes of her younger years. Throughout her later articles and autobiography she continued to stress Christian duty and the role of the church. Her anti-lynching stance evolved into a crusade of national and international scope. She held high her ideals for womanhood and was outspoken in her view of leadership.

Wells combined penetrating social analysis with decisive action. The high moral code she set for herself and others was a motivating force in her crusade for justice. Through the Black religious and social protest tradition, Wells combined a deep spirituality with a strong sense of social responsibility and witness.

CHRISTIAN DUTY

Wells expanded her early views of Christian duty to address social responsibility. In reference to lynching, she refused any attempt to paint it as a problem distinctive to the African-American community:

> Lynching is no longer "Our Problem," it is the problem of the civilized world, and Tennessee could not afford to refuse the legal measures which Christianity demands shall be used for the punishment of crime.[25]

While acknowledging that Blacks are capable of committing crimes, she refused to accept that the thousands who were hanged, shot, and burned alive were guilty in each case.

For her, Blacks as well as whites, had to take responsibility for eradicating lynching and mob rule from the American scene. Wells believed in the power of truth. For her, facts wore well in the face of misrepresentation and deception.

> "What can I do to help the cause?" The answer is always this, "Tell the world the facts." When the Christian world knows the alarming growth and extent of outlawry in our land, some means will be found to stop it.[26]

She assumed the moral rectitude of the representatives of Christianity:

> When I present our cause to a minister, editor, lecturer, or representative of any moral agency, the first demand is for facts and figures. . . . The preachers, teachers, editors and humanitarians of the white race, at home and abroad, must have facts laid before them, and it is our duty to supply these facts.[27]

In *A Red Record,* Wells offered five lines of responsible action.[28] First, the reader should make known the facts of lynching which Wells-Barnett presented in the pamphlet itself.

Second, the reader should be active in getting "churches, missionary societies, Y.M.C.A.'s, W.C.T.U's and all Christian and moral forces in connection with your religious and social life" to pass resolutions of condemnation and protest every time a lynching takes place. Further, such resolutions must be sent to the places where lynchings occur.[29] She was clear about the duty of the church and other religious institutions regarding lynching. These organizations were to take the lead in agitating for an end to mob rule and violence. Wells assumed the moral agency of religious institutions as voices of protest in the face of injustice.

Third, Wells used an economic argument. She suggested that the reader protest the loss of capital in any given area where lynch law and mob violence occur.[30]

Fourth, she urged the reader to think and act for "it is the white man's civilization and the white man's government which are on trial."[31] She maintained that the eradication of lynching was key to whether civilization or anarchy would prevail in the United States. Wells was sharp in her estimate of Christianity and:

> . . . whether the precepts and theories of Christianity are professed and practiced by American white people as Golden Rules of thought and action, or adopted as a system of morals to be preached to heathen until they attain to the intelligence which needs the system of Lynch Law.[32]

Finally, she urged agitation on behalf of a bill in Congress that would create a commission to study the charges of rape and the cases of lynching. She ended with a strong statement of the responsibility of the people and the government to maintain law and order and reminded the reader:

> The colored people of this country who have been loyal to the flag believe the same, and strong in that belief have begun this crusade.[33]

ROLE OF INSTITUTIONAL RELIGION

Wells maintained a living faith. Christianity was not a concept for her, it was her faith. She could not suffer in silence as the religion that gave her strength and comfort was abused and mocked. She wrote:

> Civilization cannot burn human beings alive or justify others who do so; neigh can it refuse a trial by jury for black men accused of crime, without making a mock-

ery of the respect for law which is the safeguard of the liberties of white men. The nation cannot profess Christianity, which makes the golden rule its foundation stone, and continue to deny equal opportunity for life, liberty and the pursuit of happiness to the black race.[34]

Wells' estimate of the church was as stringent as her standards for its clergy. In an article in the *Daily Inter Ocean,* Wells was scathing in her estimate of white Christianity in the face of unbridled and rampant lynchings. She wrote with an impassioned pen:

> they are too busy saving the souls of white Christians from future burning in hell-fire to save the lives of black ones from present burning in the flames kindled by the white Christians. The feelings of the people who do these acts must not be hurt by protesting against this sort of thing, and so the bodies of the victims of mob hate must be sacrificed, and the country disgraced, because of that fear to speak out.[35]

With incredulity, she attacked segregated worship by relating the story of a young mulatto man who was dragged from "one of the leading churches in Memphis, Tenn., by a policeman and shut up in the station-house all day Sunday for taking a seat in the church . . ."[36]

Her *Daily Inter Ocean* articles did not allow Wells' British audience to succumb to the false belief that this behavior was confined to the South. She related similar cases in the North and the North's tacit approval of southern behavior. She remarked, "as far as I knew the principle has always yielded to prejudice in the hope of gaining the good will of the south."[37] Wells extended her judgment to the YMCA and the WCTU and noted that these organizations bent to the rule of expediency as well:

> He [a clergy from England attending a national YMCA convention in the United States] was told that there had been a few [Blacks] in previous meetings, but this particular year (I forget which one) special effort had been made to get Southern delegates to be present, so no colored ones had been invited. These were the only terms upon which the YMCA and WCTU had obtained a foothold in the South, and they had consented to the arrangement which shut the negro out. They continually declared the negro degraded, intemperate, and wicked and yet shut him out from all influences in which he might become better.[38]

Convinced that religion must be put into action if it is to have any impact on the social fabric of society, she again voiced the theme of a living faith:

> When our Christian and moral influences not only concede these principles theoretically but work for them practically, lynching will become a thing of the past, and no governor will again make a mockery of all the nation holds dear in defense of lynching for any cause.[39]

Arguments grounded in the rationale of expediency held no force or persuasion for Wells. Her religious faith remained simple, plain and natural. She had no use of, or belief in, a God or a faith that was distant. The God she knew, felt, experienced, and sought to embody "came to earth to seek and save that which was lost."[40] Wells viewed lynching and the toleration, if not justification, of it as supreme social evil.

ANTI-LYNCHING CRUSADE

Wells did not tolerate apathy or difference by African-Americans any more than the apathy of the religious institutions of her day. In 1893, as the toll for lynching mounted, Wells did not disguise her outrage and anger with the lack of unity or protest by Blacks.

> Our race still sits and does nothing about it and says little except to doubt the expediency of or find fault with the remedy proposed, no plan of raising money by which the things can be investigated, the country aroused and the temple of justice, the pulpit and the press besieged until public opinion shall demand a cessation of the reign of barbarism, lynch law and stake burning.[41]

The proposed remedy was the creation of a federal commission to study the lynch law and to make recommendations for its eradication. Wells was a supporter of this plan and used her column to give it a national voice among the Negro press of her day. Wells criticized the nascent Black accommodationist movement with its call to

> sacrifice its [the race] political rights for the sake of peace. They honestly believed the Negro should fit himself for government and when he should do so, the objection to his participation in politics would be removed. This sacrifice did not remove the trouble nor move the South to do justice. One by one the Southern states have legally disfranchised the Negro.[42]

Her estimate of the effectiveness of the accommodationist stance is clear from the passage. Wells saw no benefit resulting from the forfeiture of rights or dignity. She was unwilling to deem the position as resulting from lack of thought, but wished to point out the bankruptcy of such an approach.

Unequivocal in her judgment of the motives of white lynchers, Wells noted that "white men down there [the South] do not think any more of killing a negro than they do of slaying a mad dog." The lynching she referred to in the article involved the lynching of Black men charged with burning barns. The incident proved that Blacks were lynched for crimes other than rape or alleged rape of white women. She closed the article with "An excuse is made by the whites for the purpose of shielding themselves and leaving them free to murder all the negroes they wish."[43]

Further Wells-Barnett saw lynching as representing

> the cool, calculating deliberation of intelligent people who openly vow that there is an "unwritten law" that justifies them in putting human beings to death without complaint under oath, without trial by jury, without opportunity to make defense, and without right of appeal.[44]

In this, her most systematic and thorough article on lynching, Wells-Barnett was eloquent in her outrage as she recounted the rationale for lynching. She attributed its beginning to Reconstruction and gains made by Black people during the period. Wells noted that "one Southern State after another raised the cry against 'negro domination' and proclaimed there was an 'unwritten law' that justified any means to resist it."[45] She went on to equate the horrors of lynching with that of the Spanish Inquisition and the barbarism of the Middle Ages.

Wells rejected the notion that Blacks were naturally immoral and incapable of civilized behavior. Rather, she developed an interesting twist on the ability of whites to model proper conduct or misconduct by noting that "the negro has been too long associated with the white man not to have copied his vices as well as his virtues."[46] Wells further noted that Black women have long been the victim of rape at the hands of white men. She ends with the piercing observation that "what becomes a crime deserving capital punishment when the tables are turned is a matter of small moment when the negro woman is the accusing party."[47] In short, what Blacks asked for was equal justice.

Four viewpoints in regard to lynching were proposed by Wells. The first centered on consistency.[48] She appealed to the national record of speaking out on behalf of "the Armenian Christian, the Russian Jew, the Irish Home Ruler, the native women of India, the Siberian exile, and the Cuban patriot."[49]

Second, Wells appealed to economy. She noted that the United States must pay compensation to other countries for any of their citizens who are lynched because the government was unable to protect the populace or serve justice.[50]

Third, she regarded the country's honor. She abhorred the government's acceptance that it cannot protect "its women save by hanging, shooting, and burning alleged offenders."[51]

Finally, she appealed to love of country:

> With all the powers of government in control; with all laws made by white men, administered by white judges, jurors, prosecuting attorneys, and sheriffs; with every office of the executive department filled by white men—no excuse can be offered for exchanging the orderly administration of justice for barbarous lynchings and "unwritten laws." Our country should be placed speedily above the plan of confessing herself a failure at self-government.[52]

Ultimately, Wells rested her argument on moral agency. In response to Jane Addams' article, which condemned lynching but accepted the argument that Black men were guilty of rape, Wells called for Christian and moral forces to insist that "truth, swift-winged and courageous, summon this nation to do its duty to exalt justice and preserve inviolate the sacredness of human life."[53]

Again, she did not allow the North to escape its moral responsibility. She accused the North of surrendering its position of moral rectitude. She condemned the North's

> lethargic attitude toward the lynching evil. The belief is often expressed that if the North would stand as firmly for principle as the South does for prejudice, lynching and many other evils would be checked.[54]

Wells believed in the country's ideals and considered them to be one with Christian belief and doctrine.

> In the celebration of the fiftieth year of the Negro's freedom, does it seem too much to ask white civilization, Christianity and Democracy to be true to themselves on this as all other questions? They can not then be false to any man or race of men. Our democracy asserted that the people are fighting for the time when all men shall be brothers and the liberty of each shall be the concern of all. If this is true, the struggle is about to take in the Negro.[55]

Throughout her writings, Wells was clear to note the responsibilities of the United States as a Christian nation. Wells wrote during a period in which the nation was considered the political expression of Christianity, nationally and internationally. There was no real separation between public religion and the government. Wells drew no such distinction in her writings.

Her strong sense of moral conduct grew not only from her early experiences in the church and her religious upbringing, but was a product of the national, religious, and political consciousness of her era. She sought justice and the equal application of the law for Blacks and whites alike. She did not doubt that some African-Americans committed crimes which demanded punishment. However, she held firmly to the principle of due process. The guilty must be punished, the innocent must be set free. The courts of this nation must be allowed to carry out justice.

A 1891 article in *The Free Speech* showed yet another facet of her moral code. The article defended the use of retaliatory violence by Blacks to the crime of lynching. It is not certain that Wells was the writer, but it is most certain that such an article would not appear in the paper without her knowledge or approval. In part, the article noted:

> The whites control all the machinery of government of the South. It is systematically used against the blacks. As if this were not enough, irresponsible parties lynch black men for and without provocation, a party of Alabamians recently lynched a black man for the fun of the thing. The way to prevent retaliation is to prevent lynching. Human nature is human nature.[56]

Hence, in the absence of law and order and an effective judicial system, retaliatory violence may be the only solution to lynching. Wells noted in her autobiography that she bought a pistol after the lynching of a close family friend, Tom Moss, because of the threat to her when she refused to stop calling attention to the lynching and the need to bring the lynchers to justice.[57]

Although her preference was to work through the established systems of government and due process, Wells was pragmatic in the face of social evil. When faced with a complete rejection of her rights, she prepared to defend herself. She was not so caught up in the United States ideal that she could not intuit the personal danger to herself and to others who sought justice in "the land of the free and the home of the brave."

WOMANHOOD

As strong of character as Wells was, she remained wedded to the ideal of the cult of true womanhood. She believed, as did countless Black and white women of her day, that women were the repositories of moral integrity and virtue. Writing in *The New York Age,* she painted the picture of the ideal southern Black woman:

> As a miser hoards and guards his gold, so does she guard her virtue and good name. For the sake of the noble womanhood to which she aspires, and the race whose name bears the stigma of immorality—her soul scorns each temptation to sin and guilt. She knows that our people, as a whole, are charged with immorality and vice; that it depends largely on the woman of today to refute such charges by her stainless life. . . . She strives to encourage them [men] all things honest, noble and manly . . .[58]

The themes of the cult are captured in these few phrases: a woman's virtue and good name, a woman's responsibility to be the paragon of moral conduct, her duty to encourage men to a higher moral life. Over thirty years later, Well-Barnett had not lost these standards. She passed them on to her two young daughters, Ida and Alfreda:

> I know my girls are true to me, to themselves and their God wherever they are, and my heart is content. I have had many troubles and much disappointment in life, but I felt that in you I have an abiding joy. I feel that whatever others may do, my girls are now and will be shining examples of noble true womanhood. And so mother's heart is glad and happy when she thinks of her daughters, for she knows that wherever they are and whatever they are doing they are striving to please her and reach the ideal of true womanhood.[59]

Wells-Barnett blended the strong influence of the cult of true womanhood with an equally strong sense of Christian duty. Her views on motherhood reveal the strong influence of its ideals. Writing after the birth of her children, Wells stated:

> . . . I had to become a mother before I realized what a wonderful place in the scheme of things the Creator has given woman. She it is upon whom rests the joint share of the work of creation, and I wonder if women who shirk their duties in that respect truly realize that they have not only deprived humanity of their contribu-

tion to perpetuity, but that they have robbed themselves of one of the most glorious advantages in the development of their own womanhood.[60]

Later, she wrote with pride of Madame C. J. Walker who amassed a fortune selling Black hair care products. Wells-Barnett was among Walker's doubters when she predicted her success in the hair care industry. Wells-Barnett noted Walker's meager education, but also that Walker "was never ashamed of having been a washer-woman earning a dollar and a half a day. To see her phenomenal rise made me take pride anew in Negro womanhood."[61]

As late as March of 1930, she spent time "reviewing [her] campaign and urging women voters to do their Christian duty and vote for race women on Primary Day April 8th."[62] Christian duty and womanhood were tied to justice and moral agency. True womanhood meant virtue and right action both in the private and public realms. Wells did not believe that woman's moral influence could be limited. A woman must never content herself with her own salvation. She was responsible for her race as well.

LEADERSHIP

Wells was moving in her appeals to the conscience of the leaders of the land. She held "men who stand high in the esteem of the public for christian character, for moral and physical courage, for devotion to the principles of equal and exact justice to all, and for great sagacity,"[63] accountable for the continued lawlessness in the land as the death toll from lynching mounted.

> [They] stand as cowards who fear to open their mouths before this great outrage. . . . their tacit encouragement, their silent acquiescence, the black shadow of lawlessness in the form of lynch law is spreading its wings over the whole country.[64]

Wells held African-American leadership responsible. She believed that if Blacks possessed self-respect, the friction between the races would be reduced.[65] She disapproved of Black compromise in the face of lawlessness and lynching. Referring to the Tom Moss lynching, she believed that "the Afo-American ministers, newspapers, and leaders counselled obedience to the law which did not protect them. Their counsel was heeded and not a hand was uplifted to resent the outrage."[66]

She had no patience for cowardice and believed that part of racial pride and leadership was tied to defending life and limb against racist hostility. Expanding on this theme, Wells wrote:

> . . . a Winchester rifle should have a place of honor in every black home, and it should be used for that protection which the law refuses to give. When the white man who is always the aggressor knows he runs as great a risk of biting the dust every time his Afro-American victim does, he will have greater respect for Afro-American life. The more the Afro-American yield and cringes and begs, the more he has to do so, the more he is insulted, outraged and lynched.[67]

Writing in May of 1893, Wells held the ideal that the United States had a distinct place within civilization as a Christian nation. She referred to the United States as "this Christian nation, the flower of the nineteenth century civilization" that could not stop the slaughter of Blacks.[68] Wells saw the irony of a federal government that maintained it was powerless, but state troops could shoot Blacks "like cattle, when in desperation the black men attempt to defend themselves, and then tell the world that it was necessary to put down a 'race war.'"[69]

Wells was making a moral appeal based upon the ideals of the country. By referring to the United States as both a Christian nation and the flower of civilization, she addressed the conscience of the country and its duty to provide moral leadership. She was certain that when the people and the government of the land lived up to the established social mores "a sentiment against lynch law as strong, deep and mighty as that roused against slavery prevails." She concluded "I have no fear of the result."[70]

Later, in 1900, Wells again appealed to the national character and the Christian and moral forces of the nation. She pointed out that Blacks were denied access to newspapers, religious periodicals, and magazines to refute the slander that appeared on their pages from white authorities from the South. She even noted that the "leading pulpits of the country are open to stories of the negro's degradation and ignorance but not to his defense from slander."[71]

Wells was clear about the locus of leadership in the African-American community. She commissioned Black preachers, editors and teachers to "charge themselves with the responsibility" of agitating for a restoration of the peace and due process along with their white counterparts.[72] She placed responsibility squarely in the hands of white leaders, as they worked within their spheres of influence, just as Black leadership worked within its domain.

> Not until the white editors, preachers and teachers of the country join with him [the Negro] in his fight for justice and protection by law can there be any hope of success.[73]

Wells-Barnett could not tolerate Booker T. Washington's model of leadership. She decried his proclivity for telling "chicken jokes" which she, and other Black leaders, felt were detrimental to Black social uplift. When Julius Rosenwald asked Wells-Barnett if African-Americans had accepted Washington as their leader, she responded that although he was respected, not everyone agreed with Washington's accomodationist position. She likened Washington's remarks to Rabbi Hirsch, who was a leading Jew in the city of Chicago, telling Gentile audiences stories about Jews burning down their stores to collect the insurance. She ended their exchange:

> I am sure you would not, and a great many of us cannot approve Mr. Washington's plan of telling chicken-stealing stories on his own people in order to amuse his audiences and get money for Tuskegee.[74]

School teachers, press, and pulpit provided the key leadership positions in United States society. Wells earnestly believed that persons in these areas of leadership must be united in a "vigorous denunciation of all forms of lawlessness and earnest, constant demand for the rigid enforcement of the law of the land."[75] Wells clearly saw moral agency and justice as the responsibility of leadership. Anyone or any group which did not have the dignity of the person and respect for the law as part of its agenda could not provide valid leadership.

Notes

1. Ida B. Wells, Diary, 8 February 1885, Special Collections, Joseph Regenstein Library, University of Chicago, Chicago.

2. Ibid., 1 January 1886.

3. William John Faulkner, ed., "How The Slaves Worshipped" in *The Days When the Animals Talked: Black American Folktales and How they Came to Be* (Chicago: Follett Publishing, 1977), 54.

4. Wells, Diary, 14 September 1886.

5. Ibid., 3 January 1887.

6. Ibid., 18 January 1887.

7. Ibid., 14 February 1887

8. Ibid., 20 February 1887.

9. Ibid., 28 March 1887.

10. Ibid., 16 July 1887.

11. Dwight Lyman Moody (1837-99) was one of the greatest revivalists of the nineteenth century. His theology was a blend of optimism and a strong evangelical impulse.

12. Ibid., 8 February 1885.

13. Faulkner, 52.

14. Wells, Diary, 28 November 1886.

15. Ibid., 1 February 1886.

16. Ibid.

17. Ibid.

18. Ibid., 24 April 1887.

19. Ibid., 18 March 1885.

20. Ibid., 4 September 1886.

21. Ibid., 18 April 1887.

22. Ibid., 4 December 1886.

23. Ibid., 8 February 1887.

24. Ibid., 12 August 1887. This convention was composed of writers, editors, and publishers of Negro papers. It was held in Louisville, Kentucky. In her autobiography, Wells writes "I went to Louisville to the

first press convention I had ever attended and was tickled pink over the attention I received from those veterans of the press." *Crusade,* 32. She also notes that she was the first woman representative at the convention. In 1889, Wells was elected secretary to the National Press Association.

25. Wells, *A Red Record: Tabulated Statistics and Alleged Causes of Lynching in the United States, 1892-1893-1894* (Chicago: Donohue and Henneberry, Printers, Binders and Publishers, 1894; reprint, New York: Arno Press, *On Lynching: Southern Horrors, A Red Record, Mob Rule in New Orleans,* 1969), 73.

26. Ibid., 101.

27. Ibid. A strong argument can be made that Wells placed extremely high expectations on the role of religion and Christianity in shaping public opinion. However, when viewed within her context, her heavy reliance on the "Christian and moral forces" of society to shape, change, and motivate public moral agency is in consonance with the impact of evangelical religion in her era.

28. Ibid., 97-99.

29. Ibid., 97.

30. Ibid.

31. Ibid., 98.

32. Ibid.

33. Ibid., 99.

34. Ida B. Wells-Barnett, "Our Country's Lynching Record," *Survey,* 1 February 1913, 574.

35. Wells, *Daily Inter Ocean,* 19 May 1894.

36. Ibid.

37. Ibid.

38. Ibid.

39. Wells, "Our Country's Lynching Record," 574.

40. Wells, Diary, 8 February 1885. Wells makes these observations after hearing Dwight Moody preach at a revival in Memphis.

41. Wells, "The Reign of Mob Law, Iola's Opinion of Doings in the Southern Field," *New York Age,* 18 February 1893. TMs, Special Collections, Joseph Regenstein Library, University of Chicago, Chicago.

42. Wells, *The Weekly Call* (Topeka, Kansas), 22 April 1893.

43. Wells, "Ida B. Wells Speaks" handwritten draft dated 2 September. No year given, no paper cited. Special Collections, Joseph Regenstein Library, University of Chicago, Chicago.

44. Wells, "Lynch Law in America," *The Arena,* January 1900, 15.

45. Ibid., 17.

46. Ibid., 21.

47. Ibid.

48. Ibid., 22.

49. Ibid.

50. Ibid., 23.

51. Ibid.

52. Ibid., 24.

53. Wells-Barnett, "Lynching and the Excuse For It," *The Independent,* 16 May 1901, 1136.

54. Wells-Barnett, "Our Country's Lynching Record," 574.

55. Ibid.

56. *The New York Age,* 19 September 1891 and *Weekly Avalanche* (Memphis), 6 September 1891.

57. Wells, *Crusade,* 62. "I felt that one had better die fighting against injustice than to die like a dog or a rat in a trap. I had already determined to sell my life as dearly as possible if attacked. I felt if I could take one lyncher with me, this would even up the score a little bit."

58. Wells, *New York Age,* 18 February 1888.

59. Wells, Handwritten letter to her daughters regretting her inability to be with them to help celebrate Halloween, 30 October 1920, Special Collections, Joseph Regenstein Library, University of Chicago, Chicago.

60. Wells, *Crusade,* 251.

61. Ibid., 378.

62. Wells, Diary, 25 March 1930.

63. Wells, *Southern Horrors,* 14.

64. Ibid.

65. Ibid., 18.

66. Ibid., 19.

67. Ibid., 23.

68. Wells, "Lynch Law in All Its Phases," *Our Day,* 11, no. 65. (May 1893): 344.

69. Ibid.

70. Ibid., 346.

71. Wells, "The Negro's Case in Equity," *The Independent* 26 (April 1900): 1010.

72. Ibid., 1011.

73. Ibid.

74. Wells, *Crusade,* 331.

75. Wells-Barnett, "How Enfranchisement Stops Lynchings," *Original Rights Magazine,* June 1910, 46.

Melba Joyce Boyd (essay date winter 1994)

SOURCE: Boyd, Melba Joyce. "Canon Configuration for Ida B. Wells-Barnett." *Black Scholar* 24, no. 1 (winter 1994): 8-13.

[*In the following essay, Boyd reviews two books and one film which have helped to revive interest in Wells-Barnett's life and works.*]

One hundred and one years ago, the Worlds Congress of Representative Women, a black women's organization, was founded in order for black Americans to levy some representation at the 1893 World's Columbian Exposition in Chicago. As a response to another blatant act of racial discrimination, F. L. Barnett, J. Garland Penn, Frederick Douglass, and Ida B. Wells wrote and published *The Reason Why the Colored American Is Not in the World's Columbian Exposition.* The introduction was translated into French and German, and the pamphlet was distributed to patrons of the exposition.

"Lynch Law" by Ida B. Wells was included in the pamphlet, an essay that explains the racist psychology of American society, as it details the horrors and provides the statistics that amplify this national shame. In her condemnation of the media's complicity with the perpetrators, she asserts:

> The men who make these charges encourage or lead the mobs which do the lynching. They belong to the race which holds Negro life cheap, which owns the telegraph wires, newspapers, and all other communication with the outside world. They write the reports which justify lynching by painting the Negro as black as possible, and those reports are accepted by the press associations without question or investigation. The mob spirit has increased with alarming frequency and violence. Over a thousand black men, women and children have been thus sacrificed in the past ten years.

> *(Selected Works of Ida B. Wells,* p. 75)

Shortly thereafter, a derivative women's club in Boston began publishing the journal, *Women's Era,* inscribed by the speech Frances Harper delivered at the Congress in Chicago. It became the voice of black feminism in the U.S. Ida B. Wells-Barnett, known internationally for her fight against lynching, significantly influenced the ideological direction of the black women's organizations, which embraced the anti-lynching crusade as a major issue in their political agenda.

Almost a century later, a full range of literature has emerged that resurrects and contextualizes the literary voices of Afroamerican women, which for too long were either ignored, obscured or dismissed. Undoubtedly, the presence of women scholars and writers has altered the political dynamics and the intellectual axiom of the current intellectual era. Notwithstanding, Ida B. Wells-Barnett, who endured political and gender discrimination from within and from outside the Afroamerican community, has, to a large extent, been vindicated in the advent of black women's studies. The reprinting of her essays, *Selected Works,* and her autobiography, *Crusade for Justice,* revives her voice; while a new biography by Mildred Thompson and a documentary illuminate a contemporary need for her ideological integrity and tenacity during these contemporary times.

For the most part, the three recent works, *Ida B. Wells: An Exploratory Study of an American Black Woman, Selected Works of Ida B. Wells,* and the film, *A Passion for Justice,* explain how legislated discrimination and racial terrorism beset the Reconstruction Era. And, each of these works considers Wells' response to these historical circumstances, while individually each work serves a particular purpose appropriate to the medium or the purposes of the text.

The film, *Passion for Justice,* provides a general outline of Wells era, and integrates her voice and other contemporary authorities into the telling of her story. The biography by Mildred Thompson is more detailed and intricate and therefore provides a more complex presentation of the historical dynamics that affected Wells. Trudier Harris, on the other hand, does not critique Wells' life in her introductory essay to *Selected Works,* but presents a description of related historical events and biographical issues.

Thompson's text includes essays and even a short story by Wells, which adds the unedited perspective of her subject. This presentation provides autobiography, literature, biography and historical context. If it were not for the high cost of this hardcover, it would be an excellent textbook. *Selected Works by Ida B. Wells* contains original writings by Wells, but the selections do not extend beyond 1900 because the book is a part of The Schomburg Library of Nineteenth-Century Black Women Writers Series.

Harris' overview of Wells' life touches on the nuances of Wells' political conflicts with prominent "race" leaders of the times. Thompson's book, and Wells' autobiography *Crusade for Justice,* edited by her daughter, Alfreda Duster, reveal why Wells is so highly regarded by many black Americans, though her essays remained out of print for decades. Thompson's work interrelates Wells' autobiographical voice with historical incidents and political controversy, and thereby demonstrates the impact of Wells' radicalism.

In any discussion of Wells' life, two historical incidents are relayed as essential to Ida B. Wells' destiny as an activist leader. One incident involved a direct confrontation with a Jim Crow Law, and the other involved three of her friends, who were lynched.

In May 1884, Wells was asked to leave her seat in the ladies car and to go to the smoking car because she was black. Wells refused. The conductor, with the help of other white men, forcibly removed her. Shortly thereafter she sued the Chesapeake, Ohio and Southwestern Rail Road Company. Though she won the decision in the lower court, the Court of Appeals overturned the ruling. Yet her suit against Jim Crow propelled her into national attention, and identified her as a dissident. She later wrote about the case; launching her journalism career. Regarded only as a racial being, this incident demonstrated how race and sex converge as class in the experience of black women in the United States.

Wells exerted a powerful political influence during her lifetime. Her articles in *The Free Speech* provided ideological clarity and served as an organizing tool locally, nationally and internationally. After the brutal lynching of three of her friends on March 9, 1892 in Memphis, Tennessee, she instigated a mass exodus of blacks from that city. Her open attack on white patriarchal chivalry, and the suggestion that white women might desire black male companionship, so offended the white citizenry that the press office was destroyed, and the white newspaper of Memphis called for her lynching. Fortunately, she was attending an African Methodist Episcopal Church convention in Philadelphia and was safe as a guest in the home of Frances E. W. Harper.

Hence, the fight against lynching became her particular crusade. This subject dominated her writing and her lectures, as she documented and protested this terrorism. She exposed lynching as a tactic to repress the political, social and economic ambitions of Afroamericans and forthrightly denounced the lame confabulations of "white" law and order, a subject that warrants contemporary study during the current hysterical response to urban crime.

THE DOCUMENTARY FILM

Ida B. Wells: A Passion for Justice, a William Greaves Production, has received many film awards including, First Place Documentary award from the Black Filmmakers Hall of Fame, the Silver Apple at the National Educational Film and Video Festival, and the Silver Plaque at the Chicago International Film Festival among others. The sixty minute film opens with a discussion about the Civil War and the birth of Ida B. Wells into slavery in 1862 in Holly Springs, Mississippi.

Historical photographs, drawings and authentic documents outline the visual imagery as the narrator informs the audience of dates, places, and events that move the history forward. The film traces the personal difficulties, the political issues and the key historical events which challenged Ida B. Wells, and how her determination and activism, in turn, affected the politics and history of many Afroamericans.

But more impressively, when Toni Morrison reads from Wells' autobiography, *Crusade for Justice,* the film experience becomes more personal. Morrison conveys the vitality of Wells' voice, as we learn about Wells' struggle to raise her siblings after the death of her parents. Wells' devotion to family extends to her marriage to F. L. Barnett when she retreats from active political life to devote most of her time to raising their children. But this decision should not be viewed in simple, conservative terms. Wells' children often accompanied her to political events and activities, and when the children reached maturity she returned to her activist lifestyle. These excerpts from Wells' autobiography, articles and essays also function as transitions from setting to subject. Moreover, Morrison reading Wells suggests a literary legacy in black women's history.

A series of interviews with prominent historians including Paula Giddings, John De Mott, Rosalyn Terborg-Penn, and David Tucker constructs the historical context of the Wells' legacy. What is especially effective about these historical discussions is that the details of events and instances are enhanced by critical analysis and feminist insight. These interviews explain the political relationship between Jim Crow legislation and lynching and how Ida B. Wells was personally affected and politically motivated by these dynamics. Their discussions also consider the repressive sexism in the black community and its ambivalence about female leadership.

The film also includes a brief interview with Troy Duster, a professor of sociology and the grandson of Ida B. Wells. Dr. Duster's interview includes personal reflections that reiterate his grandmother's strong character and radical convictions. Through him, family oral history enhances the film's narrative.

If there is one thematic incongruity in the film, it is the narration. Since the man behind the voice, Al Freeman, Jr., is never shown in the film, the narration avails the film like an omniscient eye. Consequently, even though this is a film about a black woman, the subliminal affect of the male voice, which gives the first and the last words on the subject, suggests that the larger intelligence and the broader view of history is male. Possibly, the interviews could have been extended to include those scripted historical accounts supplied by the narrator. Additionally, the film could have opened and closed in Ida B. Wells' words.

However, the film does indicate the key points of ideological conflict and provides a firm historical outline and critical details of Wells' life. The film also does an excellent job of conveying the complexity of her life by relaying the various conflicts that affected her, including radicalism versus conservatism, race issues versus women's rights, and private versus public life.

The film takes a more personal approach to Wells' relationships with prominent activist of the times, such as Frederick Douglass and Susan B. Anthony, demonstrating how these more amiable associates were politically aligned with Wells' outspoken radicalism. Throughout, the film maintains Wells' radical perspective as its primary focus.

The film complements the writings by Wells found in the reader, edited by Harris, while more detailed research and documentation is constructed in the biography by Thompson. Thompson, however, concludes her historical study of Wells with a comment about the film:

> National Educational Television has just aired an entire program devoted to her accomplishments. She would have been excited and pleased at this acknowledgment of her place in history.
>
> (p. 130)

THE BIOGRAPHY

Mildred Thompson's book is a part of the comprehensive sixteen volume series, Black Women in United States History, edited by Darlene Clark Hine. *Ida B. Wells-Barnett: An Exploratory Study of an American Black Woman, 1893-1930* contains a valuable biographical analysis of Wells' life and times. The creative structure of biography is the strongest dimension of the work, as the biography interacts with Wells' personality and perception through excerpts in Wells' voice. Thompson's detailed historical account should be considered a seminal text. It reconstructs the broader framework of Afroamerican history with autobiographical comments from particular personalities of the times, juxtaposing various perspectives on particular events and analyzing Wells' philosophical and political position therein. Thompson explains:

> This study of Ida Wells-Barnett reveals the complexity of a woman who was not merely engaged in almost constant civil rights activity, but who initiated many of these reform efforts. It points out some of the factors that motivated her daring and steadfastness in a climate of blatant racial prejudice, national indifference, and changing black ideologies. It also shows the relationship between her declining influence and the increasing significance of organizational powers in the black community. Ida Wells-Barnett was a militant civil rights activist during most of her adult life, but in her mature years when she was out of step with her time, attuned to a drummer whom she had heard earlier, a drummer whose beat would not be heard again for another generation.
>
> (p. 9)

Though the biography engages the traditional scholarly approach, (the text was initially written as her doctoral dissertation), the attempt to "objectify" Wells' life sometimes misconstrues Wells' radicalism. Thompson often employs the language of Wells' political critics, referring to her as an "extremist." This subjective term is derived from the prevailing conservatism that alienated Wells and dominated black politics at the turn of the century. Hence, Thompson concludes that Wells was out of step with her times, while others might conclude that Wells was on time because she extended the progressive vision of the nineteenth century radicals despite the political regression of her peers.

An analysis of Wells' political perspective is more squarely secured in Bettina Aptheker's introduction for the monograph, "Lynching and Rape: An Exchange of Views" by Jane Addams and Ida B. Wells:

> Wells determined to reveal the exact details of all lynching which came to her attention. She believed that the concrete circumstances surrounding each case would show that the overwhelming majority of lynch victims were killed for economic and political reasons. She believed further, that if the political causes of lynching could be demonstrated, political opposition could be generated. This, coupled with a moral appeal to Christian ethics, might succeed in building an effective movement to halt the atrocities.
>
> (p. 15-16)

Aptheker's discussion on Wells is more focused on political thought and considers that thought relative to historical reality (approximately 10,000 lynchings by the 1900) rather than relative to political trends. Wells never apologized for her frankness or retreated from a position that invigorated free thought. She did not compromise her principles whether it be the racist power brokers of government or the "colored accommodationists" fraternizing with the "fat cats" of big business. What becomes even more apparent as one reads about the emerging black politics during the post-reconstruction era, is that true radicalism runs against the grain of orthodoxy.

Wells was never misled by organizations beleaguered by opportunists or dilettantes. Wells' role was to identify the true intentions and motivations of oppressive forces and to dispel the projections of a corrupt democracy that believed in and practiced white male supremacy. At the same time, the principles she applied to the ruling culture were not altered to excuse the foibles of black leadership.

Wells' work not only identified the horrors of lynching and the evil and hatred of the blood-thirsty crowds, but it also carried this fight to her own community. She challenged the leadership of Booker T. Washington because she believed his political strategy was complicit with covert racists. Thompson discusses this conflict, and the inclusion of Wells' essay, **"Booker T. Washington and His Critics,"** provides the reader with the primary text. Wells squarely addresses Washington's theoretical contradictions and denotes the reactionary ramifications of his apologist appeal to racist subterfuge:

> Does some one ask a solution of the lynching evil? Mr. Washington says in substance: Give me money to educate the Negro and when he is taught how to work, he will not commit the crime for which lynching is done. Mr. Washington knows when he says this that lynching is not invoked to punish crime but color, and not even industrial education will change that.
>
> Again he sets up the dogma that when the race becomes taxpayers, produces of something the white man wants, landowners, business, etc., the Anglo-Saxon will forget all about color and respect that race's manhood. One of the leading southern papers said editorially, in discussing the separate street car law which was to go into effect last winter in Memphis, Tennessee, that it

was not the servant or working class of Negroes, who know their places, with whom the white people objected to riding, but the educated, property-owning Negro who thought himself the white man's equal.

(p. 258-59)

Wells' political integrity and strong sense of social urgency was compatible with her earliest associates, but during the more conservative era of the early twentieth century, this radicalism distanced her from the new leadership on the left. Other biographers mention this paradox that rendered Wells to a marginal position in national politics during the latter years of her political life, and Thompson provides the details of her conflict with W. E. B. Du Bois and the NAACP.

Because Wells was outspoken and questioned Du Bois' organizational appeal for white liberal leadership, she was exempted by Du Bois from the Committee of Forty, the founding membership of the NAACP. When she took exception to this, Du bois explained that her perspective would be represented by another member of the committee. Wells consulted Charles Edward Russell, one of the principal organizers of the National Negro Conference, and he overruled Du Bois and appointed her to the committee.

But Thompson explains: "Being named to the Committee by Russell did not assuage the hostility that Wells-Barnett continued to feel toward Du Bois. He, in turn, ignored her activity entirely in the pages of the Crisis, the official organ of the NAACP." Thompson extends the discussion in Wells' own words, "Both Mr. Villard and Prof. Du Bois gave me the impression that they rather feared some interference [sic] from me in the Chicago arrangements. They also gave me very clearly to understand at the executive meeting there in New York that I was not expected to do anything save to be a member" (p. 83).

Wells encountered similar difficulties with some of the leadership in the black women's movement. Hallie Q. Brown, who was instrumental in organizing the World Congress of Representative Women at the 1893 Chicago Centennial, viewed Wells as an "extremist" as well. And like Du Bois, Brown felt that Wells' political strategy was too confrontational. But the issue of lynching was the issue that distinguished the Women's Club Movement, and it was Wells' valiant fight against ghastly assaults on black women, men, and children that challenged the consciousness of the American public and that gave black women a clearer vision in establishing their organizational character.

Throughout her activist years Wells was criticized for "speaking out like a man." To some extent Wells was sensitive to this opinion. However, she refused to temper her style to the narrow perceptions of a growing conservative climate. Her class consciousness exceeded the more bourgeois motivations of the women's organizations and the Chicago black elite. Indeed, her work with the Ida B. Wells Club and the Negro Fellowship League focused on the needs of poor blacks and engaged practical problems like employment, food, housing and education.

The essays by Ida B. Wells that follow the biography carry the breath and fire of her radicalism. Unlike the more pretentious Victorian prose that resulted from the constraints of conventional intellectualism, Wells' direct and impassioned language is appropriate to her tasks and her themes. The selections about lynching demonstrate how her detailed and extensive research expose the collusion between klansmen and "upstanding citizens."

What hindsight also gives our contemporary reading of Wells is that her writing and her political thought was linked to the nineteenth century rhetorical style of black women radicals like Frances Harper. In fact, Harper named her main character after Ida B. Wells' pen name, Iola, in Harper's 1892 feminist novel, *Iola Leroy: Or Shadows Uplifted*. Likewise, Harper's essays and speeches focus on political issues, especially abolition, woman's rights and lynching.

Their urgency for justice produced literature that was not content for intellectual fodder, but rather, insight for political activism. The candid language and direct appeal were drafted to instigate change and to reach a mass audience. For example, in "Duty to Dependent Races," Harper asserts:

> A government which has power to tax its citizens from wrong and outrage and does not is vicious. A government which would do it and cannot is weak; and where human life is insecure through either weakness or viciousness in the administration of law, there must be a lack of justice, and where this is wanting nothing can make up the deficiency.

(p. 91)

Likewise, in **"Lynching Our National Crime,"** Wells charges:

> Why is the mob murder permitted by a Christian nation? What is the cause of this awful slaughter? This question is answered almost daily—always the same shameless falsehood that "Negroes are lynched to protect womanhood." Standing before a Chautauqua assemblage, John Temple Graves, at once champion of lynching and apologist for lynchers, said: "The mob stands today as the most potential bulwark between the women of the South and such a carnival of crime as would infuriate the world precipitate the annihilation of the Negro race." This is the never varying answer of lynchers and their apologists. All know that it is untrue. The cowardly lyncher revels in murder, then seeks to shield himself from public execration by claiming devotion to woman. But truth is mighty and the lynching record discloses the hypocrisy of the lyncher as well as his crime.

(p. 262)

For additional reading, *The Selected Works of Ida B. Wells-Barnett* includes all of the chapters from the pamphlet, *The Reason Why the Colored American Is Not in the World's Columbian Exposition* (1892) (including prefaces in French and German); *A Red Record: Tabulated Statistics and Alleged Causes of Lynching in the United States, 1892-1893-1894*; and *Mob Rule in New Orleans: Robert Charles and His Fight to the Death* (1900). For the most part, *Selected Works* is a reprinting of Well's essays and the text serves this essential need, but again, an expensive price tag of $32.50 will send the mass reading audience to the library for a copy.

The Black Women in the United States Series is a comprehensive attempt to historicize black women lives, but the Schomburg Series is a literary collection. By aligning Wells with Frances Harper, Charlotte Forten, Harriett Jacobs, Ann Plato and Phillis Wheatley, among others, Wells' historical and political insight can thereby be valued as cultural expression and appreciated as literature. Reading Ida B. Wells supplies an ideological context for our contemporary setting because she reveals how race hatred is linked to historical guilt and how oppressive beliefs and deeds are enacted to deny responsibility. Her analysis of lynching moves us to an understanding of the critical issue of miscegenation, and why patriarchal rule depends on the control of women.

Furthermore, her perspective and system of analysis can and should be extended to contemporary social issues that confound the public, i.e. Clarence Thomas and Anita Hill. Thomas' collusion with the Republican administration should be linked to Booker T. Washington's complicity with the ruling aristocracy, while Anita Hill's treatment by the Senate committee during the judicial hearings should be considered historically consistent with the public disdain for black women who speak up for themselves and for the conscience of the nation.

> The utterances of leading white men show that with them it is not the crime but the class. Bishop Fitzgerald has become apologist for lynchers of the rapists of white women only. Governor Tillman, of South Carolina, in the month of June, standing under the tree in Barnwell, S.C., on which eight Afro-Americans were hung last year, declared that he would ["]lead a mob to lynch a negro who raped a white woman." So say the pulpits, officials and newspapers of the South. But when the victim is a colored woman it is different.
>
> (Ida B. Wells, **"Southern Horrors,"** 1892)

In the study of Wells' life and words, we find insight into the complex and peculiar predicament of the black female experience.

Works Cited

Aptheker, Bettina. ed. "Lynching and Rape: An Exchange of Views, by Jane Addams and Ida B. Wells." The American Institute for Marxist Studies, 1977.

Duster, Alfreda M. ed. *Crusade for Justice: The Autobiography of Ida B. Wells.* Chicago: University of Chicago Press, 1970.

Harper, Frances E. W. "Duty to Dependent Races," National Council of Women in the United States, Philadelphia, 1891, (pp. 86-91).

Trudier Harris, ed. *Selected Works of Ida B. Wells.* New York: Oxford University Press, 1991.

Mildred I. Thompson. *Ida B. Wells-Barnett: An Exploratory Study of an American Black Woman.* Brooklyn, N.Y.: Carlson Publishing, Inc., 1990.

Ida B. Wells: A Passion for Justice, a film, written and directed by William Greaves Productions: New York: William Greaves Productions, Inc.

P. Gabrielle Foreman (review date summer 1997)

SOURCE: Foreman, P. Gabrielle. Review of *The Memphis Diary of Ida B. Wells,* by Ida B. Wells-Barnett. *African American Review* 31 (summer 1997): 363-65.

[*In the following review, Foreman gives a favorable assessment of a published edition of Wells-Barnett's diary.*]

To know Ida B. Wells, more than a hundred years after she launched her journalistic career, is to love her. We admire the courageous newspaper editor who in the same year her friend Thomas Moss was lynched in Memphis published an editorial that declared: "Nobody in this section believes that old threadbare lie that Negro men assault white women. If Southern white men are not careful they will overreach themselves and a conclusion will be reached which will be very damaging to the moral reputation of their women." Those of us who know of Ida B. Wells tend to think of a woman of almost mythic proportions, an unflinching anti-lynching activist who challenged new railway segregation laws in the 1880s and won (though the case was soon overturned), who in 1892, the year she began her crusade and published **Southern Horrors: Lynch Law in All Its Phases**, almost single-handedly turned back the flow of lynchings in the U.S. When we think of Wells we imagine a founding member of the NAACP who also insisted that every African American family should own a Winchester, a fiery woman who vowed that in the face of white violence she would "sell her life dearly."

Miriam DeCosta-Willis's *The Memphis Diary of Ida B. Wells: An Intimate Portrait of the Activist as a Young Woman* sets out to introduce the private side of Ida B. Wells to those already acquainted with her public persona. Flanked by a foreword and afterward by prominent scholars of African American women's literature and history, Mary Helen Washington and Dorothy Sterling, DeCosta-Willis presents three separate sets of Wells's journals: the 1885-87 diary written when the to-be activist, only twenty-four, launched her career as the prominent journalist "Iola"; a short and humorous 1893 travel log drafted as the activist set out to England to rally public support and direct international pressure against lynching; and a 1930 diary, composed from the vantage point of an elder Wells, just a year before her death. DeCosta-Willis also includes selected articles penned by "Iola," Wells's nom de plume, that coincide with the first and longest diary. Like the journals themselves, the articles reveal Wells's concerns with "race uplift," a cause that other published Black women diarists of that era, Charlotte Forten and Alice Dunbar-Nelson, shared with race women of that era, Frances E. W. Harper and Mrs. Gertrude Mossell, for example.

The collaborative trilogy, DeCosta-Willis/Washington/Sterling, could not be more appropriate to this project. The latter two have edited landmark collections of Black women's writing, and DeCosta-Willis builds on their models of structuring an interplay between primary texts and critical commentary. She presents Wells's words and also provides a backdrop that breathes into Wells's writing new life for 20th-century readers. DeCosta-Willis paints the landscape of Wells's social and political interactions with both broad strokes and meticulous detail. In the italicized commentary that precedes most entries, DeCosta-Willis identifies the players in Wells's life and provides a context for them. DeCosta-Willis suggests that she takes "an active role in interpreting the text and even in creating its meaning." Her annotations are illuminating rather than intrusive; even at the moments that she "makes meaning" she leaves room for her readers to take a different interpretative path.

Wells's writing, as a single and almost singularly accomplished young Black woman without family in the 1890s, often reveals the gender tensions between the oft-noted and problematized public and private spheres. Wells ruminates—in an abbreviated fashion—on her sometimes conflicting desire for professional success and domestic stability. Mary Helen Washington contends that, "if there is a single recurring theme in Wells's diary, it is that of a highly gifted and talented woman who is in constant conflict with conventional female roles, which undermine and restrict a woman's desire for work and achievement" in certain spheres. Indeed, in the diaries Wells stresses her ambitions rather than her dialy responsibilities; though she spends her days in the classroom, she sees journalism as her trade, and rarely spends time or energy reflecting on her responsibilities as a teacher. In the life presented to us in the diaries, then, Wells travels in a world of men. In 1888, for example, T. Thomas Fortune, editor of the powerful *New York Age,* wrote:

> I met "Iola" at the conference. She has become famous as one of the few women who handles [sic] a goose quill with diamond point as handily as any of us men in newspaper work. Her name is Ida B. Wells. She is smart as a steel trap, and she has no sympathy with humbug.

As an ambitious budding journalist who dismissed the humbug of minding her steel-trap tongue, Wells often found herself, or perhaps placed herself, as one of the "few women" among "us men." Almost all of her correspondence is with men; she reads the writings of men. Moreover, she often dates men in whom she has little romantic interest because she doesn't want to lose the intellectual camaraderie they bring, and knows that there is little room for such interaction outside of romantic paradigms set up by late-nineteenth-century gender conventions.

While DeCosta-Willis emphasizes that the diaries reveal in great detail "the courtship rituals that prevailed among the Black middle class" in that period, more interesting to me is Wells's description of the reading habits of a growing Black middle class. Wells describes a reading network that spanned geographical area and displayed the overlapping arenas of secular and religious Black writings. She reveals the social and discursive interconnections of the Black press on multiple levels: Newspaper editors publish in, and freely reprint articles from, each other's papers. Wells exchanges personal letters with many of these editors: T. Thomas Fortune, William Simmons, and J. A. Arneaux, among others. Many of Wells's correspondents enclose with their missives papers from the Black press in Arkansas, Boston, New York, Kansas, from the *A.M.E. Church Review* and the *Living Way.* Wells and her cohorts go to each other's homes specifically to borrow or discuss recent issues of Black periodicals. Reading and the Black press became central to the social activity of this class. As Wells describes it, popular literary clubs—their events themselves reported in the Black press—"consisted of recitations, essays, and debates interspersed with music. The exercises always closed with the reading of the *Evening Star*—a spicy journal prepared and read by the editor." Wells's diary not only affirms the existence of a large Black readership but reveals a powerful and pervasive African American reading culture.

We learn much about Wells's social interactions, but the diaries themselves rarely yield the private Wells; nor does Wells's style assume the kind of correlation between Wells the writer and Wells the reflector that readers often expect from private and thus ostensibly unguarded writing. We do learn about what she perceives to be her faults: her penchant for spending money she doesn't have, her quick and sharp tongue. But she logs these rather than explores them. She seems to use her diary as a memo where she assiduously notes her expenditures and debts, the photos or "cabinets" she's exchanged with her correspondents, and how many letters she has written or received that day. Despite their more public nature, one suspects that the portrait of a more psychologically complex Wells might be found in a collection of her letters to her many friends, suitors, and professional contacts, the contents of which she sometimes alludes to in her diary.

The scope of Miriam DeCosta-Willis's primary research and the skill of her editorial hand greatly overshadow the few shortcomings of *The Memphis Diaries.* If any one thing could be strengthened it would be the editor's analysis of the "Victorian script" Wells ostensibly followed in her personal life as opposed to her "male-related career." This is the only theme DeCosta-Willis follows throughout the diary without its benefitting from her commentary. Throughout the text, "Victorian social customs" remain undifferentiated and uninterrogated in relation to class, race, and decade. But this one cavil does not diminish the signal accomplishment of DeCosta-Willis's contribution. With care and consummate skill, she has made an important contribution to Wells scholarship and to the field of early Black women's writing.

Linda O. McMurry (essay date 1998)

SOURCE: McMurry, Linda O. "Antilynching Lectures." In *To Keep the Waters Troubled: The Life of Ida B. Wells,* pp. 169-87. New York: Oxford University Press, 1998.

[*In the following chapter from her biography of Wells-Barnett, McMurry discusses the social and rhetorical contexts of her subject's early anti-lynching lectures.*]

Soon after moving to Memphis, Ida B. Wells had become active in the literary and dramatic circles of that city's vibrant black community. Almost immediately she had discovered her love of the platform and stage. Although she toyed with the idea of becoming an actress, like other young women of her era, Wells soon realized that the stage could not provide adequate respectability or remuneration. Very few women speakers could support themselves on the lecture circuits either; for a long time, women had rarely been allowed to speak out in public at all. Nevertheless, while earning her living teaching and writing, Wells utilized the available forums in Memphis and spent scarce dollars on elocution lessons.

Her journalistic ties eventually provided Wells with opportunities to exercise her oratorical skills beyond her home town, at regional and national meetings. Her first lectures outside of Memphis were at National Press Association conferences. Her speeches there and at the meeting of the Afro-American League at Knoxville in July 1891 gained favorable coverage in the press. After moving to New York, her first public speech appears to have been **"The Afro-American in Literature,"** given before the Concord Literary Circle of Brooklyn, New York, on 15 September 1892. Wells was said to have "completely captivated the large and cultivated audience."[1]

At the end of that month, Wells attended the National Press Association convention in Philadelphia. Usually a center of attention whenever she attended these meetings, Wells was proclaimed the "star of the convention," elected treasurer of the group, and called on to speak. Described as "modest in appearance," she was said to have "shone with intellectual brilliancy" and to have been "moved to grief" in relating the story of her exile. Before adjourning, the seventy-five delegates adopted a resolution to establish a fund "to prevent outrages on the Negroes in the South."[2]

The National Press Association was notorious for failing to follow up resolutions with positive action. Prior to the meeting, the *Atchison Blade* predicted, "Now they will go to Philadelphia, read ably written papers on 'The Race

Problem,' denounce southern lynchings, give a ball, drink wine, eat a delicious dinner, and then go to their various homes feeling good and as though they had actually accomplished something worth talking about." Although the prophecy of the delegates' actions apparently proved true, the convention actually did lead to concrete action by a visitor at the meeting—Catherine Impey. An English Quaker, Impey was the editor of *Anti-Caste,* which was "Devoted to the Interests of the Coloured Races." She not only attended the sessions at the convention but also was the guest of honor at a tea given by Fannie J. Coppin, at whose house Wells had previously stayed. Impey left the meeting with a pledge to help the antilynching cause and with the memory of meeting Wells. Several months later she would find a way to aid both the cause and Wells.[3]

Meeting Wells now was undeniably memorable. As capable as her earlier speeches may have been, the subject of lynching was decidedly more suited to the fire and drama of Wells's temperament. With the rape myth as the centerpiece of her antilynching arguments, however, she was in danger of being scandalized for speaking so openly about sexual matters. Although forces of urbanization and industrialism were lessening sexual taboos, the Comstock Law of 1873 still barred distribution of loosely defined "obscene literature and articles of immoral use," and Margaret Sanger was forced to flee the country for giving out contraceptive information as late as 1914. Wells faced the dual suspicions of women speaking in public and of anyone speaking openly of rape. Fortunately, her first widely publicized address on lynching was made under the auspices of some of the most respectable women of her race. According to Wells, soon after her article in the *New York Age,* "two women remarked on my revelations during a visit with each other and said that the women of New York and Brooklyn should do something to show appreciation of my work and to protest the treatment I had received."[4]

The two women were Victoria Earle Matthews, a fellow journalist, and Maritcha Lyons, a schoolteacher. They called a meeting, where the group decided to rally the women of New York and Brooklyn through a series of meetings held in churches. Out of those meetings emerged a plan to raise enough money to allow Wells to start a newspaper of her own. A group of these women, called the Ida B. Wells Testimonial Reception Committee, then organized a meeting in honor of Wells that was held at Lyric Hall on 5 October 1892.

The meeting was a huge success. Not only did most of the leading black women of New York and Brooklyn attend, but sizable delegations also came from Boston and Philadelphia—swelling the audience to over two hundred. Among the members of the black elite who attended were fellow journalist Gertrude Mossell, physician Susan McKinney, social activist Josephine St. Pierre Ruffin, and the widow of the famous Episcopal clergyman, Henry Highland Garnet. In her autobiography, Wells recalled that these women "were all there on the platform, a solid array behind a lonely, homesick girl who was in exile because she had tried to defend the manhood of her race." As Wells was thirty at the time and had traveled widely, her portrait of herself as a "lonely, homesick girl" reflects a desire to cast herself as a tragic heroine—perhaps like the heroic literary characters she had always read about.[5]

The event was well planned and executed. Advertising was provided free of charge by the black press; the *New York Age* and the *New York Review* gave extensive attention and support to the preparations. The committee spent over $150 to make the event successful and memorable. Gas jets spelled out "Iola" at the back of the stage, and programs were printed on miniature copies of the *Free Speech*. The ushers and committee members wore white silk badges lettered with "Iola." Floral arrangements included a horn of plenty donated by the ushers. Victoria Earle Matthews presided over what Wells called "a beautiful program of speeches, resolutions, and music."[6]

In her memoirs Wells recalled being terrified of giving her address to the assemblage. She admitted, "I had some little reputation as an essayist from schoolgirl days, and had recited many times in public recitations which I had committed to memory." She also confessed to having made talks asking for subscriptions to her paper, but she insisted that this was the first time she "had ever been called on to deliver an honest-to-goodness address." Wells avowed that although "every detail of that horrible lynching affair was imprinted on my memory," she had "to commit it all to paper" so she would only have to read the words. Again, Wells appears to have played down her maturity and experience for dramatic effect. Her account portrayed a poignant pathos:

> As I described the cause of the trouble at home and my mind went back to the scenes of the struggle, to the thought of the friends who were scattered throughout the country, a feeling of loneliness and homesickness for the days and the friends that were gone came over me and I felt the tears coming.
>
> A panic seized me. I was afraid that I was going to make a scene and spoil all those dear good women had done for me. I kept saying to myself that whatever happened I must not break down, and so I kept on reading. I had left my handkerchief on the seat behind me and therefore could not wipe away the tears which were coursing down my cheeks.

Wells continued to describe her attempts to signal behind her back to the women on the platform who could not see her face or tears, until finally Matthews brought her a handkerchief. "I kept on reading the story which they had come to hear," Wells proclaimed.[7]

Wells remembered being "mortified" to have "not been able to prevent such an exhibition of weakness." Her consternation appears genuine; over thirty years later she went to some length to explain why it happened. "It came on me unawares," she declared. "It was the only time in all those trying months that I had yielded to personal feel-

ings." Wells noted that she had especially wanted to "be at my best in order to show my appreciation of the splendid things those women had done!" Their very kindness seems to have been the stimulus. Wells explained, "They were giving me tangible evidence that although my environment had changed I was still surrounded by kind hearts."[8]

It is likely that the expression of acceptance by these black elite women did have a profound impact on Wells. Since the death of her parents, Wells had been a frequent target of salacious rumors, expelled from Rust College, fired from teaching, and run out of town. Respectability was among the highest goals of middle-class black women after the degrading experiences of slavery, and for Wells it had been especially elusive. Despite her religious devotion and high moral standards, something always seemed to happen to tarnish the reputation she worked so hard to maintain. While in Memphis, she had also despaired of her seeming inability to sustain close relationships with women. Without the backing of wealth and family, Wells had probably felt at times like an outsider in the elite social circles of Memphis. The endorsement of so many women—some of whom were undisputed members of the elite—was a precious gift at that point in her life.

One reason scandal haunted Wells was her frequent outbursts of anger, which led her to say things she soon regretted. Not surprisingly, emotional control came to be very important to Wells in her quest for respectability. "After all these years," she wrote late in life, "I still have a feeling of chagrin over that exhibition of weakness. Whatever my feelings, I am not given to public demonstrations." Interestingly, in the handwritten autobiography manuscript, she concluded the same paragraph, "And only once before in all my life have the tears forced their way uncontrollably to the surface when I was before the public." In her final version, however, Wells changed the second half of the sentence to "had I given way to woman's weakness in public."[9] Accounts of her later speeches bear out this assertion; her oratory was usually described as forceful, earnest, and effective but also as quiet, educated, and unimpassioned.

Her reasons for ascribing what she considered "weakness" to her gender were as complex and contradictory as her own self-image often was. Even after overcoming numerous obstacles for more than a half century, Wells still blamed her infrequent moments of "weakness"—but not her strength—on her womanhood. When a woman as independent, liberated, and strong-willed as Wells could still belittle her sex, the power of patriarchy in the socialization of nineteenth-century women is abundantly evident. However, in the particular setting of her Lyric Hall speech, a failure to display emotion may have led the audience to question Wells's credibility or her femininity. Among her "sisters" Wells may have seemed unnaturally cold if she had not wept. Wells noted, "But the women didn't feel that I had spoiled things by my breakdown. They seemed to think that it made an impression on the audience favorable to the cause and me."[10]

The reception was a financial success. The committee eventually tabulated the receipts as $613.90, out of which $150.75 was deducted to cover expenses. One of those expenditures was the purchase of a brooch in the shape of "a beautiful gold pen engraved with the legend 'Mizpah,'" which was presented to Wells at the reception. On the back of the pen, according to the *American Citizen,* were engraved the words "Afro-American women of New York and Brooklyn Oct. 5 1892." Wells prized this "emblem of my chosen profession" and claimed to have worn it "for the next twenty years on all occasions." She was probably even more grateful, however, for the $450 that the women deposited in an account for her.[11]

The meeting received favorable attention in the black press. The *Washington Bee* called it "one of the finest testimonials ever rendered an Afro-American." The *American Citizen* described it as "one of the most successful affairs ever managed by the 'fairer sex'" and proclaimed Wells worthy of the honor, declaring: "She is a heroine; would we had more with such zeal and nobility of womanhood."[12] The New York speech brought not only praise but also invitations to speak. Indeed, Wells soon embarked on a frantic tour of eastern cities, where she lectured and was toasted and entertained. Her schedule caused the *Atchison Blade* to remark, "It's a wonder the eastern women haven't become jealous of the banquetting Miss Ida B. Wells is receiving. . . . Miss Wells tells our people to go west and grow up with the country and at the same time she goes east and grows up with beneficial banquets and fulsome adulation."[13]

Somewhere along the way, in such cities as Boston; Wilmington, Delaware; Chester, Pennsylvania; New Bedford, Massachusetts; Providence, and Newport, Rhode Island; New York; and Washington, D.C., Wells encountered Frederick Douglass. He apparently praised her article on lynching because on 17 October, Wells wrote to ask him "to put in writing the encomiums you were pleased to lavish on my article on Lynch Law in June 25 issue of the Age." She explained that she was preparing that article for publication as a pamphlet and would "feel highly honored" if Douglass would write his opinion of it to serve as an introduction.[14]

Douglass promptly replied. His 25 October letter was included in Wells's pamphlet *Southern Horrors, Lynch Law in All Its Phases,* which was released soon afterward. Douglass strongly praised Wells's work:

> Let me give you thanks for your faithful paper on the lynch abomination now generally practiced against colored people in the South. There has been no word equal to it in convincing power. I have spoken, but my word is feeble in comparison. You give what you know and testify from actual knowledge. You have dealt with the facts with painstaking fidelity and left those naked and uncontradicted facts to speak for themselves.
>
> Brave woman! you have done your people and mine a service which can neither be weighed nor measured. If American conscience were only half alive, if the Ameri-

can clergy were only half christianized, if American sensibility were not hardened by persistent infliction of outrage and crime against colored people, a scream of horror, shame and indignation would rise to heaven wherever your pamphlet shall be read.[15]

Douglass clearly recognized the power of personal experience; his accounts of his life as a slave had been among the most potent antislavery tools. He also highlighted an effective component of Wells's talks and writings—her decision to use white sources for "naked and uncontradicted facts."

Southern Horrors was dedicated to the women who had given the New York testimonial. Their contributions paid for its printing, so she did not have to engage in extensive fund-raising activities for printing costs, as she often did for later pamphlets. Wells was also grateful to be able to borrow some of their respectability. In her preface the assertion, "It is with no pleasure I have dipped my hands in the corruption here exposed," acknowledged that the subject was not totally proper for a woman. "Somebody must show that the Afro-American race is more sinned against than sinning," Wells explained, "and it seems to have fallen upon me to do so." The black press praised the pamphlet. The *Chicago Conservator* wrote, "We commend it to all who desire to give this phase of the Southern question serious thought."[16] Wells must have been exhilarated by the show of support by Douglass, the New York women, and the press; nevertheless, her next speech was a disappointment.

On 31 October Wells spoke at the Metropolitan A.M.E. Church in Washington, D.C. Although the meeting was given extensive advertising and support by the *Washington Bee* as well as by Frederick Douglass and T. Thomas Fortune, the turnout was quite small. An advertisement noted that Mary Church Terrell would preside and Fortune would introduce Wells. The lecture was scheduled for 8:00 P.M., and the cost of admission was set at twenty-five cents. Though the *Bee* called for a turnout of "three to four thousand" and proclaimed it "the duty of every citizen to go and hear her," the *Cleveland Gazette* reported that the meeting "was not a financial success" and noted that "fashionable colored society did not turn out *en masse*." Some blamed the failure on Fortune's connection with the event, because of his unpopular political support of the Democrats. J. E. Bruce, however, declared that "the Washington Negro is no good." Douglass was embarrassed by the reception Wells had received and promised to reschedule and deliver a larger crowd.[17]

Before Washington hosted Wells again, however, she returned to Philadelphia for the November convention of the A.M.E. Church. After a number of bishops had spoken, including Henry McNeal Turner, Wells went to the podium. Her efforts won effusive praise. In his account of the convention, *A.M.E. Church Review* editor Dr. H. T. Johnson noted,

> the climax of which was capped by the dauntless but exited "Iola," whose unique and inimitable speech won the conference, and so excited sympathy in her behalf

that it were [sic] well for her Memphian adversaries that they were in their distant safety in the lower regions of the Mississippi Valley.[18]

In a later account of this Philadelphia visit, Wells recalled that she had stayed at the home of William Still, the great operator and chronicler of the "Underground Railroad," which had aided slaves escaping to freedom. While Wells was at the Still house, Catherine Impey came to call, and they discussed the lynching plague. Impey expressed shock over Wells's lynching stories and white indifference to such occurrences. Wells noted, "She was especially hurt that this should be the fact among those of her own sect and kin. We deplored the situation and agreed that there seemed nothing to do but keep plugging away at the evils both of us were fighting."[19] Thus another link was forged in the chain that would tie their efforts together and move their labors across the sea.

News of the testimonials for Wells and her lectures on the Memphis lynching trickled back to the white community of Memphis. Retaliation was vicious. In December the *Memphis Commercial* launched an attack on her credibility and morality. The paper claimed "this Wells wench" had not even written the infamous editorial bringing her such attention. Instead it depicted her as "the mistress of the scoundrel" who authored it and implied she was raising money for personal gain under false premises. The lowest blow was the charge that she was a "black harlot" seeking a white husband.[20]

The *Commercial* described her audience as members of Boston's "effete civilization" made up of "thin-legged scholars" and "glass-eyed females." The reference to Boston was natural. Of all the towns Wells visited, none welcomed her more warmly. She made at least three visits to Boston from November 1892 to March 1893. On Thanksgiving morning, Wells spoke at the Women's Department of the Mechanics' Fair, and she returned in January to address the Moral Educational Association at the Ladies' Physiological Institute. That month she also lectured a large crowd at Wesleyan Hall on "Sufferings of the Colored People of the South." The next month, in response to the *Commercial*'s attack on Wells, the black women of the city organized to show their support for her. They formed a local branch of the National Colored Women's League, chose Josephine St. Pierre Ruffin as president, and unanimously adopted resolutions condemning "the foulest aspersion of one of the daily papers of Memphis." They recorded "our indignation at the slander" and asserted "our confidence in Miss Wells' purity of purpose and character."[21]

Her visit to Boston in mid-February 1893, however, was her greatest triumph. "It was during this visit to Boston," Wells recalled, "that I had my first opportunity to address a white audience." A famous preacher of that day, Joseph Cook, sponsored a lecture series titled the "Boston Monday Lectures" at Tremont Temple and invited Wells to speak on 13 February. Her speech was covered in the white newspapers of the city and later printed in the May 1893 edition of *Our Day*. As the only known talk preserved in full text, it illumines Wells's oratorical approach for speeches on lynching for white audiences. Regarding her lecture tour, Wells later claimed, "In these meetings I read my paper, the same one that I had read at the first meeting in New York."[22] While this is *substantially* true, the Tremont Temple speech shows that the talk was updated as new lynchings occurred and was modified to suit the various audiences.

Wells began with her standard disclaimer that she approached the subject "through no inclination of my own, but because of a deep-seated conviction that the country at large does not know the extent to which lynch law prevails." She proclaimed faith in the decency of white Americans by asserting that "the apathy and indifference" over mob rule had to be the result of "ignorance of the true situation." As Martin Luther King, Jr., would later do, Wells appealed to both whites' consciences and self-interests—by holding up American ideals.

> Repeated attacks on the life, liberty and happiness of any citizen or class of citizens are attacks on distinctive American institutions; such attacks imperiling as they do the foundation of government, law and order, merit the thoughtful consideration of far-sighted Americans; not from a standpoint of sentiment, not even so much from the standpoint of justice to a weak race, as from a desire to preserve our institutions.[23]

Wells then described the "omnipresent and all-pervading" impact of the "race problem or negro question," calling it "Banquo's ghost of politics, religion, and sociology."[24]

With the sentence, "Born and raised in the South, I had never expected to live elsewhere," Wells moved into the body of her speech—an account of her life, the triple lynchings, and her exile. She recognized the emotional impact of a well-told story and infused it with details that gave the narrative richness and texture. She told of how she had worked as a teacher and journalist in the faith that the "doctrine of self-help, thrift and economy" provided the key to acceptance and justice for her people. In the beginning, Wells asserted, "This sentiment bore good fruit in Memphis. We had nice homes, representatives in almost every branch of business and profession, and refined society." Although proscribed by segregation, black Memphians believed the city would remain free of lynchings. "But there was a rude awakening," Wells continued, launching into her account of the lynchings. One of her longest descriptions of those events, it was filled with heartrending details. "The baby daughter of Tom Moss," Wells declared, "too young to express how she misses her father, toddles to the wardrobe, seizes the legs of the trousers of his letter-carrier uniform, hugs and kisses them with evident delight and stretches up her little hands to be taken up into the arms which will nevermore clasp his daughter's form."[25]

Wells further described the responses of the black community to the lynchings. She admitted that they considered vengeance but realized it would mean "certain death for the men, and horrible slaughter for the women and children." She reminded her audience, "The power of the State, county and city, the civil authorities and the strong arm of the military power were all on the side of the mob and lawlessness." Instead they decided to leave, and white Memphians felt the impact of their departure. "There were a number of business failures and blocks of houses were for rent," Wells explained. "To restore the equilibrium and put a stop to the great financial loss," she continued, "the next move was to get rid of the *Free Speech,*—the disturbing element which kept the waters troubled."[26]

After detailing the events that led to her exile, Wells assured her audience, "The lawlessness here described is not confined to one locality. In the past over a thousand colored men, women and children have been butchered, murdered and burnt in all parts of the South." She then described a number of grisly lynchings and listed the statistics from 1882 to 1892. Her account made clear that "neither age, sex nor decency are spared" and that in only one-third of lynchings were charges of rape even made. Lynchers had come to believe nothing would be done to punish them. Wells cried that:

> So bold have the lynchers become, masks are laid aside, the temples of justice and strongholds of law are invaded in broad daylight and prisoners taken out and lynched, while governors of states and officers of law stand by and see the work well done.
>
> And yet this Christian nation, the flower of the nineteenth century civilization, says it can do nothing to stop this inhuman slaughter. The general government is willingly powerless to send troops to protect the lives of its black citizens, but the state governments are free to use state troops to shoot them down like cattle, when in desperation the black men attempt to defend themselves, and then tell all the world that it was necessary to put down a "race war."[27]

Wells then compared slavery with lynching and the nation's reaction to it. She noted that few had been willing to confront the evil of human bondage for many years. Only the martyrdom of white abolitionists and threats to freedom of speech convinced the nation "that slavery was not only a monster [but also] a tyrant." Wells proclaimed, *"The very same forces are at work now as then."* After appealing to the abolitionist sentiment of white Bostonians, Wells blamed the North's current moral blindness on a desire to prevent another Civil War. However, the efforts to win back the allegiance of the South had failed, she explained:

> With all the country's disposition to condone and temporize with the South and its methods; with its many instances of sacrificing principle to prejudice for the sake of making friends and healing the breach made by the late war; of going into the lawless country with capital to build up its waste places and remaining silent in the presence of outrage and wrong—the South is as vindictive and bitter as ever.[28]

Wells not only defined the problem for her audience but also provided a solution. "Do you ask a remedy?", she

asked, then answered, "A public sentiment strong against lawlessness must be aroused. Every individual can contribute to this awakening. When a sentiment against lynch law as strong, deep and mighty as that aroused against slavery prevails, I have no fear of the result." Wells then appealed to Republican party strength in Boston by blaming the party's defeat in the 1892 presidential election on its failure to meet "the issues squarely for human rights." She closed with a ringing appeal and reference to white abolitionists.

> The voice of the people is the voice of God, and I long with all the intensity of my soul for the Garrison, Douglas [sic], Sumner, Wittier, and Phillips who shall rouse this nation to a demand that from Greenland's icy mountains to the coral reefs of the Southern seas, mob rule shall be put down and equal and exact justice be accorded to every citizen, who finds a home within the borders of the land of the free and the home of the brave.
>
> Then no longer will our national hymn be sounding brass and tinkling cymbal, but every member of this great composite nation will be a living, harmonious illustration of the words, and all can honestly and gladly join in singing:
>
> My country! 'tis of thee,
> Sweet land of liberty
>   Of thee I sing.
> Land where our fathers died,
> Land of the Pilgrim's pride,
> From every mountain side
>   Freedom does ring.[29]

Her words are eerily prophetic of King's "I Have a Dream" speech during the "March on Washington" in 1963. Both orators, like Thomas Jefferson, realized that effective propaganda appeals to deeply felt values and "self-evident truths." Both drew from the Bible and hymns as well as patriotic songs and literature. Wells's description of "this great composite nation" celebrates the cultural diversity with which the United States continues to struggle.

Following her speech, the audience at Tremont Temple passed resolutions of support and pledged to work "to arouse public sentiment in indignant condemnation of the increasing prevalence of lynch law in our land." The resolutions referred to Wells's "pathetic and unimpassioned recital of the horrible atrocities perpetuated in various parts of the South" and expressed "thanks to this cultivated Christian lady for the important information she has imparted." The audience further declared "our admiration for her intelligent, reasonable and heroic advocacy of the rights of American Citizens and our sympathy with her and her people in the injustice they are suffering." Such a public display of support helped rehabilitate Wells's reputation of respectability after the attack by the Memphis *Commercial*. During the next three days, Joseph Cook continued to demonstrate his approval by accompanying Wells at her lectures at Charles Street A.M.E. Church and at Malden.[30]

The black press also came to the defense of Wells. The *Topeka Weekly Call* criticized the *Commercial* for "wantonly and ruthlessly slandering the good name of Miss Ida B. Wells." It labeled the attack on her as "evidence that boasted southern chivalry is a thing of the past." The *Weekly Call* proclaimed, "Miss Wells is a lady, the peer of any in the land and the *superior of many whose only stock in trade is a white skin.*" Whites, not Wells, were guilty of "inhuman brutality and insensate laciviouness [sic] and lecherousness."[31]

Wells was not only personally outraged by the *Commercial* article but also recognized that besmirching the morality of black women was an important component of the racist ideology used to justify white Southerner's actions. She decided to confront the *Commercial*'s aspersions with legal action. As she began her search for an attorney to file libel charges, Wells remembered her disappointment with the representation of black lawyer T. F. Cassells during her suit against the railroad in 1884. She also felt that the leading attorneys of Memphis—both black and white—were hostile to her. Cassells had not forgiven her for replacing him with a white lawyer, and J. T. Settle continued to resent her criticisms of him in the *Free Speech.*

When Wells realized the need to go outside of Memphis for representation, she thought of Albion Tourgee. In her twenties she had read his book, *Bricks without Straw,* about Reconstruction and race relations. A white Chicago lawyer, Tourgee was well-known among African Americans for founding a civil rights organization and for confronting racial issues in his "Bystander" column in the Chicago *Inter-Ocean.* Wells had been pleased to receive a congratulatory letter from him about her lynching article in the *New York Age.* She had also distributed information about Tourgee's National Citizens' Rights Association among the black women of New York.[32]

When Wells wrote Tourgee in February, she referred to her dilemma in obtaining representation by Memphis attorneys. He evidently questioned her about it, for she later explained the situation more fully and noted of Settle and Cassells, "Both are sycophants and do not half defend their clients." Wells asked whether Tourgee believed she could succeed in getting "vindication" of her character. Although Tourgee declined to represent Wells because of financial constraints, he did give her advice. He thought that filing her complaint in Chicago would give her a better chance of a fair trial and a *"very large verdict."* To win, however, he noted her need to prove she had not engaged in an affair with Taylor Nightingale, and also to "deny and sustain a denial of impropriety *with any man.*"[33]

Most important to Wells, Tourgee recommended another Chicago attorney to handle the case—Ferdinand L. Barnett. A native of Nashville, Barnett was a graduate of Union College of Law in Chicago. He owned the *Chicago Conservator,* practiced law with S. Laing Williams, was active in Republican party affairs, and held a number of government appointments.[34] Although he had been a supporter of the antilynching movement and Wells, he apparently knew little of her personally when he took the case.

After Tourgee cautioned him to be sure of the facts before he proceeded, Barnett expressed faith that "the libelous article was entirely without foundation" but assured Tourgee he would "find out before we take any steps in the matter." His conversations with her friends from Memphis and Wells's willingness for him to consult such "enemies" as Cassells, convinced Barnett of her integrity; however, he and Wells eventually decided not to pursue the case because they feared the damage that a loss would cause.[35] Nevertheless, working on the case together proved to be the start of a relationship that would flower into romance.

Perhaps because of the attack on Wells, the black community of Washington, D.C., rallied to support her return engagement at the Metropolitan A.M.E. Church on 3 February. Douglass's promise to Wells that if she came back, he would guarantee a large crowd came true; the church filled with what Wells called "one of the biggest audiences I had ever seen." Douglass's success was partially due to his recruitment of the city's prominent black women to take a role in the event. Douglass presided, aided by Anna J. Cooper, the principal of Washington's black high school, and Lucy Moten, the head of Miner Normal School. Mary Church Terrell, perhaps the city's most prominent black woman, introduced each speaker.[36]

The daughter of Robert Church of Memphis, Terrell had first met Wells while they were both in their twenties. Wells had thought them kindred spirits before Mollie had left to tour Europe and then married Robert Terrell, who became a judge in Washington. Although the two women did share many interests and goals, the friendship never blossomed—but rivalry grew abundantly. Many years later Terrell considered Wells an ingrate and claimed to a friend, "I did everything I could for that lady years ago when she had very few friends." Terrell's words that night in Washington were certainly supportive: "We admire Miss Wells for her undaunted courage, and laud her zeal in so worthy a cause, we encourage her ambition to enlighten the mind and touch the heart by a thrilling . . . recital of the wrongs heaped upon her oppressed people in the South." Terrell continued to extend Wells "a cordial welcome" and to "offer her our hearty support." Nevertheless, the bulk of her introduction was comprised of her own indictment of lynching as well as more fulsome and extensive praise for the other speaker, T. Thomas Fortune.[37]

In her autobiography, Wells did not allude to their rivalry and noted that Terrell "was president of the Bethel Literary and was just beginning her public career" at the time of the introduction. She also noted that Terrell was the daughter of Robert Church, "who had shown himself a friend while I was a teacher in Memphis," which was probably an allusion to his loan to her when she was in California. All in all, Wells was thrilled by the event, writing that it "ended in a blaze of glory and a donation of nearly two hundred dollars to aid the cause."[38]

Wells soon found a use for the purse. While she was in Washington, she learned of a particularly gruesome lynching in Paris, Texas. The *New York Times* provided the grisly details of the death of Henry Smith, who was accused of assaulting a four-year-old girl. After his capture, the train carrying the prisoner was met by a "mass of humanity 10,000 strong." Smith was placed on a scaffold "within view of all beholders" and "tortured for fifty minutes by red-hot irons being thrust against his quivering body." Thinking him dead, the crowd doused him with kerosene and set him on fire. When Smith "wriggled and tossed out" of the fire, he was shoved back in, twice. The *Times* further noted "the vast crowd still looked calmly on" and reported the presence of participants from eight other cities, including Dallas, Fort Worth, and Texarkana.[39]

In her autobiography, Wells elaborated on the lynching. She told of how "the mob fought over the hot ashes for bones, buttons, and teeth for souvenirs" and recounted a mother's calm response to her eight-year-old daughter's words, "I saw them burn the nigger, didn't I Mamma?" (Wells also described the lynching during her Boston speech in mid-February as evidence of the corrupting influence of mob law.) Suspicious of the charges against Smith, she decided to use the money raised at the Washington meeting to investigate the lynching. "I had said in newspaper articles and public speeches," Wells declared, "that we should be in a position to investigate every lynching and get the facts for ourselves." She used the money "to have Pinkerton's [detective agency] send an honest, unprejudiced man from the Chicago office to bring unbiased facts." Although Wells was disappointed with the quality of the report, the Paris lynching launched another phase of her antilynching crusade, and she continued to investigate lynchings for many years.[40]

The visit to the nation's capital also raised Wells's hopes that she might get the attention of the men who governed the nation. In May 1892, President Benjamin Harrison had penned a timid reply to a memorial against lynching from the black Virginia Baptist Convention. Some began to look to Congress. Before Wells's lecture, the *Washington Bee* predicted, "Several members of Congress will be present." Immediately afterwards, the *Christian Banner* noted that Wells "is stiring [sic] up the country" about lynching and reported, "it is possible she will get a hearing before a Congress committee appointed for that purpose." The report probably referred to an unsuccessful attempt by Frederick Douglass and some Washington women to get Wells a hearing before the Senate Judiciary Committee.[41] The inability to get the federal government to move against lynching continued to frustrate the antilynching movement until its death.

By this time Frederick Douglass had become an important ally to Wells. She visited his home on several occasions and won his gratitude by treating his second wife with respect. Following the death of his first wife in 1882, Douglass married a white coworker, Helen Pitts, in 1884. Many African Americans echoed the words of a writer in the *Pittsburgh Weekly News*: "We have no further use for him. His picture hangs in our parlor, we will hang it in the

stables."[42] According to Wells, Douglass told her that except for Charlotte Forten Grimke, whose husband Francis had married the Douglasses, Wells was the only black woman to treat Helen "as a hostess has a right to be treated by her guest." "I, too," Wells wrote, "would have preferred that Mr. Douglass had chosen one of the beautiful, charming colored women of my race for his second wife. But he loved Helen Pitts . . . and it was outrageous that they should be crucified by both white and black people for doing so."[43]

Well's support for the couple is easily understandable because she had also felt the sting of public disapproval by both whites and African Americans. Their union also upheld her contentions about interracial sex: She noted that they sought to "live together in the holy bonds of matrimony rather than in the illicit relationship that was the cause of so many of the lynchings I had noted and protested against."[44] Finally, like Douglass, Wells remained at heart an integrationist. Militancy was often coupled with support for integration in that era. Only in the next century would militancy become synonymous with separatism.

Perhaps the criticism he received made Douglass more sensitive to the plight of Wells. At any rate, their relationship seems to have flowered after the slanders in the *Commercial*. A year later, Wells reminded Douglass, "At that juncture you comforted me with your counsel and gave me your protection."[45] Although sometimes disappointed in the extent of protection and defense provided by Douglass, Wells appears to have reciprocated his support. In several instances, Wells sought to counter rumors critical of Douglass. In February 1893, she wrote Douglass that "many people in Boston asked me as to the truth of the published account that you had given a thousand dollars toward Will Cook's World's Fair Concert Co." After assuring Douglass that to have done so would be all right, Wells continued, "if not, the use of your name is misleading many." Eight months later, the Indianapolis *Freeman* noted, "Ida B. Wells denies that Frederick Douglass is an applicant for political office." Wells lamented, "I think this nagging of Mr. Douglass should cease."[46]

Wells's reference to Will Cook reflects a common interest that drew her closer to Douglass. To celebrate the voyage of Christopher Columbus, a world's fair, the World's Columbian Exposition, opened in Chicago on 12 October 1892. From its beginning, the fair provoked anger and controversy among African Americans. Issues included the fair's omission of black contributions to the United States, its failure to note racist activities, and the holding of a segregated "Negro Day"—at which the celebrated black violinist Will Cook was to perform. According to the *Cleveland Gazette,* it was at Wells's October lecture in Washington that Douglass conceived the idea of "an exposition, by paintings, drawing and written accounts of lynchings, hangings, burnings at the stake, whippings and all southern atrocities" to be held concurrently with the Chicago fair.[47] Wells wholeheartedly agreed, and the result would be a joint pamphlet, but first Wells was sidetracked by an offer too appealing to refuse.

The gruesome nature of the lynching in Paris, Texas, had drawn attention abroad. Among those who reacted was Isabelle Fyvie Mayo, a Scottish author who provided shelter to students from Ceylon and India. She and *Anti-Caste* editor Catherine Impey had been corresponding for some time about racial issues. In March 1893, Mayo invited Impey to Scotland to get to know a fellow opponent of the caste system in India. Having just received news of the Paris lynching, Mayo asked Impey, as Wells told it, if she had learned during her American travels "why the United States of America was burning human beings alive in the nineteenth century as the red Indians were said to have done three hundred years before."[48]

Impey's reply caused Mayo to inform the British public of the outrages. Impey asserted, "The chief difficulty over here is that people *don't know* & therefore *don't care* about the matter." As a remedy, the two women decided to form an "Emancipation" organization to attack all the evils of caste. Although they intended to "declare war against it any & everywhere," they agreed to begin combat against lynching in America, because the "evil is so *glaring, so terrible.*" Some asserted that lynching was "purely an American question," but Impey proclaimed, "where evils of such magnitude exist—& helpless people suffer wrongs unspeakable—we can't stand on ceremony." Based on Impey's contacts with Wells in Philadelphia, they decided to ask Wells to come and help them launch their movement. Mayo agreed to pay Wells's expenses, and Impey drafted the invitation on 19 March 1893.[49]

In her letter Impey declared, "Our English press has been getting hold of some of those Texas lynchings, and our people are beginning to feel that there is something very wrong somewhere." She urged Wells to aid them "to set on foot a living effort to remedy the cruel wrongs now suffered." The letter reached Wells while she was visiting Frederick Douglass. According to Wells's autobiography, Impey noted that Douglass was too old to come and asked Wells to do so or to ask Douglass to suggest someone else. Douglass told Wells, "You go, my child; you are the one to go, for you have a story to tell."[50]

Wells already recognized the potential of drawing the English and Scots into the antilynching movement—as Douglass had once done for the abolitionist movement. Her pamphlet **Southern Horrors** had been republished in London in 1892 as **U.S. Atrocities.** The invitation was "like an open door in a stone wall" to Wells. She had despaired the failure of white northern newspapers to mention her movement; all had ignored her except those in Boston. She hated to interrupt her work on the world's fair pamphlet, and she also had to cancel plans to confront a meeting of southern governors in Richmond that month.[51] Nevertheless, she felt compelled to respond to the call. On 5 April 1893, Wells embarked on a journey across the sea that would catapult her and the antilynching movement to widespread prominence.

Notes

1. *Washington Bee,* 29 October 1892. This speech is noted in the advertisement for another lecture to be held in Washington on 31 October 1892.

2. *Cleveland Gazette,* 15 October 1892; *Washington Bee,* 29 October 1892; Indianapolis *Freeman,* 8 October 1892.

3. *Atchison Blade,* 24 September 1892; Detroit *Plaindealer,* 14 October 1892; Indianapolis *Freeman,* 15 October 1892.

4. Alfreda M. Duster, ed., *Crusade for Justice, The Autobiography of Ida B. Wells* (Chicago: University of Chicago Press, 1970), p. 78.

5. Ibid., p. 79.

6. Ibid.; Detroit *Plaindealer,* 1 October, 16 December 1892.

7. Duster, *Crusade,* pp. 79-80.

8. Ibid., p. 80.

9. Ibid.; holograph manuscript in Ida B. Wells Papers, University of Chicago Library.

10. Duster, *Crusade,* p. 80.

11. (Kansas City) *American Citizen,* 21 October 1892; Mrs. N. F. Mossell, *The Work of the Afro-American Woman,* 2d ed. (Philadelphia: Geo. S. Ferguson, 1908), p. 34; Duster, *Crusade,* p. 80; Detroit *Plaindealer,* 16 December 1892.

12. *Washington Bee,* 29 October 1892; *American Citizen,* 21 October 1892.

13. *Atchison Blade,* 10 December 1892.

14. Ida B. Wells to Frederick Douglass, 17 October 1892, Frederick Douglass Papers, Library of Congress.

15. Ida B. Wells, *Southern Horrors, Lynch Law in All Its Phases,* reprinted in Trudier Harris, comp., *Selected Works of Ida B. Wells-Barnett* (New York: Oxford University Press, 1993), pp. 15-16.

16. Ibid., pp. 14-15; as reported in *Parsons* (Kansas) *Weekly Blade,* 4 February 1893.

17. *Washington Bee,* 29 October 1892; *Cleveland Gazette,* 19 November 1892; Duster, *Crusade,* p. 82.

18. Monroe A. Majors, *Noted Negro Women, Their Triumphs and Activities* (Chicago: Donohue & Henneberry, 1893), p. 193.

19. Duster, *Crusade,* p. 82. At about this time, Wells sent a copy of *Anti-Caste* to a woman in Texas who requested a copy. Mrs. M. R. Rogers Webb to Albion Tourgee, 25 November 1892, Albion Tourgee Papers, microfilm edition, University of North Carolina, Chapel Hill.

20. Memphis *Commercial,* 15 December 1892.

21. Memphis *Commercial,* 15 December 1892; Mossell, *The Work of the Afro-American Woman,* p. 34; Majors, *Noted Negro Women,* p. 193; Indianapolis *Freeman,* 25 February 1893; *American Citizen,* 25 November 1892; *Cleveland Gazette,* 11 February 1893.

22. Duster, *Crusade,* pp. 81-82.

23. Ida B. Wells, "Lynch Law in all Its Phases," *Our Day* (May 1893), pp. 333-337, reprinted in Mildred I. Thompson, *Ida B. Wells-Barnett: An Exploratory Study of an American Black Woman, 1893-1930* (New York: Carlson Publishing, 1990), p. 171.

24. Ibid., p. 172.

25. Ibid., pp. 172-176.

26. Ibid., pp. 176-177.

27. Ibid., pp. 177-183.

28. Ibid., pp. 183-185.

29. Ibid., pp. 185-187.

30. *American Citizen,* 24 February 1893; Indianapolis *Freeman,* 25 February 1893.

31. *Topeka Weekly Call,* 8 January 1893.

32. Ida B. Wells to Albion Tourgee, 2 July, 3 November 1892, Tourgee Papers.

33. Ida B. Wells to Albion Tourgee, 10, 22 February 1893; Albion Tourgee to Ida B. Wells, undated draft, Tourgee Papers.

34. *Cleveland Gazette,* 26 February 1887; Indianapolis *Freeman,* 22 June 1895.

35. Ferdinand Barnett to Albion Tourgee, 23 February, 4 March 1893, Tourgee Papers.

36. Duster, *Crusade,* p. 83; Mary Church Terrell, "Introducing Ida Wells Barnett—To deliver an Address on Lynching, ca. 1893," holograph manuscript, Mary Church Terrell Papers, Library of Congress.

37. Ibid.; Mary Church Terrell to Lethia Fleming, 19 October 1920, Terrell Papers. For the context of that letter see the letter from Fleming to Terrell, 16 October 1920.

38. Duster, *Crusade,* p. 83.

39. *New York Times,* 2 February 1893.

40. Duster, *Crusade,* pp. 84-85.

41. *Washington Bee,* 28 January 1893; *Christian Banner,* quoted in *American Citizen,* 17 February 1893; *New York Times,* 28 May 1892; *Cleveland Gazette,* 4 June 1892; Ida B. Wells to Frederick Douglass, 14 November 1894, Frederick Douglass Papers.

42. William S. McFeely, *Frederick Douglass* (New York: Norton, 1991), p. 320.

43. Duster, *Crusade,* pp. 72-73.

44. Ibid., p. 72.

45. Ida B. Wells to Frederick Douglass, 20 December 1893, Frederick Douglass Papers.

46. Ida B. Wells to Frederick Douglass, 24 February 1893, Frederick Douglass Papers; Indianapolis *Freeman,* 21 October 1893; *Cleveland Gazette,* 21 October 1893.

47. *Cleveland Gazette,* 26 November 1892; McFeely, *Frederick Douglass,* pp. 366, 370; Indianapolis *Freeman,* 26 November 1892.

48. Duster, *Crusade,* pp. 85-86.

49. Catherine Impey to "My dear Friends," 21 March 1893, Tourgee Papers; Catherine Impey to Mrs. Tourgee, 12 April 1893, Tourgee Papers.

50. Letter published in Topeka *Weekly Call,* 15 April 1893; Duster, *Crusade,* pp. 85-86.

51. Duster, *Crusade,* pp. 85-86. Portions of this pamphlet have been reprinted in Bert James Loewenberg's and Ruth Bogin's, *Black Women in Nineteenth-Century Life* (University Park: Pennsylvania State University Press, 1976), pp. 253-262.

FURTHER READING

Bibliographies

Campbell, Karlyn Kohrs, ed. *Women Public Speakers in the United States, 1800-1925,* pp. 462-75. Westport, Conn.: Greenwood Press, 1993.

    Listing of biographical and critical sources relating to Wells-Barnett as an orator.

Deegan, Mary Jo, ed. "Ida B. Wells-Barnett." In *Women in Sociology: A Bio-Bibliographical Sourcebook,* pp. 432-39. Westport, Conn.: Greenwood Press, 1991.

    List of primary and secondary works, focused mostly on Wells-Barnett as a social reformer.

Harris, Vergie Nobles. "Wells-Barnett, Ida." In *African-American Orators: A Bio-Critical Sourcebook,* edited by Richard W. Leeman, pp. 367-69. Westport, Conn.: Greenwood Press, 1996.

    Overview of biographical and critical sources on Wells-Barnett.

Nelson, Emmanuel S., ed. "Ida B. Wells-Barnett." In *African American Authors, 1745-1945: Bio-Bibliographical Sourcebook.* Westport, Conn.: Greenwood Press, 2000, 465 p.

    Biographical, thematic, and bibliographical overview.

Shockley, Ann Allen. *Afro-American Women Writers, 1746-1933: An Anthology and Critical Guide.* Westport, Conn.: Greenwood Press, 2000, 465 p.

> List of works relevant to Wells-Barnett's life and times.

Biographies

Brantley, Ben, et al. "Irritating Women." *New York Times Magazine* 148, no. 51524 (16 May 1999): 122.

> Profiles of several women in history, including Wells-Barnett, who have called attention to themselves or to important issues by making trouble.

DeCosta-Willis, Miriam. "Ida B. Wells-Barnett." In *The Oxford Companion to African American Literature,* edited by William L. Andrews, Frances Smith Foster, and Trudier Harris, pp. 763-64. New York: Oxford University Press, 1997.

> Brief biographical sketch.

Franklin, V. P. "Ida B. Wells-Barnett: To Tell the Truth Freely." In *Living Our Stories, Telling Our Truths,* pp. 59-93. New York: Oxford University Press, 1995.

> Somewhat lengthy account of Wells-Barnett's life and works.

Giddings, Paula. "Ida Wells-Barnett." In *Portraits of American Women,* pp. 367-85. New York: St. Martin's Press, 1991.

> Biographical sketch.

Hardy, Gayle J. "Wells-Barnett, Ida B." In *American Women Civil Rights Activists: Biobibliographies of 68 Leaders,* pp. 403-08. Jefferson, N.C.: McFarland & Co., 1993.

> Brief biography of Wells-Barnett as a journalist and civil rights reformer.

Moreau, Shannon. "Crusader for Justice." *American History* 35, no. 6 (February 2001): 18.

> One-page sketch of Wells-Barnett as a reformer.

Salzman, Jack, ed. "Wells-Barnett, Ida B." In *African-American History: Selections from the Five-Volume Macmillan Encyclopedia of African-American Culture and History,* pp. 1069-70. New York: Macmillan Library Reference, 1998.

> Brief biographical sketch.

Sterling, Dorothy. *Black Foremothers: Three Lives.* New York: Feminist Press, 1979, 174 p.

> A study of three prominent African-American women: Wells-Barnett, Ellen Craft, and Mary Church Terrell.

Thompson, Mildred. *Ida B. Wells-Barnett: An Exploratory Study of an American Black Woman, 1893-1930.* Brooklyn, N.Y.: Carlson Publishing, 1990, 289 p.

> Biography of Wells-Barnett in the context of her times; part of Black Women in U. S. History series.

Criticism

Royster, Jacqueline Jones. "Introduction." In *Southern Horrors and Other Writings: The Anti-Lynching Campaign of Ida B. Wells, 1892-1900,* pp. 1-13. Boston: Bedford Books, 1997.

> Introduction to a collection of anti-lynching writings by Wells-Barnett and others.

Schechter, Patricia Ann. *Ida B. Wells-Barnett and American Reform, 1880-1930.* Chapel Hill: University of North Carolina Press, 2001, 386 p.

> Study focusing on Wells-Barnett's activism, as well as her ideological mind-set and self-representation.

Additional coverage of Wells-Barnett's life and career is contained in the following sources published by the Gale Group: *Contemporary Authors,* Vol. 182; *Dictionary of Literary Biography,* Vols. 23, 221; **and** *Literature Resource Center.*

How to Use This Index

The main references

list all author entries in the following Gale Literary Criticism series:

BLC = *Black Literature Criticism*
CLC = *Contemporary Literary Criticism*
CLR = *Children's Literature Review*
CMLC = *Classical and Medieval Literature Criticism*
DA = *DISCovering Authors*
DAB = *DISCovering Authors: British*
DAC = *DISCovering Authors: Canadian*
DAM = *DISCovering Authors: Modules*
    DRAM: *Dramatists Module;* **MST:** *Most-Studied Authors Module;*
    MULT: *Multicultural Authors Module;* **NOV:** *Novelists Module;*
    POET: *Poets Module;* **POP:** *Popular Fiction and Genre Authors Module*
DC = *Drama Criticism*
HLC = *Hispanic Literature Criticism*
LC = *Literature Criticism from 1400 to 1800*
NCLC = *Nineteenth-Century Literature Criticism*
NNAL = *Native North American Literature*
PC = *Poetry Criticism*
SSC = *Short Story Criticism*
TCLC = *Twentieth-Century Literary Criticism*
WLC = *World Literature Criticism, 1500 to the Present*

The cross-references

list all author entries in the following Gale biographical and literary sources:

AAYA = *Authors & Artists for Young Adults*
AITN = *Authors in the News*
BEST = *Bestsellers*
BW = *Black Writers*
CA = *Contemporary Authors*
CAAS = *Contemporary Authors Autobiography Series*
CABS = *Contemporary Authors Bibliographical Series*
CANR = *Contemporary Authors New Revision Series*
CAP = *Contemporary Authors Permanent Series*
CDALB = *Concise Dictionary of American Literary Biography*
CDBLB = *Concise Dictionary of British Literary Biography*
DLB = *Dictionary of Literary Biography*
DLBD = *Dictionary of Literary Biography Documentary Series*
DLBY = *Dictionary of Literary Biography Yearbook*
HW = *Hispanic Writers*
JRDA = *Junior DISCovering Authors*
MAICYA = *Major Authors and Illustrators for Children and Young Adults*
MTCW = *Major 20th-Century Writers*
SAAS = *Something about the Author Autobiography Series*
SATA = *Something about the Author*
YABC = *Yesterday's Authors of Books for Children*

Literary Criticism Series
Cumulative Author Index

Aherne, Owen
See Cassill, R(onald) V(erlin)

Ai 1947- .... **CLC 4, 14, 69**
See also CA 85-88; CAAS 13; CANR 70;
DLB 120

Aickman, Robert (Fordyce)
1914-1981 .... **CLC 57**
See also CA 5-8R; CANR 3, 72, 100; DLB
261; HGG; SUFW

Aiken, Conrad (Potter) 1889-1973 .... **CLC 1,
3, 5, 10, 52; PC 26; SSC 9**
See also AMW; CA 5-8R; 45-48; CANR 4,
60; CDALB 1929-1941; DAM NOV,
POET; DLB 9, 45, 102; EXPS; HGG;
MTCW 1, 2; RGAL 4; RGSF 2; SATA 3,
30; SSFS 8; TUS

Aiken, Joan (Delano) 1924- .... **CLC 35**
See also AAYA 1, 25; CA 9-12R, 182;
CAAE 182; CANR 4, 23, 34, 64; CLR 1,
19; DLB 161; FANT; HGG; JRDA; MAI-
CYA 1, 2; MTCW 1; RHW; SAAS 1;
SATA 2, 30, 73; SATA-Essay 109; WYA;
YAW

Ainsworth, William Harrison
1805-1882 .... **NCLC 13**
See also DLB 21; HGG; RGEL 2; SATA
24; SUFW

Aitmatov, Chingiz (Torekulovich)
1928- .... **CLC 71**
See also CA 103; CANR 38; MTCW 1;
RGSF 2; SATA 56

Akers, Floyd
See Baum, L(yman) Frank

Akhmadulina, Bella Akhatovna
1937- .... **CLC 53**
See also CA 65-68; CWP; CWW 2; DAM
POET

Akhmatova, Anna 1888-1966 ..... **CLC 11, 25,
64, 126; PC 2**
See also CA 19-20; 25-28R; CANR 35;
CAP 1; DA3; DAM POET; EW 10;
MTCW 1, 2; RGWL 2

Aksakov, Sergei Timofeyvich
1791-1859 .... **NCLC 2**
See also DLB 198

Aksenov, Vassily
See Aksyonov, Vassily (Pavlovich)

Akst, Daniel 1956- .... **CLC 109**
See also CA 161; CANR 110

Aksyonov, Vassily (Pavlovich)
1932- .... **CLC 22, 37, 101**
See also CA 53-56; CANR 12, 48, 77;
CWW 2

Akutagawa Ryunosuke
1892-1927 .... **TCLC 16; SSC 44**
See also CA 117; 154; DLB 180; MJW;
RGSF 2; RGWL 2

Alain 1868-1951 .... **TCLC 41**
See also CA 163; GFL 1789 to the Present

Alain de Lille c. 1116-c. 1203 .... **CMLC 53**
See also DLB 208

Alain-Fournier .... **TCLC 6**
See also Fournier, Henri Alban
See also DLB 65; GFL 1789 to the Present;
RGWL 2

Alanus de Insluis
See Alain de Lille

Alarcon, Pedro Antonio de
1833-1891 .... **NCLC 1**

Alas (y Urena), Leopoldo (Enrique Garcia)
1852-1901 .... **TCLC 29**
See also CA 113; 131; HW 1; RGSF 2

Albee, Edward (Franklin III) 1928- . **CLC 1,
2, 3, 5, 9, 11, 13, 25, 53, 86, 113; DC
11; WLC**
See also AITN 1; AMW; CA 5-8R; CABS
3; CAD; CANR 8, 54, 74; CD 5; CDALB
1941-1968; DA; DA3; DAB; DAC; DAM
DRAM, MST; DFS 2, 3, 8, 10, 13, 14;

DLB 7, 266; INT CANR-8; LAIT 4;
MTCW 1, 2; RGAL 4; TUS

Alberti, Rafael 1902-1999 .... **CLC 7**
See also CA 85-88; 185; CANR 81; DLB
108; HW 2; RGWL 2

Albert the Great 1193(?)-1280 ...... **CMLC 16**
See also DLB 115

Alcala-Galiano, Juan Valera y
See Valera y Alcala-Galiano, Juan

Alcayaga, Lucila Godoy
See Godoy Alcayaga, Lucila

Alcott, Amos Bronson 1799-1888 .... **NCLC 1**
See also DLB 1, 223

Alcott, Louisa May 1832-1888 . **NCLC 6, 58,
83; SSC 27; WLC**
See also AAYA 20; AMWS 1; BPFB 1;
BYA 2; CDALB 1865-1917; CLR 1, 38;
DA; DA3; DAB; DAC; DAM MST, NOV;
DLB 1, 42, 79, 223, 239, 242; DLBD 14;
FW; JRDA; LAIT 2; MAICYA 1, 2; NFS
12; RGAL 4; SATA 100; TUS; WCH;
WYA; YABC 1; YAW

Aldanov, M. A.
See Aldanov, Mark (Alexandrovich)

Aldanov, Mark (Alexandrovich)
1886(?)-1957 .... **TCLC 23**
See also CA 118; 181

Aldington, Richard 1892-1962 .... **CLC 49**
See also CA 85-88; CANR 45; DLB 20, 36,
100, 149; RGEL 2

Aldiss, Brian W(ilson) 1925- . **CLC 5, 14, 40;
SSC 36**
See also AAYA 42; CA 5-8R; CAAE 190;
CAAS 2; CANR 5, 28, 64; CN 7; DAM
NOV; DLB 14, 261; MTCW 1, 2; SATA
34; SFW 4

Aldrich, Bess Streeter
1881-1954 .... **TCLC 125**
See also CLR 70

Alegria, Claribel 1924- .... **CLC 75; HLCS 1;
PC 26**
See also CA 131; CAAS 15; CANR 66, 94;
CWW 2; DAM MULT; DLB 145; HW 1;
MTCW 1

Alegria, Fernando 1918- .... **CLC 57**
See also CA 9-12R; CANR 5, 32, 72; HW
1, 2

Aleichem, Sholom .... **TCLC 1, 35; SSC 33**
See also Rabinovitch, Sholem
See also TWA

Aleixandre, Vicente 1898-1984 ... **TCLC 113;
HLCS 1**
See also CANR 81; DLB 108; HW 2;
RGWL 2

Aleman, Mateo 1547-1615(?) .... **LC 81**

Alencon, Marguerite d'
See de Navarre, Marguerite

Alepoudelis, Odysseus
See Elytis, Odysseus
See also CWW 2

Aleshkovsky, Joseph 1929-
See Aleshkovsky, Yuz
See also CA 121; 128

Aleshkovsky, Yuz .... **CLC 44**
See also Aleshkovsky, Joseph

Alexander, Lloyd (Chudley) 1924- ... **CLC 35**
See also AAYA 1, 27; BPFB 1; BYA 5, 6,
7, 9, 10, 11; CA 1-4R; CANR 1, 24, 38,
55; CLR 1, 5, 48; CWRI 5; DLB 52;
FANT; JRDA; MAICYA 1, 2; MAICYAS
1; MTCW 1; SAAS 19; SATA 3, 49, 81,
129; SUFW; TUS; WYA; YAW

Alexander, Meena 1951- .... **CLC 121**
See also CA 115; CANR 38, 70; CP 7;
CWP; FW

Alexander, Samuel 1859-1938 .... **TCLC 77**

Alexie, Sherman (Joseph, Jr.)
1966- .... **CLC 96, 154**
See also AAYA 28; CA 138; CANR 95;
DA3; DAM MULT; DLB 175, 206;
MTCW 1; NNAL

Alfau, Felipe 1902-1999 .... **CLC 66**
See also CA 137

Alfieri, Vittorio 1749-1803 .... **NCLC 101**
See also EW 4; RGWL 2

Alfred, Jean Gaston
See Ponge, Francis

Alger, Horatio, Jr. 1832-1899 .... **NCLC 8, 83**
See also DLB 42; LAIT 2; RGAL 4; SATA
16; TUS

Al-Ghazali, Muhammad ibn Muhammad
1058-1111 .... **CMLC 50**
See also DLB 115

Algren, Nelson 1909-1981 ..... **CLC 4, 10, 33;
SSC 33**
See also AMWS 9; BPFB 1; CA 13-16R;
103; CANR 20, 61; CDALB 1941-1968;
DLB 9; DLBY 1981, 1982, 2000; MTCW
1, 2; RGAL 4; RGSF 2

Ali, Ahmed 1908-1998 .... **CLC 69**
See also CA 25-28R; CANR 15, 34

Alighieri, Dante
See Dante

Allan, John B.
See Westlake, Donald E(dwin)

Allan, Sidney
See Hartmann, Sadakichi

Allan, Sydney
See Hartmann, Sadakichi

Allard, Janet .... **CLC 59**

Allen, Edward 1948- .... **CLC 59**

Allen, Fred 1894-1956 .... **TCLC 87**

Allen, Paula Gunn 1939- .... **CLC 84**
See also AMWS 4; CA 112; 143; CANR
63; CWP; DA3; DAM MULT; DLB 175;
FW; MTCW 1; NNAL; RGAL 4

Allen, Roland
See Ayckbourn, Alan

Allen, Sarah A.
See Hopkins, Pauline Elizabeth

Allen, Sidney H.
See Hartmann, Sadakichi

Allen, Woody 1935- .... **CLC 16, 52**
See also AAYA 10; CA 33-36R; CANR 27,
38, 63; DAM POP; DLB 44; MTCW 1

Allende, Isabel 1942- . **CLC 39, 57, 97; HLC
1; WLCS**
See also AAYA 18; CA 125; 130; CANR
51, 74; CDWLB 3; CWW 2; DA3; DAM
MULT, NOV; DLB 145; DNFS 1; FW;
HW 1, 2; INT CA-130; LAIT 5; LAWS
1; MTCW 1, 2; NCFS 1; NFS 6; RGSF
2; SSFS 11; WLIT 1

Alleyn, Ellen
See Rossetti, Christina (Georgina)

Alleyne, Carla D. .... **CLC 65**

Allingham, Margery (Louise)
1904-1966 .... **CLC 19**
See also CA 5-8R; 25-28R; CANR 4, 58;
CMW 4; DLB 77; MSW; MTCW 1, 2

Allingham, William 1824-1889 ...... **NCLC 25**
See also DLB 35; RGEL 2

Allison, Dorothy E. 1949- .... **CLC 78, 153**
See also CA 140; CANR 66, 107; CSW;
DA3; FW; MTCW 1; NFS 11; RGAL 4

Alloula, Malek .... **CLC 65**

Allston, Washington 1779-1843 .... **NCLC 2**
See also DLB 1, 235

Almedingen, E. M. .... **CLC 12**
See also Almedingen, Martha Edith von
See also SATA 3

Antoine, Marc
See Proust, (Valentin-Louis-George-Eugene-
)Marcel

Antoninus, Brother
See Everson, William (Oliver)

Antonioni, Michelangelo 1912- .... **CLC 20,
144**
See also CA 73-76; CANR 45, 77

Antschel, Paul 1920-1970
See Celan, Paul
See also CA 85-88; CANR 33, 61; MTCW
1

Anwar, Chairil 1922-1949 .... **TCLC 22**
See also CA 121

Anzaldua, Gloria (Evanjelina) 1942-
See also CA 175; CSW; CWP; DLB 122;
FW; HLCS 1; RGAL 4

Apess, William 1798-1839(?) .... **NCLC 73**
See also DAM MULT; DLB 175, 243;
NNAL

Apollinaire, Guillaume 1880-1918 .. **TCLC 3,
8, 51; PC 7**
See also Kostrowitzki, Wilhelm Apollinaris
de
See also CA 152; DAM POET; DLB 258;
EW 9; GFL 1789 to the Present; MTCW
1; RGWL 2; TWA; WP

Apollonius of Rhodes
See Apollonius Rhodius
See also AW 1; RGWL 2

Apollonius Rhodius c. 300 B.C.-c. 220
B.C. .... **CMLC 28**
See also Apollonius of Rhodes
See also DLB 176

Appelfeld, Aharon 1932- ... **CLC 23, 47; SSC
42**
See also CA 112; 133; CANR 86; CWW 2;
RGSF 2

Apple, Max (Isaac) 1941- .... **CLC 9, 33; SSC
50**
See also CA 81-84; CANR 19, 54; DLB
130

Appleman, Philip (Dean) 1926- .... **CLC 51**
See also CA 13-16R; CAAS 18; CANR 6,
29, 56

Appleton, Lawrence
See Lovecraft, H(oward) P(hillips)

Apteryx
See Eliot, T(homas) S(tearns)

Apuleius, (Lucius Madaurensis)
125(?)-175(?) .... **CMLC 1**
See also AW 2; CDWLB 1; DLB 211;
RGWL 2; SUFW

Aquin, Hubert 1929-1977 .... **CLC 15**
See also CA 105; DLB 53

Aquinas, Thomas 1224(?)-1274 ..... **CMLC 33**
See also DLB 115; EW 1; TWA

Aragon, Louis 1897-1982 .... **CLC 3, 22**
See also CA 69-72; 108; CANR 28, 71;
DAM NOV, POET; DLB 72, 258; EW 11;
GFL 1789 to the Present; GLL 2; MTCW
1, 2; RGWL 2; TCLC 123

Arany, Janos 1817-1882 .... **NCLC 34**

Aranyos, Kakay 1847-1910
See Mikszath, Kalman

Arbuthnot, John 1667-1735 .... **LC 1**
See also DLB 101

Archer, Herbert Winslow
See Mencken, H(enry) L(ouis)

Archer, Jeffrey (Howard) 1940- .... **CLC 28**
See also AAYA 16; BEST 89:3; BPFB 1;
CA 77-80; CANR 22, 52, 95; CPW; DA3;
DAM POP; INT CANR-22

Archer, Jules 1915- .... **CLC 12**
See also CA 9-12R; CANR 6, 69; SAAS 5;
SATA 4, 85

Archer, Lee
See Ellison, Harlan (Jay)

Archilochus c. 7th cent. B.C.- .... **CMLC 44**
See also DLB 176

Arden, John 1930- .... **CLC 6, 13, 15**
See also BRWS 2; CA 13-16R; CAAS 4;
CANR 31, 65, 67; CBD; CD 5; DAM
DRAM; DFS 9; DLB 13, 245; MTCW 1

Arenas, Reinaldo 1943-1990 .. **CLC 41; HLC
1**
See also CA 124; 128; 133; CANR 73, 106;
DAM MULT; DLB 145; GLL 2; HW 1;
LAW; LAWS 1; MTCW 1; RGSF 2;
WLIT 1

Arendt, Hannah 1906-1975 .... **CLC 66, 98**
See also CA 17-20R; 61-64; CANR 26, 60;
DLB 242; MTCW 1, 2

Aretino, Pietro 1492-1556 .... **LC 12**
See also RGWL 2

Arghezi, Tudor -1967 .... **CLC 80**
See also Theodorescu, Ion N.
See also CA 167; CDWLB 4; DLB 220

Arguedas, Jose Maria 1911-1969 .... **CLC 10,
18; HLCS 1**
See also CA 89-92; CANR 73; DLB 113;
HW 1; LAW; RGWL 2; WLIT 1

Argueta, Manlio 1936- .... **CLC 31**
See also CA 131; CANR 73; CWW 2; DLB
145; HW 1

Arias, Ron(ald Francis) 1941-
See also CA 131; CANR 81; DAM MULT;
DLB 82; HLC 1; HW 1, 2; MTCW 2

Ariosto, Ludovico 1474-1533 .... **LC 6; PC 42**
See also EW 2; RGWL 2

Aristides
See Epstein, Joseph

Aristophanes 450 B.C.-385 B.C. .... **CMLC 4,
51; DC 2; WLCS**
See also AW 1; CDWLB 1; DA; DA3;
DAB; DAC; DAM DRAM, MST; DFS
10; DLB 176; RGWL 2; TWA

Aristotle 384 B.C.-322 B.C. .... **CMLC 31;
WLCS**
See also AW 1; CDWLB 1; DA; DA3;
DAB; DAC; DAM MST; DLB 176;
RGEL 2; TWA

Arlt, Roberto (Godofredo Christophersen)
1900-1942 .... **TCLC 29; HLC 1**
See also CA 123; 131; CANR 67; DAM
MULT; HW 1, 2; LAW

Armah, Ayi Kwei 1939- .... **CLC 5, 33, 136;
BLC 1**
See also AFW; BW 1; CA 61-64; CANR
21, 64; CDWLB 3; CN 7; DAM MULT,
POET; DLB 117; MTCW 1; WLIT 2

Armatrading, Joan 1950- .... **CLC 17**
See also CA 114; 186

Armitage, Frank
See Carpenter, John (Howard)

Arnette, Robert
See Silverberg, Robert

**Arnim, Achim von (Ludwig Joachim von
Arnim)** 1781-1831 ..... **NCLC 5; SSC 29**
See also DLB 90

Arnim, Bettina von 1785-1859 .... **NCLC 38**
See also DLB 90; RGWL 2

Arnold, Matthew 1822-1888 ..... **NCLC 6, 29,
89; PC 5; WLC**
See also BRW 5; CDBLB 1832-1890; DA;
DAB; DAC; DAM MST, POET; DLB 32,
57; EXPP; PAB; PFS 2; TEA; WP

Arnold, Thomas 1795-1842 .... **NCLC 18**
See also DLB 55

Arnow, Harriette (Louisa) Simpson
1908-1986 .... **CLC 2, 7, 18**
See also BPFB 1; CA 9-12R; 118; CANR
14; DLB 6; FW; MTCW 1, 2; RHW;
SATA 42; SATA-Obit 47

Arouet, Francois-Marie
See Voltaire

Arp, Hans
See Arp, Jean

Arp, Jean 1887-1966 .... **CLC 5**
See also CA 81-84; 25-28R; CANR 42, 77;
EW 10; TCLC 115

Arrabal
See Arrabal, Fernando

Arrabal, Fernando 1932- ... **CLC 2, 9, 18, 58**
See also CA 9-12R; CANR 15

Arreola, Juan Jose 1918-2001 .... **CLC 147;
HLC 1; SSC 38**
See also CA 113; 131; 200; CANR 81;
DAM MULT; DLB 113; DNFS 2; HW 1,
2; LAW; RGSF 2

Arrian c. 89(?)-c. 155(?) .... **CMLC 43**
See also DLB 176

Arrick, Fran .... **CLC 30**
See also Gaberman, Judie Angell
See also BYA 6

Artaud, Antonin (Marie Joseph)
1896-1948 .... **TCLC 3, 36; DC 14**
See also CA 104; 149; DA3; DAM DRAM;
DLB 258; EW 11; GFL 1789 to the
Present; MTCW 1; RGWL 2

Arthur, Ruth M(abel) 1905-1979 ..... **CLC 12**
See also CA 9-12R; 85-88; CANR 4; CWRI
5; SATA 7, 26

Artsybashev, Mikhail (Petrovich)
1878-1927 .... **TCLC 31**
See also CA 170

Arundel, Honor (Morfydd)
1919-1973 .... **CLC 17**
See also CA 21-22; 41-44R; CAP 2; CLR
35; CWRI 5; SATA 4; SATA-Obit 24

Arzner, Dorothy 1900-1979 .... **CLC 98**

Asch, Sholem 1880-1957 .... **TCLC 3**
See also CA 105; GLL 2

Ash, Shalom
See Asch, Sholem

Ashbery, John (Lawrence) 1927- .. **CLC 2, 3,
4, 6, 9, 13, 15, 25, 41, 77, 125; PC 26**
See also Berry, Jonas
See also AMWS 3; CA 5-8R; CANR 9, 37,
66, 102; CP 7; DA3; DAM POET; DLB
5, 165; DLBY 1981; INT CANR-9;
MTCW 1, 2; PAB; PFS 11; RGAL 4; WP

Ashdown, Clifford
See Freeman, R(ichard) Austin

Ashe, Gordon
See Creasey, John

Ashton-Warner, Sylvia (Constance)
1908-1984 .... **CLC 19**
See also CA 69-72; 112; CANR 29; MTCW
1, 2

Asimov, Isaac 1920-1992 ..... **CLC 1, 3, 9, 19,
26, 76, 92**
See also AAYA 13; BEST 90:2; BPFB 1;
BYA 4, 6, 7, 9; CA 1-4R; 137; CANR 2,
19, 36, 60; CLR 12, 79; CMW 4; CPW;
DA3; DAM POP; DLB 8; DLBY 1992;
INT CANR-19; JRDA; LAIT 5; MAICYA
1, 2; MTCW 1, 2; RGAL 4; SATA 1, 26,
74; SCFW 2; SFW 4; TUS; YAW

Askew, Anne 1521(?)-1546 .... **LC 81**
See also DLB 136

Assis, Joaquim Maria Machado de
See Machado de Assis, Joaquim Maria

Astell, Mary 1666-1731 .... **LC 68**
See also DLB 252; FW

Astley, Thea (Beatrice May) 1925- .. **CLC 41**
See also CA 65-68; CANR 11, 43, 78; CN
7

Astley, William 1855-1911
See Warung, Price

Aston, James
See White, T(erence) H(anbury)

Asturias, Miguel Angel 1899-1974 .... **CLC 3, 8, 13; HLC 1**
See also CA 25-28; 49-52; CANR 32; CAP 2; CDWLB 3; DA3; DAM MULT, NOV; DLB 113; HW 1; LAW; MTCW 1, 2; RGWL 2; WLIT 1

Atares, Carlos Saura
See Saura (Atares), Carlos

Athanasius c. 295-c. 373 .... **CMLC 48**

Atheling, William
See Pound, Ezra (Weston Loomis)

Atheling, William, Jr.
See Blish, James (Benjamin)

Atherton, Gertrude (Franklin Horn)
1857-1948 .... **TCLC 2**
See also CA 104; 155; DLB 9, 78, 186; HGG; RGAL 4; SUFW; TCWW 2

Atherton, Lucius
See Masters, Edgar Lee

Atkins, Jack
See Harris, Mark

Atkinson, Kate .... **CLC 99**
See also CA 166; CANR 101

Attaway, William (Alexander)
1911-1986 .... **CLC 92; BLC 1**
See also BW 2, 3; CA 143; CANR 82; DAM MULT; DLB 76

Atticus
See Fleming, Ian (Lancaster); Wilson, (Thomas) Woodrow

Atwood, Margaret (Eleanor) 1939- ... **CLC 2, 3, 4, 8, 13, 15, 25, 44, 84, 135; PC 8; SSC 2, 46; WLC**
See also AAYA 12; BEST 89:2; BPFB 1; CA 49-52; CANR 3, 24, 33, 59, 95; CN 7; CP 7; CPW; CWP; DA; DA3; DAB; DAC; DAM MST, NOV, POET; DLB 53, 251; EXPN; FW; INT CANR-24; LAIT 5; MTCW 1, 2; NFS 4, 12, 13, 14; PFS 7; RGSF 2; SATA 50; SSFS 3, 13; TWA; YAW

Aubigny, Pierre d'
See Mencken, H(enry) L(ouis)

Aubin, Penelope 1685-1731(?) .... **LC 9**
See also DLB 39

Auchincloss, Louis (Stanton) 1917- .. **CLC 4, 6, 9, 18, 45; SSC 22**
See also AMWS 4; CA 1-4R; CANR 6, 29, 55, 87; CN 7; DAM NOV; DLB 2, 244; DLBY 1980; INT CANR-29; MTCW 1; RGAL 4

Auden, W(ystan) H(ugh) 1907-1973 . **CLC 1, 2, 3, 4, 6, 9, 11, 14, 43, 123; PC 1; WLC**
See also AAYA 18; AMWS 2; BRW 7; BRWR 1; CA 9-12R; 45-48; CANR 5, 61, 105; CDBLB 1914-1945; DA; DA3; DAB; DAC; DAM DRAM, MST, POET; DLB 10, 20; EXPP; MTCW 1, 2; PAB; PFS 1, 3, 4, 10; TUS; WP

Auberti, Jacques 1900-1965 .... **CLC 38**
See also CA 25-28R; DAM DRAM

Audubon, John James 1785-1851 . **NCLC 47**
See also ANW; DLB 248

Auel, Jean M(arie) 1936- .... **CLC 31, 107**
See also AAYA 7; BEST 90:4; BPFB 1; CA 103; CANR 21, 64; CPW; DA3; DAM POP; INT CANR-21; NFS 11; RHW; SATA 91

Auerbach, Erich 1892-1957 .... **TCLC 43**
See also CA 118; 155

Augier, Emile 1820-1889 .... **NCLC 31**
See also DLB 192; GFL 1789 to the Present

August, John
See De Voto, Bernard (Augustine)

Augustine, St. 354-430 .... **CMLC 6; WLCS**
See also DA; DA3; DAB; DAC; DAM MST; DLB 115; EW 1; RGWL 2

Aunt Belinda
See Braddon, Mary Elizabeth

Aunt Weedy
See Alcott, Louisa May

Aurelius
See Bourne, Randolph S(illiman)

Aurelius, Marcus 121-180 .... **CMLC 45**
See also Marcus Aurelius
See also RGWL 2

Aurobindo, Sri
See Ghose, Aurabinda

Austen, Jane 1775-1817 ...... **NCLC 1, 13, 19, 33, 51, 81, 95; WLC**
See also AAYA 19; BRW 4; BRWR 2; BYA 3; CDBLB 1789-1832; DA; DA3; DAB; DAC; DAM MST, NOV; DLB 116; EXPN; LAIT 2; NFS 1, 14; TEA; WLIT 3; WYAS 1

Auster, Paul 1947- .... **CLC 47, 131**
See also CA 69-72; CANR 23, 52, 75; CMW 4; CN 7; DA3; DLB 227; MTCW 1

Austin, Frank
See Faust, Frederick (Schiller)
See also TCWW 2

Austin, Mary (Hunter) 1868-1934 . **TCLC 25**
See also Stairs, Gordon
See also ANW; CA 109; 178; DLB 9, 78, 206, 221; FW; TCWW 2

Averroes 1126-1198 .... **CMLC 7**
See also DLB 115

Avicenna 980-1037 .... **CMLC 16**
See also DLB 115

Avison, Margaret 1918- .... **CLC 2, 4, 97**
See also CA 17-20R; CP 7; DAC; DAM POET; DLB 53; MTCW 1

Axton, David
See Koontz, Dean R(ay)

Aydy, Catherine
See Tennant, Emma (Christina)

Ayme, Marcel (Andre) 1902-1967 ... **CLC 11; SSC 41**
See also CA 89-92; CANR 67; CLR 25; DLB 72; EW 12; GFL 1789 to the Present; RGSF 2; RGWL 2; SATA 91

Ayrton, Michael 1921-1975 .... **CLC 7**
See also CA 5-8R; 61-64; CANR 9, 21

Azorin .... **CLC 11**
See also Martinez Ruiz, Jose
See also EW 9

Azuela, Mariano 1873-1952 .. **TCLC 3; HLC 1**
See also CA 104; 131; CANR 81; DAM MULT; HW 1, 2; LAW; MTCW 1, 2

Baastad, Babbis Friis
See Friis-Baastad, Babbis Ellinor

Bab
See Gilbert, W(illiam) S(chwenck)

Babbis, Eleanor
See Friis-Baastad, Babbis Ellinor

Babel, Isaac
See Babel, Isaak (Emmanuilovich)
See also EW 11; SSFS 10

Babel, Isaak (Emmanuilovich)
1894-1941(?) .... **TCLC 2, 13; SSC 16**
See also Babel, Isaac
See also CA 104; 155; MTCW 1; RGSF 2; RGWL 2; TWA

Babits, Mihaly 1883-1941 .... **TCLC 14**
See also CA 114; CDWLB 4; DLB 215

Babur 1483-1530 .... **LC 18**

Babylas 1898-1962
See Ghelderode, Michel de

Baca, Jimmy Santiago 1952- .... **PC 41**
See also CA 131; CANR 81, 90; CP 7; DAM MULT; DLB 122; HLC 1; HW 1, 2

Baca, Jose Santiago
See Baca, Jimmy Santiago

Bacchelli, Riccardo 1891-1985 .... **CLC 19**
See also CA 29-32R; 117; DLB 264

Bach, Richard (David) 1936- .... **CLC 14**
See also AITN 1; BEST 89:2; BPFB 1; BYA 5; CA 9-12R; CANR 18, 93; CPW; DAM NOV, POP; FANT; MTCW 1; SATA 13

Bache, Benjamin Franklin
1769-1798 .... **LC 74**
See also DLB 43

Bachman, Richard
See King, Stephen (Edwin)

Bachmann, Ingeborg 1926-1973 .... **CLC 69**
See also CA 93-96; 45-48; CANR 69; DLB 85; RGWL 2

Bacon, Francis 1561-1626 .... **LC 18, 32**
See also BRW 1; CDBLB Before 1660; DLB 151, 236, 252; RGEL 2; TEA

Bacon, Roger 1214(?)-1294 .... **CMLC 14**
See also DLB 115

Bacovia, George 1881-1957 .... **TCLC 24**
See also Vasiliu, Gheorghe
See also CDWLB 4; DLB 220

Badanes, Jerome 1937- .... **CLC 59**

Bagehot, Walter 1826-1877 .... **NCLC 10**
See also DLB 55

Bagnold, Enid 1889-1981 .... **CLC 25**
See also BYA 2; CA 5-8R; 103; CANR 5, 40; CBD; CWD; CWRI 5; DAM DRAM; DLB 13, 160, 191, 245; FW; MAICYA 1, 2; RGEL 2; SATA 1, 25

Bagritsky, Eduard 1895-1934 .... **TCLC 60**

Bagrjana, Elisaveta
See Belcheva, Elisaveta Lyubomirova

Bagryana, Elisaveta -1991 .... **CLC 10**
See also Belcheva, Elisaveta Lyubomirova
See also CA 178; CDWLB 4; DLB 147

Bailey, Paul 1937- .... **CLC 45**
See also CA 21-24R; CANR 16, 62; CN 7; DLB 14; GLL 2

Baillie, Joanna 1762-1851 .... **NCLC 71**
See also DLB 93; RGEL 2

Bainbridge, Beryl (Margaret) 1934- . **CLC 4, 5, 8, 10, 14, 18, 22, 62, 130**
See also BRWS 6; CA 21-24R; CANR 24, 55, 75, 88; CN 7; DAM NOV; DLB 14, 231; MTCW 1, 2

Baker, Carlos (Heard)
1909-1987 .... **TCLC 119**
See also CA 5-8R; 122; CANR 3, 63; DLB 103

Baker, Elliott 1922- .... **CLC 8**
See also CA 45-48; CANR 2, 63; CN 7

Baker, Jean H. .... **TCLC 3, 10**
See also Russell, George William

Baker, Nicholson 1957- .... **CLC 61**
See also CA 135; CANR 63; CN 7; CPW; DA3; DAM POP; DLB 227

Baker, Ray Stannard 1870-1946 .... **TCLC 47**
See also CA 118

Baker, Russell (Wayne) 1925- .... **CLC 31**
See also BEST 89:4; CA 57-60; CANR 11, 41, 59; MTCW 1, 2

Bakhtin, M.
See Bakhtin, Mikhail Mikhailovich

Bakhtin, M. M.
See Bakhtin, Mikhail Mikhailovich

Bakhtin, Mikhail
See Bakhtin, Mikhail Mikhailovich

Bakhtin, Mikhail Mikhailovich
1895-1975 .... **CLC 83**
See also CA 128; 113; DLB 242

Bakshi, Ralph 1938(?)- .... **CLC 26**
See also CA 112; 138; IDFW 3

Bakunin, Mikhail (Alexandrovich)
1814-1876 .... **NCLC 25, 58**

Baldwin, James (Arthur) 1924-1987 . **CLC 1, 2, 3, 4, 5, 8, 13, 15, 17, 42, 50, 67, 90, 127; BLC 1; DC 1; SSC 10, 33; WLC**
See also AAYA 4, 34; AFAW 1, 2; AMWS 1; BPFB 1; BW 1; CA 1-4R; 124; CABS 1; CAD; CANR 3, 24; CDALB 1941-1968; CPW; DA; DA3; DAB; DAC; DAM MST, MULT, NOV, POP; DFS 15; DLB 2, 7, 33, 249; DLBY 1987; EXPS; LAIT 5; MTCW 1, 2; NCFS 4; NFS 4; RGAL 4; RGSF 2; SATA 9; SATA-Obit 54; SSFS 2; TUS

Bale, John 1495-1563 .... **LC 62**
See also DLB 132; RGEL 2; TEA

Ball, Hugo 1886-1927 .... **TCLC 104**

Ballard, J(ames) G(raham) 1930- . **CLC 3, 6, 14, 36, 137; SSC 1, 53**
See also AAYA 3; BRWS 5; CA 5-8R; CANR 15, 39, 65, 107; CN 7; DA3; DAM NOV, POP; DLB 14, 207, 261; HGG; MTCW 1, 2; NFS 8; RGEL 2; RGSF 2; SATA 93; SFW 4

Balmont, Konstantin (Dmitriyevich)
1867-1943 .... **TCLC 11**
See also CA 109; 155

Baltausis, Vincas 1847-1910
See Mikszath, Kalman

Balzac, Honore de 1799-1850 ... **NCLC 5, 35, 53; SSC 5; WLC**
See also DA; DA3; DAB; DAC; DAM MST, NOV; DLB 119; EW 5; GFL 1789 to the Present; RGSF 2; RGWL 2; SSFS 10; SUFW; TWA

Bambara, Toni Cade 1939-1995 ...... **CLC 19, 88; BLC 1; SSC 35; WLCS**
See also AAYA 5; AFAW 2; AMWS 11; BW 2, 3; BYA 12, 14; CA 29-32R; 150; CANR 24, 49, 81; CDALBS; DA; DA3; DAC; DAM MST, MULT; DLB 38, 218; EXPS; MTCW 1, 2; RGAL 4; RGSF 2; SATA 112; SSFS 4, 7, 12; TCLC 116

Bamdad, A.
See Shamlu, Ahmad

Banat, D. R.
See Bradbury, Ray (Douglas)

Bancroft, Laura
See Baum, L(yman) Frank

Banim, John 1798-1842 .... **NCLC 13**
See also DLB 116, 158, 159; RGEL 2

Banim, Michael 1796-1874 .... **NCLC 13**
See also DLB 158, 159

Banjo, The
See Paterson, A(ndrew) B(arton)

Banks, Iain
See Banks, Iain M(enzies)

Banks, Iain M(enzies) 1954- .... **CLC 34**
See also CA 123; 128; CANR 61, 106; DLB 194, 261; HGG; INT 128; SFW 4

Banks, Lynne Reid .... **CLC 23**
See also Reid Banks, Lynne
See also AAYA 6; BYA 7

Banks, Russell 1940- .... **CLC 37, 72; SSC 42**
See also AMWS 5; CA 65-68; CAAS 15; CANR 19, 52, 73; CN 7; DLB 130; NFS 13

Banville, John 1945- .... **CLC 46, 118**
See also CA 117; 128; CANR 104; CN 7; DLB 14; INT 128

Banville, Theodore (Faullain) de
1832-1891 .... **NCLC 9**
See also DLB 217; GFL 1789 to the Present

Baraka, Amiri 1934- . **CLC 1, 2, 3, 5, 10, 14, 33, 115; BLC 1; DC 6; PC 4; WLCS**
See also Jones, LeRoi
See also AFAW 1, 2; AMWS 2; BW 2, 3; CA 21-24R; CABS 3; CAD; CANR 27, 38, 61; CD 5; CDALB 1941-1968; CP 7;

CPW; DA; DA3; DAC; DAM MST, MULT, POET, POP; DFS 3, 11; DLB 5, 7, 16, 38; DLBD 8; MTCW 1, 2; PFS 9; RGAL 4; TUS; WP

Baratynsky, Evgenii Abramovich
1800-1844 .... **NCLC 103**
See also DLB 205

Barbauld, Anna Laetitia
1743-1825 .... **NCLC 50**
See also DLB 107, 109, 142, 158; RGEL 2

Barbellion, W. N. P. .... **TCLC 24**
See also Cummings, Bruce F(rederick)

Barber, Benjamin R. 1939- .... **CLC 141**
See also CA 29-32R; CANR 12, 32, 64

Barbera, Jack (Vincent) 1945- .... **CLC 44**
See also CA 110; CANR 45

Barbey d'Aurevilly, Jules-Amedee
1808-1889 .... **NCLC 1; SSC 17**
See also DLB 119; GFL 1789 to the Present

Barbour, John c. 1316-1395 .... **CMLC 33**
See also DLB 146

Barbusse, Henri 1873-1935 .... **TCLC 5**
See also CA 105; 154; DLB 65; RGWL 2

Barclay, Bill
See Moorcock, Michael (John)

Barclay, William Ewert
See Moorcock, Michael (John)

Barea, Arturo 1897-1957 .... **TCLC 14**
See also CA 111; 201

Barfoot, Joan 1946- .... **CLC 18**
See also CA 105

Barham, Richard Harris
1788-1845 .... **NCLC 77**
See also DLB 159

Baring, Maurice 1874-1945 .... **TCLC 8**
See also CA 105; 168; DLB 34; HGG

Baring-Gould, Sabine 1834-1924 ... **TCLC 88**
See also DLB 156, 190

Barker, Clive 1952- .... **CLC 52; SSC 53**
See also AAYA 10; BEST 90:3; BPFB 1; CA 121; 129; CANR 71; CPW; DA3; DAM POP; DLB 261; HGG; INT 129; MTCW 1, 2

Barker, George Granville
1913-1991 .... **CLC 8, 48**
See also CA 9-12R; 135; CANR 7, 38; DAM POET; DLB 20; MTCW 1

Barker, Harley Granville
See Granville-Barker, Harley
See also DLB 10

Barker, Howard 1946- .... **CLC 37**
See also CA 102; CBD; CD 5; DLB 13, 233

Barker, Jane 1652-1732 .... **LC 42**
See also DLB 39, 131

Barker, Pat(ricia) 1943- ...... **CLC 32, 94, 146**
See also BRWS 4; CA 117; 122; CANR 50, 101; CN 7; INT 122

Barlach, Ernst (Heinrich)
1870-1938 .... **TCLC 84**
See also CA 178; DLB 56, 118

Barlow, Joel 1754-1812 .... **NCLC 23**
See also AMWS 2; DLB 37; RGAL 4

Barnard, Mary (Ethel) 1909- .... **CLC 48**
See also CA 21-22; CAP 2

Barnes, Djuna 1892-1982 .... **CLC 3, 4, 8, 11, 29, 127; SSC 3**
See Steptoe, Lydia
See also AMWS 3; CA 9-12R; 107; CAD; CANR 16, 55; CWD; DLB 4, 9, 45; GLL 1; MTCW 1, 2; RGAL 4; TUS

Barnes, Julian (Patrick) 1946- . **CLC 42, 141**
See also BRWS 4; CA 102; CANR 19, 54; CN 7; DAB; DLB 194; DLBY 1993; MTCW 1

Barnes, Peter 1931- .... **CLC 5, 56**
See also CA 65-68; CAAS 12; CANR 33, 34, 64; CBD; CD 5; DFS 6; DLB 13, 233; MTCW 1

Barnes, William 1801-1886 .... **NCLC 75**
See also DLB 32

Baroja (y Nessi), Pio 1872-1956 ..... **TCLC 8; HLC 1**
See also CA 104; EW 9

Baron, David
See Pinter, Harold

Baron Corvo
See Rolfe, Frederick (William Serafino Austin Lewis Mary)

Barondess, Sue K(aufman)
1926-1977 .... **CLC 8**
See also Kaufman, Sue
See also CA 1-4R; 69-72; CANR 1

Baron de Teive
See Pessoa, Fernando (Antonio Nogueira)

Baroness Von S.
See Zangwill, Israel

Barres, (Auguste-)Maurice
1862-1923 .... **TCLC 47**
See also CA 164; DLB 123; GFL 1789 to the Present

Barreto, Afonso Henrique de Lima
See Lima Barreto, Afonso Henrique de

Barrett, Andrea 1954- .... **CLC 150**
See also CA 156; CANR 92

Barrett, Michele .... **CLC 65**

Barrett, (Roger) Syd 1946- .... **CLC 35**

Barrett, William (Christopher)
1913-1992 .... **CLC 27**
See also CA 13-16R; 139; CANR 11, 67; INT CANR-11

Barrie, J(ames) M(atthew)
1860-1937 .... **TCLC 2**
See also BRWS 3; BYA 4, 5; CA 104; 136; CANR 77; CDBLB 1890-1914; CLR 16; CWRI 5; DA3; DAB; DAM DRAM; DFS 7; DLB 10, 141, 156; FANT; MAICYA 1, 2; MTCW 1; SATA 100; SUFW; WCH; WLIT 4; YABC 1

Barrington, Michael
See Moorcock, Michael (John)

Barrol, Grady
See Bograd, Larry

Barry, Mike
See Malzberg, Barry N(athaniel)

Barry, Philip 1896-1949 .... **TCLC 11**
See also CA 109; 199; DFS 9; DLB 7, 228; RGAL 4

Bart, Andre Schwarz
See Schwarz-Bart, Andre

Barth, John (Simmons) 1930- ... **CLC 1, 2, 3, 5, 7, 9, 10, 14, 27, 51, 89; SSC 10**
See also AITN 1, 2; AMW; BPFB 1; CA 1-4R; CABS 1; CANR 5, 23, 49, 64; CN 7; DAM NOV; DLB 2, 227; FANT; MTCW 1; RGAL 4; RGSF 2; RHW; SSFS 6; TUS

Barthelme, Donald 1931-1989 ... **CLC 1, 2, 3, 5, 6, 8, 13, 23, 46, 59, 115; SSC 2, 55**
See also AMWS 4; BPFB 1; CA 21-24R; 129; CANR 20, 58; DA3; DAM NOV; DLB 2, 234; DLBY 1980, 1989; FANT; MTCW 1, 2; RGAL 4; RGSF 2; SATA 7; SATA-Obit 62; SSFS 3

Barthelme, Frederick 1943- ...... **CLC 36, 117**
See also AMWS 11; CA 114; 122; CANR 77; CN 7; CSW; DLB 244; DLBY 1985; INT CA-122

Barthes, Roland (Gerard)
1915-1980 .... **CLC 24, 83**
See also CA 130; 97-100; CANR 66; EW 13; GFL 1789 to the Present; MTCW 1, 2; TWA

Barzun, Jacques (Martin) 1907- ..... **CLC 51, 145**
See also CA 61-64; CANR 22, 95

Bashevis, Isaac
See Singer, Isaac Bashevis

Bethlen, T. D.
See Silverberg, Robert

Beti, Mongo .... **CLC 27; BLC 1**
See also Biyidi, Alexandre
See also AFW; CANR 79; DAM MULT;
WLIT 2

Betjeman, John 1906-1984 ...... **CLC 2, 6, 10, 34, 43**
See also BRW 7; CA 9-12R; 112; CANR
33, 56; CDBLB 1945-1960; DA3; DAB;
DAM MST, POET; DLB 20; DLBY 1984;
MTCW 1, 2

Bettelheim, Bruno 1903-1990 .... **CLC 79**
See also CA 81-84; 131; CANR 23, 61;
DA3; MTCW 1, 2

Betti, Ugo 1892-1953 .... **TCLC 5**
See also CA 104; 155; RGWL 2

Betts, Doris (Waugh) 1932- ..... **CLC 3, 6, 28; SSC 45**
See also CA 13-16R; CANR 9, 66, 77; CN
7; CSW; DLB 218; DLBY 1982; INT
CANR-9; RGAL 4

Bevan, Alistair
See Roberts, Keith (John Kingston)

Bey, Pilaff
See Douglas, (George) Norman

Bialik, Chaim Nachman
1873-1934 .... **TCLC 25**
See also CA 170

Bickerstaff, Isaac
See Swift, Jonathan

Bidart, Frank 1939- .... **CLC 33**
See also CA 140; CANR 106; CP 7

Bienek, Horst 1930- .... **CLC 7, 11**
See also CA 73-76; DLB 75

Bierce, Ambrose (Gwinett)
1842-1914(?) ..... **TCLC 1, 7, 44; SSC 9; WLC**
See also AMW; BYA 11; CA 104; 139;
CANR 78; CDALB 1865-1917; DA;
DA3; DAC; DAM MST; DLB 11, 12, 23,
71, 74, 186; EXPS; HGG; LAIT 2; RGAL
4; RGSF 2; SSFS 9; SUFW

Biggers, Earl Derr 1884-1933 .... **TCLC 65**
See also CA 108; 153

Billings, Josh
See Shaw, Henry Wheeler

Billington, (Lady) Rachel (Mary)
1942- .... **CLC 43**
See also AITN 2; CA 33-36R; CANR 44;
CN 7

Binchy, Maeve 1940- .... **CLC 153**
See also BEST 90:1; BPFB 1; CA 127; 134;
CANR 50, 96; CN 7; CPW; DA3; DAM
POP; INT CA-134; MTCW 1; RHW

Binyon, T(imothy) J(ohn) 1936- .... **CLC 34**
See also CA 111; CANR 28

Bion 335 B.C.-245 B.C. .... **CMLC 39**

Bioy Casares, Adolfo 1914-1999 ... **CLC 4, 8, 13, 88; HLC 1; SSC 17**
See also Casares, Adolfo Bioy; Miranda,
Javier; Sacastru, Martin
See also CA 29-32R; 177; CANR 19, 43,
66; DAM MULT; DLB 113; HW 1, 2;
LAW; MTCW 1, 2

Birch, Allison .... **CLC 65**

Bird, Cordwainer
See Ellison, Harlan (Jay)

Bird, Robert Montgomery
1806-1854 .... **NCLC 1**
See also DLB 202; RGAL 4

Birkerts, Sven 1951- .... **CLC 116**
See also CA 128; 133, 176; CAAE 176;
CAAS 29; INT 133

Birney, (Alfred) Earle 1904-1995 .. **CLC 1, 4, 6, 11**
See also CA 1-4R; CANR 5, 20; CP 7;
DAC; DAM MST, POET; DLB 88;
MTCW 1; PFS 8; RGEL 2

Biruni, al 973-1048(?) .... **CMLC 28**

Bishop, Elizabeth 1911-1979 ..... **CLC 1, 4, 9, 13, 15, 32; PC 3, 34**
See also AMWS 1; CA 5-8R; 89-92; CABS
2; CANR 26, 61, 108; CDALB 1968-
1988; DA; DA3; DAC; DAM MST,
POET; DLB 5, 169; GLL 2; MAWW;
MTCW 1, 2; PAB; PFS 6, 12; RGAL 4;
SATA-Obit 24; TCLC 121; TUS; WP

Bishop, John 1935- .... **CLC 10**
See also CA 105

Bishop, John Peale 1892-1944 ..... **TCLC 103**
See also CA 107; 155; DLB 4, 9, 45; RGAL
4

Bissett, Bill 1939- .... **CLC 18; PC 14**
See also CA 69-72; CAAS 19; CANR 15;
CCA 1; CP 7; DLB 53; MTCW 1

Bissoondath, Neil (Devindra)
1955- .... **CLC 120**
See also CA 136; CN 7; DAC

Bitov, Andrei (Georgievich) 1937- ... **CLC 57**
See also CA 142

Biyidi, Alexandre 1932-
See Beti, Mongo
See also BW 1, 3; CA 114; 124; CANR 81;
DA3; MTCW 1, 2

Bjarme, Brynjolf
See Ibsen, Henrik (Johan)

Bjoernson, Bjoernstjerne (Martinius)
1832-1910 .... **TCLC 7, 37**
See also CA 104

Black, Robert
See Holdstock, Robert P.

Blackburn, Paul 1926-1971 .... **CLC 9, 43**
See also CA 81-84; 33-36R; CANR 34;
DLB 16; DLBY 1981

Black Elk 1863-1950 .... **TCLC 33**
See also CA 144; DAM MULT; MTCW 1;
NNAL; WP

Black Hobart
See Sanders, (James) Ed(ward)

Blacklin, Malcolm
See Chambers, Aidan

Blackmore, R(ichard) D(oddridge)
1825-1900 .... **TCLC 27**
See also CA 120; DLB 18; RGEL 2

Blackmur, R(ichard) P(almer)
1904-1965 .... **CLC 2, 24**
See also AMWS 2; CA 11-12; 25-28R;
CANR 71; CAP 1; DLB 63

Black Tarantula
See Acker, Kathy

Blackwood, Algernon (Henry)
1869-1951 .... **TCLC 5**
See also CA 105; 150; DLB 153, 156, 178;
HGG; SUFW

Blackwood, Caroline 1931-1996 .... **CLC 6, 9, 100**
See also CA 85-88; 151; CANR 32, 61, 65;
CN 7; DLB 14, 207; HGG; MTCW 1

Blade, Alexander
See Hamilton, Edmond; Silverberg, Robert

Blaga, Lucian 1895-1961 .... **CLC 75**
See also CA 157; DLB 220

Blair, Eric (Arthur) 1903-1950 .... **TCLC 123**
See also Orwell, George
See also CA 104; 132; DA; DA3; DAB;
DAC; DAM MST, NOV; MTCW 1, 2;
SATA 29

Blair, Hugh 1718-1800 .... **NCLC 75**

Blais, Marie-Claire 1939- .... **CLC 2, 4, 6, 13, 22**
See also CA 21-24R; CAAS 4; CANR 38,
75, 93; DAC; DAM MST; DLB 53; FW;
MTCW 1, 2; TWA

Blaise, Clark 1940- .... **CLC 29**
See also AITN 2; CA 53-56; CAAS 3;
CANR 5, 66, 106; CN 7; DLB 53; RGSF 2

Blake, Fairley
See De Voto, Bernard (Augustine)

Blake, Nicholas
See Day Lewis, C(ecil)
See also DLB 77; MSW

Blake, William 1757-1827 .... **NCLC 13, 37, 57; PC 12; WLC**
See also BRW 3; BRWR 1; CDBLB 1789-
1832; CLR 52; DA; DA3; DAB; DAC;
DAM MST, POET; DLB 93, 163; EXPP;
MAICYA 1, 2; PAB; PFS 2, 12; SATA
30; TEA; WCH; WLIT 3; WP

Blanchot, Maurice 1907- .... **CLC 135**
See also CA 117; 144; DLB 72

Blasco Ibanez, Vicente 1867-1928 . **TCLC 12**
See also BPFB 1; CA 110; 131; CANR 81;
DA3; DAM NOV; EW 8; HW 1, 2;
MTCW 1

Blatty, William Peter 1928- .... **CLC 2**
See also CA 5-8R; CANR 9; DAM POP;
HGG

Bleeck, Oliver
See Thomas, Ross (Elmore)

Blessing, Lee 1949- .... **CLC 54**
See also CAD; CD 5

Blight, Rose
See Greer, Germaine

Blish, James (Benjamin) 1921-1975 . **CLC 14**
See also BPFB 1; CA 1-4R; 57-60; CANR
3; DLB 8; MTCW 1; SATA 66; SCFW 2;
SFW 4

Bliss, Reginald
See Wells, H(erbert) G(eorge)

Blixen, Karen (Christentze Dinesen)
1885-1962
See Dinesen, Isak
See also CA 25-28; CANR 22, 50; CAP 2;
DA3; DLB 214; MTCW 1, 2; SATA 44

Bloch, Robert (Albert) 1917-1994 .... **CLC 33**
See also AAYA 29; CA 5-8R; 179; 146;
CAAE 179; CAAS 20; CANR 5, 78;
DA3; DLB 44; HGG; INT CANR-5;
MTCW 1; SATA 12; SATA-Obit 82; SFW
4; SUFW

Blok, Alexander (Alexandrovich)
1880-1921 .... **TCLC 5; PC 21**
See also CA 104; 183; EW 9; RGWL 2

Blom, Jan
See Breytenbach, Breyten

Bloom, Harold 1930- .... **CLC 24, 103**
See also CA 13-16R; CANR 39, 75, 92;
DLB 67; MTCW 1; RGAL 4

Bloomfield, Aurelius
See Bourne, Randolph S(illiman)

Blount, Roy (Alton), Jr. 1941- .... **CLC 38**
See also CA 53-56; CANR 10, 28, 61;
CSW; INT CANR-28; MTCW 1, 2

Bloy, Leon 1846-1917 .... **TCLC 22**
See also CA 121; 183; DLB 123; GFL 1789
to the Present

Bluggage, Oranthy
See Alcott, Louisa May

Blume, Judy (Sussman) 1938- .... **CLC 12, 30**
See also AAYA 3, 26; BYA 1, 8, 12; CA 29-
32R; CANR 13, 37, 66; CLR 2, 15, 69;
CPW; DA3; DAM NOV, POP; DLB 52;
JRDA; MAICYA 1, 2; MAICYAS 1;
MTCW 1, 2; SATA 2, 31, 79; WYA; YAW

Blunden, Edmund (Charles)
1896-1974 .... **CLC 2, 56**
See also BRW 6; CA 17-18; 45-48; CANR
54; CAP 2; DLB 20, 100, 155; MTCW 1;
PAB

Bly, Robert (Elwood) 1926- .... **CLC 1, 2, 5, 10, 15, 38, 128; PC 39**
See also AMWS 4; CA 5-8R; CANR 41,
73; CP 7; DA3; DAM POET; DLB 5;
MTCW 1, 2; RGAL 4

Bradbury, Edward P.
See Moorcock, Michael (John)
See also MTCW 2

Bradbury, Malcolm (Stanley)
1932-2000 .... **CLC 32, 61**
See also CA 1-4R; CANR 1, 33, 91, 98;
CN 7; DA3; DAM NOV; DLB 14, 207;
MTCW 1, 2

Bradbury, Ray (Douglas) 1920- .... **CLC 1, 3,
10, 15, 42, 98; SSC 29, 53; WLC**
See also AAYA 15; AITN 1, 2; AMWS 4;
BPFB 1; BYA 4, 5, 11; CA 1-4R; CANR
2, 30, 75; CDALB 1968-1988; CN 7;
CPW; DA; DA3; DAB; DAC; DAM MST,
NOV, POP; DLB 2, 8; EXPN; EXPS;
HGG; LAIT 3, 5; MTCW 1, 2; NFS 1;
RGAL 4; RGSF 2; SATA 11, 64, 123;
SCFW 2; SFW 4; SSFS 1; SUFW; TUS;
YAW

Braddon, Mary Elizabeth
1837-1915 .... **TCLC 111**
See also Aunt Belinda
See also BRWS 8; CA 108; 179; CMW 4;
DLB 18, 70, 156; HGG

Bradford, Gamaliel 1863-1932 .... **TCLC 36**
See also CA 160; DLB 17

Bradford, William 1590-1657 .... **LC 64**
See also DLB 24, 30; RGAL 4

Bradley, David (Henry), Jr. 1950- ... **CLC 23,
118; BLC 1**
See also BW 1, 3; CA 104; CANR 26, 81;
CN 7; DAM MULT; DLB 33

Bradley, John Ed(mund, Jr.) 1958- . **CLC 55**
See also CA 139; CANR 99; CN 7; CSW

Bradley, Marion Zimmer
1930-1999 .... **CLC 30**
See also Chapman, Lee; Dexter, John; Gard-
ner, Miriam; Ives, Morgan; Rivers, Elfrida
See also AAYA 40; BPFB 1; CA 57-60; 185;
CAAS 10; CANR 7, 31, 51, 75, 107;
CPW; DA3; DAM POP; DLB 8; FANT;
FW; MTCW 1, 2; SATA 90; SATA-Obit
116; SFW 4; YAW

Bradshaw, John 1933- .... **CLC 70**
See also CA 138; CANR 61

Bradstreet, Anne 1612(?)-1672 ...... **LC 4, 30;
PC 10**
See also AMWS 1; CDALB 1640-1865;
DA; DA3; DAC; DAM MST, POET; DLB
24; EXPP; FW; PFS 6; RGAL 4; TUS;
WP

Brady, Joan 1939- .... **CLC 86**
See also CA 141

Bragg, Melvyn 1939- .... **CLC 10**
See also BEST 89:3; CA 57-60; CANR 10,
48, 89; CN 7; DLB 14; RHW

Brahe, Tycho 1546-1601 .... **LC 45**

Braine, John (Gerard) 1922-1986 . **CLC 1, 3,
41**
See also CA 1-4R; 120; CANR 1, 33; CD-
BLB 1945-1960; DLB 15; DLBY 1986;
MTCW 1

Bramah, Ernest 1868-1942 .... **TCLC 72**
See also CA 156; CMW 4; DLB 70; FANT

Brammer, William 1930(?)-1978 ...... **CLC 31**
See also CA 77-80

Brancati, Vitaliano 1907-1954 .... **TCLC 12**
See also CA 109; DLB 264

Brancato, Robin F(idler) 1936- .... **CLC 35**
See also AAYA 9; BYA 6; CA 69-72; CANR
11, 45; CLR 32; JRDA; MAICYA 2;
MAICYAS 1; SAAS 9; SATA 97; WYA;
YAW

Brand, Max
See Faust, Frederick (Schiller)
See also BPFB 1; TCWW 2

Brand, Millen 1906-1980 .... **CLC 7**
See also CA 21-24R; 97-100; CANR 72

Branden, Barbara .... **CLC 44**
See also CA 148

Brandes, Georg (Morris Cohen)
1842-1927 .... **TCLC 10**
See also CA 105; 189

Brandys, Kazimierz 1916-2000 .... **CLC 62**

Branley, Franklyn M(ansfield)
1915- .... **CLC 21**
See also CA 33-36R; CANR 14, 39; CLR
13; MAICYA 1, 2; SAAS 16; SATA 4, 68

Brathwaite, Edward Kamau 1930- . **CLC 11;
BLCS**
See also BW 2, 3; CA 25-28R; CANR 11,
26, 47, 107; CDWLB 3; CP 7; DAM
POET; DLB 125

Brathwaite, Kamau
See Brathwaite, Edward Kamau

Brautigan, Richard (Gary)
1935-1984 ..... **CLC 1, 3, 5, 9, 12, 34, 42**
See also BPFB 1; CA 53-56; 113; CANR
34; DA3; DAM NOV; DLB 2, 5, 206;
DLBY 1980, 1984; FANT; MTCW 1;
RGAL 4; SATA 56

Brave Bird, Mary
See Crow Dog, Mary (Ellen)
See also NNAL

Braverman, Kate 1950- .... **CLC 67**
See also CA 89-92

Brecht, (Eugen) Bertolt (Friedrich)
1898-1956 ..... **TCLC 1, 6, 13, 35; DC 3;
WLC**
See also CA 104; 133; CANR 62; CDWLB
2; DA; DA3; DAB; DAC; DAM DRAM,
MST; DFS 4, 5, 9; DLB 56, 124; EW 11;
IDTP; MTCW 1, 2; RGWL 2; TWA

Brecht, Eugen Berthold Friedrich
See Brecht, (Eugen) Bertolt (Friedrich)

Bremer, Fredrika 1801-1865 .... **NCLC 11**
See also DLB 254

Brennan, Christopher John
1870-1932 .... **TCLC 17**
See also CA 117; 188; DLB 230

Brennan, Maeve 1917-1993 .... **CLC 5**
See also CA 81-84; CANR 72, 100; TCLC
124

Brent, Linda
See Jacobs, Harriet A(nn)

Brentano, Clemens (Maria)
1778-1842 .... **NCLC 1**
See also DLB 90; RGWL 2

Brent of Bin Bin
See Franklin, (Stella Maria Sarah) Miles
(Lampe)

Brenton, Howard 1942- .... **CLC 31**
See also CA 69-72; CANR 33, 67; CBD;
CD 5; DLB 13; MTCW 1

Breslin, James 1930-
See Breslin, Jimmy
See also CA 73-76; CANR 31, 75; DAM
NOV; MTCW 1, 2

Breslin, Jimmy .... **CLC 4, 43**
See also Breslin, James
See also AITN 1; DLB 185; MTCW 2

Bresson, Robert 1901(?)-1999 .... **CLC 16**
See also CA 110; 187; CANR 49

Breton, Andre 1896-1966 .. **CLC 2, 9, 15, 54;
PC 15**
See also CA 19-20; 25-28R; CANR 40, 60;
CAP 2; DLB 65, 258; EW 11; GFL 1789
to the Present; MTCW 1, 2; RGWL 2;
TWA; WP

Breytenbach, Breyten 1939(?)- .. **CLC 23, 37,
126**
See also CA 113; 129; CANR 61; CWW 2;
DAM POET; DLB 225

Bridgers, Sue Ellen 1942- .... **CLC 26**
See also AAYA 8; BYA 7, 8; CA 65-68;
CANR 11, 36; CLR 18; DLB 52; JRDA;

MAICYA 1, 2; SAAS 1; SATA 22, 90;
SATA-Essay 109; WYA; YAW

Bridges, Robert (Seymour)
1844-1930 .... **TCLC 1; PC 28**
See also BRW 6; CA 104; 152; CDBLB
1890-1914; DAM POET; DLB 19, 98

Bridie, James .... **TCLC 3**
See also Mavor, Osborne Henry
See also DLB 10

Brin, David 1950- .... **CLC 34**
See also AAYA 21; CA 102; CANR 24, 70;
INT CANR-24; SATA 65; SCFW 2; SFW
4

Brink, Andre (Philippus) 1935- . **CLC 18, 36,
106**
See also AFW; BRWS 6; CA 104; CANR
39, 62, 109; CN 7; DLB 225; INT CA-
103; MTCW 1, 2; WLIT 2

Brinsmead, H. F.
See Brinsmead, H(esba) F(ay)

Brinsmead, H. F(ay)
See Brinsmead, H(esba) F(ay)

Brinsmead, H(esba) F(ay) 1922- ...... **CLC 21**
See also CA 21-24R; CANR 10; CLR 47;
CWRI 5; MAICYA 1, 2; SAAS 5; SATA
18, 78

Brittain, Vera (Mary) 1893(?)-1970 . **CLC 23**
See also CA 13-16; 25-28R; CANR 58;
CAP 1; DLB 191; FW; MTCW 1, 2

Broch, Hermann 1886-1951 .... **TCLC 20**
See also CA 117; CDWLB 2; DLB 85, 124;
EW 10; RGWL 2

Brock, Rose
See Hansen, Joseph
See also GLL 1

Brod, Max 1884-1968 .... **TCLC 115**
See also CA 5-8R; 25-28R; CANR 7; DLB
81

Brodkey, Harold (Roy) 1930-1996 ... **CLC 56**
See also CA 111; 151; CANR 71; CN 7;
DLB 130; TCLC 123

Brodskii, Iosif
See Brodsky, Joseph
See also RGWL 2

Brodsky, Iosif Alexandrovich 1940-1996
See Brodsky, Joseph
See also AITN 1; CA 41-44R; 151; CANR
37, 106; DA3; DAM POET; MTCW 1, 2

Brodsky, Joseph . **CLC 4, 6, 13, 36, 100; PC
9**
See also Brodsky, Iosif Alexandrovich
See also AMWS 8; CWW 2; MTCW 1

Brodsky, Michael (Mark) 1948- .... **CLC 19**
See also CA 102; CANR 18, 41, 58; DLB
244

Brodzki, Bella ed. .... **CLC 65**

Brome, Richard 1590(?)-1652 .... **LC 61**
See also DLB 58

Bromell, Henry 1947- .... **CLC 5**
See also CA 53-56; CANR 9

Bromfield, Louis (Brucker)
1896-1956 .... **TCLC 11**
See also CA 107; 155; DLB 4, 9, 86; RGAL
4; RHW

Broner, E(sther) M(asserman)
1930- .... **CLC 19**
See also CA 17-20R; CANR 8, 25, 72; CN
7; DLB 28

Bronk, William (M.) 1918-1999 .... **CLC 10**
See also CA 89-92; 177; CANR 23; CP 7;
DLB 165

Bronstein, Lev Davidovich
See Trotsky, Leon

Bronte, Anne 1820-1849 ..... **NCLC 4, 71, 102**
See also BRW 5; BRWR 1; DA3; DLB 21,
199; TEA

Chabon, Michael 1963- .... **CLC 55, 149**
See also AMWS 11; CA 139; CANR 57, 96

Chabrol, Claude 1930- .... **CLC 16**
See also CA 110

Challans, Mary 1905-1983
See Renault, Mary
See also CA 81-84; 111; CANR 74; DA3;
MTCW 2; SATA 23; SATA-Obit 36; TEA

Challis, George
See Faust, Frederick (Schiller)
See also TCWW 2

Chambers, Aidan 1934- .... **CLC 35**
See also AAYA 27; CA 25-28R; CANR 12,
31, 58; JRDA; MAICYA 1, 2; SAAS 12;
SATA 1, 69, 108; WYA; YAW

Chambers, James 1948-
See Cliff, Jimmy
See also CA 124

Chambers, Jessie
See Lawrence, D(avid) H(erbert Richards)
See also GLL 1

Chambers, Robert W(illiam)
1865-1933 .... **TCLC 41**
See also CA 165; DLB 202; HGG; SATA
107; SUFW

Chamisso, Adelbert von
1781-1838 .... **NCLC 82**
See also DLB 90; RGWL 2; SUFW

Chance, John T.
See Carpenter, John (Howard)

Chandler, Raymond (Thornton)
1888-1959 .... **TCLC 1, 7; SSC 23**
See also AAYA 25; AMWS 4; BPFB 1; CA
104; 129; CANR 60, 107; CDALB 1929-
1941; CMW 4; DA3; DLB 226, 253;
DLBD 6; MSW; MTCW 1, 2; RGAL 4;
TUS

Chang, Eileen 1921-1995 .... **SSC 28**
See also CA 166; CWW 2

Chang, Jung 1952- .... **CLC 71**
See also CA 142

Chang Ai-Ling
See Chang, Eileen

Channing, William Ellery
1780-1842 .... **NCLC 17**
See also DLB 1, 59, 235; RGAL 4

Chao, Patricia 1955- .... **CLC 119**
See also CA 163

Chaplin, Charles Spencer
1889-1977 .... **CLC 16**
See also Chaplin, Charlie
See also CA 81-84; 73-76

Chaplin, Charlie
See Chaplin, Charles Spencer
See also DLB 44

Chapman, George 1559(?)-1634 .... **LC 22**
See also BRW 1; DAM DRAM; DLB 62,
121; RGEL 2

Chapman, Graham 1941-1989 .... **CLC 21**
See also Monty Python
See also CA 116; 129; CANR 35, 95

Chapman, John Jay 1862-1933 .... **TCLC 7**
See also CA 104; 191

Chapman, Lee
See Bradley, Marion Zimmer
See also GLL 1

Chapman, Walker
See Silverberg, Robert

Chappell, Fred (Davis) 1936- .... **CLC 40, 78,
162**
See also CA 5-8R; CAAE 198; CAAS 4;
CANR 8, 33, 67, 110; CN 7; CP 7; CSW;
DLB 6, 105; HGG

Char, Rene(-Emile) 1907-1988 .... **CLC 9, 11,
14, 55**
See also CA 13-16R; 124; CANR 32; DAM
POET; DLB 258; GFL 1789 to the
Present; MTCW 1, 2; RGWL 2

Charby, Jay
See Ellison, Harlan (Jay)

Chardin, Pierre Teilhard de
See Teilhard de Chardin, (Marie Joseph)
Pierre

Chariton fl. 1st cent. (?)- .... **CMLC 49**

Charlemagne 742-814 .... **CMLC 37**

Charles I 1600-1649 .... **LC 13**

Charriere, Isabelle de 1740-1805 .. **NCLC 66**

Chartier, Emile-Auguste
See Alain

Charyn, Jerome 1937- .... **CLC 5, 8, 18**
See also CA 5-8R; CAAS 1; CANR 7, 61,
101; CMW 4; CN 7; DLBY 1983; MTCW
1

Chase, Adam
See Marlowe, Stephen

Chase, Mary (Coyle) 1907-1981 .... **DC 1**
See also CA 77-80; 105; CAD; CWD; DFS
11; DLB 228; SATA 17; SATA-Obit 29

Chase, Mary Ellen 1887-1973 .... **CLC 2**
See also CA 13-16; 41-44R; CAP 1; SATA
10; TCLC 124

Chase, Nicholas
See Hyde, Anthony
See also CCA 1

Chateaubriand, Francois Rene de
1768-1848 .... **NCLC 3**
See also DLB 119; EW 5; GFL 1789 to the
Present; RGWL 2; TWA

Chatterje, Sarat Chandra 1876-1936(?)
See Chatterji, Saratchandra
See also CA 109

Chatterji, Bankim Chandra
1838-1894 .... **NCLC 19**

Chatterji, Saratchandra .... **TCLC 13**
See also Chatterje, Sarat Chandra
See also CA 186

Chatterton, Thomas 1752-1770 .... **LC 3, 54**
See also DAM POET; DLB 109; RGEL 2

Chatwin, (Charles) Bruce
1940-1989 .... **CLC 28, 57, 59**
See also AAYA 4; BEST 90:1; BRWS 4;
CA 85-88; 127; CPW; DAM POP; DLB
194, 204

Chaucer, Daniel
See Ford, Ford Madox
See also RHW

Chaucer, Geoffrey 1340(?)-1400 .. **LC 17, 56;
PC 19; WLCS**
See also BRW 1; BRWR 2; CDBLB Before
1660; DA; DA3; DAB; DAC; DAM MST,
POET; DLB 146; LAIT 1; PAB; PFS 14;
RGEL 2; TEA; WLIT 3; WP

Chavez, Denise (Elia) 1948-
See also CA 131; CANR 56, 81; DAM
MULT; DLB 122; FW; HLC 1; HW 1, 2;
MTCW 2

Chaviaras, Strates 1935-
See Haviaras, Stratis
See also CA 105

Chayefsky, Paddy .... **CLC 23**
See also Chayefsky, Sidney
See also CAD; DLB 7, 44; DLBY 1981;
RGAL 4

Chayefsky, Sidney 1923-1981
See Chayefsky, Paddy
See also CA 9-12R; 104; CANR 18; DAM
DRAM

Chedid, Andree 1920- .... **CLC 47**
See also CA 145; CANR 95

Cheever, John 1912-1982 ..... **CLC 3, 7, 8, 11,
15, 25, 64; SSC 1, 38; WLC**
See also AMWS 1; BPFB 1; CA 5-8R; 106;
CABS 1; CANR 5, 27, 76; CDALB 1941-
1968; CPW; DA; DA3; DAB; DAC;
DAM MST, NOV, POP; DLB 2, 102, 227;

DLBY 1980, 1982; EXPS; INT CANR-5;
MTCW 1, 2; RGAL 4; RGSF 2; SSFS 2,
14; TUS

Cheever, Susan 1943- .... **CLC 18, 48**
See also CA 103; CANR 27, 51, 92; DLBY
1982; INT CANR-27

Chekhonte, Antosha
See Chekhov, Anton (Pavlovich)

Chekhov, Anton (Pavlovich)
1860-1904 . **TCLC 3, 10, 31, 55, 96; DC
9; SSC 2, 28, 41, 51; WLC**
See also BYA 14; CA 104; 124; DA; DA3;
DAB; DAC; DAM DRAM, MST; DFS 1,
5, 10, 12; EW 7; EXPS; LAIT 3; RGSF
2; RGWL 2; SATA 90; SSFS 5, 13, 14;
TWA

Cheney, Lynne V. 1941- .... **CLC 70**
See also CA 89-92; CANR 58

Chernyshevsky, Nikolai Gavrilovich
See Chernyshevsky, Nikolay Gavrilovich
See also DLB 238

Chernyshevsky, Nikolay Gavrilovich
1828-1889 .... **NCLC 1**
See also Chernyshevsky, Nikolai Gavrilov-
ich

Cherry, Carolyn Janice 1942-
See Cherryh, C. J.
See also CA 65-68; CANR 10

Cherryh, C. J. .... **CLC 35**
See also Cherry, Carolyn Janice
See also AAYA 24; BPFB 1; DLBY 1980;
FANT; SATA 93; SCFW 2; SFW 4; YAW

Chesnutt, Charles W(addell)
1858-1932 .... **TCLC 5, 39; BLC 1; SSC
7, 54**
See also AFAW 1, 2; BW 1, 3; CA 106;
125; CANR 76; DAM MULT; DLB 12,
50, 78; MTCW 1, 2; RGAL 4; RGSF 2;
SSFS 11

Chester, Alfred 1929(?)-1971 .... **CLC 49**
See also CA 196; 33-36R; DLB 130

Chesterton, G(ilbert) K(eith)
1874-1936 . **TCLC 1, 6, 64; PC 28; SSC
1, 46**
See also BRW 6; CA 104; 132; CANR 73;
CDBLB 1914-1945; CMW 4; DAM NOV,
POET; DLB 10, 19, 34, 70, 98, 149, 178;
FANT; MSW; MTCW 1, 2; RGEL 2;
RGSF 2; SATA 27; SUFW

Chiang, Pin-chin 1904-1986
See Ding Ling
See also CA 118

Ch'ien, Chung-shu 1910-1998 .... **CLC 22**
See also CA 130; CANR 73; MTCW 1, 2

Chikamatsu Monzaemon 1653-1724 ... **LC 66**
See also RGWL 2

Child, L. Maria
See Child, Lydia Maria

Child, Lydia Maria 1802-1880 .. **NCLC 6, 73**
See also DLB 1, 74, 243; RGAL 4; SATA
67

Child, Mrs.
See Child, Lydia Maria

Child, Philip 1898-1978 .... **CLC 19, 68**
See also CA 13-14; CAP 1; DLB 68; RHW;
SATA 47

Childers, (Robert) Erskine
1870-1922 .... **TCLC 65**
See also CA 113; 153; DLB 70

Childress, Alice 1920-1994 .. **CLC 12, 15, 86,
96; BLC 1; DC 4**
See also AAYA 8; BW 2, 3; BYA 2; CA 45-
48; 146; CAD; CANR 3, 27, 50, 74; CLR
14; CWD; DA3; DAM DRAM, MULT,
NOV; DFS 2, 8, 14; DLB 7, 38, 249;
JRDA; LAIT 5; MAICYA 1, 2; MAIC-
YAS 1; MTCW 1, 2; RGAL 4; SATA 7,
48, 81; TCLC 116; TUS; WYA; YAW

Cook, Robin 1940- .... **CLC 14**
See also AAYA 32; BEST 90:2; BPFB 1;
CA 108; 111; CANR 41, 90, 109; CPW;
DA3; DAM POP; HGG; INT CA-111

Cook, Roy
See Silverberg, Robert

Cooke, Elizabeth 1948- .... **CLC 55**
See also CA 129

Cooke, John Esten 1830-1886 .... **NCLC 5**
See also DLB 3, 248; RGAL 4

Cooke, John Estes
See Baum, L(yman) Frank

Cooke, M. E.
See Creasey, John

Cooke, Margaret
See Creasey, John

Cooke, Rose Terry 1827-1892 ...... **NCLC 110**
See also DLB 12, 74

Cook-Lynn, Elizabeth 1930- .... **CLC 93**
See also CA 133; DAM MULT; DLB 175;
NNAL

Cooney, Ray .... **CLC 62**
See also CBD

Cooper, Douglas 1960- .... **CLC 86**

Cooper, Henry St. John
See Creasey, John

Cooper, J(oan) California (?)- .... **CLC 56**
See also AAYA 12; BW 1; CA 125; CANR
55; DAM MULT; DLB 212

Cooper, James Fenimore
1789-1851 .... **NCLC 1, 27, 54**
See also AAYA 22; AMW; BPFB 1;
CDALB 1640-1865; DA3; DLB 3, 183,
250, 254; LAIT 1; NFS 9; RGAL 4; SATA
19; TUS; WCH

Coover, Robert (Lowell) 1932- ...... **CLC 3, 7,
15, 32, 46, 87, 161; SSC 15**
See also AMWS 5; BPFB 1; CA 45-48;
CANR 3, 37, 58; CN 7; DAM NOV; DLB
2, 227; DLBY 1981; MTCW 1, 2; RGAL
4; RGSF 2

Copeland, Stewart (Armstrong)
1952- .... **CLC 26**

Copernicus, Nicolaus 1473-1543 .... **LC 45**

Coppard, A(lfred) E(dgar)
1878-1957 .... **TCLC 5; SSC 21**
See also BRWS 8; CA 114; 167; DLB 162;
HGG; RGEL 2; RGSF 2; SUFW; YABC
1

Coppee, Francois 1842-1908 .... **TCLC 25**
See also CA 170; DLB 217

Coppola, Francis Ford 1939- ... **CLC 16, 126**
See also AAYA 39; CA 77-80; CANR 40,
78; DLB 44

Corbiere, Tristan 1845-1875 .... **NCLC 43**
See also DLB 217; GFL 1789 to the Present

Corcoran, Barbara (Asenath)
1911- .... **CLC 17**
See also AAYA 14; CA 21-24R; CAAE 191;
CAAS 2; CANR 11, 28, 48; CLR 50;
DLB 52; JRDA; MAICYA 2; MAICYAS
1; RHW; SAAS 20; SATA 3, 77, 125

Cordelier, Maurice
See Giraudoux, Jean(-Hippolyte)

Corelli, Marie .... **TCLC 51**
See also Mackay, Mary
See also DLB 34, 156; RGEL 2; SUFW

Corman, Cid .... **CLC 9**
See also Corman, Sidney
See also CAAS 2; DLB 5, 193

Corman, Sidney 1924-
See Corman, Cid
See also CA 85-88; CANR 44; CP 7; DAM
POET

Cormier, Robert (Edmund)
1925-2000 .... **CLC 12, 30**
See also AAYA 3, 19; BYA 1, 2, 6, 8, 9;
CA 1-4R; CANR 5, 23, 76, 93; CDALB
1968-1988; CLR 12, 55; DA; DAB; DAC;

DAM MST, NOV; DLB 52; EXPN; INT
CANR-23; JRDA; LAIT 5; MAICYA 1,
2; MTCW 1, 2; NFS 2; SATA 10, 45, 83;
SATA-Obit 122; WYA; YAW

Corn, Alfred (DeWitt III) 1943- .... **CLC 33**
See also CA 179; CAAE 179; CAAS 25;
CANR 44; CP 7; CSW; DLB 120; DLBY
1980

Corneille, Pierre 1606-1684 .... **LC 28**
See also DAB; DAM MST; EW 3; GFL Be-
ginnings to 1789; RGWL 2; TWA

Cornwell, David (John Moore)
1931- .... **CLC 9, 15**
See also le Carre, John
See also CA 5-8R; CANR 13, 33, 59, 107;
DA3; DAM POP; MTCW 1, 2

Cornwell, Patricia (Daniels) 1956- . **CLC 155**
See also AAYA 16; BPFB 1; CA 134;
CANR 53; CMW 4; CPW; CSW; DAM
POP; MSW; MTCW 1

Corso, (Nunzio) Gregory 1930-2001 . **CLC 1,
11; PC 33**
See also CA 5-8R; 193; CANR 41, 76; CP
7; DA3; DLB 5, 16, 237; MTCW 1, 2;
WP

Cortazar, Julio 1914-1984 ... **CLC 2, 3, 5, 10,
13, 15, 33, 34, 92; HLC 1; SSC 7**
See also BPFB 1; CA 21-24R; CANR 12,
32, 81; CDWLB 3; DA3; DAM MULT,
NOV; DLB 113; EXPS; HW 1, 2; LAW;
MTCW 1, 2; RGSF 2; RGWL 2; SSFS 3;
TWA; WLIT 1

Cortes, Hernan 1485-1547 .... **LC 31**

Corvinus, Jakob
See Raabe, Wilhelm (Karl)

Corvo, Baron
See Rolfe, Frederick (William Serafino Aus-
tin Lewis Mary)
See also GLL 1; RGEL 2

Corwin, Cecil
See Kornbluth, C(yril) M.

Cosic, Dobrica 1921- .... **CLC 14**
See also CA 122; 138; CDWLB 4; CWW
2; DLB 181

Costain, Thomas B(ertram)
1885-1965 .... **CLC 30**
See also BYA 3; CA 5-8R; 25-28R; DLB 9;
RHW

Costantini, Humberto 1924(?)-1987 . **CLC 49**
See also CA 131; 122; HW 1

Costello, Elvis 1955- .... **CLC 21**

Costenoble, Philostene 1898-1962
See Ghelderode, Michel de

Costenoble, Philostene 1898-1962
See Ghelderode, Michel de

Cotes, Cecil V.
See Duncan, Sara Jeannette

Cotter, Joseph Seamon Sr.
1861-1949 .... **TCLC 28; BLC 1**
See also BW 1; CA 124; DAM MULT; DLB
50

Couch, Arthur Thomas Quiller
See Quiller-Couch, Sir Arthur (Thomas)

Coulton, James
See Hansen, Joseph

Couperus, Louis (Marie Anne)
1863-1923 .... **TCLC 15**
See also CA 115; RGWL 2

Coupland, Douglas 1961- .... **CLC 85, 133**
See also AAYA 34; CA 142; CANR 57, 90;
CCA 1; CPW; DAC; DAM POP

Court, Wesli
See Turco, Lewis (Putnam)

Courtenay, Bryce 1933- .... **CLC 59**
See also CA 138; CPW

Courtney, Robert
See Ellison, Harlan (Jay)

Cousteau, Jacques-Yves 1910-1997 .. **CLC 30**
See also CA 65-68; 159; CANR 15, 67;
MTCW 1; SATA 38, 98

Coventry, Francis 1725-1754 .... **LC 46**

Coverdale, Miles c. 1487-1569 .... **LC 77**
See also DLB 167

Cowan, Peter (Walkinshaw) 1914- .... **SSC 28**
See also CA 21-24R; CANR 9, 25, 50, 83;
CN 7; DLB 260; RGSF 2

Coward, Noel (Peirce) 1899-1973 . **CLC 1, 9,
29, 51**
See also AITN 1; BRWS 2; CA 17-18; 41-
44R; CANR 35; CAP 2; CDBLB 1914-
1945; DA3; DAM DRAM; DFS 3, 6;
DLB 10, 245; IDFW 3, 4; MTCW 1, 2;
RGEL 2; TEA

Cowley, Abraham 1618-1667 .... **LC 43**
See also BRW 2; DLB 131, 151; PAB;
RGEL 2

Cowley, Malcolm 1898-1989 .... **CLC 39**
See also AMWS 2; CA 5-8R; 128; CANR
3, 55; DLB 4, 48; DLBY 1981, 1989;
MTCW 1, 2

Cowper, William 1731-1800 ..... **NCLC 8, 94;
PC 40**
See also BRW 3; DA3; DAM POET; DLB
104, 109; RGEL 2

Cox, William Trevor 1928-
See Trevor, William
See also CA 9-12R; CANR 4, 37, 55, 76,
102; DAM NOV; INT CANR-37; MTCW
1, 2; TEA

Coyne, P. J.
See Masters, Hilary

Cozzens, James Gould 1903-1978 . **CLC 1, 4,
11, 92**
See also AMW; BPFB 1; CA 9-12R; 81-84;
CANR 19; CDALB 1941-1968; DLB 9;
DLBD 2; DLBY 1984, 1997; MTCW 1,
2; RGAL 4

Crabbe, George 1754-1832 .... **NCLC 26**
See also BRW 3; DLB 93; RGEL 2

Crace, Jim 1946- .... **CLC 157**
See also CA 128; 135; CANR 55, 70; CN
7; DLB 231; INT CA-135

Craddock, Charles Egbert
See Murfree, Mary Noailles

Craig, A. A.
See Anderson, Poul (William)

Craik, Mrs.
See Craik, Dinah Maria (Mulock)
See also RGEL 2

Craik, Dinah Maria (Mulock)
1826-1887 .... **NCLC 38**
See also Craik, Mrs.; Mulock, Dinah Maria
See also DLB 35, 163; MAICYA 1, 2;
SATA 34

Cram, Ralph Adams 1863-1942 ..... **TCLC 45**
See also CA 160

Cranch, Christopher Pearse
1813-1892 .... **NCLC 115**
See also DLB 1, 42, 243

Crane, (Harold) Hart 1899-1932 .... **TCLC 2,
5, 80; PC 3; WLC**
See also AMW; CA 104; 127; CDALB
1917-1929; DA; DA3; DAB; DAC; DAM
MST, POET; DLB 4, 48; MTCW 1, 2;
RGAL 4; TUS

Crane, R(onald) S(almon)
1886-1967 .... **CLC 27**
See also CA 85-88; DLB 63

Crane, Stephen (Townley)
1871-1900 ...... **TCLC 11, 17, 32; SSC 7;
WLC**
See also AAYA 21; AMW; BPFB 1; BYA 3;
CA 109; 140; CANR 84; CDALB 1865-
1917; DA; DA3; DAB; DAC; DAM MST,
NOV, POET; DLB 12, 54, 78; EXPN;

EXPS; LAIT 2; NFS 4; PFS 9; RGAL 4;
RGSF 2; SSFS 4; TUS; WYA; YABC 2

Cranshaw, Stanley
See Fisher, Dorothy (Frances) Canfield

Crase, Douglas 1944- .... **CLC 58**
See also CA 106

Crashaw, Richard 1612(?)-1649 .... **LC 24**
See also BRW 2; DLB 126; PAB; RGEL 2

Cratinus c. 519 B.C.-c. 422 B.C. ... **CMLC 54**

Craven, Margaret 1901-1980 .... **CLC 17**
See also BYA 2; CA 103; CCA 1; DAC;
LAIT 5

Crawford, F(rancis) Marion
1854-1909 .... **TCLC 10**
See also CA 107; 168; DLB 71; HGG;
RGAL 4; SUFW

Crawford, Isabella Valancy
1850-1887 .... **NCLC 12**
See also DLB 92; RGEL 2

Crayon, Geoffrey
See Irving, Washington

Creasey, John 1908-1973 .... **CLC 11**
See also Marric, J. J.
See also CA 5-8R; 41-44R; CANR 8, 59;
CMW 4; DLB 77; MTCW 1

Crebillon, Claude Prosper Jolyot de (fils)
1707-1777 .... **LC 1, 28**
See also GFL Beginnings to 1789

Credo
See Creasey, John

Credo, Alvaro J. de
See Prado (Calvo), Pedro

Creeley, Robert (White) 1926- .. **CLC 1, 2, 4,
8, 11, 15, 36, 78**
See also AMWS 4; CA 1-4R; CAAS 10;
CANR 23, 43, 89; CP 7; DA3; DAM
POET; DLB 5, 16, 169; DLBD 17;
MTCW 1, 2; RGAL 4; WP

Crevecoeur, Hector St. John de
See Crevecoeur, Michel Guillaume Jean de
See also ANW

Crevecoeur, Michel Guillaume Jean de
1735-1813 .... **NCLC 105**
See also Crevecoeur, Hector St. John de
See also AMWS 1; DLB 37

Crevel, Rene 1900-1935 .... **TCLC 112**
See also GLL 2

Crews, Harry (Eugene) 1935- ..... **CLC 6, 23,
49**
See also AITN 1; AMWS 11; BPFB 1; CA
25-28R; CANR 20, 57; CN 7; CSW; DA3;
DLB 6, 143, 185; MTCW 1, 2; RGAL 4

Crichton, (John) Michael 1942- .... **CLC 2, 6,
54, 90**
See also AAYA 10; AITN 2; BPFB 1; CA
25-28R; CANR 13, 40, 54, 76; CMW 4;
CN 7; CPW; DA3; DAM NOV, POP;
DLBY 1981; INT CANR-13; JRDA;
MTCW 1, 2; SATA 9, 88; SFW 4; YAW

Crispin, Edmund .... **CLC 22**
See also Montgomery, (Robert) Bruce
See also DLB 87; MSW

Cristofer, Michael 1945(?)- .... **CLC 28**
See also CA 110; 152; CAD; CD 5; DAM
DRAM; DFS 15; DLB 7

Croce, Benedetto 1866-1952 .... **TCLC 37**
See also CA 120; 155; EW 8

Crockett, David 1786-1836 .... **NCLC 8**
See also DLB 3, 11, 183, 248

Crockett, Davy
See Crockett, David

Crofts, Freeman Wills 1879-1957 .. **TCLC 55**
See also CA 115; 195; CMW 4; DLB 77;
MSW

Croker, John Wilson 1780-1857 .... **NCLC 10**
See also DLB 110

Crommelynck, Fernand 1885-1970 .. **CLC 75**
See also CA 189; 89-92

Cromwell, Oliver 1599-1658 .... **LC 43**

Cronenberg, David 1943- .... **CLC 143**
See also CA 138; CCA 1

Cronin, A(rchibald) J(oseph)
1896-1981 .... **CLC 32**
See also BPFB 1; CA 1-4R; 102; CANR 5;
DLB 191; SATA 47; SATA-Obit 25

Cross, Amanda
See Heilbrun, Carolyn G(old)
See also BPFB 1; CMW; CPW; MSW

Crothers, Rachel 1878-1958 .... **TCLC 19**
See also CA 113; 194; CAD; CWD; DLB
7, 266; RGAL 4

Croves, Hal
See Traven, B.

Crow Dog, Mary (Ellen) (?)- .... **CLC 93**
See also Brave Bird, Mary
See also CA 154

Crowfield, Christopher
See Stowe, Harriet (Elizabeth) Beecher

Crowley, Aleister .... **TCLC 7**
See also Crowley, Edward Alexander
See also GLL 1

Crowley, Edward Alexander 1875-1947
See Crowley, Aleister
See also CA 104; HGG

Crowley, John 1942- .... **CLC 57**
See also BPFB 1; CA 61-64; CANR 43, 98;
DLBY 1982; SATA 65; SFW 4

Crud
See Crumb, R(obert)

Crumarums
See Crumb, R(obert)

Crumb, R(obert) 1943- .... **CLC 17**
See also CA 106; CANR 107

Crumbum
See Crumb, R(obert)

Crumski
See Crumb, R(obert)

Crum the Bum
See Crumb, R(obert)

Crunk
See Crumb, R(obert)

Crustt
See Crumb, R(obert)

Crutchfield, Les
See Trumbo, Dalton

Cruz, Victor Hernandez 1949- .... **PC 37**
See also BW 2; CA 65-68; CAAS 17;
CANR 14, 32, 74; CP 7; DAM MULT,
POET; DLB 41; DNFS 1; EXPP; HLC 1;
HW 1, 2; MTCW 1; WP

Cryer, Gretchen (Kiger) 1935- .... **CLC 21**
See also CA 114; 123

Csath, Geza 1887-1919 .... **TCLC 13**
See also CA 111

Cudlip, David R(ockwell) 1933- .... **CLC 34**
See also CA 177

Cullen, Countee 1903-1946 .... **TCLC 4, 37;
BLC 1; PC 20; WLCS**
See also AFAW 2; AMWS 4; BW 1; CA
108; 124; CDALB 1917-1929; DA; DA3;
DAC; DAM MST, MULT, POET; DLB 4,
48, 51; EXPP; MTCW 1, 2; PFS 3; RGAL
4; SATA 18; WP

Cum, R.
See Crumb, R(obert)

Cummings, Bruce F(rederick) 1889-1919
See Barbellion, W. N. P.
See also CA 123

Cummings, E(dward) E(stlin)
1894-1962 .. **CLC 1, 3, 8, 12, 15, 68; PC
5; WLC**
See also AAYA 41; AMW; CA 73-76;
CANR 31; CDALB 1929-1941; DA;
DA3; DAB; DAC; DAM MST, POET;
DLB 4, 48; EXPP; MTCW 1, 2; PAB;
PFS 1, 3, 12, 13; RGAL 4; TUS; WP

Cunha, Euclides (Rodrigues Pimenta) da
1866-1909 .... **TCLC 24**
See also CA 123; LAW; WLIT 1

Cunningham, E. V.
See Fast, Howard (Melvin)

Cunningham, J(ames) V(incent)
1911-1985 .... **CLC 3, 31**
See also CA 1-4R; 115; CANR 1, 72; DLB
5

Cunningham, Julia (Woolfolk)
1916- .... **CLC 12**
See also CA 9-12R; CANR 4, 19, 36; CWRI
5; JRDA; MAICYA 1, 2; SAAS 2; SATA
1, 26, 132

Cunningham, Michael 1952- .... **CLC 34**
See also CA 136; CANR 96; GLL 2

Cunninghame Graham, R. B.
See Cunninghame Graham, Robert
(Gallnigad) Bontine

**Cunninghame Graham, Robert (Gallnigad)
Bontine** 1852-1936 .... **TCLC 19**
See also Graham, R(obert) B(ontine) Cun-
ninghame
See also CA 119; 184

Currie, Ellen 19(?)- .... **CLC 44**

Curtin, Philip
See Lowndes, Marie Adelaide (Belloc)

Curtis, Price
See Ellison, Harlan (Jay)

Cusanus, Nicolaus
See Nicholas of Cusa
See also LC 80

Cutrate, Joe
See Spiegelman, Art

Cynewulf c. 770- .... **CMLC 23**
See also DLB 146; RGEL 2

Cyrano de Bergerac, Savinien de
1619-1655 .... **LC 65**
See also GFL Beginnings to 1789; RGWL
2

Czaczkes, Shmuel Yosef Halevi
See Agnon, S(hmuel) Y(osef Halevi)

Dabrowska, Maria (Szumska)
1889-1965 .... **CLC 15**
See also CA 106; CDWLB 4; DLB 215

Dabydeen, David 1955- .... **CLC 34**
See also BW 1; CA 125; CANR 56, 92; CN
7; CP 7

Dacey, Philip 1939- .... **CLC 51**
See also CA 37-40R; CAAS 17; CANR 14,
32, 64; CP 7; DLB 105

Dagerman, Stig (Halvard)
1923-1954 .... **TCLC 17**
See also CA 117; 155; DLB 259

D'Aguiar, Fred 1960- .... **CLC 145**
See also CA 148; CANR 83, 101; CP 7;
DLB 157

Dahl, Roald 1916-1990 .... **CLC 1, 6, 18, 79**
See also AAYA 15; BPFB 1; BRWS 4; BYA
5; CA 1-4R; 133; CANR 6, 32, 37, 62;
CLR 1, 7, 41; CPW; DA3; DAB; DAC;
DAM MST, NOV, POP; DLB 139, 255;
HGG; JRDA; MAICYA 1, 2; MTCW 1,
2; RGSF 2; SATA 1, 26, 73; SATA-Obit
65; SSFS 4; TEA; YAW

Dahlberg, Edward 1900-1977 .. **CLC 1, 7, 14**
See also CA 9-12R; 69-72; CANR 31, 62;
DLB 48; MTCW 1; RGAL 4

Daitch, Susan 1954- .... **CLC 103**
See also CA 161

Dale, Colin .... **TCLC 18**
See also Lawrence, T(homas) E(dward)

Dale, George E.
See Asimov, Isaac

Dalton, Roque 1935-1975(?) .... **PC 36**
See also CA 176; HLCS 1; HW 2

Daly, Elizabeth 1878-1967 .... **CLC 52**
See also CA 23-24; 25-28R; CANR 60;
CAP 2; CMW 4

Dickey, James (Lafayette)
1923-1997 .... **CLC 1, 2, 4, 7, 10, 15, 47, 109; PC 40**
See also AITN 1, 2; AMWS 4; BPFB 1; CA 9-12R; 156; CABS 2; CANR 10, 48, 61, 105; CDALB 1968-1988; CP 7; CPW; CSW; DA3; DAM NOV, POET, POP; DLB 5, 193; DLBD 7; DLBY 1982, 1993, 1996, 1997, 1998; INT CANR-10; MTCW 1, 2; NFS 9; PFS 6, 11; RGAL 4; TUS

Dickey, William 1928-1994 .... **CLC 3, 28**
See also CA 9-12R; 145; CANR 24, 79; DLB 5

Dickinson, Charles 1951- .... **CLC 49**
See also CA 128

Dickinson, Emily (Elizabeth)
1830-1886 ... **NCLC 21, 77; PC 1; WLC**
See also AAYA 22; AMW; AMWR 1; CDALB 1865-1917; DA; DA3; DAB; DAC; DAM MST, POET; DLB 1, 243; EXPP; MAWW; PAB; PFS 1, 2, 3, 4, 5, 6, 8, 10, 11, 13; RGAL 4; SATA 29; TUS; WP; WYA

Dickinson, Mrs. Herbert Ward
See Phelps, Elizabeth Stuart

Dickinson, Peter (Malcolm) 1927- .. **CLC 12, 35**
See also AAYA 9; BYA 5; CA 41-44R; CANR 31, 58, 88; CLR 29; CMW 4; DLB 87, 161; JRDA; MAICYA 1, 2; SATA 5, 62, 95; SFW 4; WYA; YAW

Dickson, Carr
See Carr, John Dickson

Dickson, Carter
See Carr, John Dickson

Diderot, Denis 1713-1784 .... **LC 26**
See also EW 4; GFL Beginnings to 1789; RGWL 2

Didion, Joan 1934- . **CLC 1, 3, 8, 14, 32, 129**
See also AITN 1; AMWS 4; CA 5-8R; CANR 14, 52, 76; CDALB 1968-1988; CN 7; DA3; DAM NOV; DLB 2, 173, 185; DLBY 1981, 1986; MAWW; MTCW 1, 2; NFS 3; RGAL 4; TCWW 2; TUS

Dietrich, Robert
See Hunt, E(verette) Howard, (Jr.)

Difusa, Pati
See Almodovar, Pedro

Dillard, Annie 1945- .... **CLC 9, 60, 115**
See also AAYA 6, 43; AMWS 6; ANW; CA 49-52; CANR 3, 43, 62, 90; DA3; DAM NOV; DLBY 1980; LAIT 4, 5; MTCW 1, 2; NCFS 1; RGAL 4; SATA 10; TUS

Dillard, R(ichard) H(enry) W(ilde)
1937- .... **CLC 5**
See also CA 21-24R; CAAS 7; CANR 10; CP 7; CSW; DLB 5, 244

Dillon, Eilis 1920-1994 .... **CLC 17**
See also CA 9-12R; 182; 147; CAAE 182; CAAS 3; CANR 4, 38, 78; CLR 26; MAICYA 1, 2; MAICYAS 1; SATA 2, 74; SATA-Essay 105; SATA-Obit 83; YAW

Dimont, Penelope
See Mortimer, Penelope (Ruth)

Dinesen, Isak .... **CLC 10, 29, 95; SSC 7**
See also Blixen, Karen (Christentze Dinesen)
See also EW 10; EXPS; FW; HGG; LAIT 3; MTCW 1; NCFS 2; NFS 9; RGSF 2; RGWL 2; SSFS 3, 6, 13; WLIT 2

Ding Ling .... **CLC 68**
See also Chiang, Pin-chin

Diphusa, Patty
See Almodovar, Pedro

Disch, Thomas M(ichael) 1940- ... **CLC 7, 36**
See also AAYA 17; BPFB 1; CA 21-24R; CAAS 4; CANR 17, 36, 54, 89; CLR 18; CP 7; DA3; DLB 8; HGG; MAICYA 1, 2; MTCW 1, 2; SAAS 15; SATA 92; SCFW; SFW 4

Disch, Tom
See Disch, Thomas M(ichael)

d'Isly, Georges
See Simenon, Georges (Jacques Christian)

Disraeli, Benjamin 1804-1881 ... **NCLC 2, 39, 79**
See also BRW 4; DLB 21, 55; RGEL 2

Ditcum, Steve
See Crumb, R(obert)

Dixon, Paige
See Corcoran, Barbara (Asenath)

Dixon, Stephen 1936- .... **CLC 52; SSC 16**
See also CA 89-92; CANR 17, 40, 54, 91; CN 7; DLB 130

Doak, Annie
See Dillard, Annie

Dobell, Sydney Thompson
1824-1874 .... **NCLC 43**
See also DLB 32; RGEL 2

Doblin, Alfred .... **TCLC 13**
See also Doeblin, Alfred
See also CDWLB 2; RGWL 2

Dobrolyubov, Nikolai Alexandrovich
1836-1861 .... **NCLC 5**

Dobson, Austin 1840-1921 .... **TCLC 79**
See also DLB 35, 144

Dobyns, Stephen 1941- .... **CLC 37**
See also CA 45-48; CANR 2, 18, 99; CMW 4; CP 7

Doctorow, E(dgar) L(aurence)
1931- .... **CLC 6, 11, 15, 18, 37, 44, 65, 113**
See also AAYA 22; AITN 2; AMWS 4; BEST 89:3; BPFB 1; CA 45-48; CANR 2, 33, 51, 76, 97; CDALB 1968-1988; CN 7; CPW; DA3; DAM NOV, POP; DLB 2, 28, 173; DLBY 1980; LAIT 3; MTCW 1, 2; NFS 6; RGAL 4; RHW; TUS

Dodgson, Charles L(utwidge) 1832-1898
See Carroll, Lewis
See also CLR 2; DA; DA3; DAB; DAC; DAM MST, NOV, POET; MAICYA 1, 2; SATA 100; YABC 2

Dodson, Owen (Vincent)
1914-1983 .... **CLC 79; BLC 1**
See also BW 1; CA 65-68; 110; CANR 24; DAM MULT; DLB 76

Doeblin, Alfred 1878-1957 .... **TCLC 13**
See also Doblin, Alfred
See also CA 110; 141; DLB 66

Doerr, Harriet 1910- .... **CLC 34**
See also CA 117; 122; CANR 47; INT 122

Domecq, H(onorio Bustos)
See Bioy Casares, Adolfo

Domecq, H(onorio) Bustos
See Bioy Casares, Adolfo; Borges, Jorge Luis

Domini, Rey
See Lorde, Audre (Geraldine)
See also GLL 1

Dominique
See Proust, (Valentin-Louis-George-Eugene-)Marcel

Don, A
See Stephen, Sir Leslie

Donaldson, Stephen R(eeder)
1947- .... **CLC 46, 138**
See also AAYA 36; BPFB 1; CA 89-92; CANR 13, 55, 99; CPW; DAM POP; FANT; INT CANR-13; SATA 121; SFW 4; SUFW

Donleavy, J(ames) P(atrick) 1926- .... **CLC 1, 4, 6, 10, 45**
See also AITN 2; BPFB 1; CA 9-12R; CANR 24, 49, 62, 80; CBD; CD 5; CN 7; DLB 6, 173; INT CANR-24; MTCW 1, 2; RGAL 4

Donne, John 1572-1631 ..... **LC 10, 24; PC 1; WLC**
See also BRW 1; BRWR 2; CDBLB Before 1660; DA; DAB; DAC; DAM MST, POET; DLB 121, 151; EXPP; PAB; PFS 2, 11; RGEL 2; TEA; WLIT 3; WP

Donnell, David 1939(?)- .... **CLC 34**
See also CA 197

Donoghue, P. S.
See Hunt, E(verette) Howard, (Jr.)

Donoso (Yanez), Jose 1924-1996 ... **CLC 4, 8, 11, 32, 99; HLC 1; SSC 34**
See also CA 81-84; 155; CANR 32, 73; CD-WLB 3; DAM MULT; DLB 113; HW 1, 2; LAW; LAWS 1; MTCW 1, 2; RGSF 2; WLIT 1

Donovan, John 1928-1992 .... **CLC 35**
See also AAYA 20; CA 97-100; 137; CLR 3; MAICYA 1, 2; SATA 72; SATA-Brief 29; YAW

Don Roberto
See Cunninghame Graham, Robert (Gallnigad) Bontine

Doolittle, Hilda 1886-1961 . **CLC 3, 8, 14, 31, 34, 73; PC 5; WLC**
See also H. D.
See also AMWS 1; CA 97-100; CANR 35; DA; DAC; DAM MST, POET; DLB 4, 45; FW; GLL 1; MAWW; MTCW 1, 2; PFS 6; RGAL 4

Doppo, Kunikida .... **TCLC 99**
See also Kunikida Doppo

Dorfman, Ariel 1942- .... **CLC 48, 77; HLC 1**
See also CA 124; 130; CANR 67, 70; CWW 2; DAM MULT; DFS 4; HW 1, 2; INT CA-130; WLIT 1

Dorn, Edward (Merton)
1929-1999 .... **CLC 10, 18**
See also CA 93-96; 187; CANR 42, 79; CP 7; DLB 5; INT 93-96; WP

Dor-Ner, Zvi .... **CLC 70**

Dorris, Michael (Anthony)
1945-1997 .... **CLC 109**
See also AAYA 20; BEST 90:1; BYA 12; CA 102; 157; CANR 19, 46, 75; CLR 58; DA3; DAM MULT, NOV; DLB 175; LAIT 5; MTCW 2; NFS 3; NNAL; RGAL 4; SATA 75; SATA-Obit 94; TCWW 2; YAW

Dorris, Michael A.
See Dorris, Michael (Anthony)

Dorsan, Luc
See Simenon, Georges (Jacques Christian)

Dorsange, Jean
See Simenon, Georges (Jacques Christian)

Dos Passos, John (Roderigo)
1896-1970 ... **CLC 1, 4, 8, 11, 15, 25, 34, 82; WLC**
See also AMW; BPFB 1; CA 1-4R; 29-32R; CANR 3; CDALB 1929-1941; DA; DA3; DAB; DAC; DAM MST, NOV; DLB 4, 9; DLBD 1, 15; DLBY 1996; MTCW 1, 2; NFS 14; RGAL 4; TUS

Dossage, Jean
See Simenon, Georges (Jacques Christian)

Dostoevsky, Fedor Mikhailovich
1821-1881 . **NCLC 2, 7, 21, 33, 43; SSC 2, 33, 44; WLC**
See also Dostoevsky, Fyodor
See also AAYA 40; DA; DA3; DAB; DAC; DAM MST, NOV; EW 7; EXPN; NFS 3, 8; RGSF 2; RGWL 2; SSFS 8; TWA

Dostoevsky, Fyodor
See Dostoevsky, Fedor Mikhailovich
See also DLB 238

Doughty, Charles M(ontagu)
1843-1926 .... **TCLC 27**
See also CA 115; 178; DLB 19, 57, 174

CYA 1, 2; MAICYAS 1; SAAS 2; SATA
1, 36, 75, 133; WYA; YAW

Duncan, Robert (Edward)
1919-1988 .... **CLC 1, 2, 4, 7, 15, 41, 55;
PC 2**
See also CA 9-12R; 124; CANR 28, 62;
DAM POET; DLB 5, 16, 193; MTCW 1,
2; PFS 13; RGAL 4; WP

Duncan, Sara Jeannette
1861-1922 .... **TCLC 60**
See also CA 157; DLB 92

Dunlap, William 1766-1839 .... **NCLC 2**
See also DLB 30, 37, 59; RGAL 4

Dunn, Douglas (Eaglesham) 1942- .... **CLC 6,
40**
See also CA 45-48; CANR 2, 33; CP 7;
DLB 40; MTCW 1

Dunn, Katherine (Karen) 1945- .... **CLC 71**
See also CA 33-36R; CANR 72; HGG;
MTCW 1

Dunn, Stephen (Elliott) 1939- .... **CLC 36**
See also AMWS 11; CA 33-36R; CANR
12, 48, 53, 105; CP 7; DLB 105

Dunne, Finley Peter 1867-1936 ...... **TCLC 28**
See also CA 108; 178; DLB 11, 23; RGAL
4

Dunne, John Gregory 1932- .... **CLC 28**
See also CA 25-28R; CANR 14, 50; CN 7;
DLBY 1980

Dunsany, Lord .... **TCLC 2, 59**
See also Dunsany, Edward John Moreton
Drax Plunkett
See also DLB 77, 153, 156, 255; FANT;
IDTP; RGEL 2; SFW 4; SUFW

**Dunsany, Edward John Moreton Drax
Plunkett** 1878-1957
See Dunsany, Lord
See also CA 104; 148; DLB 10; MTCW 1

du Perry, Jean
See Simenon, Georges (Jacques Christian)

Durang, Christopher (Ferdinand)
1949- .... **CLC 27, 38**
See also CA 105; CAD; CANR 50, 76; CD
5; MTCW 1

Duras, Marguerite 1914-1996 . **CLC 3, 6, 11,
20, 34, 40, 68, 100; SSC 40**
See also BPFB 1; CA 25-28R; 151; CANR
50; CWW 2; DLB 83; GFL 1789 to the
Present; IDFW 4; MTCW 1, 2; RGWL 2;
TWA

Durban, (Rosa) Pam 1947- .... **CLC 39**
See also CA 123; CANR 98; CSW

Durcan, Paul 1944- .... **CLC 43, 70**
See also CA 134; CP 7; DAM POET

Durkheim, Emile 1858-1917 .... **TCLC 55**

Durrell, Lawrence (George)
1912-1990 ..... **CLC 1, 4, 6, 8, 13, 27, 41**
See also BPFB 1; BRWS 1; CA 9-12R; 132;
CANR 40, 77; CDBLB 1945-1960; DAM
NOV; DLB 15, 27, 204; DLBY 1990;
MTCW 1, 2; RGEL 2; SFW 4; TEA

Durrenmatt, Friedrich
See Duerrenmatt, Friedrich
See also CDWLB 2; EW 13; RGWL 2

Dutt, Toru 1856-1877 .... **NCLC 29**
See also DLB 240

Dwight, Timothy 1752-1817 .... **NCLC 13**
See also DLB 37; RGAL 4

Dworkin, Andrea 1946- .... **CLC 43, 123**
See also CA 77-80; CAAS 21; CANR 16,
39, 76, 96; FW; GLL 1; INT CANR-16;
MTCW 1, 2

Dwyer, Deanna
See Koontz, Dean R(ay)

Dwyer, K. R.
See Koontz, Dean R(ay)

Dwyer, Thomas A. 1923- .... **CLC 114**
See also CA 115

Dybek, Stuart 1942- .... **CLC 114; SSC 55**
See also CA 97-100; CANR 39; DLB 130

Dye, Richard
See De Voto, Bernard (Augustine)

Dyer, Geoff 1958- .... **CLC 149**
See also CA 125; CANR 88

Dylan, Bob 1941- .... **CLC 3, 4, 6, 12, 77; PC
37**
See also CA 41-44R; CANR 108; CP 7;
DLB 16

Dyson, John 1943- .... **CLC 70**
See also CA 144

E. V. L.
See Lucas, E(dward) V(errall)

Eagleton, Terence (Francis) 1943- .. **CLC 63,
132**
See also CA 57-60; CANR 7, 23, 68; DLB
242; MTCW 1, 2

Eagleton, Terry
See Eagleton, Terence (Francis)

Early, Jack
See Scoppettone, Sandra
See also GLL 1

East, Michael
See West, Morris L(anglo)

Eastaway, Edward
See Thomas, (Philip) Edward

Eastlake, William (Derry)
1917-1997 .... **CLC 8**
See also CA 5-8R; 158; CAAS 1; CANR 5,
63; CN 7; DLB 6, 206; INT CANR-5;
TCWW 2

Eastman, Charles A(lexander)
1858-1939 .... **TCLC 55**
See also CA 179; CANR 91; DAM MULT;
DLB 175; NNAL; YABC 1

Eberhart, Richard (Ghormley)
1904- .... **CLC 3, 11, 19, 56**
See also AMW; CA 1-4R; CANR 2;
CDALB 1941-1968; CP 7; DAM POET;
DLB 48; MTCW 1; RGAL 4

Eberstadt, Fernanda 1960- .... **CLC 39**
See also CA 136; CANR 69

**Echegaray (y Eizaguirre), Jose (Maria
Waldo)** 1832-1916 .... **TCLC 4; HLCS 1**
See also CA 104; CANR 32; HW 1; MTCW
1

Echeverria, (Jose) Esteban (Antonino)
1805-1851 .... **NCLC 18**
See also LAW

Echo
See Proust, (Valentin-Louis-George-Eugene-
)Marcel

Eckert, Allan W. 1931- .... **CLC 17**
See also AAYA 18; BYA 2; CA 13-16R;
CANR 14, 45; INT CANR-14; MAICYA
2; MAICYAS 1; SAAS 21; SATA 29, 91;
SATA-Brief 27

Eckhart, Meister 1260(?)-1327(?) ... **CMLC 9**
See also DLB 115

Eckmar, F. R.
See de Hartog, Jan

Eco, Umberto 1932- .... **CLC 28, 60, 142**
See also BEST 90:1; BPFB 1; CA 77-80;
CANR 12, 33, 55, 110; CPW; CWW 2;
DA3; DAM NOV, POP; DLB 196, 242;
MSW; MTCW 1, 2

Eddison, E(ric) R(ucker)
1882-1945 .... **TCLC 15**
See also CA 109; 156; DLB 255; FANT;
SFW 4; SUFW

Eddy, Mary (Ann Morse) Baker
1821-1910 .... **TCLC 71**
See also CA 113; 174

Edel, (Joseph) Leon 1907-1997 .. **CLC 29, 34**
See also CA 1-4R; 161; CANR 1, 22; DLB
103; INT CANR-22

Eden, Emily 1797-1869 .... **NCLC 10**

Edgar, David 1948- .... **CLC 42**
See also CA 57-60; CANR 12, 61; CBD;
CD 5; DAM DRAM; DFS 15; DLB 13,
233; MTCW 1

Edgerton, Clyde (Carlyle) 1944- ...... **CLC 39**
See also AAYA 17; CA 118; 134; CANR
64; CSW; INT 134; YAW

Edgeworth, Maria 1768-1849 .... **NCLC 1, 51**
See also BRWS 3; DLB 116, 159, 163; FW;
RGEL 2; SATA 21; TEA; WLIT 3

Edmonds, Paul
See Kuttner, Henry

Edmonds, Walter D(umaux)
1903-1998 .... **CLC 35**
See also BYA 2; CA 5-8R; CANR 2; CWRI
5; DLB 9; LAIT 1; MAICYA 1, 2; RHW;
SAAS 4; SATA 1, 27; SATA-Obit 99

Edmondson, Wallace
See Ellison, Harlan (Jay)

Edson, Russell 1935- .... **CLC 13**
See also CA 33-36R; DLB 244; WP

Edwards, Bronwen Elizabeth
See Rose, Wendy

Edwards, G(erald) B(asil)
1899-1976 .... **CLC 25**
See also CA 201; 110

Edwards, Gus 1939- .... **CLC 43**
See also CA 108; INT 108

Edwards, Jonathan 1703-1758 .... **LC 7, 54**
See also AMW; DA; DAC; DAM MST;
DLB 24; RGAL 4; TUS

Efron, Marina Ivanovna Tsvetaeva
See Tsvetaeva (Efron), Marina (Ivanovna)

Egoyan, Atom 1960- .... **CLC 151**
See also CA 157

Ehle, John (Marsden, Jr.) 1925- ...... **CLC 27**
See also CA 9-12R; CSW

Ehrenbourg, Ilya (Grigoryevich)
See Ehrenburg, Ilya (Grigoryevich)

Ehrenburg, Ilya (Grigoryevich)
1891-1967 .... **CLC 18, 34, 62**
See also CA 102; 25-28R

Ehrenburg, Ilyo (Grigoryevich)
See Ehrenburg, Ilya (Grigoryevich)

Ehrenreich, Barbara 1941- .... **CLC 110**
See also BEST 90:4; CA 73-76; CANR 16,
37, 62; DLB 246; FW; MTCW 1, 2

Eich, Guenter 1907-1972 .... **CLC 15**
See also Eich, Gunter
See also CA 111; 93-96; DLB 69, 124

Eich, Gunter
See Eich, Guenter
See also RGWL 2

Eichendorff, Joseph 1788-1857 .... **NCLC 8**
See also DLB 90; RGWL 2

Eigner, Larry .... **CLC 9**
See also Eigner, Laurence (Joel)
See also CAAS 23; DLB 5; WP

Eigner, Laurence (Joel) 1927-1996
See Eigner, Larry
See also CA 9-12R; 151; CANR 6, 84; CP
7; DLB 193

Einhard c. 770-840 .... **CMLC 50**
See also DLB 148

Einstein, Albert 1879-1955 .... **TCLC 65**
See also CA 121; 133; MTCW 1, 2

Eiseley, Loren Corey 1907-1977 .... **CLC 7**
See also AAYA 5; ANW; CA 1-4R; 73-76;
CANR 6; DLBD 17

Eisenstadt, Jill 1963- .... **CLC 50**
See also CA 140

Eisenstein, Sergei (Mikhailovich)
1898-1948 .... **TCLC 57**
See also CA 114; 149

Eisner, Simon
See Kornbluth, C(yril) M.

Erickson, Steve .... **CLC 64**
See also Erickson, Stephen Michael
See also CANR 60, 68

Ericson, Walter
See Fast, Howard (Melvin)

Eriksson, Buntel
See Bergman, (Ernst) Ingmar

Ernaux, Annie 1940- .... **CLC 88**
See also CA 147; CANR 93; NCFS 3

Erskine, John 1879-1951 .... **TCLC 84**
See also CA 112; 159; DLB 9, 102; FANT

Eschenbach, Wolfram von
See Wolfram von Eschenbach

Eseki, Bruno
See Mphahlele, Ezekiel

Esenin, Sergei (Alexandrovich)
1895-1925 .... **TCLC 4**
See also CA 104; RGWL 2

Eshleman, Clayton 1935- .... **CLC 7**
See also CA 33-36R; CAAS 6; CANR 93;
CP 7; DLB 5

Espriella, Don Manuel Alvarez
See Southey, Robert

Espriu, Salvador 1913-1985 .... **CLC 9**
See also CA 154; 115; DLB 134

Espronceda, Jose de 1808-1842 ..... **NCLC 39**

Esquivel, Laura 1951(?)- ... **CLC 141; HLCS 1**
See also AAYA 29; CA 143; CANR 68;
DA3; DNFS 2; LAIT 3; MTCW 1; NFS 5; WLIT 1

Esse, James
See Stephens, James

Esterbrook, Tom
See Hubbard, L(afayette) Ron(ald)

Estleman, Loren D. 1952- .... **CLC 48**
See also AAYA 27; CA 85-88; CANR 27, 74; CMW 4; CPW; DA3; DAM NOV, POP; DLB 226; INT CANR-27; MTCW 1, 2

Etherege, Sir George 1636-1692 .... **LC 78**
See also BRW 2; DAM DRAM; DLB 80; PAB; RGEL 2

Euclid 306 B.C.-283 B.C. .... **CMLC 25**

Eugenides, Jeffrey 1960(?)- .... **CLC 81**
See also CA 144

Euripides c. 484 B.C.-406 B.C. .... **CMLC 23, 51; DC 4; WLCS**
See also AW 1; CDWLB 1; DA; DA3; DAB; DAC; DAM DRAM, MST; DFS 1, 4, 6; DLB 176; LAIT 1; RGWL 2

Evan, Evin
See Faust, Frederick (Schiller)

Evans, Caradoc 1878-1945 ... **TCLC 85; SSC 43**
See also DLB 162

Evans, Evan
See Faust, Frederick (Schiller)
See also TCWW 2

Evans, Marian
See Eliot, George

Evans, Mary Ann
See Eliot, George

Evarts, Esther
See Benson, Sally

Everett, Percival
See Everett, Percival L.
See also CSW

Everett, Percival L. 1956- .... **CLC 57**
See also Everett, Percival
See also BW 2; CA 129; CANR 94

Everson, R(onald) G(ilmour)
1903-1992 .... **CLC 27**
See also CA 17-20R; DLB 88

Everson, William (Oliver)
1912-1994 .... **CLC 1, 5, 14**
See also CA 9-12R; 145; CANR 20; DLB 5, 16, 212; MTCW 1

Evtushenko, Evgenii Aleksandrovich
See Yevtushenko, Yevgeny (Alexandrovich)
See also RGWL 2

Ewart, Gavin (Buchanan)
1916-1995 .... **CLC 13, 46**
See also BRWS 7; CA 89-92; 150; CANR 17, 46; CP 7; DLB 40; MTCW 1

Ewers, Hanns Heinz 1871-1943 ..... **TCLC 12**
See also CA 109; 149

Ewing, Frederick R.
See Sturgeon, Theodore (Hamilton)

Exley, Frederick (Earl) 1929-1992 .... **CLC 6, 11**
See also AITN 2; BPFB 1; CA 81-84; 138; DLB 143; DLBY 1981

Eynhardt, Guillermo
See Quiroga, Horacio (Sylvestre)

Ezekiel, Nissim 1924- .... **CLC 61**
See also CA 61-64; CP 7

Ezekiel, Tish O'Dowd 1943- .... **CLC 34**
See also CA 129

Fadeyev, A.
See Bulgya, Alexander Alexandrovich

Fadeyev, Alexander .... **TCLC 53**
See also Bulgya, Alexander Alexandrovich

Fagen, Donald 1948- .... **CLC 26**

Fainzilberg, Ilya Arnoldovich 1897-1937
See Ilf, Ilya
See also CA 120; 165

Fair, Ronald L. 1932- .... **CLC 18**
See also BW 1; CA 69-72; CANR 25; DLB 33

Fairbairn, Roger
See Carr, John Dickson

Fairbairns, Zoe (Ann) 1948- .... **CLC 32**
See also CA 103; CANR 21, 85; CN 7

Fairfield, Flora
See Alcott, Louisa May

Fairman, Paul W. 1916-1977
See Queen, Ellery
See also CA 114; SFW 4

Falco, Gian
See Papini, Giovanni

Falconer, James
See Kirkup, James

Falconer, Kenneth
See Kornbluth, C(yril) M.

Falkland, Samuel
See Heijermans, Herman

Fallaci, Oriana 1930- .... **CLC 11, 110**
See also CA 77-80; CANR 15, 58; FW; MTCW 1

Faludi, Susan 1959- .... **CLC 140**
See also CA 138; FW; MTCW 1; NCFS 3

Faludy, George 1913- .... **CLC 42**
See also CA 21-24R

Faludy, Gyoergy
See Faludy, George

Fanon, Frantz 1925-1961 .... **CLC 74; BLC 2**
See also BW 1; CA 116; 89-92; DAM MULT; WLIT 2

Fanshawe, Ann 1625-1680 .... **LC 11**

Fante, John (Thomas) 1911-1983 ..... **CLC 60**
See also AMWS 11; CA 69-72; 109; CANR 23, 104; DLB 130; DLBY 1983

Farah, Nuruddin 1945- .. **CLC 53, 137; BLC 2**
See also AFW; BW 2, 3; CA 106; CANR 81; CDWLB 3; CN 7; DAM MULT; DLB 125; WLIT 2

Fargue, Leon-Paul 1876(?)-1947 .... **TCLC 11**
See also CA 109; CANR 107; DLB 258

Farigoule, Louis
See Romains, Jules

Farina, Richard 1936(?)-1966 .... **CLC 9**
See also CA 81-84; 25-28R

Farley, Walter (Lorimer)
1915-1989 .... **CLC 17**
See also BYA 14; CA 17-20R; CANR 8, 29, 84; DLB 22; JRDA; MAICYA 1, 2; SATA 2, 43, 132; YAW

Farmer, Philip Jose 1918- .... **CLC 1, 19**
See also AAYA 28; BPFB 1; CA 1-4R; CANR 4, 35; DLB 8; MTCW 1; SATA 93; SCFW 2; SFW 4

Farquhar, George 1677-1707 .... **LC 21**
See also BRW 2; DAM DRAM; DLB 84; RGEL 2

Farrell, J(ames) G(ordon)
1935-1979 .... **CLC 6**
See also CA 73-76; 89-92; CANR 36; DLB 14; MTCW 1; RGEL 2; RHW; WLIT 4

Farrell, James T(homas) 1904-1979 . **CLC 1, 4, 8, 11, 66; SSC 28**
See also AMW; BPFB 1; CA 5-8R; 89-92; CANR 9, 61; DLB 4, 9, 86; DLBD 2; MTCW 1, 2; RGAL 4

Farrell, Warren (Thomas) 1943- ...... **CLC 70**
See also CA 146

Farren, Richard J.
See Betjeman, John

Farren, Richard M.
See Betjeman, John

Fassbinder, Rainer Werner
1946-1982 .... **CLC 20**
See also CA 93-96; 106; CANR 31

Fast, Howard (Melvin) 1914- ... **CLC 23, 131**
See also AAYA 16; BPFB 1; CA 1-4R; 181; CAAE 181; CAAS 18; CANR 1, 33, 54, 75, 98; CMW 4; CN 7; CPW; DAM NOV; DLB 9; INT CANR-33; MTCW 1; RHW; SATA 7; SATA-Essay 107; TCWW 2; YAW

Faulcon, Robert
See Holdstock, Robert P.

Faulkner, William (Cuthbert)
1897-1962 .... **CLC 1, 3, 6, 8, 9, 11, 14, 18, 28, 52, 68; SSC 1, 35, 42; WLC**
See also AAYA 7; AMW; AMWR 1; BPFB 1; BYA 5; CA 81-84; CANR 33; CDALB 1929-1941; DA; DA3; DAB; DAC; DAM MST, NOV; DLB 9, 11, 44, 102; DLBD 2; DLBY 1986, 1997; EXPN; EXPS; LAIT 2; MTCW 1, 2; NFS 4, 8, 13; RGAL 4; RGSF 2; SSFS 2, 5, 6, 12; TUS

Fauset, Jessie Redmon
1882(?)-1961 .... **CLC 19, 54; BLC 2**
See also AFAW 2; BW 1; CA 109; CANR 83; DAM MULT; DLB 51; FW; MAWW

Faust, Frederick (Schiller)
1892-1944(?) .... **TCLC 49**
See also Austin, Frank; Brand, Max; Challis, George; Dawson, Peter; Dexter, Martin; Evans, Evan; Frederick, John; Frost, Frederick; Manning, David; Silver, Nicholas
See also CA 108; 152; DAM POP; DLB 256; TUS

Fawkes, Guy
See Benchley, Robert (Charles)

Fearing, Kenneth (Flexner)
1902-1961 .... **CLC 51**
See also CA 93-96; CANR 59; CMW 4; DLB 9; RGAL 4

Fecamps, Elise
See Creasey, John

Federman, Raymond 1928- .... **CLC 6, 47**
See also CA 17-20R; CAAS 8; CANR 10, 43, 83, 108; CN 7; DLBY 1980

Federspiel, J(uerg) F. 1931- .... **CLC 42**
See also CA 146

Feiffer, Jules (Ralph) 1929- ...... **CLC 2, 8, 64**
See also AAYA 3; CA 17-20R; CAD; CANR 30, 59; CD 5; DAM DRAM; DLB 7, 44; INT CANR-30; MTCW 1; SATA 8, 61, 111

Fleur, Paul
See Pohl, Frederik

Flooglebuckle, Al
See Spiegelman, Art

Flora, Fletcher 1914-1969
See Queen, Ellery
See also CA 1-4R; CANR 3, 85

Flying Officer X
See Bates, H(erbert) E(rnest)

Fo, Dario 1926- .... **CLC 32, 109; DC 10**
See also CA 116; 128; CANR 68; CWW 2;
DA3; DAM DRAM; DLBY 1997; MTCW
1, 2

Fogarty, Jonathan Titulescu Esq.
See Farrell, James T(homas)

Follett, Ken(neth Martin) 1949- .... **CLC 18**
See also AAYA 6; BEST 89:4; BPFB 1; CA
81-84; CANR 13, 33, 54, 102; CMW 4;
CPW; DA3; DAM NOV, POP; DLB 87;
DLBY 1981; INT CANR-33; MTCW 1

Fontane, Theodor 1819-1898 .... **NCLC 26**
See also CDWLB 2; DLB 129; EW 6;
RGWL 2; TWA

Fontenot, Chester .... **CLC 65**

Fonvizin, Denis Ivanovich
1744(?)-1792 .... **LC 81**
See also DLB 150; RGWL 2

Foote, Horton 1916- .... **CLC 51, 91**
See also CA 73-76; CAD; CANR 34, 51,
110; CD 5; CSW; DA3; DAM DRAM;
DLB 26, 266; INT CANR-34

Foote, Mary Hallock 1847-1938 .. **TCLC 108**
See also DLB 186, 188, 202, 221

Foote, Shelby 1916- .... **CLC 75**
See also AAYA 40; CA 5-8R; CANR 3, 45,
74; CN 7; CPW; CSW; DA3; DAM NOV,
POP; DLB 2, 17; MTCW 2; RHW

Forbes, Cosmo
See Lewton, Val

Forbes, Esther 1891-1967 .... **CLC 12**
See also AAYA 17; BYA 2; CA 13-14; 25-
28R; CAP 1; CLR 27; DLB 22; JRDA;
MAICYA 1, 2; RHW; SATA 2, 100; YAW

Forche, Carolyn (Louise) 1950- .... **CLC 25,
83, 86; PC 10**
See also CA 109; 117; CANR 50, 74; CP 7;
CWP; DA3; DAM POET; DLB 5, 193;
INT CA-117; MTCW 1; RGAL 4

Ford, Elbur
See Hibbert, Eleanor Alice Burford

Ford, Ford Madox 1873-1939 ... **TCLC 1, 15,
39, 57**
See also Chaucer, Daniel
See also BRW 6; CA 104; 132; CANR 74;
CDBLB 1914-1945; DA3; DAM NOV;
DLB 34, 98, 162; MTCW 1, 2; RGEL 2;
TEA

Ford, Henry 1863-1947 .... **TCLC 73**
See also CA 115; 148

Ford, John 1586-1639 .... **LC 68; DC 8**
See also BRW 2; CDBLB Before 1660;
DA3; DAM DRAM; DFS 7; DLB 58;
IDTP; RGEL 2

Ford, John 1895-1973 .... **CLC 16**
See also CA 187; 45-48

Ford, Richard 1944- .... **CLC 46, 99**
See also AMWS 5; CA 69-72; CANR 11,
47, 86; CN 7; CSW; DLB 227; MTCW 1;
RGAL 4; RGSF 2

Ford, Webster
See Masters, Edgar Lee

Foreman, Richard 1937- .... **CLC 50**
See also CA 65-68; CAD; CANR 32, 63;
CD 5

Forester, C(ecil) S(cott) 1899-1966 ... **CLC 35**
See also CA 73-76; 25-28R; CANR 83;
DLB 191; RGEL 2; RHW; SATA 13

Forez
See Mauriac, Francois (Charles)

Forman, James
See Forman, James D(ouglas)

Forman, James D(ouglas) 1932- .... **CLC 21**
See also AAYA 17; CA 9-12R; CANR 4,
19, 42; JRDA; MAICYA 1, 2; SATA 8,
70; YAW

Fornes, Maria Irene 1930- . **CLC 39, 61; DC
10; HLCS 1**
See also CA 25-28R; CAD; CANR 28, 81;
CD 5; CWD; DLB 7; HW 1, 2; INT
CANR-28; MTCW 1; RGAL 4

Forrest, Leon (Richard) 1937-1997 .. **CLC 4;
BLCS**
See also AFAW 2; BW 2; CA 89-92; 162;
CAAS 7; CANR 25, 52, 87; CN 7; DLB
33

Forster, E(dward) M(organ)
1879-1970 ...... **CLC 1, 2, 3, 4, 9, 10, 13,
15, 22, 45, 77; SSC 27; TCLC 125;
WLC**
See also AAYA 2, 37; BRW 6; BRWR 2;
CA 13-14; 25-28R; CANR 45; CAP 1;
CDBLB 1914-1945; DA; DA3; DAB;
DAC; DAM MST, NOV; DLB 34, 98,
162, 178, 195; DLBD 10; EXPN; LAIT
3; MTCW 1, 2; NCFS 1; NFS 3, 10, 11;
RGEL 2; RGSF 2; SATA 57; SUFW;
TEA; WLIT 4

Forster, John 1812-1876 .... **NCLC 11**
See also DLB 144, 184

Forster, Margaret 1938- .... **CLC 149**
See also CA 133; CANR 62; CN 7; DLB
155

Forsyth, Frederick 1938- .... **CLC 2, 5, 36**
See also BEST 89:4; CA 85-88; CANR 38,
62; CMW 4; CN 7; CPW; DAM NOV,
POP; DLB 87; MTCW 1, 2

Forten, Charlotte L. 1837-1914 .... **TCLC 16;
BLC 2**
See also Grimke, Charlotte L(ottie) Forten
See also DLB 50, 239

Foscolo, Ugo 1778-1827 .... **NCLC 8, 97**
See also EW 5

Fosse, Bob .... **CLC 20**
See also Fosse, Robert Louis

Fosse, Robert Louis 1927-1987
See Fosse, Bob
See also CA 110; 123

Foster, Hannah Webster
1758-1840 .... **NCLC 99**
See also DLB 37, 200; RGAL 4

Foster, Stephen Collins
1826-1864 .... **NCLC 26**
See also RGAL 4

Foucault, Michel 1926-1984 . **CLC 31, 34, 69**
See also CA 105; 113; CANR 34; DLB 242;
EW 13; GFL 1789 to the Present; GLL 1;
MTCW 1, 2; TWA

**Fouque, Friedrich (Heinrich Karl) de la
Motte** 1777-1843 .... **NCLC 2**
See also DLB 90; RGWL 2; SUFW

Fourier, Charles 1772-1837 .... **NCLC 51**

Fournier, Henri Alban 1886-1914
See Alain-Fournier
See also CA 104; 179

Fournier, Pierre 1916- .... **CLC 11**
See also Gascar, Pierre
See also CA 89-92; CANR 16, 40

Fowles, John (Robert) 1926- . **CLC 1, 2, 3, 4,
6, 9, 10, 15, 33, 87; SSC 33**
See also BPFB 1; BRWS 1; CA 5-8R;
CANR 25, 71, 103; CDBLB 1960 to
Present; CN 7; DA3; DAB; DAC; DAM
MST; DLB 14, 139, 207; HGG; MTCW
1, 2; RGEL 2; RHW; SATA 22; TEA;
WLIT 4

Fox, Paula 1923- .... **CLC 2, 8, 121**
See also AAYA 3, 37; BYA 3, 8; CA 73-76;
CANR 20, 36, 62, 105; CLR 1, 44; DLB
52; JRDA; MAICYA 1, 2; MTCW 1; NFS
12; SATA 17, 60, 120; WYA; YAW

Fox, William Price (Jr.) 1926- .... **CLC 22**
See also CA 17-20R; CAAS 19; CANR 11;
CSW; DLB 2; DLBY 1981

Foxe, John 1517(?)-1587 .... **LC 14**
See also DLB 132

Frame, Janet .. **CLC 2, 3, 6, 22, 66, 96; SSC
29**
See also Clutha, Janet Paterson Frame
See also CN 7; CWP; RGEL 2; RGSF 2;
TWA

France, Anatole .... **TCLC 9**
See also Thibault, Jacques Anatole Francois
See also DLB 123; GFL 1789 to the Present;
MTCW 1; RGWL 2; SUFW

Francis, Claude .... **CLC 50**
See also CA 192

Francis, Dick 1920- .... **CLC 2, 22, 42, 102**
See also AAYA 5, 21; BEST 89:3; BPFB 1;
CA 5-8R; CANR 9, 42, 68, 100; CDBLB
1960 to Present; CMW 4; CN 7; DA3;
DAM POP; DLB 87; INT CANR-9;
MSW; MTCW 1, 2

Francis, Robert (Churchill)
1901-1987 .... **CLC 15; PC 34**
See also AMWS 9; CA 1-4R; 123; CANR
1; EXPP; PFS 12

Francis, Lord Jeffrey
See Jeffrey, Francis
See also DLB 107

Frank, Anne(lies Marie)
1929-1945 .... **TCLC 17; WLC**
See also AAYA 12; BYA 1; CA 113; 133;
CANR 68; DA; DA3; DAB; DAC; DAM
MST; LAIT 4; MAICYA 2; MAICYAS 1;
MTCW 1, 2; NCFS 2; SATA 87; SATA-
Brief 42; WYA; YAW

Frank, Bruno 1887-1945 .... **TCLC 81**
See also CA 189; DLB 118

Frank, Elizabeth 1945- .... **CLC 39**
See also CA 121; 126; CANR 78; INT 126

Frankl, Viktor E(mil) 1905-1997 ...... **CLC 93**
See also CA 65-68; 161

Franklin, Benjamin
See Hasek, Jaroslav (Matej Frantisek)

Franklin, Benjamin 1706-1790 .... **LC 25;
WLCS**
See also AMW; CDALB 1640-1865; DA;
DA3; DAB; DAC; DAM MST; DLB 24,
43, 73, 183; LAIT 1; RGAL 4; TUS

**Franklin, (Stella Maria Sarah) Miles
(Lampe)** 1879-1954 .... **TCLC 7**
See also CA 104; 164; DLB 230; FW;
MTCW 2; RGEL 2; TWA

Fraser, (Lady) Antonia (Pakenham)
1932- .... **CLC 32, 107**
See also CA 85-88; CANR 44, 65; CMW;
MTCW 1, 2; SATA-Brief 32

Fraser, George MacDonald 1925- ...... **CLC 7**
See also CA 45-48; 180; CAAE 180; CANR
2, 48, 74; MTCW 1; RHW

Fraser, Sylvia 1935- .... **CLC 64**
See also CA 45-48; CANR 1, 16, 60; CCA
1

Frayn, Michael 1933- .... **CLC 3, 7, 31, 47**
See also BRWS 7; CA 5-8R; CANR 30, 69;
CBD; CD 5; CN 7; DAM DRAM, NOV;
DLB 13, 14, 194, 245; FANT; MTCW 1,
2; SFW 4

Fraze, Candida (Merrill) 1945- .... **CLC 50**
See also CA 126

Frazer, Andrew
See Marlowe, Stephen

Frazer, J(ames) G(eorge)
1854-1941 .... **TCLC 32**
See also BRWS 3; CA 118

Frazer, Robert Caine
See Creasey, John

Frazer, Sir James George
See Frazer, J(ames) G(eorge)

Frazier, Charles 1950- .... **CLC 109**
See also AAYA 34; CA 161; CSW

Frazier, Ian 1951- .... **CLC 46**
See also CA 130; CANR 54, 93

Frederic, Harold 1856-1898 .... **NCLC 10**
See also AMW; DLB 12, 23; DLBD 13; RGAL 4

Frederick, John
See Faust, Frederick (Schiller)
See also TCWW 2

Frederick the Great 1712-1786 .... **LC 14**

Fredro, Aleksander 1793-1876 .... **NCLC 8**

Freeling, Nicolas 1927- .... **CLC 38**
See also CA 49-52; CAAS 12; CANR 1, 17, 50, 84; CMW 4; CN 7; DLB 87

Freeman, Douglas Southall
1886-1953 .... **TCLC 11**
See also CA 109; 195; DLB 17; DLBD 17

Freeman, Judith 1946- .... **CLC 55**
See also CA 148; DLB 256

Freeman, Mary E(leanor) Wilkins
1852-1930 .... **TCLC 9; SSC 1, 47**
See also CA 106; 177; DLB 12, 78, 221; EXPS; FW; HGG; MAWW; RGAL 4; RGSF 2; SSFS 4, 8; SUFW; TUS

Freeman, R(ichard) Austin
1862-1943 .... **TCLC 21**
See also CA 113; CANR 84; CMW 4; DLB 70

French, Albert 1943- .... **CLC 86**
See also BW 3; CA 167

French, Marilyn 1929- .... **CLC 10, 18, 60**
See also BPFB 1; CA 69-72; CANR 3, 31; CN 7; CPW; DAM DRAM, NOV, POP; FW; INT CANR-31; MTCW 1, 2

French, Paul
See Asimov, Isaac

Freneau, Philip Morin 1752-1832 .. **NCLC 1, 111**
See also AMWS 2; DLB 37, 43; RGAL 4

Freud, Sigmund 1856-1939 .... **TCLC 52**
See also CA 115; 133; CANR 69; EW 8; MTCW 1, 2; NCFS 3; TWA

Freytag, Gustav 1816-1895 .... **NCLC 109**
See also DLB 129

Friedan, Betty (Naomi) 1921- .... **CLC 74**
See also CA 65-68; CANR 18, 45, 74; DLB 246; FW; MTCW 1, 2

Friedlander, Saul 1932- .... **CLC 90**
See also CA 117; 130; CANR 72

Friedman, B(ernard) H(arper)
1926- .... **CLC 7**
See also CA 1-4R; CANR 3, 48

Friedman, Bruce Jay 1930- ...... **CLC 3, 5, 56**
See also CA 9-12R; CAD; CANR 25, 52, 101; CD 5; CN 7; DLB 2, 28, 244; INT CANR-25

Friel, Brian 1929- .... **CLC 5, 42, 59, 115; DC 8**
See also BRWS 5; CA 21-24R; CANR 33, 69; CBD; CD 5; DFS 11; DLB 13; MTCW 1; RGEL 2; TEA

Friis-Baastad, Babbis Ellinor
1921-1970 .... **CLC 12**
See also CA 17-20R; 134; SATA 7

Frisch, Max (Rudolf) 1911-1991 ... **CLC 3, 9, 14, 18, 32, 44**
See also CA 85-88; 134; CANR 32, 74; CD-WLB 2; DAM DRAM, NOV; DLB 69, 124; EW 13; MTCW 1, 2; RGWL 2; TCLC 121

Fromentin, Eugene (Samuel Auguste)
1820-1876 .... **NCLC 10**
See also DLB 123; GFL 1789 to the Present

Frost, Frederick
See Faust, Frederick (Schiller)
See also TCWW 2

Frost, Robert (Lee) 1874-1963 .. **CLC 1, 3, 4, 9, 10, 13, 15, 26, 34, 44; PC 1, 39; WLC**
See also AAYA 21; AMW; AMWR 1; CA 89-92; CANR 33; CDALB 1917-1929; CLR 67; DA; DA3; DAB; DAC; DAM MST, POET; DLB 54; DLBD 7; EXPP; MTCW 1, 2; PAB; PFS 1, 2, 3, 4, 5, 6, 7, 10, 13; RGAL 4; SATA 14; TUS; WP; WYA

Froude, James Anthony
1818-1894 .... **NCLC 43**
See also DLB 18, 57, 144

Froy, Herald
See Waterhouse, Keith (Spencer)

Fry, Christopher 1907- .... **CLC 2, 10, 14**
See also BRWS 3; CA 17-20R; CAAS 23; CANR 9, 30, 74; CBD; CD 5; CP 7; DAM DRAM; DLB 13; MTCW 1, 2; RGEL 2; SATA 66; TEA

Frye, (Herman) Northrop
1912-1991 .... **CLC 24, 70**
See also CA 5-8R; 133; CANR 8, 37; DLB 67, 68, 246; MTCW 1, 2; RGAL 4; TWA

Fuchs, Daniel 1909-1993 .... **CLC 8, 22**
See also CA 81-84; 142; CAAS 5; CANR 40; DLB 9, 26, 28; DLBY 1993

Fuchs, Daniel 1934- .... **CLC 34**
See also CA 37-40R; CANR 14, 48

Fuentes, Carlos 1928- .. **CLC 3, 8, 10, 13, 22, 41, 60, 113; HLC 1; SSC 24; WLC**
See also AAYA 4; AITN 2; BPFB 1; CA 69-72; CANR 10, 32, 68, 104; CDWLB 3; CWW 2; DA; DA3; DAB; DAC; DAM MST, MULT, NOV; DLB 113; DNFS 2; HW 1, 2; LAIT 3; LAW; LAWS 1; MTCW 1, 2; NFS 8; RGSF 2; RGWL 2; TWA; WLIT 1

Fuentes, Gregorio Lopez y
See Lopez y Fuentes, Gregorio

Fuertes, Gloria 1918-1998 .... **PC 27**
See also CA 178; 180; DLB 108; HW 2; SATA 115

Fugard, (Harold) Athol 1932- . **CLC 5, 9, 14, 25, 40, 80; DC 3**
See also AAYA 17; AFW; CA 85-88; CANR 32, 54; CD 5; DAM DRAM; DFS 3, 6, 10; DLB 225; DNFS 1, 2; MTCW 1; RGEL 2; WLIT 2

Fugard, Sheila 1932- .... **CLC 48**
See also CA 125

Fukuyama, Francis 1952- .... **CLC 131**
See also CA 140; CANR 72

Fuller, Charles (H., Jr.) 1939- .... **CLC 25; BLC 2; DC 1**
See also BW 2; CA 108; 112; CAD; CANR 87; CD 5; DAM DRAM, MULT; DFS 8; DLB 38, 266; INT CA-112; MTCW 1

Fuller, Henry Blake 1857-1929 .... **TCLC 103**
See also CA 108; 177; DLB 12; RGAL 4

Fuller, John (Leopold) 1937- .... **CLC 62**
See also CA 21-24R; CANR 9, 44; CP 7; DLB 40

Fuller, Margaret
See Ossoli, Sarah Margaret (Fuller)
See also AMWS 2; DLB 183, 223, 239

Fuller, Roy (Broadbent) 1912-1991 ... **CLC 4, 28**
See also BRWS 7; CA 5-8R; 135; CAAS 10; CANR 53, 83; CWRI 5; DLB 15, 20; RGEL 2; SATA 87

Fuller, Sarah Margaret
See Ossoli, Sarah Margaret (Fuller)

Fuller, Sarah Margaret
See Ossoli, Sarah Margaret (Fuller)
See also DLB 1, 59, 73

Fulton, Alice 1952- .... **CLC 52**
See also CA 116; CANR 57, 88; CP 7; CWP; DLB 193

Furphy, Joseph 1843-1912 .... **TCLC 25**
See also CA 163; DLB 230; RGEL 2

Fuson, Robert H(enderson) 1927- .... **CLC 70**
See also CA 89-92; CANR 103

Fussell, Paul 1924- .... **CLC 74**
See also BEST 90:1; CA 17-20R; CANR 8, 21, 35, 69; INT CANR-21; MTCW 1, 2

Futabatei, Shimei 1864-1909 .... **TCLC 44**
See also Futabatei Shimei
See also CA 162; MJW

Futabatei Shimei
See Futabatei, Shimei
See also DLB 180

Futrelle, Jacques 1875-1912 .... **TCLC 19**
See also CA 113; 155; CMW 4

Gaboriau, Emile 1835-1873 .... **NCLC 14**
See also CMW 4; MSW

Gadda, Carlo Emilio 1893-1973 .... **CLC 11**
See also CA 89-92; DLB 177

Gaddis, William 1922-1998 ... **CLC 1, 3, 6, 8, 10, 19, 43, 86**
See also AMWS 4; BPFB 1; CA 17-20R; 172; CANR 21, 48; CN 7; DLB 2; MTCW 1, 2; RGAL 4

Gaelique, Moruen le
See Jacob, (Cyprien-)Max

Gage, Walter
See Inge, William (Motter)

Gaines, Ernest J(ames) 1933- ...... **CLC 3, 11, 18, 86; BLC 2**
See also AAYA 18; AFAW 1, 2; AITN 1; BPFB 2; BW 2, 3; BYA 6; CA 9-12R; CANR 6, 24, 42, 75; CDALB 1968-1988; CLR 62; CN 7; CSW; DA3; DAM MULT; DLB 2, 33, 152; DLBY 1980; EXPN; LAIT 5; MTCW 1, 2; NFS 5, 7; RGAL 4; RGSF 2; RHW; SATA 86; SSFS 5; YAW

Gaitskill, Mary 1954- .... **CLC 69**
See also CA 128; CANR 61; DLB 244

Galdos, Benito Perez
See Perez Galdos, Benito
See also EW 7

Gale, Zona 1874-1938 .... **TCLC 7**
See also CA 105; 153; CANR 84; DAM DRAM; DLB 9, 78, 228; RGAL 4

Galeano, Eduardo (Hughes) 1940- . **CLC 72; HLCS 1**
See also CA 29-32R; CANR 13, 32, 100; HW 1

Galiano, Juan Valera y Alcala
See Valera y Alcala-Galiano, Juan

Galilei, Galileo 1564-1642 .... **LC 45**

Gallagher, Tess 1943- .... **CLC 18, 63; PC 9**
See also CA 106; CP 7; CWP; DAM POET; DLB 120, 212, 244

Gallant, Mavis 1922- . **CLC 7, 18, 38; SSC 5**
See also CA 69-72; CANR 29, 69; CCA 1; CN 7; DAC; DAM MST; DLB 53; MTCW 1, 2; RGEL 2; RGSF 2

Gallant, Roy A(rthur) 1924- .... **CLC 17**
See also CA 5-8R; CANR 4, 29, 54; CLR 30; MAICYA 1, 2; SATA 4, 68, 110

Gallico, Paul (William) 1897-1976 ..... **CLC 2**
See also AITN 1; CA 5-8R; 69-72; CANR 23; DLB 9, 171; FANT; MAICYA 1, 2; SATA 13

Gallo, Max Louis 1932- .... **CLC 95**
See also CA 85-88

Gallois, Lucien
See Desnos, Robert

Gallup, Ralph
See Whitemore, Hugh (John)

Galsworthy, John 1867-1933 .... **TCLC 1, 45; SSC 22; WLC**
See also BRW 6; CA 104; 141; CANR 75; CDBLB 1890-1914; DA; DA3; DAB; DAC; DAM DRAM, MST, NOV; DLB 10, 34, 98, 162; DLBD 16; MTCW 1; RGEL 2; SSFS 3; TEA

Gogarty, Oliver St. John
1878-1957 .... **TCLC 15**
See also CA 109; 150; DLB 15, 19; RGEL 2

Gogol, Nikolai (Vasilyevich)
1809-1852 .... **NCLC 5, 15, 31; DC 1; SSC 4, 29, 52; WLC**
See also DA; DAB; DAC; DAM DRAM, MST; DFS 12; DLB 198; EW 6; EXPS; RGSF 2; RGWL 2; SSFS 7; TWA

Goines, Donald 1937(?)-1974 . **CLC 80; BLC 2**
See also AITN 1; BW 1, 3; CA 124; 114; CANR 82; CMW 4; DA3; DAM MULT, POP; DLB 33

Gold, Herbert 1924- ... **CLC 4, 7, 14, 42, 152**
See also CA 9-12R; CANR 17, 45; CN 7; DLB 2; DLBY 1981

Goldbarth, Albert 1948- .... **CLC 5, 38**
See also CA 53-56; CANR 6, 40; CP 7; DLB 120

Goldberg, Anatol 1910-1982 .... **CLC 34**
See also CA 131; 117

Goldemberg, Isaac 1945- .... **CLC 52**
See also CA 69-72; CAAS 12; CANR 11, 32; HW 1; WLIT 1

Golding, William (Gerald)
1911-1993 ..... **CLC 1, 2, 3, 8, 10, 17, 27, 58, 81; WLC**
See also AAYA 5; BPFB 2; BRWR 1; BRWS 1; BYA 2; CA 5-8R; 141; CANR 13, 33, 54; CDBLB 1945-1960; DA; DA3; DAB; DAC; DAM MST, NOV; DLB 15, 100, 255; EXPN; HGG; LAIT 4; MTCW 1, 2; NFS 2; RGEL 2; RHW; SFW 4; TEA; WLIT 4; YAW

Goldman, Emma 1869-1940 .... **TCLC 13**
See also CA 110; 150; DLB 221; FW; RGAL 4; TUS

Goldman, Francisco 1954- .... **CLC 76**
See also CA 162

Goldman, William (W.) 1931- ...... **CLC 1, 48**
See also BPFB 2; CA 9-12R; CANR 29, 69, 106; CN 7; DLB 44; FANT; IDFW 3, 4

Goldmann, Lucien 1913-1970 .... **CLC 24**
See also CA 25-28; CAP 2

Goldoni, Carlo 1707-1793 .... **LC 4**
See also DAM DRAM; EW 4; RGWL 2

Goldsberry, Steven 1949- .... **CLC 34**
See also CA 131

Goldsmith, Oliver 1730-1774 .. **LC 2, 48; DC 8; WLC**
See also BRW 3; CDBLB 1660-1789; DA; DAB; DAC; DAM DRAM, MST, NOV, POET; DFS 1; DLB 39, 89, 104, 109, 142; IDTP; RGEL 2; SATA 26; TEA; WLIT 3

Goldsmith, Peter
See Priestley, J(ohn) B(oynton)

Gombrowicz, Witold 1904-1969 .... **CLC 4, 7, 11, 49**
See also CA 19-20; 25-28R; CANR 105; CAP 2; CDWLB 4; DAM DRAM; DLB 215; EW 12; RGWL 2; TWA

Gomez de Avellaneda, Gertrudis
1814-1873 .... **NCLC 111**
See also LAW

Gomez de la Serna, Ramon
1888-1963 .... **CLC 9**
See also CA 153; 116; CANR 79; HW 1, 2

Goncharov, Ivan Alexandrovich
1812-1891 .... **NCLC 1, 63**
See also DLB 238; EW 6; RGWL 2

Goncourt, Edmond (Louis Antoine Huot) de
1822-1896 .... **NCLC 7**
See also DLB 123; EW 7; GFL 1789 to the Present; RGWL 2

Goncourt, Jules (Alfred Huot) de
1830-1870 .... **NCLC 7**
See also DLB 123; EW 7; GFL 1789 to the Present; RGWL 2

Gongora (y Argote), Luis de
1561-1627 .... **LC 72**
See also RGWL 2

Gontier, Fernande 19(?)- .... **CLC 50**

Gonzalez Martinez, Enrique
1871-1952 .... **TCLC 72**
See also CA 166; CANR 81; HW 1, 2

Goodison, Lorna 1947- .... **PC 36**
See also CA 142; CANR 88; CP 7; CWP; DLB 157

Goodman, Paul 1911-1972 ..... **CLC 1, 2, 4, 7**
See also CA 19-20; 37-40R; CAD; CANR 34; CAP 2; DLB 130, 246; MTCW 1; RGAL 4

Gordimer, Nadine 1923- ...... **CLC 3, 5, 7, 10, 18, 33, 51, 70, 123, 160, 161; SSC 17; WLCS**
See also AAYA 39; AFW; BRWS 2; CA 5-8R; CANR 3, 28, 56, 88; CN 7; DA; DA3; DAB; DAC; DAM MST, NOV; DLB 225; EXPS; INT CANR-28; MTCW 1, 2; NFS 4; RGEL 2; RGSF 2; SSFS 2, 14; TWA; WLIT 2; YAW

Gordon, Adam Lindsay
1833-1870 .... **NCLC 21**
See also DLB 230

Gordon, Caroline 1895-1981 . **CLC 6, 13, 29, 83; SSC 15**
See also AMW; CA 11-12; 103; CANR 36; CAP 1; DLB 4, 9, 102; DLBD 17; DLBY 1981; MTCW 1, 2; RGAL 4; RGSF 2

Gordon, Charles William 1860-1937
See Connor, Ralph
See also CA 109

Gordon, Mary (Catherine) 1949- .... **CLC 13, 22, 128**
See also AMWS 4; BPFB 2; CA 102; CANR 44, 92; CN 7; DLB 6; DLBY 1981; FW; INT CA-102; MTCW 1

Gordon, N. J.
See Bosman, Herman Charles

Gordon, Sol 1923- .... **CLC 26**
See also CA 53-56; CANR 4; SATA 11

Gordone, Charles 1925-1995 .. **CLC 1, 4; DC 8**
See also BW 1, 3; CA 93-96; 180; 150; CAAE 180; CAD; CANR 55; DAM DRAM; DLB 7; INT 93-96; MTCW 1

Gore, Catherine 1800-1861 .... **NCLC 65**
See also DLB 116; RGEL 2

Gorenko, Anna Andreevna
See Akhmatova, Anna

Gorky, Maxim .... **TCLC 8; SSC 28; WLC**
See also Peshkov, Alexei Maximovich
See also DAB; DFS 9; EW 8; MTCW 2; TWA

Goryan, Sirak
See Saroyan, William

Gosse, Edmund (William)
1849-1928 .... **TCLC 28**
See also CA 117; DLB 57, 144, 184; RGEL 2

Gotlieb, Phyllis Fay (Bloom) 1926- .. **CLC 18**
See also CA 13-16R; CANR 7; DLB 88, 251; SFW 4

Gottesman, S. D.
See Kornbluth, C(yril) M.; Pohl, Frederik

Gottfried von Strassburg fl. c.
1170-1215 .... **CMLC 10**
See also CDWLB 2; DLB 138; EW 1; RGWL 2

Gotthelf, Jeremias 1797-1854 .... **NCLC 115**
See also DLB 133; RGWL 2

Gould, Lois 1932(?)-2002 .... **CLC 4, 10**
See also CA 77-80; CANR 29; MTCW 1

Gould, Stephen Jay 1941-2002 .... **CLC 163**
See also AAYA 26; BEST 90:2; CA 77-80; CANR 10, 27, 56, 75; CPW; INT CANR-27; MTCW 1, 2

Gourmont, Remy(-Marie-Charles) de
1858-1915 .... **TCLC 17**
See also CA 109; 150; GFL 1789 to the Present; MTCW 2

Govier, Katherine 1948- .... **CLC 51**
See also CA 101; CANR 18, 40; CCA 1

Gower, John c. 1330-1408 .... **LC 76**
See also BRW 1; DLB 146; RGEL 2

Goyen, (Charles) William
1915-1983 .... **CLC 5, 8, 14, 40**
See also AITN 2; CA 5-8R; 110; CANR 6, 71; DLB 2, 218; DLBY 1983; INT CANR-6

Goytisolo, Juan 1931- .... **CLC 5, 10, 23, 133; HLC 1**
See also CA 85-88; CANR 32, 61; CWW 2; DAM MULT; GLL 2; HW 1, 2; MTCW 1, 2

Gozzano, Guido 1883-1916 .... **PC 10**
See also CA 154; DLB 114

Gozzi, (Conte) Carlo 1720-1806 .... **NCLC 23**

Grabbe, Christian Dietrich
1801-1836 .... **NCLC 2**
See also DLB 133; RGWL 2

Grace, Patricia Frances 1937- .... **CLC 56**
See also CA 176; CN 7; RGSF 2

Gracian y Morales, Baltasar
1601-1658 .... **LC 15**

Gracq, Julien .... **CLC 11, 48**
See also Poirier, Louis
See also CWW 2; DLB 83; GFL 1789 to the Present

Grade, Chaim 1910-1982 .... **CLC 10**
See also CA 93-96; 107

Graduate of Oxford, A
See Ruskin, John

Grafton, Garth
See Duncan, Sara Jeannette

Grafton, Sue 1940- .... **CLC 163**
See also AAYA 11; BEST 90:3; CA 108; CANR 31, 55; CMW 4; CPW; CSW; DA3; DAM POP; DLB 226; FW; MSW

Graham, John
See Phillips, David Graham

Graham, Jorie 1951- .... **CLC 48, 118**
See also CA 111; CANR 63; CP 7; CWP; DLB 120; PFS 10

Graham, R(obert) B(ontine) Cunninghame
See Cunninghame Graham, Robert (Gallnigad) Bontine
See also DLB 98, 135, 174; RGEL 2; RGSF 2

Graham, Robert
See Haldeman, Joe (William)

Graham, Tom
See Lewis, (Harry) Sinclair

Graham, W(illiam) S(idney)
1918-1986 .... **CLC 29**
See also BRWS 7; CA 73-76; 118; DLB 20; RGEL 2

Graham, Winston (Mawdsley)
1910- .... **CLC 23**
See also CA 49-52; CANR 2, 22, 45, 66; CMW 4; CN 7; DLB 77; RHW

Grahame, Kenneth 1859-1932 .... **TCLC 64**
See also BYA 5; CA 108; 136; CANR 80; CLR 5; CWRI 5; DA3; DAB; DLB 34, 141, 178; FANT; MAICYA 1, 2; MTCW 2; RGEL 2; SATA 100; TEA; WCH; YABC 1

Granger, Darius John
See Marlowe, Stephen

Grisham, John 1955- .... **CLC 84**
See also AAYA 14; BPFB 2; CA 138;
CANR 47, 69; CMW 4; CN 7; CPW;
CSW; DA3; DAM POP; MSW; MTCW 2
Grossman, David 1954- .... **CLC 67**
See also CA 138; CWW 2
Grossman, Vasily (Semenovich)
1905-1964 .... **CLC 41**
See also CA 124; 130; MTCW 1
Grove, Frederick Philip .... **TCLC 4**
See also Greve, Felix Paul (Berthold
Friedrich)
See also DLB 92; RGEL 2
Grubb
See Crumb, R(obert)
Grumbach, Doris (Isaac) 1918- . **CLC 13, 22,**
64
See also CA 5-8R; CAAS 2; CANR 9, 42,
70; CN 7; INT CANR-9; MTCW 2
Grundtvig, Nicolai Frederik Severin
1783-1872 .... **NCLC 1**
Grunge
See Crumb, R(obert)
Grunwald, Lisa 1959- .... **CLC 44**
See also CA 120
Guare, John 1938- .... **CLC 8, 14, 29, 67**
See also CA 73-76; CAD; CANR 21, 69;
CD 5; DAM DRAM; DFS 8, 13; DLB 7,
249; MTCW 1, 2; RGAL 4
Gubar, Susan (David) 1944- .... **CLC 145**
See also CA 108; CANR 45, 70; FW;
MTCW 1; RGAL 4
Gudjonsson, Halldor Kiljan 1902-1998
See Laxness, Halldor
See also CA 103; 164; CWW 2
Guenter, Erich
See Eich, Guenter
Guest, Barbara 1920- .... **CLC 34**
See also CA 25-28R; CANR 11, 44, 84; CP
7; CWP; DLB 5, 193
Guest, Edgar A(lbert) 1881-1959 ... **TCLC 95**
See also CA 112; 168
Guest, Judith (Ann) 1936- .... **CLC 8, 30**
See also AAYA 7; CA 77-80; CANR 15,
75; DA3; DAM NOV, POP; EXPN; INT
CANR-15; LAIT 5; MTCW 1, 2; NFS 1
Guevara, Che .... **CLC 87; HLC 1**
See also Guevara (Serna), Ernesto
Guevara (Serna), Ernesto
1928-1967 .... **CLC 87; HLC 1**
See also Guevara, Che
See also CA 127; 111; CANR 56; DAM
MULT; HW 1
Guicciardini, Francesco 1483-1540 ..... **LC 49**
Guild, Nicholas M. 1944- .... **CLC 33**
See also CA 93-96
Guillemin, Jacques
See Sartre, Jean-Paul
Guillen, Jorge 1893-1984 . **CLC 11; HLCS 1;**
PC 35
See also CA 89-92; 112; DAM MULT,
POET; DLB 108; HW 1; RGWL 2
Guillen, Nicolas (Cristobal)
1902-1989 .... **CLC 48, 79; BLC 2; HLC**
1; PC 23
See also BW 2; CA 116; 125; 129; CANR
84; DAM MST, MULT, POET; HW 1;
LAW; RGWL 2; WP
Guillen y Alavarez, Jorge
See Guillen, Jorge
Guillevic, (Eugene) 1907-1997 .... **CLC 33**
See also CA 93-96; CWW 2
Guillois
See Desnos, Robert
Guillois, Valentin
See Desnos, Robert
Guimaraes Rosa, Joao
See Rosa, Joao Guimaraes
See also LAW

Guimaraes Rosa, Joao 1908-1967
See also CA 175; HLCS 2; LAW; RGSF 2;
RGWL 2
Guiney, Louise Imogen
1861-1920 .... **TCLC 41**
See also CA 160; DLB 54; RGAL 4
Guinizelli, Guido c. 1230-1276 ...... **CMLC 49**
Guiraldes, Ricardo (Guillermo)
1886-1927 .... **TCLC 39**
See also CA 131; HW 1; LAW; MTCW 1
Gumilev, Nikolai (Stepanovich)
1886-1921 .... **TCLC 60**
See also CA 165
Gunesekera, Romesh 1954- .... **CLC 91**
See also CA 159; CN 7
Gunn, Bill .... **CLC 5**
See also Gunn, William Harrison
See also DLB 38
Gunn, Thom(son William) 1929- .. **CLC 3, 6,**
18, 32, 81; PC 26
See also BRWS 4; CA 17-20R; CANR 9,
33; CDBLB 1960 to Present; CP 7; DAM
POET; DLB 27; INT CANR-33; MTCW
1; PFS 9; RGEL 2
Gunn, William Harrison 1934(?)-1989
See Gunn, Bill
See also AITN 1; BW 1, 3; CA 13-16R;
128; CANR 12, 25, 76
Gunn Allen, Paula
See Allen, Paula Gunn
Gunnars, Kristjana 1948- .... **CLC 69**
See also CA 113; CCA 1; CP 7; CWP; DLB
60
Gurdjieff, G(eorgei) I(vanovich)
1877(?)-1949 .... **TCLC 71**
See also CA 157
Gurganus, Allan 1947- .... **CLC 70**
See also BEST 90:1; CA 135; CN 7; CPW;
CSW; DAM POP; GLL 1
Gurney, A. R.
See Gurney, A(lbert) R(amsdell), Jr.
See also DLB 266
Gurney, A(lbert) R(amsdell), Jr.
1930- .... **CLC 32, 50, 54**
See also Gurney, A. R.
See also AMWS 5; CA 77-80; CAD; CANR
32, 64; CD 5; DAM DRAM
Gurney, Ivor (Bertie) 1890-1937 ... **TCLC 33**
See also BRW 6; CA 167; PAB; RGEL 2
Gurney, Peter
See Gurney, A(lbert) R(amsdell), Jr.
Guro, Elena 1877-1913 .... **TCLC 56**
Gustafson, James M(oody) 1925- ... **CLC 100**
See also CA 25-28R; CANR 37
Gustafson, Ralph (Barker)
1909-1995 .... **CLC 36**
See also CA 21-24R; CANR 8, 45, 84; CP
7; DLB 88; RGEL 2
Gut, Gom
See Simenon, Georges (Jacques Christian)
Guterson, David 1956- .... **CLC 91**
See also CA 132; CANR 73; MTCW 2;
NFS 13
Guthrie, A(lfred) B(ertram), Jr.
1901-1991 .... **CLC 23**
See also CA 57-60; 134; CANR 24; DLB 6,
212; SATA 62; SATA-Obit 67
Guthrie, Isobel
See Grieve, C(hristopher) M(urray)
Guthrie, Woodrow Wilson 1912-1967
See Guthrie, Woody
See also CA 113; 93-96
Guthrie, Woody .... **CLC 35**
See also Guthrie, Woodrow Wilson
See also LAIT 3
Gutierrez Najera, Manuel 1859-1895
See also HLCS 2; LAW

Guy, Rosa (Cuthbert) 1925- .... **CLC 26**
See also AAYA 4, 37; BW 2; CA 17-20R;
CANR 14, 34, 83; CLR 13; DLB 33;
DNFS 1; JRDA; MAICYA 1, 2; SATA 14,
62, 122; YAW
Gwendolyn
See Bennett, (Enoch) Arnold
H. D. .... **CLC 3, 8, 14, 31, 34, 73; PC 5**
See also Doolittle, Hilda
H. de V.
See Buchan, John
Haavikko, Paavo Juhani 1931- .. **CLC 18, 34**
See also CA 106
Habbema, Koos
See Heijermans, Herman
Habermas, Juergen 1929- .... **CLC 104**
See also CA 109; CANR 85; DLB 242
Habermas, Jurgen
See Habermas, Juergen
Hacker, Marilyn 1942- . **CLC 5, 9, 23, 72, 91**
See also CA 77-80; CANR 68; CP 7; CWP;
DAM POET; DLB 120; FW; GLL 2
Hadrian 76-138 .... **CMLC 52**
Haeckel, Ernst Heinrich (Philipp August)
1834-1919 .... **TCLC 83**
See also CA 157
Hafiz c. 1326-1389(?) .... **CMLC 34**
See also RGWL 2
Haggard, H(enry) Rider
1856-1925 .... **TCLC 11**
See also BRWS 3; BYA 4, 5; CA 108; 148;
DLB 70, 156, 174, 178; FANT; MTCW
2; RGEL 2; RHW; SATA 16; SCFW; SFW
4; SUFW; WLIT 4
Hagiosy, L.
See Larbaud, Valery (Nicolas)
Hagiwara, Sakutaro 1886-1942 .... **TCLC 60;**
PC 18
See also CA 154
Haig, Fenil
See Ford, Ford Madox
Haig-Brown, Roderick (Langmere)
1908-1976 .... **CLC 21**
See also CA 5-8R; 69-72; CANR 4, 38, 83;
CLR 31; CWRI 5; DLB 88; MAICYA 1,
2; SATA 12
Hailey, Arthur 1920- .... **CLC 5**
See also AITN 2; BEST 90:3; BPFB 2; CA
1-4R; CANR 2, 36, 75; CCA 1; CN 7;
CPW; DAM NOV, POP; DLB 88; DLBY
1982; MTCW 1, 2
Hailey, Elizabeth Forsythe 1938- ..... **CLC 40**
See also CA 93-96; CAAE 188; CAAS 1;
CANR 15, 48; INT CANR-15
Haines, John (Meade) 1924- .... **CLC 58**
See also CA 17-20R; CANR 13, 34; CSW;
DLB 5, 212
Hakluyt, Richard 1552-1616 .... **LC 31**
See also DLB 136; RGEL 2
Haldeman, Joe (William) 1943- .... **CLC 61**
See also Graham, Robert
See also AAYA 38; CA 53-56, 179; CAAE
179; CAAS 25; CANR 6, 70, 72; DLB 8;
INT CANR-6; SCFW 2; SFW 4
Hale, Sarah Josepha (Buell)
1788-1879 .... **NCLC 75**
See also DLB 1, 42, 73, 243
Halevy, Elie 1870-1937 .... **TCLC 104**
Haley, Alex(ander Murray Palmer)
1921-1992 .... **CLC 8, 12, 76; BLC 2**
See also AAYA 26; BPFB 2; BW 2, 3; CA
77-80; 136; CANR 61; CDALBS; CPW;
CSW; DA; DA3; DAB; DAC; DAM MST,
MULT, POP; DLB 38; LAIT 5; MTCW
1, 2; NFS 9
Haliburton, Thomas Chandler
1796-1865 .... **NCLC 15**
See also DLB 11, 99; RGEL 2; RGSF 2

Harriss, Will(ard Irvin) 1922- .... CLC 34
  See also CA 111
Harson, Sley
  See Ellison, Harlan (Jay)
Hart, Ellis
  See Ellison, Harlan (Jay)
Hart, Josephine 1942(?)- .... CLC 70
  See also CA 138; CANR 70; CPW; DAM
  POP
Hart, Moss 1904-1961 .... CLC 66
  See also CA 109; 89-92; CANR 84; DAM
  DRAM; DFS 1; DLB 7, 266; RGAL 4
Harte, (Francis) Bret(t)
  1836(?)-1902 .... TCLC 1, 25; SSC 8;
  WLC
  See also AMWS 2; CA 104; 140; CANR
  80; CDALB 1865-1917; DA; DA3; DAC;
  DAM MST; DLB 12, 64, 74, 79, 186;
  EXPS; LAIT 2; RGAL 4; RGSF 2; SATA
  26; SSFS 3; TUS
Hartley, L(eslie) P(oles) 1895-1972 ... CLC 2,
  22
  See also BRWS 7; CA 45-48; 37-40R;
  CANR 33; DLB 15, 139; HGG; MTCW
  1, 2; RGEL 2; RGSF 2; SUFW
Hartman, Geoffrey H. 1929- .... CLC 27
  See also CA 117; 125; CANR 79; DLB 67
Hartmann, Sadakichi 1869-1944 ... TCLC 73
  See also CA 157; DLB 54
Hartmann von Aue c. 1170-c.
  1210 .... CMLC 15
  See also CDWLB 2; DLB 138; RGWL 2
Hartog, Jan de
  See de Hartog, Jan
Haruf, Kent 1943- .... CLC 34
  See also CA 149; CANR 91
Harwood, Ronald 1934- .... CLC 32
  See also CA 1-4R; CANR 4, 55; CBD; CD
  5; DAM DRAM, MST; DLB 13
Hasegawa Tatsunosuke
  See Futabatei, Shimei
Hasek, Jaroslav (Matej Frantisek)
  1883-1923 .... TCLC 4
  See also CA 104; 129; CDWLB 4; DLB
  215; EW 9; MTCW 1, 2; RGSF 2; RGWL
  2
Hass, Robert 1941- ... CLC 18, 39, 99; PC 16
  See also AMWS 6; CA 111; CANR 30, 50,
  71; CP 7; DLB 105, 206; RGAL 4; SATA
  94
Hastings, Hudson
  See Kuttner, Henry
Hastings, Selina .... CLC 44
Hathorne, John 1641-1717 .... LC 38
Hatteras, Amelia
  See Mencken, H(enry) L(ouis)
Hatteras, Owen .... TCLC 18
  See also Mencken, H(enry) L(ouis); Nathan,
  George Jean
Hauptmann, Gerhart (Johann Robert)
  1862-1946 .... TCLC 4; SSC 37
  See also CA 104; 153; CDWLB 2; DAM
  DRAM; DLB 66, 118; EW 8; RGSF 2;
  RGWL 2; TWA
Havel, Vaclav 1936- ..... CLC 25, 58, 65, 123;
  DC 6
  See also CA 104; CANR 36, 63; CDWLB
  4; CWW 2; DA3; DAM DRAM; DFS 10;
  DLB 232; MTCW 1, 2
Haviaras, Stratis .... CLC 33
  See also Chaviaras, Strates
Hawes, Stephen 1475(?)-1529(?) .... LC 17
  See also DLB 132; RGEL 2
Hawkes, John (Clendennin Burne, Jr.)
  1925-1998 .. CLC 1, 2, 3, 4, 7, 9, 14, 15,
  27, 49
  See also BPFB 2; CA 1-4R; 167; CANR 2,
  47, 64; CN 7; DLB 2, 7, 227; DLBY
  1980, 1998; MTCW 1, 2; RGAL 4

Hawking, S. W.
  See Hawking, Stephen W(illiam)
Hawking, Stephen W(illiam) 1942- . CLC 63,
  105
  See also AAYA 13; BEST 89:1; CA 126;
  129; CANR 48; CPW; DA3; MTCW 2
Hawkins, Anthony Hope
  See Hope, Anthony
Hawthorne, Julian 1846-1934 .... TCLC 25
  See also CA 165; HGG
Hawthorne, Nathaniel 1804-1864 ... NCLC 2,
  10, 17, 23, 39, 79, 95; SSC 3, 29, 39;
  WLC
  See also AAYA 18; AMW; AMWR 1; BPFB
  2; BYA 3; CDALB 1640-1865; DA; DA3;
  DAB; DAC; DAM MST, NOV; DLB 1,
  74, 183, 223; EXPN; EXPS; HGG; LAIT
  1; NFS 1; RGAL 4; RGSF 2; SSFS 1, 7,
  11, 15; SUFW; TUS; WCH; YABC 2
Haxton, Josephine Ayres 1921-
  See Douglas, Ellen
  See also CA 115; CANR 41, 83
Hayaseca y Eizaguirre, Jorge
  See Echegaray (y Eizaguirre), Jose (Maria
  Waldo)
Hayashi, Fumiko 1904-1951 .... TCLC 27
  See also Hayashi Fumiko
  See also CA 161
Hayashi Fumiko
  See Hayashi, Fumiko
  See also DLB 180
Haycraft, Anna (Margaret) 1932-
  See Ellis, Alice Thomas
  See also CA 122; CANR 85, 90; MTCW 2
Hayden, Robert E(arl) 1913-1980 . CLC 5, 9,
  14, 37; BLC 2; PC 6
  See also AFAW 1, 2; AMWS 2; BW 1, 3;
  CA 69-72; 97-100; CABS 2; CANR 24,
  75, 82; CDALB 1941-1968; DA; DAC;
  DAM MST, MULT, POET; DLB 5, 76;
  EXPP; MTCW 1, 2; PFS 1; RGAL 4;
  SATA 19; SATA-Obit 26; WP
Hayek, F(riedrich) A(ugust von)
  1899-1992 .... TCLC 109
  See also CA 93-96; 137; CANR 20; MTCW
  1, 2
Hayford, J(oseph) E(phraim) Casely
  See Casely-Hayford, J(oseph) E(phraim)
Hayman, Ronald 1932- .... CLC 44
  See also CA 25-28R; CANR 18, 50, 88; CD
  5; DLB 155
Hayne, Paul Hamilton 1830-1886 . NCLC 94
  See also DLB 3, 64, 79, 248; RGAL 4
Hays, Mary 1760-1843 .... NCLC 114
  See also DLB 142, 158; RGEL 2
Haywood, Eliza (Fowler)
  1693(?)-1756 .... LC 1, 44
  See also DLB 39; RGEL 2
Hazlitt, William 1778-1830 ...... NCLC 29, 82
  See also BRW 4; DLB 110, 158; RGEL 2;
  TEA
Hazzard, Shirley 1931- .... CLC 18
  See also CA 9-12R; CANR 4, 70; CN 7;
  DLBY 1982; MTCW 1
Head, Bessie 1937-1986 .... CLC 25, 67; BLC
  2; SSC 52
  See also AFW; BW 2, 3; CA 29-32R; 119;
  CANR 25, 82; CDWLB 3; DA3; DAM
  MULT; DLB 117, 225; EXPS; FW;
  MTCW 1, 2; RGSF 2; SSFS 5, 13; WLIT
  2
Headon, (Nicky) Topper 1956(?)- ..... CLC 30
Heaney, Seamus (Justin) 1939- ..... CLC 5, 7,
  14, 25, 37, 74, 91; PC 18; WLCS
  See also BRWR 1; BRWS 2; CA 85-88;
  CANR 25, 48, 75, 91; CDBLB 1960 to
  Present; CP 7; DA3; DAB; DAM POET;

DLB 40; DLBY 1995; EXPP; MTCW 1,
  2; PAB; PFS 2, 5, 8; RGEL 2; TEA;
  WLIT 4
Hearn, (Patricio) Lafcadio (Tessima Carlos)
  1850-1904 .... TCLC 9
  See also CA 105; 166; DLB 12, 78, 189;
  HGG; RGAL 4
Hearne, Vicki 1946-2001 .... CLC 56
  See also CA 139; 201
Hearon, Shelby 1931- .... CLC 63
  See also AITN 2; AMWS 8; CA 25-28R;
  CANR 18, 48, 103; CSW
Heat-Moon, William Least .... CLC 29
  See also Trogdon, William (Lewis)
  See also AAYA 9
Hebbel, Friedrich 1813-1863 .... NCLC 43
  See also CDWLB 2; DAM DRAM; DLB
  129; EW 6; RGWL 2
Hebert, Anne 1916-2000 .... CLC 4, 13, 29
  See also CA 85-88; 187; CANR 69; CCA
  1; CWP; CWW 2; DA3; DAC; DAM
  MST, POET; DLB 68; GFL 1789 to the
  Present; MTCW 1, 2
Hecht, Anthony (Evan) 1923- ...... CLC 8, 13,
  19
  See also AMWS 10; CA 9-12R; CANR 6,
  108; CP 7; DAM POET; DLB 5, 169; PFS
  6; WP
Hecht, Ben 1894-1964 .... CLC 8
  See also CA 85-88; DFS 9; DLB 7, 9, 25,
  26, 28, 86; FANT; IDFW 3, 4; RGAL 4;
  TCLC 101
Hedayat, Sadeq 1903-1951 .... TCLC 21
  See also CA 120; RGSF 2
Hegel, Georg Wilhelm Friedrich
  1770-1831 .... NCLC 46
  See also DLB 90; TWA
Heidegger, Martin 1889-1976 .... CLC 24
  See also CA 81-84; 65-68; CANR 34;
  MTCW 1, 2
Heidenstam, (Carl Gustaf) Verner von
  1859-1940 .... TCLC 5
  See also CA 104
Heifner, Jack 1946- .... CLC 11
  See also CA 105; CANR 47
Heijermans, Herman 1864-1924 .... TCLC 24
  See also CA 123
Heilbrun, Carolyn G(old) 1926- .... CLC 25
  See also Cross, Amanda
  See also CA 45-48; CANR 1, 28, 58, 94;
  FW
Hein, Christoph 1944- .... CLC 154
  See also CA 158; CANR 108; CDWLB 2;
  CWW 2; DLB 124
Heine, Heinrich 1797-1856 .... NCLC 4, 54;
  PC 25
  See also CDWLB 2; DLB 90; EW 5; RGWL
  2; TWA
Heinemann, Larry (Curtiss) 1944- .. CLC 50
  See also CA 110; CAAS 21; CANR 31, 81;
  DLBD 9; INT CANR-31
Heiney, Donald (William) 1921-1993
  See Harris, MacDonald
  See also CA 1-4R; 142; CANR 3, 58; FANT
Heinlein, Robert A(nson) 1907-1988 . CLC 1,
  3, 8, 14, 26, 55; SSC 55
  See also AAYA 17; BPFB 2; BYA 4, 13;
  CA 1-4R; 125; CANR 1, 20, 53; CLR 75;
  CPW; DA3; DAM POP; DLB 8; EXPS;
  JRDA; LAIT 5; MAICYA 1, 2; MTCW 1,
  2; RGAL 4; SATA 9, 69; SATA-Obit 56;
  SCFW; SFW 4; SSFS 7; YAW
Helforth, John
  See Doolittle, Hilda
Heliodorus fl. 3rd cent. - .... CMLC 52
Hellenhofferu, Vojtech Kapristian z
  See Hasek, Jaroslav (Matej Frantisek)

Hildesheimer, Wolfgang 1916-1991 .. **CLC 49**
See also CA 101; 135; DLB 69, 124

Hill, Geoffrey (William) 1932- ...... **CLC 5, 8, 18, 45**
See also BRWS 5; CA 81-84; CANR 21, 89; CDBLB 1960 to Present; CP 7; DAM POET; DLB 40; MTCW 1; RGEL 2

Hill, George Roy 1921- .... **CLC 26**
See also CA 110; 122

Hill, John
See Koontz, Dean R(ay)

Hill, Susan (Elizabeth) 1942- ...... **CLC 4, 113**
See also CA 33-36R; CANR 29, 69; CN 7; DAB; DAM MST, NOV; DLB 14, 139; HGG; MTCW 1; RHW

Hillard, Asa G. III .... **CLC 70**

Hillerman, Tony 1925- .... **CLC 62**
See also AAYA 40; BEST 89:1; BPFB 2; CA 29-32R; CANR 21, 42, 65, 97; CMW 4; CPW; DA3; DAM POP; DLB 206; MSW; RGAL 4; SATA 6; TCWW 2; YAW

Hillesum, Etty 1914-1943 .... **TCLC 49**
See also CA 137

Hilliard, Noel (Harvey) 1929-1996 ... **CLC 15**
See also CA 9-12R; CANR 7, 69; CN 7

Hillis, Rick 1956- .... **CLC 66**
See also CA 134

Hilton, James 1900-1954 .... **TCLC 21**
See also CA 108; 169; DLB 34, 77; FANT; SATA 34

Himes, Chester (Bomar) 1909-1984 .. **CLC 2, 4, 7, 18, 58, 108; BLC 2**
See also AFAW 2; BPFB 2; BW 2; CA 25-28R; 114; CANR 22, 89; CMW 4; DAM MULT; DLB 2, 76, 143, 226; MSW; MTCW 1, 2; RGAL 4

Hinde, Thomas .... **CLC 6, 11**
See also Chitty, Thomas Willes

Hine, (William) Daryl 1936- .... **CLC 15**
See also CA 1-4R; CAAS 15; CANR 1, 20; CP 7; DLB 60

Hinkson, Katharine Tynan
See Tynan, Katharine

Hinojosa(-Smith), Rolando (R.) 1929-
See also CA 131; CAAS 16; CANR 62; DAM MULT; DLB 82; HLC 1; HW 1, 2; MTCW 2; RGAL 4

Hinton, S(usan) E(loise) 1950- .. **CLC 30, 111**
See also AAYA 2, 33; BPFB 2; BYA 2, 3; CA 81-84; CANR 32, 62, 92; CDALBS; CLR 3, 23; CPW; DA; DAB; DAC; DAM MST, NOV; JRDA; LAIT 5; MAICYA 1, 2; MTCW 1, 2; NFS 5, 9, 15; SATA 19, 58, 115; WYA; YAW

Hippius, Zinaida .... **TCLC 9**
See also Gippius, Zinaida (Nikolayevna)

Hiraoka, Kimitake 1925-1970
See Mishima, Yukio
See also CA 97-100; 29-32R; DA3; DAM DRAM; MTCW 1, 2

Hirsch, E(ric) D(onald), Jr. 1928- .... **CLC 79**
See also CA 25-28R; CANR 27, 51; DLB 67; INT CANR-27; MTCW 1

Hirsch, Edward 1950- .... **CLC 31, 50**
See also CA 104; CANR 20, 42, 102; CP 7; DLB 120

Hitchcock, Alfred (Joseph)
1899-1980 .... **CLC 16**
See also AAYA 22; CA 159; 97-100; SATA 27; SATA-Obit 24

Hitchens, Christopher (Eric)
1949- .... **CLC 157**
See also CA 149; CANR 89

Hitler, Adolf 1889-1945 .... **TCLC 53**
See also CA 117; 147

Hoagland, Edward 1932- .... **CLC 28**
See also ANW; CA 1-4R; CANR 2, 31, 57, 107; CN 7; DLB 6; SATA 51; TCWW 2

Hoban, Russell (Conwell) 1925- ... **CLC 7, 25**
See also BPFB 2; CA 5-8R; CANR 23, 37, 66; CLR 3, 69; CN 7; CWRI 5; DAM NOV; DLB 52; FANT; MAICYA 1, 2; MTCW 1, 2; SATA 1, 40, 78; SFW 4

Hobbes, Thomas 1588-1679 .... **LC 36**
See also DLB 151, 252; RGEL 2

Hobbs, Perry
See Blackmur, R(ichard) P(almer)

Hobson, Laura Z(ametkin)
1900-1986 .... **CLC 7, 25**
See also Field, Peter
See also BPFB 2; CA 17-20R; 118; CANR 55; DLB 28; SATA 52

Hoccleve, Thomas c. 1368-c. 1437 ...... **LC 75**
See also DLB 146; RGEL 2

Hoch, Edward D(entinger) 1930-
See Queen, Ellery
See also CA 29-32R; CANR 11, 27, 51, 97; CMW 4; SFW 4

Hochhuth, Rolf 1931- .... **CLC 4, 11, 18**
See also CA 5-8R; CANR 33, 75; CWW 2; DAM DRAM; DLB 124; MTCW 1, 2

Hochman, Sandra 1936- .... **CLC 3, 8**
See also CA 5-8R; DLB 5

Hochwaelder, Fritz 1911-1986 .... **CLC 36**
See also Hochwalder, Fritz
See also CA 29-32R; 120; CANR 42; DAM DRAM; MTCW 1

Hochwalder, Fritz
See Hochwaelder, Fritz
See also RGWL 2

Hocking, Mary (Eunice) 1921- .... **CLC 13**
See also CA 101; CANR 18, 40

Hodgins, Jack 1938- .... **CLC 23**
See also CA 93-96; CN 7; DLB 60

Hodgson, William Hope
1877(?)-1918 .... **TCLC 13**
See also CA 111; 164; CMW 4; DLB 70, 153, 156, 178; HGG; MTCW 2; SFW 4; SUFW

Hoeg, Peter 1957- .... **CLC 95, 156**
See also CA 151; CANR 75; CMW 4; DA3; DLB 214; MTCW 2

Hoffman, Alice 1952- .... **CLC 51**
See also AAYA 37; AMWS 10; CA 77-80; CANR 34, 66, 100; CN 7; CPW; DAM NOV; MTCW 1, 2

Hoffman, Daniel (Gerard) 1923- . **CLC 6, 13, 23**
See also CA 1-4R; CANR 4; CP 7; DLB 5

Hoffman, Stanley 1944- .... **CLC 5**
See also CA 77-80

Hoffman, William 1925- .... **CLC 141**
See also CA 21-24R; CANR 9, 103; CSW; DLB 234

Hoffman, William M(oses) 1939- ..... **CLC 40**
See also CA 57-60; CANR 11, 71

Hoffmann, E(rnst) T(heodor) A(madeus)
1776-1822 .... **NCLC 2; SSC 13**
See also CDWLB 2; DLB 90; EW 5; RGSF 2; RGWL 2; SATA 27; SUFW; WCH

Hofmann, Gert 1931- .... **CLC 54**
See also CA 128

Hofmannsthal, Hugo von
1874-1929 .... **TCLC 11; DC 4**
See also CA 106; 153; CDWLB 2; DAM DRAM; DFS 12; DLB 81, 118; EW 9; RGWL 2

Hogan, Linda 1947- .... **CLC 73; PC 35**
See also AMWS 4; ANW; BYA 12; CA 120; CANR 45, 73; CWP; DAM MULT; DLB 175; NNAL; SATA 132; TCWW 2

Hogarth, Charles
See Creasey, John

Hogarth, Emmett
See Polonsky, Abraham (Lincoln)

Hogg, James 1770-1835 .... **NCLC 4, 109**
See also DLB 93, 116, 159; HGG; RGEL 2; SUFW

Holbach, Paul Henri Thiry Baron
1723-1789 .... **LC 14**

Holberg, Ludvig 1684-1754 .... **LC 6**
See also RGWL 2

Holcroft, Thomas 1745-1809 .... **NCLC 85**
See also DLB 39, 89, 158; RGEL 2

Holden, Ursula 1921- .... **CLC 18**
See also CA 101; CAAS 8; CANR 22

Holderlin, (Johann Christian) Friedrich
1770-1843 .... **NCLC 16; PC 4**
See also CDWLB 2; DLB 90; EW 5; RGWL 2

Holdstock, Robert
See Holdstock, Robert P.

Holdstock, Robert P. 1948- .... **CLC 39**
See also CA 131; CANR 81; DLB 261; FANT; HGG; SFW 4

Holinshed, Raphael fl. 1580- .... **LC 69**
See also DLB 167; RGEL 2

Holland, Isabelle (Christian)
1920-2002 .... **CLC 21**
See also AAYA 11; CA 21-24R; 181; CAAE 181; CANR 10, 25, 47; CLR 57; CWRI 5; JRDA; LAIT 4; MAICYA 1, 2; SATA 8, 70; SATA-Essay 103; SATA-Obit 132; WYA

Holland, Marcus
See Caldwell, (Janet Miriam) Taylor (Holland)

Hollander, John 1929- .... **CLC 2, 5, 8, 14**
See also CA 1-4R; CANR 1, 52; CP 7; DLB 5; SATA 13

Hollander, Paul
See Silverberg, Robert

Holleran, Andrew 1943(?)- .... **CLC 38**
See also Garber, Eric
See also CA 144; GLL 1

Holley, Marietta 1836(?)-1926 .... **TCLC 99**
See also CA 118; DLB 11

Hollinghurst, Alan 1954- .... **CLC 55, 91**
See also CA 114; CN 7; DLB 207; GLL 1

Hollis, Jim
See Summers, Hollis (Spurgeon, Jr.)

Holly, Buddy 1936-1959 .... **TCLC 65**

Holmes, Gordon
See Shiel, M(atthew) P(hipps)

Holmes, John
See Souster, (Holmes) Raymond

Holmes, John Clellon 1926-1988 ...... **CLC 56**
See also CA 9-12R; 125; CANR 4; DLB 16, 237

Holmes, Oliver Wendell, Jr.
1841-1935 .... **TCLC 77**
See also CA 114; 186

Holmes, Oliver Wendell
1809-1894 .... **NCLC 14, 81**
See also AMWS 1; CDALB 1640-1865; DLB 1, 189, 235; EXPP; RGAL 4; SATA 34

Holmes, Raymond
See Souster, (Holmes) Raymond

Holt, Victoria
See Hibbert, Eleanor Alice Burford
See also BPFB 2

Holub, Miroslav 1923-1998 .... **CLC 4**
See also CA 21-24R; 169; CANR 10; CDWLB 4; CWW 2; DLB 232

Homer c. 8th cent. B.C.- .... **CMLC 1, 16; PC 23; WLCS**
See also AW 1; CDWLB 1; DA; DA3; DAB; DAC; DAM MST, POET; DLB 176; EFS 1; LAIT 1; RGWL 2; TWA; WP

Hongo, Garrett Kaoru 1951- .... **PC 23**
See also CA 133; CAAS 22; CP 7; DLB 120; EXPP; RGAL 4

Huidobro Fernandez, Vicente Garcia
1893-1948 .... **TCLC 31**
See also Huidobro, Vicente
See also CA 131; HW 1

Hulme, Keri 1947- .... **CLC 39, 130**
See also CA 125; CANR 69; CN 7; CP 7;
CWP; FW; INT 125

Hulme, T(homas) E(rnest)
1883-1917 .... **TCLC 21**
See also BRWS 6; CA 117; 203; DLB 19

Hume, David 1711-1776 .... **LC 7, 56**
See also BRWS 3; DLB 104, 252; TEA

Humphrey, William 1924-1997 .... **CLC 45**
See also AMWS 9; CA 77-80; 160; CANR
68; CN 7; CSW; DLB 6, 212, 234;
TCWW 2

Humphreys, Emyr Owen 1919- .... **CLC 47**
See also CA 5-8R; CANR 3, 24; CN 7;
DLB 15

Humphreys, Josephine 1945- ..... **CLC 34, 57**
See also CA 121; 127; CANR 97; CSW;
INT 127

Huneker, James Gibbons
1860-1921 .... **TCLC 65**
See also CA 193; DLB 71; RGAL 4

Hungerford, Hesba Fay
See Brinsmead, H(esba) F(ay)

Hungerford, Pixie
See Brinsmead, H(esba) F(ay)

Hunt, E(verette) Howard, (Jr.)
1918- .... **CLC 3**
See also AITN 1; CA 45-48; CANR 2, 47,
103; CMW 4

Hunt, Francesca
See Holland, Isabelle (Christian)

Hunt, Howard
See Hunt, E(verette) Howard, (Jr.)

Hunt, Kyle
See Creasey, John

Hunt, (James Henry) Leigh
1784-1859 .... **NCLC 1, 70**
See also DAM POET; DLB 96, 110, 144;
RGEL 2; TEA

Hunt, Marsha 1946- .... **CLC 70**
See also BW 2, 3; CA 143; CANR 79

Hunt, Violet 1866(?)-1942 .... **TCLC 53**
See also CA 184; DLB 162, 197

Hunter, E. Waldo
See Sturgeon, Theodore (Hamilton)

Hunter, Evan 1926- .... **CLC 11, 31**
See also McBain, Ed
See also AAYA 39; BPFB 2; CA 5-8R;
CANR 5, 38, 62, 97; CMW 4; CN 7;
CPW; DAM POP; DLBY 1982; INT
CANR-5; MSW; MTCW 1; SATA 25;
SFW 4

Hunter, Kristin 1931-
See Lattany, Kristin (Elaine Eggleston)
Hunter

Hunter, Mary
See Austin, Mary (Hunter)

Hunter, Mollie 1922- .... **CLC 21**
See also McIlwraith, Maureen Mollie
Hunter
See also AAYA 13; BYA 6; CANR 37, 78;
CLR 25; DLB 161; JRDA; MAICYA 1,
2; SAAS 7; SATA 54, 106; WYA; YAW

Hunter, Robert (?)-1734 .... **LC 7**

Hurston, Zora Neale 1891-1960 .. **CLC 7, 30,**
61; BLC 2; DC 12; SSC 4; WLCS
See also AAYA 15; AFAW 1, 2; AMWS 6;
BW 1, 3; BYA 12; CA 85-88; CANR 61;
CDALBS; DA; DA3; DAC; DAM MST,
MULT, NOV; DFS 6; DLB 51; EXPN;
EXPS; FW; LAIT 3; MAWW; MTCW 1,
2; NFS 3; RGAL 4; RGSF 2; SSFS 1, 6,
11; TCLC 121; TUS; YAW

Husserl, E. G.
See Husserl, Edmund (Gustav Albrecht)

Husserl, Edmund (Gustav Albrecht)
1859-1938 .... **TCLC 100**
See also CA 116; 133

Huston, John (Marcellus)
1906-1987 .... **CLC 20**
See also CA 73-76; 123; CANR 34; DLB
26

Hustvedt, Siri 1955- .... **CLC 76**
See also CA 137

Hutten, Ulrich von 1488-1523 .... **LC 16**
See also DLB 179

Huxley, Aldous (Leonard)
1894-1963 .... **CLC 1, 3, 4, 5, 8, 11, 18,**
35, 79; SSC 39; WLC
See also AAYA 11; BPFB 2; BRW 7; CA
85-88; CANR 44, 99; CDBLB 1914-1945;
DA; DA3; DAB; DAC; DAM MST, NOV;
DLB 36, 100, 162, 195, 255; EXPN;
LAIT 5; MTCW 1, 2; NFS 6; RGEL 2;
SATA 63; SCFW 2; SFW 4; TEA; YAW

Huxley, T(homas) H(enry)
1825-1895 .... **NCLC 67**
See also DLB 57; TEA

Huysmans, Joris-Karl 1848-1907 ... **TCLC 7,**
69
See also CA 104; 165; DLB 123; EW 7;
GFL 1789 to the Present; RGWL 2

Hwang, David Henry 1957- .. **CLC 55; DC 4**
See also CA 127; 132; CAD; CANR 76;
CD 5; DA3; DAM DRAM; DFS 11; DLB
212, 228; INT CA-132; MTCW 2; RGAL
4

Hyde, Anthony 1946- .... **CLC 42**
See also Chase, Nicholas
See also CA 136; CCA 1

Hyde, Margaret O(ldroyd) 1917- ..... **CLC 21**
See also CA 1-4R; CANR 1, 36; CLR 23;
JRDA; MAICYA 1, 2; SAAS 8; SATA 1,
42, 76

Hynes, James 1956(?)- .... **CLC 65**
See also CA 164; CANR 105

Hypatia c. 370-415 .... **CMLC 35**

Ian, Janis 1951- .... **CLC 21**
See also CA 105; 187

Ibanez, Vicente Blasco
See Blasco Ibanez, Vicente

Ibarbourou, Juana de 1895-1979
See also HLCS 2; HW 1; LAW

Ibarguengoitia, Jorge 1928-1983 ...... **CLC 37**
See also CA 124; 113; HW 1

Ibsen, Henrik (Johan) 1828-1906 ... **TCLC 2,**
8, 16, 37, 52; DC 2; WLC
See also CA 104; 141; DA; DA3; DAB;
DAC; DAM DRAM, MST; DFS 15; EW
7; LAIT 2; RGWL 2

Ibuse, Masuji 1898-1993 .... **CLC 22**
See also Ibuse Masuji
See also CA 127; 141; MJW

Ibuse Masuji
See Ibuse, Masuji
See also DLB 180

Ichikawa, Kon 1915- .... **CLC 20**
See also CA 121

Ichiyo, Higuchi 1872-1896 .... **NCLC 49**
See also MJW

Idle, Eric 1943-2000 .... **CLC 21**
See also Monty Python
See also CA 116; CANR 35, 91

Ignatow, David 1914-1997 .... **CLC 4, 7, 14,**
40; PC 34
See also CA 9-12R; 162; CAAS 3; CANR
31, 57, 96; CP 7; DLB 5

Ignotus
See Strachey, (Giles) Lytton

Ihimaera, Witi 1944- .... **CLC 46**
See also CA 77-80; CN 7; RGSF 2

Ilf, Ilya .... **TCLC 21**
See also Fainzilberg, Ilya Arnoldovich

Illyes, Gyula 1902-1983 .... **PC 16**
See also CA 114; 109; CDWLB 4; DLB
215; RGWL 2

Immermann, Karl (Lebrecht)
1796-1840 .... **NCLC 4, 49**
See also DLB 133

Ince, Thomas H. 1882-1924 .... **TCLC 89**
See also IDFW 3, 4

Inchbald, Elizabeth 1753-1821 ...... **NCLC 62**
See also DLB 39, 89; RGEL 2

Inclan, Ramon (Maria) del Valle
See Valle-Inclan, Ramon (Maria) del

Infante, G(uillermo) Cabrera
See Cabrera Infante, G(uillermo)

Ingalls, Rachel (Holmes) 1940- .... **CLC 42**
See also CA 123; 127

Ingamells, Reginald Charles
See Ingamells, Rex

Ingamells, Rex 1913-1955 .... **TCLC 35**
See also CA 167; DLB 260

Inge, William (Motter) 1913-1973 ..... **CLC 1,**
8, 19
See also CA 9-12R; CDALB 1941-1968;
DA3; DAM DRAM; DFS 1, 5, 8; DLB 7,
249; MTCW 1, 2; RGAL 4; TUS

Ingelow, Jean 1820-1897 .... **NCLC 39, 107**
See also DLB 35, 163; FANT; SATA 33

Ingram, Willis J.
See Harris, Mark

Innaurato, Albert (F.) 1948(?)- ... **CLC 21, 60**
See also CA 115; 122; CAD; CANR 78;
CD 5; INT CA-122

Innes, Michael
See Stewart, J(ohn) I(nnes) M(ackintosh)
See also MSW

Innis, Harold Adams 1894-1952 .... **TCLC 77**
See also CA 181; DLB 88

Insluis, Alanus de
See Alain de Lille

Iola
See Wells-Barnett, Ida B(ell)

Ionesco, Eugene 1912-1994 ... **CLC 1, 4, 6, 9,**
11, 15, 41, 86; DC 12; WLC
See also CA 9-12R; 144; CANR 55; CWW
2; DA; DA3; DAB; DAC; DAM DRAM,
MST; DFS 4, 9; EW 13; GFL 1789 to the
Present; MTCW 1, 2; RGWL 2; SATA 7;
SATA-Obit 79; TWA

Iqbal, Muhammad 1877-1938 .... **TCLC 28**

Ireland, Patrick
See O'Doherty, Brian

Irenaeus St. 130- .... **CMLC 42**

Iron, Ralph
See Schreiner, Olive (Emilie Albertina)

Irving, John (Winslow) 1942- ... **CLC 13, 23,**
38, 112
See also AAYA 8; AMWS 6; BEST 89:3;
BPFB 2; CA 25-28R; CANR 28, 73; CN
7; CPW; DA3; DAM NOV, POP; DLB 6;
DLBY 1982; MTCW 1, 2; NFS 12, 14;
RGAL 4; TUS

Irving, Washington 1783-1859 . **NCLC 2, 19,**
95; SSC 2, 37; WLC
See also AMW; CDALB 1640-1865; DA;
DA3; DAB; DAC; DAM MST; DLB 3,
11, 30, 59, 73, 74, 183, 186, 250, 254;
EXPS; LAIT 1; RGAL 4; RGSF 2; SSFS
1, 8; SUFW; TUS; WCH; YABC 2

Irwin, P. K.
See Page, P(atricia) K(athleen)

Isaacs, Jorge Ricardo 1837-1895 ... **NCLC 70**
See also LAW

Isaacs, Susan 1943- .... **CLC 32**
See also BEST 89:1; BPFB 2; CA 89-92;
CANR 20, 41, 65; CPW; DA3; DAM
POP; INT CANR-20; MTCW 1, 2

Kraus, Karl 1874-1936 .... TCLC **5**
See also CA 104; DLB 118

Kreve (Mickevicius), Vincas
1882-1954 .... TCLC **27**
See also CA 170; DLB 220

Kristeva, Julia 1941- .... CLC **77, 140**
See also CA 154; CANR 99; DLB 242; FW

Kristofferson, Kris 1936- .... CLC **26**
See also CA 104

Krizanc, John 1956- .... CLC **57**
See also CA 187

Krleza, Miroslav 1893-1981 .... CLC **8, 114**
See also CA 97-100; 105; CANR 50; CD-
WLB 4; DLB 147; EW 11; RGWL 2

Kroetsch, Robert 1927- .. CLC **5, 23, 57, 132**
See also CA 17-20R; CANR 8, 38; CCA 1;
CN 7; CP 7; DAC; DAM POET; DLB 53;
MTCW 1

Kroetz, Franz
See Kroetz, Franz Xaver

Kroetz, Franz Xaver 1946- .... CLC **41**
See also CA 130

Kroker, Arthur (W.) 1945- .... CLC **77**
See also CA 161

Kropotkin, Peter (Alekseievich)
1842-1921 .... TCLC **36**
See also CA 119

Krotkov, Yuri 1917-1981 .... CLC **19**
See also CA 102

Krumb
See Crumb, R(obert)

Krumgold, Joseph (Quincy)
1908-1980 .... CLC **12**
See also BYA 1, 2; CA 9-12R; 101; CANR
7; MAICYA 1, 2; SATA 1, 48; SATA-Obit
23; YAW

Krumwitz
See Crumb, R(obert)

Krutch, Joseph Wood 1893-1970 ..... CLC **24**
See also ANW; CA 1-4R; 25-28R; CANR
4; DLB 63, 206

Krutzch, Gus
See Eliot, T(homas) S(tearns)

Krylov, Ivan Andreevich
1768(?)-1844 .... NCLC **1**
See also DLB 150

Kubin, Alfred (Leopold Isidor)
1877-1959 .... TCLC **23**
See also CA 112; 149; CANR 104; DLB 81

Kubrick, Stanley 1928-1999 .... CLC **16**
See also AAYA 30; CA 81-84; 177; CANR
33; DLB 26; TCLC 112

Kueng, Hans 1928-
See Kung, Hans
See also CA 53-56; CANR 66; MTCW 1, 2

Kumin, Maxine (Winokur) 1925- ..... CLC **5,
13, 28; PC 15**
See also AITN 2; AMWS 4; ANW; CA
1-4R; CAAS 8; CANR 1, 21, 69; CP 7;
CWP; DA3; DAM POET; DLB 5; EXPP;
MTCW 1, 2; PAB; SATA 12

Kundera, Milan 1929- . CLC **4, 9, 19, 32, 68,
115, 135; SSC 24**
See also AAYA 2; BPFB 2; CA 85-88;
CANR 19, 52, 74; CDWLB 4; CWW 2;
DA3; DAM NOV; DLB 232; EW 13;
MTCW 1, 2; RGSF 2; SSFS 10

Kunene, Mazisi (Raymond) 1930- ... CLC **85**
See also BW 1, 3; CA 125; CANR 81; CP
7; DLB 117

Kung, Hans .... CLC **130**
See also Kueng, Hans

Kunikida Doppo 1869(?)-1908
See Doppo, Kunikida
See also DLB 180

Kunitz, Stanley (Jasspon) 1905- .. CLC **6, 11,
14, 148; PC 19**
See also AMWS 3; CA 41-44R; CANR 26,
57, 98; CP 7; DA3; DLB 48; INT CANR-
26; MTCW 1, 2; PFS 11; RGAL 4

Kunze, Reiner 1933- .... CLC **10**
See also CA 93-96; CWW 2; DLB 75

Kuprin, Aleksander Ivanovich
1870-1938 .... TCLC **5**
See also CA 104; 182

Kureishi, Hanif 1954(?)- .... CLC **64, 135**
See also CA 139; CBD; CD 5; CN 7; DLB
194, 245; GLL 2; IDFW 4; WLIT 4

Kurosawa, Akira 1910-1998 ..... CLC **16, 119**
See also AAYA 11; CA 101; 170; CANR
46; DAM MULT

Kushner, Tony 1957(?)- .... CLC **81; DC 10**
See also AMWS 9; CA 144; CAD; CANR
74; CD 5; DA3; DAM DRAM; DFS 5;
DLB 228; GLL 1; LAIT 5; MTCW 2;
RGAL 4

Kuttner, Henry 1915-1958 .... TCLC **10**
See also CA 107; 157; DLB 8; FANT;
SCFW 2; SFW 4

Kuzma, Greg 1944- .... CLC **7**
See also CA 33-36R; CANR 70

Kuzmin, Mikhail 1872(?)-1936 ...... TCLC **40**
See also CA 170

Kyd, Thomas 1558-1594 .... LC **22; DC 3**
See also BRW 1; DAM DRAM; DLB 62;
IDTP; RGEL 2; TEA; WLIT 3

Kyprianos, Iossif
See Samarakis, Antonis

Labrunie, Gerard
See Nerval, Gerard de

La Bruyere, Jean de 1645-1696 .... LC **17**
See also EW 3; GFL Beginnings to 1789

Lacan, Jacques (Marie Emile)
1901-1981 .... CLC **75**
See also CA 121; 104; TWA

Laclos, Pierre Ambroise Francois
1741-1803 .... NCLC **4, 87**
See also EW 4; GFL Beginnings to 1789;
RGWL 2

Lacolere, Francois
See Aragon, Louis

La Colere, Francois
See Aragon, Louis

La Deshabilleuse
See Simenon, Georges (Jacques Christian)

Lady Gregory
See Gregory, Lady Isabella Augusta (Persse)

Lady of Quality, A
See Bagnold, Enid

**La Fayette, Marie-(Madelaine Pioche de la
Vergne)** 1634-1693 .... LC **2**
See also GFL Beginnings to 1789; RGWL
2

Lafayette, Rene
See Hubbard, L(afayette) Ron(ald)

La Fontaine, Jean de 1621-1695 .... LC **50**
See also EW 3; GFL Beginnings to 1789;
MAICYA 1, 2; RGWL 2; SATA 18

Laforgue, Jules 1860-1887 . NCLC **5, 53; PC
14; SSC 20**
See also DLB 217; EW 7; GFL 1789 to the
Present; RGWL 2

Layamon
See Layamon
See also DLB 146

Lagerkvist, Paer (Fabian)
1891-1974 .... CLC **7, 10, 13, 54**
See also Lagerkvist, Par
See also CA 85-88; 49-52; DA3; DAM
DRAM, NOV; MTCW 1, 2; TWA

Lagerkvist, Par .... SSC **12**
See also Lagerkvist, Paer (Fabian)
See also DLB 259; EW 10; MTCW 2;
RGSF 2; RGWL 2

Lagerloef, Selma (Ottiliana Lovisa)
1858-1940 .... TCLC **4, 36**
See also Lagerlof, Selma (Ottiliana Lovisa)
See also CA 108; MTCW 2; SATA 15

Lagerlof, Selma (Ottiliana Lovisa)
See Lagerloef, Selma (Ottiliana Lovisa)
See also CLR 7; SATA 15

La Guma, (Justin) Alex(ander)
1925-1985 .... CLC **19; BLCS**
See also AFW; BW 1, 3; CA 49-52; 118;
CANR 25, 81; CDWLB 3; DAM NOV;
DLB 117, 225; MTCW 1, 2; WLIT 2

Laidlaw, A. K.
See Grieve, C(hristopher) M(urray)

Lainez, Manuel Mujica
See Mujica Lainez, Manuel
See also HW 1

Laing, R(onald) D(avid) 1927-1989 . CLC **95**
See also CA 107; 129; CANR 34; MTCW 1

Lamartine, Alphonse (Marie Louis Prat) de
1790-1869 .... NCLC **11; PC 16**
See also DAM POET; DLB 217; GFL 1789
to the Present; RGWL 2

Lamb, Charles 1775-1834 ..... NCLC **10, 113;
WLC**
See also BRW 4; CDBLB 1789-1832; DA;
DAB; DAC; DAM MST; DLB 93, 107,
163; RGEL 2; SATA 17; TEA

Lamb, Lady Caroline 1785-1828 ... NCLC **38**
See also DLB 116

Lamming, George (William) 1927- ... CLC **2,
4, 66, 144; BLC 2**
See also BW 2, 3; CA 85-88; CANR 26,
76; CDWLB 3; CN 7; DAM MULT; DLB
125; MTCW 1, 2; NFS 15; RGEL 2

L'Amour, Louis (Dearborn)
1908-1988 .... CLC **25, 55**
See also Burns, Tex; Mayo, Jim
See also AAYA 16; AITN 2; BEST 89:2;
BPFB 2; CA 1-4R; 125; CANR 3, 25, 40;
CPW; DA3; DAM NOV, POP; DLB 206;
DLBY 1980; MTCW 1, 2; RGAL 4

Lampedusa, Giuseppe (Tomasi) di
.... TCLC **13**
See also Tomasi di Lampedusa, Giuseppe
See also CA 164; EW 11; MTCW 2; RGWL
2

Lampman, Archibald 1861-1899 ... NCLC **25**
See also DLB 92; RGEL 2; TWA

Lancaster, Bruce 1896-1963 .... CLC **36**
See also CA 9-10; CANR 70; CAP 1; SATA
9

Lanchester, John .... CLC **99**
See also CA 194

Landau, Mark Alexandrovich
See Aldanov, Mark (Alexandrovich)

Landau-Aldanov, Mark Alexandrovich
See Aldanov, Mark (Alexandrovich)

Landis, Jerry
See Simon, Paul (Frederick)

Landis, John 1950- .... CLC **26**
See also CA 112; 122

Landolfi, Tommaso 1908-1979 .... CLC **11, 49**
See also CA 127; 117; DLB 177

Landon, Letitia Elizabeth
1802-1838 .... NCLC **15**
See also DLB 96

Landor, Walter Savage
1775-1864 .... NCLC **14**
See also BRW 4; DLB 93, 107; RGEL 2

Landwirth, Heinz 1927-
See Lind, Jakov
See also CA 9-12R; CANR 7

Lane, Patrick 1939- .... CLC **25**
See also CA 97-100; CANR 54; CP 7; DAM
POET; DLB 53; INT 97-100

Maeterlinck, Maurice 1862-1949 ..... **TCLC 3**
See also CA 104; 136; CANR 80; DAM
DRAM; DLB 192; EW 8; GFL 1789 to
the Present; RGWL 2; SATA 66; TWA

Maginn, William 1794-1842 .... **NCLC 8**
See also DLB 110, 159

Mahapatra, Jayanta 1928- .... **CLC 33**
See also CA 73-76; CAAS 9; CANR 15,
33, 66, 87; CP 7; DAM MULT

Mahfouz, Naguib (Abdel Aziz Al-Sabilgi)
1911(?)- .... **CLC 153**
See also Mahfuz, Najib (Abdel Aziz al-
Sabilgi)
See also BEST 89:2; CA 128; CANR 55,
101; CWW 2; DA3; DAM NOV; MTCW
1, 2; RGWL 2; SSFS 9

Mahfuz, Najib (Abdel Aziz al-Sabilgi)
.... **CLC 52, 55**
See also Mahfouz, Naguib (Abdel Aziz Al-
Sabilgi)
See also AFW; DLBY 1988; RGSF 2;
WLIT 2

Mahon, Derek 1941- .... **CLC 27**
See also BRWS 6; CA 113; 128; CANR 88;
CP 7; DLB 40

Maiakovskii, Vladimir
See Mayakovski, Vladimir (Vladimirovich)
See also IDTP; RGWL 2

Mailer, Norman 1923- ... **CLC 1, 2, 3, 4, 5, 8,
11, 14, 28, 39, 74, 111**
See also AAYA 31; AITN 2; AMW; BPFB
2; CA 9-12R; CABS 1; CANR 28, 74, 77;
CDALB 1968-1988; CN 7; CPW; DA;
DA3; DAB; DAC; DAM MST, NOV,
POP; DLB 2, 16, 28, 185; DLBD 3;
DLBY 1980, 1983; MTCW 1, 2; NFS 10;
RGAL 4; TUS

Maillet, Antonine 1929- .... **CLC 54, 118**
See also CA 115; 120; CANR 46, 74, 77;
CCA 1; CWW 2; DAC; DLB 60; INT
120; MTCW 2

Mais, Roger 1905-1955 .... **TCLC 8**
See also BW 1, 3; CA 105; 124; CANR 82;
CDWLB 3; DLB 125; MTCW 1; RGEL 2

Maistre, Joseph 1753-1821 .... **NCLC 37**
See also GFL 1789 to the Present

Maitland, Frederic William
1850-1906 .... **TCLC 65**

Maitland, Sara (Louise) 1950- .... **CLC 49**
See also CA 69-72; CANR 13, 59; FW

Major, Clarence 1936- . **CLC 3, 19, 48; BLC
2**
See also AFAW 2; BW 2, 3; CA 21-24R;
CAAS 6; CANR 13, 25, 53, 82; CN 7;
CP 7; CSW; DAM MULT; DLB 33; MSW

Major, Kevin (Gerald) 1949- .... **CLC 26**
See also AAYA 16; CA 97-100; CANR 21,
38; CLR 11; DAC; DLB 60; INT CANR-
21; JRDA; MAICYA 1, 2; MAICYAS 1;
SATA 32, 82; WYA; YAW

Maki, James
See Ozu, Yasujiro

Malabaila, Damiano
See Levi, Primo

Malamud, Bernard 1914-1986 .. **CLC 1, 2, 3,
5, 8, 9, 11, 18, 27, 44, 78, 85; SSC 15;
WLC**
See also AAYA 16; AMWS 1; BPFB 2; CA
5-8R; 118; CABS 1; CANR 28, 62;
CDALB 1941-1968; CPW; DA; DA3;
DAB; DAC; DAM MST, NOV, POP;
DLB 2, 28, 152; DLBY 1980, 1986;
EXPS; LAIT 4; MTCW 1, 2; NFS 4, 9;
RGAL 4; RGSF 2; SSFS 8, 13; TUS

Malan, Herman
See Bosman, Herman Charles; Bosman,
Herman Charles

Malaparte, Curzio 1898-1957 .... **TCLC 52**
See also DLB 264

Malcolm, Dan
See Silverberg, Robert

Malcolm X .... **CLC 82, 117; BLC 2; WLCS**
See also Little, Malcolm
See also LAIT 5

Malherbe, Francois de 1555-1628 .... **LC 5**
See also GFL Beginnings to 1789

Mallarme, Stephane 1842-1898 ...... **NCLC 4,
41; PC 4**
See also DAM POET; DLB 217; EW 7;
GFL 1789 to the Present; RGWL 2; TWA

Mallet-Joris, Francoise 1930- .... **CLC 11**
See also CA 65-68; CANR 17; DLB 83;
GFL 1789 to the Present

Malley, Ern
See McAuley, James Phillip

Mallowan, Agatha Christie
See Christie, Agatha (Mary Clarissa)

Maloff, Saul 1922- .... **CLC 5**
See also CA 33-36R

Malone, Louis
See MacNeice, (Frederick) Louis

Malone, Michael (Christopher)
1942- .... **CLC 43**
See also CA 77-80; CANR 14, 32, 57

Malory, Sir Thomas 1410(?)-1471(?) . **LC 11;
WLCS**
See also BRW 1; BRWR 2; CDBLB Before
1660; DA; DAB; DAC; DAM MST; DLB
146; EFS 2; RGEL 2; SATA 59; SATA-
Brief 33; TEA; WLIT 3

Malouf, (George Joseph) David
1934- .... **CLC 28, 86**
See also CA 124; CANR 50, 76; CN 7; CP
7; MTCW 2

Malraux, (Georges-)Andre
1901-1976 .... **CLC 1, 4, 9, 13, 15, 57**
See also BPFB 2; CA 21-22; 69-72; CANR
34, 58; CAP 2; DA3; DAM NOV; DLB
72; EW 12; GFL 1789 to the Present;
MTCW 1, 2; RGWL 2; TWA

Malzberg, Barry N(athaniel) 1939- ... **CLC 7**
See also CA 61-64; CAAS 4; CANR 16;
CMW 4; DLB 8; SFW 4

Mamet, David (Alan) 1947- .. **CLC 9, 15, 34,
46, 91; DC 4**
See also AAYA 3; CA 81-84; CABS 3;
CANR 15, 41, 67, 72; CD 5; DA3; DAM
DRAM; DFS 15; DLB 7; IDFW 4;
MTCW 1, 2; RGAL 4

Mamoulian, Rouben (Zachary)
1897-1987 .... **CLC 16**
See also CA 25-28R; 124; CANR 85

Mandelshtam, Osip
See Mandelstam, Osip (Emilievich)
See also EW 10; RGWL 2

Mandelstam, Osip (Emilievich)
1891(?)-1943(?) .... **TCLC 2, 6; PC 14**
See also Mandelshtam, Osip
See also CA 104; 150; MTCW 2; TWA

Mander, (Mary) Jane 1877-1949 ... **TCLC 31**
See also CA 162; RGEL 2

Mandeville, Sir John fl. 1350- ...... **CMLC 19**
See also DLB 146

Mandiargues, Andre Pieyre de .... **CLC 41**
See also Pieyre de Mandiargues, Andre
See also DLB 83

Mandrake, Ethel Belle
See Thurman, Wallace (Henry)

Mangan, James Clarence
1803-1849 .... **NCLC 27**
See also RGEL 2

Maniere, J.-E.
See Giraudoux, Jean(-Hippolyte)

Mankiewicz, Herman (Jacob)
1897-1953 .... **TCLC 85**
See also CA 120; 169; DLB 26; IDFW 3, 4

Manley, (Mary) Delariviere
1672(?)-1724 .... **LC 1, 42**
See also DLB 39, 80; RGEL 2

Mann, Abel
See Creasey, John

Mann, Emily 1952- .... **DC 7**
See also CA 130; CAD; CANR 55; CD 5;
CWD; DLB 266

Mann, (Luiz) Heinrich 1871-1950 ... **TCLC 9**
See also CA 106; 164, 181; DLB 66, 118;
EW 8; RGWL 2

Mann, (Paul) Thomas 1875-1955 ... **TCLC 2,
8, 14, 21, 35, 44, 60; SSC 5; WLC**
See also BPFB 2; CA 104; 128; CDWLB 2;
DA; DA3; DAB; DAC; DAM MST, NOV;
DLB 66; EW 9; GLL 1; MTCW 1, 2;
RGSF 2; RGWL 2; SSFS 4, 9; TWA

Mannheim, Karl 1893-1947 .... **TCLC 65**

Manning, David
See Faust, Frederick (Schiller)
See also TCWW 2

Manning, Frederic 1887(?)-1935 ... **TCLC 25**
See also CA 124; DLB 260

Manning, Olivia 1915-1980 .... **CLC 5, 19**
See also CA 5-8R; 101; CANR 29; FW;
MTCW 1; RGEL 2

Mano, D. Keith 1942- .... **CLC 2, 10**
See also CA 25-28R; CAAS 6; CANR 26,
57; DLB 6

Mansfield, Katherine ... **TCLC 2, 8, 39; SSC
9, 23, 38; WLC**
See also Beauchamp, Kathleen Mansfield
See also BPFB 2; BRW 7; DAB; DLB 162;
EXPS; FW; GLL 1; RGEL 2; RGSF 2;
SSFS 2, 8, 10, 11

Manso, Peter 1940- .... **CLC 39**
See also CA 29-32R; CANR 44

Mantecon, Juan Jimenez
See Jimenez (Mantecon), Juan Ramon

Mantel, Hilary (Mary) 1952- .... **CLC 144**
See also CA 125; CANR 54, 101; CN 7;
RHW

Manton, Peter
See Creasey, John

Man Without a Spleen, A
See Chekhov, Anton (Pavlovich)

Manzoni, Alessandro 1785-1873 ... **NCLC 29,
98**
See also EW 5; RGWL 2; TWA

Map, Walter 1140-1209 .... **CMLC 32**

Mapu, Abraham (ben Jekutiel)
1808-1867 .... **NCLC 18**

Mara, Sally
See Queneau, Raymond

Marat, Jean Paul 1743-1793 .... **LC 10**

Marcel, Gabriel Honore 1889-1973 . **CLC 15**
See also CA 102; 45-48; MTCW 1, 2

March, William 1893-1954 .... **TCLC 96**

Marchbanks, Samuel
See Davies, (William) Robertson
See also CCA 1

Marchi, Giacomo
See Bassani, Giorgio

Marcus Aurelius
See Aurelius, Marcus
See also AW 2

Marguerite
See de Navarre, Marguerite

Marguerite d'Angouleme
See de Navarre, Marguerite
See also GFL Beginnings to 1789

Marguerite de Navarre
See de Navarre, Marguerite
See also RGWL 2

Margulies, Donald 1954- .... **CLC 76**
See also CA 200; DFS 13; DLB 228

Meyrink, Gustav .... **TCLC 21**
See also Meyer, Gustav
See also DLB 81

Michaels, Leonard 1933- .... **CLC 6, 25; SSC 16**
See also CA 61-64; CANR 21, 62; CN 7; DLB 130; MTCW 1

Michaux, Henri 1899-1984 .... **CLC 8, 19**
See also CA 85-88; 114; DLB 258; GFL 1789 to the Present; RGWL 2

Micheaux, Oscar (Devereaux) 1884-1951 .... **TCLC 76**
See also BW 3; CA 174; DLB 50; TCWW 2

Michelangelo 1475-1564 .... **LC 12**
See also AAYA 43

Michelet, Jules 1798-1874 .... **NCLC 31**
See also EW 5; GFL 1789 to the Present

Michels, Robert 1876-1936 .... **TCLC 88**

Michener, James A(lbert)
1907(?)-1997 .. **CLC 1, 5, 11, 29, 60, 109**
See also AAYA 27; AITN 1; BEST 90:1; BPFB 2; CA 5-8R; 161; CANR 21, 45, 68; CN 7; CPW; DA3; DAM NOV, POP; DLB 6; MTCW 1, 2; RHW

Mickiewicz, Adam 1798-1855 . **NCLC 3, 101; PC 38**
See also EW 5; RGWL 2

Middleton, Christopher 1926- .... **CLC 13**
See also CA 13-16R; CANR 29, 54; CP 7; DLB 40

Middleton, Richard (Barham)
1882-1911 .... **TCLC 56**
See also CA 187; DLB 156; HGG

Middleton, Stanley 1919- .... **CLC 7, 38**
See also CA 25-28R; CAAS 23; CANR 21, 46, 81; CN 7; DLB 14

Middleton, Thomas 1580-1627 .... **LC 33; DC 5**
See also BRW 2; DAM DRAM, MST; DLB 58; RGEL 2

Migueis, Jose Rodrigues 1901- .... **CLC 10**

Mikszath, Kalman 1847-1910 .... **TCLC 31**
See also CA 170

Miles, Jack .... **CLC 100**
See also CA 200

Miles, John Russiano
See Miles, Jack

Miles, Josephine (Louise)
1911-1985 .... **CLC 1, 2, 14, 34, 39**
See also CA 1-4R; 116; CANR 2, 55; DAM POET; DLB 48

Militant
See Sandburg, Carl (August)

Mill, Harriet (Hardy) Taylor
1807-1858 .... **NCLC 102**
See also FW

Mill, John Stuart 1806-1873 .... **NCLC 11, 58**
See also CDBLB 1832-1890; DLB 55, 190, 262; FW 1; RGEL 2; TEA

Millar, Kenneth 1915-1983 .... **CLC 14**
See also Macdonald, Ross
See also CA 9-12R; 110; CANR 16, 63, 107; CMW 4; CPW; DA3; DAM POP; DLB 2, 226; DLBD 6; DLBY 1983; MTCW 1, 2

Millay, E. Vincent
See Millay, Edna St. Vincent

Millay, Edna St. Vincent
1892-1950 ... **TCLC 4, 49; PC 6; WLCS**
See also Boyd, Nancy
See also AMW; CA 104; 130; CDALB 1917-1929; DA; DA3; DAB; DAC; DAM MST, POET; DLB 45, 249; EXPP; MAWW; MTCW 1, 2; PAB; PFS 3; RGAL 4; TUS; WP

Miller, Arthur 1915- ...... **CLC 1, 2, 6, 10, 15, 26, 47, 78; DC 1; WLC**
See also AAYA 15; AITN 1; AMW; CA 1-4R; CABS 3; CAD; CANR 2, 30, 54, 76; CD 5; CDALB 1941-1968; DA; DA3; DAB; DAC; DAM DRAM, MST; DFS 1, 3; DLB 7, 266; LAIT 1, 4; MTCW 1, 2; RGAL 4; TUS; WYAS 1

Miller, Henry (Valentine)
1891-1980 .... **CLC 1, 2, 4, 9, 14, 43, 84; WLC**
See also AMW; BPFB 2; CA 9-12R; 97-100; CANR 33, 64; CDALB 1929-1941; DA; DA3; DAB; DAC; DAM MST, NOV; DLB 4, 9; DLBY 1980; MTCW 1, 2; RGAL 4; TUS

Miller, Jason 1939(?)-2001 .... **CLC 2**
See also AITN 1; CA 73-76; 197; CAD; DFS 12; DLB 7

Miller, Sue 1943- .... **CLC 44**
See also BEST 90:3; CA 139; CANR 59, 91; DA3; DAM POP; DLB 143

Miller, Walter M(ichael, Jr.)
1923-1996 .... **CLC 4, 30**
See also BPFB 2; CA 85-88; CANR 108; DLB 8; SCFW; SFW 4

Millett, Kate 1934- .... **CLC 67**
See also AITN 1; CA 73-76; CANR 32, 53, 76, 110; DA3; DLB 246; FW; GLL 1; MTCW 1, 2

Millhauser, Steven (Lewis) 1943- .... **CLC 21, 54, 109**
See also CA 110; 111; CANR 63; CN 7; DA3; DLB 2; FANT; INT CA-111; MTCW 2

Millin, Sarah Gertrude 1889-1968 ... **CLC 49**
See also CA 102; 93-96; DLB 225

Milne, A(lan) A(lexander)
1882-1956 .... **TCLC 6, 88**
See also BRWS 5; CA 104; 133; CLR 1, 26; CMW 4; CWRI 5; DA3; DAB; DAC; DAM MST; DLB 10, 77, 100, 160; FANT; MAICYA 1, 2; MTCW 1, 2; RGEL 2; SATA 100; WCH; YABC 1

Milner, Ron(ald) 1938- .... **CLC 56; BLC 3**
See also AITN 1; BW 1; CA 73-76; CAD; CANR 24, 81; CD 5; DAM MULT; DLB 38; MTCW 1

Milnes, Richard Monckton
1809-1885 .... **NCLC 61**
See also DLB 32, 184

Milosz, Czeslaw 1911- ...... **CLC 5, 11, 22, 31, 56, 82; PC 8; WLCS**
See also CA 81-84; CANR 23, 51, 91; CD-WLB 4; CWW 2; DA3; DAM MST, POET; DLB 215; EW 13; MTCW 1, 2; RGWL 2

Milton, John 1608-1674 ..... **LC 9, 43; PC 19, 29; WLC**
See also BRW 2; BRWR 2; CDBLB 1660-1789; DA; DA3; DAB; DAC; DAM MST, POET; DLB 131, 151; EFS 1; EXPP; LAIT 1; PAB; PFS 3; RGEL 2; TEA; WLIT 3; WP

Min, Anchee 1957- .... **CLC 86**
See also CA 146; CANR 94

Minehaha, Cornelius
See Wedekind, (Benjamin) Frank(lin)

Miner, Valerie 1947- .... **CLC 40**
See also CA 97-100; CANR 59; FW; GLL 2

Minimo, Duca
See D'Annunzio, Gabriele

Minot, Susan 1956- .... **CLC 44, 159**
See also AMWS 6; CA 134; CN 7

Minus, Ed 1938- .... **CLC 39**
See also CA 185

Miranda, Javier
See Bioy Casares, Adolfo
See also CWW 2

Mirbeau, Octave 1848-1917 .... **TCLC 55**
See also DLB 123, 192; GFL 1789 to the Present

Miro (Ferrer), Gabriel (Francisco Victor)
1879-1930 .... **TCLC 5**
See also CA 104; 185

Misharin, Alexandr .... **CLC 59**

Mishima, Yukio ... **CLC 2, 4, 6, 9, 27; DC 1; SSC 4**
See also Hiraoka, Kimitake
See also BPFB 2; DLB 182; GLL 1; MJW; MTCW 2; RGSF 2; RGWL 2; SSFS 5, 12

Mistral, Frederic 1830-1914 .... **TCLC 51**
See also CA 122; GFL 1789 to the Present

Mistral, Gabriela
See Godoy Alcayaga, Lucila
See also DNFS 1; LAW; RGWL 2; WP

Mistry, Rohinton 1952- .... **CLC 71**
See also CA 141; CANR 86; CCA 1; CN 7; DAC; SSFS 6

Mitchell, Clyde
See Ellison, Harlan (Jay); Silverberg, Robert

Mitchell, James Leslie 1901-1935
See Gibbon, Lewis Grassic
See also CA 104; 188; DLB 15

Mitchell, Joni 1943- .... **CLC 12**
See also CA 112; CCA 1

Mitchell, Joseph (Quincy)
1908-1996 .... **CLC 98**
See also CA 77-80; 152; CANR 69; CN 7; CSW; DLB 185; DLBY 1996

Mitchell, Margaret (Munnerlyn)
1900-1949 .... **TCLC 11**
See also AAYA 23; BPFB 2; BYA 1; CA 109; 125; CANR 55, 94; CDALBS; DA3; DAM NOV, POP; DLB 9; LAIT 2; MTCW 1, 2; NFS 9; RGAL 4; RHW; TUS; WYAS 1; YAW

Mitchell, Peggy
See Mitchell, Margaret (Munnerlyn)

Mitchell, S(ilas) Weir 1829-1914 .... **TCLC 36**
See also CA 165; DLB 202; RGAL 4

Mitchell, W(illiam) O(rmond)
1914-1998 .... **CLC 25**
See also CA 77-80; 165; CANR 15, 43; CN 7; DAC; DAM MST; DLB 88

Mitchell, William 1879-1936 .... **TCLC 81**

Mitford, Mary Russell 1787-1855 ... **NCLC 4**
See also DLB 110, 116; RGEL 2

Mitford, Nancy 1904-1973 .... **CLC 44**
See also CA 9-12R; DLB 191; RGEL 2

Miyamoto, (Chujo) Yuriko
1899-1951 .... **TCLC 37**
See also Miyamoto Yuriko
See also CA 170, 174

Miyamoto Yuriko
See Miyamoto, (Chujo) Yuriko
See also DLB 180

Miyazawa, Kenji 1896-1933 .... **TCLC 76**
See also CA 157

Mizoguchi, Kenji 1898-1956 .... **TCLC 72**
See also CA 167

Mo, Timothy (Peter) 1950(?)- ... **CLC 46, 134**
See also CA 117; CN 7; DLB 194; MTCW 1; WLIT 4

Modarressi, Taghi (M.) 1931-1997 ... **CLC 44**
See also CA 121; 134; INT 134

Modiano, Patrick (Jean) 1945- .... **CLC 18**
See also CA 85-88; CANR 17, 40; CWW 2; DLB 83

Mofolo, Thomas (Mokopu)
1875(?)-1948 .... **TCLC 22; BLC 3**
See also AFW; CA 121; 153; CANR 83; DAM MULT; DLB 225; MTCW 2; WLIT 2

Mohr, Nicholasa 1938- .... **CLC 12; HLC 2**
See also AAYA 8; CA 49-52; CANR 1, 32, 64; CLR 22; DAM MULT; DLB 145; HW

Morris, William 1834-1896 .... **NCLC 4**
See also BRW 5; CDBLB 1832-1890; DLB
18, 35, 57, 156, 178, 184; FANT; RGEL
2; SFW 4; SUFW

Morris, Wright 1910-1998 .. **CLC 1, 3, 7, 18,
37**
See also AMW; CA 9-12R; 167; CANR 21,
81; CN 7; DLB 2, 206, 218; DLBY 1981;
MTCW 1, 2; RGAL 4; TCLC 107;
TCWW 2

Morrison, Arthur 1863-1945 .... **TCLC 72;
SSC 40**
See also CA 120; 157; CMW 4; DLB 70,
135, 197; RGEL 2

Morrison, Chloe Anthony Wofford
See Morrison, Toni

Morrison, James Douglas 1943-1971
See Morrison, Jim
See also CA 73-76; CANR 40

Morrison, Jim .... **CLC 17**
See also Morrison, James Douglas

Morrison, Toni 1931- . **CLC 4, 10, 22, 55, 81,
87; BLC 3**
See also AAYA 1, 22; AFAW 1, 2; AMWS
3; BPFB 2; BW 2, 3; CA 29-32R; CANR
27, 42, 67; CDALB 1968-1988; CN 7;
CPW; DA; DA3; DAB; DAC; DAM MST,
MULT, NOV, POP; DLB 6, 33, 143;
DLBY 1981; EXPN; FW; LAIT 2, 4;
MAWW; MTCW 1, 2; NFS 1, 6, 8, 14;
RGAL 4; RHW; SATA 57; SSFS 5; TUS;
YAW

Morrison, Van 1945- .... **CLC 21**
See also CA 116; 168

Morrissy, Mary 1958- .... **CLC 99**

Mortimer, John (Clifford) 1923- ..... **CLC 28,
43**
See also CA 13-16R; CANR 21, 69, 109;
CD 5; CDBLB 1960 to Present; CMW 4;
CN 7; CPW; DA3; DAM DRAM, POP;
DLB 13, 245; INT CANR-21; MSW;
MTCW 1, 2; RGEL 2

Mortimer, Penelope (Ruth)
1918-1999 .... **CLC 5**
See also CA 57-60; 187; CANR 45, 88; CN
7

Mortimer, Sir John
See Mortimer, John (Clifford)

Morton, Anthony
See Creasey, John

Morton, Thomas 1579(?)-1647(?) .... **LC 72**
See also DLB 24; RGEL 2

Mosca, Gaetano 1858-1941 .... **TCLC 75**

Mosher, Howard Frank 1943- .... **CLC 62**
See also CA 139; CANR 65

Mosley, Nicholas 1923- .... **CLC 43, 70**
See also CA 69-72; CANR 41, 60, 108; CN
7; DLB 14, 207

Mosley, Walter 1952- .... **CLC 97; BLCS**
See also AAYA 17; BPFB 2; BW 2; CA
142; CANR 57, 92; CMW 4; CPW; DA3;
DAM MULT, POP; MSW; MTCW 2

Moss, Howard 1922-1987 . **CLC 7, 14, 45, 50**
See also CA 1-4R; 123; CANR 1, 44; DAM
POET; DLB 5

Mossgiel, Rab
See Burns, Robert

Motion, Andrew (Peter) 1952- .... **CLC 47**
See also BRWS 7; CA 146; CANR 90; CP
7; DLB 40

Motley, Willard (Francis)
1912-1965 .... **CLC 18**
See also BW 1; CA 117; 106; CANR 88;
DLB 76, 143

Motoori, Norinaga 1730-1801 .... **NCLC 45**

Mott, Michael (Charles Alston)
1930- .... **CLC 15, 34**
See also CA 5-8R; CAAS 7; CANR 7, 29

Mountain Wolf Woman 1884-1960 .. **CLC 92**
See also CA 144; CANR 90; NNAL

Moure, Erin 1955- .... **CLC 88**
See also CA 113; CP 7; CWP; DLB 60

Mowat, Farley (McGill) 1921- .... **CLC 26**
See also AAYA 1; BYA 2; CA 1-4R; CANR
4, 24, 42, 68, 108; CLR 20; CPW; DAC;
DAM MST; DLB 68; INT CANR-24;
JRDA; MAICYA 1, 2; MTCW 1, 2; SATA
3, 55; YAW

Mowatt, Anna Cora 1819-1870 ..... **NCLC 74**
See also RGAL 4

Moyers, Bill 1934- .... **CLC 74**
See also AITN 2; CA 61-64; CANR 31, 52

Mphahlele, Es'kia
See Mphahlele, Ezekiel
See also AFW; CDWLB 3; DLB 125, 225;
RGSF 2; SSFS 11

Mphahlele, Ezekiel 1919- .... **CLC 25, 133;
BLC 3**
See also Mphahlele, Es'kia
See also BW 2, 3; CA 81-84; CANR 26,
76; CN 7; DA3; DAM MULT; MTCW 2;
SATA 119

Mqhayi, S(amuel) E(dward) K(rune Loliwe)
1875-1945 .... **TCLC 25; BLC 3**
See also CA 153; CANR 87; DAM MULT

Mrozek, Slawomir 1930- .... **CLC 3, 13**
See also CA 13-16R; CAAS 10; CANR 29;
CDWLB 4; CWW 2; DLB 232; MTCW 1

Mrs. Belloc-Lowndes
See Lowndes, Marie Adelaide (Belloc)

M'Taggart, John M'Taggart Ellis
See McTaggart, John McTaggart Ellis

Mtwa, Percy (?)- .... **CLC 47**

Mueller, Lisel 1924- .... **CLC 13, 51; PC 33**
See also CA 93-96; CP 7; DLB 105; PFS 9,
13

Muggeridge, Malcolm (Thomas)
1903-1990 .... **TCLC 120**
See also AITN 1; CA 101; CANR 33, 63;
MTCW 1, 2

Muir, Edwin 1887-1959 .... **TCLC 2, 87**
See also Moore, Edward
See also BRWS 6; CA 104; 193; DLB 20,
100, 191; RGEL 2

Muir, John 1838-1914 .... **TCLC 28**
See also AMWS 9; ANW; CA 165; DLB
186

Mujica Lainez, Manuel 1910-1984 ... **CLC 31**
See also Lainez, Manuel Mujica
See also CA 81-84; 112; CANR 32; HW 1

Mukherjee, Bharati 1940- .... **CLC 53, 115;
AAL; SSC 38**
See also BEST 89:2; CA 107; CANR 45,
72; CN 7; DAM NOV; DLB 60, 218;
DNFS 1, 2; FW; MTCW 1, 2; RGAL 4;
RGSF 2; SSFS 7; TUS

Muldoon, Paul 1951- .... **CLC 32, 72**
See also BRWS 4; CA 113; 129; CANR 52,
91; CP 7; DAM POET; DLB 40; INT 129;
PFS 7

Mulisch, Harry 1927- .... **CLC 42**
See also CA 9-12R; CANR 6, 26, 56, 110

Mull, Martin 1943- .... **CLC 17**
See also CA 105

Muller, Wilhelm .... **NCLC 73**

Mulock, Dinah Maria
See Craik, Dinah Maria (Mulock)
See also RGEL 2

Munford, Robert 1737(?)-1783 .... **LC 5**
See also DLB 31

Mungo, Raymond 1946- .... **CLC 72**
See also CA 49-52; CANR 2

Munro, Alice 1931- .... **CLC 6, 10, 19, 50, 95;
SSC 3; WLCS**
See also AITN 2; BPFB 2; CA 33-36R;
CANR 33, 53, 75; CCA 1; CN 7; DA3;

DAC; DAM MST, NOV; DLB 53; MTCW
1, 2; RGEL 2; RGSF 2; SATA 29; SSFS
5, 13

Munro, H(ector) H(ugh) 1870-1916
See Saki
See also CA 104; 130; CANR 104; CDBLB
1890-1914; DA; DA3; DAB; DAC; DAM
MST, NOV; DLB 34, 162; EXPS; MTCW
1, 2; RGEL 2; SSFS 15; WLC

Murakami, Haruki 1949- .... **CLC 150**
See also Murakami Haruki
See also CA 165; CANR 102; MJW; SFW
4

Murakami Haruki
See Murakami, Haruki
See also DLB 182

Murasaki, Lady
See Murasaki Shikibu

Murasaki Shikibu 978(?)-1026(?) ... **CMLC 1**
See also EFS 2; RGWL 2

Murdoch, (Jean) Iris 1919-1999 ... **CLC 1, 2,
3, 4, 6, 8, 11, 15, 22, 31, 51**
See also BRWS 1; CA 13-16R; 179; CANR
8, 43, 68, 103; CDBLB 1960 to Present;
CN 7; DA3; DAB; DAC; DAM MST,
NOV; DLB 14, 194, 233; INT CANR-8;
MTCW 1, 2; RGEL 2; TEA; WLIT 4

Murfree, Mary Noailles 1850-1922 ... **SSC 22**
See also CA 122; 176; DLB 12, 74; RGAL
4

Murnau, Friedrich Wilhelm
See Plumpe, Friedrich Wilhelm

Murphy, Richard 1927- .... **CLC 41**
See also BRWS 5; CA 29-32R; CP 7; DLB
40

Murphy, Sylvia 1937- .... **CLC 34**
See also CA 121

Murphy, Thomas (Bernard) 1935- ... **CLC 51**
See also CA 101

Murray, Albert L. 1916- .... **CLC 73**
See also BW 2; CA 49-52; CANR 26, 52,
78; CSW; DLB 38

Murray, James Augustus Henry
1837-1915 .... **TCLC 117**

Murray, Judith Sargent
1751-1820 .... **NCLC 63**
See also DLB 37, 200

Murray, Les(lie Allan) 1938- .... **CLC 40**
See also BRWS 7; CA 21-24R; CANR 11,
27, 56, 103; CP 7; DAM POET; DLBY
01; RGEL 2

Murry, J. Middleton
See Murry, John Middleton

Murry, John Middleton
1889-1957 .... **TCLC 16**
See also CA 118; DLB 149

Musgrave, Susan 1951- .... **CLC 13, 54**
See also CA 69-72; CANR 45, 84; CCA 1;
CP 7; CWP

Musil, Robert (Edler von)
1880-1942 .... **TCLC 12, 68; SSC 18**
See also CA 109; CANR 55, 84; CDWLB
2; DLB 81, 124; EW 9; MTCW 2; RGSF
2; RGWL 2

Muske, Carol .... **CLC 90**
See also Muske-Dukes, Carol (Anne)

Muske-Dukes, Carol (Anne) 1945-
See Muske, Carol
See also CA 65-68; CAAE 203; CANR 32,
70; CWP

Musset, (Louis Charles) Alfred de
1810-1857 .... **NCLC 7**
See also DLB 192, 217; EW 6; GFL 1789
to the Present; RGWL 2; TWA

Mussolini, Benito (Amilcare Andrea)
1883-1945 .... **TCLC 96**
See also CA 116

My Brother's Brother
See Chekhov, Anton (Pavlovich)

Nishida, Kitaro 1870-1945 .... **TCLC 83**
Nishiwaki, Junzaburo 1894-1982 .... **PC 15**
 See also Nishiwaki, Junzaburo
 See also CA 194; 107; MJW
Nishiwaki, Junzaburo 1894-1982
 See Nishiwaki, Junzaburo
 See also CA 194
Nissenson, Hugh 1933- .... **CLC 4, 9**
 See also CA 17-20R; CANR 27, 108; CN
 7; DLB 28
Niven, Larry .... **CLC 8**
 See also Niven, Laurence Van Cott
 See also AAYA 27; BPFB 2; BYA 10; DLB
 8; SCFW 2
Niven, Laurence Van Cott 1938-
 See Niven, Larry
 See also CA 21-24R; CAAS 12; CANR 14,
 44, 66; CPW; DAM POP; MTCW 1, 2;
 SATA 95; SFW 4
Nixon, Agnes Eckhardt 1927- .... **CLC 21**
 See also CA 110
Nizan, Paul 1905-1940 .... **TCLC 40**
 See also CA 161; DLB 72; GFL 1789 to the
 Present
Nkosi, Lewis 1936- .... **CLC 45; BLC 3**
 See also BW 1, 3; CA 65-68; CANR 27,
 81; CBD; CD 5; DAM MULT; DLB 157,
 225
Nodier, (Jean) Charles (Emmanuel)
 1780-1844 .... **NCLC 19**
 See also DLB 119; GFL 1789 to the Present
Noguchi, Yone 1875-1947 .... **TCLC 80**
Nolan, Christopher 1965- .... **CLC 58**
 See also CA 111; CANR 88
Noon, Jeff 1957- .... **CLC 91**
 See also CA 148; CANR 83; SFW 4
Norden, Charles
 See Durrell, Lawrence (George)
Nordhoff, Charles (Bernard)
 1887-1947 .... **TCLC 23**
 See also CA 108; DLB 9; LAIT 1; RHW 1;
 SATA 23
Norfolk, Lawrence 1963- .... **CLC 76**
 See also CA 144; CANR 85; CN 7
Norman, Marsha 1947- .... **CLC 28; DC 8**
 See also CA 105; CABS 3; CAD; CANR
 41; CD 5; CSW; CWD; DAM DRAM;
 DFS 2; DLB 266; DLBY 1984; FW
Normyx
 See Douglas, (George) Norman
Norris, (Benjamin) Frank(lin, Jr.)
 1870-1902 .... **TCLC 24; SSC 28**
 See also AMW; BPFB 2; CA 110; 160;
 CDALB 1865-1917; DLB 12, 71, 186;
 NFS 12; RGAL 4; TCWW 2; TUS
Norris, Leslie 1921- .... **CLC 14**
 See also CA 11-12; CANR 14; CAP 1; CP
 7; DLB 27, 256
North, Andrew
 See Norton, Andre
North, Anthony
 See Koontz, Dean R(ay)
North, Captain George
 See Stevenson, Robert Louis (Balfour)
North, Captain George
 See Stevenson, Robert Louis (Balfour)
North, Milou
 See Erdrich, Louise
Northrup, B. A.
 See Hubbard, L(afayette) Ron(ald)
North Staffs
 See Hulme, T(homas) E(rnest)
Northup, Solomon 1808-1863 ...... **NCLC 105**
Norton, Alice Mary
 See Norton, Andre
 See also MAICYA 1; SATA 1, 43

Norton, Andre 1912- .... **CLC 12**
 See also Norton, Alice Mary
 See also AAYA 14; BPFB 2; BYA 4, 10,
 12; CA 1-4R; CANR 68; CLR 50; DLB
 8, 52; JRDA; MAICYA 2; MTCW 1;
 SATA 91; SUFW; YAW
Norton, Caroline 1808-1877 .... **NCLC 47**
 See also DLB 21, 159, 199
Norway, Nevil Shute 1899-1960
 See Shute, Nevil
 See also CA 102; 93-96; CANR 85; MTCW
 2
Norwid, Cyprian Kamil
 1821-1883 .... **NCLC 17**
Nosille, Nabrah
 See Ellison, Harlan (Jay)
Nossack, Hans Erich 1901-1978 .... **CLC 6**
 See also CA 93-96; 85-88; DLB 69
Nostradamus 1503-1566 .... **LC 27**
Nosu, Chuji
 See Ozu, Yasujiro
Notenburg, Eleanora (Genrikhovna) von
 See Guro, Elena
Nova, Craig 1945- .... **CLC 7, 31**
 See also CA 45-48; CANR 2, 53
Novak, Joseph
 See Kosinski, Jerzy (Nikodem)
Novalis 1772-1801 .... **NCLC 13**
 See also CDWLB 2; DLB 90; EW 5; RGWL
 2
Novis, Emile
 See Weil, Simone (Adolphine)
Nowlan, Alden (Albert) 1933-1983 ... **CLC 15**
 See also CA 9-12R; CANR 5; DAC; DAM
 MST; DLB 53; PFS 12
Noyes, Alfred 1880-1958 ...... **TCLC 7; PC 27**
 See also CA 104; 188; DLB 20; EXPP;
 FANT; PFS 4; RGEL 2
Nunn, Kem .... **CLC 34**
 See also CA 159
Nwapa, Flora 1931-1993 .... **CLC 133; BLCS**
 See also BW 2; CA 143; CANR 83; CD-
 WLB 3; CWRI 5; DLB 125; WLIT 2
Nye, Robert 1939- .... **CLC 13, 42**
 See also CA 33-36R; CANR 29, 67, 107;
 CN 7; CP 7; CWRI 5; DAM NOV; DLB
 14; FANT; HGG; MTCW 1; RHW; SATA
 6
Nyro, Laura 1947-1997 .... **CLC 17**
 See also CA 194
Oates, Joyce Carol 1938- .. **CLC 1, 2, 3, 6, 9,
 11, 15, 19, 33, 52, 108, 134; SSC 6;
 WLC**
 See also AAYA 15; AITN 1; AMWS 2;
 BEST 89:2; BPFB 2; BYA 11; CA 5-8R;
 CANR 25, 45, 74; CDALB 1968-1988;
 CN 7; CP 7; CPW; CWP; DA; DA3;
 DAB; DAC; DAM MST, NOV, POP;
 DLB 2, 5, 130; DLBY 1981; EXPS; FW;
 HGG; INT CANR-25; LAIT 4; MAWW;
 MTCW 1, 2; NFS 8; RGAL 4; RGSF 2;
 SSFS 1, 8; TUS
O'Brian, E. G.
 See Clarke, Arthur C(harles)
O'Brian, Patrick 1914-2000 .... **CLC 152**
 See also CA 144; 187; CANR 74; CPW;
 MTCW 2; RHW
O'Brien, Darcy 1939-1998 .... **CLC 11**
 See also CA 21-24R; 167; CANR 8, 59
O'Brien, Edna 1936- ..... **CLC 3, 5, 8, 13, 36,
 65, 116; SSC 10**
 See also BRWS 5; CA 1-4R; CANR 6, 41,
 65, 102; CDBLB 1960 to Present; CN 7;
 DA3; DAM NOV; DLB 14, 231; FW;
 MTCW 1, 2; RGSF 2; WLIT 4
O'Brien, Fitz-James 1828-1862 ..... **NCLC 21**
 See also DLB 74; RGAL 4; SUFW

O'Brien, Flann .... **CLC 1, 4, 5, 7, 10, 47**
 See also O Nuallain, Brian
 See also BRWS 2; DLB 231; RGEL 2
O'Brien, Richard 1942- .... **CLC 17**
 See also CA 124
O'Brien, (William) Tim(othy) 1946- . **CLC 7,
 19, 40, 103**
 See also AAYA 16; AMWS 5; CA 85-88;
 CANR 40, 58; CDALBS; CN 7; CPW;
 DA3; DAM POP; DLB 152; DLBD 9;
 DLBY 1980; MTCW 2; RGAL 4; SSFS
 5, 15
Obstfelder, Sigbjoern 1866-1900 .... **TCLC 23**
 See also CA 123
O'Casey, Sean 1880-1964 .... **CLC 1, 5, 9, 11,
 15, 88; DC 12; WLCS**
 See also BRW 7; CA 89-92; CANR 62;
 CBD; CDBLB 1914-1945; DA3; DAB;
 DAC; DAM DRAM, MST; DLB 10;
 MTCW 1, 2; RGEL 2; TEA; WLIT 4
O'Cathasaigh, Sean
 See O'Casey, Sean
Occom, Samson 1723-1792 .... **LC 60**
 See also DLB 175; NNAL
Ochs, Phil(ip David) 1940-1976 .... **CLC 17**
 See also CA 185; 65-68
O'Connor, Edwin (Greene)
 1918-1968 .... **CLC 14**
 See also CA 93-96; 25-28R
O'Connor, (Mary) Flannery
 1925-1964 .... **CLC 1, 2, 3, 6, 10, 13, 15,
 21, 66, 104; SSC 1, 23; WLC**
 See also AAYA 7; AMW; BPFB 3; CA
 1-4R; CANR 3, 41; CDALB 1941-1968;
 DA; DA3; DAB; DAC; DAM MST, NOV;
 DLB 2, 152; DLBD 12; DLBY 1980;
 EXPS; LAIT 5; MAWW; MTCW 1, 2;
 NFS 3; RGAL 4; RGSF 2; SSFS 2, 7, 10;
 TUS
O'Connor, Frank .... **CLC 23; SSC 5**
 See also O'Donovan, Michael John
 See also DLB 162; RGSF 2; SSFS 5
O'Dell, Scott 1898-1989 .... **CLC 30**
 See also AAYA 3; BPFB 3; BYA 1, 2, 3, 5;
 CA 61-64; 129; CANR 12, 30; CLR 1,
 16; DLB 52; JRDA; MAICYA 1, 2; SATA
 12, 60; WYA; YAW
Odets, Clifford 1906-1963 ..... **CLC 2, 28, 98;
 DC 6**
 See also AMWS 2; CA 85-88; CAD; CANR
 62; DAM DRAM; DFS 3; DLB 7, 26;
 MTCW 1, 2; RGAL 4; TUS
O'Doherty, Brian 1928- .... **CLC 76**
 See also CA 105; CANR 108
O'Donnell, K. M.
 See Malzberg, Barry N(athaniel)
O'Donnell, Lawrence
 See Kuttner, Henry
O'Donovan, Michael John
 1903-1966 .... **CLC 14**
 See also O'Connor, Frank
 See also CA 93-96; CANR 84
Oe, Kenzaburo 1935- .. **CLC 10, 36, 86; SSC
 20**
 See also Oe Kenzaburo
 See also CA 97-100; CANR 36, 50, 74;
 DA3; DAM NOV; DLBY 1994; MTCW
 1, 2
Oe Kenzaburo
 See Oe, Kenzaburo
 See also CWW 2; DLB 182; EWL 3; MJW;
 RGSF 2; RGWL 2
O'Faolain, Julia 1932- .... **CLC 6, 19, 47, 108**
 See also CA 81-84; CAAS 2; CANR 12,
 61; CN 7; DLB 14, 231; FW; MTCW 1;
 RHW

EXPS; INT CANR-23; MTCW 1, 2;
RGAL 4; RGSF 2; SSFS 3, 12

Ozu, Yasujiro 1903-1963 .... **CLC 16**
See also CA 112

Pacheco, C.
See Pessoa, Fernando (Antonio Nogueira)

Pacheco, Jose Emilio 1939-
See also CA 111; 131; CANR 65; DAM
MULT; HLC 2; HW 1, 2; RGSF 2

Pa Chin .... **CLC 18**
See also Li Fei-kan

Pack, Robert 1929- .... **CLC 13**
See also CA 1-4R; CANR 3, 44, 82; CP 7;
DLB 5; SATA 118

Padgett, Lewis
See Kuttner, Henry

Padilla (Lorenzo), Heberto
1932-2000 .... **CLC 38**
See also AITN 1; CA 123; 131; 189; HW 1

Page, Jimmy 1944- .... **CLC 12**

Page, Louise 1955- .... **CLC 40**
See also CA 140; CANR 76; CBD; CD 5;
CWD; DLB 233

Page, P(atricia) K(athleen) 1916- ...... **CLC 7,
18; PC 12**
See also Cape, Judith
See also CA 53-56; CANR 4, 22, 65; CP 7;
DAC; DAM MST; DLB 68; MTCW 1;
RGEL 2

Page, Stanton
See Fuller, Henry Blake

Page, Stanton
See Fuller, Henry Blake

Page, Thomas Nelson 1853-1922 .... **SSC 23**
See also CA 118; 177; DLB 12, 78; DLBD
13; RGAL 4

Pagels, Elaine Hiesey 1943- .... **CLC 104**
See also CA 45-48; CANR 2, 24, 51; FW;
NCFS 4

Paget, Violet 1856-1935
See Lee, Vernon
See also CA 104; 166; GLL 1; HGG

Paget-Lowe, Henry
See Lovecraft, H(oward) P(hillips)

Paglia, Camille (Anna) 1947- .... **CLC 68**
See also CA 140; CANR 72; CPW; FW;
GLL 2; MTCW 2

Paige, Richard
See Koontz, Dean R(ay)

Paine, Thomas 1737-1809 .... **NCLC 62**
See also AMWS 1; CDALB 1640-1865;
DLB 31, 43, 73, 158; LAIT 1; RGAL 4;
RGEL 2; TUS

Pakenham, Antonia
See Fraser, (Lady) Antonia (Pakenham)

Palamas, Kostes 1859-1943 .... **TCLC 5**
See also CA 105; 190; RGWL 2

Palazzeschi, Aldo 1885-1974 .... **CLC 11**
See also CA 89-92; 53-56; DLB 114, 264

Pales Matos, Luis 1898-1959
See Pales Matos, Luis
See also HLCS 2; HW 1; LAW

Paley, Grace 1922- .. **CLC 4, 6, 37, 140; SSC
8**
See also AMWS 6; CA 25-28R; CANR 13,
46, 74; CN 7; CPW; DA3; DAM POP;
DLB 28, 218; EXPS; FW; INT CANR-
13; MAWW; MTCW 1, 2; RGAL 4;
RGSF 2; SSFS 3

Palin, Michael (Edward) 1943- .... **CLC 21**
See also Monty Python
See also CA 107; CANR 35, 109; SATA 67

Palliser, Charles 1947- .... **CLC 65**
See also CA 136; CANR 76; CN 7

Palma, Ricardo 1833-1919 .... **TCLC 29**
See also CA 168; LAW

Pancake, Breece Dexter 1952-1979
See Pancake, Breece D'J
See also CA 123; 109

Pancake, Breece D'J .... **CLC 29**
See also Pancake, Breece Dexter
See also DLB 130

Panchenko, Nikolai .... **CLC 59**

Pankhurst, Emmeline (Goulden)
1858-1928 .... **TCLC 100**
See also CA 116; FW

Panko, Rudy
See Gogol, Nikolai (Vasilyevich)

Papadiamantis, Alexandros
1851-1911 .... **TCLC 29**
See also CA 168

Papadiamantopoulos, Johannes 1856-1910
See Moreas, Jean
See also CA 117

Papini, Giovanni 1881-1956 .... **TCLC 22**
See also CA 121; 180; DLB 264

Paracelsus 1493-1541 .... **LC 14**
See also DLB 179

Parasol, Peter
See Stevens, Wallace

Pardo Bazan, Emilia 1851-1921 .... **SSC 30**
See also FW; RGSF 2; RGWL 2

Pareto, Vilfredo 1848-1923 .... **TCLC 69**
See also CA 175

Paretsky, Sara 1947- .... **CLC 135**
See also AAYA 30; BEST 90:3; CA 125;
129; CANR 59, 95; CMW 4; CPW; DA3;
DAM POP; INT CA-129; MSW; RGAL 4

Parfenie, Maria
See Codrescu, Andrei

Parini, Jay (Lee) 1948- .... **CLC 54, 133**
See also CA 97-100; CAAS 16; CANR 32,
87

Park, Jordan
See Kornbluth, C(yril) M.; Pohl, Frederik

Park, Robert E(zra) 1864-1944 ..... **TCLC 73**
See also CA 122; 165

Parker, Bert
See Ellison, Harlan (Jay)

Parker, Dorothy (Rothschild)
1893-1967 .. **CLC 15, 68; PC 28; SSC 2**
See also AMWS 9; CA 19-20; 25-28R; CAP
2; DA3; DAM POET; DLB 11, 45, 86;
EXPP; FW; MAWW; MTCW 1, 2; RGAL
4; RGSF 2; TUS

Parker, Robert B(rown) 1932- .... **CLC 27**
See also AAYA 28; BEST 89:4; BPFB 3;
CA 49-52; CANR 1, 26, 52, 89; CMW 4;
CPW; DAM NOV, POP; INT CANR-26;
MSW; MTCW 1

Parkin, Frank 1940- .... **CLC 43**
See also CA 147

Parkman, Francis, Jr. 1823-1893 .. **NCLC 12**
See also AMWS 2; DLB 1, 30, 183, 186,
235; RGAL 4

Parks, Gordon (Alexander Buchanan)
1912- .... **CLC 1, 16; BLC 3**
See also AAYA 36; AITN 2; BW 2, 3; CA
41-44R; CANR 26, 66; DA3; DAM
MULT; DLB 33; MTCW 2; SATA 8, 108

Parks, Tim(othy Harold) 1954- ...... **CLC 147**
See also CA 126; 131; CANR 77; DLB 231;
INT CA-131

Parmenides c. 515 B.C.-c. 450
B.C. .... **CMLC 22**
See also DLB 176

Parnell, Thomas 1679-1718 .... **LC 3**
See also DLB 95; RGEL 2

Parra, Nicanor 1914- ... **CLC 2, 102; HLC 2;
PC 39**
See also CA 85-88; CANR 32; CWW 2;
DAM MULT; HW 1; LAW; MTCW 1

Parra Sanojo, Ana Teresa de la 1890-1936
See de la Parra, (Ana) Teresa (Sonojo)
See also HLCS 2; LAW

Parrish, Mary Frances
See Fisher, M(ary) F(rances) K(ennedy)

Parshchikov, Aleksei .... **CLC 59**

Parson, Professor
See Coleridge, Samuel Taylor

Parson Lot
See Kingsley, Charles

Parton, Sara Payson Willis
1811-1872 .... **NCLC 86**
See also DLB 43, 74, 239

Partridge, Anthony
See Oppenheim, E(dward) Phillips

Pascal, Blaise 1623-1662 .... **LC 35**
See also EW 3; GFL Beginnings to 1789;
RGWL 2; TWA

Pascoli, Giovanni 1855-1912 .... **TCLC 45**
See also CA 170; EW 7

Pasolini, Pier Paolo 1922-1975 .. **CLC 20, 37,
106; PC 17**
See also CA 93-96; 61-64; CANR 63; DLB
128, 177; MTCW 1; RGWL 2

Pasquini
See Silone, Ignazio

Pastan, Linda (Olenik) 1932- .... **CLC 27**
See also CA 61-64; CANR 18, 40, 61; CP
7; CSW; CWP; DAM POET; DLB 5; PFS
8

Pasternak, Boris (Leonidovich)
1890-1960 ...... **CLC 7, 10, 18, 63; PC 6;
SSC 31; WLC**
See also BPFB 3; CA 127; 116; DA; DA3;
DAB; DAC; DAM MST, NOV, POET;
EW 10; MTCW 1, 2; RGSF 2; RGWL 2;
TWA; WP

Patchen, Kenneth 1911-1972 .... **CLC 1, 2, 18**
See also CA 1-4R; 33-36R; CANR 3, 35;
DAM POET; DLB 16, 48; MTCW 1;
RGAL 4

Pater, Walter (Horatio) 1839-1894 . **NCLC 7,
90**
See also BRW 5; CDBLB 1832-1890; DLB
57, 156; RGEL 2; TEA

Paterson, A(ndrew) B(arton)
1864-1941 .... **TCLC 32**
See also CA 155; DLB 230; RGEL 2; SATA
97

Paterson, Katherine (Womeldorf)
1932- .... **CLC 12, 30**
See also AAYA 1, 31; BYA 1, 2, 7; CA 21-
24R; CANR 28, 59; CLR 7, 50; CWRI 5;
DLB 52; JRDA; LAIT 4; MAICYA 1, 2;
MAICYAS 1; MTCW 1; SATA 13, 53, 92,
133; WYA; YAW

Patmore, Coventry Kersey Dighton
1823-1896 .... **NCLC 9**
See also DLB 35, 98; RGEL 2; TEA

Paton, Alan (Stewart) 1903-1988 ...... **CLC 4,
10, 25, 55, 106; WLC**
See also AAYA 26; AFW; BPFB 3; BRWS
2; BYA 1; CA 13-16; 125; CANR 22;
CAP 1; DA; DA3; DAB; DAC; DAM
MST, NOV; DLB 225; DLBD 17; EXPN;
LAIT 4; MTCW 1, 2; NFS 3, 12; RGEL
2; SATA 11; SATA-Obit 56; TWA; WLIT
2

Paton Walsh, Gillian 1937- .... **CLC 35**
See also Paton Walsh, Jill; Walsh, Jill Paton
See also AAYA 11; CANR 38, 83; CLR 2,
65; DLB 161; JRDA; MAICYA 1, 2;
SAAS 3; SATA 4, 72, 109; YAW

Paton Walsh, Jill
See Paton Walsh, Gillian
See also BYA 1, 8

Patton, George S(mith), Jr.
1885-1945 .... **TCLC 79**
See also CA 189

Paulding, James Kirke 1778-1860 ... **NCLC 2**
See also DLB 3, 59, 74, 250; RGAL 4

Paulin, Thomas Neilson 1949-
See Paulin, Tom
See also CA 123; 128; CANR 98; CP 7

Pure, Simon
See Swinnerton, Frank Arthur
Pushkin, Aleksandr Sergeevich
See Pushkin, Alexander (Sergeyevich)
See also DLB 205
Pushkin, Alexander (Sergeyevich)
1799-1837 .... **NCLC 3, 27, 83; PC 10; SSC 27, 55; WLC**
See also DA; DA3; DAB; DAC; DAM DRAM, MST, POET; EW 5; EXPS; RGSF 2; RGWL 2; SATA 61; SSFS 9; TWA
P'u Sung-ling 1640-1715 .... **LC 49; SSC 31**
Putnam, Arthur Lee
See Alger, Horatio, Jr.
Puzo, Mario 1920-1999 .... **CLC 1, 2, 6, 36, 107**
See also BPFB 3; CA 65-68; 185; CANR 4, 42, 65, 99; CN 7; CPW; DA3; DAM NOV, POP; DLB 6; MTCW 1, 2; RGAL 4
Pygge, Edward
See Barnes, Julian (Patrick)
Pyle, Ernest Taylor 1900-1945
See Pyle, Ernie
See also CA 115; 160
Pyle, Ernie .... **TCLC 75**
See also Pyle, Ernest Taylor
See also DLB 29; MTCW 2
Pyle, Howard 1853-1911 .... **TCLC 81**
See also BYA 2, 4; CA 109; 137; CLR 22; DLB 42, 188; DLBD 13; LAIT 1; MAICYA 1, 2; SATA 16, 100; WCH; YAW
Pym, Barbara (Mary Crampton)
1913-1980 .... **CLC 13, 19, 37, 111**
See also BPFB 3; BRWS 2; CA 13-14; 97-100; CANR 13, 34; CAP 1; DLB 14, 207; DLBY 1987; MTCW 1, 2; RGEL 2; TEA
Pynchon, Thomas (Ruggles, Jr.)
1937- ...... **CLC 2, 3, 6, 9, 11, 18, 33, 62, 72, 123; SSC 14; WLC**
See also AMWS 2; BEST 90:2; BPFB 3; CA 17-20R; CANR 22, 46, 73; CN 7; CPW 1; DA; DA3; DAB; DAC; DAM MST, NOV, POP; DLB 2, 173; MTCW 1, 2; RGAL 4; SFW 4; TUS
Pythagoras c. 582 B.C.-c. 507 B.C. .... **CMLC 22**
See also DLB 176

Q
See Quiller-Couch, Sir Arthur (Thomas)
Qian, Chongzhu
See Ch'ien, Chung-shu
Qian Zhongshu
See Ch'ien, Chung-shu
Qroll
See Dagerman, Stig (Halvard)
Quarrington, Paul (Lewis) 1953- ..... **CLC 65**
See also CA 129; CANR 62, 95
Quasimodo, Salvatore 1901-1968 ..... **CLC 10**
See also CA 13-16; 25-28R; CAP 1; DLB 114; EW 12; MTCW 1; RGWL 2
Quatermass, Martin
See Carpenter, John (Howard)
Quay, Stephen 1947- .... **CLC 95**
See also CA 189
Quay, Timothy 1947- .... **CLC 95**
See also CA 189
Queen, Ellery .... **CLC 3, 11**
See also Dannay, Frederic; Davidson, Avram (James); Deming, Richard; Fairman, Paul W.; Flora, Fletcher; Hoch, Edward D(entinger); Kane, Henry; Lee, Manfred B(ennington); Marlowe, Stephen; Powell, (Oval) Talmage; Sheldon, Walter J(ames); Sturgeon, Theodore (Hamilton); Tracy, Don(ald Fiske); Vance, John Holbrook
See also BPFB 3; CMW 4; MSW; RGAL 4

Queen, Ellery, Jr.
See Dannay, Frederic; Lee, Manfred B(ennington)
Queneau, Raymond 1903-1976 ..... **CLC 2, 5, 10, 42**
See also CA 77-80; 69-72; CANR 32; DLB 72, 258; EW 12; GFL 1789 to the Present; MTCW 1, 2; RGWL 2
Quevedo, Francisco de 1580-1645 .... **LC 23**
Quiller-Couch, Sir Arthur (Thomas)
1863-1944 .... **TCLC 53**
See also CA 118; 166; DLB 135, 153, 190; HGG; RGEL 2; SUFW
Quin, Ann (Marie) 1936-1973 .... **CLC 6**
See also CA 9-12R; 45-48; DLB 14, 231
Quinn, Martin
See Smith, Martin Cruz
Quinn, Peter 1947- .... **CLC 91**
See also CA 197
Quinn, Simon
See Smith, Martin Cruz
Quintana, Leroy V. 1944- .... **PC 36**
See also CA 131; CANR 65; DAM MULT; DLB 82; HLC 2; HW 1, 2
Quiroga, Horacio (Sylvestre)
1878-1937 .... **TCLC 20; HLC 2**
See also CA 117; 131; DAM MULT; HW 1; LAW; MTCW 1; RGSF 2; WLIT 1
Quoirez, Francoise 1935- .... **CLC 9**
See also Sagan, Francoise
See also CA 49-52; CANR 6, 39, 73; CWW 2; MTCW 1, 2; TWA
Raabe, Wilhelm (Karl) 1831-1910 . **TCLC 45**
See also CA 167; DLB 129
Rabe, David (William) 1940- .. **CLC 4, 8, 33; DC 16**
See also CA 85-88; CABS 3; CAD; CANR 59; CD 5; DAM DRAM; DFS 3, 8, 13; DLB 7, 228
Rabelais, Francois 1494-1553 .... **LC 5, 60; WLC**
See also DA; DAB; DAC; DAM MST; EW 2; GFL Beginnings to 1789; RGWL 2; TWA
Rabinovitch, Sholem 1859-1916
See Aleichem, Sholom
See also CA 104
Rabinyan, Dorit 1972- .... **CLC 119**
See also CA 170
Rachilde
See Vallette, Marguerite Eymery
Racine, Jean 1639-1699 .... **LC 28**
See also DA3; DAB; DAM MST; EW 3; GFL Beginnings to 1789; RGWL 2; TWA
Radcliffe, Ann (Ward) 1764-1823 ... **NCLC 6, 55, 106**
See also DLB 39, 178; HGG; RGEL 2; SUFW; WLIT 3
Radclyffe-Hall, Marguerite
See Hall, (Marguerite) Radclyffe
Radiguet, Raymond 1903-1923 ...... **TCLC 29**
See also CA 162; DLB 65; GFL 1789 to the Present; RGWL 2
Radnoti, Miklos 1909-1944 .... **TCLC 16**
See also CA 118; CDWLB 4; DLB 215; RGWL 2
Rado, James 1939- .... **CLC 17**
See also CA 105
Radvanyi, Netty 1900-1983
See Seghers, Anna
See also CA 85-88; 110; CANR 82
Rae, Ben
See Griffiths, Trevor
Raeburn, John (Hay) 1941- .... **CLC 34**
See also CA 57-60
Ragni, Gerome 1942-1991 .... **CLC 17**
See also CA 105; 134

Rahv, Philip .... **CLC 24**
See also Greenberg, Ivan
See also DLB 137
Raimund, Ferdinand Jakob
1790-1836 .... **NCLC 69**
See also DLB 90
Raine, Craig (Anthony) 1944- .. **CLC 32, 103**
See also CA 108; CANR 29, 51, 103; CP 7; DLB 40; PFS 7
Raine, Kathleen (Jessie) 1908- ..... **CLC 7, 45**
See also CA 85-88; CANR 46, 109; CP 7; DLB 20; MTCW 1; RGEL 2
Rainis, Janis 1865-1929 .... **TCLC 29**
See also CA 170; CDWLB 4; DLB 220
Rakosi, Carl .... **CLC 47**
See also Rawley, Callman
See also CAAS 5; CP 7; DLB 193
Ralegh, Sir Walter
See Raleigh, Sir Walter
See also BRW 1; RGEL 2; WP
Raleigh, Richard
See Lovecraft, H(oward) P(hillips)
Raleigh, Sir Walter 1554(?)-1618 .... **LC 31, 39; PC 31**
See also Ralegh, Sir Walter
See also CDBLB Before 1660; DLB 172; EXPP; PFS 14; TEA
Rallentando, H. P.
See Sayers, Dorothy L(eigh)
Ramal, Walter
See de la Mare, Walter (John)
Ramana Maharshi 1879-1950 .... **TCLC 84**
Ramoacn y Cajal, Santiago
1852-1934 .... **TCLC 93**
Ramon, Juan
See Jimenez (Mantecon), Juan Ramon
Ramos, Graciliano 1892-1953 .... **TCLC 32**
See also CA 167; HW 2; LAW; WLIT 1
Rampersad, Arnold 1941- .... **CLC 44**
See also BW 2, 3; CA 127; 133; CANR 81; DLB 111; INT 133
Rampling, Anne
See Rice, Anne
See also GLL 2
Ramsay, Allan 1686(?)-1758 .... **LC 29**
See also DLB 95; RGEL 2
Ramsay, Jay
See Campbell, (John) Ramsey
Ramuz, Charles-Ferdinand
1878-1947 .... **TCLC 33**
See also CA 165
Rand, Ayn 1905-1982 ...... **CLC 3, 30, 44, 79; WLC**
See also AAYA 10; AMWS 4; BPFB 3; BYA 12; CA 13-16R; 105; CANR 27, 73; CDALBS; CPW; DA; DA3; DAC; DAM MST, NOV, POP; DLB 227; MTCW 1, 2; NFS 10; RGAL 4; SFW 4; TUS; YAW
Randall, Dudley (Felker) 1914-2000 . **CLC 1, 135; BLC 3**
See also BW 1, 3; CA 25-28R; 189; CANR 23, 82; DAM MULT; DLB 41; PFS 5
Randall, Robert
See Silverberg, Robert
Ranger, Ken
See Creasey, John
Rank, Otto 1884-1939 .... **TCLC 115**
Ransom, John Crowe 1888-1974 .. **CLC 2, 4, 5, 11, 24**
See also AMW; CA 5-8R; 49-52; CANR 6, 34; CDALBS; DA3; DAM POET; DLB 45, 63; EXPP; MTCW 1, 2; RGAL 4; TUS
Rao, Raja 1909- .... **CLC 25, 56**
See also CA 73-76; CANR 51; CN 7; DAM NOV; MTCW 1, 2; RGEL 2; RGSF 2

Richardson (Robertson), Ethel Florence Lindesay 1870-1946
See Richardson, Henry Handel
See also CA 105; 190; DLB 230; RHW

Richardson, Henry Handel .... **TCLC 4**
See also Richardson (Robertson), Ethel Florence Lindesay
See also DLB 197; RGEL 2; RGSF 2

Richardson, John 1796-1852 .... **NCLC 55**
See also CCA 1; DAC; DLB 99

Richardson, Samuel 1689-1761 ...... **LC 1, 44; WLC**
See also BRW 3; CDBLB 1660-1789; DA; DAB; DAC; DAM MST, NOV; DLB 39; RGEL 2; TEA; WLIT 3

Richler, Mordecai 1931-2001 .... **CLC 3, 5, 9, 13, 18, 46, 70**
See also AITN 1; CA 65-68; 201; CANR 31, 62; CCA 1; CLR 17; CWRI 5; DAC; DAM MST, NOV; DLB 53; MAICYA 1, 2; MTCW 1, 2; RGEL 2; SATA 44, 98; SATA-Brief 27; TWA

Richter, Conrad (Michael)
1890-1968 .... **CLC 30**
See also AAYA 21; BYA 2; CA 5-8R; 25-28R; CANR 23; DLB 9, 212; LAIT 1; MTCW 1, 2; RGAL 4; SATA 3; TCWW 2; TUS; YAW

Ricostranza, Tom
See Ellis, Trey

Riddell, Charlotte 1832-1906 .... **TCLC 40**
See also Riddell, Mrs. J. H.
See also CA 165; DLB 156

Riddell, Mrs. J. H.
See Riddell, Charlotte
See also HGG; SUFW

Ridge, John Rollin 1827-1867 .... **NCLC 82**
See also CA 144; DAM MULT; DLB 175; NNAL

Ridgeway, Jason
See Marlowe, Stephen

Ridgway, Keith 1965- .... **CLC 119**
See also CA 172

Riding, Laura .... **CLC 3, 7**
See also Jackson, Laura (Riding)
See also RGAL 4

Riefenstahl, Berta Helene Amalia 1902-
See Riefenstahl, Leni
See also CA 108

Riefenstahl, Leni .... **CLC 16**
See also Riefenstahl, Berta Helene Amalia

Riffe, Ernest
See Bergman, (Ernst) Ingmar

Riggs, (Rolla) Lynn 1899-1954 .... **TCLC 56**
See also CA 144; DAM MULT; DLB 175; NNAL

Riis, Jacob A(ugust) 1849-1914 ..... **TCLC 80**
See also CA 113; 168; DLB 23

Riley, James Whitcomb
1849-1916 .... **TCLC 51**
See also CA 118; 137; DAM POET; MAICYA 1, 2; RGAL 4; SATA 17

Riley, Tex
See Creasey, John

Rilke, Rainer Maria 1875-1926 .. **TCLC 1, 6, 19; PC 2**
See also CA 104; 132; CANR 62, 99; CDWLB 2; DA3; DAM POET; DLB 81; EW 9; MTCW 1, 2; RGWL 2; TWA; WP

Rimbaud, (Jean Nicolas) Arthur
1854-1891 .... **NCLC 4, 35, 82; PC 3; WLC**
See also DA; DA3; DAB; DAC; DAM MST, POET; DLB 217; EW 7; GFL 1789 to the Present; RGWL 2; TWA; WP

Rinehart, Mary Roberts
1876-1958 .... **TCLC 52**
See also BPFB 3; CA 108; 166; RGAL 4; RHW

Ringmaster, The
See Mencken, H(enry) L(ouis)

Ringwood, Gwen(dolyn Margaret) Pharis
1910-1984 .... **CLC 48**
See also CA 148; 112; DLB 88

Rio, Michel 1945(?)- .... **CLC 43**
See also CA 201

Ritsos, Giannes
See Ritsos, Yannis

Ritsos, Yannis 1909-1990 .... **CLC 6, 13, 31**
See also CA 77-80; 133; CANR 39, 61; EW 12; MTCW 1; RGWL 2

Ritter, Erika 1948(?)- .... **CLC 52**
See also CD 5; CWD

Rivera, Jose Eustasio 1889-1928 ... **TCLC 35**
See also CA 162; HW 1, 2; LAW

Rivera, Tomas 1935-1984
See also CA 49-52; CANR 32; DLB 82; HLCS 2; HW 1; RGAL 4; SSFS 15; TCWW 2; WLIT 1

Rivers, Conrad Kent 1933-1968 .... **CLC 1**
See also BW 1; CA 85-88; DLB 41

Rivers, Elfrida
See Bradley, Marion Zimmer
See also GLL 1

Riverside, John
See Heinlein, Robert A(nson)

Rizal, Jose 1861-1896 .... **NCLC 27**

Roa Bastos, Augusto (Antonio)
1917- .... **CLC 45; HLC 2**
See also CA 131; DAM MULT; DLB 113; HW 1; LAW; RGSF 2; WLIT 1

Robbe-Grillet, Alain 1922- .... **CLC 1, 2, 4, 6, 8, 10, 14, 43, 128**
See also BPFB 3; CA 9-12R; CANR 33, 65; DLB 83; EW 13; GFL 1789 to the Present; IDFW 3, 4; MTCW 1, 2; RGWL 2; SSFS 15

Robbins, Harold 1916-1997 .... **CLC 5**
See also BPFB 3; CA 73-76; 162; CANR 26, 54; DA3; DAM NOV; MTCW 1, 2

Robbins, Thomas Eugene 1936-
See Robbins, Tom
See also CA 81-84; CANR 29, 59, 95; CN 7; CPW; CSW; DA3; DAM NOV, POP; MTCW 1, 2

Robbins, Tom .... **CLC 9, 32, 64**
See also Robbins, Thomas Eugene
See also AAYA 32; AMWS 10; BEST 90:3; BPFB 3; DLBY 1980; MTCW 2

Robbins, Trina 1938- .... **CLC 21**
See also CA 128

Roberts, Charles G(eorge) D(ouglas)
1860-1943 .... **TCLC 8**
See also CA 105; 188; CLR 33; CWRI 5; DLB 92; RGEL 2; RGSF 2; SATA 88; SATA-Brief 29

Roberts, Elizabeth Madox
1886-1941 .... **TCLC 68**
See also CA 111; 166; CWRI 5; DLB 9, 54, 102; RGAL 4; RHW; SATA 33; SATA-Brief 27; WCH

Roberts, Kate 1891-1985 .... **CLC 15**
See also CA 107; 116

Roberts, Keith (John Kingston)
1935-2000 .... **CLC 14**
See also CA 25-28R; CANR 46; DLB 261; SFW 4

Roberts, Kenneth (Lewis)
1885-1957 .... **TCLC 23**
See also CA 109; 199; DLB 9; RGAL 4; RHW

Roberts, Michele (Brigitte) 1949- ..... **CLC 48**
See also CA 115; CANR 58; CN 7; DLB 231; FW

Robertson, Ellis
See Ellison, Harlan (Jay); Silverberg, Robert

Robertson, Thomas William
1829-1871 .... **NCLC 35**
See also Robertson, Tom
See also DAM DRAM

Robertson, Tom
See Robertson, Thomas William
See also RGEL 2

Robeson, Kenneth
See Dent, Lester

Robinson, Edwin Arlington
1869-1935 .... **TCLC 5, 101; PC 1, 35**
See also AMW; CA 104; 133; CDALB 1865-1917; DA; DAC; DAM MST, POET; DLB 54; EXPP; MTCW 1, 2; PAB; PFS 4; RGAL 4; WP

Robinson, Henry Crabb
1775-1867 .... **NCLC 15**
See also DLB 107

Robinson, Jill 1936- .... **CLC 10**
See also CA 102; INT 102

Robinson, Kim Stanley 1952- .... **CLC 34**
See also AAYA 26; CA 126; CN 7; SATA 109; SCFW 2; SFW 4

Robinson, Lloyd
See Silverberg, Robert

Robinson, Marilynne 1944- .... **CLC 25**
See also CA 116; CANR 80; CN 7; DLB 206

Robinson, Smokey .... **CLC 21**
See also Robinson, William, Jr.

Robinson, William, Jr. 1940-
See Robinson, Smokey
See also CA 116

Robison, Mary 1949- .... **CLC 42, 98**
See also CA 113; 116; CANR 87; CN 7; DLB 130; INT 116; RGSF 2

Rochester
See Wilmot, John
See also RGEL 2

Rod, Edouard 1857-1910 .... **TCLC 52**

Roddenberry, Eugene Wesley 1921-1991
See Roddenberry, Gene
See also CA 110; 135; CANR 37; SATA 45; SATA-Obit 69

Roddenberry, Gene .... **CLC 17**
See also Roddenberry, Eugene Wesley
See also AAYA 5; SATA-Obit 69

Rodgers, Mary 1931- .... **CLC 12**
See also BYA 5; CA 49-52; CANR 8, 55, 90; CLR 20; CWRI 5; INT CANR-8; JRDA; MAICYA 1, 2; SATA 8, 130

Rodgers, W(illiam) R(obert)
1909-1969 .... **CLC 7**
See also CA 85-88; DLB 20; RGEL 2

Rodman, Eric
See Silverberg, Robert

Rodman, Howard 1920(?)-1985 .... **CLC 65**
See also CA 118

Rodman, Maia
See Wojciechowska, Maia (Teresa)

Rodo, Jose Enrique 1871(?)-1917
See also CA 178; HLCS 2; HW 2; LAW

Rodolph, Utto
See Ouologuem, Yambo

Rodriguez, Claudio 1934-1999 .... **CLC 10**
See also CA 188; DLB 134

Rodriguez, Richard 1944- .... **CLC 155; HLC 2**
See also CA 110; CANR 66; DAM MULT; DLB 82, 256; HW 1, 2; LAIT 5; NCFS 3; WLIT 1

Roelvaag, O(le) E(dvart) 1876-1931
See Rolvaag, O(le) E(dvart)
See also CA 117; 171

Roethke, Theodore (Huebner)
1908-1963 .... **CLC 1, 3, 8, 11, 19, 46, 101; PC 15**
See also AMW; CA 81-84; CABS 2; CDALB 1941-1968; DA3; DAM POET;

DLB 5, 206; EXPP; MTCW 1, 2; PAB; PFS 3; RGAL 4; WP

Rogers, Carl R(ansom)
1902-1987 .... **TCLC 125**
See also CA 1-4R; 121; CANR 1, 18; MTCW 1

Rogers, Samuel 1763-1855 .... **NCLC 69**
See also DLB 93; RGEL 2

Rogers, Thomas Hunton 1927- .... **CLC 57**
See also CA 89-92; INT 89-92

Rogers, Will(iam Penn Adair)
1879-1935 .... **TCLC 8, 71**
See also CA 105; 144; DA3; DAM MULT; DLB 11; MTCW 2; NNAL

Rogin, Gilbert 1929- .... **CLC 18**
See also CA 65-68; CANR 15

Rohan, Koda
See Koda Shigeyuki

Rohlfs, Anna Katharine Green
See Green, Anna Katharine

Rohmer, Eric .... **CLC 16**
See also Scherer, Jean-Marie Maurice

Rohmer, Sax .... **TCLC 28**
See also Ward, Arthur Henry Sarsfield
See also DLB 70; MSW; SUFW

Roiphe, Anne (Richardson) 1935- .. **CLC 3, 9**
See also CA 89-92; CANR 45, 73; DLBY 1980; INT 89-92

Rojas, Fernando de 1475-1541 .... **LC 23; HLCS 1**
See also RGWL 2

Rojas, Gonzalo 1917-
See also CA 178; HLCS 2; HW 2; LAWS 1

Rolfe, Frederick (William Serafino Austin Lewis Mary) 1860-1913 .... **TCLC 12**
See also Corvo, Baron
See also CA 107; DLB 34, 156; RGEL 2

Rolland, Romain 1866-1944 .... **TCLC 23**
See also CA 118; 197; DLB 65; GFL 1789 to the Present; RGWL 2

Rolle, Richard c. 1300-c. 1349 ...... **CMLC 21**
See also DLB 146; RGEL 2

Rolvaag, O(le) E(dvart) .... **TCLC 17**
See also Roelvaag, O(le) E(dvart)
See also DLB 9, 212; NFS 5; RGAL 4

Romain Arnaud, Saint
See Aragon, Louis

Romains, Jules 1885-1972 .... **CLC 7**
See also CA 85-88; CANR 34; DLB 65; GFL 1789 to the Present; MTCW 1

Romero, Jose Ruben 1890-1952 .... **TCLC 14**
See also CA 114; 131; HW 1; LAW

Ronsard, Pierre de 1524-1585 . **LC 6, 54; PC 11**
See also EW 2; GFL Beginnings to 1789; RGWL 2; TWA

Rooke, Leon 1934- .... **CLC 25, 34**
See also CA 25-28R; CANR 23, 53; CCA 1; CPW; DAM POP

Roosevelt, Franklin Delano
1882-1945 .... **TCLC 93**
See also CA 116; 173; LAIT 3

Roosevelt, Theodore 1858-1919 .... **TCLC 69**
See also CA 115; 170; DLB 47, 186

Roper, William 1498-1578 .... **LC 10**

Roquelaure, A. N.
See Rice, Anne

Rosa, Joao Guimaraes 1908-1967 ... **CLC 23; HLCS 1**
See also Guimaraes Rosa, Joao
See also CA 89-92; DLB 113; WLIT 1

Rose, Wendy 1948- .... **CLC 85; PC 13**
See also CA 53-56; CANR 5, 51; CWP; DAM MULT; DLB 175; NNAL; PFS 13; RGAL 4; SATA 12

Rosen, R. D.
See Rosen, Richard (Dean)

Rosen, Richard (Dean) 1949- .... **CLC 39**
See also CA 77-80; CANR 62; CMW 4; INT CANR-30

Rosenberg, Isaac 1890-1918 .... **TCLC 12**
See also BRW 6; CA 107; 188; DLB 20, 216; PAB; RGEL 2

Rosenblatt, Joe .... **CLC 15**
See also Rosenblatt, Joseph

Rosenblatt, Joseph 1933-
See Rosenblatt, Joe
See also CA 89-92; CP 7; INT 89-92

Rosenfeld, Samuel
See Tzara, Tristan

Rosenstock, Sami
See Tzara, Tristan

Rosenstock, Samuel
See Tzara, Tristan

Rosenthal, M(acha) L(ouis)
1917-1996 .... **CLC 28**
See also CA 1-4R; 152; CAAS 6; CANR 4, 51; CP 7; DLB 5; SATA 59

Ross, Barnaby
See Dannay, Frederic

Ross, Bernard L.
See Follett, Ken(neth Martin)

Ross, J. H.
See Lawrence, T(homas) E(dward)

Ross, John Hume
See Lawrence, T(homas) E(dward)

Ross, Martin 1862-1915
See Martin, Violet Florence
See also DLB 135; GLL 2; RGEL 2; RGSF 2

Ross, (James) Sinclair 1908-1996 ... **CLC 13; SSC 24**
See also CA 73-76; CANR 81; CN 7; DAC; DAM MST; DLB 88; RGEL 2; RGSF 2; TCWW 2

Rossetti, Christina (Georgina)
1830-1894 .... **NCLC 2, 50, 66; PC 7; WLC**
See also BRW 5; BYA 4; DA; DA3; DAB; DAC; DAM MST, POET; DLB 35, 163, 240; EXPP; MAICYA 1, 2; PFS 10, 14; RGEL 2; SATA 20; TEA; WCH

Rossetti, Dante Gabriel 1828-1882 . **NCLC 4, 77; WLC**
See also BRW 5; CDBLB 1832-1890; DA; DAB; DAC; DAM MST, POET; DLB 35; EXPP; RGEL 2; TEA

Rossi, Cristina Peri
See Peri Rossi, Cristina

Rossi, Jean Baptiste 1931-
See Japrisot, Sebastien
See also CA 201

Rossner, Judith (Perelman) 1935- . **CLC 6, 9, 29**
See also AITN 2; BEST 90:3; BPFB 3; CA 17-20R; CANR 18, 51, 73; CN 7; DLB 6; INT CANR-18; MTCW 1, 2

Rostand, Edmond (Eugene Alexis)
1868-1918 .... **TCLC 6, 37; DC 10**
See also CA 104; 126; DA; DA3; DAB; DAC; DAM DRAM, MST; DFS 1; DLB 192; LAIT 1; MTCW 1; RGWL 2; TWA

Roth, Henry 1906-1995 ..... **CLC 2, 6, 11, 104**
See also AMWS 9; CA 11-12; 149; CANR 38, 63; CAP 1; CN 7; DA3; DLB 28; MTCW 1, 2; RGAL 4

Roth, (Moses) Joseph 1894-1939 ... **TCLC 33**
See also CA 160; DLB 85; RGWL 2

Roth, Philip (Milton) 1933- ... **CLC 1, 2, 3, 4, 6, 9, 15, 22, 31, 47, 66, 86, 119; SSC 26; WLC**
See also AMWS 3; BEST 90:3; BPFB 3; CA 1-4R; CANR 1, 22, 36, 55, 89; CDALB 1968-1988; CN 7; CPW 1; DA; DA3; DAB; DAC; DAM MST, NOV,

POP; DLB 2, 28, 173; DLBY 1982; MTCW 1, 2; RGAL 4; RGSF 2; SSFS 12; TUS

Rothenberg, Jerome 1931- .... **CLC 6, 57**
See also CA 45-48; CANR 1, 106; CP 7; DLB 5, 193

Rotter, Pat ed. .... **CLC 65**

Roumain, Jacques (Jean Baptiste)
1907-1944 .... **TCLC 19; BLC 3**
See also BW 1; CA 117; 125; DAM MULT

Rourke, Constance (Mayfield)
1885-1941 .... **TCLC 12**
See also CA 107; YABC 1

Rousseau, Jean-Baptiste 1671-1741 ...... **LC 9**

Rousseau, Jean-Jacques 1712-1778 .... **LC 14, 36; WLC**
See also DA; DA3; DAB; DAC; DAM MST; EW 4; GFL Beginnings to 1789; RGWL 2; TWA

Roussel, Raymond 1877-1933 .... **TCLC 20**
See also CA 117; 201; GFL 1789 to the Present

Rovit, Earl (Herbert) 1927- .... **CLC 7**
See also CA 5-8R; CANR 12

Rowe, Elizabeth Singer 1674-1737 ..... **LC 44**
See also DLB 39, 95

Rowe, Nicholas 1674-1718 .... **LC 8**
See also DLB 84; RGEL 2

Rowlandson, Mary 1637(?)-1678 .... **LC 66**
See also DLB 24, 200; RGAL 4

Rowley, Ames Dorrance
See Lovecraft, H(oward) P(hillips)

Rowling, J(oanne) K(athleen)
1965(?)- .... **CLC 137**
See also AAYA 34; BYA 13, 14; CA 173; CLR 66, 80; SATA 109

Rowson, Susanna Haswell
1762(?)-1824 .... **NCLC 5, 69**
See also DLB 37, 200; RGAL 4

Roy, Arundhati 1960(?)- .... **CLC 109**
See also CA 163; CANR 90; DLBY 1997

Roy, Gabrielle 1909-1983 .... **CLC 10, 14**
See also CA 53-56; 110; CANR 5, 61; CCA 1; DAB; DAC; DAM MST; DLB 68; MTCW 1; RGWL 2; SATA 104

Royko, Mike 1932-1997 .... **CLC 109**
See also CA 89-92; 157; CANR 26; CPW

Rozanov, Vassili 1856-1919 .... **TCLC 104**

Rozewicz, Tadeusz 1921- ...... **CLC 9, 23, 139**
See also CA 108; CANR 36, 66; CWW 2; DA3; DAM POET; DLB 232; MTCW 1, 2

Ruark, Gibbons 1941- .... **CLC 3**
See also CA 33-36R; CAAS 23; CANR 14, 31, 57; DLB 120

Rubens, Bernice (Ruth) 1923- .... **CLC 19, 31**
See also CA 25-28R; CANR 33, 65; CN 7; DLB 14, 207; MTCW 1

Rubin, Harold
See Robbins, Harold

Rudkin, (James) David 1936- .... **CLC 14**
See also CA 89-92; CBD; CD 5; DLB 13

Rudnik, Raphael 1933- .... **CLC 7**
See also CA 29-32R

Ruffian, M.
See Hasek, Jaroslav (Matej Frantisek)

Ruiz, Jose Martinez .... **CLC 11**
See also Martinez Ruiz, Jose

Rukeyser, Muriel 1913-1980 . **CLC 6, 10, 15, 27; PC 12**
See also AMWS 6; CA 5-8R; 93-96; CANR 26, 60; DA3; DAM POET; DLB 48; FW; GLL 2; MTCW 1, 2; PFS 10; RGAL 4; SATA-Obit 22

Rule, Jane (Vance) 1931- .... **CLC 27**
See also CA 25-28R; CAAS 18; CANR 12, 87; CN 7; DLB 60; FW

Schreber, Daniel 1842-1911 .... **TCLC 123**

Schreiner, Olive (Emilie Albertina)
1855-1920 .... **TCLC 9**
See also AFW; BRWS 2; CA 105; 154;
DLB 18, 156, 190, 225; FW; RGEL 2;
TWA; WLIT 2

Schulberg, Budd (Wilson) 1914- .. **CLC 7, 48**
See also BPFB 3; CA 25-28R; CANR 19,
87; CN 7; DLB 6, 26, 28; DLBY 1981,
2001

Schulman, Arnold
See Trumbo, Dalton

Schulz, Bruno 1892-1942 .. **TCLC 5, 51; SSC
13**
See also CA 115; 123; CANR 86; CDWLB
4; DLB 215; MTCW 2; RGSF 2; RGWL
2

Schulz, Charles M(onroe)
1922-2000 .... **CLC 12**
See also AAYA 39; CA 9-12R; 187; CANR
6; INT CANR-6; SATA 10; SATA-Obit
118

Schumacher, E(rnst) F(riedrich)
1911-1977 .... **CLC 80**
See also CA 81-84; 73-76; CANR 34, 85

Schuyler, James Marcus 1923-1991 .. **CLC 5,
23**
See also CA 101; 134; DAM POET; DLB
5, 169; INT 101; WP

Schwartz, Delmore (David)
1913-1966 ... **CLC 2, 4, 10, 45, 87; PC 8**
See also AMWS 2; CA 17-18; 25-28R;
CANR 35; CAP 2; DLB 28, 48; MTCW
1, 2; PAB; RGAL 4; TUS

Schwartz, Ernst
See Ozu, Yasujiro

Schwartz, John Burnham 1965- .... **CLC 59**
See also CA 132

Schwartz, Lynne Sharon 1939- .... **CLC 31**
See also CA 103; CANR 44, 89; DLB 218;
MTCW 2

Schwartz, Muriel A.
See Eliot, T(homas) S(tearns)

Schwarz-Bart, Andre 1928- .... **CLC 2, 4**
See also CA 89-92; CANR 109

Schwarz-Bart, Simone 1938- . **CLC 7; BLCS**
See also BW 2; CA 97-100

Schwerner, Armand 1927-1999 .... **PC 42**
See also CA 9-12R; 179; CANR 50, 85; CP
7; DLB 165

**Schwitters, Kurt (Hermann Edward Karl
Julius)** 1887-1948 .... **TCLC 95**
See also CA 158

Schwob, Marcel (Mayer Andre)
1867-1905 .... **TCLC 20**
See also CA 117; 168; DLB 123; GFL 1789
to the Present

Sciascia, Leonardo 1921-1989 .. **CLC 8, 9, 41**
See also CA 85-88; 130; CANR 35; DLB
177; MTCW 1; RGWL 2

Scoppettone, Sandra 1936- .... **CLC 26**
See also Early, Jack
See also AAYA 11; BYA 8; CA 5-8R;
CANR 41, 73; GLL 1; MAICYA 2; MAI-
CYAS 1; SATA 9, 92; WYA; YAW

Scorsese, Martin 1942- .... **CLC 20, 89**
See also AAYA 38; CA 110; 114; CANR
46, 85

Scotland, Jay
See Jakes, John (William)

Scott, Duncan Campbell
1862-1947 .... **TCLC 6**
See also CA 104; 153; DAC; DLB 92;
RGEL 2

Scott, Evelyn 1893-1963 .... **CLC 43**
See also CA 104; 112; CANR 64; DLB 9,
48; RHW

Scott, F(rancis) R(eginald)
1899-1985 .... **CLC 22**
See also CA 101; 114; CANR 87; DLB 88;
INT CA-101; RGEL 2

Scott, Frank
See Scott, F(rancis) R(eginald)

Scott, Joan .... **CLC 65**

Scott, Joanna 1960- .... **CLC 50**
See also CA 126; CANR 53, 92

Scott, Paul (Mark) 1920-1978 ...... **CLC 9, 60**
See also BRWS 1; CA 81-84; 77-80; CANR
33; DLB 14, 207; MTCW 1; RGEL 2;
RHW

Scott, Sarah 1723-1795 .... **LC 44**
See also DLB 39

Scott, Sir Walter 1771-1832 .... **NCLC 15, 69,
110; PC 13; SSC 32; WLC**
See also AAYA 22; BRW 4; BYA 2; CD-
BLB 1789-1832; DA; DAB; DAC; DAM
MST, NOV, POET; DLB 93, 107, 116,
144, 159; HGG; LAIT 1; RGEL 2; RGSF
2; SSFS 10; SUFW; TEA; WLIT 3; YABC
2

Scribe, (Augustin) Eugene
1791-1861 .... **NCLC 16; DC 5**
See also DAM DRAM; DLB 192; GFL
1789 to the Present; RGWL 2

Scrum, R.
See Crumb, R(obert)

Scudery, Georges de 1601-1667 .... **LC 75**
See also GFL Beginnings to 1789

Scudery, Madeleine de 1607-1701 .. **LC 2, 58**
See also GFL Beginnings to 1789

Scum
See Crumb, R(obert)

Scumbag, Little Bobby
See Crumb, R(obert)

Seabrook, John
See Hubbard, L(afayette) Ron(ald)

Sealy, I(rwin) Allan 1951- .... **CLC 55**
See also CA 136; CN 7

Search, Alexander
See Pessoa, Fernando (Antonio Nogueira)

Sebastian, Lee
See Silverberg, Robert

Sebastian Owl
See Thompson, Hunter S(tockton)

Sebestyen, Igen
See Sebestyen, Ouida

Sebestyen, Ouida 1924- .... **CLC 30**
See also AAYA 8; BYA 7; CA 107; CANR
40; CLR 17; JRDA; MAICYA 1, 2; SAAS
10; SATA 39; WYA; YAW

Secundus, H. Scriblerus
See Fielding, Henry

Sedges, John
See Buck, Pearl S(ydenstricker)

Sedgwick, Catharine Maria
1789-1867 .... **NCLC 19, 98**
See also DLB 1, 74, 183, 239, 243, 254;
RGAL 4

Seelye, John (Douglas) 1931- .... **CLC 7**
See also CA 97-100; CANR 70; INT 97-
100; TCWW 2

Seferiades, Giorgos Stylianou 1900-1971
See Seferis, George
See also CA 5-8R; 33-36R; CANR 5, 36;
MTCW 1

Seferis, George .... **CLC 5, 11**
See also Seferiades, Giorgos Stylianou
See also EW 12; RGWL 2

Segal, Erich (Wolf) 1937- .... **CLC 3, 10**
See also BEST 89:1; BPFB 3; CA 25-28R;
CANR 20, 36, 65; CPW; DAM POP;
DLBY 1986; INT CANR-20; MTCW 1

Seger, Bob 1945- .... **CLC 35**

Seghers, Anna -1983 .... **CLC 7**
See also Radvanyi, Netty
See also CDWLB 2; DLB 69

Seidel, Frederick (Lewis) 1936- .... **CLC 18**
See also CA 13-16R; CANR 8, 99; CP 7;
DLBY 1984

Seifert, Jaroslav 1901-1986 .. **CLC 34, 44, 93**
See also CA 127; CDWLB 4; DLB 215;
MTCW 1, 2

Sei Shonagon c. 966-1017(?) .... **CMLC 6**

Sejour, Victor 1817-1874 .... **DC 10**
See also DLB 50

Sejour Marcou et Ferrand, Juan Victor
See Sejour, Victor

Selby, Hubert, Jr. 1928- .... **CLC 1, 2, 4, 8;
SSC 20**
See also CA 13-16R; CANR 33, 85; CN 7;
DLB 2, 227

Selzer, Richard 1928- .... **CLC 74**
See also CA 65-68; CANR 14, 106

Sembene, Ousmane
See Ousmane, Sembene
See also AFW; CWW 2; WLIT 2

Senancour, Etienne Pivert de
1770-1846 .... **NCLC 16**
See also DLB 119; GFL 1789 to the Present

Sender, Ramon (Jose) 1902-1982 ...... **CLC 8;
HLC 2**
See also CA 5-8R; 105; CANR 8; DAM
MULT; HW 1; MTCW 1; RGWL 2

Seneca, Lucius Annaeus c. 4 B.C.-c.
65 .... **CMLC 6; DC 5**
See also AW 2; CDWLB 1; DAM DRAM;
DLB 211; RGWL 2; TWA

Senghor, Leopold Sedar 1906-2001 . **CLC 54,
130; BLC 3; PC 25**
See also AFW; BW 2; CA 116; 125; 203;
CANR 47, 74; DAM MULT, POET;
DNFS 2; GFL 1789 to the Present;
MTCW 1, 2; TWA

Senna, Danzy 1970- .... **CLC 119**
See also CA 169

Serling, (Edward) Rod(man)
1924-1975 .... **CLC 30**
See also AAYA 14; AITN 1; CA 162; 57-
60; DLB 26; SFW 4

Serna, Ramon Gomez de la
See Gomez de la Serna, Ramon

Serpieres
See Guillevic, (Eugene)

Service, Robert
See Service, Robert W(illiam)
See also BYA 4; DAB; DLB 92

Service, Robert W(illiam)
1874(?)-1958 .... **TCLC 15; WLC**
See also Service, Robert
See also CA 115; 140; CANR 84; DA;
DAC; DAM MST, POET; PFS 10; RGEL
2; SATA 20

Seth, Vikram 1952- .... **CLC 43, 90**
See also CA 121; 127; CANR 50, 74; CN
7; CP 7; DA3; DAM MULT; DLB 120;
INT 127; MTCW 2

Seton, Cynthia Propper 1926-1982 .. **CLC 27**
See also CA 5-8R; 108; CANR 7

Seton, Ernest (Evan) Thompson
1860-1946 .... **TCLC 31**
See also ANW; BYA 3; CA 109; CLR 59;
DLB 92; DLBD 13; JRDA; SATA 18

Seton-Thompson, Ernest
See Seton, Ernest (Evan) Thompson

Settle, Mary Lee 1918- .... **CLC 19, 61**
See also BPFB 3; CA 89-92; CAAS 1;
CANR 44, 87; CN 7; CSW; DLB 6; INT
89-92

Seuphor, Michel
See Arp, Jean

Sevigne, Marie (de Rabutin-Chantal)
1626-1696 .... **LC 11**
See also GFL Beginnings to 1789; TWA

Sewall, Samuel 1652-1730 .... **LC 38**
See also DLB 24; RGAL 4

Sexton, Anne (Harvey) 1928-1974 ..... **CLC 2, 4, 6, 8, 10, 15, 53, 123; PC 2; WLC**
See also AMWS 2; CA 1-4R; 53-56; CABS 2; CANR 3, 36; CDALB 1941-1968; DA; DA3; DAB; DAC; DAM MST, POET; DLB 5, 169; EXPP; FW; MAWW; MTCW 1, 2; PAB; PFS 4, 14; RGAL 4; SATA 10; TUS

Shaara, Jeff 1952- .... **CLC 119**
See also CA 163; CANR 109

Shaara, Michael (Joseph, Jr.) 1929-1988 .... **CLC 15**
See also AITN 1; BPFB 3; CA 102; 125; CANR 52, 85; DAM POP; DLBY 1983

Shackleton, C. C.
See Aldiss, Brian W(ilson)

Shacochis, Bob .... **CLC 39**
See also Shacochis, Robert G.

Shacochis, Robert G. 1951-
See Shacochis, Bob
See also CA 119; 124; CANR 100; INT 124

Shaffer, Anthony (Joshua) 1926-2001 .... **CLC 19**
See also CA 110; 116; 200; CBD; CD 5; DAM DRAM; DFS 13; DLB 13

Shaffer, Peter (Levin) 1926- .. **CLC 5, 14, 18, 37, 60; DC 7**
See also BRWS 1; CA 25-28R; CANR 25, 47, 74; CBD; CD 5; CDBLB 1960 to Present; DA3; DAB; DAM DRAM, MST; DFS 5, 13; DLB 13, 233; MTCW 1, 2; RGEL 2; TEA

Shakey, Bernard
See Young, Neil

Shalamov, Varlam (Tikhonovich) 1907(?)-1982 .... **CLC 18**
See also CA 129; 105; RGSF 2

Shamlu, Ahmad 1925-2000 .... **CLC 10**
See also CWW 2

Shammas, Anton 1951- .... **CLC 55**
See also CA 199

Shandling, Arline
See Berriault, Gina

Shange, Ntozake 1948- .... **CLC 8, 25, 38, 74, 126; BLC 3; DC 3**
See also AAYA 9; AFAW 1, 2; BW 2; CA 85-88; CABS 3; CAD; CANR 27, 48, 74; CD 5; CP 7; CWD; CWP; DA3; DAM DRAM, MULT; DFS 2, 11; DLB 38, 249; FW; LAIT 5; MTCW 1, 2; NFS 11; RGAL 4; YAW

Shanley, John Patrick 1950- .... **CLC 75**
See also CA 128; 133; CAD; CANR 83; CD 5

Shapcott, Thomas W(illiam) 1935- .. **CLC 38**
See also CA 69-72; CANR 49, 83, 103; CP 7

Shapiro, Jane 1942- .... **CLC 76**
See also CA 196

Shapiro, Karl (Jay) 1913-2000 ...... **CLC 4, 8, 15, 53; PC 25**
See also AMWS 2; CA 1-4R; 188; CAAS 6; CANR 1, 36, 66; CP 7; DLB 48; EXPP; MTCW 1, 2; PFS 3; RGAL 4

Sharp, William 1855-1905 .... **TCLC 39**
See also Macleod, Fiona
See also CA 160; DLB 156; RGEL 2

Sharpe, Thomas Ridley 1928-
See Sharpe, Tom
See also CA 114; 122; CANR 85; INT CA-122

Sharpe, Tom .... **CLC 36**
See also Sharpe, Thomas Ridley
See also CN 7; DLB 14, 231

Shatrov, Mikhail .... **CLC 59**

Shaw, Bernard
See Shaw, George Bernard
See also DLB 190

Shaw, G. Bernard
See Shaw, George Bernard

Shaw, George Bernard 1856-1950 .. **TCLC 3, 9, 21, 45; WLC**
See also Shaw, Bernard
See also BRW 6; BRWR 2; CA 104; 128; CDBLB 1914-1945; DA; DA3; DAB; DAC; DAM DRAM, MST; DFS 1, 3, 6, 11; DLB 10, 57; LAIT 3; MTCW 1, 2; RGEL 2; TEA; WLIT 4

Shaw, Henry Wheeler 1818-1885 .. **NCLC 15**
See also DLB 11; RGAL 4

Shaw, Irwin 1913-1984 .... **CLC 7, 23, 34**
See also AITN 1; BPFB 3; CA 13-16R; 112; CANR 21; CDALB 1941-1968; CPW; DAM DRAM, POP; DLB 6, 102; DLBY 1984; MTCW 1, 21

Shaw, Robert 1927-1978 .... **CLC 5**
See also AITN 1; CA 1-4R; 81-84; CANR 4; DLB 13, 14

Shaw, T. E.
See Lawrence, T(homas) E(dward)

Shawn, Wallace 1943- .... **CLC 41**
See also CA 112; CAD; CD 5; DLB 266

Shchedrin, N.
See Saltykov, Mikhail Evgrafovich

Shea, Lisa 1953- .... **CLC 86**
See also CA 147

Sheed, Wilfrid (John Joseph) 1930- . **CLC 2, 4, 10, 53**
See also CA 65-68; CANR 30, 66; CN 7; DLB 6; MTCW 1, 2

Sheldon, Alice Hastings Bradley 1915(?)-1987
See Tiptree, James, Jr.
See also CA 108; 122; CANR 34; INT 108; MTCW 1

Sheldon, John
See Bloch, Robert (Albert)

Sheldon, Walter J(ames) 1917-1996
See Queen, Ellery
See also AITN 1; CA 25-28R; CANR 10

Shelley, Mary Wollstonecraft (Godwin) 1797-1851 ...... **NCLC 14, 59, 103; WLC**
See also AAYA 20; BPFB 3; BRW 3; BRWS 3; BYA 5; CDBLB 1789-1832; DA; DA3; DAB; DAC; DAM MST, NOV; DLB 110, 116, 159, 178; EXPN; HGG; LAIT 1; NFS 1; RGEL 2; SATA 29; SCFW; SFW 4; TEA; WLIT 3

Shelley, Percy Bysshe 1792-1822 .. **NCLC 18, 93; PC 14; WLC**
See also BRW 4; BRWR 1; CDBLB 1789-1832; DA; DA3; DAB; DAC; DAM MST, POET; DLB 96, 110, 158; EXPP; PAB; PFS 2; RGEL 2; TEA; WLIT 3; WP

Shepard, Jim 1956- .... **CLC 36**
See also CA 137; CANR 59, 104; SATA 90

Shepard, Lucius 1947- .... **CLC 34**
See also CA 128; 141; CANR 81; HGG; SCFW 2; SFW 4

Shepard, Sam 1943- .... **CLC 4, 6, 17, 34, 41, 44; DC 5**
See also AAYA 1; AMWS 3; CA 69-72; CABS 3; CAD; CANR 22; CD 5; DA3; DAM DRAM; DFS 3, 6, 7, 14; DLB 7, 212; IDFW 3, 4; MTCW 1, 2; RGAL 4

Shepherd, Michael
See Ludlum, Robert

Sherburne, Zoa (Lillian Morin) 1912-1995 .... **CLC 30**
See also AAYA 13; CA 1-4R; 176; CANR 3, 37; MAICYA 1, 2; SAAS 18; SATA 3; YAW

Sheridan, Frances 1724-1766 .... **LC 7**
See also DLB 39, 84

Sheridan, Richard Brinsley 1751-1816 .... **NCLC 5, 91; DC 1; WLC**
See also BRW 3; CDBLB 1660-1789; DA; DAB; DAC; DAM DRAM, MST; DFS 15; DLB 89; WLIT 3

Sherman, Jonathan Marc .... **CLC 55**

Sherman, Martin 1941(?)- .... **CLC 19**
See also CA 116; 123; CANR 86

Sherwin, Judith Johnson
See Johnson, Judith (Emlyn)
See also CANR 85; CP 7; CWP

Sherwood, Frances 1940- .... **CLC 81**
See also CA 146

Sherwood, Robert E(mmet) 1896-1955 .... **TCLC 3**
See also CA 104; 153; CANR 86; DAM DRAM; DFS 15; DLB 7, 26, 249; IDFW 3, 4; RGAL 4

Shestov, Lev 1866-1938 .... **TCLC 56**

Shevchenko, Taras 1814-1861 .... **NCLC 54**

Shiel, M(atthew) P(hipps) 1865-1947 .... **TCLC 8**
See also Holmes, Gordon
See also CA 106; 160; DLB 153; HGG; MTCW 2; SFW 4; SUFW

Shields, Carol 1935- .... **CLC 91, 113**
See also AMWS 7; CA 81-84; CANR 51, 74, 98; CCA 1; CN 7; CPW; DA3; DAC; MTCW 2

Shields, David 1956- .... **CLC 97**
See also CA 124; CANR 48, 99

Shiga, Naoya 1883-1971 ..... **CLC 33; SSC 23**
See also Shiga Naoya
See also CA 101; 33-36R; MJW

Shiga Naoya
See Shiga, Naoya
See also DLB 180

Shilts, Randy 1951-1994 .... **CLC 85**
See also AAYA 19; CA 115; 127; 144; CANR 45; DA3; GLL 1; INT 127; MTCW 2

Shimazaki, Haruki 1872-1943
See Shimazaki Toson
See also CA 105; 134; CANR 84

Shimazaki Toson .... **TCLC 5**
See also Shimazaki, Haruki
See also DLB 180

Sholokhov, Mikhail (Aleksandrovich) 1905-1984 .... **CLC 7, 15**
See also CA 101; 112; MTCW 1, 2; RGWL 2; SATA-Obit 36

Shone, Patric
See Hanley, James

Shreve, Susan Richards 1939- .... **CLC 23**
See also CA 49-52; CAAS 5; CANR 5, 38, 69, 100; MAICYA 1, 2; SATA 46, 95; SATA-Brief 41

Shue, Larry 1946-1985 .... **CLC 52**
See also CA 145; 117; DAM DRAM; DFS 7

Shu-Jen, Chou 1881-1936
See Lu Hsun
See also CA 104

Shulman, Alix Kates 1932- .... **CLC 2, 10**
See also CA 29-32R; CANR 43; FW; SATA 7

Shusaku, Endo
See Endo, Shusaku

Shuster, Joe 1914-1992 .... **CLC 21**

Shute, Nevil .... **CLC 30**
See also Norway, Nevil Shute
See also BPFB 3; DLB 255; NFS 9; RHW; SFW 4

Shuttle, Penelope (Diane) 1947- .... **CLC 7**
See also CA 93-96; CANR 39, 84, 92, 108; CP 7; CWP; DLB 14, 40

Sidney, Mary 1561-1621 .... **LC 19, 39**
See also Sidney Herbert, Mary

9, 212; DLBD 2; EXPS; LAIT 3; MTCW
1, 2; NFS 1, 5, 7; RGAL 4; RGSF 2;
RHW; SATA 9; SSFS 3, 6; TCWW 2;
TUS; WYA; YAW

Steinem, Gloria 1934- .... **CLC 63**
See also CA 53-56; CANR 28, 51; DLB
246; FW; MTCW 1, 2

Steiner, George 1929- .... **CLC 24**
See also CA 73-76; CANR 31, 67, 108;
DAM NOV; DLB 67; MTCW 1, 2; SATA
62

Steiner, K. Leslie
See Delany, Samuel R(ay), Jr.

Steiner, Rudolf 1861-1925 .... **TCLC 13**
See also CA 107

Stendhal 1783-1842 .. **NCLC 23, 46; SSC 27;**
WLC
See also DA; DA3; DAB; DAC; DAM
MST, NOV; DLB 119; EW 5; GFL 1789
to the Present; RGWL 2; TWA

Stephen, Adeline Virginia
See Woolf, (Adeline) Virginia

Stephen, Sir Leslie 1832-1904 .... **TCLC 23**
See also BRW 5; CA 123; DLB 57, 144,
190

Stephen, Sir Leslie
See Stephen, Sir Leslie

Stephen, Virginia
See Woolf, (Adeline) Virginia

Stephens, James 1882(?)-1950 .... **TCLC 4;**
SSC 50
See also CA 104; 192; DLB 19, 153, 162;
FANT; RGEL 2; SUFW

Stephens, Reed
See Donaldson, Stephen R(eeder)

Steptoe, Lydia
See Barnes, Djuna
See also GLL 1

Sterchi, Beat 1949- .... **CLC 65**
See also CA 203

Sterling, Brett
See Bradbury, Ray (Douglas); Hamilton,
Edmond

Sterling, Bruce 1954- .... **CLC 72**
See also CA 119; CANR 44; SCFW 2; SFW
4

Sterling, George 1869-1926 .... **TCLC 20**
See also CA 117; 165; DLB 54

Stern, Gerald 1925- .... **CLC 40, 100**
See also AMWS 9; CA 81-84; CANR 28,
94; CP 7; DLB 105; RGAL 4

Stern, Richard (Gustave) 1928- ... **CLC 4, 39**
See also CA 1-4R; CANR 1, 25, 52; CN 7;
DLB 218; DLBY 1987; INT CANR-25

Sternberg, Josef von 1894-1969 .... **CLC 20**
See also CA 81-84

Sterne, Laurence 1713-1768 .... **LC 2, 48;**
WLC
See also BRW 3; CDBLB 1660-1789; DA;
DAB; DAC; DAM MST, NOV; DLB 39;
RGEL 2; TEA

Sternheim, (William Adolf) Carl
1878-1942 .... **TCLC 8**
See also CA 105; 193; DLB 56, 118; RGWL
2

Stevens, Mark 1951- .... **CLC 34**
See also CA 122

Stevens, Wallace 1879-1955 ...... **TCLC 3, 12,**
45; PC 6; WLC
See also AMW; AMWR 1; CA 104; 124;
CDALB 1929-1941; DA; DA3; DAB;
DAC; DAM MST, POET; DLB 54; EXPP;
MTCW 1, 2; PAB; PFS 13; RGAL 4;
TUS; WP

Stevenson, Anne (Katharine) 1933- .. **CLC 7,**
33
See also BRWS 6; CA 17-20R; CAAS 9;
CANR 9, 33; CP 7; CWP; DLB 40;
MTCW 1; RHW

Stevenson, Robert Louis (Balfour)
1850-1894 ...... **NCLC 5, 14, 63; SSC 11,**
51; WLC
See also AAYA 24; BPFB 3; BRW 5;
BRWR 1; BYA 1, 2, 4, 13; CDBLB 1890-
1914; CLR 10, 11; DA; DA3; DAB;
DAC; DAM MST, NOV; DLB 18, 57,
141, 156, 174; DLBD 13; HGG; JRDA;
LAIT 1, 3; MAICYA 1; NFS 11; RGEL
2; RGSF 2; SATA 100; SUFW; TEA;
WCH; WLIT 4; WYA; YABC 2; YAW

Stewart, J(ohn) I(nnes) M(ackintosh)
1906-1994 .... **CLC 7, 14, 32**
See also Innes, Michael
See also CA 85-88; 147; CAAS 3; CANR
47; CMW 4; MTCW 1, 2

Stewart, Mary (Florence Elinor)
1916- .... **CLC 7, 35, 117**
See also AAYA 29; BPFB 3; CA 1-4R;
CANR 1, 59; CMW 4; CPW; DAB;
FANT; RHW; SATA 12; YAW

Stewart, Mary Rainbow
See Stewart, Mary (Florence Elinor)

Stifle, June
See Campbell, Maria

Stifter, Adalbert 1805-1868 .. **NCLC 41; SSC**
28
See also CDWLB 2; DLB 133; RGSF 2;
RGWL 2

Still, James 1906-2001 .... **CLC 49**
See also CA 65-68; 195; CAAS 17; CANR
10, 26; CSW; DLB 9; DLBY 01; SATA
29; SATA-Obit 127

Sting 1951-
See Sumner, Gordon Matthew
See also CA 167

Stirling, Arthur
See Sinclair, Upton (Beall)

Stitt, Milan 1941- .... **CLC 29**
See also CA 69-72

Stockton, Francis Richard 1834-1902
See Stockton, Frank R.
See also CA 108; 137; MAICYA 1, 2; SATA
44; SFW 4

Stockton, Frank R. .... **TCLC 47**
See also Stockton, Francis Richard
See also BYA 4, 13; DLB 42, 74; DLBD
13; EXPS; SATA-Brief 32; SSFS 3;
SUFW; WCH

Stoddard, Charles
See Kuttner, Henry

Stoker, Abraham 1847-1912 .... **SSC 55**
See also Stoker, Bram
See also CA 105; 150; DA; DA3; DAC;
DAM MST, NOV; HGG; SATA 29

Stoker, Bram .... **TCLC 8; WLC**
See also Stoker, Abraham
See also AAYA 23; BPFB 3; BRWS 3; BYA
5; CDBLB 1890-1914; DAB; DLB 36, 70,
178; RGEL 2; SUFW; TEA; WLIT 4

Stolz, Mary (Slattery) 1920- .... **CLC 12**
See also AAYA 8; AITN 1; CA 5-8R;
CANR 13, 41; JRDA; MAICYA 1, 2;
SAAS 3; SATA 10, 71, 133; YAW

Stone, Irving 1903-1989 .... **CLC 7**
See also AITN 1; BPFB 3; CA 1-4R; 129;
CAAS 3; CANR 1, 23; CPW; DA3; DAM
POP; INT CANR-23; MTCW 1, 2; RHW;
SATA 3; SATA-Obit 64

Stone, Oliver (William) 1946- .... **CLC 73**
See also AAYA 15; CA 110; CANR 55

Stone, Robert (Anthony) 1937- ... **CLC 5, 23,**
42
See also AMWS 5; BPFB 3; CA 85-88;
CANR 23, 66, 95; CN 7; DLB 152; INT
CANR-23; MTCW 1

Stone, Zachary
See Follett, Ken(neth Martin)

Stoppard, Tom 1937- ... **CLC 1, 3, 4, 5, 8, 15,**
29, 34, 63, 91; DC 6; WLC
See also BRWR 2; BRWS 1; CA 81-84;
CANR 39, 67; CBD; CD 5; CDBLB 1960
to Present; DA; DA3; DAB; DAC; DAM
DRAM, MST; DFS 2, 5, 8, 11, 13; DLB
13, 233; DLBY 1985; MTCW 1, 2; RGEL
2; TEA; WLIT 4

Storey, David (Malcolm) 1933- . **CLC 2, 4, 5,**
8
See also BRWS 1; CA 81-84; CANR 36;
CBD; CD 5; CN 7; DAM DRAM; DLB
13, 14, 207, 245; MTCW 1; RGEL 2

Storm, Hyemeyohsts 1935- .... **CLC 3**
See also CA 81-84; CANR 45; DAM
MULT; NNAL

Storm, Theodor 1817-1888 .... **SSC 27**
See also CDWLB 2; RGSF 2; RGWL 2

Storm, (Hans) Theodor (Woldsen)
1817-1888 .... **NCLC 1; SSC 27**
See also DLB 129; EW

Storni, Alfonsina 1892-1938 .. **TCLC 5; HLC**
2; PC 33
See also CA 104; 131; DAM MULT; HW
1; LAW

Stoughton, William 1631-1701 .... **LC 38**
See also DLB 24

Stout, Rex (Todhunter) 1886-1975 ..... **CLC 3**
See also AITN 2; BPFB 3; CA 61-64;
CANR 71; CMW 4; MSW; RGAL 4

Stow, (Julian) Randolph 1935- ... **CLC 23, 48**
See also CA 13-16R; CANR 33; CN 7;
DLB 260; MTCW 1; RGEL 2

Stowe, Harriet (Elizabeth) Beecher
1811-1896 .... **NCLC 3, 50; WLC**
See also AMWS 1; CDALB 1865-1917;
DA; DA3; DAB; DAC; DAM MST, NOV;
DLB 1, 12, 42, 74, 189, 239, 243; EXPN;
JRDA; LAIT 2; MAICYA 1, 2; NFS 6;
RGAL 4; TUS; YABC 1

Strabo c. 64 B.C.-c. 25 .... **CMLC 37**
See also DLB 176

Strachey, (Giles) Lytton
1880-1932 .... **TCLC 12**
See also BRWS 2; CA 110; 178; DLB 149;
DLBD 10; MTCW 2; NCFS 4

Strand, Mark 1934- .... **CLC 6, 18, 41, 71**
See also AMWS 4; CA 21-24R; CANR 40,
65, 100; CP 7; DAM POET; DLB 5; PAB;
PFS 9; RGAL 4; SATA 41

Stratton-Porter, Gene(va Grace) 1863-1924
See Porter, Gene(va Grace) Stratton
See also ANW; CA 137; DLB 221; DLBD
14; MAICYA 1, 2; SATA 15

Straub, Peter (Francis) 1943- ... **CLC 28, 107**
See also BEST 89:1; BPFB 3; CA 85-88;
CANR 28, 65, 109; CPW; DAM POP;
DLBY 1984; HGG; MTCW 1, 2

Strauss, Botho 1944- .... **CLC 22**
See also CA 157; CWW 2; DLB 124

Streatfeild, (Mary) Noel
1897(?)-1986 .... **CLC 21**
See also CA 81-84; 120; CANR 31; CLR
17, 82; CWRI 5; DLB 160; MAICYA 1,
2; SATA 20; SATA-Obit 48

Stribling, T(homas) S(igismund)
1881-1965 .... **CLC 23**
See also CA 189; 107; CMW 4; DLB 9;
RGAL 4

Strindberg, (Johan) August
1849-1912 ... **TCLC 1, 8, 21, 47; DC 18;**
WLC
See also CA 104; 135; DA; DA3; DAB;
DAC; DAM DRAM, MST; DFS 4, 9;
DLB 259; EW 7; IDTP; MTCW 2; RGWL
2; TWA

Stringer, Arthur 1874-1950 .... **TCLC 37**
See also CA 161; DLB 92

Stringer, David
See Roberts, Keith (John Kingston)

FW; LAIT 3, 5; MTCW 2; NFS 1, 13; RGAL 4; SATA 75; SSFS 9; YAW

Tandem, Felix
See Spitteler, Carl (Friedrich Georg)

Tanizaki, Jun'ichiro 1886-1965 ... **CLC 8, 14, 28; SSC 21**
See also Tanizaki Jun'ichiro
See also CA 93-96; 25-28R; MJW; MTCW 2; RGSF 2; RGWL 2

Tanizaki Jun'ichiro
See Tanizaki, Jun'ichiro
See also DLB 180

Tanner, William
See Amis, Kingsley (William)

Tao Lao
See Storni, Alfonsina

Tarantino, Quentin (Jerome) 1963- .... **CLC 125**
See also CA 171

Tarassoff, Lev
See Troyat, Henri

Tarbell, Ida M(inerva) 1857-1944 . **TCLC 40**
See also CA 122; 181; DLB 47

Tarkington, (Newton) Booth 1869-1946 .... **TCLC 9**
See also BPFB 3; BYA 3; CA 110; 143; CWRI 5; DLB 9, 102; MTCW 2; RGAL 4; SATA 17

Tarkovsky, Andrei (Arsenyevich) 1932-1986 .... **CLC 75**
See also CA 127

Tartt, Donna 1964(?)- .... **CLC 76**
See also CA 142

Tasso, Torquato 1544-1595 .... **LC 5**
See also EFS 2; EW 2; RGWL 2

Tate, (John Orley) Allen 1899-1979 .. **CLC 2, 4, 6, 9, 11, 14, 24**
See also AMW; CA 5-8R; 85-88; CANR 32, 108; DLB 4, 45, 63; DLBD 17; MTCW 1, 2; RGAL 4; RHW

Tate, Ellalice
See Hibbert, Eleanor Alice Burford

Tate, James (Vincent) 1943- ..... **CLC 2, 6, 25**
See also CA 21-24R; CANR 29, 57; CP 7; DLB 5, 169; PFS 10, 15; RGAL 4; WP

Tauler, Johannes c. 1300-1361 ...... **CMLC 37**
See also DLB 179

Tavel, Ronald 1940- .... **CLC 6**
See also CA 21-24R; CAD; CANR 33; CD 5

Taviani, Paolo 1931- .... **CLC 70**
See also CA 153

Taylor, Bayard 1825-1878 .... **NCLC 89**
See also DLB 3, 189, 250, 254; RGAL 4

Taylor, C(ecil) P(hilip) 1929-1981 .... **CLC 27**
See also CA 25-28R; 105; CANR 47; CBD

Taylor, Edward 1642(?)-1729 .... **LC 11**
See also AMW; AW; DAB; DAC; DAM MST, POET; DLB 24; EXPP; RGAL 4; TUS

Taylor, Eleanor Ross 1920- .... **CLC 5**
See also CA 81-84; CANR 70

Taylor, Elizabeth 1932-1975 ..... **CLC 2, 4, 29**
See also CA 13-16R; CANR 9, 70; DLB 139; MTCW 1; RGEL 2; SATA 13

Taylor, Frederick Winslow 1856-1915 .... **TCLC 76**
See also CA 188

Taylor, Henry (Splawn) 1942- .... **CLC 44**
See also CA 33-36R; CAAS 7; CANR 31; CP 7; DLB 5; PFS 10

Taylor, Kamala (Purnaiya) 1924-
See Markandaya, Kamala
See also CA 77-80; NFS 13

Taylor, Mildred D(elois) 1943- .... **CLC 21**
See also AAYA 10; BW 1; BYA 3, 8; CA 85-88; CANR 25; CLR 9, 59; CSW; DLB 52; JRDA; LAIT 3; MAICYA 1, 2; SAAS 5; SATA 15, 70; WYA; YAW

Taylor, Peter (Hillsman) 1917-1994 .. **CLC 1, 4, 18, 37, 44, 50, 71; SSC 10**
See also AMWS 5; BPFB 3; CA 13-16R; 147; CANR 9, 50; CSW; DLB 218; DLBY 1981, 1994; EXPS; INT CANR-9; MTCW 1, 2; RGSF 2; SSFS 9; TUS

Taylor, Robert Lewis 1912-1998 .... **CLC 14**
See also CA 1-4R; 170; CANR 3, 64; SATA 10

Tchekhov, Anton
See Chekhov, Anton (Pavlovich)

Tchicaya, Gerald Felix 1931-1988 .. **CLC 101**
See also CA 129; 125; CANR 81

Tchicaya U Tam'si
See Tchicaya, Gerald Felix

Teasdale, Sara 1884-1933 .... **TCLC 4; PC 31**
See also CA 104; 163; DLB 45; GLL 1; PFS 14; RGAL 4; SATA 32; TUS

Tegner, Esaias 1782-1846 .... **NCLC 2**

Teilhard de Chardin, (Marie Joseph) Pierre 1881-1955 .... **TCLC 9**
See also CA 105; GFL 1789 to the Present

Temple, Ann
See Mortimer, Penelope (Ruth)

Tennant, Emma (Christina) 1937- .. **CLC 13, 52**
See also CA 65-68; CAAS 9; CANR 10, 38, 59, 88; CN 7; DLB 14; SFW 4

Tenneshaw, S. M.
See Silverberg, Robert

Tennyson, Alfred 1809-1892 ... **NCLC 30, 65, 115; PC 6; WLC**
See also BRW 4; CDBLB 1832-1890; DA; DA3; DAB; DAC; DAM MST, POET; DLB 32; EXPP; PAB; PFS 1, 2, 4, 11, 15; RGEL 2; TEA; WLIT 4; WP

Teran, Lisa St. Aubin de .... **CLC 36**
See also St. Aubin de Teran, Lisa

Terence c. 184 B.C.-c. 159 B.C. ... **CMLC 14; DC 7**
See also AW 1; CDWLB 1; DLB 211; RGWL 2; TWA

Teresa de Jesus, St. 1515-1582 .... **LC 18**

Terkel, Louis 1912-
See Terkel, Studs
See also CA 57-60; CANR 18, 45, 67; DA3; MTCW 1, 2

Terkel, Studs .... **CLC 38**
See also Terkel, Louis
See also AAYA 32; AITN 1; MTCW 2; TUS

Terry, C. V.
See Slaughter, Frank G(ill)

Terry, Megan 1932- .... **CLC 19; DC 13**
See also CA 77-80; CABS 3; CAD; CANR 43; CD 5; CWD; DLB 7, 249; GLL 2

Tertullian c. 155-c. 245 .... **CMLC 29**

Tertz, Abram
See Sinyavsky, Andrei (Donatevich)
See also CWW 2; RGSF 2

Tesich, Steve 1943(?)-1996 .... **CLC 40, 69**
See also CA 105; 152; CAD; DLBY 1983

Tesla, Nikola 1856-1943 .... **TCLC 88**

Teternikov, Fyodor Kuzmich 1863-1927
See Sologub, Fyodor
See also CA 104

Tevis, Walter 1928-1984 .... **CLC 42**
See also CA 113; SFW 4

Tey, Josephine .... **TCLC 14**
See also Mackintosh, Elizabeth
See also DLB 77; MSW

Thackeray, William Makepeace 1811-1863 .... **NCLC 5, 14, 22, 43; WLC**
See also BRW 5; CDBLB 1832-1890; DA; DA3; DAB; DAC; DAM MST, NOV; DLB 21, 55, 159, 163; NFS 13; RGEL 2; SATA 23; TEA; WLIT 3

Thakura, Ravindranatha
See Tagore, Rabindranath

Thames, C. H.
See Marlowe, Stephen

Tharoor, Shashi 1956- .... **CLC 70**
See also CA 141; CANR 91; CN 7

Thelwell, Michael Miles 1939- .... **CLC 22**
See also BW 2; CA 101

Theobald, Lewis, Jr.
See Lovecraft, H(oward) P(hillips)

Theocritus c. 310 B.C.- .... **CMLC 45**
See also AW 1; DLB 176; RGWL 2

Theodorescu, Ion N. 1880-1967
See Arghezi, Tudor
See also CA 116

Theriault, Yves 1915-1983 .... **CLC 79**
See also CA 102; CCA 1; DAC; DAM MST; DLB 88

Theroux, Alexander (Louis) 1939- .... **CLC 2, 25**
See also CA 85-88; CANR 20, 63; CN 7

Theroux, Paul (Edward) 1941- ..... **CLC 5, 8, 11, 15, 28, 46**
See also AAYA 28; AMWS 8; BEST 89:4; BPFB 3; CA 33-36R; CANR 20, 45, 74; CDALBS; CN 7; CPW 1; DA3; DAM POP; DLB 2, 218; HGG; MTCW 1, 2; RGAL 4; SATA 44, 109; TUS

Thesen, Sharon 1946- .... **CLC 56**
See also CA 163; CP 7; CWP

Thespis fl. 6th cent. B.C.- .... **CMLC 51**

Thevenin, Denis
See Duhamel, Georges

Thibault, Jacques Anatole Francois 1844-1924
See France, Anatole
See also CA 106; 127; DA3; DAM NOV; MTCW 1, 2; TWA

Thiele, Colin (Milton) 1920- .... **CLC 17**
See also CA 29-32R; CANR 12, 28, 53, 105; CLR 27; MAICYA 1, 2; SAAS 2; SATA 14, 72, 125; YAW

Thistlethwaite, Bel
See Wetherald, Agnes Ethelwyn

Thomas, Audrey (Callahan) 1935- .... **CLC 7, 13, 37, 107; SSC 20**
See also AITN 2; CA 21-24R; CAAS 19; CANR 36, 58; CN 7; DLB 60; MTCW 1; RGSF 2

Thomas, Augustus 1857-1934 .... **TCLC 97**

Thomas, D(onald) M(ichael) 1935- . **CLC 13, 22, 31, 132**
See also BPFB 3; BRWS 4; CA 61-64; CAAS 11; CANR 17, 45, 75; CDBLB 1960 to Present; CN 7; CP 7; DA3; DLB 40, 207; HGG; INT CANR-17; MTCW 1, 2; SFW 4

Thomas, Dylan (Marlais) 1914-1953 ... **TCLC 1, 8, 45, 105; PC 2; SSC 3, 44; WLC**
See also BRWS 1; CA 104; 120; CANR 65; CDBLB 1945-1960; DA; DA3; DAB; DAC; DAM DRAM, MST, POET; DLB 13, 20, 139; EXPP; LAIT 3; MTCW 1, 2; PAB; PFS 1, 3, 8; RGEL 2; RGSF 2; SATA 60; TEA; WLIT 4; WP

Thomas, (Philip) Edward 1878-1917 .... **TCLC 10**
See also BRW 6; BRWS 3; CA 106; 153; DAM POET; DLB 19, 98, 156, 216; PAB; RGEL 2

Thomas, Joyce Carol 1938- .... **CLC 35**
See also AAYA 12; BW 2, 3; CA 113; 116; CANR 48; CLR 19; DLB 33; INT CA-116; JRDA; MAICYA 1, 2; MTCW 1, 2; SAAS 7; SATA 40, 78, 123; WYA; YAW

Thomas, Lewis 1913-1993 .... **CLC 35**
See also ANW; CA 85-88; 143; CANR 38, 60; MTCW 1, 2

Thomas, M. Carey 1857-1935 .... **TCLC 89**
See also FW

Thomas, Paul
See Mann, (Paul) Thomas

Thomas, Piri 1928- .... **CLC 17; HLCS 2**
See also CA 73-76; HW 1

Thomas, R(onald) S(tuart)
1913-2000 .... **CLC 6, 13, 48**
See also CA 89-92; 189; CAAS 4; CANR
30; CDBLB 1960 to Present; CP 7; DAB;
DAM POET; DLB 27; MTCW 1; RGEL
2

Thomas, Ross (Elmore) 1926-1995 .. **CLC 39**
See also CA 33-36R; 150; CANR 22, 63;
CMW 4

Thompson, Francis (Joseph)
1859-1907 .... **TCLC 4**
See also BRW 5; CA 104; 189; CDBLB
1890-1914; DLB 19; RGEL 2; TEA

Thompson, Francis Clegg
See Mencken, H(enry) L(ouis)

Thompson, Hunter S(tockton)
1937(?)- .... **CLC 9, 17, 40, 104**
See also BEST 89:1; BPFB 3; CA 17-20R;
CANR 23, 46, 74, 77; CPW; CSW; DA3;
DAM POP; DLB 185; MTCW 1, 2; TUS

Thompson, James Myers
See Thompson, Jim (Myers)

Thompson, Jim (Myers)
1906-1977(?) .... **CLC 69**
See also BPFB 3; CA 140; CMW 4; CPW;
DLB 226; MSW

Thompson, Judith .... **CLC 39**
See also CWD

Thomson, James 1700-1748 .... **LC 16, 29, 40**
See also BRWS 3; DAM POET; DLB 95;
RGEL 2

Thomson, James 1834-1882 .... **NCLC 18**
See also DAM POET; DLB 35; RGEL 2

Thoreau, Henry David 1817-1862 .. **NCLC 7,
21, 61; PC 30; WLC**
See also AAYA 42; AMW; ANW; BYA 3;
CDALB 1640-1865; DA; DA3; DAB;
DAC; DAM MST; DLB 1, 183, 223;
LAIT 2; NCFS 3; RGAL 4; TUS

Thorndike, E. L.
See Thorndike, Edward L(ee)

Thorndike, Edward L(ee)
1874-1949 .... **TCLC 107**
See also CA 121

Thornton, Hall
See Silverberg, Robert

Thubron, Colin (Gerald Dryden)
1939- .... **CLC 163**
See also CA 25-28R; CANR 12, 29, 59, 95;
CN 7; DLB 204, 231

Thucydides c. 455 B.C.-c. 395
B.C. .... **CMLC 17**
See also AW 1; DLB 176; RGWL 2

Thumboo, Edwin Nadason 1933- .... **PC 30**
See also CA 194

Thurber, James (Grover)
1894-1961 .. **CLC 5, 11, 25, 125; SSC 1,
47**
See also AMWS 1; BPFB 3; BYA 5; CA
73-76; CANR 17, 39; CDALB 1929-1941;
CWRI 5; DA; DA3; DAB; DAC; DAM
DRAM, MST, NOV; DLB 4, 11, 22, 102;
EXPS; FANT; LAIT 3; MAICYA 1, 2;
MTCW 1, 2; RGAL 4; RGSF 2; SATA
13; SSFS 1, 10; SUFW; TUS

Thurman, Wallace (Henry)
1902-1934 .... **TCLC 6; BLC 3**
See also BW 1, 3; CA 104; 124; CANR 81;
DAM MULT; DLB 51

Tibullus c. 54 B.C.-c. 18 B.C. .... **CMLC 36**
See also AW 2; DLB 211; RGWL 2

Ticheburn, Cheviot
See Ainsworth, William Harrison

Tieck, (Johann) Ludwig
1773-1853 .... **NCLC 5, 46; SSC 31**
See also CDWLB 2; DLB 90; EW 5; IDTP;
RGSF 2; RGWL 2; SUFW

Tiger, Derry
See Ellison, Harlan (Jay)

Tilghman, Christopher 1948(?)- .... **CLC 65**
See also CA 159; CSW; DLB 244

Tillich, Paul (Johannes)
1886-1965 .... **CLC 131**
See also CA 5-8R; 25-28R; CANR 33;
MTCW 1, 2

Tillinghast, Richard (Williford)
1940- .... **CLC 29**
See also CA 29-32R; CAAS 23; CANR 26,
51, 96; CP 7; CSW

Timrod, Henry 1828-1867 .... **NCLC 25**
See also DLB 3, 248; RGAL 4

Tindall, Gillian (Elizabeth) 1938- ...... **CLC 7**
See also CA 21-24R; CANR 11, 65, 107;
CN 7

Tiptree, James, Jr. .... **CLC 48, 50**
See also Sheldon, Alice Hastings Bradley
See also DLB 8; SCFW 2; SFW 4

Tirso de Molina
See Tirso de Molina
See also RGWL 2

Tirso de Molina 1580(?)-1648 ..... **LC 73; DC
13; HLCS 2**
See also Tirso de Molina

Titmarsh, Michael Angelo
See Thackeray, William Makepeace

**Tocqueville, Alexis (Charles Henri Maurice
Clerel Comte) de** 1805-1859 .. **NCLC 7,
63**
See also EW 6; GFL 1789 to the Present;
TWA

Toibin, Colm 1955- .... **CLC 162**
See also CA 142; CANR 81

Tolkien, J(ohn) R(onald) R(euel)
1892-1973 .... **CLC 1, 2, 3, 8, 12, 38;
WLC**
See also AAYA 10; AITN 1; BPFB 3;
BRWS 2; CA 17-18; 45-48; CANR 36;
CAP 2; CDBLB 1914-1945; CLR 56;
CPW 1; CWRI 5; DA; DA3; DAB; DAC;
DAM MST, NOV, POP; DLB 15, 160,
255; EFS 2; FANT; JRDA; LAIT 1; MAI-
CYA 1, 2; MTCW 1, 2; NFS 8; RGEL 2;
SATA 2, 32, 100; SATA-Obit 24; SFW 4;
SUFW; TEA; WCH; WYA; YAW

Toller, Ernst 1893-1939 .... **TCLC 10**
See also CA 107; 186; DLB 124; RGWL 2

Tolson, M. B.
See Tolson, Melvin B(eaunorus)

Tolson, Melvin B(eaunorus)
1898(?)-1966 .... **CLC 36, 105; BLC 3**
See also AFAW 1, 2; BW 1, 3; CA 124; 89-
92; CANR 80; DAM MULT, POET; DLB
48, 76; RGAL 4

Tolstoi, Aleksei Nikolaevich
See Tolstoy, Alexey Nikolaevich

Tolstoi, Lev
See Tolstoy, Leo (Nikolaevich)
See also RGSF 2; RGWL 2

Tolstoy, Alexey Nikolaevich
1882-1945 .... **TCLC 18**
See also CA 107; 158; SFW 4

Tolstoy, Leo (Nikolaevich)
1828-1910 .. **TCLC 4, 11, 17, 28, 44, 79;
SSC 9, 30, 45, 54; WLC**
See also Tolstoi, Lev
See also CA 104; 123; DA; DA3; DAB;
DAC; DAM MST, NOV; DLB 238; EFS
2; EW 7; EXPS; IDTP; LAIT 2; NFS 10;
SATA 26; SSFS 5; TWA

Tolstoy, Count Leo
See Tolstoy, Leo (Nikolaevich)

Tomasi di Lampedusa, Giuseppe 1896-1957
See Lampedusa, Giuseppe (Tomasi) di
See also CA 111; DLB 177

Tomlin, Lily .... **CLC 17**
See also Tomlin, Mary Jean

Tomlin, Mary Jean 1939(?)-
See Tomlin, Lily
See also CA 117

Tomlinson, (Alfred) Charles 1927- .... **CLC 2,
4, 6, 13, 45; PC 17**
See also CA 5-8R; CANR 33; CP 7; DAM
POET; DLB 40

Tomlinson, H(enry) M(ajor)
1873-1958 .... **TCLC 71**
See also CA 118; 161; DLB 36, 100, 195

Tonson, Jacob
See Bennett, (Enoch) Arnold

Toole, John Kennedy 1937-1969 ..... **CLC 19,
64**
See also BPFB 3; CA 104; DLBY 1981;
MTCW 2

Toomer, Eugene
See Toomer, Jean

Toomer, Eugene Pinchback
See Toomer, Jean

Toomer, Jean 1892-1967 .... **CLC 1, 4, 13, 22;
BLC 3; PC 7; SSC 1, 45; WLCS**
See also AFAW 1, 2; AMWS 3, 9; BW 1;
CA 85-88; CDALB 1917-1929; DA3;
DAM MULT; DLB 45, 51; EXPP; EXPS;
MTCW 1, 2; NFS 11; RGAL 4; RGSF 2;
SSFS 5

Toomer, Nathan Jean
See Toomer, Jean

Toomer, Nathan Pinchback
See Toomer, Jean

Torley, Luke
See Blish, James (Benjamin)

Tornimparte, Alessandra
See Ginzburg, Natalia

Torre, Raoul della
See Mencken, H(enry) L(ouis)

Torrence, Ridgely 1874-1950 .... **TCLC 97**
See also DLB 54, 249

Torrey, E(dwin) Fuller 1937- .... **CLC 34**
See also CA 119; CANR 71

Torsvan, Ben Traven
See Traven, B.

Torsvan, Benno Traven
See Traven, B.

Torsvan, Berick Traven
See Traven, B.

Torsvan, Berwick Traven
See Traven, B.

Torsvan, Bruno Traven
See Traven, B.

Torsvan, Traven
See Traven, B.

Tourneur, Cyril 1575(?)-1626 .... **LC 66**
See also BRW 2; DAM DRAM; DLB 58;
RGEL 2

Tournier, Michel (Edouard) 1924- .... **CLC 6,
23, 36, 95**
See also CA 49-52; CANR 3, 36, 74; DLB
83; GFL 1789 to the Present; MTCW 1,
2; SATA 23

Tournimparte, Alessandra
See Ginzburg, Natalia

Towers, Ivar
See Kornbluth, C(yril) M.

Towne, Robert (Burton) 1936(?)- ..... **CLC 87**
See also CA 108; DLB 44; IDFW 3, 4

Townsend, Sue .... **CLC 61**
See also Townsend, Susan Elaine
See also AAYA 28; CBD; CWD; SATA 55,
93; SATA-Brief 48

Unsworth, Barry (Forster) 1930- .... **CLC 76, 127**
See also BRWS 7; CA 25-28R; CANR 30, 54; CN 7; DLB 194

Updike, John (Hoyer) 1932- . **CLC 1, 2, 3, 5, 7, 9, 13, 15, 23, 34, 43, 70, 139; SSC 13, 27; WLC**
See also AAYA 36; AMW; AMWR 1; BPFB 3; BYA 12; CA 1-4R; CABS 1; CANR 4, 33, 51, 94; CDALB 1968-1988; CN 7; CP 7; CPW 1; DA; DA3; DAB; DAC; DAM MST, NOV, POET, POP; DLB 2, 5, 143, 218, 227; DLBD 3; DLBY 1980, 1982, 1997; EXPP; HGG; MTCW 1, 2; NFS 12; RGAL 4; RGSF 2; SSFS 3; TUS

Upshaw, Margaret Mitchell
See Mitchell, Margaret (Munnerlyn)

Upton, Mark
See Sanders, Lawrence

Upward, Allen 1863-1926 .... **TCLC 85**
See also CA 117; 187; DLB 36

Urdang, Constance (Henriette)
1922-1996 .... **CLC 47**
See also CA 21-24R; CANR 9, 24; CP 7; CWP

Uriel, Henry
See Faust, Frederick (Schiller)

Uris, Leon (Marcus) 1924- .... **CLC 7, 32**
See also AITN 1, 2; BEST 89:2; BPFB 3; CA 1-4R; CANR 1, 40, 65; CN 7; CPW 1; DA3; DAM NOV, POP; MTCW 1, 2; SATA 49

Urista, Alberto H. 1947- .... **PC 34**
See also Alurista
See also CA 45-48, 182; CANR 2, 32; HLCS 1; HW 1

Urmuz
See Codrescu, Andrei

Urquhart, Guy
See McAlmon, Robert (Menzies)

Urquhart, Jane 1949- .... **CLC 90**
See also CA 113; CANR 32, 68; CCA 1; DAC

Usigli, Rodolfo 1905-1979
See also CA 131; HLCS 1; HW 1; LAW

Ustinov, Peter (Alexander) 1921- .... **CLC 1**
See also AITN 1; CA 13-16R; CANR 25, 51; CBD; CD 5; DLB 13; MTCW 2

U Tam'si, Gerald Felix Tchicaya
See Tchicaya, Gerald Felix

U Tam'si, Tchicaya
See Tchicaya, Gerald Felix

Vachss, Andrew (Henry) 1942- .... **CLC 106**
See also CA 118; CANR 44, 95; CMW 4

Vachss, Andrew H.
See Vachss, Andrew (Henry)

Vaculik, Ludvik 1926- .... **CLC 7**
See also CA 53-56; CANR 72; CWW 2; DLB 232

Vaihinger, Hans 1852-1933 .... **TCLC 71**
See also CA 116; 166

Valdez, Luis (Miguel) 1940- ..... **CLC 84; DC 10; HLC 2**
See also CA 101; CAD; CANR 32, 81; CD 5; DAM MULT; DFS 5; DLB 122; HW 1; LAIT 4

Valenzuela, Luisa 1938- .... **CLC 31, 104; HLCS 2; SSC 14**
See also CA 101; CANR 32, 65; CDWLB 3; CWW 2; DAM MULT; DLB 113; FW; HW 1, 2; LAW; RGSF 2

Valera y Alcala-Galiano, Juan
1824-1905 .... **TCLC 10**
See also CA 106

Valery, (Ambroise) Paul (Toussaint Jules)
1871-1945 .... **TCLC 4, 15; PC 9**
See also CA 104; 122; DA3; DAM POET; DLB 258; EW 8; GFL 1789 to the Present; MTCW 1, 2; RGWL 2; TWA

Valle-Inclan, Ramon (Maria) del
1866-1936 .... **TCLC 5; HLC 2**
See also CA 106; 153; CANR 80; DAM MULT; DLB 134; EW 8; HW 2; RGSF 2; RGWL 2

Vallejo, Antonio Buero
See Buero Vallejo, Antonio

Vallejo, Cesar (Abraham)
1892-1938 .... **TCLC 3, 56; HLC 2**
See also CA 105; 153; DAM MULT; HW 1; LAW; RGWL 2

Valles, Jules 1832-1885 .... **NCLC 71**
See also DLB 123; GFL 1789 to the Present

Vallette, Marguerite Eymery
1860-1953 .... **TCLC 67**
See also CA 182; DLB 123, 192

Valle Y Pena, Ramon del
See Valle-Inclan, Ramon (Maria) del

Van Ash, Cay 1918- .... **CLC 34**

Vanbrugh, Sir John 1664-1726 .... **LC 21**
See also BRW 2; DAM DRAM; DLB 80; IDTP; RGEL 2

Van Campen, Karl
See Campbell, John W(ood, Jr.)

Vance, Gerald
See Silverberg, Robert

Vance, Jack .... **CLC 35**
See also Vance, John Holbrook
See also DLB 8; FANT; SCFW 2; SFW 4; SUFW

Vance, John Holbrook 1916-
See Queen, Ellery; Vance, Jack
See also CA 29-32R; CANR 17, 65; CMW 4; MTCW 1

Van Den Bogarde, Derek Jules Gaspard
Ulric Niven 1921-1999 .... **CLC 14**
See also Bogarde, Dirk
See also CA 77-80; 179

Vandenburgh, Jane .... **CLC 59**
See also CA 168

Vanderhaeghe, Guy 1951- .... **CLC 41**
See also BPFB 3; CA 113; CANR 72

van der Post, Laurens (Jan)
1906-1996 .... **CLC 5**
See also AFW; CA 5-8R; 155; CANR 35; CN 7; DLB 204; RGEL 2

van de Wetering, Janwillem 1931- ... **CLC 47**
See also CA 49-52; CANR 4, 62, 90; CMW 4

Van Dine, S. S. .... **TCLC 23**
See also Wright, Willard Huntington
See also MSW

Van Doren, Carl (Clinton)
1885-1950 .... **TCLC 18**
See also CA 111; 168

Van Doren, Mark 1894-1972 .... **CLC 6, 10**
See also CA 1-4R; 37-40R; CANR 3; DLB 45; MTCW 1, 2; RGAL 4

Van Druten, John (William)
1901-1957 .... **TCLC 2**
See also CA 104; 161; DLB 10; RGAL 4

Van Duyn, Mona (Jane) 1921- ...... **CLC 3, 7, 63, 116**
See also CA 9-12R; CANR 7, 38, 60; CP 7; CWP; DAM POET; DLB 5

Van Dyne, Edith
See Baum, L(yman) Frank

van Itallie, Jean-Claude 1936- .... **CLC 3**
See also CA 45-48; CAAS 2; CAD; CANR 1, 48; CD 5; DLB 7

Van Loot, Cornelius Obenchain
See Roberts, Kenneth (Lewis)

van Ostaijen, Paul 1896-1928 .... **TCLC 33**
See also CA 163

Van Peebles, Melvin 1932- .... **CLC 2, 20**
See also BW 2, 3; CA 85-88; CANR 27, 67, 82; DAM MULT

van Schendel, Arthur(-Francois-Emile)
1874-1946 .... **TCLC 56**

Vansittart, Peter 1920- .... **CLC 42**
See also CA 1-4R; CANR 3, 49, 90; CN 7; RHW

Van Vechten, Carl 1880-1964 .... **CLC 33**
See also AMWS 2; CA 183; 89-92; DLB 4, 9; RGAL 4

van Vogt, A(lfred) E(lton) 1912-2000 . **CLC 1**
See also BPFB 3; BYA 13, 14; CA 21-24R; 190; CANR 28; DLB 8, 251; SATA 14; SATA-Obit 124; SCFW; SFW 4

Varda, Agnes 1928- .... **CLC 16**
See also CA 116; 122

Vargas Llosa, (Jorge) Mario (Pedro)
1936- .... **CLC 3, 6, 9, 10, 15, 31, 42, 85; HLC 2**
See also Llosa, (Jorge) Mario (Pedro) Vargas
See also BPFB 3; CA 73-76; CANR 18, 32, 42, 67; CDWLB 3; DA; DA3; DAB; DAC; DAM MST, MULT, NOV; DLB 145; DNFS 2; HW 1, 2; LAIT 5; LAW; LAWS 1; MTCW 1, 2; RGWL 2; SSFS 14; TWA; WLIT 1

Vasiliu, George
See Bacovia, George

Vasiliu, Gheorghe
See Bacovia, George
See also CA 123; 189

Vassa, Gustavus
See Equiano, Olaudah

Vassilikos, Vassilis 1933- .... **CLC 4, 8**
See also CA 81-84; CANR 75

Vaughan, Henry 1621-1695 .... **LC 27**
See also BRW 2; DLB 131; PAB; RGEL 2

Vaughn, Stephanie .... **CLC 62**

Vazov, Ivan (Minchov) 1850-1921 . **TCLC 25**
See also CA 121; 167; CDWLB 4; DLB 147

Veblen, Thorstein B(unde)
1857-1929 .... **TCLC 31**
See also AMWS 1; CA 115; 165; DLB 246

Vega, Lope de 1562-1635 .... **LC 23; HLCS 2**
See also EW 2; RGWL 2

Vendler, Helen (Hennessy) 1933- ... **CLC 138**
See also CA 41-44R; CANR 25, 72; MTCW 1, 2

Venison, Alfred
See Pound, Ezra (Weston Loomis)

Verdi, Marie de
See Mencken, H(enry) L(ouis)

Verdu, Matilde
See Cela, Camilo Jose

Verga, Giovanni (Carmelo)
1840-1922 .... **TCLC 3; SSC 21**
See also CA 104; 123; CANR 101; EW 7; RGSF 2; RGWL 2

Vergil 70 B.C.-19 B.C. . **CMLC 9, 40; PC 12; WLCS**
See also Virgil
See also AW 2; DA; DA3; DAB; DAC; DAM MST, POET; EFS 1

Verhaeren, Emile (Adolphe Gustave)
1855-1916 .... **TCLC 12**
See also CA 109; GFL 1789 to the Present

Verlaine, Paul (Marie) 1844-1896 .. **NCLC 2, 51; PC 2, 32**
See also DAM POET; DLB 217; EW 7; GFL 1789 to the Present; RGWL 2; TWA

Verne, Jules (Gabriel) 1828-1905 ... **TCLC 6, 52**
See also AAYA 16; BYA 4; CA 110; 131; DA3; DLB 123; GFL 1789 to the Present; JRDA; LAIT 2; MAICYA 1, 2; RGWL 2; SATA 21; SCFW; SFW 4; TWA; WCH

Verus, Marcus Annius
See Aurelius, Marcus

1968-1988; CN 7; CPW; CSW; DA; DA3; DAB; DAC; DAM MST, MULT, NOV, POET, POP; DLB 6, 33, 143; EXPN; EXPS; FW; INT CANR-27; LAIT 3; MAWW; MTCW 1, 2; NFS 5; RGAL 4; RGSF 2; SATA 31; SSFS 2, 11; TUS; YAW

Walker, David Harry 1911-1992 ...... **CLC 14**
See also CA 1-4R; 137; CANR 1; CWRI 5; SATA 8; SATA-Obit 71

Walker, Edward Joseph 1934-
See Walker, Ted
See also CA 21-24R; CANR 12, 28, 53; CP 7

Walker, George F. 1947- .... **CLC 44, 61**
See also CA 103; CANR 21, 43, 59; CD 5; DAB; DAC; DAM MST; DLB 60

Walker, Joseph A. 1935- .... **CLC 19**
See also BW 1, 3; CA 89-92; CAD; CANR 26; CD 5; DAM DRAM, MST; DFS 12; DLB 38

Walker, Margaret (Abigail)
1915-1998 .... **CLC 1, 6; BLC; PC 20**
See also AFAW 1, 2; BW 2, 3; CA 73-76; 172; CANR 26, 54, 76; CN 7; CP 7; CSW; DAM MULT; DLB 76, 152; EXPP; FW; MTCW 1, 2; RGAL 4; RHW

Walker, Ted .... **CLC 13**
See also Walker, Edward Joseph
See also DLB 40

Wallace, David Foster 1962- ..... **CLC 50, 114**
See also AMWS 10; CA 132; CANR 59; DA3; MTCW 2

Wallace, Dexter
See Masters, Edgar Lee

Wallace, (Richard Horatio) Edgar
1875-1932 .... **TCLC 57**
See also CA 115; CMW 4; DLB 70; MSW; RGEL 2

Wallace, Irving 1916-1990 .... **CLC 7, 13**
See also AITN 1; BPFB 3; CA 1-4R; 132; CAAS 1; CANR 1, 27; CPW; DAM NOV, POP; INT CANR-27; MTCW 1, 2

Wallant, Edward Lewis 1926-1962 ... **CLC 5, 10**
See also CA 1-4R; CANR 22; DLB 2, 28, 143; MTCW 1, 2; RGAL 4

Wallas, Graham 1858-1932 .... **TCLC 91**

Walley, Byron
See Card, Orson Scott

Walpole, Horace 1717-1797 .... **LC 2, 49**
See also BRW 3; DLB 39, 104, 213; HGG; RGEL 2; SUFW; TEA

Walpole, Hugh (Seymour)
1884-1941 .... **TCLC 5**
See also CA 104; 165; DLB 34; HGG; MTCW 2; RGEL 2; RHW

Walser, Martin 1927- .... **CLC 27**
See also CA 57-60; CANR 8, 46; CWW 2; DLB 75, 124

Walser, Robert 1878-1956 .... **TCLC 18; SSC 20**
See also CA 118; 165; CANR 100; DLB 66

Walsh, Gillian Paton
See Paton Walsh, Gillian

Walsh, Jill Paton .... **CLC 35**
See also Paton Walsh, Gillian
See also CLR 2, 65; WYA

Walter, Villiam Christian
See Andersen, Hans Christian

Walton, Izaak 1593-1683 .... **LC 72**
See also BRW 2; CDBLB Before 1660; DLB 151, 213; RGEL 2

Wambaugh, Joseph (Aloysius, Jr.)
1937- .... **CLC 3, 18**
See also AITN 1; BEST 89:3; BPFB 3; CA 33-36R; CANR 42, 65; CMW 4; CPW 1; DA3; DAM NOV, POP; DLB 6; DLBY 1983; MSW; MTCW 1, 2

Wang Wei 699(?)-761(?) .... **PC 18**
See also TWA

Ward, Arthur Henry Sarsfield 1883-1959
See Rohmer, Sax
See also CA 108; 173; CMW 4; HGG

Ward, Douglas Turner 1930- .... **CLC 19**
See also BW 1; CA 81-84; CAD; CANR 27; CD 5; DLB 7, 38

Ward, E. D.
See Lucas, E(dward) V(errall)

Ward, Mrs. Humphry 1851-1920
See Ward, Mary Augusta
See also RGEL 2

Ward, Mary Augusta 1851-1920 ... **TCLC 55**
See also Ward, Mrs. Humphry
See also DLB 18

Ward, Peter
See Faust, Frederick (Schiller)

Warhol, Andy 1928(?)-1987 .... **CLC 20**
See also AAYA 12; BEST 89:4; CA 89-92; 121; CANR 34

Warner, Francis (Robert le Plastrier)
1937- .... **CLC 14**
See also CA 53-56; CANR 11

Warner, Marina 1946- .... **CLC 59**
See also CA 65-68; CANR 21, 55; CN 7; DLB 194

Warner, Rex (Ernest) 1905-1986 ...... **CLC 45**
See also CA 89-92; 119; DLB 15; RGEL 2; RHW

Warner, Susan (Bogert)
1819-1885 .... **NCLC 31**
See also DLB 3, 42, 239, 250, 254

Warner, Sylvia (Constance) Ashton
See Ashton-Warner, Sylvia (Constance)

Warner, Sylvia Townsend
1893-1978 .... **CLC 7, 19; SSC 23**
See also BRWS 7; CA 61-64; 77-80; CANR 16, 60, 104; DLB 34, 139; FANT; FW; MTCW 1, 2; RGEL 2; RGSF 2; RHW

Warren, Mercy Otis 1728-1814 ..... **NCLC 13**
See also DLB 31, 200; RGAL 4; TUS

Warren, Robert Penn 1905-1989 ... **CLC 1, 4, 6, 8, 10, 13, 18, 39, 53, 59; PC 37; SSC 4; WLC**
See also AITN 1; AMW; BPFB 3; BYA 1; CA 13-16R; 129; CANR 10, 47; CDALB 1968-1988; DA; DA3; DAB; DAC; DAM MST, NOV, POET; DLB 2, 48, 152; DLBY 1980, 1989; INT CANR-10; MTCW 1, 2; NFS 13; RGAL 4; RGSF 2; RHW; SATA 46; SATA-Obit 63; SSFS 8; TUS

Warshofsky, Isaac
See Singer, Isaac Bashevis

Warton, Thomas 1728-1790 .... **LC 15**
See also DAM POET; DLB 104, 109; RGEL 2

Waruk, Kona
See Harris, (Theodore) Wilson

Warung, Price .... **TCLC 45**
See also Astley, William
See also DLB 230; RGEL 2

Warwick, Jarvis
See Garner, Hugh
See also CCA 1

Washington, Alex
See Harris, Mark

Washington, Booker T(aliaferro)
1856-1915 .... **TCLC 10; BLC 3**
See also BW 1; CA 114; 125; DA3; DAM MULT; LAIT 2; RGAL 4; SATA 28

Washington, George 1732-1799 .... **LC 25**
See also DLB 31

Wassermann, (Karl) Jakob
1873-1934 .... **TCLC 6**
See also CA 104; 163; DLB 66

Wasserstein, Wendy 1950- .. **CLC 32, 59, 90; DC 4**
See also CA 121; 129; CABS 3; CAD; CANR 53, 75; CD 5; CWD; DA3; DAM DRAM; DFS 5; DLB 228; FW; INT CA-129; MTCW 2; SATA 94

Waterhouse, Keith (Spencer) 1929- . **CLC 47**
See also CA 5-8R; CANR 38, 67, 109; CBD; CN 7; DLB 13, 15; MTCW 1, 2

Waters, Frank (Joseph) 1902-1995 .. **CLC 88**
See also CA 5-8R; 149; CAAS 13; CANR 3, 18, 63; DLB 212; DLBY 1986; RGAL 4; TCWW 2

Waters, Mary C. .... **CLC 70**

Waters, Roger 1944- .... **CLC 35**

Watkins, Frances Ellen
See Harper, Frances Ellen Watkins

Watkins, Gerrold
See Malzberg, Barry N(athaniel)

Watkins, Gloria Jean 1952(?)-
See hooks, bell
See also BW 2; CA 143; CANR 87; MTCW 2; SATA 115

Watkins, Paul 1964- .... **CLC 55**
See also CA 132; CANR 62, 98

Watkins, Vernon Phillips
1906-1967 .... **CLC 43**
See also CA 9-10; 25-28R; CAP 1; DLB 20; RGEL 2

Watson, Irving S.
See Mencken, H(enry) L(ouis)

Watson, John H.
See Farmer, Philip Jose

Watson, Richard F.
See Silverberg, Robert

Waugh, Auberon (Alexander)
1939-2001 .... **CLC 7**
See also CA 45-48; 192; CANR 6, 22, 92; DLB 14, 194

Waugh, Evelyn (Arthur St. John)
1903-1966 .. **CLC 1, 3, 8, 13, 19, 27, 44, 107; SSC 41; WLC**
See also BPFB 3; BRW 7; CA 85-88; 25-28R; CANR 22; CDBLB 1914-1945; DA; DA3; DAB; DAC; DAM MST, NOV, POP; DLB 15, 162, 195; MTCW 1, 2; NFS 13; RGEL 2; RGSF 2; TEA; WLIT 4

Waugh, Harriet 1944- .... **CLC 6**
See also CA 85-88; CANR 22

Ways, C. R.
See Blount, Roy (Alton), Jr.

Waystaff, Simon
See Swift, Jonathan

Webb, Beatrice (Martha Potter)
1858-1943 .... **TCLC 22**
See also CA 117; 162; DLB 190; FW

Webb, Charles (Richard) 1939- .... **CLC 7**
See also CA 25-28R

Webb, James H(enry), Jr. 1946- ...... **CLC 22**
See also CA 81-84

Webb, Mary Gladys (Meredith)
1881-1927 .... **TCLC 24**
See also CA 182; 123; DLB 34; FW

Webb, Mrs. Sidney
See Webb, Beatrice (Martha Potter)

Webb, Phyllis 1927- .... **CLC 18**
See also CA 104; CANR 23; CCA 1; CP 7; CWP; DLB 53

Webb, Sidney (James) 1859-1947 .. **TCLC 22**
See also CA 117; 163; DLB 190

Webber, Andrew Lloyd .... **CLC 21**
See also Lloyd Webber, Andrew
See also DFS 7

Weber, Lenora Mattingly
1895-1971 .... **CLC 12**
See also CA 19-20; 29-32R; CAP 1; SATA 2; SATA-Obit 26

FANT; MAICYA 1, 2; MTCW 1, 2;
RGAL 4; SATA 2, 29, 100; SATA-Obit
44; TUS

White, Edmund (Valentine III)
1940- .... **CLC 27, 110**
See also AAYA 7; CA 45-48; CANR 3, 19,
36, 62, 107; CN 7; DA3; DAM POP; DLB
227; MTCW 1, 2

White, Hayden V. 1928- .... **CLC 148**
See also CA 128; DLB 246

White, Patrick (Victor Martindale)
1912-1990 ...... **CLC 3, 4, 5, 7, 9, 18, 65,
69; SSC 39**
See also BRWS 1; CA 81-84; 132; CANR
43; DLB 260; MTCW 1; RGEL 2; RGSF
2; RHW; TWA

White, Phyllis Dorothy James 1920-
See James, P. D.
See also CA 21-24R; CANR 17, 43, 65;
CMW 4; CN 7; CPW; DA3; DAM POP;
MTCW 1, 2; TEA

White, T(erence) H(anbury)
1906-1964 .... **CLC 30**
See also AAYA 22; BPFB 3; BYA 4, 5; CA
73-76; CANR 37; DLB 160; FANT;
JRDA; LAIT 1; MAICYA 1, 2; RGEL 2;
SATA 12; SUFW; YAW

White, Terence de Vere 1912-1994 ... **CLC 49**
See also CA 49-52; 145; CANR 3

White, Walter
See White, Walter F(rancis)

White, Walter F(rancis)
1893-1955 .... **TCLC 15; BLC 3**
See also BW 1; CA 115; 124; DAM MULT;
DLB 51

White, William Hale 1831-1913
See Rutherford, Mark
See also CA 121; 189

Whitehead, Alfred North
1861-1947 .... **TCLC 97**
See also CA 117; 165; DLB 100, 262

Whitehead, E(dward) A(nthony)
1933- .... **CLC 5**
See also CA 65-68; CANR 58; CBD; CD 5

Whitehead, Ted
See Whitehead, E(dward) A(nthony)

Whitemore, Hugh (John) 1936- .... **CLC 37**
See also CA 132; CANR 77; CBD; CD 5;
INT CA-132

Whitman, Sarah Helen (Power)
1803-1878 .... **NCLC 19**
See also DLB 1, 243

Whitman, Walt(er) 1819-1892 .. **NCLC 4, 31,
81; PC 3; WLC**
See also AAYA 42; AMW; AMWR 1;
CDALB 1640-1865; DA; DA3; DAB;
DAC; DAM MST, POET; DLB 3, 64,
224, 250; EXPP; LAIT 2; PAB; PFS 2, 3,
13; RGAL 4; SATA 20; TUS; WP; WYAS
1

Whitney, Phyllis A(yame) 1903- .... **CLC 42**
See also AAYA 36; AITN 2; BEST 90:3;
CA 1-4R; CANR 3, 25, 38, 60; CLR 59;
CMW 4; CPW; DA3; DAM POP; JRDA;
MAICYA 1, 2; MTCW 2; RHW; SATA 1,
30; YAW

Whittemore, (Edward) Reed (Jr.)
1919- .... **CLC 4**
See also CA 9-12R; CAAS 8; CANR 4; CP
7; DLB 5

Whittier, John Greenleaf
1807-1892 .... **NCLC 8, 59**
See also AMWS 1; DLB 1, 243; RGAL 4

Whittlebot, Hernia
See Coward, Noel (Peirce)

Wicker, Thomas Grey 1926-
See Wicker, Tom
See also CA 65-68; CANR 21, 46

Wicker, Tom .... **CLC 7**
See also Wicker, Thomas Grey

Wideman, John Edgar 1941- ...... **CLC 5, 34,
36, 67, 122; BLC 3**
See also AFAW 1, 2; AMWS 10; BPFB 4;
BW 2, 3; CA 85-88; CANR 14, 42, 67,
109; CN 7; DAM MULT; DLB 33, 143;
MTCW 2; RGAL 4; RGSF 2; SSFS 6, 12

Wiebe, Rudy (Henry) 1934- .. **CLC 6, 11, 14,
138**
See also CA 37-40R; CANR 42, 67; CN 7;
DAC; DAM MST; DLB 60; RHW

Wieland, Christoph Martin
1733-1813 .... **NCLC 17**
See also DLB 97; EW 4; RGWL 2

Wiene, Robert 1881-1938 .... **TCLC 56**

Wieners, John 1934- .... **CLC 7**
See also CA 13-16R; CP 7; DLB 16; WP

Wiesel, Elie(zer) 1928- .... **CLC 3, 5, 11, 37;
WLCS**
See also AAYA 7; AITN 1; CA 5-8R; CAAS
4; CANR 8, 40, 65; CDALBS; DA; DA3;
DAB; DAC; DAM MST, NOV; DLB 83;
DLBY 1987; INT CANR-8; LAIT 4;
MTCW 1, 2; NCFS 4; NFS 4; SATA 56;
YAW

Wiggins, Marianne 1947- .... **CLC 57**
See also BEST 89:3; CA 130; CANR 60

Wiggs, Susan .... **CLC 70**
See also CA 201

Wight, James Alfred 1916-1995
See Herriot, James
See also CA 77-80; SATA 55; SATA-Brief
44

Wilbur, Richard (Purdy) 1921- ..... **CLC 3, 6,
9, 14, 53, 110**
See also AMWS 3; CA 1-4R; CABS 2;
CANR 2, 29, 76, 93; CDALBS; CP 7;
DA; DAB; DAC; DAM MST, POET;
DLB 5, 169; EXPP; INT CANR-29;
MTCW 1, 2; PAB; PFS 11, 12; RGAL 4;
SATA 9, 108; WP

Wild, Peter 1940- .... **CLC 14**
See also CA 37-40R; CP 7; DLB 5

Wilde, Oscar (Fingal O'Flahertie Wills)
1854(?)-1900 ..... **TCLC 1, 8, 23, 41; DC
17; SSC 11; WLC**
See also BRW 5; BRWR 2; CA 104; 119;
CDBLB 1890-1914; DA; DA3; DAB;
DAC; DAM DRAM, MST, NOV; DFS 4,
8, 9; DLB 10, 19, 34, 57, 141, 156, 190;
EXPS; FANT; RGEL 2; RGSF 2; SATA
24; SSFS 7; SUFW; TEA; WCH; WLIT 4

Wilder, Billy .... **CLC 20**
See also Wilder, Samuel
See also DLB 26

Wilder, Samuel 1906-2002
See Wilder, Billy
See also CA 89-92

Wilder, Stephen
See Marlowe, Stephen

Wilder, Thornton (Niven)
1897-1975 .. **CLC 1, 5, 6, 10, 15, 35, 82;
DC 1; WLC**
See also AAYA 29; AITN 2; AMW; CA 13-
16R; 61-64; CAD; CANR 40; CDALBS;
DA; DA3; DAB; DAC; DAM DRAM,
MST, NOV; DFS 1, 4; DLB 4, 7, 9, 228;
DLBY 1997; LAIT 3; MTCW 1, 2; RGAL
4; RHW; WYAS 1

Wilding, Michael 1942- ...... **CLC 73; SSC 50**
See also CA 104; CANR 24, 49, 106; CN
7; RGSF 2

Wiley, Richard 1944- .... **CLC 44**
See also CA 121; 129; CANR 71

Wilhelm, Kate .... **CLC 7**
See also Wilhelm, Katie (Gertrude)
See also AAYA 20; CAAS 5; DLB 8; INT
CANR-17; SCFW 2

Wilhelm, Katie (Gertrude) 1928-
See Wilhelm, Kate
See also CA 37-40R; CANR 17, 36, 60, 94;
MTCW 1; SFW 4

Wilkins, Mary
See Freeman, Mary E(leanor) Wilkins

Willard, Nancy 1936- .... **CLC 7, 37**
See also BYA 5; CA 89-92; CANR 10, 39,
68, 107; CLR 5; CWP; CWRI 5; DLB 5,
52; FANT; MAICYA 1; MTCW 1;
SATA 37, 71, 127; SATA-Brief 30

William of Ockham 1290-1349 ..... **CMLC 32**

Williams, Ben Ames 1889-1953 ..... **TCLC 89**
See also CA 183; DLB 102

Williams, C(harles) K(enneth)
1936- .... **CLC 33, 56, 148**
See also CA 37-40R; CAAS 26; CANR 57,
106; CP 7; DAM POET; DLB 5

Williams, Charles
See Collier, James Lincoln

Williams, Charles (Walter Stansby)
1886-1945 .... **TCLC 1, 11**
See also CA 104; 163; DLB 100, 153, 255;
FANT; RGEL 2; SUFW

Williams, (George) Emlyn
1905-1987 .... **CLC 15**
See also CA 104; 123; CANR 36; DAM
DRAM; DLB 10, 77; MTCW 1

Williams, Hank 1923-1953 .... **TCLC 81**

Williams, Hugo 1942- .... **CLC 42**
See also CA 17-20R; CANR 45; CP 7; DLB
40

Williams, J. Walker
See Wodehouse, P(elham) G(renville)

Williams, John A(lfred) 1925- ..... **CLC 5, 13;
BLC 3**
See also AFAW 2; BW 2, 3; CA 53-56;
CAAE 195; CAAS 3; CANR 6, 26, 51;
CN 7; CSW; DAM MULT; DLB 2, 33;
INT CANR-6; RGAL 4; SFW 4

Williams, Jonathan (Chamberlain)
1929- .... **CLC 13**
See also CA 9-12R; CAAS 12; CANR 8,
108; CP 7; DLB 5

Williams, Joy 1944- .... **CLC 31**
See also CA 41-44R; CANR 22, 48, 97

Williams, Norman 1952- .... **CLC 39**
See also CA 118

Williams, Sherley Anne 1944-1999 . **CLC 89;
BLC 3**
See also AFAW 2; BW 2, 3; CA 73-76; 185;
CANR 25, 82; DAM MULT, POET; DLB
41; INT CANR-25; SATA 78; SATA-Obit
116

Williams, Shirley
See Williams, Sherley Anne

Williams, Tennessee 1911-1983 . **CLC 1, 2, 5,
7, 8, 11, 15, 19, 30, 39, 45, 71, 111; DC
4; WLC**
See also AAYA 31; AITN 1, 2; AMW; CA
5-8R; 108; CABS 3; CAD; CANR 31;
CDALB 1941-1968; DA; DA3; DAB;
DAC; DAM DRAM, MST; DFS 1, 3, 7,
12; DLB 7; DLBD 4; DLBY 1983; GLL
1; LAIT 4; MTCW 1, 2; RGAL 4; TUS

Williams, Thomas (Alonzo)
1926-1990 .... **CLC 14**
See also CA 1-4R; 132; CANR 2

Williams, William C.
See Williams, William Carlos

Williams, William Carlos
1883-1963 .... **CLC 1, 2, 5, 9, 13, 22, 42,
67; PC 7; SSC 31**
See also AMW; AMWR 1; CA 89-92;
CANR 34; CDALB 1917-1929; DA;
DA3; DAB; DAC; DAM MST, POET;
DLB 4, 16, 54, 86; EXPP; MTCW 1, 2;
NCFS 4; PAB; PFS 1, 6, 11; RGAL 4;
RGSF 2; TUS; WP

Woolrich, Cornell .... **CLC 77**
See also Hopley-Woolrich, Cornell George
See also MSW

Woolson, Constance Fenimore
1840-1894 .... **NCLC 82**
See also DLB 12, 74, 189, 221; RGAL 4

Wordsworth, Dorothy 1771-1855 .. **NCLC 25**
See also DLB 107

Wordsworth, William 1770-1850 .. **NCLC 12, 38, 111; PC 4; WLC**
See also BRW 4; CDBLB 1789-1832; DA; DA3; DAB; DAC; DAM MST, POET; DLB 93, 107; EXPP; PAB; PFS 2; RGEL 2; TEA; WLIT 3; WP

Wotton, Sir Henry 1568-1639 .... **LC 68**
See also DLB 121; RGEL 2

Wouk, Herman 1915- .... **CLC 1, 9, 38**
See also BPFB 2, 3; CA 5-8R; CANR 6, 33, 67; CDALBS; CN 7; CPW; DA3; DAM NOV, POP; DLBY 1982; INT CANR-6; LAIT 4; MTCW 1, 2; NFS 7; TUS

Wright, Charles (Penzel, Jr.) 1935- .. **CLC 6, 13, 28, 119, 146**
See also AMWS 5; CA 29-32R; CAAS 7; CANR 23, 36, 62, 88; CP 7; DLB 165; DLBY 1982; MTCW 1, 2; PFS 10

Wright, Charles Stevenson 1932- ... **CLC 49; BLC 3**
See also BW 1; CA 9-12R; CANR 26; CN 7; DAM MULT, POET; DLB 33

Wright, Frances 1795-1852 .... **NCLC 74**
See also DLB 73

Wright, Frank Lloyd 1867-1959 .... **TCLC 95**
See also AAYA 33; CA 174

Wright, Jack R.
See Harris, Mark

Wright, James (Arlington)
1927-1980 .... **CLC 3, 5, 10, 28; PC 36**
See also AITN 2; AMWS 3; CA 49-52; 97-100; CANR 4, 34, 64; CDALBS; DAM POET; DLB 5, 169; EXPP; MTCW 1, 2; PFS 7, 8; RGAL 4; TUS; WP

Wright, Judith (Arundell)
1915-2000 .... **CLC 11, 53; PC 14**
· See also CA 13-16R; 188; CANR 31, 76, 93; CP 7; CWP; DLB 260; MTCW 1, 2; PFS 8; RGEL 2; SATA 14; SATA-Obit 121

Wright, L(aurali) R. 1939- .... **CLC 44**
See also CA 138; CMW 4

Wright, Richard (Nathaniel)
1908-1960 ... **CLC 1, 3, 4, 9, 14, 21, 48, 74; BLC 3; SSC 2; WLC**
See also AAYA 5, 42; AFAW 1, 2; AMW; BPFB 3; BW 1; BYA 2; CA 108; CANR 64; CDALB 1929-1941; DA; DA3; DAB; DAC; DAM MST, MULT, NOV; DLB 76, 102; DLBD 2; EXPN; LAIT 3, 4; MTCW 1, 2; NCFS 1; NFS 1, 7; RGAL 4; RGSF 2; SSFS 3, 9, 15; TUS; YAW

Wright, Richard B(ruce) 1937- .... **CLC 6**
See also CA 85-88; DLB 53

Wright, Rick 1945- .... **CLC 35**

Wright, Rowland
See Wells, Carolyn

Wright, Stephen 1946- .... **CLC 33**

Wright, Willard Huntington 1888-1939
See Van Dine, S. S.
See also CA 115; 189; CMW 4; DLBD 16

Wright, William 1930- .... **CLC 44**
See also CA 53-56; CANR 7, 23

Wroth, Lady Mary 1587-1653(?) .... **LC 30; PC 38**
See also DLB 121

Wu Ch'eng-en 1500(?)-1582(?) .... **LC 7**

Wu Ching-tzu 1701-1754 .... **LC 2**

Wurlitzer, Rudolph 1938(?)- .... **CLC 2, 4, 15**
See also CA 85-88; CN 7; DLB 173

Wyatt, Sir Thomas c. 1503-1542 . **LC 70; PC 27**
See also BRW 1; DLB 132; EXPP; RGEL 2; TEA

Wycherley, William 1640-1716 .... **LC 8, 21**
See also BRW 2; CDBLB 1660-1789; DAM DRAM; DLB 80; RGEL 2

Wylie, Elinor (Morton Hoyt)
1885-1928 .... **TCLC 8; PC 23**
See also AMWS 1; CA 105; 162; DLB 9, 45; EXPP; RGAL 4

Wylie, Philip (Gordon) 1902-1971 ... **CLC 43**
See also CA 21-22; 33-36R; CAP 2; DLB 9; SFW 4

Wyndham, John .... **CLC 19**
See also Harris, John (Wyndham Parkes Lucas) Beynon
See also DLB 255; SCFW 2

Wyss, Johann David Von
1743-1818 .... **NCLC 10**
See also JRDA; MAICYA 1, 2; SATA 29; SATA-Brief 27

Xenophon c. 430 B.C.-c. 354
B.C. .... **CMLC 17**
See also AW 1; DLB 176; RGWL 2

Yakumo Koizumi
See Hearn, (Patricio) Lafcadio (Tessima Carlos)

Yamamoto, Hisaye 1921- .... **SSC 34; AAL**
See also DAM MULT; LAIT 4; SSFS 14

Yanez, Jose Donoso
See Donoso (Yanez), Jose

Yanovsky, Basile S.
See Yanovsky, V(assily) S(emenovich)

Yanovsky, V(assily) S(emenovich)
1906-1989 .... **CLC 2, 18**
See also CA 97-100; 129

Yates, Richard 1926-1992 .... **CLC 7, 8, 23**
See also AMWS 11; CA 5-8R; 139; CANR 10, 43; DLB 2, 234; DLBY 1981, 1992; INT CANR-10

Yeats, W. B.
See Yeats, William Butler

Yeats, William Butler 1865-1939 .... **TCLC 1, 11, 18, 31, 93, 116; PC 20; WLC**
See also BRW 6; BRWR 1; CA 104; 127; CANR 45; CDBLB 1890-1914; DA; DA3; DAB; DAC; DAM DRAM, MST, POET; DLB 10, 19, 98, 156; EXPP; MTCW 1, 2; NCFS 3; PAB; PFS 1, 2, 5, 7, 13, 15; RGEL 2; TEA; WLIT 4; WP

Yehoshua, A(braham) B. 1936- .. **CLC 13, 31**
See also CA 33-36R; CANR 43, 90; RGSF 2

Yellow Bird
See Ridge, John Rollin

Yep, Laurence Michael 1948- .... **CLC 35**
See also AAYA 5, 31; BYA 7; CA 49-52; CANR 1, 46, 92; CLR 3, 17, 54; DLB 52; FANT; JRDA; MAICYA 1, 2; MAICYAS 1; SATA 7, 69, 123; WYA; YAW

Yerby, Frank G(arvin) 1916-1991 . **CLC 1, 7, 22; BLC 3**
See also BPFB 3; BW 1, 3; CA 9-12R; 136; CANR 16, 52; DAM MULT; DLB 76; INT CANR-16; MTCW 1; RGAL 4; RHW

Yesenin, Sergei Alexandrovich
See Esenin, Sergei (Alexandrovich)

Yevtushenko, Yevgeny (Alexandrovich)
1933- ...... **CLC 1, 3, 13, 26, 51, 126; PC 40**
See also Evtushenko, Evgenii Aleksandrovich
See also CA 81-84; CANR 33, 54; CWW 2; DAM POET; MTCW 1

Yezierska, Anzia 1885(?)-1970 .... **CLC 46**
See also CA 126; 89-92; DLB 28, 221; FW; MTCW 1; RGAL 4; SSFS 15

Yglesias, Helen 1915- .... **CLC 7, 22**
See also CA 37-40R; CAAS 20; CANR 15, 65, 95; CN 7; INT CANR-15; MTCW 1

Yokomitsu, Riichi 1898-1947 .... **TCLC 47**
See also CA 170

Yonge, Charlotte (Mary)
1823-1901 .... **TCLC 48**
See also CA 109; 163; DLB 18, 163; RGEL 2; SATA 17; WCH

York, Jeremy
See Creasey, John

York, Simon
See Heinlein, Robert A(nson)

Yorke, Henry Vincent 1905-1974 ..... **CLC 13**
See also Green, Henry
See also CA 85-88; 49-52

Yosano Akiko 1878-1942 .... **TCLC 59; PC 11**
See also CA 161

Yoshimoto, Banana .... **CLC 84**
See also Yoshimoto, Mahoko
See also NFS 7

Yoshimoto, Mahoko 1964-
See Yoshimoto, Banana
See also CA 144; CANR 98

Young, Al(bert James) 1939- . **CLC 19; BLC 3**
See also BW 2, 3; CA 29-32R; CANR 26, 65, 109; CN 7; CP 7; DAM MULT; DLB 33

Young, Andrew (John) 1885-1971 ...... **CLC 5**
See also CA 5-8R; CANR 7, 29; RGEL 2

Young, Collier
See Bloch, Robert (Albert)

Young, Edward 1683-1765 .... **LC 3, 40**
See also DLB 95; RGEL 2

Young, Marguerite (Vivian)
1909-1995 .... **CLC 82**
See also CA 13-16; 150; CAP 1; CN 7

Young, Neil 1945- .... **CLC 17**
See also CA 110; CCA 1

Young Bear, Ray A. 1950- .... **CLC 94**
See also CA 146; DAM MULT; DLB 175; NNAL

Yourcenar, Marguerite 1903-1987 ... **CLC 19, 38, 50, 87**
See also BPFB 3; CA 69-72; CANR 23, 60, 93; DAM NOV; DLB 72; DLBY 1988; EW 12; GFL 1789 to the Present; GLL 1; MTCW 1, 2; RGWL 2

Yuan, Chu 340(?) B.C.-278(?)
B.C. .... **CMLC 36**

Yurick, Sol 1925- .... **CLC 6**
See also CA 13-16R; CANR 25; CN 7

Zabolotsky, Nikolai Alekseevich
1903-1958 .... **TCLC 52**
See also CA 116; 164

Zagajewski, Adam 1945- .... **PC 27**
See also CA 186; DLB 232

Zalygin, Sergei -2000 .... **CLC 59**

Zamiatin, Evgenii
See Zamyatin, Evgeny Ivanovich
See also RGSF 2; RGWL 2

Zamiatin, Yevgenii
See Zamyatin, Evgeny Ivanovich

Zamora, Bernice (B. Ortiz) 1938- .. **CLC 89; HLC 2**
See also CA 151; CANR 80; DAM MULT; DLB 82; HW 1, 2

Zamyatin, Evgeny Ivanovich
1884-1937 .... **TCLC 8, 37**
See also Zamiatin, Evgenii
See also CA 105; 166; EW 10; SFW 4

Zangwill, Israel 1864-1926 ... **TCLC 16; SSC 44**
See also CA 109; 167; CMW 4; DLB 10, 135, 197; RGEL 2

Zappa, Francis Vincent, Jr. 1940-1993
See Zappa, Frank
See also CA 108; 143; CANR 57

Literary Criticism Series
Cumulative Topic Index

This index lists all topic entries in Gale's *Classical and Medieval Literature Criticism, Contemporary Literary Criticism, Drama Criticism, Literature Criticism from 1400 to 1800, Nineteenth-Century Literature Criticism,* and *Twentieth-Century Literary Criticism.*

TCLC Cumulative Nationality Index

AMERICAN

Adams, Andy **56**
Adams, Brooks **80**
Adams, Henry (Brooks) **4, 52**
Addams, Jane **76**
Agee, James (Rufus) **1, 19**
Aldrich, Bess (Genevra) Streeter **125**
Allen, Fred **87**
Anderson, Maxwell **2**
Anderson, Sherwood **1, 10, 24, 123**
Anthony, Susan B(rownell) **84**
Atherton, Gertrude (Franklin Horn) **2**
Austin, Mary (Hunter) **25**
Baker, Ray Stannard **47**
Baker, Carlos (Heard) **119**
Bambara, Toni Cade **116**
Barry, Philip **11**
Baum, L(yman) Frank **7**
Beard, Charles A(ustin) **15**
Becker, Carl (Lotus) **63**
Belasco, David **3**
Bell, James Madison **43**
Benchley, Robert (Charles) **1, 55**
Benedict, Ruth (Fulton) **60**
Benét, Stephen Vincent **7**
Benét, William Rose **28**
Bierce, Ambrose (Gwinett) **1, 7, 44**
Biggers, Earl Derr **65**
Bishop, Elizabeth **121**
Bishop, John Peale **103**
Black Elk **33**
Boas, Franz **56**
Bodenheim, Maxwell **44**
Bok, Edward W. **101**
Bourne, Randolph S(illiman) **16**
Boyd, James **115**
Boyd, Thomas (Alexander) **111**
Bradford, Gamaliel **36**
Brennan, Christopher John **17**
Brennan, Maeve **124**
Brodkey, Harold (Roy) **123**
Bromfield, Louis (Brucker) **11**
Broun, Heywood **104**
Bryan, William Jennings **99**
Burroughs, Edgar Rice **2, 32**
Burroughs, William S(eward) **121**
Cabell, James Branch **6**
Cable, George Washington **4**
Cahan, Abraham **71**
Caldwell, Erskine (Preston) **117**
Cardozo, Benjamin N(athan) **65**
Carnegie, Dale **53**
Cather, Willa (Sibert) **1, 11, 31, 99, 125**
Chambers, Robert W(illiam) **41**
Chandler, Raymond (Thornton) **1, 7**
Chapman, John Jay **7**
Chase, Mary Ellen **124**
Chesnutt, Charles W(addell) **5, 39**
Childress, Alice **116**
Cobb, Irvin S(hrewsbury) **77**
Coffin, Robert P(eter) Tristram **95**
Cohan, George M(ichael) **60**

Comstock, Anthony **13**
Cotter, Joseph Seamon Sr. **28**
Cram, Ralph Adams **45**
Crane, (Harold) Hart **2, 5, 80**
Crane, Stephen (Townley) **11, 17, 32**
Crawford, F(rancis) Marion **10**
Crothers, Rachel **19**
Cullen, Countée **4, 37**
Darrow, Clarence (Seward) **81**
Davis, Rebecca (Blaine) Harding **6**
Davis, Richard Harding **24**
Day, Clarence (Shepard Jr.) **25**
Dent, Lester **72**
De Voto, Bernard (Augustine) **29**
Dewey, John **95**
Dreiser, Theodore (Herman Albert) **10, 18, 35, 83**
Dulles, John Foster **72**
Dunbar, Paul Laurence **2, 12**
Duncan, Isadora **68**
Dunne, Finley Peter **28**
Eastman, Charles A(lexander) **55**
Eddy, Mary (Ann Morse) Baker **71**
Einstein, Albert **65**
Erskine, John **84**
Faust, Frederick (Schiller) **49**
Fenollosa, Ernest (Francisco) **91**
Fields, W. C. **80**
Fisher, Dorothy (Frances) Canfield **87**
Fisher, Rudolph **11**
Fitzgerald, F(rancis) Scott (Key) **1, 6, 14, 28, 55**
Fitzgerald, Zelda (Sayre) **52**
Fletcher, John Gould **35**
Foote, Mary Hallock **108**
Ford, Henry **73**
Forten, Charlotte L. **16**
Freeman, Douglas Southall **11**
Freeman, Mary E(leanor) Wilkins **9**
Fuller, Henry Blake **103**
Futrelle, Jacques **19**
Gale, Zona **7**
Garland, (Hannibal) Hamlin **3**
Gilman, Charlotte (Anna) Perkins (Stetson) **9, 37, 117**
Ginsberg, Allen **120**
Glasgow, Ellen (Anderson Gholson) **2, 7**
Glaspell, Susan **55**
Goldman, Emma **13**
Green, Anna Katharine **63**
Grey, Zane **6**
Griffith, D(avid Lewelyn) W(ark) **68**
Griggs, Sutton (Elbert) **77**
Guest, Edgar A(lbert) **95**
Guiney, Louise Imogen **41**
Hall, James Norman **23**
Handy, W(illiam) C(hristopher) **97**
Harper, Frances Ellen Watkins **14**
Harris, Joel Chandler **2**
Harte, (Francis) Bret(t) **1, 25**
Hartmann, Sadakichi **73**
Hatteras, Owen **18**
Hawthorne, Julian **25**

Hearn, (Patricio) Lafcadio (Tessima Carlos) **9**
Hecht, Ben **101**
Hellman, Lillian (Florence) **119**
Hemingway, Ernest (Miller) **115**
Henry, O. **1, 19**
Hergesheimer, Joseph **11**
Heyward, (Edwin) DuBose **59**
Higginson, Thomas Wentworth **36**
Holley, Marietta **99**
Holly, Buddy **65**
Holmes, Oliver Wendell Jr. **77**
Hopkins, Pauline Elizabeth **28**
Horney, Karen (Clementine Theodore Danielsen) **71**
Howard, Robert E(rvin) **8**
Howe, Julia Ward **21**
Howells, William Dean **7, 17, 41**
Huneker, James Gibbons **65**
Hurston, Zora Neale **121**
Ince, Thomas H. **89**
James, Henry **2, 11, 24, 40, 47, 64**
James, William **15, 32**
Jewett, (Theodora) Sarah Orne **1, 22**
Johnson, James Weldon **3, 19**
Johnson, Robert **69**
Kerouac, Jack **117**
Kinsey, Alfred C(harles) **91**
Kirk, Russell (Amos) **119**
Kornbluth, C(yril) M. **8**
Korzybski, Alfred (Habdank Skarbek) **61**
Kubrick, Stanley **112**
Kuttner, Henry **10**
Lardner, Ring(gold) W(ilmer) **2, 14**
Lewis, (Harry) Sinclair **4, 13, 23, 39**
Lewisohn, Ludwig **19**
Lewton, Val **76**
Lindsay, (Nicholas) Vachel **17**
Locke, Alain (Le Roy) **43**
Lockridge, Ross (Franklin) Jr. **111**
London, Jack **9, 15, 39**
Lovecraft, H(oward) P(hillips) **4, 22**
Lowell, Amy **1, 8**
Mankiewicz, Herman (Jacob) **85**
March, William **96**
Markham, Edwin **47**
Marquis, Don(ald Robert Perry) **7**
Masters, Edgar Lee **2, 25**
Matthews, (James) Brander **95**
Matthiessen, F(rancis) O(tto) **100**
McAlmon, Robert (Menzies) **97**
McCoy, Horace (Stanley) **28**
Mead, George Herbert **89**
Mencken, H(enry) L(ouis) **13**
Micheaux, Oscar (Devereaux) **76**
Millay, Edna St. Vincent **4, 49**
Mitchell, Margaret (Munnerlyn) **11**
Mitchell, S(ilas) Weir **36**
Mitchell, William **81**
Monroe, Harriet **12**
Moody, William Vaughan **105**
Morley, Christopher (Darlington) **87**
Morris, Wright **107**
Muir, John **28**

Nationality Index

TCLC-125 Title Index

ISBN 0-7876-5939-8

90000

9 780787 659394